W9-CXC-461

Econometric Methods with Applications in Business and Economics

Econometric Methods with Applications in Business and Economics

Christiaan Heij
Paul de Boer
Philip Hans Franses
Teun Kloek
Herman K. van Dijk

OXFORD
UNIVERSITY PRESS

Great Clarendon Street, Oxford OX2 6DP

Oxford University Press is a department of the University of Oxford.
It furthers the University's objective of excellence in research, scholarship,
and education by publishing worldwide in

Oxford New York

Auckland Bangkok Buenos Aires Cape Town Chennai
Dar es Salaam Delhi Hong Kong Istanbul Karachi Kolkata
Kuala Lumpur Madrid Melbourne Mexico City Mumbai Nairobi
São Paulo Shanghai Taipei Tokyo Toronto

Oxford is a registered trade mark of Oxford University Press
in the UK and certain other countries

Published in the United States
by Oxford University Press Inc., New York

First published 2004

British Library Cataloguing in Publication Data
Data available

Library of Congress Cataloging in Publication Data
Data available

ISBN 0–19–926801–0

1 3 5 7 9 10 8 6 4 2

Typeset by Kolam Information Services Pvt. Ltd, Pondicherry, India
Printed in Great Britain
on acid-free paper by Antony Rowe Ltd, Chippenham, Wiltshire

Preface

Econometric models and methods are applied in the daily practice of virtually all disciplines in business and economics like finance, marketing, microeconomics, and macroeconomics. This book is meant for anyone interested in obtaining a solid understanding and active working knowledge of this field. The book provides the reader both with the required insight in econometric methods and with the practical training needed for successful applications. The guiding principle of the book is to stimulate the reader to work actively on examples and exercises, so that econometrics is learnt the way it works in practice—that is, practical methods for solving questions in business and economics, based on a solid understanding of the underlying methods. In this way the reader gets trained to make the proper decisions in econometric modelling.

This book has grown out of half a century of experience in teaching undergraduate econometrics at the Econometric Institute in Rotterdam. With the support of Jan Tinbergen, Henri Theil founded the institute in 1956 and he developed Econometrics into a full-blown academic programme. Originally, econometrics was mostly concerned with national and international macroeconomic policy; the required computing power to estimate econometric models was expensive and scarcely available, so that econometrics was almost exclusively applied in public (statistical) agencies. Much has changed, and nowadays econometrics finds widespread application in a rich variety of fields. The two major causes of this increased role of econometrics are the information explosion in business and economics (with large data sets—for instance, in finance and marketing) and the enormous growth in cheap computing power and user-friendly software for a wide range of econometric methods.

This development is reflected in the book, as it presents econometric methods as a collection of very useful tools to address issues in a wide range of application areas. First of all, students should learn the essentials of econometrics in a rigorous way, as this forms the indispensable basis for all valid practical work. These essentials are treated in Chapters 1–5, after which two major application areas are discussed in Chapter 6 (on individual choice data with applications in marketing and microeconomics) and Chapter 7 (on time series data with applications in finance and international economics). The Introduction provides more information on the motivation and contents of the book, together with advice for students and instructors, and the Guide to the Book explains the structure and use of the book.

We thank our students, who always stimulate our enthusiasm to teach and who make us feel proud by their achievements in their later careers in econometrics, economics, and business management. We also thank both current and former members of the Econometric Institute in Rotterdam who have inspired our econometric work.

Several people helped us in the process of writing the book and the solutions manual. First of all we should mention our colleague Zsolt Sandor and our (current and former) Ph.D.

students Charles Bos, Lennart Hoogerheide, Rutger van Oest, and Björn Vroomen, who all contributed substantially in producing the solutions manual. Further we thank our (current and former) colleagues at the Econometric Institute, Bas Donkers, Rinse Harkema, Johan Kaashoek, Frank Kleibergen, Richard Kleijn, Peter Kooiman, Marius Ooms, and Peter Schotman. We were assisted by our (former) students Arjan van Dijk, Alex Hoogendoorn, and Jesse de Klerk, and we obtained very helpful feedback from our students, in particular from Simone Jansen, Martijn de Jong, Mariëlle Non, Arnoud Pijls, and Gerard Voskuil. Special thanks are for Aletta Henderiks, who never lost her courage in giving us the necessary secretarial support in processing the manuscript. Finally we wish to thank the delegates and staff of Oxford University Press for their assistance, in particular Andrew Schuller, Arthur Attwell, and Hilary Walford.

Christiaan Heij, Paul de Boer, Philip Hans Franses, Teun Kloek, Herman K. van Dijk

Rotterdam, 2004

From left to right: Christiaan Heij, Paul de Boer, Philip Hans Franses, Teun Kloek, and Herman K. van Dijk

Contents

Detailed Contents

List of Exhibits

Abbreviations

Apart from abbreviations that are common in econometrics, the list also contains the abbreviations (in italics) used to denote the data sets of examples and exercises, but not the abbreviations used to denote the variables in these data sets (see Appendix B for the meaning of the abbreviated variable names).

2SLS	two-stage least squares
3SLS	three-stage least squares
ACF	autocorrelation function
ADF	augmented Dickey–Fuller
ADL	autoregressive distributed lag
AIC	Akaike information criterion
AR	autoregressive
ARCH	autoregressive conditional heteroskedasticity
ARIMA	autoregressive integrated moving average
ARMA	autoregressive moving average
BHHH	method of Berndt, Hall, Hall, and Hausman
BIC	Bayes information criterion
BLUE	best linear unbiased estimator
BWA	bank wages (data set 2)
CAPM	capital asset pricing model
CAR	car production (data set 18)
CDF	cumulative distribution function
CL	conditional logit
COF	coffee sales (data set 4)
CUSUM	cumulative sum
CUSUMSQ	cumulative sum of squares
DGP	data generating process
DJI	Dow-Jones index (data set 15)
DMF	direct marketing for financial product (data set 13)
DUS	duration of strikes (data set 14)
ECM	error correction model
EWMA	exponentially weighted moving average
EXR	exchange rates (data set 21)
FAS	fashion sales (data set 8)
FEX	food expenditure (data set 7)
FGLS	feasible generalized least squares
FWLS	feasible weighted least squares
GARCH	generalized autoregressive conditional heteroskedasticity
GLS	generalized least squares
GMM	generalized method of moments
GNP	gross national product (data set 20)
HAC	heteroskedasticity and autocorrelation consistent
IBR	interest and bond rates (data set 9)
IID	identically and independently distributed
INP	industrial production (data set 10)
IV	instrumental variable
LAD	least absolute deviation
LM	Lagrange multiplier
LOG	natural logarithm
LR	likelihood ratio
MA	moving average
MAE	mean absolute error
MGC	motor gasoline consumption (data set 6)
ML	maximum likelihood
MNL	multinomial logit
MOM	mortality and marriages (data set 16)
MOR	market for oranges (data set 23)
MSE	mean squared error
NEP	nuclear energy production (data set 19)
NID	normally and independently distributed
NLS	non-linear least squares
OLS	ordinary least squares
P	probability (*P*-value)
PACF	partial autocorrelation function
PMI	primary metal industries (data set 5)
QML	quasi-maximum likelihood
RESET	regression specification error test
RMSE	root mean squared error
SACF	sample autocorrelation function
SCDF	sample cumulative distribution function
SEM	simultaneous equation model
SIC	Schwarz information criterion
SMR	stock market returns (data set 3)

SPACF	sample partial autocorrelation function
SSE	explained sum of squares
SSR	sum of squared residuals
SST	total sum of squares
STAR	smooth transition autoregressive
STP	standard and poor index (data set 22)
STU	student learning (data set 1)
SUR	seemingly unrelated regression
TAR	threshold autoregressive
TBR	Treasury Bill rates (data set 17)
TMSP	total mean squared prediction error
TOP	salaries of top managers (data set 11)
USP	US presidential elections (data set 12)
VAR	vector autoregressive
VECM	vector error correction model
W	Wald
WLS	weighted least squares

Guide to the Book

This guide describes the organization and use of the book. We refer to the Introduction for the purpose of the book, for a synopsis of the contents of the book, for study advice, and for suggestions for instructors as to how the book can be used in different courses.

Learning econometrics: Why, what, and how

The learning student is confronted with three basic questions: Why should I study this? What knowledge do I need? How can I apply this knowledge in practice? Therefore the topics of the book are presented in the following manner:

- explanation by motivating examples;
- discussion of appropriate econometric models and methods;
- illustrative applications in practical examples;
- training by empirical exercises (using an econometric software package);
- optional deeper understanding (theory text parts and theory and simulation exercises).

The book can be used for applied courses that focus on the 'how' of econometrics and also for more advanced courses that treat both the 'how' and the 'what' of econometrics. The user is free to choose the desired balance between econometric applications and econometric theory.

- In applied courses, the theory parts (clearly marked in the text) and the theory and simulation exercises can be skipped without any harm. Even without these parts, the text still provides a good understanding of the 'what' of econometrics that is required in sound applied work, as there exist no standard 'how-to-do' recipes that can be applied blindly in practice.
- In more advanced courses, students get a deeper understanding of econometrics — in addition to the practical skills of applied courses — by studying also the theory parts and by doing the theory and simulation exercises. This allows them to apply econometrics in new situations that require a creative mind in developing alternative models and methods.

Text structure

The required background material is covered in Chapter 1 (which reviews statistical methods that are fundamental in econometrics) and in Appendix A (which summarizes useful matrix methods, together with computational examples). The core material on econometrics is in Chapters 2–7; Chapters 2–5 treat fundamental econometric methods that are needed for the topics discussed in Chapters 6 and 7. Each chapter has the following structure.

- The chapter starts with a brief statement of the purpose of the chapter, followed by sections and subsections that are divided into manageable parts with clear headings.
- Examples, theory parts, and computational schemes are clearly indicated in the text.
- Summaries are included at many points — especially at the end of all sections in Chapters 5–7.
- The chapter concludes with a brief summary, further reading, and a keyword list that summarizes the treated topics.
- A varied set of exercises is included at the end of each chapter.

To facilitate the use of the book, the required preliminary knowledge is indicated at the start of subsections.

- In Chapters 2–4 we refer to the preliminary knowledge needed from Chapter 1 (on statistics) and Appendix A (on matrix methods). Therefore, it is not necessary to cover all Chapter 1 before starting on the other chapters, as Chapter 1 can be reviewed along the way as one progresses through Chapters 2–4, and the same holds true for the material of Appendix A.
- In Chapters 6 and 7 we indicate which parts of the earlier chapters are needed at each stage. Most of the sections of Chapter 5 can be read independently of each other, and in Chapters 6 and 7 some sections can be skipped depending on the topics of interest for the reader.
- Further details of the text structure are discussed in the Introduction (see the section 'Teaching suggestions' — in particular, Exhibit 0.3).

Examples and data sets

The econometric models and methods are motivated by means of fully worked-out examples using real-world data sets from a variety of applications in business and economics. The examples are clearly marked in the text because they play a crucial role in explaining the application of econometric methods.

The corresponding data sets are available from the web site of the book, and Appendix B explains the type and source of the data and the meaning of the variables in the data files (see p. 748 for a list of all the data sets used in the book). The names of the data sets consist of three parts:

- XM (for examples) and XR (for exercises);
- three digits, indicating the example or exercise number;
- three letters, indicating the data topic.

For example, the file XM101STU contains the data for Example 1.1 on student learning, and the file XR111STU contains the data for Exercise 1.11 on student learning.

Exercises

Students will enhance their understanding and acquire practical skills by working through the exercises, which are of three types.

- *Theory exercises on derivations and model extensions*. These exercises deepen the theoretical understanding of the 'what' of econometrics. The desired level of the course will determine how many of the theory exercises should be covered.
- *Simulation exercises illustrating statistical properties of econometric models and methods*. These exercises provide more intuitive understanding of some of the central theoretical results.
- *Empirical exercises on applications with business and economic data sets to solve questions of practical interest*. These exercises focus on the 'how' of econometrics, so that the student learns to construct appropriate models from real-world data and to draw sound conclusions from the obtained results. Actively working through these empirical exercises is essential to gaining a proper understanding of econometrics and to getting hands-on experience with applications to solve practical problems. The web site of the book contains the data sets of all empirical exercises, and Appendix B contains information on these data sets.

The choice of appropriate exercises is facilitated by cross-references.

- Each subsection concludes with a list of exercises related to the material of that subsection (where T denotes theory exercises, S simulation exercises, and E empirical exercises).
- Every exercise refers to the parts of the chapter that are needed for doing the exercise.
- An asterisk (∗) denotes advanced (parts of) exercises.

Web site and software

The web site of the book contains all the data sets used in the book, in three formats:

- EViews;
- Excel;
- ASCII.

All the examples and all the empirical and simulation exercises in the book can be done with EViews version 3.1 and higher (Quantitative Micro Software, 1994–8), but other econometric software packages can also be used in most cases. The student version of the EViews package suffices for most of the book, but this version has some limitations—for example, it does not support the programs required for the simulation exercises (see the web site of the book for further details). The exhibits for the empirical examples in the text have been obtained by using EViews version 3.1.

Instructor material

Instructors who adopt the book can receive the Solutions Manual of the book for free.

- The manual contains over 350 pages with fully worked-out text solutions of all exercises, both of the theory questions and of the empirical and simulation questions; this will assist instructors in selecting material for exercise sessions and computer sessions as part of their course.
- The manual contains a CD-ROM with solution files (EViews work files with the solutions of all empirical exercises and EViews programs for all simulation exercises).
- This CD-ROM also contains all the exhibits of the book (in Word format) to facilitate lecture presentations.

The printed solutions manual and CD-ROM can be obtained from Oxford University Press, upon request by adopting instructors. For further information and additional material we refer readers to the Oxford University Press web site of the book.

Remarks on notation

In the text we follow the notational conventions commonly used in econometrics.

- Scalar variables and vectors are denoted by lower-case italic letters (x, y, and so on); however, in Section 7.6 vectors of variables are denoted by upper-case italic letters, such as Y_t, in accordance with most of the literature on this topic.
- Matrices are denoted by upper-case italic letters (X, A, and so on).

- The element in row i and column j of a matrix A is generally denoted by a_{ij}, except for the regressor matrix X, where this element is denoted by x_{ji}, which is observation i of variable j (see Section 3.1.2).
- x_i denotes the vector containing the values of all the explanatory variables x_{ji} for observation i (including the value 1 as first element of x_i if the model contains a constant term).
- Transposition is denoted by a prime (X', x', and so on).
- Unknown parameters are denoted by Greek italic letters (β, ε, σ, and so on).
- Estimated quantities are denoted by Latin italic letters (b, e, s, and so on), or sometimes by imposing a hat ($\hat{\beta}$, $\hat{\varepsilon}$, $\hat{\sigma}$, and so on).
- Expected values are denoted by $E[\cdot]$—for instance, $E[b]$.
- $\log(x)$ denotes the natural logarithm of x (with base $e = 2.71828\ \ldots$).

In many of the exhibits—for instance, the ones related to empirical examples—we show the output as generated by the software program EViews. The notation in these exhibits may differ from the above conventions.

- Scalar variables are denoted by capital letters (X, Y, instead of x, y, and so on).
- Statistics are denoted by text (R-squared, Std. Dev., instead of R^2, s, and so on).

In most cases this does not lead to any confusion, and otherwise the notation is explained in the text or in the caption of the exhibits.

Introduction

Econometrics

Decision making in business and economics is often supported by the use of quantitative information. Econometrics is concerned with summarizing relevant data information by means of a model. Such econometric models help to understand the relation between economic and business variables and to analyse the possible effects of decisions.

Econometrics was founded as a scientific discipline around 1930. In the early years, most applications dealt with macroeconomic questions to help governments and large firms in making their long-term decisions. Nowadays econometrics forms an indispensable tool to model empirical reality in almost all economic and business disciplines. There are three major reasons for this increasing attention for factual data and econometric models.

- Economic theory often does not give the quantitative information that is needed in practical decision making.
- Relevant quantitative data are available in many economic and business disciplines.
- Realistic models can easily be solved by modern econometric techniques to support everyday decisions of economists and business managers.

In areas such as finance and marketing, quantitative data (on price movements, sales patterns, and so on) are collected on a regular basis, weekly, daily, or even every split second. Much information is also available in microeconomics (for instance, on the spending behaviour of households). Econometric techniques have been developed to deal with all such kinds of information.

Econometrics is an interdisciplinary field. It uses insights from economics and business in selecting the relevant variables and models, it uses computer-science methods to collect the data and to solve econometric models, and it uses statistics and mathematics to develop econometric methods that are appropriate for the data and the problem at hand. The interplay of these disciplines in econometric modelling is summarized in Exhibit 0.1.

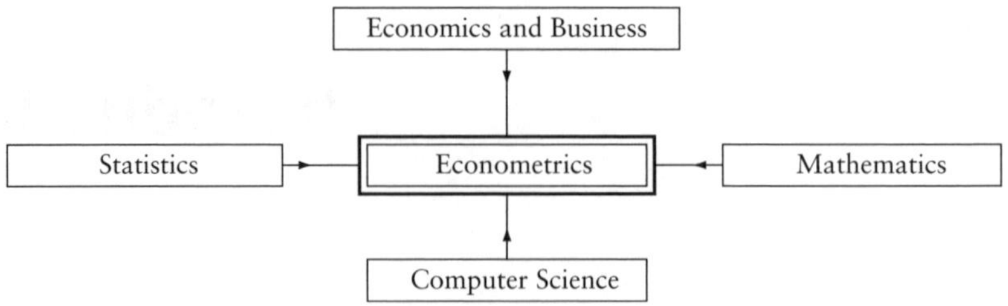

Exhibit 0.1 Econometrics as an interdisciplinary field

Purpose of the book

The book gives the student a sound introduction into modern econometrics. The student obtains a solid understanding of econometric methods and an active training in econometrics as it is applied in practice. This involves the following steps.

1. *Question.* Formulate the economic and business questions of central interest.
2. *Information.* Collect and analyse relevant statistical data.
3. *Model.* Formulate and estimate an appropriate econometric model.
4. *Analysis.* Analyse the empirical validity of the model.
5. *Application.* Apply the model to answer the questions and to support decisions.

These steps are shown in Exhibit 0.2. Steps 1, 2, and 5 form the applied part of econometrics and steps 3 and 4 the theoretical part. Although econometric models and methods differ according to the nature of the data and the type of questions under investigation, all applications share this common structure.

As the title of the book indicates, it discusses econometric methods (tools for the formulation, estimation, and diagnostic analysis of econometric models) that are motivated and illustrated by applications in business and economics (to answer practical questions that support decisions by means of relevant quantitative data information). The book provides a rigorous and self-contained treatment of the central methods in econometrics in Chapters 1–5. This provides the student with a thorough understanding of the central ideas and their practical application. Two major application areas are discussed in more detail—that is, models for individual economic behaviour (with applications in marketing and microeconomics) in Chapter 6 and models for time series data (with applications in finance and macroeconomics) in Chapter 7.

The book is selective, as its purpose is not to give an exhaustive encyclopaedic overview of all available methods. The thorough treatment of the selected topics not only enables the student to apply these methods successfully in practice; it also gives an excellent preparation for understanding and applying econometrics in other application areas.

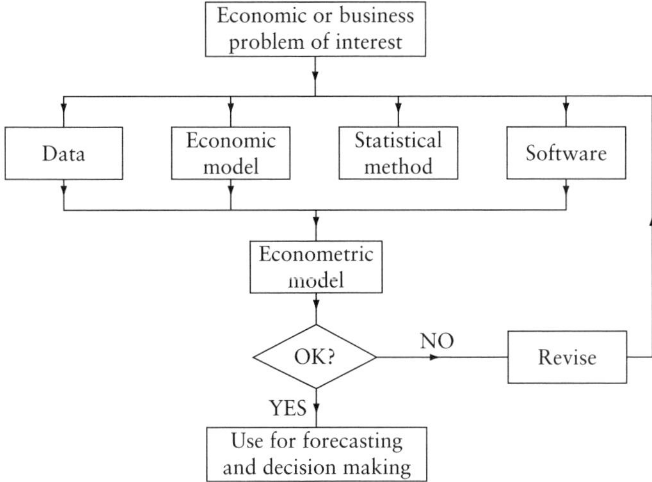

Exhibit 0.2 Econometric modelling

Characteristic features of the book

Over recent years several new and refreshing econometric textbooks have appeared. Our book is characterized by its thorough discussion of core econometrics motivated and illustrated by real-world examples from a broad range of economic and business applications. In all our discussions of econometric topics we stress the interplay between real-world applications and the practical need for econometric models and methods. This twofold serious attention for methods and applications is also reflected in the extensive exercise sections at the end of each chapter, which contain both theory questions and empirical questions. Some characteristic features of the book follow.

- The book is of an academic level and it is rigorous and self-contained. Preliminary topics in statistics are reviewed in Chapter 1, and required matrix methods are summarized in Appendix A.
- The book gives a sound and solid training in basic econometric thinking and working in Chapters 1–5, the basis of all econometric work.
- The book presents deep coverage of key econometric topics rather than exhaustive coverage of all topics. Two major application areas are discussed in detail—namely, choice data (in marketing and microeconomics) in Chapter 6 and time series data (in finance and international economics) in Chapter 7.
- All topics are treated thoroughly and are illustrated with up-to-date real-world applications to solve practical economic and business questions.
- The book stimulates active learning by the examples, which show econometrics as it works in practice, and by extensive exercise sets. The theory and simulation exercises provide a deeper understanding, and the

empirical examples provide the student with a working understanding and hands-on experience with econometrics in a broad set of real-world economic and business data sets.

- The book can be used both in more advanced (graduate) courses and in introductory applied (undergraduate) courses, because the more theoretical parts can easily be skipped without loss of coherence of the exposition.
- The book supports the learning process in many ways (see the Guide to the Book for further details).

Target audience and required background knowledge

As stated in the Preface, the book is directed at anyone interested in obtaining a solid understanding and active working knowledge of econometrics as it works in the daily practice of business and economics.

The book builds up econometrics from its fundamentals in simple models to modern applied research. It does not require any prior course in econometrics. The book assumes a good working knowledge of basic statistics and some knowledge of matrix algebra. An overview of the required statistical concepts and methods is given in Chapter 1, which is meant as a refresher and which requires a preliminary course in statistics. The required matrix methods are summarized in Appendix A.

Brief contents of the book

The contents can be split into four parts: Chapter 1 (review of statistics), Chapters 2–4 (model building), Chapter 5 (model evaluation), and Chapters 6 and 7 (selected application areas).

Chapter 1 reviews the statistical material needed in later chapters. It serves as a refresher for students with some background in statistics. The chapter discusses the concepts of random variables and probability distributions and methods of estimation and testing.

Basic econometric methods are described in Chapters 2–4. Chapters 2 and 3 treat a relatively simple yet very useful model that is much applied in practice — namely, the linear regression model. The statistical properties of the least squares method are derived under a number of assumptions. The multiple regression model in Chapter 3 is formulated in matrix terms, because this enables an analysis by means of transparent and efficient matrix methods (summarized in Appendix A). In Chapter 4 we extend Chapters 2 and 3 to non-linear models and we discuss the maximum likelihood method and the generalized method of moments. The corresponding estimates can be computed by numerical optimization procedures and statistical properties can be derived under the assumption that a sufficient number of observations are available.

Chapter 5 discusses a set of diagnostic instruments that play a crucial role in obtaining empirically valid models. Along with tests on the correct specification of the regression model, we also discuss several extensions that are often used in practice. This involves, for instance, models with varying parameters, the use of dummy variables in regression models, robust estimation methods, instrumental variables methods, models for changing variance (heteroskedasticity), and dynamic models (serial correlation). Our motivation for the extensive treatment of these topics is that regression is by far the most popular method for applied work. The applied researcher should check whether the required regression assumptions are valid and, if some of the assumptions are not acceptable, he or she should know how to proceed to improve the model. Chapter 5 forms the bridge between the basic methods in Chapters 2–4 and the application areas discussed in Chapters 6 and 7. The sections of Chapter 5 can be read independently from each other, and it is not necessary to study all Chapter 5 before proceeding with the applications in Chapters 6 and 7.

In Chapters 6 and 7 we discuss econometric models and methods for two major application areas — namely, discrete choice models and models for time series data. These two chapters can be read independently from each other. Chapter 6 concerns individual decision making with applications in marketing and microeconomics. We discuss logit and probit models and models for truncated and censored data and duration data. Chapter 7 discusses univariate and multivariate time series methods, which find many applications in finance and international economics. We pay special attention to forecasting methods and to the modelling of trends and changing variance in time series.

The book discusses core econometrics and selected key topics. It does not provide an exhaustive treatment of all econometric topics — for instance, we discuss only parametric models and we pay hardly any attention to non-parametric or semi-parametric techniques. Our models are relatively simple and can be optimized in a relatively straightforward way — for example, we do not discuss optimization by means of simulation techniques. We pay only brief attention to panel data models, simultaneous equation models, and models with latent variables, to mention a few. Also some aspects of significant practical importance, such as data collection and report writing, are not discussed in the book. As stated before, our purpose is to give the student a profound working knowledge of core econometrics needed in good applied work. We are confident that, with the views and skills acquired after studying the book, the student will be well prepared to master the other topics on his or her own.

Study advice

In Chapters 2–4 it is assumed that the student understands the statistical topics of Chapter 1. The student can check this by means of the keyword list at the end of Chapter 1. The subsections of Chapters 2–4 contain references to the corresponding relevant parts of Chapter 1, so that statistical topics that are unknown or partly forgotten can be studied along the way. The further reading list in Chapter 1 contains references to statistical textbooks that treat the required topics in much more detail. Chapter 2 is a fundamental chapter that prepares the ground for all later chapters. It discusses the concept of an econometric model and the role of random variables and it treats statistical methods for estimation, testing, and forecasting. This is extended in Chapters 3 and 4 to more general models and methods. The best way to study is as follows.

1. Understand the general nature of the practical question of interest.
2. Understand the model formulation and the main methods of analysis, including the model properties and assumptions.
3. Train the practical understanding by working through the text examples (preferably using a software package to analyse the example data sets).
4. Obtain active understanding by doing the empirical exercises, using EViews or a similar econometric software package (the data sets can be downloaded from the web site of the book).
5. Deepen the understanding by studying the theoretical parts in the main text and by doing the theory and simulation exercises. This provides a better understanding of the various model assumptions that are needed to justify the econometric analysis.

After studying Chapters 2–4 in this way, the student is ready for more. Several options for further chapters are open, and we refer to the teaching suggestions and Exhibit 0.3 below for further details.

Teaching suggestions

The book is suitable both for advanced undergraduate courses and for introductory graduate courses in business and economics programmes. In applied courses much of the underlying theory can easily be skipped without loss of coherence of the exposition (by skipping the theory sections in the text and the theory and simulation exercises). In more advanced courses, the theory parts in the text clarify the structure of econometric models and the role of model assumptions needed to justify econometric methods. The book can be used in three types of courses.

- *Advanced Undergraduate Course on Econometrics*. Focus on Chapters 2–4, and possibly on parts of Chapter 5. This material can be covered in one trimester or semester.
- *Introductory Graduate Course on Econometrics*. Focus on Chapters 2–4, and on some parts of Chapters 5–7. This requires one or two trimesters or

semesters, depending on the background of the students and on the desired coverage of topics.

- *Intermediate Graduate Course on Econometrics*. Focus on Chapters 5–7, and possibly on some parts of Chapters 3–4 as background material. This requires one or two trimesters or semesters, depending on background and coverage.

In all cases it is necessary for the students to understand the statistical topics reviewed in Chapter 1. The keyword list at the end of Chapter 1 summarizes the required topics and the further reading contains references to textbooks that treat the topics in more detail. Chapters 2–4 treat concepts and methods that are of fundamental importance in all econometric work. This material can be skipped only if the students have already followed an introductory course in econometrics. Chapters 5–7 can be treated selectively, according to the purposes of the course. Exhibit 0.3 gives an overview of the dependencies between topics. For instance, if the aim is to cover GARCH models (Section 7.4) in the course, then it will be necessary to include the main topics of Sections 5.4–5.6 and 7.1–7.3.

The book is suitable for different entrance levels. Students starting in econometrics will have to begin at the top of Exhibit 0.3, and the basics (Chapters 2–4 and possibly selected parts of Chapter 5) can be treated in one trimester or semester. Students with a preliminary background in econometrics can start somewhere lower in Exhibit 0.3 and select different routes to applied econometric areas, which can be treated thoroughly in one trimester or semester.

The book leaves the teacher a lot of freedom to select topics, as long as the logical dependencies between the topics in Exhibit 0.3 are respected. Our advice is always to pay particular attention to the motivation of models and methods; the examples in the main text serve this purpose, and the students can get further training by working on the empirical exercises at the end of each chapter. In our own programme in Rotterdam, the students work together in groups of four to perform small-scale projects on the computer by analysing data sets from the book. We advise teachers always to include the following three ingredients in the course.

- *Lectures* on the book material to discuss econometric models and methods with illustrative text examples, preferably supported by a lecture room PC to show the data and selected results of the analysis.
- *Computer sessions* treating selected empirical and simulation exercises to get hands-on experience by applying econometrics to real-world economic and business data.
- *Exercise sessions* treating selected theory exercises to train mathematical and statistical econometric methods on paper.

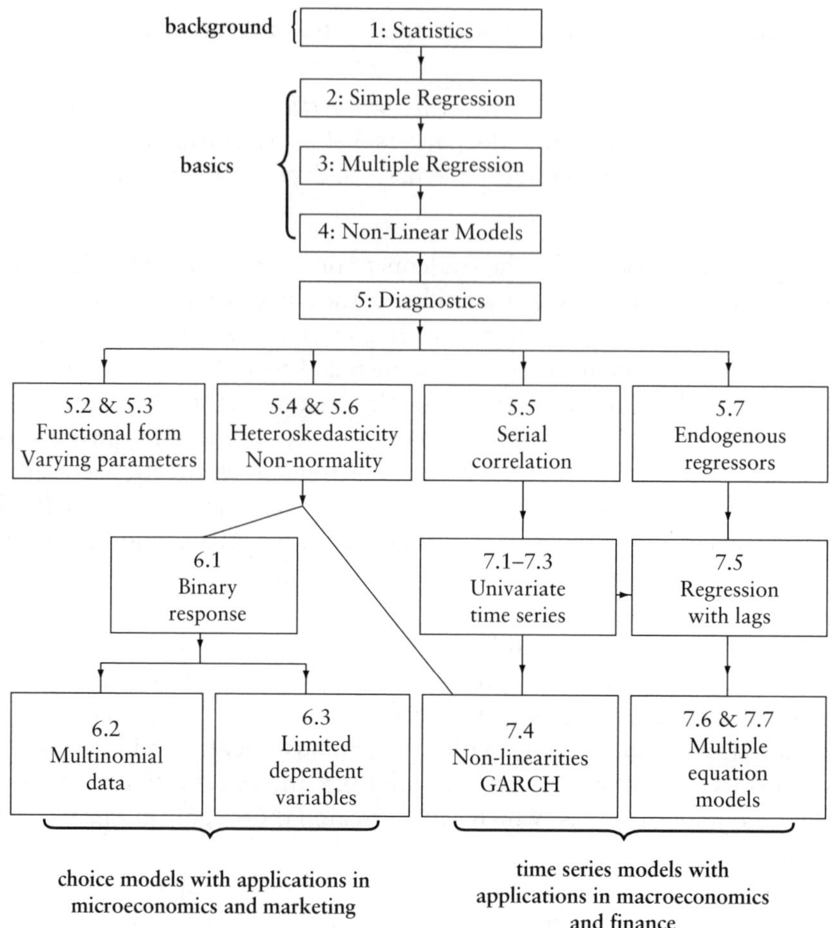

Exhibit 0.3 Book structure

Some possible course structures

For all courses we suggest reserving approximately the following relative time load for the students' different activities:

- 20 per cent for attending lectures;
- 20 per cent for computer sessions (10 per cent guided, 10 per cent group work);
- 20 per cent for exercise sessions (10 per cent guided, 10 per cent individual work);
- 40 per cent self-study of the book, including preparation of computer and paper exercises.

For instance, in a twelve-week trimester course with a student load of 120 hours, this corresponds basically to two lecture hours per week and two exercise hours per week (half on computer and half on paper). Taking this type of course as our basis, we mention the following possible course structures for students without previous knowledge of econometrics.

(*a*) *Introductory Econometrics* (single course on basics, 120 hours): Chapters 2–4.

(*b*) *Introductory Econometrics* (extended course on basics, 180 hours): Chapters 2–5.

(*c*) *Econometrics with Applications in Marketing and Microeconomics* (double course, 240 hours): Chapters 2–4, Sections 5.4 and 5.6, and Chapter 6.

(*d*) *Econometrics with Applications in Finance and Macroeconomics* (double course, 240 hours): Chapters 2–4, Sections 5.4–5.7, and Chapter 7.

(*e*) *Econometrics with Applications* (double course, 240 hours): Chapters 2–4 and Sections 5.4–5.7, 6.1 and 6.2, 7.1–7.6.

(*f*) *Econometrics with Applications* (extended double course, 300 hours): Chapters 2–7.

The book is also suitable for a second course, after an undergraduate introductory course in econometrics. The book can then be used as a graduate text by skipping most of Chapters 2–4 and choosing one of the options (*c*)–(*f*) above.

(*c*2) *Econometric Applications in Marketing and Microeconomics* (single course, 120 hours): parts of Chapters 3 and 4, Sections 5.4 and 5.6, and Chapter 6.

(*d*2) *Econometric Applications in Finance and Macroeconomics* (single course, 120 hours): parts of Chapters 3 and 4, Sections 5.4–5.7, and Chapter 7.

(*e*2) *Econometric Applications* (single course, 120 hours): parts of Chapters 3 and 4 and Sections 5.4–5.7, 6.1 and 6.2, 7.1–7.6.

(*f*2) *Econometric Applications* (extended or double course, 180–240 hours): parts of Chapters 3 and 4, and Chapters 5–7.

In Rotterdam we use the book for undergraduate students in econometrics and we basically follow option (*e*) above. This is a second-year course for students who followed introductory courses in statistics and linear algebra in their first year. We also use the book for first-year graduate students in economics in Rotterdam and Amsterdam. Here we also basically follow option (*e*), but, as the course load is 160 hours, we focus on practical aspects and skip most of the theory parts.

1

Review of Statistics

A first step in the econometric analysis of economic data is to get an idea of the general pattern of the data. Graphs and sample statistics such as mean, standard deviation, and correlation are helpful tools. In general, economic data are partly systematic and partly random. This motivates the use of random variables and distribution functions to describe the data. This chapter pays special attention to data obtained by random sampling, where the observations are mutually independent and come from an underlying population with fixed mean and standard deviation. The concepts and methods for this relatively simple situation form the building blocks for dealing with more complex models that are relevant in practice and that will be discussed in later chapters.

1.1 Descriptive statistics

1.1.1 Data graphs

☞ First used in Section 2.1.1.

Data

Economic data sets may contain a large number of observations for many variables. For instance, financial investors can analyse the patterns of many individual stocks traded on the stock exchange; marketing departments get very detailed information on individual buyers from scanner data; and national authorities have detailed data on import and export flows for many kinds of goods. It is often useful to summarize the information in some way. In this section we discuss some simple graphical methods and in the next section some summary statistics.

Example 1.1: **Student Learning**

As an example, we consider in this chapter a data set on student learning. These data were analysed by J. S. Butler, T. A. Finegan, and J. J. Siegfried in their paper 'Does More Calculus Improve Student Learning in Intermediate Micro- and Macroeconomic Theory' (*Journal of Applied Econometrics*, 13/2 (1998), 185–202). This data set contains information on 609 students of the Vanderbilt University in the USA. In total there are thirty-one observed variables, so that the data set consists of 18,879 numbers. In this chapter we restrict the attention to four variables — that is, FGPA (the overall grade point average at the end of the freshman year, on a scale from 0 to 4), SATM (the score on the SAT mathematics test divided by 100, on a scale from 0 to 10), SATV (the score on the SAT verbal test divided by 100, on a scale from 0 to 10), and FEM (with value 1 for females and value 0 for males). A part of the corresponding data table is given in Exhibit 1.1. (We refer readers to Appendix B for further details on the data sets and corresponding notation of variables used in this book.)

Graphs

The data can be visualized by means of various possible graphs. A *histogram* of a variable consists of a two-dimensional plot. On the horizontal axis, the

Obs.	FGPA	SATM	SATV	FEM
1	3.125	6.6	5.5	0
2	1.500	6.7	7.0	0
3	2.430	6.6	6.0	0
4	3.293	6.1	5.4	1
5	2.456	6.5	5.2	0
6	2.806	6.5	5.4	1
7	2.455	6.2	4.8	0
8	3.168	6.2	4.6	0
9	2.145	4.3	4.7	0
10	2.700	6.1	5.6	0
11	3.296	5.8	5.1	1
12	2.240	6.4	5.5	1
⋮	⋮	⋮	⋮	⋮
608	2.996	6.6	6.5	1
609	2.133	6.9	6.2	0

Exhibit 1.1 Student Learning (Example 1.1)

Part of data on 609 students on FGPA (grade point average at the end of the freshman year), SATM (scaled score on SAT mathematics test), SATV (scaled score on SAT verbal test), and FEM (1 for females, 0 for males).

outcome range of the variable is divided into a number of intervals. In the case of intervals with equal width, the value on the vertical axis measures the number of observations of the variable that have an outcome in that particular interval. The *sample cumulative distribution function* (SCDF) is represented by a two-dimensional plot with the outcome range of the variable on the horizontal axis. For each value v in this range, the function value on the vertical axis is the fraction of the observations with an outcome smaller than or equal to v. To investigate possible dependencies between two variables one can draw a *scatter diagram*. One variable is measured along the horizontal axis, the other along the vertical axis, and the plot consists of points representing the joint outcomes of the two variables that occur in the data set.

Example 1.2: **Student Learning (continued)**

Exhibit 1.2 shows histograms (a, c, e) and SCDFs (b, d, f) of the variables FGPA, SATM, and SATV, and scatter diagrams of FGPA against SATM (g), FGPA against SATV (h), and SATM against SATV (i). The scatter diagrams show much variation in the outcomes. In this example it is not so easy to determine from the diagrams whether the variables are related or not.

More than two variables

For three variables it is possible to plot a three-dimensional scatter cloud, but such graphs are often difficult to read. Instead three two-dimensional scatter

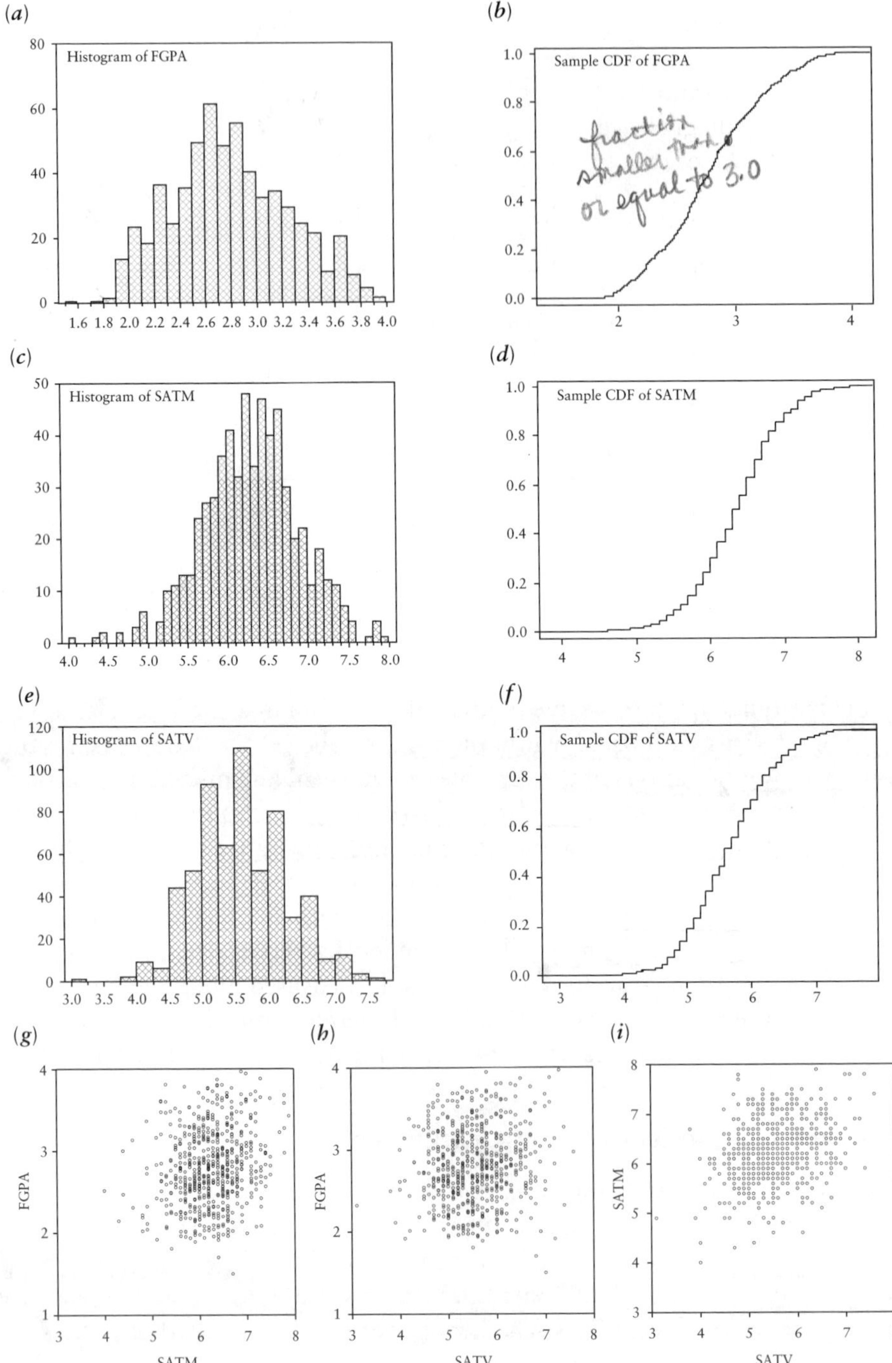

Exhibit 1.2 Student Learning (Example 1.2)

Histograms and sample cumulative distribution functions of FGPA ((*a*)–(*b*)), SATM ((*c*)–(*d*)), and SATV ((*e*)–(*f*)), and scatter diagrams ((*g*)–(*i*)) of FGPA against SATM (*g*), of FGPA against SATV (*h*), and of SATM against SATV (*i*).

diagrams can be used. The same idea applies for four or more variables. It should be realized, however, that histograms and scatter diagrams provide only partial information if there are more than one or two variables. The shape of these diagrams will partly be determined by the neglected variables, but the influence of these variables cannot be detected from the diagrams. In Example 1.3 we give an illustration of the possible effects of such a partial analysis. One of the main purposes of econometric modelling is to disentangle the mutual dependencies between a group of variables.

Example 1.3: **Student Learning (continued)**

The histogram of FGPA shows a spread that is partly caused by differences in the learning abilities of the students. If they had differed less on their SATM and SATV scores, then they would possibly have had less different FGPA outcomes. As an example, Exhibit 1.3 shows histograms for two groups of students. The 609 students are ordered by their average SAT score, defined as SATA = 0.5(SATM + SATV). The first group consists of students with low or high SATA scores (rank numbers between 1 and 100 and between 510 and 609) and the second group with middle SATA scores (rank numbers between 205 and 405). As expected, the spread of the FGPA scores in the first group (see Exhibit 1.3 (*a*)) is somewhat larger than that in the second group (see Exhibit 1.3 (*b*)). The difference is small, though, and cannot easily be detected from Exhibit 1.3. In the next section we describe numerical measures for the spread of data that will simplify the comparison.

In general, the variation in one variable may be partly caused by another variable, which of course cannot be detected from a histogram.

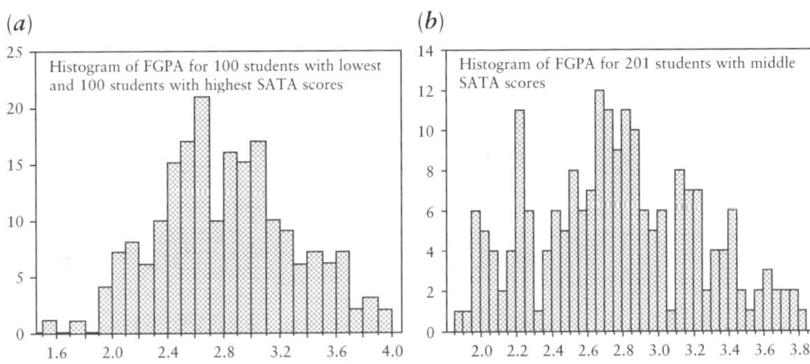

Exhibit 1.3 Student Learning (Example 1.3)

Histograms for FGPA scores of students with 100 lowest and 100 highest average SATA scores (*a*) and for FGPA scores of 201 students with middle average SATA scores (*b*).

☞ Exercises: E: 1.11c, 1.13a, d.

1.1.2 Sample statistics

☞ First used in Section 2.1.1; uses Appendix A.1.

Sample moments

For a single variable, the shape of the histogram is often summarized by measures of location and dispersion. Let the number of observations be denoted by n and let the observed data points be denoted by y_i with $i = 1, 2, \cdots, n$. The *sample mean* is defined as the average of the observations over the sample — that is,

$$\bar{y} = \frac{1}{n} \sum_{i=1}^{n} y_i. \tag{1.1}$$

The sample mean is also called the first sample moment. An alternative measure of location is the *median*. Let the observations be ordered so that $y_i \le y_{i+1}$ for $i = 1, \cdots, n-1$; then the median is equal to the middle observation $y_{\frac{n+1}{2}}$ if n is odd and equal to $\frac{1}{2}(y_{\frac{n}{2}} + y_{\frac{n}{2}+1})$ if n is even.

A measure of dispersion is the second sample moment, defined by

$$m_2 = \frac{1}{n} \sum_{i=1}^{n} (y_i - \bar{y})^2. \tag{1.2}$$

For reasons that will become clear later (see Example 1.9), in practice one often uses a slightly different measure of dispersion defined by

$$s^2 = \frac{1}{n-1} \sum_{i=1}^{n} (y_i - \bar{y})^2. \tag{1.3}$$

This is called the *sample variance*, and the *sample standard deviation* is equal to s (the square root of s^2). The rth (centred) sample moment is defined by $m_r = \frac{1}{n}\sum_{i=1}^{n}(y_i - \bar{y})^r$ and the standardized rth moment is defined by m_r/s^r. In particular, m_3/s^3 is called the *skewness* and m_4/s^4 the *kurtosis*. The skewness is zero if the observations are distributed symmetrically around the mean, negative if the left tail is longer than the right tail, and positive if the right tail is longer than the left tail. If the mean is larger (smaller) than the median, this is an indication of positive (negative) skewness. The kurtosis measures the relative amount of observations in the tails as compared to the amount of observations around the mean. The kurtosis is larger for distributions with fatter tails.

Example 1.4: **Student Learning (continued)**

XM101STU

Exhibit 1.4 shows the sample mean, median, standard deviation, skewness, and kurtosis of the data on FGPA (*a*), SATM (*b*), and SATV (*c*). Both the mean and the median of the SATV scores are lower than those of the SATM scores. The tails of the SATM scores are somewhat fatter on the left, and the mean is smaller than the median. The tails of FGPA and SATV are somewhat fatter on the right, and the mean exceeds the median. Of the three variables, FGPA has the smallest kurtosis, as it contains somewhat less observations in the tails as compared to SATM and SATV. Further, returning to our discussion in Example 1.3 on two groups of students, we measure the spread of the FGPA scores in both groups by the sample standard deviation. The first group of students (with either low or high average SATA scores) has $s = 0.485$, whereas the second group of students (with middle average SATA scores) has $s = 0.449$. As expected, the standard deviation is larger for the first, more heterogeneous group of students, but the difference is small.

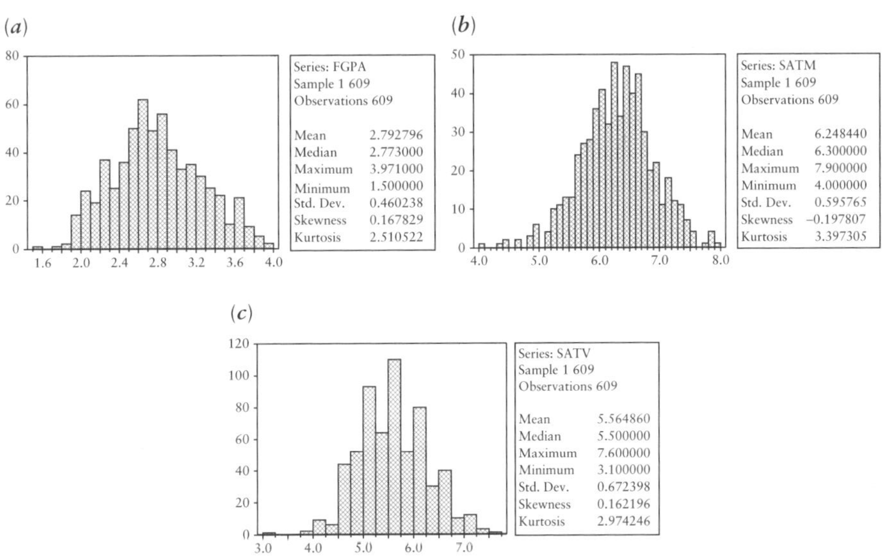

Exhibit 1.4 Student Learning (Example 1.4)

Summary statistics of FGPA (*a*), SATM (*b*), and SATV (*c*) of 609 students.

Covariance and correlation

The *dependence* between two variables can be measured by their common variation. Let the two variables be denoted by x and y, with observed outcome pairs (x_i, y_i) for $i = 1, \cdots, n$. Let $\bar{x}$ be the sample mean of x and $\bar{y}$ that of y, and let s_x be the standard deviation of x and s_y that of y. Then the *sample covariance* between x and y is defined by

$$s_{xy} = \frac{1}{n-1}\sum_{i=1}^{n}(x_i - \bar{x})(y_i - \bar{y}) \tag{1.4}$$

and the *sample correlation coefficient* by

$$r_{xy} = \frac{s_{xy}}{s_x s_y}. \tag{1.5}$$

When two variables are positively correlated, this means that, on average, relatively large observations on x correspond with relatively large observations on y and small observations on x with small observations on y. The correlation coefficient r_{xy} always lies between -1 and $+1$ and it does not depend on the units of measurement (see Exercise 1.1).

In the case of two or more variables, the first and second moments can be summarized in vectors and matrices (see Appendix A for an overview of results on matrices that are used in this book). When there are p variables, the corresponding sample means can be collected in a $p \times 1$ vector, and when s_{jk} denotes the sample covariance between the jth and kth variable, then the $p \times p$ *sample covariance matrix* S is defined by

$$S = \begin{pmatrix} s_{11} & s_{12} & \cdots & s_{1p} \\ s_{21} & s_{22} & \cdots & s_{2p} \\ \vdots & \vdots & \vdots & \vdots \\ s_{p1} & s_{p2} & \cdots & s_{pp} \end{pmatrix}.$$

The diagonal elements are the sample variances of the variables. The sample correlation coefficients are given by $r_{jk} = s_{jk}/\sqrt{s_{jj}s_{kk}}$, and the $p \times p$ *correlation matrix* is defined similar to the covariance matrix by replacing the elements s_{jk} by r_{jk}. As $r_{jj} = 1$, this matrix contains unit elements on the diagonal.

Example 1.5: **Student Learning (continued)**

Exhibit 1.5 shows the sample covariance matrix (Panel 1) and the sample correlation matrix (Panel 2) for the four variables FGPA, SATM, SATV, and FEM. The covariances are scale dependent. The correlations do not depend on the scale of measurement and are therefore easier to interpret. The scores on FGPA, SATM, and SATV are all positively correlated. As compared with males, females have on average somewhat better scores on FGPA and SATV and somewhat lower scores on SATM.

Panel 1	FGPA	SATM	SATV	FEM
FGPA	0.211	0.053	0.028	0.040
SATM	0.053	0.354	0.115	−0.047
SATV	0.028	0.115	0.451	0.011
FEM	0.040	−0.047	0.011	0.237

Panel 2	FGPA	SATM	SATV	FEM
FGPA	1.000	0.195	0.092	0.176
SATM	0.195	1.000	0.288	−0.163
SATV	0.092	0.288	1.000	0.034
FEM	0.176	−0.163	0.034	1.000

Exhibit 1.5 Student Learning (Example 1.5)

Sample covariances (Panel 1) and sample correlations (Panel 2) of FGPA, SATM, SATV, and FEM for 609 students.

☞ **Exercises:** T: 1.1; E: **1.11a, b, d, 1.13b.**

1.2 Random variables

1.2.1 Single random variables

☞ First used in Section 2.2.3.

Randomness

The observed outcomes of variables are often partly systematic and partly random. One of the causes of randomness is sampling. For instance, the data on student scores in Example 1.1 concern a group of 609 students. Other data would have been obtained if another group of students (at another university or in another year) had been observed.

Distributions

A variable y is called *random* if, prior to observation, its outcome cannot be predicted with certainty. The uncertainty about the outcome is described by a *probability distribution*. If the set of possible outcome values is discrete, say $V = \{v_1, v_2, \cdots\}$, then the distribution is given by the set of probabilities $p_i = P[y = v_i]$, the probability of the outcome v_i. These probabilities have the properties that $p_i \geq 0$ and $\sum p_i = 1$. The corresponding *cumulative distribution function* (CDF) is given by $F(v) = P[y \leq v] = \sum_{\{i;v_i \leq v\}} p_i$, which is a non-decreasing function with $\lim_{v \to -\infty} F(v) = 0$ and $\lim_{v \to \infty} F(v) = 1$. If the set of possible outcomes is continuous, then the CDF is again defined by $P[y \leq v]$, and, if this function is differentiable, then the derivative $f(v) = \frac{dF(v)}{dv}$ is called the probability *density function*. It has the properties that $f(v) \geq 0$ and $\int_{-\infty}^{\infty} f(v)dv = 1$. Interval probabilities are obtained from $P[a < y \leq b] = F(b) - F(a) = \int_a^b f(v)dv$.

The CDF of a random variable is also called the population CDF, as it represents the distribution of all the possible outcomes of the variable. For observed data $y_1, \cdots, y_n$, the *sample cumulative distribution function* (SCDF) of Section 1.1.1 is given by $F_s(v) = \frac{1}{n}$ (number of $y_i \leq v$).

Remarks on notation

Some remarks on notation are in order. In statistics one usually denotes random variables by capital letters (for instance, Y) and observed outcomes of random variables by lower-case letters (for instance, y). However, in econometrics it is usual to reserve capital letters for matrices only, so that the notation in econometrics differs from the usual one in statistics. To avoid confusion with the notation in later chapters, we use lower-case letters (like y) to denote random variables. Further, for the random variable y we denoted the set of possible outcome values by V and the observed outcome by v. However, in a sample of n observed data, the observations are usually denoted by y_i with $i = 1, \cdots, n$. Prior to observation, the outcome of y_i can be seen as a random variable. After observation, the realized values could be denoted by say $v(y_i)$, the outcome value of the random variable y_i, but for simplicity of notation we write y_i both for the random variables and for the observed outcomes. This notation is common in econometrics. We will make sure that it is always clear from the context what the notation y_i means, a random variable (prior to observation) or an observed outcome.

Mean

The distribution of a random variable can be summarized by measures of location and dispersion. If y has a discrete distribution, then the (population) *mean* is defined as a weighted average over the outcome set V with weights equal to the probabilities p_i of the different outcomes v_i—that is,

$$\mu = E[y] = \sum v_i p_i \qquad (1.6)$$

The operator E that determines the mean of a random variable is also called the *expectation* operator. Note that the sample mean is obtained when the SCDF is used. When y has a continuous distribution with density function f, the mean is defined by

$$\mu = E[y] = \int v f(v) dv \qquad (1.7)$$

(if an integral runs from $-\infty$ to $+\infty$, we delete this for simplicity of notation).

Variance

The (population) *variance* is defined as the mean of $(y - \mu)^2$. For a discrete distribution this gives

$$\sigma^2 = E[(y - \mu)^2] = \sum (v_i - \mu)^2 p_i \qquad (1.8)$$

and for a continuous distribution

$$\sigma^2 = E[(y-\mu)^2] = \int (v-\mu)^2 f(v)dv. \qquad (1.9)$$

The *standard deviation* σ is the square root of the variance σ^2. The mean is also called the (population) first moment, and the variance the second (centred) moment.

Higher moments

The rth centred moment is defined as the mean of $(y-\mu)^r$ —that is (in the case of a continuous distribution), $\mu_r = E[(y-\mu)^r] = \int (v-\mu)^r f(v)dv$. The standardized rth moment is given by μ_r/σ^r. For $r = 3$ this gives the skewness and for $r = 4$ the kurtosis. The sample moments of Section 1.1.2 are obtained by replacing the CDF by the sample CDF. Although the sample moments always exist, this is not always the case for the population moments. If $E[|y-\mu|^c] < \infty$, then all the moments μ_r with $r \leq c$ exist. In particular, a random variable with a finite variance also has a finite mean.

Transformations of random variables

Now we consider the statistical properties of functions of random variables. If y is a random variable and g is a given function, then $z = g(y)$ is also a random variable. Suppose that g is invertible with inverse function $y = h(z)$. If y has a discrete distribution with outcomes $\{v_1, v_2, \cdots\}$, then z also has a discrete distribution with outcomes $\{w_i = g(v_i), i = 1, 2, \cdots\}$ and probabilities $P[z = w_i] = P[y = h(w_i)] = p_i$. When y has a continuous distribution with density function f_y and h is differentiable with derivative h', then z has density function

$$f_z(w) = f_y(h(w))|h'(w)| \qquad (1.10)$$

(see Exercise 1.3 for a special case). The mean of z is given by $E[z] = E[g(y)] = \sum p_i g(v_i)$ in the discrete case and by $E[g(y)] = \int f(v)g(v)dv$ in the continuous case. If g is linear, so that $g(y) = ay + b$ for some constants a and b, then $E[ay+b] = aE[y] + b$, but if g is not linear then $E[g(y)] \neq g(E[y])$ in general.

☞ Exercises: T: 1.3a.

1.2.2 Joint random variables

☞ First used in Section 3.1.4; uses Appendix A.2–A.4.

Two random variables

When there are two or more variables of interest, one can consider their joint distribution. For instance, the data set on 609 student scores in Example 1.1 contains the outcomes of mathematics and verbal tests. The uncertainty about the pair of outcomes (x, y) on these two tests can be described by a joint probability distribution. If the sets of possible outcome values for x and y are both discrete, say $V = \{v_1, v_2, \cdots\}$ and $W = \{w_1, w_2, \cdots\}$, then the joint distribution is given by the set of probabilities $p_{ij} = P[x = v_i, y = w_j]$. The corresponding cumulative distribution function (CDF) is given by $F(v, w) = P[x \leq v, y \leq w] = \sum_{\{(i,j); v_i \leq v, w_j \leq w\}} p_{ij}$. If the sets of possible outcomes are continuous, then the CDF is also defined as $F(v, w) = P[x \leq v, y \leq w]$, and if the second derivative of this function exists, then the corresponding density function is defined by $f(v, w) = \frac{\partial^2 F(v,w)}{\partial v \partial w}$. The density function has the properties $f(v, w) \geq 0$ and $\int\int f(v, w)dvdw = 1$, and every function with these two properties describes a joint probability distribution.

When the joint distribution of x and y is given, the individual distributions of x and y (also called the *marginal distributions*) can be derived. The CDF F_y of y is obtained from the CDF of (x, y) by $F_y(w) = P[y \leq w] = F(\infty, w)$. For continuous distributions, the corresponding densities are related by $f_y(w) = \int f(v, w)dv$. Mean and variance of x and y can also be determined in this way—for instance, $\mu_y = \int f_y(w)wdw = \int\int f(v, w)wdvdw$.

Covariance and correlation

The *covariance* between x and y is defined (for continuous distributions) by

$$\text{cov}(x, y) = E[(x - \mu_x)(y - \mu_y)] = \int\int (v - \mu_x)(w - \mu_y)f(v, w)dvdw.$$

The *correlation coefficient* between x and y is defined by

$$\rho_{xy} = \frac{\text{cov}(x, y)}{\sigma_x \sigma_y} \qquad (1.11)$$

where σ_x and σ_y are the standard deviations of x and y. The two random variables are called *uncorrelated* if $\rho_{xy} = 0$. This is equivalent to the condition that $E[xy] = E[x]E[y]$.

Conditional distribution

The *conditional distribution* of y for given value of x is defined as follows. When the distribution is discrete and the outcome $x = v_i$ is given, with $P[x = v_i] > 0$, the conditional probabilities are given by

$$P[y = w_j|x = v_i] = \frac{P[x = v_i, y = w_j]}{P[x = v_i]} = \frac{p_{ij}}{\sum_j p_{ij}}. \tag{1.12}$$

This gives a new distribution for y, as the conditional probabilities sum up (over j) to unity. For continuous distributions, the conditional density $f_{y|x=v}$ is defined as follows (for values of v for which $f_x(v) > 0$).

$$f_{y|x=v}(w) = \frac{f(v, w)}{f_x(v)} = \frac{f(v, w)}{\int f(v, w)dw}. \tag{1.13}$$

Conditional mean and variance

The conditional mean and variance of y for given value $x = v$ are the mean and variance with respect to the corresponding conditional distribution. For instance, for continuous distributions the *conditional expectation* is given by

$$E[y|x = v] = \int f_{y|x=v}(w)wdw = \frac{\int f(v, w)wdw}{\int f(v, w)dw}. \tag{1.14}$$

Note that the conditional expectation is a function of v, so that $E[y|x]$ is a random variable with density $f_x(v)$. The mean of this conditional expectation is (see Exercise 1.2)

$$E[E[y|x]] = \int E[y|x = v]f_x(v)dv = E[y]. \tag{1.15}$$

In words, the conditional expectation $E[y|x]$ (a function of the random variable x) has the same mean as the unconditional random variable y. The conditional variance $\text{var}(y|x = v)$ is the variance of y with respect to the conditional distribution $f_{y|x=v}$. This variance depends on the value of v, and the mean of this variance satisfies (see Exercise 1.2)

$$E[\text{var}(y|x)] = \int f_x(v)\left(\int f_{y|x=v}(w)(w - E[y|x = v])^2 dw\right)dv \leq \text{var}(y). \tag{1.16}$$

So, on average, the conditional random variable $y|x = v$ has a smaller variance than the unconditional random variable y. That is, knowledge of the outcome of the variable x helps to reduce the uncertainty about the outcome of y. This is an important motivation for econometric models with explanatory variables. In such models, the differences in the outcomes of the variable of interest (y) are explained in terms of underlying factors (x) that influence this variable. For instance, the variation in the FGPA scores of students can be related to differences in student abilities as measured by their SATM and SATV scores. Such econometric models with explanatory variables are further discussed in Chapters 2 and 3.

Independence

A special situation occurs when the conditional distribution is always equal to the marginal distribution. For discrete distributions this is the case if and only if $P[y = w_j|x = v_i] = P[y = w_j]$ for all (v_i, w_j)—that is,

$$P[x = v_i, y = w_j] = P[x = v_i]P[y = w_j]$$

for all (v_i, w_j). For continuous distributions the condition is that

$$f(v, w) = f_x(v)f_y(w)$$

for all (v, w). If this holds true, then x and y are called *independent* random variables. So in this case the joint distribution is simply obtained by multiplying the marginal distributions with each other. It follows from (1.12) and (1.13) that for independent variables $E[y|x = v] = E[y]$ is independent of the value v of x. Further, for independent variables there holds $\text{var}(y|x = v) = \text{var}(y)$ for all values $x = v$, and hence also $E[\text{var}(y|x)] = \text{var}(y)$. If x and y are independent, then the uncertainty of y is not diminished by conditioning on x, that is, the variable x does not contain information on the variable y. Independent variables are always uncorrelated, but the reverse does not hold true (see Exercise 1.2).

More than two random variables

The definitions of joint, marginal, and conditional distributions are easily extended to the case of more than two random variables. For instance, the joint density function of p continuous random variables $y_1, \cdots, y_p$ is a function $f(v_1, \cdots, v_p)$ that is non-negative everywhere and that integrates (over the p-dimensional space) to unity. Means, variances, and covariances can be determined from the joint distribution. For instance, for continuous distributions the covariance between y_1 (with mean μ_1) and y_2 (with mean μ_2) is given by $\sigma_{12} = \text{cov}(y_1, y_2) = E[(y_1 - \mu_1)(y_2 - \mu_2)]$—that is, the p-dimensional integral

$$\sigma_{12} = \int \cdots \int (v_1 - \mu_1)(v_2 - \mu_2) f(v_1, \cdots, v_p) dv_1 \cdots dv_p.$$

These variances and covariances can be collected in the $p \times p$ symmetric covariance matrix

$$\Sigma = \begin{pmatrix} \text{var}(y_1) & \text{cov}(y_1, y_2) & \cdots & \text{cov}(y_1, y_p) \\ \text{cov}(y_2, y_1) & \text{var}(y_2) & \cdots & \text{cov}(y_2, y_p) \\ \vdots & \vdots & \vdots & \vdots \\ \text{cov}(y_p, y_1) & \text{cov}(y_p, y_2) & \cdots & \text{var}(y_p) \end{pmatrix} = \begin{pmatrix} \sigma_{11} & \sigma_{12} & \cdots & \sigma_{1p} \\ \sigma_{21} & \sigma_{22} & \cdots & \sigma_{2p} \\ \vdots & \vdots & \vdots & \vdots \\ \sigma_{p1} & \sigma_{p2} & \cdots & \sigma_{pp} \end{pmatrix}.$$

The correlation matrix is defined in an analogous way, replacing the elements σ_{ij} in Σ by the correlations $\rho_{ij} = \frac{\sigma_{ij}}{\sqrt{\sigma_{ii}\sigma_{jj}}}$. The variables are independent if and only if the joint density f is equal to the product of the p individual marginal densities f_{y_i} of y_i—that is,

$$f(v_1, \cdots, v_p) = \prod_{j=1}^{p} f_{y_i}(v_i).$$

Independent variables are uncorrelated, so that in this case $\sigma_{ij} = 0$ for all $i \neq j$. If in addition all the variables have equal variance $\sigma_{ii} = \sigma^2$, then the covariance matrix is of the form $\Sigma = \sigma^2 I$ where I is the $p \times p$ identity matrix.

Linear transformations of random variables

For our statistical analysis in later chapters we now consider the distribution of functions of random variables. For linear transformations the first and second moments of the transformed variables can be determined in a simple way. Let $y_1, \cdots, y_p$ be given random variables and let $z = b + \sum_{j=1}^{p} a_j y_j$ be a linear function of these random variables, for given (non-random) constants b and a_j. Then the mean and variance of z are given by

$$E[z] = b + \sum_{j=1}^{p} a_j E[y_j], \quad \text{var}(z) = \sum_{j=1}^{p} \sum_{k=1}^{p} a_j a_k \text{cov}(y_j, y_k)$$

where $\text{cov}(y_j, y_j) = \text{var}(y_j)$. When the random variables y_j are uncorrelated and have identical mean μ and variance σ^2, it follows that $E[z] = b + \mu \sum a_j$ and $\text{var}(z) = \sigma^2 \sum a_j^2$. For instance, when $\bar{y} = \frac{1}{n}\sum_{i=1}^{n} y_i$ is the mean of n uncorrelated random variables, then it follows that

$$E[\bar{y}] = \mu, \quad \text{var}(\bar{y}) = \frac{\sigma^2}{n}. \tag{1.17}$$

Now let $z = Ay + b$ be a vector of random variables, where A and b are a given (non-random) $m \times p$ matrix and $m \times 1$ vector respectively and where y is a $p \times 1$ vector of random variables with vector of means μ and covariance matrix Σ. Then the vector of means of z and its covariance matrix Σ_z are given by

$$E[z] = A\mu + b, \quad \Sigma_z = A\Sigma A' \tag{1.18}$$

where A' denotes the transpose of the matrix A (see Exercise 1.3).

Arbitrary transformations of random variables

The distribution of non-linear functions of random variables can be derived from the joint distribution of these variables. For example, let $z_1 = g_1(y_1, y_2)$ and $z_2 = g_2(y_1, y_2)$ be two functions of given random variables y_1 and y_2. Suppose that the mapping $g = (g_1, g_2)$ from (y_1, y_2) to (z_1, z_2) is invertible with inverse $h = (h_1, h_2)$. The Jacobian J is defined as the determinant of the 2×2 matrix with elements $\frac{\partial h_i(z)}{\partial z_j}$ for $i, j = 1, 2$. For discrete random variables, the distribution of (z_1, z_2) is given by $P[z_1 = w_1, z_2 = w_2] = P[y_1 = v_1, y_2 = v_2]$ where $(v_1, v_2) = h(w_1, w_2)$. For continuous random variables, the joint density function of (z_1, z_2) is given by

$$f_{z_1,z_2}(w_1, w_2) = f_{y_1,y_2}(h(w_1, w_2))\,|J(w_1, w_2)|. \tag{1.19}$$

That is, the density of (y_1, y_2) should be evaluated at the point $h(w_1, w_2)$ and the result should be multiplied by the absolute value of the Jacobian J in (w_1, w_2). This result generalizes to the case of more than two functions. When $z_1 = g_1(y_1)$ and $z_2 = g_2(y_2)$ and y_1 and y_2 are independent, then it follows from (1.10) and (1.19) that z_1 and z_2 are also independent (see Exercise 1.3). So in this case z_1 and z_2 are uncorrelated, so that $E[g_1(y_1)g_2(y_2)] = E[g_1(y_1)]E[g_2(y_2)]$ when y_1 and y_2 are independent. If y_1 and y_2 are uncorrelated but not independent, then z_1 and z_2 are in general not uncorrelated, unless g_1 and g_2 are linear functions (see Exercise 1.3).

XM101STU

Example 1.6: **Student Learning (continued)**

As an illustration we consider again the data on student learning of 609 students. In this example we will consider these 609 students as the population of interest and we will analyse the effect of the gender of the student by conditioning with respect to this variable. Exhibit 1.6 shows histograms of the variable FGPA for male students (*a*) and female students (*b*) separately. Of the 609 students in the population, 373 are male and 236 are female. The two means and standard deviations in Exhibit 1.6 are conditional on the gender of the student and they differ in the two groups. The mean and standard deviation of the unconditional (full) population are in Exhibit 1.4 (*a*). The relations (1.15) and (1.16) (more precisely, their analogue for the current discrete distributions) are easily verified, using the fact that the conditioning variable x in this case is a discrete random variable with probabilities 373/609 for a male and 236/609 for a female student. Indeed, denoting males by M and females by F, we can verify the result (1.15) for the mean because

$$E[E[y|x]] = \frac{373}{609}E[y|M] + \frac{236}{609}E[y|F] = \frac{373}{609}(2.728) + \frac{236}{609}(2.895) = 2.793 = E[y],$$

and we can verify the result (1.16) for the variance because

$$E[\text{var}(y|x)] = \frac{373}{609}\text{var}(y|M) + \frac{236}{609}\text{var}(y|F) = \frac{373}{609}(0.441)^2 + \frac{236}{609}(0.472)^2 = 0.206 < 0.212 = (0.460)^2 = \text{var}(y).$$

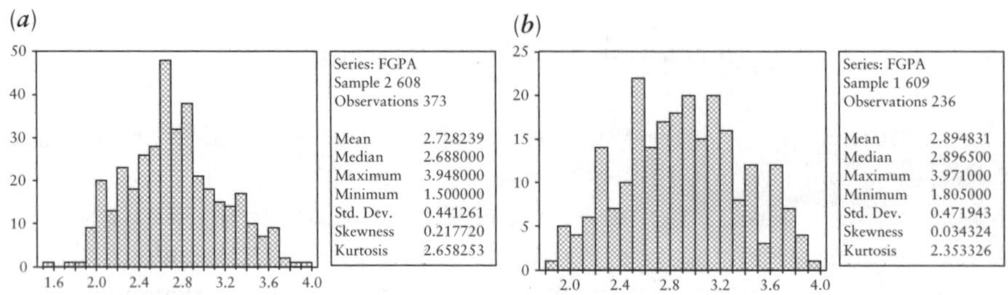

Exhibit 1.6 Student Learning (Example 1.6)

Histograms for FGPA scores of males (*a*) and females (*b*).

☞ Exercises: T: 1.2, 1.3**b–d**; E: 1.11e.

1.2.3 **Probability distributions**

☞ First used in Section 2.2.3; uses Appendix A.2–A.5.

Bernoulli distribution and binomial distribution

In this section we consider some probability distributions that are often used in econometrics. The simplest case of a random variable is a discrete variable y with only two possible outcomes, denoted by 0 (failure) and 1 (success). The probability distribution is completely described by the probability $p = P[y = 1]$ of success, as $P[y = 0] = 1 - P[y = 1] = 1 - p$. This is called the *Bernoulli distribution*. It has mean p and variance $p(1 - p)$ (see Exercise 1.4). Suppose that the n random variables y_i, $i = 1, \cdots, n$, are independent and identically distributed, with the Bernoulli distribution with probability p of success. Let $y = \sum_{i=1}^{n} y_i$ be the total number of successes. The set of possible outcome values of y is $V = \{0, 1, \cdots, n\}$, and

$$P[y = v] = \binom{n}{v} p^v (1 - p)^{n-v}$$

(the first term, 'n over v', is the number of possibilities to locate v successes over n positions). This is called the *binomial distribution*. It has mean np and variance $np(1 - p)$ (see Exercise 1.4).

Normal distribution

The *normal distribution* is the most widely used distribution in econometrics. One of the reasons is the central limit theorem (to be discussed later), which says that many distributions can be approximated by normal distributions if the sample size is large enough. Another reason is that the normal distribution has a number of attractive properties. A normal random variable is a continuous random variable that can take on any value. Its density function is given by

$$f(v) = \frac{1}{\sigma\sqrt{2\pi}} e^{-\frac{1}{2\sigma^2}(v-\mu)^2}, \quad -\infty < v < \infty. \tag{1.20}$$

This function is symmetric around μ and it is shaped like a bell (see Exhibit 1.7). The distribution contains two *parameters*, μ and σ^2, and the distribution is denoted by $N(\mu, \sigma^2)$. This notation is motivated by the fact that μ is the mean and σ^2 the variance of this distribution. The third and fourth moments of this distribution are 0 and $3\sigma^4$ respectively (see Exercise 1.4), so that the skewness is zero and the kurtosis is equal to 3. As the normal distribution is

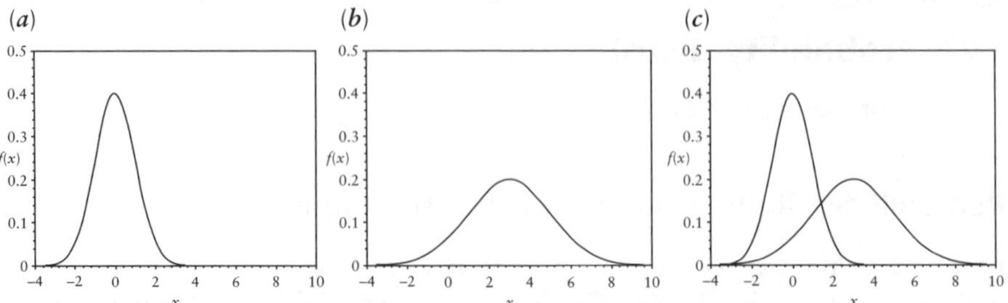

Exhibit 1.7 Normal distribution

Density functions of two normal distributions, one with mean 0 and variance 1 (*a*) and another one with mean 3 and variance 2 (*b*). The plot in (*c*) shows the two densities in one diagram for comparison.

often taken as a benchmark, distributions with kurtosis larger than three are called fat-tailed.

When y follows the $\mathrm{N}(\mu, \sigma^2)$ distribution, this is written as $y \sim \mathrm{N}(\mu, \sigma^2)$. The result in (1.10) implies (see Exercise 1.4) that the linear function $ay + b$ (with a and b fixed numbers) is also normally distributed and

$$ay + b \sim \mathrm{N}(a\mu + b, a^2\sigma^2).$$

In particular, when y is standardized by subtracting its mean and dividing by its standard deviation, it follows that

$$\frac{y - \mu}{\sigma} \sim \mathrm{N}(0, 1).$$

This is called the *standard normal distribution*. Its density function is denoted by ϕ, so that

$$\phi(v) = \frac{1}{\sqrt{2\pi}} e^{-\frac{1}{2}v^2},$$

and the cumulative distribution function is denoted by $\Phi(v) = \int_{-\infty}^{v} \phi(u)du$.

Multivariate normal distribution

In later chapters we will often consider jointly normally distributed random variables. It is very convenient to use matrix notation to describe the multivariate normal distribution. The *multivariate normal distribution* of n random variables has density function

$$f(v) = \frac{1}{(2\pi)^{n/2}(\det(\Sigma))^{1/2}} e^{-\frac{1}{2}(v-\mu)'\Sigma^{-1}(v-\mu)}, \tag{1.21}$$

where v denotes the n variables, μ is an $n \times 1$ vector, and Σ an $n \times n$ positive definite matrix ($\det(\Sigma)$ denotes the determinant of this matrix). This notation is motivated by the fact that this distribution has mean μ and covariance matrix Σ. The distribution is written as $\mathrm{N}(\mu, \Sigma)$.

Properties of the multivariate normal distribution

Marginal and conditional distributions of normal distributions remain normal. If $y \sim \mathrm{N}(\mu, \Sigma)$, then the ith component y_i is also normally distributed and $y_i \sim \mathrm{N}(\mu_i, \sigma_{ii})$ where μ_i is the ith component of μ and σ_{ii} the ith diagonal element of Σ. For the conditional distribution, let the vector y be split in two parts (with sub-vectors y_1 and y_2) and let the mean vector and covariance matrix be split accordingly. Then the conditional distribution of y_1, given that $y_2 = v_2$, is given by

$$y_1|y_2 = v_2 \sim \mathrm{N}\left(\mu_1 + \Sigma_{12}\Sigma_{22}^{-1}(v_2 - \mu_2), \Sigma_{11} - \Sigma_{12}\Sigma_{22}^{-1}\Sigma_{21}\right) \tag{1.22}$$

where Σ_{11} is the covariance matrix of y_1, Σ_{22} is the covariance matrix of y_2, Σ_{12} is the covariance matrix between y_1 and y_2, and Σ_{21} is the transpose of Σ_{12} (see Exercise 1.4). Note that the conditional variance does not depend on the value of y_2 in this case. That is, knowledge of the value of y_2 always leads to the same reduction in the uncertainty of y_1 if the variables are normally distributed.

For arbitrary random variables, independence implies being uncorrelated but not the other way round. However, when jointly normally distributed variables are uncorrelated, so that Σ is a diagonal matrix, then the joint density (1.21) reduces to the product of the individual densities. That is, when normally distributed variables are uncorrelated they are also independent. This also follows from (1.22), as $\Sigma_{12} = 0$ if y_1 and y_2 are uncorrelated so that the conditional distribution of y_1 becomes independent of y_2.

If the $n \times 1$ vector y is normally distributed, then the linear function $Ay + b$ (with A a given $m \times n$ matrix and b a given $m \times 1$ vector) is also normally distributed and (see Exercise 1.4)

$$Ay + b \sim \mathrm{N}(A\mu + b, A\Sigma A'). \tag{1.23}$$

Chi-square (χ^2) distribution

In the rest of this section we consider the distribution of some other functions of normally distributed random variables that will be used later on. Suppose that $y_1, \cdots, y_n$ are independent and all follow the standard normal distribution. Then the distribution of the sum of squares $\sum_{i=1}^{n} y_i^2$ is called the *chi-square distribution* with n degrees of freedom, denoted by $\chi^2(n)$. This can be generalized to other quadratic forms in the vector of random variables $y = (y_1, \cdots, y_n)'$. Let A be an $n \times n$ matrix that is symmetric (that is, $A' = A$), idempotent (that is, $A^2 = A$) and that has rank r (which in this case is equal to the trace of A—that is, the sum of the n diagonal elements of this matrix). Then

$$y'Ay \sim \chi^2(r) \tag{1.24}$$

(see Exercise 1.5). For a symmetric idempotent matrix A there always holds that $y'Ay \geq 0$. The density of the $\chi^2(r)$ distribution is given by

$$\begin{aligned} f(v) &\propto v^{\frac{r}{2}-1}e^{-\frac{v}{2}}, \; v \geq 0, \\ &= 0, \qquad\quad v < 0, \end{aligned} \tag{1.25}$$

where $\propto$ means 'proportional to'—that is, $f(v)$ is equal to the given expression up to a scaling constant that does not depend on v. This scaling constant is defined by the condition that $\int f(v)dv = 1$. The $\chi^2(r)$ distribution has mean r and variance $2r$ (see Exercise 1.5). Exhibit 1.8 shows chi-square densities for varying degrees of freedom. The distributions have a positive skewness.

Student *t*-distribution

If $y_1 \sim \mathrm{N}(0, 1)$ and $y_2 \sim \chi^2(r)$ and y_1 and y_2 are independently distributed, then the distribution of $y_1/\sqrt{y_2/r}$ is called the *Student t-distribution* with r degrees of freedom, written as

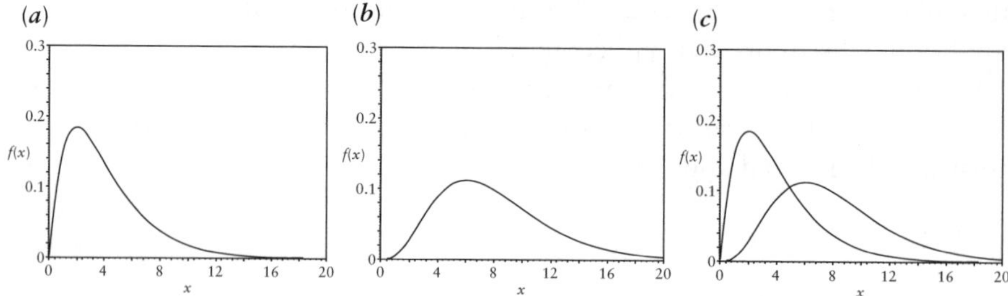

Exhibit 1.8 χ^2-distribution

Density functions of two chi-squared distributions, one with 4 degrees of freedom (*a*) and another one with 8 degrees of freedom (*b*). The plot in (*c*) shows the two densities in one diagram for comparison.

$$\frac{y_1}{\sqrt{y_2/r}} \sim t(r). \tag{1.26}$$

Up to a scaling constant, the density of the $t(r)$-distribution is given by

$$f(v) \propto \frac{1}{\left(1+\frac{v^2}{r}\right)^{\frac{r+1}{2}}}, \qquad -\infty < v < \infty. \tag{1.27}$$

For $r > 1$ the mean is equal to 0, and for $r > 2$ the variance is equal to $\frac{r}{r-2}$. Exhibit 1.9 shows t-distributions for varying degrees of freedom. These distributions are symmetric (the skewness is zero) and have fat tails (the kurtosis is larger than three). For $r = 1$, the $t(1)$-distribution (also called the Cauchy distribution) has density

$$f(v) = \frac{1}{\pi(1+v^2)}.$$

This distribution is so much dispersed that it does not have finite moments—in particular, the mean and the variance do not exist. On the other hand, if $r \to \infty$ then the $t(r)$ density converges to the standard normal density (see Exercise 1.5).

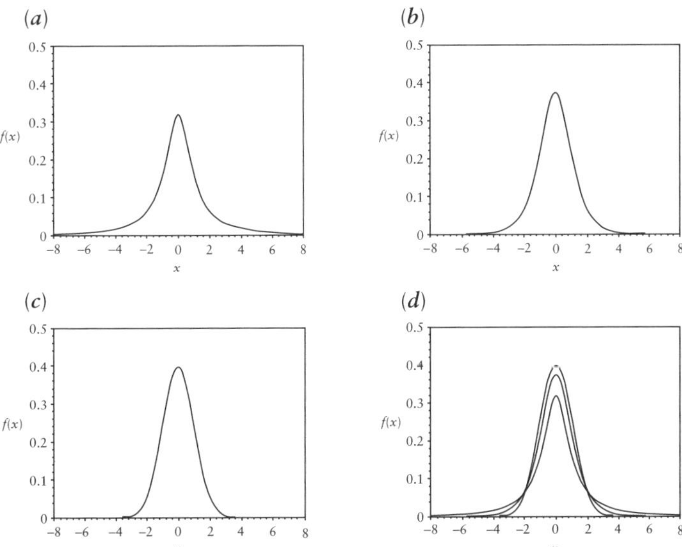

Exhibit 1.9 *t*-distribution

Density functions of three t-distributions, with number of degrees of freedom equal to 1 (*a*), 4 (*b*), and 100 (*c*). The plot in (*d*) shows the three densities in one diagram for comparison. For more degrees of freedom the density is more concentrated around zero and has less fat tails.

F-distribution

If $y_1 \sim \chi^2(r_1)$ and $y_2 \sim \chi^2(r_2)$ and y_1 and y_2 are independently distributed, then the distribution of $(y_1/r_1)/(y_2/r_2)$ is called the *F-distribution* with r_1 and r_2 degrees of freedom. This is written as

$$\frac{y_1/r_1}{y_2/r_2} \sim F(r_1, r_2). \tag{1.28}$$

Exhibit 1.10 shows F-distributions for varying degrees of freedom. If $r_2 \to \infty$, then $r_1 \cdot F(r_1, r_2)$ converges to the $\chi^2(r_1)$-distribution (see Exercise 1.5).

Conditions for independence

In connection with the t- and F-distributions, it is for later purposes helpful to use simple checks for the independence between linear and quadratic forms of normally distributed random variables. Let $y \sim \mathrm{N}(0, I)$ be a vector

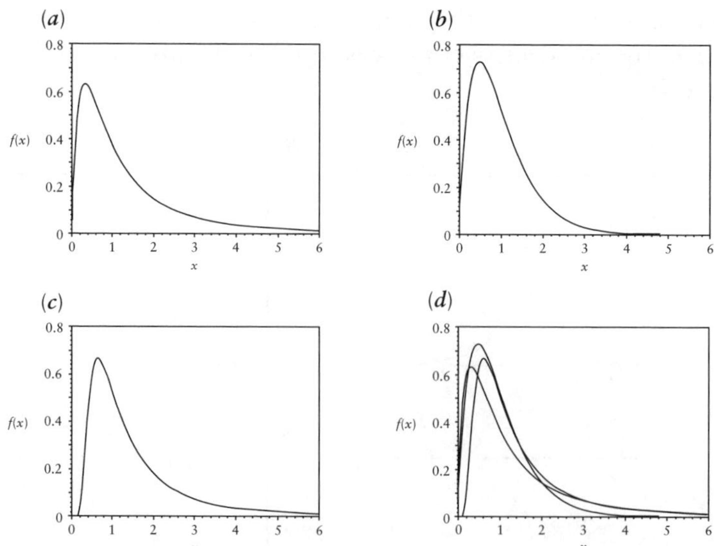

Exhibit 1.10 *F*-distribution

Density functions of three F-distributions, with numbers of degrees of freedom in numerator and denominator respectively (4,4) (*a*), (4,100) (*b*), and (100,4) (*c*). The plot in (*d*) shows the three densities in one diagram for comparison. For more degrees of freedom in the numerator the density shifts more to the right, and for more degrees of freedom in the denominator it gets less fat tails.

of independent standard normal random variables, and let $z_0 = Ay$, $z_1 = y'Q_1y$ and $z_2 = y'Q_2y$ be respectively a linear form (with A an $m \times n$ matrix) and two quadratic forms (with Q_1 and Q_2 symmetric and idempotent $n \times n$ matrices). The two following results are left as an exercise (see Exercise 1.5). The random variables z_0 (with normal distribution) and z_1 (with χ^2-distribution) are independently distributed if

$$AQ_1 = 0, \tag{1.29}$$

and the random variables z_1 and z_2 (both with χ^2-distribution) are independently distributed if

$$Q_1Q_2 = 0. \tag{1.30}$$

☞ **Exercises:** T: 1.4, 1.5**a–e**, 1.13**f**, 1.15**b**.

1.2.4 Normal random samples

☞ First used in Section 2.2.3; uses Appendix A.2–A.5.

To illustrate some of the foregoing results, we consider the situation where $y_1, \cdots, y_n$ are normally and independently distributed random variables with the same mean μ and variance σ^2. This is written as

$$y_i \sim \text{NID}(\mu, \sigma^2), \quad i = 1, \cdots, n, \tag{1.31}$$

where NID stands for normally and independently distributed. One also says that $y_1, \cdots, y_n$ is a *random sample* (that is, with independent observations) from $\text{N}(\mu, \sigma^2)$. We are interested in the distributions of the sample mean $\overline{y}$ in (1.1) and of the sample variance s^2 in (1.3).

Sample mean

Let y be the $n \times 1$ vector with elements $y_1, \cdots, y_n$, so that

$$y \sim \text{N}(\mu\imath, \sigma^2 I) \tag{1.32}$$

where ι is the $n \times 1$ vector with all its elements equal to 1 and I is the $n \times n$ identity matrix. The sample mean is given by $\bar{y} = \frac{1}{n}\sum y_i = \frac{1}{n}\iota' y$, and as $\iota'\iota = n$ and $\iota' I \iota = n$ it follows from (1.23) that

$$\bar{y} = \frac{1}{n}\iota' y \sim \mathrm{N}\left(\mu, \frac{\sigma^2}{n}\right). \tag{1.33}$$

Sample variance

To derive the distribution of the sample variance s^2, let

$$z_i = (y_i - \mu)/\sigma$$

so that $z_i \sim \mathrm{NID}(0, 1)$. Then s^2 can be written as $s^2 = \frac{1}{n-1}\sum_{i=1}^n (y_i - \bar{y})^2 = \frac{\sigma^2}{n-1}\sum_{i=1}^n (z_i - \bar{z})^2$. Now $\sum_{i=1}^n (z_i - \bar{z})^2 = z' M z$ where the matrix M is defined by

$$M = I - \frac{1}{n}\iota\iota'. \tag{1.34}$$

The matrix M is symmetric and idempotent and has rank $n - 1$ (see Exercise 1.5). Then (1.24) shows that

$$\frac{(n-1)s^2}{\sigma^2} = z' M z \sim \chi^2(n-1). \tag{1.35}$$

The *t*-value of the sample mean

Using the notation introduced above, the result (1.33) implies that $\frac{1}{\sqrt{n}}\iota' z = \sqrt{n}\bar{z} = \sqrt{n}(\bar{y} - \mu)/\sigma \sim \mathrm{N}(0, 1)$. As $\iota' M = 0$, it follows from (1.29) that this standard normal random variable is independent from the $\chi^2(n-1)$ random variable in (1.35). By definition,

$$\frac{\sqrt{n}(\bar{y} - \mu)/\sigma}{\sqrt{\frac{(n-1)s^2}{\sigma^2}/(n-1)}} = \frac{\bar{y} - \mu}{s/\sqrt{n}} \sim t(n-1). \tag{1.36}$$

Note that the random variable in (1.36) has a distribution that does not depend on σ^2. Such a random variable (in this case, a function of the data and of the parameter μ that does not depend on σ^2) is called *pivotal* for the parameter μ. The result in (1.35) shows that $(n-1)s^2/\sigma^2$ is pivotal for σ^2. Such pivotal random variables are helpful in statistical hypothesis testing, as will become clear in Section 1.4.2.

If it is assumed that the population mean is zero—that is, $\mu = 0$—it follows that

$$\frac{\bar{y}}{s/\sqrt{n}} \sim t(n-1). \tag{1.37}$$

This is called the *t-value* of the sample mean.

☞ Exercises: T: 1.5f, 1.15a.

1.3 Parameter estimation

1.3.1 Estimation methods

☞ First used in Section 4.3.2; uses Appendix A.1, A.7.

Concepts: model, parameters, estimator, estimate

Suppose that n available observations y_i, $i = 1, \cdots, n$ are considered as the outcomes of random variables with a joint probability distribution $f_\theta(y_1, \cdots, y_n)$. Here it is assumed that the general shape of the distribution is known up to one or more unknown *parameters* that are denoted by θ. A set of distributions $\{f_\theta; \theta \in \Theta\}$ is called a *model* for the observations—that is, it specifies the general shape of the distribution together with a set Θ of possible values for the unknown parameters. The numerical values of θ are unknown, but they can be estimated from the observed data. Estimated parameters are denoted by $\hat{\theta}$. As an example, if it is supposed that $y_i \sim \text{NID}(\mu, \sigma^2)$ with unknown mean μ and variance σ^2, then the joint distribution is given by (1.32) with parameter set $\Theta = \{(\mu, \sigma^2); \sigma^2 > 0\}$. The parameters can be estimated, for instance, by the sample mean and sample variance discussed in Section 1.1.2.

In this section we consider a general framework for estimation with corresponding concepts and terminology that are used throughout this book. In all that follows, we use the notation y_i both for the random variable and for the observed outcome of this variable. A *statistic* is any given function $g(y_1, \cdots, y_n)$—that is, any numerical expression that can be evaluated from the observed data alone. An *estimator* is a statistic that is used to make a guess about an unknown parameter. For instance, the sample mean (1.1) is a statistic that provides an intuitively appealing guess for the population mean μ. An estimator is a random variable, as it depends on the random variables y_i. For given observed outcomes, the resulting numerical value of the estimator is called the *estimate* of the parameter. So an estimator is a numerical expression in terms of random variables, and an estimate is a number. Several methods have been developed for the construction of estimators. We discuss three methods—that is, the method of moments, least squares, and maximum likelihood.

The method of moments

In the *method of moments* the parameters are estimated as follows. Suppose that θ contains k unknown parameters. The specified model (that is, the general shape of the distribution) implies expressions for the population moments in terms of θ. If k such moments are selected, the parameters θ can in general be solved from these k expressions. Now θ is estimated by replacing the unknown population moments by the corresponding sample moments. An advantage of this method is that it is based on moments that are often easy to compute. However, it should be noted that the obtained estimates depend on the chosen moments.

Example 1.7: **Student Learning (continued)**

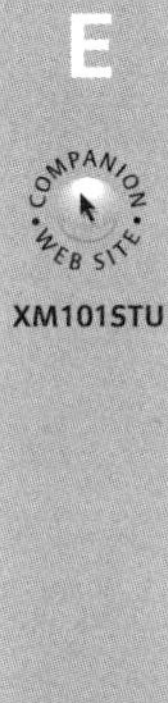

To illustrate the method of moments, we consider the FGPA scores of 609 students in Example 1.4. Summary statistics of this sample are in Exhibit 1.4 (*a*), with mean $\bar{y} = 2.793$, standard deviation $s = 0.460$, skewness 0.168, and kurtosis 2.511. So the first moment is 2.793 and the second moment (1.2) is equal to $m_2 = (n-1)s^2/n = 0.211$. If these scores are assumed to be normally and independently distributed with mean μ and variance σ^2, the first and second moment of this distribution are equal to μ and σ^2 respectively. So the moment estimates then become $\hat{\mu} = 2.793$ and $\hat{\sigma}^2 = 0.211$.

Instead of using the second moment, one could also use the fourth moment to estimate σ^2. The fourth (population) moment of the normal distribution is equal to $3\sigma^4$. To obtain the fourth sample moment from the summary statistics presented in Exhibit 1.4 (*a*), note that the sample kurtosis (K) is equal to the sample fourth moment (m_4) divided by s^4, so that $m_4 = Ks^4 = 2.511(0.460)^4 = 0.112$. The estimate $\hat{\sigma}^2$ of the parameter σ^2 based on the fourth moment is then obtained by solving $3\hat{\sigma}^4 = m_4$, so that $\hat{\sigma}^2 = \sqrt{m_4/3} = 0.194$. The above results show that the parameter estimates may be different for different choices of the fitted moments. In our example the differences are not so large.

Least squares

Another method for parameter estimation is *least squares*. We illustrate this method for the estimation of the population mean from a random sample $y_1, \cdots, y_n$ of a distribution with unknown mean μ and unknown variance σ^2. Let $\varepsilon_i = y_i - \mu$; then it follows that $\varepsilon_1, \cdots, \varepsilon_n$ are identically and independently distributed with mean zero and variance σ^2. This is written as $\varepsilon_i \sim \mathrm{IID}(0, \sigma^2)$. The model can now be written as

$$y_i = \mu + \varepsilon_i, \quad \varepsilon_i \sim \mathrm{IID}(0, \sigma^2). \tag{1.38}$$

The least squares estimate is that value of μ that minimizes the sum of squared errors

$$S(\mu) = \sum_{i=1}^{n} (y_i - \mu)^2.$$

Taking the first derivative of this expression with respect to μ gives the first order condition $\sum_{i=1}^{n} (y_i - \mu) = 0$. Solving this for μ gives the least squares estimate $\hat{\mu} = \bar{y}$, the sample mean. Instead of least squares one could also use other estimation criteria—for instance, the sum of absolute errors

$$\sum_{i=1}^{n} |y_i - \mu|.$$

As will be seen in Chapter 5 (see Exercise 5.14), the resulting estimate is then given by the median of the sample.

Maximum likelihood

A third method is that of *maximum likelihood*. Recall that a model consists of a set $\{f_\theta; \theta \in \Theta\}$ of joint probability distributions for $y_1, \cdots, y_n$. For every value of θ, the distribution gives a certain value $f_\theta(y_1, \cdots, y_n)$ for the given observations. When seen as a function of θ, this is called the *likelihood function*, denoted by $L(\theta)$, so that

$$L(\theta) = f_\theta(y_1, \cdots, y_n), \quad \theta \in \Theta. \tag{1.39}$$

For discrete distributions, the likelihood $L(\theta)$ is equal to the probability (with respect to the distribution f_θ) of the actually observed outcome. The maximum likelihood estimate is the value of θ for which this probability is maximal (over the set of all possible values $\theta \in \Theta$). Similarly, for a continuous distribution the maximum likelihood estimate is obtained by maximizing $L(\theta)$ over Θ.

An attractive property of this method is that the estimates are *invariant* with respect to changes in the definition of the parameters. Suppose that, instead of using the parameters θ, one describes the model in terms of another set of parameters ψ and that the relation between ψ and θ is given by $\psi = h(\theta)$, where h is an invertible transformation. The model is then expressed as the set of distributions $\{\tilde{f}_\psi; \psi \in \Psi\}$ where $\tilde{f}_\psi = f_{h^{-1}(\psi)}$ and $\Psi = h(\Theta)$. Let $\hat{\theta}$ and $\hat{\psi}$ be the maximum likelihood estimates of θ and ψ respectively. Then $\hat{\theta} = h^{-1}(\hat{\psi})$, so that both models lead to the same estimated probability distribution (see Exercise 1.6 for an example).

Comparison of methods

In later chapters we will encounter each of the above three estimation methods. It depends on the application which method is the most attractive one. If the model is expressed in terms of an equation, as in (1.38), then least squares is intuitively appealing, as it optimizes the fit of the model with respect to the observations. Sometimes the model is expressed in terms of moment conditions, so that the method of moments is a natural way of estimation.

Least squares and the method of moments are both based on the idea of minimizing a distance function. For least squares the distance is measured directly in terms of the observed data, whereas for the method of moments the distance is measured in terms of the sample and population moments. The maximum likelihood method, on the other hand, is based not on a distance function, but on the likelihood function that expresses the likelihood or 'credibility' of parameter values with respect to the observed data. This method can be applied only if the joint probability distribution of the observations is completely specified so that the likelihood function (1.39) is a known function of θ. In this case maximum likelihood estimators have optimal properties in large samples, as will be discussed in Section 1.3.3.

Example 1.8: **Normal Random Sample**

E

We will illustrate the method of maximum likelihood by considering data generated by a random sample from a normal distribution. Suppose that $y_i \sim \text{NID}(\mu, \sigma^2)$, $i = 1, \cdots, n$, with unknown parameters $\theta = (\mu, \sigma^2)$. Then the likelihood function is given by

$$L(\mu, \sigma^2) = \prod_{i=1}^{n} \left(\frac{1}{\sigma\sqrt{2\pi}} e^{-\frac{1}{2\sigma^2}(y_i - \mu)^2} \right).$$

As the logarithm is a monotonically increasing function, the likelihood function and its logarithm $\log(L(\mu, \sigma^2))$ obtain their maximum for the same values of μ and σ^2. As $\log(L(\mu, \sigma^2))$ is easier to work with, we maximize

$$\log(L(\mu, \sigma^2)) = -\frac{n}{2}\log(2\pi) - \frac{n}{2}\log(\sigma^2) - \frac{1}{2\sigma^2}\sum_{i=1}^{n}(y_i - \mu)^2. \tag{1.40}$$

The first order conditions (with respect to μ and σ^2) for a maximum are given by

$$\frac{\partial \log(L)}{\partial \mu} = \frac{1}{\sigma^2}\sum_{i=1}^{n}(y_i - \mu) = 0, \tag{1.41}$$

$$\frac{\partial \log(L)}{\partial \sigma^2} = -\frac{n}{2\sigma^2} + \frac{1}{2\sigma^4}\sum_{i=1}^{n}(y_i - \mu)^2 = 0. \tag{1.42}$$

The solutions of these two equations are given by

$$\hat{\mu}_{ML} = \frac{1}{n}\sum y_i = \bar{y}, \quad \hat{\sigma}^2_{ML} = \frac{1}{n}\sum (y_i - \bar{y})^2 = \frac{n-1}{n}s^2.$$

So μ is estimated by the sample mean and σ^2 by $(1 - \frac{1}{n})$ times the sample variance. For large sample sizes the difference with the sample variance s^2 becomes negligible.

To check whether the estimated values indeed correspond to a maximum of the likelihood function we compute the matrix of second order derivatives (the Hessian matrix) and check whether this matrix (evaluated at $\hat{\mu}_{ML}$ and $\hat{\sigma}^2_{ML}$) is negative definite. By differentiating the above two first order conditions, it follows that the Hessian matrix is equal to

$$H(\theta) = \begin{pmatrix} \frac{\partial^2 \log(L)}{\partial \mu^2} & \frac{\partial^2 \log(L)}{\partial \mu \partial \sigma^2} \\ \frac{\partial^2 \log(L)}{\partial \sigma^2 \partial \mu} & \frac{\partial^2 \log(L)}{\partial (\sigma^2)^2} \end{pmatrix} = \begin{pmatrix} -\frac{n}{\sigma^2} & -\frac{1}{\sigma^4}\sum (y_i - \mu) \\ -\frac{1}{\sigma^4}\sum (y_i - \mu) & \frac{n}{2\sigma^4} - \frac{1}{\sigma^6}\sum (y_i - \mu)^2 \end{pmatrix}. \tag{1.43}$$

Evaluating this at the values of $\hat{\mu}_{ML}$ and $\hat{\sigma}^2_{ML}$ shows that $H(\hat{\mu}, \hat{\sigma}^2)$ is a diagonal matrix with elements $-n/\hat{\sigma}^2_{ML}$ and $-n/2\hat{\sigma}^4_{ML}$ on the diagonal, which is indeed a negative definite matrix.

Note that we expressed the model and the likelihood function in terms of the parameters μ and σ^2. We could equally well use the parameters μ and σ. We leave it as an exercise (see Exercise 1.6) to show that solving the first order conditions with respect to μ and σ gives the same estimators as before, which illustrates the invariance property of maximum likelihood estimators.

☞ **Exercises:** T: 1.6a, b, 1.9d, 1.10a, c.

1.3.2 Statistical properties

☞ First used in Section 2.2.4; uses Appendix A.2–A.5.

Data generating process

To evaluate the quality of estimators, suppose that the data are generated by a particular distribution that belongs to the specified model. That is, the *data generating process* (DGP) of $y_1, \cdots, y_n$ has a distribution f_{θ_0} where $\theta_0 \in \Theta$.

An estimator $\hat{\theta}$ is a function of the random variables $y_1, \cdots, y_n$, so that $\hat{\theta}$ is itself a random variable with a distribution that depends on θ_0. The estimator would be perfect if $P[\hat{\theta} = \theta_0] = 1$, as it would always infer the correct parameter value from the sample. However, as the observations are partly random, θ_0 can in general not be inferred with certainty from the information in the data. To evaluate the quality of an estimator we therefore need statistical measures for the distance of the distribution of $\hat{\theta}$ from θ_0.

Variance and bias

First assume that θ consists of a single parameter. The *mean squared error* (MSE) of an estimator is defined by $E[(\hat{\theta} - \theta_0)^2]$, which can be decomposed in two terms as

$$\mathrm{MSE}(\hat{\theta}) = E[(\hat{\theta} - \theta_0)^2] = \mathrm{var}(\hat{\theta}) + (E[\hat{\theta}] - \theta_0)^2. \tag{1.44}$$

Here all expectations are taken with respect to the underlying distribution f_{θ_0} of the data generating process. The first term is the variance of the estimator, and if this is small this means that the estimator is not so much affected by the randomness in the data. The second term is the square of the *bias* $E[\hat{\theta}] - \theta_0$, and if this is small this means that the estimator has a distribution that is centred around θ_0. The mean squared error provides a trade-off between the variance and the bias of an estimator.

Unbiased and efficient estimators

The practical use of the MSE criterion is limited by the fact that $\mathrm{MSE}(\hat{\theta})$ depends in general on the value of θ_0. As θ_0 is unknown (else there would be no reason to estimate it), one often uses other criteria that can be evaluated without knowing θ_0. For instance, one can restrict the attention to *unbiased* estimators—that is, with the property that

$$E[\hat{\theta}] = \theta_0,$$

and try to minimize the variance $\mathrm{var}(\hat{\theta})$ within the class of unbiased estimators. Assume again that θ consists of a single parameter. An estimator that minimizes the variance over a class of estimators is called *efficient* within that class. The Cramér–Rao lower bound states that for every unbiased estimator $\hat{\theta}$ there holds

$$\mathrm{var}(\hat{\theta}) \geq \left(E\left[\left(\frac{d \log (L(\theta))}{d\theta} \right)^2 \right] \right)^{-1} = -\left(E\left[\frac{d^2 \log (L(\theta))}{d\theta^2} \right] \right)^{-1} \tag{1.45}$$

where $L(\theta)$ is the likelihood function and, as before, the expectations are taken with respect to the distribution with parameter θ_0. The proof of the equality in (1.45) is left as an exercise (see Exercise 1.7). The inequality in (1.45) implies that a sufficient condition for the efficiency of an estimator $\hat{\theta}$ in the class of unbiased estimators with $E[\hat{\theta}] = \theta_0$ is that $\text{var}(\hat{\theta})$ is equal to the Cramér–Rao lower bound. This condition is not necessary, however, because in some situations the lower bound on the variance cannot be attained by any unbiased estimator.

Warning on terminology

A comment on the terminology is in order. Although the property of unbiasedness is an attractive one, this does not mean that biased estimators should automatically be discarded. Exhibit 1.11 shows the density functions of two estimators, one that is unbiased but that has a relatively large variance and another that has a small bias and a relatively small variance. In practice we have a *single sample* $y_1, \cdots, y_n$ at our disposal, and corresponding single outcomes of the estimators. As is clear from Exhibit 1.11, the outcome of the biased estimator will in general be closer to the correct parameter value than the outcome of the unbiased estimator. This shows that unbiasedness should not be imposed blindly.

More than one parameter

Now suppose that θ consists of a vector of parameters, and that $\hat{\theta}$ is a vector of estimators where each component is an estimator of the corresponding component of θ. Then $\hat{\theta}$ is unbiased if $E[\hat{\theta}] = \theta_0$ — that is, if all components are unbiased. For unbiased estimators, the covariance matrix is given by

$$\text{var}(\hat{\theta}) = E\Big[(\hat{\theta} - E[\hat{\theta}])(\hat{\theta} - E[\hat{\theta}])'\Big] = E\Big[(\hat{\theta} - \theta_0)(\hat{\theta} - \theta_0)'\Big].$$

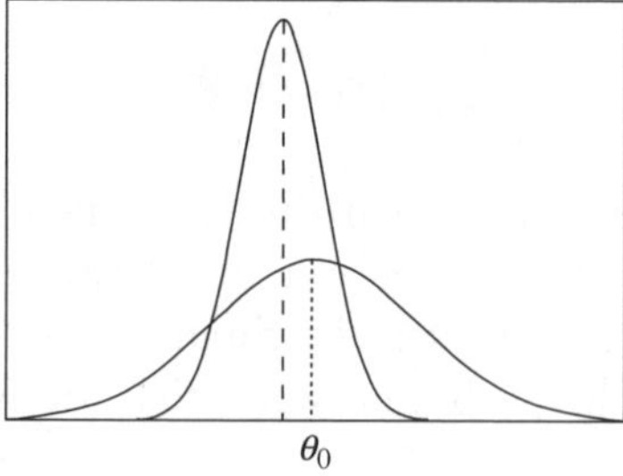

Exhibit 1.11 Bias and variance

Densities of two estimators, one that is unbiased but that has a larger variance and another one that is biased (downwards) but that has a smaller variance (θ_0 denotes the parameter of the data generating process).

An estimator $\hat{\theta}_1$ is called more efficient than another estimator $\hat{\theta}_2$ if $\text{var}(\hat{\theta}_2) - \text{var}(\hat{\theta}_1)$ is a positive semidefinite matrix. This means in particular that every component of $\hat{\theta}_2$ has a variance that is at least as large as that of the corresponding component of $\hat{\theta}_1$. The Cramér–Rao lower bound for the variance of unbiased estimators is given by the inverse of the so-called *information matrix*. This matrix is defined as follows, where the expectations are taken with respect to the probability distribution with parameters θ_0 and where the derivatives are evaluated at θ_0.

$$\mathcal{I}_0 = E\left[\left(\frac{\partial \log (L(\theta))}{\partial \theta}\right)\left(\frac{\partial \log (L(\theta))}{\partial \theta}\right)'\right] = -E\left[\frac{\partial^2 \log (L(\theta))}{\partial \theta \partial \theta'}\right]. \qquad (1.46)$$

So, for every unbiased estimator there holds that $\text{var}(\hat{\theta}) - \mathcal{I}_0^{-1}$ is positive semidefinite. A sufficient condition for efficiency of an unbiased estimator of the kth component of θ is that its variance is equal to the kth diagonal element of $\mathcal{I}_0^{-1}$.

Example 1.9: **Normal Random Sample (continued)**

E

As in Example 1.8, we consider the case of data consisting of a random sample from the normal distribution. We suppose that $y_i \sim \text{NID}(\mu, \sigma^2)$, $i = 1, \cdots, n$, with unknown parameters $\theta = (\mu, \sigma^2)$. The maximum likelihood estimators are given by $\hat{\mu}_{ML} = \bar{y}$ and $\hat{\sigma}^2_{ML} = (n-1)s^2/n$ where s^2 is the sample variance. We will investigate (i) the unbiasedness of the ML estimators $\hat{\mu}_{ML}$ and $\hat{\sigma}^2_{ML}$, (ii) the variance and efficiency of these two estimators, (iii) simulated sample distributions of these two estimators and of two alternative estimators, the median (for μ) and the sample variance s^2 (for σ^2), and (iv) the interpretation of the outcomes of this simulation experiment.

(i) Means of the ML estimators $\hat{\mu}_{ML}$ and $\hat{\sigma}^2_{ML}$

As was shown in Section 1.2.4, $\hat{\mu} \sim \text{N}(\mu, \sigma^2/n)$ and $(n-1)s^2/\sigma^2 \sim \chi^2(n-1)$. It follows that $E[\hat{\mu}_{ML}] = \mu$ and that $E[\hat{\sigma}^2_{ML}] = (n-1)\sigma^2/n$—that is, $\hat{\mu}_{ML}$ is unbiased but $\hat{\sigma}^2_{ML}$ not. An unbiased estimator of σ^2 is given by the sample variance s^2. This is the reason to divide by $(n-1)$ in (1.3) instead of by n. Unless the sample size n is small, the difference between s^2 and $\hat{\sigma}^2_{ML}$ is small.

(ii) Variance and efficiency of the ML estimators

Now we evaluate the efficiency of the estimators $\bar{y}$ and s^2 in the class of all unbiased estimators. The variance of $\bar{y}$ is equal to σ^2/n. As the $\chi^2(n-1)$ distribution has variance $2(n-1)$, it follows that s^2 has variance $2\sigma^4/(n-1)$. The information matrix is equal to $\mathcal{I}_0 = -E[H(\theta_0)]$, where

$\theta_0 = (\mu, \sigma^2)$ and $H(\theta_0)$ is the Hessian matrix in (1.43). As $E[y_i - \mu] = 0$ and $E[(y_i - \mu)^2] = \sigma^2$, it follows that

$$\mathcal{I}_0 = \begin{pmatrix} \frac{n}{\sigma^2} & 0 \\ 0 & \frac{n}{2\sigma^4} \end{pmatrix}.$$

By taking the inverse, it follows that the Cramér–Rao lower bounds for the variance of unbiased estimators of μ and σ^2 are respectively σ^2/n and $2\sigma^4/n$. So $\bar{y}$ is efficient, but the variance of s^2 does not attain the lower bound. We mention that s^2 is nonetheless efficient—that is, there exists no unbiased estimator of σ^2 with variance smaller than $2\sigma^4/(n-1)$.

(iii) Simulated sample distributions

To illustrate the sampling aspect of estimators, we perform a small *simulation experiment*. To perform a simulation we have to specify the data generating process. We consider $n = 10$ independent random variables $y_1, \cdots, y_n$ that are all normally distributed with mean $\mu = 0$ and variance $\sigma^2 = 1$. A *simulation run* then consists of the outcomes of the variables $y_1, \cdots, y_{10}$ obtained by ten random drawings from N(0, 1). Statistical and econometric software packages contain random number generators for this purpose. For such a simulated set of ten data points, we compute the following statistics: the sample mean $\bar{y}$, the sample median med(y), the sample variance s^2, and the second sample moment $m_2 = \hat{\sigma}^2_{ML}$. The values of these statistics depend on the simulated data, so that the outcomes will be different for different simulation runs. To get an idea of this variation we perform 10,000 runs. Exhibit 1.12 shows histograms for the resulting 10,000 outcomes of the statistics $\bar{y}$ in (*a*), med(y) in (*b*), s^2 in (*c*), and $\hat{\sigma}^2_{ML}$ in (*d*), together with their averages and standard deviations over the 10,000 runs.

(iv) Interpretation of simulation outcomes

Both the sample mean and the median have an average close to the mean $\mu = 0$ of the data generating process, but the sample mean has a smaller standard deviation than the median. This is in line with the fact that the sample mean is the efficient estimator. Also note that the sample standard deviation of the sample mean over the 10,000 runs (0.3159, see (*a*)) is close to the theoretical standard deviation of the sample mean (which is $\sigma/\sqrt{n} = 1/\sqrt{10} = 0.3162$). The estimates $\hat{\sigma}^2_{ML}$ show a downward bias, whereas s^2 has an average that is close to the variance $\sigma^2 = 1$ of the data generating process. This is in line with the fact that $\hat{\sigma}^2_{ML}$ is biased and s^2 is unbiased. The theoretical expected value of $\hat{\sigma}^2$ is equal to $\frac{n-1}{n}\sigma^2 = 0.9$, which is close to the sample average of the estimates over the 10,000

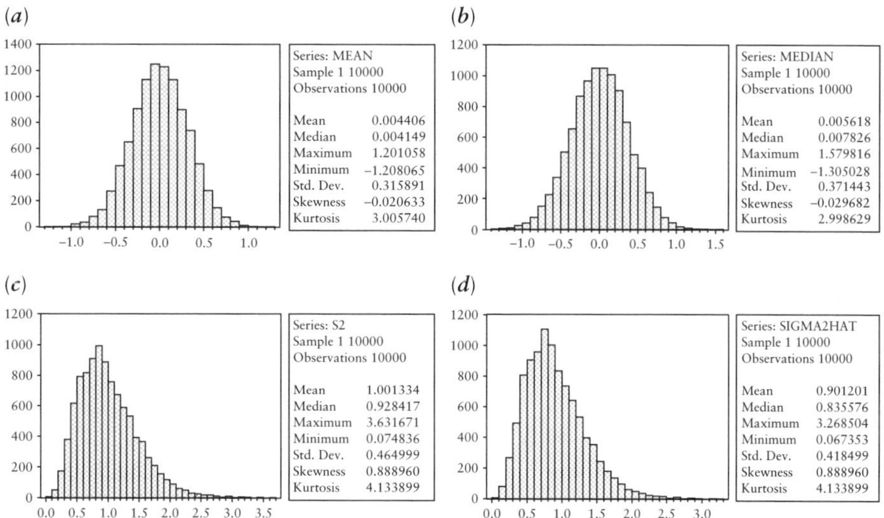

Exhibit 1.12 Normal Random Sample (Example 1.9)

Histograms of sample mean (*a*), sample median (*b*), sample variance (*c*), and second sample moment (*d*) obtained in 10,000 simulation runs. Each simulation run consists of ten random drawings from the standard normal distribution and provides one outcome of the four sample statistics.

simulation runs (0.901). The standard deviations of $\hat{\sigma}^2_{ML}$ and s^2 over the 10,000 runs are in line with the theoretical standard deviations of $\sqrt{2(n-1)/n^2} = 0.424$ for $\hat{\sigma}^2_{ML}$ (as compared to a value of 0.418 in (*d*) over the 10,000 simulation runs) and $\sqrt{2/(n-1)} = 0.471$ for s^2 (as compared to a value of 0.465 in (*c*) over the 10,000 simulation runs).

☞ Exercises: T: 1.6c, 1.7a, 1.8a–c, 1.9a–c, e, 1.10a.

1.3.3 Asymptotic properties

☞ First used in Section 4.1; uses Appendix A.2–A.5.

Motivation

In some situations the sample distribution of an estimator is known exactly. For instance, for random samples from the normal distribution, the sample mean and variance have distributions given by (1.33) and (1.35). In other cases, however, the exact finite sample distribution of estimators is not known. This is the case for many estimators used in econometrics, as will become clear in later chapters. Basically two methods can be followed in such situations. One method is to simulate the distribution of the estimator for a range of data generating processes. A possible disadvantage is that the results depend on the chosen parameters of the data generating process. Another method is to consider the *asymptotic properties* of the estimator—that is, the properties if the sample size n tends to infinity. Asymptotic properties give an indication of the distribution of the estimator in large enough finite samples. A possible disadvantage is that it may be less clear whether the actual sample size is large enough to use the asymptotic properties as an approximation.

Consistency

In this section we discuss some asymptotic properties that are much used in econometrics. Let θ be a parameter of interest and let $\hat{\theta}_n$ be an estimator of θ that is based on a sample of n observations. We are interested in the properties of this estimator when $n \to \infty$, under the assumption that the data are generated by a process with parameter θ_0. The estimator is called *consistent* if it converges in probability to θ_0—that is, if for all $\delta > 0$ there holds

$$\lim_{n \to \infty} P[|\hat{\theta}_n - \theta_0| < \delta] = 1. \tag{1.47}$$

In this case θ_0 is called the *probability limit* of $\hat{\theta}_n$, written as $\text{plim}(\hat{\theta}_n) = \theta_0$. If θ is a vector of parameters, an estimator $\hat{\theta}_n$ is called consistent if each component of $\hat{\theta}_n$ is a consistent estimator of the corresponding component of θ. Consistency is illustrated graphically in Exhibit 1.13. The distribution of the estimator becomes more and more concentrated around the correct parameter value θ_0 if the sample size increases. A sufficient (but not necessary) condition for consistency is that

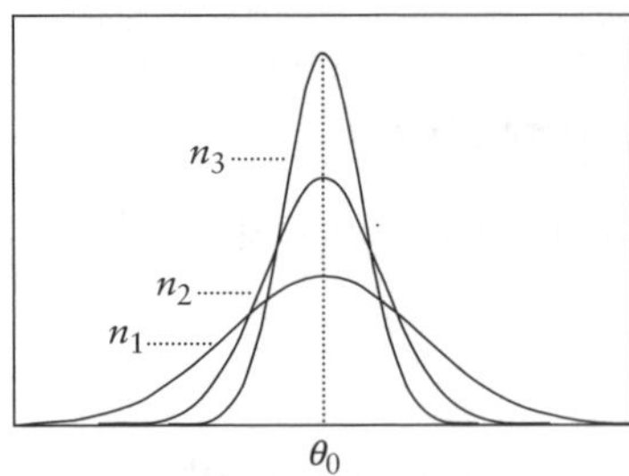

Exhibit 1.13 Consistency

Distribution of a consistent estimator for three sample sizes, with $n_1 < n_2 < n_3$. If the sample size gets larger, then the distribution becomes more concentrated around the parameter θ_0 of the data generating process.

$$\lim_{n\to\infty} E[\hat{\theta}_n] = \theta_0 \text{ and } \lim_{n\to\infty} \text{var}(\hat{\theta}_n) = 0, \tag{1.48}$$

that is, if the estimator is asymptotically unbiased and its variance tends to zero (see Exercise 1.7).

Calculation rules for probability limits

Probability limits are easy to work with, as they have similar properties as ordinary limits of functions. Suppose that y_n and z_n are two sequences of random variables with probability limits $\text{plim}(y_n) = c_1$ and $\text{plim}(z_n) = c_2$ $(\neq 0)$, then there holds, for instance, that

$$\text{plim}\,(y_n + z_n) = c_1 + c_2, \quad \text{plim}\,(y_n z_n) = c_1 c_2, \quad \text{plim}\,(y_n/z_n) = c_1/c_2$$

(see Exercise 1.7). Note that for expectations there holds $E[y + z] = E[y] + E[z]$, but $E[yz] = E[y]E[z]$ holds only if y and z are uncorrelated, and in general $E[y/z] \neq E[y]/E[z]$ (even when y and z are independent). If g is a continuous function that does not depend on n, then

$$\text{plim}\,(g(y_n)) = g(c_1)$$

(see Exercise 1.7), so that, for instance, $\text{plim}(y_n^2) = c_1^2$. Again, for expectations this does in general not hold true (unless g is linear)—for instance, $E[y_n^2] \neq (E[y_n])^2$ in general. This result implies that, if $\hat{\theta}_n$ is a consistent estimator of θ_0, then $g(\hat{\theta}_n)$ is a consistent estimator of $g(\theta_0)$.

Similar results hold true for vector or matrix sequences of random variables. Let A_n be a sequence of $p \times q$ matrices of random variables $a_n(i, j)$; then we write $\text{plim}\,(A_n) = A$ if all the elements converge so that $\text{plim}\,(a_n(i, j)) = a(i, j)$ for all $i = 1, \cdots, p$, $j = 1, \cdots, q$. For two matrix sequences A_n and B_n with $\text{plim}\,(A_n) = A$ and $\text{plim}\,(B_n) = B$ there holds

$$\text{plim}\,(A_n + B_n) - A + B, \ \text{plim}\,(A_n B_n) = AB, \ \text{plim}\,(A_n^{-1} B_n) = A^{-1}B,$$

provided that the matrices have compatible dimensions and, for the last equality, that the matrix A is invertible.

Law of large numbers

When the data consist of a random sample from a population, sample moments provide consistent estimators of the population moments. The reason is that the uncertainty in the individual observations cancels out in the limit by taking averages. That is, if $y_i \sim \text{IID}$, $i = 1, \cdots, n$, with finite population mean $E[y_i] = \mu$, then

$$\text{plim}\left(\frac{1}{n}\sum_{i=1}^{n} y_i\right) = \mu. \tag{1.49}$$

This is called the *law of large numbers*. To get the idea, assume for simplicity that the population variance σ^2 is finite. Then the sample mean of n observations $\bar{y}_n = \frac{1}{n}\sum_{i=1}^{n} y_i$ is a random variable with mean μ and variance σ^2/n, and (1.49) follows from (1.48). Similarly, if $y_i \sim \text{IID}$, $i = 1, \cdots, n$, and the rth population moment $\mu_r = E[(y_i - \mu)^r] < \infty$, then

$$\text{plim}\left(\frac{1}{n}\sum_{i=1}^{n} (y_i - \bar{y}_n)^r\right) = \mu_r.$$

For instance, the sample variance converges in probability to the population variance. Also the sample covariance between two variables converges in probability to the population covariance, and so on.

Central limit theorem

A sequence of random variables y_n with cumulative distribution functions F_n is said to *converge in distribution* to a random variable y with distribution function F if $\lim_{n\to\infty} F_n(v) = F(v)$ at all points v where F is continuous. This is written as

$$y_n \xrightarrow{d} y$$

and F is also called the *asymptotic distribution* of y_n. A central result in statistics is that, under very general conditions, sample averages from arbitrary distributions are *asymptotically normally distributed.* Let y_i, $i = 1, \cdots, n$ be independently and identically distributed random variables with mean μ and finite variance σ^2. Then

$$z_n = \sqrt{n}\frac{\bar{y}_n - \mu}{\sigma} \xrightarrow{d} z \sim \text{N}(0, 1) \tag{1.50}$$

This is called the *central limit theorem*. This means that (after standardization by subtracting the mean, dividing by the standard deviation, and multiplying by the square root of the sample size) the sample mean of a random sample from an arbitrary distribution has an asymptotic standard normal distribution. For large enough sample sizes, the finite sample distribution of z_n can be approximated by the standard normal distribution N(0, 1). It follows that $\overline{y}_n$ is approximately distributed as $\mathrm{N}(\mu, \frac{\sigma^2}{n})$, which we write as

$$\overline{y}_n \approx \mathrm{N}\left(\mu, \frac{\sigma^2}{n}\right).$$

Note that an exact distribution is denoted by $\sim$ and an approximate distribution by $\approx$.

Generalized central limit theorems

The above central limit theorem for the IID case can be generalized in several directions. We mention three generalizations that are used later in this book. When y_i are independent random variables with common mean μ and different variances σ_i^2 for which the average variance $\sigma^2 = \lim_{n\to\infty} \frac{1}{n}\sum_{i=1}^n \sigma_i^2$ is finite, then

$$\sqrt{n}\left(\frac{1}{n}\sum_{i=1}^n y_i - \mu\right) \xrightarrow{d} \mathrm{N}(0, \sigma^2).$$

When y_i, $i = 1, \cdots, n$ is a random sample from a p-dimensional distribution with finite vector of means μ and finite covariance matrix Σ, then

$$\sqrt{n}\left(\frac{1}{n}\sum_{i=1}^n y_i - \mu\right) \xrightarrow{d} \mathrm{N}(0, \Sigma).$$

Now suppose that A_n is a sequence of $p \times p$ matrices of random variables and that y_n is a sequence of $p \times 1$ vectors of random variables. When $\mathrm{plim}(A_n) = A$ where A is a given (non-random) matrix and $y_n \xrightarrow{d} \mathrm{N}(0, \Sigma)$, then

$$A_n y_n \xrightarrow{d} \mathrm{N}(0, A\Sigma A').$$

Asymptotic properties of maximum likelihood estimators

The law of large numbers shows that moment estimators are consistent in case of random samples. However, maximum likelihood estimators are consistent and (asymptotically) efficient. Suppose that the likelihood function (1.39) is correctly specified, in the sense that the data are generated by a distribution f_{θ_0} with $\theta_0 \in \Theta$. Then, under certain regularity conditions, maximum likelihood estimators are consistent, asymptotically efficient, and asymptotically normally distributed. More in particular, under these conditions there holds

$$\sqrt{n}(\hat{\theta}_{ML} - \theta_0) \xrightarrow{d} \mathrm{N}(0, \mathcal{I}_0^{-1}). \tag{1.51}$$

Here $\hat{\theta}_{ML}$ denotes the maximum likelihood estimator (based on n observations) and $\mathcal{I}_0$ is the asymptotic information matrix evaluated at θ_0—that is,

$$\mathcal{I}_0 = \lim_{n\to\infty}\left(\frac{1}{n}\mathcal{I}_n\right),$$

where $\mathcal{I}_n$ is the information matrix for sample size n defined in (1.46). Asymptotic efficiency means that $\sqrt{n}(\hat{\theta}_{ML} - \theta_0)$ has, for $n \to \infty$, the smallest covariance matrix among all consistent estimators, in the following sense. Let $\hat{\theta}$ be a consistent estimator (based on n observations) and let $\Sigma = \lim_{n\to\infty} \mathrm{var}(\sqrt{n}(\hat{\theta} - \theta_0))$ and $\Sigma_{ML} = \lim_{n\to\infty} \mathrm{var}(\sqrt{n}(\hat{\theta}_{ML} - \theta_0))$, then $\Sigma - \Sigma_{ML}$ is a positive semidefinite matrix. For finite samples we obtain from (1.51) the approximation

$$\hat{\theta}_{ML} \approx \mathrm{N}(\theta_0, \hat{\mathcal{I}}_n^{-1}),$$

where $\hat{\mathcal{I}}_n$ is the information matrix (1.46) evaluated at $\hat{\theta}_{ML}$. The result in (1.51) can be seen as a generalization of the central limit theorem.

T

Intuitive argument for the consistency of $\hat{\theta}_{ML}$

Although a formal proof of consistency falls outside the scope of this book, it may be of interest to provide some intuition for this result, without being precise about the required regularity conditions. Suppose that y_i, $i = 1, \cdots, n$ are IID with common probability density function f_{θ_0}. The ML estimator $\hat{\theta}_{ML}$ is obtained by maximizing the likelihood function $L(\theta) = \prod_{i=1}^n f_\theta(y_i)$ or equivalently by maximizing the *log-likelihood* $\frac{1}{n}\log(L(\theta)) = \frac{1}{n}\sum_{i=1}^n \log(f_\theta(y_i))$. The first order conditions for a maximum of this function can be expressed as

$$\frac{\partial}{\partial\theta}\left(\frac{1}{n}\sum_{i=1}^n \log(f_\theta(y_i))\right) = \frac{1}{n}\sum_{i=1}^n \frac{\partial \log(f_\theta(y_i))}{\partial\theta} = \frac{1}{n}\sum_{i=1}^n \frac{1}{f_\theta(y_i)}\frac{\partial f_\theta(y_i)}{\partial\theta} = 0.$$

Under suitable regularity conditions, the law of large numbers applies to the IID random variables $\frac{1}{f_\theta(y_i)}\frac{\partial f_\theta(y_i)}{\partial\theta}$, so that the first order conditions converge in probability (for $n \to \infty$) to

$$\text{plim}\left(\frac{1}{n}\sum_{i=1}^{n}\frac{1}{f_\theta(y_i)}\frac{\partial f_\theta(y_i)}{\partial\theta}\right) = E_0\left[\frac{1}{f_\theta(y_i)}\frac{\partial f_\theta(y_i)}{\partial\theta}\right],$$

where E_0 means that the expectation should be evaluated according to the density f_{θ_0} of the DGP. We will show below that the DGP parameter θ_0 solves the above asymptotic first order condition for a maximum. Intuitively, the estimator $\hat{\theta}_{ML}$ (which solves the equations for finite n) will then converge to θ_0 (which solves the equations asymptotically) in case $n \to \infty$. This intuition is correct under suitable regularity conditions. Then $\text{plim}(\hat{\theta}_{ML}) = \theta_0$, so that $\hat{\theta}_{ML}$ is consistent.

To prove that θ_0 is a solution of the asymptotic first order conditions, note that f_θ is a density function, so that $\int f_\theta(y_i)dy_i = 1$. Using this result, and substituting $\theta = \theta_0$ in the asymptotic first order conditions, we get

$$\begin{aligned} E_0\left[\frac{1}{f_{\theta_0}(y_i)}\frac{\partial f_\theta(y_i)}{\partial\theta}\right] &= \int \frac{1}{f_{\theta_0}(y_i)}\frac{\partial f_\theta(y_i)}{\partial\theta} f_{\theta_0}(y_i)dy_i = \int \frac{\partial f_\theta(y_i)}{\partial\theta}dy_i \\ &= \frac{\partial}{\partial\theta}\left(\int f_\theta(y_i)dy_i\right) = \frac{\partial}{\partial\theta}(1) = 0. \end{aligned}$$

This shows that θ_0 solves the asymptotic first order conditions.

Example 1.10: **Simulated Normal Random Sample**

E

To illustrate the consistency and asymptotic normality of maximum likelihood, we consider the following simulation experiment. We generate a sample of n observations $(y_1, \cdots, y_n)$ by independent drawings from the standard normal distribution N(0, 1) and we compute the corresponding maximum likelihood estimate $\hat{\sigma}^2_{ML} = \frac{1}{n}\sum_{i=1}^{n}(y_i - \overline{y})^2$. The results in Section 1.3.2 and Example 1.9 (for $n = 10$) showed that $\hat{\sigma}^2_{ML}$ is a biased estimator of $\sigma^2 = 1$. For each of the sample sizes $n = 10$, $n = 100$, and $n = 1000$, we perform 10,000 simulation runs.

Exhibits 1.14 (*a*), (*c*), and (*e*) show three histograms of the resulting 10,000 estimates of $\hat{\sigma}^2_{ML}$ for the three sample sizes. As the histograms become strongly concentrated around the value $\sigma^2 = 1$ for large sample size ($n = 1000$), this illustrates the consistency of this estimator. Exhibit 1.4 (*b*, *d*, and *f*) show three histograms of the resulting 10,000 values of $\sqrt{n}(\hat{\sigma}^2_{ML} - 1)$ for the three sample sizes. Whereas for $n = 10$ the skewness of the χ^2 distribution is still visible, for $n = 1000$ the distribution is much more symmetric and approaches a normal distribution. This illustrates the asymptotic normality of the maximum likelihood estimator of σ^2.

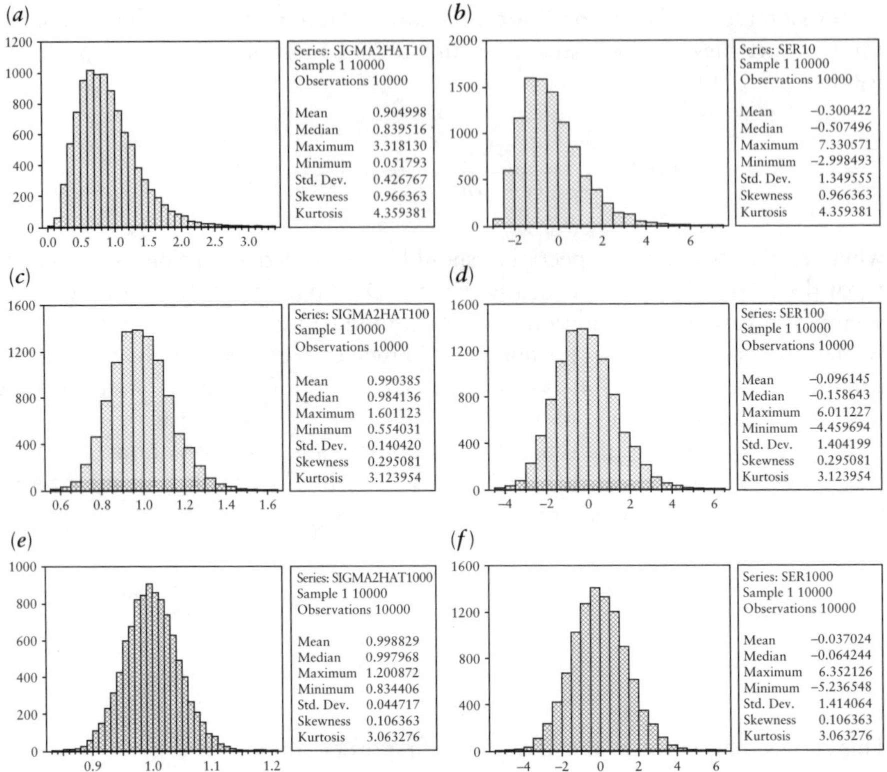

Exhibit 1.14 Simulated Normal Random Sample (Example 1.10)

Histograms of the maximum likelihood estimates $\hat{\sigma}^2_{ML}$ of the error variance (denoted by SIGMA2HAT, shown in (*a*), (*c*), and (*e*)) and of a scaled version (defined by $\sqrt{n}(\hat{\sigma}^2_{ML} - 1)$ and denoted by SER, shown in (*b*), (*d*), and (*f*)) for random drawings of the standard normal distribution, with sample size $n = 10$ in ((*a*)–(*b*)), $n = 100$ in ((*c*)–(*d*)), and $n = 1000$ in ((*e*)–(*f*)).

☞ Exercises: T: 1.7b–e, 1.8d, 1.10b–d, 1.12d.

1.4 Tests of hypotheses

1.4.1 Size and power

☞ First used in Section 2.3.1.

Null hypothesis and alternative hypothesis

When observations are affected by random influences, the same holds true for all inference that is based on these data. If one wishes to evaluate hypotheses concerning the data generating process, one should take the random nature of the data into account. For instance, consider the hypothesis that the data are generated by a probability distribution with mean zero. In general, the sample mean of the observed data will not be (exactly) equal to zero, even if the hypothesis is correct. The question is whether the difference between the sample mean and the hypothetical population mean is due only to randomness in the data. If this seems unlikely, then the hypothesis is possibly not correct.

Now we introduce some terminology. A statistical *hypothesis* is an assertion about the distribution of one or more random variables. If the functional form of the distribution is known up to a parameter (or vector of parameters), then the hypothesis is parametric; otherwise it is non-parametric. If the hypothesis specifies the distribution completely, then it is called a simple hypothesis; otherwise, a composite hypothesis. We restrict the attention to parametric hypotheses where one assertion, called the *null hypothesis* and denoted by H_0, is tested against another one, called the *alternative hypothesis* and denoted by H_1. Let the specified set of distributions be given by $\{f_\theta; \theta \in \Theta\}$; then H_0 corresponds to the assertion that $\theta \in \Theta_0$ and H_1 to the assertion that $\theta \in \Theta_1$, where Θ_0 and Θ_1 are disjoint subsets of Θ. For instance, if θ is the (unknown) population mean, then we can test the hypothesis of zero mean against the alternative of non-zero mean. In this case $\Theta_0 = \{0\}$ and $\Theta_1 = \{\theta \in \Theta; \theta \neq 0\}$.

Test statistic and critical region

Let θ_0 be the parameter (or vector of parameters) of the data generating process. The observed data $(y_1, \cdots, y_n)$ are used to decide which of the two hypotheses (H_0 and H_1) seems to be the most appropriate one. This decision is made by means of a *test statistic* $t(y_1, \cdots, y_n)$—that is, an expression that can be computed from the observed data. The possible outcomes of this statistic are divided into two regions, the *critical region* (denoted by C) and the complement of this region. The null hypothesis is rejected if $t \in C$ and it is not rejected if $t \notin C$. Note that we say that H_0 is not rejected, instead of saying that H_0 is accepted. For instance, to test the null hypothesis that the population mean $\theta = 0$ against the alternative that $\theta \neq 0$, the sample mean $\bar{y}$ provides an intuitively appealing test statistic. The null hypothesis will be rejected if $\bar{y}$ is 'too far away' from zero. For instance, one can choose a value $c > 0$ and reject the null hypothesis if $|\bar{y}| > c$. If the sample is such that $|\bar{y}| \leq c$, then the hypothesis is not rejected, but this does not mean that we accept the null hypothesis as a factual truth.

Size and power

In general, to test a hypothesis one has to decide about the test statistic and about the critical region. These should be selected in such a way that one can discriminate well between the null and alternative hypotheses. The quality of a test can be evaluated in terms of the probability $\pi(\theta) = P[t \in C]$ to reject the null hypothesis. We restrict the attention to *similar tests*—that is, test statistics $t(y_1, \cdots, y_n)$ that are pivotal in the sense that the distribution under the null hypothesis does not depend on any unknown parameters. This means that, for every given critical region C, the rejection probability $\pi(\theta)$ can be calculated for $\theta \in \Theta_0$ and that (in case the set Θ_0 contains more than one element) this probability is independent of the value of $\theta \in \Theta_0$. If the null hypothesis is valid (so that the data generating process satisfies $\theta_0 \in \Theta_0$) but the observed data lead to rejection of the null hypothesis (because $t \in C$), this is called an *error of the first type*. The probability of this error is called the *size* or also the *significance level* of the test. For similar tests, the size can be computed for every given critical region. On the other hand, if the null hypothesis is false (as $\theta \notin \Theta_0$) but the observed data do not lead to rejection of the null hypothesis (because $t \notin C$), this is called an *error of the second type*. The rejection probability $\pi(\theta)$ for $\theta \notin \Theta_0$ is called the *power* of the test. A test is called *consistent* if the power $\pi(\theta)$ converges to 1 for all $\theta \notin \Theta_0$ if $n \to \infty$.

Tests with a given significance level

Of course, for practical applications one prefers tests that have small size and large power in finite samples. A perfect test would be one where the probability to make a mistake is zero—that is, with $\pi(\theta) = 0$ for $\theta \in \Theta_0$ and $\pi(\theta) = 1$ for $\theta \notin \Theta_0$. This is possible only if the parameter values can be inferred with absolute certainty from the observed data, but then there is, of course, no need for tests anymore. In practice one often fixes a maximally tolerated size—for instance, 5 per cent—to control for errors of the first type. It then remains to choose a test statistic and a critical region with good power properties—that is, with small probabilities of errors of the second type. In this book we mostly use intuitive arguments to construct econometric tests of a given size, and we pay relatively little attention to their power properties. However, many of the standard econometric tests can be shown to have reasonably good power properties.

Note that the null and alternative hypotheses play different roles in testing, because a small size is taken as a starting point. This means that an econometrician should try to formulate tests in such a way that errors of the first type are more serious than errors of the second type.

The meaning of significance

One should distinguish *statistical significance* from *practical significance.* In empirical econometrics we analyse data that are the result of economic processes that are often relatively involved. The purpose of an econometric model is to capture the main aspects of interest of these processes. Tests can help to find a model that is reasonable, given the information at hand. Hereby the less relevant details are neglected on purpose. One should not always blindly follow rules of thumb like significance levels of 5 per cent in testing. For example, in large samples nearly every null hypothesis will be rejected at the 5 per cent significance level. In many cases the relevant question is not so much whether the null hypothesis is exactly correct, but whether it is a reasonable approximation. This means, for instance, that significance levels should in practice be taken as a decreasing function of the sample size.

Example 1.11: **Simulated Normal Random Sample (continued)**

E

To illustrate the power of tests, we consider a simulation experiment where the data $y_i, i = 1, \cdots, n$ are generated by independent drawings from $\mathrm{N}(\mu, 1)$. We assume that the modeller knows that the data are generated by an NID process with known variance $\sigma^2 = 1$ but that the mean μ is unknown. We will test the null hypothesis $H_0 : \mu = 0$ against the alternative $H_1 : \mu \neq 0$. We will now discuss (i) two alternative test statistics (the mean and the median), (ii) the choice of critical regions (for fixed significance level), (iii) the set-up of the simulation experiment, and (iv) the outcomes of this experiment.

(i) Two test statistics: mean and median

We will analyse the properties of two alternative estimators of μ—namely, the sample mean $\bar{y}$ and the sample median $\mathrm{med}(y)$. Both estimators can be used to construct test statistics to test the null hypothesis.

(ii) Choice of critical regions

As both statistics (sample mean and sample median) have a distribution that is symmetric around the population mean, intuition suggests that we should reject the null hypothesis if $|\bar{y}| > c_1$ (if we use the sample mean) or if $|\text{med}(y)| > c_2$ (if we use the sample median). We fix the size of the tests at 5 per cent in all cases. The critical values c_1 and c_2 are determined by the condition that $P[-c_1 \leq \bar{y} \leq c_1] = P[-c_2 \leq \text{med}(y) \leq c_2] = 0.95$ when $\mu = 0$. We consider sample sizes of $n = 10, n = 100$, and $n = 1000$, for which $c_1 = 1.96/\sqrt{n}$ (because σ is known to the modeller) and c_2 is approximately 0.73, 0.24, and 0.08 respectively. The values of c_2 are obtained from a simulation experiment with 100,000 runs, where in each run the median of a sample $y_i \sim \text{N}(0, 1), i = 1, \cdots, n$ is determined.

(iii) Simulation experiment

To investigate the power properties of the two test statistics, we consider as data generating processes $y_i \sim \text{N}(\mu, 1)$ for a range of eleven values for μ between $\mu = -2$ and $\mu = 2$, including $\mu = 0$ (see Exhibit 1.15 for the precise values of μ in the eleven experiments). This leads to in total thirty-three simulation experiments (three sample sizes $n = 10, 100$, or 1000, for each of the eleven values of μ). For each experiment we perform 10,000 simulation runs and determine the frequency of rejection of the null hypothesis, both for the sample mean and for the sample median.

Population mean	$n = 10$		$n = 100$		$n = 1000$	
	Mean	Median	Mean	Median	Mean	Median
$\mu = -2$	100.0	100.0	100.0	100.0	100.0	100.0
$\mu = -1$	89.0	77.2	100.0	100.0	100.0	100.0
$\mu = -0.2$	9.7	8.8	51.2	35.9	100.0	99.9
$\mu = -0.1$	6.4	5.9	17.3	13.2	88.5	70.7
$\mu = -0.05$	5.4	5.5	7.3	6.9	35.5	23.6
$\mu = 0$	5.0	5.0	4.7	5.0	4.8	4.8
$\mu = 0.05$	5.2	5.0	7.7	7.5	34.4	24.1
$\mu = 0.1$	6.4	6.1	16.7	12.5	88.3	71.1
$\mu = 0.2$	9.5	7.8	51.6	37.2	100.0	99.9
$\mu = 1$	88.4	76.7	100.0	100.0	100.0	100.0
$\mu = 2$	100.0	100.0	100.0	100.0	100.0	100.0

Exhibit 1.15 Simulated Normal Random Sample (Example 1.11)

Results of simulation experiments with random samples of different sizes and with different means of the data generating process. The numbers in the table report the rejection percentages (over 10,000 simulation runs) of the null hypothesis that $\mu = 0$, using tests of size 5% based on the sample mean and on the sample median.

(iv) Outcomes of the simulation experiment

The results are in Exhibit 1.15. For $\mu = 0$ this indicates that the size is indeed around 5 per cent. For $\mu \neq 0$ the power of the tests increases for larger samples, indicating that both tests are consistent. The sample mean has higher power than the sample median. This means that, for the normal distribution, the sample mean is to be preferred above the sample median to perform tests on the population mean. Note that for $n = 1000$ the null hypothesis that $\mu = 0$ is rejected nearly always (both by the mean and by the median) if the data generating process has $\mu = 0.2$. It depends on the particular investigation whether the distinction between $\mu = 0$ and $\mu = 0.2$ is really of interest — that is, whether this difference is of practical significance.

1.4.2 Tests for mean and variance

☞ First used in Section 2.3.1.

Two-sided test for the mean

To illustrate the general principles discussed in Section 1.4.1, we consider tests for the mean and variance of a population. It is assumed that the data $y_i, i = 1, \cdots, n$ consist of a random sample from a normal distribution, so that $y_i \sim \text{NID}(\mu, \sigma^2), i = 1, \cdots, n$. Both the mean μ and the variance σ^2 of the population are unknown, so that $\theta = (\mu, \sigma^2)$. First we test a hypothesis about the mean — for instance,

$$H_0 : \mu = \mu_0, \quad H_1 : \mu \neq \mu_0,$$

where μ_0 is a given value. This is called a *two-sided* test, as the alternative contains values $\mu > \mu_0$ as well as values $\mu < \mu_0$. As test statistic we consider the sample mean $\bar{y}$ and we reject the null hypothesis if $|\bar{y} - \mu_0| > c$. This defines the critical region of the test, and c determines the size of the test. According to (1.33), for $\mu = \mu_0$ we get

$$\frac{\bar{y} - \mu_0}{\sigma/\sqrt{n}} \sim \text{N}(0, 1).$$

However, the expression on the left-hand side is not a statistic, as σ^2 is unknown. If this is replaced by the unbiased estimator s^2, we obtain, according to (1.36),

$$t = \frac{\bar{y} - \mu_0}{s/\sqrt{n}} \sim t(n-1). \tag{1.52}$$

Because all the terms in this expression are known (μ_0 is given and $\bar{y}$ and s can be computed from the data), this is a test statistic. It is also a similar test statistic, as the statistic t is pivotal in the sense that the distribution does not depend on the unknown variance σ^2. The test (1.52) is called the *t-test for the mean.* The null hypothesis is rejected if $|t| > c$, where the value of c is chosen in accordance with the desired size of the test. So the null hypothesis is rejected if $\bar{y}$ falls in the critical region

$$\bar{y} < \mu_0 - c\frac{s}{\sqrt{n}} \text{ or } \bar{y} > \mu_0 + c\frac{s}{\sqrt{n}}. \tag{1.53}$$

The size of this test is equal to $P[|t| > c]$, where t follows the $t(n-1)$ distribution. For size 5 per cent, the critical value for $n = 20$ is around 2.09; for $n = 60$ it is around 2.00, and for $n \to \infty$ it converges to 1.96. As a rule of thumb, one often takes $c \approx 2$. Note that $s/\sqrt{n}$ is the estimated standard deviation of the sample mean; see (1.33), where σ is replaced by s. The estimated standard deviation $s/\sqrt{n}$ is called the *standard error* of the sample mean. So the null hypothesis is rejected if the sample mean is more than two standard errors away from the postulated mean μ_0. In this case one says that the sample mean differs significantly from μ_0, or (when $\mu_0 = 0$) that the sample mean is *significant* at the 5 per cent significance level.

One-sided test for the mean

In some cases it is of interest to test the null hypothesis $H_0 : \mu = \mu_0$ against the one-sided alternative $H_1 : \mu > \mu_0$. This is called a *one-sided test.* The test statistic is again as given in (1.52), but now the null hypothesis is rejected if $t > c$ with size equal to $P[t > c]$ where $t \sim t(n-1)$. The critical value for $n = 20$ is around 1.73 in this case; for $n = 60$ it is around 1.67, and for $n \to \infty$ it approaches 1.645. This test can also be used for the null hypothesis $H_0 : \mu \leq \mu_0$ against the alternative $H_1 : \mu > \mu_0$. Tests for $H_0 : \mu = \mu_0$ or $H_0 : \mu \geq \mu_0$ against $H_1 : \mu < \mu_0$ are performed in a similar fashion, where H_0 is rejected for small values of t.

Probability value (*P*-value)

In practice it may not be clear how to choose the size. In principle this depends on the consequences of making errors of the first and second type, but such errors are often difficult to determine. Instead of fixing the size — for instance, at 5 per cent — one can also leave the size unspecified and compute the value of the test statistic from the observed sample. One can then ask for which sizes this test outcome would lead to rejection of the null hypothesis. As larger sizes correspond to larger rejection probabilities, there will be a minimal value of the size for which the null hypothesis is rejected. This is called the *probability value* or *P-value* of the test outcome. That is, the null hypothesis should be rejected for all sizes larger than P, and it should not be rejected for all sizes smaller than P. Stated otherwise, the null hypothesis should be rejected for small values of P and it should not be rejected for large values of P.

P-value for the mean

As an example, let t_0 be the calculated value of the t-test for the null hypothesis $H_0 : \mu = \mu_0$ against the two-sided alternative $H_1 : \mu \neq \mu_0$; then the P-value is given by $P = P[t < t_0 \text{ or } t > t_0]$. If this P-value is small, this means that outcomes of the test statistic so far away from zero are improbable under the null hypothesis, so that the null hypothesis should be rejected. Note that the P-value depends on the form of the (one-sided or two-sided) alternative hypothesis. For instance, when $H_0 : \mu = \mu_0$ is tested against $H_1 : \mu > \mu_0$, then $P = P[t > t_0]$. This is illustrated graphically in Exhibit 1.16. In general, the P-value can be defined as the probability (under the null hypothesis) of getting the observed outcome of the test statistic or a more extreme outcome—that is, the P-value is the corresponding (one-sided or two-sided) tail probability.

Chi-square test for the variance

Next we consider tests on the variance. Again it is assumed that the data consist of a random sample $y_i \sim \mathrm{N}(\mu, \sigma^2)$, $i = 1, \cdots, n$, with μ and σ^2 unknown. Let the null hypothesis be $H_0 : \sigma^2 = \sigma_0^2$ and the (one-sided) alternative $H_1 : \sigma^2 > \sigma_0^2$. If the null hypothesis holds true, then $(y_i - \mu)/\sigma_0 \sim \mathrm{N}(0, 1)$ are independent, so that

$$\sum_{i=1}^{n} (y_i - \mu)^2 / \sigma_0^2 \sim \chi^2(n).$$

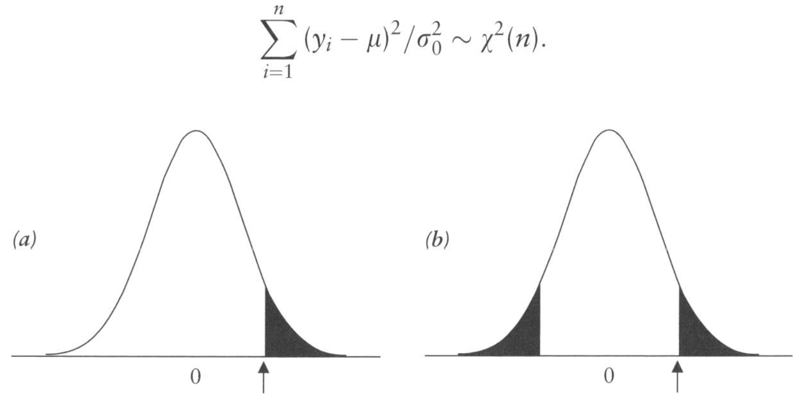

Exhibit 1.16 *P*-value

P-value of a one-sided test ((*a*), for the one-sided alternative that the parameter is larger than zero) and of a two-sided test ((*b*), for the two-sided alternative that the parameter is not zero, with equal areas in both tails). The arrow indicates the outcome of the test statistic calculated from the observed sample. In (*a*) the P-value is equal to the surface of the shaded area, and in (*b*) the P-value is equal to the sum of the surfaces of the two shaded areas.

However, this is not a test statistic, as μ is unknown. When this parameter is replaced by its estimate $\bar{y}$, we obtain, according to (1.35),

$$\frac{1}{\sigma_0^2}\sum_{i=1}^{n}(y_i - \bar{y})^2 = \frac{(n-1)s^2}{\sigma_0^2} \sim \chi^2(n-1). \tag{1.54}$$

The null hypothesis is rejected for large values of this test statistic, with critical value determined from the $\chi^2(n-1)$ distribution. For other hypotheses—for instance, $H_0: \sigma^2 = \sigma_0^2$ against $H_1: \sigma^2 \neq \sigma_0^2$—the same test statistic can be used with appropriate modifications of the critical regions.

F-test for equality of two variances

Finally we discuss a test to compare the variances of two populations. Suppose that the data consist of two independent samples, one of n_1 observations distributed as $\text{NID}(\mu_1, \sigma_1^2)$ and the other of n_2 observations distributed as $\text{NID}(\mu_2, \sigma_2^2)$. Consider the null hypothesis $H_0: \sigma_1^2 = \sigma_2^2$ of equal variances against the alternative $H_1: \sigma_1^2 \neq \sigma_2^2$ that the variances are different. Let s_1^2 be the sample variance in the first sample and s_2^2 that in the second sample. As the two samples are assumed to be independent, the same holds true for s_1^2 and s_2^2. Further (1.35) implies that $(n_i - 1)s_i^2/\sigma_i^2 \sim \chi^2(n_i - 1)$ for $i = 1, 2$, so that $(s_2^2/\sigma_2^2)/(s_1^2/\sigma_1^2) \sim F(n_2 - 1, n_1 - 1)$. When the null hypothesis $\sigma_1^2 = \sigma_2^2$ is true, it follows that

$$\frac{s_2^2}{s_1^2} \sim F(n_2 - 1, n_1 - 1) \tag{1.55}$$

and the null hypothesis is rejected if this test statistic differs significantly from 1. The critical values can be obtained from the $F(n_2 - 1, n_1 - 1)$ distribution. Note that this test statistic is similar, as its distribution does not depend on the unknown parameters μ_1 and μ_2.

The testing problem $H_0: \mu_1 = \mu_2$ against the alternative $H_1: \mu_1 \neq \mu_2$ is more complicated and will be discussed later (see Exercise 3.10).

Example 1.12: **Student Learning (continued)**

We illustrate tests for the mean and variance by considering the random variable consisting of the FGPA score of students at the Vanderbilt University (see Example 1.1). We will discuss (i) a test for the mean and (ii) a test for the equality of two variances.

(i) **Test for the mean**

Suppose that the mean value of this score over a sequence of previous years is equal to 2.70 (this is a hypothetical, non-random value). Further suppose that the individual FGPA scores of students in the current year are independently and normally distributed with unknown mean μ and unknown variance σ^2. The university wishes to test the null hypothesis $H_0 : \mu = 2.70$ of average scores against the alternative hypothesis $H_1 : \mu > 2.70$ that the scores in the current year are above average.

The FGPA scores in the current year of 609 students of this university are summarized in Exhibit 1.4 (*a*). The sample mean and standard deviation are $\bar{y} = 2.793$ and $s = 0.460$ (after rounding; see Exhibit 1.4 (*a*) for the more precise numbers). So the sample average is above 2.70. The question is whether this should be attributed to random fluctuations in student scores or whether the student scores are above average in the current year. Under the null hypothesis that $\mu = 2.70$, it follows from (1.52) that $(\bar{y} - 2.70)/(s/\sqrt{609}) \sim t(608)$. The one-sided critical value for size 5 per cent is (approximately) 1.645. If we substitute the values of $\bar{y}$ and s as calculated from the sample, this gives the value $t = 4.97$. As this outcome is well above 1.645, this leads to rejection of the null hypothesis. The *P*-value of this test outcome is around 10^{-6}. It seems that the current students have better scores on average than the students in previous years.

(ii) Test for equality of two variances

Next we split the sample into two parts, males and females, and we assume that all scores are independently distributed with distribution $N(\mu_1, \sigma_1^2)$ for males and $N(\mu_2, \sigma_2^2)$ for females. The sample means and standard deviations for both sub-samples are in Exhibit 1.6—that is, $n_1 = 373$ and $n_2 = 236$, the sample means are $\bar{y}_1 = 2.728$ and $\bar{y}_2 = 2.895$, and the sample standard deviations are $s_1 = 0.441$ and $s_2 = 0.472$. We test whether $\sigma_1^2 = \sigma_2^2$ against the alternative that $\sigma_1^2 \neq \sigma_2^2$ by means of (1.55). The outcome is $F = s_2^2/s_1^2 = (0.472)^2/(0.441)^2 = 1.14$, and for the corresponding $F(235, 372)$ distribution this gives a (two-sided) *P*-value of around 0.26. The null hypothesis of equal variances is not rejected (at 5 per cent significance level). That is, there is no significant difference in the variance of the scores for male and female students.

☞ Exercises: E: 1.12a–c, e.

1.4.3 Interval estimates and the bootstrap

☞ First used in Section 2.3.1.

Interval estimates

Although a point estimate may suggest a high precision, this neglects the random nature of estimators. Because estimates depend on data that are partly random, it is sometimes preferred to give an *interval estimate* of the parameter instead of a point estimate. This interval indicates the uncertainty about the actual value of the parameter. When the interval is constructed in such a way that it contains the true parameter value with probability $1-\alpha$, then it is called a $(1-\alpha)\times 100$ per cent interval estimate. One method to construct such an interval is to use a test of size α and to include all parameter values θ_* for which the null hypothesis $H_0: \theta = \theta_*$ is not rejected. Indeed, if the true parameter value is θ_0, then for a test of size α the probability that $H_0: \theta = \theta_0$ is rejected is precisely α, so that the probability that the constructed interval contains θ_0 is $1-\alpha$. For example, assuming that the observations are $\text{NID}(\mu, \sigma^2)$, a 95 per cent interval estimate for the mean is given by all values μ for which

$$\bar{y} - c\frac{s}{\sqrt{n}} \leq \mu \leq \bar{y} + c\frac{s}{\sqrt{n}}, \tag{1.56}$$

where c is such that $P[-c \leq t \leq c] = 0.95$ when t has the $t(n-1)$ distribution. If μ_0 is the true population mean, the complementary set of outcomes in (1.53) has a probability of 5 per cent, so that the interval in (1.56) has a probability of 95 per cent to contain μ_0. In a similar way, using (1.54), a 95 per cent interval estimate for the variance σ^2 is given by

$$\frac{(n-1)s^2}{c_2} \leq \sigma^2 \leq \frac{(n-1)s^2}{c_1},$$

where $c_1 < c_2$ are chosen such that $P[c_1 \leq t \leq c_2] = 0.95$ when t has the $\chi^2(n-1)$ distribution. For instance, one can take these values so that $P[t \leq c_1] = P[t \geq c_2] = 0.025$.

Approximate tests and approximate interval estimators

Until now the attention has been restricted to data consisting of random samples from the normal distribution. In this case, tests can be constructed for the mean and variance that have a known distribution in finite samples. In other cases, the distribution of the estimator $\hat{\theta}$ in finite samples is not known. When the asymptotic distribution is known, this can be used to construct asymptotic tests and corresponding interval estimates. For instance, if a maximum likelihood estimator $\hat{\theta}_n$ is asymptotically normally distributed

$$\sqrt{n}(\hat{\theta}_n - \theta_0) \xrightarrow{d} \text{N}(0, \sigma^2),$$

then in finite samples we can take as an approximation $\hat{\theta}_n \approx \text{N}(\theta_0, \hat{\sigma}^2/n)$, where $\hat{\sigma}^2$ is a consistent estimator of σ^2. This means that

$$\frac{\hat{\theta}_n - \theta_0}{\hat{\sigma}/\sqrt{n}} \approx \mathrm{N}(0, 1).$$

This is very similar to (1.52). For instance, let $H_0 : \theta = \theta_0$ and $H_1 : \theta \neq \theta_0$; then the null hypothesis is rejected if

$$\hat{\theta} < \theta_0 - c\frac{\hat{\sigma}}{\sqrt{n}} \text{ or } \hat{\theta} > \theta_0 + c\frac{\hat{\sigma}}{\sqrt{n}},$$

where $P[|t| > c]$ with $t \sim \mathrm{N}(0, 1)$ is the approximate size of the test. For a 5 per cent size there holds $c \approx 2$. An approximate 95 per cent interval estimate of θ is given by all values in the interval

$$\hat{\theta} - 2\frac{\hat{\sigma}}{\sqrt{n}} \leq \theta \leq \hat{\theta} + 2\frac{\hat{\sigma}}{\sqrt{n}}.$$

Bootstrap method

An alternative to asymptotic approximations is to use the *bootstrap* method. This method has the attractive property that it does not require knowledge of the shape of the probability distribution of the data or of the estimator. It is, therefore, said to be distribution free. The bootstrap method uses the sample distribution to construct an interval estimate. We discuss this for the case of random samples. If the observations all have different values (that is, $y_i \neq y_j$ for $i \neq j$, $i, j = 1, \cdots, n$), then the bootstrap probability distribution of the random variable y is the discrete distribution with outcome set $V = \{y_1, \cdots, y_n\}$ and with probabilities

$$P[y = y_i] = \frac{1}{n}. \tag{1.57}$$

The distribution of a statistic $t(y_1, \cdots, y_n)$ is simulated as follows. In one simulation run, n observations are randomly drawn (with replacement) from the distribution (1.57) and the corresponding value of t is calculated. Repeating this in a large number of runs (always with the same distribution (1.57), which is based on the original data), this provides an accurate approximation of the distribution of t if (1.57) would be the data generating process. In reality it will, of course, be only an approximation of the data generating process. However, the bootstrap is a simple method to get an idea of possible random variations when there is little information about the probability distribution that generates the data.

XM101STU

Example 1.13: **Student Learning (continued)**

We will construct two interval estimates of the mean of the FGPA scores—namely, (i) based on the assumed normal distribution of FGPA scores, and (ii) obtained by the bootstrap method.

(i) **Interval based on normal distribution**

We construct interval estimates of the mean of FGPA, both for the combined population (denoted by μ) and for males (μ_1) and females (μ_2) separately. If we assume that the scores are in all three cases normally distributed, the interval estimates can be computed from (1.56). The resulting 95 per cent interval estimates are

$$2.76 \leq \mu \leq 2.83, \; 2.68 \leq \mu_1 \leq 2.77, \; 2.83 \leq \mu_2 \leq 2.96.$$

Note that the interval estimate of μ_1 is below that of μ_2, which suggests that the two means differ significantly. If we do not assume that the individual scores are normally distributed but apply the asymptotic normal approximation for the sample means, then the corresponding asymptotic interval estimates for the mean are the same as before.

(ii) **Interval obtained by the bootstrap method**

Although the sample sizes are relatively large in all three cases, we will consider the bootstrap as an alternative to construct an interval estimate for μ_2 (as the corresponding sample size $n_2 = 236$ is the smallest of the three cases). For this purpose, the bootstrap distribution (1.57) consists of the 236 FGPA scores of female students. We perform 10,000 simulation runs. In each

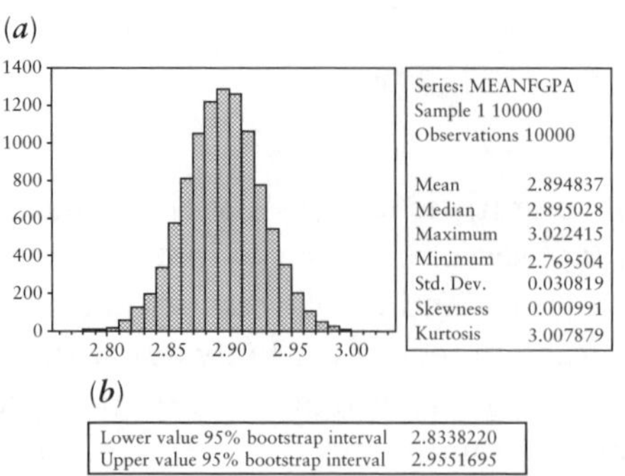

Exhibit 1.17 Student Learning (Example 1.13)

Bootstrap distribution (*a*) of the sample mean obtained by 10,000 simulation runs (each of sample size 236) from the bootstrap distribution of the FGPA scores of female students, and 95% bootstrap interval estimate for the population mean μ_2 (*b*).

run, 236 IID observations are drawn from the bootstrap distribution and the corresponding sample mean is calculated. This gives a set of 10,000 simulated values of the sample mean, with histogram given in Exhibit 1.17 (*a*). Deleting the 250 smallest and the 250 largest values of the sample mean, we obtain the 95 per cent bootstrap interval estimate $2.83 \leq \mu_2 \leq 2.96$ (see Exhibit 1.17 (*b*)). This interval coincides (within this precision) with the earlier interval that was based on the normal distribution, but this is a coincidence, as in general the two intervals will be different. Here the outcomes are very close, because the sample size ($n = 236$) is large enough to use the normal distribution of the sample mean as a reasonable approximation.

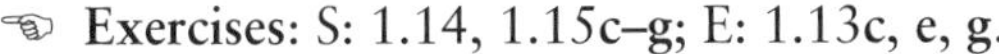
Exercises: S: 1.14, 1.15c–g; E: 1.13c, e, g.

Summary, further reading, and keywords

SUMMARY

This chapter gives a concise review of the main statistical concepts and methods that are used in the rest of this book. We discussed methods to describe observed data by means of graphs and sample statistics. Random variables provide a means to describe the random nature of economic data. The normal distribution and distributions related to the normal distribution play a central role. We considered different methods to estimate the parameters of distributions from observed data and we discussed statistical properties such as unbiasedness, efficiency, consistency, and asymptotic distributions of estimators. Further we discussed hypothesis testing and related concepts such as size, power, significance, and P-values.

FURTHER READING

For a more extensive treatment of statistics the reader is referred to the literature. We mention only a few key references from the large collection of good textbooks in statistics. As concerns the technical level, Aczel and Sounderpandian (2002), Keller and Warrack (2003), and Moore and McCabe (1999) are introductory; Arnold (1990), Bain and Engelhardt (1992), Hogg and Craig (1995), and Mood, Graybill, and Boes (1987) are intermediate; and Kendall and Stuart (1977–83) and Spanos (1995) are advanced.

Aczel, A. D., and Sounderpandian, J. (2002). *Complete Business Statistics*. Boston: McGraw-Hill.

Arnold, S. F. (1990). *Mathematical Statistics*. Englewood Cliffs, NJ: Prentice Hall.

Bain, L. J., and Engelhardt, M. (1992). *Introduction to Probability and Mathematical Statistics*. Boston: Duxbury Press.

Hogg, R. V., and Craig, A. T. (1995). *Introduction to Mathematical Statistics*. Englewood Cliffs, NJ: Prentice Hall.

Keller, G., and Warrack, B. (2003). *Statistics for Management and Economics*. Pacific Grove, Calif.: Brooks/Cole-Thomson Learning.

Kendall, M. G., and Stuart, A. (1977–83). *The Advanced Theory of Statistics*. 3 vols. London: Griffin.

Mood, A. M., Graybill, F. A., and Boes, D. C. (1987). *Introduction to the Theory of Statistics*. Auckland: McGraw-Hill.

Moore, D. S., and McCabe, G. P. (1999). *Introduction to the Practice of Statistics*. New York: Freeman.

Spanos, A. (1995). *Statistical Foundations of Econometric Modelling*. Cambridge: Cambridge University Press.

KEYWORDS

alternative hypothesis 55
asymptotic distribution 50
asymptotic normal distribution 50
asymptotic properties 48
Bernoulli distribution 29
bias 43
binomial distribution 29
bootstrap 65
central limit theorem 50
chi-square distribution 32
conditional distribution 24
conditional expectation 24
consistent estimator 48
consistent test 56
convergence in distribution 50
correlation coefficient 23
correlation matrix 18
covariance 23
critical region 56
cumulative distribution function 20
data generating process 42
density function 20
dependence 17
efficient 43
error of the first type 56
error of the second type 56
estimate 38
estimator 38
expectation 21
F-distribution 34
histogram 12
hypothesis 55
independence 25
information matrix 45
interval estimate 64
invariant 40
kurtosis 16
law of large numbers 50
least squares 39
likelihood function 40
log-likelihood 52
marginal distribution 23
maximum likelihood 40
mean 21
mean squared error 43
median 16
method of moments 39
model 38
multivariate normal distribution 30
normal distribution 29
null hypothesis 55
one-sided test 60
P-value 60
parameters 29, 38
pivotal 36
power 56
practical significance 57
probability distribution 20
probability limit 48
probability value 60
random 20
random sample 35
sample correlation coefficient 18
sample covariance 18
sample covariance matrix 18
sample cumulative distribution function 13, 20
sample mean 16
sample standard deviation 16
sample variance 16
scatter diagram 13
significance level 56
significant 60
similar test 56
simulation experiment 46
simulation run 46

Exercises

THEORY QUESTIONS

1.1 (☞ Section 1.1.2)
Suppose that n pairs of outcomes (x_i, y_i) of the variables x and y have been observed.

a. Prove that the sample correlation coefficient between the variables x and y always lies between -1 and $+1$. It may be helpful to consider the function $S(b) = \sum_{i=1}^{n} (y_i - \bar{y} - b(x_i - \bar{x}))^2$ and to use the fact that the minimal value of this function is non-negative.

b. Prove that the sample correlation coefficient is invariant under the linear transformation $x_i^* = a_1 x_i + b_1$ and $y_i^* = a_2 y_i + b_2$ for all $i = 1, \cdots, n$, with $a_1 > 0$ and $a_2 > 0$ positive constants.

c. Show, by means of an example, that the sample correlation coefficient is in general not invariant under non-linear transformations.

d*. Prove that the sample correlation coefficient is equal to 1 or -1 if and only if y is a linear function of x—that is, $y_i = a + bx_i, i = 1, \cdots, n$, for some numbers a and b that do not depend on i.

1.2 (☞ Section 1.2.2)

a*. Prove the results in (1.15) and (1.16).

b. Suppose that x and y are independent random variables. Prove that the conditional distribution of $y|x = v$ then does not depend on the value of v and that therefore the conditional mean and variance of $y|x = v$ also do not depend on v.

c. Prove that independent variables are uncorrelated.

d. Give an example of two random variables that are uncorrelated but not independent.

1.3 (☞ Sections 1.2.1, 1.2.2)

a. Prove the result in (1.10) for the case of a linear transformation $z = ay + b$ with $a \neq 0$.

b. Prove the two results in (1.18).

c. Suppose that y_1 and y_2 are independent random variables and that $z_1 = g_1(y_1)$ and $z_2 = g_2(y_2)$. Use the results in (1.10) and (1.19) to prove that z_1 and z_2 are independent.

d. Show, by means of an example, that the result in **c** does not generally hold true when 'independent' is replaced by 'uncorrelated'.

1.4 (☞ Section 1.2.3)

a. Show that the mean and variance of the Bernoulli distribution are equal to p and $p(1 - p)$ respectively.

b. Show that the mean and variance of the binomial distribution are equal to np and $np(1 - p)$ respectively.

c. Show the result in (1.23) for the case that A is an $n \times n$ non-singular matrix, by using the generalization of the result in (1.19) to the case of n functions.

d. Show that, when two jointly normally distributed random variables are uncorrelated, they are also independent.

e*. Show that the first four moments of the normal distribution $N(\mu, \sigma^2)$ are equal to $\mu_1 = \mu$, $\mu_2 = \sigma^2$, $\mu_3 = 0$, and $\mu_4 = 3\sigma^4$. Show that the skewness and kurtosis are equal to zero and three respectively.

f. Let $y \sim N(\mu, \sigma^2)$ and let $z = ay + b$ with $a \neq 0$; then prove that $z \sim N(a\mu + b, a^2\sigma^2)$.

g*. Show the result in (1.22).

1.5 (☞ Sections 1.2.3, 1.2.4)
Let $y \sim N(0, I)$ be an $n \times 1$ vector of independent standard normal random variables and let $z_0 = Ay$, $z_1 = y'Q_1 y$ and $z_2 = y'Q_2 y$ with A a given $m \times n$ matrix and with Q_1 and Q_2 given symmetric idempotent $n \times n$ matrices.

a. If the rank of Q_1 is equal to r, then $Q_1 = UU'$ for an $n \times r$ matrix U with the property that $U'U = I$ (the $r \times r$ identity matrix). Use this result to prove that $y'Q_1y \sim \chi^2(r)$.

b. Show that the mean and variance of the $\chi^2(r)$ distribution are r and $2r$ respectively.

c. Prove the results in (1.29) and (1.30), using the fact that jointly normally distributed random variables are independent if and only if they are uncorrelated.

d. Let $y_r \sim t(r)$; then show that for $r \to \infty$ the random variables y_r converge in distribution to the standard normal distribution.

e. Let $y_r \sim F(r_1, r)$ with r_1 fixed; then show that for $r \to \infty$ the random variables $r_1 \cdot y_r$ converge in distribution to the $\chi^2(r_1)$ distribution.

f. Show that the matrix M in (1.34) is symmetric and idempotent and that it has rank $(n-1)$.

1.6 (☞ Sections 1.3.1, 1.3.2)
Let $y_i \sim \text{NID}(\mu, \sigma^2)$, $i = 1, \cdots, n$. In Example 1.8 the log-likelihood function (1.40) was analysed in terms of the parameters $\theta = (\mu, \sigma^2)$, but now we consider as an alternative the parameters $\psi = (\mu, \sigma)$.

a. Determine gradient and Hessian matrix of the log-likelihood function $\log(L(\psi))$.

b. Check that the maximum likelihood estimates are invariant under this change of parameters. In particular, show that the estimated value of σ is the square root of the estimated value of σ^2 in Example 1.8.

c. Check the equality in (1.46) for the log-likelihood function $\log(L(\psi))$.

1.7 (☞ Sections 1.3.2, 1.3.3)

a. Prove the equality in (1.45) for arbitrary distributions.

b. Prove the inequality of Chebyshev, which states that for a random variable y with mean μ and variance σ^2 there holds $P[|y - \mu| \geq c\sigma] \leq 1/c^2$ for every $c > 0$.

c. Use the inequality of Chebyshev to prove that the two conditions in (1.48) imply consistency.

d. Use this result to prove that the maximum likelihood estimators $\hat{\mu}_{ML}$ and $\hat{\sigma}^2_{ML}$ in Example 1.8 are consistent.

e*. Prove the four rules for probability limits that are stated in the text below formula (1.48)—that is, for the sum, the product, the quotient, and arbitrary continuous functions of sequences of random variables.

1.8 (☞ Sections 1.3.2, 1.3.3)
Let $y_1, \cdots, y_n$ be a random sample from a Bernoulli distribution.

a. Derive the maximum likelihood estimator of the parameter $p = P[y_i = 1]$. Investigate whether this estimator is unbiased and consistent.

b. Derive the Cramér–Rao lower bound.

c. Investigate whether the estimator in **a** is efficient in the class of unbiased estimators.

d. Suppose that the odds ratio $P[y = 1]/P[y = 0]$ is estimated by $\hat{p}/(1 - \hat{p})$ with $\hat{p}$ the estimator in **a**. Investigate whether this estimator of the odds ratio is unbiased and consistent.

1.9 (☞ Sections 1.3.1, 1.3.2)
Let $y_i \sim \text{IID}(\mu, \sigma^2)$, $i = 1, \cdots, n$, and consider linear estimators of the mean μ of the form $\hat{\mu} = \sum_{i=1}^{n} a_i y_i$.

a. Derive the restriction on a_i needed to guarantee that the estimator $\hat{\mu}$ is unbiased.

b. Derive the expression for the variance of the estimator $\hat{\mu}$.

c. Derive the linear unbiased estimator that has the minimal variance in this class of estimators.

d. Suppose that the distribution of each observation is given by the double exponential density $f(v) = \frac{1}{2}e^{-|v-\mu|}$ with $-\infty < v < \infty$. Show that in this case the maximum likelihood estimator of μ is the median.

e. Discuss whether the estimator of **c** will be asymptotically efficient in the class of all unbiased estimators if the data are generated by the double exponential density.

1.10 (☞ Sections 1.3.1, 1.3.2, 1.3.3)
Let $y_1, \cdots, y_n$ be a random sample from a population with density function $f_\theta(v) = e^{\theta - v}$ for $v \geq \theta$ and $f(v) = 0$ for $v < \theta$, where θ is an unknown parameter.

a. Determine the method of moments estimator of θ, based on the first moment. Determine the mean and variance of this estimator.

b. Prove that this estimator is consistent.

c. Prove that the maximum likelihood estimator of θ is given by the minimum value of $y_1, \cdots, y_n$. Give explicit proofs that this estimator is biased but consistent.

d. Discuss which of the two estimators in **a** and **c** you would prefer. Consider in particular the two extreme cases of a single observation ($n = 1$) and the asymptotic case (for $n \to \infty$).

EMPIRICAL AND SIMULATION QUESTIONS

1.11 (☞ Sections 1.1.1, 1.1.2, 1.2.2)

In this exercise we consider data of ten randomly drawn students (the observation index i indicates the position of the students in the file of all 609 students of Example 1.1). The values of FGPA, SATM, and FEM of these students are as follows.

i	FGPA	SATM	FEM
8	3.168	6.2	0
381	3.482	5.4	0
186	2.592	5.7	1
325	2.566	6.0	0
290	2.692	5.9	1
138	1.805	5.4	1
178	2.264	6.2	1
108	3.225	6.0	1
71	2.074	5.3	0
594	3.020	6.2	1

a. Compute for each of the three variables the sample mean, median, standard deviation, skewness, and kurtosis.

b. Compute the sample covariances and sample correlation coefficients between these three variables.

c. Make three histograms and three scatter plots for these three variables.

d. Relate the outcomes in **a** and **b** with the results in **c**.

e. Compute the conditional means of FGPA and SATM for the four male students and also for the six female students. Check the relation (1.15) (applied to the 'population' of the ten students considered here) for the two variables FGPA and SATM.

1.12 (☞ Sections 1.3.3, 1.4.2)

Consider the data set of ten observations used in Exercise 1.11. The FGPA scores are assumed to be independently normally distributed with mean μ and variance σ^2, and the gender variable FEM is assumed to be independently Bernoulli distributed with parameter $p = P[\text{FEM} = 1]$. These ten students are actually drawn from a larger data set consisting of 236 female and 373 male students where the FGPA scores have mean 2.79 and standard deviation 0.46.

a. On the basis of the ten observations, test the null hypothesis that the mean is $\mu = 2.79$ against the alternative that $\mu < 2.79$. Use a statistical package to compute the corresponding (one-sided) P-value of this test outcome.

b. Repeat **a**, but now for the two-sided alternative that $\mu \neq 2.79$. What is the relation between the P-values of the one-sided and the two-sided tests?

c. Answer the questions in **a** and **b** for testing the null hypothesis $\sigma = 0.46$ against the one-sided alternative $\sigma > 0.46$.

d. Let $\hat{p}$ denote the random variable consisting of the fraction of successes in a random sample of size n from the Bernoulli distribution. Use the central limit theorem to argue that the approximate distribution of $\hat{p}$ is $\hat{p} \approx \mathrm{N}(p, \frac{1}{n}p(1-p))$.

e. In the sample there are six female and four male students. Test the null hypothesis that $p = 236/609$ against the alternative that $p \neq 236/609$, based on the asymptotic approximation in **d**.

1.13 (☞ Sections 1.1.1, 1.1.2, 1.2.3, 1.4.3)

In this exercise we consider data of 474 employees (working in the banking sector) on the variables y (the yearly salary in dollars) and x (the number of finished years of education).

a. Make histograms of the variables x and y and make a scatter plot of y against x.

b. Compute mean, median, and standard deviation of the variables x and y and compute the correlation between x and y. Check that the distribution of the salaries y is very skewed and has excess kurtosis.

c. Compute a 95% interval estimate of the mean of the variable y, assuming that the salaries are $\text{NID}(\mu, \sigma^2)$.

d. Define the random variable $z = \log(y)$. Make a histogram of the resulting 474 values of z and compute the mean, median, standard deviation, skewness and kurtosis of z. Check that $\bar{z} \neq \log(\bar{y})$ but that $\text{med}(z) = \log(\text{med}(y))$. Explain this last result.

e. Compute a 95% interval estimate of the mean of the variable z, assuming that the observations on z are $\text{NID}(\mu_z, \sigma_z^2)$.

f. If $z \sim \text{N}(\mu_z, \sigma_z^2)$, then $y = e^z$ is said to be log-normally distributed. Show that the mean of y is given by $\mu = e^{\mu_z + \frac{1}{2}\sigma_z^2}$.

g. Compute a 95% interval estimate of μ, based on the results in **d**, **e**, and **f**. Compare this interval with that obtained in **c**. Which interval do you prefer?

1.14 (☞ Section 1.4.3)
In this simulation exercise we consider the quality of the asymptotic interval estimates discussed in Section 1.4.3. As data generating process we consider the $t(3)$ distribution that has mean equal to zero and variance equal to three. We focus on the construction of interval estimates of the mean and on corresponding tests.

a. Generate a sample of $n = 10$ independent drawings from the $t(3)$ distribution. Let $\bar{y}$ be the sample mean and s the sample standard deviation. Compute the interval $\bar{y} \pm 2s/\sqrt{n}$. Reject the null hypothesis of zero mean if and only if this interval does not include zero.

b. Repeat the simulation run of **a** 10,000 times and compute the number of times that the null hypothesis of zero mean is rejected.

c. Repeat the simulation experiment of **a** and **b** for sample sizes $n = 100$ and $n = 1000$ instead of $n = 10$.

d. Give an explanation for the simulated rejection frequencies of the null hypothesis for sample sizes $n = 10$, $n = 100$, and $n = 1000$.

1.15 (☞ Sections 1.2.3, 1.2.4, 1.4.3)
In this simulation exercise we consider an example of the use of the bootstrap in constructing an interval estimate of the median. If the median is taken as a measure of location of a distribution f, this can be estimated by the sample median. For a random sample of size n, the sample median has a standard deviation of $(2f(m)\sqrt{n})^{-1}$ where m is the median of the density f. When the distribution f is unknown, this expression cannot be used to construct an interval estimate.

a. Show that for random samples from the normal distribution the standard deviation of the sample median is $\sigma\sqrt{\pi}/\sqrt{2n}$ whereas the standard deviation of the sample mean is $\sigma/\sqrt{n}$. Comment on these results.

b. Show that for random samples from the Cauchy distribution (that is, the $t(1)$ distribution) the standard deviation of the sample mean does not exist, but that the standard deviation of the sample median is finite and equal to $\pi/(2\sqrt{n})$.

c. Simulate a data set of $n = 1000$ observations $y_1, \cdots, y_{1000}$ by independent drawings from the $t(1)$ distribution.

d. Use the bootstrap method (based on the data of **c**) to construct a 95% interval estimate of the median, as follows. Generate a new set of 1000 observations by IID drawings from the bootstrap distribution and compute the median. Repeat this 10,000 times. The 95% interval estimate of the median can be obtained by ordering the 10,000 computed sample medians. The lower bound is then the 251st value and the upper bound is the 9750th value in this ordered sequence of sample medians (this interval contains 9500 of the 10,000 medians—that is, 95%).

e. Compute the standard deviation of the median over the 10,000 simulations in **d**, and compare this with the theoretical standard deviation in **b**.

f. Repeat **c** 10,000 times. Construct a corresponding 95% interval estimate of the median and compare this with the result in **d**. Also compute the standard deviation of the median over these 10,000 simulations and compare this with the result in **b**.

g. Comment on the differences between the methods in **d** and **f** and their usefulness in practice if we do not know the true data generating process.

2

Simple Regression

Econometrics is concerned with relations between economic variables. The simplest case is a linear relation between two variables. This relation can be estimated by the method of least squares. We discuss this method and we describe conditions under which this method performs well. We also describe tests for the statistical significance of models and their use in making predictions.

2.1 Least squares

2.1.1 Scatter diagrams

☞ Uses Sections 1.1.1, 1.1.2; Appendix A.1.

Data

Data form the basic ingredient for every applied econometric study. Therefore we start by introducing three data sets, one taken from the financial world, the second one from the field of labour economics, and the third one from a marketing experiment. These examples are helpful to understand the methods that we will discuss in this chapter.

XR201SMR

Example 2.1: **Stock Market Returns**

Exhibit 2.1 shows two histograms (in (*a*) and (*b*)) and a scatter plot (in (*c*)) of monthly excess returns in the UK over the period January 1980 to December 1999. The data are taken from the data bank DataStream. One variable, which we denote by y_i, corresponds to the excess returns on an index of stocks in the sector of cyclical consumer goods. This index is composed on the basis of 104 firms in the areas of household durables, automobiles, textiles, and sports. The consumption of these goods is relatively sensitive to economic fluctuations, for which reason they are said to be cyclical. The other variable, which we denote by x_i, corresponds to the excess returns on an overall stock market index. The index i denotes the observation number and runs from $i = 1$ (for 1980.01) to $i = 240$ (for 1999.12). The excess returns are obtained by subtracting the return on a riskless asset from the asset returns. Here we used the one-month interest rate as riskless asset. In Exhibit 2.1, y_i is denoted by RENDMARK and x_i by RENDCYCO (see Appendix B for an explanation of the data sets and corresponding notation of variables used in the book).

The histograms indicate that the excess returns in the sector of cyclical consumer goods are on average lower than those in the total market and that they show a relatively larger variation over time. The extremely large negative returns (of around −36 per cent and −28 per cent) correspond to the stock market crash in October 1987. The scatter diagram shows that the two variables are positively related, since the top right and

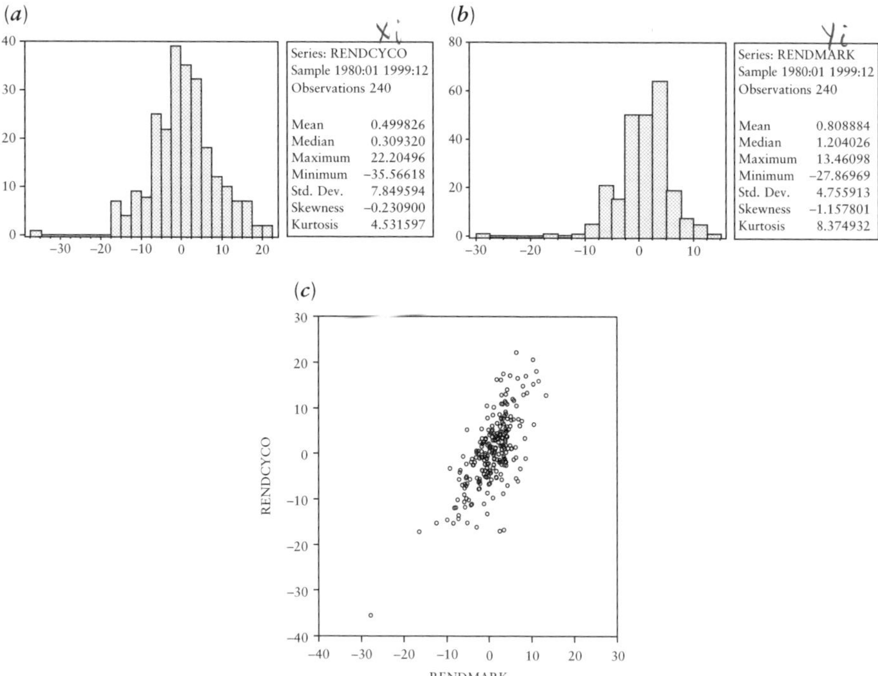

Exhibit 2.1 Stock Market Returns (Example 2.1)

Histograms of monthly returns in the sector of cyclical consumer goods (*a*) and monthly total market returns (*b*) in the UK, and corresponding scatter diagram (*c*).

bottom left of the diagram contain relatively many observations. However, the relationship is not completely linear. If we were to draw a straight line through the scatter of points, then there would be clear deviations from the line.

The further analysis of these data is left as an exercise (see Exercises 2.11, 2.12, and 2.15).

Example 2.2: **Bank Wages**

Exhibit 2.2 shows two histograms (in (*a*) and (*b*)) and a scatter diagram (in (*c*)) of 474 observations on education (in terms of finished years of education) and salary (in (natural) logarithms of the yearly salary S in dollars). The salaries are measured in logarithms for reasons to be discussed later (see Example 2.6). The data are taken from one of the standard data files of the statistical software package SPSS and concern the employees of a US bank. Each point in the scatter diagram corresponds to the education and salary of an employee. On average, salaries are higher for higher educated people. However, for a fixed level of education there remains much variation in salaries. This can be seen in the scatter diagram (*c*), as for a fixed value of

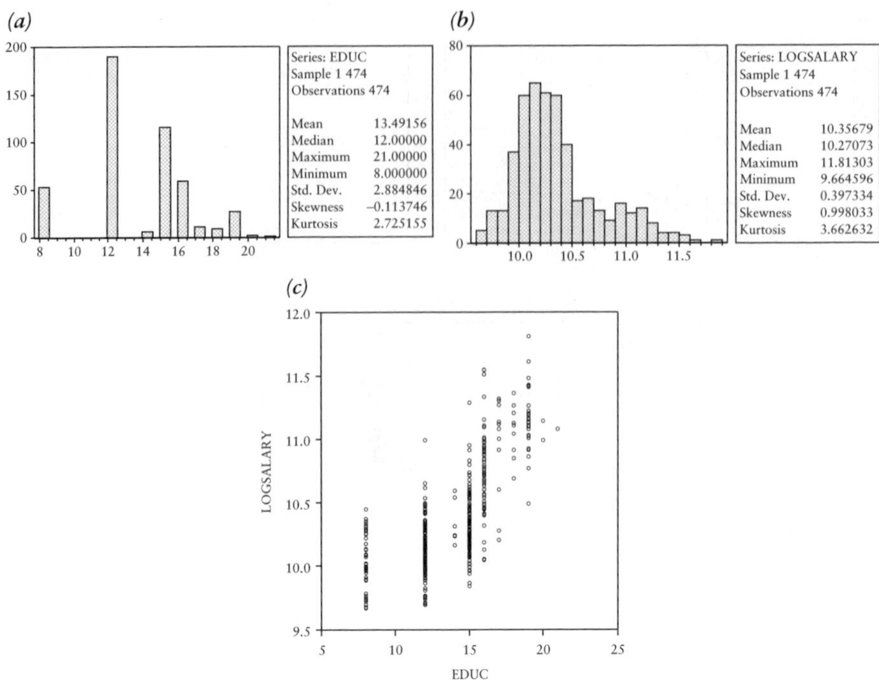

Exhibit 2.2 Bank Wages (Example 2.2)

Histograms of education (in years (*a*)) and salary (in logarithms (*b*)) of 474 bank employees, and corresponding scatter diagram (*c*).

education (on the horizontal axis) there remains variation in salaries (on the vertical axis).

In the sequel we will take this as the leading example to illustrate the theory of this chapter.

E

XR210COF

Example 2.3: **Coffee Sales**

Exhibit 2.3 shows a scatter diagram with twelve observations (x_i, y_i) on price and quantity sold of a brand of coffee. The data are taken from A. C. Bemmaor and D. Mouchoux, 'Measuring the Short-Term Effect of In-Store Promotion and Retail Advertising on Brand Sales: A Factorial Experiment', *Journal of Marketing Research*, 28 (1991), 202–14, and were obtained from a controlled marketing experiment in stores in Paris. The price is indexed, with value one for the usual price. Two price actions are investigated, with reductions of 5 per cent or 15 per cent of the usual price. The quantity sold is in units of coffee per week. Clearly, lower prices result in higher sales. Further, for a fixed price (on the horizontal axis) there remains variation in sales (different values on the vertical axis).

The further analysis of these data is left as an exercise (see Exercise 2.10).

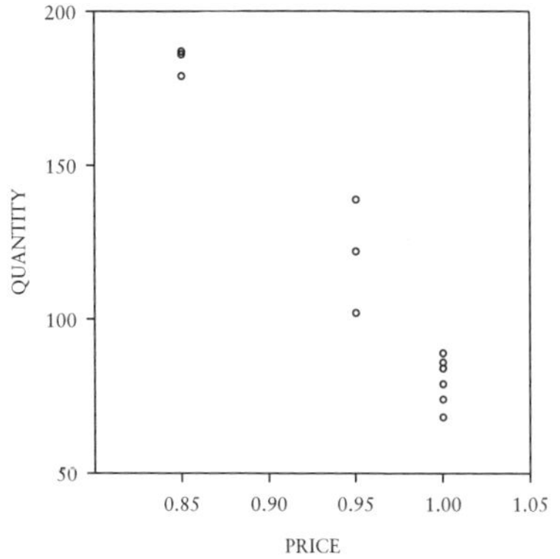

Exhibit 2.3 Coffee Sales (Example 2.3)

Scatter diagram of quantity sold against price index of a brand of coffee (the data set consists of twelve observations; in the top left part of the diagram two observations nearly coincide).

2.1.2 Least squares

☞ Uses Appendix A.1, A.7.

Fitting a line to a scatter of data

Our starting point is a set of points in a *scatter diagram* corresponding to n paired observations (x_i, y_i), $i = 1, \cdots, n$, and we want to find the line that gives the best fit to these points. We describe the line by the formula

$$y = a + bx. \tag{2.1}$$

Here b is called the slope of the line and a the intercept. The idea is to explain the differences in the outcomes of the variable y in terms of differences in the corresponding values of the variable x. To evaluate the fit, we assume that our purpose is to explain or predict the value of y that is associated with a given value of x. In the three examples in Section 2.1.1, this means that the monthly variation in sector returns is explained by the market returns, that differences in salaries are explained by education, and that variations in sales are explained by prices.

Terminology

The variable y in (2.1) is called the *variable to be explained* (or also the *dependent* variable or the *endogenous* variable) and the variable x is called the *explanatory variable* (or also the *independent* variable, the *exogenous* variable, the *regressor*, or the *covariate*). We measure the deviations e_i of the observations from the line vertically—that is,

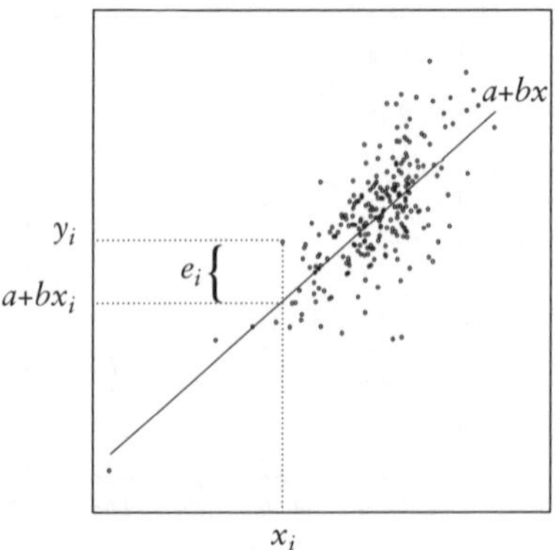

Exhibit 2.4 Scatter diagram with fitted line

Scatter diagram with observed data (x_i, y_i), regression line $(a + bx)$, fitted value $(a + bx_i)$, and residual (e_i).

$$e_i = y_i - a - bx_i. \tag{2.2}$$

So e_i is the error that we make in predicting y_i by means of the variable x_i using the linear relation (2.1) (see Exhibit 2.4).

The least squares criterion

Now we have to make precise what we mean by the fit of a line. We will do this by specifying a criterion function—that is, a function of a and b that takes smaller values if the deviations are smaller. In many situations we dislike positive deviations as much as negative deviations, in which case the criterion function depends on a and b via the absolute values of the deviations e_i. There are several ways to specify such a function—for instance,

$$S_{\text{abs}}(a, b) = \sum |e_i|,$$
$$S(a, b) = \sum e_i^2.$$

In both cases the summation index runs from 1 through n (where no misunderstanding can arise we simply write $\sum$). The second of these functions, the *least squares criterion* that measures the sum of squared deviations, is by far the most frequently used. The reason is that its minimization is much more convenient than that of other functions. This method is also called *ordinary least squares* (abbreviated as OLS). However, we will meet other criterion functions in later chapters. In this chapter we restrict our attention to the minimization of $S(a, b)$.

Computation of the least squares estimates *a* and *b*

By substituting (2.2) in the least squares criterion we obtain

$$S(a, b) = \sum (y_i - a - bx_i)^2. \tag{2.3}$$

Here the n observations (x_i, y_i) are given, and we minimize the function $S(a, b)$ with respect to a and b. The first order conditions for a minimum are given by

$$\frac{\partial S}{\partial a} = -2\sum (y_i - a - bx_i) = 0, \tag{2.4}$$

$$\frac{\partial S}{\partial b} = -2\sum x_i(y_i - a - bx_i) = 0. \tag{2.5}$$

From the condition in (2.4) we obtain, after dividing by $2n$, that

$$a = \overline{y} - b\overline{x} \tag{2.6}$$

where $\overline{y} = \sum y_i/n$ and $\overline{x} = \sum x_i/n$ denote the sample means of the variables y and x respectively. Because $\overline{x}$ is fixed (that is, independent of i) so that $\sum \overline{x}(y_i - a - bx_i) = \overline{x}\sum (y_i - a - bx_i) = 0$ according to (2.4), we can rewrite (2.5) as

$$\sum (x_i - \overline{x})(y_i - a - bx_i) = 0. \tag{2.7}$$

Now we substitute (2.6) in (2.7) and solve this expression for b, so that

$$b = \frac{\sum (x_i - \overline{x})(y_i - \overline{y})}{\sum (x_i - \overline{x})^2}. \tag{2.8}$$

To check whether the values of a and b in (2.6) and (2.8) indeed provide the minimum of $S(a, b)$, it suffices to check whether the Hessian matrix is positive definite. From (2.4) and (2.5) the Hessian matrix is obtained as

$$\begin{pmatrix} \partial^2 S/\partial a^2 & \partial^2 S/\partial a \partial b \\ \partial^2 S/\partial b \partial a & \partial^2 S/\partial b^2 \end{pmatrix} = \begin{pmatrix} 2n & 2\sum x_i \\ 2\sum x_i & 2\sum x_i^2 \end{pmatrix}.$$

This matrix is positive definite if $n > 0$ and the determinant $4n\sum x_i^2 -4(\sum x_i)^2 > 0$—that is,

$$\sum (x_i - \overline{x})^2 > 0.$$

The condition that $n > 0$ is evident, and the condition that $\sum (x_i - \overline{x})^2 > 0$ means that there should be some variation in the explanatory variable x. If this condition does not hold true, then all the points in the scatter diagram are situated on a vertical line. Of course, it makes little sense to try to explain variations in y by variations in x if x does not vary in the sample.

Normal equations

We can rewrite the two first order conditions in (2.4) and (2.5) as

$$an + b\sum x_i = \sum y_i, \tag{2.9}$$

$$a\sum x_i + b\sum x_i^2 = \sum x_i y_i. \tag{2.10}$$

These are called the *normal equations*. The expressions in (2.6) and (2.8) show that the least squares estimates depend solely on the first and second sample moments of the data.

Remark on notation

Now that we have completed our minimization procedure, we make a remark on the notation. When minimizing (2.3) we have treated the x_i and y_i as fixed numbers and a and b as independent variables that could be chosen freely. After completing the minimization procedure, we have found specific values of a and b by (2.6) and (2.8). Strict mathematicians would stress the difference by using different symbols. From now on, we no longer need a and b as independent variables and for convenience we will use the notation a and b only for the expressions in (2.6) and (2.8). That is, from now on a and b are uniquely defined as the numbers that can be computed from the observed data (x_i, y_i), $i = 1, \cdots, n$, by means of these two formulas.

☞ Exercises: T: 2.1a, b; E: 2.10b, 2.12a, c.

2.1.3 Residuals and R^2

Least squares residuals

Given the observations $(x_1, y_1), \cdots, (x_n, y_n)$, and the corresponding unique values of a and b given by (2.6) and (2.8), we obtain the *residuals*

$$e_i = y_i - a - bx_i.$$

Because a and b satisfy the first order conditions (2.4) and (2.7), we find two properties of these residuals

$$\sum e_i = 0, \quad \sum (x_i - \overline{x})e_i = 0. \tag{2.11}$$

So (in the language of descriptive statistics) the residuals have zero mean and they are uncorrelated with the explanatory variable.

Three sums of squares

A traditional way to measure the performance of least squares is to compare the sum of squared residuals with the sum of squares of $(y_i - \overline{y})$. We can rewrite (2.2) as

$$y_i = a + bx_i + e_i$$

and we obtain from (2.6) that

$$y_i - \overline{y} = b(x_i - \overline{x}) + e_i.$$

So the difference from the mean $(y_i - \overline{y})$ can be decomposed as a sum of two components, a component corresponding to the difference from the mean of the explanatory variable $(x_i - \overline{x})$ and an unexplained component described by the residual e_i. The sum of squares of $(y_i - \overline{y})$ also consists of two components

$$\sum (y_i - \overline{y})^2 = b^2 \sum (x_i - \overline{x})^2 + \sum e_i^2 \qquad (2.12)$$

$$SST = SSE + SSR. \qquad (2.13)$$

Note that the cross product term $\sum (x_i - \overline{x})e_i$ vanishes as a consequence of (2.11). Here SST is called the total sum of squares, SSE the explained sum of squares, and SSR the sum of squared residuals.

Coefficient of determination: R^2

The above three sums of squares depend on the scale of measurement of the variable y. To get a performance measure that is independent of scale we divide through by SST. The *coefficient of determination*, denoted by the symbol R^2, is defined as the relative explained sum of squares

$$R^2 = \frac{SSE}{SST} = \frac{b^2 \sum (x_i - \overline{x})^2}{\sum (y_i - \overline{y})^2}. \qquad (2.14)$$

By substituting (2.8) in (2.14) we obtain

$$R^2 = \frac{\left(\sum (x_i - \overline{x})(y_i - \overline{y})\right)^2}{\sum (x_i - \overline{x})^2 \sum (y_i - \overline{y})^2}.$$

So R^2 is equal to the square of the correlation coefficient between y and x. By using (2.12) it follows that (2.14) can be rewritten as

$$R^2 = 1 - \frac{\sum e_i^2}{\sum (y_i - \bar{y})^2}. \tag{2.15}$$

The expressions (2.14) and (2.15) show that $0 \leq R^2 \leq 1$ and that the least squares criterion is equivalent to the maximization of R^2.

R^2 in model without intercept

Until now we have assumed that an intercept term (the coefficient a) is included in the model. If the model does not contain an intercept—that is, if the fitted line is of the form $y = bx$—then R^2 is still defined as in (2.14). However, the results in (2.11), (2.12), and (2.15) no longer hold true (see Exercise 2.4).

☞ **Exercises:** T: 2.2; E: 2.10c, 2.11.

2.1.4 Illustration: Bank Wages

E

XM202BWA

We illustrate the results in Sections 2.1.2 and 2.1.3 with the data on bank wages discussed before in Example 2.2. We will discuss (i) the precision of reported results in this book, (ii) the least squares estimates, (iii) the sums of squares and R^2, and (iv) the outcome of a regression package (we used the package EViews).

(i) Precision of reported results

For readers who want to check the numerical outcomes, we first comment on the precision of the reported results. In all our examples, we report intermediary and final results with a much lower precision than the software packages used to compute the outcomes. Therefore, to check the outcomes, the reader should also use a software package and should not work with our intermediary outcomes, which involve *rounding errors*.

(ii) Least squares estimates

Continuing the discussion in Example 2.2 on bank wages, we report the following sample statistics for the $n = 474$ observations of the variables x (education) and y (natural logarithm of salary).

$$\sum x_i = 6395, \ \sum y_i = 4909, \ \sum x_i^2 = 90215,$$
$$\sum y_i^2 = 50917, \ \sum x_i y_i = 66609.$$

To compute the slope (2.8), we use

$$\sum (x_i - \bar{x})(y_i - \bar{y}) = \sum x_i y_i - n\bar{x}\,\bar{y} = \sum x_i y_i - \frac{1}{n}\sum x_i \sum y_i = 378.9,$$
$$\sum (x_i - \bar{x})^2 = \sum x_i^2 - n\bar{x}^2 = \sum x_i^2 - \frac{1}{n}\left(\sum x_i\right)^2 = 3936.5,$$

so that $b = 0.096$. The formula (2.6) for the intercept gives $a = 9.06$. We leave it as an exercise to check that these values satisfy the normal equations (2.9) and (2.10) (up to rounding errors). The regression line is given by $a + bx = 9.06 + 0.096x$ and is shown in Exhibit 2.5 (*a*). In the sense of least squares, this line gives an optimal fit to the cloud of points. The histogram of the residuals is shown in Exhibit 2.5 (*b*).

(iii) Sums of squares and R^2

The sums of squares are

$$SST = \sum y_i^2 - n\bar{y}^2 = \sum y_i^2 - \frac{1}{n}\left(\sum y_i\right)^2 = 74.7,$$
$$SSE = b^2\left(\sum x_i^2 - n\bar{x}^2\right) = b^2\left(\sum x_i^2 - \frac{1}{n}\left(\sum x_i\right)^2\right) = 36.3,$$
$$SSR = SST - SSE = 38.4,$$

with a corresponding coefficient of determination $R^2 = 0.49$.

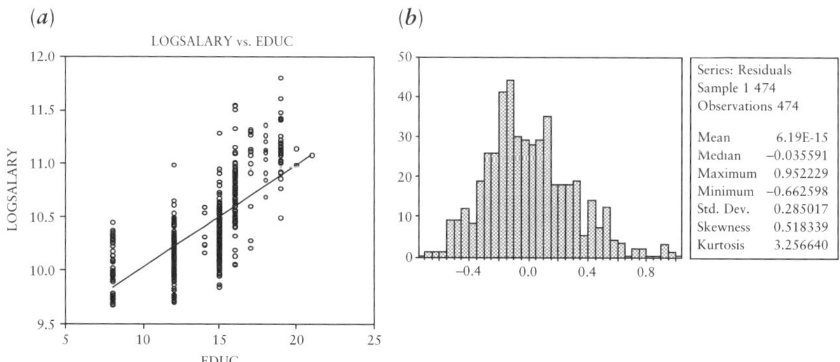

Exhibit 2.5 Bank Wages (Section 2.1.4)

Scatter diagram of salary (in logarithms) against education with least squares line (*a*) and histogram of the residuals (*b*).

(iv) Outcome of regression package

The outcome of a regression package is given in Exhibit 2.6. The two values in the column denoted by 'coefficient' show the values of a (the constant term) and b (the coefficient of the explanatory variable). The table reports R^2, SSR, and also $\bar{y}$ and $\sqrt{SST/(n-1)}$ (the sample mean and sample standard deviation of the dependent variable). We conclude that there is an indication of a positive effect of education on salary and that around 50 per cent of the variation in (logarithmic) salaries can be attributed to differences in education.

Dependent Variable: LOGSALARY Method: Least Squares Sample: 1 474			
Variable	Coefficient		
C	9.062102		
EDUC	0.095963		
R-squared	0.485447	Mean dependent var	10.35679
Sum squared resid	38.42407	S.D. dependent var	0.397334

Exhibit 2.6 Bank Wages (Section 2.1.4)

Results of regression of salary (in logarithms) on a constant (denoted by C) and education, based on data of 474 bank employees.

2.2 Accuracy of least squares

2.2.1 Data generating processes

☞ Uses Appendix A.1.

The helpful fiction of a 'true model' in statistical analysis

Before discussing the statistical properties of least squares, we pay attention to the meaning of some of the terminology that is used in this context. This concerns in particular the meaning of 'data generating process' and 'true model'.

Economic data are the outcome of economic processes. For instance, the stock market data in Example 2.1 result from developments in the production and value of many firms (in this case firms in the sector of cyclical consumer goods) in the UK, and the sales data in Example 2.3 result from the purchase decisions of many individual buyers in a number of stores in Paris. The reported figures may further depend on the method of measurement. For the stock market data, this depends on the firms that are included in the analysis, and for the sales data this depends on the chosen shops and the periods of measurement. It is common to label the combined economic and measurement process as the *data generating process* (DGP). An econometric model aims to provide a concise and reasonably accurate reflection of the data generating process. By disregarding less relevant aspects of the data, the model helps to obtain a better understanding of the main aspects of the data generating process. This implies that, in practice, an econometric model will never provide a completely accurate description of the data generating process. Therefore, if taken literally, the concept of a 'true model' does not make much practical sense. Still, in discussing statistical properties, we sometimes use the notion of a 'true model'. This reflects an idealized situation that allows us to obtain mathematically exact results. The idea is that similar results hold approximately true if the model is a reasonably accurate approximation of the data generating process.

Simulation as a tool in statistical analysis

The ideal situation of a 'true model' will never hold in practice, but we can imitate this situation by means of computer simulations. In this case the data are generated by means of a computer program that satisfies the assumptions of the model. Then the model is indeed 'true', as the data generating process satisfies all the model assumptions. So, for illustrative purposes, we will start not by analysing a set of empirical data, but by generating a set of data ourselves. For that purpose we shall write a small computer program in which we shall carry out a number of steps.

Example of a simulation experiment

We start by choosing a value for the number n of observations — for instance, $n = 20$. Then we fix n numbers for the explanatory variable x — for instance, $x_1 = 1, x_2 = 2, \cdots, x_n = n$. We choose a constant term α — say, $\alpha = 10$ — and a slope coefficient β — say, $\beta = 1$. Finally we choose a value σ^2 for the variance of the *disturbance* or *error term* — for instance, $\sigma^2 = 25$. Then we generate n random disturbances $\varepsilon_1, \cdots, \varepsilon_n$. For this purpose we use a generator of normally distributed random numbers. Many computer packages contain such a generator. As the computer usually generates random numbers with zero mean and unit variance, we have to multiply them by $\sigma = 5$ to obtain disturbances with variance $\sigma^2 = 25$. Finally we generate values for the dependent variable according to

$$y_i = \alpha + \beta x_i + \varepsilon_i \quad (i = 1, \cdots, n). \tag{2.16}$$

The role of the disturbances is to ensure that our data points are around the line $\alpha + \beta x$ instead of exactly on this line. In practice, simple relations like $y_i = \alpha + \beta x_i$ will not hold exactly true for the observed data, and the disturbances ε_i summarize the effect of all the other variables (apart from x_i) on y_i. This completes our data generating process (DGP).

Use of simulated data in statistical analysis

Now consider the situation of an econometrician whose only information consists of a data set (x_i, y_i), $i = 1, \cdots, n$, which is generated by this process, but that this econometrician does not know the underlying values of α, β, σ, and ε_i, $i = 1, \cdots, n$. The observed data are partly random because of the effects of the disturbance terms ε_i in (2.16). If this econometrician now applies the formulas of Section 2.1.2 to this data set to compute a and b, we can interpret them as estimates of α and β, respectively, and we can compare them with the original values of α and β, which are known to us. Because of the disturbance terms, the outcomes of a and b are random and in general $a \neq \alpha$ and $b \neq \beta$. The estimates are accurate if they do not differ much from the values of α and β of the DGP. So this experiment is useful for assessing the accuracy of the method of least squares.

We can repeat this simulation, say m times. The values of a and b obtained in the jth simulation run are denoted by a_j and b_j, $j = 1, \cdots, m$. The accuracy of least squares estimates can be evaluated in terms of the means $\bar{a} = \sum a_j/m$ and $\bar{b} = \sum b_j/m$ and the mean squared errors

$$\text{MSE}_b = \frac{1}{m}\sum (b_j - \beta)^2, \ \text{MSE}_a = \frac{1}{m}\sum (a_j - \alpha)^2.$$

Example 2.4: **Simulated Regression Data**

E

We will consider outcomes of the above simulation experiment. The data are generated by the equation (2.16) with $n = 20$, $x_i = i$ for $i = 1, \cdots, 20$, $\alpha = 10$, $\beta = 1$, and with $\varepsilon_1, \cdots, \varepsilon_{20}$ a random sample from a normal distribution with mean zero and variance $\sigma^2 = 25$. The results of two simulation runs are shown in Exhibit 2.7. As the two series of disturbance terms are different in the two simulation runs (see (*b*) and (*c*)), the values of the dependent variable are also different. This is also clear from the two scatter diagrams in Exhibit 2.7 (*d*) and (*e*). As a result, the obtained regression line $a + bx$ is different in the two simulation runs.

This simulation is repeated $m = 10{,}000$ times. Histograms of the resulting estimates a and b are in Exhibit 2.8 (*a*) and (*b*). The means of the outcomes are close to the values $\alpha = 10$ and $\beta = 1$ of the DGP. We see that the variation

(*a*)

X	YSYS = 10+X	EPS1	Y1 = YSYS+EPS1	EPS2	Y2 = YSYS+EPS2
1.000000	11.00000	−1.550532	9.449468	2.234083	13.23408
2.000000	12.00000	−2.385784	9.614216	−2.767494	9.232506
3.000000	13.00000	−0.577481	12.42252	9.072153	22.07215
4.000000	14.00000	1.973480	15.97348	−8.105329	5.894671
5.000000	15.00000	−4.845870	10.15413	−10.94552	4.054479
6.000000	16.00000	−5.324765	10.67523	0.572068	16.57207
7.000000	17.00000	−0.929291	16.07071	6.152398	23.15240
8.000000	18.00000	12.00469	30.00469	−5.419486	12.58051
9.000000	19.00000	−10.93570	8.064299	7.506255	26.50625
10.00000	20.00000	0.267976	20.26798	5.855825	25.85582
11.00000	21.00000	−1.136992	19.86301	5.656347	26.65635
12.00000	22.00000	4.090115	26.09012	0.413848	22.41385
13.00000	23.00000	−5.915039	17.08496	−0.160951	22.83905
14.00000	24.00000	−6.685956	17.31404	1.584349	25.58435
15.00000	25.00000	6.563120	31.56312	2.285183	27.28518
16.00000	26.00000	−2.506565	23.49344	13.43999	39.43999
17.00000	27.00000	−9.757085	17.24291	7.935698	34.93570
18.00000	28.00000	2.295170	30.29517	3.045441	31.04544
19.00000	29.00000	3.536910	32.53691	−4.568719	24.43128
20.00000	30.00000	8.769024	38.76902	6.649318	36.64932

Exhibit 2.7 Stimulated Regression Data (Example 2.4)

Data generated by $y = 10 + x + \varepsilon$ with $\varepsilon \sim \text{N}(0, 25)$; shown are two simulations of sample size 20 (*a*).

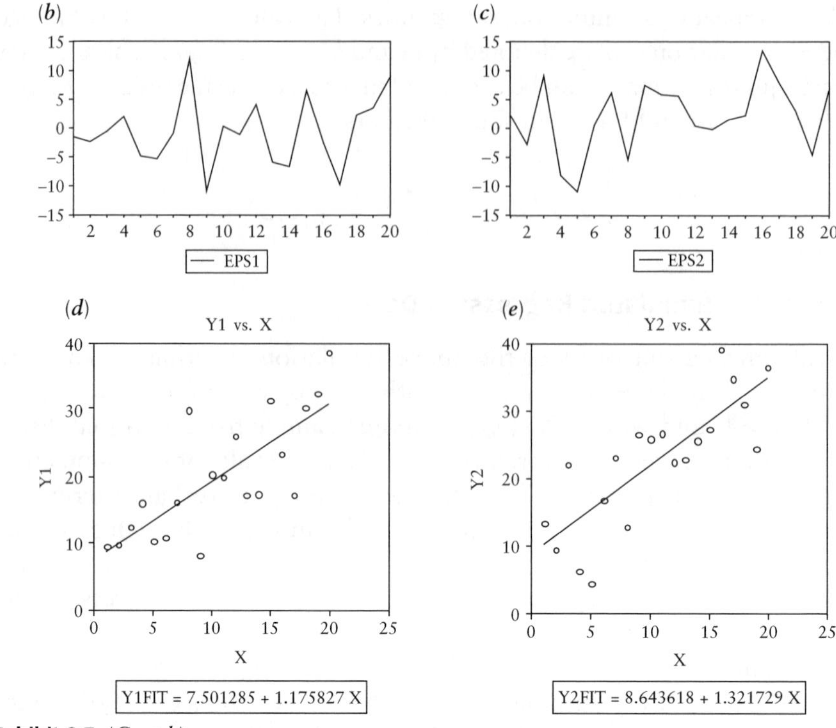

Exhibit 2.7 (*Contd.*)

Graphs corresponding to the two simulations in (*a*), with series of disturbances (EPS1 and EPS2 ((*b*)–(*c*))), and scatter diagrams (of y_1 against x and of y_2 against x) and fitted regressions (Y1FIT and Y2FIT ((*d*)–(*e*))).

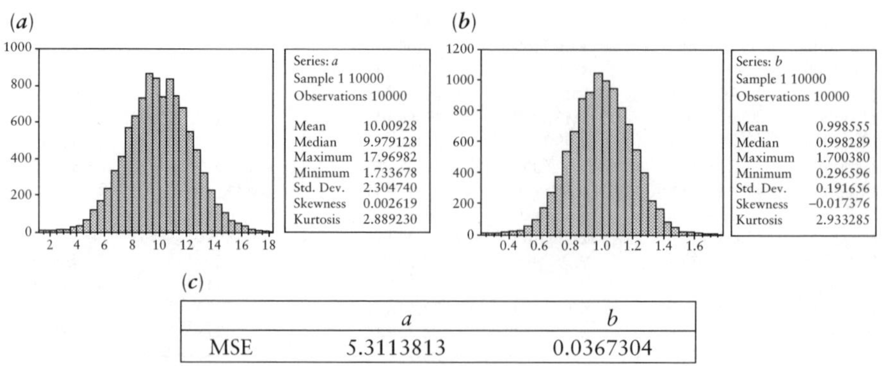

	a	b
MSE	5.3113813	0.0367304

Exhibit 2.8 Simulated Regression Data (Example 2.4)

Histograms of least squares estimates (a in (*a*) and b in (*b*)) in 10,000 simulations (the DGP has $\alpha = 10$ and $\beta = 1$), and mean squared error of these estimates (*c*).

of the outcomes in b (measured by the standard deviation) is much smaller than that of a, and the same holds true for the MSE (see (c)). Intuitively speaking, the outcomes of the slope estimates b differ significantly from zero. This will be made more precise in Section 2.3.1, where we discuss the situation of a single data set, which is the usual situation in practice.

2.2.2 Examples of regression models

Notation: we do not know Greek but we can compute Latin

One of the virtues of the computer experiment in the foregoing section is that it helps to explain the usual notation and terminology. We follow the convention to denote the parameters of the DGP by Greek letters (α, β, σ^2) and the estimates by Latin letters (a, b, s^2). When we analyse empirical data we do not know 'true' values of α and β, but we can compute estimates a and b from the observed data.

Example 2.5: **Stock Market Returns (continued)**

A well-known model of financial economics, the capital asset pricing model (CAPM), relates the excess returns x_i (on the market) and y_i (of an individual asset or a portfolio of assets in a sector) by the model (2.16). So the CAPM assumes that the data in Example 2.1 in Section 2.1.1 are generated by the linear model $y_i = \alpha + \beta x_i + \varepsilon_i$ for certain (unknown) values of α and β. The disturbance terms ε_i are needed because the linear dependence between the returns is only an approximation, as is clear from Exhibit 2.1. It is one of the tasks of the econometrician to estimate α and β as well as possible. The formulas for a and b in (2.6) and (2.8) can be used for this purpose. The residuals e_i in (2.2) can be seen as estimates of the disturbances ε_i in (2.16). The further analysis of this data set is left as an exercise (see Exercises 2.11, 2.12, and 2.15).

Example 2.6: **Bank Wages (continued)**

We consider again Example 2.2 and assume that the model (2.16) applies for the data on logarithmic salary and education. Let S be the salary; then the model states that $y_i = \log(S_i) = \alpha + \beta x_i + \varepsilon_i$. Here β can be interpreted as the relative increase in salary due to one year of additional education, which is given by $\frac{dS/S}{dx} = \frac{d\log(S)}{dx} = \frac{dy}{dx}$. In the model (2.16) this derivative is assumed to be constant. A careful inspection of Exhibit 2.2 (c) may cast some doubt on this assumption, but for the time being we will accept it as a working hypothesis. Again, the disturbance terms ε_i are needed because the linear dependence between the y_i and x_i is only an approximation. For every individual there

will be many factors, apart from education, that affect the salary. In the next chapter we will introduce some of these factors explicitly. This data set is further analysed in Example 2.9 (p. 102) and in Example 2.11 (p. 107).

Example 2.7: **Coffee Sales (continued)**

The data on prices and quantities sold of Example 2.3 show that demand increases if the price is decreased. If this effect is supposed to be proportional to the price decrease, then the demand curve can be described by the model (2.16) with y_i for the quantity sold and with x_i for the price. The scatter diagram in Exhibit 2.3 clearly shows that, for fixed prices, the sales still fluctuate owing to unobserved causes. The variations in sales that are not related to price variations are summarized by the disturbance terms ε_i in (2.16). The analysis of this data set is left as an exercise (see Exercise 2.10).

2.2.3 Seven assumptions

☞ Uses Sections 1.2.1, 1.2.3, 1.2.4.

The purpose of assumptions: simpler analysis

Data generating experiments as described in Section 2.2.1 are often performed in applied econometrics, in particular in complicated cases where little is known about the accuracy of the estimation procedures used. In the case of the linear model and the method of least squares, however, we can obtain accuracy measures by means of analytical methods. For this purpose, we introduce the following assumptions on the data generating process.

Assumption on the regressors

- *Assumption 1: fixed regressors.* The n observations on the explanatory variable $x_1, \cdots, x_n$ are fixed numbers. They satisfy $\sum (x_i - \overline{x})^2 > 0$.

This means that the values x_i of the explanatory variable are assumed to be non-random. This describes the situation of *controlled experiments*. For instance, the price reductions in Example 2.3 were performed in a controlled marketing experiment. However, in economics the possibilities for experiments are often quite limited. For example, the data on salaries and education in Example 2.2 are obtained from a sample of individuals. Here the x variable, education, is not determined by a controlled experiment. It is influenced by many factors—for instance, the different opportunities and situational characteristics of the individuals—and these factors are not observed in this sample.

Assumptions on the disturbances

- *Assumption 2: random disturbances, zero mean.* The n disturbances $\varepsilon_1, \cdots, \varepsilon_n$ are random variables with zero mean, $E[\varepsilon_i] = 0$ $(i = 1, \cdots, n)$.
- *Assumption 3: homoskedasticity.* The variances of the n disturbances $\varepsilon_1, \cdots, \varepsilon_n$ exist and are all equal, $E[\varepsilon_i^2] = \sigma^2$ $(i = 1, \cdots, n)$.
- *Assumption 4: no correlation.* All pairs of disturbances $(\varepsilon_i, \varepsilon_j)$ are uncorrelated, $E[\varepsilon_i \varepsilon_j] = 0$ $(i, j = 1, \cdots, n,\ i \neq j)$.

Assumptions 2–4 concern properties of the disturbance terms. Note that they say nothing about the shape of the distribution, except that extreme distributions (such as the Cauchy distribution) are excluded because it is assumed that the means and variances exist. When the variances are equal the disturbances are called *homoskedastic*, and when the variances differ they are called *heteroskedastic*. Assumption 4 is also called the *absence of serial correlation* across the observations.

Assumptions on model and model parameters

- *Assumption 5: constant parameters.* The parameters α, β, and σ are fixed unknown numbers with $\sigma > 0$.

This means that, although the parameters of the DGP are unknown, we assume that all the n observations are generated with the same values of the parameters.

- *Assumption 6: linear model.* The data on $y_1, \cdots, y_n$ have been generated by

$$y_i = \alpha + \beta x_i + \varepsilon_i \qquad (i = 1, \cdots, n). \tag{2.17}$$

The model is called *linear* because it postulates that y_i depends in a linear way on the *parameters* α and β. Together with Assumptions 1–4, it follows that

$$E[y_i] = \alpha + \beta x_i, \qquad \text{var}(y_i) = \sigma^2, \qquad \text{cov}(y_i, y_j) = 0 \qquad (i \neq j).$$

So the observed values of the dependent variable are uncorrelated and have the same variance. However, the mean value of y_i varies across the observations and depends on x_i.

Assumption on the probability distribution

- *Assumption 7: normality.* The disturbances $\varepsilon_1, \cdots, \varepsilon_n$ are jointly normally distributed.

Together with Assumptions 2–4, this assumption specifies a precise distribution for the disturbance terms and it implies that the disturbances are mutually independent.

Interpretation of the simple regression model

Under Assumptions 1–7, the values y_i are normally and independently distributed with varying means $\alpha + \beta x_i$ and constant variance σ^2. This can be written as

$$y_i \sim \mathrm{NID}(\alpha + \beta x_i, \sigma^2) \qquad (i = 1, \cdots, n).$$

If $\beta = 0$, this reduces to the case of random samples from a fixed population described in Chapter 1. The essential characteristic of the current model is that variations in y_i are not seen purely as the effect of randomness, but partly as the effect of variations in the explanatory variable x_i.

Several of the results to be given below are proved under Assumptions 1–6, but sometimes we also need Assumption 7. This is the case, for instance, in Section 2.3.1, when we test whether the estimated slope parameter b is significantly different from zero.

☞ Exercises: E: 2.10a.

2.2.4 Statistical properties

☞ Uses Sections 1.2.1, 1.3.2; Appendix A.1.

T

Derivation: Some helpful notation and results

Using Assumptions 1–6 we now derive some statistical properties of the least squares estimators a and b as defined in (2.6) and (2.8). For this purpose, it is convenient to express the random part of a and b as explicit functions of the random variables ε_i, as the properties of these disturbances are given by Assumptions 2–4. To express b in (2.8) in terms of ε_i, first note that

$$\sum (x_i - \overline{x})\overline{y} = \overline{y} \sum (x_i - \overline{x}) = 0, \qquad \sum (x_i - \overline{x})\overline{x} = \overline{x} \sum (x_i - \overline{x}) = 0. \quad (2.18)$$

Using this result, (2.8) can be written as

$$b = \frac{\sum (x_i - \overline{x}) y_i}{\sum (x_i - \overline{x}) x_i}.$$

Because of Assumption 6 we may substitute (2.17) for y_i, and by using $\sum (x_i - \overline{x})\alpha = 0$ it follows that

$$b = \beta + \frac{\sum (x_i - \overline{x})\varepsilon_i}{\sum (x_i - \overline{x}) x_i} = \beta + \sum c_i \varepsilon_i \qquad (2.19)$$

where the coefficients c_i are non-random (because of Assumption 1) and given by

$$c_i = \frac{x_i - \overline{x}}{\sum (x_i - \overline{x})x_i} = \frac{x_i - \overline{x}}{\sum (x_i - \overline{x})^2}. \tag{2.20}$$

To express a in (2.6) in terms of ε_i, (2.17) implies that $\overline{y} = \alpha + \beta\overline{x} + \overline{\varepsilon}$ (where $\overline{\varepsilon} = \frac{1}{n}\sum \varepsilon_i$) and (2.19) that $b\overline{x} = \beta\overline{x} + \overline{x}\sum c_i\varepsilon_i$. This shows that

$$a = \overline{y} - b\overline{x} = \alpha + \frac{1}{n}\sum \varepsilon_i - \overline{x}\sum c_i\varepsilon_i = \alpha + \sum d_i\varepsilon_i \tag{2.21}$$

where the coefficients d_i are non-random and given by

$$d_i = \frac{1}{n} - \overline{x}c_i = \frac{1}{n} - \frac{\overline{x}(x_i - \overline{x})}{\sum (x_i - \overline{x})^2}. \tag{2.22}$$

From (2.20) and (2.22) we directly obtain the following properties:

$$\sum c_i = 0, \qquad \sum c_i^2 = \frac{1}{\sum (x_i - \overline{x})^2}, \tag{2.23}$$

$$\sum d_i = 1, \qquad \sum d_i^2 = \frac{1}{n} + \frac{\overline{x}^2}{\sum (x_i - \overline{x})^2}. \tag{2.24}$$

Least squares is unbiased

If we use the rules of the calculus of expectations (see Section 1.2), it follows from (2.19) that

$$E[b] = E\left[\beta + \sum c_i\varepsilon_i\right] = \beta + \sum c_i E[\varepsilon_i] = \beta, \tag{2.25}$$

because β is non-random (Assumption 5), the c_i are non-random (Assumption 1), and $E[\varepsilon_i] = 0$ (Assumption 2). Summarizing, under Assumptions 1, 2, 5, and 6 the estimator b has expected value β and hence b is an *unbiased* estimator of β. Under the same assumptions we get from (2.21)

$$E[a] = E\left[\alpha + \sum d_i\varepsilon_i\right] = \alpha + \sum d_i E[\varepsilon_i] = \alpha, \tag{2.26}$$

so that a is also an unbiased estimator of α. So the least squares estimates will, on average, be equal to the correct parameter values.

The variance of least squares estimators

Although the property of being unbiased is nice, it tells us only that the estimators a and b will on average be equal to α and β. However, in practice we often have only a single data set at our disposal. Then it is important that the deviations $(b - \beta)^2$ and $(a - \alpha)^2$ are expected to be small. We measure the accuracy by the mean squared errors $E[(b - \beta)^2]$ and $E[(a - \alpha)^2]$. As the estimators are unbiased, these MSEs are equal to the variances var(b) and var(a) respectively. It follows from (2.19) that

$$\text{var}(b) = \sum\sum c_i c_j E[\varepsilon_i \varepsilon_j],$$

and Assumptions 3 and 4 and (2.23) give

$$\text{var}(b) = \sum c_i^2 \sigma^2 = \frac{\sigma^2}{\sum (x_i - \overline{x})^2}. \tag{2.27}$$

The variance of a follows from (2.21) and (2.24) with result

$$\text{var}(a) = \sum d_i^2 \sigma^2 = \sigma^2 \left(\frac{1}{n} + \frac{\overline{x}^2}{\sum (x_i - \overline{x})^2} \right). \tag{2.28}$$

Graphical illustration

In Exhibit 2.9 we show four scatters generated with simulations of the type described in Section 2.2.1, with different values for the error variance σ^2 and for the systematic variance $\sum (x_i - \overline{x})^2$. The shapes of the scatters give a good impression of the possibilities to determine the regression line accurately. The best case is small error variance and large systematic variance (shown in (b)), and the worst case is large error variance and small systematic variance (shown in (c)).

Mean and variance of residuals

In a similar way we can derive the mean and variance of the residuals e_i, where $e_i = y - a - bx_i$. There holds $E[e_i] = 0$ and

$$\text{var}(e_i) = \sigma^2 \left(1 - \frac{1}{n} - \frac{(x_i - \overline{x})^2}{\sum (x_j - \overline{x})^2} \right) \tag{2.29}$$

(see Exercise 2.7). Note that this variance is smaller than the variance σ^2 of the disturbances ε_i. The reason is that the method of least squares tries to minimize the sum of squares of the residuals. Note also that the difference is small if n and $\sum (x_j - \overline{x})^2$ are large. If both n and $\sum (x_j - \overline{x})^2$ tend to infinity, then var(e_i) tends to σ^2.

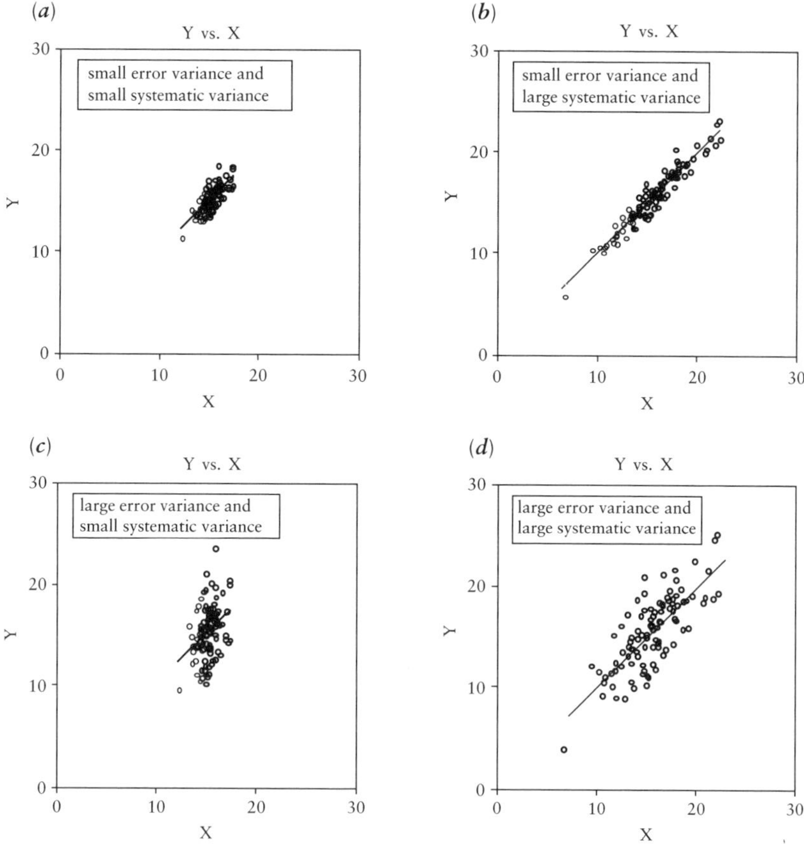

Exhibit 2.9 Accuracy of least squares

Scatter diagrams of y against x; the standard deviation of x in (*b*) and (*d*) is three times as large as in (*a*) and (*c*), and the standard deviation of the error terms in (*c*) and (*d*) is three times as large as in (*a*) and (*b*).

☞ Exercises: T: 2.4, 2.5, 2.6, 2.9.

2.2.5 Efficiency

☞ Uses Section 1.2.1.

Best linear unbiased estimators (BLUE)

The least squares estimators a and b given in (2.6) and (2.8) are linear expressions in $y_1, \cdots, y_n$. Such estimators are called linear estimators. We have shown that they are unbiased. Now we will show that, under Assumptions 1–6, the estimators a and b are the *best linear unbiased estimators* (BLUE)—that is, they have the smallest possible variance in the class of all linear unbiased estimators. Stated otherwise, the least squares estimators are efficient in this respect. This is called the Gauss–Markov theorem. Note that the assumption of normality is not needed for this result.

Proof of BLUE

We will prove this result for b (the result for a follows from a more general result treated in Section 3.1.4). Let $\hat{\beta}$ be an arbitrary linear estimator of β. This means that it can be written as $\hat{\beta} = \sum d_i y_i$ for certain fixed coefficients $d_1, \cdots, d_n$. The least squares estimator can be written as $b = \sum c_i y_i$ with c_i as defined in (2.20). Now define $w_i = d_i - c_i$; then it follows that $d_i = c_i + w_i$ and

$$\hat{\beta} = \sum (c_i + w_i) y_i = b + \sum w_i y_i. \tag{2.30}$$

Under Assumptions 1–6, the expected value of $\hat{\beta}$ is given by

$$E[\hat{\beta}] = E[b] + \sum w_i E[y_i] = \beta + \alpha \sum w_i + \beta \sum w_i x_i.$$

We require unbiasedness, irrespective of the values taken by α and β. So the two conditions on $w_1, \cdots, w_n$ are that

$$\sum w_i = 0, \ \sum w_i x_i = 0. \tag{2.31}$$

It then follows from the assumption of the linear model (2.17) that

$$\sum w_i y_i = \alpha \sum w_i + \beta \sum w_i x_i + \sum w_i \varepsilon_i = \sum w_i \varepsilon_i, \tag{2.32}$$

and from (2.30) and (2.19) that

$$\hat{\beta} = b + \sum w_i \varepsilon_i = \beta + \sum (c_i + w_i) \varepsilon_i.$$

Because of Assumptions 3 and 4, the variance of $\hat{\beta}$ is equal to

$$\mathrm{var}(\hat{\beta}) = \sigma^2 \sum (c_i + w_i)^2. \tag{2.33}$$

Now $\sum (c_i + w_i)^2 = \sum c_i^2 + \sum w_i^2 + 2 \sum c_i w_i$, and the expression (2.20) for c_i together with the properties in (2.31) imply that $\sum c_i w_i = 0$. Therefore (2.33) reduces to

$$\mathrm{var}(\hat{\beta}) = \mathrm{var}(b) + \sigma^2 \sum w_i^2.$$

Clearly, the variance is minimal if and only if $w_i = 0$ for all $i = 1, \cdots, n$. This means that $\hat{\beta} = b$, and this proves the Gauss–Markov theorem.

☞ **Exercises:** T: 2.3.

2.3 Significance tests

2.3.1 The *t*-test

☞ Uses Sections 1.2.3, 1.4.1–1.4.3.

The significance of an estimate

The regression model aims to explain the variation in the dependent variable y in terms of variations in the explanatory variable x. This makes sense only if y is related to x—that is, if $\beta \neq 0$ in the model (2.17). In general, the least squares estimator b will be different from zero, even if $\beta = 0$. We want to apply a test for the null hypothesis $\beta = 0$ against the alternative that $\beta \neq 0$. The null hypothesis will be rejected if b differs significantly from zero. Now it is crucial to realize that, under Assumptions 1–6, the obtained value of b is the outcome of a random variable. So, to decide whether b is significant or not, we have to take the uncertainty of this random variable into account. For instance, if b has standard deviation 100, then an outcome $b = 10$ is not significantly different from zero, and if b has standard deviation 0.01 then an outcome $b = 0.1$ is significantly different from zero. Therefore we scale the outcome of b by its standard deviation. Further, to apply the testing approach discussed in Section 1.4, the distribution of b should be known.

Derivation of test statistic

To derive a test for the significance of the slope estimate b, we will assume that the disturbances ε_i are normally distributed. So we will make use of Assumptions 1–7 of Section 2.2.3. Since $b - \beta$ is linear in the disturbances (see (2.19)), it is normally distributed with mean zero and with variance given by (2.27). So the standard deviation of b is given by $\sigma_b = \sigma/\sqrt{\sum (x_i - \bar{x})^2}$ and

$$\frac{b - \beta}{\sigma_b} \sim \mathrm{N}(0, 1).$$

This expression cannot be used as a test statistic, since σ is an unknown parameter. As the residuals e_i are estimates of the disturbances ε_i, this suggests estimating the variance $\sigma^2 = E[\varepsilon_i^2]$ by $\hat{\sigma}^2 = \frac{1}{n}\sum e_i^2$. However, this estimator is biased. It is left as an exercise (see Exercise 2.7) to show that an unbiased estimator is given by

$$s^2 = \frac{1}{n-2}\sum e_i^2. \tag{2.34}$$

We also refer to Sections 3.1.5 and 3.3.1 below, where it is further proved that $\sum e_i^2/\sigma^2$ follows the $\chi^2(n-2)$ distribution and that s^2 and b are independent.

Standard error and t-value

It follows from the above results and by the definition of the t-distribution that

$$t_b = \frac{b-\beta}{s_b} = \frac{b-\beta}{s/\sqrt{\sum (x_i - \overline{x})^2}} = \frac{(b-\beta)/\sigma_b}{\sqrt{\sum \frac{e_i^2}{\sigma^2}/(n-2)}} \sim t(n-2), \tag{2.35}$$

where

$$s_b = \frac{s}{\sqrt{\sum (x_i - \overline{x})^2}}. \tag{2.36}$$

That is, t_b follows the Student t-distribution with $n-2$ degrees of freedom. For $\beta = 0$, t_b is called the *t-value* of b. Further, s_b is called the *standard error of* b, and s, the square root of (2.34), is called the *standard error of the regression.* The null hypothesis $H_0 : \beta = 0$ is rejected against the alternative $H_1 : \beta \neq 0$ if b is too far from zero—that is, if $|t_b| > c$, or equivalently, if $|b| > cs_b$. Then b is called *significant*—that is, it differs significantly from zero.

A practical rule of thumb for significance

For a given level of significance, the critical value c is obtained from the $t(n-2)$ distribution. For a 5 per cent significance level, the critical value for $n = 30$ is $c = 2.05$, for $n = 60$ it is 2.00, and for $n \to \infty$ the critical value converges to 1.96. As a rule of thumb (for the popular 5 per cent significance level), one often uses $c = 2$ as an approximation. In this case the estimate b is significant if $|b| > 2s_b$—that is, if the outcome is at least twice as large as the uncertainty in this outcome as measured by the standard deviation. That is, an estimated coefficient is significant if its t-value is (in absolute value) larger than 2.

Interval estimates

The foregoing results can also be used to construct interval estimates of β. Let c be the critical value of the t-test of size α, so that $P[|t_b| > c] = \alpha$ where t_b is defined as in (2.35). Then $P[|t_b| \leq c] = 1 - \alpha$, and an $(1-\alpha)$ interval estimate of β is given by all values for which $-c \leq t_b \leq c$—that is,

$$b - cs_b \leq \beta \leq b + cs_b. \tag{2.37}$$

☞ **Exercises:** T: 2.1**c**, **d**, 2.7; E: 2.10**d–f**, 2.12**b**, **c**, 2.13, 2.14**a–c**.

2.3.2 Examples

Example 2.8: **Simulated Regression Data (continued)**

First we consider the situation of simulated data with a known DGP. For this purpose we consider again the 10,000 simulated data sets of Example 2.4, with data generating process $y_i = 10 + x_i + \varepsilon_i$ where $x_i = i$ and ε_i are NID(0, 25), $i = 1, \cdots, 20$. So this DGP has slope parameter $\beta = 1$. The histograms and some summary statistics of the resulting 10,000 values of b, s^2, and t_b are given in Exhibit 2.10 (*a–d*). For comparison, (*d*) also contains some properties of the corresponding theoretical distributions.

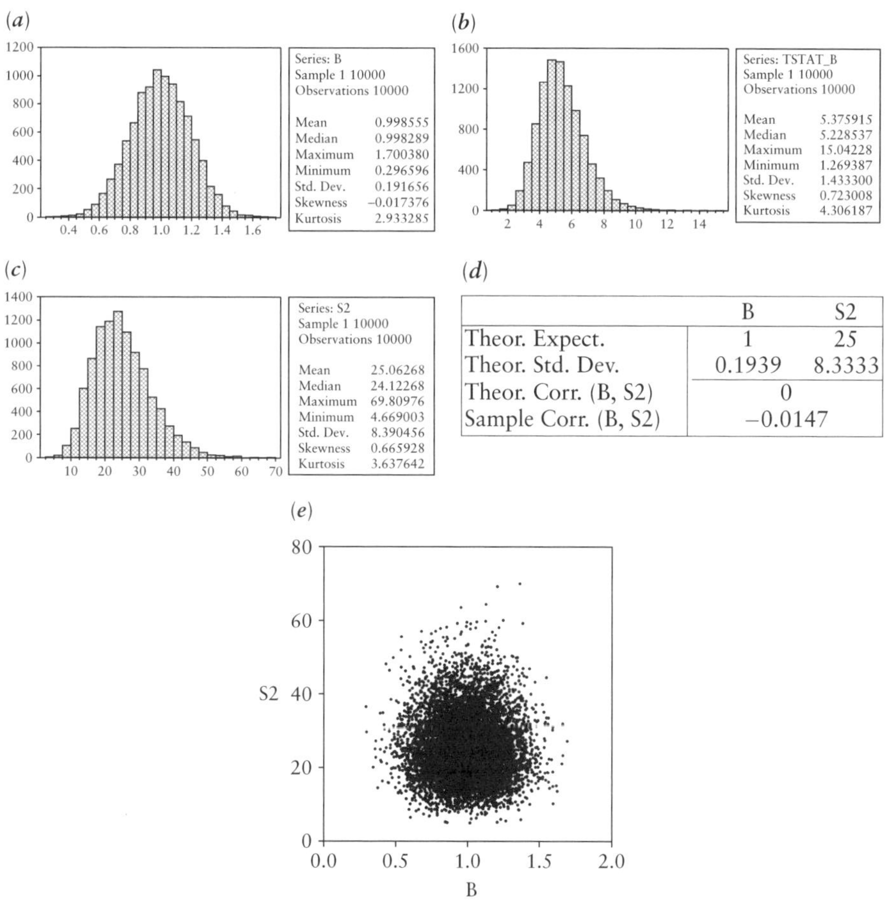

	B	S2
Theor. Expect.	1	25
Theor. Std. Dev.	0.1939	8.3333
Theor. Corr. (B, S2)	0	
Sample Corr. (B, S2)	−0.0147	

Exhibit 2.10 Simulated Regression Data (Example 2.8)

Histograms of least squares estimates of slope (b, denoted by B in (*a*)), t-value (t_b, denoted by TSTAT_B in (*b*)), and variance (s^2, denoted by S2 in (*c*)) resulting from 10,000 simulations of the data generating process in Example 2.4 (with slope $\beta = 1$ and variance $\sigma^2 = 25$). Theoretical means and standard deviations of b and s^2 and theoretical and sample correlations between b and s^2 (*d*) and scatter diagram of s^2 against b (*e*).

The histogram of b is in accordance with the normal distribution of this least squares estimator, and the histogram of s^2 is in accordance with the (scaled) χ^2 distribution. The t-statistic for the null hypothesis $H_0: \beta = 0$ does not follow the t-distribution, as this hypothesis is not correct ($\beta = 1$). In the great majority of cases the null hypothesis is rejected; only in nineteen cases it is not rejected (using the 5 per cent critical value $c = 2.1$ for the $t(18)$ distribution). This indicates a high power (of around 99.8 per cent) of the t-test in this example. The scatter diagram of s^2 against b (shown in (*e*)) illustrates the independence of these two random variables; their sample correlation over the 10,000 simulation runs is less than 1.5 per cent.

This simulation illustrates the distribution properties of b, s^2, and t_b. In this example, the t-test is very successful in detecting a significant effect of the variable x on the variable y.

E

XM202BWA

Example 2.9: **Bank Wages (continued)**

Next we consider a real data set—namely, on bank wages. For the salary and education data of bank employees discussed before in Example 2.2, the sample moments were given in Section 2.1.4. Using the results in Exhibit 2.6, the variance of the disturbance terms is estimated by $s^2 = SSR/(n-2) = 38.424/472 = 0.0814$ and the standard error of the regression is $s = 0.285$. So the standard error of b is $s_b = 0.285/\sqrt{3937} = 0.00455$ and the t-value is $t_b = 0.096/0.00455 = 21.1$. To perform a 5 per cent significance test of $H_0: \beta = 0$ against $H_1: \beta \neq 0$, the (two-sided) critical value of the $t(472)$ distribution is given by 1.96, so that the null hypothesis is clearly rejected. This means that education has a very significant effect on wages. These outcomes are also given in Exhibit 2.11, together with the P-value for the test of $H_0: \beta = 0$ against $H_1: \beta \neq 0$. The P-value is reported as 0.0000, which actually means that it is smaller than 0.00005. Note that this P-value is not exactly zero, as even for $\beta = 0$ the probability of getting t-values larger than 21.1 is non-zero. However, the null hypothesis that $\beta = 0$ is rejected for all sizes $\alpha > 0.00005$. For such a low P-value as in this example we will always reject the null hypothesis.

The regression results are often presented in the following way, where the numbers in parentheses denote the t-values and e denotes the residuals of the regression (the equation without e is not valid, as the data do not lie exactly on the estimated line).

$$\begin{aligned} y = \underset{(144)}{9.06} + \underset{(21.1)}{0.096x} + e. \end{aligned}$$

Dependent Variable: LOGSALARY				
Method: Least Squares				
Sample: 1 474				
Variable	Coefficient	Std. Error	t-Statistic	Prob.
C	9.062102	0.062738	144.4446	0.0000
EDUC	0.095963	0.004548	21.10214	0.0000
R-squared	0.485447	Mean dependent var		10.35679
Sum squared resid	38.42407	S.D. dependent var		0.397334
S.E. of regression	0.285319			

Exhibit 2.11 Bank Wages (Example 2.9)

Results of regression of salary (in logarithms) on a constant (denoted by C) and education, based on data of 474 bank employees.

2.3.3 Use under less strict conditions

Weaker assumptions on the DGP

The rather strict conditions of Assumptions 1–7 (in particular, fixed values of the x variable and normally distributed disturbances) were introduced in order to simplify the proofs. Fortunately, the same results hold approximately true under more general conditions. In Exhibit 2.12 we present the results of a number of simulation experiments where the conditions on both the explanatory variable and the disturbances have been varied. The exhibit reports some quantiles. If a random variable y has a strictly monotone cumulative distribution function $F(v) = P[y \leq v]$, then the quantile $q(p)$ is defined by the condition that $F(q(p)) = p$. In other words, the quantile function is the inverse of the cumulative distribution function. The exhibit shows quantiles for $p = 0.75$, $p = 0.90$, $p = 0.95$, and $p = 0.975$. The last quantile corresponds to the critical value for a two-sided test with significance level 5 per cent.

Row	x	ε	Result	Quantiles 0.750	0.900	0.950	0.975
1	Fixed	Normal	Exact $t(198)$	0.676	1.286	1.653	1.972
2	Fixed	Normal	Simulated	0.675	1.290	1.651	1.984
3	Fixed	Logistic	Simulated	0.678	1.289	1.656	1.986
4	Normal	Normal	Simulated	0.677	1.285	1.653	1.980
5	Normal	Logistic	Simulated	0.679	1.287	1.650	1.982

Exhibit 2.12 Quantiles of distributions of t-statistics

Rows 1 and 2 correspond to the standard model that satisfies Assumptions 1–7, in rows 3 and 5 the DGP does not satisfy Assumption 7 (normality), and in rows 4 and 5 the DGP does not satisfy Assumption 1 (fixed regressors).

Discussion of simulation results

Rows 1 and 2 of the table give the results for the classical linear model, where the x values are fixed and the disturbances are independently, identically normally distributed. The first row gives the exact results corresponding to the $t(198)$ distribution. The second row gives the results from a simulation experiment where 50,000 samples were drawn, each of $n = 200$ observations. The remaining rows give the results of further simulation experiments (each consisting of 50,000 simulation runs) under different conditions. In row 3 the disturbances are drawn from a logistic distribution with density function $f(x) = e^x/(1 + e^x)^2$ and with cumulative distribution function $F(x) = 1/(1 + e^{-x})$. This density is bell-shaped but the tails are somewhat fatter than those of the normal density. In rows 4 and 5 the values of the x variable are no longer kept fixed along the different simulation runs, but instead they are drawn from a normal distribution, independently of the disturbances. To enhance the comparability of the results the same x values were used in rows 4 and 5. Likewise, the same disturbances were used in rows 2 and 4, and in rows 3 and 5.

Conclusion

When we compare the quantiles, we see that the differences between the rows are very small. This illustrates that we may apply the formulas derived under the assumptions of the linear model also in cases where the assumptions of fixed regressors or normal disturbances are not satisfied. Under the assumptions of this simulation example this still gives reliable results.

2.4 Prediction

2.4.1 Point predictions and prediction intervals

Point prediction

We consider the use of an estimated regression model for the prediction of the outcome of the dependent variable y for a given value of the explanatory variable x.

The least squares residuals $e_i = y_i - a - bx_i$ correspond to the deviations of y_i from the fitted values $a + bx_i$, $i = 1, \cdots, n$. The regression line $a + bx$ can be interpreted as the prediction of the y-value for a given x-value, and s^2 indicates the average accuracy of these predictions. Now assume that we want to predict the outcome y_{n+1} for a given new value x_{n+1}. An obvious prediction is given by $a + bx_{n+1}$. This is called a *point prediction.*

Prediction error and variance

In order to say something about the accuracy of this prediction we need to make assumptions about the mechanism generating the value of y_{n+1}. We suppose that Assumptions 1–6 hold true for $i = 1, \cdots, n + 1$. If at a later point of time we observe y_{n+1}, we can evaluate the quality of our prediction by computing the prediction error

$$f = y_{n+1} - a - bx_{n+1}. \tag{2.38}$$

If y_{n+1} is unknown, we can get an idea of the prediction accuracy by deriving the mean and variance of the prediction error. Under Assumptions 1–6, the mean is $E[f] = 0$, so that the prediction is unbiased, and the variance is given by

$$\text{var}(f) = \sigma^2 \left(1 + \frac{1}{n} + \frac{(x_{n+1} - \overline{x})^2}{\sum (x_i - \overline{x})^2} \right). \tag{2.39}$$

Here the average $\overline{x}$ and the summation refer to the estimation sample $i = 1, \cdots, n$. The proofs are left as an exercise (see Exercise 2.8). Note that the variance of the prediction error is larger than the variance σ^2 of the disturbances. The extra terms are due to the fact that a and b are used rather

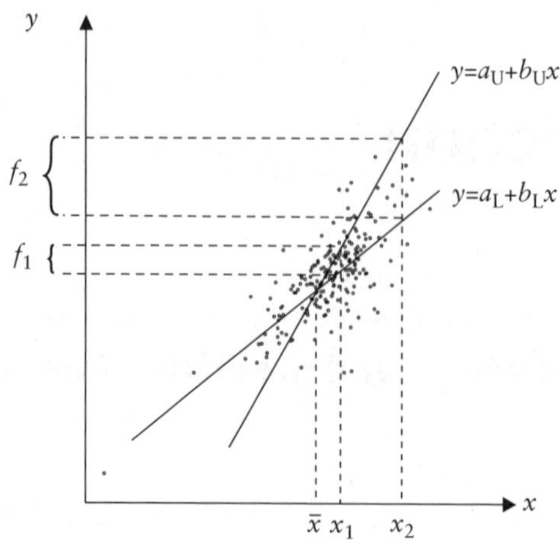

Exhibit 2.13 Prediction error

Uncertainty in the slope of the regression line (indicated by the lower value b_L and the upper value b_U of an interval estimate of the slope) results in larger forecast uncertainty for values of the explanatory variable that are further away from the sample mean (the forecast interval f_2 corresponding to x_2 is larger than the interval f_1 corresponding to x_1).

than α and β. It is also seen that the variance of the prediction error reaches its minimum for $x_{n+1} = \overline{x}$ and that the prediction errors tend to be larger for values of x_{n+1} that are further away from $\overline{x}$. By using the expression (2.6) for a, (2.38) can be written as $f = (y_{n+1} - \overline{y}) - b(x_{n+1} - \overline{x})$. So uncertainty about the slope b of the regression line leads to larger forecast uncertainty when x_{n+1} is further away from $\overline{x}$. This is illustrated in Exhibit 2.13.

Prediction interval

The above results can also be used to construct *prediction intervals*. If Assumptions 1–7 hold true for $i = 1, \cdots, n+1$, then the prediction error f is normally distributed and independent of s^2, based on the first n observations and defined in (2.34). Let

$$s_f^2 = s^2\left(1 + \frac{1}{n} + \frac{(x_{n+1} - \overline{x})^2}{\sum_{i=1}^{n}(x_i - \overline{x})^2}\right),$$

then it follows that $f/s_f \sim t(n-2)$. So a $(1-\alpha)$ prediction interval for y_{n+1} is given by

$$(a + bx_{n+1} - cs_f,\ a + bx_{n+1} + cs_f)$$

where c is such that $P[|t| > c] = \alpha$ when $t \sim t(n-2)$.

Conditional prediction

In the foregoing results the value of x_{n+1} should be known. Therefore this is called *conditional prediction*, in contrast to unconditional prediction, where the value of x_{n+1} is unknown and should also be predicted. Since our model does not contain a mechanism to predict x_{n+1}, this would require additional assumptions on the way the x-values are generated.

☞ Exercises: T: 2.8; E: 2.14d, e, 2.15.

2.4.2 Examples

Example 2.10: **Simulated Regression Data (continued)**

Consider once more the 10,000 simulated data sets of Example 2.4. We consider two situations, one where the new value of $x_{21} = 10$ is in the middle of the sample of previous x-values (that range between 1 and 20) and another where $x_{21} = 40$ lies outside this range. For both cases we generate 10,000 predictions $a + bx_{21}$, each prediction corresponding to the values of (a, b) obtained for one of the 10,000 simulated data sets. Further we also generate in both cases 10,000 new values of $y_{21} = 10 + x_{21} + \varepsilon_{21}$ by random drawings ε_{21} of the N(0, 25) distribution.

Exhibit 2.14 shows histograms and summary statistics of the resulting two sets of 10,000 predictions (in (a) and (c)) and of the prediction errors $f_{21} = y_{21} - (a + bx_{21})$ (in (b), (d), and (e)). Clearly, for $x_{21} = 10$ the predictions and forecast errors have a smaller standard deviation than for $x_{21} = 40$, as would be expected because of (2.39).

Example 2.11: **Bank Wages (continued)**

We consider again the salary and education data of bank employees. We will discuss (i) the splitting of the sample in two sub-samples, (ii) the forecasts, and (iii) the interpretation of the forecast results.

(i) Splitting of the sample in two sub-samples

To illustrate the idea of prediction we split the data set up in two parts. The first part (used in estimation) consists of 424 individuals with sixteen years of education or less, the second part (used in prediction) consists of the remaining 50 individuals with seventeen years of education or more. In this way we can investigate whether the effect of education on salary is the same for lower and higher levels of education.

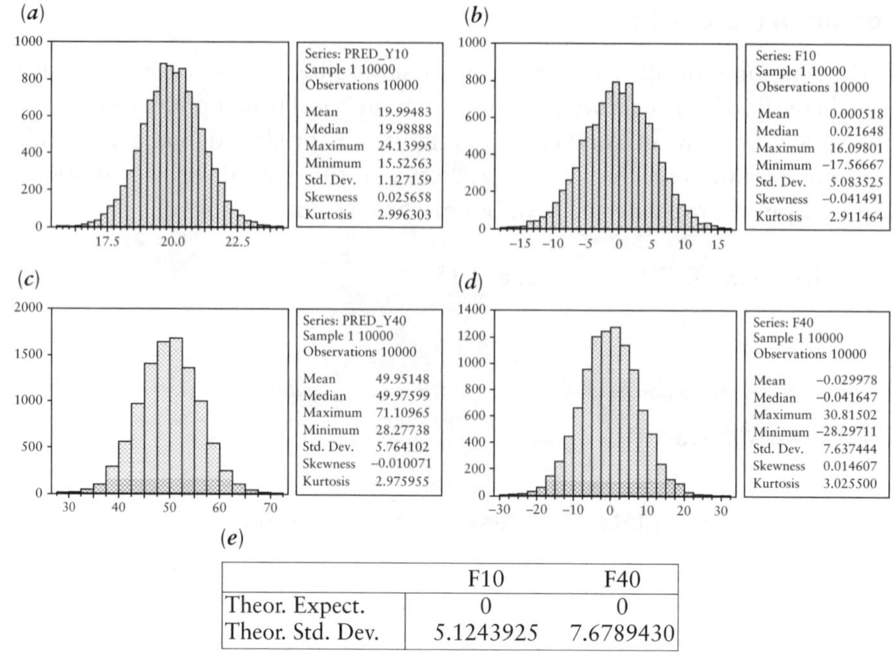

	F10	F40
Theor. Expect.	0	0
Theor. Std. Dev.	5.1243925	7.6789430

Exhibit 2.14 Simulated Regression Data (Example 2.10)

Forecasted values of y ((*a*) and (*c*)) and forecast errors f ((*b*) and (*d*)) in 10,000 simulations from the data generating process of Example 2.4 for two values of x—that is, $x = 10$ ((*a*)–(*b*)) and $x = 40$ ((*c*)–(*d*)), together with theoretical expected values and standard deviations of the forecast errors (denoted by F10 for $x = 10$ and F40 for $x = 40$ (*e*)).

(ii) Forecasts

The results of the regression over the first group of individuals are shown in Exhibit 2.15 (*a*). The estimated intercept is $a = 9.39$ and the estimated slope is $b = 0.0684$. With this model the salary of an individual in the second group with an education of x years is predicted by $a + bx = 9.39 + 0.0684x$.

(iii) Interpretation of forecast results

Exhibit 2.15 (*d*) shows that the actual salaries of these highly educated persons are systematically higher than predicted. We mention the following facts. The average squared prediction error (for the fifty highly educated employees) is equal to $\sum_{i=425}^{474} f_i^2/50 = 0.268$. This is larger than the average squared residual $\sum_{i=425}^{474} e_i^2/50 = 0.142$ if the estimates $a = 9.06$ and $b = 0.0960$ are used that were obtained from a regression over the full sample in Section 2.1.4 (see Exhibit 2.6). Moreover, the average squared prediction error is also larger than what would be expected on the basis of (2.39), which is based on Assumptions 1–7 for the DGP. If we average this expression over the fifty values of education (x) in the second group, with the estimated variance $s^2 = (0.262)^2 = 0.0688$ obtained from the regression

(*a*)

Dependent Variable: LOGSALARY				
Method: Least Squares				
Sample: 1 424 (individuals with at most 16 years of education)				
Variable	Coefficient	Std. Error	t-Statistic	Prob.
C	9.387947	0.068722	136.6081	0.0000
EDUC	0.068414	0.005233	13.07446	0.0000
R-squared	0.288294	Mean dependent var		10.27088
Sum squared resid	29.02805	S.D. dependent var		0.310519
S.E. of regression	0.262272			

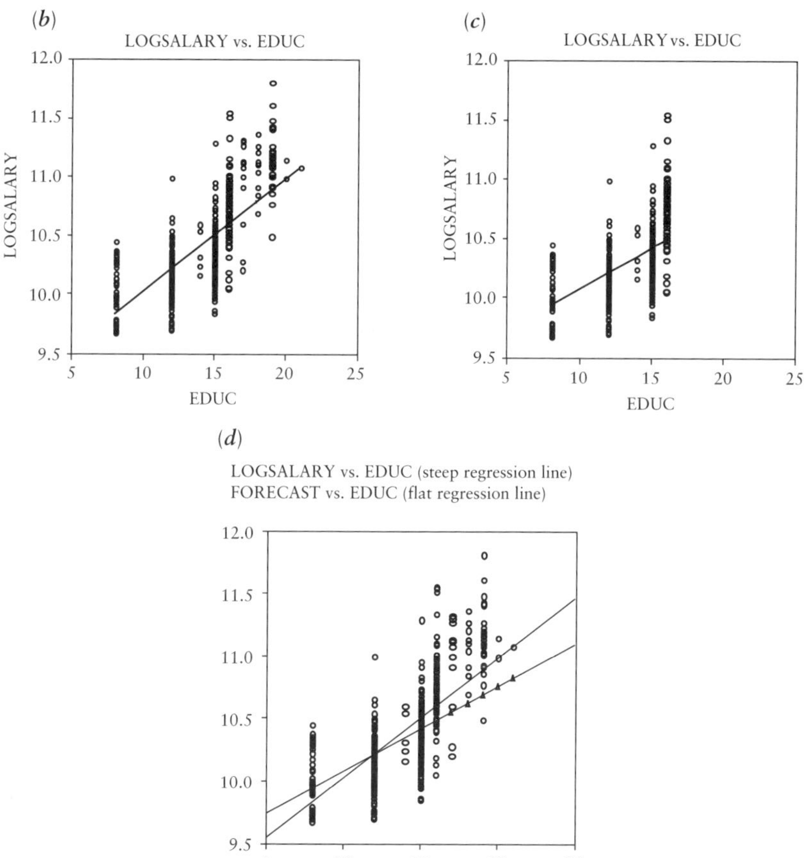

Exhibit 2.15 Bank Wages (Example 2.11)

Result of regression of salary (in logarithms) on a constant and education for 424 bank employees with at most sixteen years of education (*a*) and three scatter diagrams, one for all 474 employees (*b*), one for 424 employees with at most sixteen years of education (*c*), and one for all 474 employees together with the predicted values of employees with at least seventeen years of education ((*d*), with predictions based on the regression in (*a*)).

over the 424 individuals with sixteen years of education or less in Exhibit 2.15, then this gives the value 0.139. As the actual squared prediction errors are on average nearly twice as large (0.268 instead of 0.139), this may cast

some doubt on the working hypothesis that Assumptions 1–7 hold true for the full data set of 474 persons. It seems that the returns on education are larger for higher-educated employees than for lower-educated employees. We will return to this question in Section 5.2.1.

Summary, further reading, and keywords

SUMMARY

In this chapter we considered the simple regression model, where variations in the dependent variable are explained in terms of variations of the explanatory variable. The method of least squares can be used to estimate the parameters of this model. The statistical properties of these estimators were derived under a number of assumptions on the data generating process. Further we described methods to construct point predictions and prediction intervals.

The ideas presented in this chapter form the basis for many other types of econometric models. In Chapter 3 we consider models with more than one explanatory variable, and later chapters contain further extensions that are often needed in practice.

FURTHER READING

Most of the textbooks on statistics mentioned in Section 1.5 contain chapters on regression. Econometric textbooks go beyond the simple regression model. In the following chapters we make intensive use of matrix algebra, and references to textbooks that also follow this approach are given in Chapter 3, Further Reading (p. 178). We now mention some econometric textbooks that do not use matrix algebra.

Gujarati, D. N. (2003). *Basic Econometrics*. Boston: McGraw-Hill.
Hill, R. C., Griffiths, W. E., and Judge, G. G. (2001). *Undergraduate Econometrics*. New York: Wiley.
Kennedy, P. (1998). *A Guide to Econometrics*. Oxford: Blackwell.
Maddala, G. S. (2001). *Introduction to Econometrics*. London: Prentice Hall.
Pindyck, R. S., and Rubinfeld, D. L. (1998). *Econometric Models and Economic Forecasts*. Boston: McGraw-Hill.
Thomas, R. L. (1997). *Modern Econometrics*. Harlow: Addison-Wesley.
Wooldridge, J. M. (2000). *Introductory Econometrics*. Australia: Thomson Learning.

KEYWORDS

absence of serial correlation 93
best linear unbiased estimator 97
BLUE 97
coefficient of determination 83
conditional prediction 107
controlled experiments 92
covariate 79
data generating process 87
dependent variable 79
DGP 87
disturbance 88
endogenous variable 79
error term 88
exogenous variable 79
explanatory variable 79
fixed regressors 92
heteroskedastic 93
homoskedastic 93
independent variable 79
least squares criterion 80
linear model 93
normal equations 82
normality assumption 93
OLS 80
ordinary least squares 80
parameters 93
point prediction 105
prediction interval 106
R-squared (R^2) 83
regressor 79
residuals 82
rounding errors 84
scatter diagram 79
significant 100
standard error of b 100
standard error of the regression 100
t-value of b 100
variable to be explained 79

Exercises

THEORY QUESTIONS

2.1 (☞ Sections 2.1.2, 2.3.1)
Let two data sets (x_i, y_i) and (x_i^*, y_i^*) be related by $x_i^* = c_1 + c_2 x_i$ and $y_i^* = c_3 + c_4 y_i$ for all $i = 1, \cdots, n$. This means that the only differences between the two data sets are the location and the scale of measurement. Such data transformations are often applied in economic studies. For example, y_i may be the total variable production costs in dollars of a firm in month i and y_i^* the total production costs in millions of dollars. Then c_3 are the total fixed costs (in millions of dollars) and $c_4 = 10^{-6}$.

a. Derive the relation $y^* = \alpha^* + \beta^* x^*$ between y^* and x^* if y and x would satisfy the linear relation $y = \alpha + \beta x$.

b. For arbitrary data (x_i, y_i), $i = 1, \cdots, n$, derive the relation between the least squares estimators (a, b) for the original data and (a^*, b^*) for the transformed data.

c. Which of the statistics R^2, s^2, s_b, and t_b are invariant with respect to this transformation?

d. Check the results in **b** and **c** with the excess returns data of Example 2.1 on stock market returns. Perform two regressions, one with the original data (in percentages) and the other with transformed data with the actual excess returns—that is, with $c_1 = c_3 = 0$ and $c_2 = c_4 = 0.01$.

XR201SMR

2.2 (☞ Section 2.1.3)
In the regression model the variable y is regressed on the variable x with resulting regression line $a + bx$. Reversing the role of the two variables, x can be regressed on y with resulting regression line $c + dy$.

a. Derive formulas for the least squares estimates of c and d obtained by regressing x on y.

b. Show that $bd = R^2$, where b is the conventional least squares estimator and d the slope estimator in **a**.

c. Conclude that in general $d \neq 1/b$. Explain this in terms of the criterion functions used to obtain b and d.

d. Finally, check the results in **b** and **c** by considering again the excess returns data of Example 2.1.

2.3 (☞ Section 2.2.5)
Suppose that Assumptions 1–6 are satisfied. We consider two slope estimators, $b_1 = (y_n - y_1)/(x_n - x_1)$ and $b_2 = \sum y_i / \sum x_i$, as alternatives for the least squares estimator b.

a. Investigate whether b_1 and b_2 are unbiased estimators of β.

b. Determine expressions for the variances of b_1 and b_2.

c. Show that $\text{var}(b_1) \geq \text{var}(b)$.

d. Show that there exist data x_i, $i = 1, \cdots, n$, so that $\text{var}(b_2) < \text{var}(b)$. Is this not in contradiction with the Gauss–Markov theorem?

2.4 (☞ Section 2.2.4)
Let Assumption 6 be replaced by the assumption that the data are generated by $y_i = \beta x_i + \varepsilon_i$, so that $\alpha = 0$ is given. We wish to fit a line through the origin by means of least squares—that is, by minimizing $\sum (y_i - bx_i)^2$.

a. Adapt Assumptions 1 and 5 for this special case.

b. Prove that the value of b that minimizes this sum of squares is given by $b_* = \sum x_i y_i / \sum x_i^2$.

c. Find the mean and variance of this estimator.

d. Investigate whether the estimator b_2 of Exercise 2.3 is unbiased now, and show that $\text{var}(b_2) \geq \text{var}(b_*)$.

e. Let R^2 be defined by $R^2 = b_*^2 \sum x_i^2 / \sum y_i^2$. Show, by means of a simulation example, that the results in (2.11), (2.12), and (2.15) no longer hold true.

2.5 (☞ Section 2.2.4)
Sometimes we wish to assign different weights to the observations. This is for instance the case if the observations refer to countries and we want to give larger weights to larger countries.

a. Find the value of b that minimizes $\sum w_i e_i^2$ where the weights $w_1, \cdots, w_n$ are given positive numbers—for instance, the populations or the areas of the countries. Without loss of generality it may be assumed that the weights are scaled so that $\sum w_i = 1$.
b. Now suppose that Assumptions 1–6 are satisfied. Is the estimator of **a** unbiased?

2.6 (☞ Section 2.2.4)
Suppose that Assumptions 1, 2, and 4–6 hold but that the variances of the disturbances are given by $E[\varepsilon_i^2] = \sigma^2 g_i$ $(i = 1, \cdots, n)$, where the g_i are known and given numbers. Assume that b is computed according to (2.8).

a. Is b still unbiased under these assumptions?
b. Derive the variance of b under these assumptions.
c. Verify that this result reduces to (2.27) if $g_i = 1$ for $i = 1, \cdots, n$.

2.7 (☞ Section 2.3.1)
In this exercise we prove that the least squares estimator s^2 is unbiased. Prove the following results under Assumptions 1–6.

a. $e_i = (y_i - \bar{y}) - b(x_i - \bar{x}) = -(x_i - \bar{x})(b - \beta) + \varepsilon_i - \bar{\varepsilon}$.
b. $E[(\varepsilon_i - \bar{\varepsilon})^2] = \sigma^2(1 - \frac{1}{n})$ and $E[(b - \beta)(\varepsilon_i - \bar{\varepsilon})] = \sigma^2 \frac{(x_i - \bar{x})}{\sum (x_j - \bar{x})^2}$.
c. $E[e_i] = 0$ and $\text{var}(e_i) = \sigma^2 \left(1 - \frac{1}{n} - \frac{(x_i - \bar{x})^2}{\sum (x_j - \bar{x})^2}\right)$.
d. $E[s^2] = \sigma^2$, where s^2 is defined in (2.34).

2.8 (☞ Section 2.4.1)
Under the assumptions stated in Section 2.4.1, prove the following results for the prediction error f in (2.38). The notation $\bar{x}$, $\bar{y}$, and $\bar{\varepsilon}$ is used to denote sample averages over the estimation sample $i = 1, \cdots, n$.

a. $f = (y_{n+1} - \bar{y}) - b(x_{n+1} - \bar{x})$
$= -(x_{n+1} - \bar{x})(b - \beta) + \varepsilon_{n+1} - \bar{\varepsilon}$, and $E[f] = 0$.
b. $E[(\varepsilon_{n+1} - \bar{\varepsilon})^2] = \sigma^2(1 + \frac{1}{n})$. Explain the difference with the first result in Exercise 2.7**b**.
c. Prove the result (2.39).
d. Comment on the difference between this result and the one in Exercise 2.7**c**; in particular, explain why $\text{var}(f) > \text{var}(e_i)$.

2.9 (☞ Section 2.2.4)
Suppose that data are generated by a process that satisfies Assumptions 1 and 3–6, but that the random disturbances ε_i do not have mean zero but that $E[\varepsilon_i] = \mu_i$.

a. Show that the least squares slope estimator b remains unbiased if $\mu_i = \mu$ is constant for all $i = 1, \cdots, n$.
b. Now suppose that $\mu_i = x_i/10$ is proportional to the level of x_i. Derive the bias $E[b] - \beta$ under these assumptions.
c. Discuss whether Assumption 2 can be checked by considering the least squares residuals e_i, $i = 1, \cdots, n$. Consider in particular the situations of **a** and **b**.

EMPIRICAL AND SIMULATION QUESTIONS

2.10 (☞ Sections 2.1.2, 2.1.3, 2.2.3, 2.3.1)

Consider the set of $n = 12$ observations on price x_i and quantity sold y_i for a brand of coffee in Example 2.3. It may be instructive to perform the calculations of this exercise only with the help of a calculator. For this purpose we present the data in the following table.

a. Discuss whether the Assumptions 1–6 are plausible for these data.
b. Compute the least squares estimates of α and β in the model $y = \alpha + \beta x_i + \varepsilon_i$.
c. Compute SST, SSE, SSR, and R^2 for these data.
d. Estimate the variance σ^2 of the disturbance terms.

i	Price	Quantity
1	1.00	89
2	1.00	86
3	1.00	74
4	1.00	79
5	1.00	68
6	1.00	84
7	0.95	139
8	0.95	122
9	0.95	102
10	0.85	186
11	0.85	179
12	0.85	187

e. Compute the standard error of b and test the null hypothesis $H_0: \beta = 0$ against the alternative $H_1: \beta \neq 0$, using a 5% significance level (the corresponding two-sided critical value of the $t(10)$ distribution is $c = 2.23$).

f. Compute a 95% interval estimate of β.

2.11 (☞ Section 2.1.3)

Consider the excess returns data set described in Example 2.1 on stock market returns, with x_i the excess returns of the market index and y_i the excess returns in the sector of cyclical consumer goods.

a. Perform two regressions of y on x, one in the model $y_i = \alpha + \beta x_i + \varepsilon_i$ and the second in the model $y_i = \beta x_i + \varepsilon_i$.

b. Check the conditions (2.11) and (2.12) for both models.

c. Investigate the correlation between the two series of residuals obtained in **a**. Can you explain this outcome?

2.12 (☞ Sections 2.1.2, 2.3.1)

Consider again the stock market returns data of Example 2.1, with the x-variable for the excess returns for the whole market and with the y-variable for the excess returns for the sector of cyclical consumer goods.

a. Use a software package to compute the sample means $\overline{x}$ and $\overline{y}$ and the sample moments $\sum (x_i - \overline{x})^2/n$, $\sum (y_i - \overline{y})^2/n$, and $\sum (x_i - \overline{x})\,(y_i - \overline{y})/n$.

b. Compute a, b, s^2, and R^2 from the statistics in **a**.

c. Check the results by performing a regression of y on x by means of a software package.

2.13 (☞ Section 2.3.1)

Consider the data generating process defined in terms of Assumptions 1–7 with the following specifications. In Assumption 1 take $n = 10$ and $x_i = 100 + i$ for $i = 1, \cdots, 10$, in Assumption 3 take $\sigma^2 = 1$, and in Assumption 6 take $\alpha = -100$ and $\beta = 1$. Note that we happen to know the parameters of this DGP, but we will simulate the situation where the modeller knows only a set of data generated by the DGP, and not the parameters of the DGP.

a. Simulate one data set from this model and determine the least squares estimates a and b, the standard errors of a and b, and the t-values of a and b.

b. Determine 95% interval estimates for α and β.

c. Repeat steps **a** and **b** 100 times. Compare the resulting variances in the 100 estimates a and b with the theoretical variances. How many of the 100 computed interval estimates contain the true values of α and β?

d. Now combine the data into one large data set with 1000 observations. Estimate α and β by using all 1000 observations simultaneously and construct 95% interval estimates for α and β. Discuss the resulting outcomes.

2.14 (☞ Sections 2.3.1, 2.4.1)

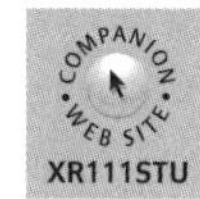

Consider the data set of Exercise 1.11 on student learning, with FGPA and SATM scores of ten students. We investigate how far the FGPA scores of these students can be explained in terms of their SATM scores.

a. Regress the FGPA scores on a constant and SATM and compute a, b, and s^2.

b. Perform 5% significance tests on a and b.

c. Construct 95% interval estimates for α and β.

d. Make a point prediction of the FGPA score for a student with SATM score equal to 6.0. Construct also a 95% prediction interval.

e. Discuss the conditions needed to be confident about these predictions.

2.15 (☞ Section 2.4.1)

Consider the CAPM of Example 2.5 for the stock market returns data on the excess returns y_i for the sector of cyclical consumer goods and x_i for the market index. This data set consists of 240 monthly returns. We pay special attention to the 'crash observation' $i = 94$

corresponding to October 1987 when a crash took place.

a. Estimate the CAPM using all the available data, and a second version where the crash observation is deleted from the sample.

b. Compare the outcomes of the two regressions.

c. Use the second model (estimated without the crash observation) to predict the value of y_{94} for the given historical value of x_{94}. Construct also four prediction intervals, with confidence levels 50%, 90%, 95%, and 99%. Does the actual value of y_{94} belong to these intervals?

d. Explain the relation between your findings in **b** and **c**.

e. Answer questions **a** and **b** also for some other sectors instead of cyclical consumer goods—that is, for the three sectors 'Noncyclical Consumer Goods', 'Information Technology', and 'Telecommunication, Media and Technology'.

f. For each of the four sectors in **a** and **e**, test the null hypothesis $H_0: \beta = 1$ against the alternative $H_1: \beta \neq 1$, using the data over the full sample (that is, including the crash observation). For which sectors should this hypothesis be rejected (at the 5% significance level)?

g. Relate the outcomes in **f** to the risk of the different sectors as compared to the total market in the UK over the period 1980–99.

3

Multiple Regression

In practice there often exists more than one variable that influences the dependent variable. This chapter discusses the regression model with multiple explanatory variables. We use matrices to describe and analyse this model. We present the method of least squares, its statistical properties, and the idea of partial regression. The F-test is the central tool for testing linear hypotheses, with a test for predictive accuracy as a special case. Particular attention is paid to the question whether additional variables should be included in the model or not.

3.1 Least squares in matrix form

☞ Uses Appendix A.2–A.4, A.6, A.7.

3.1.1 Introduction

More than one explanatory variable

In the foregoing chapter we considered the simple regression model where the dependent variable is related to one explanatory variable. In practice the situation is often more involved in the sense that there exists more than one variable that influences the dependent variable.

As an illustration we consider again the salaries of 474 employees at a US bank (see Example 2.2 (p. 77) on bank wages). In Chapter 2 the variations in salaries (measured in logarithms) were explained by variations in education of the employees. As can be observed from the scatter diagram in Exhibit 2.5(*a*) (p. 85) and the regression results in Exhibit 2.6 (p. 86), around half of the variance can be explained in this way. Of course, the salary of an employee is not only determined by the number of years of education because many other variables also play a role. Apart from salary and education, the following data are available for each employee: begin or starting salary (the salary that the individual earned at his or her first position at this bank), gender (with value zero for females and one for males), ethnic minority (with value zero for non-minorities and value one for minorities), and job category (category 1 consists of administrative jobs, category 2 of custodial jobs, and category 3 of management jobs). The begin salary can be seen as an indication of the qualities of the employee that, apart from education, are determined by previous experience, personal characteristics, and so on. The other variables may also affect the earned salary.

Simple regression may be misleading

Of course, the effect of each variable could be estimated by a simple regression of salaries on each explanatory variable separately. For the explanatory variables education, begin salary, and gender, the scatter diagrams with regression lines are shown in Exhibit 3.1 (*a*–*c*). However, these results may be misleading, as the explanatory variables are mutually related. For

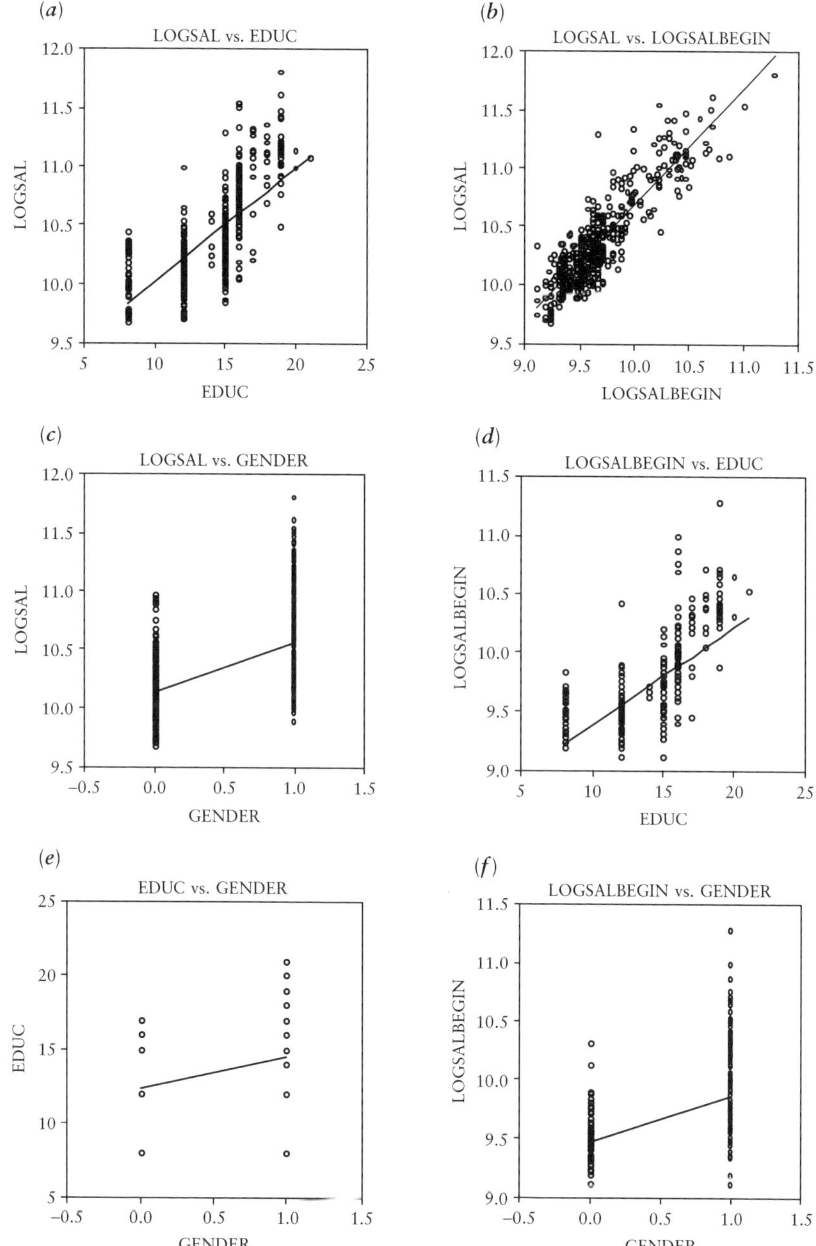

Exhibit 3.1 Scatter diagrams of Bank Wage data

Scatter diagrams with regression lines for several bivariate relations between the variables LOGSAL (logarithm of yearly salary in dollars), EDUC (finished years of education), LOGSALBEGIN (logarithm of yearly salary when employee entered the firm) and GENDER (0 for females, 1 for males), for 474 employees of a US bank.

example, the gender effect on salaries (c) is partly caused by the gender effect on education (e). Similar relations between the explanatory variables are shown in (d) and (f). This mutual dependence is taken into account by formulating a multiple regression model that contains more than one explanatory variable.

3.1.2 Least squares

☞ Uses Appendix A.7.

Regression model in matrix form

The linear model with several explanatory variables is given by the equation

$$y_i = \beta_1 + \beta_2 x_{2i} + \beta_3 x_{3i} + \cdots + \beta_k x_{ki} + \varepsilon_i \quad (i = 1, \cdots, n). \tag{3.1}$$

From now on we follow the convention that the constant term is denoted by β_1 rather than α. The first explanatory variable x_1 is defined by $x_{1i} = 1$ for every $i = 1, \cdots, n$, and for simplicity of notation we write β_1 instead of $\beta_1 x_{1i}$. For purposes of analysis it is convenient to express the model (3.1) in *matrix form*. Let

$$y = \begin{pmatrix} y_1 \\ \vdots \\ y_n \end{pmatrix}, \quad X = \begin{pmatrix} 1 & x_{21} & \cdots & x_{k1} \\ \vdots & \vdots & & \vdots \\ 1 & x_{2n} & \cdots & x_{kn} \end{pmatrix}, \quad \beta = \begin{pmatrix} \beta_1 \\ \vdots \\ \beta_k \end{pmatrix}, \quad \varepsilon = \begin{pmatrix} \varepsilon_1 \\ \vdots \\ \varepsilon_n \end{pmatrix}. \tag{3.2}$$

Note that in the $n \times k$ matrix $X = (x_{ji})$ the first index j ($j = 1, \cdots, k$) refers to the variable number (in columns) and the second index i ($i = 1, \cdots, n$) refers to the observation number (in rows). The notation in (3.2) is common in econometrics (whereas in books on linear algebra the indices i and j are often reversed). In our notation, we can rewrite (3.1) as

$$y = X\beta + \varepsilon. \tag{3.3}$$

Here β is a $k \times 1$ vector of unknown parameters and ε is an $n \times 1$ vector of unobserved disturbances.

Residuals and the least squares criterion

If b is a $k \times 1$ vector of estimates of β, then the estimated model may be written as

$$y = Xb + e. \quad (3.4)$$

Here e denotes the $n \times 1$ vector of residuals, which can be computed from the data and the vector of estimates b by means of

$$e = y - Xb. \quad (3.5)$$

We denote transposition of matrices by primes ($'$)—for instance, the transpose of the residual vector e is the $1 \times n$ matrix $e' = (e_1, \cdots, e_n)$. To determine the least squares estimator, we write the sum of squares of the residuals (a function of b) as

$$\begin{aligned} S(b) &= \sum e_i^2 = e'e = (y - Xb)'(y - Xb) \\ &= y'y - y'Xb - b'X'y + b'X'Xb. \end{aligned} \quad (3.6)$$

Derivation of least squares estimator

T

The minimum of $S(b)$ is obtained by setting the derivatives of $S(b)$ equal to zero. Note that the function $S(b)$ has scalar values, whereas b is a column vector with k components. So we have k first order derivatives and we will follow the convention to arrange them in a column vector. The second and third terms of the last expression in (3.6) are equal (a 1×1 matrix is always symmetric) and may be replaced by $-2b'X'y$. This is a linear expression in the elements of b and so the vector of derivatives equals $-2X'y$. The last term of (3.6) is a quadratic form in the elements of b. The vector of first order derivatives of this term $b'X'Xb$ can be written as $2X'Xb$. The proof of this result is left as an exercise (see Exercise 3.1). To get the idea we consider the case $k = 2$ and we denote the elements of $X'X$ by c_{ij}, $i, j = 1, 2$, with $c_{12} = c_{21}$. Then $b'X'Xb = c_{11}b_1^2 + c_{22}b_2^2 + 2c_{12}b_1b_2$. The derivative with respect to b_1 is $2c_{11}b_1 + 2c_{12}b_2$ and the derivative with respect to b_2 is $2c_{12}b_1 + 2c_{22}b_2$. When we arrange these two partial derivatives in a 2×1 vector, this can be written as $2X'Xb$. See Appendix A (especially Examples A.10 and A.11 in Section A.7) for further computational details and illustrations.

The least squares estimator

Combining the above results, we obtain

$$\frac{\partial S}{\partial b} = -2X'y + 2X'Xb. \quad (3.7)$$

The least squares estimator is obtained by minimizing $S(b)$. Therefore we set these derivatives equal to zero, which gives the *normal equations*

$$X'Xb = X'y. \quad (3.8)$$

Solving this for b, we obtain

$$b = (X'X)^{-1}X'y \tag{3.9}$$

provided that the inverse of $X'X$ exists, which means that the matrix X should have rank k. As X is an $n \times k$ matrix, this requires in particular that $n \geq k$—that is, the number of parameters is smaller than or equal to the number of observations. In practice we will almost always require that k is considerably smaller than n.

Proof of minimum

From now on, if we write b, we always mean the expression in (3.9). This is the classical formula for the *least squares estimator* in matrix notation. If the matrix X has rank k, it follows that the Hessian matrix

$$\frac{\partial^2 S}{\partial b \partial b'} = 2X'X \tag{3.10}$$

is a positive definite matrix (see Exercise 3.2). This implies that (3.9) is indeed the minimum of (3.6). In (3.10) we take the derivatives of a vector $\left(\frac{\partial S}{\partial b}\right)$ with respect to another vector (b') and we follow the convention to arrange these derivatives in a matrix (see Exercise 3.2). An alternative proof that b minimizes the sum of squares (3.6) that makes no use of first and second order derivatives is given in Exercise 3.3.

Summary of computations

The least squares estimates can be computed as follows.

Least squares estimation

- *Step 1: Choice of variables.* Choose the variable to be explained (y) and the explanatory variables ($x_1, \cdots, x_k$, where x_1 is often the constant that always takes the value 1).
- *Step 2: Collect data.* Collect n observations of y and of the related values of $x_1, \cdots, x_k$ and store the data of y in an $n \times 1$ vector and the data on the explanatory variables in the $n \times k$ matrix X.
- *Step 3: Compute the estimates.* Compute the least squares estimates by the OLS formula (3.9) by using a regression package.

☞ Exercises: T: 3.1, 3.2.

3.1.3 Geometric interpretation

☞ Uses Sections 1.2.2, 1.2.3; Appendix A.6.

Least squares seen as projection

The least squares method can be given a geometric interpretation, which we discuss now. Using the expression (3.9) for b, the residuals may be written as

$$e = y - Xb = y - X(X'X)^{-1}X'y = My \tag{3.11}$$

where

$$M = I - X(X'X)^{-1}X'. \tag{3.12}$$

The matrix M is symmetric ($M' = M$) and idempotent ($M^2 = M$). Since it also has the property $MX = 0$, it follows from (3.11) that

$$X'e = 0. \tag{3.13}$$

We may write the explained component $\hat{y}$ of y as

$$\hat{y} = Xb = Hy \tag{3.14}$$

where

$$H = X(X'X)^{-1}X' \tag{3.15}$$

is called the 'hat matrix', since it transforms y into $\hat{y}$ (pronounced: 'y-hat'). Clearly, there holds $H' = H$, $H^2 = H$, $H + M = I$ and $HM = 0$. So

$$y = Hy + My = \hat{y} + e$$

where, because of (3.11) and (3.13), $\hat{y}'e = 0$, so that the vectors $\hat{y}$ and e are orthogonal to each other. Therefore, the least squares method can be given the following interpretation. The sum of squares $e'e$ is the square of the length of the residual vector $e = y - Xb$. The length of this vector is minimized by choosing Xb as the orthogonal *projection* of y onto the space spanned by the columns of X. This is illustrated in Exhibit 3.2. The projection is characterized by the property that $e = y - Xb$ is orthogonal to all columns of X, so that $0 = X'e = X'(y - Xb)$. This gives the normal equations (3.8).

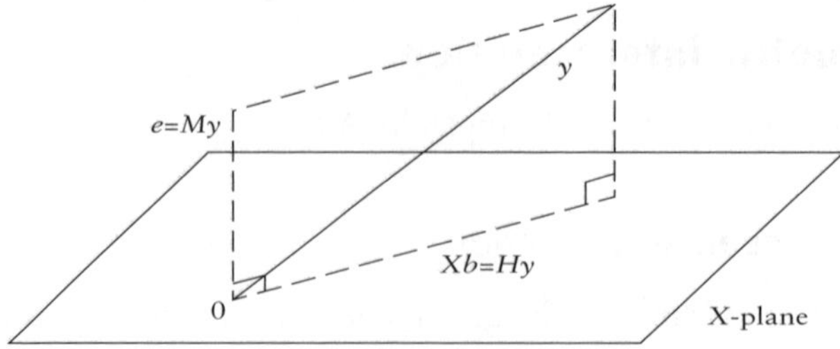

Exhibit 3.2 Least squares

Three-dimensional geometric impression of least squares, the vector of observations on the dependent variable y is projected onto the plane of the independent variables X to obtain the linear combination Xb of the independent variables that is as close as possible to y.

Geometry of least squares

Let $S(X)$ be the space spanned by the columns of X (that is, the set of all $n \times 1$ vectors that can be written as Xa for some $k \times 1$ vector a) and let $S^{\perp}(X)$ be the space orthogonal to $S(X)$ (that is, the set of all $n \times 1$ vectors z with the property that $X'z = 0$). The matrix H projects onto $S(X)$ and the matrix M projects onto $S^{\perp}(X)$. In $y = \hat{y} + e$, the vector y is decomposed into two orthogonal components, with $\hat{y} \in S(X)$ according to (3.14) and $e \in S^{\perp}(X)$ according to (3.13). The essence of this decomposition is given in Exhibit 3.3, which can be seen as a two-dimensional version of the three-dimensional picture in Exhibit 3.2.

Geometric interpretation as a tool in analysis

This geometric interpretation can be helpful to understand some of the algebraic properties of least squares. As an example we consider the effect of applying linear transformations on the set of explanatory variables. Suppose that the $n \times k$ matrix X is replaced by $X_* = XA$ where A is a $k \times k$ invertible matrix. Then the least squares fit ($\hat{y}$), the residuals (e), and the projection matrices (H and M) remain unaffected by this transformation. This is immediately evident from the geometric pictures in Exhibits 3.2 and 3.3, as $S(X_*) = S(X)$.

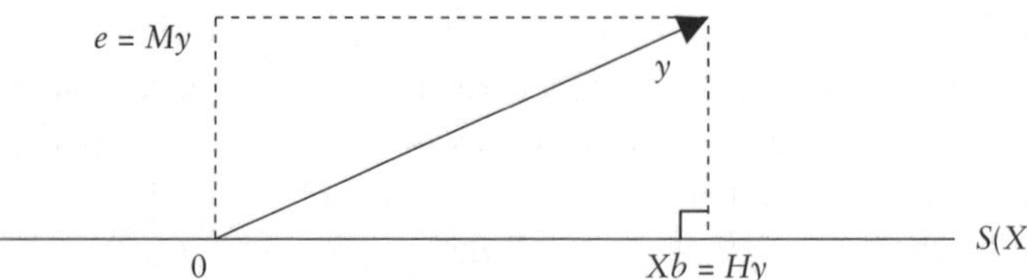

Exhibit 3.3 Least squares

Two-dimensional geometric impression of least squares where the k-dimensional plane $S(X)$ is represented by the horizontal line, the vector of observations on the dependent variable y is projected onto the space of the independent variables $S(X)$ to obtain the linear combination Xb of the independent variables that is as close as possible to y.

The properties can also be checked algebraically, by working out the expressions for $\hat{y}$, e, H, and M in terms of X_*. The least squares estimates change after the transformation, as $b_* = (X_*'X_*)^{-1}X_*'y = A^{-1}b$. For example, suppose that the variable x_k is measured in dollars and x_k^* is the same variable measured in thousands of dollars. Then $x_{ki}^* = x_{ki}/1000$ for $i = 1, \cdots, n$, and $X_* = XA$ where A is the diagonal matrix diag$(1, \cdots, 1, 0.001)$. The least squares estimates of β_j for $j \neq k$ remain unaffected—that is, $b_j^* = b_j$ for $j \neq k$, and $b_k^* = 1000b_k$. This also makes perfect sense, as one unit increase in x_k^* corresponds to an increase of a thousand units in x_k.

☞ **Exercises:** T: 3.3.

3.1.4 Statistical properties

☞ Uses Sections 1.2.2, 1.3.2.

Seven assumptions on the multiple regression model

To analyse the statistical properties of least squares estimation, it is convenient to use as conceptual background again the simulation experiment described in Section 2.2.1 (p. 87–8). We first restate the seven assumptions of Section 2.2.3 (p. 92) for the multiple regression model (3.3) and use the matrix notation introduced in Section 3.1.2.

- *Assumption 1: fixed regressors.* All elements of the $n \times k$ matrix X containing the observations on the explanatory variables are non-stochastic. It is assumed that $n \geq k$ and that the matrix X has rank k.
- *Assumption 2: random disturbances, zero mean.* The $n \times 1$ vector ε consists of random disturbances with zero mean so that $E[\varepsilon] = 0$, that is, $E[\varepsilon_i] = 0$ $(i = 1, \cdots, n)$.
- *Assumption 3: homoskedasticity.* The covariance matrix of the disturbances $E[\varepsilon\varepsilon']$ exists and all its diagonal elements are equal to σ^2, that is, $E[\varepsilon_i^2] = \sigma^2$ $(i = 1, \cdots, n)$.
- *Assumption 4: no correlation.* The off-diagonal elements of the covariance matrix of the disturbances $E[\varepsilon\varepsilon']$ are all equal to zero, that is, $E[\varepsilon_i\varepsilon_j] = 0$ for all $i \neq j$.
- *Assumption 5: constant parameters.* The elements of the $k \times 1$ vector β and the scalar σ are fixed unknown numbers with $\sigma > 0$.
- *Assumption 6: linear model.* The data on the explained variable y have been generated by the data generating process (DGP)

$$y = X\beta + \varepsilon. \tag{3.16}$$

- *Assumption 7: normality.* The disturbances are jointly normally distributed.

Assumptions 3 and 4 can be summarized in matrix notation as

$$E[\varepsilon\varepsilon'] = \sigma^2 I, \tag{3.17}$$

where I denotes the $n \times n$ identity matrix. If in addition Assumption 7 is satisfied, then ε follows the multivariate normal distribution

$$\varepsilon \sim \mathrm{N}(0, \sigma^2 I).$$

Assumptions 4 and 7 imply that the disturbances $\varepsilon_i, i = 1, \cdots, n$ are mutually independent.

Least squares is unbiased

The expected value of b is obtained by using Assumptions 1, 2, 5, and 6. Assumption 6 implies that the least squares estimator $b = (X'X)^{-1}X'y$ can be written as

$$b = (X'X)^{-1}X'(X\beta + \varepsilon) = \beta + (X'X)^{-1}X'\varepsilon.$$

Taking expectations is a linear operation—that is, if z_1 and z_2 are two random variables and A_1 and A_2 are two non-random matrices of appropriate dimensions so that $z = A_1z_1 + A_2z_2$ is well defined, then $E[z] = A_1E[z_1] + A_2E[z_2]$. From Assumptions 1, 2, and 5 we obtain

$$E[b] = E[\beta + (X'X)^{-1}X'\varepsilon] = \beta + (X'X)^{-1}X'E[\varepsilon] = \beta. \tag{3.18}$$

So b is *unbiased.*

The covariance matrix of b

Using the result (3.18), we obtain that under Assumptions 1–6 the *covariance matrix* of b is given by

$$\begin{aligned} \mathrm{var}(b) &= E[(b-\beta)(b-\beta)'] = E[(X'X)^{-1}X'\varepsilon\varepsilon'X(X'X)^{-1}] \\ &= (X'X)^{-1}X'E[\varepsilon\varepsilon']X(X'X)^{-1} = (X'X)^{-1}X'(\sigma^2 I)X(X'X)^{-1} \\ &= \sigma^2(X'X)^{-1}. \end{aligned} \tag{3.19}$$

The diagonal elements of this matrix are the variances of the estimators of the individual parameters, and the off-diagonal elements are the covariances between these estimators.

Least squares is best linear unbiased

The Gauss–Markov theorem, proved in Section 2.2.5 (p. 97–8) for the simple regression model, also holds for the more general model (3.16). It states that, among all linear unbiased estimators, b has *minimal variance*—that is, b is the best linear unbiased estimator (BLUE) in the sense that, if $\hat{\beta} = Ay$ with A a $k \times n$ non-stochastic matrix and $E[\hat{\beta}] = \beta$, then $\text{var}(\hat{\beta}) - \text{var}(b)$ is a positive semidefinite matrix. This means that for every $k \times 1$ vector c of constants there holds $c'(\text{var}(\hat{\beta}) - \text{var}(b))c \geq 0$, or, equivalently, $\text{var}(c'b) \leq \text{var}(c'\hat{\beta})$. Choosing for c the jth unit vector, this means in particular that for the jth component $\text{var}(b_j) \leq \text{var}(\hat{\beta}_j)$ so that the least squares estimators are efficient. This result holds true under Assumptions 1–6, the assumption of normality is not needed.

T

Proof of Gauss–Markov theorem

To prove the result, first note that the condition that $E[\hat{\beta}] = E[Ay] = AE[y] = AX\beta = \beta$ for all β implies that $AX = I$, the $k \times k$ identity matrix. Now define $D = A - (X'X)^{-1}X'$, then $DX = AX - (X'X)^{-1}X'X = I - I = 0$ so that

$$\text{var}(\hat{\beta}) = \text{var}(Ay) = \text{var}(A\varepsilon) = \sigma^2 AA' = \sigma^2 DD' + \sigma^2 (X'X)^{-1},$$

where the last equality follows by writing $A = D + (X'X)^{-1}X'$ and working out AA'. This shows that $\text{var}(\hat{\beta}) - \text{var}(b) = \sigma^2 DD'$, which is positive semidefinite, and zero if and only if $D = 0$—that is, $A = (X'X)^{-1}X'$. So $\hat{\beta} = b$ gives the minimal variance.

Exercises: T: 3.4.

3.1.5 Estimating the disturbance variance

T

Derivation of unbiased estimator

Next we consider the estimation of the unknown variance σ^2. As in the previous chapter we make use of the sum of squared residuals $e'e$. Intuition could suggest to estimate $\sigma^2 = E[\varepsilon_i^2]$ by the sample mean $\frac{1}{n}\sum e_i^2 = \frac{1}{n}e'e$, but this estimator is not unbiased. It follows from (3.11) and (3.16) and the fact that $MX = 0$ that $e = My = M(X\beta + \varepsilon) = M\varepsilon$. So

$$E[e] = 0, \tag{3.20}$$

$$\text{var}(e) = E[ee'] = E[M\varepsilon\varepsilon'M] = ME[\varepsilon\varepsilon']M = \sigma^2 M^2 = \sigma^2 M. \tag{3.21}$$

To evaluate $E[e'e]$ it is convenient to use the trace of a square matrix, which is defined as the sum of the diagonal elements of this matrix. Because the trace and the expectation operator can be interchanged, we find, using the property that $\mathrm{tr}(AB) = \mathrm{tr}(BA)$, that

$$E[e'e] = E[\mathrm{tr}(ee')] = \mathrm{tr}(E[ee']) = \sigma^2 \mathrm{tr}(M).$$

Using the property that $\mathrm{tr}(A + B) = \mathrm{tr}(A) + \mathrm{tr}(B)$ we can simplify this as

$$\begin{aligned}\mathrm{tr}(M) &= \mathrm{tr}(I_n - X(X'X)^{-1}X') = n - \mathrm{tr}(X(X'X)^{-1}X') \\ &= n - \mathrm{tr}(X'X(X'X)^{-1}) = n - \mathrm{tr}(I_k) = n - k,\end{aligned}$$

where the subscripts denote the order of the identity matrices.

The least squares estimator s^2 and standard errors

This shows that $E[e'e] = (n - k)\sigma^2$ so that

$$s^2 = \frac{e'e}{n - k} \tag{3.22}$$

is an unbiased estimator of σ^2. The square root s of (3.22) is called the *standard error of the regression.* If in the expression (3.19) we replace σ^2 by s^2 and if we denote the jth diagonal element of $(X'X)^{-1}$ by a_{jj}, then $s\sqrt{a_{jj}}$ is called the *standard error* of the estimated coefficient b_j. This is an estimate of the standard deviation $\sigma\sqrt{a_{jj}}$ of b_j.

Intuition for the factor $1/(n - k)$

The result in (3.22) can also be given a more intuitive interpretation. Suppose we would try to explain y by a matrix X with $k = n$ columns and rank k. Then we would obtain $e = 0$, a perfect fit, but we would not have obtained any information on σ^2. Of course this is an extreme case. In practice we confine ourselves to the case $k < n$. The very fact that we choose b in such a way that the sum of squared residuals is minimized is the cause of the fact that the squared residuals are smaller (on average) than the squared disturbances. Let us consider a diagonal element of (3.21),

$$\mathrm{var}(e_i) = \sigma^2(1 - h_i), \tag{3.23}$$

where h_i is the ith diagonal element of the matrix $H = I - M$ in (3.15). As H is positive semidefinite, it follows that $h_i \geq 0$. If the model contains a constant term (so that the matrix X contains a column of ones), then $h_i > 0$ (see Exercise 3.7). So each single element e_i of the residual vector has a variance that is smaller than σ^2, and therefore the sum of squares $\sum e_i^2$ has an expected value less than $n\sigma^2$. This effect becomes stronger when we have more parameters to obtain a good fit for the data. If one would like to use a small residual variance as a criterion for a good model, then the denominator $(n - k)$ of the estimator (3.22) gives an automatic penalty for choosing models with large k.

Intuition for the number of degrees of freedom $(n - k)$

As $e = M\varepsilon$, it follows under Assumptions 1–7 that $e'e/\sigma^2 = \varepsilon' M\varepsilon/\sigma^2$ follows the χ^2-distribution with $(n - k)$ degrees of freedom. This follows from the results in Section 1.2.3 (p. 32), using the fact that M is an idempotent matrix with rank $(n - k)$. The term *degrees of freedom* refers to the restrictions $X'e = 0$. We may partition this as $X_1'e_1 + X_2'e_2 = 0$, where X_1' is a $k \times (n - k)$ matrix and X_2' a $k \times k$ matrix. If the matrix X_2' has a rank less than k, we may rearrange the columns of X' in such a way that X_2' has rank k. The restrictions imply that, once we have freely chosen the $n - k$ elements of e_1, the remaining elements are dictated by $e_2 = -(X_2')^{-1}X_1'e_1$. This is also clear from Exhibit 3.3. For given matrix X of explanatory variables, the residual vector lies in $S^{\perp}(X)$ and this space has dimension $(n - k)$. That is, k degrees of freedom are lost because β has been estimated.

☞ Exercises: T: 3.5, 3.7a.

3.1.6 Coefficient of determination

Derivation of R^2

T

The performance of least squares can be evaluated by the *coefficient of determination* R^2—that is, the fraction of the total sample variation $\sum(y_i - \bar{y})^2$ that is explained by the model.

In matrix notation, the total sample variation can be written as $y'Ny$ with

$$N = I - \frac{1}{n}\iota\iota',$$

where $\iota = (1, \cdots, 1)'$ is the $n \times 1$ vector of ones. The matrix N has the property that it takes deviations from the mean, as the elements of Ny are $y_i - \bar{y}$. Note that N is a special case of an M-matrix (3.12) with $X = \iota$, as $\iota'\iota = n$. So Ny can be interpreted as the vector of residuals and $y'Ny = (Ny)'Ny$ as the residual sum of squares from a regression where y is explained by $X = \iota$. If X in the multiple regression model (3.3) contains a constant term, then the fact that $X'e = 0$ implies that $\iota'e = 0$ and hence $Ne = e$. From $y = Xb + e$ we then obtain $Ny = NXb + Ne = NXb + e =$ 'explained' + 'residual', and

$$y'Ny = (Ny)'Ny = (NXb + e)'(NXb + e)$$
$$= b'X'NXb + e'e.$$

Here the cross term vanishes because $b'X'Ne = 0$, as $Ne = e$ and $X'e = 0$. It follows that the total variation in y (SST) can be decomposed in an explained part $SSE = b'X'NXb$ and a residual part $SSR = e'e$.

Coefficient of determination: R^2

Therefore R^2 is given by

$$R^2 = \frac{SSE}{SST} = \frac{b'X'NXb}{y'Ny} = 1 - \frac{e'e}{y'Ny} = 1 - \frac{SSR}{SST}. \tag{3.24}$$

The third equality in (3.24) holds true if the model contains a constant term. If this is not the case, then SSR may be larger than SST (see Exercise 3.7) and R^2 is defined as SSE/SST (and not as $1 - SSR/SST$). If the model contains a constant term, then (3.24) shows that $0 \leq R^2 \leq 1$. It is left as an exercise (see Exercise 3.7) to show that R^2 is the squared sample correlation coefficient between y and its explained part $\hat{y} = Xb$. In geometric terms, R (the square root of R^2) is equal to the length of NXb divided by the length of Ny—that is, R is equal to the cosine of the angle between Ny and NXb. This is illustrated in Exhibit 3.4. A good fit is obtained when Ny is close to NXb—that is, when the angle between these two vectors is small. This corresponds to a high value of R^2.

Adjusted R^2

When explanatory variables are added to the model, then R^2 never decreases (see Exercise 3.6). The wish to penalize models with large k has motivated an adjusted R^2 defined by adjusting for the degrees of freedom.

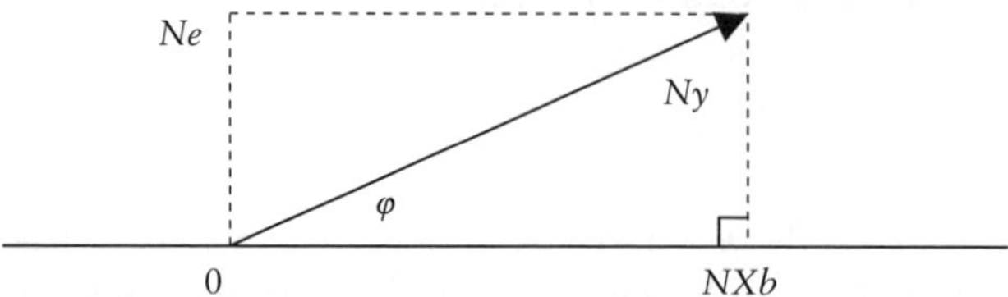

Exhibit 3.4 Geometric picture of R^2

Two-dimensional geometric impression of the coefficient of determination. The dependent variable and all the independent variables are taken in deviation from their sample means, with resulting vector of dependent variables Ny and matrix of independent variables NX. The explained part of Ny is NXb with residuals $Ne = e$, and the coefficient of determination is equal to the square of the cosine of the indicated angle φ.

$$\overline{R}^2 = 1 - \frac{e'e/(n-k)}{y'Ny/(n-1)} = 1 - \frac{n-1}{n-k}(1 - R^2). \qquad (3.25)$$

Exercises: T: 3.6a, b, 3.7b, c.

3.1.7 Illustration: Bank Wages

To illustrate the foregoing results we consider the data on salary and education discussed earlier in Chapter 2 and in Section 3.1.1. We will discuss (i) the data, (ii) the model, (iii) the normal equations and the least squares estimates, (iv) the interpretation of the estimates, (v) the sums of squares and R^2, and (vi) the orthogonality of residuals and explanatory variables.

(i) Data

The data consist of a cross section of 474 individuals working for a US bank. For each employee, the information consists of the following variables: salary (S), education (x_2), begin salary (B), gender ($x_4 = 0$ for females, $x_4 = 1$ for males), minority ($x_5 = 1$ if the individual belongs to a minority group, $x_5 = 0$ otherwise), job category ($x_6 = 1$ for clerical jobs, $x_6 = 2$ for custodial jobs, and $x_6 = 3$ for management positions), and some further job-related variables.

(ii) Model

As a start, we will consider the model with $y = \log(S)$ as variable to be explained and with x_2 and $x_3 = \log(B)$ as explanatory variables. That is, we consider the regression model

$$y_i = \beta_1 + \beta_2 x_{2i} + \beta_3 x_{3i} + \varepsilon_i \qquad (i = 1, \cdots, n).$$

(iii) Normal equations and least squares estimates

As before, to simplify the notation we define the first regressor by $x_{1i} = 1$. The normal equations (3.8) involve the cross product terms $X'X$ and $X'y$. For the data at hand they are given (after rounding) in Exhibit 3.5, Panel 1. Solving the normal equations (3.8) gives the least squares estimates shown in Panel 3 in Exhibit 3.5, so that (after rounding) $b_1 = 1.647$, $b_2 = 0.023$, and $b_3 = 0.869$. It may be checked from the cross products in Panel 1 in Exhibit 3.5 that $X'Xb = X'y$ (apart from rounding errors)—that is,

$$\begin{pmatrix} 474 & 6395 & 4583 \\ 6395 & 90215 & 62166 \\ 4583 & 62166 & 44377 \end{pmatrix} \begin{pmatrix} 1.647 \\ 0.023 \\ 0.869 \end{pmatrix} = \begin{pmatrix} 4909 \\ 66609 \\ 47527 \end{pmatrix}.$$

Panel 1	IOTA	LOGSAL	EDUC	LOGSALBEGIN
IOTA	474			
LOGSAL	4909	50917		
EDUC	6395	66609	90215	
LOGSALBEGIN	4583	47527	62166	44377

Panel 2	LOGSAL	EDUC	LOGSALBEGIN
LOGSAL	1.000000		
EDUC	0.696740	1.000000	
LOGSALBEGIN	0.886368	0.685719	1.000000

Panel 3: Dependent Variable: LOGSAL Method: Least Squares Sample: 1 474 Included observations: 474		
Variable	Coefficient	Std. Error
C	1.646916	0.274598
EDUC	0.023122	0.003894
LOGSALBEGIN	0.868505	0.031835
R-squared	0.800579	
Adjusted R-squared	0.799733	
S.E. of regression	0.177812	
Sum squared resid	14.89166	
Total sum of squares	74.67462	
Explained sum of squares	59.78296	

Panel 4: Dependent Variable: RESID Method: Least Squares Sample: 1 474 Included observations: 474	
Variable	Coefficient
C	3.10E-11
EDUC	2.47E-13
LOGSALBEGIN	−3.55E-12
R-squared	0.000000
Adjusted R-squared	−0.004246
S.E. of regression	0.177812
Sum squared resid	14.89166

Exhibit 3.5 Bank Wages (Section 3.1.7)

Panel 1 contains the cross product terms ($X'X$ and $X'y$) of the variables (iota denotes the constant term with all values equal to one), Panel 2 shows the correlations between the dependent and the two independent variables, and Panel 3 shows the outcomes obtained by regressing salary (in logarithms) on a constant and the explanatory variables education and the logarithm of begin salary. The residuals of this regression are denoted by RESID, and Panel 4 shows the result of regressing these residuals on a constant and the two explanatory variables (3.10E-11 means $3.10*10^{-11}$, and so on; these values are zero up to numerical rounding).

(iv) Interpretation of estimates

A first thing to note here is that the marginal relative effect of education on wage (that is, $\frac{dS/S}{dx_2} = \frac{d\log(S)}{dx_2} = \frac{dy}{dx_2} = \beta_2$) is estimated now as 0.023, whereas in Chapter 2 this effect was estimated as 0.096 with a standard error of 0.005 (see Exhibit 2.11, p. 103). This is a substantial difference. That is, an additional year of education corresponds on average with a 9.6 per cent increase in salary. But, if the begin salary is 'kept fixed', an additional year of education gives only a 2.3 per cent increase in salary. The cause of this difference is that the variable 'begin salary' is strongly related to the variable 'education'. This is clear from Panel 2 in Exhibit 3.5, which shows that x_2 and x_3 have a correlation of around 69 per cent. We refer also to Exhibit 3.1 (*d*), which shows a strong positive relation between x_2 and x_3. This means that in Chapter 2, where we have excluded the begin salary from the model, part of the positive association between education and salary is due to a third variable, begin salary. This explains why the estimated effect in Chapter 2 is larger.

(v) Sums of squares and R^2

The sums of squares for this model are reported in Panel 3 in Exhibit 3.5, with values $SST = 74.675$, $SSE = 59.783$, and $SSR = 14.892$, so that $R^2 = 0.801$. This is larger than the $R^2 = 0.485$ in Chapter 2 (see Exhibit 2.6, p. 86). In Section 3.4 we will discuss a method to test whether this is a significant increase in the model fit. Panel 3 in Exhibit 3.5 also reports the standard error of the regression $s = \sqrt{SSR/(474 - 3)} = 0.178$ and the standard error of b_2 0.0039.

(vi) Orthogonality of residuals and explanatory variables

Panel 4 in Exhibit 3.5 shows the result of regressing the least squares residuals on the variables x_1, x_2, and x_3. This gives an $R^2 = 0$, which is in accordance with the property that the residuals are uncorrelated with the explanatory variables in the sense that $X'e = 0$ (see Exhibits 3.2 and 3.4).

3.2 Adding or deleting variables

☞ Uses Appendix A.2–A.4.

Choice of the number of explanatory variables

To make an econometric model we have to decide which variables provide the best explanation of the dependent variable. That is, we have to decide which explanatory variables should be included in the model. In this section we analyse what happens if we add variables to our model or delete variables from our model. This is illustrated in the scheme in Exhibit 3.6, where X_1 and X_2 denote two subsets of variables. Here X_1 is included in the model, and the question is whether X_2 should be included in the model or not.

Organization of this section

The section is organized as follows. Section 3.2.1 considers the effects of including or deleting variables on the regression coefficients, and Section 3.2.2 provides an interpretation of this result in terms of *ceteris paribus* conditions. In Sections 3.2.3 and 3.2.4 we analyse the statistical consequences of omitting or including variables. Section 3.2.5 shows that, in a multiple regression model, each individual coefficient measures the effect of an explanatory variable on the dependent variable after neutralizing for the effects that are due to the other explanatory variables included in the model.

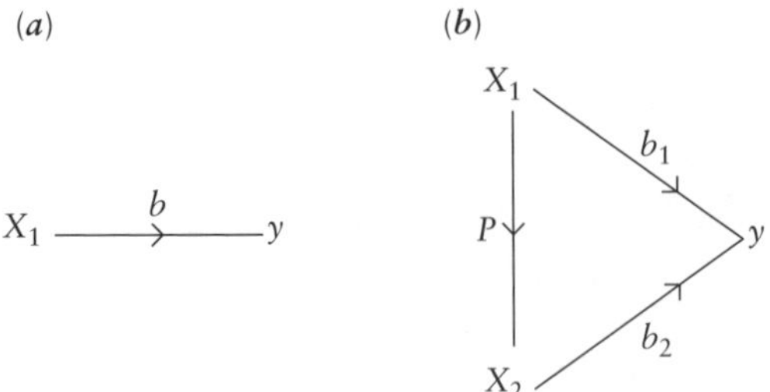

Exhibit 3.6 Direct and indirect effects

Two subsets of explanatory variables (X_1 and X_2) influence the variable to be explained (y), and one subset of explanatory variables (X_1) influences the other one (X_2). The (total) effect of X_1 on y (*a*) is denoted by b in Chapter 2 (and by b_R in Section 3.2.1), the (partial) effect of X_1 on y (*b*) for given value of X_2 is denoted by b_1 and the (partial) effect of X_2 on y for given value of X_1 is denoted by b_2. The effect of changes in X_1 on X_2 is denoted by P.

3.2.1 Restricted and unrestricted models

Two models: Notation

As before, we consider the regression model $y = X\beta + \varepsilon$ where X is the $n \times k$ matrix of explanatory variables with $\text{rank}(X) = k$. We partition the explanatory variables in two groups, one with $k - g$ variables that are certainly included in the model and another with the remaining g variables that may be included or deleted. The matrix of explanatory variables is partitioned as $X = (X_1 \quad X_2)$, where X_1 is the $n \times (k - g)$ matrix of observations of the included regressors and X_2 is the $n \times g$ matrix with observations on the variables that may be included or deleted. The $k \times 1$ vector β of unknown parameters is decomposed in a similar way in the $(k - g) \times 1$ vector β_1 and the $g \times 1$ vector β_2. Then the regression model can be written as

$$y = X_1\beta_1 + X_2\beta_2 + \varepsilon. \qquad (3.26)$$

All the assumptions on the linear model introduced in Section 3.1.4 are assumed to hold true. In this section we compare two versions of the model—namely, the unrestricted version in (3.26) and a restricted version where X_2 is deleted from the model. In particular, we investigate the consequences of deleting X_2 for the estimate of β_1 and for the residuals of the estimated model.

Least squares in the restricted model

In the restricted model we estimate β_1 by regressing y on X_1, so that

$$b_R = (X_1'X_1)^{-1}X_1'y. \qquad (3.27)$$

We use the notation

$$e_R = y - X_1 b_R \qquad (3.28)$$

for the corresponding restricted residuals.

Least squares in the unrestricted model

We may write the unrestricted model as

$$y = X\beta + \varepsilon = (\,X_1 \quad X_2\,)\begin{pmatrix}\beta_1 \\ \beta_2\end{pmatrix} + \varepsilon. \qquad (3.29)$$

The unrestricted least squares estimator is given by $b = (X'X)^{-1}X'y$. Decomposing the $k \times 1$ vector b into a $(k-g) \times 1$ vector b_1 (the unrestricted estimator of β_1) and a $g \times 1$ vector b_2 (the unrestricted estimator of β_2), we can write the unrestricted regression as

$$y = (\, X_1 \quad X_2 \,)\begin{pmatrix} b_1 \\ b_2 \end{pmatrix} + e = X_1 b_1 + X_2 b_2 + e. \tag{3.30}$$

So we continue to write e for the residuals of the unrestricted model. We have learned in the previous section that the least squares residuals are orthogonal to all regressors. So we now have $X_1' e_R = 0$ for the restricted model, and $X_1' e = 0$ and $X_2' e = 0$ for the unrestricted model. Note, however, that in general $X_2' e_R \neq 0$.

Comparison of b_R and b_1

To study the difference between the two estimators b_R and b_1 of β_1, we premultiply (3.30) by the matrix $(X_1'X_1)^{-1}X_1'$ and make use of $X_1'e = 0$ to obtain $b_R = (X_1'X_1)^{-1}X_1'y = b_1 + (X_1'X_1)^{-1}X_1'X_2 b_2$, that is,

$$b_R = b_1 + P b_2 \tag{3.31}$$

where the $(k-g) \times g$ matrix P is defined by

$$P = (X_1'X_1)^{-1}X_1'X_2. \tag{3.32}$$

So we see that the difference $b_R - b_1$ depends on both P and b_2. If either of these terms vanishes, then $b_R = b_1$. This is the case, for instance, if X_2 has no effect at all ($b_2 = 0$) or if X_1 and X_2 are orthogonal ($X_1'X_2 = 0$). In these cases it does not matter for the estimate of β_1 whether we include X_2 in the model or not. However, in general the restricted estimate b_R will be different from the unrestricted estimate b_1.

Comparison of $e_R' e_R$ and $e'e$

Next we compare the residuals of both equations—that is, the residuals e_R in the restricted regression (3.28) and the residuals e in the unrestricted regression (3.30). As the unrestricted model contains more variables to explain the dependent variable, it can be expected that it provides a better (or at least not a worse) fit than the restricted model so that $e'e \leq e_R' e_R$. This is indeed the case, as we will now show.

Derivation of sums of squares

To prove that $e'e \leq e_R'e_R$ we start with the restricted residuals and then substitute the unrestricted model (3.30) for y. We obtain

$$e_R = M_1 y = M_1(X_1 b_1 + X_2 b_2 + e) = M_1 X_2 b_2 + e. \qquad (3.33)$$

Here $M_1 = I - X_1(X_1'X_1)^{-1}X_1'$ is the projection orthogonal to the space spanned by the columns of X_1, and we used that $M_1 X_1 = 0$ and $M_1 e = e$ (as $X_1'e = 0$). So the difference between e_R and e depends on $M_1 X_2$ and b_2. We see that $e_R = e$ if, for instance, X_2 has no effect at all ($b_2 = 0$). For the sums of squared residuals, (3.33) implies that

$$e_R'e_R = b_2'X_2'M_1 X_2 b_2 + e'e \qquad (3.34)$$

where the product term vanishes as $X_2'M_1 e = X_2'e - X_2'X_1(X_1'X_1)^{-1}X_1'e = 0$ because $X_1'e = 0$ and $X_2'e = 0$.

Interpretation of result

As M_1 is a positive semidefinite matrix, it follows that $b_2'X_2'M_1X_2b_2 = (X_2b_2)'M_1(X_2b_2) \geq 0$ in (3.34), so that

$$e_R'e_R \geq e'e$$

and the inequality is strict unless $M_1X_2b_2 = 0$. This shows that adding variables to a regression model in general leads to a reduction of the sum of squared residuals. If this reduction is substantial, then this motivates to include the variables X_2 in the model, as they provide a significant additional explanation of the dependent variable. A test for the significance of the increased model fit is derived in Section 3.4.1.

Example 3.1: **Bank Wages (continued)**

To illustrate the results in this section we return to the illustration in Section 3.1.7. The dependent variable y is the yearly wage (in logarithms). In the restricted model we take as explanatory variables 'education' and a constant term, and in the notation of Section 3.2.1 these two variables are collected in the matrix X_1 with n rows and $k - g = 2$ columns. In the unrestricted model we take as explanatory variables 'education', a constant term, and the additional variable 'begin salary' (in logarithms). This additional variable is denoted by the matrix X_2 with n rows and $g = 1$ column in this case.

The results of the restricted and unrestricted regressions are given in Panels 1 and 2 of Exhibit 3.7. The unrestricted model (in Panel 2) has a larger R^2 than the restricted model (in Panel 1). As $R^2 = 1 - (e'e/\text{SST})$

Panel 1: Dependent Variable: LOGSAL Method: Least Squares		
Variable	Coefficient	Std. Error
C	9.062102	0.062738
EDUC	0.095963	0.004548
R-squared	0.485447	

Panel 2: Dependent Variable: LOGSAL Method: Least Squares		
Variable	Coefficient	Std. Error
C	1.646916	0.274598
EDUC	0.023122	0.003894
LOGSALBEGIN	0.868505	0.031835
R-squared	0.800579	

Panel 3: Dependent Variable: RESIDUNREST Method: Least Squares	
Variable	Coefficient
C	3.10E-11
EDUC	2.47E-13
LOGSALBEGIN	−3.55E-12
R-squared	0.000000

Panel 4: Dependent Variable: RESIDREST Method: Least Squares	
Variable	Coefficient
C	3.78E-13
EDUC	−2.76E-14
R-squared	0.000000

Panel 5: Dependent Variable: RESIDREST Method: Least Squares	
Variable	Coefficient
C	−4.449130
LOGSALBEGIN	0.460124
R-squared	0.324464

Panel 6: Dependent Variable: LOGSALBEGIN Method: Least Squares	
Variable	Coefficient
C	8.537878
EDUC	0.083869
R-squared	0.470211

Exhibit 3.7 Bank Wages (Example 3.1)

Regression in the restricted model (Panel 1) and in the unrestricted model (Panel 2). The residuals of the unrestricted regression (denoted by RESIDUNREST) are uncorrelated with both explanatory variables (Panel 3), but the residuals of the restricted regression (denoted by RESIDREST) are uncorrelated only with education (Panel 4) and not with the logarithm of begin salary (Panel 5). The regression in Panel 6 shows that the logarithm of begin salary is related to education.

$= 0.801 > 0.485 = 1 - (e_R'e_R)/\text{SST}$, it follows that $e'e \leq e_R'e_R$. Panels 3–5 in Exhibit 3.7 show that $X_1'e = 0$ (Panel 3), $X_1'e_R = 0$ (Panel 4), but $X_2'e_R \neq 0$ (Panel 5). Panel 6 shows the regression of X_2 on X_1 corresponding to (3.32). It follows from the outcomes in Panel 1 (for b_R), Panel 2 (for b_1 and b_2), and Panel 6 (for P) that (apart from rounding errors)

$$\begin{pmatrix} 9.062 \\ 0.096 \end{pmatrix} = \begin{pmatrix} 1.647 \\ 0.023 \end{pmatrix} + \begin{pmatrix} 8.538 \\ 0.084 \end{pmatrix} \cdot 0.869,$$

which verifies the relation $b_R = b_1 + Pb_2$ in (3.31) between restricted and unrestricted least squares estimates.

Summary of computations

In the restricted model (where y is regressed on $k - g$ regressors) the $(k - g) \times 1$ vector of least squares estimates is given by $b_R = (X_1'X_1)^{-1} X_1'y$. In the unrestricted model (where y is regressed on the same $k - g$ regressors and g additional regressors) the $k \times 1$ vector of least squares estimates is given by $b = (X'X)^{-1}X'y$.

Let b be decomposed in two parts as $b = (b_1', b_2')'$, where the $(k - g) \times 1$ vector b_1 corresponds to the regressors of the restricted model and b_2 to the g added regressors. Then the relation between b_R and b_1 is given by $b_R = b_1 + Pb_2$.

3.2.2 Interpretation of regression coefficients

Relations between regressors: The effect of X_1 on X_2

The result in (3.31) shows that the estimated effect of X_1 on y changes from b_1 to $b_R = b_1 + Pb_2$ if we delete the regressors X_2 from the model. The question arises which of these two estimates should be preferred. To investigate this question, we first give an interpretation of the matrix P in (3.32). This matrix may be interpreted in terms of regressions, where each column of X_2 is regressed on X_1. For the jth column of X_2—say, z—this gives estimated coefficients $p_j = (X_1'X_1)^{-1}X_1'z$ with explained part $\hat{z} = X_1p_j$ and residual vector $z - \hat{z} = M_1z$ where $M_1 = I - X_1(X_1'X_1)^{-1}X_1'$. Collecting the g regressions $z = \hat{z} + M_1z$ in g columns, we get

$$\begin{aligned} X_2 &= X_1P + M_1X_2 \\ &= \text{'explained part'} + \text{'residuals'} \end{aligned} \tag{3.35}$$

with $P = (X_1'X_1)^{-1}X_1'X_2$ as defined in (3.32).

Non-experimental data and the *ceteris paribus* idea

The *auxiliary regressions* (3.35) have an interesting interpretation. In experimental situations where we are free to choose the matrices X_1 and X_2, we can choose orthogonal columns so that $P = 0$. The result in (3.31) shows that neglecting the variables X_2 then has no effect on the estimate of β_1. On the other hand, if X_1 and X_2 are *uncontrolled*, then there are several possible reasons why P could be different from 0. For instance, X_1 may 'cause' X_2 or X_2 may 'cause' X_1, or there could exist a third 'cause' in the background that influences both X_1 and X_2. It may be useful to keep this in mind when interpreting the restricted estimate b_R and the unrestricted estimate b. Consider the second element of b_R (the first element is the intercept). Traditionally, in a linear relationship this measures the partial derivative $\partial y/\partial z$ (where z now denotes the second explanatory variable—that is, the second column of X_1). It answers the question how y will react on a change in z *ceteris paribus*—that is, if all other things remain equal. Now the question is: which 'other things'? In the restricted model, the 'other things' clearly are the remaining columns of the matrix X_1 and the residual e_R, and in the unrestricted model the 'other things' are the same columns of X_1 and in addition the columns of X_2 and the residual e.

Direct, indirect, and total effects

So the restricted and the unrestricted model raise different questions and one should not be surprised if different questions lead to different answers. Take the particular case that X_1 'causes' X_2. Then a change of X_1 may have two effects on y, a *direct effect* measured by b_1 and an *indirect effect* measured by Pb_2. It is seen from (3.31) that these are precisely the two components of b_R. Under these circumstances it may be hard to keep X_2 constant if X_1 changes. So in this case it may be more natural to look at the restricted model. That is, b_R gives a better idea of the *total effect* on y of changes in X_1 than b_1, as it is unnatural to assume that X_2 remains fixed.

If the variables would satisfy exact functional relationships, say $y = f(x_1, x_2)$ and $x_2 = h(x_1)$ (with $k = 2$ and $g = 1$), then the marginal effect of x_1 on y is given by

$$\frac{dy}{dx_1} = \frac{\partial f}{\partial x_1} + \frac{dh}{dx_1}\frac{\partial f}{\partial x_2}.$$

Here the total effect of x_1 on y (on the left-hand side) is decomposed as the sum of two terms (on the right-hand side), the direct effect of x_1 on y (the first term) and the indirect effect that runs via x_2 (the second term). The result in (3.31) shows that the same relation holds true when linear relationships are estimated by least squares.

Interpretation of regression coefficients in restricted and unrestricted model

If one wants to estimate only the direct effect of an explanatory variable—that is, under the assumption that all other explanatory variables remain fixed—then one should estimate the unrestricted model that includes all explanatory variables. On the other hand, if one wants to estimate the total effect of an explanatory variable—that is, the direct effect and all the indirect effects that run via the other explanatory variables—then one should estimate the restricted model where all the other explanatory variables are deleted.

Example 3.2: **Bank Wages (continued)**

To illustrate the relation between direct, indirect, and total effects, we return to Example 3.1 on bank wages. The current salary of an employee is influenced by the education and the begin salary of that employee. Clearly, the begin salary may for a large part be determined by education. The results discussed in Example 3.1 are summarized in Exhibit 3.8 and have the following interpretation. In the restricted model (without begin salary) the coefficient $b_R = 0.0960$ measures the total effect of education on salary. This effect is split up in two parts in the unrestricted model as $b_R = b + pc$.

(*a*)

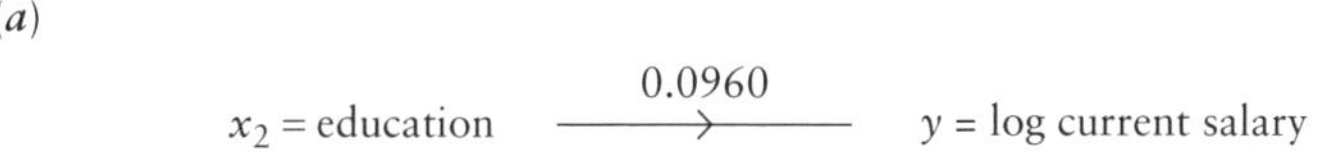

(*b*)

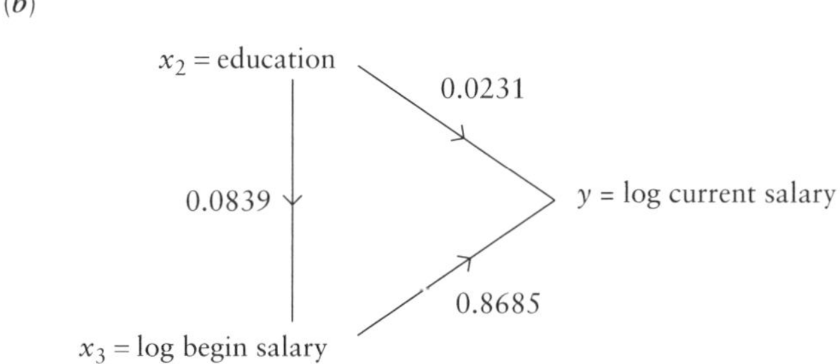

Exhibit 3.8 Bank Wages (Example 3.2)

Two variables (education and begin salary) influence the current salary, and education also influences the begin salary. The total effect of education on salary consists of two parts, a direct effect and an indirect effect that runs via the begin salary. If salary is regressed on education alone, the estimated effect is 0.0960, and if salary is regressed on education and begin salary together, then the estimated effects are respectively 0.0231 and 0.8685. If begin salary is regressed on education, the estimated effect is 0.0839. In this case the direct effect is 0.0231, the indirect effect is $0.0839 \cdot 0.8685 = 0.0729$, and the total effect is $0.0231 + 0.0729 = 0.0960$.

Here $b = 0.0231$ measures the direct effect of education on salary under the assumption that begin salary remains constant (the *ceteris paribus* condition), and $pc = 0.0839 \cdot 0.8685 = 0.0729$ measures the indirect effect of education on salary that is due to a higher begin salary.

Clearly, the estimates b_R and b have very different interpretations.

☞ **Exercises: E: 3.14a–c.**

3.2.3 Omitting variables

Choice of explanatory variables

For most economic variables to be explained, one can find a long list of possible explanatory variables. The question is which of these variables should be included in the model. It seems intuitively reasonable to include variables only if they have a clear effect on the dependent variable and to omit variables that are less important. In this section we analyse the effect of omitting variables from the model, and in the next section of including irrelevant variables. We focus on the statistical properties of the least squares estimator. When comparing the restricted and the unrestricted model, a remark about the term *true model* is in order; see also our earlier remarks in Section 2.2.1 (p. 87). Strictly speaking, the term 'true' model has a clear interpretation only in the case of simulated data. When the data are from the real world, then the DGP is unknown and can at best be approximated. Nevertheless, it helps our insight to study some of the consequences of estimating a different model from the true model.

Omitted variables bias

In this section we consider the consequences of omitting variables from the 'true model'. Suppose the 'true model' is

$$y = X_1\beta_1 + X_2\beta_2 + \varepsilon,$$

but we use the model with only X_1 as explanatory variables and with b_R as our estimator of β_1. Then we have

$$b_R = (X_1'X_1)^{-1}X_1'y = \beta_1 + (X_1'X_1)^{-1}X_1'X_2\beta_2 + (X_1'X_1)^{-1}X_1'\varepsilon.$$

This shows that

$$E[b_R] = \beta_1 + (X_1'X_1)^{-1}X_1'X_2\beta_2 = \beta_1 + P\beta_2.$$

The last term is sometimes called the *omitted variables bias*. The estimator b_R is in general a biased estimator of β_1. In the light of our discussion in Section 3.2.2 we should not be surprised by this 'bias', since b_R and b_1 have different interpretations.

Variance reduction

To compute the variance of b_R, the above two expressions show that $b_R - E[b_R] = (X_1'X_1)^{-1}X_1'\varepsilon$ so that

$$\text{var}(b_R) = E[(b_R - E[b_R])(b_R - E[b_R])'] = \sigma^2(X_1'X_1)^{-1}.$$

It is left as an exercise (see Exercise 3.7) to prove that this is smaller than the variance of the unrestricted least squares estimator b_1, that is, $\text{var}(b_1) - \text{var}(b_R)$ is positive semidefinite.

Summary

Summarizing, the omission of relevant variables leads to biased estimates but to a reduction in variance. If one is interested in estimating the 'direct' effect β_1, then omission of X_2 is undesirable unless the resulting bias is small compared to the gain in efficiency, for instance, when β_2 is small enough. This means that variables can be omitted if their effect is small, as this leads to an improved efficiency of the least squares estimator.

3.2.4 Consequences of redundant variables

Redundant variables lead to inefficiency

A variable is called redundant if it plays no role in the 'true' model. Suppose that

$$y = X_1\beta_1 + \varepsilon,$$

that is, the DGP satisfies Assumptions 1–6 with $\beta_2 = 0$. In practice we do not know that β_2 is zero. Suppose that the variables X_2 are included as additional regressors, so that the estimation results are given by

$$y = X_1b_1 + X_2b_2 + e.$$

Although the estimated model $y = X_1\beta_1 + X_2\beta_2 + \varepsilon$ neglects the fact that $\beta_2 = 0$, it is not wrongly specified as it satisfies Assumptions 1–6. The result

(3.18) shows that $E[b_1] = \beta_1$ and $E[b_2] = \beta_2 = 0$ in this case. Therefore b_1 is an unbiased estimator. However, this estimator is *inefficient* in the sense that $\text{var}(b_1) - \text{var}(b_R)$ is positive semidefinite. That is, if the model contains redundant variables, then the parameters are estimated with less precision (larger standard errors) as compared with the model that excludes the redundant variables. To prove this, we write (3.31) as $b_1 = b_R - Pb_2$. Then the result

$$\text{var}(b_1) = \text{var}(b_R) + P\text{var}(b_2)P'$$

follows from the fact that $\text{cov}(b_2, b_R) = 0$, as we will prove below. Because $\text{var}(b_2)$ is positive definite, it follows that $P\text{var}(b_2)P'$ is positive semidefinite. So the variances of the elements of b_1 are larger than those of the corresponding elements of b_R, unless the corresponding rows of P are zero. That is, if $\beta_2 = 0$, then in general we gain efficiency by deleting the irrelevant variables X_2 from the model. This shows the importance of imposing restrictions on the model.

Proof of auxiliary result $\text{cov}(b_2, b_R) = 0$

It remains to prove that $\text{cov}(b_2, b_R) = 0$. The basic step is to express b_R and b_2 in terms of ε. As $\beta_2 = 0$ it follows that

$$b_R = (X_1'X_1)^{-1}X_1'y = (X_1'X_1)^{-1}X_1'(X_1\beta_1 + \varepsilon) = \beta_1 + (X_1'X_1)^{-1}X_1'\varepsilon. \qquad (3.36)$$

To express b_2 in terms of ε we first prove as an auxiliary result that the $g \times g$ matrix $X_2'M_1X_2$ is non-singular. As $X_2'M_1X_2 = (M_1X_2)'M_1X_2$, it suffices to prove that the $n \times g$ matrix M_1X_2 has rank g. We use (3.35) and (3.32) to write

$$(X_1 \quad M_1X_2) = (X_1 \quad X_2 - X_1P) = (X_1 \quad X_2)\begin{pmatrix} I & -P \\ 0 & I \end{pmatrix}.$$

The last matrix is non-singular and Assumption 1 states that the $n \times k$ matrix $(X_1 \quad X_2)$ has rank k. So $(X_1 \quad M_1X_2)$ also has rank k—that is, all its columns are linearly independent. This means in particular that all columns of the $n \times g$ matrix M_1X_2 are linearly independent, so that this matrix has rank g. This proves that $X_2'M_1X_2$ is non-singular.

Now the result in (3.33) states that $M_1y = M_1X_2b_2 + e$. If we premultiply this by X_2', then we obtain, as $X_2'e = 0$, that $X_2'M_1y = X_2'M_1X_2b_2$. As $X_2'M_1X_2$ is non-singular, this means that

$$b_2 = (X_2'M_1X_2)^{-1}X_2'M_1y. \qquad (3.37)$$

We now substitute the 'true' model $y = X_1\beta_1 + \varepsilon$ into (3.37). Because $M_1X_1 = 0$, this gives

$$b_2 = (X_2' M_1 X_2)^{-1} X_2' M_1 \varepsilon \quad (\text{as } \beta_2 = 0). \tag{3.38}$$

Using the expressions (3.36) and (3.38) that express b_R and b_2 in terms of ε, we obtain (as $M_1 X_1 = 0$)

$$\begin{aligned} \text{cov}(b_2, b_R) &= E[(b_2 - E[b_2])(b_R - E[b_R])'] \\ &= E[(X_2' M_1 X_2)^{-1} X_2' M_1 \varepsilon \varepsilon' X_1 (X_1' X_1)^{-1}] \\ &= \sigma^2 (X_2' M_1 X_2)^{-1} X_2' M_1 X_1 (X_1' X_1)^{-1} = 0. \end{aligned}$$

Summary of results

We summarize the results of this and the foregoing section in Exhibit 3.9. If we include redundant variables ($\beta_2 = 0$) in our model, then this causes a loss of efficiency of the estimators of the parameters (β_1) of the relevant variables. That is, by excluding irrelevant variables we gain efficiency. However, if we exclude relevant variables ($\beta_2 \neq 0$), this causes a bias in the estimators. So the choice between a restricted and an unrestricted model involves a trade-off between the bias and efficiency of estimators. In practice we do not know the true parameters β_2 but we can test whether $\beta_2 = 0$. This is discussed in Sections 3.3 and 3.4.

	Data Generating Process	
Estimated Model	$y = X_1\beta_1 + X_2\beta_2 + \varepsilon$ (β_2 non-zero)	$y = X_1\beta_1 + \varepsilon$ ($\beta_2 = 0$)
$y = X_1 b_R + e_R$	b_R biased, but smaller variance than b_1	b_R best linear unbiased
$y = X_1 b_1 + X_2 b_2 + e$	b_1 unbiased, but larger variance than b_R	b_1 unbiased, but not efficient

Exhibit 3.9 Bias and efficiency

Consequences of regression in models that contain redundant variables (bottom right cell) and in models with omitted variables (top left cell). Comparisons should be made in columns — that is, for a fixed data generating process. The cells show the statistical properties of the estimators b_R (of the restricted model where X_2 is deleted, first row) and b_1 (of the unrestricted model that contains both X_1 and X_2, second row) for the model parameters β_1, under Assumptions 1–6.

☞ Exercises: 1: 3.7d.

3.2.5 Partial regression

Multiple regression and partial regression

In this section we give a further interpretation of the least squares estimates in a multiple regression model. In Section 3.2.2 we mentioned that these estimates measure direct effects under the *ceteris paribus* condition that the other variables are kept fixed. As such 'controlled experiments' are almost never possible in economics, the question arises what is the precise interpretation of this condition. As will be shown below, it means that the indirect effects that are caused by variations in the other variables are automatically removed in a multiple regression. We consider again the model where the $n \times k$ matrix of explanatory variables X is split in two parts as $X = (X_1 \quad X_2)$, where X_1 is an $n \times (k-g)$ matrix and X_2 an $n \times g$ matrix. The regression of y on X_1 and X_2 gives the result

$$y = X_1 b_1 + X_2 b_2 + e.$$

Another approach to estimate the effects of X_1 on y is the following two-step method, called *partial regression*.

Partial regression

- *Step 1: Remove the effects of* X_2. Here we remove the side effects that are caused by X_2. That is, regress y on X_2 with residuals $M_2 y$, where $M_2 = I - X_2(X_2'X_2)^{-1}X_2'$. Also regress each column of X_1 on X_2 with residuals $M_2 X_1$. Here $M_2 y$ and $M_2 X_1$ can be interpreted as the 'cleaned' variables obtained after removing the effects of X_2. Note that, as a consequence of the fact that residuals are orthogonal to explanatory variables, the 'cleaned' variables $M_2 y$ and $M_2 X_1$ are uncorrelated with X_2.
- *Step 2: Estimate the 'cleaned' effect of* X_1 *on* y. Now estimate the 'cleaned' effect of X_1 on y by regressing $M_2 y$ on $M_2 X_1$. This gives

$$M_2 y = M_2 X_1 b_* + e_*$$

where $b_* = [(M_2X_1)'M_2X_1]^{-1}(M_2X_1)'M_2y = (X_1'M_2X_1)^{-1}X_1'M_2y$ and $e_* = M_2y - M_2X_1b_*$ are the corresponding residuals.

The result of Frisch–Waugh

The result of *Frisch–Waugh* states that

$$b_* = b_1, \quad e_* = e. \tag{3.39}$$

That is, by including X_2 in the regression model, the estimated effect b_1 of X_1 on y is automatically 'cleaned' from the side effects caused by X_2.

T

Proof of the result of Frisch–Waugh

To prove the result of Frisch–Waugh, we write out the normal equations $X'Xb = X'y$ in terms of the partitioned matrix $X = (X_1 \quad X_2)$.

$$X_1'X_1b_1 + X_1'X_2b_2 = X_1'y \tag{3.40}$$

$$X_2'X_1b_1 + X_2'X_2b_2 = X_2'y \tag{3.41}$$

From (3.41) we get $b_2 = (X_2'X_2)^{-1}X_2'y - (X_2'X_2)^{-1}X_2'X_1b_1$, and by substituting this in (3.40) and arranging terms it follows that

$$X_1'M_2X_1b_1 = X_1'M_2y,$$

where $M_2 = I - X_2(X_2'X_2)^{-1}X_2'$. In Section 3.2.4 we proved that $X_2'M_1X_2$ is invertible, and a similar argument shows that also $X_1'M_2X_1$ is invertible. This shows that $b_* = b_1$. Further it follows from (3.30) and the facts that $M_2X_2 = 0$ and $M_2e = e$ that

$$M_2y = M_2X_1b_1 + e.$$

As $b_1 = b_*$, this shows that $e_* = e$.

Summary: To estimate the effect of X_1 on y, should we include X_2 or not?

Suppose that we wish to estimate the effect of a certain set of regressors (X_1) on the dependent variable (y). The question is whether certain other variables (X_2) should be added to or omitted from the regression. If the two sets of regressors X_1 and X_2 are related (in the sense that $X_1'X_2 \neq 0$), then the estimated effects $X_1 \to y$ differ in the two models. The partial effect $X_1 \to y$ (*ceteris paribus*, as if X_2 were fixed) cannot be determined if X_2 is deleted from the model, because then the indirect effect $X_1 \to X_2 \to y$ is also present.

To isolate the direct effect $X_1 \to y$ one can first remove the effects of X_2 on y and of X_2 on X_1, after which the cleaned M_2y is regressed on the cleaned M_2X_1. Instead of this partial regression, one can also include X_2 as additional regressors in the model and regress y on X_1 and X_2.

On the other hand, if one is interested in the total effect of X_1 on y, then X_2 should be deleted from the model.

Three illustrations

There are several interesting applications of the result of Frisch–Waugh, and we mention three of them.

Case 1: Deviations from sample mean

Let X_2 have only one column consisting of ones. If we premultiply by M_2, this amounts to taking deviations from means. For instance, regressing y on X_2

gives an estimated coefficient $(X_2'X_2)^{-1}X_2'y = \frac{1}{n}\sum y_i = \bar{y}$ with residuals $y_i - \bar{y}$, so that the elements of M_2y are $(y_1 - \bar{y}), \cdots, (y_n - \bar{y})$. The result of Frisch–Waugh states that inclusion of a constant term gives the same results as a regression where all variables are expressed in deviation from their means. In fact we have already met this kind of formula in Chapter 2—for instance, in formula (2.8) for the least squares slope estimator.

Case 2: Detrending

Let X_2 consist of two columns, a constant and a trend, as follows.

$$X_2 = \begin{pmatrix} 1 & 1 \\ 1 & 2 \\ \vdots & \vdots \\ 1 & n \end{pmatrix}.$$

Then the first step in partial regression amounts to removing the (linear) trends from y and the columns of X_1. This case was the subject of the article by R. Frisch and F. V. Waugh, 'Partial Time Regressions as Compared with Individual Trends', *Econometrica*, 1 (1933), 387–401.

Case 3: Single partial relation

Let X_1 consist of a single variable, so that $k - g = 1$ and X_2 contains the remaining $k - 1$ variables. Then both M_2X_1 and M_2y have one column and one can visualize the relation between these columns by drawing a scatter plot. This is called a *partial regression scatter* plot. The slope of the regression line in this plot is b_1. This equals the slope parameter of X_1 in the multiple regression equation (3.30).

Example 3.3: **Bank Wages (continued)**

Using the data on bank wages of the illustration in Section 3.1.7, we illustrate some of the foregoing results for the model

$$y_i = \beta_1 + \beta_2 x_{2i} + \beta_3 x_{3i} + \varepsilon_i,$$

where y_i denotes the logarithm of yearly salary, x_{2i} the education, and x_{3i} the logarithm of the begin salary of the ith employee. This is the regression of the illustration in Section 3.1.7, with results in Exhibit 3.5, Panel 3. We will now consider (i) the above-mentioned Case 1, and (ii) the above-mentioned Case 3.

Regression 1: Dependent Variable: LOGSAL		
Variable	Coefficient	Std. Error
C	10.35679	0.018250

Regression 2: Dependent Variable: EDUC		
Variable	Coefficient	Std. Error
C	13.49156	0.132505

Regression 3: Dependent Variable: LOGSALBEGIN		
Variable	Coefficient	Std. Error
C	9.669405	0.016207

Regression 4: Dependent Variable: DMLOGSAL		
Variable	Coefficient	Std. Error
DMEDUC	0.023122	0.003890
DMLOGSALBEGIN	0.868505	0.031801
R-squared	0.800579	
Adjusted R-squared	0.800157	
S.E. of regression	0.177624	
Sum squared resid	14.89166	

Regression 5: Dependent Variable: LOGSAL		
Variable	Coefficient	Std. Error
C	0.705383	0.232198
LOGSALBEGIN	0.998139	0.023998

Regression 6: Dependent Variable: EDUC		
Variable	Coefficient	Std. Error
C	−40.71973	2.650406
LOGSALBEGIN	5.606476	0.273920

Regression 7: Dependent Variable: RESLOGSAL		
Variable	Coefficient	Std. Error
RESEDUC	0.023122	0.003885
R-squared	0.069658	
Adjusted R-squared	0.069658	
S.E. of regression	0.177436	
Sum squared resid	14.89166	

Exhibit 3.10 Bank Wages (Example 3.3)

Two illustrations of partial regressions. Regressions 1–3 determine the effect of the constant term on the variables LOGSAL, EDUC, and LOGSALBEGIN. The residuals of these regressions (which correspond to taking the original observations in deviation from their sample mean and which are denoted by DM) are related in Regression 4. Regressions 5 and 6 determine the effect of LOGSALBEGIN on EDUC and LOGSAL. The residuals of these two regressions (which correspond to the variables LOGSAL and EDUC where the effect of LOGSALBEGIN has been eliminated and which are denoted by RESLOGSAL and RESEDUC) are related in Regression 7.

(i) Deviation from mean

We first consider Case 1 above, where the variables are expressed in deviations from their sample mean. In the first step all variables are regressed on a constant, and then the demeaned y is regressed on the two demeaned variables x_2 and x_3. This is shown in Regressions 1–4 in Exhibit 3.10. If we compare the results of Regression 4 in Exhibit 3.10 with those of the unrestricted regression in Exhibit 3.5, Panel 3, we see that the regression coefficients are equal. However, there is a small difference in the calculated standard errors (see Exercise 3.9).

(ii) Direct effect of education on salary

Next we consider Case 3 above and give a partial regression interpretation of the coefficient $b_2 = 0.023$ in Exhibit 3.5, Panel 3, for the estimated 'direct effect' of education on salary for 'fixed' begin salary. This is shown in Regressions 5–7 in Exhibit 3.10. In terms of the model $y = X_1\beta_1 + X_2\beta_2 + \varepsilon$ in (3.26), let X_2 be the 474×2 matrix with a column of ones and with the values of x_3 (begin salary) in column 2, and let X_1 be the 474×1 vector containing the values of x_2 (education). To remove the effects of the other variables, y and X_1 are first regressed on X_2 with residuals M_2y and M_2X_1, and in the second step M_2y is regressed on M_2X_1. The last regression corresponds to the model $M_2y = (M_2X_1)b_* + e_*$ in the result of Frisch–Waugh. This result states that the estimated coefficient in this

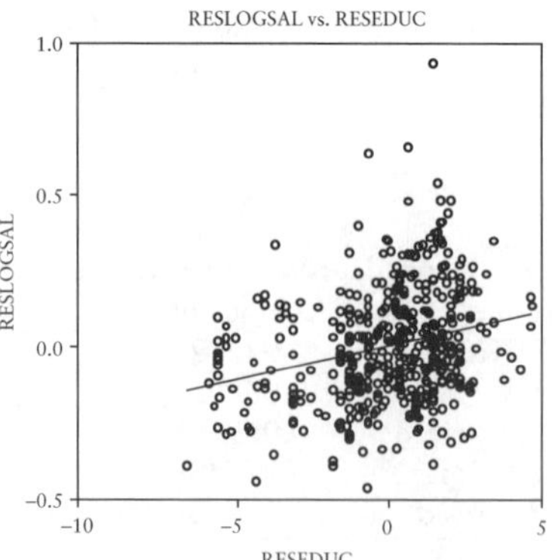

Exhibit 3.11 Bank Wages (Example 3.3)

Partial regression scatter plot of (logarithmic) salary against education, with regression line. On the vertical axis are the residuals of the regression of log salary on a constant and log begin salary and on the horizontal axis are the residuals of the regression of education on a constant and log begin salary. The slope of the regression line in the figure indicates the direct effect of education on log salary after neutralizing for the indirect effect via log begin salary.

regression is equal to the coefficient in the multiple regression model, which is verified by comparing Regression 7 in Exhibit 3.10 with the result in Exhibit 3.5, Panel 3. The corresponding partial regression scatter plot is shown in Exhibit 3.11, where RESLOGSAL denotes M_2y and RESEDUC denotes M_2X_1.

☞ **Exercises:** T: 3.9; E: 3.16, 3.18.

3.3 The accuracy of estimates

3.3.1 The *t*-test

☞ Uses Sections 1.4.1, 1.4.2.

Test of significance

To test whether we should include a variable in the model or not, we can test its statistical significance. To check whether the jth explanatory variable has a significant effect on y, we test the null hypothesis $H_0 : \beta_j = 0$ against the alternative $H_1 : \beta_j \neq 0$.

T

Derivation of *t*-test

For this purpose we suppose that Assumptions 1–7 hold true. As the least squares estimator b is a linear function of ε, it follows that, under these assumptions, b is normally distributed. Its mean and variance are given by (3.18) and (3.19), so that

$$b \sim \mathrm{N}(\beta, \sigma^2(X'X)^{-1}). \tag{3.42}$$

The variance of the jth component b_j of the least squares estimator b is equal to $\sigma^2 a_{jj}$, where a_{jj} is the jth diagonal element of $(X'X)^{-1}$. By standardization we get

$$\frac{b_j - \beta_j}{\sigma\sqrt{a_{jj}}} \sim \mathrm{N}(0, 1).$$

This expression cannot be used to test whether $\beta_j = 0$, as the variance σ^2 is unknown. Therefore σ is replaced by s, where s^2 is the unbiased estimator of σ^2 defined in (3.22).

To derive the distribution of the resulting test statistic we use the following results of Section 1.2.3 (p. 31–5). Let $w \sim \mathrm{N}(0, I)$ be a $n \times 1$ vector of independent $\mathrm{N}(0, 1)$ variables, and let A be a given $m \times n$ matrix and Q a given $n \times n$ symmetric and idempotent matrix. Then $Aw \sim \mathrm{N}(0, AA')$ and $w'Qw \sim \chi^2(r)$ where $r = \mathrm{tr}(Q)$, and these two random variables are independently distributed when $AQ = 0$. We apply these results with $w = (1/\sigma)\varepsilon$, $A = (X'X)^{-1}X'$, and $Q = M = I - X(X'X)^{-1}X'$ with $\mathrm{tr}(M) = n - k$. Note that

$b - \beta = (X'X)^{-1}X'\varepsilon = A\varepsilon$ so that $(b - \beta)/\sigma = Aw$, and that $e = My = M(X\beta + \varepsilon) = M\varepsilon$ so that $e'e/\sigma^2 = w'Mw$. As $AM = 0$, it follows that b and $e'e$ are independently distributed. Further, $e'e/\sigma^2 \sim \chi^2(n-k)$ and $(b_j - \beta_j)/(\sigma\sqrt{a_{jj}}) \sim \mathrm{N}(0, 1)$, and as both terms are independent their quotient has by definition the Student t-distribution with $(n-k)$ degrees of freedom.

The *t*-test

Let $s_j = s\sqrt{a_{jj}}$ be the standard error of b_j; then

$$t_j = \frac{b_j - \beta_j}{s_j} = \frac{b_j - \beta_j}{s\sqrt{a_{jj}}} = \frac{(b_j - \beta_j)/(\sigma\sqrt{a_{jj}})}{\sqrt{\frac{e'e}{\sigma^2}/(n-k)}} \sim t(n-k), \tag{3.43}$$

that is, t_j follows the $t(n-k)$ distribution.

The *t*-value and significance

To test whether x_j has no effect on y, which corresponds to $\beta_j = 0$, we use the above test statistic with $\beta_j = 0$. That is, to test the null hypothesis that $\beta_j = 0$ against the alternative that $\beta_j \neq 0$, we compute the *t-value*

$$t_j = \frac{b_j}{s_j} = \frac{b_j}{s\sqrt{a_{jj}}}. \tag{3.44}$$

We reject the null hypothesis if t_j differs significantly from zero. If the null hypothesis $\beta_j = 0$ is true, t_j follows the $t(n-k)$ distribution. Against the above two-sided alternative, we reject the null hypothesis if $|t| > c$ where c is the significance level defined by $P[|t| > c]$ where $t \sim t(n-k)$. This is called the *t-test*, or the test of (individual) *significance* of b_j.

Use of the *t*-test and the *P*-value

As discussed in Section 2.3.1 (p. 100), for a size of 5 per cent we can use $c = 2$ as a rule of thumb, which is accurate if $n - k$ is not very small (say $n - k > 30$). In general it is preferable to report the P-value of the test. Of course, if we want to establish an effect of x_j on y, then we hope to be able to reject the null hypothesis. However, we should do this only if there exists sufficient evidence for this effect. That is, in this case the size of the test should be chosen small enough to protect ourselves from a large probability of an error of the first type. Stated otherwise, the null hypothesis is rejected only for small enough P-values of the test. For a significance level of 5 per cent, the null hypothesis is rejected for $P < 0.05$ and it is not rejected for $P > 0.05$. In some situations smaller significance levels are used (especially in large samples), and in other situations sometimes larger significance levels are used (for instance in small samples).

Summary of computations

In regression we usually compute

- the regression coefficients $b = (X'X)^{-1}X'y$,
- the standard error of regression s,
- for each of the coefficients b_j, $j = 1, \cdots, k$, their standard error $s_j = s\sqrt{a_{jj}}$, their t-value $t_j = b_j/s_j$, and their P-value $P_j = P[|t| > |t_j|]$ where t has the $t(n-k)$-distribution.

Of particular interest are

- the significance of the regressors (measured by the P-values),
- the sign of significant coefficients (indicating whether the corresponding regressor has a positive or a negative effect on y),
- the size of the coefficients (which can only be judged properly in combination with the measurement scale of the corresponding regressor).

Other statistics like R^2 may also be of interest, as well as other statistics that will be discussed later in the book.

3.3.2 Illustration: Bank Wages

E

XM301BWA

We consider again the salary data and the linear model with $k = 3$ explanatory variables (a constant, education, and the logarithm of begin salary) discussed in Example 3.3. We will discuss (i) the regression outcomes and t-tests, (ii) presentation of the regression results, and (iii) results of the model with two additional regressors (gender and minority).

(i) Regression outcomes and *t*-tests

Panel 1 in Exhibit 3.12 shows the outcomes of regressing salary (in logarithms) on a constant and the explanatory variables education and begin salary (the last again in logarithms). The column 'Coefficient' contains the regression coefficients b_j, the column 'Std. Error' the standard errors s_j, and the column 't-Statistic' the t-values $t_j = b_j/s_j$. The column denoted by 'Prob' contains the P-values corresponding to the t-values in the preceding column—that is, the P-value of the hypothesis that $\beta_j = 0$ against the two-sided alternative that $\beta_j \neq 0$. In this example with $n = 474$ and $k = 3$, if t follows the $t(471)$ distribution and c is the outcome of the t-statistic, then the P-value is defined as the (two-sided) probability $P(|t| > |c|)$. The P-value

Panel 1: Dependent Variable: LOGSAL				
Method: Least Squares				
Sample: 1 474				
Included observations: 474				
Variable	Coefficient	Std. Error	t-Statistic	Prob.
C	1.646916	0.274598	5.997550	0.0000
EDUC	0.023122	0.003894	5.938464	0.0000
LOGSALBEGIN	0.868505	0.031835	27.28174	0.0000
R-squared	0.800579	Mean dependent var		10.35679
Adjusted R-squared	0.799733	S.D. dependent var		0.397334
S.E. of regression	0.177812			
Sum squared resid	14.89166			

Panel 2: Dependent Variable: LOGSAL				
Method: Least Squares				
Sample: 1 474				
Included observations: 474				
Variable	Coefficient	Std. Error	t-Statistic	Prob.
C	2.079647	0.314798	6.606288	0.0000
EDUC	0.023268	0.003870	6.013129	0.0000
LOGSALBEGIN	0.821799	0.036031	22.80783	0.0000
GENDER	0.048156	0.019910	2.418627	0.0160
MINORITY	−0.042369	0.020342	−2.082842	0.0378
R-squared	0.804117	Mean dependent var		10.35679
Adjusted R-squared	0.802446	S.D. dependent var		0.397334
S.E. of regression	0.176603			
Sum squared resid	14.62750			

Exhibit 3.12 Bank Wages (Section 3.3.2)

Results of two regressions. Panel 1 shows the regression of salary (in logarithms) on education and begin salary (in logarithms) and Panel 2 shows the results when gender and minority are included as additional explanatory variables. The column 'Prob' contains the P-values for the null hypothesis that the corresponding parameter is zero against the two-sided alternative that it is non-zero.

requires Assumptions 1–7 and, in addition, that the null hypothesis $\beta_j = 0$ is true. All parameters are highly significant.

(ii) Presentation of regression results

There are several conventions to present regression results in the form of an equation. For example, similar to what was done in Example 2.9 (p. 102), the parameter estimates can be reported together with their t-values (in parentheses) in the form

$$y = \underset{(5.998)}{1.647} + \underset{(5.938)}{0.023}\, x_2 + \underset{(27.282)}{0.869}\, x_3 + e.$$

Sometimes the parameter estimates are reported together with their standard errors. Many readers are interested in the question whether the estimates are significantly different from zero. These readers almost automatically start to calculate the t-values themselves. So it is friendly to them to present the t-values right away. In some cases, however, the null hypothesis of interest is different from zero. In such a case the t-values give the wrong answers and extra calculations are required. These calculations are simpler if standard errors are presented. Those who prefer interval estimates are also better served by reporting standard errors. The obvious way out seems to report both the t-values and the standard errors, but this requires more reporting space. In any case, one should always clearly mention which convention is followed.

(iii) Two additional regressors

As compared with the illustration in Section 3.1.7, we now extend the set of explanatory variables with x_4 (gender) and x_5 (minority). Panel 2 of Exhibit 3.12 shows the regression outcomes when these variables are added. On the basis of the t-test, both the variable x_4 and the variable x_5 have significant effects (at 5 per cent significance level).

Note that, if we add variables, the coefficients of the other variables change also. This is because the explanatory variables are correlated with each other—that is, in the notation of Section 3.2.1 we have $X_1'X_2 \neq 0$ (see (3.31)). For instance, the additional regressor gender is correlated with the regressors education and begin salary, with correlation coefficients 0.36 and 0.55 respectively. Using the notation of the result of Frisch–Waugh, to guarantee that $b_* = b_1$ we should not simply regress y on X_1 (as in Panel 1 of Exhibit 3.12), but instead we should regress M_2y on M_2X_1. If important variables like x_4 and x_5 are omitted from the model, this may lead to biased estimates of direct effects, as was discussed in Section 3.2.3.

3.3.3 Multicollinearity

Factors that affect significance

It may happen that $\beta_j \neq 0$ but that the t-test cannot reject the hypothesis that $\beta_j = 0$. The estimate b_j is then not accurate enough—that is, its standard error is too large. In this case the t-test does not have enough power to reject the null hypothesis. To analyse the possible causes of such a situation we decompose the variance of the least squares estimators in terms of a number of components. We will derive the result in three steps, first for the mean, then for the simple regression model, and finally for the multiple regression model.

First case: Sample mean

We start with the simplest possible example of a matrix X that consists of one column of unit elements. In this case we have $b = \overline{y}$ and

$$\mathrm{var}(b) = \frac{\sigma^2}{n}.$$

We see that for a given required accuracy there is a trade-off between σ^2 and n. If the disturbance variance σ^2 is large—that is, if there is much random variation in the outcomes of y—then we need a large sample size to obtain a precise estimate of b.

Second case: Simple regression

Next we consider the simple regression model studied in Chapter 2,

$$y_i = \alpha + \beta x_i + \varepsilon_i.$$

For the least squares estimator b discussed there, the variance is given by

$$\mathrm{var}(b) = \frac{\sigma^2}{\sum (x_i - \overline{x})^2} = \frac{\sigma^2}{(n-1)s_x^2}. \tag{3.45}$$

Here we use the expression

$$s_x^2 = \frac{\sum (x_i - \overline{x})^2}{n-1}$$

for the sample variance of x. For a given required accuracy we now see a tradeoff between three factors: a large disturbance σ^2 can be compensated for by either a large sample size n or by a large variance s_x^2 of the explanatory variable. More variation in the disturbances ε_i gives a smaller accuracy of the estimators whereas more observations and more variation in the regressor x_i lead to a higher accuracy.

General case: Multiple regression (derivation)

T

Finally we look at the general multiple regression model. We concentrate on one regression coefficient and without loss of generality we choose the last one, since it is always possible to change the order of the columns of X. We use the notation introduced in Section 3.2. In the current situation $g = 1$ so that the $n \times g$ matrix X_2 reduces to an $n \times 1$ vector that we will denote by x_2. The $n \times (k-1)$

matrix X_1 corresponds to the first $(k-1)$ regressors. We concentrate on the single parameter β_2 in the model

$$y = X_1\beta_1 + X_2\beta_2 + \varepsilon = X_1\beta_1 + \beta_2 x_2 + \varepsilon.$$

Substituting this in (3.37) and using $M_1X_1 = 0$, it follows that $b_2 = \beta_2 + (x_2'M_1x_2)^{-1}x_2'M_1\varepsilon$, so that

$$\text{var}(b_2) = \sigma^2(x_2'M_1x_2)^{-1}. \qquad (3.46)$$

Here M_1x_2 has one column and $x_2'M_1x_2$ is the residual sum of squares of the auxiliary regression $x_2 = X_1P + M_1x_2$ (see (3.35)). As $R^2 = 1 - (SSR/SST)$, we may write

$$SSR = SST(1 - R^2).$$

If we apply this result to the auxiliary regression $x_2 = X_1P + M_1x_2$ we may substitute $SSR = x_2'M_1x_2$ and $SST = \sum(x_{2i} - \overline{x}_2)^2 = (n-1)s_{x_2}^2$. Denoting the R^2 of this auxiliary regression by R_a^2 we obtain the following result.

The effect of multicollinearity

In the multiple regression model the variance of the last regression coefficient (denoted by b_2) may be decomposed as

$$\text{var}(b_2) = \frac{\sigma^2}{(n-1)s_{x_2}^2(1 - R_a^2)}.$$

If we compare this with (3.45), we see three familiar factors and a new one, $(1 - R_a^2)$. So $\text{var}(b_2)$ increases with R_a^2 and it even explodes if $R_a^2 \uparrow 1$. This is called the *multicollinearity* problem. If x_2 is closely related to the remaining regressors X_1, it is hard to estimate its isolated effect accurately. Indeed, if R_a^2 is large, then x_2 is strongly correlated with the set of variables in X_1, so that the 'direct' effect of x_2 on y (that is, β_2) is accompanied by strong side effects via X_1 on y.

Rewriting the above result for an arbitrary column of X (except the intercept), we get

$$\text{var}(b_j) = \frac{\sigma^2}{(n-1)s_{x_j}^2(1 - R_j^2)}, \quad (j = 2, \cdots, k), \qquad (3.47)$$

where R_j^2 denotes the R^2 of the auxiliary regression of the jth regressor variable on the remaining $(k-1)$ regressors (including the constant term) and $s_{x_j}^2$ is the sample variance of x_j. So, accurate estimates of 'direct' or 'partial' effects are obtained for large sample sizes, large variation in the relevant explanatory variable, small error variance, and small collinearity with the other explanatory variables. The factor $1/(1 - R_j^2)$ is called the *variance inflation factor*—that is, the factor by which the variance increases because of collinearity of the jth regressor with the other $(k - 1)$ regressors.

Interpretation of results

In many applications we hope to find significant estimates of the partial effects of the explanatory variables. If some of the t-values of the regression coefficients are small, this may possibly be caused by high correlations among the explanatory variables, measured by the coefficients of determination R_j^2. One method to improve the significance is to get more data, if this is possible. However, if the purpose of the model would be to estimate the total effects of some of the variables (as opposed to partial effects), then another solution is to drop some of the other explanatory variables. In some applications the individual parameters may not be of so much interest—for instance, in prediction. Then multicollinearity is not a very relevant issue, but it may be of interest to compare the forecast quality of the full model with that of restricted versions where some of the explanatory variables are omitted. Methods to choose the number of explanatory variables in prediction will be discussed later (see Section 5.2.1).

☞ **Exercises:** S: 3.12; E: 3.14d.

3.3.4 Illustration: Bank Wages

To illustrate the factors that affect the standard errors of least squares estimates we consider once again the bank wage data. Panel 1 of Exhibit 3.13 shows once more the regression of salary on five explanatory variables (see also Panel 2 of Exhibit 3.12). The standard errors of the estimated parameters are relatively small, but it is still of interest to decompose these errors as in (3.47) to see if this is only due to the fact that the number of observations $n = 474$ is quite large. The values R_j^2 of the auxiliary regressions are equal to $R_2^2 = 0.47$ (shown in Panel 2), $R_3^2 = 0.59$, $R_4^2 = 0.33$, and $R_5^2 = 0.07$. Recall from Section 3.1.6 that R^2 is the square of a correlation coefficient, so that these outcomes cannot directly be compared to the (bivariate) correlations that are also reported in Panel 3 of Exhibit 3.13. Therefore Panel 3 also contains the values of $R_j = \sqrt{R_j^2}$ and of the square root of the variance inflation factors $1/\sqrt{1 - R_j^2}$ that affect the standard

Panel 1: Dependent Variable: LOGSAL				
Method: Least Squares				
Sample: 1 474				
Included observations: 474				
Variable	Coefficient	Std. Error	t-Statistic	Prob.
C	2.079647	0.314798	6.606288	0.0000
EDUC	0.023268	0.003870	6.013129	0.0000
LOGSALBEGIN	0.821799	0.036031	22.80783	0.0000
GENDER	0.048156	0.019910	2.418627	0.0160
MINORITY	−0.042369	0.020342	−2.082842	0.0378
R-squared	0.804117	Mean dependent var		10.35679
Adjusted R-squared	0.802446	S.D. dependent var		0.397334
S.E. of regression	0.176603			
Sum squared resid	14.62750			

Panel 2: Dependent Variable: EDUC				
Method: Least Squares				
Variable	Coefficient	Std. Error	t-Statistic	Prob.
C	−41.59997	3.224768	−12.90014	0.0000
LOGSALBEGIN	5.707538	0.339359	16.81859	0.0000
GENDER	−0.149278	0.237237	−0.629237	0.5295
MINORITY	−0.071606	0.242457	−0.295337	0.7679
R-squared	0.470869			

Panel 3	EDUC	LOGSALBEGIN	GENDER	MINORITY
R_j^2	0.470869	0.592042	0.330815	0.071537
R_j	0.6862	0.7694	0.5752	0.2675
$1/\sqrt{(1-R_j^2)}$	1.3747	1.5656	1.2224	1.0378
EDUC	1.000000			
LOGSALBEGIN	0.685719	1.000000		
GENDER	0.355986	0.548020	1.000000	
MINORITY	−0.132889	−0.172836	0.075668	1.000000

Exhibit 3.13 Bank Wages (Section 3.3.4)

Panel 1 shows the regression of salary (in logarithms) on a constant, education, begin salary (in logarithms), gender, and minority. Panel 2 shows the regression of one of the explanatory variables (EDUC) on the other ones, with corresponding coefficient of determination. Similar regressions are performed (but not shown) and the corresponding R^2 are reported in Panel 3, together with the values of R and of the square root of the variance inflation factors. For comparison, Panel 3 also contains the pairwise sample correlations between the explanatory variables.

errors of b_j in (3.47), for $j = 2, 3, 4, 5$. The largest multiple correlation is $R_3 = 0.77$ with corresponding square root of the variance inflation factor $1/\sqrt{1 - R_3^2} = 1.57$. This shows that some collinearity exists. However, as the variance inflation factors are not so large, multicollinearity does not seem to be a very serious problem in this example.

3.4 The *F*-test

3.4.1 The *F*-test in different forms

☞ Uses Section 1.2.3, 1.4.1; Appendix A.2–A.4.

Testing the joint significance of more than one coefficient

In Section 3.2 we considered the choice between the unrestricted model

$$y = X_1\beta_1 + X_2\beta_2 + \varepsilon$$

with estimates $y = X_1b_1 + X_2b_2 + e$, and the restricted model with $\beta_2 = 0$ and estimates $y = X_1b_R + e_R$. We may prefer to work with the simpler restricted model if b_2 is small. The question is when b_2 is small enough to do so, so that a measure is needed for the distance between b_2 and 0. For this purpose the *F-test* is commonly used to test the null hypothesis that $\beta_2 = 0$. One computes the *F*-statistic to be defined below and uses the restricted model if *F* does not exceed a certain critical value.

Derivation of the *F*-test

T

To derive the *F*-test for $H_0 : \beta_2 = 0$ against $H_1 : \beta_2 \neq 0$, we use the result in (3.38), which states that, if $\beta_2 = 0$,

$$b_2 = (X_2'M_1X_2)^{-1}X_2'M_1\varepsilon.$$

Under Assumptions 1–7 we conclude that $E[b_2] = 0$ and $b_2 \sim \mathrm{N}(0, V)$, where $V = \mathrm{var}(b_2) = \sigma^2(X_2'M_1X_2)^{-1}$. Let $V^{-1/2}$ be a symmetric matrix with the property that $V^{-1/2}VV^{-1/2} = I$, the $g \times g$ identity matrix. Such a matrix $V^{-1/2}$ is called a square root of the matrix V^{-1}, and it exists because V is a positive definite matrix. As $b_2 \sim \mathrm{N}(0, V)$, it follows that $V^{-1/2}b_2 \sim \mathrm{N}(0, I)$—that is, the g components of $V^{-1/2}b_2$ are independently distributed with standard normal distribution. By definition it follows that the sum of the squares of these components $b_2'V^{-1}b_2$ has the $\chi^2(g)$ distribution. As $V^{-1} = \sigma^{-2}X_2'M_1X_2$ this means that

$$b_2'X_2'M_1X_2b_2/\sigma^2 \sim \chi^2(g), \qquad (3.48)$$

if the null hypothesis that $\beta_2 = 0$ is true. However, this still involves the unknown parameter σ^2 and hence it can not be used in practice. But if we divide it by the ratio $e'e/\sigma^2$ (which follows a $\chi^2(n-k)$ distribution (see Section 3.3.1)), and if we divide both the numerator and the denominator by their degrees of freedom, the two factors with the unknown σ^2 cancel and we obtain

$$F = \frac{b_2'X_2'M_1X_2b_2/g}{e'e/(n-k)}. \tag{3.49}$$

This follows an $F(g, n-k)$ distribution, as it was shown in Section 3.3.1 that $s^2 = e'e/(n-k)$ and the least squares estimator b (and hence also b_2) are independent (for an alternative proof see Exercise 3.7). Using (3.34) we see that $b_2'X_2'M_1X_2b_2 = e_R'e_R - e'e$, so that F may be computed as follows.

Basic form of the *F*-test

$$F = \frac{(e_R'e_R - e'e)/g}{e'e/(n-k)} \sim F(g, n-k). \tag{3.50}$$

So the smaller model with $\beta_2 = 0$ is rejected if the increase in the sum of squared residuals $e_R'e_R - e'e$ is too large. The null hypothesis that $\beta_2 = 0$ is rejected for large values of F—that is, this is a one-sided test (see Exhibit 3.14). A geometric impression of the equality of the two forms (3.49) and (3.50) of the F-test is given in Exhibit 3.15. This equality can be derived from the theorem of Pythagoras, as is explained in the text below the exhibit.

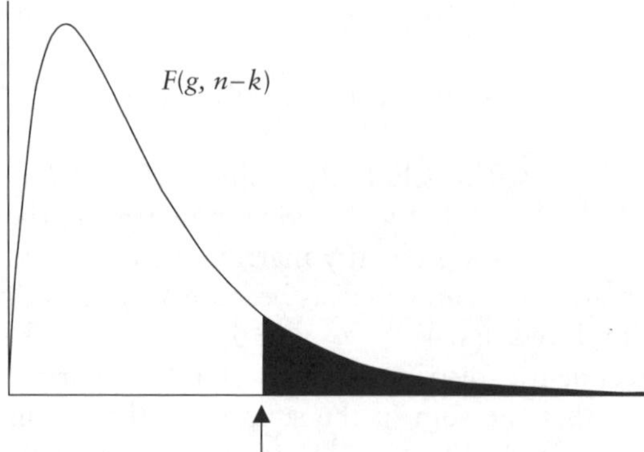

Exhibit 3.14 *P*-value

F-test on parameter restrictions, where g is the number of restrictions under the null hypothesis, n is the total number of observations, and k is the total number of regression parameters in the unrestricted model. The P-value is equal to the area of the shaded region in the right tail, and the arrow on the horizontal axis indicates the calculated F-value.

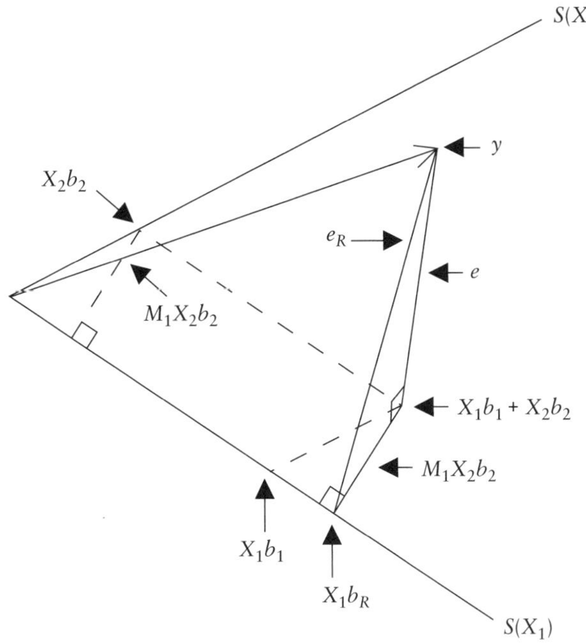

Exhibit 3.15 Geometry of *F*-test

Three-dimensional geometric impression of the *F*-test for the null hypothesis that the variables X_2 are not significant. The projection of y on the unrestricted model (which contains both X_1 and X_2) is given by $X_1b_1 + X_2b_2$ with residual vector e. The projection of y on the restricted model (which contains only X_1) is given by X_1b_R with residual vector e_R. The vectors e_R and e are both orthogonal to the variables X_1, and hence the same holds true for the difference $e_R - e$. This difference is the residual that remains after projection of $X_1b_1 + X_2b_2$ on the space of the variables X_1—that is, $e_R - e = M_1(X_1b_1 + X_2b_2) = M_1X_2b_2$. As the vector e is orthogonal to X_1 and X_2, it is also orthogonal to $M_1X_2b_2$. The theorem of Pythagoras implies that $e_R'e_R = e'e + (M_1X_2b_2)'M_1X_2b_2 = e'e + b_2'X_2'M_1X_2b_2$. The *F*-test for $\beta_2 = 0$ corresponds to testing whether the contribution $M_1X_2b_2$ of explaining y in terms of X_2 is significant—that is, it tests whether the length of e_R is significantly larger than the length of e, or, equivalently, whether $(e_R'e_R - e'e)$ differs significantly from 0.

The *F*-test with R^2

In the literature the *F*-test appears in various equivalent forms, and we now present some alternative formulations. Let R^2 and R_R^2 denote the coefficients of determination for the unrestricted model and the restricted model respectively. Then $e'e = SST(1 - R^2)$ and $e_R'e_R = SST(1 - R_R^2)$, where the total sum of squares is in both cases equal to $SST = \sum (y_i - \overline{y})^2$. Substituting this in (3.50) gives

$$F = \frac{n-k}{g} \cdot \frac{R^2 - R_R^2}{1 - R^2}. \tag{3.51}$$

So the restriction $\beta_2 = 0$ is not rejected if the R^2 does not decrease too much when this restriction is imposed. This method to compare the R^2 of two models is preferred above the use of the adjusted R^2 of Section 3.1.6. This is because the F-test can be used to compute the P-value for the null hypothesis that $\beta_2 = 0$, which provides a more explicit basis to decide whether the decrease in fit is significant or not.

The derivation of (3.51) from (3.50) makes clear that the R^2 or the adjusted R^2 can only be used to compare two models that have the same dependent variable. For instance, it makes no sense to compare the R^2 of a model where y is the measured variable with another model where y is the logarithm of the measured variable. This is because the total sum of squares (SST) of both models differ—that is, explaining the variation of y around its mean is something different from explaining the variation of $\log(y)$ around its mean.

F- and *t*-tests

The above F-statistics can be computed for every partition of the matrix X in two parts X_1 and X_2. For instance, in the particular case that X_2 consists of only one column (so that $g = 1$) $F = t^2$—that is, the F-statistic equals the square of the t-statistic and in this case the F-test and the two-sided t-test always lead to the same conclusion (see Exercise 3.7).

Test on the overall significance of the regression

Several statistical packages present for every regression the F-statistic and its associated P-value for the so-called *significance of the regression*. This corresponds to a partitioning of X in X_1 and X_2 where X_1 only contains the constant term (that is, X_1 is a single column consisting of unit elements) and X_2 contains all remaining columns (so that $g = k - 1$). If we denote the components of the $(k - 1) \times 1$ vector β_2 by the scalar parameters $\beta_2, \cdots, \beta_k$, then the null hypothesis is that $\beta_2 = \beta_3 = \cdots = \beta_k = 0$, which means that none of the explanatory variables (apart from the constant term) has effect on y. So this tests whether the model makes any sense at all. In this case, $e_R = y - \iota\bar{y}$ and $e_R'e_R = SST$, so that $R_R^2 = 0$. For this special case the F-statistic can therefore be written as

$$F = \frac{n-k}{k-1} \cdot \frac{R^2}{1-R^2}.$$

So there is a straightforward link between the F-test for the *joint significance* of all variables (except the intercept) and the coefficient of determination R^2.

Test of general linear restrictions

Until now we have tested whether certain parameters are zero and we have decomposed the regression matrix $X = (X_1 \ \ X_2)$ accordingly. An arbitrary set of *linear restrictions* on the parameters can be expressed in the form $R\beta = r$, where R is a given $g \times k$ matrix with rank g and r is a given $g \times 1$ vector. We consider the testing problem

$$y = X\beta + \varepsilon, \quad H_0 : R\beta = r, \tag{3.52}$$

which imposes g independent linear restrictions on β under the null hypothesis. Examples are given in Section 3.4.2.

T

Derivation of the *F*-test

We can test these restrictions, somewhat in the spirit of the t-test, by estimating the unrestricted model and checking whether Rb is sufficiently close to r. Under Assumptions 1–7, it follows that $b \sim \mathrm{N}(\beta, \sigma^2(X'X)^{-1})$ (see (3.42)). Therefore $Rb - r \sim \mathrm{N}(R\beta - r, \sigma^2 R(X'X)^{-1}R')$ and we reject the null hypothesis if $Rb - r$ differs significantly from zero. If the null hypothesis is true, then $Rb - r \sim \mathrm{N}(0, \sigma^2 R(X'X)^{-1}R')$ and

$$(Rb - r)'[\sigma^2 R(X'X)^{-1}R']^{-1}(Rb - r) \sim \chi^2(g). \tag{3.53}$$

The unknown σ^2 drops out again if we divide by $e'e/\sigma^2$, which has the $\chi^2(n-k)$ distribution and which is independent of b and hence also of the expression (3.53). By the definition of the F-distribution, this means that

$$\frac{(Rb - r)'[R(X'X)^{-1}R']^{-1}(Rb - r)/g}{e'e/(n-k)} \tag{3.54}$$

follows the $F(g, n-k)$ distribution if the null hypothesis is true. Expression (3.54) is not so convenient from a computational point of view. It is left as an exercise (see Exercise 3.8) that this F-test can again be written in terms of the sum of squared residuals (SSR) as in (3.50), where $e'e$ is the unrestricted SSR and $e_R'e_R$ is the SSR under the null hypothesis.

Summary of computations

A set of linear restrictions on the model parameters can be tested as follows. Let n be the number of observations, k the number of parameters of the unrestricted model, and g the number of parameter restrictions under the null hypothesis (so that there are only $(k-g)$ free parameters in the restricted model).

Testing a set of linear restrictions

- *Step 1: Estimate the unrestricted model.* Estimate the unrestricted model and compute the corresponding sum of squared residuals $e'e$.
- *Step 2: Estimate the restricted model.* Estimate the restricted model under the null hypothesis and compute the corresponding sum of squared residuals $e'_R e_R$.
- *Step 3: Perform the F-test.* Compute the F-test by means of (3.50), and reject the null hypothesis for large values of F. The P-values can be obtained from the fact that the F-test has the $F(g, n-k)$ distribution if the null hypothesis is true (provided that Assumptions 1–7 are satisfied).

☞ Exercises: T: 3.6c, d, 3.7e, f, 3.8, 3.10; E: 3.13, 3.15, 3.19a–e.

3.4.2 Illustration: Bank Wages

As an illustration, we consider again the data discussed in previous examples on salary (y, in logarithms of yearly wage), education (x_2, in years), begin salary (x_3, in logarithms of yearly wage), gender (x_4, taking the value 0 for females and 1 for males), and minority (x_5, taking the value 0 for non-minorities and 1 for minorities). We will discuss (i) the results of various models for three data sets, (ii) the significance of the variable minority, (iii) the joint significance of the regression, (iv) the joint significance of gender and minority, and (v) the test whether gender and minority have the same effect.

(i) Results of various models for three data sets

Exhibit 3.16 summarizes results (the sum of squared residuals and the coefficient of determination) of regressions in the unrestricted model

$$y = \beta_1 + \beta_2 x_2 + \beta_3 x_3 + \beta_4 x_4 + \beta_5 x_5 + \varepsilon$$

(see Panel 1) and in several restricted versions corresponding to different restrictions on the parameters β_i, $i = 1, \cdots, 5$ (see Panel 2). Most of the results of the unrestricted regression in Panel 1 of Exhibit 3.16 were already reported in Panel 1 of Exhibit 3.13 (p. 160).

In Panel 2 of Exhibit 3.16 the models are estimated for different data sets. One version uses the data of all 474 employees, a second one of the employees with custodial jobs (job category 2), and a third one of the employees with management jobs (job category 3). Some of the regressions cannot be performed for the second version. The reason is that all employees with a custodial job are male, so that $x_4 = 1$ for all employees in job category 2.

Panel 1: Dependent Variable: LOGSAL				
Method: Least Squares				
Sample: 1 474				
Included observations: 474				
Variable	Coefficient	Std. Error	t-Statistic	Prob.
C	2.079647	0.314798	6.606288	0.0000
EDUC	0.023268	0.003870	6.013129	0.0000
LOGSALBEGIN	0.821799	0.036031	22.80783	0.0000
GENDER	0.048156	0.019910	2.418627	0.0160
MINORITY	−0.042369	0.020342	−2.082842	0.0378
R-squared	0.804117	Mean dependent var		10.35679
Adjusted R-squared	0.802446	S.D. dependent var		0.397334
S.E. of regression	0.176603	F-statistic		481.3211
Sum squared resid	14.62750	Prob(F-statistic)		0.000000

Panel 2	ALL (n = 474)		JOBCAT 2 (n = 27)		JOBCAT 3 (n = 84)	
X-variables	SSR	R^2	SSR	R^2	SSR	R^2
1	74.6746	0.0000	0.1274	0.0000	5.9900	0.0000
1 2	38.4241	0.4854	0.1249	0.0197	4.8354	0.1928
1 2 3	14.8917	0.8006	0.1248	0.0204	3.1507	0.4740
1 2 3 4	14.7628	0.8023	-----	-----	3.1263	0.4781
1 2 3 5	14.8100	0.8017	0.1224	0.0391	3.0875	0.4846
1 2 3 4 5 ($\beta_4 + \beta_5 = 0$)	14.6291	0.8041	-----	-----	3.1503	0.4741
1 2 3 4 5 (unrestricted)	14.6275	0.8041	-----	-----	3.0659	0.4882

Exhibit 3.16 Bank Wages (Section 3.4.2)

Summary of outcomes of regressions where the dependent variable (logarithm of salary) is explained in terms of different sets of explanatory variables. Panel 1 shows the unrestricted regression in terms of five explanatory variables (including a constant term). In Panel 2, the explanatory variables (X) are denoted by their index 1 (the constant term), 2 (education), 3 (logarithm of begin salary), 4 (gender), and 5 (minority). The significance of explanatory variables can be tested by F-tests using the *SSR* (sum of squared residuals) or the R^2 (coefficient of determination) of the regressions. The column 'X-variables' indicates which variables are included in the model (in the sixth row all variables are included and the parameter restriction is that $\beta_4 + \beta_5 = 0$). The models are estimated for three data sets, for all 474 employees, for the twenty-seven employees in job category 2 (custodial jobs), and for the eighty-four employees in job category 3 (management jobs).

Therefore the variable x_4 should not be included in this second version of the model, as $x_4 = x_1 = 1$ and this would violate Assumption 1. With the results in Exhibit 3.16, we will perform four tests, all for the data set of all 474 employees. We refer to Exercise 3.13 for the analysis of similar questions for the sub-samples of employees with management or custodial jobs.

(ii) Significance of minority

Here the unrestricted model contains a constant term and the variables x_2, x_3, x_4, and x_5, and we test $H_0: \beta_5 = 0$ against $H_1: \beta_5 \neq 0$. This corresponds to (3.52) with $k = 5$ and $g = 1$ and with $R = (0, 0, 0, 0, 1)$ and $r = 0$. This restriction can be tested by the t-value of b_5 in Panel 1 of Exhibit 3.16. It is equal to -2.083 with P-value 0.038, so that the hypothesis is rejected at the 5 per cent level of significance.

As an alternative, we can also compare the residual sum of squares $e'e = 14.6275$ in the unrestricted model (see last row in Panel 2 of Exhibit 3.16) with the restricted sum of squares $e_R'e_R = 14.7628$ (see the row with x_1, x_2, x_3, and x_4 included in Panel 2 of Exhibit 3.16) and compute the F-test

$$F = \frac{(14.7628 - 14.6275)/1}{14.6275/(474 - 5)} = 4.338$$

with corresponding P-value of 0.038. The 5 per cent critical value of the $F(1, 469)$ distribution is 3.84, so that the null hypothesis is rejected at 5 per cent significance level. Note that $\sqrt{4.338} = 2.083$ is equal (in absolute value) to the t-value of b_5, that $\sqrt{3.84} = 1.96$ is the two-sided 5 per cent critical value of the $t(469)$ distribution, and that the P-values of the t-test and the F-test are equal. If we substitute the values $R^2 = 0.8041$ and $R_R^2 = 0.8023$ into (3.51), then the same value for F is obtained.

(iii) Significance of the regression

Now we test the joint significance of all explanatory variables by testing the null hypothesis that $\beta_2 = \beta_3 = \beta_4 = \beta_5 = 0$. In this case there are $g = 4$ independent restrictions and in terms of (3.52) we have

$$R = \begin{pmatrix} 0 & 1 & 0 & 0 & 0 \\ 0 & 0 & 1 & 0 & 0 \\ 0 & 0 & 0 & 1 & 0 \\ 0 & 0 & 0 & 0 & 1 \end{pmatrix}, \qquad r = \begin{pmatrix} 0 \\ 0 \\ 0 \\ 0 \end{pmatrix}.$$

Using the values of the sum of squared residuals in Panel 2 of Exhibit 3.16, the F-statistic becomes

$$F = \frac{(74.6746 - 14.6275)/4}{14.6275/(474 - 5)} = 481.321.$$

The 5 per cent critical value of $F(4, 469)$ is 2.39 and so this hypothesis is strongly rejected. Note that the value of this F-test has already been reported in the regression table in Panel 1 in Exhibit 3.16, with a P-value that is rounded to zero.

(iv) Joint significance of gender and minority

Next we test the null hypothesis that $\beta_4 = \beta_5 = 0$. This corresponds to (3.52) with $k = 5$ and $g = 2$ and with

$$R = \begin{pmatrix} 0 & 0 & 0 & 1 & 0 \\ 0 & 0 & 0 & 0 & 1 \end{pmatrix}, \qquad r = \begin{pmatrix} 0 \\ 0 \end{pmatrix}.$$

To perform this test for the joint significance of the variables x_4 and x_5, we use row 3 (for the restricted model) and row 7 (for the unrestricted model) in Exhibit 3.16, Panel 2, and find (using the R^2 this time)

$$F = \frac{(0.8041 - 0.8006)/2}{(1 - 0.8041)/(474 - 5)} = 4.190.$$

The P-value with respect to the $F(2, 469)$ distribution is equal to $P = 0.016$. So, at 5 per cent significance level we reject the null hypothesis.

(v) Test whether gender and minority have the same effect

In the unrestricted model the variable gender (x_4) has a positive coefficient (0.048). As $x_4 = 0$ for females and $x_4 = 1$ for males, this means that, on average, males have higher salaries than females (for the same education, begin salary, and minority classification). Further, the variable minority has a negative coefficient (-0.042). As $x_5 = 1$ for minorities and $x_5 = 0$ for non-minorities, this means that, on average, minorities have lower salaries than non-minorities (for the same education, begin salary, and gender). As the two estimated effects are nearly of equal magnitude, we will test whether the advantage of males is equally large as the advantage of non-minorities. This corresponds to the null hypothesis that $\beta_4 = -\beta_5$, or, equivalently, $\beta_4 + \beta_5 = 0$. In terms of (3.52), we have $k = 5, g = 1$, $R = (0, 0, 0, 1, 1)$, and $r = 0$. Using the last two rows in Exhibit 3.16, Panel 2, we get (in terms of SSR)

$$F = \frac{(14.6291 - 14.6275)/1}{14.6275/(474 - 5)} = 0.051$$

with a P-value of $P = 0.821$. So this hypothesis is not rejected—that is, the two factors of discrimination (gender and minority) seem to be of equal magnitude.

3.4.3 Chow forecast test

☞ Uses Appendix A.2–A.4.

Evaluation of predictive performance: Sample split

One of the possible practical uses of a multiple regression model is to produce forecasts of the dependent variable for given values of the explanatory variables. It is, therefore, of interest to evaluate an estimated regression model by studying its *predictive performance* out of sample. For this purpose

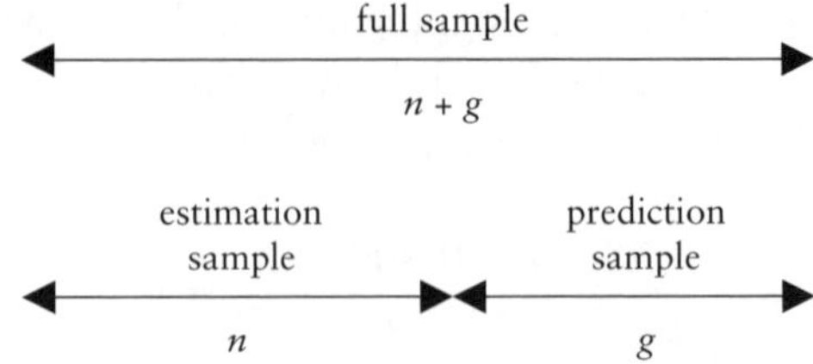

Exhibit 3.17 Prediction

The full sample is split into two non-overlapping parts, the estimation sample with observations that are used to estimate the model, and the prediction sample. The estimated model is used to forecast the values in the prediction sample, which can be compared with the actually observed values in the prediction sample.

the full sample is split into two parts, an estimation sample with n observations used to estimate the parameters, and a prediction sample with g additional observations used for the evaluation of the forecast quality of the estimated model. This is illustrated in Exhibit 3.17.

Notation

The data in the estimation sample are denoted by y_1 and X_1, where y_1 is a $n \times 1$ vector and X_1 a $n \times k$ matrix. The data in the prediction sample are denoted by y_2 and X_2, where y_2 is a $g \times 1$ vector and X_2 a $g \times k$ matrix. Note that this notation of X_1 and X_2 differs from the one used until now. That is, now the rows of the matrix X are partitioned instead of the columns. We can write

$$X = \begin{pmatrix} X_1 \\ X_2 \end{pmatrix}, \; y = \begin{pmatrix} y_1 \\ y_2 \end{pmatrix},$$

where X is a $(n+g) \times k$ matrix and y is a $(n+g) \times 1$ vector. Since we use y_1 and X_1 for estimation, we assume that $n > k$, whereas g may be any positive integer. For the DGP over the full sample we suppose that Assumptions 1–7 are satisfied, so that

$$y_1 = X_1\beta + \varepsilon_1,$$
$$y_2 = X_2\beta + \varepsilon_2,$$

with $E[\varepsilon_1\varepsilon_1'] = \sigma^2 I$, $E[\varepsilon_2\varepsilon_2'] = \sigma^2 I$, $E[\varepsilon_1\varepsilon_2'] = 0$.

Prediction and prediction error

The estimate of β is based on the estimation sample and is given by

$$b = (X_1'X_1)^{-1}X_1'y_1.$$

This estimate is used to predict the values of y_2 by means of X_2b, with resulting prediction error

$$f = y_2 - X_2b. \tag{3.55}$$

It is left as an exercise (see Exercise 3.7) to show that X_2b is the best linear unbiased predictor of y_2 in the sense that it minimizes the variance of f. We can write

$$f = X_2\beta + \varepsilon_2 - X_2(X_1'X_1)^{-1}X_1'y_1 = \varepsilon_2 - X_2(X_1'X_1)^{-1}X_1'\varepsilon_1,$$

so that the prediction error f consists of two uncorrelated components—namely, the disturbance ε_2 and a component caused by the fact that we use b rather than β in our prediction formula X_2b. As a consequence, the variance of the prediction errors is larger than the variance of the disturbances,

$$\text{var}(f) = \sigma^2(I + X_2(X_1'X_1)^{-1}X_2'). \tag{3.56}$$

Superficial observation could suggest that the prediction error covariance matrix attains it minimum if $X_2 = 0$, but in a model with an intercept this is impossible (as the elements in the first column of X_2 all have the value 1). It can be shown that the minimum is reached if all the rows of X_2 are equal to the row of column averages of X_1 (for the regression model with $k = 2$ this follows from formula (2.39) for the variance of the prediction error in Section 2.4.1 (p. 105)).

Prediction interval

If σ^2 in (3.56) is replaced by the least squares estimator $s^2 = e_1'e_1/(n-k)$, where $e_1 = y_1 - X_1b$ are the residuals over the estimation sample, then one can construct forecast intervals for y_2. It is left as an exercise (see Exercise 3.7) that a $(1-\alpha)$ *prediction interval* for y_{2j} for given values X_{2j} of the explanatory variables is given by

$$X_{2j}'b - cs\sqrt{d_{jj}} \leq y_{2j} \leq X_{2j}'b + cs\sqrt{d_{jj}},$$

where d_{jj} is the jth diagonal element of the matrix $I + X_2(X_1'X_1)^{-1}X_2'$ in (3.56) and c is such that $P[|t| > c] = \alpha$ when $t \sim t(n-k)$.

Test of constant DGP

To obtain the predicted values of y_2, we assumed that the data in the two sub-samples are generated by the same DGP. This may be tested by considering whether the predictions are sufficiently accurate. For a cross section this may mean, for example, that we check whether our model estimated using data from a number of regions may be used to predict the y variable in another region. For a time series model we check if our model estimated using data from a certain period can be used to predict the y variable in another period. In all cases we study conditional prediction—that is, we assume that the X_2 matrix required in the prediction is given. In order to test the predictive accuracy, we formulate the model

$$\begin{aligned} y_1 &= X_1\beta + \varepsilon_1 \\ y_2 &= X_2\beta + \gamma + \varepsilon_2, \end{aligned}$$

where γ is a $g \times 1$ vector of unknown parameters. The foregoing predictions of y_2 are made under the assumption that $\gamma = 0$. We can test this by means of an F-test in the model

$$\begin{pmatrix} y_1 \\ y_2 \end{pmatrix} = \begin{pmatrix} X_1 & 0 \\ X_2 & I \end{pmatrix} \begin{pmatrix} \beta \\ \gamma \end{pmatrix} + \begin{pmatrix} \varepsilon_1 \\ \varepsilon_2 \end{pmatrix}, \qquad (3.57)$$

where it is assumed, as before, that the model satisfies Assumptions 1–7 over the full sample of $n+g$ observations. To perform the F-test for $H_0: \gamma = 0$ against $H_1: \gamma \neq 0$, note that H_0 involves g restrictions. The number of observations in the model (3.57) is $n+g$ and the number of parameters is $k+g$. So the F-test in (3.50) becomes in this case

$$F = \frac{(e_R'e_R - e'e)/g}{e'e/(n+g-(k+g))} = \frac{(e_R'e_R - e'e)/g}{e'e/(n-k)},$$

which follows the $F(g, n-k)$ distribution when $\gamma = 0$. Note that n is the number of observations in the estimation sample, not in the full sample.

T

Derivation of sums of squares

To compute the F-test we still have to determine the restricted sum of squared residuals $e_R'e_R$ and the unrestricted sum of squared residuals $e'e$. Under the null hypothesis that $\gamma = 0$, the model becomes

$$\begin{pmatrix} y_1 \\ y_2 \end{pmatrix} = \begin{pmatrix} X_1 \\ X_2 \end{pmatrix} \beta + \begin{pmatrix} \varepsilon_1 \\ \varepsilon_2 \end{pmatrix}.$$

So e_R is obtained as the $(n+g) \times 1$ vector of residuals of the regression over the full sample of $(n+g)$ observations, and $e_R'e_R$ is the corresponding SSR. Under the alternative hypothesis that $\gamma \neq 0$, least squares in (3.57) is equivalent to minimizing

$$S(b, c) = \begin{pmatrix} y_1 - X_1 b \\ y_2 - X_2 b - c \end{pmatrix}' \begin{pmatrix} y_1 - X_1 b \\ y_2 - X_2 b - c \end{pmatrix}$$
$$= (y_1 - X_1 b)'(y_1 - X_1 b) + (y_2 - X_2 b - c)'(y_2 - X_2 b - c).$$

The first term is minimized by regressing y_1 on X_1—that is, for $b = (X_1'X_1)^{-1}X_1'y$, and the second term attains its minimal value zero for $c = y_2 - X_2 b$. So the unrestricted *SSR* is equal to $e'e = (y_1 - X_1 b)'\ (y_1 - X_1 b) = e_1'e_1$—that is, the SSR corresponding to a regression of the n observations in the estimation sample.

Chow forecast test

The test may therefore be performed by running two regressions, an 'unrestricted' one (the regression of y_1 on X_1 on the estimation sample with residuals e_1) and a 'restricted' one (the regression of $\begin{pmatrix} y_1 \\ y_2 \end{pmatrix}$ on $\begin{pmatrix} X_1 \\ X_2 \end{pmatrix}$ on the full sample with residuals e_R). This gives

$$F = \frac{(e_R'e_R - e_1'e_1)/g}{e_1'e_1/(n-k)}, \tag{3.58}$$

which is called the *Chow forecast test* for predictive accuracy. If we use the expression (3.49) of the *F*-test instead of (3.50), then b_2 corresponds to the estimated parameters γ in the unrestricted model. As stated before, these estimates are given by $c = y_2 - X_2 b$—that is, $c = f$ are the prediction errors in (3.55). So the Chow test may also be written as

$$F = \frac{f'Vf/g}{e_1'e_1/(n-k)},$$

where V is a $g \times g$ matrix of similar structure as in (3.49) with submatrices of explanatory variables as indicated in (3.57). This shows that the null hypothesis that $\gamma = 0$ is rejected if the prediction errors f are too large.

Comment on the two regressions in the Chow forecast test

Note that in the Chow forecast test (3.58) the regression in the 'large' (unrestricted) model corresponds to the regression over the 'small' subsample (of the first n observations), whereas the regression in the 'small' (restricted) model corresponds to the regression over the 'large' sample (of all $n + g$ observations). The unrestricted model is larger in the sense that it contains more parameters ($k+g$ instead of k). Both models apply to the same set of $n+g$ observations, and it is precisely because the large model contains g parameters for the g observations in the second sub-sample that the estimation of the large model can be reduced to a regression over the first sub-sample.

☞ **Exercises:** T: 3.7g, h, 3.11; E: 3.17, 3.19f, g.

3.4.4 Illustration: Bank Wages

As an illustration we return to the data on bank wages and we perform two forecast tests of the salary model with the explanatory variables x_1, x_2, x_3, x_4, and x_5 described in Section 3.4.2. We will discuss (i) the regression results, (ii) forecast of salaries for custodial jobs, (iii) forecast of salaries for management jobs, and (iv) a comparison of the two forecasts.

(i) Regression results

We use the results in Exhibit 3.18. This exhibit contains three regressions, one over the full sample of 474 employees (Panel 1), a second one over an estimation sample of 447 employees working in administration or management (Panel 2, the twenty-seven employees with custodial jobs form the prediction sample in this case), and a third one over an estimation sample of 390 employees with administrative or custodial jobs (Panel 3, the eighty-four employees with management jobs form the prediction sample in this case).

(ii) Forecast of salaries for custodial jobs

We first perform a Chow forecast test by predicting the salaries of the twenty-seven employees with custodial jobs. The corresponding F-statistic (3.58) can be computed from the results in Panels 1 and 2 in Exhibit 3.18:

$$F=\frac{(e_R'e_R-e_1'e_1)/g}{e_1'e_1/(n-k)}=\frac{(14.6275-13.9155)/27}{13.9155/(447-5)}=0.838.$$

The P-value of the corresponding $F(27,\,442)$ distribution is $P=0.70$, so that the predictions are sufficiently accurate. That is, the salaries for custodial jobs can be predicted by means of the model estimated for administrative and management jobs. The scatter of twenty-seven points of the actual and predicted salaries is shown in Exhibit 3.19 (*a*), and a histogram of the forecast errors is given in Exhibit 3.19 (*b*). Although the great majority of the predicted salaries are lower than the actual salaries, indicating a

Panel 1: Dependent Variable: LOGSAL Method: Least Squares Sample: 1 474 Included observations: 474				
Variable	Coefficient	Std. Error	t-Statistic	Prob.
C	2.079647	0.314798	6.606288	0.0000
EDUC	0.023268	0.003870	6.013129	0.0000
LOGSALBEGIN	0.821799	0.036031	22.80783	0.0000
GENDER	0.048156	0.019910	2.418627	0.0160
MINORITY	−0.042369	0.020342	−2.082842	0.0378
R-squared	0.804117	Mean dependent var		10.35679
Adjusted R-squared	0.802446	S.D. dependent var		0.397334
S.E. of regression	0.176603			
Sum squared resid	14.62750			

Panel 2: Dependent Variable: LOGSAL Method: Least Squares Sample: 1 474 IF JOBCAT = 1 OR JOBCAT = 3 Included observations: 447				
Variable	Coefficient	Std. Error	t-Statistic	Prob.
C	2.133639	0.323277	6.600032	0.0000
EDUC	0.029102	0.004352	6.687637	0.0000
LOGSALBEGIN	0.808688	0.037313	21.67293	0.0000
GENDER	0.028500	0.020875	1.365269	0.1729
MINORITY	−0.053989	0.021518	−2.508953	0.0125
R-squared	0.813307	Mean dependent var		10.35796
Adjusted R-squared	0.811617	S.D. dependent var		0.408806
S.E. of regression	0.177434			
Sum squared resid	13.91547			

Panel 3: Dependent Variable: LOGSAL Method: Least Squares Sample (adjusted): 2 474 IF JOBCAT = 1 OR JOBCAT = 2 Included observations: 390 after adjusting endpoints				
Variable	Coefficient	Std. Error	t-Statistic	Prob.
C	3.519694	0.517151	6.805930	0.0000
EDUC	0.018640	0.003774	4.939607	0.0000
LOGSALBEGIN	0.674293	0.056446	11.94577	0.0000
GENDER	0.071522	0.020327	3.518492	0.0005
MINORITY	−0.040494	0.019292	−2.099032	0.0365
R-squared	0.552306	Mean dependent var		10.21188
Adjusted R-squared	0.547655	S.D. dependent var		0.240326
S.E. of regression	0.161635			
Sum squared resid	10.05848			

Exhibit 3.18 Bank Wages (Section 3.4.4)

Regressions for two forecast tests. In Panel 1 a model for salaries is estimated using the data of all 474 employees; in Panel 2 this model is estimated using only the data of the employees with jobs in categories 1 and 3 (administration and management); in Panel 3 this model is estimated using only the data of the employees with jobs in categories 1 and 2 (administration and custodial jobs).

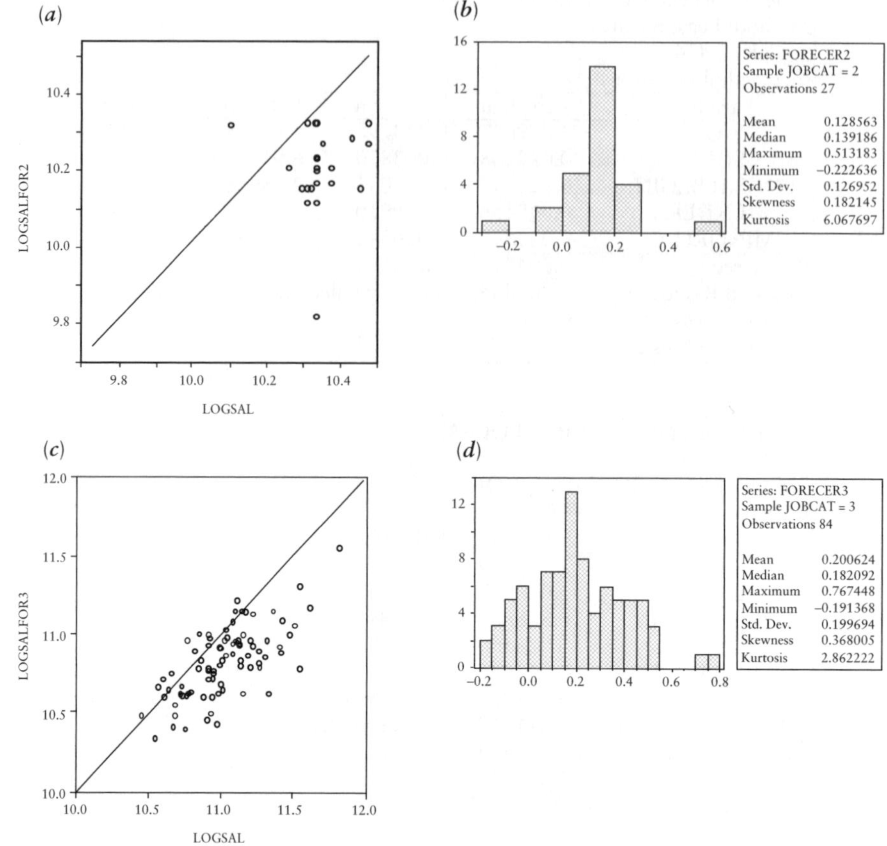

Exhibit 3.19 Bank Wages (Section 3.4.4)

Scatter diagrams of forecasted salaries against actual salaries, both in logarithms ((*a*) and (*c*)), and histograms of forecast errors ((*b*) and (*d*)), for employees in job category 2 ((*a*) and (*b*), forecasts obtained from model estimated for the data of employees in job categories 1 and 3) and for employees in job category 3 ((*c*) and (*d*), forecasts obtained from model estimated for the data of employees in job categories 1 and 2). The diagrams indicate that the salaries in a job category cannot be well predicted from the salaries in the other two job categories. In terms of the Chow forecast test, the prediction errors in (*a*) and (*b*) are acceptable, whereas those in (*c*) and (*d*) are not.

downward bias, the forecast errors are small enough for the null hypothesis not to be rejected. The mean squared error of the forecasts (that is, the sum of the squared bias and the variance) is $(0.1286)^2 + (0.1270)^2 = 0.0327$ (see Exhibit 3.19 (*b*)), whereas the estimated variance of the disturbances is $s^2 = (0.1774)^2 = 0.03125$ (see Panel 2 in Exhibit 3.18). The forecast test is based on the magnitude of the forecast errors, and these are of the same order as the random variation s^2 on the estimation sample. This explains that the Chow test does not reject the hypothesis that custodial salaries can be predicted from the model estimated on the basis of wage data for jobs in administration and management.

(iii) Forecast of salaries for management jobs

As a second test, we predict the salaries for the eighty-four employees with management positions from the model estimated for administrative and custodial jobs (job categories 1 and 2). The regression results based on the 390 observations in job categories 1 and 2 are shown in Panel 3 of Exhibit 3.18. The corresponding Chow forecast test (3.58) can be computed from the results in Panels 1 and 3 of Exhibit 3.18:

$$F = \frac{(e_R'e_R - e_1'e_1)/g}{e_1'e_1/(n-k)} = \frac{(14.6275 - 10.0585)/84}{10.0585/(390-5)} = 2.082.$$

The P-value of the corresponding $F(84, 385)$ distribution is rounded to $P = 0.0000$, so that the predictions are not accurate. That is, the salaries in job category 3 cannot be predicted well in this case.

The scatter of eighty-four points of the actual and predicted salaries is shown in Exhibit 3.19 (*c*), and the histogram of the forecast errors in Exhibit 3.19 (*d*). The values are again mostly below the 45° line, so that salaries in this category are higher than would be expected (on the basis of education, begin salary, gender, and minority) for categories 1 and 2. The standard error of the regression over the 390 individuals in categories 1 and 2 is $s = 0.1616$ (see Panel 3 in Exhibit 3.18), whereas the root mean squared forecast error over the eighty-four individuals in category 3 can be computed from Exhibit 3.19 (*d*) as $((0.2006)^2 + (0.1997)^2)^{1/2} = 0.2831$. So the forecast errors are much larger than the usual random variation in the estimation sample. Stated otherwise, people with management positions earn on average more than people with administrative or custodial jobs for given level of education, begin salary, gender, and minority.

(iv) Comparison of the two forecasts

Comparing once more Exhibit 3.19 (*a*) and (*c*), at first sight the predictive quality seems to be comparable in both cases. Note, however, that the vertical scales differ in the two scatter diagrams. Further, (*a*) contains much less observations than (*c*) (27 and 84 respectively). Forecast errors become more significant if they occur for a larger number of observations.

Summary, further reading, and keywords

SUMMARY

In this chapter we considered regression models with more than one explanatory variable. The least squares coefficients measure the direct effect of an explanatory variable on the dependent variable after neutralizing for the indirect effects that run via the other explanatory variables. These estimated effects therefore depend on the set of all explanatory variables included in the model. We paid particular attention to the question of which explanatory variables should be included in the model. For reasons of efficiency it is better to exclude variables that have only a marginal effect. The statistical properties of least squares were derived under a number of assumptions on the data generating process. Under these assumptions, the F-test can be used to test for the individual and joint significance of explanatory variables.

FURTHER READING

In our analysis we made intensive use of matrix methods. We give some references to econometric textbooks that also follow this approach. Chow (1983), Greene (2000), Johnston and DiNardo (1997), Stewart and Gill (1998), Verbeek (2000), and Wooldridge (2002) are on an intermediate level; the other books are on an advanced level. The handbooks edited by Griliches and Intriligator contain overviews of many topics that are treated in this and the next chapters.

Chow, G. G. (1983). *Econometrics*. Auckland: McGraw-Hill.

Davidson, R., and MacKinnon, J. G. (1993). *Estimation and Inference in Econometrics*. New York: Oxford University Press.

Gourieroux, C., and Monfort, A. (1995). *Statistics and Econometric Models*. 2 vols. Cambridge: Cambridge University Press.

Greene, W. H. (2000). *Econometric Analysis*. New York: Prentice Hall.

Griliches, Z., and Intriligator, M. D. (1983, 1984, 1986). *Handbook of Econometrics*. 3 vols. Amsterdam: North-Holland.

Johnston, J., and DiNardo, J. (1997). *Econometric Methods*. New York: McGraw-Hill.

Judge, G. G., Griffiths, W. E., Hill, R. C., Lütkepohl, H., and Lee, T. C. (1985). *The Theory and Practice of Econometrics*. New York: Wiley.

Malinvaud, E. (1980). *Statistical Methods of Econometrics.* Amsterdam: North Holland.
Mittelhammer, R. C., Judge, G. G., and Miller, D. J. (2000). *Econometric Foundations.* Cambridge: Cambridge University Press.
Ruud, P. A. (2000). *An Introduction to Classical Econometric Theory.* New York: Oxford University Press.
Stewart, J., and Gill, L. (1998). *Econometrics.* London: Prentice Hall.
Theil, H. (1971). *Principles of Econometrics.* New York: Wiley.
Verbeek, M. (2000). *A Guide to Modern Econometrics.* Chichester: Wiley.
Wooldridge, J. M. (2002). *Econometric Analysis of Cross Section and Panel Data.* Cambridge, MA: MIT Press.

KEYWORDS

Exercises

THEORY QUESTIONS

3.1 (☞ Section 3.1.2)
In this exercise we study the derivatives of (3.6) and prove the result in (3.7). For convenience, we write $X'y = p$ (a $k \times 1$ vector) and $X'X = Q$ (a $k \times k$ matrix), so that we have to minimize the function $f(b) = y'y - p'b - b'p + b'Qb = y'y - 2b'p + b'Qb$. Check every detail of the following argument.

a. Let b increase to $b + h$, where we may choose the elements of the $k \times 1$ vector h as small as we like. Then $f(b+h) = f(b) + h'(-2p + (Q' + Q)b) + h'Qh$.

b. This result can be interpreted as a Taylor expansion. If the elements of h are sufficiently small, the last term can be neglected, and the central term is a linear expression containing the $k \times 1$ vector of first order derivatives $\frac{\partial f}{\partial b} = -2p + (Q' + Q)b$. There are k first order derivatives and we follow the convention to arrange them in a column vector.

c. If we apply this to (3.6), this shows that $\frac{\partial S}{\partial b} = -2X'y + 2X'Xb$.

3.2 (☞ Section 3.1.2)
In this exercise we prove the result in (3.10). The vector of first order derivatives in (3.7) contains one term that depends on b. For convenience we write it as Qb and we partition the $k \times k$ matrix $Q = 2X'X$ into its columns as $Q = (q_1\ q_2\ \ldots\ q_k)$. Verify each step in the following argument.

a. Qb can be written as $Qb = q_1 b_1 + q_2 b_2 + \ldots + q_k b_k$.

b. The derivatives of the elements of Qb with respect to the scalar b_i can be written as a column q_i. To write all derivatives for $i = 1, \ldots, k$ in one formula we follow the convention to write them as a 'row of columns'—that is, we group them into a matrix, so that $\frac{\partial Qb}{\partial b'} = Q$ (note the prime in the left-hand denominator; this indicates that the separate derivatives are arranged as a row).

c. With the same conventions we get $\frac{\partial^2 S}{\partial b \partial b'} = Q$ for the Hessian.

d. Let X be an $n \times k$ matrix with rank k; then prove that the $k \times k$ matrix $X'X$ is positive definite.

3.3 (☞ Section 3.1.2)
The following steps show that the least squares estimator $b = (X'X)^{-1}X'y$ minimizes (3.6) without using the first and second order derivatives. In this exercise b_* denotes any $k \times 1$ vector.

a. Let $b_* = (X'X)^{-1}X'y + d$; then show that $y - Xb_* = e - Xd$, where e is a vector of constants that does not depend on the choice of d.

b. Show that $S(b_*) = e'e + (Xd)'(Xd)$ and that the minimum of this expression is attained if $Xd = 0$.

c. Derive the condition for uniqueness of this minimum and show that the minimum is then given by $d = 0$.

3.4 (☞ Section 3.1.4)

a. In the model $y = X\beta + \varepsilon$, the normal equations are given by $X'Xb = X'y$, the least squares estimates by $b = (X'X)^{-1}X'y$, and the variance by $\text{var}(b) = \sigma^2(X'X)^{-1}$. Work these three formulas out for the special case of the simple regression model $y_i = \alpha + \beta x_i + \varepsilon_i$ and prove that these results are respectively equal to the normal equations, the estimates a and b, and the variances of a and b obtained in Sections 2.1.2 and 2.2.4.

b. Suppose that the k random variables $y, x_2, x_3, \cdots, x_k$ are jointly normally distributed with mean μ and (non-singular) covariance matrix Σ. Let the observations be obtained by a random sample of size n from this distribution $\text{N}(\mu, \Sigma)$. Define the random variable $y_c = y|\{x_2, \cdots, x_k\}$—that is, y conditional on the values of $x_2, \cdots, x_k$. Show that the n observations y_c satisfy Assumptions 1–7 of Section 3.1.4.

3.5 (☞ Section 3.1.5)
In some software packages the user is asked to specify the variable to be explained and the explanatory variables, while an intercept is added automatically. Now suppose that you wish to compute the least squares estimates b in a regression of the type $y = X\beta + \varepsilon$ where the $n \times k$ matrix X does *not* contain an 'intercept column' consisting of unit elements. Define

$$y_* = \begin{pmatrix} y \\ -y \end{pmatrix}, \quad X_* = \begin{pmatrix} \iota & X \\ \iota & -X \end{pmatrix},$$

where the ι columns, consisting of unit elements only, are added by the computer package and the user specifies the other data.

a. Prove that the least squares estimator obtained by regressing y_* on X_* gives the desired result.

b. Prove that the standard errors of the regression coefficients of this regression must be corrected by a factor $\sqrt{(2n-k-1)/(n-k)}$.

3.6 (☞ Section 3.1.6)
Suppose we wish to explain a variable y and that the number of possible explanatory variables is so large that it is tempting to take a subset. In such a situation some researchers apply the so-called Theil criterion and maximize the adjusted R^2 defined by $\overline{R}^2 = 1 - \frac{n-1}{n-k}(1 - R^2)$, where n is the number of observations and k the number of explanatory variables.

a. Prove that R^2 never decreases by including an additional regressor in the model.

b. Prove that the Theil criterion is equivalent with minimizing s, the standard error of regression.

c. Prove that the Theil criterion implies that an explanatory variable x_j will be maintained if and only if the F-test statistic for the null hypothesis $\beta_j = 0$ is larger than one.

d. Show that the size (significance level) of such a test is larger than 0.05.

3.7 (☞ Sections 3.1.5, 3.1.6, 3.2.4, 3.4.1, 3.4.3)
Some of the following questions and arguments were mentioned in this chapter.

a. Prove the result stated in Section 3.1.5 that $h_i > 0$ if the $n \times k$ matrix X contains a column of unit elements and rank $(X) = k$.

b. Prove that R^2 (in the model with constant term) is the square of the sample correlation coefficient between y and $\hat{y} = Xb$.

c. If a regression model contains no constant term so that the matrix X contains no column of ones, then show that $1 - (SSR/SST)$ (and hence R^2 when it is computed in this way) may be negative.

d. Let $y = X_1\beta_1 + X_2\beta_2 + \varepsilon$ and let β_1 be estimated by regressing y on X_1 alone (the 'omitted variables' case of Section 3.2.3). Show that $\text{var}(b_R) \leq \text{var}(b_1)$ in the sense that $\text{var}(b_1) - \text{var}(b_R)$ is a positive semidefinite matrix. When are the two variances equal?

e. Show that the F-test for a single restriction $\beta_j = 0$ is equal to the square of the t-value of b_j. Show also that both tests lead to the same conclusion, irrespective of the chosen significance level.

f*. Consider the expression (3.49) of the F-test in terms of the random variables $b_2'X_2'M_1X_2b_2$ and $e'e$. Prove that, under the null hypothesis that $\beta_2 = 0$, these two random variables are independently distributed as $\chi^2(g)$ and $\chi^2(n-k)$ respectively by showing that (i) they can be expressed as $\varepsilon'Q_1\varepsilon$ and $\varepsilon'Q_2\varepsilon$, with (ii) $Q_1 = M_1 - M$ and $Q_2 = M$, where M is the M-matrix corresponding to X and M_1 is the M-matrix corresponding to X_1, so that (iii) Q_1 is idempotent with rank g and Q_2 is idempotent with rank $(n-k)$, and (iv) $Q_1Q_2 = 0$.

g. In Section 3.4 we considered the prediction of y_2 for given values of X_2 under the assumptions that $y_1 = X_1\beta + \varepsilon_1$ and $y_2 = X_2\beta + \varepsilon_2$ where $E[\varepsilon_1] = 0$, $E[\varepsilon_2] = 0$, $E[\varepsilon_1\varepsilon_1'] = \sigma^2 I$, $E[\varepsilon_2\varepsilon_2'] = \sigma^2 I$, and $E[\varepsilon_1\varepsilon_2'] = 0$. Prove that under Assumptions 1–6 the predictor X_2b with $b = (X_1'X_1)^{-1}X_1'y_1$ is best linear unbiased. That is, among all predictors of the form $\hat{y}_2 = Ly_1$ (with L a given matrix) with the property that $E[y_2 - \hat{y}_2] = 0$, it minimizes the variance of the forecast error $y_2 - \hat{y}_2$.

h. Using the notation introduced in Section 3.4.3, show that a $(1-\alpha)$ prediction interval for y_{2j} is given by $X_{2j}'b \pm cs\sqrt{d_{jj}}$.

3.8 (☞ Section 3.4.1)
Consider the model $y = X\beta + \varepsilon$ with the null hypothesis that $R\beta = r$ where R is a given $g \times k$ matrix of rank g and r is a given $g \times 1$ vector. Use the following steps to show that the expression (3.54) for the F-test can be written in terms of residual sums of squares as in (3.50).

a. The restricted least squares estimator b_R minimizes the sum of squares $(y - X\hat{\beta})'(y - X\hat{\beta})$ under the restriction that $R\hat{\beta} = r$. Show that

$b_R = b - A(Rb - r)$, where b is the unrestricted least squares estimator and $A = (X'X)^{-1} R'[R(X'X)^{-1}R']^{-1}$.

b. Let $e = y - Xb$ and $e_R = y - Xb_R$; then show that

$$e_R'e_R = e'e + (Rb - r)'[R(X'X)^{-1}R']^{-1}(Rb - r).$$

c. Show that the F-test in (3.54) can be written as in (3.50).

d. In Section 3.4.2 we tested the null hypothesis that $\beta_4 + \beta_5 = 0$ in the model with $k = 5$ explanatory variables. Describe a method to determine the restricted sum of squared residuals $e_R'e_R$ in this case.

3.9 (☞ Section 3.2.5)
This exercise serves to clarify a remark on standard errors in partial regressions that was made in Example 3.3 (p. 150). We use the notation of Section 3.2.5, in particular the estimated regressions

(1) $y = X_1b_1 + X_2b_2 + e$, and
(2) $M_2y = (M_2X_1)b_* + e_*$

in the result of Frisch–Waugh. Here X_1 and M_2X_1 are $n \times (k - g)$ matrices and X_2 is an $n \times g$ matrix.

a. Prove that $\text{var}(b_1) = \text{var}(b_*) = \sigma^2(X_1'M_2X_1)^{-1}$.

b. Derive expressions for the estimated variance s^2 in regression (1) and s_*^2 in regression (2), both in terms of $e'e$.

c. Prove that the standard errors of the coefficients b_1 in (1) can be obtained by multiplying the standard errors of the coefficients b_* in (2) by the factor $\sqrt{(n - k + g)/(n - k)}$.

d. Check this result by considering the standard errors of the variable education in the second regression in Exhibit 3.7 and the last regression in Exhibit 3.10. (These values are rounded; a more precise result is obtained when higher precision values from a regression package are used).

e. Derive the relation between the t-values of (1) and (2).

3.10 (☞ Section 3.4.1)
In Section 1.4.2 we mentioned the situation of two independent random samples, one of size n_1 from $N(\mu_1, \sigma^2)$ and a second one of size n_2 from $N(\mu_2, \sigma^2)$. We want to test the null hypothesis $H_0: \mu_1 = \mu_2$ against the alternative $H_1: \mu_1 \neq \mu_2$. The pooled t-test is based on the difference between the sample means $\overline{y}_1$ and $\overline{y}_2$ of the two sub-samples. Let $e_1'e_1 = \sum_{i=1}^{n_1}(y_i - \overline{y}_1)^2$ and $e_2'e_2 = \sum_{i=n_1+1}^{n_1+n_2}(y_i - \overline{y}_2)^2$ be the total sum of squares in the first and second sub-sample respectively; then the pooled estimator of the variance is defined by $s_p^2 = (e_1'e_1 + e_2'e_2)/(n_1 + n_2 - 2)$ and the pooled t-test is defined by

$$t_p = \sqrt{\frac{n_1n_2}{n_1 + n_2}} \frac{\overline{y}_2 - \overline{y}_1}{s_p}.$$

a. Formulate the testing problem of $\mu_1 = \mu_2$ against $\mu_1 \neq \mu_2$ in terms of a parameter restriction in a multivariate regression model (with parameters μ_1 and μ_2).

b. Derive the F-test for $H_0: \mu_1 = \mu_2$ in the form (3.50).

c. Prove that t_p^2 is equal to the F-test in **b** and that t_p follows the $t(n_1 + n_2 - 2)$ distribution if the null hypothesis of equal means holds true.

d. In Example 1.12 (p. 62) we considered the FGPA scores of $n_1 = 373$ male students and $n_2 = 236$ female students. Use the results reported in Exhibit 1.6 to perform a test of the null hypothesis of equal means for male and female students against the alternative that female students have on average higher scores than male students.

3.11 (☞ Section 3.4.3)
We consider the Chow forecast test (3.58) for the case $g = 1$ of a single new observation (x_{n+1}, y_{n+1}). The n preceding observations are used in the model $y_1 = X_1\beta + \varepsilon$ with least squares estimator b. We assume that Assumptions 1–4 and 7 are satisfied for the full sample $i = 1, \cdots, n + 1$, and Assumptions 5 and 6 for the estimation sample $i = 1, \cdots, n$, whereas for the $(n + 1)$st observation we write

$$y_{n+1} = x_{n+1}'\beta + \gamma + \varepsilon_{n+1}$$

with γ an unknown scalar parameter. We consider the null hypothesis that $\gamma = 0$ against the alternative that $\gamma \neq 0$.

a. Prove that the least squares estimators of β and γ over the full sample $i = 1, \cdots, n + 1$, are given by b and $c = y_{n+1} - x_{n+1}'b$. Show that the residual for the $(n + 1)$st observation is equal to zero. Provide an intuitive explanation for this result.

b. Derive the residual sum of squares over the full sample $i = 1, \cdots, n+1$ under the alternative hypothesis.

c. Derive the F-test for the hypothesis that $\gamma = 0$.

EMPIRICAL AND SIMULATION QUESTIONS

3.12 (☞ Section 3.3.3)

In this simulation exercise we consider five variables (y, z, x_1, x_2, and x_3) that are generated as follows. Let $n = 100$ and let $\varepsilon_i, \omega_i, \eta_i \sim \text{NID}(0, 1)$ be independent random samples from the standard normal distribution, $i = 1, \cdots, n$. Define

$$\begin{aligned} x_{1i} &= 5 + \omega_i + 0.3\eta_i \\ x_{2i} &= 10 + \omega_i \\ x_{3i} &= 5 + \eta_i \\ y_i &= x_{1i} + x_{2i} + \varepsilon_i \\ z_i &= x_{2i} + x_{3i} + \varepsilon_i \end{aligned}$$

a. What is the correlation between x_1 and x_3? And what is the correlation between x_2 and x_3?

b. Perform the regression of y on a constant, x_1 and x_2. Compute the regression coefficients and their t-values. Comment on the outcomes.

c. Answer the questions of **b** for the regression of z on a constant, x_2 and x_3.

d. Perform also regressions of y on a constant and x_1, and of z on a constant and x_3. Discuss the differences that arise between these two cases.

3.13 (☞ Section 3.4.1)

In Section 3.4.2 we tested four different hypotheses—that is, (i) $\beta_5 = 0$, (ii) $\beta_2 = \beta_3 = \beta_4 = \beta_5 = 0$, (iii) $\beta_4 = \beta_5 = 0$, and (iv) $\beta_4 + \beta_5 = 0$. As data set we considered the data on all 474 employees (see Exhibit 3.16). Use a significance level of 5 per cent in all tests below.

a. Test these four hypotheses also for the subset of employees working in management (job category 3), using the results in the last two columns in Exhibit 3.16.

b. Now consider the hypothesis (iii) that gender and minority have no effect on salary for employees in management. We mention that of the eighty-four employees in management, seventy are male non-minority, ten are female-non-minority, four are male-minority, and no one is female-minority. Discuss the relevance of this information with respect to the power of the test for hypothesis (iii).

c. Finally consider the subset of employees with custodial jobs (job category 2, where all employees are male). Use the results in Exhibit 3.16 to test the hypothesis that $\beta_5 = 0$. Test also the hypothesis that $\beta_2 = \beta_3 = \beta_5 = 0$.

3.14 (☞ Sections 3.2.2, 3.3.3)

In this exercise we consider the data set on student learning of Example 1.1 (p. 12) for 609 students. The dependent variable (y) is the FGPA score of a student, and the explanatory variables are x_1 (constant term), x_2 (SATM score), x_3 (SATV score), and x_4 (FEM, with $x_4 = 1$ for females and $x_4 = 0$ for males).

a. Compute the 4×4 correlation matrix for the variables (y, x_2, x_3, x_4).

b. Estimate a model for FGPA in terms of SATV by regressing y on x_1 and x_3. Estimate also a model by regressing y on x_1, x_2, x_3, and x_4.

c. Comment on the differences between the two models in **b** for the effect of SATV on FGPA.

d. Investigate the presence of collinearity between the explanatory variables by computing R_j^2 in (3.47) and the square root of the variance inflation factors, $1/\sqrt{1 - R_j^2}$, for $j = 2, 3, 4$.

3.15 (☞ Section 3.4.1)

In this exercise we consider production data for the year 1994 of $n = 26$ US firms in the sector of primary metal industries (SIC33). The data are taken from E. J. Bartelsman and W. Gray, National Bureau of Economic Research, NBER Technical Working Paper 205, 1996. For each firm, values are given of production (Y, value added in millions of dollars), labour (L, total payroll in millions of dollars), and capital (K, real capital stock in millions of 1987 dollars). A log-linear production function is estimated with the following result (standard errors are in parentheses).

$$\log(Y) = \underset{(0.415)}{0.701} + \underset{(0.091)}{0.756} \log(L) + \underset{(0.110)}{0.242} \log(K) + e$$

The model is also estimated under two alternative restrictions, the first with equal coefficients for $\log(L)$ and $\log(K)$ and the second with the sum of the coefficients of $\log(L)$ and $\log(K)$ equal to one ('constant returns to scale'). For this purpose the following two regressions are performed.

$$\log(Y) = \underset{(0.358)}{0.010} + \underset{(0.026)}{0.524}(\log(L) + \log(K)) + e_1$$

$$\log(Y) - \log(K) = \underset{(0.132)}{0.686} + \underset{(0.089)}{0.756}(\log(L) - \log(K)) + e_2$$

The residual sums of squares are respectively $e'e = 1.825544$, $e_1'e_1 = 2.371989$, and $e_2'e_2 = 1.825652$, and the R^2 are respectively equal to $R^2 = 0.956888$, $R_1^2 = 0.943984$, and $R_2^2 = 0.751397$. In the following tests use a significance level of 5%.

a. Test for the individual significance of $\log(L)$ and $\log(K)$ in the first regression. Test also for the joint significance of these two variables.

b. Test the restriction of equal coefficients by means of an F-test based on the residual sums of squares.

c. Test this restriction also by means of the R^2.

d. Test the restriction of constant returns to scale also in two ways, one with the F-test based on the residual sums of squares and the other with the F-test based on the R^2.

e. Explain why the outcomes of **b** and **c** are the same but the two outcomes in **d** are different. Which of the two tests in **d** is the correct one?

3.16 (☞ Section 3.2.5)

Consider the data on bank wages of the example in Section 3.1.7. To test for the possible effect of gender on wage, someone proposes to estimate the model $y = \beta_1 + \beta_4 x_4 + \varepsilon$, where y is the yearly wage (in logarithms) and x_4 is the variable gender (with $x_4 = 0$ for females and $x_4 = 1$ for males). As an alternative we consider the model with x_2 (education) as an additional explanatory variable.

a. Use the data to perform the two regressions.

b. Comment on the differences between the conclusions that could be drawn (without further thinking) from each of these two regressions.

c. Draw a partial regression scatter plot (with regression line) for salary (in logarithms) against gender after correction for the variable education (see Case 3 in Section 3.2.5). Draw also a scatter plot (with regression line) for the original (uncorrected) data on salary (in logarithms) and gender. Discuss how these plots help in clarifying the differences in **b**.

d. Check the results on regression coefficients and residuals in the result of Frisch–Waugh (3.39) for these data, where X_1 refers to the variable x_4, and X_2 refers to the constant term and the variable x_2.

3.17 (☞ Section 3.4.3)

In this exercise we consider data on weekly coffee sales of a certain brand of coffee. These data come from the same marketing experiment as discussed in Example 2.3 (p. 78), but for another brand of coffee and for another selection of weeks. The data provide for $n = 18$ weeks the values of the coffee sales in that week (Q, in units), the applied deal rate ($D = 1$ for the usual price, $D = 1.05$ in weeks with 5% price reduction, and $D = 1.15$ in weeks with 15% price reduction), and advertisement ($A = 1$ in weeks with advertisement, $A = 0$ otherwise). We postulate the model

$$\log(Q) = \beta_1 + \beta_2 \log(D) + \beta_3 A + \varepsilon.$$

For all tests below use a significance level of 5 %.

a. Test whether advertisement has a significant effect on sales, both by a t-test and by an F-test.

b. Test the null hypothesis that $\beta_2 = 1$ against the alternative that $\beta_2 > 1$.

c. Construct 95% interval estimates for the parameters β_2 and β_3.

d. Estimate the model using only observations in weeks without advertisement. Test whether this model produces acceptable forecasts for the sales (in logarithms) in the weeks with advertisement. Note: take special care of the fact that the estimated model can not predict the effect of advertisement.

e. Make two scatter plots, one of the actual values of $\log(Q)$ against the fitted values of **d** for the twelve observations in the estimation sample, and a second one of log (Q) against the predicted values for the six observations in the prediction sample. Relate these graphs to your conclusions in **d**.

3.18 (☞ Section 3.2.5)

In this exercise we consider yearly data (from 1970 to 1999) related to motor gasoline consumption in the USA. The data are taken from different sources (see the table). Here 'rp' refers to data in the Economic Report of the President (see w3.access.gpo.gov), 'ecocb' to data of the Census Bureau, and 'ecode' to data of the Department of Energy (see www.economagic.com). The price indices are defined so that the average value over the years 1982–4 is equal to 100. We define the variables $y = \log(SGAS/PGAS)$, $x_2 = \log(INC/PALL)$, $x_3 = \log(PGAS/PALL)$, $x_4 = \log(PPUB/PALL)$, $x_5 = \log(PNCAR/PALL)$, and $x_6 = \log(PUCAR/PALL)$. We are interested in the price elasticity of gasoline consumption — that is, the marginal relative increase in sold quantity due to a marginal relative price increase.

Variable	Definition	Units	Source
SGAS	Retail sales gasoline service stations	10^6 dollars	ecocb
PGAS	Motor gasoline retail price, US city average	cts/gallon	ecode
INC	Nominal personal disposable income	10^9 dollars	rp
PALL	Consumer price index	$(1982-4)/3 = 100$	rp
PPUB	Consumer price index of public transport	idem	rp
PNCAR	Consumer price index of new cars	idem	rp
PUCAR	Consumer price index of used cars	idem	rp

a. Estimate this price elasticity by regressing log ($SGAS$) on a constant and log ($PGAS$). Comment on the outcome, and explain why this outcome is misleading.

b. Estimate the price elasticity now by regressing y on a constant and log ($PGAS$). Explain the precise relation with the results in **a**. Why is this outcome still misleading?

c. Now estimate the price elasticity by regressing y on a constant and the variables x_2 and x_3. Provide a motivation for this choice of explained and explanatory variables and comment on the outcomes.

d. If y is regressed on a constant and the variable x_3 then the estimated elasticity is more negative than in **c**. Check this result and give an explanation in terms of partial regressions. Use the fact that, in the period 1970–99, real income has mostly gone up and the price of gasoline (as compared with other prices) has mostly gone down.

e. Perform the partial regressions needed to remove the effect of income (x_2) on the consumption (y) and on the relative price (x_3). Make a partial regression scatter plot of the 'cleaned' variables and check the validity of the result of Frisch–Waugh in this case.

f. Estimate the price elasticity by regressing y on a constant and the variables x_2, x_3, x_4, x_5, and x_6. Comment on the outcomes and compare them with the ones in **c**.

g. Transform the four price indices ($PALL$, $PPUB$, $PNCAR$, and $PUCAR$) so that they all have the value 100 in 1970. Perform the regression of **f** for the transformed data (taking logarithms again) and compare the outcomes with the ones in **f**. Which regression statistics remain the same, and which ones have changed? Explain these results.

3.19 (☞ Sections 3.4.1, 3.4.3)

We consider the same data on motor gasoline consumption as in Exercise 3.18 and we use the same notation as introduced there. For all tests below, compute sums of squared residuals of appropriate regressions, determine the degrees of freedom of the test statistic, and use a significance level of 5%.

a. Regress y on a constant and the variables x_2, x_3, x_4, x_5, and x_6. Test for the joint significance of the prices of new and used cars.

b. Regress y on a constant and the four explanatory variables log ($PGAS$), log ($PALL$), log (INC), and log ($PPUB$). Use the results to construct a 95% interval estimate for the price elasticity of gasoline consumption.

c. Test the null hypothesis that the sum of the coefficients of the four regressors in the model in **b** (except the constant) is equal to zero. Explain why this restriction is of interest by relating this regression model to the restricted regression in **a**.

d. Show that the following null hypothesis is not rejected: the sum of the coefficients of $\log(PALL)$, $\log(INC)$, and $\log(PPUB)$ in the model of **b** is equal to zero. Show that the restricted model has regressors $\log(PGAS)$, x_2 and x_4 (and a constant term), and estimate this model.

e. Use the model of **d** (with the constant, $\log(PGAS)$, x_2 and x_4 as regressors) to construct a 95% interval estimate for the price elasticity of gasoline consumption. Compare this with the result in **b** and comment.

f. Search the Internet to find the most recent year with values of the variables *SGAS*, *PGAS*, *PALL*, *INC*, and *PPUB* (make sure to use the same units as the ones mentioned in Exercise 3.18). Use the models in **b** and **d** to construct 95% forecast intervals of $y = \log(SGAS/PGAS)$ for the given most recent values of the regressors.

g. Compare the most recent value of y with the two forecast intervals of part **f**. For the two models in **b** and **d**, perform Chow forecast tests for the most recent value of y.

4 Non-Linear Methods

In the previous chapter, the finite sample statistical properties of regression methods were derived under restrictive assumptions on the data generating process. In this chapter we describe several methods that can be applied more generally. We consider models with stochastic explanatory variables, non-normal disturbances, and non-linearities in the parameters. Some of these models can be estimated by (non-linear) least squares; other models are better estimated by maximum likelihood or by the generalized method of moments. In most cases there exists no closed-form expression for the estimates, so that numerical methods are required. Often the finite sample statistical properties of the estimators cannot be derived analytically. An approximation is obtained by asymptotic analysis—that is, by considering the statistical properties if the sample size tends to infinity.

4.1 Asymptotic analysis

☞ Uses Section 1.3.3.

4.1.1 Introduction

Motivation of asymptotic analysis and use in finite samples

In the previous chapter we have seen that, given certain assumptions on the data generating process, we can derive the exact distributional properties of estimators (b and s^2) and of tests (for instance, t- and F-tests). However, these assumptions are rather strong and one might have a hard time finding practical applications where all these assumptions hold exactly true. For example, regressors typically do not tend to be 'fixed' (as we do not often do controlled experiments), but they are often stochastic (as we rely on empirical data that are for some part affected by random factors). Also, regression models need not be linear in the parameters.

An interesting question now is whether estimators and tests, which are based on the same principles as before, still make sense in this more general setting. Strictly speaking, if one or several of the standard Assumptions 1–7 in Section 3.1.4 (p. 125–6) are violated, then we do not know the statistical properties of the estimators and tests anymore. A useful tool to obtain understanding of the properties and tests in this more general setting is to pretend that we can obtain a limitless number of observations. We can then pose the question how the estimators and tests would behave when the number of observations increases without limit. This, in essence, is what is called *asymptotic analysis*. Of course, in practice our sample size is finite. However, the asymptotic properties translate into results that hold true approximately in finite samples, provided that the sample size is large enough. That is, once we know how estimators and tests behave for a limitless number of observations, we also get an approximate idea of how they perform in finite samples of usual size.

Random regressors and non-normal disturbances

As before, we consider the linear model

$$y = X\beta + \varepsilon. \tag{4.1}$$

In the previous chapter we derived the statistical properties of the least squares estimator under the seven assumptions listed in Section 3.1.4. In this chapter we relax some of these assumptions. In particular, we consider situations where the explanatory variables are random (so that Assumption 1 is not satisfied), where the disturbances are not normally distributed (so that Assumption 7 is violated), or where the model is not linear in the parameters (so that Assumption 6 is violated). Such situations often occur in practice when we analyse observed economic data. In this section we consider the properties of the least squares estimator when Assumptions 1 and 7 are violated. Non-linear regression models are discussed in Section 4.2.

Averaging to remove randomness and to obtain normality, asymptotically

The general idea is to remove randomness and non-normality asymptotically by taking averages of the observed data. In Section 1.3.3 (p. 50) we discussed the law of large numbers, which states that the (random) sample average converges in probability to the (non-random) population mean, and the central limit theorem, which states that this average (properly scaled) converges in distribution to a normal distribution. That is, if Assumptions 1 and 7 are violated, then under appropriate conditions these assumptions still hold true asymptotically—that is, if the sample size grows without limit ($n \to \infty$). The results of Chapter 3 then also hold true asymptotically, and they can be taken as an approximation in large enough finite samples.

Before discussing further details of asymptotic analysis, we give an example to illustrate that Assumptions 1 and 7 are often violated in practice.

Example 4.1: **Bank Wages (continued)**

As an illustration, suppose that we want to investigate the wage structure in the US banking sector. We will discuss (i) randomness of the regressors due to sampling, (ii) measurement errors, and (iii) non-normality of the disturbances.

(i) Sampling as a source of randomness

To estimate a wage equation for the US banking sector, we could use the data of $n = 474$ employees of a US bank (see Section 2.1.4 and Exhibit 2.5 (*a*) (p. 85), and Section 3.1.7 and Exhibit 3.5, Panel 3 (p. 132)). If we were to use data of employees of another bank, this would of course give other values for the dependent and explanatory variables. That is, both y and X in (4.1) are obtained by sampling from the full population of employees of all US banks. This means that both y and X are random, so that Assumption 1 is violated.

To illustrate this idea, suppose that our data set consisted only of a subset of the 474 employees considered before. We show the results for two such sub-samples. Exhibit 4.1 contains three histograms of the explanatory

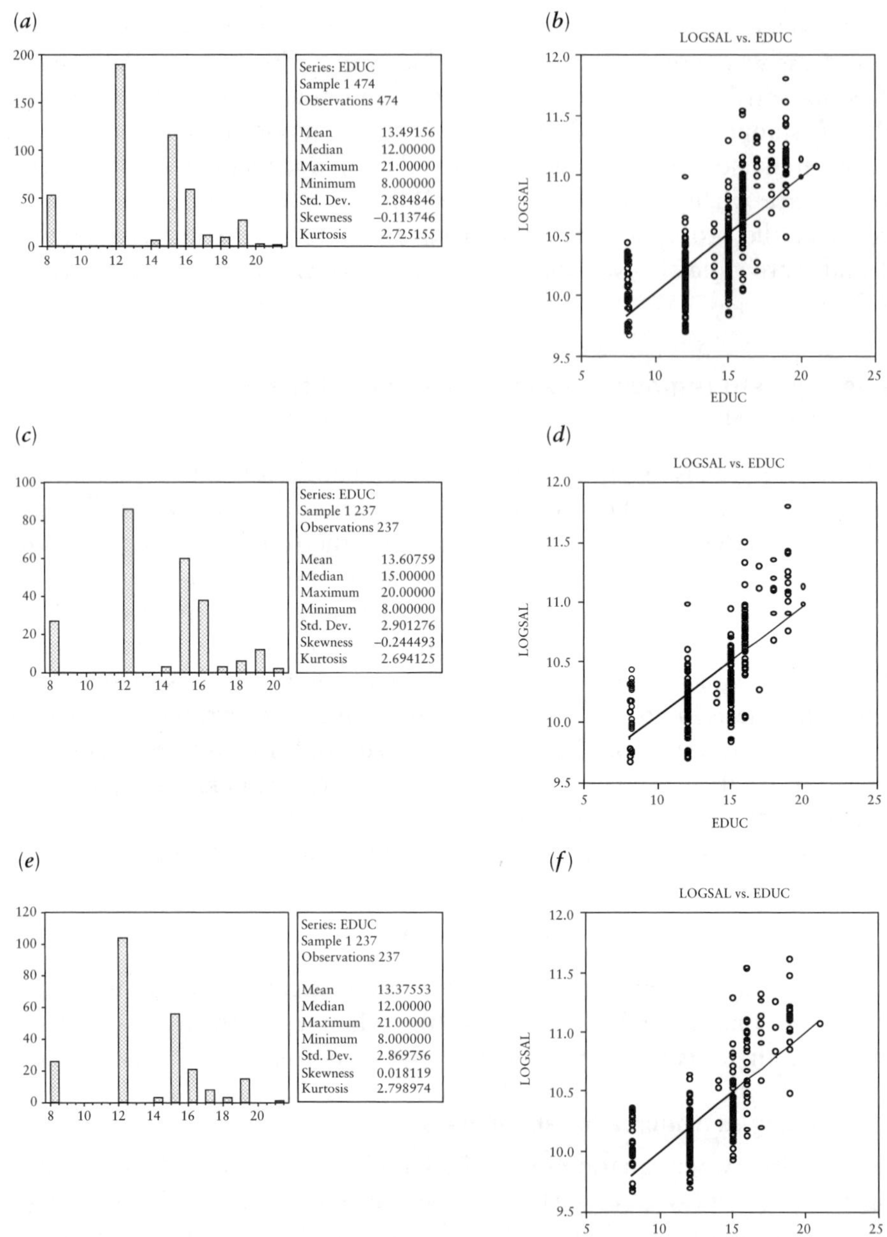

Exhibit 4.1 Bank Wages (Example 4.1)

Histograms of variable education (EDUC) ((*a*), (*c*), and (*e*)), and scatter diagrams of salary (in logarithms) against education ((*b*), (*d*), and (*f*)), for full sample ($n = 474$ ((*a*) and (*b*))), and for two (complementary) random samples of size 237 ((*c*)–(*f*)).

variable education (in (*a*), (*c*), and (*e*)) and three corresponding scatter diagrams (in (*b*), (*d*), and (*f*)). The first data set consists of the full sample; the other two are the result of a random selection of the employees in two distinct groups of size 237 each. Clearly, the outcomes depend on the chosen sample, and both y and X are random because of sampling.

(ii) Measurement errors

Apart from sampling effects, the observed explanatory variables often provide only partial information on the economic variables of interest. For example, the measured number of years of education of employees does not take the quality of the education into account. The reported data contain *measurement errors*, in the sense that they give imperfect information on the relevant underlying economic variables.

(iii) Non-normality of disturbances

As concerns the Assumption 7, an indication of the distribution of the disturbances may be obtained by considering the least squares residuals. For the simple regression model of Section 2.1.4, where salaries (in logarithms) are explained from education alone, the histogram of the residuals is given in Exhibit 2.5 (*b*). This distribution is skewed and this may cast doubt on the validity of Assumption 7.

4.1.2 Stochastic regressors

Interpretation of previous results for stochastic regressors

One way to deal with stochastic regressors is to interpret the results that are obtained under the assumption of fixed regressors as results that hold true *conditional* on the given outcomes of the regressors. The results in Chapters 2 and 3, which were obtained under Assumption 1 of fixed regressors, carry over to the case of stochastic regressors, provided that all assumptions and results are interpreted conditional on the given values of the regressors. To illustrate this idea, we consider the mean and variance of the least squares estimator b. In Section 3.1.4 (p. 126) we showed that, under Assumptions 1–6, $E[b] = \beta$ and $\text{var}(b) = \sigma^2(X'X)^{-1}$. If the regressors in the $n \times k$ matrix X are stochastic, these results are not valid anymore. However, suppose that we replace Assumption 2 that $E[\varepsilon] = 0$ and Assumptions 3 and 4 that $\text{var}(\varepsilon) = \sigma^2 I$ by the following two assumptions that are conditional on X:

$$E[\varepsilon|X] = 0, \qquad \text{var}(\varepsilon|X) = \sigma^2 I.$$

Then it holds true that

$$E[b|X] = \beta, \qquad \text{var}(b|X) = \sigma^2(X'X)^{-1},$$

so that the previous results remain true if we interpret everything conditional on X. To prove the above two results, note that

$$\begin{aligned} E[b|X] &= E[\beta + (X'X)^{-1}X'\varepsilon|X] = \beta + (X'X)^{-1}X'E[\varepsilon|X] = \beta, \\ \text{var}(b|X) &= \text{var}(\beta + (X'X)^{-1}X'\varepsilon|X) = (X'X)^{-1}X'\text{var}(\varepsilon|X)X(X'X)^{-1} \\ &= (X'X)^{-1}X'(\sigma^2 I)X(X'X)^{-1} = \sigma^2(X'X)^{-1}. \end{aligned}$$

T

Derivation of statistical properties OLS when X and ε are independent

Consider the linear model $y = X\beta + \varepsilon$ and suppose that Assumptions 2–6 (see Section 3.1.4) are satisfied, but that Assumption 1 of fixed regressors is not valid. If X is *random* but independently distributed from ε, then it follows that

$$\begin{aligned} E[b] &= E[(X'X)^{-1}X'y] \\ &= \beta + E[(X'X)^{-1}X'\varepsilon] \\ &= \beta + E[(X'X)^{-1}X']E[\varepsilon] \\ &= \beta, \end{aligned}$$

where the third equality follows because X and ε are independent. So, in this case the least squares estimator is still unbiased. To evaluate the variance $\text{var}(b) = E[(b-\beta)(b-\beta)']$ we write

$$b = (X'X)^{-1}X'y = (X'X)^{-1}X'(X\beta + \varepsilon) = \beta + (X'X)^{-1}X'\varepsilon, \qquad (4.2)$$

so that $b - \beta = (X'X)^{-1}X'\varepsilon$. Using the properties of conditional expectations (see Section 1.2.2 (p. 24)) it follows by conditioning on X (denoted by $E[\,\cdot\,|X]$) that

$$\begin{aligned} \text{var}(b) &= E[(X'X)^{-1}X'\varepsilon\varepsilon'X(X'X)^{-1}] \\ &= E[E[(X'X)^{-1}X'\varepsilon\varepsilon'X(X'X)^{-1}|X]] \\ &= E[(X'X)^{-1}X'E[\varepsilon\varepsilon'|X]X(X'X)^{-1}] \\ &= E[(X'X)^{-1}X'E[\varepsilon\varepsilon']X(X'X)^{-1}] \\ &= \sigma^2 E[(X'X)^{-1}]. \end{aligned}$$

The third equality follows because, conditional on X, X is given, and the fourth equality holds true because X and ε are independent. The last equality uses the fact that $E[\varepsilon\varepsilon'] = \sigma^2 I$ because of Assumptions 2–4. This shows that the variance of b depends on the distribution of X.

Consequences of random regressors

In general it may be difficult to estimate the joint distribution of X or to estimate $E[(X'X)^{-1}]$. The t- and F-statistics as computed in Chapter 3 will no longer exactly follow the t- and F-distributions. This also means that the P-values reported by statistical packages that are based on these distributions are no longer valid. In general, the exact finite sample distributions of b and of the t- and F-statistics cannot be determined analytically. However, the *asymptotic properties* can be determined under appropriate regularity conditions (see Section 4.1.4).

The assumption of stable regressors

In the sequel we no longer assume that X and ε are independent. In order to investigate the asymptotic properties of the least squares estimator, we make the following assumption. For the definition and calculation rules of probability limits we refer to Section 1.3.3 (p. 48–9).

- *Assumption 1**: *stability* (replaces Assumption 1 of fixed regressors). The regressors X may be stochastic and the probability limit of $\frac{1}{n}X'X$ exists and is non-singular, that is, for some non-singular $k \times k$ matrix Q there holds

$$\text{plim}\left(\frac{1}{n}X'X\right) = Q.$$

This stability assumption places restrictions on the variation in the explanatory variables—that is, the variables should vary sufficiently (so that Q is invertible) but not excessively (so that Q is finite). For example, suppose that the values of the $k \times 1$ vector of regressors are obtained by random sampling from a population with zero mean and positive definite covariance matrix Q—that is, from a population where the regressors are not perfectly collinear. The element (h, j) of the matrix $\frac{1}{n}X'X$ is given by $\frac{1}{n}\sum_{i=1}^{n} x_{hi}x_{ji}$, the (non-centred) second moment of the hth and jth explanatory variable. The law of large numbers (see Section 1.3.3 (p. 50)) implies that $\text{plim}\left(\frac{1}{n}\sum_{i=1}^{n} x_{hi}x_{ji}\right) = E[x_{hi}x_{ji}] = Q_{hj}$, so that Assumption 1* holds true under these conditions.

4.1.3 Consistency

The exogeneity condition for consistency

If X is random but independent of ε, then the least squares estimator b is unbiased. If X and ε are not independent, then b is in general no longer unbiased, because $E[b] = \beta + E[(X'X)^{-1}X'\varepsilon]$ and the last term is non-zero in general. To investigate whether b is *consistent*—that is, whether $\text{plim}(b) = \beta$—we write (4.2) as

$$b = \beta + \left(\frac{1}{n}X'X\right)^{-1}\frac{1}{n}X'\varepsilon. \tag{4.3}$$

Using the rules for probability limits, it follows from Assumption 1* that

$$\text{plim}(b) = \beta + Q^{-1}\text{plim}\left(\frac{1}{n}X'\varepsilon\right),$$

so that b is consistent if and only if

$$\text{plim}\left(\frac{1}{n}X'\varepsilon\right) = 0. \tag{4.4}$$

This last condition is called the *orthogonality condition*. If this condition is satisfied, then the explanatory variables are said to be *exogenous* (or sometimes 'weakly' exogenous, to distinguish this type of exogeneity, which is related to consistent estimation, from other types of exogeneity related to forecasting and structural breaks). The jth component of (4.4) can be written as $\text{plim}\left(\frac{1}{n}\sum_{i=1}^{n} x_{ji}\varepsilon_i\right)$, so that this condition basically means that the explanatory variables should be asymptotically uncorrelated with the disturbances.

Derivation of consistency of s^2

Under Assumption 1* and condition (4.4), s^2 (defined in (3.22)) is a consistent estimator of σ^2 provided that $\text{plim}\left(\frac{1}{n}\varepsilon'\varepsilon\right) = \text{plim}\left(\frac{1}{n}\sum_{i=1}^{n}\varepsilon_i^2\right) = \sigma^2$. This can be seen by writing (using the notation and results of Section 3.1.5)

$$\begin{aligned} s^2 &= \frac{1}{n-k}e'e = \frac{1}{n-k}\varepsilon' M\varepsilon = \frac{1}{n-k}(\varepsilon'\varepsilon - \varepsilon' X(X'X)^{-1}X'\varepsilon) \\ &= \frac{n}{n-k}\left(\frac{1}{n}\varepsilon'\varepsilon - \frac{1}{n}\varepsilon' X\left(\frac{1}{n}X'X\right)^{-1}\frac{1}{n}X'\varepsilon\right). \end{aligned}$$

For $n \to \infty$ the first term converges to 1, the second to σ^2, the third and fifth to zero because of condition (4.4), and the fourth term converges to Q^{-1} because of Assumption 1*. This shows that $\text{plim}(s^2) = \sigma^2$ under the stated conditions.

An example where OLS is consistent

As an illustration, we consider the data generating process

$$y_i = \beta x_i + \varepsilon_i,$$

where the x_i are IID(0, q) and the ε_i are IID(0, σ^2). If the explanatory variable x_i and the disturbance term ε_i are independent, it follows that

$$E\left[\frac{1}{n}X'\varepsilon\right] = E\left[\frac{1}{n}\sum_{i=1}^{n} x_i\varepsilon_i\right] = \frac{1}{n}\sum_{i=1}^{n} E[x_i]E[\varepsilon_i] = 0,$$

$$\text{var}\left(\frac{1}{n}X'\varepsilon\right) = E\left[\frac{1}{n^2}\sum_{i=1}^{n}\sum_{j=1}^{n} x_i x_j \varepsilon_i \varepsilon_j\right] = \frac{1}{n^2}\sum_{i=1}^{n}\sum_{j=1}^{n} E[x_i x_j]E[\varepsilon_i\varepsilon_j]$$
$$= \frac{1}{n^2}\sum_{i=1}^{n} E\left[x_i^2\right]\sigma^2 = \frac{\sigma^2 q}{n}.$$

It follows from the result (1.48) in Section 1.3.3 (p. 49) that in this case condition (4.4) is satisfied.

An example where OLS is not consistent

On the other hand, if x_i and ε_i are correlated then the least squares estimator is no longer consistent. This is illustrated by a simulation in Exhibit 4.2. Here the explanatory variable and the disturbance terms have positive covariance (see (*a*)), so that $\gamma = E[x_i\varepsilon_i] > 0$, and the estimated slope b is larger than the slope β of the DGP (see (*b*)). This is in line with the fact that $\text{plim}(b) = \beta + q^{-1}\text{plim}(\frac{1}{n}X'\varepsilon) = \beta + \gamma/q > \beta$. Note that the least squares

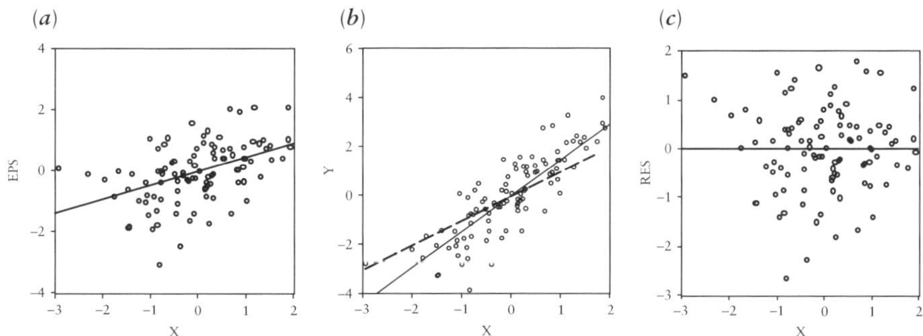

Exhibit 4.2 Inconsistency

Effect of correlation between regressor and disturbance terms. The data are generated by $y = x + \varepsilon$ (so that the DGP has slope parameter $\beta = 1$). (*a*) shows the scatter diagram of the disturbance terms ε (EPS) against the regressor x, which are positively correlated. (*b*) contains the scatter diagram of y against x with the regression line and the systematic relation $y = x$ (dashed line) of the DGP. This shows that least squares overestimates the slope parameter. (*c*) contains the scatter diagram of the least squares residuals (RES) against x, which shows that the correlation between x and the disturbances (ε) cannot be detected in this way.

estimate is obtained from the normal equation $\frac{1}{n}\sum x_i(y_i - bx_i) = \frac{1}{n}\sum x_i e_i = 0$, where $e_i = y_i - bx_i$ are the least squares residuals. This means that the positive correlation between x_i and ε_i cannot be detected from the least squares residuals (see (*c*)). Therefore, in practice this issue cannot be tested by simply looking at the residuals. Tests for exogeneity will be discussed later (see Section 5.7.3 (p. 411)).

☞ **Exercises:** T: 4.1, 4.3, 4.4; S: 4.8.

4.1.4 Asymptotic normality

Derivation of asymptotic distribution

T

To determine the *asymptotic distribution of b*, it is helpful to rewrite (4.3) as

$$\sqrt{n}(b - \beta) = \left(\frac{1}{n}X'X\right)^{-1}\frac{1}{\sqrt{n}}X'\varepsilon. \tag{4.5}$$

Under Assumption 1*, the first factor in (4.5) converges in probability to Q^{-1}, so that it remains to determine the asymptotic distribution of $\frac{1}{\sqrt{n}}X'\varepsilon$. It can be shown that, under Assumptions 1* and 2–6 and some additional weak regularity conditions, there holds

$$\frac{1}{\sqrt{n}}X'\varepsilon \xrightarrow{d} \mathrm{N}(0, \sigma^2 Q). \tag{4.6}$$

The result in (4.6) is based on generalizations of the central limit theorem. We do not discuss the precise regularity conditions needed for this general result, but we analyse the simple regression model $y_i = \beta x_i + \varepsilon_i$ in somewhat more detail.

Illustration: Simple regression model

T

Suppose that the disturbances ε_i are independently but not normally distributed and that the (single) explanatory variable x_i is non-stochastic. In this case $\frac{1}{\sqrt{n}}X'\varepsilon = \frac{1}{\sqrt{n}}\sum x_i\varepsilon_i = \frac{1}{\sqrt{n}}\sum z_i$, where the random variables $z_i = x_i\varepsilon_i$ are independently distributed with mean $E[z_i] = E[x_i\varepsilon_i] = 0$ and variance $E\left[z_i^2\right] = E\left[x_i^2\varepsilon_i^2\right] = \sigma^2 x_i^2$. In particular, if $x_i = 1$ (so that the model contains only the constant term), then $\frac{1}{\sqrt{n}}X'\varepsilon = \frac{1}{\sqrt{n}}\sum \varepsilon_i$, and, according to the central limit theorem (1.50) in Section 1.3.3 (p. 50), it follows that this converges in distribution to $\mathrm{N}(0, \sigma^2)$. As $Q = 1$ in this situation this shows (4.6) for this particular case. If x_i is not constant, we can use a generalized central limit theorem (see Section 1.3.3), which states that $\frac{1}{\sqrt{n}}\sum z_i$ converges in distribution to $\mathrm{N}(0, \sigma_*^2)$ with variance equal to $\sigma_*^2 = \lim_{n\to\infty}\frac{1}{n}\sum_{i=1}^n \mathrm{var}(z_i) = \sigma^2 \lim\left(\frac{1}{n}\sum_{i=1}^n x_i^2\right) = \sigma^2 Q$, which proves (4.6) also for this case. Note that asymptotic normality is obtained independent of the distribution of the disturbances — that is, even if the disturbances are not normally distributed. The result in (4.6) can be proved under much weaker conditions, with correlated disturbances and stochastic X, but the orthogonality condition is crucial to obtain the zero mean in (4.6).

Asymptotic distribution of OLS estimator

If the result on the asymptotic distribution in (4.6) holds true, it follows from (4.5) and Assumption 1* that

$$\sqrt{n}(b-\beta)\xrightarrow{d}\mathrm{N}(0,\sigma^2Q^{-1}QQ^{-1})=\mathrm{N}(0,\sigma^2Q^{-1}). \tag{4.7}$$

Approximate distribution in finite samples

We say that the rate of convergence of b to β is $\sqrt{n}$. If the sample size n is large enough, the finite sample distribution of b can be approximated by $\mathrm{N}\left(\beta,\ \frac{\sigma^2}{n}Q^{-1}\right)$. It depends on the application to hand which size of the sample is required to justify this approximation. For instance, for the case of random samples discussed in Section 1.3.3, the distribution of the sample mean is often well approximated by a normal distribution for small sample sizes like $n=50$. On the other hand, if the model for example contains many regressors, then larger sample sizes may be required. The situation is somewhat comparable to the discussion in Section 3.3.3 on multicollinearity (p. 158). The expression (3.47) for the variance shows that the sample size required to get a prescribed precision depends on the amount of variation in the individual regressors and on the correlations between the regressors.

Practical use of asymptotic distribution

To apply the normal approximation in practice, the (unknown) matrix Q is approximated by $\frac{1}{n}X'X$. This gives the approximate distribution

$$b\approx\mathrm{N}\left(\beta,\sigma^2(X'X)^{-1}\right). \tag{4.8}$$

This means that the statistical results of Chapter 3 — for example, the t-test and the F-test that are based on the assumption that $b\sim\mathrm{N}\left(\beta,\sigma^2(X'X)^{-1}\right)$ — remain valid as an *asymptotic approximation* under the following four assumptions.

(i) $\mathrm{plim}\left(\frac{1}{n}X'X\right)=Q$ exists and is invertible (Assumption 1*),
(ii) $E[\varepsilon]=0, \mathrm{var}(\varepsilon)=\sigma^2I$ (Assumptions 2–4),
(iii) $y=X\beta+\varepsilon$ (Assumptions 5 and 6),
(iv) $\mathrm{plim}\left(\frac{1}{n}X'\varepsilon\right)=0$ (orthogonality condition).

The standard inference methods for least squares are still valid for stochastic regressors and non-normal disturbances, provided that these four conditions are satisfied.

4.1.5 Simulation examples

As an illustration, we perform some simulation experiments with the model

$$y_i = x_i + \varepsilon_i, \quad i = 1, \cdots, n.$$

So our data generating process has parameters $\beta = 1$ and $\sigma^2 = 1$.

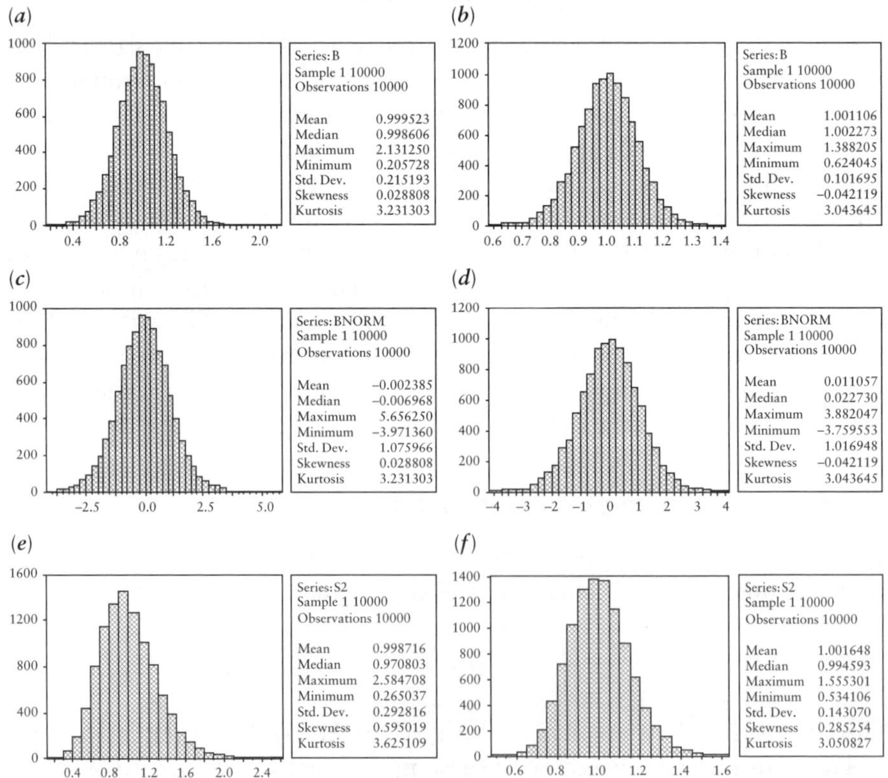

Exhibit 4.3 Simulation Example (Section 4.1.5)

Consistency and asymptotic normality. Estimates of the slope parameter (b, denoted by B in (a) and (b)), a normalized version (BNORM, i.e. $\sqrt{n}(b - 1)$ in (c) and (d)), and estimates of the disturbance variance (s^2, denoted by S2 in (e) and (f)), for simulated data that satisfy the orthogonality condition. The number of simulation runs is 10,000, and the histograms show the distribution of the resulting 10,000 estimates. The sample size is $n = 25$ in (a), (c), and (e) and $n = 100$ in (b), (d), and (f) (note the differences between the scales on the horizontal axis for both sample sizes).

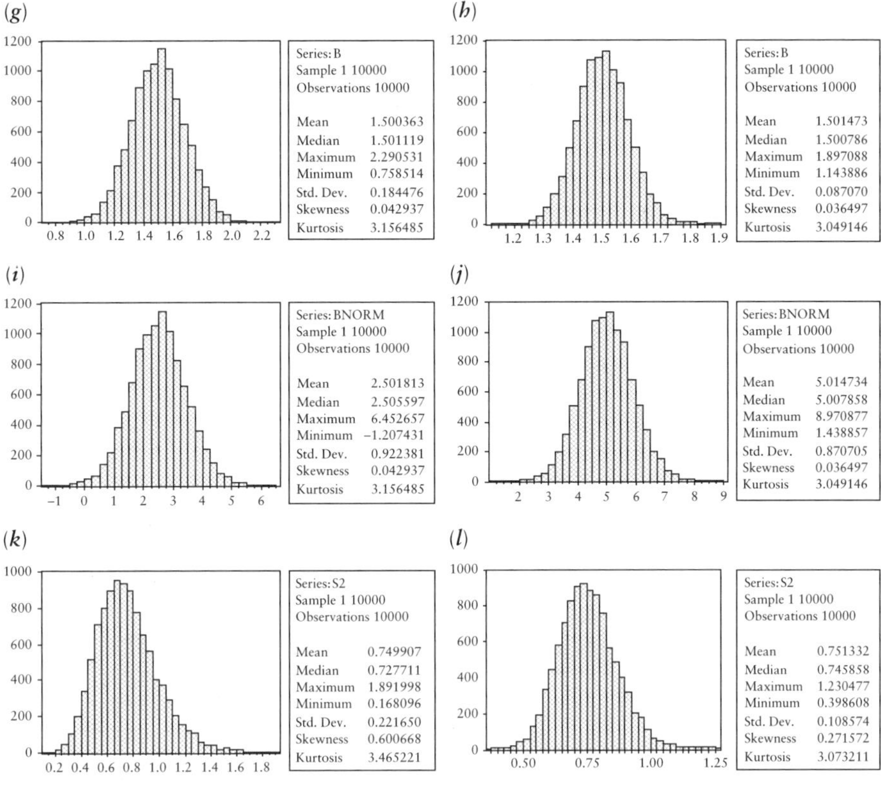

Exhibit 4.3 (*Contd.*)

Inconsistency when orthogonality is violated. Estimates of the slope parameter (b, denoted by B in (g) and (h)), a normalized version (BNORM, i.e. $\sqrt{n}\,(b-1)$ in (i) and (j)), and estimates of the disturbance variance (s^2, denoted by S2 in (k) and (l)), for simulated data that do not satisfy the orthogonality condition. The number of simulation runs is 10,000, and the histograms show the distribution of the resulting 10,000 estimates. The sample size is $n = 25$ in (g), (i), and (k) and $n = 100$ in (h), (j), and (l) (note the differences between the scales on the horizontal axis for both sample sizes).

Simulations with stable random regressors

First we consider simulations where the values of (x_i, ε_i) are obtained by a random sample of the bivariate normal distribution with mean zero, unit variances, and covariance ρ. So the regressor x_i is random, and it is also stable because the law of large numbers implies that $\text{plim}\left(\frac{1}{n}\sum_{i=1}^{n} x_i^2\right) = E[x^2] = 1$.

We consider two experiments, one experiment with $\rho = 0$ (so that the regressor satisfies the orthogonality condition) and another experiment with $\rho = 0.5$ (so that the orthogonality condition is violated). Exhibit 4.3 shows histograms (based on 10,000 simulations) of the values of b, $\sqrt{n}(b-1)$, and s^2, for sample sizes $n = 25$ (a, c, e, g, i, k) and $n = 100$ (b, d, f, h, j, l). The histograms (a–f) indicate the consistency and

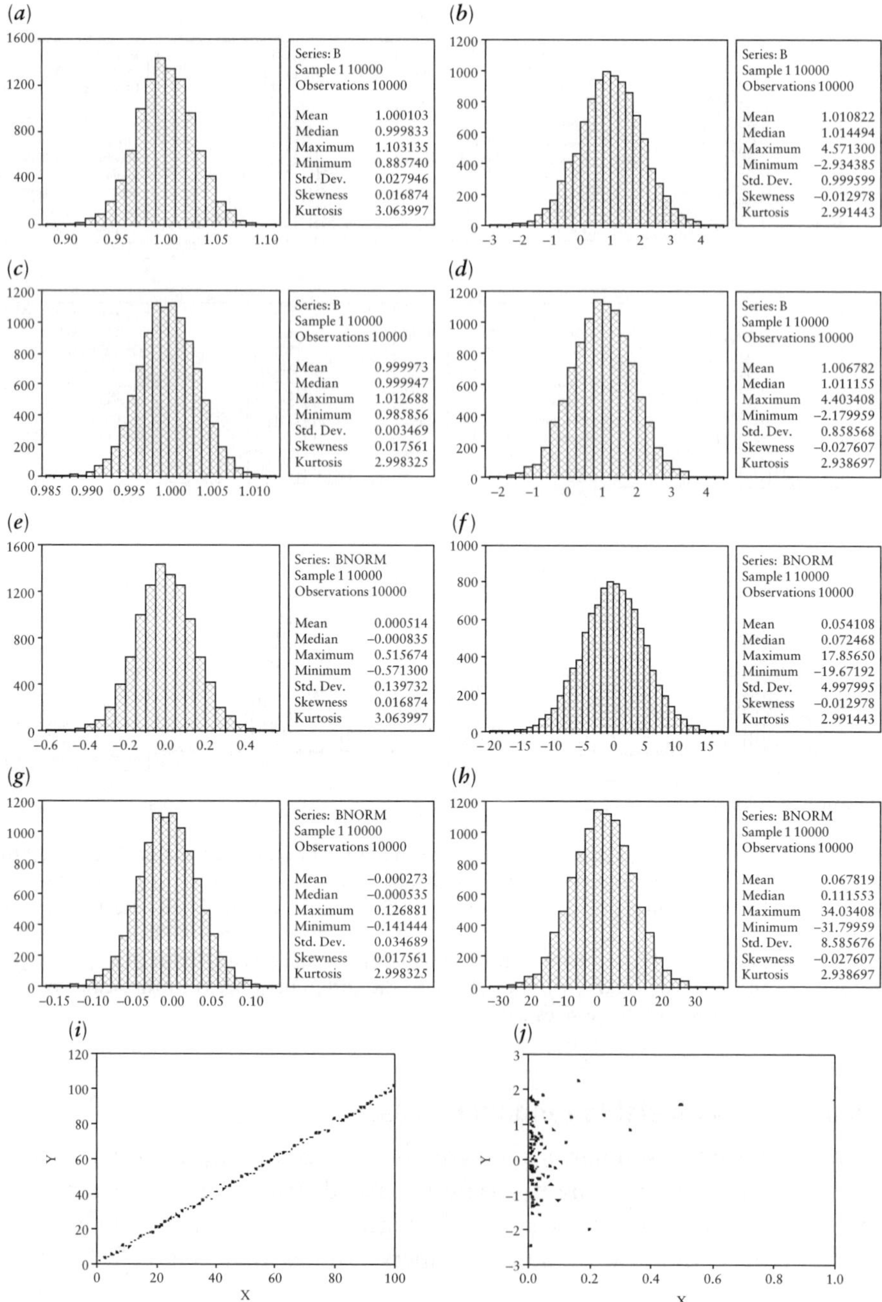

Exhibit 4.4 Simulation Example (Section 4.1.5)

Estimates of the slope parameter (b, denoted by B in (a)–(d)) and a normalized version (BNORM, i.e. $\sqrt{n}(b-1)$ in (e)–(h)) for two data generating processes that do not satisfy Assumption 1*. (a), (c), (e), (g), and (i) are for the model with linear trend and (b), (d), (f), (h), and (j) are for the model with hyperbolic trend. (a)–(b) show the estimates of b for sample size $n = 25$ and (c)–(d) for $n = 100$; (e)–(f) show the outcomes of BNORM for $n = 25$ and (g)–(h) for $n = 100$; (i)–(j) show scatter diagrams for a sample of size $n = 100$ of the models with linear trend (i) and with hyperbolic trend (j).

approximate normality when the orthogonality condition is satisfied, and the histograms (*g–l*) indicate the inconsistency of both b and s^2 when the orthogonality condition is violated. (Note that the horizontal axis differs among the different histograms, so that the width of the distributions is more easily compared by comparing the reported standard deviations of the outcomes.)

Simulations with regressors that are not stable

Next we generate data from the model $y_i = x_i + \varepsilon_i$ with $x_i = i$ (a linear trend) and with $x_i = 1/i$ (a hyperbolic trend). In both cases the disturbances ε_i are NID(0, 1), and the least squares estimator b is unbiased and efficient. Note that these trend models do not satisfy the stability Assumption 1*, as $\lim\left(\frac{1}{n}\sum_{i=1}^{n} i^2\right) = \infty$ and $\lim\left(\frac{1}{n}\sum_{i=1}^{n} i^{-2}\right) = 0$. In the linear trend model, the rate of convergence of b to β is equal to $n\sqrt{n}$ (instead of $\sqrt{n}$), and in the hyperbolic trend model the estimator b does not converge to β (the proof is left as an exercise (see Exercise 4.2)).

Exhibit 4.4 shows the histograms of b and $\sqrt{n}(b-1)$ for 10,000 simulations of both models, with sample sizes $n = 25$ (a, b, e, f) and $n = 100$ (c, d, g, h). By comparing the reported standard deviations in the histograms, it is seen that for the linear trend the distribution of $\sqrt{n}(b-1)$ shrinks to zero for $n \to \infty$ (see (e) and (g)), whereas for the hyperbolic trend the distribution of $\sqrt{n}(b-1)$ does not converge for $n \to \infty$ (see (f) and (h)). For the hyperbolic trend data the least squares estimator b is not consistent (see (b) and (d)), as the observations $x_i = \frac{1}{i}$ of the explanatory variable do not contain sufficient variation for $i \to \infty$.

☞ **Exercises:** T: 4.2.

4.2 Non-linear regression

4.2.1 Motivation

Assumptions on the data generating process

In this section we consider regression models that are non-linear in the parameters. This means that Assumption 6 in Section 3.1.4 (p. 125) no longer holds true. Throughout this section we suppose that the stability Assumption 1* of Section 4.1.2 and the Assumptions 2–5 of Section 3.1.4 are satisfied and that the regressors satisfy the orthogonality condition (4.4) in Section 4.1.3. We now present two examples motivating the use of non-linear models.

E

XM402COF

Example 4.2: **Coffee Sales (continued)**

In this example we consider marketing data on coffee sales. These data are obtained from a controlled marketing experiment in stores in suburban Paris (see A. C. Bemmaor and D. Mouchoux, 'Measuring the Short-Term Effect of In-Store Promotion and Retail Advertising on Brand Sales: A Factorial Experiment', *Journal of Marketing Research*, 28 (1991), 202–14). The question of interest is whether the sensitivity of consumers to price reductions depends on the magnitude of the price reduction. Stated in economic terms, the question is whether the price elasticity of demand for coffee is constant or whether it depends on the price. We will discuss (i) the data, (ii) the linear model with constant elasticity, and (iii) a non-linear model with varying elasticity.

(i) Data

Exhibit 4.5 shows scatter diagrams of weekly sales (q) of two brands of coffee against the applied deal rate (d) in these weeks (both variables are taken in natural logarithms). The data for brand 2 (in (***b***)) were discussed before in Example 2.3 (p. 78). The deal rate d is defined as $d = 1$ if no price reduction applies, $d = 1.05$ if the price reduction is 5 per cent, and $d = 1.15$ if the price reduction is 15 per cent. For each brand there are $n = 12$ observations, six with $d = 1$, three with $d = 1.05$, and three with $d = 1.15$. For both brands, two of the sales figures for $d = 1.15$ are nearly overlapping (the lower figure for brand 1 in (a) and the higher figure for brand 2 in (b)).

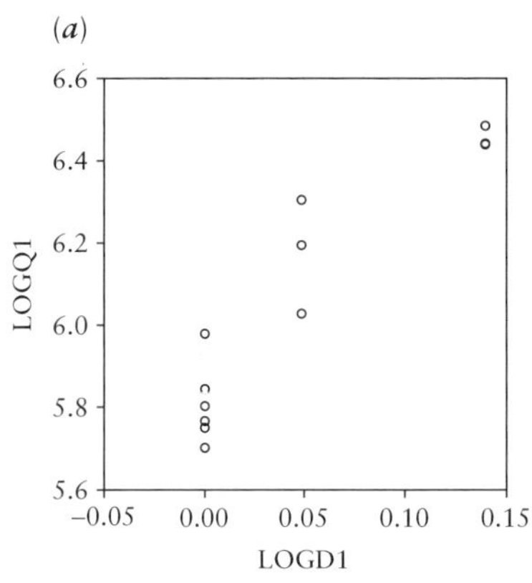

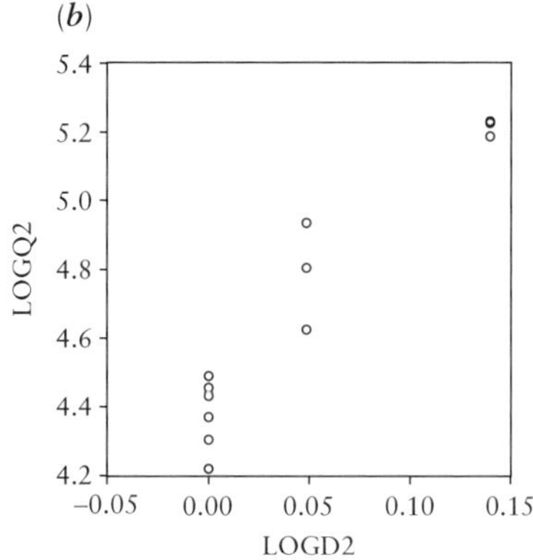

Exhibit 4.5 Coffee Sales (Example 4.2)

Scatter diagrams for two brands of coffee, brand 1 (*a*) and brand 2 (*b*). The variable on the vertical axis is the logarithm of sales (in units of coffee), the variable on the horizontal axis is the logarithm of the deal rate (deal rates of 1.05 and 1.15 correspond to price reductions of 5% and 15% respectively). Both scatter diagrams contain twelve points, but for both brands two observations for deal rate 15% are nearly overlapping (for brand 1 the ones with the lower sales and for brand 2 the ones with the higher sales).

(ii) Linear model with constant elasticity

A simple linear regression model is given by

$$\log(q) = \beta_1 + \beta_2 \log(d) + \varepsilon$$

(here we suppress the observation index i for ease of notation). In this model β_2 is the derivative of $\log(q)$ with respect to $\log(d)$—that is,

$$\beta_2 = \frac{\partial \log(q)}{\partial \log(d)} = \frac{\partial q/q}{\partial d/d},$$

which is the demand elasticity with respect to the deal rate. So the slope in the scatter diagram of $\log(q)$ against $\log(d)$ corresponds to the demand elasticity.

(iii) Non-linear model with varying elasticity

The scatter diagrams in Exhibit 4.5 suggest that for both brands the elasticity may not be constant. The slope seems to decrease for larger values of $\log(d)$, so that the elasticity may be decreasing for higher deal rates. A possible way to model such a rate-specific elasticity is given by the equation

$$\log(q) = \beta_1 + \frac{\beta_2}{\beta_3}(d^{\beta_3} - 1) + \varepsilon. \qquad (4.9)$$

As $(d^{\beta_3} - 1)/\beta_3 \to \log(d)$ for $\beta_3 \to 0$, the limiting model for $\beta_3 = 0$ is the linear model $\log(q) = \beta_1 + \beta_2 \log(d) + \varepsilon$. The deal rate elasticity in (4.9) is equal to

$$\frac{\partial \log q}{\partial \log d} = \frac{\partial \log q}{\partial d/d} = d\frac{\partial \log q}{\partial d} = d\beta_2 d^{\beta_3 - 1} = \beta_2 d^{\beta_3}.$$

The null hypothesis of constant elasticity corresponds to $\beta_3 = 0$—that is, the linear model. The non-linear model (4.9) provides a simple way to model a non-constant elasticity. This example will be further analysed in Sections 4.2.5 and 4.3.9.

XR416FEX

Example 4.3: **Food Expenditure**

As a second example we consider budget data on food expenditure of groups of households. Here the question of interest is whether the food expenditure depends linearly on household income or whether this dependence becomes weaker for higher levels of income. Such a decreasing effect of income on food consumption may be expected because households with higher incomes can afford to spend relatively more on other expenses that provide a higher marginal utility than additional food.

Exhibit 4.6 shows a scatter diagram of the fraction of consumptive expenditure of households spent on food against total consumptive expenditure (measured in \$10,000). These data are analysed (amongst others) in a special issue of the *Journal of Applied Econometrics* (12/5 (1997)). The data consist of averages over groups of households and were obtained by a budget survey

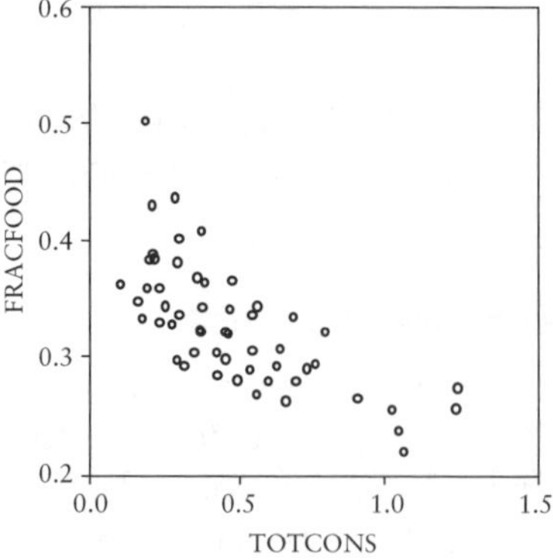

Exhibit 4.6 Food Expenditure (Example 4.3)

Scatter diagram of fifty-four data points of the fraction of expenditure spent on food against total (consumption) expenditure.

in the USA in 1950. The total consumption expenditure is taken as a measure of the household income. We denote the fraction of expenditure spent on food by y, the total consumption expenditure (in \$10,000) by x_2, and the (average) household size by x_3. The scatter diagram indicates that the effect of income on the fraction spent on food declines for higher income levels. Such a relation can be expressed by the non-linear model

$$y = \beta_1 + \beta_2 x_2^{\beta_3} + \beta_4 x_3 + \varepsilon.$$

The hypothesis that the fraction spent on food does not depend on household income corresponds to $\beta_3 = 0$, and the hypothesis that it depends linearly on income corresponds to $\beta_3 = 1$. Further analysis of this example is left as an exercise (see Exercise 4.16).

4.2.2 Non-linear least squares

☞ Uses Appendix A.7.

Non-linear regression

The linear regression model $y = X\beta + \varepsilon$ can be written as $y_i = x_i'\beta + \varepsilon_i$, where i $(i = 1, \cdots, n)$ denotes the observation and where x_i' is the ith row of the $n \times k$ matrix X (so that x_i is a $k \times 1$ vector). This model is linear in the unknown parameters β. A non-linear regression model is described by an equation of the form

$$y_i = f(x_i, \beta) + \varepsilon_i, \qquad (4.10)$$

where f is a non-linear function. If the non-linearity is only in x_i—that is, if for fixed x_i the function f is linear in β—then this can be written as $f(x_i, \beta) = \beta_1 f_1(x_i) + \cdots + \beta_k f_k(x_i)$. This is a linear regression model with explanatory variables $f_j(x_i)$, $j = 1, \cdots, k$. In this case the parameters can be estimated by regressing y on the explanatory variables $f_1, \cdots, f_k$. On the other hand, if the function is *non-linear in* β—for instance, as in (4.9)—then the least squares estimation problem to minimize

$$S(\beta) = \sum_{i=1}^{n} \left(y_i - f(x_i, \beta)\right)^2 \qquad (4.11)$$

becomes non-linear. The first order conditions are given by

$$\frac{\partial S(\beta)}{\partial \beta} = -2\sum_{i=1}^{n} (y_i - f(x_i, \beta)) \cdot \frac{\partial f(x_i, \beta)}{\partial \beta} = 0.$$

This gives a set of non-linear normal equations in β. In general the solution of these equations cannot be determined analytically, so that numerical approximations are needed. Numerical aspects are discussed in the next section.

Requirement of identified parameters

The non-linear least squares (NLS) estimator b_{NLS} is defined as the minimizing value of (4.11). We assume that this minimum exists and that it is unique. This imposes conditions on the model. For example, if there exist parameter vectors $\beta_1 \neq \beta_2$ with $f(x_i, \beta_1) = f(x_i, \beta_2)$ for all x_i, then $S(\beta_1) = S(\beta_2)$ in (4.11), in which case minima need not be unique. The parameters of the model (4.10) are said to be *identified* if for all $\beta_1 \neq \beta_2$ there exists a vector x such that $f(x, \beta_1) \neq f(x, \beta_2)$. The parameters of the linear model with $f(x, \beta) = x'\beta$ are always identified provided that the explanatory variables x are not perfectly collinear. So, if Assumption 1 is satisfied so that the regressor matrix X has rank k, then the parameters β of the linear model are identified. An example of a non-linear regression model with unidentified parameters (with a single explanatory variable x) is $f(x, \beta) = \beta_1 e^{\beta_2 + \beta_3 x}$, as two parameter vectors $(\beta_{11}, \beta_{21}, \beta_{31})$ and $(\beta_{12}, \beta_{22}, \beta_{32})$ give the same function values for all values of x if $\beta_{31} = \beta_{32}$ and $\beta_{11} e^{\beta_{21}} = \beta_{12} e^{\beta_{22}}$. To avoid problems in optimization one should work only with models with identified parameters.

Statistical properties of non-linear least squares

The estimator b_{NLS} will in general not be unbiased. Under appropriate assumptions it is a consistent estimator and its variance may be approximated in large samples by

$$\text{var}(b_{NLS}) \approx s^2 (X'X)^{-1},$$

where $s^2 = \frac{1}{n-k}\sum_{i=1}^{n} (y_i - f(x_i, b_{NLS}))^2$ is the NLS estimate of the variance of the disturbance terms ε_i. Here X is the $n \times k$ matrix of first order derivatives of the function f in (4.10) with respect to β—that is,

$$X = \begin{pmatrix} \partial f(x_1, \beta)/\partial \beta' \\ \vdots \\ \partial f(x_n, \beta)/\partial \beta' \end{pmatrix}. \tag{4.12}$$

Note that for the linear model with $f(x_i, \beta) = x_i'\beta$ this gives the matrix X as defined in (3.2) in Section 3.1.2 (p. 120).

Idea of conditions for asymptotic properties

It is beyond the scope of this book to derive the above asymptotic results for b_{NLS}. However, we give an idea of the required assumptions, which are basically the same as the ones discussed in Section 4.1.

Suppose that the data are generated by (4.10) with parameter vector $\beta = \beta_0$. Further suppose that the disturbance terms satisfy Assumptions 2–4, and that Assumption 5 (constant parameters) is also satisfied. Suppose further that Assumption 1* is satisfied with X as defined in (4.12) and evaluated at $\beta = \beta_0$. Let $f_i^0 = f(x_i, \beta_0)$ and $f_i = f(x_i, \beta)$, then the least squares criterion (4.11) can be decomposed as follows:

$$\frac{1}{n}S(\beta) = \frac{1}{n}\sum (y_i - f_i)^2 = \frac{1}{n}\sum (f_i^0 + \varepsilon_i - f_i)^2$$
$$= \frac{1}{n}\sum (f_i^0 - f_i)^2 + \frac{1}{n}\sum \varepsilon_i^2 + \frac{2}{n}\sum (f_i^0 - f_i)\varepsilon_i.$$

Of the three terms in the last expression, the middle one does not depend on β and hence it does not affect the location of the minimum of $S(\beta)$. For $n \to \infty$, the last term will tend (in probability) to zero under appropriate orthogonality conditions. For instance, in the linear model with $f_i = x_i'\beta$, we get $f_i^0 - f_i = x_i'(\beta_0 - \beta)$ and the condition $\text{plim}(\frac{1}{n}\sum x_i\varepsilon_i) = 0$ is the orthogonality condition (4.4). Finally, the first term $\frac{1}{n}\sum (f_i^0 - f_i)^2$ will not vanish for $\beta \neq \beta_0$ if the parameters are identified in the sense that for every $\beta \neq \beta_0$

$$\text{plim}\left(\frac{1}{n}\sum_{i=1}^{n} (f(x_i, \beta_0) - f(x_i, \beta))^2\right) \neq 0.$$

Under the above conditions, the minimum value of $\frac{1}{n}S(\beta)$ is asymptotically only obtained for $\beta = \beta_0$, and hence b_{NLS} is consistent. Under similar conditions b_{NLS} is also *asymptotically normally distributed* in the sense that

$$\sqrt{n}(b_{NLS} - \beta_0) \xrightarrow{d} \text{N}(0, \sigma^2 Q^{-1}) \qquad (4.13)$$

where $Q = \text{plim}(\frac{1}{n}X'X)$ with X the $n \times k$ matrix of first order derivatives defined in (4.12) and evaluated at β_0.

Approximate distribution in finite samples

Under the foregoing conditions, the result in (4.13) means that

$$b_{NLS} \approx \mathrm{N}\left(\beta_0, s^2(X'X)^{-1}\right) \tag{4.14}$$

where X is the matrix defined in (4.12) and evaluated at b_{NLS} and where $s^2 = \frac{1}{n-k}\sum_{i=1}^{n}(y_i - f(x_i, b_{NLS}))^2$ is the NLS estimate of σ^2. Under similar conditions b_{NLS} is also asymptotically efficient, in the sense that $\sqrt{n}(b_{NLS} - \beta_0)$ has the smallest covariance matrix among all consistent estimators of β_0.

The result in (4.14) motivates the use of t-tests and F-tests in a similar way as in Chapter 3. For the F-test the sums of squares are equal to the minimum value of $S(\beta)$ in (4.11) under the null hypothesis and under the alternative hypothesis. That is, let b_{NLS} be the unrestricted non-linear least squares estimator and b_{NLS}^R the restricted estimator obtained by imposing g restrictions under the null hypothesis. Then under the above assumptions the F-test is computed by

$$F = \frac{(e_R'e_R - e'e)/g}{e'e/(n-k)} \approx F(g, n-k),$$

where $e'e = S(b_{NLS})$ is the sum of squares (4.11) obtained for the unrestricted NLS estimate b_{NLS} and $e_R'e_R = S\left(b_{NLS}^R\right)$ is the sum of squares obtained for b_{NLS}^R.

Summary of computations in NLS

The non-linear least squares estimate b_{NLS} is obtained by minimizing the sum of squares (4.11)—for instance, by one of the non-linear optimization algorithms discussed in the next section. Under suitable regularity conditions, and provided that the parameters of the model are identified, the estimator b_{NLS} is consistent and asymptotically normally distributed. Asymptotic t-values and F-tests can be obtained as in the linear regression model, using the fact that in large enough samples $\mathrm{var}(b_{NLS}) \approx s^2(X'X)^{-1}$ where $s^2 = \frac{1}{n-k}\sum e_i^2$ (with $e_i = y_i - f(x_i, b_{NLS})$ the NLS residuals) and where the $n \times k$ regressor matrix X is given in (4.12), evaluated at $\beta = b_{NLS}$. Summarizing,

Computations for NLS

- *Step 1: Estimation.* Estimate β by minimizing (4.11) and determine the NLS residuals $e_i = y_i - f(x_i, b_{NLS})$.
- *Step 2: Testing.* Approximate t- and F-tests can be based on the fact that $b_{NLS} \approx \mathrm{N}(\beta, s^2(X'X)^{-1})$ where $s^2 = \frac{1}{n-k}\sum e_i^2$ and X is given in (4.12).

4.2.3 Non-linear optimization

☞ Uses Appendix A.7.

Numerical aspects

If the model (4.10) is non-linear, the objective function $S(\beta)$ in (4.11) is not quadratic and the optimal value of β cannot be written as an explicit expression in terms of the data (y_i, x_i), $i = 1, \cdots, n$. In this section we consider some numerical aspects of non-linear optimization. The vector of unknown parameters is denoted by θ and the objective function by $F(\theta)$, with column vector of gradients $G(\theta) = \partial F(\theta)/\partial\theta$ and Hessian matrix $H(\theta) = \partial^2 F(\theta)/\partial\theta\partial\theta'$. Optimal values of θ are characterized by the first order conditions

$$G(\theta) = 0.$$

Numerical procedures often involve the following steps.

Iterative optimization

- *Step 1: Start.* Determine an initial estimate of θ, say $\hat{\theta}_0$.
- *Step 2: Improve and repeat.* Determine an improved estimate of θ, say $\hat{\theta}_1$. Iterate these improvements, giving a sequence of estimates $\hat{\theta}_1, \hat{\theta}_2, \hat{\theta}_3, \cdots$.
- *Step 3: Stop.* Stop the iterations if the improvements become sufficiently small.

Remarks on numerical methods

In general there is no guarantee that the final estimate $\hat{\theta}$ is close to the global optimum. Even if $G(\hat{\theta}) \approx 0$, this may correspond to a local optimum. To prevent the calculated $\hat{\theta}$ being only a local optimum instead of a global optimum one can vary the initial estimate of θ in step 1. For instance, we can change each component of the final estimate $\hat{\theta}$ by a certain percentage and take the new values as initial estimates in a new round of iterations. For the stopping rule in step 3, one can consider the percentage changes in the estimated parameters $\hat{\theta}_h$ and $\hat{\theta}_{h+1}$ in two consecutive iterations and the relative improvement $(F(\hat{\theta}_{h+1}) - F(\hat{\theta}_h))/F(\hat{\theta}_h)$. If these changes are small enough, the iterations are stopped. If the improvements in the objective function are small but the changes in the parameters remain large in a sequence of iterations, this may be an indication of identification problems. A possible solution is to adjust the objective function or the underlying model specification.

Several methods are available for the iterations in step 2. Here we discuss two methods that are often applied — namely, Newton–Raphson and Gauss–Newton. Both methods are based on the idea of linear approximation — namely, of the gradient $G(\theta)$ in Newton–Raphson and of the non-linear function $f(x, \beta)$ in Gauss–Newton.

The Newton–Raphson method

The *Newton–Raphson* method is based on the iterative linearization of the first order condition for an optimum — that is, $G(\theta) = 0$. Around a given value $\hat{\theta}_h$, the gradient G can be linearized by $G(\theta) \approx G(\hat{\theta}_h) + H(\hat{\theta}_h)(\theta - \hat{\theta}_h)$. The condition $G(\theta) = 0$ is approximated by the condition $G(\hat{\theta}_h) + H(\hat{\theta}_h)(\theta - \hat{\theta}_h) = 0$. These equations are linear in the unknown parameter vector θ and they are easily solved, giving the next estimate

$$\hat{\theta}_{h+1} = \hat{\theta}_h - H_h^{-1} G_h, \qquad (4.15)$$

where G_h and H_h are the gradient and Hessian matrix evaluated at $\hat{\theta}_h$. Under certain regularity conditions these iterations converge to a local optimum of $F(\theta)$. It depends on the form of the function $F(\theta)$ and on the procedure to determine initial estimates $\hat{\theta}_0$ whether the limiting estimate corresponds to the global optimum. A graphical illustration of this method is given in Exhibit 4.7, which shows the (non-linear) gradient function and two iterations of the algorithm.

Regularization

Sometimes — for instance, if the Hessian matrix is nearly singular — the iterations in (4.15) are adjusted by a regularization factor so that

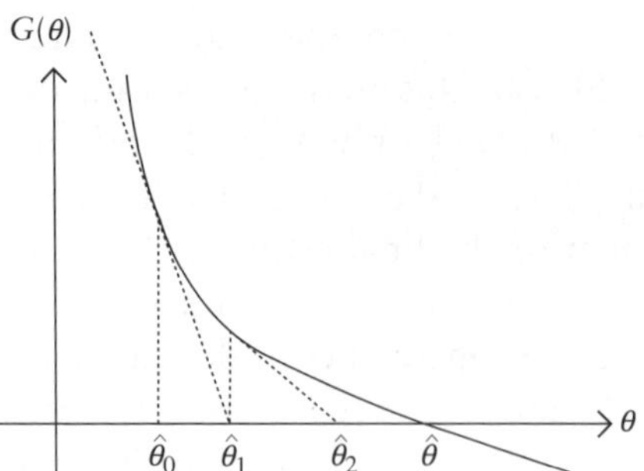

Exhibit 4.7 Newton–Raphson

Illustration of two Newton–Raphson iterations to find the optimum of an objective function. The graph shows the first derivative (G) of the objective function as a function of the parameter θ. The algorithm starts in $\hat{\theta}_0$; $\hat{\theta}_1$ and $\hat{\theta}_2$ denote the estimates obtained in the first and second iteration, and $\hat{\theta}$ is the optimal value.

$$\hat{\theta}_{h+1} = \hat{\theta}_h - (H_h + cI)^{-1} G_h,$$

where $c > 0$ is a chosen constant and I is the identity matrix. This forces the parameter adjustments more in the direction of the gradient. The Newton–Raphson method requires the computation of the gradient vector and the Hessian matrix in each iteration. In some cases these can be computed analytically; in other cases one has to use numerical methods.

The Gauss–Newton method

In many cases the computation of the Hessian matrix is cumbersome and it is much more convenient to use methods that require only the gradient. Therefore we now discuss the *Gauss–Newton* method for non-linear regression models. In this case the parameter vector is $\theta = \beta$ and the objective function is $S(\beta)$ defined in (4.11). The idea is to linearize the function f so that this objective function becomes quadratic.

Derivation of Gauss–Newton iterations

T

Assuming that the function $f(x, \beta)$ is differentiable around a given value $\hat{\beta}_h$, it can be written as

$$f(x, \beta) = f_h(x) + g_h(x)'(\beta - \hat{\beta}_h) + r_h(x),$$

where $f_h(x) = f(x, \hat{\beta}_h)$ and $g_h(x) = \partial f(x, \beta)/\partial \beta$ is the gradient, the $k \times 1$ vector of first order derivatives, evaluated at $\hat{\beta}_h$. Further $r_h(x)$ is a remainder term that becomes negligible if β is close to $\hat{\beta}_h$. If we replace the function $f(x, \beta)$ in (4.11) by its linear approximation, the least squares problem becomes to minimize

$$S_h(\beta) = \sum_{i=1}^{n} \left(y_i - f_h(x_i) - g_h(x_i)'(\beta - \hat{\beta}_h) \right)^2 = \sum_{i=1}^{n} (z_{hi} - g'_{hi}\beta)^2,$$

where $z_{hi} = y_i - f_h(x_i) + g_h(x_i)'\hat{\beta}_h$ and $g_{hi} = g_h(x_i)$ are computed at the given value of $\hat{\beta}_h$. The minimization of $S_h(\beta)$ with respect to β is an ordinary least squares problem with dependent variable z_{hi} and with independent variables g_{hi}. Let z_h be the $n \times 1$ vector with elements z_{hi} and let X_h be the $n \times k$ matrix with rows $g'_{hi} = \partial f(x_i, \beta)/\partial \beta'$ —that is, the matrix (4.12) evaluated at $\hat{\beta}_h$. Further let

$$e_{hi} = y_i - f(x_i, \hat{\beta}_h)$$

be the residuals of the non-linear regression model (4.10) corresponding to $\hat{\beta}_h$. The value of β that minimizes $S_h(\beta)$ is obtained by regressing z_h on X_h, so that $\hat{\beta}_{h+1} = (X'_h X_h)^{-1} X'_h z_h = (X'_h X_h)^{-1} X'_h (e_h + X_h \hat{\beta}_h)$, and using the fact that $z_h = e_h + X_h \hat{\beta}_h$ we get

$$\hat{\beta}_{h+1} = \hat{\beta}_h + (X'_h X_h)^{-1} X'_h e_h. \qquad (4.16)$$

So, in each Gauss–Newton iteration the parameter adjustment $\hat{\beta}_{h+1} - \hat{\beta}_h$ is obtained by regressing the residuals e_h of the last estimated model on the gradient matrix X_h evaluated at $\hat{\beta}_h$. The Gauss–Newton iterations are repeated until the estimates converge. The usual expression for the variance of least squares estimators in the final iteration is $\sigma^2(X'X)^{-1}$, where X is the gradient matrix evaluated at the final estimate $\hat{\beta}$. This is precisely the asymptotic approximation of the variance of the non-linear least squares estimator b_{NLS} in (4.14). So asymptotic standard errors of $\hat{\beta}$ are immediately obtained from the final regression in (4.16).

T

Comparison of the two methods

Finally, we compare the Gauss–Newton iterations (4.16) with those of Newton–Raphson in (4.15) for the least squares criterion $S(\beta)$ in (4.11). For the criterion function $F(\theta) = S(\beta)$, the gradient and Hessian at $\hat{\beta}_h$ are given by

$$\frac{\partial S}{\partial \beta} = -2\sum_{i=1}^{n}\left(y_i - f(x_i, \beta)\right)\frac{\partial f(x_i, \beta)}{\partial \beta} = -2X_h' e_h$$

$$\frac{\partial^2 S}{\partial \beta \partial \beta'} = 2\sum_{i=1}^{n}\frac{\partial f(x_i, \beta)}{\partial \beta}\frac{\partial f(x_i, \beta)}{\partial \beta'} - 2\sum_{i=1}^{n}\left(y_i - f(x_i, \beta)\right)\frac{\partial^2 f(x_i, \beta)}{\partial \beta \partial \beta'}$$

$$= 2X_h' X_h - 2\sum_{i=1}^{n} e_{hi}\frac{\partial^2 f(x_i, \beta)}{\partial \beta \partial \beta'}.$$

So the Newton–Raphson iterations (4.15) reduce to those of Gauss–Newton (4.16) if we neglect the last term in the above expression for the Hessian. This can also be motivated asymptotically, as $\frac{1}{n}X'X$ has a finite and non-zero limit (under Assumption 1*) and the term $\frac{1}{n}\sum e_{hi}\frac{\partial^2 f}{\partial \beta \partial \beta'}$ converges to zero for $n \to \infty$ (under appropriate orthogonality conditions).

☞ **Exercises:** S: 4.9; E: 4.13b, 4.16b, c.

4.2.4 The Lagrange Multiplier test

☞ Uses Appendix A.7, A.8.

For the computation of the F-test at the end of Section 4.2.2 we have to perform two non-linear optimizations, one in the restricted model and another one in the unrestricted model. We now discuss an alternative approach for testing parameter restrictions that needs the estimates only of the restricted model. This test is based on the method of Lagrange for minimization under restrictions.

Interpretation of the Lagrange multiplier in the linear model

For simplicity we first consider the case of a linear model with linear restrictions, so that

$$y = X_1\beta_1 + X_2\beta_2 + \varepsilon, \qquad H_0: \beta_2 = 0, \tag{4.17}$$

where β_2 contains g parameters and β_1 contains the remaining $k - g$ parameters. We assume that the restricted model contains a constant term, so that X_1 contains a column with all elements equal to 1. The *Lagrange method* states that the least squares estimates under the null hypothesis are obtained by minimization of the (unconstrained) Lagrange function

$$\Lambda(\beta_1, \beta_2, \lambda) = S(\beta_1, \beta_2) + 2\lambda'\beta_2, \tag{4.18}$$

where $S(\beta_1, \beta_2) = (y - X_1\beta_1 - X_2\beta_2)'(y - X_1\beta_1 - X_2\beta_2)$ is the least squares criterion function and λ is a vector with the g Lagrange multipliers. The first order conditions for a minimum are given by

$$\frac{\partial\Lambda}{\partial\beta_1} = -2X_1'(y - X_1b_1 - X_2b_2) = 0,$$
$$\frac{\partial\Lambda}{\partial\beta_2} = -2X_2'(y - X_1b_1 - X_2b_2) + 2\hat{\lambda} = 0,$$
$$\frac{\partial\Lambda}{\partial\lambda} = 2b_2 = 0.$$

Substituting $b_2 = 0$ in the first condition shows that $X_1'(y - X_1b_1) = 0$— that is, $b_1 = b_R = (X_1'X_1)^{-1}X_1'y$ is the restricted least squares estimate obtained by regressing y on X_1. If we write $e_R = y - X_1b_R$ for the corresponding restricted least squared residuals, then the above three first order conditions can be written as

$$X_1'e_R = 0, \qquad \hat{\lambda} = X_2'e_R, \qquad b_2 = 0. \tag{4.19}$$

In particular, $\frac{\partial\Lambda}{\partial\beta_2} = \frac{\partial S}{\partial\beta_2} + 2\lambda = 0$, so that (evaluated at the restricted estimates)

$$-2\hat{\lambda} = \frac{\partial S(b_1, 0)}{\partial\beta_2}.$$

So $\hat{\lambda}$ measures the marginal decrease of the least squares criterion S in (4.11), which can be achieved by relaxing the restriction that $\beta_2 = 0$. This is illustrated graphically in Exhibit 4.8. In (*a*) the slope $\hat{\lambda}$ is nearly zero (and the

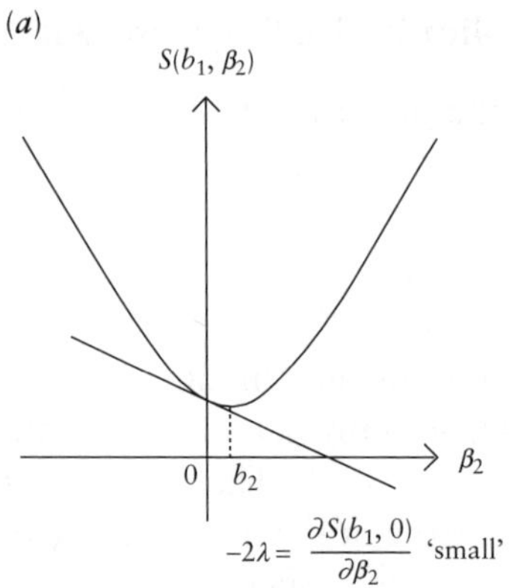

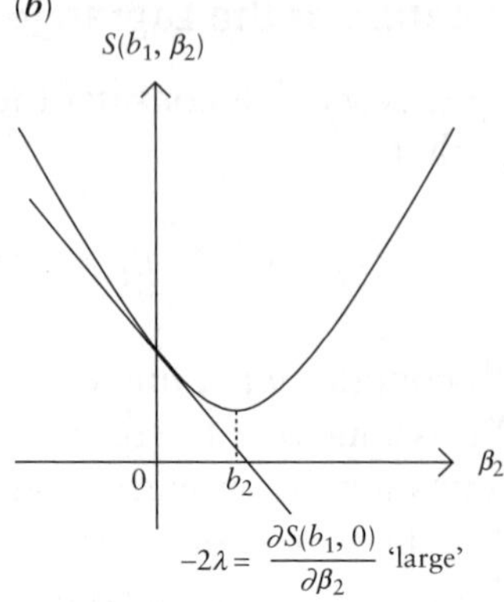

Exhibit 4.8 **Lagrange multiplier**

Graphical interpretation of the Lagrange multiplier in constrained optimization. The graphs show the objective function as a function of the parameter β_2. In (***a***) the restriction $\beta_2 = 0$ is close to the unrestricted minimizing value (b_2), whereas in (***b***) $\beta_2 = 0$ is further away from b_2.

value of S at $\beta_2 = 0$ is nearly minimal), whereas in (b) the slope $\hat{\lambda}$ is further away from zero (and the value of S at $\beta_2 = 0$ is further away from the minimum).

The hypothesis $\beta_2 = 0$ is acceptable if the sum of squares S does not increase much by imposing this restriction—that is, if $\hat{\lambda}$ is sufficiently small. This suggests that the null hypothesis can be tested by testing whether $\hat{\lambda}$ differs significantly from zero. For this purpose we need to know the distribution of $\hat{\lambda}$ under the null hypothesis that $\beta_2 = 0$.

T

Derivation of *LM*-test statistic

Under the null hypothesis that $\beta_2 = 0$, it follows that

$$e_R = y - X_1 b_R = M_1 y = M_1(X_1\beta_1 + \varepsilon) = M_1\varepsilon,$$

where $M_1 = I - X_1(X_1'X_1)^{-1}X_1'$. Under the standard Assumptions 1–7 of Section 3.1.4 (p. 125–6), there holds $\varepsilon \sim \mathrm{N}(0, \sigma^2 I)$ so that $e_R \sim \mathrm{N}(0, \sigma^2 M_1)$ and

$$\hat{\lambda} = X_2' e_R \sim \mathrm{N}(0, \sigma^2 X_2' M_1 X_2).$$

This means that $\hat{\lambda}'(X_2'M_1X_2)^{-1}\hat{\lambda}/\sigma^2$ is distributed as $\chi^2(g)$. If the unknown variance σ^2 is replaced by the consistent estimator $\hat{\sigma}^2 = \frac{1}{n}e_R'e_R$, then it follows that

$$LM = \hat{\lambda}'(X_2'M_1X_2)^{-1}\hat{\lambda}/\hat{\sigma}^2 \approx \chi^2(g). \tag{4.20}$$

This is called the *Lagrange Multiplier* test statistic. The null hypothesis is rejected for large values of LM, as the value of $\hat{\lambda}$ then differs significantly from zero. Of course we could also use the unbiased estimator $s^2 = e_R'e_R/(n-k+g)$ instead of $\hat{\sigma}^2$, but here we use $\hat{\sigma}^2$ for ease of later comparisons. The difference between s^2 and $\hat{\sigma}^2$ is small if n is sufficiently large and it disappears for $n \to \infty$.

Computation of *LM*-test by auxiliary regressions

The expression for the LM-test in (4.20) involves the inverse of the matrix $X_2'M_1X_2$. It is convenient to compute the LM-test in an alternative way by means of regressions. We will show that the value of the LM-test in (4.20) can be computed by the following steps.

Computation of *LM*-test

- *Step 1: Estimate the restricted model.* Estimate the restricted model under the null hypothesis that $\beta_2 = 0$—that is, regress y on X_1 alone, with result $y = X_1b_R + e_R$, where e_R is the vector of residuals of this regression.
- *Step 2: Auxiliary regression of residuals of step 1.* Regress the residuals e_R of step 1 on the set of all explanatory variables of the unrestricted model—that is, regress e_R on $X = (\,X_1 \quad X_2\,)$.
- *Step 3: $LM = nR^2$ of step 2.* Then $LM = nR^2$ of the regression in step 2, and $LM \approx \chi^2(g)$ if the null hypothesis β_0 holds true (where g is the number of elements of β_2—that is, the number of restrictions under the null hypothesis).

Derivation of auxiliary regressions

T

The proof of the validity of the above three-step computation of the LM-test is based on results obtained in Chapter 3. We proceed as follows. It follows from (4.19) and $\hat{\sigma}^2 = e_R'e_R/n$ that (4.20) can be written as

$$LM = n\frac{e_R'X_2(X_2'M_1X_2)^{-1}X_2'e_R}{e_R'e_R}.$$

To prove that $LM = nR^2$ of step 3, it suffices to prove that the regression in step 2 has total sum of squares $SST = e_R'e_R$ and explained sum of squares $SSE = e_R'X_2(X_2'M_1X_2)^{-1}X_2'e_R$, as by definition $R^2 = SSE/SST$.

First we consider the total sum of squares SST of the regression in step 2. By assumption, the restricted model contains a constant term, and as $X_1'e_R = 0$ it follows that the mean of the restricted residuals e_R is zero. Therefore the total sum of squares of the regresion in step 2 is equal to $SST = \sum(e_{Ri} - \bar{e}_R)^2 = \sum e_{Ri}^2 = e_R'e_R$. Next we consider the explained sum of squares of the regression in step 2. The regression of e_R on X in the model $e_R = X\gamma + \omega$ gives $\hat{\gamma} = (X'X)^{-1}X'e_R$ with explained part $\hat{e}_R = X\hat{\gamma} = X(X'X)^{-1}X'e_R$. As X contains a constant term, it follows that the mean of $\hat{e}_R$ is zero. So the explained sum of squares is

$$SSE = \hat{e}_R'\hat{e}_R = e_R'X(X'X)^{-1}X'e_R.$$

It remains to prove that this can be written as $e_R'X_2(X_2'M_1X_2)^{-1}X_2'e_R$. Now the conditions in (4.19) also imply that, with $X = (X_1 \quad X_2)$, there holds $X'e_R = \begin{pmatrix} X_1'e_R \\ X_2'e_R \end{pmatrix} = \begin{pmatrix} 0 \\ X_2'e_R \end{pmatrix}$. Further it follows from the results in Section 3.4.1 (p. 161) that the covariance matrix of b_2 (the least squares estimator of β_2 in the unrestricted model) is equal to $\text{var}(b_2) = \sigma^2(X_2'M_1X_2)^{-1}$ (see (3.46) (p. 158) for the case where X_2 contains a single column). As the covariance matrix of the unrestricted estimators (b_1, b_2) of (β_1, β_2) is equal to $\sigma^2(X'X)^{-1}$, this means that $(X_2'M_1X_2)^{-1}$ is the lower $g \times g$ diagonal block of $(X'X)^{-1}$. Combining these results gives

$$\begin{aligned} e_R'X(X'X)^{-1}X'e_R &= (0 \ e_R'X_2)(X'X)^{-1}\begin{pmatrix} 0 \\ X_2'e_R \end{pmatrix} \\ &= e_R'X_2(X_2'M_1X_2)^{-1}X_2'e_R. \end{aligned}$$

The above results prove the validity of the three-step procedure to compute the LM-test, so that

$$LM = n\frac{e_R'X(X'X)^{-1}X'e_R}{e_R'e_R} = n\frac{SSE}{SST} = nR^2, \tag{4.21}$$

where R^2 is the coefficient of determination of the *auxiliary regression*

$$e_R = X_1\gamma_1 + X_2\gamma_2 + \omega. \tag{4.22}$$

Interpretation of *LM*-test and relation with *F*-test

The null hypothesis that $\beta_2 = 0$ is rejected for large values of LM—that is, for large values of R^2 in (4.22). Stated intuitively, the restrictions are rejected if the residuals e_R under the null hypothesis can be explained by the variables X_2. The LM-test in the linear model is related to the F-test (3.50). It is left as an exercise (see Exercise 4.6) to prove that in the linear model

$$LM = \frac{ngF}{n - k + gF}. \tag{4.23}$$

This shows that for a large sample size n there holds $LM \approx gF$.

Derivation of *LM*-test in non-linear regression model

Until now we considered the linear regression model (4.17). A similar approach can be followed to perform tests in non-linear regression models. Consider the following testing problem, where β_2 contains g parameters and β_1 the remaining $k - g$ parameters in the model

$$y_i = f(x_i, \beta_1, \beta_2) + \varepsilon, \qquad H_0 : \beta_2 = 0. \tag{4.24}$$

The Lagrange function is defined as in (4.18), with S the non-linear least squares criterion in (4.11). So $S = \sum (y_i - f(x_i, \beta_1, \beta_2))^2$ and

$$\frac{\partial S}{\partial \beta_1} = -2X_1'e, \qquad \frac{\partial S}{\partial \beta_2} = -2X_2'e,$$

where $X_1 = \partial f / \partial \beta_1'$ is the $n \times (k - g)$ matrix of first order derivatives with respect to β_1, $X_2 = \partial f / \partial \beta_2'$ is the $n \times g$ matrix of derivatives with respect to β_2, and $e_i = y_i - f(x_i, \beta_1, \beta_2)$ are the residuals. It follows from (4.19) that the first order conditions $\partial \Lambda / \partial \beta_1 = 0$, $\partial \Lambda / \partial \beta_2 = 0$, and $\partial \Lambda / \partial \lambda = 0$ can be written as

$$X_{1R}'e_R = 0, \ \hat{\lambda} = X_{2R}'e_R, \ \beta_2 = 0.$$

Here X_{1R} and X_{2R} are the matrices of derivatives $X_1 = \partial f / \partial \beta_1'$ and $X_2 = \partial f / \partial \beta_2'$ evaluated at $(\beta_1, \beta_2) = (b_{NLS}^R, 0)$, with b_{NLS}^R the restricted NLS estimator of β_1 under the restriction that $\beta_2 = 0$ and $e_{Ri} = y_i - f\left(x_i, b_{NLS}^R, 0\right)$ are the corresponding residuals. The difference with (4.19) is that X_{1R} and X_{2R} depend on b_{NLS}, so that the normal equations $X_{1R}'e_R = 0$ are non-linear in β_1. As before, the restrictions that $\beta_2 = 0$ can be tested by considering whether $\hat{\lambda}$ differs significantly from zero. Under the conditions of asymptotic normality in (4.14), the test can again be computed (approximately in large enough samples) as in (4.21).

LM-test in non-linear regression model

The foregoing arguments show that the *LM*-test of the null hypothesis that $\beta_2 = 0$ can be computed as

$$LM = nR^2 \approx \chi^2(g),$$

with R^2 of the regression of the restricted residuals $e_{Ri} = y_i - f(x_i, b_{NLS}^R, 0)$ on the gradients $X_1 = \partial f / \partial \beta_1'$ and $X_2 = \partial f / \partial \beta_2'$, evaluated at $(b_{NLS}^R, 0)$. In terms of the Gauss–Newton iterations (4.16), this means that the residuals of the last iteration (in the model estimated under the null hypothesis) are regressed on the full matrix of gradients under the alternative hypothesis and evaluated at $\left(b_{NLS}^R, 0\right)$. The *LM*-test has the advantage that only the smaller model has to be estimated by NLS, followed by an auxiliary linear regression as in (4.22).

Summary of computations for the *LM*-test

The *LM*-test of the hypothesis that $\beta_2 = 0$ in the model $y = f(x, \beta_1, \beta_2) + \varepsilon$ can be computed by means of an auxiliary regression. Let β_2 consist of g components and β_1 of $(k - g)$ components.

> **Computation of *LM*-test**
>
> - *Step 1: Estimate the restricted model.* Estimate the restricted model (with $\beta_2 = 0$ imposed), with corresponding vector of residuals e_R.
> - *Step 2: Auxiliary regression of residuals on full set of regressors.* Regress the residuals e_R on the $n \times k$ matrix of first order derivatives $X = \left(\frac{\partial f}{\partial \beta_1'} \quad \frac{\partial f}{\partial \beta_2'}\right)$.
> - *Step 3: $LM = nR^2$ of the regression in step 2.* Then $LM = nR^2$ of the regression in step 2, and the null hypothesis is rejected for large enough values of the *LM*-statistic. Asymptotically, the *LM*-statistic follows the $\chi^2(g)$ distribution if the hypothesis that $\beta_2 = 0$ holds true.

☞ Exercises: T: 4.6a; S: 4.10; E: 4.13d, 4.16g.

4.2.5 Illustration: Coffee Sales

XM402COF

We illustrate the results on non-linear regression by considering the marketing data of coffee sales discussed before in Example 4.2 (p. 202). We will discuss (i) the model, (ii) the non-linear least squares estimates, (iii) results of the Gauss–Newton iterations, (iv) *t*- and *F*-tests on constant elasticity, and (v) the *LM*-test on constant elasticity.

(i) Model

In Example 4.2 in Section 4.2.1 we considered the non-linear regression model $\log(q_i) = f(d_i, \beta) + \varepsilon_i$ for coffee sales (q) in terms of the deal rate (d) where

$$f(d, \beta) = \beta_1 + \frac{\beta_2}{\beta_3}(d^{\beta_3} - 1).$$

Of special interest is the hypothesis that $\beta_3 = 0$, which corresponds to a constant demand elasticity. This case is obtained in the limit for $\beta_3 \to 0$, which gives the linear model $f(d, \beta) = \beta_1 + \beta_2 \log(d)$.

(ii) Non-linear least squares estimates

We first consider the $n = 12$ data for the first brand of coffee. For a given value of β_3 the model is linear in the parameters β_1 and β_2 and these two parameters can be estimated by regressing $\log(q_i)$ on a constant and $\frac{1}{\beta_3}(d^{\beta_3} - 1)$. Exhibit 4.9 (*a*) shows the minimal value of the least squares criterion (the sum of squared residuals SSR in (4.11)) for a grid of values of β_3. The NLS estimates correspond to the values where SSR is minimal. This grid search gives $\hat{\beta}_3 = -13.43$, with corresponding estimates $\hat{\beta}_1 = 5.81$ and $\hat{\beta}_2 = 10.30$. The SSR at $\hat{\beta}_3$ is of course lower than at $\beta_3 = 0$, and below we will test the hypothesis that $\beta_3 = 0$ by evaluating whether this difference is significant.

(iii) Gauss–Newton iterations

Next we apply the Gauss–Newton algorithm for the estimation of β. As starting values we take $\beta_1 = 0$, $\beta_2 = 1$, and $\beta_3 = 1$. The vector of gradients is given by

$$\frac{\partial f}{\partial \beta_1} = 1,$$

$$\frac{\partial f}{\partial \beta_2} = \frac{1}{\beta_3}(d^{\beta_3} - 1),$$

$$\frac{\partial f}{\partial \beta_3} = -\frac{\beta_2}{\beta_3^2}(d^{\beta_3} - 1) + \frac{\beta_2}{\beta_3} d^{\beta_3} \log(d).$$

Exhibit 4.9 shows the estimates of β_3 (in (*b*)) and the value of SSR (in (*c*)) for a number of iterations of the Gauss–Newton method. This shows that the values of SSR converge, and the same holds true for the parameter estimates. The resulting estimates of a software package are in Panel 2 in Exhibit 4.10. The outcomes are in line with the earlier results based on a grid search for β_3.

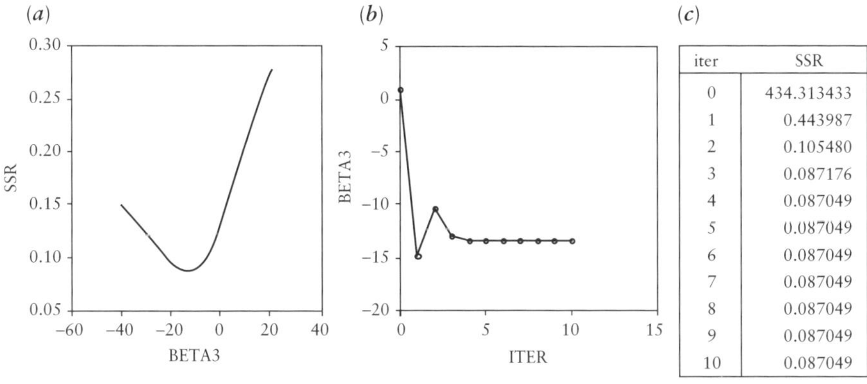

iter	SSR
0	434.313433
1	0.443987
2	0.105480
3	0.087176
4	0.087049
5	0.087049
6	0.087049
7	0.087049
8	0.087049
9	0.087049
10	0.087049

Exhibit 4.9 Coffee Sales (Section 4.2.5)

Non-linear least squares for the model for coffee sales of brand 1. (*a*) shows the minimum SSR that can be obtained for a given value of β_3, and the NLS estimate corresponds to the value of β_3 where this SSR is minimal. (*b*) shows the values of β_3 that are obtained in iterations of the Gauss–Newton algorithm, with starting values $\beta_1 = 0$ and $\beta_2 = \beta_3 = 1$. (*c*) shows the values of SSR that are obtained in the Gauss–Newton iterations.

Panel 1: Dependent Variable: LOGQ1 (brand 1, 12 observations) Method: Least Squares				
Variable	Coefficient	Std. Error	t-Statistic	Prob.
C	5.841739	0.043072	135.6284	0.0000
LOGD1	4.664693	0.581918	8.016063	0.0000
R-squared	0.865333	Sum squared resid		0.132328

Panel 2: Dependent Variable: LOGQ1 (brand 1, 12 observations) Method: Least Squares, convergence achieved after 5 iterations				
LOGQ1 = C(1) + (C(2)/C(3)) * (D1^C(3)−1)				
Parameter	Coefficient	Std. Error	t-Statistic	Prob.
C(1)	5.807118	0.040150	144.6360	0.0000
C(2)	10.29832	3.295386	3.125072	0.0122
C(3)	−13.43073	6.674812	−2.012152	0.0751
R-squared	0.911413	Sum squared resid		0.087049

Panel 3: Dependent Variable: LOGQ2 (brand 2, 12 observations) Method: Least Squares				
Variable	Coefficient	Std. Error	t-Statistic	Prob.
C	4.406561	0.043048	102.3638	0.0000
LOGD2	6.003298	0.581599	10.32206	0.0000
R-squared	0.914196	Sum squared resid		0.132183

Panel 4: Dependent Variable: LOGQ2 (brand 2, 12 observations) Method: Least Squares, convergence achieved after 5 iterations				
LOGQ2 = C(1) + (C(2)/C(3)) * (D2^C(3)−1)				
Parameter	Coefficient	Std. Error	t-Statistic	Prob.
C(1)	4.377804	0.043236	101.2540	0.0000
C(2)	10.28864	3.001698	3.427608	0.0075
C(3)	−8.595289	5.207206	−1.650653	0.1332
R-squared	0.934474	Sum squared resid		0.100944

Panel 5: Dep Var: RESLIN1 (12 residuals of Panel 1 for brand 1)				
Variable	Coefficient	Std. Error	t-Statistic	Prob.
C	−0.034622	0.040150	−0.862313	0.4109
LOGD1	4.449575	2.115810	2.103012	0.0648
LOGD1^2	−31.96557	14.77373	−2.163676	0.0587
R-squared	0.342177			

Panel 6: Dep Var: RESLIN2 (12 residuals of Panel 3 for brand 2)				
Variable	Coefficient	Std. Error	t-Statistic	Prob.
C	−0.028757	0.043236	−0.665120	0.5227
LOGD2	3.695844	2.278436	1.622097	0.1392
LOGD2^2	−26.55080	15.90927	−1.668888	0.1295
R-squared	0.236330			

Exhibit 4.10 Coffee Sales (Section 4.2.5)

Regressions for two brands of coffee, models with constant elasticity (Panels 1 and 3), models with varying elasticity (Panels 2 and 4), and auxiliary regressions for *LM*-tests on constant elasticities (Panels 5 and 6).

This table also contains the NLS estimates for the second brand of coffee (in Panel 4) and the estimates under the null hypothesis that $\beta_3 = 0$ (in Panels 1 and 3).

(iv) *t*- and *F*-tests on constant elasticity

At 5 per cent significance, the t-test fails to reject the null hypothesis that $\beta_3 = 0$ for both brands. The reported P-values (rounded to two decimals) are 0.08 for brand 1 (see Panel 2) and 0.13 for brand 2 (see Panel 4). Note, however, that these values are based on the asymptotic distribution in (4.14) and that the number of observations ($n = 12$) is quite small, so that the P-values are not completely reliable. The F-tests for brands 1 and 2 are given by

$$F_1 = \frac{(0.1323 - 0.0870)/1}{0.0870/(12-3)} = 4.68, \; F_2 = \frac{(0.1322 - 0.1009)/1}{0.1009/(12-3)} = 2.79.$$

The 5 per cent critical value of the $F(1, 9)$ distribution is equal to 5.12, so that the hypothesis that $\beta_3 = 0$ is again not rejected. As can be checked from the t-values in Panels 2 and 4 in Exhibit 4.10, the F-values are not equal to the squares of the t-value of β_3. The relation $F = t^2$ for a single parameter restriction was shown in Chapter 3 to be valid for linear models, but for non-linear models this no longer holds true.

(v) *LM*-test on constant elasticity

Next we compute the LM-test for the hypothesis that $\beta_3 = 0$. To compute this test, the residuals of the log-linear models (corresponding to $\beta_3 = 0$) are regressed on the partial derivatives $\partial f/\partial\beta_i$ (evaluated at the estimated parameters under the null hypothesis, so that limits for $\beta_3 \to 0$ should be taken). This gives

$$\frac{\partial f}{\partial \beta_1} = 1,$$
$$\frac{\partial f}{\partial \beta_2} = \lim_{\beta_3 \to 0}\left(\frac{d^{\beta_3} - 1}{\beta_3}\right) = \log(d),$$
$$\frac{\partial f}{\partial \beta_3} = \lim_{\beta_3 \to 0}\left(\frac{\beta_2}{\beta_3}\left(d^{\beta_3}\log(d) - \frac{1}{\beta_3}(d^{\beta_3} - 1)\right)\right) = \beta_2(\log(d))^2,$$

so the relevant regressors in step 2 of the LM computation scheme are 1, $\log(d)$, and $(\log(d))^2$. The results of the auxiliary regressions in (4.22) for the two brands are in Panels 5 and 6 in Exhibit 4.10. So the test statistics (rounded to two decimals) are $LM_1 = 12R_1^2 = 12 \cdot 0.34 = 4.11$ and $LM_2 = 12R_2^2 = 12 \cdot 0.24 = 2.84$. The 5 per cent critical value of the $\chi^2(1)$ distribution is equal to 3.84, so that in this case the null hypothesis is rejected for brand 1, but not for brand 2.

4.3 Maximum likelihood

4.3.1 Motivation

Two approaches in estimation

In Section 1.3.1 (p. 41) we discussed two approaches in parameter estimation. One is based on the idea of minimizing the distance between the data and the model parameters in some way. Least squares is an example of this approach. Although this is a very useful method, it is not always the most appropriate approach, and for some models it is even impossible to apply this method, as will become clear in later chapters. Another approach in parameter estimation is to maximize the likelihood of the parameters for the observed data. Then the parameters are chosen in such a way that the observed data become as likely or 'probable' as possible. In this section we will discuss the method of maximum likelihood (ML) in more detail. We will consider the general framework and we will use the linear model as an illustration. The ML method is the appropriate estimation method for a great variety of models, and applications models of special interest in business and economics will be discussed in later chapters.

Some disadvantages of least squares

If we apply least squares in the linear model $y = X\beta + \varepsilon$, then the estimator is given by

$$b = (X'X)^{-1}X'y = \beta + (X'X)^{-1}X'\varepsilon.$$

This means that the (unobserved) disturbances ε affect the outcome of b in a linear way. If some of the disturbances ε_i are large, these observations have a relatively large impact on the estimates. There are several ways to reduce the influence of such observations—for instance, by adjusting the model, by transforming the data, or by using another criterion than least squares. These methods are discussed in Chapter 5. Another approach is to replace the normal distribution of the disturbances by another distribution—for instance, one that has fatter tails. We recall from Section 3.1.4 (p. 127) that OLS is the best linear unbiased estimator under Assumptions 1–6.

However, if the disturbances are not normally distributed (so that Assumption 7 is not satisfied), there exist non-linear estimators that are more efficient. Asymptotically, the most efficient estimators are the maximum likelihood estimators.

Example 4.4: **Stock Market Returns (continued)**

XM404SMR

We investigate the assumption of normally distributed disturbances in the CAPM for stock market returns discussed before in Example 2.1 (p. 76–7). We will discuss (i) the possibility of fat tails in returns data, (ii) the least squares residuals, and (iii) choice of the distribution of the disturbances.

(i) **Possibility of fat tails in returns data**

Traders on financial markets may react relatively strongly to positive or negative news, and in particular they may react to the behaviour of fellow traders. This kind of herd behaviour may cause excessive up and down swings of stock prices, so that the returns may be larger (both positive and negative) than would normally be expected. Such periods of shared panic or euphoria among traders may lead to returns far away from the long-run mean—that is, in the tail of the distribution of returns.

(ii) **Least squares residuals**

The data consist of excess returns data for the sector of cyclical consumer goods (denoted by y) and for the whole market (denoted by x) in the UK. The CAPM postulates the linear model

$$y_i = \alpha + \beta x_i + \varepsilon_i, \quad i = 1, \cdots, n.$$

A scatter diagram of these data is given in Exhibit 2.1 (*c*) (p. 77). The parameters α and β can be estimated by least squares. The histogram of the least squares residuals is shown in Exhibit 4.11 (*a*). It seems somewhat doubtful that the disturbances are normally distributed. The sample mean and standard deviation of the residuals e_i are $\bar{e} = 0$ and $s = \sqrt{\sum e_i^2/(n-1)} = 5.53$. Two of the $n = 240$ residuals have values of around $-20 \approx -3.6\,s$. For the normal distribution, the probability of outcomes more than 3.6 standard deviations away from the mean is around 0.0003, which is much smaller than $2/240 = 0.0083$. The histogram indicates that the disturbances may have fatter tails than the normal distribution.

(iii) **Choice of distribution of the disturbances**

As an alternative, one could for instance use a t-distribution for the disturbances. Exhibit 4.11 (*b*) shows the density function of the standard normal

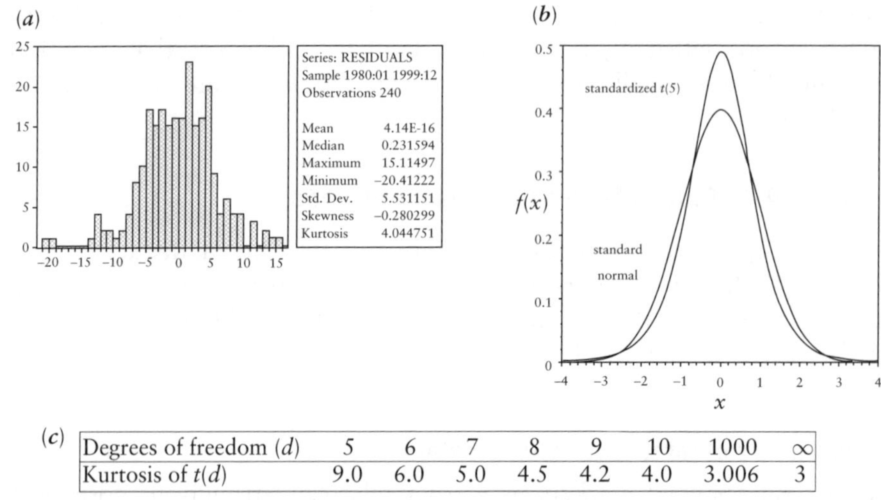

(c)

Degrees of freedom (d)	5	6	7	8	9	10	1000	∞
Kurtosis of $t(d)$	9.0	6.0	5.0	4.5	4.2	4.0	3.006	3

Exhibit 4.11 Stock Market Returns (Example 4.4)

(*a*) shows the histogram of the least squares residuals of the CAPM for the sector of cyclical consumer goods in the UK. (*b*) shows two distributions, the standard normal distribution and the $t(5)$ distribution (scaled so that it has variance 1); the t-distribution has fatter tails than the normal distribution. (*c*) shows the kurtosis of t-distributions for selected values of the number of degrees of freedom.

distribution and of the $t(5)$ distribution (scaled so that it also has variance equal to one). The table with values of the kurtosis in Exhibit 4.11 (*c*) shows that t-distributions have fatter tails than the normal distribution. In the next sections we describe the method of maximum likelihood that can be applied for any specified distribution.

4.3.2 Maximum likelihood estimation

☞ Uses Section 1.3.1; Appendix A.7.

The idea of maximum likelihood

In Section 1.3.1 we discussed the method of maximum likelihood estimation for data consisting of a random sample from a population with fixed mean and variance. The idea is illustrated in Exhibit 4.12. The observed values of the dependent variable are indicated by crosses. Clearly, this set of outcomes is much more probable for the distribution on the right side than for the distribution on the left side. This is expressed by saying that the distribution on the right side has a larger likelihood then the one on the left side. For a random sample $y_1, \cdots, y_n$ from the normal density $N(\mu, \sigma^2)$, the normal distribution with the largest likelihood is given by $\hat{\mu} = \bar{y}$ and $\hat{\sigma}^2 = \frac{1}{n}\sum (y_i - \bar{y})^2$, see Section 1.3.1.

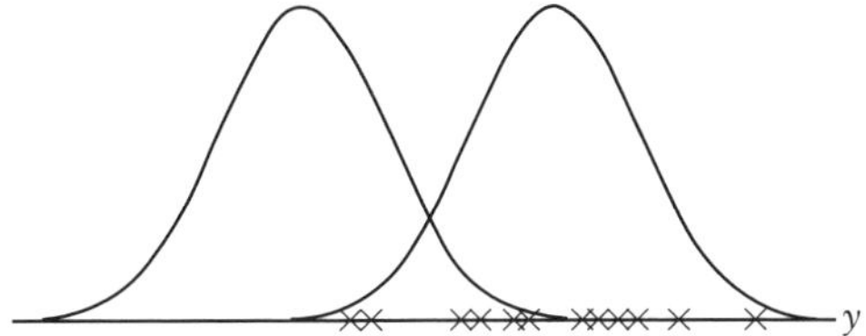

Exhibit 4.12 Maximum likelihood

The set of actually observed outcomes of y (denoted by the crosses on the horizontal axis) is less probable for the distribution on the left than for the distribution on the right; the distribution on the left therefore has a smaller likelihood than the distribution on the right.

Likelihood function and log-likelihood

We now extend the maximum likelihood (ML) method to more general models. The observed data on the dependent variable are denoted by the $n \times 1$ vector y and those on the explanatory variables by the $n \times k$ matrix X. In order to apply ML, the model is expressed in terms of a joint probability density $p(y, X, \theta)$. Here θ denotes the vector of model parameters, and for given values of θ, $p(y, X, \theta)$ is a probability density for (y, X). On the other hand, for given (y, X) the *likelihood function* is defined by

$$L(\theta) = p(y, X, \theta). \tag{4.25}$$

Stated intuitively, this measures the 'probability' of observing the data (y, X) for different values of θ. It is natural to prefer parameter values for which this 'probability' is large. The maximum likelihood estimator $\hat{\theta}_{ML}$ is defined as the value of θ that maximizes the function $L(\theta)$ over the set of allowed parameter values. In practice, for computational convenience one often maximizes the logarithmic likelihood function or *log-likelihood*

$$l(\theta) = \log(L(\theta)). \tag{4.26}$$

As the logarithm is a monotonically increasing transformation, the maximum of (4.25) and (4.26) is obtained for the same values of θ. An attractive property of ML is that it is invariant under reparametrization. That is, suppose that the model is formulated in terms of another parameter vector ψ and that ψ and θ are related by an invertible transformation $\psi = h(\theta)$. Then the ML estimates are related by $\hat{\psi}_{ML} = h(\hat{\theta}_{ML})$ (see also Section 1.3.1).

The log-likelihood can be decomposed if the observations (y_i, x_i) are mutually independent for $i = 1, \cdots, n$. If the probability density function for the ith observation is $p_\theta(y_i, x_i)$, then the joint density is $p(y, X, \theta) = \Pi_{i=1}^n p_\theta(y_i, x_i)$ so that

$$l(\theta) = \sum_{i=1}^{n} \log(p_\theta(y_i, x_i)) = \sum_{i=1}^{n} l_i(\theta), \tag{4.27}$$

where $l_i(\theta) = \log(p_\theta(y_i, x_i))$ is the contribution of the ith observation to the log-likelihood $l(\theta)$.

T

Numerical aspects of optimization

In general the computation of $\hat{\theta}_{ML}$ is a *non-linear optimization* problem. Solution methods were discussed in Section 4.2.3. For instance, the Newton–Raphson iterations in (4.15) can be performed with the gradient vector $G = \partial l(\theta)/\partial\theta$ and with the Hessian matrix $H = \partial^2 l(\theta)/\partial\theta\partial\theta'$, or equivalently with $G = \frac{1}{n}\partial l(\theta)/\partial\theta$ and $H = \frac{1}{n}\partial^2 l(\theta)/\partial\theta\partial\theta'$. If the observations are mutually independent, the result in (4.27) shows that then

$$G = \frac{1}{n}\sum_{i=1}^{n} \frac{\partial l_i}{\partial\theta} \quad , \quad H = \frac{1}{n}\sum_{i=1}^{n} \frac{\partial^2 l_i}{\partial\theta\partial\theta'}.$$

In this case it is also possible to perform the iterations in a way where only the first order derivatives (and no second order derivatives) need to be computed. In this case there holds

$$\frac{1}{n}\sum_{i=1}^{n} \frac{\partial^2 l_i}{\partial\theta\partial\theta'} \approx E\left[\frac{\partial^2 l_i}{\partial\theta\partial\theta'}\right] = -E\left[\frac{\partial l_i}{\partial\theta}\frac{\partial l_i}{\partial\theta'}\right] \approx -\frac{1}{n}\sum_{i=1}^{n} \frac{\partial l_i}{\partial\theta}\frac{\partial l_i}{\partial\theta'}. \tag{4.28}$$

The first and the last approximate equalities follow from the law of large numbers, as the terms $\partial^2 l_i/\partial\theta\partial\theta'$ are mutually independent and the same holds true for the terms $(\partial l_i/\partial\theta)(\partial l_i/\partial\theta')$. The middle equality in (4.28) follows from (1.46) in Section 1.3.2 (p. 45) (applied for each individual observation i separately). The last term in (4.28) is called the *outer product of gradients*. Using this approximation, the Newton–Raphson iterations (4.15) become

$$\hat{\theta}_{h+1} = \hat{\theta}_h + \left(\frac{1}{n}\sum_{i=1}^{n} \frac{\partial l_i}{\partial\theta}\frac{\partial l_i}{\partial\theta'}\right)^{-1}\left(\frac{1}{n}\sum_{i=1}^{n} \frac{\partial l_i}{\partial\theta}\right).$$

This is called the method of Berndt, Hall, Hall, and Hausman (abbreviated as BHHH). As discussed in Section 4.2.3, one sometimes uses a regularization factor and replaces the above matrix inverse by $\left(\frac{1}{n}\sum_{i=1}^{n} \frac{\partial l_i}{\partial\theta}\frac{\partial l_i}{\partial\theta'} + cI\right)^{-1}$ with $c > 0$ a chosen constant and I the identity matrix. This is called the Marquardt algorithm. These methods have the advantage that they require only the first order derivatives, but they may give less precise estimates as compared with methods using the second order derivatives.

ML in the linear model

In some cases the ML estimates can be computed analytically. An example is given by the linear model under Assumptions 1–7 of Section 3.1.4 (p. 125–6). In this case

$$y = X\beta + \varepsilon, \quad \varepsilon \sim \mathrm{N}(0, \sigma^2 I), \tag{4.29}$$

so that $y \sim \mathrm{N}(X\beta, \sigma^2 I)$. This model has parameters $\theta = (\beta', \sigma^2)'$. Using the expression (1.21) in Section 1.2.3 (p. 31) for the density of the multivariate normal distribution with mean $\mu = X\beta$ and covariance matrix $\Sigma = \sigma^2 I$, it follows that the log-likelihood (4.26) is given by

$$l(\beta, \sigma^2) = -\frac{n}{2}\log(2\pi) - \frac{n}{2}\log(\sigma^2) - \frac{1}{2\sigma^2}(y - X\beta)'(y - X\beta). \tag{4.30}$$

The maximum likelihood estimates are obtained from the first order conditions

$$\frac{\partial l}{\partial \beta} = \frac{1}{\sigma^2}X'(y - X\beta) = 0, \tag{4.31}$$

$$\frac{\partial l}{\partial \sigma^2} = -\frac{n}{2\sigma^2} + \frac{1}{2\sigma^4}(y - X\beta)'(y - X\beta) = 0. \tag{4.32}$$

The solutions are given by

$$b_{ML} = (X'X)^{-1}X'y = b, \tag{4.33}$$

$$s^2_{ML} = \frac{1}{n}(y - Xb)'(y - Xb) = \frac{n-k}{n}s^2, \tag{4.34}$$

where s^2 is the (unbiased) least squares estimator of σ^2 discussed in Section 3.1.5 (p. 128). This shows that b_{ML} coincides with the least squares estimator b, and that s^2_{ML} differs from the unbiased estimator s^2 by a factor that tends to 1 for $n \to \infty$.

ML in non-linear regression models

In a similar way, the ML estimates of β in the non-linear regression model $y_i = f(x_i, \beta) + \varepsilon_i$ with $\varepsilon_i \sim \mathrm{NID}(0, \sigma^2)$ are equal to the non-linear least squares estimates b_{NLS} (see Exercise 4.6).

☞ **Exercises:** T: 4.6c; S: 4.12a, b, d–f.

4.3.3 Asymptotic properties

☞ Uses Sections 1.3.2, 1.3.3; Appendix A.7.

Asymptotic distribution of ML estimators

As was discussed in Section 1.3.3 (p. 51–2), maximum likelihood estimators have asymptotically optimal statistical properties. Apart from mild regularity conditions on the log-likelihood (4.26), the main condition is that the model (that is, the joint probability distribution of the data) has been specified correctly. Then the maximum likelihood estimator is *consistent*, is *asymptotically efficient*, and has an *asymptotically normal* distribution. The model is correctly specified if there exists a parameter θ_0 so that the data are generated by the probability distribution $p(y, X, \theta_0)$. The asymptotic efficiency means that $\sqrt{n}(\hat{\theta}_{ML} - \theta_0)$ has the smallest covariance matrix among all consistent estimators of θ_0 (the reason for scaling with $\sqrt{n}$ is to get a finite, non-zero covariance matrix in the limit). Some regularity conditions are necessary for generalizations of the central limit theorem to hold true, so that

$$\sqrt{n}(\hat{\theta}_{ML} - \theta_0) \xrightarrow{d} \mathrm{N}(0, \mathcal{I}_0^{-1}). \tag{4.35}$$

Here $\mathcal{I}_0$ is the asymptotic *information matrix* evaluated at θ_0—that is, $\mathcal{I}_0 = \lim_{n\to\infty}\left(\frac{1}{n}\mathcal{I}_n(\theta_0)\right)$ where

$$\mathcal{I}_n(\theta_0) = E\left[\frac{\partial l}{\partial \theta}\frac{\partial l}{\partial \theta'}\right] = -E\left[\frac{\partial^2 l}{\partial \theta \partial \theta'}\right] \tag{4.36}$$

is the information matrix (evaluated at $\theta = \theta_0$) for sample size n of the data (y, X) in (4.25).

Approximate distribution for finite samples

This means that, asymptotically, conventional t- and F-tests can be based on the approximate distribution

$$\hat{\theta}_{ML} \approx \mathrm{N}\left(\theta_0, \mathcal{I}_n^{-1}(\hat{\theta}_{ML})\right)$$

where we used that in large enough samples $\mathrm{var}(\hat{\theta}_{ML}) \approx \frac{1}{n}\mathcal{I}_0^{-1} \approx \mathcal{I}_n^{-1}(\theta_0) \approx \mathcal{I}_n^{-1}(\hat{\theta}_{ML})$. In the following sections we discuss some alternative tests that are of much practical use—namely, the Likelihood Ratio test, the Wald test, and the Lagrange Multiplier test. These tests are compared in Section 4.3.8.

T

Illustration of asymptotic results for ML in the linear model

Now we illustrate the above asymptotic results for the linear model $y = X\beta + \varepsilon$ that satisfies Assumptions 1–7. Here the parameter vector is given by the $(k+1) \times 1$ vector $\theta = (\beta', \sigma^2)'$ and the vector of ML estimators by $\hat{\theta}_{ML} = \left(b'_{ML}, s^2_{ML}\right)'$ in (4.33) and (4.34). According to (4.35), these estimators (when measured in deviation from θ_0 and multiplied by $\sqrt{n}$) are asymptotically normally distributed with covariance matrix $\mathcal{I}_0^{-1}$. The second order derivatives of the log-likelihood in (4.30) are given by

$$\frac{\partial^2 l}{\partial\beta\partial\beta'} = -\frac{1}{\sigma^2}X'X, \tag{4.37}$$

$$\frac{\partial^2 l}{\partial\beta\partial\sigma^2} = -\frac{1}{\sigma^4}X'(y - X\beta), \tag{4.38}$$

$$\frac{\partial^2 l}{\partial\sigma^2\partial\sigma^2} = \frac{n}{2\sigma^4} - \frac{1}{\sigma^6}(y - X\beta)'(y - X\beta). \tag{4.39}$$

Using (4.29) and the assumption that X is fixed, for $\beta = \beta_0$ there holds $E[X'(y - X\beta_0)] = X'E[y - X\beta_0] = 0$ and $E[(y - X\beta_0)'(y - X\beta_0)] = n\sigma^2$, so that the $(k+1) \times (k+1)$ information matrix in (4.36) is given by

$$\mathcal{I}_n(\theta_0) = \begin{pmatrix} \frac{1}{\sigma^2}X'X & 0 \\ 0 & \frac{n}{2\sigma^4} \end{pmatrix}. \tag{4.40}$$

The asymptotic covariance matrix is obtained from $\mathcal{I}_0 = \lim\left(\frac{1}{n}\mathcal{I}_n(\theta_0)\right)$, and under Assumption 1* in Section 4.1.2 it follows that

$$\mathcal{I}_0 = \begin{pmatrix} \frac{1}{\sigma^2}Q & 0 \\ 0 & \frac{1}{2\sigma^4} \end{pmatrix}.$$

Therefore, large sample approximations of the distribution of the ML estimators (4.33) and (4.34) for the linear model are given by

$$b_{ML} \approx \mathrm{N}(\beta_0, \sigma^2(X'X)^{-1}), \tag{4.41}$$

$$s^2_{ML} \approx \mathrm{N}\left(\sigma^2, \frac{2\sigma^4}{n}\right). \tag{4.42}$$

Actually, for the model (4.29) the distribution in (4.41) holds exactly, as was shown in Section 3.3.1 (p. 152). In Section 3.4.1 we considered the F-test for the null hypothesis of g linear restrictions on the model (4.29) of the form $R\beta = r$, where R is a $g \times k$ matrix of rank g. In (3.50) this test is computed in the form

$$F = \frac{(e'_R e_R - e'e)/g}{e'e/(n-k)}, \tag{4.43}$$

where $e_R'e_R$ and $e'e$ are the sums of squared residuals under the null and alternative hypothesis respectively. Under Assumptions 1–7, the test statistic (4.43) has the $F(g, n-k)$ distribution.

Summary of computations in ML

To estimate model parameters by the method of maximum likelihood, one proceeds as follows.

> **Computations in ML**
>
> - *Step 1: Formulate the log-likelihood.* First one has to specify the form of the likelihood function—that is, the form of the joint probability function $L(\theta) = p(y, X, \theta)$. For given data y and X, this should be a known function of θ—that is, for every choice of θ the value of $L(\theta)$ can be computed. The criterion for estimation is the maximization of $L(\theta)$, or, equivalently, the maximization of the log-likelihood $l(\theta) = \log(L(\theta))$.
> - *Step 2: Maximize the log-likelihood.* For the observed data y and X, the log-likelihood $l(\theta) = \log(p(y, X, \theta))$ is maximized with respect to the parameters θ. This is often a non-linear optimization problem, and numerical aspects were discussed in Section 4.3.2.
> - *Step 3: Asymptotic tests.* Approximate t-values and F-tests for the ML estimates $\hat{\theta}_{ML}$ can be obtained from the fact that this estimator is consistent and approximately normally distributed with covariance matrix $\text{var}(\hat{\theta}_{ML}) \approx \mathcal{I}_n^{-1}(\hat{\theta}_{ML})$, where $\mathcal{I}_n$ is the information matrix defined in (4.36) and evaluated at $\hat{\theta}_{ML}$. In Section 4.3.8 we will make some comments on the actual computation of this covariance matrix.

☞ Exercises: E: 4.17a–f.

4.3.4 The Likelihood Ratio test

☞ Uses Appendix A.8.

General form of the *LR*-test

Suppose that the model is given by the likelihood function (4.25) and that the null hypothesis imposes g independent restrictions $r(\theta) = 0$ on the parameters. We denote the ML estimator under the null hypothesis by $\hat{\theta}_0$ and the ML estimator under the alternative by $\hat{\theta}_1$. The *Likelihood Ratio test* is based on the loss of log-likelihood that results if the restrictions are imposed—that is,

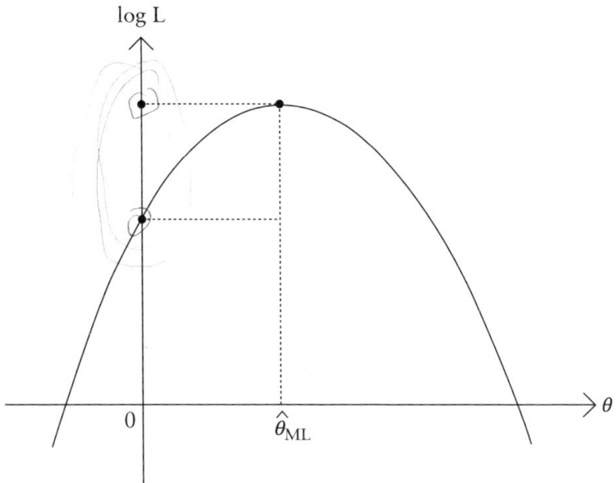

Exhibit 4.13 Likelihood Ratio test

Graphical illustration of the Likelihood Ratio test. The restrictions are rejected if the loss in the log-likelihood (measured on the vertical axis) is too large.

$$LR = 2\log(L(\hat{\theta}_1)) - 2\log(L(\hat{\theta}_0)) = 2l(\hat{\theta}_1) - 2l(\hat{\theta}_0). \tag{4.44}$$

A graphical illustration of this test is given in Exhibit 4.13. Here θ is a single parameter and the null hypothesis is that $\theta = 0$. This hypothesis is rejected if the (vertical) distance between the log-likelihoods is too large. It can be shown that, if the null hypothesis is true,

$$LR \xrightarrow{d} \chi^2(g). \tag{4.45}$$

The null hypothesis is rejected if LR is sufficiently large. For a proof of (4.45) we refer to textbooks on statistics (see Chapter 1, Further Reading (p. 68)).

LR-test in the linear model

T

As an illustration we consider the linear model $y = X\beta + \varepsilon$ with Assumptions 1–7. To compute the LR-test for the null hypothesis that $R\beta = r$ (with R a $g \times k$ matrix of rank g), we use a technique known as *concentration* of the log-likelihood. This means that the ML optimization problem is transformed into another one that involves less parameters. For a linear model it follows from (4.32) that, for given value of β, the optimal value of σ^2 is given by $\sigma^2(\beta) = \frac{1}{n}(y - X\beta)'(y - X\beta)$. Substituting this in (4.30), the optimal value of β is obtained by maximizing the concentrated log-likelihood

$$l(\beta, \sigma^2(\beta)) = -\frac{n}{2}\log(2\pi) - \frac{n}{2}\log(\sigma^2(\beta)) - \frac{n}{2}.$$

This function of β is maximal if $\sigma^2(\beta)$ is minimal, and this corresponds to least squares. The maximum likelihood estimator of β under the null hypothesis is therefore given by the restricted least squares estimator b_R, and the above expression for the log-likelihood shows that

$$LR = 2l(\hat{\theta}_1) - 2l(\hat{\theta}_0) = -n\log(\sigma^2(b)) + n\log(\sigma^2(b_R)) = n\log\left(\frac{e_R'e_R}{e'e}\right),$$

where b is the unrestricted least squares estimator. The relation between this test and the F-test in (4.43) is given by

$$LR = n\log\left(1 + \frac{e_R'e_R - e'e}{e'e}\right) = n\log\left(1 + \frac{g}{n-k}F\right). \qquad (4.46)$$

This result holds true for linear models with linear restrictions under the null hypothesis. It does not in general hold true for other types of models and restrictions.

Computational disadvantage of the *LR*-test

The LR-test (4.44) requires that ML estimates are determined both for the unrestricted model and for the restricted model. If the required computations turn out to be complicated, then it may be more convenient to estimate only one of these two models. Two of such test methods are discussed in the following two sections.

☞ **Exercises:** E: 4.13e, **4.14b**, **4.15b**, 4.16f.

4.3.5 The Wald test

Idea of Wald test (for a single parameter)

Whereas the LR-test requires two optimizations (ML under the null hypothesis and ML under the alternative hypothesis), the *Wald test* is based on the unrestricted model alone. This test considers how far the restrictions are satisfied by the unrestricted estimator $\hat{\theta}_1$. This is illustrated graphically in Exhibit 4.14 for the simple case of a single parameter θ with the restriction $\theta = 0$. The (horizontal) difference between the unrestricted estimator $\hat{\theta}_1$ and $\theta = 0$ is related to the (vertical) difference in the log-likelihoods. Because only the unrestricted model is estimated, an indication of this vertical distance is obtained by the curvature $\frac{d^2l}{d\theta^2}$ of the log-likelihood l in $\hat{\theta}_1$. The exhibit shows that this distance becomes larger for larger curvatures. Asymptotically, the curvature is equal to the inverse of the covariance matrix of $\hat{\theta}_1$, see

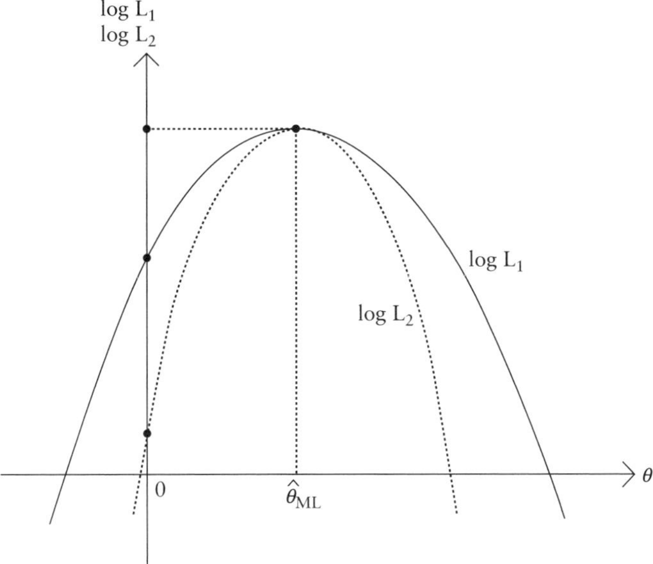

Exhibit 4.14 Wald test

Graphical illustration of the Wald test. The restrictions are rejected if the estimated parameters are too far away from the restrictions of the null hypothesis. This is taken as an indication that the loss in the log-likelihood is too large, and this 'vertical' difference is larger if the log-likelihood function has a larger curvature.

(4.35) and (4.36). This motivates to estimate the loss in log-likelihood, that results from imposing the restriction that $\theta = 0$, by the Wald test statistic

$$W = \hat{\theta}_1^2 \cdot \left(-\frac{d^2 l}{d\theta^2} \right) \approx \left(\frac{\hat{\theta}_1}{s_{\hat{\theta}1}} \right)^2 \approx \chi^2(1).$$

Here $s_{\hat{\theta}1}^2$ is an estimate of the variance of the unrestricted ML estimator $\hat{\theta}_1$ and the asymptotic distribution follows from (4.35). The expression $\hat{\theta}_1 / s_{\hat{\theta}1}$ is analogous to the t-value in a regression model (see Section 3.3.1 (p. 153)). The t-test for a single parameter restriction is also obtained by estimating the unrestricted model and evaluating whether the estimated parameter differs significantly from zero.

Derivation of Wald test for general parameter restrictions

T

Now we describe the Wald test for the general case of g non-linear restrictions $r(\theta) = 0$. Suppose that this hypothesis holds true for the DGP, so that $r(\theta_0) = 0$. Because $\hat{\theta}_1$ is consistent, it follows that in large enough samples $r(\hat{\theta}_1) \approx r(\theta_0) + R_0(\hat{\theta}_1 - \theta_0) = R_0(\hat{\theta}_1 - \theta_0)$, where $R_0 = \partial r / \partial \theta'$ evaluated at $\theta = \theta_0$. It follows from (4.35) that

$$\sqrt{n}r(\hat{\theta}_1) \xrightarrow{d} \mathrm{N}(0,\ R_0\mathcal{I}_0^{-1}R_0'). \tag{4.47}$$

Let $R_1 = \partial r/\partial\theta'$ evaluated at $\theta = \hat{\theta}_1$ and let $\mathcal{I}_n(\hat{\theta}_1)$ be the information matrix for sample size n defined in (4.36) evaluated at $\theta = \hat{\theta}_1$. Then $\mathrm{plim}(R_1) = R_0$ and $\mathrm{plim}(\frac{1}{n}\mathcal{I}_n(\hat{\theta}_1)) = \mathcal{I}_0$, and (4.47) implies that

$$r(\hat{\theta}_1) \approx \mathrm{N}(0,\ R_1\mathcal{I}_n^{-1}(\hat{\theta}_1)R_1').$$

Now recall that, if the $g \times 1$ vector z has the distribution $\mathrm{N}(0, V)$ then $z'V^{-1}z \sim \chi^2(g)$, so that under the null hypothesis

$$W = r(\hat{\theta}_1)'(R_1\mathcal{I}_n^{-1}(\hat{\theta}_1)R_1')^{-1}r(\hat{\theta}_1) \approx \chi^2(g). \tag{4.48}$$

This is an attractive test if the restricted model is difficult to estimate—for instance, if the parameter restriction $r(\theta) = 0$ is non-linear. A disadvantage is that the numerical outcome of the test may depend on the way the model and the restrictions are formulated (see Exercise 4.16 for an example).

T

Wald test in the linear model

We illustrate the Wald test by considering the linear model $y = X\beta + \varepsilon$ with Assumptions 1–7 and the linear hypothesis that $R\beta = r$ (with R a $g \times k$ matrix of rank g). The parameter vector $\theta = (\beta', \sigma^2)'$ contains $k + 1$ parameters and the restrictions are given by $r(\theta) = 0$, where $r(\theta) = R\beta - r = (R\ 0)\theta - r$. The unrestricted estimators are given by b in (4.33) and $s_{ML}^2 = e'e/n$ in (4.34), where $e = y - Xb$ are the unrestricted least squares residuals. So in (4.48) we have $r(\hat{\theta}_1) = Rb - r$ and $R_1 = \partial r/\partial\theta' = (\partial r/\partial\beta'\ \partial r/\partial\sigma^2) = (R\ 0)$. An asymptotic approximation of the inverse of the information matrix in (4.48) is obtained from (4.40)—that is,

$$\mathcal{I}_n^{-1}(\hat{\theta}_1) \approx \mathcal{I}_n^{-1}(\theta_0) = \begin{pmatrix} \sigma^2(X'X)^{-1} & 0 \\ 0 & \frac{2\sigma^4}{n} \end{pmatrix} \approx \begin{pmatrix} s_{ML}^2(X'X)^{-1} & 0 \\ 0 & \frac{2s_{ML}^4}{n} \end{pmatrix}.$$

Combining these results, we get $R_1\mathcal{I}_n^{-1}(\hat{\theta}_1)R_1' \approx s_{ML}^2R(X'X)^{-1}R'$ so that

$$\begin{aligned} W &= (Rb - r)'\left(s_{ML}^2R(X'X)^{-1}R'\right)^{-1}(Rb - r) \\ &= \frac{(Rb - r)'\left(R(X'X)^{-1}R'\right)^{-1}(Rb - r)}{e'e/n} \\ &= \frac{ng}{n-k}F. \end{aligned} \tag{4.49}$$

The last equality follows from (3.54) in Section 3.4.1 (p. 165). This formula, like the one in (4.46), holds true only for linear models with linear restrictions. (Some software packages, such as EViews, compute the Wald test with the OLS estimate

s^2 instead of the ML estimate s^2_{ML}, in which case the relation (4.49) becomes $W = gF$; in EViews, tests of coefficient restrictions are computed in two ways, one with the F-test and with P-values based on the $F(g, n-k)$ distribution, and another with the Wald test $W = gF$ and with P-values based on the $\chi^2(g)$ distribution.)

Relation between Wald test and *t*-test

For the case of a single restriction (so that $g = 1$) we obtained in Section 3.4.1 the result that $F = t^2$. Substituting this in (4.49) we get the following relation between the Wald test and the t-test for a single parameter restriction:

$$W = \frac{n}{n-k} t^2. \tag{4.50}$$

The cause of the difference lies in the different estimator of the variance σ^2 of the error terms, s^2_{ML} in the Wald test and the OLS estimator s^2 in the t-test. Because of the relation $s^2_{ML} = \frac{n-k}{n} s^2$ in (4.34), the relation (4.50) can also be written as

$$W = t^2 \cdot \frac{s^2}{s^2_{ML}}.$$

☞ **Exercises:** S: **4.11a, b, d, e**; E: 4.13c, 4.14c, **4.15b, 4.16h–j.**

4.3.6 The Lagrange Multiplier test

☞ Uses Section 1.2.3; Appendix A.8.

Formulation of parameter restrictions by means of Lagrange parameters

As a third test we discuss the *Lagrange Multiplier test*, also called the *score test*. This test considers whether the gradient (also called the 'score') of the unrestricted likelihood function is sufficiently close to zero at the restricted estimate $\hat{\theta}_0$. This test was discussed in Section 4.2.4 for regression models where we minimize the sum of squares criterion (4.11), but now we consider this within the framework of ML estimation where we maximize the log-likelihood criterion (4.26).

The null hypothesis $r(\theta) = 0$ imposes g independent restrictions on θ. For simplicity of notation we suppose that the vector of parameters θ can be split in two parts, $\theta = \begin{pmatrix} \theta_1 \\ \theta_2 \end{pmatrix}$, and that the restrictions are given by $\theta_2 = 0$, where θ_2 contains g components. Then the restricted ML estimator can be obtained by maximizing the Lagrange function

$$\Lambda(\theta_1, \theta_2, \lambda) = l(\theta_1, \theta_2) - \lambda'\theta_2.$$

Here λ is the $g \times 1$ vector of Lagrange multipliers. The restricted maximum satisfies the first order conditions

$$\frac{\partial \Lambda}{\partial \theta_1} = \frac{\partial l}{\partial \theta_1} = 0, \quad \frac{\partial \Lambda}{\partial \theta_2} = \frac{\partial l}{\partial \theta_2} - \hat{\lambda} = 0, \quad \frac{\partial \Lambda}{\partial \lambda} = \theta_2 = 0. \tag{4.51}$$

So the Lagrange multipliers $\hat{\lambda} = \partial l / \partial \theta_2$ measure the marginal increase in the log-likelihood l if the restrictions $\theta_2 = 0$ are relaxed. The idea is to reject the restrictions if these marginal effects are too large.

Idea of *LM*-test for a single parameter

This is illustrated graphically in Exhibit 4.15 for the simple case of a single parameter ($g = 1$, $\theta = \theta_2$ contains one component, and there are no additional components θ_1). The slope $\hat{\lambda} = \partial l / \partial \theta$ in $\theta = 0$ is related to the (vertical) difference in the log-likelihoods $l(\hat{\theta}) - l(0)$, where $\hat{\theta}$ is the unrestricted ML estimate. This difference is larger for smaller curvatures $\partial^2 l / \partial \theta^2$ in $\theta = 0$. This suggests evaluating the loss in log-likelihood, which results from imposing the restriction that $\theta = 0$, by the *LM*-test statistic

$$LM = \frac{(\partial l / \partial \theta)^2}{-\partial^2 l / \partial \theta^2} \quad \text{(evaluated at } \theta = 0\text{)}.$$

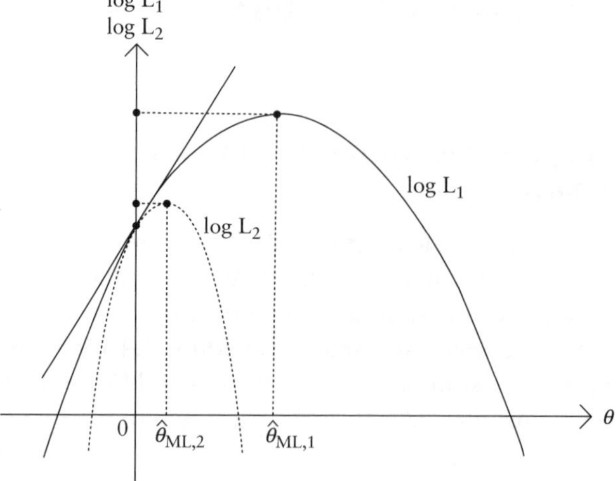

Exhibit 4.15 Lagrange Multiplier test

Graphical illustration of the Lagrange Multiplier test. The restrictions are rejected if the gradient (evaluated at the restricted parameter estimates) differs too much from zero. This is taken as an indication that the loss in the log-likelihood is too large, and this 'vertical' difference is larger if the log-likelihood has a smaller curvature.

T

Derivation of *LM*-test for general parameter restrictions

Now we return to the more general case in (4.51) and consider a test for the null hypothesis that $\theta_2 = 0$ that is based on the magnitude of the vector of Lagrange multipliers λ. To test the significance of the Lagrange multipliers we have to derive the distribution under the null hypothesis of $\hat{\lambda} = \partial l / \partial \theta_2$ (evaluated at the restricted ML estimates). This derivation (which runs till (4.54) below) goes as follows. Let

$$z(\theta) = \begin{pmatrix} \partial l / \partial \theta_1 \\ \partial l / \partial \theta_2 \end{pmatrix}$$

be the gradient vector of the log-likelihood (4.26) for n observations. Then, under weak regularity conditions, this vector evaluated at the parameter $\theta = \theta_0$ of the DGP has the property that

$$\frac{1}{\sqrt{n}} z(\theta_0) \xrightarrow{d} \mathrm{N}(0, \mathcal{I}_0). \tag{4.52}$$

The proof of asymptotic normality is beyond the scope of this book and is based on generalizations of the central limit theorem. Here we only consider the mean and variance of $z(\theta_0)$. To compute the mean, we write $l(\theta) = \log(p_\theta(y))$ with $p_\theta(y) = p(y, X, \theta)$ the density in (4.25). Then

$$\begin{aligned} E[z(\theta_0)] &= E\left[\frac{\partial \log p_\theta(y)}{\partial \theta}\right]_{|\theta=\theta_0} = E\left[\frac{1}{p_{\theta_0}(y)} \frac{\partial p_\theta(y)}{\partial \theta}\right]_{|\theta=\theta_0} \\ &= \int \left(\frac{p_{\theta_0}(y)}{p_{\theta_0}(y)} \frac{\partial p_\theta(y)}{\partial \theta} dy\right)_{|\theta=\theta_0} = \left(\frac{\partial \int p_\theta(y) dy}{\partial \theta}\right)_{|\theta=\theta_0} = 0 \end{aligned} \tag{4.53}$$

as $\int p_\theta(y) dy = 1$ for every density function function of y. Using (4.36) it then follows that

$$\mathrm{var}(z(\theta_0)) = E\left[\frac{\partial l}{\partial \theta} \frac{\partial l}{\partial \theta'}\right]_{|\theta=\theta_0} = \mathcal{I}_n(\theta_0).$$

The two foregoing results show that $\frac{1}{\sqrt{n}} z(\theta_0)$ in (4.52) has mean zero and covariance matrix $\frac{1}{n} \mathcal{I}_n(\theta_0)$. For $n \to \infty$ this covariance matrix converges to $\mathcal{I}_0$.

If the null hypothesis $\theta_2 = 0$ is true and $\hat{\theta}_0$ denotes the ML estimator of θ under this hypothesis, then $\hat{\theta}_0$ is a consistent estimator of θ_0 and (4.52) implies that

$$\frac{1}{\sqrt{n}} z(\hat{\theta}_0) \approx \mathrm{N}(0, \mathcal{I}_0).$$

Now the Lagrange multipliers $\hat{\lambda}$ in (4.51) are given by $\hat{\lambda} = \partial l / \partial \theta_2$ under the restriction that $\partial l / \partial \theta_1 = 0$. If we decompose the matrix $\mathcal{I}_0$ in (4.52) in accordance with the components $z_1 = \partial l/\partial\theta_1$ and $z_2 = \partial l/\partial\theta_2$ of z and use the result (1.22) on conditional distributions of the normal distribution, it follows that

$$\frac{1}{\sqrt{n}}\hat{\lambda} = \left(\frac{1}{\sqrt{n}}z_2|z_1 = 0\right) \approx \mathrm{N}(0, \mathcal{I}_{022} - \mathcal{I}_{021}\mathcal{I}_{011}^{-1}\mathcal{I}_{012}).$$

If we denote the above covariance matrix by W, it follows that $\hat{\lambda} \approx \mathrm{N}(0, V)$, where $V = nW \approx \mathcal{I}_{22} - \mathcal{I}_{21}\mathcal{I}_{11}^{-1}\mathcal{I}_{12}$ is defined in terms of $\mathcal{I}_n$ in (4.36) with decomposition according to that of z in z_1 and z_2. Therefore $\hat{\lambda}'V^{-1}\hat{\lambda} \approx \chi^2(g)$. As the matrix V^{-1} is equal to the lower diagonal block of the matrix $\mathcal{I}_n^{-1}$, it follows from (4.51) that

$$LM = \hat{\lambda}'V^{-1}\hat{\lambda} = \begin{pmatrix} 0 \\ \hat{\lambda} \end{pmatrix}' \mathcal{I}_n^{-1} \begin{pmatrix} 0 \\ \hat{\lambda} \end{pmatrix} = \left(\frac{\partial l}{\partial\theta}\right)' \mathcal{I}_n^{-1} \left(\frac{\partial l}{\partial\theta}\right).$$

LM-test in terms of the log-likelihood

The above result can be written as

$$LM = \left(\frac{\partial l}{\partial\theta}\right)' \left(-E\left[\frac{\partial^2 l}{\partial\theta\partial\theta'}\right]\right)^{-1} \left(\frac{\partial l}{\partial\theta}\right) \approx \chi^2(g), \qquad (4.54)$$

where the expressions $\partial l/\partial\theta$ and $E[\partial^2 l/\partial\theta\partial\theta']$ are both evaluated at $\theta = \hat{\theta}_0$, the ML estimate under the null hypothesis. The advantage of the *LM*-test is that only the restricted ML estimate $\hat{\theta}_0$ has to be computed. This estimate is then substituted in (4.54) in the gradient and the information matrix of the unrestricted model. So we need to compute the gradient and Hessian matrix of the unrestricted model, but we do not need to optimize the unrestricted likelihood function. Therefore the *LM*-test is attractive if the unrestricted likelihood function is relatively complicated.

4.3.7 *LM*-test in the linear model

Model formulation

As an illustration we apply the *LM*-test (4.54) for the linear model $y = X\beta + \varepsilon$ with Assumptions 1–7. The vector of parameters β is split in two parts $\beta = (\beta_1', \beta_2')'$, where β_2 is a $g \times 1$ vector and β_1 is a $(k-g) \times 1$ vector. The model can be written as $y = X_1\beta_1 + X_2\beta_2 + \varepsilon$ and we consider the null hypothesis that $\beta_2 = 0$.

T

Derivation of *LM*-test with auxiliary regressions

To compute the LM-test (4.54) for this hypothesis, we first note that under the null hypothesis the model is given by $y = X_1\beta_1 + \varepsilon$. According to the results in Section 4.3.2, the ML estimates of this model are given by $b_{ML} = b_R = (X_1'X_1)^{-1}X_1'y$ and $s_R^2 = \frac{1}{n}e_R'e_R$, where $e_R = y - X_1 b_R$ are the restricted least squares residuals. The gradient $\frac{\partial l}{\partial\theta}$ in (4.54), evaluated at $(\beta_1, \beta_2, \sigma^2) = (b_R, 0, s_R^2)$, is given by (4.31) and (4.32), so that

$$\begin{aligned}
\frac{\partial l}{\partial \beta_1} &= \frac{1}{s_R^2}X_1'(y - X_1 b_R) = 0,\\
\frac{\partial l}{\partial \beta_2} &= \frac{1}{s_R^2}X_2'(y - X_1 b_R) = \frac{1}{s_R^2}X_2'e_R,\\
\frac{\partial l}{\partial \sigma^2} &= -\frac{n}{2s_R^2} + \frac{1}{2s_R^4}(y - X_1 b_R)'(y - X_1 b_R) = 0.
\end{aligned}$$

To compute the information matrix in (4.54), evaluated at $(b_R, 0, s_R^2)$, we use the second order derivatives in (4.37), (4.38), and (4.39). The term in (4.37) becomes $-\frac{1}{s_R^2}X'X$. As s_R^2 is a consistent estimator of σ^2 (under the null hypothesis), the expectation of this term is approximately also equal to $-\frac{1}{s_R^2}X'X$. The term in (4.39) becomes $\frac{n}{2s_R^4} - \frac{1}{s_R^6}e_R'e_R = -\frac{n}{2s_R^4}$, and the expectation of this term is approximately the same. Finally, to evaluate (4.38), note that in Section 3.3.1 (p. 152–3) we proved that the least squares estimators b and s^2 are independent. Therefore, if the null hypothesis holds true, the restricted least squares estimators b_R and s_R^2 are also independent. The term in (4.38) is given by $-\frac{1}{s_R^4}X'(y - X_1 b_R)$, and

$$E\left[\frac{1}{s_R^4}X'(y - X_1 b_R)\right] = E\left[\frac{1}{s_R^4}\right]X'E[y - X_1 b_R] = 0,$$

as $E[y - X_1 b_R] = E[y] - X_1 E[b_R] = X_1\beta_1 - X_1\beta_1 = 0$ for $\beta_2 = 0$. Combining the above results, we get

$$-E\left[\left(\frac{\partial^2 l}{\partial\theta\partial\theta'}\right)\right]_{|\theta=\hat{\theta}_0} \approx \begin{pmatrix} \frac{1}{s_R^2}X_1'X_1 & \frac{1}{s_R^2}X_1'X_2 & 0 \\ \frac{1}{s_R^2}X_2'X_1 & \frac{1}{s_R^2}X_2'X_2 & 0 \\ 0 & 0 & \frac{n}{2s_R^4} \end{pmatrix} = \begin{pmatrix} \frac{1}{s_R^2}X'X & 0 \\ 0 & \frac{n}{2s_R^4} \end{pmatrix}.$$

With the above expressions for the gradient and the Hessian matrix, the LM-test (4.54) becomes

$$\begin{aligned}
LM &= \begin{pmatrix} 0 \\ \frac{1}{s_R^2}X_2'e_R \end{pmatrix}'\left(\frac{1}{s_R^2}X'X\right)^{-1}\begin{pmatrix} 0 \\ \frac{1}{s_R^2}X_2'e_R \end{pmatrix}\\
&= \frac{1}{s_R^2}\begin{pmatrix} X_1'e_R \\ X_2'e_R \end{pmatrix}'(X'X)^{-1}\begin{pmatrix} X_1'e_R \\ X_2'e_R \end{pmatrix}\\
&= \frac{e_R'X(X'X)^{-1}X'e_R}{s_R^2}\\
&= n\frac{e_R'X(X'X)^{-1}X'e_R}{e_R'e_R} = nR^2.
\end{aligned} \tag{4.55}$$

Computation of *LM*-test as variable addition test

This is precisely the result (4.21) that was obtained in Section 4.2.4 within the setting of non-linear regression models. This result holds true much more generally—that is, in many cases (non-linear models, non-linear restrictions, non-normal disturbances) the *LM*-test can be computed as follows.

> **Computation of *LM*-test by auxiliary regressions**
>
> - *Step 1: Estimate the restricted model.* Estimate the restricted model, with corresponding residuals e_R.
> - *Step 2: Auxiliary regression of residuals of step 1.* Perform a regression of e_R on all the variables in the unrestricted model. In non-linear models $y = f(x, \beta) + \varepsilon$, the regressors are given by $\frac{\partial f}{\partial \beta'}$; in other types of models the regressors may be of a different nature (several examples will follow in the next chapters).
> - *Step 3: $LM = nR^2$ of step 2.* Then $LM = nR^2 \approx \chi^2(g)$, where R^2 is the R^2 of the regression in step 2.

Because variables are added in step 2 to the variables that are used in step 1, this is also called a *variable addition test*. The precise nature of the variables to be used in the regression in step 2 depends on the particular testing problem at hand. In the rest of this book we will encounter several examples.

☞ Exercises: E: **4.14d**, **4.15b**.

4.3.8 Remarks on tests

☞ Uses Section 1.4.1.

Comparison of three tests

In the foregoing sections we discussed four tests on parameter restrictions (*F*, *LR*, *W*, and *LM*). In this section we give a brief summary and we comment on some computational issues.

Exhibit 4.16 (*a*) gives a graphical illustration of the relation between the *LR*-, *W*-, and *LM*-tests for the case of a single parameter θ with the null hypothesis that $\theta = 0$. The *W*- and *LM*-tests are an approximation of the *LR*-test—that is, the loss in log-likelihood caused by imposing the null hypothesis. The advantage of the *LM*- and *W*-tests is that only one model needs to be estimated. If the restricted model is the simplest to estimate, as is often the

(*a*)

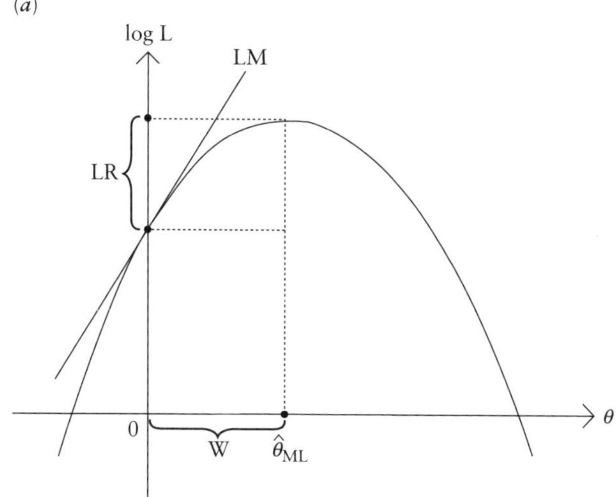

(*b*)

	Test		
	LR	*W*	*LM*
Estimated models	2 (under H_0 and H_1)	1 (under H_1)	1 (under H_0)
Advantage	Optimal power	If model under H_0 is complicated	Simple computations (auxiliary regressions)
Disadvantage	Needs 2 optimizations (ML under H_0 and H_1)	Test depends on parametrization	Power may be small
Main formula	(4.44) $2 \log L(H_1) - 2 \log L(H_0)$	(4.48) (generalizes F-test)	(4.54) and (4.55) $LM = nR^2$

Exhibit 4.16 Comparison of tests

(*a*) gives a graphical illustration of the Likelihood Ratio test, the Wald test, and the Lagrange Multiplier test. The *LR*-test is based on the indicated vertical distance, the *W*-test on the indicated horizontal distance, and the *LM*-test on the indicated gradient. (*b*) contains a summary comparison of the three tests.

case, then the *LM*-test is preferred. In situations where the unrestricted model is the simplest to estimate we can use the *W*-test. Exhibit 4.16 (*b*) gives a summary comparison of the three tests *LR*, *W*, and *LM*.

In Section 4.2.3 we discussed methods for non-linear optimization. In general this involves a number of iterations to improve the estimates and a stopping rule determines when the iterations are ended. In ML estimation one can stop the iterations if the criterion values of the log-likelihood do not change anymore (this is related to the *LR*-test), if the estimates do not change anymore (this is related to the *W*-test, which weighs the changes against the variance of the estimates), or if the gradient has become zero (this is related to the *LM*-test, which weighs the gradient against its variance).

Relations between tests

The relations of the tests LR, W, and LM with the F-test for a linear hypothesis in a linear model is given in (4.46), (4.49), and (4.23). From these expressions the following inequalities can be derived for testing a linear hypothesis in a linear model.

$$LM \leq LR \leq W. \tag{4.56}$$

This is left as an exercise (see Exercise 4.6). As all three statistics have the same asymptotic $\chi^2(g)$ distribution, it follows that the P-values based on this distribution satisfy $P(LM) \geq P(LR) \geq P(W)$. This means that, if the LM-test rejects the null hypothesis, the same holds true for the LR- and W-tests, and, if the W-test fails to reject the null hypothesis, then the same holds true for the LM- and LR-tests. It also follows from (4.23), (4.46), and (4.49) that the three tests are asymptotically (for $n \to \infty$) equivalent to $gF(g, n-k)$, and this converges in distribution to a $\chi^2(g)$ distribution. That is, all four tests are asymptotically equivalent.

χ^2- and F-distribution in testing

To perform the tests LR, W, and LM, it is sometimes preferable to use the critical values of the $gF(g, n-k)$ distribution instead of those of the $\chi^2(g)$ distribution. These critical values are somewhat larger, so that the evidence to reject the null hypothesis should be somewhat stronger than what would be required asymptotically. Exhibit 4.17 shows the 5 per cent critical values for some selected degrees of freedom $(g, n-k)$. This shows that both

g	$gF(g,10)$	$gF(g,100)$	$gF(g,1000)$	$\chi^2(g)$
1	4.96	3.94	3.85	3.84
2	8.21	6.17	6.01	5.99
3	11.12	8.09	7.84	7.81
4	13.91	9.85	9.52	9.49
5	16.63	11.53	11.12	11.07
6	19.30	13.14	12.65	12.59
7	21.95	14.72	14.13	14.07
8	24.57	16.26	15.58	15.51
9	27.18	17.77	17.00	16.92
10	29.78	19.27	18.40	18.31
20	55.48	33.53	31.62	31.41
50	131.86	73.86	68.16	67.50
100	258.84	139.17	125.96	124.34

Exhibit 4.17 F- and χ^2-distributions

The 5% critical values of the chi-squared distribution (last column) for some selected degrees of freedom (g) and the 5% critical values of the scaled F-distribution $gF(g, n-k)$ for different values of $n-k$ (10, 100, and 1000).

methods lead to the same results for large sample sizes, but that for small samples the critical values of the $gF(g, n-k)$ distribution may be considerably larger than those of the $\chi^2(g)$ distribution.

Alternative expressions for tests and information matrix

T

Sometimes the W-test and the LM-test are computed by expressions that differ from (4.48) and (4.54) by using approximations of the information matrix. Note that each of the values $\theta = \theta_0$ (of the DGP), $\theta = \hat{\theta}_1$ (ML in the unrestricted model) and $\theta = \hat{\theta}_0$ (ML under the null hypothesis) are asymptotically equal (if the null hypothesis is true), as ML estimators are consistent so that $\text{plim}(\hat{\theta}_1) = \theta_0$ and $\text{plim}(\hat{\theta}_0) = \theta_0$. For instance, for independent observations the log-likelihood is given by (4.27) and the information matrix in (4.48) and (4.54) can be approximated by using

$$\frac{1}{n}\mathcal{I}_n = -\frac{1}{n}E\left[\sum_{i=1}^{n}\frac{\partial^2 l_i}{\partial\theta\partial\theta'}\right] \approx -\frac{1}{n}\sum\frac{\partial^2 l_i}{\partial\theta\partial\theta'} \approx \frac{1}{n}\sum\frac{\partial l_i}{\partial\theta}\frac{\partial l_i}{\partial\theta'} \qquad (4.57)$$

evaluated at any of the three parameter values θ_0, $\hat{\theta}_1$, or $\hat{\theta}_0$. The last approximation was stated in (4.28) and may be convenient as it requires only the first order derivatives, but it may provide less precise estimates as compared to methods that make use of the second order derivatives. All these expressions can also be used as approximations of the asymptotic covariance matrix of the ML estimator in (4.35).

☞ Exercises: T: 4.5, 4.6**b**; E: 4.13, 4.14, 4.15, 4.16.

4.3.9 Two examples

We illustrate ML estimation and testing with two examples. The first example concerns a linear model with non-normal disturbances, the second example a non-linear regression model with normally distributed disturbances. Of course it is also of interest to apply the LR-, W-, and LM-tests for a linear hypothesis in a linear model and to compare the outcomes with the F-test of Chapter 3. This is left for the exercises (see Exercises 4.14 and 4.15). Further, ML has important applications for other types of models that cannot be expressed as a regression. Such applications will be discussed in Chapters 6 and 7.

Example 4.5: **Stock Market Returns (continued)**

We consider again the CAPM for the sector of cyclical consumer goods of Example 4.4 in Section 4.3.1. We will discuss (i) the specification of the log-likelihood for $t(5)$-distributed disturbances, (ii) outcomes of the ML estimates, and (iii) choice of the number of degrees of freedom in the t-distribution.

(i) Log-likelihood for (scaled) *t*(5)-distributed disturbances

As was discussed in Example 4.4 (p. 223–4), the disturbance terms in the CAPM may have fatter tails than the normal distribution (see also Exhibit 4.11 (*a*)). As an alternative, we consider the same linear model with disturbances that have the (scaled) $t(5)$-distribution. That is, the model is given by

$$y_i = \alpha + \beta x_i + \varepsilon_i,$$

where y_i and x_i are the excess returns in respectively the sector of cyclical consumer goods and the whole market. We suppose that Assumptions 1–6 of Section 3.1.4 (p. 125) are satisfied. In particular, the disturbance terms ε_i have zero mean, they have equal variance, and we assume that they are mutually independent. As independence implies being uncorrelated, this is stronger than Assumption 4 of uncorrelated disturbance terms. The postulated scaled $t(5)$-density of the disturbance terms is

$$p(\varepsilon_i) = c_5(1 + \varepsilon_i^2/5\sigma^2)^{-3}/\sigma,$$

where c_5 is a scaling constant (that does not depend on σ) so that $\int p(\varepsilon_i)d\varepsilon_i = 1$. The log-likelihood (4.27) is given by

$$l(\alpha, \beta, \sigma^2) = \sum_{i=1}^{n} \log(p(\varepsilon_i)) = n\log(c_5) - \frac{n}{2}\log(\sigma^2) - 3\sum_{i=1}^{n} \log\left(1 + \frac{(y_i - \alpha - \beta x_i)^2}{5\sigma^2}\right).$$

(ii) ML estimates based on (scaled) *t*(5)-distribution

The first order derivatives of the above log-likelihood are given by

$$\frac{\partial l}{\partial \alpha} = \sum_{i=1}^{n} \frac{-3}{1 + \varepsilon_i^2/5\sigma^2} \cdot (-2\varepsilon_i/5\sigma^2) = \sum_{i=1}^{n} \frac{6\varepsilon_i}{5\sigma^2 + \varepsilon_i^2},$$

$$\frac{\partial l}{\partial \beta} = \sum_{i=1}^{n} \frac{-3}{1 + \varepsilon_i^2/5\sigma^2} \cdot (-2\varepsilon_i x_i/5\sigma^2) = \sum_{i=1}^{n} \frac{6\varepsilon_i x_i}{5\sigma^2 + \varepsilon_i^2},$$

$$\frac{\partial l}{\partial \sigma^2} = -\frac{n}{2\sigma^2} - 3\sum_{i=1}^{n} \frac{1}{1 + \varepsilon_i^2/5\sigma^2} \cdot (-\varepsilon_i^2/5\sigma^4) = -\frac{n}{2\sigma^2} + \frac{3}{\sigma^2}\sum_{i=1}^{n} \frac{\varepsilon_i^2}{5\sigma^2 + \varepsilon_i^2}.$$

Substituting $\varepsilon_i = y_i - \alpha - \beta x_i$, the ML estimates are obtained by solving the above three non-linear equations $\partial l/\partial\alpha = \partial l/\partial\beta = \partial l/\partial\sigma^2 = 0$. The outcomes (a_{ML}, b_{ML}, s_{ML}) of the BHHH algorithm of Section 4.3.2 are given

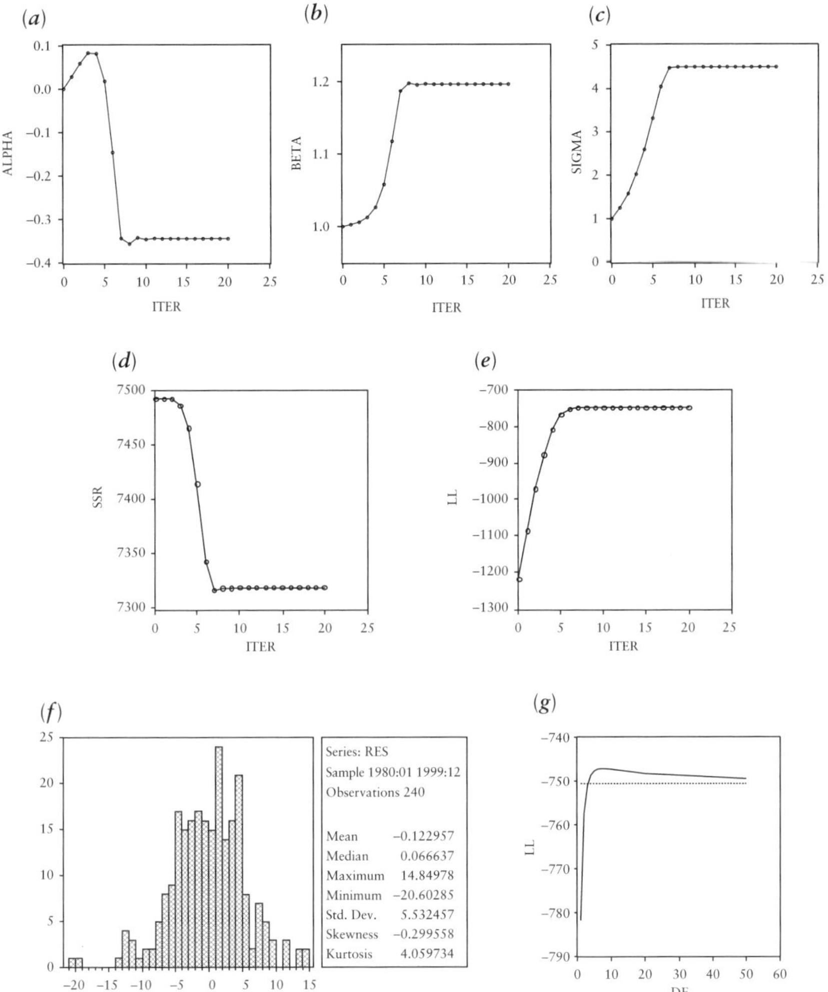

Exhibit 4.18 Stock Market Returns (Example 4.5)

ML estimates of CAPM for the sector of cyclical consumer goods in the UK, using a scaled $t(5)$ distribution for the disturbances. (*a*)–(*c*) show the estimates of the constant term α (*a*), the slope β (*b*), and the scale parameter σ (*c*) obtained by twenty iterations of the BHHH algorithm, with starting values $\alpha = 0$, $\beta = 1$, and $\sigma = 1$. (*d*)–(*e*) show the values of SSR (*d*) and of the log-likelihood values (denoted by LL (*e*)) obtained in these iterations. The value of LL increases at each iteration, but the value of SSR does not decrease always. (*f*) shows the histogram of the ML residuals, and (*g*) shows the maximum of the log-likelihood function for the $t(d)$ distribution for different degrees of freedom (the optimal value is obtained for $d = 8$, and for d infinitely large (the case of the normal distribution) the LL value is indicated by the horizontal line).

in Exhibit 4.18 (*a–c*), together with a histogram of the ML residuals $\hat{\varepsilon}_i = y_i - a_{ML} - b_{ML}x_i$ in (*f*). The iterations are started in $(\alpha, \beta, \sigma) = (0, 1, 1)$ and converge to $(a_{ML}, b_{ML}, s_{ML}) = (-0.34, 1.20, 4.49)$.

(iii) Choice of degrees of freedom of t-distribution

The motivation to use the (scaled) $t(5)$-distribution instead of the normal distribution is that the disturbance distribution may have fat tails. However, we have no special reason to take the t-distribution with $d = 5$ degrees of freedom. Therefore we estimate the CAPM also with scaled $t(d)$-distributions for selected values of d, including $d = \infty$ (which corresponds to the normal distribution, see Section 1.2.3 (p. 33)). This can be used for a grid search for d to obtain ML estimates of the parameters $(\alpha, \beta, \sigma^2, d)$. Exhibit 4.18 (g) shows the maximum of the log-likelihood for different values of d. The overall optimum is obtained for $d = 8$. The difference in the log-likelihood with $d = 5$ is rather small. We can also test for the null hypothesis of normally distributed error terms against the alternative of a $t(d)$-distribution—that is, the test of $d = \infty$ against $d < \infty$. The Likelihood Ratio test is given by

$$LR = 2l(\hat{\theta}_1) - 2l(\hat{\theta}_0) = 2(-747.16 + 750.54) = 6.77,$$

where $l(\hat{\theta}_1) = -747.16$ is the unrestricted maximal log-likelihood value (that is, for $d = 8$) and $l(\hat{\theta}_0) = -750.54$ is the log-likelihood value for the model with normally distributed disturbances. Asymptotically, LR follows the $\chi^2(1)$ distribution. The P-value of the computed LR-test is $P = 0.009$, so that the null hypothesis is rejected. Therefore we conclude that, under the stated assumptions, a t-distribution may be more convenient to model the disturbances of the CAPM than a normal distribution. In Section 4.4.6 we provide a further comparison between the models with normal and with scaled $t(5)$-disturbances.

E

XM402COF

Example 4.6: **Coffee Sales (continued)**

As a second example we consider again the data on sales of two brands of coffee discussed before in Section 4.2.5. We will discuss (i) the outcomes of ML estimation for the two brands, (ii) LR-tests on constant elasticity, (iii) LM-tests on constant elasticity, (iv) Wald tests on constant elasticity, and (v) comparison of the tests and conclusion.

(i) Outcomes of ML for the two brands

For each of the two brands separately, we use the non-linear regression model (4.9) with the assumption of normally distributed disturbances, so that

$$\log(q_i) = \beta_1 + \frac{\beta_2}{\beta_3}(d_i^{\beta_3} - 1) + \varepsilon_i, \quad \varepsilon_i \sim \text{NID}(0, \sigma^2).$$

The null hypothesis of constant demand elasticity corresponds to the parameter restriction $\beta_3 = 0$, with corresponding model $\log(q) = \beta_1 + \beta_2 \log(d) + \varepsilon$.

We perform different tests of this hypothesis for both brands of coffee. The tests are based on the results in Exhibit 4.19. Panels 1 and 3 give the results of ML estimation under the hypothesis that $\beta_3 = 0$. Because the disturbances are assumed to be normally distributed, ML corresponds to least squares (see Section 4.3.2). Panels 2 and 4 give the results of ML estimation in the unrestricted non-linear regression model (4.9). This corresponds to non-linear least squares.

(ii) *LR*-tests on constant elasticity

The Likelihood Ratio tests for the null hypothesis that $\beta_3 = 0$ against the alternative that $\beta_3 \neq 0$ can be obtained from the results in Exhibit 4.19 for brands 1 and 2. The results are as follows, with P-values based on the asymptotic $\chi^2(1)$ distribution:

$$LR_1 = 2(12.530 - 10.017) = 5.026 \quad (P = 0.025),$$
$$LR_2 = 2(11.641 - 10.024) = 3.235 \quad (P = 0.072).$$

(iii) *LM*-tests on constant elasticity

Under the null hypothesis, the model is linear with dependent variable $\log(q_i)$ and with explanatory variable $\log(d_i)$ (see Example 4.2 (p. 202–4)). The Lagrange Multiplier test for non-linear regression models has already been performed in Section 4.2.5 for both brands of coffee, with the results in Panels 5 and 6 in Exhibit 4.10. The test outcomes are

$$LM_1 = nR^2 = 12 \cdot 0.342 = 4.106 \quad (P = 0.043),$$
$$LM_2 = nR^2 = 12 \cdot 0.236 = 2.836 \quad (P = 0.092).$$

(iv) Wald tests on constant elasticity

To compute the Wald test (4.48) we use the relation (4.50) between the Wald test and the t-test—that is,

$$W = \frac{n}{n-k} t^2.$$

The non-linear regressions in Panels 2 and 4 in Exhibit 4.10 show the t-values of $\hat{\beta}_3$ with P-values based on the $t(9)$-distribution—namely,

$$t_1 = -2.012 \quad (P = 0.075),$$
$$t_2 = -1.651 \quad (P = 0.133).$$

Using (4.50) with $n = 12$ and $k = 3$, this leads to the following values for the Wald test, with corresponding P-values based on the $\chi^2(1)$ distribution:

Panel 1: Dependent Variable: LOGQ1 (brand 1)				
Method: Least Squares				
Included observations: 12				
Variable	Coefficient	Std. Error	t-Statistic	Prob.
C	5.841739	0.043072	135.6284	0.0000
LOGD1	4.664693	0.581918	8.016063	0.0000
R-squared	0.865333			
Sum squared resid	0.132328			
Log likelihood	10.01699			

Panel 2: Dependent Variable: LOGQ1 (brand 1)				
Method: Least Squares				
Included observations: 12				
Convergence achieved after 5 iterations				
LOGQ1 = C(1) + (C(2)/C(3)) * (D1^C(3)− 1)				
Parameter	Coefficient	Std. Error	t-Statistic	Prob.
C(1)	5.807118	0.040150	144.6360	0.0000
C(2)	10.29832	3.295386	3.125072	0.0122
C(3)	−13.43073	6.674812	−2.012152	0.0751
R-squared	0.911413			
Sum squared resid	0.087049			
Log likelihood	12.52991			

Panel 3: Dependent Variable: LOGQ2 (brand 2)				
Method: Least Squares				
Included observations: 12				
Variable	Coefficient	Std. Error	t-Statistic	Prob.
C	4.406561	0.043048	102.3638	0.0000
LOGD2	6.003298	0.581599	10.32206	0.0000
R-squared	0.914196			
Sum squared resid	0.132183			
Log likelihood	10.02358			

Panel 4: Dependent Variable: LOGQ2 (brand 2)				
Method: Least Squares				
Included observations: 12				
Convergence achieved after 5 iterations				
LOGQ2 = C(1) + (C(2)/C(3)) * (D2^C(3)− 1)				
Parameter	Coefficient	Std. Error	t-Statistic	Prob.
C(1)	4.377804	0.043236	101.2540	0.0000
C(2)	10.28864	3.001698	3.427608	0.0075
C(3)	−8.595289	5.207206	−1.650653	0.1332
R-squared	0.934474			
Sum squared resid	0.100944			
Log likelihood	11.64129			

Exhibit 4.19 Coffee Sales (Example 4.6)

Regressions for two brands of coffee, models with constant elasticity (Panels 1 and 3) and models with varying elasticity (Panels 2 and 4).

$$W_1 = \frac{12}{9} \cdot (-2.012)^2 = 5.398 \quad (P = 0.020),$$

$$W_2 = \frac{12}{9} \cdot (-1.651)^2 = 3.633 \quad (P = 0.057).$$

(v) Comparison of tests and conclusion

Summarizing the outcomes of the test statistics, note that for both brands of coffee $LM < LR < W$, in accordance with (4.56). If we use a 5 per cent significance level, the null hypothesis of constant demand elasticity is not rejected for brand 2, but it is rejected for brand 1 by the LR-test, the LM-test, and the W-test, but not by the t-test.

As the sample size ($n = 12$) is very small, the asymptotic $\chi^2(1)$ distribution is only a rough approximation. It is helpful to consider also the $gF(g, n-k) = F(1, 9)$ distribution with 5 per cent critical value equal to 5.12. This is considerably larger than the value 3.84 for the $\chi^2(1)$ distribution. With this critical value of 5.12, all tests fail to reject the null hypothesis, with the exception of the Wald test for brand 1. Therefore, on the basis of these data there is not so much compelling evidence to reject the null hypothesis of constant elasticity of the demand for coffee. Of course, the number of observations for the two models ($n = 12$ for both brands) is very small, and in Section 5.3.1 (p. 307–10) we will use a combined model for the two brands (so that $n = 24$ in this case). As we shall see in Section 5.3.1, the null hypothesis of constant elasticity can then be rejected for both brands by all three tests (LR, LM, and Wald).

4.4 Generalized method of moments

4.4.1 Motivation

Requirements for maximum likelihood

The results in the foregoing section show that maximum likelihood has (asymptotically) optimal properties for correctly specified models. In practice this means that the joint probability distribution (4.25) of the data should be a reasonable reflection of the data generating process. If there is much uncertainty about this distribution, then it may be preferable to use an estimation method that requires somewhat less information on the DGP. In general, by making less assumptions on the DGP, some efficiency will be lost as compared to ML in the correct model. However, this loss may be relatively small compared to the loss of using ML in a model that differs much from the DGP.

Evaluation of accuracy of estimates

The accuracy of parameter estimates is usually evaluated in terms of their standard errors and their P-values associated with tests of significance. Until now we have discussed two methods for this purpose. The expression

$$\widehat{\text{var}}(b) = s^2(X'X)^{-1}$$

provides correct P-values on the significance of least squares estimates if the seven standard Assumptions 1–7 of Section 3.1.4 are satisfied. Further, the expression

$$\widehat{\text{var}}(\hat{\theta}_{ML}) = \mathcal{I}_n^{-1}(\hat{\theta}_{ML})$$

provides asymptotically correct P-values on the significance of maximum likelihood estimates if the joint probability function $p(y, X, \theta)$ of the data is correctly specified (see Section 4.3.3).

In this section we discuss the *generalized method of moments* (GMM). In this approach the parameters are estimated by solving a set of moment conditions. As we shall see below, both OLS and ML can be seen as particular examples of estimators based on moment conditions. The GMM standard errors are computed on the basis of the moment conditions and they provide asymptotically correct P-values, provided that the specified moment conditions are valid. For instance, one can estimate the parameters by OLS and compute the GMM standard errors even if not all the Assumptions 1–7 hold true. One can also estimate the parameters by ML and compute the GMM standard errors, even if the specified probability distribution is not correct. That is, GMM can be used to compute reliable standard errors and P-values in situations where some of the assumptions of OLS or ML are not satisfied.

Example 4.7: **Stock Market Returns (continued)**

As an illustration, Exhibit 4.20 shows the OLS residuals of the CAPM discussed in Examples 2.1, 4.4, and 4.5. It seems that the disturbances have a larger variance at the beginning and near the end of the observation period as compared to the middle period. If the variances differ, then the disturbances are heteroskedastic and Assumption 3 is violated. We have already concluded (see Sections 4.3.1 and 4.3.9) that Assumption 7 of normally distributed disturbances is also doubtful. However, the alternative of ML based on t-distribution does not take the apparent heteroskedasticity of the disturbances into account either. It seems preferable to evaluate the CAPM, in particular to compute the standard errors, without making such assumptions. In Section 4.4.6 we will use GMM for this purpose.

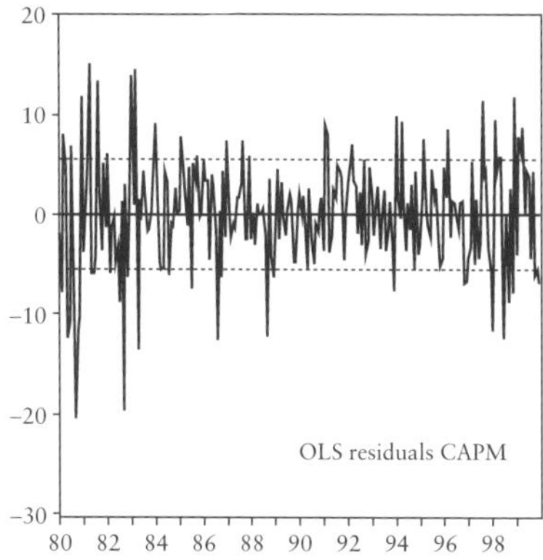

Exhibit 4.20 Stock Market Returns (Example 4.7)

Least squares residuals of CAPM for the sector of cyclical consumer goods in the UK.

4.4.2 GMM estimation

☞ Uses Section 1.3.1.

Method of moments estimator of the mean

In Section 1.3.1 (p. 39) we discussed the method of moments, which is based on estimating population moments by means of sample moments. For example, suppose that the data y_i consist of a random sample from a population with unknown mean μ, so that

$$E[y_i - \mu] = 0.$$

Then the moment estimator of μ is obtained by replacing the population mean (E) by the sample mean $(\frac{1}{n}\sum_{i=1}^{n})$, so that

$$\frac{1}{n}\sum_{i=1}^{n}(y_i - \hat{\mu}) = 0,$$

that is, $\hat{\mu} = \frac{1}{n}\sum_{i=1}^{n} y_i$.

Least squares derived by the method of moments

The least squares estimator in the linear model (4.1) can also be derived by the method of moments. The basic requirement for this estimator is the orthogonality condition (4.4). Here $\frac{1}{n}X'\varepsilon = \frac{1}{n}\sum_{i=1}^{n} x_i\varepsilon_i$, where x_i is the $k \times 1$ vector of explanatory variables for the ith observation, and condition (4.4) is satisfied (under weak regularity conditions) if $E[x_i\varepsilon_i] = 0$ for all i. As $\varepsilon_i = y_i - x_i'\beta$, this is equivalent to the condition that

$$E[x_i(y_i - x_i'\beta)] = 0, \quad i = 1, \cdots, n. \tag{4.58}$$

Note that x_i is a $k \times 1$ vector, so that this imposes k restrictions on the parameter vector β. The corresponding conditions on the sample moments (replacing the population mean E by the sample mean $\frac{1}{n}\sum_{i=1}^{n}$) gives the k equations

$$\frac{1}{n}\sum_{i=1}^{n} x_i(y_i - x_i'\hat{\beta}) = 0.$$

This can be written as $X'(y - X\hat{\beta}) = 0$, so that $\hat{\beta} = b$ is equal to the least squares estimator. This shows that OLS can be derived by the method of moments, using the orthogonality conditions (4.58) as moment conditions.

ML as methods of moments estimator

ML estimators can also be obtained from moment conditions. Suppose that the data consist of n independent observations, so that the log-likelihood is $l(\theta) = \sum_{i=1}^{n} l_i(\theta)$, as in (4.27). By the arguments in (4.53), replacing $\log p(\theta)$ by $l_i(\theta) = \log p_\theta(y_i, x_i)$, it follows that

$$E\left[\frac{\partial l_i}{\partial \theta}\right]_{|\theta=\theta_0} = 0, \quad i = 1, \cdots, n. \tag{4.59}$$

Replacing the population mean E by the sample mean $\frac{1}{n}\sum_{i=1}^{n}$, this gives

$$\frac{1}{n}\sum_{i=1}^{n}\frac{\partial l_i}{\partial \theta} = 0. \tag{4.60}$$

The solution of these equations gives the ML estimator, as this corresponds to the first order conditions for a maximum of the log-likelihood. The equations (4.60) require that the sample mean of the terms $\frac{\partial l_i}{\partial \theta}$ is equal to zero. Such equations are called 'generalized' moment conditions.

The generalized method of moments

We now describe the generalized method of moments more in general. The basic assumption is that we can formulate a set of *moment conditions*. Suppose that the parameter vector of interest, θ, contains p unknown parameters and that the DGP has parameters θ_0. Further suppose that for each observation ($i = 1, \cdots, n$) the DGP satisfies m distinct moment conditions, say

$$E[g_i(\theta_0)] = 0, \quad i = 1, \cdots, n, \tag{4.61}$$

where the g_i are known functions $g_i : R^p \to R^m$ that depend on the observed data. That is, the crucial assumption is that the DGP satisfies the m restrictions in (4.61) for the observations $i = 1, \cdots, n$. Examples are the orthogonality conditions (4.58) (which corresponds to k linear functions in the k unknown parameters) and the first order conditions (4.60) (which gives p non-linear functions in the p unknown parameters). If the number of moment conditions m is equal to the number of unknown parameters p in θ, then the model (4.61) is called *exactly identified*, and if $m > p$ then the model is called *over-identified*. The GMM estimator $\hat{\theta}$ is defined as the solution of the m equations obtained by replacing the population mean E in (4.61) by the sample mean $\frac{1}{n}\sum_{i=1}^{n}$—that is,

$$\frac{1}{n}\sum_{i=1}^{n} g_i(\hat{\theta}) = 0. \tag{4.62}$$

Numerical aspects of GMM

To obtain a solution for $\hat{\theta}$, we need in general to impose at least as many moment conditions as there are unknown parameters ($m \geq p$). In the exactly identified case ($m = p$), this system of m equations in p unknown parameters has a unique solution (under suitable regularity conditions). The numerical solution methods discussed in Section 4.2.3 can be used for this purpose. In the over-identified case ($m > p$) there are more equations than unknown parameters and there will in general exist no exact solution of this system of equations. That is, although the m (population) conditions (4.61) are satisfied (by assumption) for the DGP—that is, for $\theta = \theta_0$—there often exists no value $\hat{\theta}$ for which the sample condition (4.62) is exactly satisfied. Let the $m \times 1$ vector $G_n(\theta)$ be defined by

$$G_n(\theta) = \sum_{i=1}^{n} g_i(\theta).$$

If there exists no value of θ so that $G_n(\theta) = 0$, one can instead minimize the distance of this vector from zero, for instance by minimizing $\frac{1}{n} G_n'(\theta) G_n(\theta)$ with respect to θ. As an alternative one can also minimize a weighted sum of squares

$$\frac{1}{n} G_n' W G_n, \tag{4.63}$$

where W is an $m \times m$ symmetric and positive definite matrix. In the exactly identified case (with a solution $G_n(\hat{\theta}) = 0$) the choice of W is irrelevant, but in the over-identified case it may be chosen to take possible differences in sampling variation of the individual moment conditions into account. In general the minimization of (4.63) will be a non-linear optimization problem that can be solved by the numerical methods discussed in Section 4.2.3—for example, by Newton–Raphson.

Summary of computations in GMM estimation

Estimation by GMM proceeds in the following two steps.

GMM estimation

- *Step 1: Specify a sufficient number of moment conditions.* Identify the p parameters of interest θ and specify m ($\geq p$) moment conditions (4.61). The crucial assumption is that the DGP satisfies these moment conditions. In particular, the specified moments should exist.
- *Step 2: Estimate the parameters.* Estimate θ by GMM by solving the equations (4.62) (in the exactly identified case with $m = p$) or by minimizing (4.63) (in the over-identified case with $m > p$). The choice of the weighting matrix W (when $m > p$) will be discussed in the next section.

4.4.3 GMM standard errors

An asymptotic result

To apply tests based on GMM estimators we need to know (asymptotic) expressions for the covariance matrix of these estimators. In our analysis we will *assume* that the moment conditions are valid for the DGP, that our GMM estimator is consistent, and that the sample average $\frac{1}{n}G_n = \frac{1}{n}\sum_{i=1}^{n} g_i$ satisfies the following central limit theorem:

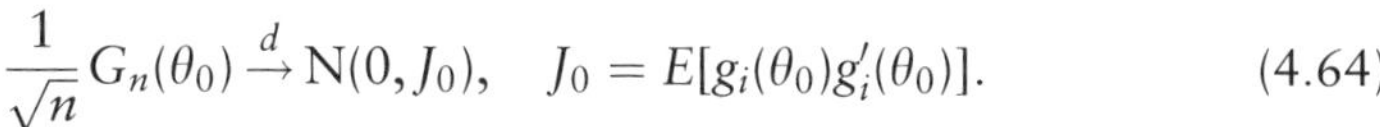

$$\frac{1}{\sqrt{n}}G_n(\theta_0) \xrightarrow{d} \mathrm{N}(0, J_0), \quad J_0 = E[g_i(\theta_0)g_i'(\theta_0)]. \tag{4.64}$$

These assumptions hold true under suitable regularity assumptions on the moment conditions (4.61) and on the correlation structure of the data generating process (in particular, the random vectors $g_i(\theta_0)$ should satisfy the moment conditions (4.61) and these random vectors should not be too strongly correlated for $i = 1, \cdots, n$ with $n \to \infty$). Note that $E[G_n(\theta_0)] = 0$ if (4.61) is valid. It falls beyond the scope of this book to treat the required assumptions for asymptotic normality in (4.64) in more detail. However, for two special cases (OLS and ML), the result (4.64) follows from earlier results in this chapter, as we shall now show.

Illustration of asymptotic result: OLS

If the moment conditions are those of OLS in (4.58), it follows that

$$G_n(\theta_0) = \sum_{i=1}^{n} x_i(y_i - x_i'\beta) = \sum_{i=1}^{n} x_i\varepsilon_i = X'\varepsilon.$$

Under appropriate conditions (Assumptions 1*, 2–6, and orthogonality between x_i and ε_i) there holds $J_0 = E[x_i\varepsilon_i^2 x_i'] = \sigma^2 E[x_i x_i'] = \sigma^2 \mathrm{plim}\left(\frac{1}{n}\sum_{i=1}^{n} x_i x_i'\right) = \sigma^2 Q$ and then (4.64) follows from (4.6) in Section 4.1.4, which states that $\frac{1}{\sqrt{n}}X'\varepsilon \xrightarrow{d} \mathrm{N}(0, \sigma^2 Q)$.

Second Illustration of asymptotic result: ML

If the moment conditions are those of ML in (4.60), it follows that

$$G_n(\theta_0) = \sum_{i=1}^{n} \frac{\partial l_i}{\partial \theta}\bigg|_{\theta=\theta_0} = \frac{\partial l}{\partial \theta}\bigg|_{\theta=\theta_0}.$$

Now (4.52) in Section 4.3.6 states that for $z(\theta_0) = \frac{\partial l}{\partial \theta}|_{\theta=\theta_0}$ there holds $\frac{1}{\sqrt{n}}z(\theta_0) \xrightarrow{d} \mathrm{N}(0, \mathcal{I}_0)$. This result is equivalent to (4.64), because $z(\theta_0) = G_n(\theta_0)$ and

$$J_0 = E\left[\frac{\partial l_i}{\partial \theta}\frac{\partial l_i}{\partial \theta'}\right] = \lim\left(-\frac{1}{n}\sum_{i=1}^{n} E\left[\frac{\partial^2 l_i}{\partial \theta \partial \theta'}\right]\right) = \mathcal{I}_0$$

(see (4.36) and (4.57)).

T

Derivation of asymptotic distribution of the GMM estimator

Assuming that (4.64) is satisfied, it follows that for large enough samples (so that $\hat{\theta}$ is close to θ_0) the minimization problem in (4.63) can be simplified by the linearization $G_n = G_n(\theta) \approx G_{n0} + H_{n0}(\theta - \theta_0)$, where $G_{n0} = G_n(\theta_0)$ and $H_{n0} = H_n(\theta_0)$ is the $m \times p$ matrix defined by $H_n = \partial G_n/\partial \theta'$. Substituting this linear approximation in (4.63) and using the fact that the derivative of $G_{n0} + H_{n0}(\theta - \theta_0)$ with respect to θ is equal to H_{n0}, the first order conditions for a minimum of (4.63) are given by

$$H'_{n0} W(G_{n0} + H_{n0}(\theta - \theta_0)) = 0.$$

The solution is given by

$$\hat{\theta} = \theta_0 - (H'_{n0} W H_{n0})^{-1} H'_{n0} W G_{n0}.$$

Suppose that $\text{plim}\left(\frac{1}{n} H_{n0}\right) = H_0$ exists, then it follows from the above expression and (4.64) that

$$\sqrt{n}(\hat{\theta} - \theta_0) \xrightarrow{d} \text{N}(0, V), \tag{4.65}$$

where $V = (H_0' W H_0)^{-1} H_0' W J_0 W H_0 (H_0' W H_0)^{-1}$.

T

Choice of weighting matrix in the over-identified case

The weighting matrix W in (4.63) can now be chosen so that this expression is minimal (in the sense of positive semidefinite matrices) to get an asymptotically efficient estimator. Intuitively, it seems reasonable to allow larger errors for estimated parameters that contain more uncertainty. We can then penalize the deviations of G_n from zero less heavily in directions that have a larger variance. This suggests choosing the weights inversely proportional to the covariance matrix $\text{var}\left(\frac{1}{\sqrt{n}} G_n(\theta_0)\right) \approx J_0$—that is, taking $W = J_0^{-1}$. It is left as an exercise (see Exercise 4.7) to show that this is indeed the optimal weighting matrix. The resulting $p \times p$ asymptotic covariance matrix is given by

$$V = \left(H_0' J_0^{-1} H_0\right)^{-1}. \tag{4.66}$$

So the estimator $\hat{\theta}$ obtained by minimizing (4.63) with $W = J_0^{-1}$ is the most efficient estimator within the class of GMM estimators obtained by minimizing (4.63) for any positive definite matrix W.

Factors that influence the variance of GMM

The efficiency of this estimator further depends on the set of moment conditions that has been specified. Stated in general terms, the best moment conditions (that is, with the smallest covariance matrix V for $\hat{\theta}$) are those for which H_0 is large and J_0 is small (all in the sense of positive definite matrices). Here $H_0 = \partial G/\partial\theta'$ is large when the violation of the moment conditions (4.61) is relatively strong for $\theta \neq \theta_0$ — that is, when the restrictions are powerful in this sense. And J_0 is small when the random variation of the moments $g_i(\theta_0)$ in (4.61) is small.

Illustration: OLS

As an illustration, for the OLS moment conditions $E[x_i(y_i - x_i'\beta)] = 0$ in (4.58) we obtain $H_n = \partial G_n/\partial\beta = -\sum_{i=1}^n x_i x_i' = -X'X$ and (under Assumptions 1*, 2–6, and orthogonality of the regressors x_i with the disturbances ε_i) $H_0 = \text{plim}(-\frac{1}{n}X'X) = -Q$. We showed earlier that $J_0 = \sigma^2 Q$ in this case, so that

$$V_{OLS} = (H_0' J_0^{-1} H_0)^{-1} = (Q\sigma^{-2}Q^{-1}Q)^{-1} = \sigma^2 Q^{-1} \approx \sigma^2\left(\frac{1}{n}X'X\right)^{-1}.$$

This agrees with (4.7) in Section 4.1.4. So this estimator is more efficient if $X'X$ is larger (more systematic variation) and if σ^2 is smaller (less random variation).

Second illustration: ML

For the ML moment conditions (4.60) we obtain $H_n = \partial G_n/\partial\theta = \sum \frac{\partial^2 l_i}{\partial\theta\partial\theta'}$ and it follows from (4.57) that $H_0 = \text{plim}(\frac{1}{n}H_{n0}) = \text{plim}(-\frac{1}{n}\mathcal{I}_n) = -\mathcal{I}_0$. We showed earlier that in this case $J_0 = \mathcal{I}_0$, so that for ML there holds $H_0 = -J_0$ and

$$V_{ML} = (H_0' J_0^{-1} H_0)^{-1} = (\mathcal{I}_0 \mathcal{I}_0^{-1} \mathcal{I}_0)^{-1} = \mathcal{I}_0^{-1}.$$

This is in line with (4.35) in Section 4.3.3. So ML estimators are efficient if the information matrix $\mathcal{I}_0$ is large, or, equivalently, if the log-likelihood has a large curvature around θ_0. This is also intuitively evident, as for $\theta \neq \theta_0$ the log-likelihood values drop quickly if the curvature is large.

Iterative choice of weights

In practice θ_0 is unknown, so that we cannot estimate θ with the criterion (4.63) with $W = J_0^{-1}$. A possible iterative method is to start, for instance, with $W = I$ (the $m \times m$ identity matrix) and to minimize (4.63). The resulting estimate $\hat{\theta}$ is then used to compute $\hat{J}_0 = \frac{1}{n}\sum_{i=1}^n g_i(\hat{\theta})g_i'(\hat{\theta})$ as an estimate of J_0. Then (4.63) is minimized with $W = \hat{J}_0^{-1}$, and this process is repeated until the estimates converge.

GMM standard errors

Consistent estimates of the *standard errors* of the GMM estimators $\hat{\theta}$ are obtained as the square roots of the diagonal elements of the estimated covariance matrix of $\hat{\theta}$—that is,

$$\widehat{\text{var}}(\hat{\theta}) = (H_n' J_n^{-1} H_n)^{-1}, \tag{4.67}$$

$$J_n = \sum_{i=1}^{n} g_i(\hat{\theta}) g_i'(\hat{\theta}), \quad H_n = \sum_{i=1}^{n} \frac{\partial g_i(\hat{\theta})}{\partial \theta'}. \tag{4.68}$$

Here we used the fact that, according to (4.65), $\hat{\theta}$ has covariance matrix approximately equal to $\frac{1}{n}V$, and H_0 and J_0 in (4.66) are approximated by $\frac{1}{n}H_n$ and $\frac{1}{n}J_n$ evaluated at $\theta = \hat{\theta}$, so that

$$\text{var}(\hat{\theta}) \approx \frac{1}{n}V = \frac{1}{n}(H_0' J_0^{-1} H_0)^{-1} \approx \frac{1}{n}\left(\frac{1}{n}H_n'\left(\frac{1}{n}J_n\right)^{-1}\frac{1}{n}H_n\right)^{-1} = (H_n' J_n^{-1} H_n)^{-1}.$$

The covariance matrix in (4.67) is called the *sandwich estimator* of the covariance matrix of the GMM estimator $\hat{\theta}$.

Test of moment conditions: The *J*-test

In the over-identified case, one can test the *over-identifying restrictions* by means of the result that, under the null hypothesis that the moment conditions (4.61) hold true,

$$G_n' J_n^{-1} G_n \approx \chi^2(m - p). \tag{4.69}$$

This is called the *J-test*. Here m is the number of moment conditions and p is the number of parameters in θ. The result of the χ^2-distribution is based on (4.64), where J_0 is approximated by $\frac{1}{n}J_n$. Note that (4.63) can be seen as a non-linear least squares problem with m 'observations' and p parameters, which explains that the number of degrees of freedom is $m - p$. In the exactly identified case ($m = p$) the moment conditions cannot be tested, as $G_n(\hat{\theta})$ will be identically zero irrespective of the question whether the imposed moment conditions are correct or not.

Summary of computations in GMM estimation and testing

Summarizing the results on GMM estimation and testing obtained in this and the foregoing section, this approach consists of the following steps.

GMM estimation and testing

- *Step 1: Specify a sufficient number of moment conditions.* Identify the p parameters of interest θ and specify m ($\geq p$) moment conditions (4.61). The crucial assumption is that the DGP satisfies these moment conditions.

(*continues*)

GMM estimation and testing (*continued*)

- *Step 2: Estimate the parameters.* Estimate θ by GMM by solving the equations (4.62) (if $m = p$) or by minimizing (4.63) (if $m > p$). The weighting matrix W can be chosen iteratively, starting with $W = I$ and (if $\hat{\theta}_h$ is the estimate obtained in the hth iteration) choosing in the $(h+1)$st iteration $W = J_h^{-1}$, where $J_h = \frac{1}{n}\sum_{i=1}^{n} g_i(\hat{\theta}_h)g_i'(\hat{\theta}_h)$.
- *Step 3: Compute the GMM standard errors.* The asymptotic covariance matrix of the GMM estimator $\hat{\theta}$ can be obtained from (4.67) and (4.68). The GMM standard errors are the square roots of the diagonal elements of this matrix.
- *Step 4: Test of moment conditions (in over-identified models).* The correctness of the moment conditions can be tested in the over-identified case $(m > p)$ by the J-test in (4.69).

☞ Exercises: T: 4.7; S: 4.11c, f, 4.12c, g.

4.4.4 Quasi-maximum likelihood

Moment conditions derived from a postulated likelihood

Considering the four steps of GMM at the end of the last section, the question remains how to find the required moment conditions in step 1. In some cases these conditions can be based on models of economic behaviour — for instance, expected utility maximization. Another possibility is the so-called *quasi-maximum likelihood* (QML) method. This method derives the moment conditions from a postulated likelihood function, as in (4.60). It is assumed that the corresponding moment conditions

$$E[g_i(\theta)] = E[\partial l_i/\partial\theta] = 0$$

hold true for the DGP, but that the likelihood function is possibly misspecified. This means that the expression (4.35) for the covariance matrix does not apply. The (asymptotically) correct covariance matrix can be computed by means of (4.67). As was discussed in Section 4.4.3, if the likelihood function is correct, then $H_0 = -J_0$, but this no longer holds true if the model is misspecified. The reason is that the equality (4.36) holds true only at $\theta = \theta_0$ — that is, for correctly specified models. On the other hand, the results in (4.65) and (4.66) always hold true as long as the moment conditions (4.61) are valid.

Comparison of ML and QML

So in QML the likelihood function is used only to obtain the first order conditions (4.60) and the standard errors are computed from (4.67). QML is consistent if the conditions $E[\partial l_i/\partial\theta] = 0$ hold true for the DGP. In practice, when one is uncertain about the correct specification of the likelihood function, it may be helpful to calculate the standard errors in both ways, with ML and with QML. If the outcomes are widely different, this is a sign of misspecification.

Summary of QML method

In quasi-maximum likelihood, the parameter estimates and their standard errors are computed in the following way. Here it is assumed that the n observations (y_i, x_i) are mutually independent for $i = 1, \cdots, n$.

Quasi-maximum likelihood

- *Step 1: Specify a probability distribution for the observed data.* Identify the p parameters of interest θ. Postulate a probability distribution $p(y_i, x_i, \theta)$ for the ith observation, and let $l_i(\theta) = \log(p(y_i, x_i, \theta))$ be the contribution of the ith observation to the log-likelihood $\log(L(\theta)) = \sum_{i=1}^{n} \log(p(y_i, x_i, \theta))$.
- *Step 2: Derive the corresponding moment conditions.* Define the p moment conditions $E[g_i(\theta)] = 0$, where the moments are defined by $g_i(\theta) = \frac{\partial l_i}{\partial\theta}, i = 1, \cdots, n$. The crucial assumption is that the DGP satisfies these moment conditions.
- *Step 3: Estimate the parameters.* Estimate θ by solving the equations (4.62) (as $m = p$, there is no need for a weighting matrix). This is equivalent to ML estimation based on the chosen probability distribution in step 1.
- *Step 4: Compute the GMM standard errors.* Approximate standard errors of the QML estimates can be obtained from the asymptotic covariance matrix in (4.67) and (4.68), with $g_i(\theta) = l_i(\theta) = \log(p(y_i, x_i, \theta))$.

☞ **Exercises: E: 4.17h.**

4.4.5 GMM in simple regression

The two moment conditions

We illustrate GMM by considering the simple regression model. The results will be used in the example in the next section. Suppose that we wish to estimate the parameters α and β in the model

$$y_i = \alpha + \beta x_i + \varepsilon_i, \quad i = 1, \cdots, n.$$

We suppose that the functional form is correctly specified in the sense that the DGP has parameters (α_0, β_0) with the property that

$$E[\varepsilon_i] = E[y_i - \alpha_0 - \beta_0 x_i] = 0, \quad i = 1, \cdots, n.$$

Further we assume that the explanatory variable x_i satisfies the orthogonality condition

$$E[x_i \varepsilon_i] = E[x_i(y_i - \alpha_0 - \beta_0 x_i)] = 0, \quad i = 1, \cdots, n.$$

This provides two moment conditions, so that the model is exactly identified.

The GMM estimators

The GMM estimates of α and β are obtained by replacing the expectation E by the sample mean $\frac{1}{n}\sum_{i=1}^{n}$, so that

$$\frac{1}{n}\sum_{i=1}^{n}\left(y_i - \hat{\alpha} - \hat{\beta}x_i\right) = 0, \quad \frac{1}{n}\sum_{i=1}^{n} x_i\left(y_i - \hat{\alpha} - \hat{\beta}x_i\right) = 0.$$

These equations are equivalent to the two normal equations (2.9) and (2.10) in Section 2.1.2 (p. 82). So the GMM estimates of α and β are the OLS estimates a and b.

GMM standard errors (allowing for heteroskedasticity)

T

The variance of the estimators a and b was derived in Section 2.2.4 (p. 96) under Assumptions 1–6 (see (2.27) and (2.28)). The above two moment conditions correspond to Assumptions 1 (exogeneity), 2 (zero mean), and 5 and 6 (linear model with constant parameters). We now suppose that Assumption 4 (no correlation) is also satisfied, but that Assumption 3 (homoskedasticity) is doubtful. If Assumption 3 is violated, then the formulas (2.27) and (2.28) for the variances of a and b do not apply. A consistent estimator of the 2×2 covariance matrix is obtained from (4.67). In our case,

$$g_i(a, b) = \begin{pmatrix} y_i - a - bx_i \\ x_i(y_i - a - bx_i) \end{pmatrix} = \begin{pmatrix} e_i \\ x_i e_i \end{pmatrix},$$

so that the estimated covariance matrix (4.67) is $\widehat{\text{var}}(\hat{\theta}) = \left(H_n' J_n^{-1} H_n\right)^{-1}$ with

$$H_n = \sum_{i=1}^{n}\begin{pmatrix} \frac{\partial g_i}{\partial a} & \frac{\partial g_i}{\partial b} \end{pmatrix} = \sum_{i=1}^{n}\begin{pmatrix} -1 & -x_i \\ -x_i & -x_i^2 \end{pmatrix} = -\sum_{i=1}^{n}\begin{pmatrix} 1 & x_i \\ x_i & x_i^2 \end{pmatrix},$$

$$J_n = \sum_{i=1}^{n} g_i g_i' = \sum_{i=1}^{n} e_i^2 \begin{pmatrix} 1 & x_i \\ x_i & x_i^2 \end{pmatrix}.$$

If the residuals are all of nearly equal magnitude so that $e_i^2 \approx \sigma^2$, then we obtain $H_n = -X'X$ and $J_n \approx \sigma^2(X'X)$, where X is the $n \times 2$ regressor matrix. The formula (4.67) then gives $\hat{V} \approx \sigma^2(X'X)^{-1}$, as in Chapter 3. However, if the residuals differ much in magnitude, then J_n may differ considerably from $\sigma^2(X'X)^{-1}$, and the (correct) GMM expression in (4.67) may differ much from the (incorrect) expression $\sigma^2(X'X)^{-1}$ for the covariance matrix.

☞ Exercises: E: 4.17g.

XM404SMR

4.4.6 Illustration: Stock Market Returns

We consider once again the excess returns data for the sector of cyclical consumer goods (y_i) and for the whole asset market (x_i) in the UK (see also Examples 4.5 (p. 243–6) and 4.7 (p. 251)). We will discuss (i) the data and the model assumptions, (ii) two estimation methods, OLS and QML with (scaled) $t(5)$-disturbances, (iii) correctness of the implied moment conditions, (iv) the estimation results, and (v) tests of two hypotheses.

(i) Data and model assumptions

The data set consists of $n = 240$ monthly data over the period 1980.01–1999.12. The CAPM is given by

$$y_i = \alpha + \beta x_i + \varepsilon_i, \quad i = 1, \cdots, n.$$

We make the following assumptions on the DGP. The disturbances have mean zero (Assumption 2). The terms x_i and ε_i are independent, so that in particular $E[x_i\varepsilon_i] = E[x_i]E[\varepsilon_i] = 0$ (compare with Assumption 1). The disturbances are independent (Assumption 4) and the DGP is described by the above simple regression model for certain (unknown) parameters (α_0, β_0) (Assumptions 5 and 6). However, we do not assume normality (Assumption 7), as the results in Example 4.4 (p. 223–4) indicate that the distribution may have fat tails. We also do not assume homoskedasticity (Assumption 3), as the variance of the disturbances may be varying over time (see Example 4.7). That is, we assume that the disturbances ε_i are independently distributed with unknown distributions $p_i(\varepsilon_i)$ with mean $E[\varepsilon_i] = 0$ and possibly different unknown variances $E[\varepsilon_i^2] = \sigma_i^2$, $i = 1, \cdots, n$. Further we assume that the density functions $p_i(\varepsilon_i)$ are symmetric around zero in the sense that $p_i(\varepsilon_i) = p_i(-\varepsilon_i)$, that is, $P[\varepsilon_i \geq c] = P[\varepsilon_i \leq -c]$ for every value of c.

(ii) Two estimation methods: OLS and QML with (scaled) *t*(5)-disturbances

As the distribution of the disturbances is unknown, we cannot estimate the parameters α and β by maximum likelihood. We consider two estimators, least squares (OLS) and quasi-maximum likelihood (QML) based on the (scaled) $t(5)$-distribution introduced in Example 4.5 (p. 244). We compute the standard errors by GMM and compare the outcomes with those obtained by the conventional expressions for OLS and ML standard errors.

(iii) Correctness of moment conditions under the stated assumptions

Under the above assumptions, the OLS and QML estimators are consistent and (asymptotic) GMM standard errors can be obtained from (4.67) and (4.68), provided that the specified moment conditions hold true for the DGP. For OLS this follows from Assumptions 1 and 2, as discussed in Section 4.4.5. For QML, the moment conditions are given by (4.59)—that is, $E[\partial l_i/\partial\theta]_{|\theta=\theta_0} = 0$. We use only the moments for α and β, with first order conditions described in Example 4.5 (p. 244). That is,

$$g_i^{QML}(\alpha_0, \beta_0) = \begin{pmatrix} \frac{\partial l_i}{\partial\alpha} \\ \frac{\partial l_i}{\partial\beta} \end{pmatrix} = \begin{pmatrix} \dfrac{6\varepsilon_i}{5\sigma^2 + \varepsilon_i^2} \\ \dfrac{6x_i\varepsilon_i}{5\sigma^2 + \varepsilon_i^2} \end{pmatrix}$$

(in QML we use the estimated value $\hat{\sigma}^2 = 4.49$ obtained in Example 4.5). It follows from Assumptions 1 and 2, together with the symmetry of the densities $p_i(\varepsilon_i)$, that $E[g_i^{QML}(\alpha_0, \beta_0)] = 0$. Therefore, under the stated assumptions the moment conditions are valid for both estimation procedures.

(iv) Estimation results

The results in Exhibit 4.21 show the estimates for OLS (Panels 1 and 2) and QML (Panels 3 and 4), with standard errors computed both in the conventional way (see Section 4.4.3, by means of V_{OLS} in Panel 1 and V_{ML} in Panel 3) and by means of GMM as in (4.67) (in Panels 2 and 4). For OLS, the matrices H_n and J_n in (4.68) were derived in Section 4.4.5. For QML, the matrices H_n and J_n can be derived from the above expression for g_i^{QML}. The differences between the OLS and QML estimates are not so large, and the same applies for the standard errors (computed in four different ways for $\hat{\alpha}$ and $\hat{\beta}$). Therefore, the effects of possible heteroskedasticity and non-normality of the disturbances seem to be relatively mild for these data. The application of OLS with conventional formulas for the standard errors seems to be reasonable for these data.

(v) Test outcomes

We finally consider tests for the hypothesis that $\alpha = 0$ against the alternative that $\alpha \neq 0$, and also for $\beta = 1$ against the alternative that $\beta \neq 1$. Based on the (asymptotic) normal distribution, the P-values of the test outcomes in Exhibit 4.21 are as follows:

$$\text{for } \alpha = 0: \quad P_{OLS} = 0.22, \quad P_{OLS}^{GMM} = 0.19, \quad P_{ML} = 0.32, \quad P_{ML}^{GMM} = 0.30,$$
$$\text{for } \beta = 1: \quad P_{OLS} = 0.023, \quad P_{OLS}^{GMM} = 0.012, \quad P_{ML} = 0.008, \quad P_{ML}^{GMM} = 0.003.$$

Panel 1: Dependent Variable: RENDCYCO Method: Least Squares Sample: 1980:01 1999:12 Included observations: 240				
Variable	Coefficient	Std. Error	t-Statistic	Prob.
C	−0.447481	0.362943	−1.232924	0.2188
RENDMARK	1.171128	0.075386	15.53500	0.0000
R-squared	0.503480			

Panel 2: Dependent Variable: RENDCYCO Method: Generalized Method of Moments Sample: 1980:01 1999:12 Included observations: 240 Moment Conditions: normal equations				
Variable	Coefficient	Std. Error	t-Statistic	Prob.
C	−0.447481	0.342143	−1.307876	0.1922
RENDMARK	1.171128	0.067926	17.24135	0.0000
R-squared	0.503480			

Panel 3: Model: RENDCYCO = C(1) + C(2)*RENDMARK + EPS EPS are IID with scaled t(5) distribution, scale parameter is C(3) Method: Maximum Likelihood (BHHH) Sample: 1980:01 1999:12 Included observations: 240 Convergence achieved after 19 iterations				
Parameter	Coefficient	Std. Error	z-Statistic	Prob.
C(1)	−0.344971	0.348223	−0.990660	0.3219
C(2)	1.196406	0.073841	16.20244	0.0000
C(3)	4.494241	0.271712	16.54049	0.0000
Log likelihood	−747.6813			

Panel 4: GMM standard errors	
a_{ML} (C(1) in Panel 3)	0.334173
b_{ML} (C(2) in Panel 3)	0.066475

Exhibit 4.21 Stock Market Returns (Section 4.4.6)

Results of different estimates of CAPM for the sector of cyclical consumer goods, estimated by OLS (Panel 1) and by ML (Panel 3, using the scaled $t(5)$ distribution for the disturbances). For OLS the standard errors are computed in two ways, as usual (Panel 1, using the expression $s^2(X'X)^{-1}$ of Chapter 3) and by means of GMM (Panel 2, using the normal equations of OLS as moment conditions). For ML the standard errors are also computed in two ways, as usual (Panel 3, using the information matrix as discussed in Section 4.3.3) and by means of GMM (Panel 4, using the first order conditions for the maximum of the log-likelihood as moment conditions).

The four computed P-values for these two tests all point in the same direction. The outcomes suggest that we should reject the hypothesis that $\beta = 1$ but not that $\alpha = 0$. The conclusions based on ML are somewhat sharper than those based on OLS.

Summary, further reading, and keywords

SUMMARY

In this chapter we considered methods that can be applied if some of the assumptions of the regression model in Chapter 3 are not satisfied. If the regressors are stochastic or the disturbances are not normally distributed, then the results of Chapter 3 are still valid asymptotically if the regressors are exogenous. If the model is non-linear in the parameters, then the least squares estimator has to be computed by numerical optimization methods and this estimator has similar asymptotic properties as the least squares estimator in the linear model. Maximum likelihood is a widely applicable estimation method that has (asymptotically) optimal properties — that is, it is consistent and it has minimal variance among all consistent estimators. This method requires that the joint probability distribution of the disturbances is correctly specified. If there is much uncertainty about this distribution, then the generalized method of moments can be applied. In this case the parameters are estimated by solving a set of moment equations, and the standard errors are computed in a way that does not require the joint probability distribution. This method requires that the specified moment conditions are valid for the data generating process.

FURTHER READING

The textbooks mentioned in Chapter 3, Further Reading (p. 178–9), all contain sections on asymptotic analysis, non-linear methods, maximum likelihood, and the generalized method of moments. We further refer in particular to Davidson and MacKinnon (1993), Gourieroux and Monfort (1995), and Hayashi (2000).

Davidson, R., and MacKinnon, J. G. (1993). *Estimation and Inference in Econometrics*. New York: Oxford University Press.

Gourieroux, C., and Monfort, A. (1995). *Statistics and Econometric Models*. 2 vols. Cambridge: Cambridge University Press.

Hayashi, F. (2000). *Econometrics*. Princeton: Princeton University Press.

KEYWORDS

Exercises

THEORY QUESTIONS

4.1 (☞ Section 4.1.3)
The consistency of b depends on the probability limits of the two terms $\frac{1}{n}X'X$ and $\frac{1}{n}X'\varepsilon$.

a. Investigate this consistency for nine cases, according to whether these limits are zero, finite, or infinite.
b. Give examples of models where $\text{plim}(\frac{1}{n}X'X)$ is zero, finite, and infinite. Give an intuitive explanation why b is (in)consistent in these cases.

4.2 (☞ Section 4.1.5)
Consider the data generating process $y_i = x_i + \varepsilon_i$ where ε_i are independently normally distributed N(0, 1) random variables. For simplicity we estimate the parameter $\beta = 1$ by regression in the model without constant term—that is, in the model $y_i = \beta x_i + \varepsilon_i$. By the speed of convergence of b to β we mean the power n^p for which the distribution of $n^p(b - \beta)$ does not diverge and also does not have limit zero if $n \to \infty$. Section 4.1 presented results with speed of convergence $\sqrt{n}$, see (4.7).

a. Let $x_i = i$. Show that this DGP does not satisfy Assumption 1*. Show that the speed of convergence is $n\sqrt{n}$ in this case. (It may be helpful to use the fact that $\sum_{i=1}^{n} i^2 = \frac{1}{6}n(n+1)(2n+1)$.)
b. Now let $x_i = 1/i$. Show that this DGP also does not satisfy Assumption 1*. Show that $\text{plim}(b)$ does not exist in this case, and that the speed of convergence is n^0. (It may be helpful to use the fact that $\sum_{i=1}^{\infty} (1/i)^2 = \frac{1}{6}\pi^2$.)

4.3 (☞ Section 4.1.3)
Consider the linear model $y = X\beta + \varepsilon$ with stochastic regressors that satisfy Assumption 1* and with $\text{plim}(\frac{1}{n}X'\varepsilon) = (0, \cdots, 0, \rho)'$, so that only the last regressor is asymptotically correlated with the error term.

a. Show that, in general, b is inconsistent with respect to all coefficients of the vector β.
b. Under which condition does only the estimator of the last coefficient become inconsistent? Provide an intuitive explanation of this result.

4.4 (☞ Section 4.1.3)
Consider the model with measurement errors, where two economic variables y^* and x^* are related by $y^* = \alpha + \beta x^*$ and where the measured variables are given by $y = y^* + \varepsilon_y$ and $x = x^* + \varepsilon_x$. The variances of the measurement errors ε_y and ε_x are denoted by σ_y^2 and σ_x^2 respectively. It is assumed that ε_y and ε_x are uncorrelated with each other and that both are also uncorrelated with the variables y^* and x^*. The variance of x^* is denoted by σ_*^2. The observed data consist of n independent observations (x_i, y_i), $i = 1, \cdots, n$.

a. Write the model in the form $y = \alpha + \beta x + \varepsilon$ and express ε in terms of ε_y and ε_x.
b. Show that the OLS estimator b is inconsistent if $\sigma_x^2 \neq 0$ and $\beta \neq 0$.
c. Express the magnitude of the inconsistency (that is, $\text{plim}(b) - \beta$) in terms of the so-called signal-to-noise ratio $\text{var}(x_*)/\text{var}(\varepsilon_x) = \sigma_*^2/\sigma_x^2$. Explain this result by means of two scatter diagrams, one with small and the other with large signal-to-noise ratio.

4.5 (☞ Section 4.3.8)
In Section 4.3 it was discussed that the *LM*-, *LR*-, and *W*-tests are asymptotically distributed as $\chi^2(g)$, but that $gF(g, n-k)$ can also be used.

a. Show that for $n \to \infty$ there holds $gF(g, n-k) \xrightarrow{d} \chi^2(g)$.
b. Check that the *P*-values (corresponding to the right tail of the distributions) of $gF(g, n-k)$ are larger than those of $\chi^2(g)$, by using a statistical package or by inspecting tables of critical values of both distributions.

c. Comment on the relevance of this result for applying the LM-, LR-, and W-tests.

4.6 (☞ Sections 4.2.4, 4.3.2, 4.3.8)

a. Prove the expression (4.23) for the relation between the LM-test and the F-test in the linear model $y = X_1\beta_1 + X_2\beta_2 + \varepsilon$ for the null hypothesis $\beta_2 = 0$. It may be helpful to prove as a first step that the numerator of R^2 in (4.21) can be written, with $M = I - X(X'X)^{-1}X'$, as $e_R'(I - M)e_R = e_R'e_R - e_R'Me_R$ and that $e_R'Me_R = e'e$.

b. Prove the inequalities in (4.56) for testing a linear hypothesis in the linear model $y = X\beta + \varepsilon$. For this purpose, make use of the expressions (4.23), (4.46), and (4.49), which express the three tests LM, LR, and W in terms of the F-test.

c. Show the statement at the end of Section 4.3.2 that ML in a non-linear regression model with normally distributed disturbances is equivalent to non-linear least squares.

4.7* (☞ Section 4.4.3)

Prove that the choice of weights $W = J_0^{-1}$ (with the notation of Section 4.4) minimizes the asymptotic covariance matrix V in (4.65) of the GMM estimator. Also prove that this choice makes the GMM estimator invariant with respect to linear transformations of the model restrictions (4.61)—that is, if g_i is replaced by Ag_i, where A is an $m \times m$ non-singular matrix.

EMPIRICAL AND SIMULATION QUESTIONS

4.8 (☞ Section 4.1.3)

Suppose that data are generated by the process $y_i = \beta_1 + \beta_2 x_{2i} + \beta_3 x_{3i} + \omega_i$, where the ω_i are $\text{IID}(0, \sigma^2)$ disturbances that are uncorrelated with the regressors x_2 and x_3. Suppose that the regressors x_2 and x_3 are positively correlated. An investigator investigates the relation between y and x_2 by regressing y on a constant and x_2—that is, x_3 is omitted. The estimator of β_2 in this restricted model is denoted by b_2^R, and the estimator of σ^2 in this model is denoted by s_R^2.

a. Investigate whether b_2^R is an unbiased and/or consistent estimator of β_2.

b. Also argue whether or not s_R^2 will be an unbiased and/or consistent estimator of σ^2.

c. Construct a data generating process that satisfies the above specifications. Generate samples of sizes $n = 10$, $n = 100$, and $n = 1000$ of this process.

d. Compute the estimates b_2^R and s_R^2 for the sample sizes $n = 10$, $n = 100$, and $n = 1000$. Compare these outcomes with the results in **a** and **b**.

4.9 (☞ Section 4.2.3)

a. Generate a sample of size 100 from the model $y_i = 2 + \sqrt{x_i} + \varepsilon_i$, where the x_i are independent and uniformly distributed on the interval [0, 20] and the ε_i are independent and distributed as N(0, 0.01).

b. Consider the non-linear regression model $y = f(x, \beta) + \varepsilon$ with $f(x, \beta) = \beta_1 + \beta_2 x^{\beta_3}$. Determine the 3×1 vector of gradients $g = \partial f / \partial \beta$ of this model.

c. Perform twenty steps of the Gauss–Newton method to estimate β, with starting values $\beta = (0, 1, 1)'$. Plot the three resulting series of twenty estimates of β_1, β_2, and β_3.

d. Now take as starting values $\beta = (0, 1, 0)$. Explain the problems that arise in this case.

e. With the final estimate in **c**, perform an F-test of the hypothesis that $\beta_3 = 1/2$. Perform also an LM-test of this hypothesis.

4.10 (☞ Sections 4.2.4, 4.3.7)

Consider the DGP $y_i = 1 + x_i^2 + \omega_i$ with $x_i \sim \text{NID}(0, 1)$ and $\omega_i \sim \text{NID}(0, 1)$ and with $(x_1, \cdots, x_n)$ independent from $(\omega_1, \cdots, \omega_n)$. The estimated model is $y_i = \beta_1 + \beta_2 x_i + \beta_3 x_i^2 + \varepsilon_i$—that is, with additional regressor x_i. Let b_2 denote the least squares estimate of β_2 in this model.

a. Generate two samples of this model, one of size $n = 10$ and another of size $n = 100$. Determine b_2 and the standard error of b_2 for these two samples.

b. Perform an LM-test for the null hypothesis that $\beta_2 = 0$ against the alternative that $\beta_2 \neq 0$ for the two samples of **a**. Use a 5% significance level (the 5% critical value of the $\chi^2(1)$ distribution is 3.84).

c. Repeat **a** and **b** 1000 times, drawing new values for x_i and ω_i in each simulation run. Make histograms of the resulting 1000 values of b_2 and of the LM-test, both for $n = 10$ and for $n = 100$.

d. What is the standard deviation of the 1000 outcomes of b_2 for $n = 10$? And for $n = 100$? How does this compare with the standard errors in **a**?

e. How many of the 1000 computed LM-values are larger than 3.84 for $n = 10$? And for $n = 100$? Comment on the outcomes.

f. Compute the asymptotic distribution (4.7) for the parameter vector $\beta = (\beta_1, \beta_2, \beta_3)'$ of this DGP. What approximation does this provide for the standard error of b_2? How does this compare with the results in **d**?

4.11 (☞ Sections 4.3.5, 4.4.3)
In this simulation exercise we generate a random sample by means of $y_i = \mu + \varepsilon_i$, where $\mu = \frac{1}{2}$ and the disturbances ε_i are independently and identically distributed with the $t(3)$ distribution. A researcher who does not know the DGP is interested in testing the hypothesis that the observations come from a population with mean zero. This hypothesis is, of course, not correct, as the DGP has mean $\frac{1}{2}$.

a. Simulate a set of $n = 50$ data from this DGP. Make a histogram of the simulated data set.

b. The researcher tests the null hypothesis of zero mean by means of the conventional (least squares based) t-test. Perform this test. What is the computed standard error of the sample mean? What is the true standard deviation of the sample mean? What is your conclusion?

c. Suppose now that the researcher uses GMM, based on the moment condition $E[y_i - \mu] = 0$ for $i = 1, \cdots, n$. What is the estimated mean? What is the corresponding GMM standard error? Give a formal proof, based on (4.67) and (4.68), of the fact that in the current model the GMM standard error is equal to the conventional OLS standard error multiplied by the factor $\sqrt{1 - \frac{1}{n}}$.

d. Now the researcher postulates the Cauchy distribution (that is, the $t(1)$ distribution) for the disturbances. Using this distribution, compute the corresponding ML estimate of μ and perform the Wald test on the hypothesis that $\mu = 0$. What is the computed standard error of this ML estimator of μ? Why is this not the true standard error of this estimator?

e. Now suppose that the researcher is so lucky to postulate the $t(3)$ distribution for the disturbances. Perform the corresponding Wald test of the hypothesis that the population mean is zero.

f. Discuss which method (of the ones used in **b–e**) the researcher would best use if he or she does not know the DGP and is uncertain about the correct disturbance distribution.

4.12 (☞ Sections 4.3.2, 4.4.3)

In this exercise we consider a simulated data set of sample size $n = 50$. The data were generated by the model

$$y_i = 0.5 + x_i + \eta_i, \qquad i = 1, \cdots, 50,$$

where the regressors x_i are IID with uniform distribution on the interval $0 \leq x \leq 2$ and the η_i are IID with $t(3)$ distribution. The estimated model is

$$y_i = \alpha + \beta x_i + \varepsilon_i,$$

so that the correct parameter values of the DGP are $\alpha = 0.5$ and $\beta = 1$. In answering the following questions, give comments on all the outcomes.

a. Estimate the parameters α and β by means of OLS.

b. Make a scatter plot of the data and make a histogram of the OLS residuals obtained in **a**.

c. Determine the GMM standard errors of the OLS estimates of α and β.

d. Estimate the parameters α and β by ML, using the (incorrect) Cauchy distribution for the disturbances ε_i. The density of the Cauchy distribution (that is, the $t(1)$ distribution) is $f(\varepsilon_i) = \frac{1}{\pi(1+\varepsilon_i^2)}$.

e. Estimate the parameters α and β now by ML using the (incorrect) $t(5)$ distribution with density $f(\varepsilon_i) \propto \frac{1}{\left(1+\frac{1}{5}\varepsilon_i^2\right)^3}$.

f. Finally estimate the parameters α and β by ML using the correct $t(3)$ distribution with density $f(\varepsilon_i) \propto \frac{1}{\left(1+\frac{1}{3}\varepsilon_i^2\right)^2}$.

g. Explain why GMM provides no help here to get a clear idea of the slope parameter β. Also explain why the (incorrect) ML estimates in **d** and **e** perform quite well in this case. State your overall conclusion for estimating models for data that are scattered in a way as depicted in **b**.

4.13 (☞ Section 4.3.8)

Consider the $n = 12$ data for coffee sales of brand 2 in Section 4.2.5. Let $y = \log(q)$ denote the logarithm of quantity sold and $x = \log(d)$ the logarithm of the deal rate. Two econometricians (A and B) estimate different models for these data—namely,

$$A: y = \alpha + \beta x + \varepsilon, \quad B: y = \gamma(1 + \delta x) + \varepsilon.$$

The least squares estimates of α and β are denoted by a and b, the (non-linear) least squares estimates of γ and δ by c and d. In the tests below use a significance level of 5%.

a. Give a mathematical proof of the fact that $c = a$ and $d = b/a$.

b. Perform the two regressions and check that the outcomes satisfy the relations in **a**.

c. Test the hypothesis that $\delta = 1$ by a Wald test.

d. Test this hypothesis also by a Lagrange Multiplier test.

e. Test this hypothesis also by a Likelihood Ratio test.

f. Test this hypothesis using the model of econometrician A.

4.14 (☞ Section 4.3.8)

In this exercise we consider the bank wage data and the model discussed before in Section 3.4.2. Here the logarithm of yearly wage (y) is explained in terms of education (x_2), logarithm of begin salary (x_3), gender (x_4), and minority (x_5), by the model

$$y = \beta_1 + \beta_2 x_2 + \beta_3 x_3 + \beta_4 x_4 + \beta_5 x_5 + \varepsilon.$$

The data set consists of observations for $n = 474$ individuals. Apart from the unrestricted model we consider three restricted models—that is, (i) $\beta_5 = 0$, (ii) $\beta_4 = \beta_5 = 0$, (iii) $\beta_4 + \beta_5 = 0$. For all tests below, compute the relevant (asymptotic) P-values.

a. For each of the four models, compute the SSR and the ML estimate s^2_{ML} of the disturbance variance.

b. Compute the log-likelihoods (4.30) of the four models. Perform LR-tests for the three restricted models against the unrestricted model.

c. Perform Wald tests for the three restricted models against the unrestricted model.

d. Perform also LM-tests for the three restricted models against the unrestricted model, by means of auxiliary regressions (4.55).

e. Compare the outcomes with the ones obtained in Section 3.4.2.

4.15 (☞ Section 4.3.8)

Use the same bank wage data set as in Exercise 4.14. Now assume that we accept the hypothesis that $\beta_5 = 0$ and that we wish to test the hypothesis that $\beta_4 = 0$, given that $\beta_5 = 0$. In the notation of Exercise 4.14, we test the restricted model (ii) against the alternative 'unrestricted' model (i). For the tests below, compute the relevant (asymptotic) P-values.

a. Perform conventional t- and F-tests for this hypothesis.

b. Compute also the LR-, W-, and LM-tests for this hypothesis.

c. Use these outcomes to discuss the difference between joint testing of multiple restrictions (as in Exercise 4.14 with the joint model restriction (ii) tested against the full model with all five regressors) and sequential testing of single hypotheses (as in the current exercise). In particular, consider the differences if one uses a significance level of 2.5% in all tests.

4.16 (☞ Section 4.3.8)

In this exercise we consider the food expenditure data on food consumption (fc, measured in \$10,000 per year), total consumption (tc, also measured in \$10,000 per year), and average household size (hs) that were discussed in Example 4.3 (p. 204–5). As dependent variable we take $y = fc/tc$, the fraction of total consumption spent on food, and as explanatory variables we take (apart from a constant term) $x_2 = tc$ and $x_3 = hs$. The estimated model is of the form $y_i = f(x_{2i}, x_{3i}, \beta) + \varepsilon_i$, where $f(x_{2i}, x_{3i}, \beta) = \beta_1 + \beta_2 x_{2i}^{\beta_3} + \beta_4 x_{3i}$. We will consider three hypotheses for the parameter β_3—namely, $\beta_3 = 0$ (so that x_2 has no effect on y), $\beta_3 = 1$ (so that the marginal effect of x_2 on y is constant), and $\beta_3 = \frac{1}{2}$ (so that the marginal effect of x_2 on y declines for higher values of x_2).

a. Exhibit 4.6 shows a scatter diagram of y against x_2. Discuss whether you can get any intuition from this diagram concerning the question which of the hypotheses $\beta_3 = 0$, $\beta_3 = 1$, and $\beta_3 = \frac{1}{2}$ could be plausible.

b. For $\beta_3 = 0$ the parameters $(\beta_1, \beta_2, \beta_4)$ of the model are not identified. Prove this. What reformulation of the restricted model (for $\beta_3 = 0$) is needed to get identified parameters in this case?

c. Estimate the unrestricted model with four regression parameters. Try out different starting values and pay attention to the convergence of the estimates.

d. Test the three hypotheses ($\beta_3 = 0$, $\beta_3 = 1$, and $\beta_3 = \frac{1}{2}$) by means of t-tests.

e. Test these three hypotheses also by means of F-tests.

f. Now test the three hypotheses by means of LR-tests.

g. Test the three hypotheses by means of LM-tests, using the result (4.21) with appropriate auxiliary regressions. The regressors in step 2 of the LM-test consist of the four partial derivatives $\frac{\partial f}{\partial \beta_j}$ for $j = 1, 2, 3, 4$.

h. Test the three hypotheses by means of the Wald test as expressed in (4.48). Formulate the parameter restriction respectively as $r(\theta) = \beta_3 = 0$, $r(\theta) = \beta_3 - 1 = 0$, and $r(\theta) = \beta_3 - \frac{1}{2} = 0$.

i. Test the three hypotheses again by means of the Wald test as expressed in (4.48), but now with the parameter restriction formulated as respectively $r(\theta) = \beta_3^2 = 0$, $r(\theta) = \beta_3^2 - 1 = 0$, and $r(\theta) = \beta_3^2 - \frac{1}{4} = 0$.

j. Compare the outcomes of the foregoing six testing methods (in d–i) for the three hypotheses on β_3. Comment on the similarities and differences of the test outcomes.

4.17 (☞ Sections 4.3.3, 4.4.4, 4.4.5)

In this exercise we consider the stock market returns data for the sector of non-cyclical consumer goods in the UK. The model is $y_i = \alpha + \beta x_i + \varepsilon_i$, where y_i are the excess returns in this sector and x_i are the market excess returns. The monthly data are given for 1980–99, giving $n = 240$ observations. The disturbances ε_i are assumed to be IID distributed, either with normal distribution $N(0, \sigma^2)$ or with the Cauchy distribution with density $f(\varepsilon_i) = \left(\pi(1 + \varepsilon_i^2)\right)^{-1}$.

a. Determine the log-likelihood for the case of Cauchy disturbances. Show that the ML estimates for α and β are obtained from the two conditions $\sum \varepsilon_i(1 + \varepsilon_i^2)^{-1} = 0$ and $\sum \varepsilon_i x_i(1 + \varepsilon_i^2)^{-1} = 0$.

b. Estimate α and β by ML, based on the Cauchy distribution. Determine also the (asymptotic) standard errors of these estimates.

c. Estimate α and β by ML, based on the normal distribution. Compute also the standard errors of these estimates. Compare the results with those obtained by OLS.

d. Test the hypothesis that $\alpha = 0$ using the results in **b**. Test this hypothesis also using the results in **c**. Use a 5% significance level.

e. Answer the questions in **d** also for the hypothesis that $\beta = 1$. Again use a 5% significance level.

f. Determine the two histograms of the residuals corresponding to the estimates in **b** and **c**. On the basis of this information, which of the two estimation methods do you prefer? Motivate your answer.

g. Compute GMM standard errors of the estimates in **c**—that is, the estimates based on the two moment conditions $E[\varepsilon_i] = 0$ and $E[\varepsilon_i x_i] = 0$. How does this compare with the (ordinary) standard errors computed in **c**? Does this alter your answers in **d** and **e** to test respectively whether $\alpha = 0$ and $\beta = 1$?

h*. Finally, consider the QML estimates based on the two Cauchy moment conditions defined by $E[\frac{\varepsilon_i}{1+\varepsilon_i^2}] = 0$ and $E[\frac{\varepsilon_i x_i}{1+\varepsilon_i^2}] = 0$. Determine the GMM standard errors of these estimates and perform the two tests of **d** and **e**. Compare the outcomes (standard errors and test results) with the outcomes in **b**, **d**, and **e** based on the Cauchy ML standard errors.

5

Diagnostic Tests and Model Adjustments

In this chapter we describe methods to test the assumptions of the regression model. If some of the assumptions are not satisfied then there are several ways to proceed. One option is to use least squares and to derive the properties of this estimator under more general conditions. Another option is to adjust the specification of the model — for instance, by changing the included variables, the functional form, or the probability distribution of the disturbance terms. We discuss alternative model specifications, including non-linear models, disturbances that are heteroskedastic or serially correlated, and the use of instrumental variables.

Most of the sections of this chapter can be read independently of each other. We refer to Exhibit 0.3 (p. 8) for the sections of this chapter that are needed for selected topics in Chapters 6 and 7.

5.1 Introduction

Modelling in practice

It is the skill of econometricians to use economic theory and statistical data in order to construct econometric models that provide an adequate summary of the available information. In most situations the relevant theoretical information is of a qualitative nature, suggesting which economic variables play a role and perhaps whether variables are positively or negatively related. Most models from economic theory describe a part of the economy in isolation from its environment (the *ceteris paribus* assumption). This means that the empirical modeller is faced with the following two questions. How should the relationships between the variables of interest be specified, and how should the other influences be taken into account?

In practice it often occurs that an initially chosen econometric model does not fit well to the data. This may happen despite genuine efforts to use economic theory and to collect data that are relevant for the investigation at hand. The model may turn out to be weak, for instance, because important aspects of the data are left unexplained or because some of the basic assumptions underlying the econometric model are violated. Examples of the latter are that the residuals may be far from normal or that the parameter estimates may differ substantially in subsamples. If the model is not correctly specified, there are various avenues to take, depending on the degree of belief one has in the employed model structure and in the observed data. In this book we describe econometric modelling from an applied point of view where we start from the data. We consider models as constructs that we can change in the light of the data information. By incorporating more of the relevant data characteristics in the model, we may improve our understanding of the underlying economic processes. The selection and adjustment of models are guided by our insight in the relevant economic and business phenomena. As economic theory does not often suggest explicit models, this leaves some freedom to choose the model specification. Several diagnostic tests have been developed that help to get clear ideas about which features of the model need improvement.

This view on econometric modelling differs from a more traditional one that has more confidence in the theory and the postulated model and less in the observed data. In this view econometrics is concerned with the measurement of theoretical relations as suggested by economic theory. In our approach, on the other hand, we are not primarily interested in testing a particular theory but in using data to get a better understanding of an observed phenomenon of interest. The major role of tests is then to find out whether the chosen model is able to represent the main characteristics of interest of the data.

Diagnostic tests

In econometrics we use empirical data to improve our understanding of economic processes. The regression model,

$$y = X\beta + \varepsilon,$$

discussed in Chapter 3 is one of the standard tools of analysis. This is a nice tool as it is simple to apply and it gives reliable information if the assumptions of Chapter 3 are satisfied. Several tests are available to test whether the proposed model is correctly specified. Such tests of the underlying model assumptions are called *misspecification tests*. Because the purpose of the analysis is to make a diagnosis of the quality of the model, this is also called *diagnostic testing*. Like a medical doctor, the econometrician tries to detect possible weaknesses of the model, to diagnose possible causes, and to propose treatments (model adjustments) to end up with a 'healthy' model. Such a model is characterized by the fact that it provides insight into the problem at hand and that it shows acceptable reactions to relevant diagnostic tests.

The regression model $y = X\beta + \varepsilon$ was analysed in Chapter 3 under the seven assumptions stated in Section 3.1.4 (p. 125–6). All these assumptions will be subjected to diagnostic tests in this chapter. In Section 5.2 we test the specification of the functional form—that is, the number of included explanatory variables in X and the way they enter into the model (Assumptions 2 and 6). Section 5.3 considers the possibility of non-constant parameters β (Assumptions 5 and 2). Next we examine the assumptions on the disturbance terms ε and we discuss alternative estimation methods in the case of heteroskedasticity (Assumption 3, in Section 5.4), serial correlation (Assumption 4, in Section 5.5), and non-normal distributions (Assumption 7, in Section 5.6). Finally, in Section 5.7 we consider models with endogenous regressors in X, in which case the orthogonality condition of Section 4.1.3 (p. 194) is violated.

The empirical cycle in model construction

In practice, econometric models are formed in a sequence of steps. First one selects the relevant data, specifies an initial model, and chooses an estimation method. The resulting estimated model is subjected to diagnostic tests. The test outcomes can help to make better choices for the model and the estimation method (and sometimes for the data). The new model is again subjected to diagnostic tests, and this process is repeated until the final model is

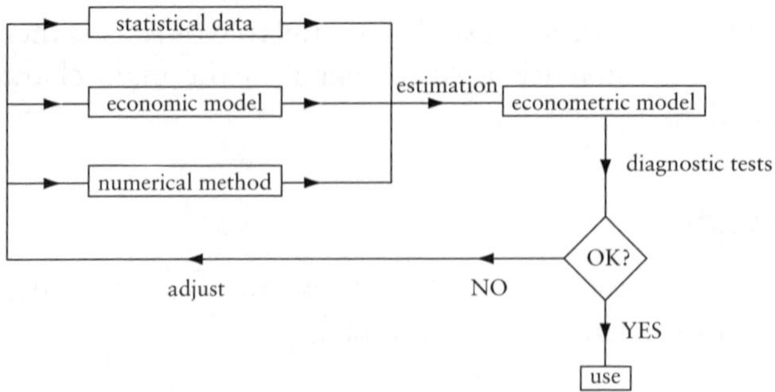

Exhibit 5.1 The empirical cycle in econometric modelling

satisfactory. This process of iterative model specification and testing is called the *empirical cycle* (see Exhibit 5.1).

This sequential method of model construction has implications for the interpretation of test outcomes. Tests are usually performed under the assumption that the model has been correctly specified. For instance, the computed standard errors of estimated coefficients and their *P*-values depend on this assumption. In practice, in initial rounds of the empirical cycle we may work with first-guess models that are not appropriately specified. This may lead, for instance, to underestimation of the standard errors. Also in this situation diagnostic tests remain helpful tools to find suitable models. However, one should not report *P*-values without providing the details of the search process that has led to the finally chosen model.

At this point we mention one diagnostic tool that is of particular importance—namely, the evaluation of the predictive quality of proposed models. It is advisable to exclude a part of the observed data in the process of model construction. The excluded data are called the *hold-out sample*. It is then possible to investigate whether the final model that is obtained in the empirical cycle is able to predict the outcomes in this hold-out sample. This provides a clear test of model quality, irrespective of the way the model has been obtained. Forecast evaluation as a diagnostic tool will be further discussed in Sections 5.2.1 (p. 280) and 7.2.4 (p. 570).

5.2 Functional form and explanatory variables

5.2.1 The number of explanatory variables

How many variables should be included?

Assume that a set of explanatory variables has been selected as possible determinants of the variable y. Even if one is interested in the effect of only one of these explanatory variables—say, x_2—it is of importance not to exclude the other variables a priori. The reason is that variation in the other variables may cause variations in the variable y, and, if these variables are excluded from the model, then all the variations in y will be attributed to the variable x_2 alone. On the other hand, the list of possibly influential variables may be very long. If all these variables are included, it may be impossible to estimate the model (if the number of parameters becomes larger than the number of observations) or the estimates may become very inefficient (owing to a lack of degrees of freedom if there are insufficient observations available). The question then is how many variables to include in the model.

Suppose that we want to estimate the effects of a set of $(k - g)$ variables X_1 on the dependent variable y, and that in addition another set of g variables X_2 is available that possibly also influence the dependent variable y. The effects of X_1 on y can be estimated in the model $y = X_1\beta_1 + \varepsilon$, with estimator $b_R = (X_1'X_1)^{-1}X_1'y$. An alternative is to include the variables X_2 and to perform a regression in the model $y = X_1\beta_1 + X_2\beta_2 + \varepsilon$, with corresponding estimators (b_1, b_2) of (β_1, β_2). Which estimator of β_1 should be preferred, b_1 or b_R?

Trade-off between bias and efficiency

The answer to the above question is easy if $\beta_2 = 0$. In Section 3.2.4 (p. 144) we showed that the inclusion of irrelevant variables leads to a loss in efficiency. More precisely, under Assumptions 1–6 and with $\beta_2 = 0$ there holds $E[b_1] = E[b_R] = \beta_1$, so that both estimators are unbiased, and $\text{var}(b_1) \geq \text{var}(b_R)$ (in the sense that $\text{var}(b_1) - \text{var}(b_R)$ is positive semidefinite). On the other hand, if $\beta_2 \neq 0$, then the situation is more complicated. In Section 3.2.3 (p. 142–3) we showed that by deleting variables we obtain an estimator that is in general biased (so that $E[b_R] \neq \beta_1$), but that it has a smaller variance than the unbiased estimator b_1 (so that $\text{var}(b_R) \leq \text{var}(b_1)$). The question then becomes whether the gain in efficiency is large enough to justify the bias that results from deleting X_2. The fact that restrictions improve the efficiency is one of the main motivations for modelling, but of course the restrictions should not introduce too much *bias*. If many observations are available, then it is better to start with a model that includes all variables that are economically meaningful, as deleting variables gives only a small gain in efficiency.

T

A prediction criterion and relation with the *F*-test

A possible criterion to find a trade-off between bias and variance is the mean squared error (MSE) of an estimator $\hat{\beta}$ of β, defined by

$$\text{MSE}(\hat{\beta}) = E[(\hat{\beta} - \beta)(\hat{\beta} - \beta)'] = \text{var}(\hat{\beta}) + (E[\hat{\beta}] - \beta)(E[\hat{\beta}] - \beta)'.$$

If β contains more than one component then the MSE is a matrix, and the last equality follows by using the definition of the variance $\text{var}(\hat{\beta}) = E[(\hat{\beta} - E[\hat{\beta}])(\hat{\beta} - E[\hat{\beta}])']$. A scalar criterion could be obtained by taking the trace of the MSE matrix. However, as the magnitude of the individual parameters β_j depends on the scales of measurement of the individual explanatory variables x_j, this addition of squared errors $(\hat{\beta}_j - \beta_j)^2$ does not make much sense in general. Instead we consider the accuracy of the prediction $\hat{y} = X\hat{\beta}$ of the vector of mean values $E[y] = X\beta$, as the prediction error $X\hat{\beta} - X\beta$ does not depend on the scales of measurement. The *total mean squared prediction error* (TMSP) is defined as the sum of the squared prediction errors $(\hat{y}_i - E[y_i])^2$—that is,

$$\text{TMSP}(\hat{\beta}) = E[(X\hat{\beta} - X\beta)'(X\hat{\beta} - X\beta)].$$

We can apply this criterion to compare the predictions $\hat{y} = X_1 b_1 + X_2 b_2$ of the larger model with the predictions $\hat{y}_R = X_1 b_R$ of the smaller model. It is left as an exercise (see Exercise 5.2) to show that $\text{TMSP}(b_R) \leq \text{TMSP}(b_1)$ if and only if

$$\beta_2' V_2^{-1} \beta_2 \leq g,$$

where V_2 is the covariance matrix of b_2 and g is the number of components of β_2. So the restricted estimator b_R has a smaller TMSP than the unbiased estimator b_1 if β_2 is sufficiently small and/or the variance V_2 of the estimator b_2 is sufficiently large. In such a situation it is also intuitively evident that it is better to reduce the uncertainty by eliminating the variables X_2 from the model. In practice, β_2 and V_2 are of course unknown. We can replace β_2 and V_2 by their least squares estimates in the model $y = X_1\beta_1 + X_2\beta_2 + \varepsilon$. That is, β_2 is replaced by b_2 and V_2 by $\hat{V}_2 = s^2(X_2'M_1X_2)^{-1}$, where s^2 is the estimated error variance in the unrestricted model and $M_1 = I - X_1(X_1'X_1)^{-1}X_1'$ (see Section 3.4.1 (p. 161)). We can prefer to delete the variables X_2 from the model if

$$b_2'\hat{V}_2^{-1}b_2/g = b_2'X_2'M_1X_2b_2/(gs^2) \leq 1.$$

According to the result (3.49) in Section 3.4.1, this is equivalent to the F-test for the null hypothesis that $\beta_2 = 0$ with a critical value of 1. This F-test can also be written as

$$F = \frac{(e_R'e_R - e'e)/g}{e'e/(n-k)}, \quad (5.1)$$

where e_R and e are the residuals of the restricted and unrestricted model, respectively. The critical value of 1 corresponds to a size of more than 5 per cent—that is, the TMSP criterion used in this way is more liberal in accepting additional regressors.

The information criteria of Akaike and Schwarz

Another method to decide whether the variables X_2 should be included in the model or not is to use information criteria that express the model fit and the number of parameters in a single criterion. The *Akaike information criterion* (AIC) and *Schwarz information criterion* (SIC) (also called the Bayes information criterion or BIC) are defined as follows, where p is the number of included regressors and s_p^2 is the maximum likelihood estimator of the error variance in the model with p regressors:

$$\text{AIC}(p) = \log\left(s_p^2\right) + \frac{2p}{n},$$

$$\text{SIC}(p) = \log\left(s_p^2\right) + \frac{p\log(n)}{n}.$$

These criteria involve a penalty term for the number of parameters, to account for the fact that the model fit always increases (that is, s_p^2 decreases) if more explanatory variables are included. The unrestricted model has $p = k$, and the restricted model obtained by deleting X_2 has $p = (k - g)$. The model with the smallest value of AIC or SIC is chosen. For $n \geq 8$, the SIC imposes a stronger penalty on extra variables than AIC, so that SIC is more inclined to choose the smaller model than AIC.

For the linear regression model, the information criteria are related to the F-test (5.1). For large enough sample size n, the comparison of AIC values corresponds to an F-test with critical value 2 and SIC corresponds to an F-test with critical value $\log(n)$ (see Exercise 5.2). For instance, the restricted model is preferred above the unrestricted model by AIC, in the sense that $\mathrm{AIC}(k-g) < \mathrm{AIC}(k)$, if the F-test in (5.1) is smaller than 2.

Criteria based on out-of-sample predictions

Another useful method for model selection is to compare the *predictive performance* of the models. For this purpose the data set is split in two parts, an 'estimation sample' (used to construct the model) and a 'prediction sample' or 'hold-out sample' for predictive evaluation. So the models are estimated using only the data in the first subsample, and the estimated models are then used to predict the y-values in the prediction sample. Possible evaluation criteria are the *root mean squared error* (RMSE) and the *mean absolute error* (MAE). These are defined by

$$\mathrm{RMSE} = \left(\frac{1}{n_f}\sum_{i=1}^{n_f}(y_i - \hat{y}_i)^2\right)^{1/2},$$

$$\mathrm{MAE} = \frac{1}{n_f}\sum_{i=1}^{n_f}|y_i - \hat{y}_i|,$$

where n_f denotes the number of observations in the prediction sample and $\hat{y}_i$ denotes the predicted values.

Iterative variable selection methods

In the foregoing we assumed that the $(k-g)$ variables in X_1 should all be included in the model and that the g variables in X_2 should either all be included or all be deleted. But how should we choose g and the decomposition of the variables in the two groups X_1 and X_2? We assume that the k regressors can be ordered in decreasing importance—that is, if the jth regressor is included in the model then also the regressors $1, 2, \cdots, j-1$ are included. It then remains to choose the number of regressor $(k-g)$ to be included in the model. This can be done, for instance, by choosing the model with the smallest value of TMSP, AIC, or SIC. Another method is to perform a sequence of t-tests.

In the *bottom-up approach* one starts with the smallest model (including only the constant term, corresponding to $g = k - 1$) and tests $H_0 : \beta_2 = 0$ against $H_1 : \beta_2 \neq 0$ (in the model with $g = k - 2$). If this hypothesis is rejected, then the second regressor is included in the model and one tests $H_0 : \beta_3 = 0$ against $H_1 : \beta_3 \neq 0$ (in the model with $g = k - 3$). Variables are added in this way until the next regressor is not significant anymore. This is also called the specific-to-general method and it is applied much in practice, as it starts from simple models.

In the *top-down approach* one starts with the largest model (with $g = 0$) and tests $H_0 : \beta_k = 0$ against $H_1 : \beta_k \neq 0$. If this hypothesis is not rejected, then one tests $H_0 : \beta_k = \beta_{k-1} = 0$ and so on. Variables are deleted until the next regressor becomes significant. This is also called the general-to-specific method and it has the attractive statistical property that all tests are performed in correctly specified models. In contrast, in the specific-to-general approach, the initial small models are in general misspecified, as they will exclude relevant regressors.

Variants of this approach can also be applied if the regressors cannot be ordered in decreasing importance. The method of *backward elimination* starts with the full model (with $g = 0$) and deletes the variable that is least significant. In the second step, the model with the remaining $k - 1$ regressors is estimated and again the least significant variable is deleted. This is repeated until all remaining regressors are significant. The method of *forward selection* starts with the smallest model (that includes only the constant term, with $g = k - 1$). Then the variable is added that has the (in absolute sense) largest t-value (this involves $k - 1$ regressions in models that contain a constant and one other regressor). This is repeated until none of the additional regressors is significant anymore.

Example 5.1: **Bank Wages (continued)**

As an illustration we consider again the data on wages and education of 474 employees of a US bank that were analysed in foregoing chapters. The relation between education and wage may be non-linear because the marginal returns of schooling may depend on the attained level of education. We will discuss (i) the data and possible nonlinearities in the wage equation, (ii) a class of polynomial models, (iii) selection of the degree of the polynomial by means of different selection criteria, and (iv) a forecast evaluation of the models.

(i) The data and possible non-linearities in the wage equation

The dependent variable (y) is the logarithm of yearly wage, and as regressors we take the variables education (x, the number of years of education), gender

($D_g = 0$ for females, $D_g = 1$ for males), and minority ($D_m = 0$ for non-minorities, $D_m = 1$ for minorities). Exhibit 5.2 (*a*) shows the partial regression scatter plot of wage against education (after regressions on a constant and the variables D_g and D_m). This plot indicates the possibility of a non-linear relation between education and wage.

(ii) Polynomial models for the wage equation

One method to incorporate non-linearities is to consider polynomial models of the form

$$y = \alpha + \gamma D_g + \mu D_m + \beta_1 x + \beta_2 x^2 + \cdots + \beta_p x^p + \varepsilon.$$

The constant term and the variables D_g and D_m are included in all models, and the question is how many powers of x to include in the model. These variables are ordered in a natural way—that is, if x^p is included in the model, then x^j is also included for all $j < p$. For evaluation purposes we leave out the fifty observations corresponding to employees with the highest education ($x \geq 17$). The remaining 424 observations (with $x \leq 16$) are used to estimate models with different values of p.

(iii) Selection of the degree of the polynomial model

Exhibit 5.2 (*b*) and (*c*) show plots for $p = 1$ of the residuals against x and of the value of y against the fitted value $\hat{y}$. Both plots indicate some non-linearities. Exhibit 5.2 (*d*) and (*e*) show the same two plots for the model with $p = 2$. There are less indications for remaining non-linearities in this case. Exhibit 5.3 summarizes the outcomes of the models with degrees $p = 1, 2, 3, 4$. If we use the adjusted R^2 as criterion, then $p = 4$ is optimal. If we use the t-test on the highest included power of x ('bottom up'), then this would suggest taking $p = 3$ (for a significance level of 5 per cent). If we perform F-tests on the significance of the highest powers in the model with $p = 4$ ('top down'), then $p = 3$ is again preferred. The AIC and SIC criteria also prefer the model with $p = 3$.

(iv) Forecast evaluation of the models

Although the foregoing results could suggest selecting the degree of the polynomial model as $p = 3$ or $p = 4$, the models with $p = 1$ and $p = 2$ provide much better forecasts. The model with degree $p = 2$ is optimal from this perspective.

This is also illustrated by the graphs in Exhibit 5.2 ($f - i$), which show that for $p = 3$ and $p = 4$ the forecasted wages of the fifty employees with the highest education are larger than the actual wages. This means that the

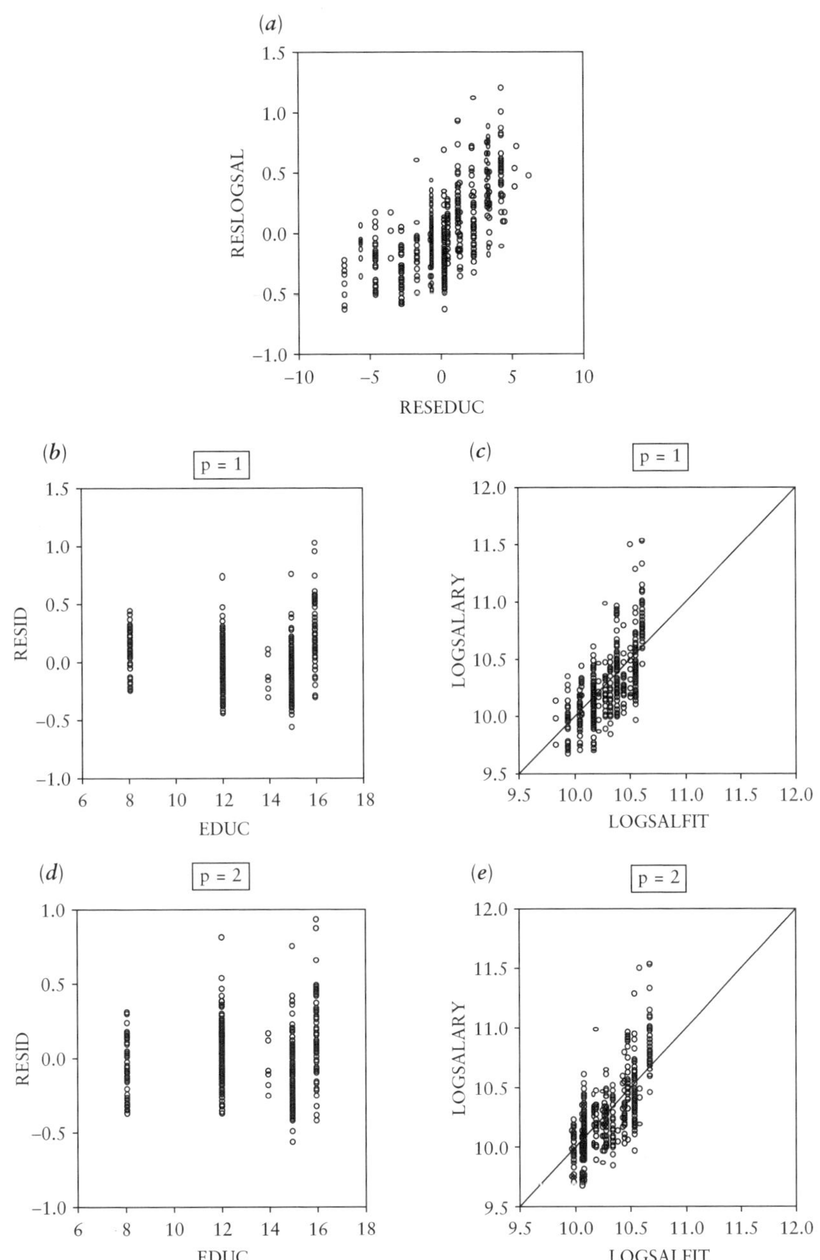

Exhibit 5.2 Bank Wages (Example 5.1)

(*a*): partial regression scatter plot of wage (in logarithms) against education (after regressions on a constant and the variables 'gender' and 'minority', 474 employees). (*b*) and (*c*): scatter diagrams of residuals against education (*b*) and of wage against fitted values for the (linear) model with $p = 1$ (*c*) using data of 424 employees with EDUC ≤ 16. (*d*) and (*e*): two similar scatter diagrams for the (quadratic) model with $p = 2$.

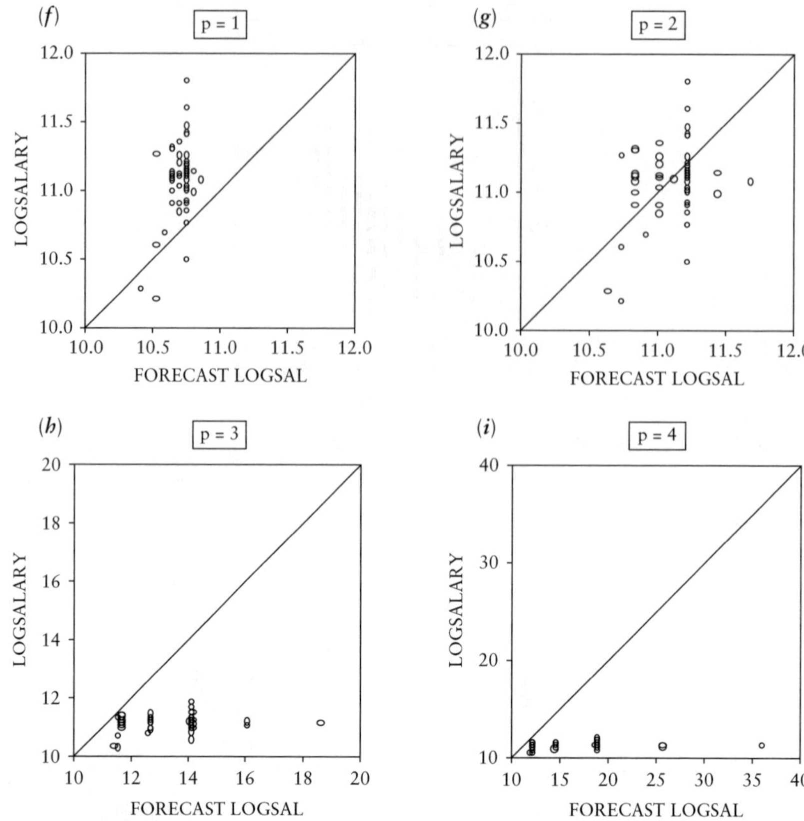

Exhibit 5.2 (*Contd.*)

Scatter diagrams of actual wages against forecasted wages (both in logarithms) for fifty employees with highest education (≥ 17 years), based on polynomial models with different values of p ($p = 1, 2, 3, 4$).

Criterion	$p = 1$	$p = 2$	$p = 3$	$p = 4$
Adjusted R^2	0.4221	0.4804	0.5620	0.5628*
P-values 'bottom up' t-test	0.0000	0.0000	0.0000*	0.1808
P-values 'top down' F-test	0.0000	0.0000	0.0000*	0.1808
AIC	−0.0400	−0.1440	−0.3125*	−0.3121
SIC	−0.0019	−0.0963	−0.2552*	−0.2452
RMSE of forecasts	0.4598	0.2965*	2.7060	7.3530
MAE of forecasts	0.4066	0.2380*	2.3269	5.9842

Exhibit 5.3 Bank Wages (Example 5.1)

Model selection criteria applied to wage data; an * indicates the optimal degree of the polynomial model for each criterion.

models with larger values of p do not reflect systematic properties of the wage–education relation for higher levels of education.

☞ Exercises: T: 5.1, 5.2a–d

5.2.2 **Non-linear functional forms**

A general misspecification test: RESET

In the foregoing chapters the functional relation between the dependent variable and the explanatory variables was assumed to be known up to a set of parameters to be estimated. The linear model is given by

$$y_i = x_i'\beta + \varepsilon_i = \beta_1 + \sum_{j=2}^{k} \beta_j x_{ji} + \varepsilon_i. \tag{5.2}$$

Instead of this linear relation, it may be that the dependent variable depends in a non-linear way on the explanatory variables. To test this, we can, for example, add quadratic and cross product terms to obtain the model

$$y_i = \beta_1 + \sum_{j=2}^{k} \beta_j x_{ji} + \sum_{j=2}^{k} \gamma_{jj} x_{ji}^2 + \sum_{j=2}^{k} \sum_{h=j+1}^{k} \gamma_{jh} x_{ji} x_{hi} + \varepsilon_i.$$

A test for non-linearity is given by the F-test for the $\frac{1}{2}k(k-1)$ restrictions that all parameters γ_{ij} are zero. This may be impractical if k is not small. A simpler test is to add a single squared term to the linear model (5.2)—for example, $\hat{y}_i^2$, where $\hat{y}_i = x_i'b$ with b the OLS estimator in (5.2). This gives the test equation

$$y_i = x_i'\beta + \gamma \hat{y}_i^2 + \varepsilon_i. \tag{5.3}$$

Under the null hypothesis of a correct linear specification in (5.2) there holds $\gamma = 0$, which can be tested by the t-test in (5.3). This is called the *regression specification error test* (RESET) of Ramsey. As b depends on y, this means that the added regressor $\hat{y}_i^2$ in (5.3) is stochastic. Therefore the t-test is valid only asymptotically under the assumptions stated in Section 4.1.4 (p. 197). To allow for higher order non-linearities we can include higher order terms in the RESET—that is,

$$y_i = x_i'\beta + \sum_{j=1}^{p} \gamma_j (\hat{y}_i)^{j+1} + \varepsilon_i. \tag{5.4}$$

The hypothesis that the linear model is correctly specified then corresponds to the $F(p, n-k-p)$ test on the joint significance of the parameters $\gamma_1, \cdots, \gamma_p$.

Some meaningful non-linear specifications

The RESET is a *misspecification test*. That is, it tests the null hypothesis of correct specification, but if the null hypothesis is rejected it does not tell us how to adjust the functional form. If possible, the choice of an alternative model should be inspired by economic insight.

In the linear model (5.2), the marginal effects of the explanatory variables on the dependent variable are constant—that is, $\frac{\partial y}{\partial x_j} = \beta_j$ for $j = 2, \cdots, k$. Alternative models can be obtained by assuming different forms for these marginal effects. We discuss some possible models, and for simplicity we assume that $k = 3$.

It may be that the marginal effect $\frac{\partial y}{\partial x_2}$ depends on the level of x_2—say, $\frac{\partial y}{\partial x_2} = \beta_2 + \gamma_2 x_2$. This can be modelled by including the squared term x_2^2 in the model so that

$$y_i = \beta_1 + \beta_2 x_{2i} + \tfrac{1}{2}\gamma_2 x_{2i}^2 + \beta_3 x_{3i} + \varepsilon_i.$$

It may also be that the marginal effect $\frac{\partial y}{\partial x_2}$ depends on the level of another variable—say, $\frac{\partial y}{\partial x_2} = \beta_2 + \gamma_3 x_3$. This can be modelled by including the product term $x_2 x_3$ in the model, so that

$$y_i = \beta_1 + \beta_2 x_{2i} + \beta_3 x_{3i} + \gamma_3 x_{2i} x_{3i} + \varepsilon_i.$$

The term $x_{2i} x_{3i}$ is called an *interaction term*. The above two specifications provide non-linear functional forms with a clear interpretation. As these models remain linear in the unknown parameters, they can be estimated by (linear) least squares. Other methods to deal with non-linearities are to use non-parametric techniques, to transform the data, or to use varying parameters. This is discussed in Sections 5.2.3, 5.2.4, and 5.3.2 respectively.

Example 5.2: **Bank Wages (continued)**

We consider again the wage data discussed in Example 5.1, with education (x), gender (D_g), and minority (D_m) as explanatory variables. The linear model is given by

$$y = \alpha + \gamma D_g + \mu D_m + \beta x + \varepsilon.$$

As was discussed in Example 5.1, the wage equation may be non-linear. We will now discuss (i) tests on non-linearities, (ii) a non-linear model with non-constant marginal returns to schooling, and (iii) the results of this model.

(i) Tests on non-linearities

Recall that y is the logarithm of yearly wage S, so that $\beta = \partial y/\partial x = \partial \log(S)/\partial x = (\partial S/\partial x)/S$ measures the relative wage increase due to an additional year of education. The above linear model assumes that this effect of education is constant for all employees. The results of two RESETs (with $p = 1$ and with $p = 2$ in (5.4)) are in Panels 2 and 3 of Exhibit 5.4. Both tests indicate that the linear model is misspecified. Note that in the model with $p = 2$, the two terms $\hat{y}_i^2$ and $\hat{y}_i^3$ are individually not significant but

Panel 1: Dependent Variable: LOGSALARY Method: Least Squares Sample: 1 474 Included observations: 474				
Variable	Coefficient	Std. Error	t-Statistic	Prob.
C	9.199980	0.058687	156.7634	0.0000
EDUC	0.077366	0.004436	17.44229	0.0000
GENDER	0.261131	0.025511	10.23594	0.0000
MINORITY	−0.132673	0.028946	−4.583411	0.0000

Panel 2: Ramsey RESET Test:				
F-statistic	77.60463	Probability		0.000000
Log likelihood ratio	72.58029	Probability		0.000000
Test Equation: Dependent Variable: LOGSALARY Method: Least Squares Sample: 1 474 Included observations: 474				
Variable	Coefficient	Std. Error	t-Statistic	Prob.
C	−69.82447	8.970686	−7.783627	0.0000
EDUC	−1.443306	0.172669	−8.358791	0.0000
GENDER	−4.877462	0.583791	−8.354812	0.0000
MINORITY	2.488307	0.298731	8.329595	0.0000
FITTED^2	0.947902	0.107602	8.809349	0.0000

Panel 3: Ramsey RESET Test:				
F-statistic	40.23766	Probability		0.000000
Log likelihood ratio	75.21147	Probability		0.000000
Test Equation: Dependent Variable: LOGSALARY Method: Least Squares Sample: 1 474 Included observations: 474				
Variable	Coefficient	Std. Error	t-Statistic	Prob.
C	827.2571	555.8566	1.488256	0.1374
EDUC	10.63188	7.483135	1.420779	0.1560
GENDER	35.89400	25.26657	1.420612	0.1561
MINORITY	−18.22389	12.83565	−1.419787	0.1563
FITTED^2	−14.11083	9.330216	−1.512380	0.1311
FITTED^3	0.483936	0.299821	1.614082	0.1072

Exhibit 5.4 Bank Wages (Example 5.2)

Panel 1: regression of wage (in logarithms) on education, gender, and minority. Panels 2 and 3: RESET, respectively with $p = 1$ and with $p = 2$.

Panel 4: Dependent Variable: LOGSALARY Method: Least Squares Sample: 1 474 Included observations: 474				
Variable	Coefficient	Std. Error	t-Statistic	Prob.
C	10.72379	0.182800	58.66402	0.0000
GENDER	0.234323	0.123432	1.898401	0.0583
MINORITY	0.315020	0.136128	2.314151	0.0211
EDUC	−0.171086	0.028163	−6.074851	0.0000
EDUC^2	0.009736	0.001117	8.717483	0.0000
GENDER*EDUC	−0.002213	0.009350	−0.236632	0.8130
MINORITY*EDUC	−0.032525	0.010277	−3.164785	0.0017

Panel 5: Dependent Variable: LOGSALARY Method: Least Squares Sample: 1 474 Included observations: 474				
Variable	Coefficient	Std. Error	t-Statistic	Prob.
C	10.72135	0.182324	58.80378	0.0000
GENDER	0.205648	0.023451	8.769373	0.0000
MINORITY	0.322841	0.131921	2.447231	0.0148
EDUC	−0.169464	0.027289	−6.209968	0.0000
EDUC^2	0.009624	0.001010	9.529420	0.0000
MINORITY*EDUC	−0.033074	0.010002	−3.306733	0.0010

Exhibit 5.4 (*Contd.*)

Non-linear models with quadratic term for education and with interaction terms for education with gender and minority (Panel 4) and with the insignificant interaction term GENDER*EDUC omitted (Panel 5).

jointly they are highly significant. This is because of multicollinearity, as the terms $\hat{y}_i^2$ and $\hat{y}_i^3$ have a correlation coefficient of 0.999871. The reason for this high correlation is that the logarithmic salaries y_i vary only between 9.66 and 10.81 in the sample (corresponding to salaries ranging from \$15,750 to \$135,000).

(ii) A non-linear model

As a possible alternative model we investigate whether the marginal returns of schooling depend on the level of (previous) education and on the variables gender and minority — that is,

$$\frac{\partial y}{\partial x} = \beta_1 + 2\beta_2 x + \beta_3 D_g + \beta_4 D_m.$$

This motivates a model with quadratic term and interaction effects

$$y = \alpha + \gamma D_g + \mu D_m + \beta_1 x + \beta_2 x^2 + \beta_3 D_g x + \beta_4 D_m x + \varepsilon.$$

(iii) Results of the non-linear model

The estimated model is in Panel 4 of Exhibit 5.4. The regression coefficient b_3 is not significant. The estimated model obtained after deleting the regressor $D_g x$ is given in Panel 5 of Exhibit 5.4. The marginal returns of schooling are estimated as

$$\frac{\partial y}{\partial x} = b_1 + 2b_2 x + b_4 D_m = -0.169 + 0.019x - 0.033D_m.$$

For instance, for an education level of $x = 16$ years an additional year of education gives an estimated wage increase of 13.8 per cent for non-minorities and of 10.5 per cent for minorities.

5.2.3 Non-parametric estimation

Non-parametric model formulation

The methods discussed in the foregoing section to deal with non-linear functional forms require that the non-linearity is explicitly modelled in terms of a limited number of variables (such as squared terms and interaction terms) and their associated parameters. Such methods are called parametric, as the non-linearity is modelled in terms of a limited number of parameters. Non-linearity can also be modelled in a more flexible way, by means of so-called non-parametric models. In this section we will discuss the main ideas by considering the situation of a scatter of points (x_i, y_i), $i = 1, \cdots, n$. Instead of the simple linear regression model that requires a linear dependence in the sense that $y = \alpha + \beta x + \varepsilon$, it is assumed that

$$y = f(x) + \varepsilon,$$

where the function f is unknown. In particular, it may be non-linear in the explanatory variable x. It is assumed that $E[\varepsilon] = 0$, or, in the case where the regressor x is stochastic, that $E[\varepsilon|x] = 0$. This means that the (parametric) assumption of the linear regression model that $E[y|x] = \alpha + \beta x$ is replaced by the (non-parametric) assumption that $E[y|x] = f(x)$. That is, $f(x)$ can be interpreted as the expectation of y for a given value of x.

Local regression with nearest neighbour fit

We now describe a procedure called *local regression* to estimate the function $f(x)$. This estimation method is called local because the function values $f(x)$ are estimated locally, for (a large number of) fixed values of x. We describe the estimation of $f(x_0)$ at a given point x_0. The function $f(x)$ can then be estimated by repeating the procedure for a grid of values of x. It is assumed that the function f is smooth, in particular, differentiable at x_0. This implies that, locally around x_0, the function f can be approximated by a linear function—that is,

$$f(x) \approx \alpha_0 + \beta_0(x - x_0),$$

where $\alpha_0 = f(x_0)$ and β_0 is the derivative of the function f at x_0. The basic idea of local regression is to use the observations (x_i, y_i) with x_i-values that are close enough to x_0 to estimate the parameters α_0 and β_0 in the model

$$y_i = \alpha_0 + \beta_0(x_i - x_0) + \omega_i.$$

As the linear function is only an approximation, we denote the error by a new disturbance term ω. If we consider a point x_0 that is present in the observed data set—say, for observation i_0 so that $x_{i_0} = x_0$—then

$$E[y_{i_0}|x_{i_0}] = f(x_{i_0}) = \alpha_0.$$

That is, in this case the estimate of the constant term α_0 can be interpreted as an estimate of the function value $f(x_{i_0})$.

The linear approximation is more accurate for values of x_i that are closer to x_0, and this motivates the use of larger weights for such observations. Therefore, instead of estimating α_0 and β_0 by ordinary least squares, the parameters are estimated by minimizing the weighted sum of squares

$$\sum_i w_i\Big(y_i - \alpha_0 - \beta_0(x_i - x_0)\Big)^2.$$

This is called *weighted least squares*. In particular, we can exclude observations with values of x_i that are too far away from x_0 (and that include no reliable information on $f(x_0)$ anymore) by choosing weights with $w_i = 0$ if $|x_i - x_0|$ is larger than a certain threshold value. In this case only the observations for which x_i lies in some sufficiently close neighbourhood of x_0 are included in the regression. This is, therefore, called a regression with *nearest neighbour fit*.

Choice of neighbourhood

To apply the above local regression method, we have to choose which observations are included in the regression (that is, the considered neighbourhood of x_0) and the weights of the included observations. We will discuss a method for choosing neighbourhoods and weights that is much applied in practice.

The neighbourhood can be chosen by selecting the *bandwidth span*, also called the *span*. This is a number $0 \leq s \leq 1$ representing the fraction of the n observations (x_i, y_i) that are included in the regression to estimate α_0 and β_0. The selected observations are the ones that are closest to x_0—that is, the sn nearest neighbours of x_0, and the other $(1-s)n$ observations with largest values of $|x_i - x_0|$ are excluded in the regression. One usually chooses the bandwidth span around $s = 0.6$ or $s = 0.7$. Smaller values may lead to estimated curves that are overly erratic, whereas larger values may lead to very smooth curves that miss relevant aspects of the function f. It is often instructive to try out some values for the bandwidth span—for instance, $s = 0.3$, $s = 0.6$, and $s = 0.9$—and then to decide which estimated curve has the best interpretation.

Choice of weights

After the selection of the relevant neighbourhood of x_0, the next step is to select the weights of the included observations. These weights decrease for observations with a larger distance between x_i and x_0. Let D be the maximal distance $|x_i - x_0|$ that occurs for the sn included observations, and let $d_i = |x_i - x_0|/D$ be the scaled distance of the ith observation from x_0 (so that $0 \leq d_i \leq 1$ for all included observations). A popular weighting function is the so-called *tricube weighting function*, defined by

$$w_i = \left(1 - d_i^3\right)^3 \quad \text{for } 0 \leq d_i \leq 1.$$

The largest weight is given when $d_i = 0$ (that is, when $x_i = x_0$) and the weights gradually decrease to zero as d_i tends to 1 (the upper bound). The graph of the tricube function is shown in Exhibit 5.5.

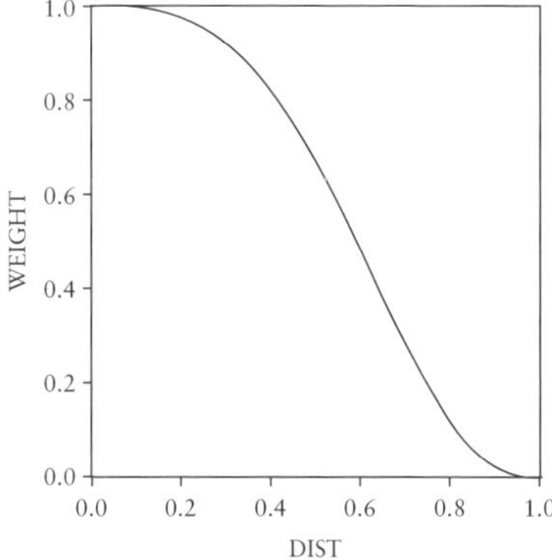

Exhibit 5.5 Tricube weights

The tricube weighting function $w = (1 - d^3)^3$ for $0 \leq d \leq 1$.

Some extensions

The tricube function is only one out of a number of possible weighting functions that are used in practice. In most cases the choice of the bandwidth span is crucial, whereas the estimates for a given bandwidth span do not depend much on the chosen weights. Note that the weights of the tricube function will in general not add up to unity, and the same holds true for other weighting functions. This is not important, as the choice of scaled weights (with weights $w_i / \sum w_j$, where the sum runs over the sn included observations) gives the same estimates of α_0 and β_0. Since the weights need not add up to unity, the weighting functions are often called *kernel functions*.

The local linear specification $y_i = \alpha_0 + \beta_0(x_i - x_0) + \omega_i$ is recommended in most cases, but sometimes one uses regressions with only a constant term

$$y_i = \alpha_0 + \omega_i,$$

or regressions with a second degree polynomial

$$y_i = \alpha_0 + \beta_0(x_i - x_0) + \gamma_0(x_i - x_0)^2 + \omega_i.$$

The version with only the constant term was the first one that was developed and is usually called the *kernel method*. It has the disadvantage that it leads to biased estimates near the left and right end of the curve, whereas the local linear regression method is unbiased.

Local regression is most often used to draw a smooth curve through a two-dimensional scatter plot. It is, however, also possible to use it with k regressors, but it is less easy to get a good graphical feeling for the obtained estimates.

Summary of local linear regression

To estimate a non-linear curve $y = f(x)$ from a scatter of points (x_i, y_i), $i = 1, \cdots, n$, by means of local linear regression, one takes the following steps.

Local regression

- *Step 1: Choice of grid of points.* Choose a grid of points for the variable x where the function $f(x)$ will be estimated. If the number of observations is not too large, one can take all the n observed values x_i; otherwise one can estimate $f(x)$ only for a selected subsample of these values.
- *Step 2: Choice of bandwidth span.* Choose the fraction s (with $0 \leq s \leq 1$) of the observations to be included in each local regression. A usual choice is $s = 0.6$, but it is advisable to try out some other values as well.
- *Step 3: Choice of weighting function.* Choose the weights w_i to be used in weighted least squares. A possible choice is the tricube weighting function.

(continues)

Local regression (*continued*)

- *Step 4: Perform weighted linear regressions.* For each point x_0 in the grid of points chosen in step 1, perform a weighted linear regression by minimizing the weighted sum of squares $\sum_i w_i(y_i - \alpha_0 - \beta_0(x_i - x_0))^2$. Here the summation runs over the sn included points of step 3.
- *Step 5: Estimated non-linear function* $y = f(x)$. For given value of x_0, estimate the function value $f(x_0)$ by $\hat{f}(x_0) = \hat{\alpha}_0$ with $\hat{\alpha}_0$ the estimated constant term in step 4. The estimated function can be visualized by means of a scatter plot of $\hat{f}(x_i)$ against x_i for the grid of points of step 1, and a continuous curve is obtained by interpolating between the points $(x_i, \hat{f}(x_i))$ in this scatter.

Example 5.3: **Simulated Data from a Non-linear Model**

E

To illustrate the idea of local regression we first apply the method to a set of simulated data. We simulate a set of $n = 200$ data from the data generating process $y_i = \sin(x_i) + \varepsilon_i$, where the x_i consist of a random sample from the uniform distribution on the interval $0 \leq x_i \leq 2.5$ and the ε_i are a random sample from the normal distribution with mean zero and standard deviation $\sigma = 0.2$, with x_i and ε_j independent for all $i, j = 1, \cdots, 200$.

Exhibit 5.6 shows the scatter of the generated data (in (*a*)) as well as four curves—namely, of the data generating process in (*b*) and of three curves that are estimated by local linear regression with three choices for the bandwidth span, $s = 0.3$ in (*c*), $s = 0.6$ in (*d*), and $s = 0.9$ in (*e*). For $s = 0.9$ the fitted curve is very smooth, but it underestimates the decline of the curve at the right end. For $s = 0.3$ this decline is picked up well, but the curve shows some erratic movements that do not correspond to properties of the data generating process. The curve obtained for $s = 0.6$ provides a reasonable compromise between smoothness and sensitivity to fluctuations that are present in the functional relationship.

Example 5.4: **Bank Wages (continued)**

As a second illustration we consider the relation between education and wages in the banking sector. In Example 5.1 we found evidence for possible non-linearities in this relation. We can also investigate this by a local linear regression of wage on education (for simplicity we exclude other explanatory variables gender and minority).

Exhibit 5.7 (*a*) shows the scatter of the $n = 474$ data, together with four fitted curves in (*b–e*). The relation does not seem to be linear, and the returns to education seem to become larger for higher levels of education. For this data set the local linear regression with bandwidth span $s = 0.9$ seems to be preferable, as it gives nearly the same results as $s = 0.6$ but without the small irregularities that do not seem to have a clear interpretation.

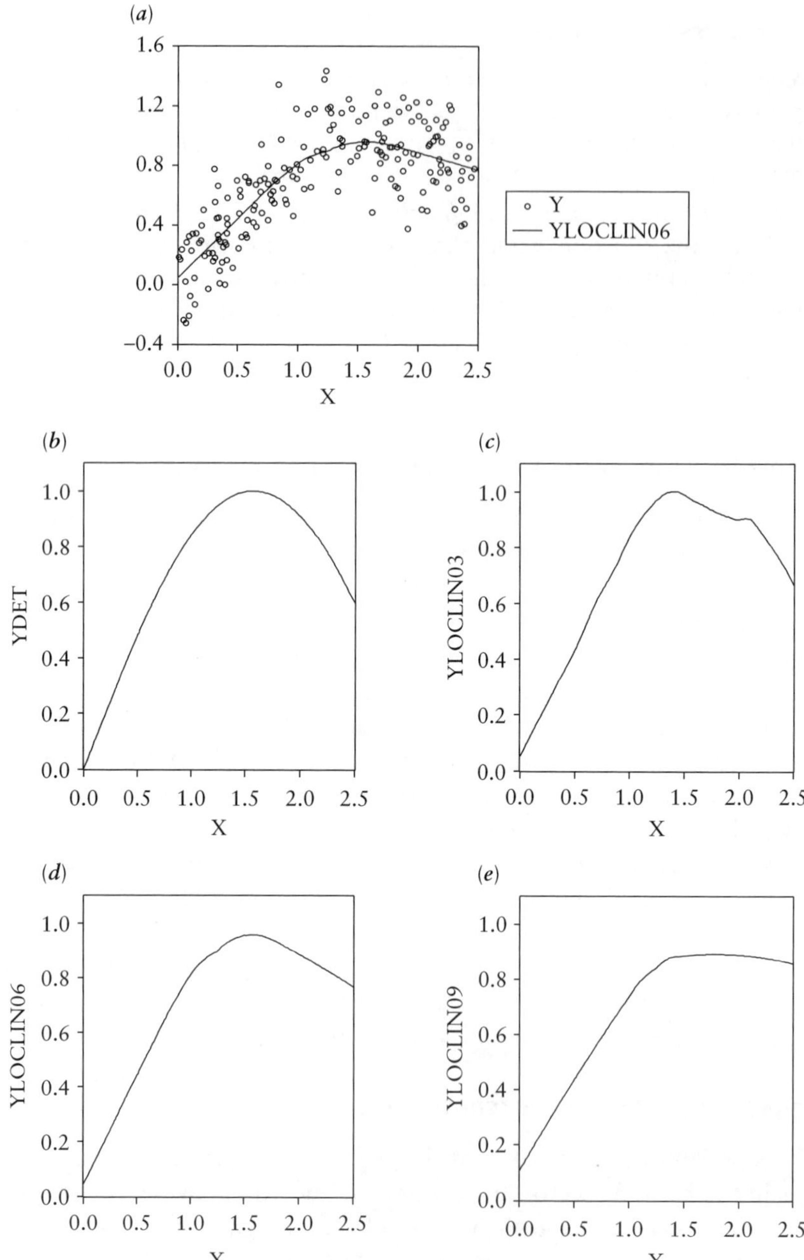

Exhibit 5.6 Simulated Data from a Non-linear Model (Example 5.3)

Simulated data with local linear regression based on nearest neighbour fit with span 0.6 (*a*), DGP curve (*b*), and three local linear regression curves with spans 0.3 (*c*), 0.6 (*d*), and 0.9 (*e*).

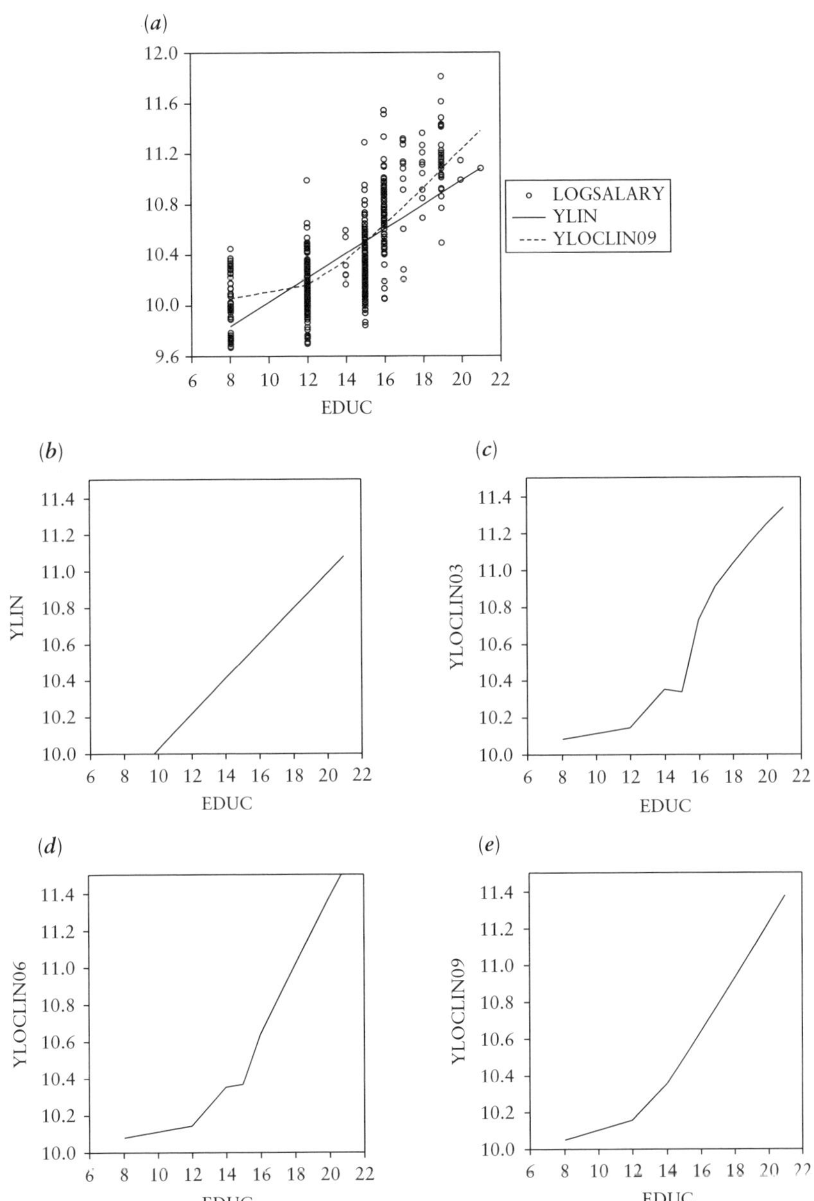

Exhibit 5.7 Bank Wages (Example 5.4)

Scatter diagram of salary (in logarithms) against education with linear fit and with local linear fit with span 0.9 (*a*) and four fitted curves, linear (*b*) and local linear with spans 0.3 (*c*), 0.6 (*d*), and 0.9 (*e*).

5.2.4 Data transformations

Data should be measured on compatible scales

If diagnostic tests indicate misspecification of the model, one can consider transformations of the data to obtain a better specification. In every empirical investigation, one of the first questions to be answered concerns the most appropriate form of the data to be used in the econometric model.

For linear models (5.2) the *scaling* of the variables is not of intrinsic importance, as was discussed at the end of Section 3.1.3 (p. 124–5), although for the computation of the inverse of $X'X$ in $b = (X'X)^{-1}X'y$, it is preferable that all explanatory variables are roughly of the same order of magnitude. What is more important is that the additive structure of the model implies that the variables should be incorporated in a compatible manner. For example, it makes sense to relate the price of one stock to the price of another stock, and also to relate the respective returns, but it makes less sense to relate the price of one stock to the returns of another stock. It also makes sense to relate the output of a firm to labour and capital, or to relate the logarithms of these variables, but it makes less sense to relate the logarithm of output to the levels of labour and capital. Of all the possible data transformations we discuss two important ones, taking logarithms and taking differences.

Use and interpretation of taking logarithms of observed data

The *logarithmic transformation* is useful for several reasons. Of course, it can only be applied if all variables take on only positive values, but this is the case for many economic variables. For instance, if the dependence of the dependent variable on the explanatory variable is multiplicative of the form $y_i = \alpha_1 x_i^{\alpha_2} e^{\varepsilon_i}$, then

$$\log(y_i) = \beta_1 + \beta_2 \log(x_i) + \varepsilon_i, \tag{5.5}$$

with $\beta_1 = \log(\alpha_1)$ and $\beta_2 = \alpha_2$. This so-called log-linear specification is of interest because the coefficient β_2 is the *elasticity* of y with respect to x—that is,

$$\beta_2 = \frac{d\log(y_i)}{d\log(x_i)} = \frac{dy_i}{dx_i}\frac{x_i}{y_i}.$$

It is often more plausible that economic agents show constant reactions to relative changes in variables like prices and income than to absolute changes. Further, the logarithmic transformation may reduce skewness and heteroskedasticity. To illustrate this idea, consider the model (5.5), where ε_i is normally distributed. Then $\log(y_i)$ is normally distributed with mean $\mu_i = \beta_1 + \beta_2 \log(x_i)$ and variance σ^2, and the original variable y_i is log-normally distributed with median e^{μ_i}, mean $E[y_i] = e^{\mu_i + \frac{1}{2}\sigma^2}$, and variance $\text{var}(y_i) = (E[y_i])^2(e^{\sigma^2} - 1)$ (see Exercise 5.2). This means that the distribution of y_i is (positively) skewed and that the standard deviation is proportional to the level. These are very common properties of economic data and then the logarithmic transformation of the data may reduce the skewness and heteroskcdasticity.

Taking differences of observed data

Many economic time series show a *trending* pattern. In such cases, the statistical assumptions of Chapters 3 and 4 may fail to hold. For instance, Assumption 1* of Section 4.1.2 (p. 193) requires the regressors to be stable in the sense that $\text{plim}\left(\frac{1}{n}\sum_{i=1}^{n} x_{ji}^2\right)$ exists and is finite for all explanatory variables x_j. In the case of a linear deterministic trend, say $x_{2i} = i$ for $i = 1, \cdots, n$, the sequence $\frac{1}{n}\sum_{i=1}^{n} i^2$ diverges. To apply conventional tests, the variables should be transformed to get stable regressors. The trend in a variable y can often be removed by taking *first differences*. This operation is denoted by Δ, which is defined by

$$\Delta y_i = y_i - y_{i-1}.$$

For instance, if $x_{2i} = i$, then $\Delta x_{2i} = 1$, which is a stable regressor. A combination of the two foregoing transformations is also of interest. Because

$$\Delta \log(y_i) = \log\left(\frac{y_i}{y_{i-1}}\right) = \log\left(1 + \frac{\Delta y_i}{y_{i-1}}\right) \approx \frac{\Delta y_i}{y_{i-1}}$$

for $\Delta y_i / y_{i-1}$ sufficiently small, this transforms the original level variables y_i into *growth rates*. The modelling of trends and the question whether variables should be differenced or not is further discussed in Chapter 7.

The Box–Cox transformation

T

If one doubts whether the variables should be included in levels or in logarithms, one can consider the more general *Box–Cox transformation* given by

$$y_i(\lambda) = \beta_1 + \sum_{j=2}^{k} \beta_j x_{ji}(\lambda) + \varepsilon_i, \tag{5.6}$$

where $y_i(\lambda) = (y_i^\lambda - 1)/\lambda$ and $x_{ji}(\lambda)$ is defined in a similar way. If $\lambda = 1$, this corresponds to a linear model, and, as $y_i(\lambda) \to \log(y_i)$ for $\lambda \to 0$, the log-linear model is obtained for $\lambda = 0$. The elasticity of y with respect to x_j in (5.6) is given by $\beta_j x_{ji}^\lambda / y_i^\lambda$. To estimate the parameters of the model (5.6) we assume that the disturbance terms ε_i satisfy Assumptions 2–4 and 7. Then the logarithm of the joint density function is given by

$$\log(p(\varepsilon_1, \cdots, \varepsilon_n)) = \sum_{i=1}^{n} \log(p(\varepsilon_i)) = -\frac{n}{2}\log(2\pi) - \frac{n}{2}\log(\sigma^2) - \frac{1}{2\sigma^2}\sum_{i=1}^{n}\varepsilon_i^2.$$

To obtain the likelihood function, we use that $\varepsilon_i = y_i(\lambda) - \beta_1 - \sum_{j=2}^{k}\beta_j x_{ji}(\lambda)$ so that $d\varepsilon_i/dy_i = y_i^{\lambda-1}$. The Jacobian corresponding to the transformation of $(\varepsilon_1, \cdots, \varepsilon_n)$ to $(y_1, \cdots, y_n)$ is therefore equal to $\Pi_{i=1}^{n} y_i^{\lambda-1}$ (see also (1.19) in Section 1.2.2 (p. 27)). The log-likelihood is equal to $l(\beta_1, \cdots, \beta_k, \lambda, \sigma^2) = \log(p(y_1, \cdots, y_n)) = (\lambda - 1)\sum_{i=1}^{n}\log(y_i) + \log(p(\varepsilon_1, \cdots, \varepsilon_n))$, so that

$$\begin{aligned} l = &-\frac{n}{2}\log(2\pi) - \frac{n}{2}\log(\sigma^2) + (\lambda - 1)\sum_{i=1}^{n}\log(y_i) \\ &- \frac{1}{2\sigma^2}\sum_{i=1}^{n}\left(y_i(\lambda) - \beta_1 - \sum_{j=2}^{k}\beta_j x_{ji}(\lambda)\right)^2. \end{aligned} \qquad (5.7)$$

The ML estimates of the parameters are obtained by maximizing this function. Note that this differs from non-linear least squares in (5.6), as in the minimization of $\sum \varepsilon_i^2$ the term $(\lambda - 1)\sum \log(y_i)$ in (5.7) would be neglected. Actually, NLS in (5.6) to estimate the parameters makes no sense. For instance, if the values of the variables satisfy $y_i \geq 1$ and $x_{ji} \geq 1$ for all $i = 1, \cdots, n$ and all $j = 1, \cdots, k$, then $\sum \varepsilon_i^2 \to 0$ by taking $\lambda \to -\infty$.

Tests for a linear model ($\lambda = 1$) or a log-linear model ($\lambda = 0$) can be based on (5.7)—for instance, by using the LR test.

XM501BWA

Example 5.5: **Bank Wages (continued)**

We consider once again the bank wage data and investigate the best way to include the dependent variable, the salary of US bank employees, in the model. Until now we have chosen to take the logarithm of salary as the dependent variable, but there are alternatives. We will discuss (i) the choice between salaries in levels or logarithms, (ii) a test of linearity and log-linearity, and (iii) the results and interpretation of an alternative relation.

(i) **Choice between levels and logarithms**

Exhibit 5.8 (*a*) and (*b*) show histograms of the salary (S) (in dollars per year) and of the natural logarithm of salary ($y = \log(S)$) of the 474 employees of

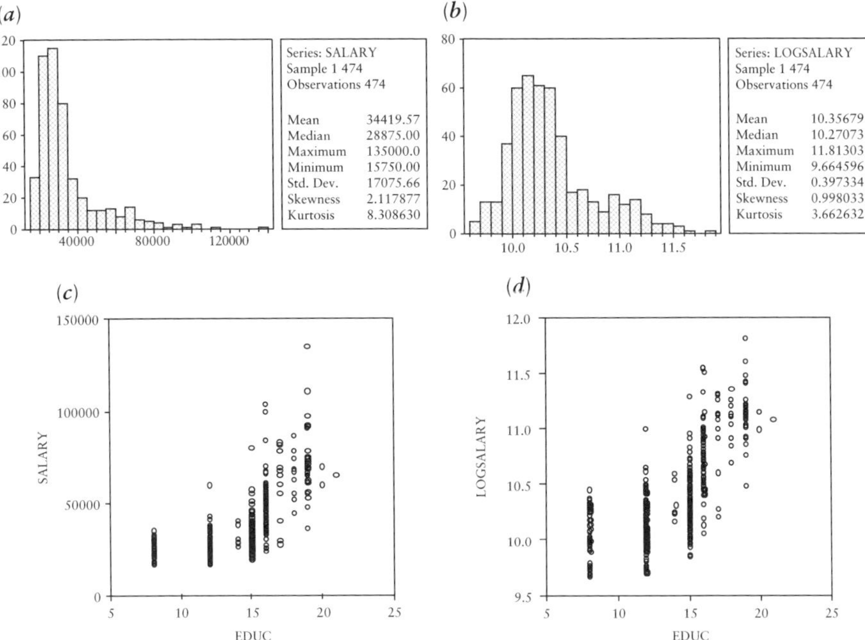

Exhibit 5.8 Bank Wages (Example 5.5)

Histograms of salary (*a*) and log salary (*b*), and scatter diagrams of salary against education (*c*) and of log salary against education (*d*).

the considered bank. The distribution of S is more skewed than that of y. Exhibits 5.8 (*c*) and (*d*) show scatter diagrams of S and y against education. As could be expected, the variation of salaries is considerably larger for higher levels of education than for lower levels of education. This effect is much less pronounced for the variable y. This provides statistical reasons to formulate models in terms of the variable y instead of the variable S. Regression models for y also have an attractive economic interpretation, as $\partial y/\partial x_j = (\partial S/\partial x_j)/S$ measures the relative increase in salary due to an increase in the explanatory variable x_j. We are often more interested in such relative effects than in absolute effects.

(ii) Tests of linearity and log-linearity

Now we consider the following model for the relation between (scaled) salary (the dependent variable is expressed in terms of $S = \text{Salary}/\$10,000$) and education ($x$). Here we scale the salary to make the two variables x and S of similar order of magnitude.

$$S(\lambda) = \frac{S^\lambda - 1}{\lambda} = \alpha + \gamma D_g + \mu D_m + \beta x + \varepsilon.$$

(*a*)

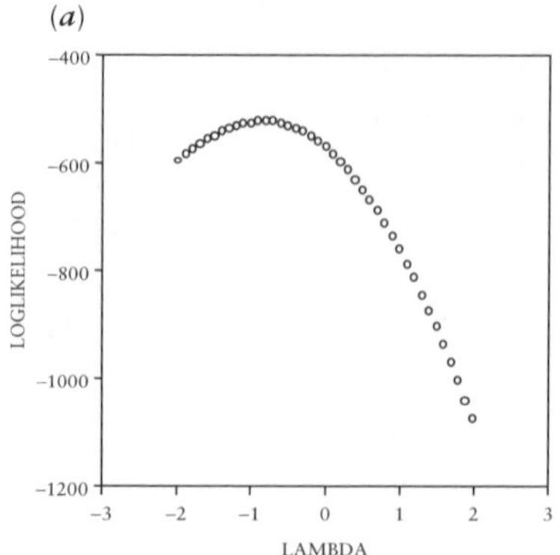

(*b*)

Panel 2: Method: Maximum Likelihood Dependent variable: (S^lambda – 1)/lambda with S = Salary/10000 Included observations: 474 Convergence achieved after 58 iterations				
Parameter	Coefficient	Std. Error	z-Statistic	Prob.
LAMBDA	−0.835898	0.111701	−7.483362	0.0000
C	0.320157	0.022535	14.20703	0.0000
GENDER	0.102712	0.014278	7.193465	0.0000
MINORITY	−0.046302	0.011135	−4.158373	0.0000
EDUCATION	0.025821	0.003656	7.062606	0.0000
VARIANCE	0.007800	0.001986	3.926990	0.0001
Log likelihood	−519.9367			

(*c*)

Panel 3: Method: Maximum Likelihood for lambda = 1 Dependent variable: S – 1 with S = Salary/10000 Included observations: 474				
Variable	Coefficient	Std. Error	z-Statistic	Prob.
C	−13314.27	2763.358	−4.818149	0.0000
GENDER	9022.212	1201.227	7.510828	0.0000
MINORITY	−5116.840	1362.978	−3.754163	0.0002
EDUCATION	3257.199	208.8534	15.59562	0.0000
Log likelihood	−759.5043			

(*d*)

Panel 4: Method: Maximum Likelihood for lambda = 0 Dependent variable: log(S) with S = Salary/10000 Included observations: 474				
Variable	Coefficient	Std. Error	z-Statistic	Prob.
C	9.199980	0.058687	156.7634	0.0000
GENDER	0.261131	0.025511	10.23594	0.0000
MINORITY	−0.132673	0.028946	−4.583411	0.0000
EDUCATION	0.077366	0.004436	17.44229	0.0000
Log likelihood	−568.5082			

Exhibit 5.9 Bank Wages (Example 5.5)

Values of log-likelihood for a grid of values of λ (*a*) and ML estimates, both unrestricted (Panel 2) and under the restriction that $\lambda = 1$ (Panel 3) or $\lambda = 0$ (Panel 4).

So we consider the transformation only of the dependent variable and not of the regressors. The log-likelihood of this model is given by (5.7), replacing the last term in parentheses of this expression by $\varepsilon_i = S_i(\lambda) - \alpha - \gamma D_{gi} - \mu D_{mi} - \beta x_i$. The ML estimates are given in Panel 2 of Exhibit 5.9 and the ML estimate of λ is $\hat{\lambda} = -0.836$. The exhibit also shows the results for $\lambda = 1$ in Panel 3 (with dependent variable $S - 1$) and for $\lambda = 0$ in Panel 4 (with dependent variable $\log(S)$). The LR-tests for linearity and log-linearity are given by

$$LR(\lambda = 1) = 2(-519.94 + 759.50) = 479.14 \ (P = 0.0000),$$
$$LR(\lambda = 0) = 2(-519.94 + 568.51) = 97.14 \ (P = 0.0000).$$

We conclude that linearity and log-linearity are rejected.

(iii) Interpretation of an alternative relation

We now use the ML estimates of the above model in Panel 2 of Exhibit 5.9 (with $\lambda = -0.836$) to determine the relative increase in salary caused by an additional year of schooling—that is, $(dS/dx)/S$. It is left as an exercise (see Exercise 5.2) to show that in this model

$$\frac{dS/dx}{S} = \frac{\beta}{1 + \lambda(\alpha + \gamma D_g + \mu D_m + \beta x + \varepsilon)}.$$

In the log-linear model that was considered in previous examples, $\lambda = 0$ and the marginal return to schooling is constant. Now, in our model with $\lambda = -0.836$, this return depends on the values of the explanatory variables. For instance, for an 'average' non-minority male employee (with $D_g = 0, D_m = 0$ and $\varepsilon = 0$), the estimated increase is

$$\frac{dS/dx}{S} = \frac{\hat{\beta}}{1 + \hat{\lambda}(\hat{\alpha} + \hat{\beta}x)} = \frac{0.0258}{0.732 - 0.022x}.$$

This means that the marginal returns of schooling increase with the previously achieved level of education. For instance, at an education level of $x = 10$ years the predicted increase in salary is 5.0 per cent, whereas for an education level of $x = 20$ years this becomes 8.6 per cent. Such a non-linear effect is in line with our previous analysis in Examples 5.1 and 5.4.

☞ Exercises: T: 5.2e, f.

5.2.5 Summary

In order to construct a model for the explanation of the dependent variable we have to make a number of decisions.

- How many explanatory variables should be included in the model? This can be investigated by means of selection criteria (such as AIC, SIC), by tests of significance (for instance, forward selection or backward elimination), and by comparing the predictive performance of competing models on a hold-out sample.
- What is the best way to incorporate the variables in the model? In many cases the model has a better economic interpretation if variables are taken in logarithms, and, if the observed data contain trends, it may be worthwhile to take first differences.
- Can the relation between explanatory variables and explained variable be expressed by a linear model or is the relationship non-linear? The method of local regression and Ramsey's RESET can be used to get an idea of possible non-linearities.

5.3 Varying parameters

5.3.1 The use of dummy variables

Relaxing the assumption of fixed parameters

In the linear model $y = X\beta + \varepsilon$, the 'direct' effect of a regressor x_j on the dependent variable y is given by $\partial y/\partial x_j = \beta_j$. The assumption of fixed parameters (Assumption 5) means that these effects are the same for all observations. If these effects differ over the sample, then this can be modelled in different ways. In Section 5.2.2 we discussed the addition of quadratic terms and product terms of regressors. In other cases the sample can be split in groups so that the parameters are constant for all observations within a group but differ between groups. For example, the sampled population may consist of several groups that are affected in different ways by the regressors. This kind of parameter variation can be modelled by means of *dummy variables.*

An example: Seasonal dummies

For example, suppose that the data consist of quarterly observations with a mean level that varies over the seasons. This can be represented by the time varying parameter model

$$y_i = \alpha_i + \sum_{j=2}^{k} \beta_j x_{ji} + \varepsilon_i, \qquad (5.8)$$

where α_i takes on four different values, according to the season of the ith observation. This means that $\alpha_i = \alpha_{i+4}$ for all i, as the observations i and $(i+4)$ fall in the same season. Now define four dummy variables D_h, $h = 1, 2, 3, 4$, where $D_{hi} = 1$ if the ith observation falls in season h and $D_{hi} = 0$ if the ith observation falls in another season. These variables are called 'dummies' because they are artificial variables that we define ourselves. With the help of these dummies, the model (5.8) can be expressed as

$$y_i = \alpha_1 D_{1i} + \alpha_2 D_{2i} + \alpha_3 D_{3i} + \alpha_4 D_{4i} + \sum_{j=2}^{k} \beta_j x_{ji} + \varepsilon_i. \qquad (5.9)$$

This is a linear regression model with constant parameters. That is, the parameter variation in (5.8) is removed by including dummy variables as additional regressors. In practice we often prefer models that include a constant term. In this case we should delete one of the dummy variables in (5.9) from the model. For instance, if we delete the variable D_1, then (5.9) can be reformulated as

$$y_i = \alpha_1 + \gamma_2 D_{2i} + \gamma_3 D_{3i} + \gamma_4 D_{4i} + \sum_{j=2}^{k} \beta_j x_{ji} + \varepsilon_i, \qquad (5.10)$$

where $\gamma_s = \alpha_s - \alpha_1$ for $s = 2, 3, 4$. The first quarter is called the reference quarter in this case and the parameters γ_s measure the incremental effects of the other quarters relative to the first quarter. Clearly, the parameters γ_s in (5.10) have a different interpretation from the parameters α_s in (5.9). For instance, suppose we want to test whether the second quarter has a significant effect on the level of y. A t-test on α_2 in (5.9) corresponds to the null hypothesis that $E[y_i] = \sum_{j=2}^{k} \beta_j x_{ji}$ in the second quarter. However, a t-test on γ_2 in (5.10) corresponds to the null hypothesis that $E[y_i] = \alpha_1 + \sum_{j=2}^{k} \beta_j x_{ji}$ in the second quarter—that is, that $\alpha_1 - \alpha_2$. The latter hypothesis is more interesting. If we delete another dummy variable from (5.9)—for instance, D_4 instead of D_1—then the dummy part in (5.10) becomes $\alpha_4 + \delta_1 D_{1i} + \delta_2 D_{2i} + \delta_3 D_{3i}$, where $\delta_s = \alpha_s - \alpha_4$ for $s = 1, 2, 3$. The interpretation of the t-test on δ_2 differs from that of the t-test on γ_2. In general, models with dummy variables can often be formulated in different ways, and we can choose the one with the most appealing interpretation.

The use of dummies for piece-wise linear relations

Dummy variables can also be used to model varying slope parameters. For instance, suppose that the dependence of y on x_2 is continuous and piece-wise linear with slope β_2 for $x_2 \leq a$ and with slope $\beta_2 + \gamma_2$ for $x > a$. This can be formulated as follows. Let D be a dummy variable with $D_i = 0$ if $x_{2i} \leq a$ and $D_i = 1$ if $x_{2i} > a$; then

$$y_i = \alpha + \beta_2 x_{2i} + \gamma_2 (x_{2i} - a) D_i + \sum_{j=3}^{k} \beta_j x_{ji} + \varepsilon_i.$$

This model has constant parameters and it is linear in the parameters, provided that the break point a is known. The null hypothesis that the marginal effect of x_2 on y does not vary over the sample can be tested by a t-test on the significance of γ_2.

E

COMPANION WEB SITE

XM506FAS

Example 5.6: Fashion Sales

We consider US retail sales data of high-priced fashion apparel. The data are taken from G.M. Allenby, L. Jen, and R.P. Leone, 'Economic Trends and Being Trendy: The Influence of Consumer Confidence on Retail Fashion Sales', *Journal of Business and Economic Statistics*, 14/1 (1996), 103–11. We may expect seasonal fluctuations in sales of fashion apparel — for instance, because of sales actions around the change of seasons. We will discuss (i) the data and the model, and (ii) estimation results and tests of seasonal effects.

(i) The data and the model

We consider quarterly data from 1986 to 1992, so that $n = 28$, and we investigate whether there exists a quarterly effect in the relation between sales (S_i, real sales per thousand square feet of retail space) and two explanatory variables, purchasing ability (A_i, real personal disposable income) and consumer confidence (C_i, an index of consumer sentiment). We define four quarterly dummies $D_{ji}, j = 1, 2, 3, 4$, where $D_{ji} = 1$ if the ith observation falls in quarter j and $D_{ji} = 0$ if the ith observation does not fall in quarter j. The general levels of sales and the effect of purchasing ability and consumer confidence on fashion sales may vary over the seasons. We suppose that the standard Assumptions 1–7 are satisfied for the model

$$\log(S_i) = \alpha_1 + \sum_{j=2}^{4} \alpha_j D_{ji} + \sum_{j=1}^{4} \beta_j D_{ji} \log(A_i) + \sum_{j=1}^{4} \gamma_j D_{ji} \log(C_i) + \varepsilon_i.$$

The variation in the coefficients α reflects the possible differences in the average level of retail fashion sales between seasons.

(ii) Estimation results and tests on seasonal effects

Exhibit 5.10 shows the results of three estimated models. The null hypothesis that the effects of the variables A_i and C_i on sales do not depend on the season corresponds to the six parameter restrictions $\beta_1 = \beta_2 = \beta_3 = \beta_4$ and $\gamma_1 = \gamma_2 = \gamma_3 = \gamma_4$. The corresponding F-test of this hypothesis can be computed from the results in Panels 1 and 2 of Exhibit 5.10 — that is,

$$F = \frac{(0.1993 - 0.1437)/6}{0.1437/(28 - 12)} = 1.03 \quad (P = 0.440).$$

Therefore, the null hypothesis of constant parameters for β and γ is not rejected. The corresponding restricted model has six parameters, and we test whether fashion sales depend on the season — that is, we test whether $\alpha_2 = \alpha_3 = \alpha_4 = 0$ in this model. The results in Panels 2 and 3 of Exhibit 5.10 give

Panel 1: Dependent Variable: LOGSALES
Method: Least Squares
Sample: 1986:1 1992:4
Included observations: 28

Variable	Coefficient	Std. Error	t-Statistic	Prob.
C	−13.20387	5.833571	−2.263429	0.0379
D2	12.75170	12.06633	1.056800	0.3063
D3	9.671240	8.959647	1.079422	0.2964
D4	8.545816	7.282290	1.173507	0.2578
LOGA*D1	2.711783	0.841984	3.220704	0.0053
LOGA*D2	1.085208	1.175397	0.923269	0.3696
LOGA*D3	0.737792	0.849956	0.868036	0.3982
LOGA*D4	1.386734	0.660245	2.100334	0.0519
LOGC*D1	0.933291	0.445010	2.097239	0.0522
LOGC*D2	0.003096	1.006677	0.003076	0.9976
LOGC*D3	0.860878	0.609848	1.411626	0.1772
LOGC*D4	0.587470	0.342052	1.717487	0.1052
R-squared	0.910259	Sum squared resid		0.143700

Panel 2: Dependent Variable: LOGSALES
Method: Least Squares
Sample: 1986:1 1992:4
Included observations: 28

Variable	Coefficient	Std. Error	t-Statistic	Prob.
C	−6.139694	2.870911	−2.138587	0.0438
D2	0.193198	0.051066	3.783329	0.0010
D3	0.313589	0.051166	6.128849	0.0000
D4	0.618763	0.052318	11.82706	0.0000
LOGA	1.488666	0.393303	3.785039	0.0010
LOGC	0.660192	0.240432	2.745860	0.0118
R-squared	0.875514	Sum squared resid		0.199337

Panel 3: Dependent Variable: LOGSALES
Method: Least Squares
Sample: 1986:1 1992:4
Included observations: 28

Variable	Coefficient	Std. Error	t-Statistic	Prob.
C	1.175230	7.073808	0.166138	0.8694
LOGA	0.774249	0.986040	0.785210	0.4397
LOGC	−0.022716	0.587800	−0.038646	0.9695
R-squared	0.044989	Sum squared resid		1.529237

Exhibit 5.10 Fashion Sales (Example 5.6)

Regressions of sales on purchasing ability and consumer confidence (all in logarithms), with seasonal variation in all parameters (Panel 1) or only in the constant term (Panel 2) or in none of the parameters (Panel 3).

$$F = \frac{(1.5292 - 0.1993)/3}{0.1993/(28 - 6)} = 48.93 \quad (P = 0.000).$$

This hypothesis is therefore clearly rejected. Exhibit 5.11 shows the residuals of the model with $\alpha_2 = \alpha_3 = \alpha_4 = 0$. The residuals show a clear seasonal pattern with peaks in the fourth quarter. This can also be interpreted as a

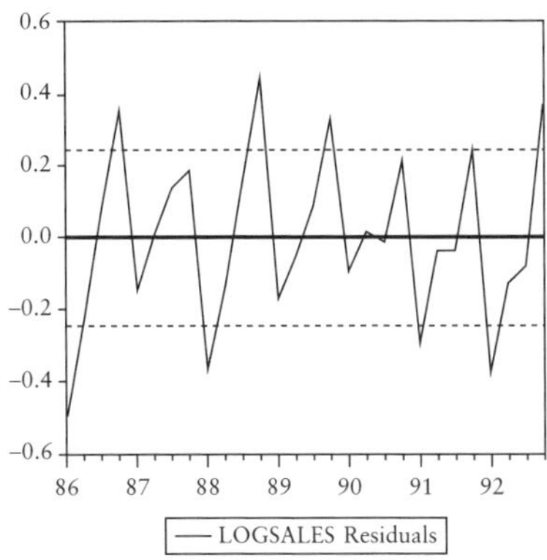

Exhibit 5.11 Fashion Sales (Example 5.6)

Residuals of the model for fashion sales where none of the parameters is allowed to vary over the seasons (note that time is measured on the horizontal axis and that the values of the residuals are measured on the vertical axis).

violation of Assumption 2 that the disturbance terms have a fixed mean. The seasonal variation of this mean is modelled by including the three dummy variables with parameters α_2, α_3, and α_4 in the model.

Example 5.7: **Coffee Sales**

As a second illustration of the use of dummy variables we return to the marketing data on coffee sales of two brands of coffee that were discussed before in Section 4.2.5 (p. 218–21). We will discuss (i) the results for the two brands separately, (ii) a combined model for the two brands, (iii) a test of constant elasticity in the combined model, and (iv) the interpretation of the results.

(i) **Results for the two brands separately**

In Section 4.2.5 we analysed the relation between coffee sales and the applied deal rate and we tested the null hypothesis of constant price elasticity for two brands of coffee. Although scatter diagrams of the data indicate a decreasing elasticity for larger deal rates (see Exhibit 4.5), we had difficulty in rejecting the null hypothesis of constant elasticity when this is tested for the two brands separately. A possible reason is the small number of observations, $n = 12$, for both brands.

(ii) **A combined model for the two brands**

We will now consider a model that combines the information of the two brands. The model for the effect of price deals (denoted by d) on coffee sales (denoted by q) in Section 4.2.5 is given by

$$\log(q_i) = \beta_1 + \frac{\beta_2}{\beta_3}\left(d_i^{\beta_3} - 1\right) + \varepsilon_i.$$

The price elasticity in this model is equal to $\beta_2 d^{\beta_3}$ (see Example 4.2, p. 204), and the null hypothesis of constant price elasticity corresponds to the parameter restriction $\beta_3 = 0$. Now we combine the data of the two brands of coffee by means of the model

$$\log(q_i) = D_{1i}\left(\beta_1 + \frac{\beta_2}{\beta_3}(d_i^{\beta_3} - 1)\right) + D_{2i}\left(\gamma_1 + \frac{\gamma_2}{\gamma_3}(d_i^{\gamma_3} - 1)\right) + \varepsilon_i, \quad i = 1, \ldots, 24,$$

where $D_{1i} = 1$ for the observations of brand one and $D_{1i} = 0$ for the observations of brand two, and where $D_{2i} = 1 - D_{1i}$. This model allows for the possibility that all regression coefficients differ between the two brands of coffee. Exhibit 5.12 shows the NLS estimates of this model in Panel 1 and of the restricted model with $\beta_2 = \gamma_2$ and $\beta_3 = \gamma_3$ in Panel 3. This corresponds to the assumption that the elasticities are the same for the two brands of coffee—that is, $\beta_2 d^{\beta_3} = \gamma_2 d^{\gamma_3}$. We do not impose the condition $\beta_1 = \gamma_1$, as the level of the sales are clearly different for the two brands (see Exhibit 4.5). The Wald test for the hypothesis that $(\beta_2, \beta_3) = (\gamma_2, \gamma_3)$ has P-value 0.249 (see Panel 2). We do not reject this hypothesis and therefore we will consider the following combined model for the two brands of coffee:

$$\log(q_i) = D_{1i}\beta_1 + D_{2i}\gamma_1 + \frac{\beta_2}{\beta_3}\left(d_i^{\beta_3} - 1\right) + \varepsilon_i, \quad i = 1, \ldots, 24.$$

(iii) Test of constant elasticity in the combined model

We now test the hypothesis of constant elasticity in the above combined model for the two brands. That is, we test whether $\beta_3 = 0$, in which case $\frac{\beta_2}{\beta_3}\left(d_i^{\beta_3} - 1\right)$ reduces to $\beta_2 \log(d_i)$, as in the Box–Cox transformation. The results in Panels 3–5 of Exhibit 5.12 are used to compute the values of the Wald test, the Likelihood Ratio test, and the Lagrange Multiplier test. For the Wald test (for a single parameter restriction) we use the relation (4.50) with the t-test, and Panel 3 gives

$$W = \frac{n}{n-k}t^2 = \frac{24}{20}(-2.520)^2 = 7.62 \quad (P = 0.006).$$

The Likelihood Ratio test is obtained from Panels 3 and 4 and is equal to

$$LR = 2(l_1 - l_0) = 2(22.054 - 18.549) = 7.01 \quad (P = 0.008).$$

The Lagrange Multiplier test is computed in a similar way as described in Sections 4.2.5 (p. 221) and 4.3.9 (p. 247), and Panel 5 gives

$$LM = nR^2 = 24(0.253) = 6.08 \quad (P = 0.014).$$

(iv) Interpretation of the results

The above test outcomes indicate that the null hypothesis of constant deal elasticity should be rejected. Our earlier results in Example 4.6 in Section 4.3.9 gave less clear conclusions. This illustrates the power of imposing model restrictions, in this example, the assumption that the functional dependence of the elasticity on the deal rate is the same for the two brands of coffee. The combined model is estimated for twenty-four observations, so that, in comparison with our analysis in Section 4.2.5, we gain twelve

Panel 1: Dependent Variable: LOGQ				
Method: Least Squares				
Sample: 1 24				
Included observations: 24				
Convergence achieved after 5 iterations				
LOGQ=C(1)*DUMRGC1+C(2)*DUMRGC2+C(3)/C(4)*DUMRGC1 *(DEAL^C(4)−1)+C(5)/C(6)*DUMRGC2*(DEAL^C(6)−1)				
Parameter	Coefficient	Std. Error	t-Statistic	Prob.
C(1)	5.807118	0.041721	139.1879	0.0000
C(2)	4.377804	0.041721	104.9294	0.0000
C(3)	10.29832	3.424515	3.007235	0.0076
C(4)	−13.43074	6.936886	−1.936133	0.0687
C(5)	10.28864	2.896461	3.552142	0.0023
C(6)	−8.595289	5.024271	−1.710753	0.1043
R-squared	0.986396	Sum squared resid		0.187993
S.E. of regression	0.102196	Log likelihood		24.13832

Panel 2: Wald Test			
Null Hypothesis:	C(3)=C(5)		
	C(4)=C(6)		
F-statistic	1.502889	Probability	0.249117
Chi-square	3.005777	Probability	0.222487

Panel 3: Dependent Variable: LOGQ				
Method: Least Squares				
Sample: 1 24				
Included observations: 24				
Convergence achieved after 5 iterations				
LOGQ=C(1)*DUMRGC1+C(2)*DUMRGC2+C(3)/C(4)*(DEAL^C(4)−1)				
Parameter	Coefficient	Std. Error	t-Statistic	Prob.
C(1)	5.778500	0.037388	154.5565	0.0000
C(2)	4.406421	0.037388	117.8577	0.0000
C(3)	10.23724	2.274838	4.500207	0.0002
C(4)	−10.67745	4.237472	−2.519770	0.0204
R-squared	0.983815	Sum squared resid		0.223654
S.E. of regression	0.105748	Log likelihood		22.05400

Exhibit 5.12 Coffee Sales (Example 5.7)

Regression of coffee sales on deal rate with all parameters different for the two brands (Panel 1), test on equal elasticities for the two brands (Panel 2), and regression model with equal elasticities (but different sales levels) for the two brands (Panel 3).

Panel 4: Dependent Variable: LOGQ				
Method: Least Squares				
Sample: 1 24				
Included observations: 24				
Variable	Coefficient	Std. Error	t-Statistic	Prob.
DUMRGC1	5.810190	0.039926	145.5240	0.0000
DUMRGC2	4.438110	0.039926	111.1584	0.0000
LOG(DEAL)	5.333995	0.427194	12.48611	0.0000
R-squared	0.978325	Sum squared resid		0.299523
S.E. of regression	0.119428	Log likelihood		18.54891

Panel 5: Dependent Variable: RESLOGDEAL				
Method: Least Squares				
Sample: 1 24				
Included observations: 24				
Variable	Coefficient	Std. Error	t-Statistic	Prob.
DUMRGC1	−0.031689	0.037388	−0.847590	0.4067
DUMRGC2	−0.031689	0.037388	−0.847590	0.4067
LOG(DEAL)	4.072710	1.608700	2.531678	0.0198
LOG(DEAL)^2	−29.25819	11.23281	−2.604707	0.0170
R-squared	0.253300	Sum squared resid		0.223654
S.E. of regression	0.105748			

Exhibit 5.12 *(Contd.)*

Regression model for coffee sales with constant elasticity (Panel 4) and regression of the residuals of this model on the gradient of the unrestricted model where the elasticity depends on the deal rate (Panel 5).

observations at the cost of one parameter. This gain of eleven degrees of freedom leads to more clear-cut conclusions.

☞ **Exercises:** E: 5.26.

5.3.2 Recursive least squares

Recursive estimation to detect parameter variations

If we want to model varying parameters by means of dummy variables, we should know the nature of this variation. In some situations the choice of dummy variables is straightforward (see for instance Examples 5.6 and 5.7 in the foregoing section). However, in other cases it may be quite difficult to specify the precise nature of the parameter variation.

Now suppose that the data can be *ordered* in a natural way. For instance, if the data consist of time series that are observed sequentially over time, then it is natural to order them with time. If the data consist of a cross section, then the observations can be ordered according to the values of one of the explanatory variables. For such ordered data sets we can detect possible break points by applying recursive least squares. For every value of t with $k+1 \leq t \leq n$, a regression is performed in the model $y_i = x_i'\beta + \varepsilon_i$ using only the $(t-1)$ observations $i = 1, \cdots, t-1$. This gives an OLS estimator b_{t-1} and a corresponding forecast $\hat{y}_t = x_t'b_{t-1}$ with forecast error

$$f_t = y_t - x_t'b_{t-1}. \tag{5.11}$$

The *recursive least squares* estimators are defined as the series of estimators b_t. It is left as an exercise (see Exercise 5.3) to show that these estimators can be calculated recursively by

$$b_t = b_{t-1} + A_t x_t f_t \tag{5.12}$$

$$A_t = A_{t-1} - \frac{1}{v_t} A_{t-1} x_t x_t' A_{t-1} \tag{5.13}$$

$$v_t = 1 + x_t' A_{t-1} x_t, \tag{5.14}$$

where $A_t = (X_t'X_t)^{-1}$ with X_t the $t \times k$ regressor matrix for the observations $i = 1, \cdots, t$. The result in (5.12) shows that the magnitude of the changes $b_t - b_{t-1}$ in the recursive estimates depends on the forecast errors f_t in (5.11). Under the standard Assumptions 1–7, the correction factor A_t is proportional to the covariance matrix of the estimator b_t, so that large uncertainty leads to large changes in the estimates.

Recursive residuals

Under Assumptions 1–7 the forecast errors have mean $E[f_t] = 0$. As $y_t = x_t'\beta + \varepsilon_t$ is independent of b_{t-1} (that depends only on $\varepsilon_1, \cdots, \varepsilon_{t-1}$), it follows that $\text{var}(f_t) = \text{var}(y_t) + \text{var}(x_t'b_{t-1}) = \sigma^2(1 + x_t'A_{t-1}x_t) = \sigma^2 v_t$. It is left as an exercise (see Exercise 5.3) to show that the forecast errors f_t are also mutually independent. This means that, if the model is valid (so that in particular the parameters are constant),

$$w_t = \frac{f_t}{\sqrt{v_t}} \sim \text{NID}(0, \sigma^2), \quad t = k+1, \cdots, n. \tag{5.15}$$

The values of w_t are called the *recursive residuals*. To detect possible parameter breaks it is helpful to plot the recursive estimates b_t and the recursive residuals w_t as a function of t. If the parameters are varying, then this is reflected in variations in the estimates b_t and in relatively large and serially correlated recursive residuals w_t after the break. Such breaks may suggest additional explanatory variables that account for the break, or the model can be adjusted by including non-linear terms or dummy variables, as discussed in Sections 5.2.2 and 5.3.1.

Example 5.8: **Bank Wages (continued)**

We continue our analysis of the bank wage data discussed in previous sections. Using the notation introduced there, the model is

$$y_i = \alpha + \gamma D_{gi} + \mu D_{mi} + \beta x_i + \varepsilon_i, \tag{5.16}$$

where y is the logarithm of yearly salary and x the number of completed years of education. We order the $n = 474$ employees according to the values of x, starting with the lowest education. The education ranges from 8 to 21 years. Employees with ranking number 365 or lower have at most 15 years of education ($x \leq 15$), those with ranking number 366–424 have $x = 16$, and those with ranking number 425–474 have $x > 16$.

Exhibit 5.13 shows the recursive least squares estimates of the constant term α (in (*a*)) and of the marginal return of schooling β (in (*b*)), together

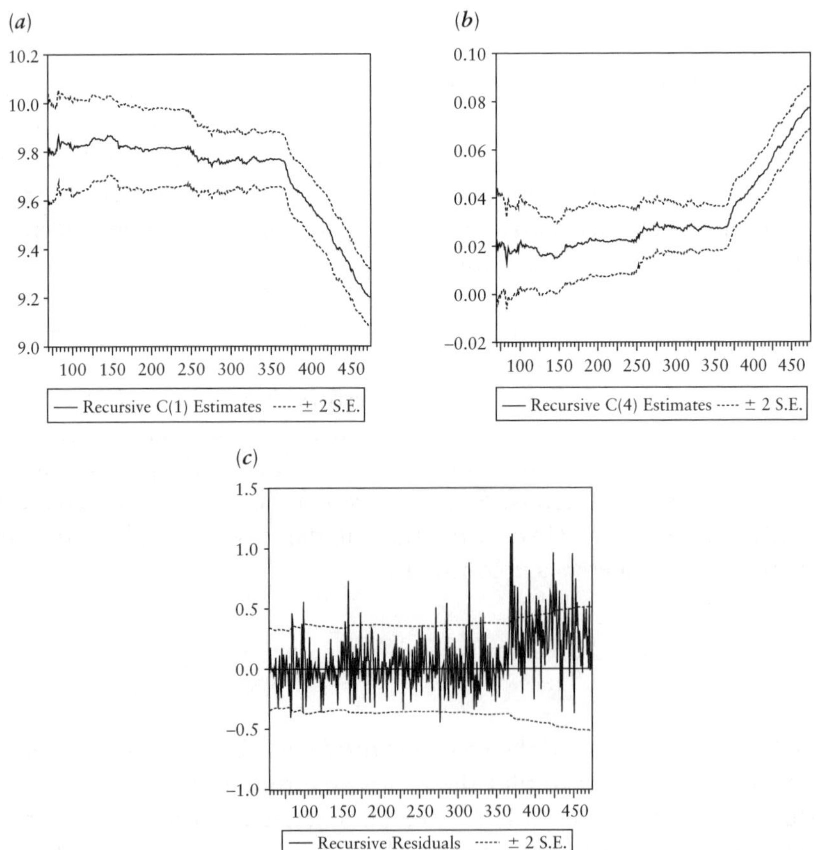

Exhibit 5.13 Bank Wages (Example 5.8)

Recursive estimates of constant term (*a*) and of slope with respect to education (*b*), together with plot of recursive residuals (*c*). The graphs also show 95% interval estimates of the parameters and 95% confidence intervals for the recursive residuals.

with 95 per cent interval estimates. The estimates of β show a break after observation 365, suggesting that the returns may be larger for higher levels of education. The plot of recursive residuals in (*c*) shows mostly positive values after observation 365. This means that for higher levels of education the wages are higher than is predicted from the estimates based on the employees with less education. These results are in line with our analysis of non-linearities in the previous examples, see Examples 5.1, 5.4, and 5.5. All these results indicate that the effect of education on salary is non-linear.

☞ Exercises: T: 5.3.

5.3.3 Tests for varying parameters

The CUSUM test for the regression parameters

Although plots of recursive estimates and recursive residuals are helpful in analysing possible parameter variations, it is also useful to perform statistical tests on the null hypothesis of constant parameters. Such tests can be based on the recursive residuals w_t defined in (5.15). Under the hypothesis of constant parameters, it follows from (5.15) that the sample mean $\overline{w} = \frac{1}{n-k}\sum_{t=k+1}^{n} w_t$ is normally distributed with mean zero and variance $\frac{\sigma^2}{n-k}$. Let $\hat{\sigma}^2 = \frac{1}{n-k-1}\sum_{t=k+1}^{n}(w_t - \overline{w})^2$ be the unbiased estimator of σ^2 based on the recursive residuals; then

$$\sqrt{n-k}\frac{\overline{w}}{\hat{\sigma}} \sim t(n-k-1).$$

A significant non-zero mean of the recursive residuals indicates possible instability of the regression parameters. The *CUSUM test* is based on the cumulative sums

$$W_r = \sum_{t=k+1}^{r} \frac{w_t}{s}, \quad r = k+1, \cdots, n,$$

where s^2 is the OLS estimate of σ^2 in the model $y = X\beta + \varepsilon$ over the full data sample using all n observations. If the model is correctly specified, then the terms w_t/σ are independent with distribution $\mathrm{N}(0, 1)$, so that W_r is approximately distributed as $\mathrm{N}(0, r-k)$. For a significance level of (approximately) 5 per cent, an individual value W_r differs significantly from zero if $|W_r| > 2\sqrt{r-k}$. It is also possible to test for the joint significance of the set of values W_r, $r = k+1, \cdots, n$. For a significance level of (approximately) 5 per cent, it can be shown that this set of values indicates misspecification of the model if there exists a point r for which $|W_r| > 0.948\left(1 + 2\frac{r-k}{n-k}\right)\sqrt{n-k}$.

The CUSUMSQ test for the variance

Large values for one or more recursive residuals are not necessarily caused by changes in the regression parameters β. Another possibility is that the variance σ^2 of the error terms is changing—that is, the amount of uncertainty or randomness in the observations may vary over time. This can be investigated by considering the sequence of squared recursive residuals $w_t^2/\hat{\sigma}^2$. If the model is correctly specified, then (5.15) shows that these values are approximately distributed as independent $\chi^2(1)$ variables. The *CUSUMSQ test* is based on the cumulative sums of squares

$$S_r = \frac{\sum_{t=k+1}^{r} w_t^2}{\sum_{t=k+1}^{n} w_t^2}, \quad r = k+1, \cdots, n.$$

For large enough sample size, $\frac{1}{n-k}\sum_{t=k+1}^{n} w_t^2 \approx \sigma^2$, so that $(n-k)S_r$ is approximately distributed as $\chi^2(r-k)$ with expected value $r-k$ and variance $2(r-k)$. So S_r has approximately a mean of $(r-k)/(n-k)$ and a variance of $2(r-k)/(n-k)^2$. This provides simple tests for the individual significance of a value of S_r (for fixed r).

Note that the values always run from $S_k = 0$ (for $r = k$) to $S_n = 1$ (for $r = n$), independent of the values of the recursive residuals. Tests on the joint significance of deviations of S_r from their mean values have been derived, where the model is said to be misspecified if there exists a point r for which $|S_r - \frac{r-k}{n-k}| > c$. The value of c depends on the significance level and on $(n-k)$.

Interpretation as general misspecification tests

Apart from the effects of changing parameters or variances, large recursive residuals may also be caused by exceptional values of the disturbance terms ε_i in the relation $y_i = x_i'\beta + \varepsilon_i$. Such observations are called outliers, and this is discussed in Section 5.6. It may also be the case that breaks occur in the explanatory variables. For instance, if one of the x_i variables shows significant growth over the sample period, then the linear approximation $y_i = x_i'\beta + \varepsilon_i$ that may be acceptable at the beginning of the sample, for small values of x_i, may cause large errors at the end of the sample. That is, the diagnostic tests CUSUM and CUSUMSQ that are introduced here as parameter stability tests are sensitive to any kind of instability of the model, not only for changes in the parameters.

The Chow break test

In some situations there may be a clear break point in the sample and we want to test whether the parameters have changed at this point. Let the n observations be split in two parts, the first part consisting of n_1 observations and the second part of the remaining $n_2 = n - n_1$ observations. In order to test the hypothesis of constant coefficients across the two subsets of data, the model can be formulated as

$$\begin{aligned} y_1 &= X_1\beta_1 + \varepsilon_1 \\ y_2 &= X_2\beta_2 + \varepsilon_2, \end{aligned} \tag{5.17}$$

where y_1 and y_2 are the $n_1 \times 1$ and $n_2 \times 1$ vectors of the dependent variable in the two subsets and X_1 and X_2 the $n_1 \times k$ and $n_2 \times k$ matrices of explanatory variables. This can also be written as

$$\begin{pmatrix} y_1 \\ y_2 \end{pmatrix} = \begin{pmatrix} X_1 & 0 \\ 0 & X_2 \end{pmatrix} \begin{pmatrix} \beta_1 \\ \beta_2 \end{pmatrix} + \begin{pmatrix} \varepsilon_1 \\ \varepsilon_2 \end{pmatrix}. \tag{5.18}$$

It is assumed that the model (5.18) satisfies all the standard Assumptions 1–7, in particular, that all the $(n_1 + n_2)$ error terms are independent and have equal variance. The null hypothesis of constant coefficients is given by

$$H_0 : \beta_1 = \beta_2. \tag{5.19}$$

This can be tested against the alternative that $\beta_1 \neq \beta_2$ by means of the F-test. The number of parameters under the alternative hypothesis is $2k$, and the number of restrictions in (5.19) is k. Least squares in the unrestricted model (5.18) gives an error sum of squares that is equal to the sum of the error sum of squares of the two separate regressions in (5.17) (see Exercise 5.4). So the F-test is given by

$$F = \frac{(S_0 - S_1 - S_2)/k}{(S_1 + S_2)/(n_1 + n_2 - 2k)}, \tag{5.20}$$

where S_0 is the error sum of squares under the null hypothesis (obtained by regression in $y = X\beta + \varepsilon$ over the full sample of $n = n_1 + n_2$ observations) and where S_1 and S_2 are obtained by the two subset regressions in (5.17). This is called the *Chow break test*, and under the null hypothesis of constant parameters it follows the $F(k, n_1 + n_2 - 2k)$ distribution. The regressions under the alternative hypothesis require that $n_1 \geq k$ and $n_2 \geq k$—that is, in both subsets the number of observations should be at least as large as the number of parameters in the model for that subset.

The Chow forecast test

The model specification (5.17) allows for a break in the parameters, but apart from this the model structure is assumed to be the same. The model structure under the alternative can also be left unspecified. Then the null hypothesis is that $y = X\beta + \varepsilon$ holds for all $n_1 + n_2$ observations and the alternative is that this model only holds for the first n_1 observations and that the last n_2 observations are generated by an unknown model. This can be expressed by the model

$$y_i = x_i'\beta + \sum_{j=n_1+1}^{n_1+n_2} \gamma_j D_{ji} + \varepsilon_i, \tag{5.21}$$

where D_j is a dummy variable with $D_{ji} = 1$ for $i = j$ and $D_{ji} = 0$ for $i \neq j$. So, for every observation $i > n_1$, the model allows for an additional effect γ_j that may differ from observation to observation. The coefficients γ_j represent all factors that are excluded under the null hypothesis—for instance, neglected variables, another functional form, or another error model. The null hypothesis of constant model structure corresponds to

$$H_0 : \gamma_j = 0 \text{ for all } j = n_1 + 1, \cdots, n_1 + n_2. \tag{5.22}$$

This can be tested by the F-test, which is called the *Chow forecast test*. Using the above notation, the Chow forecast test is computed as

$$F = \frac{(S_0 - S_1)/n_2}{S_1/(n_1 - k)}.$$

This is exactly equal to the forecast test discussed in Section 3.4.3 (p. 173) (see Exercise 5.4). This test can also be used as an alternative to the Chow break test (5.20) if one of the subsets of data contains less than k observations.

Example 5.9: **Bank Wages (continued)**

We continue our analysis of the data on wages and education where the data are ordered with increasing values of education (see Example 5.8). We will discuss (i) Chow tests on parameter variations, and (ii) CUSUM and CUSUMSQ tests.

(i) **Chow tests**

To test whether an additional year of education gives the same relative increase in wages for lower and higher levels of education, we perform a

Chow break test and a Chow forecast test. The $n = 474$ employees are split into two groups, one group with at most sixteen years of education ($n_1 = 424$) and the other with seventeen years of education or more ($n_2 = 50$). Exhibit 5.14 shows the results of regressions for the whole data set (in Panel 1) and for the two subsamples (in Panels 2 and 3). The Chow break test (5.20) is given by

$$F = \frac{(30.852 - 23.403 - 2.941)/4}{(23.403 + 2.941)/(424 + 50 - 8)} = 19.93 \quad (P = 0.000).$$

Panel 1: Dependent Variable: LOGSALARY
Method: Least Squares
Sample: 1 474
Included observations: 474

Variable	Coefficient	Std. Error	t-Statistic	Prob.
C	9.199980	0.058687	156.7634	0.0000
GENDER	0.261131	0.025511	10.23594	0.0000
MINORITY	−0.132673	0.028946	−4.583411	0.0000
EDUC	0.077366	0.004436	17.44229	0.0000
R-squared	0.586851	Sum squared resid		30.85177

Panel 2: Dependent Variable: LOGSALARY
Method: Least Squares
Sample: 1 424
Included observations: 424

Variable	Coefficient	Std. Error	t-Statistic	Prob.
C	9.463702	0.063095	149.9906	0.0000
GENDER	0.229931	0.023801	9.660543	0.0000
MINORITY	−0.111687	0.027462	−4.066947	0.0001
EDUC	0.055783	0.004875	11.44277	0.0000
R-squared	0.426202	Sum squared resid		23.40327

Panel 3: Dependent Variable: LOGSALARY
Method: Least Squares
Sample: 425 474
Included observations: 50

Variable	Coefficient	Std. Error	t-Statistic	Prob.
C	9.953242	0.743176	13.39284	0.0000
GENDER	0.830174	0.263948	3.145213	0.0029
MINORITY	−0.346533	0.126096	−2.748175	0.0085
EDUC	0.019132	0.041108	0.465418	0.6438
R-squared	0.302888	Sum squared resid		2.941173

Exhibit 5.14 Bank Wages (Example 5.9)

Regressions of salary on gender, minority, and education over full sample (Panel 1), over subsample of employees with at most sixteen years of education (Panel 2), and over subsample of employees with seventeen years of education or more (Panel 3).

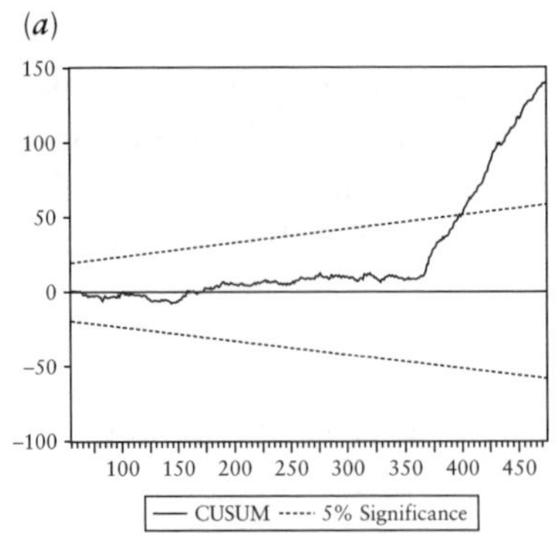

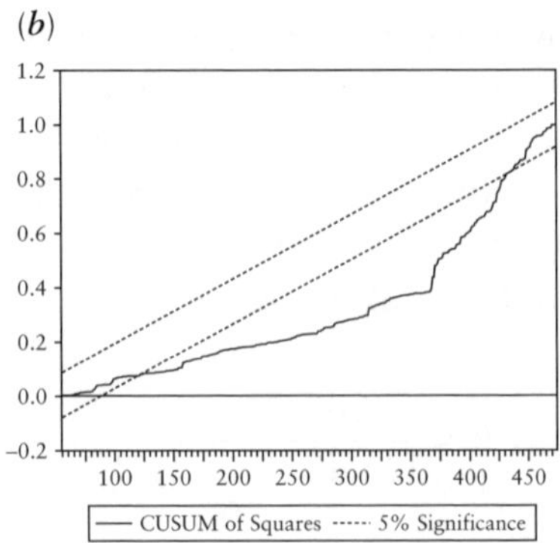

Exhibit 5.15 Bank Wages (Example 5.9)

Plots of CUSUM and CUSUMSQ for wage data, ordered with increasing education. Employees with index 365 or lower have at most fifteen years of education, those with index between 366 and 424 have sixteen years of education, and those with index 425 or higher have seventeen years of education or more.

The Chow forecast test (3.58) gives

$$F = \frac{(30.852 - 23.403)/50}{23.403/(424 - 4)} = 2.67 \quad (P = 0.000).$$

The null hypothesis of constant returns of schooling is clearly rejected.

(ii) CUSUM and CUSUMSQ tests

Exhibit 5.15 shows plots of the CUSUM and CUSUMSQ tests. This shows that, at the end of the sample, the CUSUM deviates significantly from zero. After observation $i = 366$ the recursive residuals are mostly positive, meaning that predicted wages are smaller than the actual wages. This is in agreement with the recursive slope estimate in Exhibit 5.13 (*b*), which becomes larger after observation 366. The CUSUMSQ plot shows that the squared recursive residuals in the first part of the sample are relatively small and that the sum of squares builds up faster after observation 366. This is a further sign that the returns of schooling are not constant for different levels of education.

☞ **Exercises:** T: 5.4; S: 5.19; E: 5.24, 5.31**a**, **b**, **f**, 5.33**b**, **d**.

5.3.4 Summary

An econometric model usually involves a number of parameters that are all assumed to be constant over the observation sample. It is advisable to apply tests on parameter constancy and to adjust the model if the parameters seem to vary over the sample.

- The assumption of constant parameters can be tested by applying recursive least squares, by considering plots of recursive residuals and of the CUSUM and CUSUMSQ statistics, and by means of the break and forecasts tests of Chow.
- If the parameters are not constant one has to think of meaningful adjustments of the model that do have constant parameters. This may mean that one has to adjust the specification of the model — for instance, by choosing an appropriate non-linear model or by incorporating additional relevant explanatory variables. Dummy variables are a helpful tool to remove parameter variation by incorporating additional parameters that account for this variation.

5.4 Heteroskedasticity

5.4.1 Introduction

General model for heteroskedastic error terms

For ordinary least squares, it is assumed that the error terms of the model have constant variance and that they are mutually uncorrelated. If this is not the case, then OLS is no longer efficient, so that we can possibly get more accurate esimates by applying different methods. In this section we discuss the estimation and testing of models for data that exhibit heteroskedasticity, and in the next section we discuss serial correlation.

Under Assumptions 1–6, the standard regression model is given by

$$y = X\beta + \varepsilon, \quad E[\varepsilon] = 0, \quad E[\varepsilon\varepsilon'] = \sigma^2 I.$$

In this section we suppose that Assumptions 1, 2, 4, 5, and 6 are satisfied but that Assumption 3 of constant variance is violated. Let the disturbances be heteroskedastic with $E[\varepsilon_i^2] = \sigma_i^2$, $i = 1, \cdots, n$; then

$$E[\varepsilon\varepsilon'] = \Omega = \begin{pmatrix} \sigma_1^2 & 0 & \cdots & 0 \\ 0 & \sigma_2^2 & \cdots & 0 \\ \vdots & \vdots & \ddots & \vdots \\ 0 & 0 & \cdots & \sigma_n^2 \end{pmatrix}.$$

So the covariance matrix is diagonal because of Assumption 4 of uncorrelated disturbances, but the elements on the diagonal may be different for each observation. This means that the amount of randomness in the outcome of y_i, measured by $\mathrm{var}(y_i) = \sigma_i^2$, may differ for each observation.

Implications of heteroskedasticity for estimation

In least squares we minimize $\sum_{i=1}^n (y_i - x_i'\beta)^2$, but if the variances differ it may be better to assign relatively smaller weights to observations with large variance and larger weights to observations with small variance. This is because observations with small error terms provide more information on the value of β than observations with large error terms. We can then use a weighted least squares criterion of the form

$$\sum_{i=1}^{n} w_i^2 \left(y_i - x_i'\beta\right)^2,$$

with weights w_i^2 that decrease for larger values of σ_i^2. The choice of optimal weights is one of the issues discussed below. First we give two examples.

Example 5.10: **Bank Wages (continued)**

We consider again the bank wage data of 474 bank employees. We will discuss (i) three job categories, (ii) a possible model for heteroskedasticity, and (iii) a graphical idea of the amount of variation in wages.

(i) **Three job categories**

The bank employees can be divided according to three job categories—namely, administrative jobs, custodial jobs, and management jobs. It may well be that the amount of variation in wages differs among these three categories. For instance, for a given level of education it may be expected that employees with custodial jobs earn more or less similar wages. However, two managers with the same level of education may have quite different salaries—for instance, because the job responsibilities differ or because the two employees have different management experience.

(ii) **A possible model for heteroskedasticity**

We consider the regression model

$$y_i = \beta_1 + \beta_2 x_i + \beta_3 D_{gi} + \beta_4 D_{mi} + \beta_5 D_{2i} + \beta_6 D_{3i} + \varepsilon_i,$$

where y_i is the logarithm of yearly wage, x_i is the number of years of education, D_g is a gender dummy (1 for males, 0 for females), and D_m is a minority dummy (1 for minorities, 0 otherwise). Administration is taken as reference category and D_2 and D_3 are dummy variables ($D_2 = 1$ for individuals with a custodial job and $D_2 = 0$ otherwise, and $D_3 = 1$ for individuals with a management position and $D_3 = 0$ otherwise). We sort the observations so that the first $n_1 = 363$ individuals have jobs in administration, the next $n_2 = 27$ ones have custodial jobs, and the last $n_3 = 84$ ones have jobs in management. If we allow for different variances among the three job categories, the covariance matrix can be specified as follows, where I_{n_i} denotes the $n_i \times n_i$ identity matrix for $i = 1, 2, 3$.

$$\Omega = \begin{pmatrix} \sigma_1^2 I_{n_1} & 0 & 0 \\ 0 & \sigma_2^2 I_{n_2} & 0 \\ 0 & 0 & \sigma_3^2 I_{n_3} \end{pmatrix}.$$

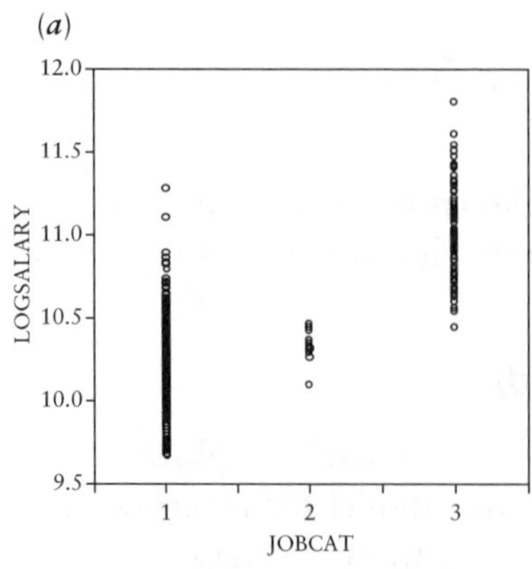

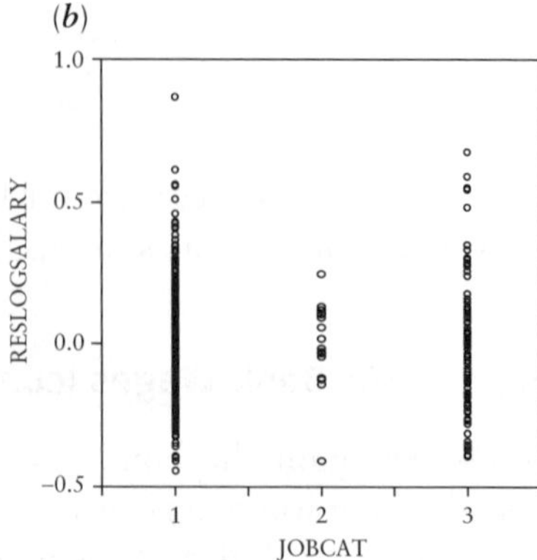

Exhibit 5.16 Bank Wages (Example 5.10)

Unconditional variation in log salary (*a*) and conditional variation of residuals of log salary (after regression on education, gender, minority, and job category dummies (*b*)). The job categories are administration (1), custodial jobs (2), and management (3), with respective sizes of the subsamples $n_1 = 363, n_2 = 27$, and $n_3 = 84$.

(iii) Graphical impression of the amount of variation

Exhibit 5.16 shows for each job category both the (unconditional) variation in y in (a) and the conditional variation (that is, the variation of the OLS residuals of the above regression model) in (b). The exhibit indicates that the variations are the smallest for custodial jobs.

XM511IBR

Example 5.11: **Interest and Bond Rates**

We now consider monthly data on the short-term interest rate (the three-month Treasury Bill rate) and on the AAA corporate bond yield in the USA. As Treasury Bill notes and AAA bonds can be seen as alternative ways of investment in low-risk securities, it may be expected that the AAA bond rate is positively related to the interest rate. It may further be that this relation holds more tightly for lower than for higher levels of the rates, as for higher rates there may be more possibilities for speculative gains. We will discuss (i) the data and the model, (ii) a graphical impression of changes in variance, and (iii) a possible model for heteroskedasticity.

(i) Data and model

The AAA bond rate is defined as an average over long-term bonds of firms with AAA rating. The data on the Treasury Bill rate are taken from the Federal Reserve Board of Governors and the data on AAA bonds from Moody's Investors Service. The data run from January 1950 to December 1999. Let x_i denote the monthly change in the Treasury Bill rate and let y_i be the monthly change in the AAA bond rate. These changes will be related to each other, and we postulate the simple regression model

$$y_i = \alpha + \beta x_i + \varepsilon_i, \quad i = 1, 2, \cdots, 600.$$

(ii) Graphical impression of changes in variance

Exhibit 5.17 (*a*) shows the residuals that are obtained from regression in the above model (the figure has time on the horizontal axis, the values of the residuals are measured on the vertical axis). The variance over the first half of the considered time period is considerably smaller than that over the second half. This suggests that the uncertainty of AAA bonds has increased over time. One of the possible causes is that the Treasury Bill rate has become more volatile. Exhibit 5.17 shows two scatter diagrams of y_i against x_i, one (*b*) for the first 300 observations (1950–74) and the other (*c*) for the last 300 observations (1975–99).

(iii) A possible model for heteroskedasticity

The magnitude of the random variations ε_i in the AAA bond rate changes may be related to the magnitude of the changes x_i in the Treasury Bill rate. For instance, if $E[\varepsilon_i^2] = \sigma^2 x_i^2$, then the covariance matrix becomes

$$\Omega = \sigma^2 \begin{pmatrix} x_1^2 & 0 & \cdots & 0 \\ 0 & x_2^2 & \cdots & 0 \\ \vdots & \vdots & \ddots & \vdots \\ 0 & 0 & \cdots & x_n^2 \end{pmatrix},$$

where $n = 600$. Observations in months with small changes in the Treasury Bill rate are then more informative about α and β than observations in months with large changes. Alternative models for the variance in these data will be considered in later sections (see Examples 5.16 and 5.18).

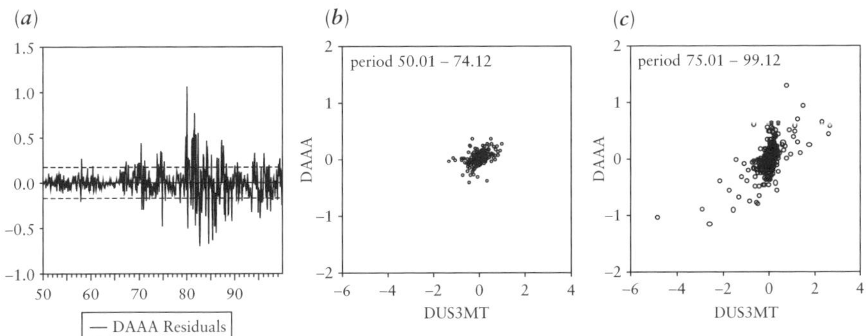

Exhibit 5.17 Interest and Bond Rates (Example 5.11)

Plot of residuals of regression of changes in AAA bond rate on changes in three-month Treasury Bill rate (*a*) and scatter diagrams of these changes over the periods 1950–74 (*b*) and 1975–99 (*c*).

5.4.2 Properties of OLS and White standard errors

Properties of OLS for heteroskedastic disturbances

Suppose that Assumptions 1, 2, 5, and 6 are satisfied but that the covariance matrix of the disturbances is not equal to $\sigma^2 I$. That is, assume that

$$y = X\beta + \varepsilon, \quad E[\varepsilon] = 0, \quad E[\varepsilon\varepsilon'] = \Omega.$$

Although ordinary least squares will no longer have all the optimality properties discussed in Chapter 3, it is still attractive, as it is simple to compute these estimates. In this section we consider the consequences of applying ordinary least squares under the above assumptions. The OLS estimator is given by $b = (X'X)^{-1}X'y$, and, substituting $y = X\beta + \varepsilon$, it follows that

$$b = \beta + (X'X)^{-1}X'\varepsilon.$$

Under the stated assumptions this means that

$$E[b] = \beta, \quad \text{var}(b) = (X'X)^{-1}X'\Omega X(X'X)^{-1}. \tag{5.23}$$

So the OLS estimator b remains unbiased. However, the usual expression $\sigma^2(X'X)^{-1}$ for the variance does not apply anymore. Therefore, if one routinely applies the usual least squares expressions for standard errors, then the outcomes misrepresent the correct standard errors, unless $\Omega = \sigma^2 I$. So the estimated coefficients b are 'correct' in the sense of being unbiased, but the OLS formulas for the standard errors are wrong.

White standard errors

In order to perform significance tests we should estimate the covariance matrix in (5.23). If the disturbances are uncorrelated but heteroskedastic, so that Ω is a diagonal matrix with elements $\sigma_1^2, \cdots, \sigma_n^2$ on the diagonal, then (5.23) can be written as

$$\text{var}(b) = (X'X)^{-1}\left(\sum_{i=1}^{n} \sigma_i^2 x_i x_i'\right)(X'X)^{-1}. \tag{5.24}$$

Here x_i is the $k \times 1$ vector of explanatory variables for the ith observation. In most situations the values σ_i^2 of the variances are unknown. A simple estimator of σ_i^2 is given by e_i^2, the square of the OLS residual $e_i = y_i - x_i'b$. This gives

$$\widehat{\text{var}}(b) = (X'X)^{-1}\left(\sum_{i=1}^{n} e_i^2 x_i x_i'\right)(X'X)^{-1}. \qquad (5.25)$$

This is called the White estimate of the covariance matrix of b, and the square roots of the diagonal elements are called the *White standard errors*. Sometimes a correction is applied. In case of homoskedastic error terms, it was derived in Section 3.1.5 (p. 127–8) that the residual vector e has covariance matrix $\sigma^2 M$, where $M = I - X(X'X)^{-1}X' = I - H$. So the residual e_i has variance $\sigma^2(1 - h_i)$ in this case, where h_i is the ith diagonal element of H. For this reason one sometimes replaces e_i^2 in (5.25) by $e_i^2/(1 - h_i)$.

Proof of consistency of White standard errors

Note that, even in the homoskedastic case and with the above correction, the estimator $e_i^2/(1 - h_i)$ of the variance σ_i^2 is unbiased but not consistent. This is because only a single observation (the ith) has information about the value of σ_i^2, so that by increasing the sample size we gain no additional information on σ_i^2. However, we will now show that the estimator (5.25) of the covariance matrix (5.24) of b is consistent, provided that

$$E[\varepsilon_i x_i] = E[(y_i - x_i'\beta)x_i] = 0.$$

That is, the orthogonality conditions should be satisfied. This is also required for the consistency of the OLS estimator b. To prove that (5.25) is a consistent estimator of the covariance matrix (5.24), we use the results in Section 4.4.3 (p. 258) on GMM estimators. Note that the GMM estimator for the above moment conditions is equal to the OLS estimator b (see Section 4.4.2 (p. 252)). The above moment conditions can be formulated as $E[g_i] = 0$ with $g_i = (y_i - x_i'\beta)x_i$. According to the results in (4.67) and (4.68), a consistent estimator of the covariance matrix of the GMM estimator is given by

$$\widehat{\text{var}}(b) = (H'J^{-1}H)^{-1},$$

where $J = \sum_{i=1}^{n} g_i g_i'$ and $H = \sum_{i=1}^{n} \partial g_i/\partial\beta'$ and with J and H evaluated at b. This means that $J = \sum e_i^2 x_i x_i'$ and $H = -\sum x_i x_i' = -X'X$. This shows that (5.25) is the *GMM estimator* of the covariance matrix, which is consistent (see Section 4.4.3).

Example 5.12: **Bank Wages; Interest and Bond Rates (continued)**

As an illustration we consider the two examples of Section 5.4.1, the first on wages (see Example 5.10) and the second on interest rates (see Example 5.11). Exhibit 5.18 shows the results of least squares with conventional OLS formulas for the standard errors (in Panels 1 and 3) and with White heteroskedasticity consistent standard errors (in Panels 2 and 4). For most coefficients, these two standard errors are quite close to each other. Note, however, that for

Panel 1: Dependent Variable: LOGSALARY
Dependent Variable: LOGSALARY
Method: Least Squares
Sample: 1 474
Included observations: 474

Variable	Coefficient	Std. Error	t-Statistic	Prob.
C	9.574694	0.054218	176.5965	0.0000
EDUC	0.044192	0.004285	10.31317	0.0000
GENDER	0.178340	0.020962	8.507685	0.0000
MINORITY	−0.074858	0.022459	−3.333133	0.0009
DUMJCAT2	0.170360	0.043494	3.916891	0.0001
DUMJCAT3	0.539075	0.030213	17.84248	0.0000
R-squared	0.760775			

Panel 2: Dependent Variable: LOGSALARY
Method: Least Squares
Sample: 1 474
Included observations: 474
White Heteroskedasticity-Consistent Standard Errors & Covariance

Variable	Coefficient	Std. Error	t-Statistic	Prob.
C	9.574694	0.054477	175.7556	0.0000
EDUC	0.044192	0.004425	9.987918	0.0000
GENDER	0.178340	0.019985	8.923848	0.0000
MINORITY	−0.074858	0.020699	−3.616538	0.0003
DUMJCAT2	0.170360	0.033025	5.158477	0.0000
DUMJCAT3	0.539075	0.035887	15.02147	0.0000
R-squared	0.760775			

Panel 3: Dependent Variable: DAAA
Method: Least Squares
Sample: 1950:01 1999:12
Included observations: 600

Variable	Coefficient	Std. Error	t-Statistic	Prob.
C	0.006393	0.006982	0.915697	0.3602
DUS3MT	0.274585	0.014641	18.75442	0.0000
R-squared	0.370346			

Panel 4: Dependent Variable: DAAA
Method: Least Squares
Sample: 1950:01 1999:12
Included observations: 600
White Heteroskedasticity-Consistent Standard Errors & Covariance

Variable	Coefficient	Std. Error	t-Statistic	Prob.
C	0.006393	0.006992	0.914321	0.3609
DUS3MT	0.274585	0.022874	12.00409	0.0000
R-squared	0.370346			

Exhibit 5.18 Bank Wages; Interest and Bond Rates (Example 5.12)

Regressions for wage data (Panels 1 and 2) and for AAA bond rate data (Panels 3 and 4), with conventional standard errors (Panels 1 and 3) and with White standard errors (Panels 2 and 4).

the interest rate data the (consistent) White standard error of the slope coefficient is 0.023, whereas according to the conventional OLS formula this standard error is computed as 0.015.

☞ Exercises: S: 5.20a.

5.4.3 **Weighted least squares**

Models for the variance

The use of OLS with White standard errors has the advantage that no model for the variances is needed. However, OLS is no longer efficient, and more efficient estimators can be obtained if one has reliable information on the variances σ_i^2. If the model explaining the heteroskedasticity is sufficiently accurate, then this will increase the efficiency of the estimators. Stated in general terms, a model for heteroskedasticity is of the form

$$\sigma_i^2 = h(z_i'\gamma), \tag{5.26}$$

where h is a known function, $z = (1, z_2, \cdots, z_p)'$ is a vector consisting of p observed variables that influence the variances, and γ is a vector of p unknown parameters. Two specifications that are often applied are the model with *additive heteroskedasticity* where $h(z'\gamma) = z'\gamma$ and the model with *multiplicative heteroskedasticity* where $h(z'\gamma) = e^{z'\gamma}$. The last model has the advantage that it always gives positive variances, whereas in the additive model we have to impose restrictions on the parameters γ.

Weighted least squares

A particularly simple model is obtained if the variance depends only on a single variable v so that

$$\sigma_i^2 = \sigma^2 v_i,$$

where $v_i > 0$ is known and where σ^2 is an unknown scalar parameter. An example is the regression model for bond rates in Example 5.11, where we proposed the model $\sigma_i^2 = \sigma^2 x_i^2$. In such cases we can transform the model

$$y_i = x_i'\beta + \varepsilon_i, \quad E[\varepsilon_i^2] = \sigma^2 v_i, \quad i = 1, \cdots, n,$$

by dividing the ith equation by $\sqrt{v_i}$. Let $y_i^* = y_i/\sqrt{v_i}$, $x_i^* = \frac{1}{\sqrt{v_i}}x_i$ and $\varepsilon_i^* = \varepsilon_i/\sqrt{v_i}$, then we obtain the *transformed model*

$$y_i^* = x_i^{*'}\beta + \varepsilon_i^*, \quad E[\varepsilon_i^{*2}] = \sigma^2, \quad i = 1, \cdots, n.$$

As the numbers v_i are known, we can calculate the transformed data y_i^* and x_i^*. Further, if the original model satisfies Assumptions 1, 2, and 4–6, then the same holds true for the transformed model. The transformed model has also homoskedastic error terms and hence it satisfies Assumptions 1–6. Therefore, the best linear (in y_i^*) unbiased estimator of β is obtained by applying least squares in the transformed model. To derive an explicit formula for this estimator, let X_* be the $n \times k$ matrix with rows $x_i^{*'}$ and let y_* be the $n \times 1$ vector with elements y_i^*. Then the estimator is given by

$$\begin{aligned} b_* = (X_*'X_*)^{-1}X_*'y_* &= \left(\sum_{i=1}^n x_i^* x_i^{*'}\right)^{-1} \sum_{i=1}^n x_i^* y_i^* \\ &= \left(\sum_{i=1}^n \frac{1}{v_i} x_i x_i'\right)^{-1} \left(\sum_{i=1}^n \frac{1}{v_i} x_i y_i\right). \end{aligned} \tag{5.27}$$

This estimator is obtained by minimizing the criterion

$$S(\beta) = \sum_{i=1}^n \left(y_i^* - x_i^{*'}\beta\right)^2 = \sum_{i=1}^n \frac{(y_i - x_i'\beta)^2}{v_i}. \tag{5.28}$$

As observations with smaller variance have a relatively larger weight in determining the estimate b_*, this is called *weighted least squares* (WLS). The intuition is that there is less uncertainty around observations with smaller variances, so that these observations are more important for estimation. We recall that in Section 5.2.3 we applied weighted least squares in local regression, where the observations get larger weight the nearer they are to a given reference value.

Illustration: Heteroskedasticity for grouped data

In research in business and economics, the original data of individual agents or individual firms are often averaged over groups for privacy reasons. The groups should be chosen so that the individuals within a group are more or less homogeneous with respect to the variables in the model. Let the individual data satisfy the model $y = X\beta + \varepsilon$ with $E[\varepsilon] = 0$ and $E[\varepsilon\varepsilon'] = \sigma^2 I$ (that is, with homoskedastic error terms). Let n_j be the number of individuals in group j, then, in terms of the reported group means, the model becomes

$$\overline{y}_j = \overline{x}_j'\beta + \overline{\varepsilon}_j,$$

where $\overline{y}_j$ and $\overline{\varepsilon}_j$ are the means of y_j and ε_j and $\overline{x}_j'$ is the row vector of the means of the explanatory variables in group j. The error terms satisfy

$E[\bar{\varepsilon}_j] = 0$, $E[\bar{\varepsilon}_j^2] = \sigma^2/n_j$ and $E[\bar{\varepsilon}_j\bar{\varepsilon}_h] = 0$ for $j \neq h$, so that grouping leads to heteroskedastic disturbances with covariance matrix

$$\Omega = \sigma^2 \begin{pmatrix} n_1^{-1} & 0 & \cdots & 0 \\ 0 & n_2^{-1} & \cdots & 0 \\ \vdots & \vdots & \ddots & \vdots \\ 0 & 0 & \cdots & n_G^{-1} \end{pmatrix},$$

where G denotes the number of groups. The WLS estimator is given by (5.27) with $v_j = 1/n_j$, so that

$$b_{WLS} = \left(\sum_{j=1}^{G} n_j \bar{x}_j \bar{x}_j' \right)^{-1} \left(\sum_{j=1}^{G} n_j \bar{x}_j \bar{y}_j \right).$$

The weighting factors show that larger groups get larger weights.

Statistical properties of the WLS estimator

The properties of the weighted least squares estimator are easily obtained from the transformed model. The covariance matrix of b_* is given by

$$\text{var}(b_*) = \sigma^2 (X_*' X_*)^{-1} = \sigma^2 \left(\sum_{i=1}^{n} \frac{1}{v_i} x_i x_i' \right)^{-1}. \tag{5.29}$$

The weighted least squares estimator is efficient, and hence its covariance matrix is smaller than that of the OLS estimator in (5.24) (see also Exercise 5.5). In terms of the residuals of the transformed model

$$e_* = y_* - X_* b_*,$$

an unbiased estimator of the variance σ^2 is given by

$$s_*^2 = \frac{1}{n-k} \sum_{i=1}^{n} \left(y_i^* - x_i^{*\prime} b_* \right)^2 = \frac{1}{n-k} \sum_{i=1}^{n} \frac{1}{v_i} (y_i - x_i b_*)^2.$$

If we add Assumption 7 that the disturbance terms are normally distributed, then the results of Chapter 3 on testing linear hypotheses can be applied directly to the transformed model. For instance, the F-test of Chapter 3 now becomes

$$F = \frac{\left(\sum e_{*Ri}^2 - \sum e_{*i}^2 \right)/g}{\sum e_{*i}^2/(n-k)} = \frac{\left(\sum \frac{e_{Ri}^2}{v_i} - \sum \frac{e_i^2}{v_i} \right)/g}{\sum \frac{e_i^2}{v_i}/(n-k)}, \tag{5.30}$$

where $e = y - Xb_*$, $e_{*R} = y_* - X_* b_{*R}$, and $e_R = y - Xb_{*R}$ with b_{*R} the restricted ordinary least squares estimator in the transformed model.

Asymptotic properties of WLS

The asymptotic results in Chapter 4 can be applied directly to the transformed model. For instance, if we drop Assumption 1 of fixed regressors and Assumption 7 of normally distributed error terms, then

$$\sqrt{n}(b_* - \beta) \xrightarrow{d} \mathrm{N}(0, \sigma^2 Q_*^{-1}), \tag{5.31}$$

that is, WLS is consistent and has an asymptotic normal distribution, under the conditions that

$$\mathrm{plim}\left(\frac{1}{n}X_*'X_*\right) = \mathrm{plim}\left(\frac{1}{n}\sum_{i=1}^{n}\frac{1}{v_i}x_i x_i'\right) = Q_* \tag{5.32}$$

$$\mathrm{plim}\left(\frac{1}{n}X_*'\varepsilon_*\right) = \mathrm{plim}\left(\frac{1}{n}\sum_{i=1}^{n}\frac{1}{v_i}x_i\varepsilon_i\right) = 0. \tag{5.33}$$

Under these assumptions, expressions like (5.29) and (5.30) remain valid asymptotically.

Summary of estimation by WLS

Estimation by weighted least squares can be performed by means of the following steps.

Weighted least squares

- *Step 1: Formulate the model.* Formulate the model regression model $y_i = x_i'\beta + \varepsilon_i$ and the model for the variances $E[\varepsilon_i^2] = \sigma^2 v_i$, where (y_i, x_i) are observed and v_i are known, $i = 1, \cdots, n$, and where β and σ^2 are unknown fixed parameters.
- *Step 2: Transform the data.* Transform the observed data y_i and x_i by dividing by $\sqrt{v_i}$, to get $y_i^* = \frac{1}{\sqrt{v_i}}y_i$ and $x_i^* = \frac{1}{\sqrt{v_i}}x_i$.
- *Step 3: Estimate and test with transformed data.* Apply the standard procedures for estimation and testing of Chapters 3 and 4 on the transformed data y_*, X_*.
- *Step 4: Transform results to original data.* The results can be rewritten in terms of the original data by substituting $y_i = \sqrt{v_i}y_i^*$ and $x_i = \sqrt{v_i}x_i^*$.

We illustrate this with two examples.

E

COMPANION WEB SITE

XM513BWA

Example 5.13: **Bank Wages (continued)**

In this example we continue our previous analysis of the bank wage data. We consider the possible heteroskedasticity that results by grouping the data. We will discuss (i) the grouped data, and (ii) the results of OLS and WLS for the grouped data.

(i) Grouped bank wage data

Suppose that for privacy reasons the individual bank wage data are grouped according to the variables gender, minority, job category, and four education groups (10 years or less, between 11 and 13 years, between 14 and 16 years, and 17 years or more). In principle this gives $2 \times 2 \times 3 \times 4 = 48$ groups. However, twenty-two combinations do not occur in the sample, so that $G = 26$ groups remain. Exhibit 5.19 shows a histogram of the resulting group sizes. Some groups consist of a single individual, and the largest group contains 101 individuals. It is intuitively clear that the averaged data in this large group should be given more weight than the data in the small groups.

(ii) Results of OLS and WLS for grouped data

Exhibit 5.20 shows the result of applying OLS to the grouped data, both with OLS standard errors (in Panel 1) and with White standard errors (in Panel 2), and efficient WLS estimates are reported in Panel 3. The WLS estimates are clearly different from the OLS estimates and the standard errors of WLS are considerably smaller than those of OLS. For WLS, the R^2 and the standard error of regression are reported both for weighted data (based on the residuals $e_* = y_* - X_* b_*$ of step 3 of WLS) and for unweighted data (based on the residuals $e = y - Xb_*$ of step 4 of WLS).

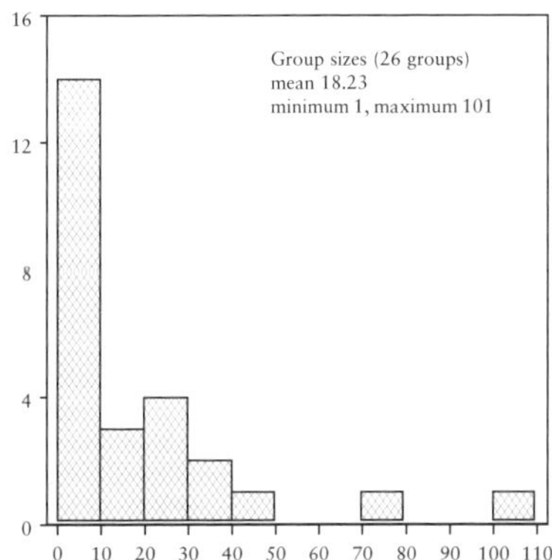

Exhibit 5.19 Bank Wages (Example 5.13)

Grouped data of 474 employees, with groups defined by gender, minority, job category, and four education groups. The histogram shows the sizes of the resulting twenty-two groups of employees (the group size is measured on the horizontal axis, and the vertical axis measures the frequency of occurrence of the group sizes in the indicated intervals on the horizontal axis).

Panel 1: Dependent Variable: MEANLOGSAL				
Method: Least Squares				
Sample(adjusted): 1 26				
Included observations: 26 after adjusting endpoints				
Variable	Coefficient	Std. Error	t-Statistic	Prob.
C	9.673440	0.141875	68.18272	0.0000
MEANEDUC	0.033592	0.010022	3.351783	0.0032
GENDER	0.249522	0.074784	3.336567	0.0033
MINORITY	−0.024444	0.062942	−0.388348	0.7019
DUMJCAT2	0.019526	0.090982	0.214610	0.8322
DUMJCAT3	0.675614	0.084661	7.980253	0.0000
R-squared	0.886690	S.E. of regression		0.157479

Panel 2: Dependent Variable: MEANLOGSAL				
Method: Least Squares				
Sample(adjusted): 1 26				
Included observations: 26 after adjusting endpoints				
White Heteroskedasticity-Consistent Standard Errors & Covariance				
Variable	Coefficient	Std. Error	t-Statistic	Prob.
C	9.673440	0.125541	77.05376	0.0000
MEANEDUC	0.033592	0.009617	3.492757	0.0023
GENDER	0.249522	0.053352	4.676939	0.0001
MINORITY	−0.024444	0.060389	−0.404766	0.6899
DUMJCAT2	0.019526	0.102341	0.190792	0.8506
DUMJCAT3	0.675614	0.104891	6.441090	0.0000
R-squared	0.886690	S.E. of regression		0.157479

Panel 3: Dependent Variable: MEANLOGSAL				
Method: Least Squares				
Sample(adjusted): 1 26				
Included observations: 26 after adjusting endpoints				
Weighting series: sq.root group size ($v_i = 1/n_i$ with n_i the group size)				
Variable	Coefficient	Std. Error	t-Statistic	Prob.
C	9.586344	0.077396	123.8604	0.0000
MEANEDUC	0.043238	0.006123	7.061221	0.0000
GENDER	0.179823	0.029525	6.090510	0.0000
MINORITY	−0.074960	0.031581	−2.373596	0.0277
DUMJCAT2	0.166985	0.061281	2.724918	0.0130
DUMJCAT3	0.542568	0.042672	12.71483	0.0000
Weighted Statistics				
R-squared	0.999903	S.E. of regression		0.077288
Unweighted Statistics				
R-squared	0.834443	S.E. of regression		0.190354

Exhibit 5.20 Bank Wages (Example 5.13)

Regressions for grouped wage data, OLS (Panel 1), OLS with White standard errors (Panel 2), and WLS with group seizes as weights (Panel 3). In Panel 3, the weighted statistics refer to the transformed data (with weighted observations) and the unweighted statistics refer to the observed (unweighted) data.

E

COMPANION WEB SITE

XM511IBR

Example 5.14: **Interest and Bond Rates (continued)**

We continue our analysis of the interest and bond rate data introduced in Example 5.11 in Section 5.4.1. We will discuss (i) the application of weighted least squares in this model, (ii) the outcomes of OLS and WLS, and (iii) comments on the outcomes.

(i) Application of weighted least squares

In Example 5.11 in Section 5.4.1 we considered the regression model $y_i = \alpha + \beta x_i + \varepsilon_i$ for the relation between changes in the AAA bond rate y_i

(*a*)

Panel 1: Dependent Variable: DAAA Method: Least Squares Sample: 1950:01 1999:12 Included observations: 600				
Variable	Coefficient	Std. Error	t-Statistic	Prob.
C	0.006393	0.006982	0.915697	0.3602
DUS3MT	0.274585	0.014641	18.75442	0.0000
R-squared	0.370346	S.E. of regression		0.171002

(*b*)

Panel 2: Dependent Variable: DAAA Method: Least Squares Sample: 1950:01 1999:12 Included observations: 583 Excluded observations: 17 Weighting series: 1/DUS3MT ($v_i = (\text{DUS3MT}_i)^2$)				
Variable	Coefficient	Std. Error	t-Statistic	Prob.
C	−0.002380	0.005143	−0.462794	0.6437
DUS3MT	0.262260	0.144280	1.817717	0.0696
Weighted Statistics				
R-squared	0.000369	S.E. of regression		7.381207
Unweighted Statistics				
R-squared	0.370293	S.E. of regression		0.172944

(*c*)

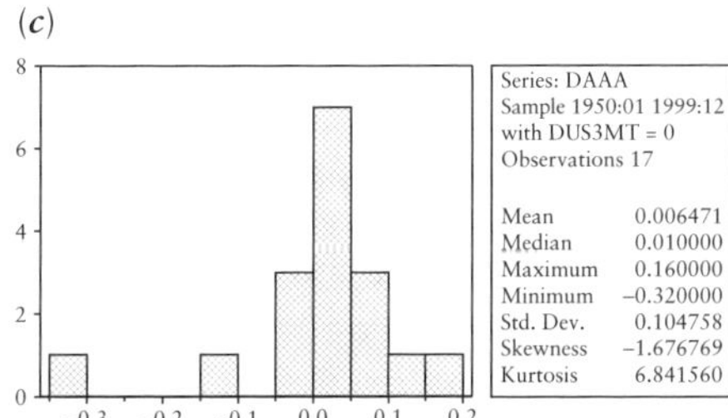

Exhibit 5.21 **Interest and Bond Rates (Example 5.14)**

Regressions for AAA bond rate data, OLS (Panel 1) and WLS (with variances proportional to the square of DUS3MT, Panel 2). (*c*) shows the histogram of the values of DAAA in the seventeen months where DUS3MT = 0 (these observations are excluded in WLS in Panel 2).

and the three-month Treasury Bill rate x_i. The plots in Exhibit 5.17 suggest $E[\varepsilon_i^2] = \sigma^2 x_i^2$ as a possible model for the variances. The WLS estimator (5.27) is obtained by ordinary least squares in the transformed model

$$\frac{y_i}{x_i} = \alpha \cdot \frac{1}{x_i} + \beta + \varepsilon_i^*,$$

where the error terms $\varepsilon_i^* = \varepsilon_i / x_i$ are homoskedastic with $E[\varepsilon_i^{*2}] = \sigma^2$.

(ii) Outcomes of OLS and WLS

Exhibit 5.21 shows the results of OLS in the original model (in Panel 1) and of WLS (in Panel 2). Note that, according to the WLS outcomes and at the 5 per cent significance level, the Treasury Bill rate changes (x_i) provide no significant explanation of AAA rate changes (y_i).

(iii) Comments on the outcomes

Panel 2 of Exhibit 5.21 indicates that, for WLS, 17 of the $n = 600$ observations are dropped. This is because in these months $x_i = 0$. This indicates a shortcoming of the model for the variance, as for $x_i = 0$ the model postulates that $\text{var}(y_i) = E[\varepsilon_i^2] = \sigma^2 x_i^2 = 0$. In reality this variance is non-zero, as the AAA rate does not always remain fixed in months where the Treasury Bill rate remains unchanged (see the histogram in Exhibit 5.21 (*c*)). In the next section we will consider alternative, less restrictive models for the variance of the disturbances (see Example 5.16).

☞ Exercises: T: 5.5; S: 5.20**b–e**; E: 5.33**c**, **e**.

5.4.4 Estimation by maximum likelihood and feasible WLS

Maximum likelihood in models with heteroskedasticity

The application of WLS requires that the variances of the disturbances are known up to a scale factor—that is, $\sigma_i^2 = \sigma^2 v_i$ with σ^2 an unknown scalar parameter and with v_i known for all $i = 1, \cdots, n$. If we are not able to specify such a type of model, then we can use the more general model (5.26) with variances $\sigma_i^2 = h(z_i'\gamma)$, where γ contains p unknown parameters. Under Assumptions 1, 2, and 4–7, the log-likelihood (in terms of the $(k + p)$ unknown parameters β and γ) is given by

$$l(\beta, \gamma) = -\frac{n}{2}\log(2\pi) - \frac{1}{2}\sum_{i=1}^{n} \log\left(h(z_i'\gamma)\right) - \frac{1}{2}\sum_{i=1}^{n} \frac{(y_i - x_i'\beta)^2}{h(z_i'\gamma)}. \qquad (5.34)$$

The ML estimators of β and γ are obtained by maximizing $l(\beta, \gamma)$, and these estimators have the usual optimal asymptotic properties. For given values of γ, the optimal values of β are obtained by WLS, replacing v_i in (5.27) by $h(z_i'\gamma)$, so that

$$b_{WLS}(\gamma) = \left(\sum_{i=1}^{n} \frac{1}{\sigma_i^2} x_i x_i'\right)^{-1} \left(\sum_{i=1}^{n} \frac{1}{\sigma_i^2} x_i y_i\right), \quad \sigma_i^2 = h(z_i'\gamma). \tag{5.35}$$

This estimator is not 'feasible'—that is, it cannot be computed because γ is unknown. However, we can substitute this formula for b_{WLS} in (5.34) to obtain the concentrated log-likelihood as a function of γ alone. Then γ can be estimated by maximizing this concentrated log-likelihood and the corresponding estimate of β follows from (5.35).

Feasible weighted least squares

An alternative and computationally simpler estimation method is to use a two-step approach. In the first step the variance parameters γ are estimated, and in the second step the regression parameters β are estimated, using the estimated variances of the first step. This method is called *(two-step) feasible weighted least squares* (FWLS).

Two-step feasible weighted least squares

- *Step 1: Estimate the variance parameters.* Determine an estimate c of the variance parameters γ in the model $\text{var}(\varepsilon_i) = h(z_i'\gamma)$ and define the estimated variances by $s_i^2 = h(z_i'c)$.
- *Step 2: Apply WLS with the estimated variances.* Compute the feasible weighted least squares estimates

$$b_{FWLS} = \left(\sum_i \frac{1}{s_i^2} x_i x_i'\right)^{-1} \left(\sum_i \frac{1}{s_i^2} x_i y_i\right). \tag{5.36}$$

Derivation of statistical properties of FWLS

T

The properties of the estimator b_{FWLS} depend on those of the used estimator c of γ in step 1. To investigate the consistency and the asymptotic distribution of b_{FWLS}, we write Ω_γ for the $n \times n$ diagonal matrix with elements $\sigma_i^2 = h(z_i'\gamma)$ and Ω_c for the $n \times n$ diagonal matrix with elements $s_i^2 = h(z_i'c)$. Writing the model $y_i = x_i'\beta + \varepsilon_i$ in matrix form $y = X\beta + \varepsilon$, we get

$$\begin{aligned} b_{FWLS} - b_{WLS}(\gamma) &= (X'\Omega_c^{-1}X)^{-1}X'\Omega_c^{-1}y - (X'\Omega_\gamma^{-1}X)^{-1}X'\Omega_\gamma^{-1}y \\ &= (X'\Omega_c^{-1}X)^{-1}X'\Omega_c^{-1}\varepsilon - (X'\Omega_\gamma^{-1}X)^{-1}X'\Omega_\gamma^{-1}\varepsilon. \end{aligned}$$

Therefore, b_{FWLS} has the same asymptotic distribution (5.31) as b_{WLS} (and hence it is consistent and asymptotically efficient) provided that

$$\text{plim}\left(\frac{1}{n}X'\left(\Omega_c^{-1} - \Omega_\gamma^{-1}\right)X\right) = \text{plim}\left(\frac{1}{n}\sum_{i=1}^{n}\left(\frac{1}{s_i^2} - \frac{1}{\sigma_i^2}\right)x_i x_i'\right) = 0, \qquad (5.37)$$

$$\text{plim}\left(\frac{1}{\sqrt{n}}X'\left(\Omega_c^{-1} - \Omega_\gamma^{-1}\right)\varepsilon\right) = \text{plim}\left(\frac{1}{\sqrt{n}}\sum_{i=1}^{n}\left(\frac{1}{s_i^2} - \frac{1}{\sigma_i^2}\right)x_i \varepsilon_i\right) = 0. \qquad (5.38)$$

Under some regularity conditions on the regressors x_i and the function h in (5.26), the above two conditions are satisfied if c is a consistent estimator of γ. If c is consistent, then the FWLS estimator has the same asymptotic covariance matrix as the WLS estimator. Under conditions (5.37), (5.38), and (5.32), (5.33), we can use the following result as an approximation in finite samples.

Approximate distribution of the FWLS estimator

Under the above conditions, in particular consistency of the estimator c of the variance parameters γ, there holds

$$b_{FWLS} \approx \text{N}(\beta, (X'\Omega_c^{-1}X)^{-1}).$$

Here c is the estimate of γ obtained in step 1 of FWLS, and Ω_c is the corresponding diagonal matrix with the estimated variances $s_i^2 = h(z_i'c)$ on the diagonal. So the covariance matrix of the FWLS estimator can be approximated by

$$\widehat{\text{var}}(b_{FWLS}) = (X'\Omega_c^{-1}X)^{-1} = \left(\sum_{i=1}^{n}\frac{1}{s_i^2}x_i x_i'\right)^{-1}.$$

If one wants to use WLS with chosen weighting factors s_i^2 but one is uncertain whether these weights correspond to the actual variances, then the above formula for the variance is in general no longer correct. In this case consistent estimates of the standard errors can be obtained by GMM. This corresponds to the White standard errors of OLS after the observations (y_i, x_i) have been transformed to (y_i^*, x_i^*), where $y_i^* = y_i/s_i$ and $x_i^* = \frac{1}{s_i}x_i$.

Two-step FWLS in the additive and multiplicative model

The foregoing shows that the two-step FWLS estimator is asymptotically equally efficient as WLS, provided that the estimator c in step 1 is a consistent estimator of γ. We consider this for the additive and the multiplicative model for heteroskedasticity. In both cases, first OLS is applied in the model $y = X\beta + \varepsilon$ with residuals e. If b is consistent, the squared residuals e_i^2 are asymptotically unbiased estimates of σ_i^2. Then γ is estimated by replacing σ_i^2 by e_i^2 and by running the regression

$$e_i^2 = z_i'\gamma + \eta_i$$

in the additive model, and in the multiplicative model

$$\log(e_i^2) = z_i'\gamma + \eta_i.$$

The error terms are given by $\eta_i = e_i^2 - \sigma_i^2$ in the additive model and by $\eta_i = \log(e_i^2/\sigma_i^2)$ in the multiplicative model. It is left as an exercise (see Exercise 5.6) to show that the above regression for the additive model gives a consistent estimate of γ, but that in the multiplicative model a correction factor is needed. In the latter model the coefficients γ_j of the variables z_j are consistently estimated for $j = 2, \ldots, p$, but the coefficient γ_1 of the constant term $z_1 = 1$ should be estimated as $\hat{\gamma}_1 + a$, where $\hat{\gamma}_1$ is the OLS estimate of γ_1 and $a = -E[\log(\chi^2(1))] \approx 1.27$.

Iterated FWLS

Instead of the above *two-step* FWLS method, we can also apply *iterated* FWLS. In this case the FWLS estimate of β in step 2 is used to construct the corresponding series of residuals, which are used again in step 1 to determine new estimates of the heteroskedasticity parameters γ. The newly estimated variances are then used in step 2 to compute the corresponding new FWLS estimates of β. This is iterated until the parameter estimates converge. These iterations can improve the efficiency of the FGLS estimator in finite samples.

Example 5.15: **Bank Wages (continued)**

We consider the bank wage data again and will discuss (i) a multiplicative model for heteroskedasticity, (ii) the two-step FWLS estimates of this model, and (iii) the ML estimates.

(i) A multiplicative model for heteroskedasticity

In Example 5.10 we considered the regression model

$$y_i = \beta_1 + \beta_2 x_i + \beta_3 D_{gi} + \beta_4 D_{mi} + \beta_5 D_{2i} + \beta_6 D_{3i} + \varepsilon_i.$$

We concluded that the unexplained variation ε_i in the (logarithmic) salaries may differ among the three job categories (see Exhibit 5.16). Suppose that the disturbance terms ε_i in the above regression model have variances σ_1^2, σ_2^2, or σ_3^2 according to whether the ith employee has a job in category 1, 2, or 3 respectively. Let the parameters be transformed by $\gamma_1 = \log(\sigma_1^2)$,

$\gamma_2 = \log(\sigma_2^2/\sigma_1^2)$, and $\gamma_3 = \log(\sigma_3^2/\sigma_1^2)$; then we can formulate the following multiplicative model for

$$\sigma_i^2 = E[\varepsilon_i^2] = e^{\gamma_1 + \gamma_2 D_{2i} + \gamma_3 D_{3i}}.$$

(ii) Two-step FWLS estimates

To apply (two-step) FWLS, the parameters of this model for the variances are estimated in Panels 1 and 2 of Exhibit 5.22. In Panel 2 the explained variable

Panel 1: Dependent Variable: LOGSALARY
Method: Least Squares
Sample: 1 474
Included observations: 474

Variable	Coefficient	Std. Error	t-Statistic	Prob.
C	9.574694	0.054218	176.5965	0.0000
EDUC	0.044192	0.004285	10.31317	0.0000
GENDER	0.178340	0.020962	8.507685	0.0000
MINORITY	−0.074858	0.022459	−3.333133	0.0009
DUMJCAT2	0.170360	0.043494	3.916891	0.0001
DUMJCAT3	0.539075	0.030213	17.84248	0.0000
R-squared	0.760775			

Panel 2: Dependent Variable: LOG(RESOLS^2)
Method: Least Squares
Sample: 1 474
Included observations: 474

Variable	Coefficient	Std. Error	t-Statistic	Prob.
C	−4.733237	0.123460	−38.33819	0.0000
DUMJCAT2	−0.289197	0.469221	−0.616335	0.5380
DUMJCAT3	0.460492	0.284800	1.616892	0.1066
R-squared	0.006882			

Panel 3: Dependent Variable: LOGSALARY
Method: Least Squares
Sample: 1 474
Included observations: 474
Weighting series: 1/STDEV ($v_i = (STDEV_i)^2$ obtained from Panel 2)

Variable	Coefficient	Std. Error	t-Statistic	Prob.
C	9.595652	0.052207	183.8011	0.0000
EDUC	0.042617	0.004128	10.32413	0.0000
GENDER	0.178389	0.020391	8.748212	0.0000
MINORITY	−0.077864	0.021358	−3.645626	0.0003
DUMJCAT2	0.166836	0.037321	4.470278	0.0000
DUMJCAT3	0.545375	0.032659	16.69933	0.0000
Weighted Statistics				
R-squared	0.936467			
Unweighted Statistics				
R-squared	0.760688			

Exhibit 5.22 Bank Wages (Example 5.15)

OLS for wage data (Panel 1), step 1 of FWLS (Panel 2, auxiliary regression of OLS residuals for estimation of the variance parameters in the multiplicative model of heteroskedasticity), and step 2 of FWLS (Panel 3, WLS with estimated variances obtained from Panel 2).

Panel 4: Dependent Variable: LOGSALARY				
Method: Maximum Likelihood (BHHH), multiplicative heteroskedasticity				
Sample: 1 474				
Included observations: 474				
Evaluation order: By observation				
Convergence achieved after 76 iterations				
Variable	Coefficient	Std. Error	z-Statistic	Prob.
Constant	9.629294	0.053441	180.1839	0.0000
EDUC	0.039782	0.004162	9.559227	0.0000
GENDER	0.182140	0.021259	8.567533	0.0000
MINORITY	−0.072756	0.023355	−3.115197	0.0018
DUMJCAT2	0.155865	0.036379	4.284448	0.0000
DUMJCAT3	0.557101	0.034005	16.38289	0.0000
Variance Equation				
Constant (γ_1)	−3.342117	0.065795	−50.79576	0.0000
DUMJCAT2 (γ_2)	−0.867102	0.259368	−3.343140	0.0008
DUMJCAT3 (γ_3)	0.452073	0.173538	2.605030	0.0092
Log likelihood	112.2237			

Exhibit 5.22 (*Contd.*)

ML estimates of model for wages with multiplicative model for heteroskedasticity (Panel 4, starting values at FWLS estimates).

is $\log(e_i^2)$, where e_i are the OLS residuals of the regression in Panel 1. With the correction factor for multiplicative models, the variances are estimated by $s_i^2 = e^{1.27+\hat{\gamma}_1+\hat{\gamma}_2 D_{2i}+\hat{\gamma}_3 D_{3i}}$—that is, $s_1^2 = e^{1.27+\hat{\gamma}_1}$, $s_2^2 = s_1^2 e^{\hat{\gamma}_2}$ and $s_3^2 = s_1^2 e^{\hat{\gamma}_3}$. The results in Panel 2 give the following estimates of the standard deviations per job category.

$$s_1 = \sqrt{e^{1.27-4.733}} = 0.177, \; s_2 = s_1\sqrt{e^{-0.289}} = 0.153,$$
$$s_3 = s_1\sqrt{e^{0.460}} = 0.223.$$

As expected, the standard deviation is smallest for custodial jobs and it is largest for management jobs. The corresponding (two-step) FWLS estimator in (5.36) is given in Panel 3 of Exhibit 5.22. The outcomes are quite close to those of OLS, so that the effect of heteroskedasticity is relatively small. Moreover, the estimates $\hat{\gamma}_2$ and $\hat{\gamma}_3$ are not significant, indicating that the homoskedasticity of the error terms need not be rejected.

(iii) ML estimates

Panel 4 of Exhibit 5.22 shows the results of ML. The ML estimates of the parameters of the regression equation are close to the (two-step) FWLS estimates. However, the ML estimates of the variance parameters γ_1, γ_2, and γ_3 are quite different from those obtained in the (two-step) FWLS method. In particular, the ML estimates of the parameters γ_2 and γ_3 differ significantly from zero. That is, the ML results indicate significant heteroskedasticity between the three job categories. As the ML estimates are efficient, this leads to sharper conclusions than FWLS (where the null hypothesis of homoskedasticity could not be rejected).

Example 5.16: **Interest and Bond Rates (continued)**

XM511IBR

We continue our analysis of the interest and bond rate data of Example 5.14. The model $E[\varepsilon_i^2] = \sigma^2 x_i^2$ that was analysed in that example did not turn out to be very realistic. We will discuss (i) two alternative models for the variance, (ii) two-step FWLS and ML estimates of both models, and (iii) our conclusion.

(i) Two alternative models for the variance

We consider again the relation between monthly changes in AAA bond rates (y_i) and monthly changes in Treasury Bill rates (x_i) given by

$$y_i = \alpha + \beta x_i + \varepsilon_i, \quad E[\varepsilon_i^2] = \sigma_i^2.$$

In Section 5.4.3 we considered WLS with the model $\sigma_i^2 = \sigma^2 x_i^2$ for the variances and we concluded that this model has its shortcomings. Exhibit 5.17 shows that the variance in the period 1950–74 is smaller than that in the period 1975–99. This can be modelled by

$$\sigma_i^2 = \gamma_1 + \gamma_2 D_i,$$

where D_i is a dummy variable with $D_i = 0$ in the months 50.01–74.12 and $D_i = 1$ in the months 75.01–99.12. In this model the variance is γ_1 until 1974 and it becomes $\gamma_1 + \gamma_2$ from 1975 onwards. However, as is clear from Exhibit 5.17 (*a*), the variance is also changing within these two subperiods. In general, large residuals tend to be followed by large residuals, and small residuals by small ones. A model for this kind of clustered variances is given by

$$\sigma_i^2 = \gamma_1 + \gamma_2 \varepsilon_{i-1}^2 = \gamma_1 + \gamma_2 (y_{i-1} - \alpha - \beta x_{i-1})^2.$$

(ii) Two-step FWLS and ML estimates

Exhibit 5.23 shows the results of two-step FWLS and ML estimates for both heteroskedasticity models. The two-step FWLS estimates are obtained as follows. In the first step, y_i is regressed on x_i with residuals $e_i = y_i - a - bx_i$ (see Panels 1 and 5). In the second step, for the dummy variable model we perform the regression (see Panel 2)

$$e_i^2 = \gamma_1 + \gamma_2 D_i + \eta_i,$$

and for the model with clustered variances we perform the regression (see Panel 6)

Panel 1: Dependent Variable: DAAA Method: Least Squares Sample: 1950:01 1999:12 Included observations: 600				
Variable	Coefficient	Std. Error	t-Statistic	Prob.
C	0.006393	0.006982	0.915697	0.3602
DUS3MT	0.274585	0.014641	18.75442	0.0000

Panel 2: Dependent Variable: RESOLS^2 Method: Least Squares Sample: 1950:01 1999:12 Included observations: 600				
Variable	Coefficient	Std. Error	t-Statistic	Prob.
C	0.009719	0.004374	2.222044	0.0267
DUM7599	0.038850	0.006186	6.280616	0.0000

Panel 3: Dependent Variable: DAAA Method: Least Squares Sample: 1950:01 1999:12 Included observations: 600 Weighting series: 1/STDEV ($v_i = (STDEV_i)^2 =$ fitted value of Panel 2)				
Variable	Coefficient	Std. Error	t-Statistic	Prob.
C	0.013384	0.005127	2.610380	0.0093
DUS3MT	0.214989	0.014079	15.27018	0.0000

Panel 4: Dependent Variable : DAAA Method: Maximum Likelihood (BHHH), dummy model heteroskedasticity Sample: 1950:01 1999:12 Included observations: 600 Convergence achieved after 18 iterations				
Variable	Coefficient	Std. Error	z-Statistic	Prob.
Constant	0.014083	0.005036	2.796224	0.0052
DUS3MT	0.205870	0.010699	19.24227	0.0000
Variance Equation				
Constant (γ_1)	0.008413	0.000393	21.38023	0.0000
DUM7599 (γ_2)	0.043714	0.002960	14.76792	0.0000

Exhibit 5.23 Interest and Bond Rates (Example 5.16)

OLS of AAA bond rate on Treasury Bill rate (Panel 1), step 1 of FWLS (Panel 2, auxiliary regression of squared residuals to estimate dummy model of heteroskedasticity), step 2 of FWLS (Panel 3, WLS with estimated variances obtained from Panel 2), and ML with dummy model for heteroskedasticity (Panel 4).

$$e_i^2 = \gamma_1 + \gamma_2 e_{i-1}^2 + \eta_i.$$

The estimated variances, $\hat{\sigma}_i^2 = \hat{\gamma}_1 + \hat{\gamma}_2 D_i$ in the first model and $\hat{\sigma}_i^2 = \hat{\gamma}_1 + \hat{\gamma}_2 e_{i-1}^2$ in the second model, are then used to compute the (two-step) FWLS estimates (5.36) of α and β (see Panels 3 and 7). The results in Panels 4 and 8 of Exhibit 5.23 show that the standard errors of the ML estimates are smaller than those of the FWLS estimates. For instance, the estimated slope parameter β in the dummy model for the variance has standard errors 0.0107 (ML, see Panel 4) and 0.0141 (FWLS, see Panel 3), and in the model with

Panel 5: Dependent Variable: DAAA Method: Least Squares Sample: 1950:01 1999:12 Included observations: 600				
Variable	Coefficient	Std. Error	t-Statistic	Prob.
C	0.006393	0.006982	0.915697	0.3602
DUS3MT	0.274585	0.014641	18.75442	0.0000

Panel 6: Dependent Variable: RESOLS^2 Method: Least Squares Sample(adjusted): 1950:02 1999:12 Included observations: 599 after adjusting endpoints				
Variable	Coefficient	Std. Error	t-Statistic	Prob.
C	0.023025	0.003336	6.901212	0.0000
RESOLS(− 1)^2	0.211512	0.039997	5.288181	0.0000

Panel 7: Dependent Variable: DAAA Method: Least Squares Sample(adjusted): 1950:02 1999:12 Included observations: 599 after adjusting endpoints Weighting series: 1/STDEV ($v_i = (STDEV_i)^2 =$ fitted value of Panel 6)				
Variable	Coefficient	Std. Error	t-Statistic	Prob.
C	0.008738	0.006354	1.375250	0.1696
DUS3MT	0.284731	0.015628	18.21882	0.0000

Panel 8: Dependent Variable: DAAA Method: Maximum Likelihood (BHHH), clustered variances Sample: 1950:01 1999:12 Included observations: 600 Convergence achieved after 14 iterations				
Variable	Coefficient	Std. Error	z-Statistic	Prob.
C	0.013154	0.003749	3.508211	0.0005
DUS3MT	0.246218	0.003566	69.04759	0.0000
Variance Equation				
Constant (γ_1)	0.010647	0.000647	16.45021	0.0000
ε_{i-1}^2 (γ_2)	1.023405	0.101769	10.05619	0.0000

Exhibit 5.23 (*Contd.*)

OLS of AAA bond rate on Treasury Bill rate (Panel 5), step 1 of FWLS (Panel 6, auxiliary regression of residuals to estimate model with clustered variances), step 2 of FWLS (Panel 7, WLS with estimated variances obtained from Panel 6), and ML for model with clustered variances (Panel 8).

clustered variances the standard errors are 0.0036 (ML, see Panel 8) and 0.0156 (FWLS, see Panel 7).

(iii) Conclusion

A natural question is which model for the variance should be preferred. To answer this question we should test the validity of the specified models for heteroskedasticity. This is further analysed in Example 5.18 at the end of the next section.

☞ **Exercises:** T: 5.6a, b; E: 5.25a, 5.28a–c.

5.4.5 Tests for homoskedasticity

Motivation of diagnostic tests for heteroskedasticity

When heteroskedasticity is present, ML and FWLS will in general offer a gain in efficiency as compared to OLS. But efficiency is lost if the disturbances are homoskedastic. In order to decide which estimation method to use, we first have to test for the presence of heteroskedasticity.

It is often helpful to make plots of the least squares residuals e_i and their squares e_i^2 as well as scatters of these variables against explanatory variables x_i or against the fitted values $\hat{y}_i = x_i'b$. This may provide a first indication of deviations from homoskedastic error terms. Diagnostic tests like the CUSUMSQ discussed in Section 5.3.3 are also helpful. Further, if the disturbances in the model $y_i = x_i'\beta + \varepsilon_i$ are heteroskedastic and a model $\sigma_i^2 = h(z_i'\gamma)$ has been postulated, then it is of interest to test whether this model for the variances is adequately specified. Let $\hat{\beta}$ be the (ML or FWLS) estimate of β with corresponding residuals $\hat{\varepsilon}_i = y_i - x_i'\hat{\beta}$ and let $\hat{\gamma}$ be the estimate of γ and $\hat{\sigma}_i^2 = h(z_i'\hat{\gamma})$. Then the standardized residuals $\hat{\varepsilon}_i/\hat{\sigma}_i$ should be (approximately) homoskedastic.

In this section we discuss some tests for homoskedasticity—that is, Goldfeld–Quandt, Likelihood Ratio, Breusch–Pagan, and White.

The Goldfeld–Quandt test

The *Goldfeld–Quandt test* requires that the data can be ordered with non-decreasing variance. The null hypothesis is that the variance is constant for all observations, and the alternative is that the variance increases. To test this hypothesis, the ordered data set is split in three groups. The first group consists of the first n_1 observations (with variance σ_1^2), the second group of the last n_2 observations (with variance σ_2^2), and the third group of the remaining $n_3 = n - n_1 - n_2$ observations in the middle. This last group is left out of the analysis, to obtain a sharper contrast between the variances in the first and second group. The null and alternative hypotheses are

$$H_0 : \sigma_1^2 = \sigma_2^2, \; H_1 : \sigma_2^2 > \sigma_1^2.$$

Now OLS is applied in groups 1 and 2 separately, with resulting sums of squared residuals SSR_1 and SSR_2 respectively and estimated variances $s_1^2 = SSR_1/(n_1 - k)$ and $s_2^2 = SSR_2/(n_2 - k)$. Under the standard Assumptions 1–7 (in particular, independently and normally distributed error terms), SSR_j/σ_j^2 follows the $\chi^2(n_j - k)$ distribution for $j = 1, 2$, and these two statistics are independent. Therefore

$$\frac{SSR_2/(n_2 - k)\sigma_2^2}{SSR_1/(n_1 - k)\sigma_1^2} = \frac{s_2^2/\sigma_2^2}{s_1^2/\sigma_1^2} \sim F(n_2 - k, n_1 - k).$$

So, under the null hypothesis of equal variances, the test statistic

$$F = s_2^2/s_1^2$$

follows the $F(n_2 - k, n_1 - k)$ distribution. The null hypothesis is rejected in favour of the alternative if F takes large values. There exists no generally accepted rule to choose the number n_3 of excluded middle observations. If the variance changes only at a single break-point, then it would be optimal to select the two groups accordingly and to take $n_3 = 0$. On the other hand, if nearly all variances are equal and only a few first observations have smaller variance and a few last ones have larger variance, then it would be best to take n_3 large. In practice one uses rules of thumb—for example, $n_3 = n/5$ if the sample size n is small and $n_3 = n/3$ if n is large.

Likelihood Ratio test

Sometimes the data can be split in several groups where the variance is assumed to be constant within groups and to vary between groups. If there are G groups and σ_j^2 denotes the variance in group j, then the null hypothesis of homoskedasticity is

$$H_0 : \sigma_1^2 = \sigma_2^2 = \cdots = \sigma_G^2,$$

and the alternative is that this restriction does not hold true. It is left as an exercise (see Exercise 5.6) to show that, under the standard Assumptions 1–7, the Likelihood Ratio test for the above hypothesis is given by

$$LR = n \log(s_{ML}^2) - \sum_{j=1}^{G} n_j \log\left(s_{j,\,ML}^2\right) \approx \chi^2(G-1). \qquad (5.39)$$

Here $s_{ML}^2 = e'e/n$ is the estimated variance over the full data set (that is, under the null hypothesis of homoskedasticity) and $s_{j,\,ML}^2 = e_j'e_j/n_j$ is the estimated variance in group j (obtained by a regression over the n_j observations in this group).

Breusch–Pagan *LM*-test

The Breusch–Pagan test is based on models of the type $\sigma_i^2 = h(z_i'\gamma)$ for the variances, with variables $z_i = (1, z_{2i}, \cdots, z_{pi})$ that explain the differences in the variances. The null hypothesis of constant variance corresponds to the $(p-1)$ parameter restrictions

$$\gamma_2 = \cdots = \gamma_p = 0.$$

The Breusch–Pagan test is equal to the LM-test

$$LM = \left(\frac{\partial l}{\partial \theta}\right)' \left(-E\left[\frac{\partial^2 l}{\partial \theta \partial \theta'}\right]\right)^{-1} \left(\frac{\partial l}{\partial \theta}\right).$$

To compute this test we should calculate the first and second order derivatives of the (unrestricted) log-likelihood (5.34) with respect to the parameters $\theta = (\beta, \gamma)$, which are then evaluated at the estimated parameter values under the null hypothesis. It is left as an exercise (see Exercise 5.7) to show that this leads to the following three-step procedure to compute the *Breusch–Pagan test* for heteroskedasticity.

Breusch–Pagan test for heteroskedasticity

- *Step 1: Apply OLS.* Apply OLS in the model $y = X\beta + \varepsilon$ and compute the residuals $e = y - Xb$.
- *Step 2: Perform auxiliary regression.* If the variances σ_i^2 are possibly affected by the $(p-1)$ variables $(z_{2i}, \cdots, z_{pi})$, then apply OLS in the auxiliary regression equation

$$e_i^2 = \gamma_1 + \gamma_2 z_{2i} + \cdots + \gamma_p z_{pi} + \eta_i. \tag{5.40}$$

- *Step 3: $LM = nR^2$ of the regression in step 2.* Then $LM = nR^2$ where R^2 is the coefficient of determination of the auxiliary regression in step 2. This is asymptotically distributed as $\chi^2(p-1)$ under the null hypothesis of homoskedasticity.

White test

An advantage of the Breusch–Pagan test is that the function h in the model (5.26) may be left unspecified. However, one should know the variables z_j $(j = 2, \cdots, p)$ that influence the variance. If these variables are unknown, then one can replace the variables z_j $(j = 2, \cdots, p)$ by functions of the explanatory variables x—for instance, $x_{2i}, \cdots, x_{ki}$ and $x_{2i}^2, \cdots, x_{ki}^2$, in which case $p - 1 = 2k - 2$. The above LM-test with this particular choice of the variables z is called the *White test* (without cross terms). An extension is the White test with cross terms, where all cross products $x_{ji}x_{hi}$ with $j \neq h$ are also included as z-variables.

Remarks on choice and interpretation of tests

If one can identify variables z_j for the model for the variances that are based on plausible economic assumptions, then the corresponding test of Breusch and Pagan is preferred. If homoskedasticity is rejected, then the variances can be modelled in terms of the variables z_j. After the model has been estimated by taking this type of heteroskedasticity into account, one can test whether the standardized residuals are homoskedastic. If not, one can try to find a better model for the variances.

Although the above tests are originally developed to test for heteroskedasticity, they can also be considered more generally as misspecification tests. For example, in the White test a significant correlation between the squared OLS residuals e_i^2 and the squares and cross products of explanatory variables may be caused by misspecification of the functional form. The hypothesis of homoskedastic error terms may also be rejected because of the presence of outliers. This is further discussed in Section 5.6.

XM501BWA
XM513BWA

Example 5.17: **Bank Wages (continued)**

We continue our analysis of the bank wage data (see Example 5.15). We will discuss (i) the Goldfeld–Quandt test, (ii) the Breusch–Pagan test, (iii) the Likelihood Ratio test, and (iv) tests for grouped data.

(i) **Goldfeld–Quandt test**

We apply tests on homoskedasticity for the Bank Wage data. Using the notation of Example 5.10, the model is given by

$$y_i = \beta_1 + \beta_2 x_i + \beta_3 D_{gi} + \beta_4 D_{mi} + \beta_5 D_{2i} + \beta_6 D_{3i} + \varepsilon_i.$$

For the Goldfeld–Quandt test we perform three regressions, one for each job category (see Panels 2–4 of Exhibit 5.24). The two job category dummies D_2 and D_3 should, of course, be dropped in these regressions. For the second job category the gender dummy D_g also has to be deleted from the model, as this subsample consists of males only. Because the results in job category 2 are not significant, possibly owing to the limited number of observations within this group, we will leave them out and test the null hypothesis that $\sigma_1^2 = \sigma_3^2$ against the alternative that $\sigma_3^2 > \sigma_1^2$. Using the results in Panels 2 and 4 of Exhibit 5.24, the corresponding test is computed as $F = (0.227/0.188)^2 = 1.46$, and this has the $F(n_2 - k, n_1 - k) = F(84 - 4, 363 - 4) = F(80, 359)$ distribution. The corresponding P-value is 0.011, which indicates that the variance in the third job category is larger than that in the first job category.

Panel 1: Dependent Variable: LOGSALARY				
Method: Least Squares; Sample: 1 474; Included observations: 474				
Variable	Coefficient	Std. Error	t-Statistic	Prob.
C	9.574694	0.054218	176.5965	0.0000
EDUC	0.044192	0.004285	10.31317	0.0000
GENDER	0.178340	0.020962	8.507685	0.0000
MINORITY	−0.074858	0.022459	−3.333133	0.0009
DUMJCAT2	0.170360	0.043494	3.916891	0.0001
DUMJCAT3	0.539075	0.030213	17.84248	0.0000
R-squared	0.760775	S.E. of regression		0.195374

Panel 2: Dependent Variable: LOGSALARY				
Method: Least Squares; Sample: JOBCAT=1; Included observations: 363				
Variable	Coefficient	Std. Error	t-Statistic	Prob.
C	9.556421	0.056544	169.0083	0.0000
EDUC	0.046360	0.004494	10.31572	0.0000
GENDER	0.169221	0.021275	7.954113	0.0000
MINORITY	−0.098557	0.023313	−4.227561	0.0000
R-squared	0.418977	S.E. of regression		0.188190

Panel 3: Dependent Variable: LOGSAL				
Method: Least Squares; Sample: JOBCAT=2; Included observations: 27				
Variable	Coefficient	Std. Error	t-Statistic	Prob.
C	10.39388	0.067739	153.4409	0.0000
EDUC	−0.004634	0.006319	−0.733397	0.4704
MINORITY	−0.019166	0.027543	−0.695845	0.4932
R-squared	0.039055	S.E. of regression		0.071427

Panel 4: Dependent Variable: LOGSAL				
Method: Least Squares; Sample: JOBCAT=3; Included observations: 84				
Variable	Coefficient	Std. Error	t-Statistic	Prob.
C	9.675982	0.274004	35.31327	0.0000
EDUC	0.066967	0.016525	4.052588	0.0001
GENDER	0.211185	0.080797	2.613780	0.0107
MINORITY	0.260611	0.119540	2.180112	0.0322
R-squared	0.308942	S.E. of regression		0.227476

Panel 5: Dependent Variable: RES^2				
Method: Least Squares; Sample: 1 474; Included observations: 474				
Variable	Coefficient	Std. Error	t-Statistic	Prob.
C	0.035166	0.003427	10.26280	0.0000
DUMJCAT2	−0.018265	0.013023	−1.402511	0.1614
DUMJCAT3	0.020103	0.007904	2.543209	0.0113
R-squared	0.019507			

Exhibit 5.24 Bank Wages (Example 5.17)

Regression for wage data of all employees (Panel 1) and for the three job categories separately (Panel 2 for category 1, Panel 3 for category 2, and Panel 4 for category 3), and Breusch–Pagan test (Panel 5, RES denotes the residuals of Panel 1).

(ii) Breusch–Pagan test

The Breusch-Pagan test for the multiplicative model $\sigma_i^2 = e^{\gamma_1+\gamma_2 D_{2i}+\gamma_3 D_{3i}}$ can be computed from the regression in Panel 5 of Exhibit 5.24. Note that in step 2 of the Breusch–Pagan test the dependent variable is e_i^2, not $\log(e_i^2)$. The explained variable in this regression consists of the squared OLS residuals of the above regression model for the wages. The test result for the hypothesis that $\gamma_2 = \gamma_3 = 0$ is $LM = nR^2 = 474(0.0195) = 9.24$. With the $\chi^2(2)$ distribution, the (asymptotic) P-value is 0.010. This again indicates that the hypothesis of homoskedastic error terms should be rejected.

(iii) Likelihood Ratio test

The Likelihood Ratio test (5.39) for equal variances in the three job categories can also be computed from the results in Exhibit 5.24. For each regression in the exhibit, the standard error of regression (s) is computed by least squares, and s_{ML}^2 can then be computed by $s_{ML}^2 = \frac{n-k}{n}s^2$. For the regression over the full sample with $n = 474$ in Panel 1, this gives $s = 0.195$ and $s_{ML}^2 = \frac{468}{474}s^2 = 0.0377$. In a similar way, using the results for the three job categories in Panels 2–4 of Exhibit 5.24, we obtain $s_{1,ML}^2 = 0.0350$, $s_{2,ML}^2 = 0.0045$, and $s_{3,ML}^2 = 0.0493$. With these values, the LR-test is computed as $LR = 474\log(0.0377) - 363\log(0.0350) - 27\log(0.0045) - 84\log(0.0493) = 61.2$. With the (asymptotic) $\chi^2(2)$ distribution the P-value is $P = 0.000$, so that homoskedasticity is again rejected.

(iv) Tests for grouped data

Next we consider the data obtained after grouping, as described in Example 5.13. The result of estimating the above regression model for the grouped data was given in Panel 1 of Exhibit 5.20, and is repeated in Panel 1 of Exhibit 5.25. Panel 2 of Exhibit 5.25 shows the corresponding White test for homoskedasticity. Note that the square of a dummy variable is equal to that dummy variable, so that the squares of dummies are not included as explanatory variables in the White test. This outcome does not lead to the rejection of homoskedasticity. However, if we use the model $\sigma_j^2 = \sigma^2/n_j$ then the Breusch–Pagan test in Panel 3 of Exhibit 5.25 gives a value of $LM = nR^2 = 26 \cdot 0.296 = 7.69$ with P-value 0.006. This leads to rejection of homoskedasticity. This test relates the variance directly to the inverse of the group size.

The foregoing results illustrate the importance of using all the available information on the variances of the disturbance terms. This also becomes evident in the scatter plot in Exhibit 5.25 (d), which relates the squared OLS residuals to the inverse of the group sizes $1/n_j$.

(*a*)

Panel 1: Dependent Variable: MEANLOGSAL				
Method: Least Squares				
Sample(adjusted): 1 26				
Included observations: 26				
Variable	Coefficient	Std. Error	t-Statistic	Prob.
C	9.673440	0.141875	68.18272	0.0000
MEANEDUC	0.033592	0.010022	3.351783	0.0032
GENDER	0.249522	0.074784	3.336567	0.0033
MINORITY	−0.024444	0.062942	−0.388348	0.7019
DUMJCAT2	0.019526	0.090982	0.214610	0.8322
DUMJCAT3	0.675614	0.084661	7.980253	0.0000

(*b*)

Panel 2: White Heteroskedasticity Test:				
F-statistic	0.839570	Probability		0.554832
Obs*R-squared	5.448711	Probability		0.487677
Test Equation:				
Dependent Variable: RES^2				
Method: Least Squares				
Sample: 1 26				
Included observations: 26				
Variable	Coefficient	Std. Error	t-Statistic	Prob.
C	−0.037059	0.112378	−0.329770	0.7452
MEANEDUC	0.002928	0.018407	0.159088	0.8753
MEANEDUC^2	−1.30E-05	0.000720	−0.018086	0.9858
GENDER	0.009429	0.018527	0.508896	0.6167
MINORITY	0.009845	0.015601	0.631018	0.5355
DUMJCAT2	0.019932	0.022435	0.888406	0.3854
DUMJCAT3	0.019311	0.020769	0.929819	0.3641
R-squared	0.209566			

(*c*)

Panel 3: Dependent Variable: RES^2				
Method: Least Squares				
Sample(adjusted): 1 26				
Included observations: 26 after adjusting endpoints				
Variable	Coefficient	Std. Error	t-Statistic	Prob.
C	0.002398	0.008236	0.291213	0.7734
1/GROUPSIZE	0.059922	0.018879	3.173942	0.0041
R-squared	0.295649			

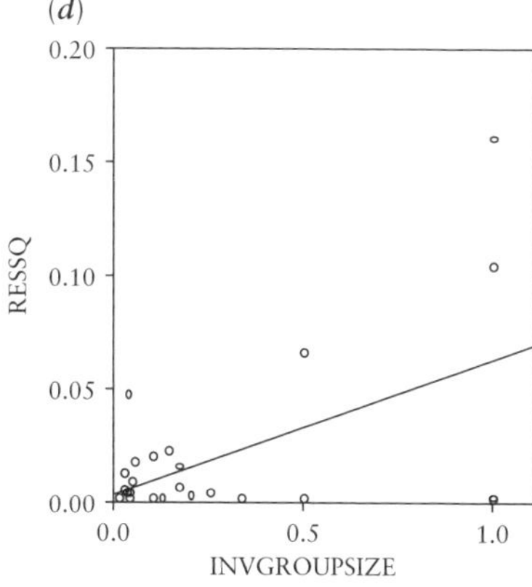

Exhibit 5.25 Bank Wages (Example 5.17)

Regression for grouped wage data (Panel 1), White heteroskedasticity test (Panel 2, RES are the residuals of Panel 1), and Breusch–Pagan test for heteroskedasticity related to group size (Panel 3) with scatter diagram of squared residuals against inverse of group size (*d*).

Example 5.18: Interest and Bond Rates (continued)

We continue our previous analysis of the interest and bond rate data (see Examples 5.14 and 5.16). We will discuss (i) heteroskedasticity tests based on different models, (ii) evaluation of the obtained results, and (iii) our conclusion.

(i) Tests on heteroskedasticity based on different models

We consider again the model $y_i = \alpha + \beta x_i + \varepsilon_i$ for the relation between the monthly changes in the AAA bond rate (y_i) and the monthly changes in the three-month Treasury Bill rate (x_i). In the foregoing we considered different possible models for the variances σ_i^2 of the disturbances—that is, (i) $\sigma_i^2 = \sigma^2 x_i^2$, (ii) $\sigma_i^2 = \gamma_1 + \gamma_2 D_i$, where D_i is a dummy variable for the second half (1975–99) of the considered time period, and (iii) $\sigma_i^2 = \gamma_1 + \gamma_2 \varepsilon_{i-1}^2$.

Now we use these models to test for the presence of heteroskedasticity. For the models (ii) and (iii) this can be done by testing whether γ_2 differs significantly from zero. The results in Panels 4 and 8 of Exhibit 5.23 show that the null hypothesis of homoskedastic disturbances is rejected for both models ($P = 0.000$). Exhibit 5.26 shows the result of the White test. The P-value of this test is $P = 0.046$ (see Panel 2). At 5 per cent significance we still reject the null hypothesis of homoskedasticity, but the tests based on the explicit models (ii) and (iii) have smaller P-values.

Panel 1: Dependent Variable: DAAA
Method: Least Squares
Sample: 1950:01 1999:12
Included observations: 600

Variable	Coefficient	Std. Error	t-Statistic	Prob.
C	0.006393	0.006982	0.915697	0.3602
DUS3MT	0.274585	0.014641	18.75442	0.0000

Panel 2: White Heteroskedasticity Test:

F-statistic	3.106338	Probability	0.045489
Obs*R-squared	6.179588	Probability	0.045511

Test Equation:
Dependent Variable: RES^2
Method: Least Squares
Sample: 1950:01 1999:12
Included observations: 600

Variable	Coefficient	Std. Error	t-Statistic	Prob.
C	0.027654	0.003246	8.518663	0.0000
DUS3MT	−0.000224	0.007073	−0.031639	0.9748
DUS3MT^2	0.006560	0.002804	2.339087	0.0197
R-squared	0.010299	Mean dependent var		0.029144

Exhibit 5.26 Interest and Bond Rates (Example 5.18)

OLS (Panel 1) and White heteroskedasticity test (Panel 2) for regression of changes in AAA bond rate on changes in Treasury Bill rate (RES in Panel 2 denotes the residuals of the regression in Panel 1).

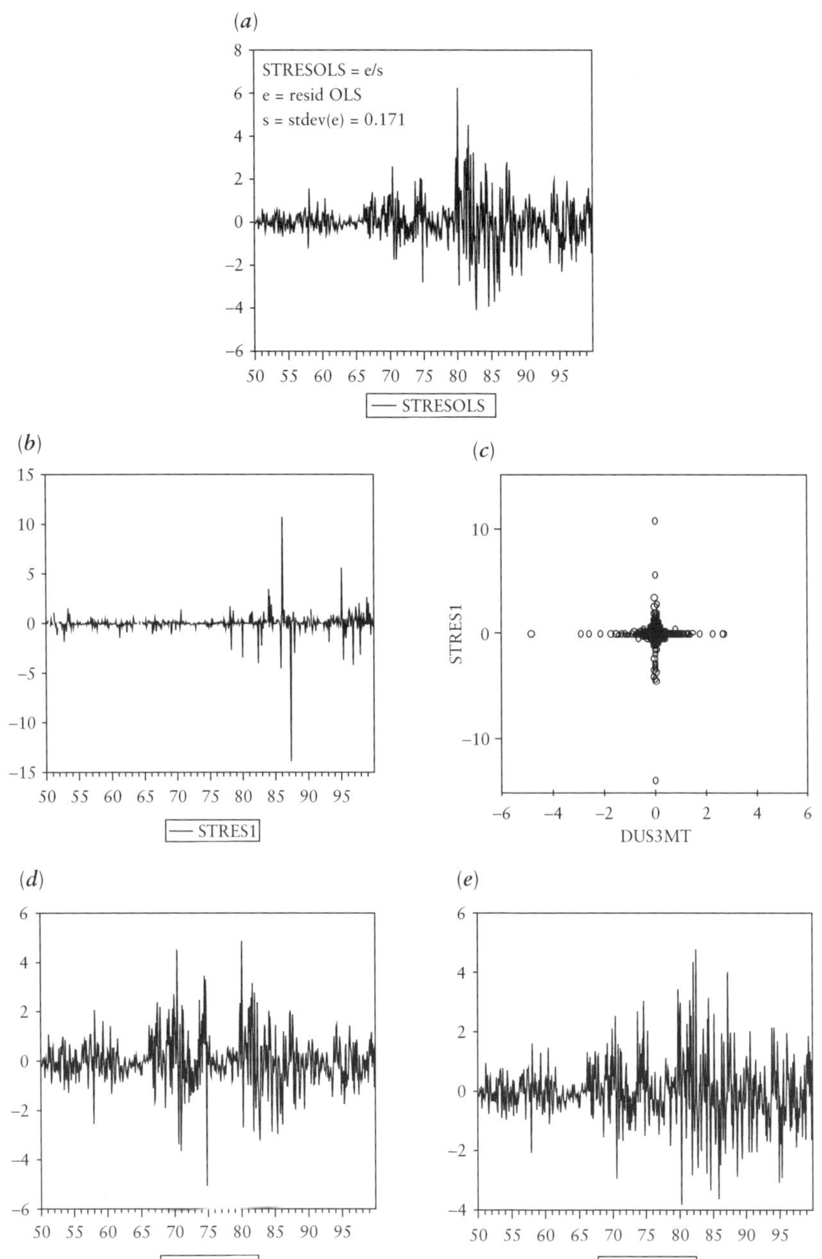

Exhibit 5.27 Interest and Bond Rates (Example 5.18)

Time plots of standardized residuals of AAA bond rate data, for OLS (STRESOLS (*a*)), for model with variance proportional to the square of DUS3MT (STRES1 (*b*), and (*c*) shows the scatter diagram of these standardized residuals against DUS3MT), for dummy variance model (STRES2 (*d*)), and for clustered variance model (STRES3 (*e*)).

(ii) Evaluation of the results

It is of interest to compare the success of the models (i), (ii), and (iii) in removing the heteroskedasticity. For this purpose we compute the standardized residuals of the three models—that is, $(y_i - \hat{\alpha} - \hat{\beta}x_i)/\hat{\sigma}_i$. Plots of the standardized residuals are in Exhibit 5.27 (b, d, e), together with the plot of the standardized OLS residuals e_i/s in (a). This shows that model (i) has some very large standardized residuals, corresponding to observations in months where x_i is close to zero, see Exhibit 5.27(c). Such observations get an excessively large weight. The standardized residuals of models (ii) and (iii) still show some changes in the variance, but somewhat less than the OLS residuals.

(iii) Conclusion

The overall conclusion is that the models considered here are not able to describe the relation between AAA bond rates and the Treasury Bill rate over the time span 1950–99. This means that we should either consider less simplistic models or restrict the attention to a shorter time period. We will return to these data in Chapter 7, where we discuss the modelling of time series data in more detail.

☞ **Exercises:** T: 5.6c, 5.7; E: 5.25b–e, 5.31c.

5.4.6 Summary

If the error terms in a regression model are heteroskedastic, this means that some observations are more informative than others for the underlying relation. Efficient estimation requires that the more informative observations get a relatively larger weight in estimation. One can proceed as follows.

- Apply a test for the possible presence of heteroskedasticity. If one has an idea what are the possible causes of heteroskedasticity, it is helpful to formulate a corresponding model for the variance of the error terms and to apply the Breusch–Pagan test. If one has no such ideas, one can apply the White test or the Goldfeld–Quandt test.
- If tests indicate the presence of significant heteroskedasticity, then OLS should not be routinely applied, as it is not efficient and the usual formulas for the standard errors (as computed by software packages) do not apply. If one sees no possibility of formulating a meaningful model for the heteroskedasticity, then one can apply GMM—that is, OLS with White standard errors.

- If one can formulate a model for the heteroskedasticity (for instance, an additive or a multiplicative model), then the model parameters can be estimated by weighted least squares if the variances are known up to a scale factor. Otherwise one can use feasible weighted least squares or maximum likelihood, with the usual approximate distributions of the estimators.
- Let $e_i = y_i - x_i'\hat{\beta}$ be the ith residual and let $\hat{\sigma}_i^2$ be the estimated variance of the ith disturbance. Then the model for heteroskedasticity may be evaluated by checking whether the scaled residuals $e_i/\hat{\sigma}_i$ are homoskedastic. If this is not the case, one can try to improve the model for the variances, or otherwise apply OLS with White standard errors.

5.5 Serial correlation

5.5.1 Introduction

Interpretation of serial correlation

As before, let the relation between the dependent variable y and the independent variables x be specified by

$$y_i = x_i'\beta + \varepsilon_i, \quad i = 1, \cdots, n. \tag{5.41}$$

The disturbances are said to be serially correlated if there exist observations $i \neq j$ so that ε_i and ε_j have a non-zero correlation. In this case the covariance matrix Ω is not diagonal. This means that, apart from the systematic parts modelled by $x_i'\beta$ and $x_j'\beta$, the observations y_i and y_j have something more in common.

In general, the purpose of (5.41) is to model all systematic factors that influence the dependent variable y. If the error terms are serially correlated, this means that the model is not successful in this respect. One should then try to detect the possible causes for serial correlation and, if possible, to adjust the model so that its disturbances become uncorrelated. For example, it may be that in (5.41) an important independent variable is missing (omitted variables), or that the functional relationship is non-linear instead of linear (functional misspecification), or that lagged values of the dependent or independent variables should be included as explanatory variables (neglected dynamics). We illustrate this by two examples.

Example 5.19: Interest and Bond Rates (continued)

We continue our analysis of the interest and bond rate data and will discuss (i) graphical evidence of serial correlation for these data, and (ii) an economic interpretation of this serial correlation.

(i) Graphical evidence for serial correlation

We consider the linear model

$$y_i = \alpha + \beta x_i + \varepsilon_i, \quad i = 1, \cdots, 600,$$

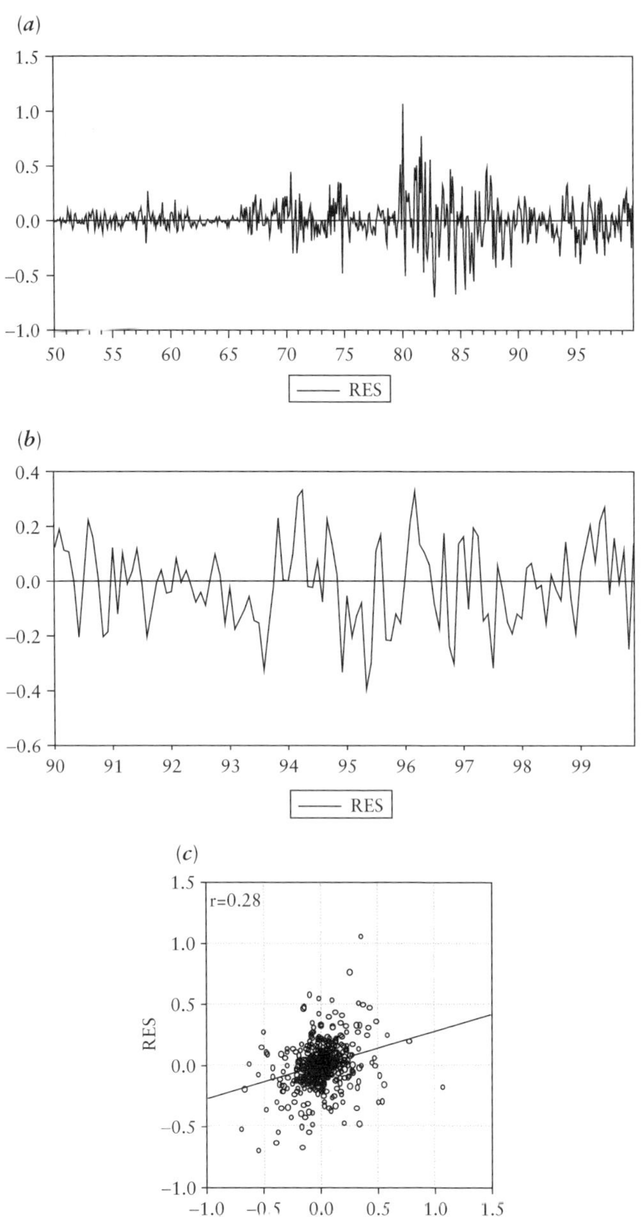

Exhibit 5.28 **Interest and Bond Rates (Example 5.19)**

Residuals of regression of changes in AAA bond rates on changes in Treasury Bill rates over the period 1950.01–1999.12 (*a*), same plot over subsample 1990.01–1999.12 (*b*), and scatter plot of residuals against their one-month lagged value (*c*).

for the monthly changes y_i in the AAA bond rate and the monthly changes x_i in the three-month Treasury Bill rate. The sample period runs from January 1950 to December 1999. Exhibit 5.28 shows graphs of the series of residuals

e_i over the whole sample period (in (*a*)) and also over the period January 1990 to December 1999 (in (*b*)). These graphs have time on the horizontal axis and the values of the residuals on the vertical axis. Exhibit 5.28 (*c*) is a scatter plot of the residuals against their lagged values—that is, the points in this plot are given by (e_{i-1}, e_i). The residuals of consecutive months are positively correlated with sample correlation coefficient $r = 0.28$. In 60 per cent of the months the residual e_i has the same sign as the residual e_{i-1} in the previous month.

(ii) Economic interpretation

These results indicate that the series of disturbances ε_i may be positively correlated over time. Suppose that in some month the change of the AAA bond rate is larger than would be predicted from the change of the Treasury Bill rate in that month, so that $\varepsilon_{i-1} = y_{i-1} - \alpha - \beta x_{i-1} > 0$. If ε_i and ε_{i-1} are positively correlated, then we expect that $\varepsilon_i > 0$—that is, that in the next month the change of the AAA rate is again larger than usual. This may be caused by the fact that deviations from an equilibrium relation between the two rates are not corrected within a single month but that this adjustment takes a longer period of time. Such dynamic adjustments require a different model from the above (static) regression model.

E

XM520FEX

Example 5.20: Food Expenditure (continued)

The investigation of serial correlation for cross section data makes sense only if the observations can be ordered in some meaningful way. We will illustrate this by considering a cross section of budget data on food expenditure for a number of households. These data were earlier discussed in Example 4.3 (p. 204). We will discuss (i) the data, (ii) a meaningful ordering of the data, and (iii) the interpretation of serial correlation for these cross section data.

(i) The data

The budget study of Example 4.3 consists of a cross section of 12,488 households that are aggregated in fifty-four groups. Exhibit 5.29 (*a*) shows a histogram of the group sizes. In all that follows we will delete the six groups with size smaller than twenty. This leaves $n = 48$ group observations for our analysis (see Exhibit 5.29 (*b*)). For each group the following data are available: the fraction of expenditure spent on food (y), the total consumption expenditure (x_2, in \$10,000 per year), and the average household size (x_3). We consider the following linear regression model:

$$y_i = \beta_1 + \beta_2 x_{2i} + \beta_3 x_{3i} + \varepsilon_i, \quad i = 1, \cdots, 48.$$

(ii) A meaningful ordering of the data

The OLS estimates of β_1, β_2, and β_3 and of the variance $\sigma^2 = E[\varepsilon_i^2]$ do not depend on the ordering of the groups. Exhibit 5.29 (*c*) shows the scatter diagram of the residuals against their lagged values—that is, the scatter of points (e_{i-1}, e_i), for a randomly chosen order of the groups. The sample correlation between e_i and e_{i-1} is very small: $r = -0.012$. Of course, it does not make much sense to compare the residual of one observation with the residual of the previous observation in such a randomly ordered sample.

To obtain a meaningful ordering we first order the data in six segments. Each segment consists of group observations with comparable household size, with $1 \leq x_3 < 2$ in the first segment to $5 \leq x_3 < 6$ in the fifth segment, and with $x_3 \geq 6$ in the last segment. The number of observations in the six segments is respectively 6, 9, 9, 8, 8, and 8. Within each segment—that is, for 'fixed' household size—the observations are ordered according to the total consumption expenditure. This ordering is indicated in Exhibit 5.29 (*d*) and (*f*). With this ordering, we make a scatter diagram of the residuals e_i against the previous residuals e_{i-1} within segments—that is, for i taking the values 2–6, 8–15, 17–24, 26–32, 34–40, and 42–48 so that residuals are compared only within the same segment and not between different segments. The scatter diagram in (*e*) shows a positive correlation between e_{i-1} and e_i, and the sample correlation coefficient is $r = 0.43$ in this case. This indicates that the series of error terms ε_i may be positively correlated within each segment.

(iii) Interpretation of serial correlation for cross section data

To obtain a better understanding, Exhibits 5.29 (*g*) and (*h*) show the actual values of y_i and the fitted values $\hat{y}_i = b_1 + b_2 x_{2i} + b_3 x_{3i}$ for the third segment of households (where $x_{3i} = 3.1$ for each observation), together with the residuals $e_i = y_i - \hat{y}_i$. Whereas the fitted relation is linear, the observed data indicate a non-linear relation with diminishing slope for higher levels of total expenditure. As a consequence, residuals tend to be positive for relatively small and for relatively large values of total expenditure and they tend to be negative for average values of total expenditure. As a consequence, the residuals are serially correlated. These results are in line with the earlier discussion in Example 4.3 (p. 204–5), as the effect of income on food expenditure declines for higher income levels. That is, the relation between x_2 and y is non-linear, so that the linear regression model is misspecified. The serial correlation of the ordered data provides a diagnostic indication of this misspecification.

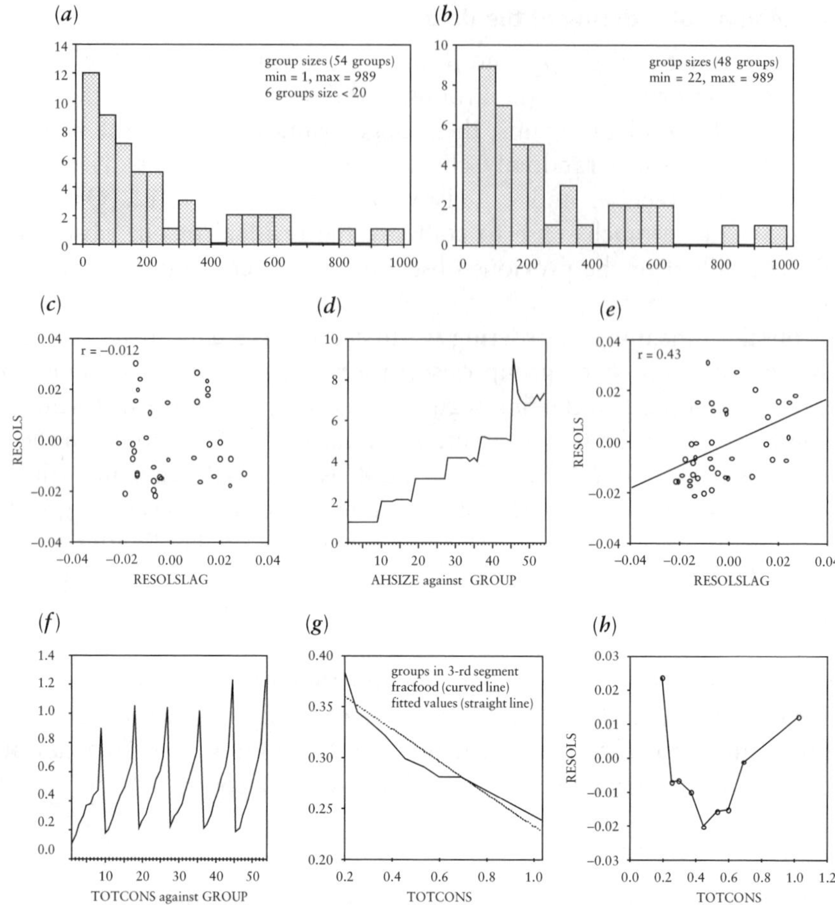

Exhibit 5.29 Food Expenditure (Example 5.20)

(*a*) and (*b*) show histograms of the group sizes ((*a*) for all 54 groups, (*b*) for the 48 groups with size ≥ 20). (*c*) and (*e*) show scatter diagrams of the OLS residuals (RESOLS) against their lagged values (RESOLSLAG) for random ordering ((*c*), $r = -0.012$) and for systematic ordering ((*e*), $r = 0.43$). The systematic ordering is in six segments according to household size (*d*), and the ordering within each segment is by total consumption (*f*). (*g*) shows the actual and fitted values in the third segment (groups 16–24, average household size 3.1) with corresponding residuals in (*h*).

☞ Exercises: E: 5.27a, b.

5.5.2 Properties of OLS

Consequences of serial correlation

Serial correlation is often a sign that the model should be adjusted. If one sees no possibilities to adjust the model to remove the serial correlation, then one can still apply OLS. Serial correlation corresponds to the case where the covariance matrix $\Omega = E[\varepsilon\varepsilon']$ of the disturbances is not diagonal, and we assume that Ω is unknown. As was discussed in Section 5.4.2, under the Assumptions 1, 2, 5, and 6, OLS remains unbiased and is consistent under appropriate conditions. In this sense OLS is still an acceptable method of estimation. However, the OLS estimator is not efficient, and its covariance matrix is not equal to $\sigma^2(X'X)^{-1}$ but it depends on the (unknown) covariance matrix Ω (see (5.23)). In many cases, the OLS expressions underestimate the standard errors of the regression coefficients and therefore t- and F-tests tend to exaggerate the significance of these coefficients (see Exercise 5.22 for an illustration).

Derivation of GMM standard errors

T

Consistent estimates of the standard errors can be obtained by GMM. That is, OLS can be expressed in terms of the k moment conditions

$$E[g_i] = 0, \quad g_i = \varepsilon_i x_i = (y_i - x_i'\beta)x_i, \quad i = 1, \cdots, n.$$

Note that the situation differs from the one considered in Section 5.4.2, as there the functions g_i are mutually independent, but this does not hold true if the ε_i are serially correlated. To describe the required modifications, we use the result (5.23) so that the variance of b is given by

$$\mathrm{var}(b) = \frac{1}{n}\left(\frac{1}{n}X'X\right)^{-1}\left(\frac{1}{n}X'\Omega X\right)\left(\frac{1}{n}X'X\right)^{-1}.$$

Let σ_{ij} denote the (i, j)th element of Ω; then $\sigma_{ij} = \sigma_{ji}$ (as Ω is symmetric) and

$$\frac{1}{n}X'\Omega X = \frac{1}{n}\sum_{i=1}^{n}\sum_{j=1}^{n}\sigma_{ij}x_i x_j' = \frac{1}{n}\sum_{i=1}^{n}\sigma_{ii}x_i x_i' + \frac{1}{n}\sum_{i=1}^{n-1}\sum_{j=i+1}^{n}\sigma_{ij}(x_i x_j' + x_j x_i').$$

In the White correction for standard errors, the unknown variances σ_i^2 in (5.24) are replaced by the squared residuals e_i^2 in (5.25). If we copy this idea for the current situation, then the variance would be estimated simply by replacing $\sigma_{ij} = E[\varepsilon_i\varepsilon_j]$ by the product $e_i e_j$ of the corresponding residuals. However, the resulting estimate of the covariance matrix of b is useless because

$$\frac{1}{n}\sum_{i=1}^{n}e_i^2 x_i x_i' + \frac{1}{n}\sum_{i=1}^{n-1}\sum_{j=i+1}^{n}e_i e_j(x_i x_j' + x_j x_i') = \frac{1}{n}X'ee'X = 0.$$

A consistent estimator of the variance of b can be obtained by weighting the contributions of the terms $e_i e_j$ to give the estimate

$$\hat{V} = \frac{1}{n}X'\widehat{\Omega}X = \frac{1}{n}\sum_{i=1}^{n}e_i^2 x_i x_i' + \frac{1}{n}\sum_{i=1}^{n-1}\sum_{j=i+1}^{n}w_{j-i}e_i e_j\left(x_i x_j' + x_j x_i'\right). \tag{5.42}$$

The terms on the diagonal (with $i = j$) have weight 1, and the terms with $i \neq j$ are given weights with $0 \leq w_{j-i} \leq 1$. The weighting function w is also called the *kernel*. For example, the Bartlett kernel has weights $w_h = 1 - \frac{h}{B}$ for $h < B$ and $w_h = 0$ for $h \geq B$. To get consistent estimates, the bandwidth B should depend on the sample size n in such a way that $B \to \infty$ for $n \to \infty$, but at the same time B should be sufficiently small so that the double summation in (5.42) converges. Rules that are applied in practice are to take $B \approx n^{1/3}$ or, in large samples, $B \approx n^{1/5}$.

Newey–West standard errors

The above method with weighting kernels is due to Newey and West. The corresponding estimates of the standard errors of the OLS estimator b are called HAC—that is, they are heteroskedasticity and autocorrelation consistent. So the *Newey–West standard errors* of b are given by the square roots of the diagonal elements of the matrix

$$\widehat{\text{var}}(b) = \frac{1}{n}(X'X)^{-1}\hat{V}(X'X)^{-1}$$

with the matrix $\hat{V}$ as defined in (5.42).

XM511IBR

Example 5.21: **Interest and Bond Rates (continued)**

We continue our analysis of the interest and bond rate data (see Example 5.19). Exhibit 5.30 shows the result of regressing the changes in AAA bond

Panel 1: Dependent Variable: DAAA
Method: Least Squares
Sample: 1950:01 1999:12
Included observations: 600

Variable	Coefficient	Std. Error	t-Statistic	Prob.
C	0.006393	0.006982	0.915697	0.3602
DUS3MT	0.274585	0.014641	18.75442	0.0000
R-squared	0.370346			

Panel 2: Dependent Variable: DAAA
Method: Least Squares
Sample: 1950:01 1999:12
Included observations: 600
Newey-West HAC Standard Errors & Covariance (lag truncation=5)

Variable	Coefficient	Std. Error	t-Statistic	Prob.
C	0.006393	0.008309	0.769436	0.4419
DUS3MT	0.274585	0.021187	12.95993	0.0000
R-squared	0.370346			

Exhibit 5.30 Interest and Bond Rates (Example 5.21)

Regression of changes in AAA bond rates on changes in Treasury Bill rates with conventional OLS standard errors (Panel 1) and with Newey–West standard errors (Panel 2).

rates on the changes in the Treasury Bill rates. The HAC standard errors in Panel 2 are larger than the standard errors computed by the conventional OLS formulas in Panel 1. However, these differences do not affect the significance of the relationship. The residual correlation is relatively mild ($r = 0.28$ (see Exhibit 5.28 (*c*))). In situations with more substantial serial correlation the differences may be much more dramatic (see Exercise 5.22 for an illustration).

Exercises: S: 5.22.

5.5.3 Tests for serial correlation

Autocorrelation coefficients

Serial correlation tests require that the observations can be ordered in a natural way. For time series data, where the variables are observed sequentially over time, such a natural ordering is given by the time index i. For cross section data the observations can be ordered according to one of the explanatory variables. In the foregoing sections we considered the correlation between consecutive residuals. The sample correlation coefficient of the residuals is defined by

$$r = \frac{\sum_{i=2}^{n} e_i e_{i-1}}{\sqrt{\sum_{i=2}^{n} e_i^2 \sum_{i=1}^{n-1} e_i^2}}.$$

In practice one often considers a slightly different (but asymptotically equivalent) expression, the *first order autocorrelation coefficient* defined by

$$r_1 = \frac{\sum_{i=2}^{n} e_i e_{i-1}}{\sum_{i=1}^{n} e_i^2}. \tag{5.43}$$

Large values of r_1 may be an indication of dynamic misspecification (for time series data) or of functional misspecification (for cross section data). To consider the possibility of more general forms of misspecification, it is informative to consider also the *kth order autocorrelation coefficients*

$$r_k = \frac{\sum_{i=k+1}^{n} e_i e_{i-k}}{\sum_{i=1}^{n} e_i^2}. \tag{5.44}$$

This measures the correlation between residuals that are k observations apart. A plot of the autocorrelations r_k against the lag k is called the *correlogram*. This plot provides a first idea of possible serial correlation.

We will now discuss three tests for serial correlation, Durbin–Watson, Breusch–Godfrey, and Ljung–Box.

The Durbin–Watson test

The Durbin–Watson test is based on the following idea. Let σ^2 be the variance of the disturbances and let ρ be the correlation between ε_i and ε_{i-1}; then $E[(\varepsilon_i - \varepsilon_{i-1})^2] = 2\sigma^2(1-\rho)$. So if successive error terms are positively (negatively) correlated, then the differences $\varepsilon_i - \varepsilon_{i-1}$ tend to be relatively small (large). The *Durbin–Watson statistic* is defined as

$$d = \frac{\sum_{i=2}^{n}(e_i - e_{i-1})^2}{\sum_{i=1}^{n} e_i^2}.$$

This statistic satisfies $0 \leq d \leq 4$, and

$$d \approx 2(1 - r_1)$$

with r_1 the first order autocorrelation coefficient defined in (5.43). In the absence of first order serial correlation $r_1 \approx 0$ so that $d \approx 2$. Values of d close to zero indicate positive serial correlation, and values close to four indicate negative serial correlation. Critical values to test the null hypothesis $\rho = 0$ depend on the matrix X of explanatory variables. However, lower and upper bounds for the critical values that do not depend on X have been calculated by Durbin and Watson. The use of these bounds requires that the model contains a constant term, that the disturbances are normally distributed, and that the regressors are non-stochastic—for instance, lagged values of the dependent variable y_i are not allowed. The Durbin–Watson test is nowadays mostly used informally as a diagnostic tool to indicate the possible existence of serial correlation.

Derivation of the Breusch–Godfrey *LM*-test

The Breusch–Godfrey test is an *LM*-test on serial correlation. The model is given by

$$y_i = x_i'\beta + \varepsilon_i \tag{5.45}$$

$$\varepsilon_i = \gamma_1\varepsilon_{i-1} + \cdots + \gamma_p\varepsilon_{i-p} + \eta_i, \tag{5.46}$$

where η_i satisfies Assumptions 2–4 and 7. That is, the $n \times 1$ vector η is distributed as $\mathrm{N}(0, \sigma_\eta^2 I)$ so that the η_i are homoskedastic and serially uncorrelated. The equation (5.46) is called an *autoregressive model* of order p (written as AR(p)) for the error terms. For simplicity we consider in our analysis below only the case of an AR(1) model for the error terms. In this case we have

$$\varepsilon_i = \gamma \varepsilon_{i-1} + \eta_i, \tag{5.47}$$

and we assume that $-1 < \gamma < 1$. By repetitive substitution we get

$$\varepsilon_i = \eta_i + \gamma \eta_{i-1} + \gamma^2 \eta_{i-2} + \cdots + \gamma^{i-2}\eta_2 + \gamma^{i-1}\varepsilon_1.$$

So the error term for observation i is composed of independent terms with weights that decrease geometrically. The absence of serial correlation corresponds to the null hypothesis that

$$\mathrm{H}_0: \quad \gamma = 0.$$

We derive the LM-test for this hypothesis by using the results in Section 4.2.4 (p. 217–8) for non-linear regression models (the ML approach of Section 4.3.6 is left as an exercise (see Exercise 5.8)). As a first step in the derivation of the LM-test we use (5.45) and (5.47) to obtain

$$y_i = \gamma y_{i-1} + x_i'\beta - \gamma x_{i-1}'\beta + \eta_i. \tag{5.48}$$

This model contains $2k+1$ regressors but only $k+1$ parameters—that is, the parameters satisfy k (non-linear) restrictions. The model (5.48) can be written as a non-linear regression model

$$y_i = f(z_i, \beta, \gamma) + \eta_i,$$

where $z_i = (y_{i-1}, x_i', x_{i-1}')'$. According to the results for non-linear regression models in Section 4.2.4, the LM-test can be computed by auxiliary regressions provided that the regressors z_i satisfy the two conditions that $\mathrm{plim}(\frac{1}{n}\sum z_i z_i') = Q_z$ exists (and is non-singular) and that $\mathrm{plim}(\frac{1}{n}\sum \eta_i z_i) = 0$ (orthogonality). Under the null hypothesis that $\gamma = 0$ in (5.47), we get $\varepsilon_i = \eta_i$ and (5.45) shows that z_i is a linear function of $(\eta_{i-1}, x_i', x_{i-1}')'$. The above two limit conditions are satisfied if $\mathrm{plim}(\frac{1}{n}\sum \eta_i x_i) = \mathrm{plim}(\frac{1}{n}\sum \eta_i x_{i-1}) = \mathrm{plim}(\frac{1}{n}\sum \eta_{i-1} x_i) = 0$ and

$$\mathrm{plim}\left(\frac{1}{n}\begin{pmatrix} \sum x_i x_i' & \sum x_i x_{i-1}' \\ \sum x_{i-1} x_i' & \sum x_{i-1} x_{i-1}' \end{pmatrix}\right) = Q$$

with Q a non-singular $(2k) \times (2k)$ matrix. According to the results in Section 4.2.4, the LM-test for $\gamma = 0$ can then be computed as

$$LM = nR^2.$$

Here R^2 is obtained from the regression of the OLS residuals $e = y - Xb$ on the gradient of the function f—that is, the vector of first order derivatives $\partial f / \partial \beta$ and $\partial f / \partial \gamma$ evaluated in the point $(\beta, \gamma) = (b, 0)$. The model (5.48) gives, when evaluated at $\beta = b$ and $\gamma = 0$,

$$\partial f/\partial \beta = x_i - \gamma x_{i-1} = x_i$$
$$\partial f/\partial \gamma = y_{i-1} - x'_{i-1}\beta = y_{i-1} - x'_{i-1}b = e_{i-1}.$$

The Breusch–Godfrey test

The foregoing arguments show that the *Breusch–Godfrey test* is obtained as $LM = nR^2$ of the auxiliary regression

$$e_i = x_i'\delta + \gamma e_{i-1} + \omega_i, \quad i = 2, \cdots, n. \tag{5.49}$$

This test has an asymptotic $\chi^2(1)$ distribution under the null hypothesis of absence of serial correlation. The LM-test for the null hypothesis of absence of serial correlation against the alternative of AR(p) errors in (5.46) can be derived in a similar way. This leads to the following test procedure.

Breusch–Godfrey test for serial correlation of order p

- *Step 1: Apply OLS.* Apply OLS in the model $y = X\beta + \varepsilon$ and compute the residuals $e = y - Xb$.
- *Step 2: Perform auxiliary regression.* Apply OLS in the auxiliary regression equation

$$e_i = x_i'\delta + \gamma_1 e_{i-1} + \cdots + \gamma_p e_{i-p} + \omega_i, \quad i = p+1, \cdots, n.$$

- *Step 3: $LM = nR^2$ of the regression in step 2.* Then $LM = nR^2$ where R^2 is the coefficient of determination of the auxiliary regression in step 2. This is asymptotically distributed as $\chi^2(p)$ under the null hypothesis of no serial correlation, that is, if $\gamma_1 = \cdots = \gamma_p = 0$.

An asymptotically equivalent test is given by the usual F-test on the joint significance of the parameters $(\gamma_1, \cdots, \gamma_p)$ in the above auxiliary regression. To choose the value of p in the Breusch–Godfrey test, it may be helpful to draw the correlogram of the residuals e_i. In practice one usually selects small values for p ($p = 1$ or $p = 2$) and includes selective additional lags according to the data structure. For instance, if the data consist of time series that are observed every month, then one can include all lags up to order twelve to incorporate monthly effects.

Box–Pierce and Ljung–Box tests

As a third test for serial correlation we consider the *Box–Pierce test* for the joint significance of the first p autocorrelation coefficients defined in (5.44). The test statistic is given by

$$BP = n \sum_{k=1}^{p} r_k^2. \qquad (5.50)$$

It is left as an exercise (see Exercise 5.9) to show that this test is asymptotically equivalent to the Breusch–Godfrey test. In particular, $BP \approx \chi^2(p)$ under the null hypothesis of no serial correlation.

Sometimes the correlations in (5.50) are weighted because higher order autocorrelations are based on less observations — that is, r_k in (5.44) is based on $(n-k)$ products of residuals $e_i e_{i-k}$. This gives the *Ljung–Box test* (also denoted as the Q-test)

$$LB = n \sum_{k=1}^{p} \frac{n+2}{n-k} r_k^2 \approx \chi^2(p).$$

Similar to the Durbin–Watson test, the Box–Pierce test and the Ljung–Box test also require that the regressors x_i in the model (5.45) are non-stochastic. Otherwise it is better to apply the Breusch–Godfrey LM-test.

Example 5.22: **Interest and Bond Rates (continued)**

We perform serial correlation tests for the interest and bond rate data discussed before in Examples 5.19 and 5.21. Exhibit 5.31, Panel 1, shows the results of regressing the changes in the AAA bond rate on the changes in the Treasury Bill rate. The Durbin–Watson statistic is equal to $d = 1.447$, so that the first order autocorrelation coefficient is $r_1 \approx 1 - \frac{1}{2}d = 0.277$. Exhibit 5.31, Panel 2, contains the first twelve autocorrelation coefficients of the residuals. The first order autocorrelation coefficient is significant. The Q-test in Panel 2 corresponds to the Ljung–Box test (with p ranging from $p = 1$ to $p = 12$). Panels 3 and 4 show the results of the Breusch–Godfrey test with one or two lags of the residuals. All tests lead to a clear rejection of the null hypothesis of no serial correlation.

Example 5.23: **Food Expenditure (continued)**

Next we perform tests on serial correlation for the data on food expenditure discussed before in Example 5.20. Exhibit 5.32 shows the results of different tests for serial correlation for the budget data of forty-eight groups of households. For a randomly chosen ordering of the groups, the correlogram, the Ljung–Box test, and the Breusch–Godfrey test indicate that there is no serial correlation (see Panels 1 and 2).

Now we consider a meaningful ordering of the groups in six segments, as discussed in Example 5.20. Each segment consists of groups of households of

Panel 1: Dependent Variable: DAAA Method: Least Squares Sample: 1950:01 1999:12 Included observations: 600				
Variable	Coefficient	Std. Error	t-Statistic	Prob.
C	0.006393	0.006982	0.915697	0.3602
DUS3MT	0.274585	0.014641	18.75442	0.0000
R-squared	0.370346	Durbin-Watson stat		1.446887

Panel 2: Correlogram of residuals			
Lag	AC	Q-Stat	Prob
1	0.276	45.932	0.000
2	−0.076	49.398	0.000
3	0.008	49.441	0.000
4	0.034	50.126	0.000
5	0.055	51.939	0.000
6	0.101	58.189	0.000
7	0.035	58.934	0.000
8	0.049	60.412	0.000
9	0.044	61.610	0.000
10	0.008	61.646	0.000
11	0.032	62.289	0.000
12	−0.062	64.624	0.000

Panel 3: Breusch–Godfrey Serial Correlation LM Test:				
F-statistic	51.91631	Probability		0.000000
Obs*R-squared	48.00277	Probability		0.000000
Dependent Variable: RESID				
Variable	Coefficient	Std. Error	t-Statistic	Prob.
C	0.000222	0.006702	0.033123	0.9736
DUS3MT	−0.022449	0.014396	−1.559364	0.1194
RESID(−1)	0.289879	0.040231	7.205297	0.0000
R-squared	0.080005			

Panel 4: Breusch–Godfrey Serial Correlation LM Test:				
F-statistic	36.01114	Probability		0.000000
Obs*R-squared	64.68852	Probability		0.000000
Dependent Variable: RESID				
Variable	Coefficient	Std. Error	t-Statistic	Prob.
C	0.000311	0.006606	0.047153	0.9624
DUS3MT	−0.029051	0.014271	−2.035626	0.0422
RESID(−1)	0.342590	0.041495	8.256187	0.0000
RESID(−2)	−0.175063	0.040616	−4.310152	0.0000
R-squared	0.107814			

Exhibit 5.31 Interest and Bond Rates (Example 5.22)

Regression of AAA bond rates (Panel 1) with correlogram of residuals (Panel 2, 'Q-Stat' is the Ljung–Box test) and Breusch–Godfrey tests on serial correlation (with order $p = 1$ in Panel 3 and $p = 2$ in Panel 4; these panels also show the auxiliary regression of step 2 of this *LM*-test).

Panel 1: Correlogram RESRAND (randomly ordered data, 48 observations)			
Lag	AC	Q-Stat	Prob
1	−0.096	0.4697	0.493
2	0.093	0.9237	0.630
3	0.066	1.1560	0.764
4	0.012	1.1643	0.884
5	0.031	1.2165	0.943
6	−0.134	2.2497	0.895
7	0.207	4.7566	0.690
8	−0.256	8.6744	0.370
9	0.183	10.729	0.295
10	−0.019	10.752	0.377

Panel 2: Breusch–Godfrey test, Dependent Variable: RESRAND Sample(adjusted): 2 48 (included observations: 47)				
Variable	Coefficient	Std. Error	t-Statistic	Prob.
C	−8.66E-05	0.005750	−0.015064	0.9881
TOTCONS	−0.000470	0.008724	−0.053863	0.9573
AHSIZE	9.38E-05	0.001248	0.075099	0.9405
RESRAND(−1)	−0.101757	0.156142	−0.651694	0.5181
R-squared	0.009857			

Panel 3: Correlogram RESORD (systematically ordered data) Sample: 1–6, 8–15, 17–24, 26–32, 34–40, 42–48 (43 obs)			
Lag	AC	Q-Stat	Prob
1	0.327	4.9124	0.027
2	0.115	5.5369	0.063
3	−0.039	5.6113	0.132
4	−0.340	11.362	0.023
5	−0.253	14.618	0.012
6	0.007	14.620	0.023
7	0.087	15.031	0.036
8	0.353	21.912	0.005
9	0.213	24.503	0.004
10	0.076	24.842	0.006

Panel 4: Breusch–Godfrey test, Dependent Variable: RESORD Sample: 2–6, 8–15, 17–24, 26–32, 34–40, 42–48 (included obs 42)				
Variable	Coefficient	Std. Error	t-Statistic	Prob.
C	−0.007112	0.005876	−1.210341	0.2336
TOTCONS	0.016883	0.009605	1.757771	0.0868
AHSIZE	−0.000463	0.001233	−0.375160	0.7096
RESORD(−1)	0.480625	0.168762	2.847947	0.0071
R-squared	0.183146			

Exhibit 5.32 Food Expenditure (Example 5.23)

Correlograms of residuals and auxiliary regressions of step 2 of Breusch–Godfrey test for budget data with randomly ordered data (Panels 1 and 2, residuals RESRAND) and with systematically ordered data (Panels 3 and 4, residuals RESORD).

comparable size, and the observations within a segment are ordered according to the total consumption expenditure. The six segments consist of the observations with index 1–6, 7–15, 16–24, 25–32, 33–40, and 41–48. We investigate the presence of first order serial correlation within these segments. At the observations $i = 7, 16, 25, 33$, and 41, the residuals e_i and e_{i-1} correspond to different segments and the correlations between these residuals are excluded from the analysis. This leaves forty-two pairs of residuals (e_i, e_{i-1}) for analysis. The results are in Panels 3 and 4 of Exhibit 5.32. The correlogram, the Ljung–Box test, and the Breusch–Godfrey test (with $LM = nR^2 = 42 \cdot 0.18 = 7.69$ with $P = 0.006$) all reject the absence of serial correlation. This indicates misspecification of the linear model—that is, the fraction of expenditure spent on food depends in a non-linear way on total expenditure (see also Example 5.20 (p. 356–8)).

☞ **Exercises:** T: 5.8, 5.9, 5.11; S: 5.21; E: 5.30**a**, **b**, 5.31**d**.

5.5.4 Model adjustments

Regression models with lagged variables

If the residuals of an estimated equation are serially correlated, this indicates that the model is not correctly specified. For (ordered) cross section data this may be caused by non-linearities in the functional form, and we refer to Section 5.2 for possible adjustments of the model. For time series data, serial correlation means that some of the dynamic properties of the data are not captured by the model. In this case one can adjust the model—for instance, by including lagged values of the explanatory variables and of the explained variable as additional regressors. As an example, suppose that the model

$$y_i = \beta_1 + \beta_2 x_i + \varepsilon_i$$

is estimated by OLS and that the residuals are serially correlated. This suggests that $\varepsilon_i = y_i - \beta_1 - \beta_2 x_i$ is correlated with $\varepsilon_{i-1} = y_{i-1} - \beta_1 - \beta_2 x_{i-1}$. This may be caused by correlation of y_i with y_{i-1} and x_{i-1}, which can be expressed by the model

$$y_i = \gamma_1 + \gamma_2 x_i + \gamma_3 x_{i-1} + \gamma_4 y_{i-1} + \eta_i. \qquad (5.51)$$

When the disturbances η_i of this model are identically and independently distributed (IID), then the model is said to have a correct dynamic specification. The search for correct dynamic specifications of time series models is discussed in Chapter 7.

Regression model with autoregressive disturbances

In this section we consider only a special case that is often applied as a first step in modelling serial correlation. Here it is assumed that the dynamics can be modelled by means of the disturbances ε_i, and more in particular that ε_i satisfies the AR(1) model (5.47) so that $\varepsilon_i = \gamma\varepsilon_{i-1} + \eta_i$. This is called the regression model with AR(1) errors. If one substitutes $\varepsilon_i = y_i - \beta_1 - \beta_2 x_i$ and $\varepsilon_{i-1} = y_{i-1} - \beta_1 - \beta_2 x_{i-1}$, it follows that (5.47) can be written as

$$y_i = \beta_1(1-\gamma) + \beta_2 x_i - \beta_2\gamma x_{i-1} + \gamma y_{i-1} + \eta_i. \tag{5.52}$$

This is of the form (5.51) with $\gamma_1 = \beta_1(1-\gamma)$, $\gamma_2 = \beta_2$, $\gamma_3 = -\beta_2\gamma$, and $\gamma_4 = \gamma$, so that the parameters satisfy the restriction

$$\gamma_2\gamma_4 + \gamma_3 = \beta_2\gamma - \beta_2\gamma = 0.$$

Estimation by Cochrane–Orcutt

If the terms η_i are IID and normally distributed, then the parameters β_1, β_2, and γ can be estimated by NLS. An alternative is to use the following iterative two-step method. Note that for a given value of γ the parameters β_1 and β_2 can be estimated by OLS in

$$y_i - \gamma y_{i-1} = \beta_1(1-\gamma) + \beta_2(x_i - \gamma x_{i-1}) + \eta_i.$$

On the other hand, if the values of β_1 and β_2 are given, then $e_i = y_i - \beta_1 - \beta_2 x_i$ can be computed and hence γ can be estimated by OLS in

$$e_i = \gamma e_{i-1} + \eta_i.$$

We can exploit this as follows. As a first step take $\gamma = 0$ and estimate β_1 and β_2, by OLS. This estimator is consistent (provided that $-1 < \gamma < 1$ (see Chapter 7)), but it is not efficient. Let $e_i = y_i - b_1 - b_2 x_i$ be the OLS residuals; then in the second step γ is estimated by regressing e_i on e_{i-1}. This estimator (say $\hat{\gamma}$) is also consistent. To improve the efficiency we can repeat these two steps. First a new estimate of β_1 and β_2 is obtained by regressing $y_i - \hat{\gamma} y_{i-1}$ on a constant and $x_i - \hat{\gamma} x_{i-1}$. Second, if $\tilde{e}_i$ are the new residuals, then a new estimate of γ is obtained by regressing $\tilde{e}_i$ on $\tilde{e}_{i-1}$. This process is iterated till the estimates of β_1, β_2, and γ converge. This is called the *Cochrane–Orcutt method* for the estimation of regression models with AR(1) errors. The estimates converge to a local minimum of the sum-of-squares criterion function, and it may be worthwhile to redo the iterations with different initial values for the parameters β_1, β_2, and γ.

As the regression model with AR(1) errors is a restriction of the more general model (5.51), this restriction can be tested in the usual way—for instance, by the Wald test. The regression model with AR(1) errors has been popular because it is simple and because the Cochrane–Orcutt estimator can be computed by iterated regressions. Nowadays more general dynamic models like (5.51) are often preferred, as will be discussed in Chapter 7.

XM511IBR

Example 5.24: **Interest and Bond Rates (continued)**

We continue our analysis of the interest and bond rate data. In Example 5.22 in the previous section we found clear evidence for the presence of serial correlation for these data. We now estimate the adjusted model (5.51), with the result shown in Panel 2 of Exhibit 5.33. Both lagged terms (x_{i-1} and y_{i-1}) are significant, and $\hat{\gamma}_2\hat{\gamma}_4 + \hat{\gamma}_3 = 0.252 \cdot 0.290 - 0.080 = -0.007$ is close to zero. The Wald test on the restriction $\gamma_2\gamma_4 + \gamma_3 = 0$ in Panel 3 has a P-value of $P = 0.64$, so that this restriction is not rejected. The regression model with AR(1) errors is therefore not rejected, and the estimation results of this model are shown in Panel 4 of Exhibit 5.33. To evaluate this last model, Panel 1 contains for comparison the results of OLS. Including AR(1) errors leads to an increase of R^2, but this should not be a surprise. The Durbin–Watson statistic is more close to 2 (1.90 as compared with 1.45), but recall that for models with lags this statistic does not provide consistent estimates of the correlation between the residuals. Panel 5 contains the correlogram of the OLS residuals and of the residuals of the model with AR(1) errors—that is, of (5.52). The residuals of the model (5.52) still contains some significant correlations. Other models are needed for these data, and this will be further discussed in Chapter 7.

XM520FEX

Example 5.25: **Food Expenditure (continued)**

In Example 5.23 we concluded that there exists significant serial correlation for the residuals of the linear food expenditure model of Example 5.20. This is an indication that this linear model is not correctly specified. As it makes no sense to include 'lagged' variables for cross section data, we consider instead another specification of the functional relation between income and food expenditure. We will discuss (i) a non-linear model, (ii) the Breusch–Godfrey test for this non-linear model, and (iii) the outcome and interpretation of the test.

Panel 1: Dependent Variable: DAAA (1950.01 – 1999.12)				
Variable	Coefficient	Std. Error	t-Statistic	Prob.
C	0.006393	0.006982	0.915697	0.3602
DUS3MT	0.274585	0.014641	18.75442	0.0000
R-squared	0.370346	Durbin–Watson stat		1.446887

Panel 2: Dependent Variable: DAAA (1950.01 – 1999.12)				
Variable	Coefficient	Std. Error	t-Statistic	Prob.
C	0.004780	0.006712	0.712171	0.4766
DUS3MT	0.252145	0.015007	16.80237	0.0000
DUS3MT(−1)	−0.079636	0.017800	−4.473948	0.0000
DAAA(−1)	0.289881	0.040344	7.185151	0.0000
R-squared	0.420728	Durbin–Watson stat		1.897040

Panel 3: Wald Test			
Null Hypothesis: C(2)*C(4) + C(3) = 0			
F-statistic	0.215300	Probability	0.642814
Chi-square	0.215300	Probability	0.642645

Panel 4: Dependent Variable: DAAA (1950.01 – 1999.12) Convergence achieved after 3 iterations				
Variable	Coefficient	Std. Error	t-Statistic	Prob.
C	0.006668	0.009423	0.707620	0.4795
DUS3MT	0.252361	0.014989	16.83586	0.0000
AR(1)	0.288629	0.040228	7.174887	0.0000
R-squared	0.420519	Durbin–Watson stat		1.896645

Panel 5: Correlograms							
OLS residuals				AR(1) residuals			
Lag	AC	Q-Stat	Prob	Lag	AC	Q-Stat	Prob
1	0.276	45.932	0.000	1	0.050	1.5232	0.217
2	−0.076	49.398	0.000	2	−0.181	21.402	0.000
3	0.008	49.441	0.000	3	0.013	21.509	0.000
4	0.034	50.126	0.000	4	0.023	21.829	0.000
5	0.055	51.939	0.000	5	0.036	22.622	0.000
6	0.101	58.189	0.000	6	0.090	27.510	0.000
7	0.035	58.934	0.000	7	−0.011	27.582	0.000
8	0.049	60.412	0.000	8	0.030	28.136	0.000
9	0.044	61.610	0.000	9	0.036	28.926	0.001
10	0.008	61.646	0.000	10	−0.005	28.938	0.001
11	0.032	62.289	0.000	11	0.058	31.023	0.001
12	−0.062	64.624	0.000	12	−0.044	32.189	0.001

Exhibit 5.33 Interest and Bond Rates (Example 5.24)

Regression models for AAA bond rates, simple regression model (Panel 1), dynamic model with single lags (Panel 2) with Wald test for AR(1) errors (Panel 3), simple regression model with AR(1) errors (Panel 4), and correlograms of residuals (Panel 5, for residuals of Panel 1 on the left and for residuals of Panel 4 on the right).

(i) Non-linear food expenditure model

In Example 4.3 (p. 205) we considered a non-linear functional form for the budget data. That is,

$$y_i = \beta_1 + \beta_2 x_{2i}^{\beta_3} + \beta_4 x_{3i} + \varepsilon_i,$$

where y_i is the fraction of total expenditure spent on food, x_2 is total expenditure (in \$10,000 per year), and x_3 is the (average) household size of households in group i.

Panel 1 of Exhibit 5.34 shows the resulting estimates and a scatter diagram (in (b)) of the NLS residuals e_i against their lagged values e_{i-1}, with correlation $r = 0.167$ (as compared to $r = 0.43$ for the residuals of the linear model in Example 5.20 (see Exhibit 5.29 (g))).

(ii) Breusch–Godfrey test for the non-linear model

To test whether the residual correlation is significant we apply the Breusch–Godfrey LM-test for the non-linear model. Step 1 of this test consists of NLS, with NLS residuals e_i. To perform step 2 of this test, we first reformulate the non-linear model with AR(1) error terms as a non-linear regression model, similar to (5.48) for the linear model. The AR(1) model is $\varepsilon_i = \gamma\varepsilon_{i-1} + \eta_i$, where $\eta_i \sim \text{NID}(0, \sigma_\eta^2)$, and the non-linear model can be written in terms of the independent error terms η_i as

$$y_i = \beta_1(1-\gamma) + \gamma y_{i-1} + \beta_2 x_{2i}^{\beta_3} - \gamma\beta_2 x_{2,i-1}^{\beta_3} + \beta_4 x_{3i} - \gamma\beta_4 x_{3,i-1} + \eta_i.$$

This is a non-linear regression model $y_i = f(x_i, \theta) + \eta_i$ with 6×1 vector of regressors given by $x_i = (1, y_{i-1}, x_{2i}, x_{2,i-1}, x_{3i}, x_{3,i-1})'$ and with 5×1 parameter vector $\theta = (\beta_1, \beta_2, \beta_3, \beta_4, \gamma)'$. Now step 2 of the Breusch–Godfrey test can be performed as described in Section 4.2.4 (p. 217–8) for LM-tests—that is, the NLS residuals e_i are regressed on the gradient $\frac{\partial f}{\partial \theta}$, evaluated at the restricted NLS estimates $\hat{\theta} = (b_1, b_2, b_3, b_4, 0)$, with $\gamma = 0$ and with the NLS estimates of the other parameters, as given in Panel 1 of Exhibit 5.34. The regressors in step 2 are therefore (for $\gamma = 0$) given by

$$\frac{\partial f}{\partial \beta_1} = 1 - \gamma = 1,$$

$$\frac{\partial f}{\partial \beta_2} = x_{2i}^{\beta_3} - \gamma x_{2,i-1}^{\beta_3} = x_{2i}^{b_3},$$

$$\frac{\partial f}{\partial \beta_3} = \beta_2 x_{2i}^{\beta_3} \log(x_{2i}) - \gamma\beta_2 x_{2,i-1}^{\beta_3} \log(x_{2,i-1}) = b_2 x_{2i}^{b_3} \log(x_{2i}),$$

(a)

Panel 1: Dependent Variable: FRACFOOD				
Method: Least Squares				
Sample: 1 48 (groups with size ≥ 20)				
Included observations: 48				
Convergence achieved after 7 iterations				
FRACFOOD=C(1)+C(2)*TOTCONS^C(3)+C(4)*AHSIZE				
Parameter	Coefficient	Std. Error	t-Statistic	Prob.
C(1)	0.453923	0.054293	8.360611	0.0000
C(2)	−0.271015	0.053437	−5.071693	0.0000
C(3)	0.412584	0.115538	3.570982	0.0009
C(4)	0.016961	0.000991	17.11004	0.0000
R-squared	0.939246			
Durbin–Watson stat	1.957808			

(b)

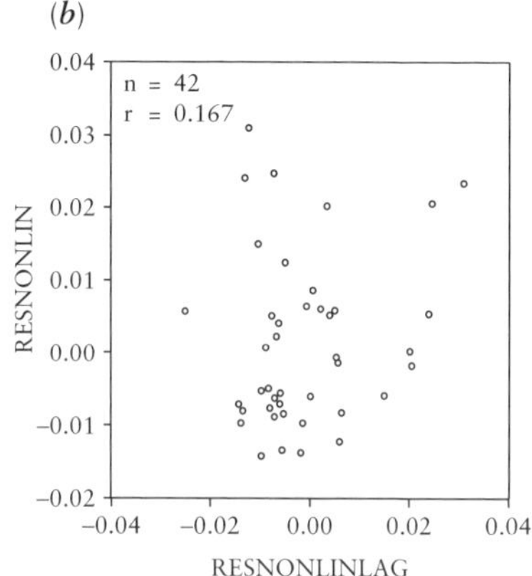

(c)

Panel 3: Dependent Variable: RESNONLIN				
Method: Least Squares				
Sample: 2–6, 8–15, 17–24, 26–32, 34–40, 42–48 (included obs 42)				
Variable	Coefficient	Std. Error	t-Statistic	Prob.
C	0.154181	0.070516	2.186478	0.0352
TOTCONS^(0.412584)	−0.155027	0.070053	−2.212985	0.0331
TOTCONS^(0.412584)* LOG(TOTCONS)	0.078232	0.038573	2.028173	0.0498
AHSIZE	0.000423	0.001012	0.418210	0.6782
RESNONLIN(−1)	0.195965	0.152414	1.285746	0.2065
R-squared	0.157982			

Exhibit 5.34 Food Expenditure (Example 5.25)

Non-linear regression model for budget data (Panel 1), scatter plot of residuals against their lags (within segments (*b*)), and auxiliary regression of step 2 of Breusch–Godfrey test on serial correlation (Panel 3).

$$\frac{\partial f}{\partial \beta_4} = x_{3i} - \gamma x_{3,i-1} = x_{3i},$$

$$\frac{\partial f}{\partial \gamma} = y_{i-1} - \beta_1 - \beta_2 x_{2,i-1}^{\beta_3} - \beta_4 x_{3,i-1} = y_{i-1} - b_1 - b_2 x_{2,i-1}^{b_3} - b_4 x_{3,i-1} = e_{i-1}.$$

Therefore the required regression in step 2 is

$$e_i = \delta_1 + \delta_2 x_{2i}^{b_3} + \delta_3 x_{2i}^{b_3} \log(x_{2i}) + \delta_4 x_{3i} + \gamma e_{i-1} + \omega_i.$$

The Breusch–Godfrey test is $LM = nR^2$ of this regression.

(iii) Outcome and interpretation of the test

The results in Panel 3 of Exhibit 5.34 show that $LM = nR^2 = 42 \cdot 0.158 = 6.64$ with P-value $P = 0.010$ (there are forty-two relevant observations because residuals in different segments should not be compared to each other (see Example 5.23)). This indicates that there still exists significant serial correlation, although the coefficient of e_{i-1} is not significant ($P = 0.207$ (see Panel 3 of Exhibit 5.34), as compared to $P = 0.007$ for the linear model in Panel 4 of Exhibit 5.32). So the above simple non-linear model does not capture all the non-linear effects of the variable x_2 on y, but it is an improvement as compared to the linear model.

This example shows that serial correlation tests can be applied as diagnostic tools for cross section data, provided that the observations are ordered in a meaningful way.

E

XM526INP

Example 5.26: **Industrial Production**

Whereas the two foregoing examples were concerned with data from finance and microeconomics, serial correlation is also often a relevant issue for macroeconomic time series. For instance, serial correlation may result because of prolonged up- and downswings of macroeconomic variables from their long-term growth path. Although the discussion of time series models is postponed till Chapter 7, we will now give a brief illustration. We will discuss (i) the data, (ii) a simple trend model, (iii) tests on serial correlation, and (iv) interpretation of the result.

(i) The data

We consider quarterly data on industrial production in the USA over the period 1950.1 until 1998.3. The data are taken from the OECD main economic indicators.

(ii) A simple trend model

We denote the series of industrial production by *INP*. In order to model the exponential growth of this series, we fit a linear trend to the logarithm of this series. We estimate the simple regression model

$$\log(INP_i) = \alpha + \beta i + \varepsilon_i,$$

where $x_i = i$ denotes the linear trend. The result is shown in Panel 1 of Exhibit 5.35. The estimated quarterly growth rate is around 0.8 per cent, corresponding to a yearly growth rate of around 3.3 per cent.

(iii) Tests on serial correlation

The Durbin–Watson statistic is very close to zero, indicating a strong positive serial correlation in the residuals. This is also clear from the autocorrelations of the residuals in Panel 2 of Exhibit 5.35. Both the Ljung–Box test in Panel 2

Panel 1: Dependent Variable: LOG(IP)
Method: Least Squares
Sample(adjusted): 1950:1 1998:3
Included observations: 195 after adjusting endpoints

Variable	Coefficient	Std. Error	t-Statistic	Prob.
C	3.321756	0.012141	273.6052	0.0000
@TREND(1950.1)	0.008197	0.000108	75.71580	0.0000
R-squared	0.967431			
S.E. of regression	0.085094			
Durbin–Watson stat	0.084571			

Panel 2: Correlogram of residuals

Lag	AC	Q-Stat	Prob
1	0.941	175.36	0.000
2	0.875	327.80	0.000
3	0.813	459.89	0.000
4	0.768	578.37	0.000
5	0.716	681.88	0.000
6	0.686	777.61	0.000
7	0.649	863.63	0.000
8	0.632	945.73	0.000
9	0.609	1022.4	0.000
10	0.589	1094.5	0.000
11	0.556	1159.2	0.000
12	0.548	1222.2	0.000

Panel 3: Breusch–Godfrey Serial Correlation LM Test:

F-statistic	747.5207	Probability	0.000000
Obs*R-squared	172.9098	Probability	0.000000

Test Equation:
Dependent Variable: RESID
Method: Least Squares

Variable	Coefficient	Std. Error	t-Statistic	Prob.
C	0.000138	0.004108	0.033538	0.9733
@TREND(1950.1)	−2.13E-06	3.66E-05	−0.058197	0.9537
RESID(−1)	1.026273	0.072090	14.23600	0.0000
RESID(−2)	−0.090350	0.072114	−1.252877	0.2118
R-squared	0.886717			

Exhibit 5.35 Industrial Production (Example 5.26)

Linear trend model for industrial production (in logarithms) (Panel 1, @TREND denotes the linear trend), correlogram of residuals (Panel 2), and Breusch–Godfrey test (Panel 3).

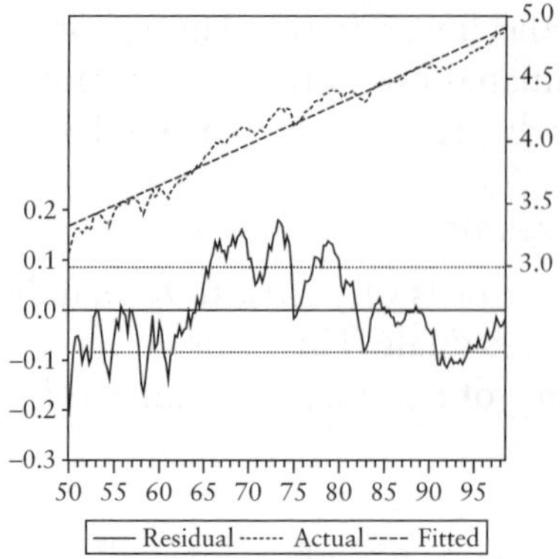

Exhibit 5.36 Industrial Production (Example 5.26)

Actual and fitted values of US quarterly industrial production (in logarithms, right vertical axis) and plot of residuals with 95% confidence interval (left vertical axis).

and the Breusch–Godfrey test in Panel 3 (with $p = 2$) strongly reject the absence of serial correlation.

(iv) Interpretation

The time plot of the residuals in Exhibit 5.36 shows that the growth was above average for a long period from around 1965 to 1980. Such prolonged deviations from the linear trend line indicate that this simple linear trend model misses important dynamical aspects of the time series. More realistic models for this series will be presented in Chapter 7.

Exercises: T: 5.10; E: 5.27c, d, 5.29a, b.

5.5.5 Summary

If the error terms in a regression model are serially correlated, this means that the model misses some of the systematic factors that influence the dependent variable. One should then try to find the possible causes and to adjust the model accordingly. The following steps may be helpful in the diagnostic analysis.

- Order the observations in a natural way. The ordering is evident for time series data, and serial correlation is one of the major issues for such data (see Chapter 7). In the case of cross section data, the analysis of serial correlation makes sense only if the observations are ordered in some meaningful way.
- Check whether serial correlation is present, by drawing the correlogram of the residuals and by performing tests, in particular the Breusch–Godfrey *LM*-test.

- If serial correlation is present, OLS is no longer efficient and the usual formulas for the standard errors do not apply. If it is not possible to adjust the model to remove the serial correlation, then OLS can be applied with Newey–West standard errors.
- The best way to deal with serial correlation is to adjust the model so that the correlation disappears. This may sometimes be achieved by adjusting the specification of the functional relation—for instance, by including lagged variables in the model (this is further discussed in Chapter 7).

5.6 Disturbance distribution

5.6.1 Introduction

Weighted influence of individual observations

In ordinary least squares, the regression parameters are estimated by minimizing the criterion

$$S(\beta) = \sum_{i=1}^{n} (y_i - x_i'\beta)^2.$$

This means that errors are penalized in the same way for all observations and that large errors are penalized more than proportionally. An alternative is to apply weighted least squares where the errors are not all penalized in the same way. For instance, for time series data the criterion

$$S_w(\beta) = \sum_{t=1}^{n} w^{n-t} (y_t - x_t'\beta)^2 \qquad (5.53)$$

(with $0 < w < 1$) assigns larger weights to more recent observations. This criterion may be useful, for instance, when the parameters β vary over time so that the most recent observations contain more information on the current parameter values than the older observations. In Section 5.4 the use of weighted least squares was motivated by heteroskedastic error terms. For time-varying parameters the criterion (5.53) allows for relatively larger residuals for older observations.

Overview

In Section 5.6.2 we investigate the question of which observations are the most influential ones in determining the outcomes of an ordinary least squares regression. If the outcomes depend heavily on only a few observations, it is advisable to investigate the validity of these data. If the explanation of outlying data falls within the purpose of the analysis, then the specification of the model should be reconsidered.

Section 5.6.3 contains a test for normality of the disturbances. It may be that outlying observations are caused by special circumstances that fall outside the scope of the model. The influence of such data can be reduced by using a less sensitive criterion function—for example,

$$S_{\text{abs}}(\beta) = \sum_{i=1}^{n} |y_i - x_i'\beta|.$$

If the outcomes of estimation and testing methods are less sensitive to individual observations and to the underlying model assumptions, then such methods are called robust. Robust methods are discussed in Section 5.6.4.

5.6.2 Regression diagnostics

The leverage of an observation

To characterize *influential data* in the regression model $y = X\beta + \varepsilon$, we use the hat-matrix H defined by (see Section 3.1.3 (p. 123))

$$H = X(X'X)^{-1}X'.$$

The explained part $\hat{y}$ of the dependent variable y is given by $\hat{y} = Xb = Hy$. The jth diagonal element of H is denoted by

$$h_j = x_j'(X'X)^{-1}x_j, \tag{5.54}$$

where the $1 \times k$ vector x_j' is the jth row of the $n \times k$ matrix X. The value h_j is called the *leverage* of the jth observation. The leverages satisfy $0 \leq h_j \leq 1$ and $\sum_{j=1}^{n} h_j = k$ (see Exercise 5.12). So the mean leverage is equal to k/n. A large leverage h_j means that the values of the explanatory variables x_j are somewhat unusual as compared to the average of these values over the sample.

Characterization of outliers

An observation is called an *outlier* if the value of the dependent variable y_j differs substantially from what would be expected from the general pattern of the other observations. To test whether the jth observation is an outlier, we consider the model with a dummy variable for the jth observation—that is,

$$y_i = x_i'\beta + \gamma D_{ji} + \varepsilon_i, \quad i = 1, \cdots, n, \tag{5.55}$$

with $D_{jj} = 1$ and $D_{ji} = 0$ for $i \neq j$. The null hypothesis that the jth observation fits in the general pattern of the data corresponds to the null hypothesis that $\gamma = 0$, and this can be tested by the t-test.

Derivation of studentized residuals

Let D_j denote the $n \times 1$ vector with elements D_{ji}, $i = 1, \cdots, n$; then the model in (5.55) can be written as $y = X\beta + D_j\gamma + \varepsilon$. According to the result of Frisch–Waugh in Section 3.2.5 (p. 146), the OLS estimator of γ is given by

$$\begin{aligned}\hat{\gamma} &= (D_j'MD_j)^{-1}D_j'My = (D_j'D_j - D_j'X(X'X)^{-1}X'D_j)^{-1}D_j'e \\ &= (1 - x_j'(X'X)^{-1}x_j)^{-1}e_j = \frac{e_j}{1-h_j}.\end{aligned}$$

Here $M = I - H$ and $e = My$ is the usual vector of OLS residuals in the model $y = X\beta + \varepsilon$—that is, in (5.55) with $\gamma = 0$. If $\varepsilon \sim \mathrm{N}(0, \sigma^2 I)$, then $e = M\varepsilon \sim \mathrm{N}(0, \sigma^2 M)$ and $e_j = D_j'e \sim \mathrm{N}(0, \sigma^2(1 - h_j))$, so that $\hat{\gamma} \sim \mathrm{N}(0, \sigma^2/(1 - h_j))$. Let s_j^2 be the OLS estimator of σ^2 based on the model (5.55), including the dummy. Then the t-value of $\hat{\gamma}$ in (5.55) is given by

$$e_j^* = \frac{\hat{\gamma}}{s_j/\sqrt{1-h_j}} = \frac{e_j}{s_j\sqrt{1-h_j}}. \tag{5.56}$$

This statistic follows the $t(n - k - 1)$ distribution under the null hypothesis that $\gamma = 0$. The jth observation is an outlier if $\hat{\gamma}$ is significant—that is, if the residual e_j or the leverage h_j is sufficiently large. The residuals e_j^* are called the *studentized residuals*. Note that the dummy variable is included only to compute the studentized residual. This should not be interpreted as an advice to include dummies in the model for each outlier. Indeed, if one uses the rule of thumb $|t| > 2$ for significance, then one may expect that 5 per cent of all observations are 'outliers'. Such 'ordinary' outliers are of no concern, but one should pay attention to large outliers (with t-values further away from zero) and try to understand the cause of such outliers, as this may help to improve the model.

The 'leave-one-out' interpretation of studentized residuals

The jth studentized residual can also be obtained by leaving out the jth observation. That is, perform a regression in the model $y_i = x_i'\beta + \varepsilon_i$ using the $(n - 1)$ observations with $i \neq j$, so that the jth observation is excluded. Let $b(j)$ and $s^2(j)$ be the corresponding OLS estimators of β and σ^2. It is left as an exercise (see Exercise 5.12) to show that $b(j)$ is the OLS estimator of β in (5.55) (for n observations), that $s^2(j) = s_j^2$ (that is, the OLS estimator of σ^2 in (5.55)), and that $y_j - x_j'b(j) = \hat{\gamma}$ in (5.55). With these results it follows from (5.56) that the studentized residuals can be computed as

$$e_j^* = \frac{y_j - x_j' b(j)}{s(j)/\sqrt{1 - h_j}}.$$

The studentized residual can be interpreted in terms of the Chow forecast test of observation j, where the forecast is based on the model estimated from the $(n-1)$ observations $i \neq j$ (see Exercise 5.12). If e_j^* is large, this means that y_j cannot be predicted well from the other observations, so that the jth observation does not fit the general pattern of the other observations. In this sense the jth observation then is an outlier.

OLS may not detect outliers

It should be noted that outliers may not always be detected from the plot of OLS residuals e_i. This is because OLS tries to prevent very large residuals, so that e_j may be small even if e_j^* is large. Because of (5.56), this can occur if the leverage of the observation is large. This is illustrated by a simulation in Exhibit 5.37. The outlier (corresponding to the first observation, with $j = 1$) is not detected from the residuals if we include all observations (*a–b*), but it is revealed very clearly if the outlier observation is excluded from the regression (*c–e*).

Panels 7 and 8 of Exhibit 5.37 illustrate that the estimates of β and σ^2 and the sum of squared residuals (SSR) in (5.55) are the same as the estimates obtained by deleting the outlier observation. The R^2 of (5.55) is much larger, however. This is simply caused by the fact that the total sum of squares is much larger for the set of all observations ($SST = 1410$ in Panel 8) than for the set of observations excluding the outlier ($SST = 285$ in Panel 7).

Influence on parameter estimates: 'dfbetas'

T

The influence of individual observations on the estimates of β can be evaluated as follows. Let b be the usual OLS estimator in (5.55) under the restriction that $\gamma = 0$, with residuals e, and let $b(j)$ and $\hat{\gamma}$ be the OLS estimators in (5.55) with the dummy included, with residuals $e(j)$. Then $y = Xb + e = Xb(j) + D_j\hat{\gamma} + e(j)$, so that

$$X(b - b(j)) - D_j\hat{\gamma} - e(j) + e = 0.$$

If we premultiply this with X' and use that $X'e = 0$, $X'e(j) = 0$, and $X'D_j = x_j'$, then we obtain

$$b - b(j) = (X'X)^{-1}X'D_j\hat{\gamma} = \frac{1}{1 - h_j}(X'X)^{-1}x_j e_j. \qquad (5.57)$$

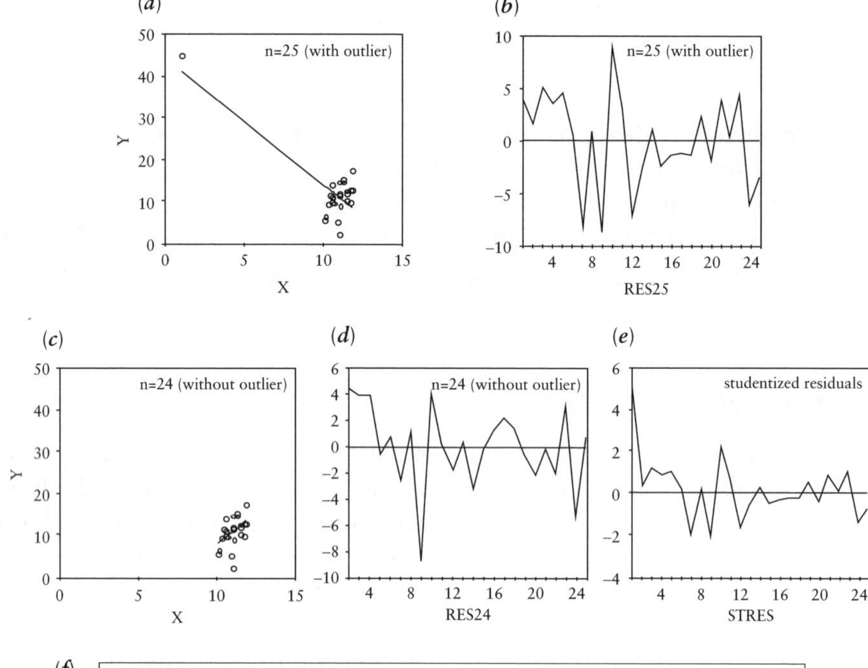

(f)

Panel 6: Dependent Variable: Y Included observations: 25				
Variable	Coefficient	Std. Error	t-Statistic	Prob.
C	43.99717	4.873317	9.028179	0.0000
X	−2.988136	0.448928	−6.656161	0.0000
R-squared	0.658269	Sum squared resid		481.7315
S.E. of regression	4.576554	Total sum of squares		1409.682

(g)

Panel 7: Dependent Variable: Y Included observations: 24 (first observation, outlier, removed)				
Variable	Coefficient	Std. Error	t-Statistic	Prob.
C	−22.73838	13.66355	−1.664163	0.1103
X	3.028141	1.233459	2.454999	0.0225
R-squared	0.215043	Sum squared resid		223.4754
S.E. of regression	3.187157	Total sum of squares		284.6977

(h)

Panel 8: Dependent Variable: Y Included observations: 25 (DUM1 is dummy for first observation)				
Variable	Coefficient	Std. Error	t-Statistic	Prob.
C	−22.73838	13.66355	−1.664163	0.1103
X	3.028141	1.233459	2.454999	0.0225
DUM1	64.71023	12.83368	5.042220	0.0000
R-squared	0.841471	Sum squared resid		223.4754
S.E. of regression	3.187157	Total sum of squares		1409.682

Exhibit 5.37 Outliers and OLS

Scatter diagrams and residuals ((*a*)–(*d*)), studentized residuals (*e*), regressions with outlier (Panel 6), without outlier (Panel 7) and with outlier dummy (Panel 8).

It is preferable to make the difference $b_l - b_l(j)$ in the lth estimated parameter, owing to the jth observation, invariant with respect to the measurement scale of the explanatory variable x_l. Therefore this difference is scaled with an estimate of the standard deviation of b_l—for example, $s_j\sqrt{a_{ll}}$ where a_{ll} is the lth diagonal element of $(X'X)^{-1}$. This gives the *dfbetas* defined by

$$\text{dfbetas}_{lj} = \frac{b_l - b_l(j)}{s_j\sqrt{a_{ll}}}. \tag{5.58}$$

It is left as an exercise (see Exercise 5.13) to show that (under appropriate conditions) the variance of the 'dfbetas' is approximately $1/n$. So the difference in the parameter estimates can be stated to be significant if the value of (5.58) is (in absolute value) larger than $2/\sqrt{n}$.

Influence on fitted values: 'dffits'

T

The influence of the jth observation on the fitted values is given by $\hat{y} - \hat{y}(j)$, where $\hat{y} = Xb$ and $\hat{y}(j) = Xb(j)$. In particular, by using (5.57) the difference in the fitted values for y_j is given by

$$\hat{y}_j - \hat{y}_j(j) = x_j'(b - b(j)) = \frac{h_j}{1 - h_j}e_j.$$

As $e_j = y_j - \hat{y}_j$ it follows that

$$\hat{y}_j = h_j y_j + (1 - h_j)\hat{y}_j(j).$$

Therefore, the leverage h_j gives the relative weight of the observation y_j itself in constructing the predicted value for the jth observation. That is, if h_j is large, then the jth observation may be difficult to fit from the other observations. Because the variance of $\hat{y}_j$ is equal to $E[(x_j'b - x_j'\beta)^2] = \sigma^2 x_j'(X'X)^{-1}x_j = \sigma^2 h_j$, a scale invariant measure for the difference in fitted values is given by the *dffits* defined by

$$\text{dffits}_j = \frac{\hat{y}_j - \hat{y}_j(j)}{s_j\sqrt{h_j}} = \frac{e_j}{s_j}\frac{\sqrt{h_j}}{1 - h_j} = e_j^*\sqrt{\frac{h_j}{1 - h_j}}.$$

Also in this respect, the jth observation is influential if the studentized residual or the leverage is large. As $\text{var}(e_j^*) \approx 1$ and h_j is generally very small for large enough sample sizes, it follows that 'dffits' has a variance of approximately $\text{var}(\text{'dffits'}) \approx \text{var}(e_j^*\sqrt{h_j}) = h_j$. As $\sum_{j=1}^n h_j = k$, the average variance is approximately $\frac{k}{n}$. Therefore, differences in fitted values can be stated to be significant if 'dffits' is larger (in absolute value) than $2\sqrt{k/n}$.

What to do with influential observations?

If the most influential observations in the data set are detected, the question arises what to do with these observations. They can be the most important pieces of information, in which case their large influence is justified. If the influential observations do not fit well in the general pattern of the data, one may be tempted to delete them from the analysis. However, one should be careful not to remove important sample information. In any case one should check whether these observations are correctly reported and one should investigate whether outliers can possibly be explained in terms of additional explanatory variables.

XM527SMR

Example 5.27: **Stock Market Returns (continued)**

As an illustration we consider the stock market returns data that were introduced in Example 2.1 (p. 76–7). We will discuss (i) the data and the possibility of outliers and (ii) the analysis of influential data.

(i) The data and the possibility of outliers

Financial markets are characterized by sudden deviations from normal operation caused by crashes or moments of excessive growth. Here we consider data on excess returns in the sector of cyclical consumer goods and in the whole market in the UK. These data were previously analysed in Examples 2.1, 4.4 (p. 223–4), and 4.5 (p. 243–6), and in Section 4.4.6 (p. 262–5). In Examples 4.4 and 4.5 we analysed the possibility of fat tails and now we will apply regression diagnostics on these data.

(ii) Analysis of influential data

The data consist of monthly observations over the period from January 1980 to December 1999. The CAPM corresponds to the simple regression model $y_i = \alpha + \beta x_i + \varepsilon_i$, where y_i is the excess return of the sector and x_i that of the market. Exhibit 5.38 provides graphical information (leverages, studentized residuals, dfbetas, and dffits, among others) and Exhibit 5.39 displays the characteristics for some of the data points. The observation in October 1987 (when a crash took place) has a very large leverage but a small studentized residual, so that this is not an outlier. Such observations are helpful in estimation, as they fit well in the estimated model and reduce the standard errors of the estimated parameters. On the other hand, the observations in September 1980 and September 1982 are outliers, but the leverages of these observations are small.

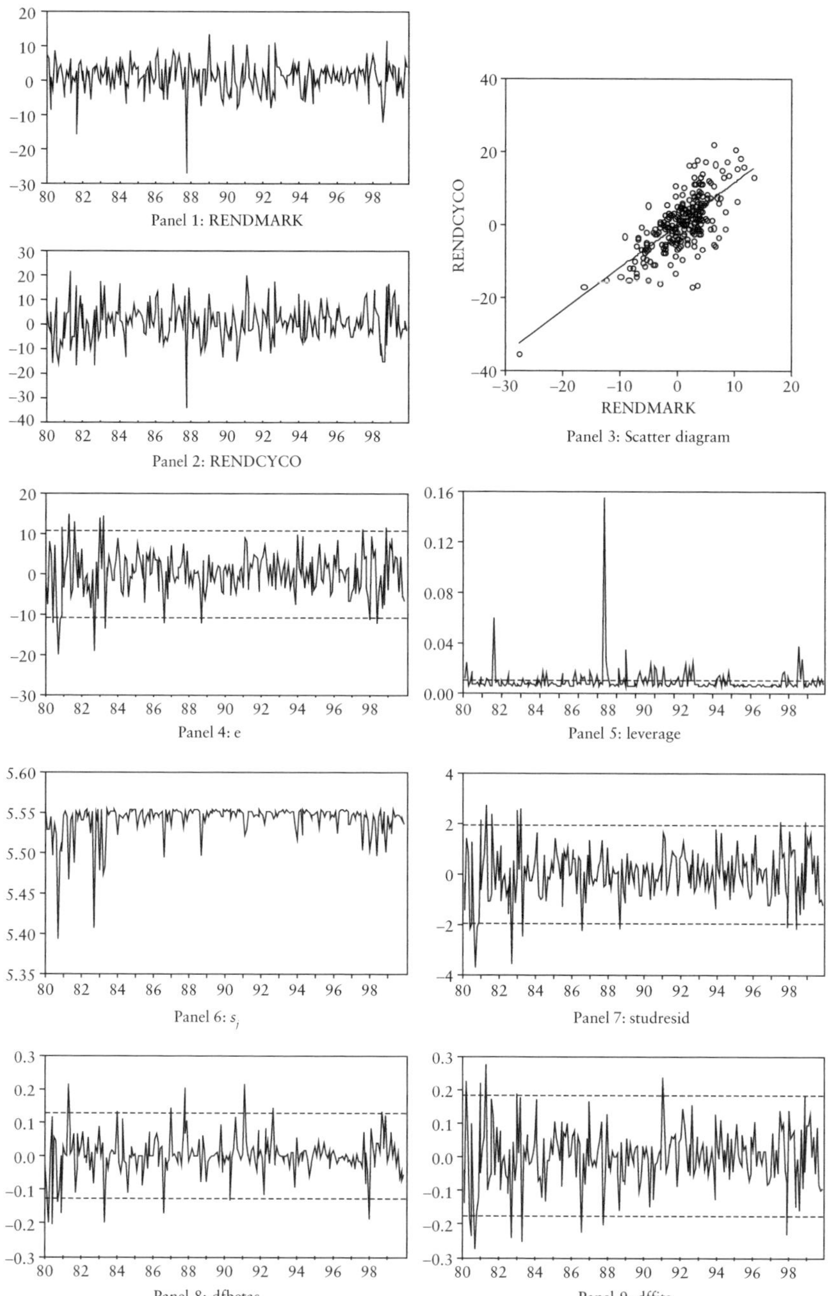

Exhibit 5.38 Stock Market Returns (Example 5.27)

Time plots of excess returns in market (Panel 1) and in sector of cyclical consumer goods (Panel 2), scatter diagram of excess returns in sector against market (Panel 3), regression of excess sector returns on excess market returns with corresponding residuals (e, Panel 4), leverages (Panel 5), standard deviations (s_j, Panel 6), studentized residuals (Panel 7), dfbetas (Panel 8), and dffits (Panel 9). The dashed horizontal lines in Panels 4 and 7–9 denote 95% confidence intervals.

Characteristic	Residual e_j	Leverage h_j	St. Resid. e_j^*	dfbetas	dffits
5% crit. value	$\pm 2s =$ ± 11.086	$\pm 2/n =$ ± 0.008	± 2	$\pm 2/\sqrt{n} =$ ± 0.129	$\pm 2\sqrt{(2/n)} =$ ± 0.183
1980:06	−10.694	0.015*	−1.956	−0.209*	−0.245*
1980:09	−20.412*	0.005	−3.795*	−0.139*	−0.282*
1981:04	15.115*	0.010*	2.779*	0.214*	0.280*
1981:09	2.551	0.059*	0.474	−0.115	0.119
1982:09	−19.558*	0.005	−3.626*	−0.086	−0.250*
1983:04	−13.588*	0.011*	−2.492*	−0.204*	−0.260*
1987:10	−2.480	0.156*	−0.486	0.206*	−0.209*
1991:02	8.930	0.021*	1.634	0.215*	0.240*

Exhibit 5.39 Stock Market Returns (Example 5.27)

Characteristics of some selected influential observations in CAPM over the period 1980.01–1999.12 ($n = 240$ observations). An * indicates values that differ significantly from zero (at 5% significance).

☞ Exercises: T: 5.12a–c, 5.13; E: 5.29c, d, 5.30c, d, 5.31e, 5.33a.

5.6.3 Test for normality

Skewness and kurtosis

As was discussed in Chapter 4, OLS is equivalent to maximum likelihood if the error terms are normally distributed. So under this assumption OLS is an optimal estimation method, in the sense that it is consistent and (asymptotically) efficient. For this reason it is of interest to test Assumption 7 of normally distributed error terms. It is also of interest for other reasons—for example, because many econometric tests (like the t-test and the F-test) are based on the assumption of normally distributed error terms.

Suppose that the standard Assumptions 1–6 of the regression model are satisfied. This means that

$$y_i = x_i'\beta + \varepsilon_i, \quad i = 1, \cdots, n,$$

where $E[\varepsilon_i] = 0$, $E[\varepsilon_i^2] = \sigma^2$, and $E[\varepsilon_i \varepsilon_j] = 0$ for all $i \neq j$. Then Assumption 7 of normally distributed disturbances can be tested by means of the OLS residuals $e_i = y_i - x_i'b$. In particular, we can compare the sample moments of the residuals with the theoretical moments of the disturbances under the null hypothesis of the normal distribution. In this case there holds $E[\varepsilon_i^3] = 0$ and $E[\varepsilon_i^4] = 3\sigma^4$, so that the *skewness* (S) and *kurtosis* (K) are equal to

$$S = E[\varepsilon_i^3]/\sigma^3 = 0, \quad K = E[\varepsilon_i^4]/\sigma^4 = 3.$$

If the null hypothesis of normality is true, then the residuals e_i should have a skewness close to 0 and a kurtosis close to 3. We suppose that the model contains a constant term, so that the sample mean of the residuals is zero. Then the jth moment of the residuals is given by $m_j = \sum_{i=1}^n e_i^j / n$ and the skewness and kurtosis are computed as

$$S = m_3/(m_2)^{3/2}, \quad K = m_4/m_2^2.$$

It can be shown that, under the null hypothesis of normality, $\sqrt{n/6}S$ and $\sqrt{n/24}(K-3)$ are asymptotically independently distributed as N(0, 1). These results can be used to perform individual tests for the skewness and kurtosis.

Jarque–Bera test on normality

The skewness and kurtosis can also be used jointly to test for normality. The normal distribution has skewness $S = 0$ and kurtosis $K = 3$, and the deviation from normality can be measured by

$$JB = \left(\sqrt{\frac{n}{6}}S\right)^2 + \left(\sqrt{\frac{n}{24}}(K-3)\right)^2 = n\left(\frac{1}{6}S^2 + \frac{1}{24}(K-3)^2\right) \approx \chi^2(2).$$

This is the *Jarque–Bera test* on normality, and the null hypothesis is rejected for large values of JB. Here we will not derive the asymptotic $\chi^2(2)$ distribution, but note that the null hypothesis poses two conditions ($S = 0$ and $K = 3$), so that the test statistic has two degrees of freedom.

Example 5.28: **Stock Market Returns (continued)**

We continue our analysis of Example 5.27 in the previous section and consider the Capital Asset Pricing Model (CAPM) of Example 2.5 (p. 91) for the sector of cyclical consumer goods. The data consist of monthly observations over the period 1980–99 ($n = 240$). Exhibit 5.40 (a, b) shows the time series plot and the histogram of the residuals. The skewness and kurtosis are equal to $S = -0.28$ and $K = 4.04$. This gives values of $\sqrt{n/6}S = -1.77$ and $\sqrt{n/24}(K-3) = 3.30$. The corresponding (two-sided) P-value for the hypothesis that $S = 0$ is $P = 0.08$, and for the hypothesis that $K = 3$ it is $P = 0.001$. So the residuals have a considerably larger kurtosis than the normal distribution. The Jarque–Bera test has value $JB = (-1.77)^2 + (3.30)^2 = 14.06$ with P-value 0.001. So the assumption of normality is rejected. Exhibit 5.40 (c) shows the histogram that results when two extremely large negative residuals (in the months of September 1980 and September 1982) are removed. This has a large effect on the skewness and kurtosis, and the assumption of normality is no longer rejected. This indicates that for the majority of the sample period the assumption of

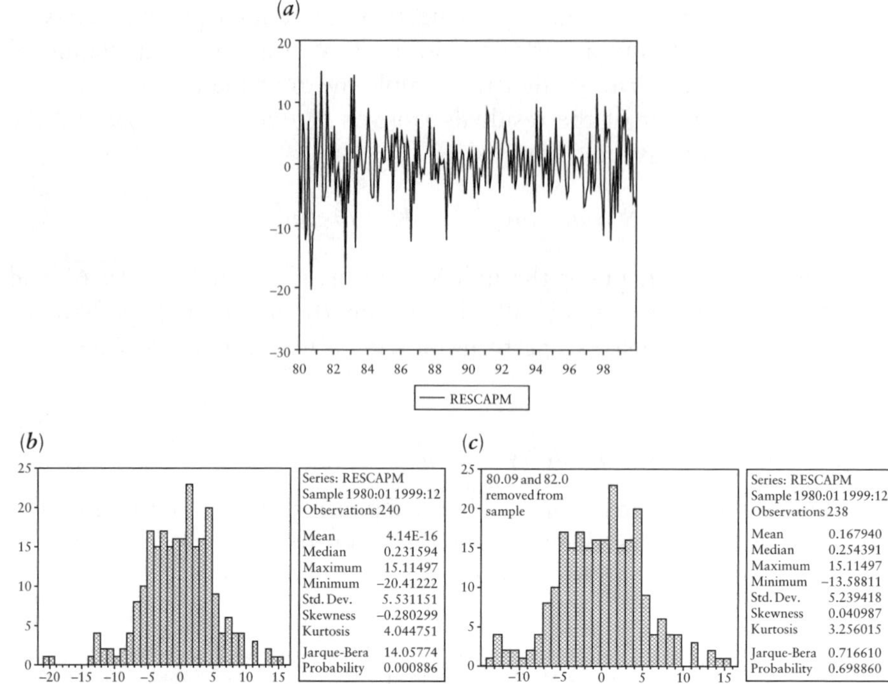

Exhibit 5.40 Stock Market Returns (Example 5.28)

Time plot of residuals of CAPM (*a*) and histograms of all residuals ($n = 240$ (*b*)) and of residuals with two outliers removed ($n = 238$ (*c*)).

normality is a reasonable one. The two extreme observations were detected as outliers in Example 5.27.

☞ Exercises: E: 5.28d, 5.31e.

5.6.4 Robust estimation

Motivation of robust methods

If we apply OLS, then all the observations are weighted in a similar way. On the other hand, the regression model (5.55) with the dummy variable D_j effectively removes all effects of the jth observation on the estimate of β. If this observation is very influential but not very reliable, it may indeed make sense to remove it. Sometimes there are several or even a large number of outlying data points, and it may be undesirable to neglect them completely.

An alternative is to use another estimation criterion that assigns relatively less weight to extreme observations as compared to OLS. Such estimation methods are called *robust*, because the estimation results are relatively insensitive to changes in the data.

As a simple illustration, we first consider the situation where the data consist of a random sample y_i, $i = 1, \cdots, n$, and we want to estimate the centre of location of the population. This centre is more robustly estimated by the sample median than by the sample mean, as the following simulation example illustrates.

Example 5.29: Simulated Data of Normal and Student t(2) Distributions

To illustrate the idea of robust estimation we consider two data generating processes. The first one is the standard normal distribution N(0, 1). In this case the sample mean is an efficient estimator, and the median is inefficient. The second one is the Student t-distribution with two degrees of freedom, $t(2)$. This distribution has mean zero and infinite variance. It has very fat tails so that outliers occur frequently, and the mean is an inefficient estimator. Exhibit 5.41 shows summary statistics of simulated data from the two distributions. The sample sizes are $n = 10$, 25, 100, and 400, with 1000 replications for each sample size. For every replication the mean and median of the sample are computed as estimates of the centre of location, $\mu = 0$. The exhibit reports the range (the difference between the maximum and minimum values of these estimates over the 1000 replications) and the (non-centred) sample standard deviation $\sqrt{\sum \hat{\mu}_j^2/1000}$ over the replications. It clearly shows that the mean is the best estimator if the population

n	DGP	N(0, 1)	N(0, 1)	$t(2)$	$t(2)$
	Estimator	Mean	Median	Mean	Median
10	St. Dev.	0.322	0.383	1.015	0.445
	Range	2.092	3.145	18.903	3.457
25	St. Dev.	0.200	0.255	0.880	0.290
	Range	1.254	1.630	20.599	1.925
100	St. Dev.	0.098	0.126	0.325	0.135
	Range	0.617	0.795	4.720	0.984
400	St. Dev.	0.050	0.063	0.203	0.070
	Range	0.322	0.383	4.542	0.440

Exhibit 5.41 Simulated Data of Normal and Student $t(2)$ Distribution (Example 5.29)

Sample standard deviation and range of sample mean and sample median over 1000 simulation runs of two DGPs (N(0, 1) and $t(2)$) for different sample sizes ($n = 10$, 25, 100, and 400).

is normally distributed and that the median is best if the population has the $t(2)$ distribution. That is, for distributions with fat tails the median is a more robust estimator than the mean.

Robust estimation criteria

Now we consider the model $y_i = x_i'\beta + \varepsilon_i$ and we suppose that Assumptions 1–6 are satisfied. Further we suppose that β is estimated by minimizing a criterion function of the form

$$S(\hat{\beta}) = \sum_{i=1}^{n} G\left(y_i - x_i'\hat{\beta}\right) = \sum_{i=1}^{n} G(e_i), \tag{5.59}$$

where we write $e_i = y_i - x_i'\hat{\beta}$ for the residuals. The function G is assumed to be differentiable with derivative $g(e_i) = dG(e_i)/de_i$. The first order conditions for a minimum of (5.59) are given by

$$\frac{\partial S(\hat{\beta})}{\partial \hat{\beta}} = -\sum_{i=1}^{n} g(e_i)x_i = 0. \tag{5.60}$$

If one defines the weights $w_i = g(e_i)/e_i$, this can also be written as

$$\sum_{i=1}^{n} w_i e_i x_i = 0. \tag{5.61}$$

Ordinary least squares corresponds to the choice

$$G(e_i) = \frac{1}{2}e_i^2, \quad g(e_i) = e_i, \quad w_i = 1.$$

The function $g(e_i)$ measures the influence of outliers in the first order conditions (5.60) for the estimator $\hat{\beta}$. In ordinary least squares this influence is a linear function of the residuals. A more robust estimator—that is, an estimator that is less sensitive to outliers—is obtained by choosing

$$G(e_i) = |e_i|, \quad g(e_i) = \begin{cases} -1 & \text{for} \quad e_i < 0, \\ +1 & \text{for} \quad e_i > 0. \end{cases}$$

We call this criterion function the *least absolute deviation* (LAD). If the observations consist of a random sample—that is, $y_i = \mu + \varepsilon_i$ for $i = 1, \cdots, n$—then OLS gives $\hat{\mu} = \sum y_i/n$ and LAD gives $\hat{\mu} = \text{med}(y_i)$, the median of the observations (see Exercise 5.14). As our simulation in Example 5.29 illustrates, LAD is more robust than OLS, but some efficiency is lost if the disturbances are normally distributed. The attractive properties of both methods (OLS and LAD) can be combined by using, for instance, the following criterion:

$$G(e_i) = \begin{cases} \frac{1}{2}e_i^2 & \text{if} \quad |e_i| \leq c, \\ c|e_i| - \frac{1}{2}c^2 & \text{if} \quad |e_i| > c. \end{cases} \tag{5.62}$$

This criterion was proposed by Huber. The derivative of G is given by

$$g(e_i) = \begin{cases} -c & \text{if} \quad e_i < -c, \\ e_i & \text{if} \quad -c \leq e_i \leq c, \\ c & \text{if} \quad e_i > c. \end{cases} \tag{5.63}$$

The corresponding estimator of $\hat{\beta}$ gives a compromise between the efficiency (for normally distributed errors) of OLS (obtained for $c \to \infty$) and the robustness of LAD (obtained for $c \downarrow 0$). In Exhibit 5.42 the Huber criterion is compared with OLS and LAD. Relatively small residuals have a linear influence and constant weights, and large residuals have constant influence and declining weights. The influence of outliers is reduced because (5.63) imposes a threshold on the function $g(e_i)$.

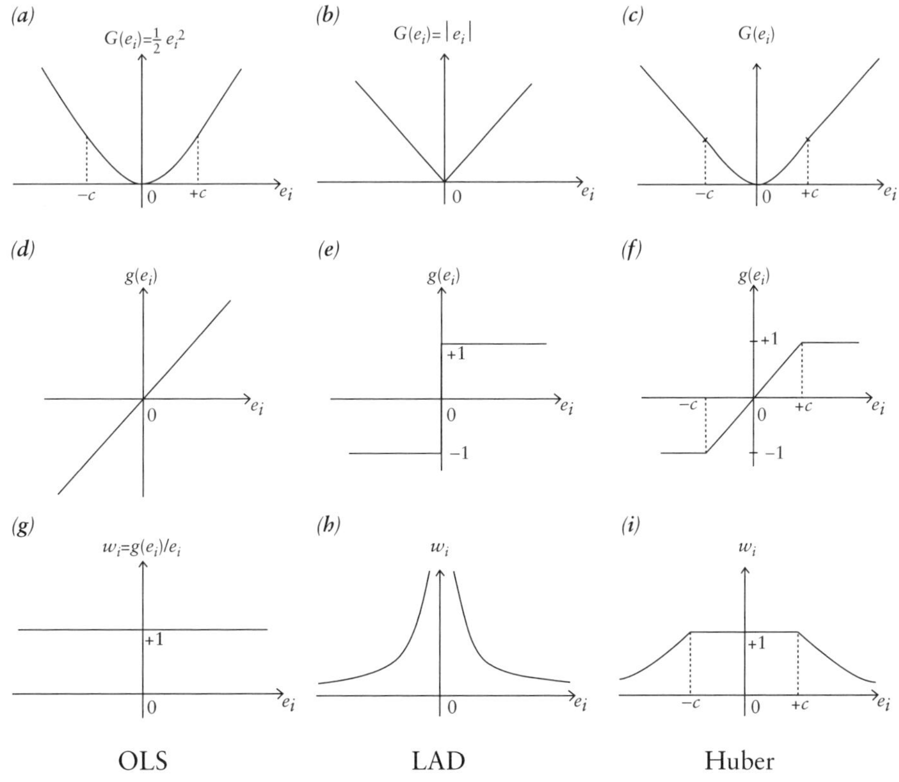

Exhibit 5.42 Three estimation criteria

Criterion functions (G in (a–c)), first order derivatives (influence functions g in (d–f)), and weights (w_i in $\Sigma w_i e_i x_i = 0$ in (g–i)) of three criteria, OLS ((a), (d), (g)), LAD ((b), (e), (h)), and Huber ((c), (f), (i)).

Remarks on statistical properties

In general, the equations (5.60) to compute the estimator $\hat{\beta}$ are non-linear and should be solved by numerical methods. The initial estimate is of importance and it is advisable to use a robust initial estimate, even if this may be inefficient. The statistical properties of this estimator can be derived by noting that (5.60) corresponds to a GMM estimator with moment functions $g_i = -g(e_i)x_i$ (see Section 4.4.2 (p. 253–4)). The estimator is consistent and, in large enough samples, approximate standard errors can be obtained from the asymptotic results on GMM in Section 4.4.3 (p. 258), provided that $E[g(\varepsilon_i)x_i] = 0$, see (4.61) (p. 253). If the regressors x_i are not stochastic this gives the condition

$$E[g(\varepsilon_i)] = 0.$$

For OLS, with $g(\varepsilon_i) = \varepsilon_i$, this is guaranteed by Assumption 2, as this states that $E[\varepsilon_i] = 0$. For LAD this condition means that $P(\varepsilon_i > 0) = P(\varepsilon_i < 0)$—that is, that the median of the distribution of ε_i is zero.

Interpretation of robust estimation in terms of ML

Robust estimation can also be interpreted in terms of maximum likelihood estimation by an appropriate choice of the probability distribution of the error terms ε_i. Let ε_i have density function f and let $l_i = \log(f(e_i))$, where $e_i = y_i - x_i'\hat{\beta}$ for a given estimate $\hat{\beta}$ of β. Then the log-likelihood is given by $\log L = \sum l_i = \sum \log(f(e_i))$, and ML corresponds to the minimization of $(-\log L)$ with first order conditions

$$-\frac{\partial \log L}{\partial \hat{\beta}} = -\sum_{i=1}^{n} \frac{\partial \log(f(e_i))}{\partial \hat{\beta}} = -\sum_{i=1}^{n} \frac{d \log(f(e_i))}{de_i} \frac{\partial e_i}{\partial \beta} = \sum_{i=1}^{n} \frac{f'(e_i)}{f(e_i)} x_i,$$

where $f'(e_i) = df(e_i)/de_i$ is the derivative of f. This corresponds to the equations (5.60) with

$$g(e_i) = -f'(e_i)/f(e_i).$$

In practice the density f of the disturbances is unknown. A criterion of the type (5.59) can be interpreted as postulating that $-f'(e_i)/f(e_i) = g(e_i)$ is a reasonable assumption to estimate β. For OLS this leads to $-f'(e_i)/f(e_i) = e_i$, with solution $f(e_i) = \frac{1}{\sqrt{2\pi}} e^{-\frac{1}{2}e_i^2}$, the standard normal distribution. For LAD this gives $-f'(e_i)/f(e_i) = \pm 1$ (the sign of e_i), with solution $f(e_i) = \frac{1}{2} e^{-|e_i|}$ (see also Exercise 5.14).

Interpretation of robust estimation in terms of WLS

The estimator $\hat{\beta}$ that minimizes (5.59) can also be interpreted in terms of weighted least squares. If the weights w_i in (5.61) are fixed, then these equations correspond to the first order conditions for minimizing the weighted least squares criterion $\sum_{i=1}^{n} w_i e_i^2$. So the weights w_i measure the relative importance of the squared errors e_i^2 in determining $\hat{\beta}$. This also motivates a simple iterative method for estimating β by means of the (robust) criterion (5.59). Start with weights $w_i = 1, i - 1, \cdots, n$, and estimate β by OLS with residuals e_i. Then compute $w_i = g(e_i)$ and estimate β by WLS. Iterate the computation of residuals e_i, weights w_i, and WLS estimates of β, until convergence.

Appropriate scaling in robust estimation

It is of course preferable that the results do not depend on the chosen scales of measurement of the variables. Let us consider the effect of rescaling the dependent variable y_i. If this variable is replaced by $y_i^* = ay_i$, with a a given constant, then we would like the estimates $\hat{\beta}$ to be replaced by $\hat{\beta}^* = a\hat{\beta}$, as in this case the fitted values are related by $\hat{y}_i^* = x_i'\hat{\beta}^* = ax_i'\hat{\beta} = a\hat{y}_i$. The criteria OLS and LAD satisfy this requirement. For other criterion functions this requirement is satisfied by replacing (5.59) by

$$S(\hat{\beta}) = \sum_{i=1}^{n} G\left(\frac{y_i - x_i'\hat{\beta}}{\sigma}\right),$$

where $\sigma^2 = E[\varepsilon_i^2] = \text{var}(y_i)$. For instance, for the Huber criterion (5.62) this means that c should be replaced by $c\sigma$.

In practice σ is unknown and has to be estimated. The usual OLS estimator of the variance may be sensitive for outliers. Let m denote the median of the n residuals $e_1, \cdots, e_n$; then a robust estimator of the standard deviation is given by

$$\hat{\sigma} = 1.483 \cdot \text{med}(|e_j - m|, j = 1, \cdots, n), \tag{5.64}$$

where 'med' denotes the median of the n values $|e_j - m|$. It is left as an exercise (see Exercise 5.12) to prove (for a simple case) that this gives a consistent estimator of σ if the observations are normally distributed.

This can be used to estimate the parameters β and σ by an iterative two-step method. In the first step σ is fixed and β is estimated robustly, with corresponding residuals e_i. In the second step, $\hat{\sigma}$ is estimated from the residuals e_i. This new estimate of σ can be used to compute new robust estimates of β, and so on, until the estimates converge.

Limiting the influence of observations with large leverage

Finally we note that by an appropriate choice of the function g in the criterion (5.60) the influence of large residuals can be limited, but the explanatory variables can still be influential because of the linear term x_i. This influence may also be bounded—for example, by replacing the 'normal equations' (5.60) by

$$\sum_{i=1}^{n} g_1(x_i) g_2\left(\frac{y_i - x_i'\hat{\beta}}{\hat{\sigma}}\right) = 0.$$

For instance, one can take $g_1(x_i) = g(x_i'(X'X)^{-1}x_i) = g(h_i)$ with h_i the leverage in (5.54) and with g chosen as in (5.63) with $c = k/n$ (the mean value of the leverages).

☞ **Exercises:** T: 5.12d, 5.14, 5.15; E: 5.29e.

5.6.5 Summary

In least squares the deviations from the postulated relation between dependent and independent variables are penalized in a quadratic way. This means that observations that deviate much from the general pattern may have an excessive influence on the parameter estimates. To investigate the presence of such influential observations and to reduce their influence, one can proceed as follows.

- A first impression may be obtained by inspecting the histogram of the least squares residuals and by the Jarque–Bera test on normality. Note, however, that OLS is not a reliable method to detect influential observations.
- Influential data may be detected by considering the leverages, studentized residuals, dffits, and dfbetas of the individual observations.
- If some of the observations deviate a lot from the overall pattern, one should try to understand the possible causes. This may suggest, for instance, additional relevant explanatory variables or another choice for the distribution of the disturbances. In some cases it may also be that some of the reported data are unreliable, so that they should be excluded in estimation.
- If the deviating observations are a realistic aspect of the data (as is the case in many situations), one may wish to limit their influence by applying a robust estimation method.

- The choice of the robust estimation method (corresponding to solving the equations $\sum g(e_i)x_i = 0$) can be based on ideas concerning appropriate weights w_i of the individual observations (by taking $g(e_i) = w_i e_i$) or on ideas concerning the probability distribution f of the disturbances (by taking $g(e_i) = -f'(e_i)/f(e_i)$ where $f'(e_i) = df(e_i)/de_i$).

5.7 Endogenous regressors and instrumental variables

5.7.1 Instrumental variables and two-stage least squares

Motivation

Until now we have assumed either that the regressors x_i are fixed or that they are stochastic and exogenous in the sense that there is no correlation between the regressors and the disturbance terms. It is intuitively clear that, if x_i and ε_i are mutually correlated, it will be hard to distinguish their individual contributions to the outcome of the dependent variable $y_i = x_i'\beta + \varepsilon_i$. In Section 4.1.3 (p. 194–6) we showed that OLS is inconsistent in this situation.

We briefly discuss two examples that will be treated in greater detail later in this section. The first example is concerned with price movements on financial markets. If we relate the returns of one financial asset y (in our example AAA bonds) to the returns of another asset x (in our example Treasury Bill notes) by means of the simple regression model

$$y_i = \alpha + \beta x_i + \varepsilon_i,$$

then x_i and ε_i may well be correlated. This is the case if the factors ε_i that affect the bond rate, such as the general sentiment in the market, also affect the Treasury Bill rate. For instance, unforeseen increased uncertainties in international trade may have a simultaneous upward effect both on bond rates and on interest rates. We will consider this possible endogeneity of Treasury Bill rates in later examples in this section (see Examples 5.30, 5.32, and 5.33).

As a second example, for many goods the price and traded quantity are determined jointly in the market. A higher price may lead to lower demand, whereas a higher demand may lead to higher prices. If we relate price x and quantity y by the simple regression model $y_i = \alpha + \beta x_i + \varepsilon_i$, then x_i and ε_i may well be correlated. For instance, the demand may increase because of higher wealth of consumers, and this may at the same time increase the price. We will consider this possible endogeneity of the price by considering the market for motor gasoline consumption in later examples (see Examples 5.31 and 5.34).

OLS requires exogenous regressors

In the multivariate regression model $y_i = x_i'\beta + \varepsilon_i$, the dependent variable y_i is modelled in terms of k explanatory variables $x_i' = (1, x_{2i}, \cdots, x_{ki})$. Under the standard Assumptions 1–6 of Section 3.1.4 (p. 125), it is assumed that y_i is a random variable, but that the values of x_i are 'fixed'. In many situations the outcomes of the variables x_i are partly random. This was analysed in Section 4.1 under Assumption 1* of stability — that is,

$$\text{plim}\left(\frac{1}{n}X'X\right) = Q \tag{5.65}$$

exists with Q a $k \times k$ invertible matrix. In Section 4.1.3 (p. 194) we derived that OLS is consistent in this case if and only if the explanatory variables are (weakly) exogenous — that is, the variables should satisfy the orthogonality condition $\text{plim}(\frac{1}{n}X'\varepsilon) = 0$. In this case the results that were obtained under the assumption of fixed regressors (including the diagnostic analysis in Sections 5.1–5.6) carry over to the case of stochastic exogenous regressors, by interpreting the results conditional on the given outcomes of the regressors in the $n \times k$ matrix X. For instance, the statistical properties $E[b] = \beta$ and $\text{var}(b) = \sigma^2(X'X)^{-1}$ should then be interpreted as $E[b|X] = \beta$ and $\text{var}(b|X) = \sigma^2(X'X)^{-1}$. This was also discussed in Section 4.1.2 (p. 191–2).

Consequences of endogenous regressors

We will now consider the situation where one or more of the regressors is *endogenous* in the sense that

$$\text{plim}\left(\frac{1}{n}X'\varepsilon\right) \neq 0. \tag{5.66}$$

This means that the random variation in X is correlated with the random variation ε in y. In such a situation it is difficult to isolate the effect of X on y because variations in X are related to variations in y in two ways, directly via the term $X\beta$ but also indirectly via changes in the term ε. For instance, in a cross section of cities the per capita crime (y) may very well be positively correlated with the per capita police force (x), in which case a regression of y on x gives a positive OLS estimate of the effect of police on crime. The reason is that in the model $y_i = \alpha + \beta x_i + \varepsilon_i$ cities with high crime rates ($\varepsilon_i > 0$) tend to have larger police forces (values of x_i larger than average). Clearly, in such a situation the effect of police on crime cannot be estimated reliably by OLS (see also Exercise 5.23). Stated in statistical terms, if one or more of the regressors is endogenous, then OLS is no longer consistent and the conventional results (t-test, F-tests, diagnostic tests in previous sections of this chapter) are no longer valid.

The use of instruments

A consistent estimator can be obtained if one can identify *instruments*. A set of m observed variables $z_i' = (z_{1i}, \cdots, z_{mi})$ is called a set of instruments if the following three conditions are satisfied, where Z denotes the $n \times m$ matrix with rows $z_i', i = 1, \cdots, n$:

$$\text{plim}\left(\frac{1}{n}Z'\varepsilon\right) = 0, \tag{5.67}$$

$$\text{plim}\left(\frac{1}{n}Z'X\right) = Q_{zx}, \qquad \text{rank}(Q_{zx}) = k, \tag{5.68}$$

$$\text{plim}\left(\frac{1}{n}Z'Z\right) = Q_{zz}, \qquad \text{rank}(Q_{zz}) = m. \tag{5.69}$$

The condition (5.67) means that the instruments should be exogenous. For example, this is satisfied (under weak additional conditions) when the instruments are uncorrelated with the disturbances in the sense that

$$E[z_i\varepsilon_i] = 0, \qquad i = 1, \cdots, n. \tag{5.70}$$

The condition (5.68) means that the instruments should be sufficiently correlated with the regressors. This is called the *rank condition*. As Q_{zx} is an $m \times k$ matrix, this requires that $m \geq k$—that is, the number of instruments should be at least as large as the number of regressors. This is called the *order condition* for the instruments. The stability condition (5.69) is similar to (5.65).

How to find instruments?

Before we describe the instrumental variable estimator (below) and its statistical properties (in the next section), we first discuss the question of how to find instruments. First of all, one should analyse which of the explanatory variables are endogenous. If the jth explanatory variable is exogenous, so that $\text{plim}\left(\frac{1}{n}\sum_{i=1}^{n} x_{ji}\varepsilon_i\right) = 0$, then this variable should be included in the set of instruments. For instance, the constant term should always be included, together with all other exogenous regressors. If k_0 of the regressors are endogenous, one should find at least k_0 additional instruments. One option is to formulate additional equations that explain the dependence of the endogenous variables in terms of exogenous variables. This leads to simultaneous equation models that are discussed in Chapter 7. In many cases it is too demanding to specify such additional equations, and instead one selects a number of variables that are supposed to satisfy the conditions (5.67)–(5.69). In Section 5.7.3 we describe a test for the validity of these conditions.

In practice the choice of instruments is often based on economic insight, as we will illustrate by means of two examples at the end of this section.

Derivation of IV estimator

T

To describe the *instrumental variable (IV) estimator*, we assume that condition (5.70) is satisfied. This corresponds to m moment conditions. The IV estimator is defined as the GMM estimator corresponding to these moment conditions. In the exactly identified case ($m = k$), the IV estimator b_{IV} is given by the solution of the m equations $\frac{1}{n}\sum_{i=1}^{n} z_i(y_i - x_i' b_{IV}) = 0$—that is,

$$b_{IV} = \left(\sum_{i=1}^{n} z_i x_i'\right)^{-1} \sum_{i=1}^{n} z_i y_i = (Z'X)^{-1}Z'y.$$

In the over-identified case ($m > k$), the results in Section 4.4.3 (p. 256) show that the efficient estimator corresponding to these moment conditions is obtained by weighted least squares. More particularly, the GMM criterion function $\frac{1}{n}G_n' W G_n$ in (4.63) with $G_n = \sum_{i=1}^{n} z_i(y_i - x_i'\beta) = Z'(y - X\beta)$ leads to the criterion function

$$S(\beta) = \frac{1}{n}(y - X\beta)' Z W Z'(y - X\beta),$$

where the weighting matrix W is equal to the inverse of the covariance matrix $J_* = E[z_i\varepsilon_i(z_i\varepsilon_i)'] = E[\varepsilon_i^2 z_i z_i']$. Under weak regularity conditions, a consistent estimator of these weights is given by $W = J^{-1}$, where $J = \frac{\sigma^2}{n}\sum_{i=1}^{n} z_i z_i' = \frac{\sigma^2}{n} Z'Z$. As the scale factor σ^2 has no effect on the location of the minimum of $S(\beta)$, we obtain the criterion function

$$S_{IV}(\beta) = (y - X\beta)' Z(Z'Z)^{-1} Z'(y - X\beta) = (y - X\beta)' P_Z (y - X\beta), \qquad (5.71)$$

where $P_Z = Z(Z'Z)^{-1}Z'$ is the projection matrix corresponding to regression on the instruments Z. The first order conditions for a minimum are given by

$$\frac{\partial S_{IV}(\beta)}{\partial \beta} = -2X'P_Z(y - X\beta) = 0.$$

The IV estimator and two-stage least squares

The foregoing analysis shows that the IV estimator is given by

$$b_{IV} = (X'P_Z X)^{-1} X'P_Z y. \tag{5.72}$$

This estimator has an interesting interpretation. We are interested in the coefficients β in $y = X\beta + \varepsilon$, but OLS is inconsistent because of (5.66). If the regressors would have been Z instead of X, then (5.67) means that OLS is consistent. The idea is to replace X by linear combinations of Z that approximate X as well as possible. This best approximation is obtained by regressing every column of X on the instruments matrix Z. The fitted values of this regression are

$$\hat{X} = Z(Z'Z)^{-1}Z'X = P_Z X. \tag{5.73}$$

Then β is estimated by regressing y on $\hat{X}$, which gives the following estimator of β:

$$(\hat{X}'\hat{X})^{-1}\hat{X}'y = (X'P_Z X)^{-1}X'P_Z y = b_{IV}. \tag{5.74}$$

So the IV estimator can be computed by two successive regressions. The IV estimator is therefore also called the *two-stage least squares* estimator, abbreviated as 2SLS.

> **Two-stage least squares estimates of the parameters β (2SLS)**
>
> - *Stage 1.* Regress each column of X on Z, with fitted values $\hat{X} = Z(Z'Z)^{-1}Z'X$.
> - *Stage 2.* Regress y on $\hat{X}$, with parameter estimates $b_{IV} = (\hat{X}'\hat{X})^{-1}\hat{X}'y$.

Example 5.30: **Interest and Bond Rates (continued)**

As an illustration we consider the interest and bond rate data introduced in Example 5.11. We will discuss (i) the possible endogeneity of the explanatory variable (the interest rate), (ii) a suggestion for possible instruments, and (iii) the results of IV estimation with these instruments.

(i) Possible endogeneity of the interest rate

In foregoing sections we analysed the relation between monthly changes in the AAA bond rate (y_i) and in the short-term interest rate (the three-month Treasury Bill rate, (x_i)) by the model

$$y_i = \alpha + \beta x_i + \varepsilon_i, \quad i = 1, \cdots, n.$$

It may very well be that the factors ε_i that cause changes in the AAA bond rate reflect general financial conditions that also affect the Treasury Bill rate. If this is the case, then x_i is not exogenous and OLS is not consistent.

Panel 1: Correlogram of explanatory var. DUS3MT
Sample 1980.01–1999.12 (240 observations)

Lag	AC	Q-Stat	Prob
1	0.279	18.938	0.000
2	−0.185	27.259	0.000
3	−0.155	33.156	0.000
4	−0.102	35.713	0.000
5	0.037	36.056	0.000
6	−0.167	42.972	0.000
7	−0.157	49.110	0.000
8	0.155	55.157	0.000
9	0.264	72.725	0.000
10	0.048	73.318	0.000
11	−0.110	76.382	0.000
12	−0.247	91.897	0.000

Panel 2: Dependent Variable: DUS3MT
Method: Least Squares
Sample: 1980:01 1999:12
Included observations: 240

Variable	Coefficient	Std. Error	t-Statistic	Prob.
C	−0.026112	0.039009	−0.669400	0.5039
DUS3MT(−1)	0.358145	0.062307	5.748060	0.0000
DUS3MT(−2)	−0.282601	0.062266	−4.538625	0.0000
R-squared	0.151651			

Panel 3: Dependent Variable: DAAA
Method: Least Squares
Sample: 1980:01 1999:12
Included observations: 240

Variable	Coefficient	Std. Error	t-Statistic	Prob.
C	−0.004558	0.015440	−0.295200	0.7681
DUS3MT	0.306453	0.023692	12.93503	0.0000
R-squared	0.412803			

Panel 4: Dependent Variable: DAAA
Method: Instrumental Variables
Sample: 1980:01 1999:12
Included observations: 240
Instrument list: C DUS3MT(−1) DUS3MT(−2)

Variable	Coefficient	Std. Error	t-Statistic	Prob.
C	−0.008453	0.016572	−0.510085	0.6105
DUS3MT	0.169779	0.064952	2.613906	0.0095
R-squared	0.330694			

Exhibit 5.43 Interest and Bond Rates (Example 5.30)

Correlations of explanatory variable (DUS3MT) with its lagged values (Panels 1 and 2) and regression model estimated by OLS (Panel 3) and by IV (Panel 4).

(ii) Possible instruments

If financial markets are efficient, this means that all past information is processed in the current prices. In this case the current value of ε_i is uncorrelated with the past values of both y_{i-j} and x_{i-j} for all $j \geq 1$. We will assume that the disturbance term ε_i is correlated with the current change x_i in the Treasury Bill rate, but not with past changes x_{i-1}, x_{i-2}, and so on. Then these past changes can serve as instruments. In Example 5.33 we will test the exogeneity condition (5.67)—that is, the condition that $E[x_{i-1}\varepsilon_i] = E[x_{i-2}\varepsilon_i] = 0$.

(iii) Results of IV estimation

We now analyse the interest and bond rate data over the period from January 1980 to December 1999 ($n = 240$). To check the rank condition (5.68), Panel 1 of Exhibit 5.43 shows that the variable x_i is correlated with its past values. As instruments we take x_{i-1} and x_{i-2}, the one- and two-month lagged changes in the Treasury Bill rate. The regression of x_i on x_{i-1} and x_{i-2} has an $R^2 = 0.15$ (see Panel 2 of Exhibit 5.43). The condition (5.68) is satisfied, although the correlations are not so large. Panel 4 reports the IV estimates with instruments $z_i' = (1, x_{i-1}, x_{i-2})$, and for comparison Panel 3 reports the OLS estimates. The estimates of the slope parameter β differ quite substantially. A further analysis is given in Example 5.33 at the end of Section 5.7.3.

XM531MGC

Example 5.31: Motor Gasoline Consumption

For many goods, the price and traded quantities are determined jointly in the market process. It may well be that price and quantity influence each other, with higher prices leading to lower demand and with higher demand leading to higher prices. We will analyse this for the market of motor gasoline in the USA. We will discuss (i) the data and (ii) possible instruments and corresponding IV estimates.

(i) The data

We consider the relation between gasoline consumption, gasoline price, and disposable income in the USA. Yearly data on these variables and three price indices (of public transport, new cars, and used cars) are available over the period 1970–99. Exhibit 5.44 (*a*–*c*) shows time plots of these three variables (all in logarithms), and a scatter diagram (*d*) and a partial scatter diagram (*e*) (after removing the influence of income) of consumption against price.

We are interested in the demand equation for motor gasoline, in particular, in the effects of price and income on demand. We postulate the linear demand function

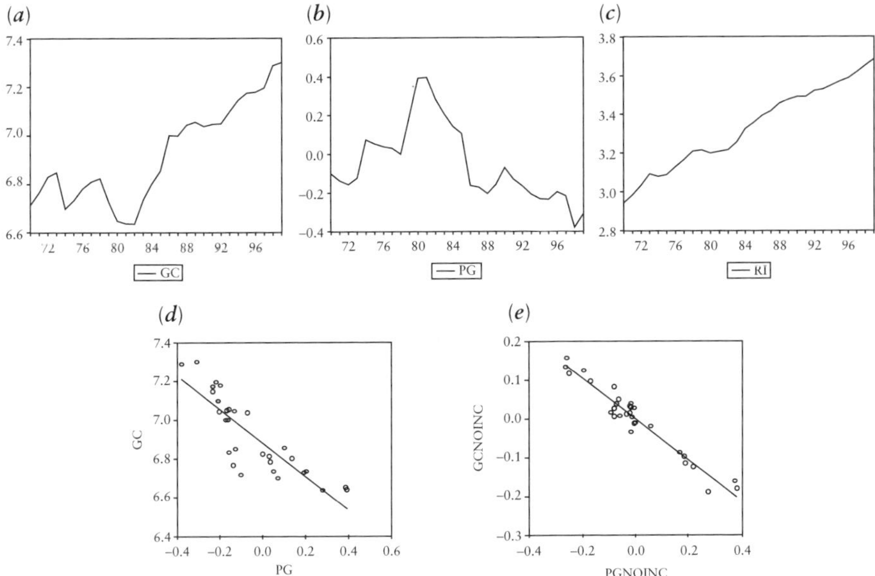

Exhibit 5.44 Motor Gasoline Consumption (Example 5.31)

Time plots of real gasoline consumption (GC (*a*)), real gasoline price (PG (*b*)) and real income (RI (*c*)), all in logarithms, and scatter diagram of consumption against price (*d*) and partial scatter diagram after removing the influence of income (*e*).

$$GC_i = \alpha + \beta PG_i + \gamma RI_i + \varepsilon_i, \quad i = 1, \cdots, 30,$$

where GC stands for gasoline consumption, PG for the gasoline price index, and RI for disposable income (all measured in real terms and taken in logarithms).

The USA is a major player on the world oil market, so that the fluctuations ε_i in US gasoline consumption could affect the gasoline price. If this is the case, then PG is not exogenous, and OLS provides inconsistent estimates.

(ii) Possible instruments and corresponding IV estimates

As possible instruments we consider (apart from the constant term and the regressor RI) the real price indices of public transport (RPT), of new cars (RPN), and of used cars (RPU). In Example 5.34 we will test whether these variables are indeed exogenous.

Exhibit 5.45 shows the results of OLS (in Panel 1) and IV (in Panel 2). The estimates do not differ much, which can be taken as an indication that the gasoline price can be considered as an exogenous variable for gasoline consumption in the US. In Example 5.34 we will formally test whether the price is exogenous or endogenous.

Panel 1: Dependent Variable: GC
Method: Least Squares
Sample: 1970 1999
Included observations: 30

Variable	Coefficient	Std. Error	t-Statistic	Prob.
C	4.985997	0.081101	61.47914	0.0000
PG	−0.527578	0.026319	−20.04565	0.0000
RI	0.573220	0.024511	23.38644	0.0000
R-squared	0.987155			

Panel 2: Dependent Variable: GC
Method: Instrumental Variables
Sample: 1970 1999
Included observations: 30
Instrument list: C RPT RPN RPU RI

Variable	Coefficient	Std. Error	t-Statistic	Prob.
C	5.013700	0.083911	59.75035	0.0000
PG	−0.544450	0.028950	−18.80669	0.0000
RI	0.564662	0.025389	22.24005	0.0000
R-squared	0.986959			

Panel 3: Dependent Variable: PG
Method: Least Squares
Sample: 1970 1999
Included observations: 30

Variable	Coefficient	Std. Error	t-Statistic	Prob.
C	7.740963	0.833698	9.285095	0.0000
RPT	−0.808004	0.191221	−4.225499	0.0003
RPN	−3.527853	0.351973	−10.02308	0.0000
RPU	0.233078	0.183108	1.272898	0.2148
RI	−2.298421	0.247071	−9.302668	0.0000
R-squared	0.886815			

Exhibit 5.45 Motor Gasoline Consumption (Example 5.31)

OLS of gasoline consumption (GC) on price of gasoline (PG) and income (RI) (Panel 1), IV of consumption on price and income using five instruments, the constant term, income, and three real price indices (of public transport (RPT), new cars (RPN), and used cars (RPU) (Panel 2)), and relation between gasoline price and the five instruments (Panel 3).

 Exercises: T: 5.16a, b, 5.18; S: 5.23a–d.

5.7.2 Statistical properties of IV estimators

Derivation of consistency of IV estimators

T

We consider the properties of the IV estimator (5.72) for the model $y = X\beta + \varepsilon$ with $n \times m$ instrument matrix Z. Referring to Section 3.1.4 (p. 125–6), we suppose that Assumptions 2–6 are satisfied and that Assumption 1 is replaced by the five (asymptotic) conditions (5.65)–(5.69). Under these conditions the IV estimator is consistent. To prove this, we write (5.72) as

$$b_{IV} = \left(X'Z(Z'Z)^{-1}Z'X\right)^{-1}X'Z(Z'Z)^{-1}Z'(X\beta+\varepsilon)$$
$$= \beta + \left(\frac{1}{n}X'Z\left(\frac{1}{n}Z'Z\right)^{-1}\frac{1}{n}Z'X\right)^{-1}\frac{1}{n}X'Z\left(\frac{1}{n}Z'Z\right)^{-1}\frac{1}{n}Z'\varepsilon. \qquad (5.75)$$

Because of the conditions (5.67)–(5.69) we obtain the probability limit of b_{IV} as

$$\text{plim}(b_{IV}) = \beta + (Q'_{zx}Q_{zz}^{-1}Q_{zx})^{-1}Q'_{zx}Q_{zz}^{-1}0 = \beta.$$

This shows that the exogeneity of the instruments Z is crucial to obtain consistency. Note that the IV estimator is also consistent if Assumptions 3 and 4 are not satisfied (that is, for heteroskedastic or serially correlated errors), as long as the instruments are exogenous. However, Assumptions 3 and 4 are needed in our derivation of the asymptotic distribution of b_{IV}.

Derivation of asymptotic distribution

T

We will assume (in analogy with (4.6) in Section 4.1.4 (p. 196)) that

$$\frac{1}{\sqrt{n}}Z'\varepsilon \xrightarrow{d} \text{N}(0, \sigma^2 Q_{zz}).$$

Using the notation $b_{IV} = \beta + A_n(\frac{1}{n}Z'\varepsilon)$ for the last expression in (5.75), we can rewrite (5.75) as $\sqrt{n}(b_{IV} - \beta) = A_n \cdot \frac{1}{\sqrt{n}}Z'\varepsilon$, where A_n has probability limit $A = (Q'_{zx}Q_{zz}^{-1}Q_{zx})^{-1}Q'_{zx}Q_{zz}^{-1}$. Combining these results and using $AQ_{zz}A' = (Q'_{zx}Q_{zz}^{-1}Q_{zx})^{-1}$ gives

$$\sqrt{n}(b_{IV} - \beta) \xrightarrow{d} \text{N}\left(0, \sigma^2\left(Q'_{zx}Q_{zz}^{-1}Q_{zx}\right)^{-1}\right).$$

In large enough finite samples, b_{IV} is approximately normally distributed with mean β and covariance matrix $\frac{\sigma^2}{n}(\frac{1}{n}X'Z(\frac{1}{n}Z'Z)^{-1}\frac{1}{n}Z'X)^{-1} = \sigma^2(X'P_ZX)^{-1}$. With the notation (5.73) this gives

$$b_{IV} \approx \text{N}\left(\beta, \sigma^2(X'P_ZX)^{-1}\right) = \text{N}\left(\beta, \sigma^2(\hat{X}'\hat{X})^{-1}\right). \qquad (5.76)$$

The instrumental variable estimator is relatively more efficient if the instruments Z are more highly correlated with the explanatory variables. In practice, the exogeneity condition (5.67) is often satisfied only for variables that are relatively weakly correlated with the explanatory variables. Such *weak instruments* lead to relatively large variances of the IV estimator.

To use the above results in testing we need a consistent estimator of the variance σ^2. Let $e_{IV} = y - Xb_{IV}$ be the IV residuals; then a consistent estimator is given by

$$s_{IV}^2 = \frac{1}{n-k} e'_{IV} e_{IV} = \frac{1}{n-k} (y - Xb_{IV})'(y - Xb_{IV}). \qquad (5.77)$$

If the IV estimator is computed as in (5.74)—that is, by regressing y on $\hat{X}$—then the conventional OLS expression for the covariance matrix is not correct. This would give $\hat{s}^2(\hat{X}'\hat{X})^{-1}$ with $\hat{s}^2 = \frac{1}{n-k}(y - \hat{X}b_{IV})'(y - \hat{X}b_{IV})$, and this estimator of σ^2 is not consistent (see Exercise 5.16).

T

Remark on finite sample statistical properties

The above analysis is based on asymptotic results. As concerns finite sample properties, we mention that in finite samples the pth moments of b_{IV} exist if and only if $p < m - k + 1$. In the exactly identified case there holds $m = k$, so that the finite sample probability distribution of b_{IV} does not have a well-defined mean or variance. The covariance matrix of b_{IV} exists if and only if $m \geq k + 2$. This result could suggest that it is always best to incorporate as many instruments as possible. Adding instruments also leads to asymptotically smaller variances, provided that all additional instruments are exogenous. However, if the additional instruments are weak, then the finite sample distribution may very well deteriorate. In practice it is often better to search for a sufficient number of good instruments than for a large number of relatively weak instruments.

Derivation of the *F*-test in IV estimation

Tests on the individual significance of coefficients can be performed by conventional t-tests based on (5.76) and (5.77). An F-test for joint linear restrictions can be performed along the lines of Section 3.4.1 (p. 161–2). To derive the expression for this test we use some results of matrix algebra (see Appendix A, Section A.6 (p. 737)). There it is proved that the $n \times n$ projection matrix $P_Z = Z(Z'Z)^{-1}Z'$ of rank m can be written in terms of an $m \times n$ matrix K as

$$P_Z = K'K, \quad \text{with } KK' = I_m,$$

where I_m is the $m \times m$ identity matrix. Define the $m \times 1$ vector $y^* = Ky$ and the $m \times k$ matrix $X^* = KX$. The instrumental variable criterion (5.71) can then be written as

$$S_{IV}(\beta) = (y - X\beta)'K'K(y - X\beta) = (y^* - X^*\beta)'(y^* - X^*\beta).$$

If $y = X\beta + \varepsilon$ with $\varepsilon \sim \mathrm{N}(0, \sigma^2 I_n)$, then

$$y^* = X^*\beta + \varepsilon^*, \quad \varepsilon^* \sim \mathrm{N}(0, \sigma^2 KK') = \mathrm{N}(0, \sigma^2 I_m).$$

This shows that IV estimation in the model $y = X\beta + \varepsilon$ is equivalent to applying OLS in the transformed model $y^* = X^*\beta + \varepsilon^*$. Let the unrestricted IV estimator be denoted by b_{IV} and the restricted IV estimator by b_{RIV}, with corresponding residuals $e^* = y^* - X^* b_{IV} = K(y - Xb_{IV}) = Ke_{IV}$ and $e_R^* = y^* - X^* b_{RIV} = K(y - Xb_{RIV}) = Ke_{RIV}$. If the g restrictions of the null hypothesis hold true, then the results in Section 3.4.1 (p. 161–2) imply that

$$\left(e_R^{*\prime} e_R^* - e^{*\prime} e^*\right)/\sigma^2 = \left(e'_{RIV} K' K e_{RIV} - e'_{IV} K' K e_{IV}\right)/\sigma^2$$
$$= \left(e'_{RIV} P_Z e_{RIV} - e'_{IV} P_Z e_{IV}\right)/\sigma^2 \approx \chi^2(g).$$

If we replace σ^2 by the consistent estimator (5.77), then we get

$$F = \frac{\left(e'_{RIV} P_Z e_{RIV} - e'_{IV} P_Z e_{IV}\right)/g}{e'_{IV} e_{IV}/(n-k)} \approx F_{(g,\, n-k)}.$$

This differs from the standard expression (3.50) for the F-test, as in the numerator the IV residuals are weighted with P_Z.

Computation of the *F*-test

It is computationally more convenient to perform the following regressions. First regress every column of X on Z with fitted values $\hat{X}$ as in (5.73). Then perform two regressions of y on $\hat{X}$, one without restrictions (with residuals denoted by $\hat{e}$) and one with the restrictions of the null hypothesis imposed (with residuals denoted by $\hat{e}_R$). Then

$$F = \frac{\left(\hat{e}'_R \hat{e}_R - \hat{e}'\hat{e}\right)/g}{e'_{IV} e_{IV}/(n-k)}. \tag{5.78}$$

The proof that this leads to the same F-value as the foregoing expression is left as an exercise (see Exercise 5.16).

Example 5.32: **Interest and Bond Rates (continued)**

We continue our previous analysis of the interest and bond rate data in Example 5.30. The model is

$$y_i = \alpha + \beta x_i + \varepsilon_i,$$

with y_i the monthly AAA bond rate changes and x_i the monthly Treasury Bill rate changes. As instruments we take again $z'_i = (1, x_{i-1}, x_{i-2})$. Now we test whether the AAA bond rate will on average remain the same if the Treasury Bill rate is fixed. This seems to be a natural assumption. So we test the null hypothesis that $\alpha = 0$. Panel 1 of Exhibit 5.46 shows the t-value obtained by IV—that is, $t_{IV}(\hat{\alpha}) = -0.510$. So the null hypothesis is not rejected. Note that if we compute the IV estimate by regressing y on $\hat{X}$ as in (5.74), then the reported t-value becomes -0.42 (see Panel 3 of Exhibit 5.46), so this t-value is not correct. Exhibit 5.46 also contains the regressions needed for (5.78), with sums of squared residuals $\hat{e}'_R\hat{e}_R = 22.717$ (Panel 4), $\hat{e}'\hat{e} = 22.700$ (Panel 3), and $e'_{IV}e_{IV} = 15.491$ (Panel 1). So the F-test for $\alpha = 0$ becomes

Panel 1: Dependent Variable: DAAA
Method: Instrumental Variables
Sample: 1980:01 1999:12
Included observations: 240
Instrument list: C DUS3MT(−1) DUS3MT(−2)

Variable	Coefficient	Std. Error	t-Statistic	Prob.
C	−0.008453	0.016572	−0.510085	0.6105
DUS3MT	0.169779	0.064952	2.613906	0.0095
R-squared	0.330694	Sum squared resid		15.49061

Panel 2: Dependent Variable: DUS3MT
Method: Least Squares
Sample: 1980:01 1999:12
Included observations: 240

Variable	Coefficient	Std. Error	t-Statistic	Prob.
C	−0.026112	0.039009	−0.669400	0.5039
DUS3MT(−1)	0.358145	0.062307	5.748060	0.0000
DUS3MT(−2)	−0.282601	0.062266	−4.538625	0.0000
R-squared	0.151651	Sum squared resid		86.30464

Panel 3: Dependent Variable: DAAA
Method: Least Squares
Sample: 1980:01 1999:12
Included observations: 240

Variable	Coefficient	Std. Error	t-Statistic	Prob.
C	−0.008453	0.020060	−0.421374	0.6739
XHAT	0.169779	0.078626	2.159311	0.0318
R-squared	0.019214	Sum squared resid		22.69959

Panel 4: Dependent Variable: DAAA
Method: Least Squares
Sample: 1980:01 1999:12
Included observations: 240

Variable	Coefficient	Std. Error	t-Statistic	Prob.
XHAT	0.173480	0.078000	2.224107	0.0271
R-squared	0.018483	Sum squared resid		22.71653

Exhibit 5.46 Interest and Bond Rates (Example 5.32)

Model for AAA bond rates estimated by IV (Panel 1), first step of 2SLS (Panel 2, construction of $\hat{X}$, denoted by XHAT, by regressing DUS3MT on three instruments—that is, the constant term and the 1 and 2 lagged values of DUS3MT), second step of 2SLS (Panel 3, regression of AAA bond rates on XHAT), and regression of AAA bond rates on XHAT in restricted model without constant term (Panel 4). The sum of squared residuals in Panels 1, 3, and 4 is used in the F-test for the significance of the constant term.

$$F = \frac{(22.717 - 22.700)/1}{15.491/(240 - 2)} = 0.261, \quad P = 0.611.$$

This is equal to the square of the IV t-value in Panel 1, $F = t_{IV}^2(\hat{\alpha})$, and both tests do not lead to rejection of the hypothesis that $\alpha = 0$.

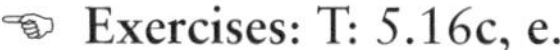

Exercises: T: 5.16c, e.

5.7.3 Tests for exogeneity and validity of instruments

Motivation of exogeneity tests

If some of the regressors are endogenous, then OLS is not consistent but IV is consistent. On the other hand, if the regressors are exogenous, then OLS is consistent and (under the usual assumptions) more efficient than IV in the sense that $\text{var}(b_{IV}) \geq \text{var}(b)$, because $(X'P_Z X)^{-1} \geq (X'X)^{-1}$ (see Exercise 5.16). So OLS will be preferred if the regressors are exogenous (or weakly endogenous in the sense that the correlations in (5.66) are small) and IV will be better if the regressors are (too strongly) endogenous. The choice between these two estimators can be based on a test for the exogeneity of the regressors. So we want to test the null hypothesis of *exogeneity*—that is,

$$\text{plim}\left(\frac{1}{n} X'\varepsilon\right) = 0, \tag{5.79}$$

against the alternative of endogeneity (5.66) that $\text{plim}(\frac{1}{n} X'\varepsilon) \neq 0$. If the assumption of exogeneity is not rejected, we can apply OLS, otherwise it may be better to use IV to prevent large biases due to the inconsistency of OLS for endogenous regressors.

Derivation of test based on comparison of OLS and IV

A simple idea is the following. If the regressors in $y = X\beta + \varepsilon$ are exogenous, then OLS and IV are both consistent and the respective estimators b and b_{IV} of β should not differ very much (in large enough samples). This suggests basing the test on the difference $d = b_{IV} - b$. Using (5.74) and the fact that $\hat{X}'X = X'P_Z X = \hat{X}'\hat{X}$, we get

$$b = (X'X)^{-1}X'y = \beta + (X'X)^{-1}X'\varepsilon,$$

$$b_{IV} = (\hat{X}'\hat{X})^{-1}\hat{X}'y = \beta + (\hat{X}'\hat{X})^{-1}\hat{X}'\varepsilon.$$

So $d = b_{IV} - b = (\frac{1}{n}\hat{X}'\hat{X})^{-1}\frac{1}{n}\hat{X}'\varepsilon - (\frac{1}{n}X'X)^{-1}\frac{1}{n}X'\varepsilon$. If the null hypothesis (5.79) holds true, then $E[d] \approx 0$ and

$$\begin{aligned}\mathrm{var}(d) &\approx \mathrm{var}\big((\hat{X}'\hat{X})^{-1}\hat{X}'\varepsilon - (X'X)^{-1}X'\varepsilon\big)\\ &\approx \sigma^2\big((\hat{X}'\hat{X})^{-1}\hat{X}' - (X'X)^{-1}X'\big)\big((\hat{X}'\hat{X})^{-1}\hat{X}' - (X'X)^{-1}X'\big)'\\ &= \sigma^2\big((\hat{X}'\hat{X})^{-1} - (X'X)^{-1}\big) \approx \mathrm{var}(b_{IV}) - \mathrm{var}(b),\end{aligned}$$

where we used that $\mathrm{var}(\varepsilon) = \sigma^2 I$ and $\hat{X}'X = \hat{X}'\hat{X}$. Under the usual assumptions, d is also asymptotically normally distributed so that (under the null hypothesis of exogeneity)

$$(b_{IV} - b)'\big(\mathrm{var}(b_{IV}) - \mathrm{var}(b)\big)^{-1}(b_{IV} - b) \approx \chi^2(k).$$

This test is easy to apply, as OLS of y on X gives b and an estimate of $\mathrm{var}(b)$, and OLS of y on $\hat{X}$ gives b_{IV} and an estimate of $\mathrm{var}(b_{IV})$ (see (5.76)). However, in finite samples the estimated covariances may be such that $(\widehat{\mathrm{var}}(b_{IV}) - \widehat{\mathrm{var}}(b))$ is not positive semidefinite, in which case the variance of d is very badly estimated and the test as computed above does not have a good interpretation.

T

Derivation of exogeneity test of Durbin, Wu, and Hausman

Usually exogeneity is tested in another way. We will now describe an exogeneity test associated with Durbin, Wu, and Hausman, commonly known as the *Hausman test*. This test corresponds to the Lagrange Multiplier test. The main idea is to reformulate the exogeneity condition (5.79) in terms of a parameter restriction. For this purpose we split the regressors into two parts, the k_0 variables that are possibly endogenous and the other $(k - k_0)$ variables that are exogenous (for instance, the constant term). We order the regressors so that the first $(k - k_0)$ ones are exogenous and the last k_0 ones are potentially endogenous. The null hypothesis of exogeneity of these regressors is formulated as

$$E[x_{ji}\varepsilon_i] = 0, \quad j = k - k_0 + 1, \cdots, k.$$

By assumption, the m instruments z_i satisfy the exogeneity condition (5.70) that $E[z_i\varepsilon_i] = 0$. Now we consider the auxiliary regression model explaining the jth regressor in terms of these m instruments—that is,

$$x_{ji} = z_i'\gamma_j + v_{ji}, \quad i = 1, \cdots, n. \tag{5.80}$$

Here γ_j is an $m \times 1$ vector of parameters and v_{ji} are error terms. Because of (5.70) it follows that $E[x_{ji}\varepsilon_i] = E[v_{ji}\varepsilon_i]$, and the null hypothesis of exogeneity is equivalent to $E[v_{ji}\varepsilon_i] = 0$ for $j = k - k_0 + 1, \cdots, k$. Let v_i be the $k_0 \times 1$ vector with components v_{ji}; then the condition is that ε_i is uncorrelated with all components of v_i. If we assume that all error terms are normally distributed, the condition becomes more specific, in that v_i and ε_i are independent—that is, that in the conditional expectation $E[\varepsilon_i|v_i] = v_i'\alpha$ there holds $\alpha = 0$. Let $w_i = \varepsilon_i - E[\varepsilon_i|v_i]$; then $\varepsilon_i = v_i'\alpha + w_i$, where w_i is independent of v_i, and the condition of exogeneity can be expressed as follows:

$$\varepsilon_i = v_i'\alpha + w_i, \quad H_0 : \alpha = 0. \tag{5.81}$$

Substituting the results (5.81) and (5.80) in the original model $y_i = x_i'\beta + \varepsilon_i$ gives

$$y_i = \sum_{j=1}^{k} \beta_j x_{ji} + \sum_{j=k-k_0+1}^{k} \alpha_j (x_{ji} - z_i'\gamma_j) + w_i. \tag{5.82}$$

This is a non-linear regression model, as it involves products of the unknown parameters α_j and γ_j. Assuming a joint normal distribution for the error terms w_i in (5.82) and v_{ji} in (5.80), the *LM*-test for the hypothesis that $\alpha = 0$ can be derived along the lines of Section 4.3.6 (p. 238) in terms of the score vector and the Hessian matrix (see (4.54)). The computations are straightforward but tedious and are left as an exercise for the interested reader (see Exercise 5.17 for the derivation).

The Hausman *LM*-test on exogeneity

The Hausman *LM*-test on exogeneity can be computed as follows.

Hausman text on exogeneity

- *Step 1: Perform preliminary regressions.* Regress y on X, with $n \times 1$ residual vector $e = y - Xb$. Regress every possibly endogenous regressor x_j on Z in (5.80), with $n \times 1$ residual vector $\hat{v}_j = x_j - Z\hat{\gamma}_j$.
- *Step 2: Perform the auxiliary regression.* Regress e on X (the $n \times k$ matrix including both the $(k - k_0)$ exogenous and the k_0 possibly endogenous regressors) and on the k_0 series of residuals $\hat{v}_{k-k_0+1}, \cdots, \hat{v}_k$—that is, perform OLS in the model

$$e_i = \sum_{j=1}^{k} \delta_j x_{ji} + \sum_{j=k-k_0+1}^{k} \alpha_j \hat{v}_{ji} + \eta_i. \tag{5.83}$$

- *Step 3: $LM = nR^2$ of the regression in step 2.* Then $LM = nR^2$ where R^2 is the coefficient of determination of the regression in step 2. Under the hypothesis that all k_0 regressors $x_j, j = k - k_0 + 1, \cdots, k$, are exogenous, *LM* has asymptotically the $\chi^2(k_0)$ distribution.

This three-step method to compute the LM-test by means of auxiliary regressions is similar to the LM-test procedure described in Section 4.3.7 (p. 238–40) for the linear model. In step 1 the model (5.82) is estimated under the null hypothesis—that is, with $\alpha = 0$. In step 2, the residuals of step 1 are regressed on all explanatory variables in the unrestricted model (5.82). Because the regressors $v_{ji} = x_{ji} - z_i'\gamma_j$ are unknown (as the parameters γ_j are unknown), they are replaced by the residuals $\hat{v}_{ji}$ obtained by regressing the jth regressor on the m instruments.

T

Comments on the *LM*-test

The null hypothesis of exogeneity—that is, $\alpha_j = 0$ for $j = k - k_0 + 1, \cdots, k$ in (5.82)—can also be tested by the usual F-test on the joint significance of these parameters in the regression (5.83). Under the null hypothesis, this test statistic is asymptotically distributed as $F(k_0, n - k - k_0)$. This F-test and the LM-test of step 3 above are asymptotically equivalent. That is, in large enough samples they provide (nearly) the same P-value and hence both tests lead to the same conclusion (rejection or not) concerning the exogeneity of the last k_0 regressors.

In another version of the F-test on exogeneity, the 'explained' variable e_i in (5.83) is replaced by the dependent variable y_i. As $e = y - Xb$, both regressions (with e_i or with y_i on the left-hand side) have the same residual sum of squares (as all k regressors x_i are included on the right-hand side). That is, the F-test on the joint significance of the parameters α_j can be equivalently performed in the regression equation (5.83) or in the same equation with e_i replaced by y_i.

Summarizing, exogeneity is equivalent to the condition that $E[v_{ji}\varepsilon_i] = 0$, where ε_i are the error terms in the model $y_i = x_i'\beta + \varepsilon_i$ and v_{ji} are the error terms in (5.80). As error terms are not observed, they are replaced by residuals in step 1 and the correlation between the residuals e_i and $\hat{v}_{ji}$ is evaluated by the regression (5.83). Endogeneity of the regressors is indicated by significant correlations—that is, by a significant R^2 and significant estimates of the parameters α_j.

Sargan test on validity of instruments

Finally we consider the question whether the instruments are valid. That is, we test whether the instruments are exogenous in the sense that condition (5.70) is satisfied. This assumption is critical in all the foregoing results. If the instruments are not exogenous, then IV is not consistent and also the Hausman test is not correct anymore. In some cases the exogeneity of the instruments is reasonable from an economic point of view, but in other situations this may be less clear. We illustrate this later with two examples. A simple idea to test (5.70) is to replace the (unobserved) error terms ε_i by reliable estimates of these error terms. As the regressors may be endogenous, we should take not the OLS residuals but the IV residuals $e_{IV} = y - Xb_{IV}$. Under the null hypothesis that the instruments are exogenous, b_{IV} is consistent and e_{IV} provides reliable estimates of the vector of error terms ε. We test (5.70) by testing whether z_i is uncorrelated with e_{IVi}, the ith component of e_{IV}. This suggests the following test, which is called the *Sargan test* on the *validity of instruments*.

Sargan test on the validity of instruments

- *Step 1: Apply IV.* Estimate $y = X\beta + \varepsilon$ by IV, with $n \times 1$ residual vector $e_{IV} = y - Xb_{IV}$.
- *Step 2: Perform auxiliary regression.* Regress e_{IV} on Z in the model

$$e_{IVi} = z_i'\gamma + \eta_i.$$

- *Step 3: $LM = nR^2$ of the regression in step 2.* Compute $LM = nR^2$ of the regression in step 2. Under the null hypothesis that the instruments are exogenous, LM asymptotically has the $\chi^2(m-k)$ distribution, where m is the number of instruments (the number of variables in z_i) and k is the number of regressors (the number of variables in x_i).

Derivation of the distribution of the Sargan test

T

To derive the distribution under the null hypothesis, in particular that the degrees of freedom is equal to $(m-k)$, we recall that IV corresponds to GMM with moment conditions (5.70). If $m > k$—that is, in the over-identified case—we can apply the GMM test on over-identifying restrictions of Section 4.4.3 (p. 258). Using the notation of Section 4.4.3 (p. 253), the moment functions corresponding to (5.70) are

$$g_i = z_i\varepsilon_i = z_i(y_i - x_i'\beta),$$

and $G_n = \sum_{i=1}^n g_i = \sum_{i=1}^n z_i\varepsilon_i = Z'\varepsilon$ and $J_n = \sum_{i=1}^n g_ig_i' = \sum_{i=1}^n \varepsilon_i^2 z_iz_i'$. Evaluated at the GMM estimator b_{IV}, we get $G_n = Z'e_{IV}$ and $\text{plim}(\frac{1}{n}J_n) = \text{plim}\left(\frac{1}{n}\sum_{i=1}^n \varepsilon_i^2 z_iz_i'\right) = \sigma^2 Q_{zz}$. If we approximate Q_{zz} by $\frac{1}{n}Z'Z$ and σ^2 by $\frac{1}{n}e_{IV}'e_{IV}$, we get $J_n \approx \frac{1}{n}e_{IV}'e_{IV}Z'Z$. Then the test on over-identifying restrictions—that is, the J-test (4.69)—is given by

$$G_n'J_n^{-1}G_n = n\frac{e_{IV}'Z(Z'Z)^{-1}Z'e_{IV}}{e_{IV}'e_{IV}} = nR^2$$

with the R^2 of the regression in step 2 above. So our intuitive arguments for the Sargan test can be justified by the GMM test on over-identifying restrictions. According to Section 4.4.3 (p. 258), under the null hypothesis of exogenous instruments there holds

$$LM = nR^2 \approx \chi^2(m-k).$$

The validity of the instruments is rejected for large values of this test statistic. Note that the validity can be checked only if $m > k$—that is, if the number of instruments exceeds the number of regressors. In the exactly identified case ($m = k$) the validity of the instruments cannot be tested.

E

XM511IBR

Example 5.33: **Interest and Bond Rates (continued)**

We continue our previous analysis of the interest and bond rate data in Example 5.30. We will discuss (i) a comparison of the IV and OLS estimates, (ii) the Hausman test on exogeneity, and (iii) the Sargan test on the validity of the lagged Treasury Bill rate changes as instruments.

(i) Comparison of IV and OLS estimates

In Section 5.7.1 we estimated the relation between changes in the AAA bond rate (y_i) and the Treasury Bill rate (x_i) by instrumental variables, with the lagged values x_{i-1} and x_{i-2} as instruments. Exhibit 5.43, Panels 3 and 4 (p. 401), shows the results of OLS and of IV. Denoting the estimates of α and β in $y_i = \alpha + \beta x_i + \varepsilon_i$ by a and b, respectively, we see that $a_{IV} - a = -0.004$ and $b_{IV} - b = -0.137$. The covariance matrices of these estimates are

$$\widehat{\text{var}}_{OLS} = s^2(X'X)^{-1} = 10^{-5}\begin{pmatrix} 23.8 & 1.6 \\ 1.6 & 56.1 \end{pmatrix},$$

$$\widehat{\text{var}}_{IV} = s_{IV}^2(\hat{X}'\hat{X})^{-1} = 10^{-5}\begin{pmatrix} 27.5 & 12.0 \\ 12.0 & 421.9 \end{pmatrix}.$$

If one uses these results to test for exogeneity, it follows that

$$\begin{pmatrix} a_{IV} - a \\ b_{IV} - b \end{pmatrix}' (\widehat{\text{var}}_{IV} - \widehat{\text{var}}_{OLS})^{-1} \begin{pmatrix} a_{IV} - a \\ b_{IV} - b \end{pmatrix} = 5.11.$$

This is smaller than the 5 per cent critical value of the $\chi^2(2)$ distribution (5.99), so that at this significance level this test does not lead to rejection of the hypothesis that x_i is exogenous.

(ii) Hausman test on exogeneity

As the above test is not so reliable, we now perform the Hausman test. As in the model $y_i = \alpha + \beta x_i + \varepsilon_i$ we have $k = 2$ and as the constant term is exogenous, it follows that $k_0 = 1$. The result of step 2 of the Hausman test is in Panel 1 of Exhibit 5.47, where 'resaux' stands for the residuals obtained

(*a*)

Panel 1: Step 2 of Hausman test; Dependent Variable: RESOLS				
Method: Least Squares				
Sample: 1980:01 1999:12				
Included observations: 240				
Variable	Coefficient	Std. Error	t-Statistic	Prob.
C	−0.003895	0.015359	−0.253610	0.8000
DUS3MT	−0.136674	0.060199	−2.270359	0.0241
RESAUX	0.161106	0.065359	2.464945	0.0144
R-squared	0.024996			

(*b*)

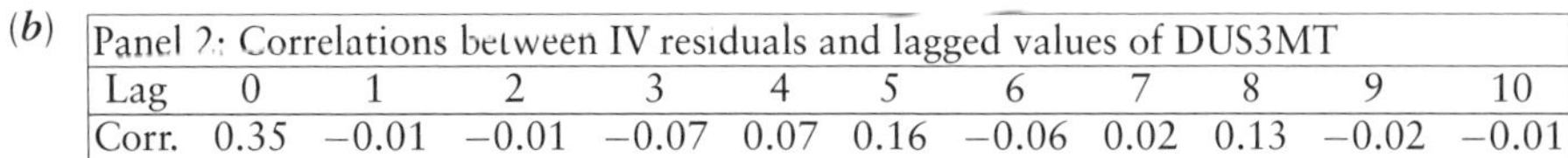

Panel 2: Correlations between IV residuals and lagged values of DUS3MT											
Lag	0	1	2	3	4	5	6	7	8	9	10
Corr.	0.35	−0.01	−0.01	−0.07	0.07	0.16	−0.06	0.02	0.13	−0.02	−0.01

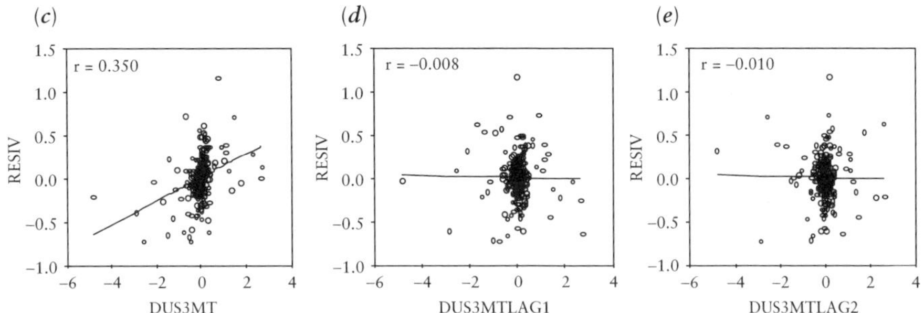

(*f*)

Panel 6: Step 2 of Sargan test; Dependent Variable: RESIV				
Method: Least Squares				
Sample: 1980:01 1999:12				
Included observations: 240				
Variable	Coefficient	Std. Error	t-Statistic	Prob.
C	−0.000156	0.016525	−0.009431	0.9925
DUS3MT(−1)	−0.002218	0.026395	−0.084042	0.9331
DUS3MT(−2)	−0.003387	0.026378	−0.128395	0.8979
R-squared	0.000135			

Exhibit 5.47 Interest and Bond Rates (Example 5.33)

Panel 1 contains the regression of step 2 of the Hausman test on exogeneity of the explanatory variable DUS3MT (RESOLS and RESAUX are the residuals obtained in step 1 of the Hausman test, RESOLS are the residuals of the regression in Panel 3 of Exhibit 5.43, and RESAUX are the residuals of the regression in Panel 2 of Exhibit 5.46). Panel 2 shows the correlations of the IV residuals with lags of the explanatory variable for lags 0–10, and the three scatter diagrams are for lags 0 (*c*), 1 (*d*), and 2 (*e*). Panel 6 contains the regression for step 2 of the Sargan test on validity of instruments (RESIV are the IV residuals obtained in step 1 of this test; this regression is shown in Panel 1 of Exhibit 5.46).

by regressing x_i on the instruments x_{i-1}, x_{i-2} and a constant term. The t-test on the significance of 'resaux' has a P-value of 0.014, and the Hausman LM-test gives $LM = nR^2 = 240 \cdot 0.024996 = 6.00$, with P-value (corresponding to the $\chi^2(1)$ distribution) $P = 0.014$. This indicates that the assumption of exogeneity should be rejected, and that the OLS estimator may be considerably biased. The IV estimate of the slope is much smaller than the OLS estimate and it has a much larger standard error (0.065 instead of the computed value of 0.024 for OLS (see Panels 3 and 4 of Exhibit 5.43)).

(iii) Sargan test on validity of instruments

The IV estimates can be trusted only if the instruments x_{i-1} and x_{i-2} are exogenous—that is, this requires that $E[x_{i-1}\varepsilon_i] = E[x_{i-2}\varepsilon_i] = 0$. Exhibit 5.47 shows the correlations between lagged values of x_i and the IV residuals e_{IV} (in Panel 2) and scatters of the IV residuals against x_i, x_{i-1}, and x_{i-2} (see (*c*), (*d*), and (*e*)). This indicates that x_i is indeed not exogenous but that x_{i-1} and x_{i-2} are exogenous (with correlations of around -0.01, both between x_{i-1} and e_{IV} and between x_{i-2} and e_{IV}).

Panel 6 of Exhibit 5.47 shows the regression of step 2 of the Sargan test. This gives $LM = nR^2 = 240 \cdot 0.000135 = 0.032$. As there are $m = 3$ instruments (the constant term and x_{i-1} and x_{i-2}) and $k = 2$ regressors (the constant term and x_i), it follows that the χ^2-distribution has $(m - k) = 1$ degree of freedom. The P-value of the LM-test, corresponding to the $\chi^2(1)$ distribution, is $P = 0.86$. This indicates that the lagged values of x_i are valid instruments.

E

XM531MGC

Example 5.34: Motor Gasoline Consumption (continued)

Next we consider the data on motor gasoline consumption introduced in Example 5.31. We will discuss (i) the Hausman test on exogeneity of the gasoline price, (ii) the Sargan test on the validity of the price indices as instruments, and (iii) a remark on the required model assumptions.

(i) Hausman test on the exogeneity of the gasoline price

In Example 5.31 we considered the relation between gasoline consumption (GC), gasoline price (PG), and disposable income (RI) in the USA. We postulated the demand equation

$$GC_i = \alpha + \beta PG_i + \gamma RI_i + \varepsilon_i.$$

We supposed that RI is exogenous and considered the possible endogeneity of PG. The outcomes of OLS and IV estimates (with five instruments—that is, a constant, RI, and the three price indices RPT, RPN, and RPU) in Panels 1 and 2 of Exhibit 5.45 turned out to be close together, suggesting that PG is exogenous. Panel 1 of Exhibit 5.48 shows the regression of step 2 of the Hausman test, with outcome $LM = nR^2 = 2.38$. Since the constant and the income are assumed to be exogenous and the price PG is the only possibly endogenous variable, we have $k_0 = 1$. So the distribution of the LM-test

Panel 1: Step 2 of Hausman test; Dependent Variable: RESOLS				
Method: Least Squares				
Sample: 1970 1999				
Included observations: 30				
Variable	Coefficient	Std. Error	t-Statistic	Prob.
C	0.027703	0.081429	0.340209	0.7364
PG	−0.016872	0.028093	−0.600566	0.5533
RI	−0.008558	0.024638	−0.347347	0.7311
RESAUX	0.104845	0.070032	1.497107	0.1464
R-squared	0.079363			

Panel 2: Step 2 of Sargan test; Dependent Variable: RESIV				
Method: Least Squares				
Sample: 1970 1999				
Included observations: 30				
Variable	Coefficient	Std. Error	t-Statistic	Prob.
C	−0.209753	0.271047	−0.773862	0.4463
RPT	−0.051202	0.062169	−0.823606	0.4180
RPN	0.020409	0.114431	0.178352	0.8599
RPU	−0.070229	0.059531	−1.179698	0.2492
RI	0.060410	0.080326	0.752055	0.4590
R-squared	0.104159			

Exhibit 5.48 Motor Gasoline Consumption (Example 5.34)

Panel 1 shows the regression for step 2 of the Hausman test on exogeneity of the explanatory variable PG (RESOLS and RESAUX are the residuals obtained in step 1 of the Hausman test, RESOLS are the residuals of the regression in Panel 1 of Exhibit 5.45 and RESAUX are the residuals of the regression in Panel 3 of Exhibit 5.45). Panel 2 shows the regression for step 2 of the Sargan test on validity of instruments (RESIV are the IV residuals obtained in step 1 of this test; this regression is shown in Panel 2 of Exhibit 5.45).

(under the null hypothesis of exogeneity) is $\chi^2(1)$, which gives a P-value of $P = 0.12$. This does not lead to rejection of the exogeneity of the variable PG.

(ii) Sargan test on validity of instruments

Panel 2 of Exhibit 5.48 shows the regression of step 2 of the Sargan test. Here we test whether the five instruments are exogenous. In this case $k = 3$ and $m = 5$, so that $LM = nR^2 = 3.12$ should be compared with the $\chi^2(2)$ distribution. The corresponding P-value is $P = 0.21$, so that the exogeneity of the instruments is not rejected. However, note that IV estimation is not required as the regressor PG seems to be exogenous. For these data we therefore prefer OLS, as OLS is consistent and gives (somewhat) smaller standard errors (see the results in Exhibit 5.45, Panel 1 for OLS and Panel 2 for IV).

(iii) Remark on required model assumptions

We conclude by mentioning that the above tests require that the standard Assumptions 2–6 of the regression model are satisfied. It is left as an exercise (see Exercise 5.31) to show that the residuals of the above demand equation for motor gasoline consumption show significant serial correlation. Therefore we should give the above test outcomes on exogeneity and validity of instruments the correct interpretation — that is, as diagnostic tests indicating possible problems with OLS. In particular, the OLS estimates are not efficient, as they neglect the serial correlation of the disturbances. Similar remarks apply to our analysis of the interest and bond rate data in Example 5.33, as in Examples 5.27 and 5.28 we concluded that these data contain some outliers.

☞ **Exercises:** T: 5.16d, 5.17; S: 5.23e.

5.7.4 **Summary**

The OLS method becomes inconsistent if the regressors are not exogenous. In this case the OLS estimates may provide very misleading information. One may proceed as follows.

- First of all, try to use economic intuition to guess whether endogeneity might play a role for the investigation at hand. If it does, one should find a sufficient number of instruments that are exogenous and that carry information on the possibly endogenous regressors (that is, the order and rank conditions should be satisfied).
- Investigate the possible endogeneity of 'suspect' regressors by means of the Hausman test. If one has a sufficiently large number of instruments, then perform the Sargan test to check whether the proposed instruments are indeed exogenous.
- If some of the regressors are endogenous and the instruments are valid, then consistent estimates are obtained by the instrumental variables estimation method. The t- and F-tests can be performed as usual, although some care is needed to use the correct formulas (see (5.77) and (5.78)).
- If the endogeneity is only weak, then OLS may be considered as an alternative, provided that the resulting bias is compensated by a sufficiently large increase in efficiency as compared to IV.

5.8 Illustration: Salaries of top managers

The discussion in this chapter could lead one to think that ordinary least squares is threatened from so many sides that it never works in practice. This is not true. OLS is a natural first step in estimating economic relations and in many cases it provides valuable insight in the nature of such relations. By means of the following example we will illustrate that in some cases OLS provides a reasonable model that performs well under various relevant diagnostic tests.

Example 5.35: **Salaries of Top Managers**

As an example we analyse the relation between salaries of top managers and profits of firms. The data set consists of 100 large firms in the Netherlands in 1999. The 100 firms are ordered with increasing profits. Let y_i be the logarithm of the average yearly salary (in thousands of Dutch guilders) of top managers of firm i and let x_i be the logarithm of the profit (in millions of Dutch guilders) of firm i. Results of OLS in the model

$$y_i = \alpha + \beta x_i + \varepsilon_i$$

are in Panel 3 of Exhibit 5.49, and this exhibit also shows the outcomes of various diagnostic tests discussed in this chapter. The tests in Exhibits 5.49 (e–q) do not indicate any misspecification of the model, so that we are satisfied with this simple relation. The estimated elasticity β is around 16 per cent, so that salaries of top managers tend to be rather inelastic with respect to profits when compared over this cross section of firms.

(a)

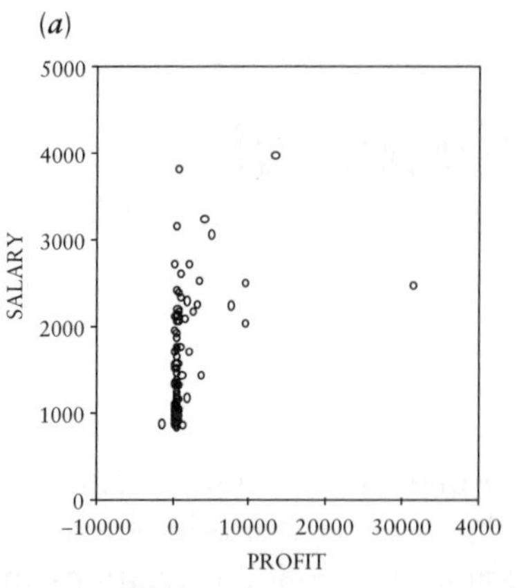

(b)

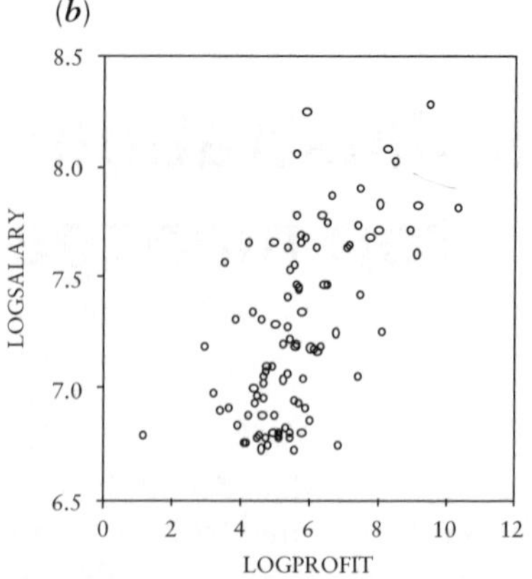

(c)

Panel 3: Dependent Variable: LOGSALARY
Method: Least Squares
Sample(adjusted): 5 100
Included observations: 96 after adjusting endpoints

Variable	Coefficient	Std. Error	t-Statistic	Prob.
C	6.350338	0.128961	49.24249	0.0000
LOGPROFIT	0.162212	0.021984	7.378765	0.0000
R-squared	0.366774	Mean dependent var		7.269493
Adjusted R-squared	0.360037	S.D. dependent var		0.408740
S.E. of regression	0.326982	Akaike info criterion		0.622791
Sum squared resid	10.05023	Schwarz criterion		0.676215
Log likelihood	−27.89396	F-statistic		54.44617
Durbin–Watson stat	2.233248	Prob(F-statistic)		0.000000

(d)

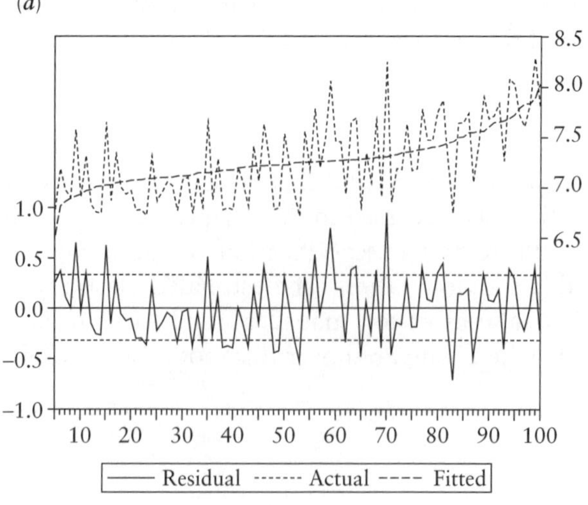

Exhibit 5.49 Salaries of Top Managers (Example 5.35)

Scatter diagrams of salary against profit (in levels (*a*) and in logarithms (*b*)), regression table (with variables in logarithms, Panel 3), and graph of actual and fitted (logarithmic) salaries and corresponding least squares residuals ((*d*); the data are ordered with increasing values of profits; the original number of observations is 100, but the number of observations in estimation is 96, as 4 firms have negative profits).

(*e*)

Panel 5: Ramsey RESET Test:				
F-statistic	0.878905	Probability		0.350930
Log likelihood ratio	0.902997	Probability		0.341979
Test Equation: Dependent Variable: LOGSALARY				
Method: Least Squares				
Sample: 5 100; Included observations: 96				
Variable	Coefficient	Std. Error	t-Statistic	Prob.
C	−5.981640	13.15475	−0.454713	0.6504
LOGPROFIT	−0.582640	0.794813	−0.733053	0.4654
FITTED^2	0.312867	0.333725	0.937499	0.3509

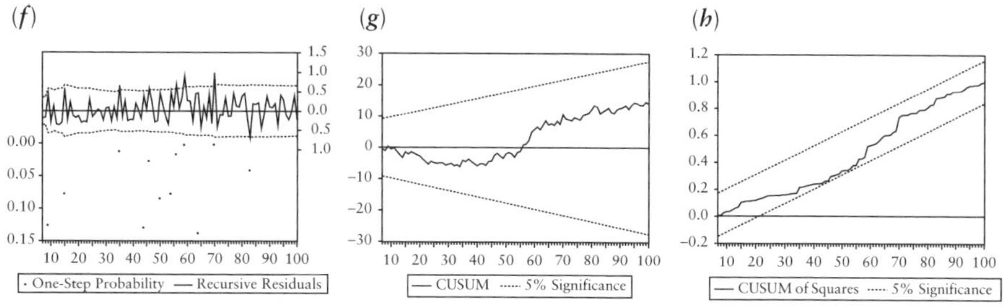

(*i*)

Panel 9: Chow Breakpoint Test: 77			
F-statistic	0.845556	Probability	0.432627
Log likelihood ratio	1.748622	Probability	0.417149

(*j*)

Panel 10: Chow Forecast Test: Forecast from 77 to 100				
F-statistic	0.873523	Probability		0.634024
Log likelihood ratio	25.14958	Probability		0.397669
Test Equation: Dependent Variable: LOGSALARY				
Method: Least Squares				
Sample: 5 76; Included observations: 72				
Variable	Coefficient	Std. Error	t-Statistic	Prob.
C	6.521363	0.222507	29.30862	0.0000
LOGPROFIT	0.124737	0.044001	2.834870	0.0060
R-squared	0.102984	Mean dependent var		7.142288
Adjusted R-squared	0.090169	S.D. dependent var		0.348475
S.E. of regression	0.332393	Akaike info criterion		0.662387
Sum squared resid	7.733956	Schwarz criterion		0.725628
Log likelihood	−21.84593	F-statistic		8.036490
Durbin–Watson stat	2.306228	Prob(F-statistic)		0.005988

Exhibit 5.49 (*Contd.*)

Diagnostic tests, RESET (Panel 5), recursive residuals with CUSUM and CUSUMSQ tests ((*f*)–(*h*)), Chow break test (Panel 9), and Chow forecast test (Panel 10), both with 72 firms (those with lower profits) in the first subsample and with 24 firms (those with higher profits) in the second subsample. The test outcomes do not give reason to adjust the functional specification of the model (Assumptions 2, 5, and 6).

(*k*)

Panel 11: White Heteroskedasticity Test:				
F-statistic	0.589335	Probability		0.556754
Obs*R-squared	1.201465	Probability		0.548410
Test Equation: Dependent Variable: RESOLS^2				
Method: Least Squares				
Sample: 5 100; Included observations: 96				
Variable	Coefficient	Std. Error	t-Statistic	Prob.
C	−0.032151	0.140858	−0.228249	0.8200
LOGPROFIT	0.048798	0.046586	1.047494	0.2976
LOGPROFIT^2	−0.004059	0.003746	−1.083502	0.2814
R-squared	0.012515			

(*l*)

Panel 12: Breusch-Godfrey Serial Correlation LM Test:				
F-statistic	0.759000	Probability		0.471043
Obs*R-squared	1.558288	Probability		0.458798
Test Equation: Dependent Variable: RESOLS				
Method: Least Squares				
Variable	Coefficient	Std. Error	t-Statistic	Prob.
C	−0.005453	0.129438	−0.042130	0.9665
LOGPROFIT	0.001021	0.022068	0.046281	0.9632
RESOLS(−1)	−0.119031	0.104460	−1.139490	0.2575
RESOLS(−2)	0.035061	0.105207	0.333255	0.7397
R-squared	0.016232			

(*m*)

Panel 13: CORRELATIONS OF RESOLS			
Lag	AC	Ljung-Box	Prob
1	−0.122	1.4799	0.224
2	0.048	1.7100	0.425
3	−0.095	2.6321	0.452
4	0.262	9.6293	0.047
5	0.019	9.6656	0.085
6	−0.060	10.045	0.123
7	0.006	10.049	0.186
8	−0.111	11.368	0.182
9	0.172	14.571	0.103
10	0.106	15.792	0.106

(*n*)

Series: Residuals	
Sample 5 100	
Observations 96	
Mean	−2.87E-15
Median	−0.040238
Maximum	0.946792
Minimum	−0.714197
Std. Dev.	0.325257
Skewness	0.388016
Kurtosis	2.743717
Jarque-Bera	2.671623
Probability	0.262945

Exhibit 5.49 (*Contd.*)

Diagnostic tests, White test on heteroskedasticity (Panel 11), tests on serial correlation (Breusch–Godfrey *LM*-test in Panel 12 and Ljung–Box test in Panel 13), and test on normality (histogram and Jarque–Bera test (*n*)). RESOLS denotes the OLS residuals of the regression in Panel 3. The test outcomes do not give reason to adjust the standard probability model for the disturbance terms (Assumptions 3, 4, and 7).

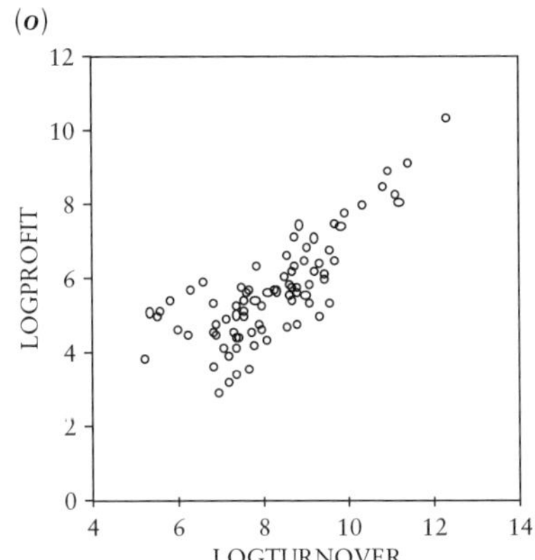

(p)

Panel 16: Dependent Variable: LOGSALARY				
Method: Instrumental Variables				
Included observations: 84				
Excluded observations: 16 (missing values of turnover)				
Instrument list: C LOGTURNOVER				
Variable	Coefficient	Std. Error	t-Statistic	Prob.
C	6.253435	0.182995	34.17263	0.0000
LOGPROFIT	0.181561	0.031937	5.685017	0.0000
R-squared	0.385981			

(q)

Panel 17: Dependent Variable: RESOLS				
Method: Least Squares				
Included observations: 84				
Excluded observations: 16 (missing values of turnover)				
Variable	Coefficient	Std. Error	t-Statistic	Prob.
C	−0.096903	0.184116	−0.526314	0.6001
LOGPROFIT	0.019349	0.032132	0.602173	0.5487
V	−0.002833	0.052095	−0.054385	0.9568
R-squared	0.006438			

Exhibit 5.49 (*Contd.*)

Diagnostic tests, instrumental variable estimate of the wage equation (with LOGTURNOVER as instrument, Panel 16; the scatter diagram of the explanatory variable against the instrument is shown in (*o*)) and step 2 of the Hausman test on exogeneity of the explanatory variable (LOGPROFIT) in the wage equation (Panel 17; RESOLS denotes the OLS residuals of the regression in Panel 3 and V denotes the residuals of the regression of LOGPROFIT on a constant and LOGTURNOVER). The sample size in estimation is 84 because the turnover of some of the firms is unknown. The test outcomes do not give reason to reject the assumption of exogeneity of profits in the wage equation for top managers (Assumption 1).

☞ Exercises: E: 5.32.

Summary, further reading, and keywords

SUMMARY

In this chapter the seven standard assumptions of the regression model were subjected to diagnostic tests. The exogeneity of the regressors (Assumption 1) is required for OLS to be consistent, and this was investigated in Section 5.7. If the regressors are endogenous, then consistent estimates can be obtained by using instrumental variables. The functional specification of the model (linear model with constant parameters, Assumptions 2, 5, and 6) was discussed in Sections 5.2 and 5.3. A correct specification is required to get consistent estimators. In practice it may be worthwhile excluding the less relevant variables—namely, if the resulting bias is compensated by an increased efficiency of the estimators. We also discussed methods for the specification and estimation of non-linear models and models with varying parameters. If the disturbances of the model are heteroskedastic or serially correlated (so that Assumptions 3 or 4 are not satisfied), then OLS is consistent but not efficient. The efficiency can be increased by using weighted least squares (based on a model for the variances of the disturbances) or by transforming the model (to remove the serial correlation of the disturbances). This was discussed in Sections 5.4 and 5.5. In Section 5.6 we considered the assumption of normally distributed disturbances (Assumption 7). If the disturbances are not normally distributed, then OLS is consistent but not efficient. Regression diagnostics can be used to detect influential observations, and if there are relatively many outliers then robust methods can improve the efficiency of the estimators.

FURTHER READING

The textbooks mentioned in Chapter 3, Further Reading (p. 178–9), contain chapters on most of the topics discussed in this chapter. For a more extensive treatment of some of these topics we refer to the three volumes of the *Handbook of Econometrics* mentioned in Chapter 3. We mention some further references: Belsley, Kuh, and Welsch (1980) for regression diagnostics; Cleveland (1993) and Fan and Gijbels (1996) for non-parametric methods; Godfrey (1988) for diagnostic tests; Rousseeuw and Leroy (1987) for robust methods.

Belsley, D. A., Kuh, E., and Welsch, R. E. (1980). *Regression Diagnostics: Identifying Influential Data and Sources of Collinearity*. New York: Wiley.
Cleveland, W. S. (1993). *Visualizing Data*. Summit, NJ: Hobart Press.
Fan, J., and Gijbels, I. (1996). *Local Polynomial Modelling and its Applications*. London: Chapman and Hall.
Godfrey, L. G. (1988). *Misspecification Tests in Econometrics*. Cambridge: Cambridge University Press.
Rousseeuw, P. J., and Leroy, A. M. (1987). *Robust Regression and Outlier Detection*. New York: Wiley.

KEYWORDS

Exercises

THEORY QUESTIONS

5.1 (☞ Section 5.2.1)
Consider the model $y = X_1\beta_1 + X_2\beta_2 + \varepsilon$ with $\beta_2 \neq 0$. It was shown in Section 3.2.3 (p. 143) that the restricted least squares estimator $b_R = (X_1'X_1)^{-1}X_1'y$ has a variance that is smaller than that of the unrestricted least squares estimator b_1 in the model that includes both X_1 and X_2.

a. Show that the standard error of the regression s may be larger in the restricted model. Is the standard error in the restricted model always larger?

b. Show that, as a consequence, the estimates b_R need not be more significant (in the sense of having larger t-values) than the estimates b_1.

c. Verify the results in **a** and **b** by simulating a data set with sample size $n = 100$ by means of the model $y = \beta_1 + \beta_2 x + \varepsilon$, where $x_{1i} = 1$ is the constant term and x_{2i} and ε_i are two independent samples from the standard normal distribution. As parameter values take $\beta_1 = 1$ and $\beta_2 = 10$.

d. Discuss the relevance of your findings for the 'bottom-up' strategy in model selection, which starts with small models and performs sequential tests on the significance of additional variables.

5.2 (☞ Sections 5.2.1, 5.2.4)

a. Using the notation of Section 5.2.1, show that $MSE(b_1) - MSE(b_R) = P(V_2 - \beta_2\beta_2')P'$, where $P = (X_1'X_1)^{-1}X_1'X_2$ and where $V_2 = \text{var}(b_2)$ is the $g \times g$ covariance matrix of b_2 in the model $y = X_1\beta_1 + X_2\beta_2 + \varepsilon$.

b. Using again the notation of Section 5.2.1, prove that $\text{TMSP}(b_R) \leq \text{TMSP}(b_1)$ if and only if $\beta_2'V_2^{-1}\beta_2 \leq g$.

c. Prove that, for n sufficiently large, AIC corresponds to an F-test with critical value approximately equal to 2.

d. Prove that SIC corresponds to an F-test with critical value approximately equal to $\log(n)$.

e. Suppose that $\log(y) \sim \text{N}(\mu, \sigma^2)$; then prove that y has mean $e^{\mu+\frac{1}{2}\sigma^2}$, median e^{μ}, and variance $e^{2\mu+\sigma^2}(e^{\sigma^2} - 1)$.

f. Consider the non-linear wage model $S(\lambda) = \alpha + \gamma D_g + \mu D_m + \beta x + \varepsilon$ in Example 5.5, where $S(\lambda) = (S^{\lambda} - 1)/\lambda$. Prove that in this model $(dS/dx)/S = \beta/(1 + \lambda(\alpha + \gamma D_g + \mu D_m + \beta x + \varepsilon))$.

5.3 (☞ Section 5.3.2)

a. Prove the expressions (5.12)–(5.14). It is helpful to write out the normal equations $X_{t+1}'X_{t+1}b_{t+1} = X_{t+1}'Y_{t+1}$, where $Y_{t+1} = (y_1, \cdots, y_{t+1})'$ and $X_{t+1} = (x_1, \cdots, x_{t+1})' = (X_t', x_{t+1})'$.

b. Prove that the variances of the forecast errors f_t in (5.11) are equal to $\sigma^2 v_t$.

c. Prove that the forecast errors f_t are independent under the standard Assumptions 1–7.

5.4 (☞ Section 5.3.3)

a. Prove the result (5.20) for the hypothesis (5.19).

b. The F-test requires that the disturbance vectors ε_1 and ε_2 in (5.18) are uncorrelated with mean zero and covariance matrices $\sigma_1^2 I_{n_1}$ and $\sigma_2^2 I_{n_2}$, where $\sigma_1^2 = \sigma_2^2$. Derive a test for the hypothesis (5.19) for the case that $\sigma_1^2 \neq \sigma_2^2$.

c. Prove that the F-test for the hypothesis (5.22) in the model (5.21) is equal to the forecast test in Section 3.4.3.

5.5 (☞ Section 5.4.3)
Consider the model $y_i = \beta x_i + \varepsilon_i$ (without constant term and with $k = 1$), where $E[\varepsilon_i] = 0$, $E[\varepsilon_i\varepsilon_j] = 0$ for $i \neq j$, and $E[\varepsilon_i^2] = \sigma_i^2$.

a. Consider the following three estimators of β: $b_1 = \sum x_i y_i / \sum x_i^2$, $b_2 = \sum y_i / \sum x_i$, and $b_3 = \frac{1}{n}\sum (y_i/x_i)$. For each estimator, derive a model for the variances σ_i^2 for which this estimator is the best linear unbiased estimator of β.

b. Let $\sigma_i^2 = \sigma^2 x_i^2$. Show that the OLS estimator is unbiased. Derive expressions for the variance of the OLS estimator and also for the WLS estimator.

c. Use the results in **b** to show that the OLS estimator has a variance that is at least as large as that of the WLS estimator.

d*. For the general case, show that the OLS variance in (5.24) is always at least as large as the WLS variance (5.29) in the sense that $\text{var}(b) - \text{var}(b_*)$ is positive semidefinite.

5.6 (☞ Sections 5.4.4, 5.4.5)

a. In the additive heteroskedasticity model with $\sigma_i^2 = z_i'\gamma$, the variances are estimated by the regression $e_i^2 = z_i'\gamma + \eta_i$ with error terms $\eta_i = e_i^2 - \sigma_i^2$ (see Section 5.4.4). Now assume that $\text{plim}(\frac{1}{n}\sum z_i z_i') = Q_{zz}$ exists with Q_{zz} an invertible matrix, and assume that the variables z_i are exogenous in the sense that $\text{plim}(\frac{1}{n}\sum z_i(\varepsilon_i^2 - \sigma_i^2)) = 0$. Show that γ is estimated consistently under this assumption.

b*. Prove the results that are stated in Section 5.4.4 for the consistent estimation of the parameters of the multiplicative model for heteroskedasticity.

c. Derive the expression (5.39) for the LR-test for groupwise heteroskedasticity in the model $y = X\beta + \varepsilon$.

5.7* (☞ Section 5.4.5)

In this exercise we derive the three-step method for the computation of the Breusch–Pagan test on homoskedasticity. Consider the model $y = X\beta + \varepsilon$, which satisfies the standard regression Assumptions 1–7, except for Assumption 3, which is replaced by the model (5.26).

a. Let $\sigma_i^2 = \sigma^2 z_i^\alpha$, where z_i is a single explanatory variable that takes on only positive values. Derive the log-likelihood for this model, with parameter vector $\theta = (\beta', \alpha, \sigma^2)'$, and determine the first order conditions (for ML) and the information matrix.

b. Derive the LM-test for homoskedasticity ($\alpha = 0$), using the results in **a**. Show in particular that this can be written as $LM = SSE/2$, where SSE is the explained sum of squares of the regression of e_i^2/s_{ML}^2 on a constant and $\log(z_i)$ and where $s_{ML}^2 = e'e/n$.

c. Show that, in large enough samples, the result in **b** can also be written as $LM = nR^2$ of the regression of e_i^2 on a constant and $\log(z_i)$.

d. Now consider the general model (5.26). Derive the log-likelihood and its first order derivatives. Show that the LM-test for $\gamma_2 = \cdots = \gamma_p = 0$ is given by $LM = SSE/2$, where SSE is the explained sum of squares of the regression of e_i^2/s_{ML}^2 on z.

e. Show that the result in **d** can be written as $LM = nR^2$ of the auxiliary regression (5.40).

5.8* (☞ Section 5.5.3)

In this exercise we consider an alternative derivation of the Breusch–Godfrey test—that is, the auxiliary regression (5.49). In the text this test was derived by using the results of Section 4.2.4 (p. 218) on non-linear regression models, and now we will consider the ML-based version of this test. The model is given by (5.45) with AR(1) errors (5.47) where $\eta_i \sim \text{NID}(0, \sigma_\eta^2)$. The parameter vector is $\theta = (\beta', \gamma, \sigma_\eta^2)'$ and the null hypothesis of no serial correlation corresponds to $\gamma = 0$.

a. Determine the log-likelihood of this model (for the observations $(y_2, \cdots, y_n)$, treating y_1 as a fixed, non-random value).

b. Determine the first and second order derivatives of the log-likelihood with respect to the parameter vector θ.

c. Use the results in **a** and **b** to compute the LM-test by means of the definition in (4.54) in Section 4.3.6 (p. 238).

d. Prove that the result in **c** can be written as nR^2 of the auxiliary regression (5.49). It may be assumed that the model (5.45) contains a constant term—that is, $x_{1,i} = 1$ for $i = 1, \cdots, n$—and that $\text{plim}(\frac{1}{n}\sum x_i e_{i-1}) = 0$, where e is the vector of OLS residuals.

5.9* (☞ Section 5.5.3)

In this exercise we show that the Box–Pierce (BP) test (5.50) is asymptotically equivalent to the Breusch–Godfrey (BG) test obtained by the regression of the OLS residuals e_i on x_i and the lagged values $e_{i-1}, \cdots, e_{i-p}$. We assume that the explanatory variables x include a constant term and that they satisfy the conditions that $\text{plim}(\frac{1}{n}\sum_{i=1}^n x_i x_i') = Q$ is invertible and that $\text{plim}(\frac{1}{n}\sum_{i=p+1}^n e_{i-j} x_i) = 0$ for all $j = 1, \cdots, p$. Further we assume that under the null hypothesis of absence of serial correlation there also holds $\text{plim}(\frac{1}{n}\sum_{i=p+1}^{n} e_{i-j}e_i) = 0$ for all $j = 1, \cdots, p$, and $\text{plim}(\frac{1}{n}\sum e_i^2) = \sigma^2$.

a. Write the regression of e_i on x_i and $e_{i-1}, \cdots, e_{i-p}$, as $e = X\delta + E\gamma + \omega$, where the columns of E consist of lagged values of the OLS residuals. Let $\hat{\delta}$ and $\hat{\gamma}$ be the OLS estimators obtained from this model; then show that (under the null hypothesis of no serial correlation) $\sqrt{n}\hat{\delta} \approx 0$ and $\sqrt{n}\hat{\gamma} \approx \frac{1}{\sigma^2}\frac{1}{\sqrt{n}}E'e$ (where we write $a \approx b$ if $\text{plim}(a - b) = 0$).

b. Show that the explained sum of squares SSE of the regression in **a** satisfies $SSE \approx \frac{1}{n}\sum_{k=1}^{p} [\sum_i e_i e_{i-k}]^2/\sigma^2$.

c. Use the result in **b** to prove that for the regression in **a** there holds $nR^2 = \frac{SSE}{SST/n} \approx n\sum_{k=1}^{p} r_k^2$.

5.10 (☞ Section 5.5.4)
Consider the model $y_i = \mu + \varepsilon_i$, where μ is the unknown mean of the variable y and the ε_i are error terms. It is assumed that $\varepsilon_1 = (1 - \gamma^2)^{-1/2}\eta_1$ and $\varepsilon_i = \gamma\varepsilon_{i-1} + \eta_i$ for $i = 2, \cdots, n$, where the terms η_i (with mean zero) are uncorrelated and homoskedastic and where $-1 < \gamma < 1$.

a. Show that the error terms ε_i are homoskedastic but that all autocorrelations are non-zero. Describe in detail how μ can be estimated by the Cochrane–Orcutt method.

b. Investigate whether the estimator of **a** is unbiased. Investigate also whether it is consistent.

c. Now suppose that the error terms are not generated by the above process, but that instead $\varepsilon_1 = \eta_1$ and $\varepsilon_i = \varepsilon_{i-1} + \eta_i$ for $i = 2, \cdots, n$. Derive the best linear unbiased estimator for μ in this model.

d. Investigate whether the estimator of **c** is unbiased. Investigate also whether it is consistent.

e. Try to give an intuitive explanation of the result in **d**.

5.11 (☞ Section 5.5.3)
Let $y_i = \beta y_{i-1} + \varepsilon_i$ and $\varepsilon_i = \gamma\varepsilon_{i-1} + \eta_i$, where $-1 < \beta < 1$ and $-1 < \gamma < 1$ and the terms η_i are homoskedastic and uncorrelated. By b we denote the OLS estimator of β and by r the estimator of γ obtained by regressing the OLS residuals e_i on their lagged values e_{i-1}.

a. Show that the above model can be rewritten as $y_i = (\beta + \gamma)y_{i-1} - \beta\gamma y_{i-2} + \eta_i$ and that the two transformed parameters ($\beta + \gamma$ and $\beta\gamma$) can be estimated consistently by OLS. Can this result be used to estimate β and γ?

b. Prove that $\text{plim}(b) = \beta + \frac{\gamma(1-\beta^2)}{1+\beta\gamma}$.

c. Prove that $\text{plim}(b) + \text{plim}(r) = \beta + \gamma$.

d. What is the implication of these results for the Durbin–Watson test when lagged values of the dependent variable are used as explanatory variables in a regression model?

5.12 (☞ Sections 5.6.2, 5.6.4)
In this exercise we use the notation of Sections 5.6.2 and 5.6.4.

a. Prove that the leverages h_j in (5.54) satisfy $0 \leq h_j \leq 1$ and $\sum_{j=1}^{n} h_j = k$.

b. Let $b(j)$ and $s^2(j)$ be the estimators of β and the disturbance variance σ^2 obtained by the regression $y_i = x_i'\beta + \varepsilon_i, i \neq j$—that is, by leaving out the jth observation. Further let $\hat{\beta}$ and $\hat{\gamma}$ be the OLS estimators of β and γ in the model (5.55)—that is, OLS for all observations but with a dummy for the jth observation included in the model—and let s_j^2 be the corresponding estimated disturbance variance. Prove that $\hat{\beta} = b(j)$, $\hat{\gamma} = y_j - x_j'b(j)$, and $s_j^2 = s^2(j)$.

c. The studentized residual in (5.56) can be interpreted as a Chow forecast test for the jth observation, where the forecast is based on the $(n - 1)$ observations $i \neq j$. Prove this, using the results of **b** and of Exercise 3.11.

d. Show that (5.64) is a consistent estimator of σ in the simple case that $y_i = \mu + \varepsilon_i$, where the ε_i are $\text{NID}(0, \sigma^2)$.

5.13 (☞ Section 5.6.2)
Consider the simple regression model $y_i = \alpha + \beta x_i + \varepsilon_i$. The following results are helpful in computing regression diagnostics for this model by means of a single regression including all n observations. We use the notation of Section 5.6.2.

a. Show that the leverages are equal to $h_j = \frac{1}{n} + \frac{(x_j - \bar{x})^2}{\sum (x_i - \bar{x})^2}$.

b. Show that $s_j^2 = \frac{n-k}{n-k-1}s^2 - \frac{e_j^2}{(n-k-1)(1-h_j)}$.

c. Show that the 'dfbetas' (for β) are equal to $\frac{e_j^*}{\sqrt{1-h_j}}\frac{x_j - \bar{x}}{\sqrt{\sum (x_i - \bar{x})^2}}$.

d. Give an interpretation of the results in **a** and **c** by drawing scatter plots.

e. Show that the variance of the 'dfbetas' for the slope parameter β is approximately $\frac{(x_i-\bar{x})^2}{\sum(x_i-\bar{x})^2}$, with average value $1/n$.

f. Now consider the multiple regression model. Show that the average variance of the 'dfbetas' in (5.58) in this case is approximately equal to $1/n$ if the terms a_{ll} are approximately constant—that is, if all least squares coefficients have approximately the same standard error.

5.14 (☞ Section 5.6.4)
Consider estimation of the mean μ from a random sample $y_i = \mu + \varepsilon_i, i = 1, \cdots, n$.

a. Let μ be estimated by minimizing the criterion $\sum |y_i - \mu|$. Show that the median $m = \text{med}(y_i, i = 1, \cdots, n)$ is optimal for this criterion (distinguish the cases n odd and n even).

b. Show that the median is the maximum likelihood estimator if the disturbances are independently distributed with the double-exponential distribution with density function $f(\varepsilon_i) = \frac{1}{2\alpha} e^{-|\varepsilon_i|/\alpha}$. Compare this distribution with the normal distribution, and give an intuitive motivation why the median will be a better estimator than the sample mean in this case.

c. Now suppose that the disturbances are independently $t(d)$ distributed with density $f(\varepsilon_i) = c_d \left(1 + \frac{\varepsilon_i^2}{d}\right)^{-\frac{d+1}{2}}$, where d is positive and c_d is a scaling constant. Show that the ML estimator is relatively insensitive to outliers (for small values of d) by writing out the first order condition $d \log(L)/d\mu = 0$.

d. Show this also by computing the weights w_i in (5.61) for the t-distribution.

5.15 (☞ Section 5.6.4)
As estimation criterion we consider expressions of the form $S(\theta) = \sum_{i=1}^n G(e_i(\theta))$, where $e_i(\theta)$ are the residuals corresponding to θ. We impose the following conditions on the function G: $G(0) = 0$, $G(e) = G(-e)$, G is non-decreasing in $|e|$ and constant for $|e| > c$ for a given constant $c > 0$, and the Hessian of G is continuous.

a. Discuss possible motivations for each of these five conditions.

b. Let G be a non-zero polynomial of degree m—say, $G(e) = \sum_{j=0}^m G_k e^k$ for $|e| \leq c$; then prove that $m \geq 6$ is required to satisfy the five conditions.

c. Show that, up to an arbitrary multiplicative scaling constant, the only polynomial of degree six, $G(e) = \sum_{j=0}^6 G_k e^k$, that satisfies the five conditions has a derivative $g(e) = dG(e)/de = e(1 - \frac{e^2}{c^2})^2$ for $|e| \leq c$, the so-called bisquare function.

d. Make plots of the functions $G(e)$ and $g(e)$ and of the weights w_i in (5.61) corresponding to this criterion, similar to the plots shown in Exhibit 5.42. Discuss the outcomes.

5.16 (☞ Sections 5.7.1–5.7.3)
In this exercise we consider the two-step method (5.73) and (5.74) for the computation of the IV estimator. We assume that Z contains a constant term, and we denote the jth column of X by X_j and the jth column of $\hat{X}$ by $\hat{X}_j$. So X_j and $\hat{X}_j$ are $n \times 1$ vectors, with elements denoted by x_{ji} and $\hat{x}_{ji}$, $j = 1, \cdots, k$, $i = 1, \cdots, n$.

a. Prove that of all linear combinations of the instruments (that is, of all vectors of the form $v = Zc$ for some $m \times 1$ vector c), $\hat{X}_j$ is the linear combination that has the largest 'correlation' with X_j, in the sense that it maximizes $\frac{\sum_{i=1}^n x_{ji} v_i}{\sqrt{\sum_{i=1}^n x_{ji}^2 \sum_{i=1}^n v_i^2}}$.

b. If X_j is exogenous, then it is included in the set of instruments. Prove that in this case $\hat{X}_j$ in (5.73) is equal to X_j.

c. Show that the usual OLS estimator of the variance based on the regression in (5.74)—that is, $\hat{s}^2 = (y - \hat{X}b_{IV})'(y - \hat{X}b_{IV})/(n-k)$—is not a consistent estimator of σ^2.

d. If all the regressors in X are exogenous, then prove that $(\text{var}(b_{IV}) - \text{var}(b))$ is positive semidefinite. For this purpose, show first that $X'X - X'P_Z X$ is positive semidefinite.

e. Prove that the F-test on linear restrictions can be computed by (5.78). It is helpful to prove first that $\hat{e}_R'\hat{e}_R - e_{RIV}'P_Z e_{RIV} = y'y - y'P_Z y$ and also that $\hat{e}'\hat{e} - e_{IV}'P_Z e_{IV} = y'y - y'P_Z y$.

5.17* (☞ Section 5.7.3)
This exercise is concerned with the derivation of the Hausman test for the null hypothesis that all regressors are exogenous against the alternative that the last k_0 regressors are endogenous. We use the notation of Section 5.7.3, and we write v_i for the $k_0 \times 1$ vector with elements v_{ji}, X_e for the $n \times k_0$ matrix of possibly endogenous regressors, x_{ei}' for the ith row

of X_e, α for the $k_0 \times 1$ vector with elements α_j, and Γ for the $k_0 \times m$ matrix with rows γ_j'. In the equations $x_{ei} = \Gamma z_i + v_i$ it is assumed that $v_i \sim \text{NID}(0, \Omega)$, where Ω is the $k_0 \times k_0$ covariance matrix of v_i, and in the equation $\varepsilon_i = v_i'\alpha + w_i$ (where $v_i'\alpha = E[\varepsilon_i|v_i]$) it is assumed that $w_i \sim \text{NID}(0, \sigma^2)$. The null hypothesis of exogeneity is that $\alpha = 0$, in which case $\varepsilon_i = w_i \sim \text{NID}(0, \sigma^2)$. With this notation, the model (5.82) can be written as

$$\begin{aligned} y_i &= x_i'\beta + \varepsilon_i = x_i'\beta + v_i'\alpha + w_i \\ &= x_i'\beta + (x_{ei} - \Gamma z_i)'\alpha + w_i. \end{aligned}$$

This model is non-linear in the parameters $\theta = (\alpha, \beta, \Gamma, \sigma^2, \Omega^{-1})$, because of the product term $\Gamma'\alpha$.

a. Show that the log-likelihood is given by $l(\theta) = -n\log(2\pi) + \frac{n}{2}\log\det(\Omega^{-1}) - \frac{1}{2}\sum_{i=1}^{n} v_i'\Omega^{-1}v_i - \frac{n}{2}\log(\sigma^2) - \frac{1}{2\sigma^2}\sum_{i=1}^{n} w_i^2$.

b. Show that the ML estimators obtained under the null hypothesis that $\alpha = 0$, are given by $\hat{\beta} = b$, $\hat{\Gamma}' = (Z'Z)^{-1}Z'X_e$, $\hat{\sigma}^2 = e'e/n$, and $\hat{\Omega} = \frac{1}{n}\sum \hat{v}_i\hat{v}_i'$, where $\hat{v}_i = x_{ei} - \hat{\Gamma}z_i$.

c. Show that the score vector $\partial l/\partial\theta$ of the unrestricted log-likelihood, evaluated at the estimates of **b**, is zero, with the exception of $\partial l/\partial\alpha$, which is equal to $\frac{1}{\hat{\sigma}^2}\hat{V}'e$.

d. The Hessian matrix $(-\frac{\partial^2 l}{\partial\theta\partial\theta'})$ is a 5×5 block matrix with blocks B_{rs}. Let sub-index 1 indicate the blocks related to α and sub-index 2 the blocks related to β, then show that $B_{11} = \frac{1}{\hat{\sigma}^2}\hat{V}'\hat{V}$, that $B_{12} = B_{21}' = \frac{1}{\hat{\sigma}^2}\hat{V}'X$, and that $B_{22} = \frac{1}{\hat{\sigma}^2}X'X$. Further the following approximations may be used in **e**, but these results need not be proved: $B_{rs} = 0$ for all (r, s) with $r = 1, 2$ and $s = 3, 4, 5$, and also for all (r, s) with $r = 3, 4, 5$ and $s = 1, 2$.

e. Use the results in **c** and **d** to prove that the LM-test computed according to $LM = (\frac{\partial l}{\partial\theta})'(-\frac{\partial^2 l}{\partial\theta\partial\theta'})^{-1}(\frac{\partial l}{\partial\theta})$ can be written as $LM = \frac{1}{\hat{\sigma}^2}e'U(U'U)^{-1}U'e$, where U is the $n \times (k_0 + k)$ matrix $U = (\hat{V}\ \ X)$.

f. Prove that **e** implies that $LM = nR^2$ of the regression in (5.83).

5.18 (☜ Section 5.7.1)
Consider the following model for the relation between macroeconomic consumption (C), disposable income (D), and non-consumptive expenditures (Z): $C_i = \alpha + \beta D_i + \varepsilon_i$ (the consumption equation) and $D_i = C_i + Z_i$ (the income equation). Here Z is assumed to be exogenous in the sense that $E[Z_i\varepsilon_i] = 0$ for all $i = 1, \cdots, n$.

a. Prove that the application of OLS in the consumption equation gives an inconsistent estimator of the parameter β.

b. Give a graphical illustration of the result in **a** by drawing a scatter plot of C against D, and use this graph to explain why OLS is not consistent.

c. Consider two cases in **b**, one where Z does not vary at all and another where Z has a very large variance.

d. Derive an explicit expression for the IV estimator of β in terms of the observed variables C, D, and Z.

e. Use the expression of **d** to prove that this IV estimator is consistent.

EMPIRICAL AND SIMULATION QUESTIONS

5.19 (☜ Section 5.3.3)

a. Generate a sample of size 100 from the model $y_i = 2 + \sqrt{x_i} + \varepsilon_i$ where the x_i are independent and uniformly distributed on the interval [0, 20] and the ε_i are independent and distributed as N(0, 0.01).

b. Regress y on a constant and x. Perform a RESET test and a Chow forecast test. Analyse the recursive residuals and the CUSUM and CUSUMSQ plots.

c. Answer the same questions after the data have been ordered with increasing values of x.

d. Estimate the model $y = \alpha + \beta x(\lambda) + \varepsilon$ by ML, where $x(\lambda) = (x^\lambda - 1)/\lambda$.

e. For the estimated value of λ, regress y on a constant and $x(\lambda)$ and analyse the corresponding recursive residuals and CUSUM and CUSUMSQ plots. Perform also a RESET test and a Chow forecast test.

5.20 (☞ Sections 5.4.2, 5.4.3)
Simulate $n = 100$ data points as follows. Let x_i consist of 100 random drawings from the standard normal distribution, let η_i be a random drawing from the distribution $N(0, x_i^2)$, and let $y_i = x_i + \eta_i$. We will estimate the model $y_i = \beta x_i + \varepsilon_i$.

a. Estimate β by OLS. Estimate the standard error of b both in the conventional way and by White's method.

b. Estimate β by WLS using the knowledge that $\sigma_i^2 = \sigma^2 x_i^2$. Compare the estimate and the standard error obtained for this WLS estimator with the results for OLS in **a**.

c. Now estimate β by WLS using the (incorrect) heteroskedasticity model $\sigma_i^2 = \sigma^2/x_i^2$. Compute the standard error of this estimate in three ways—that is, by the WLS expression corresponding to this (incorrect) model, by the White method for OLS on the (incorrectly) weighted data, and also by deriving the correct formula for the standard deviation of WLS with this incorrect model for the variances.

d. Perform 1000 simulations, where the $n = 100$ values of x_i remain the same over all simulations but the 100 values of η_i are different drawings from the $N(0, x_i^2)$ distributions and where the values of $y_i = x_i + \eta_i$ differ accordingly between the simulations. Determine the sample standard deviations over the 1000 simulations of the three estimators of β in **a**, **b**, and **c**—that is, OLS, WLS (with correct weights), and WLS (with incorrect weights).

e. Compare the three sample standard deviations in **d** with the estimated standard errors in **a**, **b**, and **c**, and comment on the outcomes. Which standard errors are reliable, and which ones are not?

5.21 (☞ Section 5.5.3)

a. Generate a sample of size $n = 100$ from the model $y_i = 2 + \sqrt{x_i} + \varepsilon_i$, where the x_i are independent and uniformly distributed on the interval [0, 20] and the ε_i are independent and distributed as $N(0, 0.01)$. Regress y on a constant and x and apply tests on serial correlation.

b. Sort the data of **a** with increasing values of x. Again regress y on a constant and x and apply tests on serial correlation. Save the residual series for later use in **e**.

c. Generate a sample of size $n = 100$ from the linear model $y_i = 2 + x_i + \varepsilon_i$, where the x_i are independent and uniformly distributed on the interval [0, 20] and the ε_i are independent and distributed as $N(0, 0.01)$. Regress y on a constant and x and apply tests on serial correlation.

d. Sort the data of **c** with increasing values of the residuals e. Again regress y on a constant and x and apply tests on serial correlation.

e. Explain the results in **b** and **d** by considering relevant scatter diagrams.

f. Discuss the relevance of your findings for the interpretation of serial correlation tests (like Durbin–Watson) for cross section data.

5.22* (☞ Section 5.5.2)
In this exercise we simulate data with the model $y_i = \beta x_i + \varepsilon_i$, $i = 1, \cdots, n$, where x_i and ε_i are both generated by an AR(1) model. That is, $x_i = \rho x_{i-1} + \omega_i$ (with $x_0 = 0$) and $\varepsilon_i = \gamma \varepsilon_{i-1} + \eta_i$ (with $\varepsilon_0 = 0$), where ω_i and η_i are both NID(0,1) with ω_i and η_j independent for all i, j. The parameters ρ and γ satisfy $-1 < \rho < 1$ and $-1 < \gamma < 1$. The OLS estimator of β is given by $b = \sum_{i=1}^n x_i y_i / \sum_{i=1}^n x_i^2$, and the conventional OLS formula for the variance is $\widehat{\text{var}}(b) = s^2/\sum_{i=1}^n x_i^2$ where $s^2 = \sum_{i=1}^n (y_i - b x_i)^2/(n-1)$.

a. Prove that, for $i \to \infty$, the correlation between x_i and x_{i-k} converges to ρ^k and the correlation between ε_i and ε_{i-k} to γ^k. Prove also that, for $i \to \infty$, the variance of x_i converges to $1/(1-\rho^2)$ and the variance of ε_i to $1/(1-\gamma^2)$.

b. Prove that, although the regressors are stochastic here, the OLS estimator b is unbiased and consistent in this case.

c. Prove that, for $n \to \infty$, the true variance of b is not given by the OLS formula $\widehat{\text{var}}(b) = s^2/\sum_{i=1}^n x_i^2$, but that it is approximately equal to $\widehat{\text{var}}(b)\frac{1+\rho\gamma}{1-\rho\gamma}$. Use the fact that s^2 is a consistent estimator of the variance $1/(1-\gamma^2)$ of the disturbances ε_i.

d. Simulate two data sets of size $n = 100$, one in the model with $\beta = 0$ and the other one in the model with $\beta = 1$. For both simulations, take $\rho = \gamma = 0.7$. For both data sets, regress y on x and compute the OLS standard error of b and also the HAC standard error of b. For the data generated with $\beta = 0$, test the null hypothesis that $\beta = 0$ against the (two-sided) alternative that $\beta \neq 0$ (at 5% significance), using the two t-values obtained by the OLS and the HAC standard errors of b.

e. Repeat the simulation of **d** 1000 times. For the model with $\beta = 0$, compute the frequency of rejection of the null hypothesis that $\beta = 0$ for the t-tests based on the OLS and the HAC standard errors of **b**.

f. For each of the two data generating processes, compute the standard deviation of the estimates b over the 1000 simulations and also the mean of the 1000 reported OLS standard errors and of the 1000 reported HAC standard errors. Compare these values and relate them to the outcomes in **e**.

g. Relate the outcomes in **f** also to the result obtained in **c**.

h. Comment on the relevance of your findings for significance tests of regression coefficients if serial correlation is neglected.

5.23 (☞ Sections 5.7.1, 5.7.3)

In this exercise we consider simulated data on the relation between police (x) and crime (y). Some of the data refer to election years ($z = 1$), the other data to non-election years ($z = 0$). We want to estimate the effect of police on crime—that is, the parameter β in the model $y_i = \alpha + \beta x_i + \varepsilon_i$.

a. Regress 'crime' on a constant and 'police'. Give a possible explanation of the estimated positive effect.

b. Give a verbal motivation why the election dummy z could serve as an instrument.

c. Show that the IV estimator of β is given by $(\overline{y}_1 - \overline{y}_0)/(\overline{x}_1 - \overline{x}_0)$, where $\overline{y}_1$ denotes the sample mean of y over election years and $\overline{y}_0$ over non-election years and where $\overline{x}_1$ and $\overline{x}_0$ are defined in a similar way. Give also an intuitive motivation for this estimator of β.

d. Use the data to estimate β by instrumental variables, using z (and a constant) as instruments. Check that the result of **c** holds true. Give an interpretation of the resulting estimate.

e. Perform the Hausman test on the exogeneity of the variable x.

5.24 (☞ Section 5.3.3)

Consider the data of Example 5.9 (ordered with education), which showed a break at observation 366 (education at least 16 years) in the marginal effect β of education on salaries (see Exhibit 5.15).

a. Check the outcomes on a break (at observation 425 for the Chow tests) discussed in Example 5.9.

b. Formulate a model with two different values of β in (5.16), one for education levels less than 16 years (observations $i \leq 365$) and another for education levels of 16 years or more (observations $i \geq 366$). Estimate this model, and give an interpretation of the outcomes.

c. Perform Chow break tests and Chow forecast tests (with the break now located at observation 366).

d. Perform a sequence of Chow break tests for all segments where the variable 'education' changes. This variable takes on ten different values, so that there are nine possible break points. Comment on the outcomes.

e. Perform also a sequence of Chow forecast tests and give an interpretation of the outcomes.

5.25 (☞ Sections 5.4.4, 5.4.5)

Consider the salary data of Example 5.15 with the regression model discussed in that example. In this exercise we adjust the model for the variances as follows: $E[\varepsilon_i^2] = \gamma_1 + \gamma_2 D_{2i} + \gamma_3 D_{3i} + \gamma_4 x_i + \gamma_5 x_i^2$—that is, the model for the variances is additive and contains also effects of the level of education.

a. Estimate the eleven parameters (six regression parameters and five variance parameters) by (two-step) FWLS and compare the outcomes with the results in Exhibit 5.22.

b. Sort the data with increasing values of x_i. Inspect the histogram of x_i and choose two subsamples to perform the Goldfeld–Quandt test on possible heteroskedasticity due to the variable x_i.

c. Perform the Breusch–Pagan test on heteroskedasticity, using the specified model for the variances.

d. Also perform the White test on heteroskedasticity.

e. Comment on the similarities and differences between the test outcomes in **b–d**.

5.26 (☞ Section 5.3.1)

In this exercise we consider data on weekly coffee sales (for brand 1). In total there are $n = 18$ weekly observations, namely six weeks without any marketing actions, six weeks with price reductions without advertisement, and six weeks with joint price reductions and advertisement. In Example 5.7 we considered similar coffee data, but only for the twelve weeks without advertisement. Now we will shift the attention to another subset of the data, and we restrict the attention to sales in the twelve weeks with marketing actions. As there are no advertisements without simultaneous price reductions, we formulate the model

$$y = \beta_1 + \beta_2 D_p + \beta_3 D_a + \beta_4 D_p D_a + \varepsilon,$$

where y denotes the logarithm of weekly sales, D_p is a dummy variable with the value 0 if the price reduction is 5% and the value 1 if this reduction is 15%, and D_a is a dummy variable that is 0 if there is no advertisement and 1 if there is advertisement.

a. Give an economic motivation for the above model. Estimate this model and test the null hypothesis that $\beta_2 = 0$. What is the P-value of this test?
b. Estimate the above model, replacing D_a by the alternative dummy variable D_a^*, which has the value 0 if there is advertisement and 1 if there is not. The model then becomes $y = \beta_1^* + \beta_2^* D_p + \beta_3^* D_a + \beta_4^* D_p D_a^* + \varepsilon$. Compare the estimated price coefficient and its t-value and P-value with the results obtained in **a**.
c. Explain why the two results for the price dummy differ in **a** and **b**. Discuss the relevance of this fact for the interpretation of coefficients of dummy variables in regression models.
d. Derive the four relations between the parameters β_i and $\beta_i^*, i = 1, \cdots, 4$, in the two models. Check that the two sets of regression parameters satisfy the same relations. Relate this result to **c**.

5.27 (☞ Sections 5.5.1, 5.5.4)

In this exercise we consider the budget data of Example 5.20, ordered in segments as discussed in Example 5.20. We consider both the linear model of Section 5.5.1 and the non-linear model of Section 5.5.4 for the relation between the fraction of expenditures spent on food (y), the total consumption expenditures (x_2, in \$10,000 per year), and the average household size (x_3).

a. Apply OLS in the linear model and perform a RESET.
b. Apply recursive least squares in the linear model and perform a CUSUM test.
c. Investigate whether the disturbances in the non-linear model are heteroskedastic. In particular, investigate whether the disturbance variance is related to the group size.
d. Discuss how the non-linear model can be estimated in case of heteroskedasticity related to the group size. Estimate this model and compare the outcomes (especially the regression coefficients and the standard errors) with the results in Example 5.25 (see Exhibit 5.34).

5.28 (☞ Sections 5.4.4, 5.6.3)

In this exercise we consider monthly data of the three-month Treasury Bill rate (r_i) in the USA from January 1985 to December 1999. In Example 5.11 we considered the monthly changes $x_i = r_i - r_{i-1}$. We consider the following simple model for the relation of these changes to the level of this interest rate: $r_i - r_{i-1} = \alpha + \beta r_{i-1} + \varepsilon_i$. In financial economics, several models are proposed for the variance of the unpredicted changes ε_i. We consider models of the form $E[\varepsilon_i^2] = \sigma^2 r_{i-1}^{2\gamma}$, so that the vector of unknown parameters is given by $\theta = (\alpha, \beta, \gamma, \sigma^2)'$. The Vasicek model postulates that $\gamma = 0$, the Cox–Ingersoll–Ross model that $\gamma = 1/2$, and the Brennan–Schwartz model that $\gamma = 1$.

a. Estimate the four parameters in θ by (two-step) FWLS.
b. Estimate θ by maximum likelihood, assuming that the error terms ε_i are normally distributed. Compare the estimates with the ones obtained in **a**.
c. Test the three hypotheses that $\gamma = 0, \gamma = 1/2$, and $\gamma = 1$, both by the Wald test and by the Likelihood Ratio test. What is your conclusion?
d. Test the hypothesis of normally distributed error terms ε_i by means of the ML residuals of **b**. What is your conclusion?

5.29 (☞ Sections 5.5.4, 5.6.2, 5.6.4)

In this exercise we consider the quarterly series of industrial production (y_i, in logarithms) for the USA over the period 1950.1–1998.3. These data were discussed in Example 5.26 (see Exhibit 5.36 to get an idea of this series).

a. Estimate the linear trend model $y_i = \alpha + \beta i + \varepsilon_i$ and test whether the slope β is constant over the sample.

b. Now include seasonal dummies to account for possible seasonal effects. Test for the individual and joint significance of the seasonal dummies.

c. Investigate the presence of outliers in this model.

d. Let $\Delta_4 y_i = y_i - y_{i-4}$ be the yearly growth rate; then estimate the model $\Delta_4 y_i = \mu + \varepsilon_i$ by OLS. What are the leverages in this model? Investigate the presence of outliers in this model.

e. How would you estimate the yearly growth rate of industrial production, by the sample mean, by the median, or in another way? Motivate your answer.

5.30 (☞ Sections 5.5.3, 5.6.2)

In Example 5.27 we considered the CAPM for the sector of cyclical consumer goods. In addition we now also consider the sector of non-cyclical consumer goods.

a. Perform tests for heteroskedasticity and serial correlation in the CAPM for the sector of cyclical consumer goods.

b. Answer **a** also for the sector of non-cyclical consumer goods.

c. Investigate the presence and nature of influential observations in the CAPM for the sector of non-cyclical consumer goods.

d. Discuss the relevance of the possible presence of heteroskedasticity and serial correlation on the detection of influential observations.

5.31 (☞ Sections 5.3.3, 5.4.5, 5.5.3, 5.6.2, 5.6.3)

In Example 5.31 we considered data on gasoline consumption (GC), price of gasoline (PG), and real income (RI) over the years 1970–99. In all tests below use a significance level of 5%.

a. Estimate the model $GC_i = \alpha + \beta PG_i + \gamma RI_i + \varepsilon_i$, using the data over the period 1970–95.

b. Perform a test on parameter constancy over this period.

c. Perform a test for heteroskedasticity over this period.

d. Perform a test for serial correlation over this period.

e. Perform a test on outliers and a test on normality of the disturbances over this period.

f. Perform a Chow forecast test for the quality of the model in **a** in forecasting the gasoline consumption in the years 1996–99, for given values of the explanatory variables over this period.

5.32 (☞ Section 5.8)

In Section 5.8 we considered the relation between the salary of top managers and the profits of firms for the 100 largest firms in the Netherlands in 1999. We postulated the model $y_i = \alpha + \beta x_i + \varepsilon_i$, where y_i is the average salary of top managers of firm i and x_i is the profit of firm i (both in logarithms).

a. Discuss whether you find the seven standard assumptions of the regression model intuitively plausible.

b. Check the results of diagnostic tests reported in Exhibit 5.49 (for the sample of $n = 96$ firms with positive profits).

c. When the model is estimated for the forty-eight firms with the smallest (positive) profits, then no significant relation is found. Check this, and discuss the importance of this finding for a top manager of a firm with small profits who wishes to predict his or her salary.

5.33 (☞ Sections 5.3.3, 5.4.3, 5.6.2)

In this exercise we consider data on the US presidential election in 2000. The data file contains the number of votes on the different candidates in the $n = 67$ counties of the state Florida, before recounting. The county Palm Beach is observation number $i = 50$. The recounts in Florida were motivated in part by possible mistakes of voters in Palm Beach who wanted to vote for Gore (the second candidate, but third punch hole on the ballot paper) but by accident first selected Buchanan (second punch hole on the ballot paper). This resulted in ballot papers with multiple punch holes. The difference (before recounts) between Bush and Gore in the state Florida was 975 votes in favour of Bush.

a. Perform a regression of the number of votes on Buchanan on a constant and the number of votes on Gore. Investigate for the presence of outliers.

b. Estimate the number of votes v in Palm Beach county that are accidentally given to Buchanan by including a dummy variable for this county in the regression model of **a**. Test the hypothesis that $v < 975$ against the alternative that $v \geq 975$.

c. The counties differ in size so that the error terms in the regression in **a** may be heteroskedastic. Perform the Breusch–Pagan test on heteroskedasticity of the form $\sigma_i^2 = h(\gamma_1 + \gamma_2 n_i)$, where n_i denotes the total number of votes on all candidates in county *i*.

d. Answer **b** and **c** also for the model where the fraction of votes (instead of the number of votes) on Buchanan in each county is explained in terms of the fraction of votes on Gore in that county. For the Breusch–Pagan test consider heteroskedasticity of the form $\sigma_i^2 = h(\gamma_1 + \gamma_2 \frac{1}{n_i})$.

e. Formulate an intuitively plausible model for the variance of the disturbance terms in the regression model of **a**, using the results of the Breusch–Pagan tests in **c** and **d**. Answer **b** using a regression equation with appropriately weighted data.

f. Discuss and investigate whether the assumptions that are needed for the (politically important) conclusion of **e** are plausible for these data.

6

Qualitative and Limited Dependent Variables

In this chapter we consider dependent variables with a restricted domain of possible outcomes. Binary variables have only two possible outcomes ('yes' and 'no'); other qualitative variables can have more than two but a finite number of possible outcomes (for example, the choice between a limited number of alternatives). It may also be that the outcomes of the dependent variable are restricted to an interval. For instance, for individual agents the amount of money spent on luxury goods or the duration of unemployment is non-negative, with a positive probability for the outcome 'zero'. For all such types of dependent variables, the linear regression model with normally distributed error terms is not suitable. We discuss probit and logit models for qualitative data, tobit models for limited dependent variables, and models for duration data.

Section 6.1 is the basic section of this chapter and it is required for the material discussed in Sections 6.2 and 6.3. These last two sections can be read independently from each other.

6.1 Binary response

6.1.1 Model formulation

☞ Uses Chapters 1–4; Sections 5.4 and 5.6.

Motivation

Students may succeed in finishing their studies or they may drop out, households may buy a trendy new product or not, and individuals may respond to a direct mailing or not. In all such cases the variable of interest can take only two possible values. Such variables are called *binary.* The two outcomes will be labelled as 1 ('success') and 0 ('failure'). The simplest statistical model to describe a binary variable y is the Bernoulli distribution with $P[y = 1] = p$ and $P[y = 0] = 1 - p$. However, it may well be that the probability of success differs among individuals, and in this section we are interested in modelling the possible causes of these differences. For instance, the probability of success for students in their studies will depend on their intelligence, the probability of buying a new trendy product will depend on income and age, and the probability of a response to a direct mailing will depend on relevant interests of the individuals.

Assumptions on explanatory variables

As before, for individual i the values of k explanatory variables are denoted by the $k \times 1$ vector x_i and the outcome of the binary dependent variable is denoted by y_i. We will always assume that the model contains a constant term and that $x_{1i} = 1$ for all individuals. Throughout this chapter we will treat the explanatory variables as fixed values, in accordance with Assumption 1 in Section 3.1.4 (p. 125). However, as was discussed in Section 4.1, in practice all data (both y_i and x_i) are often stochastic. This is the case, for instance, when the observations are obtained by random sampling from an underlying population, and this is the usual situation for the types of data considered in this chapter. All the results of this chapter carry over to the case of exogenous stochastic regressors, by interpreting the results conditional on the given outcomes of $x_i, i = 1, \cdots, n$. This kind of interpretation was also discussed in Section 4.1.2 (p. 191).

The linear probability model

For a binary dependent variable, the regression model

$$y_i = x_i'\beta + \varepsilon_i = \beta_1 + \sum_{j=2}^{k} \beta_j x_{ji} + \varepsilon_i, \quad E[\varepsilon_i] = 0 \tag{6.1}$$

is called the *linear probability model*. As $E[\varepsilon_i] = 0$ and y_i can take only the values zero and one, it follows that $x_i'\beta = E[y_i] = 0 \cdot P[y_i = 0] + 1 \cdot P[y_i = 1]$, so that

$$P[y_i = 1] = E[y_i] = x_i'\beta. \tag{6.2}$$

Note that we write $P[y_i = 1] = x_i'\beta$—that is, the subindex i of y_i indicates that we deal with an individual with characteristics x_i. This can be written more explicitly as $P[y_i = 1|x_i]$, but for simplicity of notation we delete the conditioning on x_i. Similar shorthand notations will be used throughout this chapter. In the linear probability model, $x_i'\beta$ measures the probability that an individual with characteristics x_i will make the choice $y_i = 1$, so that the marginal effect of the jth explanatory variable is equal to

$$\partial P[y_i = 1]/\partial x_{ji} = \beta_j, \ j = 2, \cdots, k.$$

Disadvantages of the linear model

The linear probability model has several disadvantages. It places implicit restrictions on the parameters β, as (6.2) requires that $0 \leq x_i'\beta \leq 1$ for all $i = 1, \cdots, n$. Further, the error terms ε_i are not normally distributed. This is because the variable y_i can take only the values zero and one, so that ε_i is a random variable with discrete distribution given by

$$\begin{aligned} \varepsilon_i &= 1 - x_i'\beta \quad \text{with probability} \quad x_i'\beta \\ \varepsilon_i &= -x_i'\beta \qquad \text{with probability} \quad 1 - x_i'\beta. \end{aligned}$$

The distribution of ε_i depends on x_i and has variance equal to $\text{var}(\varepsilon_i) = x_i'\beta(1 - x_i'\beta)$, so that the error terms are heteroskedastic with variances that depend on β. The assumption that $E[\varepsilon_i] = 0$ in (6.1) implies that OLS is an unbiased estimator of β (provided that the regressors are exogenous), but clearly it is not efficient and the conventional OLS formulas for the standard errors do not apply. Further, if the OLS estimates b are used to compute the estimated probabilities $\hat{P}[y_i = 1] = x_i'b$, then this may give values smaller than zero or larger than one, in which case they are not real 'probabilities'. This may occur because OLS neglects the implicit restrictions $0 \leq x_i'\beta \leq 1$.

Non-linear model for probabilities

The probabilities can be confined to values between zero and one by using a non-linear model. Let F be a function with values ranging between zero and one, and let

$$P[y_i = 1] = F(x_i'\beta). \tag{6.3}$$

For the ease of interpretation of this model, the function F is always taken to be monotonically non-decreasing. In this case, if $\beta_j > 0$, then an increase in x_{ji} leads to an increase (or at least not to a decrease) of the probability that $y_i = 1$. That is, positive (negative) coefficients correspond to positive (negative) effects on the probability of success. An obvious choice for the function F is a cumulative distribution function. This is illustrated in Exhibit 6.1.

Marginal effects on probabilities

In the model (6.3) $x_i'\beta$ can be interpreted as the strength of the stimulus for the outcome $y_i = 1$, with $P[y_i = 1] = F(x_i'\beta) \to 1$ if $x_i'\beta \to \infty$ and $P[y_i = 1] \to 0$ if $x_i'\beta \to -\infty$. Assuming that F is differentiable with derivative f (the density function corresponding to F), the *marginal effect* of the jth explanatory variable is given by

$$\frac{\partial P[y_i = 1]}{\partial x_{ji}} = f(x_i'\beta)\beta_j, \quad j = 2, \cdots, k. \tag{6.4}$$

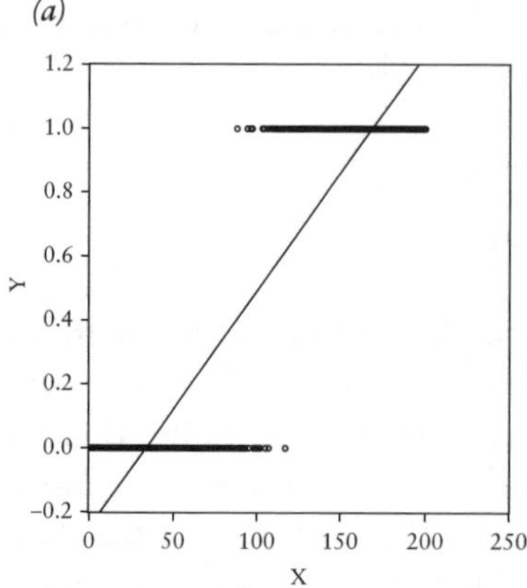

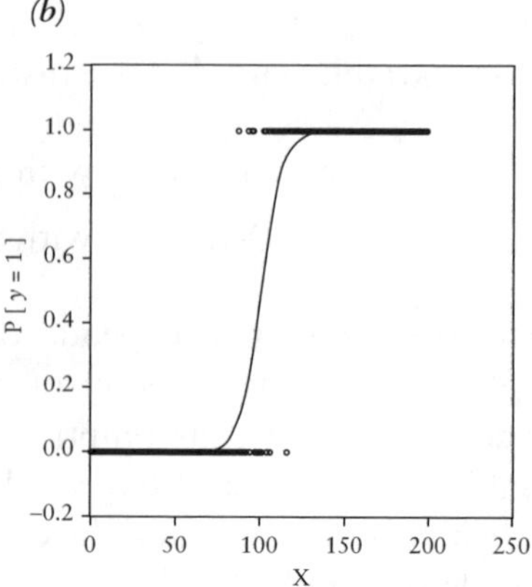

Exhibit 6.1 Probability Models

Binary dependent variable (y takes value 0 or 1) with linear probability model (*a*) and with non-linear probability model in terms of a cumulative distribution function (*b*), for a single explanatory variable (x).

This shows that the marginal effect of changes in the explanatory variables depends on the level of these variables. Usually, the density function f has relatively smaller values in the tails and relatively larger values near the mean, so that the effects are smallest for individuals for which $P[y_i = 1]$ is near zero (in the left tail of f) or near one (in the right tail of f). This conforms with the intuition that individuals with clear-cut preferences are less affected by changes in the explanatory variables. The sensitivity of decisions to changes in the explanatory variables depends on the shape of the density function f. It is usually assumed that this density has mean zero, which is no loss of generality, because the explanatory variables include a constant term. Further it is usually assumed that the density is unimodal and symmetric, so that $f(t)$ is maximal for $t = 0$ and $f(t) = f(-t)$ for all t. Then the marginal effects are maximal for values of $x_i'\beta$ around zero, where $P[y_i = 1]$ is around 1/2.

Restriction needed for parameter identification

The standard deviation of the density f should be specified beforehand. Indeed, if $g(t) = \sigma f(\sigma t)$, then the cumulative distribution functions (G of g and F of f) are related by $G(t) = F(\sigma t)$, so that $P[y_i = 1] = F(x_i'\beta) = G(x_i'\beta/\sigma)$. That is, the model (6.3) with function F and parameter vector β is equivalent to the model with function G and parameter vector β/σ. So the variance of the distribution f should be fixed, independent of the data, as otherwise the parameter vector β is not identified.

Interpretation of model in terms of latent variables

The model (6.3) can be given an interpretation in terms of an unobserved variable y_i^* that represents the latent preference of individual i for the choice $y_i = 1$. It is assumed that

$$y_i^* = x_i'\beta + \varepsilon_i, \quad \varepsilon_i \sim \text{IID}, \quad E[\varepsilon_i] = 0.$$

This is the so-called *index function*, where $x_i'\beta$ is the systematic preference and ε_i the individual–specific effect. This takes the possibility into account that individuals with the same observed characteristics x may make different choices because of unobserved individual effects. The observed choice y is related to the index y^* by means of the equation

$$\begin{aligned} y_i &= 1 \ \text{ if } \ y_i^* \geq 0, \\ y_i &= 0 \ \text{ if } \ y_i^* < 0. \end{aligned}$$

It is assumed that the individual effects ε_i are independent and identically distributed with symmetric density f—that is, $f(\varepsilon_i) = f(-\varepsilon_i)$. It then follows that $P[\varepsilon_i \geq -t] = \int_{-t}^{\infty} f(s)ds = \int_{-\infty}^{t} f(s)ds = P[\varepsilon_i \leq t]$, so that $P[y_i = 1] = P[\varepsilon_i \geq -x_i'\beta] = P[\varepsilon_i \leq x_i'\beta] = F(x_i'\beta)$, where F is the cumulative distribution function of ε_i. This provides an interpretation of the model (6.3) in terms of differences in the individual effects ε_i over the population.

Interpretation of model in terms of utilities

Another possible interpretation of the model (6.3) is in terms of the *utilities* U^0 and U^1 of the two alternative choices. The utilities for individual i are defined by

$$U_i^0 = x_i'\beta_0 + \varepsilon_{0i}, \quad U_i^1 = x_i'\beta_1 + \varepsilon_{1i}.$$

The alternative with maximal utility is chosen, so that

$$\begin{aligned} y_i &= 1 \text{ if } U_i^0 \leq U_i^1, \\ y_i &= 0 \text{ if } U_i^0 > U_i^1. \end{aligned}$$

In this case the choice depends on the difference in the utilities $U_i^1 - U_i^0 = x_i'\beta + \varepsilon_i$, where $\beta = \beta_1 - \beta_0$ and $\varepsilon_i = \varepsilon_{1i} - \varepsilon_{0i}$. Again, if the individual-specific terms ε_i are assumed to be independent and identically distributed with symmetric density f, it follows that $P[y_i = 1] = P[\varepsilon_i \geq -x_i'\beta] = P[\varepsilon_i \leq x_i'\beta] = F(x_i'\beta)$. So this motivates the model (6.3) in terms of unobserved individual effects in the utilities of the two alternatives.

Example 6.1: **Direct Marketing for Financial Product**

To illustrate the modelling of binary response data, we consider data that were collected in a marketing campaign for a new financial product of a commercial investment firm (Robeco). We will discuss (i) the motivation of the marketing campaign, and (ii) the data set.

(i) **Motivation of the marketing campaign**

The campaign consisted of a direct mailing to customers of the firm. The firm is interested in identifying characteristics that might explain which customers are interested in the new product and which ones are not. In particular, there may be differences between male and female customers and between active and inactive customers (where active means that the customer already invests in other products of the firm). Also the age of customers may be of importance, as relatively young and relatively old customers may have less interest in investing in this product than middle-aged people.

(ii) The data set

The variable to be explained is whether a customer is interested in the new financial product or not. This is denoted by the binary variable y_i, with $y_i = 1$ if the ith customer is interested and $y_i = 0$ otherwise. Apart from a constant term (denoted by $x_{1i} = 1$), the explanatory variables are gender (denoted by $x_{2i} = 0$ for females and $x_{2i} = 1$ for males), activity (denoted by $x_{3i} = 1$ for customers that are already active investors and $x_{3i} = 0$ for customers that do not yet invest in other products of the firm), age (in years, denoted by x_{4i}) and the square of age (divided by hundred, denoted by $x_{5i} = x_{4i}^2/100$).

The data set considered in this chapter is drawn from a much larger database that contains more than 100,000 observations. A sample of 1000 observations is drawn from this database, and 75 observations are omitted because of missing data (on the age of the customer). This leaves a data set of $n = 925$ customers. Of these customers, 470 responded positively (denoted by $y_i = 1$) and the remaining 455 did not respond (denoted by $y_i = 0$). The original data set of more than 100,000 observations contains only around 5000 respondents. So our sample contains relatively many more positive responses (470 out of 925) than the original database. The effect of this selection is analysed in Exercises 6.2 and 6.11. For further background on the data we refer to the research report by P. H. Franses, 'On the Econometrics of Modelling Marketing Response', RIBES Report 97-15, Rotterdam, 1997. This data set will be further analysed in Examples 6.2 and 6.3.

6.1.2 Probit and logit models

Model formulation

The model (6.3) depends not only on the choice of the explanatory variables x but also on the shape of the distribution function F. This choice corresponds to assuming a specific distribution for the unobserved individual effects (in the index function or in the utilities) and it determines the shape of the marginal response function (6.4) via the corresponding density function f. In practice one often chooses either the standard normal density

$$f(t) = \phi(t) = \frac{1}{\sqrt{2\pi}} e^{-\frac{1}{2}t^2}$$

or the logistic density

$$f(t) = \lambda(t) = \frac{e^t}{(1 + e^t)^2}.$$

The model (6.3) with the standard normal distribution is called the *probit model*, and that with the logistic distribution is called the *logit model*.

Comparison of probit and logit model

Both the standard normal density and the logistic density have mean zero and are unimodal and symmetric. The standard deviation of both distributions is fixed, for reasons explained before. The logistic distribution has standard deviation $\sigma = \pi/\sqrt{3} \approx 1.8$, whereas the standard normal distribution has standard deviation 1. In order to compare the two models, the graphs of the density $\phi(t)$ and the standardized logistic density $\sigma\lambda(\sigma t)$ are given in Exhibit 6.2. This shows that, as compared to the probit model, the logit model has marginal effects (6.4) that are relatively somewhat larger around the mean and in the tails but somewhat smaller in the two regions in between. There are often no compelling reasons to choose between the logit and probit model. An advantage of the logit model is that the cumulative distribution function $F = \Lambda$ can be computed explicitly, as

$$\Lambda(t) = \int_{-\infty}^{t} \lambda(s)ds = \frac{e^t}{1+e^t} = \frac{1}{1+e^{-t}}, \qquad (6.5)$$

whereas the cumulative distribution function $F = \Phi$ of the probit model should be computed numerically by approximating the integral

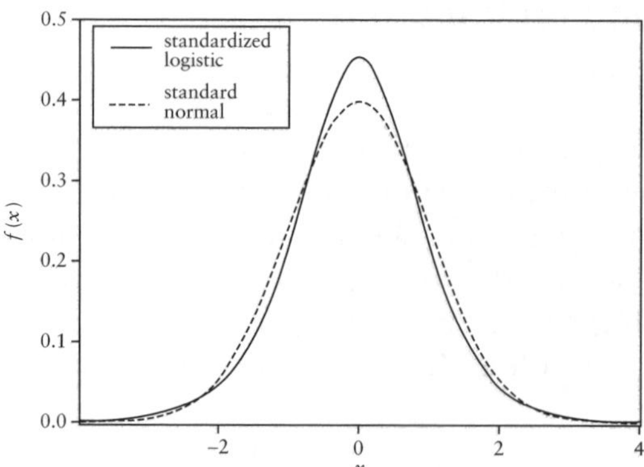

Exhibit 6.2 Normal and logistic densities

Densities of the standard normal distribution (dashed line) and of the logistic distribution (solid line, scaled so that both densities have standard deviation equal to 1). As compared with the normal density, the logistic density has larger values around the mean ($x = 0$) and also in both tails (for values of x far away from 0).

$$\Phi(t) = \int_{-\infty}^{t} \phi(s)ds = \frac{1}{\sqrt{2\pi}} \int_{-\infty}^{t} e^{-\frac{1}{2}s^2}\, ds. \qquad (6.6)$$

In practice this poses no real problems, however, as there exist very accurate numerical integration algorithms. In general the differences between the two models are not so large, unless the tails of the distributions are of importance. This is the case when the choices are very unbalanced, in the sense that the fraction of individuals with $y_i = 1$ differs considerably from $\frac{1}{2}$.

Comparison of parameters of the two models: scaling

One can, of course, always estimate both the logit and the probit model and compare the outcomes. The parameters of the two models should be *scaled* for such a comparison. Instead of the scaling factor 1.8, which gives the two densities the same variance, one often uses another correction factor. The marginal effects (6.4) of the explanatory variables are maximal around zero, so that these effects are of special interest. As $\phi(0)/\lambda(0) = 4/\sqrt{2\pi} \approx 1.6$, the estimated probit parameters β can be multiplied by 1.6 to compare them with the estimated logit parameters. In terms of Exhibit 6.2 this means that, after scaling, the two densities have the same function value in $t = 0$.

Marginal effects of explanatory variables

As concerns the interpretation of the parameters β, (6.4) shows that the signs of the coefficients β_j and the relative magnitudes β_j/β_h have a direct interpretation in terms of the sign and the relative magnitude of the marginal effects of the explanatory variables on the chance of success ($y_i = 1$). Since the marginal effects depend on the values of x_i, these effects vary among the different individuals. The effects of the jth explanatory variable can be summarized by the *mean marginal effects* over the sample of n individuals—that is,

$$\frac{1}{n}\sum_{i=1}^{n} \frac{\partial P[y_i = 1]}{\partial x_{ji}} = \beta_j \frac{1}{n}\sum_{i=1}^{n} f(x_i'\beta), \quad j - 2, \cdots, k.$$

Sometimes the effect at the mean values of the explanatory variables is reported instead—that is, (6.4) evaluated at $\overline{x} = \frac{1}{n}\sum_{i=1}^{n} x_i$. This is a bit simpler to compute, but the interpretation is somewhat less clear. When the jth explanatory variable is a dummy variable, it remains possible to compute 'marginal' effects in this way. Instead, it is also possible to compare the two situations $x_{ji} = 0$ and $x_{ji} = 1$ by comparing

$P[y_i = 1] = F\left(\sum_{l \neq j} \beta_l x_{li}\right)$ (for individuals with $x_{ji} = 0$) with $P[y_i = 1] = F\left(\beta_j + \sum_{l \neq j} \beta_l x_{li}\right)$ (for individuals with $x_{ji} = 1$). This may reveal differences in the effect of the dummy variable for different ranges of the other explanatory variables (x_{li} with $l \neq j$).

Comparison of probabilities and the odds ratio

It may further be informative to consider the predicted probabilities $p_i = P[y_i = 1] = F(x_i'\beta)$, $i = 1, \cdots, n$—for instance, the mean, variance, minimum, and maximum of these probabilities. The individuals may also be split into groups, after which the values of p_i can be compared within and between groups. Of special interest is the *odds ratio*, which is defined by

$$\frac{P[y_i = 1]}{P[y_i = 0]} = \frac{F(x_i'\beta)}{1 - F(x_i'\beta)}.$$

So the odds ratio is the relative preference of option 1 as compared to option 0. This preference depends on the values x_i of the explanatory variables. The *log-odds* is the natural logarithm of the odds ratio. In the logit model with $F = \Lambda$ there holds $\Lambda(t) = e^t/(1 + e^t)$ and $1 - \Lambda(t) = 1/(1 + e^t)$, so that $\Lambda(t)/(1 - \Lambda(t)) = e^t$ and

$$\log\left(\frac{\Lambda(x_i'\beta)}{1 - \Lambda(x_i'\beta)}\right) = x_i'\beta.$$

That is, in the logit model the log-odds is a linear function of the explanatory variables.

As a constant term is included in the model, we can transform the data by measuring all other explanatory variables $(x_2, \cdots, x_k)$ in deviation from their sample mean. After this transformation, the odds ratio, evaluated at the sample mean of the explanatory variables, becomes $F(\beta_1)/(1 - F(\beta_1))$, and this provides the following interpretation of the constant term. If $\beta_1 = 0$, then the odds ratio evaluated at the sample mean is equal to 1 (as $F(0) = \frac{1}{2}$, both for the probit and for the logit model), so that for an 'average' individual both choices are equally likely. If $\beta_1 > 0$, then $F(\beta_1) > F(0) = \frac{1}{2}$, so that an 'average' individual has a relative preference for alternative 1 above alternative 0, and, if $\beta_1 < 0$, an 'average' individual has a relative preference for alternative 0 above alternative 1.

☞ Exercises: T: 6.2a–c; S: 6.7a–c.

6.1.3 Estimation and evaluation

The likelihood function

The logit and probit models are non-linear and the parameters can be estimated by maximum likelihood. Suppose that a random sample of n outcomes of the binary variable y_i is available. If the probability of success is the same for all observations—say, $P[y_i = 1] = p$—then the probability distribution of the ith observation is given by $p^{y_i}(1-p)^{1-y_i}$. If the observations are mutually independent, then the likelihood function is given by $L(p) = \Pi_{i=1}^{n} p^{y_i}(1-p)^{1-y_i}$ and the log-likelihood by

$$\begin{aligned}\log(L(p)) &= \sum_{\{i;\, y_i=1\}} \log(p) + \sum_{\{i;\, y_i=0\}} \log(1-p) \\ &= \sum_{i=1}^{n} y_i \log(p) + \sum_{i=1}^{n} (1-y_i)\log(1-p).\end{aligned}$$

Maximizing this with respect to p we get the ML estimator $\hat{p} = \sum_{i=1}^{n} y_i/n$. Now suppose that the observations $y_1, \cdots, y_n$ are mutually independent but that the probability of success differs among the observations according to the model (6.3), all with the same function F but with differences in the values of the explanatory variables x_i. Then the variable y_i follows a Bernoulli distribution with probability

$$p_i = P[y_i = 1] = F(x_i'\beta)$$

on the outcome $y_i = 1$ and with probability $(1 - p_i)$ on the outcome $y_i = 0$. The probability distribution is then given by $p(y_i) = p_i^{y_i}(1-p_i)^{1-y_i}$, $y_i = 0, 1$. The log-likelihood is therefore equal to

$$\begin{aligned}\log(L(\beta)) &= \sum_{i=1}^{n} y_i \log(p_i) + \sum_{i=1}^{n} (1-y_i)\log(1-p_i) \\ &= \sum_{i=1}^{n} y_i \log(F(x_i'\beta)) + \sum_{i=1}^{n} (1-y_i)\log(1-F(x_i'\beta)) \\ &= \sum_{\{i;\, y_i=1\}} \log(F(x_i'\beta)) + \sum_{\{i;\, y_i=0\}} \log(1-F(x_i'\beta)). \qquad (6.7)\end{aligned}$$

The terms p_i depend on β, but for simplicity of notation we will in the sequel often write p_i instead of the more explicit expression $F(x_i'\beta)$.

Maximization of the log-likelihood

The maximum likelihood estimates are obtained by solving the first order conditions. Using the fact that the density function $f(t)$ is the derivative of the cumulative distribution function $F(t)$, the k first order conditions are given by

$$\begin{aligned} g(\beta) = \frac{\partial \log(L)}{\partial \beta} &= \sum_{i=1}^{n} \frac{y_i}{p_i} \frac{\partial p_i}{\partial \beta} + \sum_{i=1}^{n} \frac{(1-y_i)}{1-p_i} \frac{\partial (1-p_i)}{\partial \beta} \\ &= \sum_{i=1}^{n} \frac{y_i}{p_i} f_i x_i - \sum_{i=1}^{n} \frac{(1-y_i)}{1-p_i} f_i x_i = \sum_{i=1}^{n} \frac{y_i - p_i}{p_i(1-p_i)} f_i x_i = 0. \end{aligned} \tag{6.8}$$

Here $f_i = f(x_i'\beta)$ is the density function corresponding to the cumulative distribution function F. These first order conditions can be seen as a variation of the normal equations $\sum_{i=1}^{n} e_i x_i = 0$ of the linear regression model. In a binary response model, $y_i - p_i = y_i - P[y_i = 1]$ is the residual of the model (6.3) with respect to the actually observed outcome of y_i. The weighting factor $p_i(1 - p_i)$ is equal to the variance of y_i, so that this corresponds to the usual correction for heteroskedasticity in weighted least squares (see Section 5.4.3 (p. 327–8)). Finally, the factor f_i reflects the fact that the marginal effects (6.4) are not constant over the sample (as is the case in a linear regression model) but depend on the value of $f(x_i'\beta)$. The set of k non-linear equations $g(\beta) = 0$ can be solved numerically—for instance, by Newton–Raphson—to give the estimate b. To get an idea of the effects of the different explanatory variables it can be helpful to plot the predicted probabilities $\hat{P}[y = 1] = F(x'b)$ and the corresponding odds ratio or log-odds against each individual explanatory variable, fixing the other variables at their sample means.

Approximate distribution of the ML estimator

The general properties of ML estimators were discussed in Section 4.3.3 (p. 228)—for instance, large sample standard errors can be obtained from the inverse of the information matrix. It is often convenient to use the outer product of gradients expression for this (see Sections 4.3.2 and 4.3.3 and formula (4.57) in Section 4.3.8). With the notation introduced there, we have $\partial l_i/\partial \beta = (y_i - p_i) f_i x_i/(p_i(1 - p_i))$, so that the covariance matrix of b can be estimated by

$$\text{var}(b) \approx \hat{V} = \left[\sum_{i=1}^{n} \frac{\partial l_i}{\partial \beta} \frac{\partial l_i}{\partial \beta'} \right]^{-1} = \left[\sum_{i=1}^{n} \frac{(y_i - \hat{p}_i)^2}{\hat{p}_i^2 (1 - \hat{p}_i)^2} \hat{f}_i^2 x_i x_i' \right]^{-1}, \tag{6.9}$$

where $\hat{p}_i = F(x_i'b)$ and $\hat{f}_i = f(x_i'b)$. Under the stated assumptions—that is, that the observations y_i are independently distributed with $P[y_i = 1] = F(x_i'\beta)$ with the same cumulative distribution function F for all observations—the ML estimator b has an asymptotic normal distribution in the sense that $\sqrt{n}(b - \beta)$ converges in distribution to the normal distribution with mean zero and covariance matrix $\text{plim}(n\hat{V})$. This probability limit exists under weak regularity conditions on the explanatory variables x_i. In finite samples this gives

$$b \approx \mathrm{N}(\beta, \hat{V}). \tag{6.10}$$

These results can be used to perform t- and F-tests in the usual way, and of course the Likelihood Ratio test (4.44) can also be applied.

Results for the logit model

T

The foregoing expressions apply for any choice of the distribution function F. As an illustration we consider the logit model with $F = \Lambda$ in (6.5) in more detail. The expression for the gradient (6.8) simplifies in this case as

$$\lambda_i = \frac{e^{x_i'\beta}}{(1 + e^{x_i'\beta})^2} = \frac{e^{x_i'\beta}}{1 + e^{x_i'\beta}}\left(1 - \frac{e^{x_i'\beta}}{1 + e^{x_i'\beta}}\right) = \Lambda_i(1 - \Lambda_i),$$

so that $f_i = p_i(1 - p_i)$ in this case. Therefore the logit estimates are obtained by solving the k equations

$$g(\beta) = \sum_{i=1}^{n} (y_i - p_i)x_i = \sum_{i=1}^{n}\left(y_i - \frac{1}{1 + e^{-x_i'\beta}}\right)x_i = 0.$$

As the first explanatory variable is the constant term with $x_{1i} = 1$ for all $i = 1, \cdots, n$, it follows that $\sum_{i=1}^{n} (y_i - \hat{p}_i) = 0$, so that

$$\frac{1}{n}\sum_{i=1}^{n} \hat{p}_i = \frac{1}{n}\sum_{i=1}^{n} y_i.$$

So the logit model has the property that the average predicted probabilities of success and failure are equal to the observed fractions of successes and failures in the sample. The ML first order conditions (6.11) have a unique solution, because the Hessian matrix

$$\frac{\partial^2 \log(L)}{\partial\beta\partial\beta'} = \frac{\partial g(\beta)}{\partial\beta'} = -\sum_{i=1}^{n} f_i x_i x_i' = -\sum_{i=1}^{n} p_i(1 - p_i)x_i x_i'$$

is negative definite. This simplifies the numerical optimization, and in general the Newton–Raphson iterations will converge rather rapidly to the global maximum. The information matrix (for given values of the explanatory variables) is given by

$$\mathcal{I}_n = -E\left[\frac{\partial^2 \log(L)}{\partial\beta\partial\beta'}\right] = \sum_{i=1}^{n} p_i(1 - p_i)x_i x_i'. \tag{6.11}$$

Large sample standard errors of the logit parameters can be obtained, as discussed in Section 4.3.3 (p. 228)—that is, by substituting the logit estimate b for β in the above expression and by taking the square roots of the diagonal elements of the inverse of (6.11). Expression (6.9) for the covariance matrix can be obtained from (6.11) by replacing the terms $p_i(1 - p_i)$ in (6.11) by $(y_i - p_i)^2$, since for the logit model $\hat{f}_i^2 = \hat{p}_i^2(1 - \hat{p}_i^2)$, so that these terms cancel in (6.9). As $E[(y_i - p_i)^2] = \text{var}(y_i) = p_i(1 - p_i)$, the two expressions (6.9) and $\mathcal{I}_n^{-1}$ of (6.11) for the covariance matrix are asymptotically equivalent.

Remarks on the probit model

The analysis of the probit model is technically somewhat more involved. The Hessian matrix is again negative definite, and the numerical optimization poses no problems in general. With suitable software, the practical usefulness of probit and logit models is very much alike.

E

XM601DMF

Example 6.2: **Direct Marketing for Financial Product (continued)**

We continue our analysis of the direct mailing data introduced in Example 6.1. We will discuss (i) the outcomes of estimated logit and probit models for the probability that a customer is interested in the product, and (ii) the odds ratios (depending on the age of the customer) of the two models.

(i) Outcomes of logit and probit models

The dependent variable is y_i with $y_i = 1$ if the ith individual is interested and $y_i = 0$ otherwise. The explanatory variables are gender, activity, and age (with a linear and a squared term) (see Example 6.1). The results of logit and probit models are given in Panels 2 and 3 of Exhibit 6.3. For comparison the results of the linear probability model are also given (see Panel 1). All models indicate that the variables 'gender' and 'activity' are statistically the most significant ones. As the corresponding two parameters are positive, these variables have a positive impact on the probability of responding to the mailing. That is, male customers and active customers tend to be more interested than female and inactive customers. The effects of 'gender' and 'activity' are almost the same.

The numerical values of the coefficients of the three models can be compared by determining the mean marginal effects of the explanatory variables in the three models. As discussed in Section 6.1.2, the mean marginal effect of the jth explanatory variable is $\beta_j \frac{1}{n}\sum_{i=1}^n f(x_i'\beta)$, so we take as correction factor $\frac{1}{n}\sum_{i=1}^n f(x_i'b)$. For our data, in the logit model this correction factor is 0.230 and in the probit model it is 0.373. For instance, the mean marginal effect of the variable gender is 0.224 in the linear probability model (see Panel 1), $0.954 \cdot 0.230 = 0.219$ in the logit model, and $0.588 \cdot 0.373 = 0.219$ in the probit model. So the coefficients of the variable gender differs in the three models (0.224, 0.954, 0.588), but their interpretation in terms of mean marginal effects is very much the same. This also holds true for the coefficients of the other explanatory variables.

The variable 'age' has an effect that first increases and then decreases, although the effects are only marginally significant (at 5 per cent significance level). However, the possible effect of age is of great practical importance for the firm.

(*a*)

Panel 1: Dependent Variable: RESPONSE
Method: Least Squares
Sample: 1 1000
Included observations: 925; Excluded observations: 75

Variable	Coefficient	Std. Error	t-Statistic	Prob.
C	−0.060888	0.195906	−0.310802	0.7560
GENDER	0.224002	0.035809	6.255535	0.0000
ACTIVITY	0.208268	0.040669	5.121010	0.0000
AGE	0.015494	0.007861	1.971057	0.0490
AGE^2/100	−0.015209	0.007507	−2.026048	0.0430
R-squared	0.081542			
S.E. of regression	0.480418			

(*b*)

Panel 2: Dependent Variable: RESPONSE
Method: ML - Binary Logit
Sample: 1 1000
Included observations: 925; Excluded observations: 75
Convergence achieved after 5 iterations

Variable	Coefficient	Std. Error	z-Statistic	Prob.
C	−2.488358	0.889992	−2.795932	0.0052
GENDER	0.953694	0.158183	6.029070	0.0000
ACTIVITY	0.913748	0.184779	4.945090	0.0000
AGE	0.069945	0.035605	1.964455	0.0495
AGE^2/100	−0.068692	0.034096	−2.014643	0.0439
S.E. of regression	0.480195	Scale factor	(marg. eff.)	0.229533
Log likelihood	−601.8624			

(*c*)

Panel 3: Dependent Variable: RESPONSE
Method: ML - Binary Probit
Sample: 1 1000
Included observations: 925; Excluded observations: 75
Convergence achieved after 5 iterations

Variable	Coefficient	Std. Error	z-Statistic	Prob.
C	1.497584	0.536822	−2.789720	0.0053
GENDER	0.588114	0.096684	6.082811	0.0000
ACTIVITY	0.561167	0.111572	5.029656	0.0000
AGE	0.041680	0.021544	1.934636	0.0530
AGE^2/100	−0.040982	0.020607	−1.988730	0.0467
S.E. of regression	0.480242	Scale factor	(marg. eff.)	0.372705
Log likelihood	−601.9497			

Exhibit 6.3 Direct Marketing for Financial Product (Example 6.2)

Responses to direct mailing (1 = response, 0 = no response) explained by gender, activity dummy, and age (quadratic function). Estimates obtained from the linear probability model (Panel 1), the logit model (Panel 2), and the probit model (Panel 3). The reported scale factors are the averages of $f(x_i'b)$ over the sample, with f the logistic density (Panel 2) or the standard normal density (Panel 3).

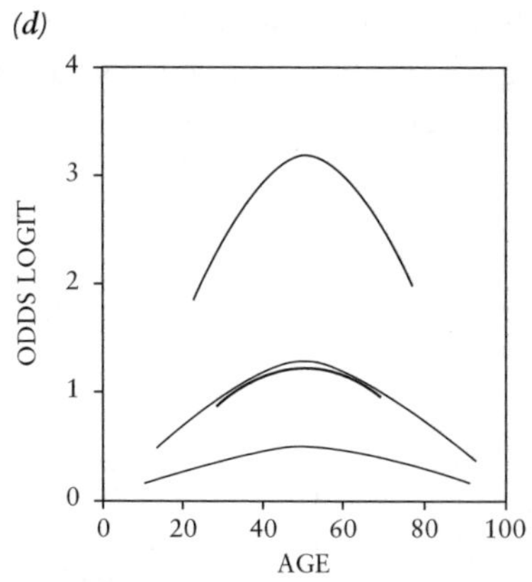

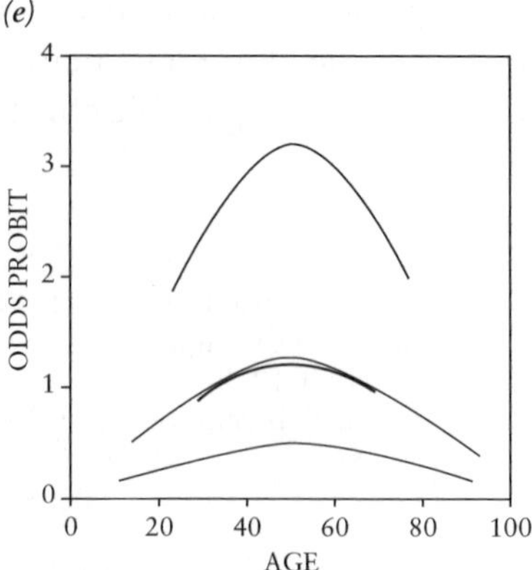

Exhibit 6.3 (*Contd.*)

Estimated odds ratios for logit model (*d*) and for probit model (*e*) against age. In both diagrams, the top curve is for active males, the second one for non-active males, the (nearly coinciding) third one for active females, and the lowest one for non-active females.

(ii) Odds ratios depending on age

To give an impression of the age effect, Exhibit 6.3 shows the estimated odds ratios (for the logit model in (*d*) and for the probit model in (*e*)) against the variable 'age'. All odds ratios are highest around an age of 50 years. In each diagram, the top curve shows that males who are already active investors have a probability of responding to the direct mailing that is two to three times as large as the probability of not responding. The opposite odds ratios apply for females who are not yet investing. As the coefficients of 'gender' and 'activity' are almost equal, the odds ratios for inactive males and active females coincide approximately.

☞ Exercises: T: 6.2d, e; S: 6.7d–f, 6.8a, b; E: 6.11, 6.13a, b.

6.1.4 Diagnostics

In this section we discuss some diagnostic tools for logit and probit models — namely, the goodness of fit (LR-test and R^2), the predictive quality (classification table and hit rate), and analysis of the residuals (in particular an LM-test for heteroskedasticity).

Goodness of fit

The significance of individual explanatory variables can be tested by the usual t-test based on (6.10). The sample size should be sufficiently large to rely on the asymptotic expressions for the standard errors, and the t-test statistic then follows approximately the standard normal distribution. Joint parameter restrictions can be tested by the Likelihood Ratio test. For logit and probit models it is no problem to estimate the unrestricted and restricted models, at least if the restrictions are not too involved. The overall *goodness of fit* of the model can be tested by the LR-test on the null hypothesis that all coefficients (except the constant term) are zero—that is, $\beta_2 = \cdots = \beta_k = 0$. This test follows (asymptotically) the $\chi^2(k-1)$ distribution. Sometimes one reports measures similar to the R^2 of linear regression models—for instance, *McFadden's* R^2 defined by

$$R^2 = 1 - \frac{\log(L_1)}{\log(L_0)},$$

where L_1 is the maximum value of the unrestricted likelihood function and L_0 that of the restricted likelihood function. It follows from (6.7) that $L_0 \leq L_1 < 0$, so that $0 \leq R^2 < 1$ and higher values of R^2 correspond to a relatively higher overall significance of the model. Note, however, that this R^2 cannot be used, for example, to choose between a logit and a probit model, as these two models have different likelihood functions.

Predictive quality

Alternative specifications of the model may be compared by evaluating whether the model gives a good classification of the data into the two categories $y_i = 1$ and $y_i = 0$. The estimated model gives predicted probabilities $\hat{p}_i$ for the choice $y_i = 1$, and this can be transformed into predicted choices by predicting that $\hat{y}_i = 1$ if $\hat{p}_i \geq c$ and $\hat{y}_i = 0$ if $\hat{p}_i < c$. The choice of c can sometimes be based on the costs of misclassification. In practice one often takes $c = \frac{1}{2}$, or, if the fraction $\hat{p}$ of successes differs much from 50 per cent, one sometimes takes $c = \hat{p}$. This leads to a 2×2 *classification table* of the predicted responses $\hat{y}_i$ against the actually observed responses y_i. The *hit rate* is defined as the fraction of correct predictions in the sample. Formally, let w_i be the random variable indicating a correct prediction—that is, $w_i = 1$ if $y_i = \hat{y}_i$ and $w_i = 0$ if $y_i \neq \hat{y}_i$; then the hit rate is defined by $h = \frac{1}{n}\sum_{i=1}^{n} w_i$.

In the population the fraction of successes is p. If we randomly make the prediction 1 with probability p and 0 with probability $(1-p)$, then we make a correct prediction with probability $q = p^2 + (1-p)^2$. Using the properties of the binomial distribution for the number of correct random predictions, it follows that the 'random' hit rate h_r has expected value $E[h_r] = E[w] = q$ and variance $\text{var}(h_r) = \text{var}(w)/n = q(1-q)/n$. The predictive quality of our model can be evaluated by comparing our hit rate h with the random hit rate h_r. Under the null hypothesis that the predictions of the model are no better than pure random predictions, the hit rate h is approximately normally distributed with mean q and variance $q(1-q)/n$. Therefore we reject the null hypothesis of random predictions in favour of the (one-sided) alternative of better-than-random predictions if

$$z = \frac{h-q}{\sqrt{q(1-q)/n}} = \frac{nh-nq}{\sqrt{nq(1-q)}}$$

is large enough (larger than 1.645 at 5 per cent significance level). In practice, $q = p^2 + (1-p)^2$ is unknown and estimated by $\hat{p}^2 + (1-\hat{p})^2$, where $\hat{p}$ is the fraction of successes in the sample. In the above expression for the z-test, nh is the total number of correct predictions in the sample and nq is the expected number of correct random predictions.

Description may be more relevant than prediction

Although the comparison of the classification success of alternative models may be of interest, it should be realized that the parameters of binary response models are chosen to maximize the likelihood function, and not directly to maximize a measure of fit between the observed outcomes y_i and the predicted outcomes $\hat{y}_i$. This is another distinction with the linear regression model, where maximizing the (normal) likelihood function is equivalent to maximizing the (least squares) fit. A binary response model may be preferred over another one because it gives a more useful description, for example, of the marginal effects (6.4), even if it performs worse in terms of classification.

Standardized residuals and consequences of heteroskedasticity

The residuals e_i of a binary response model are defined as the differences between the observed outcomes y_i and the fitted probabilities $\hat{p}_i$. As the variance of y_i (for given values of x_i) is $p_i(1-p_i)$, the *standardized residuals* are defined by

$$e_i^* = \frac{y_i - \hat{p}_i}{\sqrt{\hat{p}_i(1-\hat{p}_i)}}. \qquad (6.12)$$

A histogram of the standardized residuals may be of interest, for example, to detect outliers. Further, scatter diagrams of these residuals against explanatory variables are useful to investigate the possible presence of *heteroskedasticity*. Heteroskedasticity can be due to different kinds of misspecification of the model. It may be, for instance, that a relevant explanatory variable is missing or that the function F is misspecified. In contrast with the linear regression model, where OLS remains consistent under heteroskedasticity, maximum likelihood estimators of binary response models become inconsistent under this kind of misspecification. For instance, if the data generating process is a probit model but one estimates a logit model, then the estimated parameters and marginal effects are inconsistent and the calculated standard errors are not correct. However, as the differences between the probit function Φ and the logit function Λ are not so large, the outcomes may still be reasonably reliable. If one has doubts on the correct choice of the distribution function F, it may be helpful to compute the standard errors in two ways—that is, by the ML expression (6.9) and also by GMM based on the 'moment' conditions (6.8). If the two sets of computed standard errors differ significantly, then this is a sign of misspecification.

Likelihood Ratio test on heteroskedasticity

A formal test for heteroskedasticity can be based on the index model $y_i^* = x_i'\beta + \varepsilon_i$. Until now it was assumed that the error terms ε_i all follow the same distribution (described by F). As an alternative we consider the model where all ε_i/σ_i follow the same distribution F where

$$\sigma_i = e^{z_i'\gamma},$$

with z_i a vector of observed variables. The constant term should not be included in this vector because (as was discussed in Section 6.1.1) the scale parameter of a binary response model should be fixed, independent of the data. We assume again that the density function f (the derivative of F) is symmetric—that is, $f(t) = f(-t)$. It then follows that $P[y_i = 1] = P[y_i^* \geq 0]$ $= P[\varepsilon_i \geq -x_i'\beta] = P[(\varepsilon_i/\sigma) \geq -x_i'\beta/\sigma] = P[(\varepsilon_i/\sigma) \leq x_i'\beta/\sigma] = F(x_i'\beta/\sigma)]$, so that

$$P[y_i = 1] = F\left(x_i'\beta/e^{z_i'\gamma}\right). \tag{6.13}$$

The null hypothesis of homoskedasticity corresponds to the parameter restriction $H_0: \gamma = 0$. This hypothesis can be tested by the LR-test. The unrestricted likelihood function is obtained from the log-likelihood (6.7) by replacing the terms $p_i = F(x_i'\beta)$ by $p_i = F(x_i'\beta/e^{z_i'\gamma})$.

Lagrange Multiplier test on heteroskedasticity

An alternative is to use the LM-test, so that only the model under the null hypothesis (with $\gamma = 0$) needs to be estimated. By working out the formulas for the gradient and the Hessian of the unrestricted likelihood, it can be shown that the LM-test can be performed as if (6.13) were a non-linear regression model. The correctness of the following steps to compute the LM-test is left as an exercise (see Exercise 6.1).

First estimate the model without heteroskedasticity—that is, under the null hypothesis that $\gamma = 0$. This amounts to estimating the model $p[y_i = 1] = F(x_i'\beta)$ by ML, as discussed in Section 6.1.3. The residuals of this model are denoted by $e_i = y_i - \hat{p}_i = y_i - F(x_i'b)$. As a second step, regress the residuals e_i on the gradient of the non-linear model $P[y_i = 1] = F(x_i'\beta/e^{z_i'\gamma})$, taking into account that the residuals are heteroskedastic. This amounts to applying (feasible) weighted least squares—that is, OLS after division for the ith observation by the (estimated) standard deviation. The variance of the 'error term' $y_i - p_i$ is $\text{var}(y_i - p_i) = \text{var}(y_i) = p_i(1 - p_i)$. We replace p_i by $\hat{p}_i$ obtained in the first step, so that the weight of the ith observation in WLS is given by $1/\sqrt{\hat{p}_i(1 - \hat{p}_i)}$. Further, the gradient of the function $F(x_i'\beta/e^{z_i'\gamma})$ in the model (6.13), when evaluated at $\gamma = 0$, is given by

$$\frac{\partial F(x'\beta/e^{z'\gamma})}{\partial \beta} = f(x'\beta)x, \qquad \frac{\partial F(x'\beta/e^{z'\gamma})}{\partial \gamma} = -f(x'\beta)x'\beta z.$$

Therefore, the required auxiliary regression in this second step can be written in terms of the standardized residuals (6.12) as

$$e_i^* = \frac{y_i - \hat{p}_i}{\sqrt{\hat{p}_i(1 - \hat{p}_i)}} = \frac{f(x_i'b)}{\sqrt{\hat{p}_i(1 - \hat{p}_i)}} x_i'\delta_1 + \frac{f(x_i'b)x_i'b}{\sqrt{\hat{p}_i(1 - \hat{p}_i)}} z_i'\delta_2 + \eta_i. \qquad (6.14)$$

Under the null hypothesis of homoskedasticity, there holds that $LM = nR_{nc}^2$ of this regression, where R_{nc}^2 denotes the non-centred R^2—that is, the explained sum of squares of (6.14) is divided by the non-centred total sum of squares $\sum_{i=1}^{n} (e_i^*)^2$. As the regression in (6.14) does not contain a constant term on the right-hand side, one should take here the non-centred R^2 defined by $R_{nc}^2 = \sum (\hat{e}_i^*)^2 / \sum (e_i^*)^2$, where $\hat{e}_i^*$ denote the fitted values of the regression in (6.14). We reject the null hypothesis for large values of the LM-test, and under the null hypothesis of homoskedasticity ($\gamma = 0$) it is asymptotically distributed as $\chi^2(g)$, where g is the number of variables in z_i—that is, the number of parameters in γ.

This can be summarized as follows.

Computation of *LM*-test on heteroskedasticity

- *Step 1: Estimate the restricted model.* Estimate the homoskedastic model $P[y_i = 1] = F(x_i'\beta)$ by ML. Let $\hat{p}_i = F(x_i'b)$ and define the generalized residuals e_i^* by (6.12).
- *Step 2: Auxiliary regression of generalized residuals of step 1.* Regress the generalized residuals e_i^* of step 1 on the (scaled) gradient of the heteroskedastic model $P[y_i = 1] = F(x_i'\beta/e^{z_i'\gamma})$ — that is, perform OLS in (6.14).
- *Step 3: $LM = nR_{nc}^2$ of step 2.* Then $LM = nR_{nc}^2$, where R_{nc}^2 is the non-centred R^2 of the regression in step 2. If the null hypothesis of homoskedasticity ($\gamma = 0$) holds true, then $LM \approx \chi^2(g)$, where g is the number of parameters in γ.

Example 6.3: Direct Marketing for Financial Product (continued)

E

XM601DMF

We perform some diagnostic checks on the logit and probit models that were estimated for the direct mailing data in Example 6.2. We will discuss (i) the significance of the explanatory variables, (ii) the investigation of the possible presence of outliers and heteroskedasticity, and (iii) the predictive performance of the models. Exhibit 6.4 reports the results of these diagnostic checks.

(i) Significance of the explanatory variables

In Example 6.2 we concluded that the variables 'gender' and 'activity' are significant but that the linear and quadratic age variables are individually only marginally significant. Panel 1 of Exhibit 6.4 contains the result of the *LR*-test for the joint significance of the two age variables. This indicates that they are jointly not significant, as $P = 0.12$ in the logit model and $P = 0.13$ in the probit model. The two models have nearly equal and not so large values of R^2 (0.061), but the *LR*-test for the joint significance of the variables $(x_2, \cdots, x_5)$ in Panel 1 of Exhibit 6.4 shows that the models have explanatory power. The combination of statistical significance with relatively low fit is typical for models explaining individual behaviour. This means that the model may have difficulty in describing individual decisions but that it gives insight into the overall pattern of behaviour.

(ii) Investigation of possible outliers and heteroskedasticity

The maximum and minimum values of the standardized residuals reported in Panel 1 of Exhibit 6.4 for the logit and probit model do not indicate the presence of outliers. To test for the possible presence of heteroskedasticity, we consider the model $\sigma_i = e^{\gamma z_i}$, where z_i is the total amount of money that individual i has already invested in other products of the bank. The test outcomes provide some evidence for the presence of heteroskedasticity ($P = 0.01$).

(iii) Predictive performance

Panels 2 and 3 of Exhibit 6.4 also contain results on the predictive performance of the logit and probit models. The hit rates are 0.616 for the logit model and 0.622 for the probit model. This is well above the expected hit rate of around 0.5 of random predictions (more precisely, of the 925 observations there are 470 with $y_i = 1$ and 455 with $y_i = 0$ so that $\hat{p} = \frac{470}{925}$ and $\hat{p}^2 + (1 - \hat{p})^2 = 0.5001$). The test whether the predictions are better than

Panel 1: DIAGNOSTIC TEST RESULTS	LOGIT	PROBIT
Standardized residuals: maximum	2.123	2.135
minimum	−1.786	−1.787
Heteroskedasticity LM test value (df = 1)	6.237	6.186
corresponding P-value	0.0125	0.0129
LR test for significance of explanatory variables (df = 4)	78.35	78.18
corresponding P-value	0.0000	0.0000
LR test for significance of age variables (df = 2)	4.247	4.089
corresponding P-value	0.1196	0.1294
R-squared	0.061	0.061

Panel 2: LOGIT: Prediction Evaluation (success cutoff C = 0.5)						
	Estimated Equation			Constant Probability		
	Dep = 0	Dep = 1	Total	Dep = 0	Dep = 1	Total
P(Dep = 1)<=C	196	96	292	0	0	0
P(Dep=1)>C	259	374	633	455	470	925
Total	455	470	925	455	470	925
Correct	196	374	570	0	470	470
% Correct	43.08	79.57	61.62	0.00	100.00	50.81
% Incorrect	56.92	20.43	38.38	100.00	0.00	49.19
p = 470/925 = 0.508, random hit rate $p^2 + (1 - p)^2 = 0.5001$						
Z-value = $(570 - 462.5)/\sqrt{(925*0.5001*0.4999)} = 7.07$, P = 0.0000						

Panel 3: PROBIT: Prediction Evaluation (success cutoff C = 0.5)						
	Estimated Equation			Constant Probability		
	Dep = 0	Dep = 1	Total	Dep = 0	Dep = 1	Total
P(Dep=1)<=C	190	85	275	0	0	0
P(Dep=1)>C	265	385	650	455	470	925
Total	455	470	925	455	470	925
Correct	190	385	575	0	470	470
% Correct	41.76	81.91	62.16	0.00	100.00	50.81
% Incorrect	58.24	18.09	37.84	100.00	0.00	49.19
p = 470/925 = 0.508, random hit rate $p^2 + (1 - p)^2 = 0.5001$						
Z-value = $(575 - 462.5)/\sqrt{(925*0.5001*0.4999)} = 7.40$, P = 0.0000						

Exhibit 6.4 Direct Marketing for Financial Product (Example 6.3)

Outcomes of various diagnostic tests for logit and probit models for responses to direct mailing (Panel 1) and predictive performance of logit model (Panel 2) and of probit model (Panel 3).

random gives values of $z = 7.07$ for the logit model and $z = 7.40$ for the probit model, with P-value $P = 0.00$ (see Panels 2 and 3 of Exhibit 6.4). This shows that the classification of respondents by the logit and probit models is better than what would have been achieved by random predictions. The models are more successful in predicting positive responses (around 80 per cent is predicted correctly) than in predicting no response (of which a bit more than 40 per cent is predicted correctly).

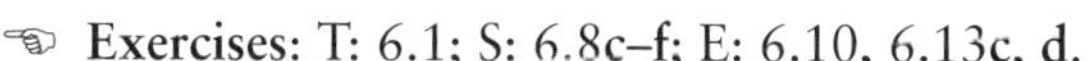

Exercises: T: 6.1; S: 6.8c–f; E: 6.10, 6.13c, d.

6.1.5 Model for grouped data

Grouped data

Sometimes—for instance, for reasons of confidentiality—the individual data are not given and only the average values of the variables over *groups* of individuals are reported. For instance, the investment decisions of customers of a bank may be averaged over residential areas (zip codes) or over age groups. Suppose that the individual data satisfy the binary response model (6.3)—that is, $P[y_i = 1] = F(x_i'\beta)$ with the same function F for all $i = 1, \cdots, n$. Let the data be grouped into G groups, with n_j individuals in group j. The groups should be chosen so that the values of the explanatory variables x are reasonably constant within each group. Let $\bar{x}_j$ denote the vector of group means of the explanatory variables for the n_j individuals in this group. Let $\bar{y}_j$ be the fraction of individuals in group j that have chosen alternative 1, so that a fraction $1 - \bar{y}_j$ has chosen the alternative 0. The data consist of the G values of $(\bar{y}_j, \ \bar{x}_j)$, and the group sizes n_j are assumed to be known, $j = 1, \cdots, G$.

Estimation by maximum likelihood

It is assumed that $\bar{x}_j$ is a close enough approximation of the characteristics of all individuals in group j so that their probabilities to choose alternative 1 are constant and given by $p_j = F(\bar{x}_j'\beta)$. Then the joint contribution of the individuals in group j to the log-likelihood (6.7) is given by $n_{j1} \log(p_j) + (n_j - n_{j1}) \log(1 - p_j)$, where $n_{j1} = n_j\bar{y}_j$ is the number of individuals in group j that chooses alternative 1. So, in terms of the observed fractions $\bar{y}_j$, the log-likelihood becomes

$$\log(L) = \sum_{j=1}^{G} n_j\Big(\bar{y}_j \log(p_j) + (1 - \bar{y}_j)\log(1 - p_j)\Big). \tag{6.15}$$

It is required that $k \leq G$—that is, the number of explanatory variables may not be larger than the number of groups. The model parameters can be estimated by maximum likelihood, much in the same way as was discussed in Section 6.1.3 for the case of individual binary response data. The model imposes restrictions if the decisions of G groups are modelled in terms of $k < G$ parameters. To test the specification of the model, one can consider as an alternative the model that contains a dummy for each group, that is, with $p_j = F(\delta_j)$ for $j = 1, \cdots, G$. This model contains G parameters and allows for arbitrary different specific probabilities for each group. The corresponding maximum likelihood estimates are given by $\hat{\delta}_j = \overline{y}_j$. The model $p_j = F(\overline{x}_j'\beta)$ imposes $(G - k)$ parameter restrictions $\delta_j = \overline{x}_j'\beta$. This can be tested by the LR-test that follows a $\chi^2(G - k)$ distribution under the null hypothesis of correct specification.

T

Estimation by feasible weighted least squares

Instead of using the above maximum likelihood approach, one can also use feasible weighted least squares (FWLS) to estimate the parameters β. This is based on the fact that $\overline{y}_j$ is the sample mean of n_j independent drawings from the Bernoulli distribution with mean p_j and variance $p_j(1 - p_j)$. If n_j is sufficiently large, it follows from the central limit theorem that

$$\overline{y}_j \approx \mathrm{N}\left(p_j, \frac{p_j(1 - p_j)}{n_j}\right).$$

If F is continuous and monotonically increasing (as is the case for logit and probit models), then the inverse function F^{-1} exists. We define transformed observations

$$z_j = F^{-1}(\overline{y}_j).$$

Using the facts that $F^{-1}(p_j) = \overline{x}_j'\beta$ and that $F^{-1}(p)$ has derivative $1/f(F^{-1}(p))$, it follows that in large enough samples

$$z_j \approx \mathrm{N}\left(\overline{x}_j'\beta, \frac{p_j(1 - p_j)}{n_j f_j^2}\right),$$

where $f_j = f(\overline{x}_j'\beta)$. This can be written as a regression equation

$$z_j = \overline{x}_j'\beta + \varepsilon_j, \quad j = 1, \cdots, G.$$

Here the error terms ε_j are independent and approximately normally distributed with mean zero and variances $\sigma_j^2 = p_j(1 - p_j)/\left(n_j f_j^2\right)$. So the error terms are heteroskedastic. Then β can be estimated by FWLS—for instance, as follows. In the first step β is estimated by OLS, regressing z_j on $\overline{x}_j$ for the G groups. Let b be the OLS estimate; then the variance σ_j^2 of ε_j can be estimated by replacing p_j by $\hat{p}_j = F(\overline{x}_j'b)$ and f_j by $f(\overline{x}_j'b)$, so that

$$s_j^2 = \hat{p}_j(1-\hat{p}_j)/(n_j f^2(\overline{x}_j b)).$$

In the second step β is estimated by WLS, using the estimated standard deviations of ε_j to obtain the appropriate weighting factors. That is, in the second step OLS is applied in the transformed model

$$\frac{z_j}{s_j} = \left(\frac{1}{s_j}x_j\right)'\beta + \omega_j, \quad j = 1, \cdots, G.$$

FWLS in the logit model

T

We specify the above general method in more detail for the logit model. In this case the required regressions simplify somewhat, because the logit model has the property that $f_j = \lambda_j = \Lambda_j(1-\Lambda_j) = p_j(1-p_j)$ (see Section 6.1.3). So $s_j^2 = 1/(n_j\hat{p}_j(1-\hat{p}_j))$ and the FWLS estimates are obtained by performing OLS in the following regression model.

$$\sqrt{n_j\hat{p}_j(1-\hat{p}_j)}\, z_j = \sqrt{n_j\hat{p}_j(1-\hat{p}_j)}\, \overline{x}_j'\beta + \omega_j, \quad \hat{p}_j = \Lambda(\overline{x}_j b) = \frac{1}{1+e^{-\overline{x}_j' b}}.$$

So, for the logit model the FWLS estimates are obtained by regressing z_j on $\overline{x}_j$ (with OLS estimate b) followed by a regression of $w_j z_j$ on $w_j \overline{x}_j$ with weights

$$w_j = \sqrt{n_j\hat{p}_j(1-\hat{p}_j)} = \sqrt{n_j}\frac{e^{-\frac{1}{2}\overline{x}_j' b}}{1+e^{-\overline{x}_j' b}} = \sqrt{n_j}\frac{e^{\frac{1}{2}\overline{x}_j' b}}{1+e^{\overline{x}_j' b}}.$$

FWLS is asymptotically equivalent to ML (see also Section 5.4.4 (p. 336)). However, if n_j is relatively small for some groups, it may be preferable to use ML. An example using grouped data is left as an exercise: see Exercise 6.12, which considers the direct mailing data averaged over ten age groups.

☞ Exercises: E: 6.12.

6.1.6 Summary

To model the underlying factors that influence the outcome of a binary dependent variable we take the following steps.

- Determine the possibly relevant explanatory variables and formulate a model of the form $P[y=1] = F(x'\beta)$, where y is the dependent variable (with possible outcomes 0 and 1) and x is the vector of explanatory variables. The function F is chosen as a cumulative distribution function, in most cases $F = \Lambda$ of (6.5) (the logit model) or $F = \Phi$ of (6.6) (the probit model).

- Estimate the parameters β of the model by maximum likelihood. For logit and probit models, the required non-linear optimization can be solved without any problems by standard numerical methods.
- The estimated model can be interpreted in terms of the signs and significance of the estimated coefficients β and in terms of the mean marginal effects and odds ratios discussed in Section 6.1.2.
- The model can be evaluated in different ways, by diagnostic tests (standardized residuals, test on heteroskedasticity) and by measuring the model quality (goodness of fit and predictive performance).
- The approach for grouped (instead of individual) data is similar; the main distinction is that the log-likelihood is now given by (6.15) instead of (6.7).

6.2 Multinomial data

6.2.1 Unordered response

☞ Uses Chapters 1–4; Section 5.4; Section 6.1.

Multinomial data

When the dependent variable has a finite number of possible outcomes, the data are called *multinomial*. This occurs, for instance, when individuals can choose among more than two options. In some cases the options can be *ordered* (for example, how much one agrees or disagrees with a statement), in other cases the different options are *unordered* (for example the choice of travel mode for urban commuters). In this section and the next one we discuss models for unordered data and in Section 6.2.3 we consider ordered data.

Multinomial model for individual-specific data

Let m be the number of alternatives. These alternatives (for example, to travel by bicycle, bus, car or train) are supposed to have no natural ordering. However, for ease of reference the alternatives are labeled by an index $j = 1, \cdots, m$, so that the response $y_i = j$ is a *nominal* (not an ordinal) variable. Let n_j be the number of observations with response $y_i = j$ and let $n = \sum_{j=1}^{m} n_j$ be the total number of observations. Suppose that, apart from the choices y_i, also the values x_i of k explanatory variables are observed, $i = 1, \cdots, n$. The first element of x_i is the constant term $x_{1i} = 1$, and the other elements of x_i represent characteristics of the ith individual. A possible model in terms of stochastic utilities is given by

$$U_i^j = u_{ij} + \varepsilon_{ij} = x_i'\beta_j + \varepsilon_{ij}. \quad (6.16)$$

Here x_i is a $k \times 1$ vector of explanatory variables for individual i and β_j is a $k \times 1$ vector of parameters for alternative j. Further, $u_{ij} = x_i'\beta_j$ represents the systematic utility of alternative j for an individual with characteristics x_i, and β_j measures the relative weights of the characteristics in the derived utility. The differences between the alternatives are modelled by differences in the weights, and $\beta_{jl} - \beta_{hl}$ measures the marginal increase of the utility of alternative j as compared to alternative h when the lth explanatory variable raises by one unit. The terms ε_{ij} are individual-specific and represent unmodelled factors in individual preferences.

The model (6.16) is called the *multinomial model*. This model can be used if data are available on the individual-specific values of the k explanatory variables $x_i, i = 1, \cdots, n$, and there is no data information on the characteristics of the alternatives $j = 1, \cdots, m$. The differences between the alternatives are modelled by the unknown $k \times 1$ parameter vectors $\beta_j, j = 1, \cdots, m$.

Conditional model for individual- and alternative-specific data

Another type of model is obtained when aspects of the alternatives are measured for each individual—for example, the travel times for alternative transport modes. Let x_{ij} be the vector of values of the explanatory variables that apply for individual i and alternative j. A possible model for the utilities is

$$U_i^j = u_{ij} + \varepsilon_{ij} = x'_{ij}\beta + \varepsilon_{ij}, \qquad (6.17)$$

where x_{ij} and β are $m \times 1$ vectors. This is called the *conditional model*. This model can be used if relevant characteristics x_{ij} of the m alternatives can be measured for the n individuals. The difference with the multinomial model (6.16) is that the differences between the alternatives j and h are measured now by $(x_{ij} - x_{ih})$, which may vary between individuals, whereas in (6.16) these differences are $(\beta_j - \beta_h)$, which are unknown and the same for all individuals.

Choice model and log-likelihood

Both in the multinomial model and in the conditional model, it is assumed that the ith individual chooses the alternative j for which the utility U_i^j is maximal. It then follows that

$$p_{ij} = P[y_i = j] = P[u_{ij} + \varepsilon_{ij} > u_{ih} + \varepsilon_{ih} \text{ for all } h \neq j], \qquad (6.18)$$

where $u_{ij} = x'_i\beta_j$ or $u_{ij} = x'_{ij}\beta$ depending on which of the two above models is chosen.

In order to estimate the parameters, the joint distribution of the terms ε_{ij} has to be specified. It is assumed that (conditional on the given values of the explanatory variables) the individuals make independent choices, so that ε_{ij} and ε_{gh} are independent for all $i \neq g$ and all $j, h = 1, \cdots, m$. The log-likelihood can then be written as follows, where $y_{ij} = 1$ if $y_i = j$ and $y_{ij} = 0$ otherwise, and where $p_{ij} = p_{iy_i}$ for the actually chosen alternative $j = y_i$.

$$\log(L) = \sum_{i=1}^{n}\sum_{j=1}^{m} y_{ij}\log(p_{ij}) = \sum_{i=1}^{n}\log(p_{iy_i}). \tag{6.19}$$

So this consists of the sum over the n terms $\log(p_{ij})$, where $j = y_i$ is the alternative chosen by individual i. For the binary choice model with $m = 2$ alternatives, (6.19) reduces to the log-likelihood (6.7).

Multinomial and conditional probit models

The ML estimates of the parameters of the model can be obtained by maximizing (6.19) after the joint distribution of the terms ε_{ij}, $j = 1, \cdots, m$, in (6.18) has been specified. For example, suppose that these terms are jointly normally distributed with mean zero and (unknown) $m \times m$ covariance matrix V, so that

$$\begin{pmatrix} \varepsilon_{i1} \\ \vdots \\ \varepsilon_{im} \end{pmatrix} \sim \text{NID}(0, V).$$

If $u_{ij} = x_i'\beta_j$, as in the multinomial model (6.16), then the model (6.18) for the choice probabilities p_{ij} with $\varepsilon_i \sim \text{NID}(0, V)$ is called the *multinomial probit model*. And if $u_{ij} = x_{ij}'\beta$, as in the conditional model (6.17), then (6.18) with $\varepsilon_i \sim \text{NID}(0, V)$ is called the *conditional probit model*. An important advantage of incorporating the covariance matrix V in the model is the following. When two alternatives j and h are perceived as being close together, then a typical preference $\varepsilon_{ij} = U_i^j - u_{ij} > 0$ (meaning that the ith individual derives a larger utility from alternative j than is usual for individuals with the same values of the explanatory variables) will mostly correspond to a preference $\varepsilon_{ih} = U_i^h - u_{ih} > 0$ as well. That is, if in the multinomial probit model $\beta_j \approx \beta_h$ or in the conditional probit model $x_{ij} \approx x_{ih}$ (so that the utilities derived from the alternatives j and h are close together), then it may be expected that ε_{ij} and ε_{ih} are positively correlated. Such correlations can be modelled by the off-diagonal elements (j, h) of the covariance matrix V.

Estimation of multinomial and conditional probit models

T

The multinomial and conditional probit models can be estimated by ML. For fixed values of the parameters, the log-likelihood (6.19) can be evaluated by numerical integration of the probabilities p_{ij} in (6.18). As the probability p_{ij} involves the $(m-1)$ conditions $\varepsilon_{ij} - \varepsilon_{ih} > u_{ih} - u_{ij}$ (for $h \neq j$), this probability is expressed as an $(m-1)$ dimensional integral in terms of the $(m-1)$ random variables $(\varepsilon_{ij} - \varepsilon_{ih})$. The evaluation of this integral (for given values of $(u_{ih} - u_{ij})$, that is, of $x_i'(\beta_h - \beta_j)$ in the multinomial model and of $(x_{ih} - x_{ij})'\beta$ in the conditional model) requires appropriate numerical integration techniques. Numerically simpler likelihood functions can be obtained by choosing other distributions for the error terms ε_{ij}, as is discussed in the next section.

Parameter restrictions needed for identification

Some parameter restrictions have to be imposed, as the probabilities p_{ij} depend only on the differences $u_{ih} - u_{ij}$ and as they are invariant under multiplication of the utilities U_i' by a constant. The last problem can be solved by fixing one of the variances—for instance, by setting $E[\varepsilon_{i1}^2] = V_{11} = 1$. Further, for the multinomial probit model $u_{ih} - u_{ij} = x_i'(\beta_h - \beta_j)$, so that one of the parameter vectors can be chosen arbitrarily—for instance, $\beta_1 = 0$, which corresponds to choosing the first alternative as reference. In the conditional probit model $u_{ih} - u_{ij} = (x_{ih} - x_{ij})'\beta$, so that the vector of explanatory variables should not include a constant term in this case.

6.2.2 Multinomial and conditional logit

Model formulation

Although multinomial and conditional probit models can be estimated by suitable numerical integration methods, it is in practice often preferred to use simpler models. A considerable simplification is obtained by assuming that all the mn error terms ε_{ij} are independently and identically distributed (for all individuals and all alternatives) with the so-called *extreme value distribution*. It can be shown (see Exercise 6.3) that in this case the multinomial and the conditional probabilities in (6.18) become

$$\begin{aligned} \text{multinomial logit:} \quad p_{ij} &= \frac{e^{x_i'\beta_j}}{\sum_{h=1}^{m} e^{x_i'\beta_h}} = \frac{e^{x_i'\beta_j}}{1 + \sum_{h=2}^{m} e^{x_i'\beta_h}}, \\ \text{conditional logit:} \quad p_{ij} &= \frac{e^{x_{ij}'\beta}}{\sum_{h=1}^{m} e^{x_{ih}'\beta}}. \end{aligned} \qquad (6.20)$$

For the multinomial model we used the identification convention to choose $\beta_1 = 0$ for the first (reference) category. The first model for the choice probabilities p_{ij} is called the *multinomial logit model*, the second model the *conditional logit model*. For the case of $m = 2$ alternatives, both models boil down to a binary logit model. Indeed, for the multinomial model we get $p_{i2} = e^{x_i'\beta_2}/(1 + e^{x_i'\beta_2})$, which is a binary logit model with parameter vector $\beta = \beta_2$. In the conditional logit model we get for $m = 2$ that

$$p_{i2} = \frac{e^{x'_{i2}\beta}}{e^{x'_{i1}\beta} + e^{x'_{i2}\beta}} = \frac{e^{(x_{i2}-x_{i1})'\beta}}{1 + e^{(x_{i2}-x_{i1})'\beta}},$$

which is a binary logit model with explanatory variables $x_i = x_{i2} - x_{i1}$.

Estimation of the multinomial logit model

T

The multinomial logit (MNL) model can be estimated by maximum likelihood—that is, by maximizing (6.19) with respect to the parameters β_j, $j = 2, \cdots, m$. It is left as an exercise (see Exercise 6.3) to show the following results. If we substitute (6.20) in (6.19), the log-likelihood becomes

$$\log\left(L_{MNL}(\beta_2, \cdots, \beta_m)\right) = \sum_{i=1}^{n}\left(\sum_{j=2}^{m} y_{ij}x'_i\beta_j - \log\left(1 + \sum_{h=2}^{m} e^{x'_i\beta_h}\right)\right). \qquad (6.21)$$

The gradient of the log-likelihood consists of the $(m-1)$ stacked $k \times 1$ vectors

$$\frac{\partial \log\left(L_{MNL}\right)}{\partial \beta_h} = \sum_{i=1}^{n}(y_{ih} - p_{ih})x_i, \quad h = 2, \cdots, m,$$

with p_{ih} as specified above for the multinomial model. Further, the $(m-1)k \times (m-1)k$ Hessian matrix is negative definite with $k \times k$ blocks $-\sum_{i=1}^{n} p_{ih}(1 - p_{ih})x_i x'_i$ on the diagonal $(h = 2, \cdots, m)$ and $k \times k$ blocks $\sum_{i=1}^{n} p_{ih}p_{ig}x_i x'_i$ off the diagonal $(g, h = 2, \cdots, m, g \neq h)$.

Estimation of the conditional logit model

T

For the conditional logit (CL) model the results are as follows (see Exercise 6.3). The log-likelihood is given by

$$\log\left(L_{CL}(\beta)\right) = \sum_{i=1}^{n}\left(\sum_{j=1}^{m} y_{ij}x'_{ij}\beta - \log\left(\sum_{h=1}^{m} e^{x'_{ih}\beta}\right)\right). \qquad (6.22)$$

The gradient of the log-likelihood is

$$\frac{\partial \log\left(L_{CL}\right)}{\partial \beta} = \sum_{i=1}^{n}\sum_{j=1}^{m}(y_{ij} - p_{ij})x_{ij}.$$

Finally, the Hessian is $-\sum_{i=1}^{n}\sum_{j=1}^{m} p_{ij}x_{ij}\left(x_{ij} - \sum_{h=1}^{m} p_{ih}x_{ih}\right)'$.

Numerical aspects

The first order conditions for a maximum can be solved numerically—for instance, by using the above expressions for the gradient and the Hessian in the Newton–Raphson algorithm. In both the multinomial and the conditional logit model the Hessian matrix is negative definite, so that in general the iterations converge relatively fast to the global maximum. As usual, approximate standard errors of the ML estimates can be obtained from the inverse of the Hessian matrix.

Marginal effects of explanatory variables

The parameters of the model can be interpreted in terms of the *marginal effects* of the explanatory variables on the choice probabilities. The following results are left as an exercise (see Exercise 6.3). In the multinomial logit model, the $k \times 1$ vector of marginal effects is given by

$$\frac{\partial P_{MNL}[y_i = j]}{\partial x_i} = p_{ij}\left(\beta_j - \sum_{h=2}^{m} p_{ih}\beta_h\right). \tag{6.23}$$

In the conditional logit model the marginal effects are

$$\frac{\partial P_{CL}[y_i = j]}{\partial x_{ij}} = p_{ij}(1 - p_{ij})\beta, \quad \frac{\partial P_{CL}[y_i = j]}{\partial x_{ih}} = -p_{ij}p_{ih}\beta \quad \text{for } h \neq j.$$

Note that, in the multinomial logit model, all the parameters β_h, $h = 2, \cdots, m$, together determine the marginal effect of x_i on the probability to choose the jth alternative. It may even be the case that the marginal effect of the lth variable x_{li} on $P[y_i = j]$ has the opposite sign of the parameter β_{jl}. So the sign of the parameter β_{jl} cannot always be interpreted directly as the sign of the effect of the lth explanatory variable on the probability to choose the jth alternative. Therefore the individual parameters of a multinomial logit model do not always have an easy direct interpretation. On the other hand, in the conditional logit model the sign of β_l is equal to the sign of the marginal effect of the lth explanatory variable $(x_{ij,l})$ on the probability to choose each alternative since $0 < p_{ij}(1 - p_{ij}) < 1$.

Odds ratios and the 'independence of irrelevant alternatives'

The above multinomial and conditional logit models are based on the assumption that the error terms ε_{ij} are independent not only among different individuals i but also among the different alternatives j. That is, the unmodelled individual preferences ε_{ij} of a given individual i are independent for the different alternatives j. This requires that the alternatives should be sufficiently different from each other. This can be further clarified by considering the log-odds between two alternatives j and h. In the multinomial and conditional logit model, the log-odds for alternatives j and h is given respectively by

$$\log\left(\frac{P_{MNL}[y_i = j]}{P_{MNL}[y_i = h]}\right) = x_i'(\beta_j - \beta_h),$$

$$\log\left(\frac{P_{CL}[y_i = j]}{P_{CL}[y_i = h]}\right) = (x_{ij} - x_{ih})'\beta.$$

So the relative odds to choose between the alternatives j and h is not affected by the other alternatives. This property of the multinomial and conditional logit model is called the '*independence of irrelevant alternatives*'. That is, in comparing the alternatives j and h, the other options are irrelevant. As an example, suppose that consumers can choose between ten brands of a certain product, with two strong leading brands ($j = 1, 2$) and with eight other much smaller brands. Suppose that the owner of the first leading brand is interested in the odds of his product compared with the other leading brand—that is, in $\log(P[y_i = 1]/P[y_i = 2])$. Clearly, it should make little difference whether this is modelled as a choice between ten alternative brands or as a choice between three alternatives (the two leading brands and the rest, taken as one category). In such situations the 'independence of irrelevant alternatives' is a reasonable assumption. The odds ratio between two alternatives then does not change when other alternatives are added to or deleted from the model. In other situations, especially if some of the alternatives are very similar, the independence of irrelevant alternatives is not realistic, so that the discussed logit models are not appropriate. In this case it is better to use multinomial or conditional probit models to incorporate the dependencies between the error terms ε_{ij} for the different alternatives j.

Diagnostic tests

One can apply similar diagnostic checks on multinomial and conditional models, as discussed before in Section 6.1.4 for binary models. For instance, the overall significance of the model can again be tested by means of the likelihood ratio test on the null hypothesis that all parameters are zero. One can further evaluate the success of classification—for instance, by predicting that the ith individual chooses the alternative h for which $\hat{p}_{ih}$ is maximal. These predicted choices can be compared with the actual observed choices y_i in an $m \times m$ classification table. Let n_{jj} be the number of individuals for which $y_i = \hat{y}_i = j$ is predicted correctly, and let $p_{jj} = n_{jj}/n$. Then $h = \sum_{j=1}^{m} p_{jj}$ is the hit rate—that is, the success rate of the model predictions. This may be compared to random predictions, where for each individual the alternative j

is predicted with probability $\hat{p}_j = n_j/n$, the observed fractions in the sample. The expected hit rate of these random predictions is $\hat{q} = \sum_{j=1}^{m} \hat{p}_j^2$. The model provides better-than-random predictions if

$$z = \frac{h - \hat{q}}{\sqrt{\hat{q}(1 - \hat{q})/n}} = \frac{nh - n\hat{q}}{\sqrt{n\hat{q}(1 - \hat{q})}}$$

is large enough (larger than 1.645 at 5 per cent significance level). An *LR*-test for heteroskedasticity may be performed, for instance, by specifying a model for the error terms ε_{ij} in the utility function (6.16) or (6.17) by $E[\varepsilon_{ij}^2] = \sigma_j^2, j = 2, \cdots, m$, where $E[\varepsilon_{i1}^2] = 1$ is fixed. This allows for the possibility that the utilities of some of the alternatives are better captured by the explanatory variables than other ones.

XM604BWA

Example 6.4: **Bank Wages (continued)**

We return to data of employees of a bank considered in earlier chapters. The jobs in the bank are divided into three categories. One category (which is given the label '1') consists of administrative jobs, a second category (with label '2') of custodial jobs, and a third category (with label '3') of management jobs. We consider the job category (1, 2, 3) as nominal variable and we estimate a multinomial logit model to explain the attained job category in terms of observed characteristics of the employees. We will discuss (i) the data and the model, (ii) the estimation results, (iii) an analysis of the marginal effects of education, (iv) the average marginal effects of education, (v) the predictive performance of the model, and (vi) the odds ratios.

(i) The data and the model

The dependent variable is the attained job category (1, 2, or 3) of the bank employee. As there are no women with custodial jobs, we restrict the attention to the 258 male employees of the bank (a model for all 474 employees of the bank is left as an exercise (see Exercise 6.14)). As explanatory variables we use the education level (x_2, in years) and the variable 'minority' ($x_3 = 1$ for minorities and $x_3 = 0$ otherwise). The multinomial model logit model (6.20) for the $m = 3$ job categories has $k = 3$ explanatory variables (the constant term and x_2 and x_3). We take the first job category (administration) as reference category. The model contains in total six parameters, a 3×1 vector β_2 for job category 2 (custodial jobs) and a 3×1 vector β_3 for job category 3 (management). For an individual with characteristics x_i, the probabilities for the three job categories are then given by

$$p_{i1} = \frac{1}{1 + e^{x_i'\beta_2} + e^{x_i'\beta_3}}, \quad p_{i2} = \frac{e^{x_i'\beta_2}}{1 + e^{x_i'\beta_2} + e^{x_i'\beta_3}}, \quad p_{i3} = \frac{e^{x_i'\beta_3}}{1 + e^{x_i'\beta_2} + e^{x_i'\beta_3}}.$$

(ii) Estimation results

The results of the multinomial logit model are in Panel 1 of Exhibit 6.5. The outcomes show that the minority effect is significant for management jobs, but not for custodial jobs. The education effect is significant for both job categories, with a positive coefficient of 1.63 for management jobs and a negative coefficient of -0.55 for custodial jobs. Note, however, that these coefficients do not have the interpretation of marginal effects, not even their signs, see (6.23). The marginal effects are analysed below in part (iii). Panel 2 of Exhibit 6.5 contains the results of the model without the variables education and minority. The corresponding LR-test on the joint significance of education and minority has value $LR = 2(-118.7 + 231.3) = 225.2$ (see Exhibit 6.5, Panels 1 and 2). This test corresponds to four restrictions, and the 5 per cent critical value of the corresponding $\chi^2(4)$ distribution is 9.49, so that the two explanatory variables are clearly jointly significant.

(iii) Analysis of the marginal effects of education

In multinomial logit models the sign of the marginal effect of an explanatory variable is not always the same as the sign of the corresponding coefficient. We will now analyse the marginal effect of education on the probabilities to attain a job in the three job categories. The coefficient of education (x_2) is $\hat{\beta}_{22} = -0.55$ for custodial jobs and $\hat{\beta}_{32} = 1.63$ for management jobs. For administrative jobs the coefficient of education is by definition $\beta_{12} = 0$, as this is the reference category. For an individual with characteristics $x_i = (1, x_{2i}, x_{3i})'$, the estimated marginal effects of education are obtained from (6.23), with the following results.

$$\frac{\partial P_{MNL}[y_i = 1]}{\partial x_{2i}} = \hat{p}_{i1}\left(\hat{\beta}_{12} - \sum_{h=2}^{3} \hat{p}_{ih}\hat{\beta}_{h2}\right) = \hat{p}_{i1}(0.55\hat{p}_{i2} - 1.63\hat{p}_{i3}),$$

$$\frac{\partial P_{MNL}[y_i = 2]}{\partial x_{2i}} = \hat{p}_{i2}\left(\hat{\beta}_{22} - \sum_{h=2}^{3} \hat{p}_{ih}\hat{\beta}_{h2}\right) = \hat{p}_{i2}(-0.55(1 - \hat{p}_{i2}) - 1.63\hat{p}_{i3}) < 0,$$

$$\frac{\partial P_{MNL}[y_i = 3]}{\partial x_{2i}} = \hat{p}_{i3}\left(\hat{\beta}_{32} - \sum_{h=2}^{3} \hat{p}_{ih}\hat{\beta}_{h2}\right) = \hat{p}_{i3}(0.55\hat{p}_{i2} + 1.63(1 - \hat{p}_{i3})) > 0.$$

Here we used the fact that the probabilities $\hat{p}_{ij}$ satisfy $0 < \hat{p}_{ij} < 1$. So we conclude that additional education leads to a lower probability of getting a custodial job and a higher probability of getting a management job, as could be expected. The effect on the probability of attaining an administrative job is positive if and only if $0.55\hat{p}_{i2} - 1.63\hat{p}_{i3} > 0$—that is, as long as the probability of a custodial job for this individual is at least $1.63/0.55 \approx 3$

times as large as the probability of a management job. The interpretation is as follows. If someone is most suited to a custodial job, then additional education may lead more quickly to a job in administration. On the other hand, if someone already has some chances of a management job, then additional education decreases the chance of an administrative job in favour of a management job.

(*a*)

Panel 1: MULTINOMIAL LOGIT						
Method: Maximum Likelihood (Marquardt)						
Sample: 1 474 IF (GENDER=1)						
Included observations: 258						
Convergence achieved after 33 iterations						
Cat	Variable	Beta	Coefficient	Std. Error	z-Statistic	Prob.
Cat 2 :	C	B2(1)	4.760717	1.268015	3.754465	0.0002
	EDUC	B2(2)	−0.553399	0.114211	−4.845405	0.0000
	MINORITY	B2(3)	0.426952	0.488181	0.874578	0.3818
Cat 3 :	C	B3(1)	−26.01435	2.717261	−9.573738	0.0000
	EDUC	B3(2)	1.633386	0.168697	9.682362	0.0000
	MINORITY	B3(3)	−2.109115	0.636723	−3.312454	0.0009
Log likelihood			−118.7360	Akaike info criterion		0.966946
Avg. log likelihood			−0.460217	Schwarz criterion		1.049573
Number of Coefs.			6			

(*b*)

Panel 2: MULTINOMIAL LOGIT						
Method: Maximum Likelihood (Marquardt)						
Sample: 1 474 IF (GENDER=1)						
Included observations: 258						
Convergence achieved after 10 iterations						
Cat	Variable	Beta	Coefficient	Std. Error	z-Statistic	Prob.
Cat 2:	C	B2(1)	−1.760409	0.208342	−8.449604	0.0000
Cat 3:	C	B3(1)	−0.752181	0.141007	−5.334355	0.0000
Log likelihood			−231.3446	Akaike info criterion		1.808873
Avg. log likelihood			−0.896684	Schwarz criterion		1.836415
Number of Coefs.			2			

(*c*)

Panel 3: MARGINAL EFFECTS OF EDUCATION ON PROBABILITIES JOBCAT			
	JOBCAT = 1	JOBCAT = 2	JOBCAT = 3
NON - MINORITIES	−0.127	−0.030	0.157
MINORITIES	0.012	−0.062	0.049

Exhibit 6.5 Bank Wages (Example 6.4)

Multinomial logit model for attained job category of male employees (Panel 1: category 1 (administration) is the reference category, category 2 (custodial jobs) has coefficients B2(1), B2(2), and B2(3), and category 3 (management) has coefficients B3(1), B3(2), and B3(3)), multinomial model without explanatory variables (except constant terms for each job category, Panel 2), and the marginal effects of education on the probability of attaining the three job categories (Panel 3: the reported numbers are averages over the two subsamples of non-minority males and minority males).

(*d*)

Panel 4: PREDICTION-REALIZATION TABLE					
		Actual			predicted
		jobcat = 1	jobcat = 2	jobcat = 3	total
	jobcat = 1	138	14	7	159
predicted	jobcat = 2	10	13	0	23
	jobcat = 3	9	0	67	76
actual total		157	27	74	258

random hit rate $(157/258)^2 + (27/258)^2 + (74/258)^2 = 0.464$
Z-value $= (218–119.6)/\sqrt{(258 * 0.464 * 0.536)} = 12.28$, $P = 0.0000$

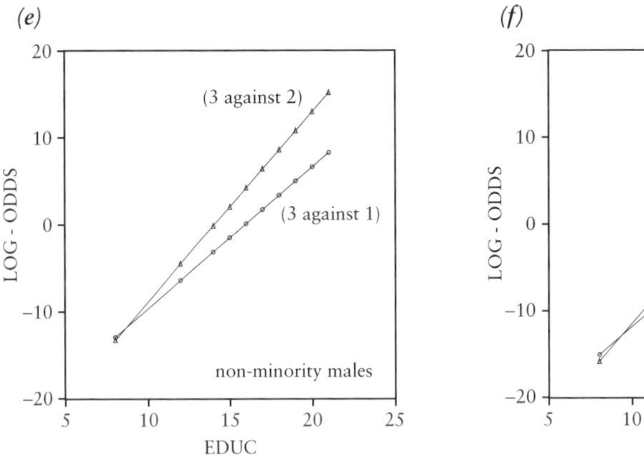

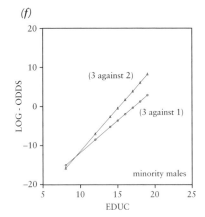

Exhibit 6.5 (*Contd.*)

Prediction–realization table of the predicted and actual job categories for the multinomial model of Panel 1 (Panel 4), and relation between the logarithm of the odds ratio (on the vertical axis) against education (on the horizontal axis) for non-minority males (*e*) and for minority males (*f*).

(iv) Average marginal effects of education

Panel 3 of Exhibit 6.5 shows the average marginal effect of education on the probabilities of having a job in each of the three categories. The estimated marginal effects are averaged over the relevant subsamples of minority males and non-minority males. With more education the chance of getting a management job increases and of getting a custodial job decreases. For management, the effects are much larger for non-minority males (around 16 per cent more chance for one additional year of education) than for minority males (around 5 per cent more chance).

(v) Predictive performance

Panel 4 of Exhibit 6.5 shows actual against predicted job categories, where an individual is predicted of having a job in the category with the highest estimated probability. The predictions are quite successful for jobs in administration and management but somewhat less so for custodial jobs, as for around half the people with custodial jobs it is predicted that they will work in administration. If the estimated probabilities of having a custodial job are added over all $n = 258$ individuals, then the predicted total number is equal to 27, but for fourteen individuals in job category 2 it is predicted to be more likely that they belong to job category 1. The hit rate is equal to $(138 + 13 + 67)/258 = 218/258 = 0.845$, whereas the expected hit rate of random predictions is equal to $(157/258)^2 + (27/258)^2 + (74/258)^2 = 0.464$. To test the classification success of the model, these hit rates can be compared by

$$z = (0.845 - 0.464)/\sqrt{0.464(1 - 0.464)/258} = 12.28, \qquad P = 0.0000.$$

This shows that the model indeed provides significantly better predictions than would be obtained by random predictions.

(vi) Odds ratios

Exhibit 6.5 gives the log-odds (as a function of education) of job category 3 against job categories 1 and 2, for non-minority male employees (e) and for male employees belonging to minorities (f). The odds ratios are higher for non-minority males, and the odds ratios are larger with respect to category 2 than with respect to category 1. Recall that in the logit model the log-odds is a linear function of the explanatory variables. The odds ratios become very large for high levels of education. This corresponds to relatively large probabilities for a management job, as could be expected.

☞ **Exercises: T: 6.3; E: 6.13e, 6.14, 6.15c, d.**

6.2.3 Ordered response

Model formulation

In some situations the alternatives can be *ordered*—for instance, if the dependent variable measures opinions (degree of agreement or disagreement with a statement) or rankings (quality of products). Such a variable is called *ordinal*—that is, the outcomes are ordered, although their numerical values have no further meaning. We follow the convention of labelling the m ordered alternatives by integers ranging from 1 to m. In the *ordered response* model, the outcome y_i is related to the index function

$$y_i^* = x_i'\beta + \varepsilon_i, \qquad E[\varepsilon_i] = 0.$$

The observed outcome of y_i is related to the index y_i^* by means of $(m-1)$ unknown threshold values $\tau_1 < \tau_2 < \cdots < \tau_{m-1}$ in the sense that

$$\begin{aligned} y_i &= 1 \text{ if } -\infty < y_i^* \leq \tau_1, \\ y_i &= j \text{ if } \tau_{j-1} < y_i^* \leq \tau_j, \, j = 2, \cdots, m-1, \\ y_i &= m \text{ if } \tau_{m-1} < y_i^* < \infty. \end{aligned}$$

The index y_i^* is not observed, and the measured response is $y_i = j$ if the index falls between the threshold values τ_{j-1} and τ_j. The unknown parameters of this model are β and the $(m-1)$ threshold values. The constant term should be excluded from the explanatory variables x_i, as otherwise the threshold parameters are not identified. When there are only $m = 2$ alternatives, this gives the binary response model of Section 6.1.1, where the unknown threshold value plays the role of the unknown constant term. Indeed, for $m = 2$ we get $P[y_i = 1] = P[y_i^* \leq \tau_1] = P[\varepsilon_i \leq \tau_1 - x_i'\beta] = F(\tau_1 - x_i'\beta)$, where F is the cumulative distribution of ε_i.

As compared with the multinomial model (6.16) with $U_i^j = x_i'\beta_j + \varepsilon_{ij}$, the ordered response model has the advantage that it uses only a single index function. Whereas the multinomial model contains $(m-1)k$ parameters, the ordered response model has $k + m - 2$ parameters and this is considerably less (for $k \geq 2$) if the number of alternatives m is large.

Marginal effects in ordered response models

Let F be the cumulative distribution function of ε_i, then

$$\begin{aligned} p_{ij} = P[y_i = j] &= P[\tau_{j-1} < y_i^* \leq \tau_j] = P[y_i^* \leq \tau_j] - P[y_i^* \leq \tau_{j-1}] \\ &= F(\tau_j - x_i'\beta) - F(\tau_{j-1} - x_i'\beta), \, j = 1, \cdots, m. \end{aligned} \tag{6.24}$$

Here we use the notation $\tau_0 = -\infty$ and $\tau_m = \infty$, so that $P[y_i = 1] = F(\tau_1 - x_i'\beta)$ and $P[y_i = m] = 1 - F(\tau_{m-1} - x_i'\beta)$. The marginal effects of changes in the explanatory variables are given by

$$\frac{\partial P[y_i = j]}{\partial x_i} = \left(f(\tau_{j-1} - x_i'\beta) - f(\tau_j - x_i'\beta)\right)\beta,$$

where f is the density function of ε_i. When $x_i'\beta$ increases, this leads to larger values of the index y_i^*, so that the outcome of y_i tends to become larger. The probability of the outcome $y_i = 1$ will decrease, that of $y_i = m$ will

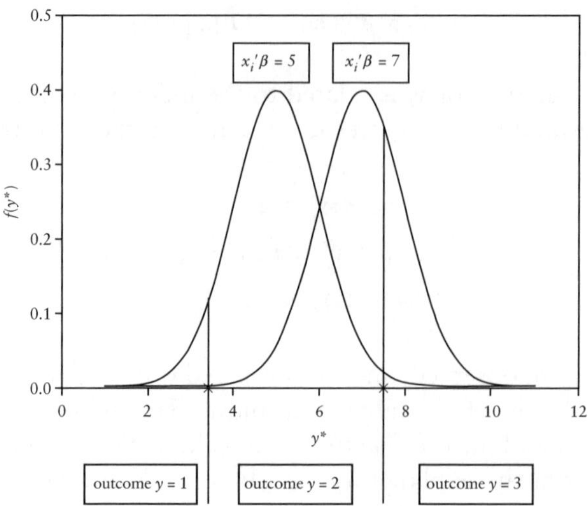

Exhibit 6.6 Ordered response

Effect of changes in the x-variables (measured by $y^* = x'\beta + \varepsilon$ on the horizontal axis) on the choice probabilities ($y = 1$ if $y^* \leq 3.5$, $y = 2$ if $3.5 < y^* \leq 7.5$, and $y = 3$ if $y^* > 7.5$).

increase, and that of $y_i = j$ for $j = 2, \cdots, m$ can increase or decrease, as at the same time $P[y_i \leq j-1] = F(\tau_{j-1} - x_i'\beta)$ decreases and $P[y_i \geq j+1] = 1 - F(\tau_j - x_i'\beta)$ increases.

This is illustrated in Exhibit 6.6 for the case of $m = 3$ possible outcomes and two threshold values for index values 3.5 and 7.5. The left density in the figure corresponds to $x_i'\beta = 5$, in which case the probabilities for the outcomes 1 and 3 are both quite small. The right density in the figure corresponds to $x_i'\beta = 7$, in which case the probability of the outcome 1 is nearly zero. As compared with $x_i'\beta = 5$, the probability of the outcome 3 for $x_i'\beta = 7$ has become much larger. And the probability of the outcome 2 has decreased, because the loss in the right tail (to alternative 3) is larger than the gain in the left tail (from alternative 1).

Estimation of ordered logit and probit models

The parameters in an ordered response model can be estimated by maximum likelihood. The log-likelihood is

$$\log(L(\beta, \tau_1, \cdots, \tau_{m-1})) = \sum_{i=1}^{n}\sum_{j=1}^{m} y_{ij}\log(p_{ij}) = \sum_{i=1}^{n}\log(p_{iy_i}),$$

with p_{ij} as defined in (6.24) and with $y_{ij} = 1$ if $y_i = j$ and $y_{ij} = 0$ if $y_i \neq j$. The function F should be specified, and in practice one often takes the standard normal or the logistic distribution. These are called the *ordered probit* and the *ordered logit* model respectively.

Diagnostic tests

Diagnostic tests for the ordered response model are similar to those for the multinomial and conditional models discussed in Section 6.2.2. The joint significance of the explanatory variables x_i can be tested by the LR-test for the hypothesis that $\beta = 0$. The predictive quality can be evaluated by a classification table. If an alternative is relatively rarely chosen in the sample, then the corresponding estimated threshold values will have large standard errors. Such an alternative can sometimes be better combined with neighbouring alternatives.

Additional diagnostic tests can be obtained by dividing the ordered alternatives into two groups and by applying the diagnostic tools discussed in Section 6.1.4 on the resulting two (groups of) alternatives.

Example 6.5: **Bank Wages (continued)**

We continue the analysis in Example 6.4 concerning the three job categories of male employees of a bank. We will now treat the job category as an ordinal variable and we discuss (i) the ordering of the three job categories, (ii) the outcomes of the ordered logit model, (iii) the outcomes of the ordered probit model, and (iv) the effect of additional education.

(i) Ordering of the three job categories

Instead of the multinomial logit model estimated in Example 6.4, we now consider an ordered logit model. The three alternative job categories are ordered so that $y_i = 1$ for custodial jobs (the former 'second' category), $y_i = 2$ for administrative jobs (the former 'first' category), and $y_i = 3$ for management jobs (the former 'third' category). This ordering is chosen as this corresponds to increasing average wages.

(ii) Outcomes of the ordered logit model

The estimation results are in Panel 1 of Exhibit 6.7. The ML estimates show a positive effect (0.87) of education and a negative effect ($-$ 1.06) of minority. The LR-test ($LR = 202$ with $P = 0.0000$) shows that the variables are jointly significant. Exhibit 6.7, Panel 2, is a classification table comparing actual and predicted job categories. The predictions are quite successful on average, although too many employees are predicted of having a job in administration (189 instead of 157) and too few in the other two categories. The estimated probabilities sum up to the actual numbers of individuals in the three categories. This always holds true for logit models.

(iii) Outcomes of the ordered probit model

For comparison, Panels 3 and 4 of Exhibit 6.7 show the results of the ordered probit model. The estimates are in line with those obtained for the ordered logit model, taking into account the scaling factor of around 1.6 to compare probit with logit estimates. The classifications in Panel 4 are also very similar to those of the ordered logit model in Panel 2. However, the estimated probabilities no longer sum up to the actual totals per job category, although the differences are very small.

(iv) Effect of additional education

The effect of having 16 instead of 12 years of education (approximately that of having a university degree) for non-minority males in the probit model is represented graphically in Exhibit 6.7 (*e*). The index $y_i^* = x_i'\beta + \varepsilon_i$ is on the horizontal axis. The left density is for 12 years of education and the right density for 16 years of education. In the probit model $\varepsilon_i \sim \mathrm{N}(0, 1)$, so that

(*a*)

Panel 1: Dependent Variable: ORDERJOBCAT Method: ML – ORDERED LOGIT; Number of ordered outcomes: 3 Sample(adjusted): 1 472 IF GENDER=1; Included observations: 258 Convergence achieved after 9 iterations				
Variable	Coefficient	Std. Error	z-Statistic	Prob.
EDUC	0.870026	0.089099	9.764700	0.0000
MINORITY	−1.056442	0.375384	−2.814296	0.0049
Limit Points				
LIMIT_2:C(3)	7.952259	1.004817	7.914141	0.0000
LIMIT_3:C(4)	14.17223	1.429637	9.913163	0.0000
Log likelihood	−130.3198	Akaike info criterion		1.041239
Restr. log likelihood	−231.3446	Schwarz criterion		1.096323
LR statistic (2 df)	202.0495			
Probability (LR stat)	0.000000			

(*b*)

Panel 2: Dependent Variable: ORDERJOBCAT Method: ML – ORDERED LOGIT Sample(adjusted): 1 472 IF GENDER=1; Included observations: 258 Prediction table for ordered dependent variable					
Value	Count	Count of obs with Max Prob	Error	Sum of all Probabilities	Error
1	27	23	4	27	0
2	157	189	−32	157	0
3	74	46	28	74	0

Exhibit 6.7 Bank Wages (Example 6.5)

Ordered logit model (Panel 1) for achieved job categories, ranked by the variable ORDERJOBCAT (with value 1 for 'custodial' jobs, 2 for 'administrative' jobs, and 3 for 'management' jobs), with classification table of predicted job categories (Panel 2).

(*c*)

Panel 3: Dependent Variable: ORDERJOBCAT				
Method: ML – ORDERED PROBIT; Number of ordered outcomes: 3				
Sample(adjusted): 1 472 IF GENDER=1; Included observations: 258				
Convergence achieved after 5 iterations				
Variable	Coefficient	Std.Error	z-Statistic	Prob.
EDUC	0.479043	0.046617	10.27624	0.0000
MINORITY	−0.509259	0.213978	−2.379963	0.0173
Limit Points				
LIMIT_2:C(3)	4.443056	0.556591	7.982620	0.0000
LIMIT_3:C(4)	7.843644	0.744473	10.53583	0.0000
Log likelihood	−131.2073	Akaike info criterion		1.048119
Restr. log likelihood	−231.3446	Schwarz criterion		1.103203
LR statistic (2 df)	200.2746			
Probability(LR stat)	0.000000			

(*d*)

Panel 4: Dependent Variable: ORDERJOBCAT					
Method: MI – ORDERED PROBIT					
Sample(adjusted): 1 472 IF GENDER=1; Included observations: 258					
Prediction table for ordered dependent variable					
Value	Count	Count of obs with Max Prob	Error	Sum of all Probabilities	Error
1	27	23	4	27.626	−0.626
2	157	189	−32	156.600	0.400
3	74	46	28	73.773	0.227

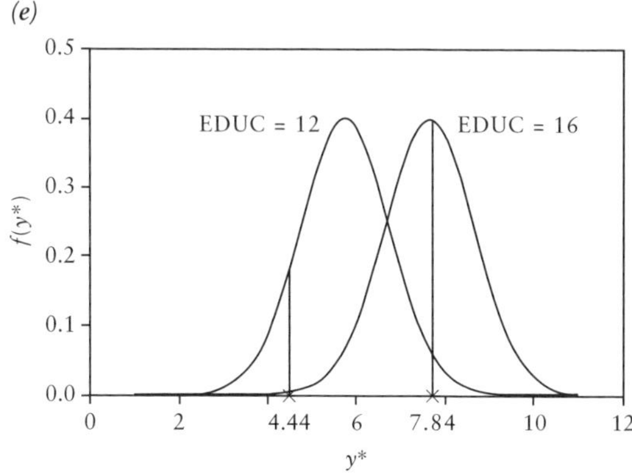

Exhibit 6.7 (*Contd.*)

Ordered probit model (Panel 3) for achieved job categories, ranked by the variable ORDERJOBCAT (with value 1 for 'custodial' jobs, 2 for 'administrative' jobs, and 3 for 'management' jobs), with classification table of predicted job categories (Panel 4). (*e*) shows the graphs of two probability distributions (corresponding to the ordered probit model) for non-minority males, the left one for an education level of 12 years and the right one for an education level of 16 years, with the index y^* on the horizontal axis (the limit points 4.44 and 7.84 for the three job categories are taken from Panel 3).

$y_i^* \sim \mathrm{N}(x_i'\beta, 1)$, that is, both densities are normal with standard deviation 1, the left density has mean $x_i'\beta = 0.479 \cdot 12 - 0.509 \cdot 0 = 5.75$ and the right density has mean $x_i'\beta = 0.479 \cdot 16 = 7.66$. The estimated threshold value between custodial and administrative jobs is 4.44 and that between administrative and management jobs is 7.84. For 12 years of education the probability of having an administrative job is by far the largest, whereas for 16 years of education the probabilities of having a management job or an administrative job are nearly equally large. In Exercise 6.13 some further aspects of these data are investigated where we also consider a binary logit model obtained by joining administrative and custodial jobs into a single category.

☞ **Exercises:** E: 6.13f, 6.15a.

6.2.4 Summary

We summarize the steps to model the underlying factors that influence the outcome of a multinomial dependent variable. Note that, if the dependent variable is a quantitative variable (so that the outcome values are not simply qualitative labels but the actual quantitative measurement of some quantity of interest), we should not use the methods discussed in this section, as regression-based methods may be more informative. This is discussed in Section 6.3, for instance, for quantitative dependent variables that take only non-negative values.

- Determine whether the dependent multinomial variable is a nominal variable (without a natural ordering of the outcomes) or an ordinal variable (with a natural ordering).
- Determine the possibly relevant explanatory variables.
- For a nominal dependent variable, one can formulate either a multinomial model (if no characteristics of the alternative choices are measured) or a conditional model (in case the characteristics of the alternatives can be measured for each individual).
- Multinomial and conditional logit models are easily estimated by maximum likelihood. However, the use of the logit model requires that the alternatives are sufficiently distinct from each other (the 'independence of irrelevant alternatives'). Otherwise one can estimate a multinomial or conditional probit model by maximum likelihood, at the expense of more involved numerical integration and optimization techniques.
- For an ordinal dependent variable, one can estimate an ordered logit or ordered probit model. As these models are easier to estimate and interpret than multinomial logit and probit models, it is advantageous to exploit the ordered nature of the outcomes of the dependent variable.

- All mentioned models can be evaluated in a similar way as binary dependent variable models—for instance, by testing the individual and joint significance of parameters, by determining (mean) marginal effects of the explanatory variables, by plotting odds ratios, by evaluating the predictive performance, and so on. Some care is needed in interpreting individual coefficients, especially in multinomial logit models, and one often gets a better interpretation of the model by computing the (mean) marginal effects instead.

6.3 Limited dependent variables

6.3.1 Truncated samples

☞ Uses Chapters 1–4; Section 5.6; Section 6.1.

Different types of limited dependent variables

In the two foregoing sections we considered models for qualitative, discrete-valued (nominal or ordinal) dependent variables. Now we will investigate models for limited dependent variables — that is, quantitative, continuous-valued variables with outcomes that are restricted in some way. So the dependent variable is an interval variable, in the sense that the numerical differences in observed values have a quantitative meaning. However, in contrast with the regression model discussed in Chapters 2–5, the dependent variable cannot take any arbitrary real value, as there exist some restrictions on the possible outcomes. We analyse four types of limited dependent variables. In this section we consider truncated samples where the observations can be obtained only from a limited part of the underlying population. If the selection mechanism can be modelled in some way, one can employ the methods discussed in Section 6.3.3. Section 6.3.2 treats models for censored data where the possible observed outcomes are limited to an interval. A special case consists of duration data, discussed in Section 6.3.4. Although least squares is not appropriate for these types of data, in Sections 6.3.1 and 6.3.2 we will pay detailed attention to the properties of least squares estimators as this analysis provides suggestions for better estimation methods.

Truncated observations

Suppose that the dependent variable y_i and the independent variables x_i are related by $y_i = x_i'\beta + \varepsilon_i$. A sample is called *truncated* if we know beforehand that the observations can come only from a restricted part of the underlying population distribution.

For instance, suppose that the data concern the purchases of new cars, with y_i the price of the car and x_i characteristics of the buyer like age and income class. Then no observations on y_i can be below the price of the cheapest new car. Some households may want to buy a new car but find it too expensive, in which case they do not purchase a new car and are not part of the observed data. This truncation effect should be taken into account, for instance, if one wants to predict the potential sales of a cheaper new type of car, because most potential buyers will not be part of the observed sample.

A model for truncated data

The truncation can be from below (as in the above example of prices of new cars), from above (so that y_i cannot take values above a certain threshold), or from both sides. We will consider the situation that the truncation is from below with known truncation point. Other types of truncation can be treated in a similar way (see Exercise 6.5). We further assume that the truncation point is equal to zero, which can always be achieved by measuring y_i in deviation from the known truncation point. It is assumed that, in the untruncated population, the relation between the dependent variable (y_i^*) and the explanatory variables (x_i) is linear. For later purposes it is convenient to write the model as

$$y_i^* = x_i'\beta + \sigma\varepsilon_i, \quad \varepsilon_i \sim \text{IID}, \quad E[\varepsilon_i] = 0.$$

Here σ is a scale parameter and ε_i is an error term with known symmetric and continuous density function f. For example, if ε_i follows the standard normal distribution, then σ is the unknown standard deviation of the error terms. The above formulation of the regression equation differs from the usual one in Chapters 2–5, as it explicitly contains the scale factor σ. This is convenient in what follows, since by extracting the scale factor σ we can now assume that the density function f of the (normalized) error terms ε_i is completely known. The observed data are assumed to satisfy this model, but the sample is truncated in the sense that individuals with $y_i^* \leq 0$ are not observed. In the car sales example, y_i^* may be interpreted as the amount of money that an individual wants to spend on a new car, and, if this is less than the price of the cheapest car, then this individual will not buy a new car. So the sample comes from a subpopulation—that is,

$$\begin{aligned} y_i &= y_i^* = x_i'\beta + \sigma\varepsilon_i && \text{if } y_i^* > 0, \\ y_i &\text{ is not observed} && \text{if } y_i^* \leq 0. \end{aligned} \qquad (6.25)$$

A graphical illustration of truncation

The effect of truncation is illustrated graphically in Exhibit 6.8. This corresponds to the above truncated regression model, with $y_i^* = x_i + \varepsilon_i$ and $\varepsilon_i \sim \text{NID}(0, 1)$. If $x_i = 1$, then the corresponding value of y_i is observed if and only if $\varepsilon_i > -1$—that is, the error term comes from the standard normal distribution truncated on the left at the value -1. In general, for a given value

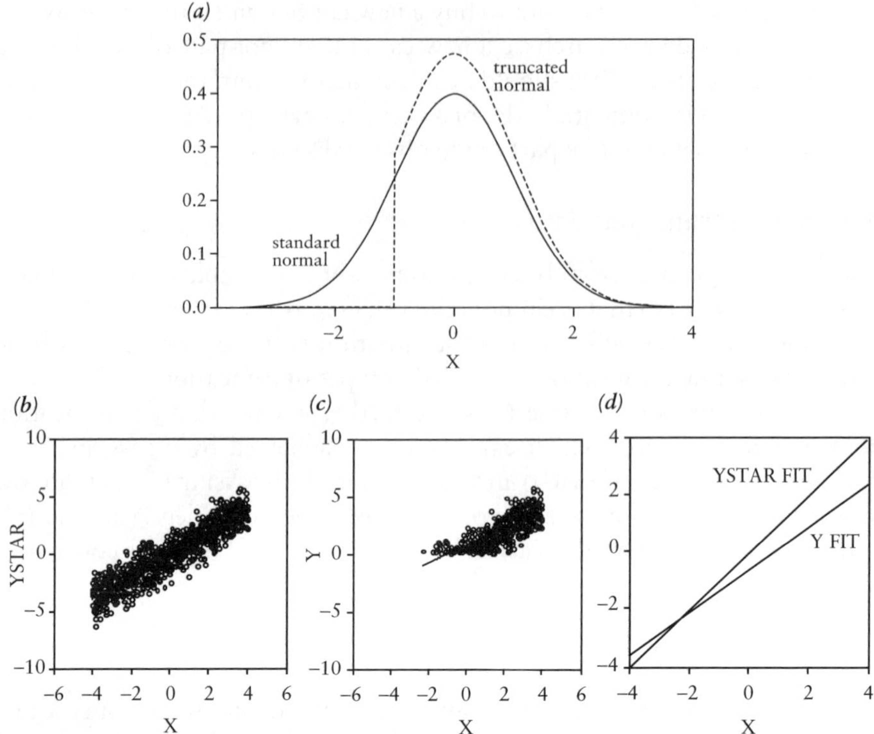

Exhibit 6.8 Truncated data

(a) shows a truncated normal density with truncation from below (at $x = -1$). (b)–(d) show scatter diagrams illustrating the effect of truncation on the OLS estimates; (b) is the untruncated scatter of y^* against x, (c) is the truncated scatter of y against x, and (d) contains the two regression lines (the DGP has slope $\beta = 1$).

of x_i, the density of ε_i is truncated at the value $-x_i$. The scatter diagrams in Exhibit 6.8 (b) and (c) illustrate that the truncation effect is large for small values of x_i and small for large values of x_i. For small values of x_i we get observations only for relatively large values of the disturbances. This means that, on the left part of the scatter diagram, the observed values tend to lie above the model relation $y = x$, whereas on the right part the observations are scattered more symmetrically around this line. This leads, in this model with a positive slope $\beta = 1$, to a downward bias of the OLS estimator (see Exhibit 6.8 (d)).

T

The truncated density function of the error terms

We now analyse the effect of truncation more generally for the model (6.25). In the observed sample there holds $y_i^* > 0$, so that ε_i comes from the truncation of the distribution f with $\varepsilon_i > -x_i'\beta/\sigma$. The cumulative distribution of the error term of the ith observation is therefore given by

$$P[\varepsilon_i \leq t | \varepsilon_i > -x_i'\beta/\sigma] = 0 \quad \text{if } t \leq -x_i'\beta/\sigma,$$
$$= \frac{P[\varepsilon_i \leq t]}{P[\varepsilon_i > -x_i'\beta/\sigma]} = \frac{F(t)}{F(x_i'\beta/\sigma)} \quad \text{if } t > -x_i'\beta/\sigma.$$

Here F denotes the cumulative distribution corresponding to the density f, and we used the continuity and symmetry of f so that $P[\varepsilon_i > -a] = P[\varepsilon_i < a] = P[\varepsilon_i \leq a] = F(a)$. The density function of the error terms ε_i of the data generating process (that is, with observations $y_i > 0$) is obtained by differentiating the above cumulative distribution function with respect to the argument t. This gives the truncated density function f_i defined by

$$f_i(t) = 0 \qquad \text{for } t \leq -x_i'\beta/\sigma,$$
$$f_i(t) = \frac{f(t)}{F(x_i'\beta/\sigma)} \qquad \text{for } t > -x_i'\beta/\sigma.$$

So the truncated density of the error terms is proportional to the 'right part' (with $t > -x_i'\beta/\sigma$) of the original density f. The scaling factor $F(x_i'\beta/\sigma)$ is needed to get a density—that is, with $\int f_i(t)dt = 1$.

Derivation of the truncated density function of the dependent variable

T

The foregoing results for the density function of the error terms ε_i can be used to derive the density function $p(y_i)$ of the dependent variable $y_i = x_i'\beta + \varepsilon_i$. As y_i is observed, this means that $y_i > 0$, so that the error term comes from the truncated distribution with $\varepsilon_i > -x_i'\beta/\sigma$. Let F_{y_i} denote the cumulative density of y_i; then for $t > 0$ we get

$$F_{y_i}(t) = P[y_i \leq t \mid \varepsilon_i > -x_i'\beta/\sigma] = P[x_i'\beta + \sigma\varepsilon_i \leq t \mid \varepsilon_i > -x_i'\beta/\sigma]$$
$$= P[\varepsilon_i \leq (t - x_i'\beta)/\sigma \mid \varepsilon_i > -x_i'\beta/\sigma] = \frac{F((t - x_i'\beta)/\sigma)}{F(x_i'\beta/\sigma)}.$$

The density function is obtained by differentiating with respect to t so that

$$p(y_i) = \frac{1}{\sigma}\frac{f((y_i - x_i'\beta)/\sigma)}{F(x_i'\beta/\sigma)}. \qquad (6.26)$$

This result can also be obtained by applying (1.10) (p. 22) for the transformation $y_i = x_i'\beta + \sigma\varepsilon_i = g(\varepsilon_i)$, where ε_i has density $f(t)/F(x_i'\beta/\sigma)$ for $t > -x_i'\beta/\sigma$. The inverse transformation is $\varepsilon_i = h(y_i) = (y_i - x_i'\beta)/\sigma$ with derivative $h'(y_i) = (1/\sigma)$. Then (6.26) follows directly from (1.10).

Derivation of systematic bias of OLS

The estimates of β obtained by applying OLS to (6.25) (for observations $y_i > 0$ in the sample) are not consistent. Exhibit 6.8 illustrates this graphically. More formally, inconsistency follows from the fact that the error terms with distribution f_i do not have zero mean, as $E[\varepsilon_i|y_i^* > 0] = E[\varepsilon_i|\varepsilon_i > -x_i'\beta/\sigma] > 0$. For instance, if $f = \phi$ is the standard normal distribution with cumulative distribution Φ, then (using the notation $z_i = x_i'\beta/\sigma$) we get

$$\begin{aligned} E[\varepsilon_i|y_i^* > 0] &= \int_{-z_i}^{\infty} t\frac{\phi(t)}{\Phi(z_i)}dt = \frac{1}{\Phi(z_i)}\int_{-z_i}^{\infty}\frac{1}{\sqrt{2\pi}}te^{-\frac{1}{2}t^2}dt \\ &= -\frac{1}{\Phi(z_i)}\frac{1}{\sqrt{2\pi}}e^{-\frac{1}{2}t^2}\Big|_{-z_i}^{\infty} = \frac{1}{\Phi(z_i)}\frac{1}{\sqrt{2\pi}}e^{-\frac{1}{2}z_i^2} \\ &= \frac{\phi(z_i)}{\Phi(z_i)} = \frac{\phi(x_i'\beta/\sigma)}{\Phi(x_i'\beta/\sigma)} = \lambda_i > 0. \end{aligned} \tag{6.27}$$

The term λ_i is called the *inverse Mills ratio*, and this expression for the truncation bias is specific for the normal distribution of the error terms ε_i. For observations in the sample, the mean value of $y_i = x_i'\beta + \varepsilon_i$ is not $x_i'\beta$ (as in the untruncated regression model) but it is

$$E[y_i|y_i^* > 0] = x_i'\beta + \sigma E[\varepsilon_i|y_i^* > 0] = x_i'\beta + \sigma\lambda_i. \tag{6.28}$$

Let $\omega_i = y_i - E[y_i|y_i^* > 0] = \varepsilon_i - \sigma\lambda_i$, then $E[\omega_i|y_i^* > 0] = 0$ and in the observed sample (with $y_i^* > 0$) we can write

$$y_i = x_i'\beta + \sigma\lambda_i + \omega_i, \qquad E[\omega_i] = 0.$$

If we regress y_i on x_i, then the (unobserved) regressor λ_i is neglected. This makes OLS biased and inconsistent (see also Section 3.2.3 (p. 142–3) on omitted variables bias). Formally, the OLS estimator is

$$b = \left(\sum x_i x_i'\right)^{-1}\left(\sum x_i y_i\right) = \beta + \left(\frac{1}{n}\sum x_i x_i'\right)^{-1}\left(\frac{1}{n}\sum(\sigma\lambda_i + \omega_i)x_i\right).$$

OLS is inconsistent because the probability limit $\text{plim}(\frac{1}{n}\sum \lambda_i x_i) \neq 0$, as λ_i is a function of x_i. That is, the orthogonality condition is violated so that OLS is inconsistent. The bias of OLS will be small if the terms λ_i are small—that is, if the terms $x_i'\beta/\sigma$ are large (as $\phi(z_i) \to 0$ and $\Phi(z_i) \to 1$ so that $\lambda_i \to 0$ for $z_i \to \infty$). In this case the truncation has only a small effect, as the condition that $\varepsilon_i > -x_i'\beta/\sigma$ is then hardly a restriction anymore.

Estimation by maximum likelihood

Consistent estimates of β are obtained by applying maximum likelihood, using the correct truncated density functions f_i for the error terms ε_i and the corresponding truncated density (6.26) of the observations y_i. For the normal distribution, the corresponding truncated density (6.26) is equal to

$$p(y_i) = \frac{1}{\sigma}\frac{\phi((y_i - x_i'\beta)/\sigma)}{\Phi(x_i'\beta/\sigma)}.$$

As the observations y_i are assumed to be mutually independent, the log-likelihood $\log(L(\beta, \sigma)) = \log(p(y_1, \cdots, y_n)) = \sum_{i=1}^{n} \log(p(y_i))$ becomes

$$\log(L) = -\frac{n}{2}\log(2\pi) - \frac{n}{2}\log(\sigma^2) - \frac{1}{2\sigma^2}\sum_{i=1}^{n}(y_i - x_i'\beta)^2 - \sum_{i=1}^{n}\log(\Phi(x_i'\beta/\sigma)). \tag{6.29}$$

The last term comes in addition to the usual terms in a linear regression model (see (4.30) in Section 4.3.2 (p. 227)) and represents the truncation effect. This last term is non-linear in β and σ, and the first order conditions for a maximum of $\log(L)$ involve the terms λ_i so that numerical integration is needed.

Marginal effects in truncated models

Some care is needed in interpreting the parameters β. They measure the marginal effects on $E[y]$ of the explanatory variables x in the (untruncated) population. Therefore they are the parameters of interest for out-of-sample predictions—that is, to estimate effects for unobserved values $y^* \leq 0$. If one is instead interested in within-sample effects—that is, in the truncated population with $y^* > 0$—then for the normal distribution the relevant marginal effects are

$$\frac{\partial E[y_i | y_i^* > 0]}{\partial x_i} = (1 - \lambda_i^2 - \lambda_i x_i'\beta/\sigma)\beta. \tag{6.30}$$

This measures the effect of each explanatory variable on the expected value of the response of an individual in the sample. The correction term in front of β in (6.30) lies between zero and one (see Exercise 6.4). So the marginal effects in the truncated population are closer to zero than those in the untruncated population. For purposes of interpretation, the averages of these effects over the sample can be reported. Note that the ratios β_j/β_h continue to have the interpretation of the relative effect of the jth and hth explanatory variables on the dependent variable (as the scalar factor in front of β in (6.30) is the same for all the k elements of the vector of explanatory variables x_i). This implies that these relative effects are the same for the untruncated and the truncated population.

XM601DMF

Example 6.6: **Direct Marketing for Financial Product (continued)**

In Example 6.1 we described direct marketing data concerning a new financial product. Of the 925 customers, 470 responded to the mailing by investing in the new product. Now we analyse the truncated sample consisting of these 470 customers. We will discuss (i) a truncated model for the invested amount of money, (ii) results of OLS and ML, and (iii) some comments on the obtained results.

(i) A truncated model for the invested amount of money

We relate the amount of invested money to characteristics of the customer—that is, gender (1 for males, 0 for females), activity (1 if the customer already invests in other products of the bank, 0 otherwise), and age (including also a squared term to allow for non-linear effects). We consider the truncated data set of 470 customers who invested a positive amount of money. As the variable to be explained we take $y_i = \log(1 + \text{invest})$, where 'invest' is the amount of money invested. We take logarithms because the distribution of the amount of invested money is very skewed. In the sample the investments are positive, so that $y_i > 0$. Let y^* be the 'inclination to invest'; then the model is given by (6.25), where x_i is the 5×1 vector of explanatory variables (constant, gender, activity, age, and squared age). This is a truncated regression model.

(ii) Results of OLS and ML

Exhibit 6.9 shows the results of OLS (without taking the truncation into account, in Panel 1) and of ML in (6.29) (that is, using the truncated normal density, in Panel 2). The outcomes suggest that the variables 'gender' and 'activity' do not have significant effects on the amount of invested money and that age has a significant effect, with a maximum at an age of around 62 years (namely, where $0.0698 - 2 \cdot 0.0559 \cdot (\text{age}/100) = 0$). This is somewhat surprising, as one would normally expect the variable 'activity' to have a positive effect on the invested amount and the effect of age to be maximal at an earlier age.

(iii) Comments on the obtained results

The results of OLS and of ML are nearly equal. Exhibit 6.9 (*c*) and (*d*) show the histogram of the values of $z_i = x_i'b/s$, where b and s are the ML estimates of β and σ, and the histogram of the corresponding values of the inverse Mills ratio $\lambda_i = \phi(z_i)/\Phi(z_i)$. The z_i values are positive and lie far away from the truncation point zero, with minimal value 4.06. Consequently, the values of λ_i are very close to zero, with maximal value 0.0001. This means that the correction term in the log-likelihood (6.29) is very small (for $z_i \geq 4.06$ there holds $\Phi(z_i) \approx 1$ and hence $\log(\Phi(z_i)) \approx 0$). This explains that ML and OLS are nearly equivalent for these data. As the estimates by OLS (neglecting the truncation) and ML (with truncation) are close together, it is tempting to

(*a*)

Panel 1: Dependent Variable: LOGINV = LOG(1 + INVEST)				
Method: Least Squares				
Sample(adjusted): 1 1000 IF INVEST>0				
Included observations: 470				
Variable	Coefficient	Std. Error	t-Statistic	Prob.
C	2.854243	0.611331	4.668900	0.0000
GENDER	−0.214029	0.115786	−1.848499	0.0652
ACTIVITY	−0.132122	0.099673	−1.325556	0.1856
AGE	0.069782	0.024903	2.802193	0.0053
AGE^2/100	−0.055928	0.024156	−2.315258	0.0210
R-squared	0.047838			
S.E. of regression	0.944256			

(*b*)

Panel 2: Dependent Variable: LOGINVEST = LOG(1 + INVEST)				
Method: ML - Truncated Normal				
Sample(adjusted): 1 1000 IF INVEST>0				
Included observations: 470; truncated sample with left censoring value 0				
Convergence achieved after 11 iterations				
Variable	Coefficient	Std. Error	z-Statistic	Prob.
C	2.854157	0.608105	4.693525	0.0000
GENDER	−0.214033	0.115170	−1.858412	0.0631
ACTIVITY	−0.132126	0.099144	−1.332676	0.1826
AGE	0.069785	0.024771	2.817203	0.0048
AGE^2/100	−0.055931	0.024029	−2.327683	0.0199
Error Distribution				
SCALE: SIGMA	0.939228	0.030637	30.65627	0.0000
R-squared	0.047838			
S.E. of regression	0.945272			

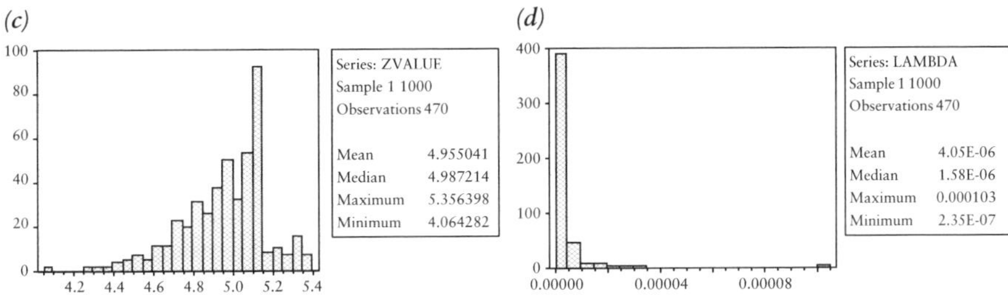

Exhibit 6.9 Direct Marketing for Financial Product (Example 6.6)

Models for invested amount of money based on data of 470 individuals who made an investment, OLS (Panel 1) and ML in truncated model (Panel 2). (*c*) and (*d*) show histograms of the values of $z = (x'b_{ML})/s_{ML}$ (in (*c*)) and of the inverse Mills ratio $\lambda = \phi(z)/\Phi(z)$ (in (*d*)).

conclude that the truncation has no serious effects. However, this need not be correct. To investigate these effects in a proper way we need further information on the individuals who are excluded from the sample, here the customers who did not invest. In the next section we consider the situation where we also know the characteristics of the individuals who did not invest.

As we will see in Example 6.7, we then get quite different conclusions (for instance, on the sign of the effect of the variable activity and on the question at what age the effect is maximal).

Exercises: T: 6.4a, b; S: 6.9a, b.

6.3.2 Censored data

Tobit model for censored data

The dependent variable is called *censored* when the response cannot take values below (left censored) or above (right censored) a certain threshold value. For instance, in the example on investments in a new financial product, the investments are either zero or positive. And, in deciding about a new car, one has either to pay the cost of the cheapest car or abstain from buying a new car. The so-called *tobit model* relates the observed outcomes of $y_i \geq 0$ to an index function

$$y_i^* = x_i'\beta + \sigma\varepsilon_i$$

by means of

$$\begin{aligned} y_i &= \ y_i^* = x_i'\beta + \sigma\varepsilon_i \text{ if } y_i^* > 0, \\ y_i &= \ 0 \qquad\qquad\qquad \text{if } y_i^* \leq 0. \end{aligned} \tag{6.31}$$

Here σ is a scale parameter and the error terms ε_i have a known symmetric density function f (so that $f(t) = f(-t)$ for all t) with cumulative distribution function F, so that

$$E[\varepsilon_i] = 0.$$

In the tobit model, the functions f and F are usually chosen in accordance with the standard normal distribution (with $f = \varphi$ and $F = \Phi$). The above model for censored data is sometimes called the tobit type 1 model, to distinguish it from the tobit type 2 model that will be discussed in the next section for data with selection effects. In contrast with a truncated sample, where only the responses for $y_i^* > 0$ are observed, it is now assumed that responses $y_i = 0$ corresponding to $y_i^* \leq 0$ are also observed and that the values of x_i for such observations are also known. In practice these zero-responses are of interest, as they provide relevant information on economic behaviour. For instance, it is of interest to know which individuals decided not to invest (as other financial products could be developed for this group) or which individuals did not buy a new car (as one could design other cars that appeal more to this group). The tobit model can be seen as a variation of the probit model, with one discrete option ('failure', $y_i = 0$) and where the option 'success' is replaced by the continuous variable $y_i > 0$.

A graphical illustration of censoring

If one simply applies OLS by regressing y_i (including the zero observations) on x_i, then this leads to inconsistent estimators. The reason is the same as in the case of truncated samples—that is, $E[y_i] \neq x_i'\beta$.

Exhibit 6.10 provides a graphical illustration of the effect of censoring. Here the data are generated by $y_i^* = x_i + \varepsilon_i$ with $\varepsilon_i \sim \mathrm{N}(0, 1)$ and $y_i = y_i^*$ if $y_i^* > 0$ and $y_i = 0$ if $y_i^* \leq 0$. For a given value of x_i, the probability distribution of y_i is mixed continuous-discrete. For instance, for $x_i = 0$, the probability on the outcome $y_i = 0$ is $P[\varepsilon_i \leq 0] = 0.5$, outcomes $y_i > 0$ have a standard normal density, and outcomes $y_i < 0$ are not possible. Observed values y_i correspond to the uncensored model $y_i = x_i + \varepsilon_i$ if and only if $y_i = y_i^*$—that is, if and only if $y_i^* = x_i + \varepsilon_i > 0$. Clearly, the condition $\varepsilon_i > -x_i$ is hardly a

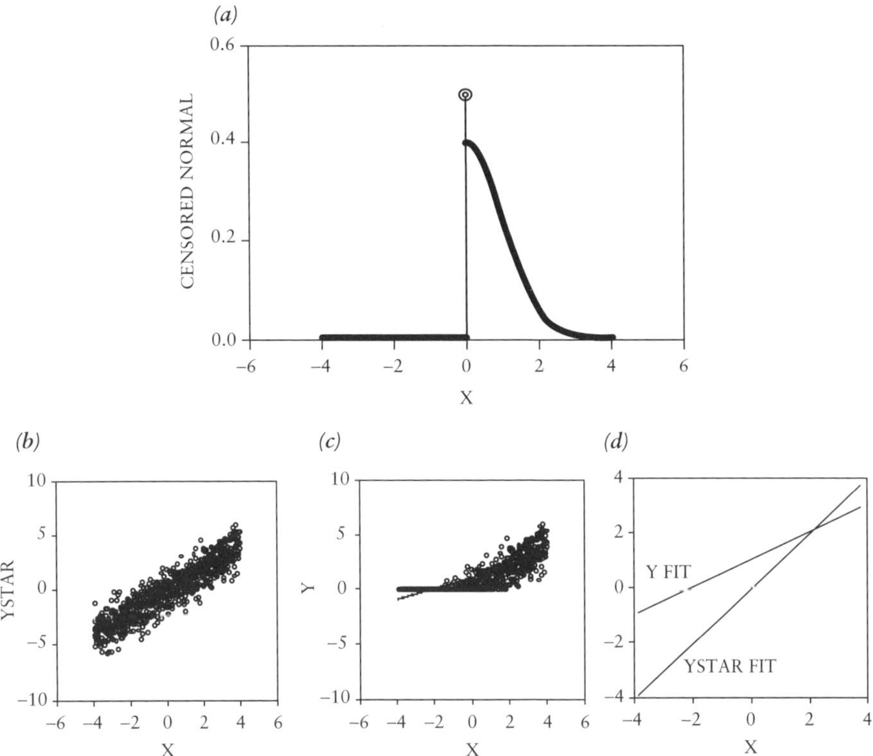

Exhibit 6.10 Censored data

(*a*) shows a censored normal density with censoring from below (at $x = 0$), with a point mass $P[x = 0] = 0.5$. (*b*)–(*d*) show scatter diagrams illustrating the effect of censoring on the OLS estimates: (*b*) is the uncensored scatter of y^* against x, (*c*) is the censored scatter of y against x, and (*d*) contains the two regression lines (the DGP has slope $\beta = 1$).

restriction if x_i takes large positive values, but it is a strong restriction if x_i takes large negative values. In Exhibit 6.10 (*c*) the observed values y_i (with $y_i > 0$ always) for small values of x_i are systematically larger than the corresponding values of the index y_i^* in (*b*) (which are often negative for negative values of x_i). This upward bias in the observations y_i in the left part of the scatter diagram in Exhibit 6.10 (*c*) leads to a downward bias in the OLS estimator (see (*d*)).

T

Derivation of the distribution of a censored dependent variable

For given values of x_i, the distribution of y_i in the tobit model is mixed continuous-discrete, with continuous density $p_{y_i}(t)$ for outcomes $t > 0$ and with a positive probability on the discrete outcome $y_i = 0$. We will now derive the explicit expression for the probability distribution. First we consider the discrete part. As the density f of the error terms is assumed to be symmetric, it follows that $F(-t) = 1 - F(t)$, so that

$$P[y_i = 0] = P[\varepsilon_i \leq -x_i'\beta/\sigma] = F(-x_i'\beta/\sigma) = 1 - F(x_i'\beta/\sigma).$$

Second, we consider the continuous part for $y_i = t > 0$. For $t > 0$ there holds

$$F_{y_i}(t) = P[y_i \leq t] = P[x_i'\beta + \sigma\varepsilon_i \leq t] = P\left[\varepsilon_i \leq \frac{t - x_i'\beta}{\sigma}\right] = F\left(\frac{t - x_i'\beta}{\sigma}\right).$$

The density $p_{y_i}(t)$ of $y_i > 0$ is the derivative of this expression with respect to t—that is, $(1/\sigma)f((t - x_i'\beta)/\sigma)$. Summarizing the above results, the probability distribution of a censored variable is equal to

$$\begin{aligned} P[y_i = 0] &= 1 - F(x_i'\beta/\sigma), \\ p_{y_i}(t) &= \frac{1}{\sigma} f\left(\frac{t - x_i'\beta}{\sigma}\right) \quad \text{for } y_i = t > 0. \end{aligned} \qquad (6.32)$$

Derivation of systematic bias of OLS for censored data

We now investigate the effect of censoring in the model (6.31). In the standard (uncensored) regression model there holds $x_i'\beta = E[y_i]$, but this does not hold true for the censored regression model. In this case the model (6.31) implies (as before, we interpret all expressions conditional on the given values of x_i)

$$\begin{aligned} E[y_i] &= 0 \cdot P[y_i = 0] + P[y_i > 0]E[y_i|y_i > 0] \\ &= F(x_i'\beta/\sigma)\left(x_i'\beta + \sigma E[\varepsilon_i|y_i > 0]\right). \end{aligned} \qquad (6.33)$$

Here we used $P[y_i > 0] = 1 - P[y_i = 0] = F(x_i'\beta/\sigma)$, see (6.32). In the expression (6.33) there holds $E[\varepsilon_i|y_i > 0] > 0$ (as in the case of truncated samples) and $0 \leq F(x_i'\beta/\sigma) \leq 1$. So $E[y_i]$ may be larger or smaller than $x_i'\beta$—that is, the sign of the bias term $(E[y_i] - x_i'\beta)$ may depend on x_i. As an example, let $f = \phi$ be the standard normal distribution. Then the results in (6.27) and (6.33) imply that, in this case,

$$E[y_i] = \Phi(x_i'\beta/\sigma)\big(x_i'\beta + \sigma\lambda_i\big) = \Phi_i x_i'\beta + \sigma\phi_i, \tag{6.34}$$

where

$$\lambda_i = \phi(x_i'\beta/\sigma)/\Phi(x_i'\beta/\sigma)$$

is the inverse Mills ratio and we used the shorthand notation $\phi_i = \phi(x_i'\beta/\sigma)$ and $\Phi_i = \Phi(x_i'\beta/\sigma)$. Now the model (6.31) can be written as the regression equation $y_i = x_i'\beta + \sigma\eta_i$, where $\eta_i = \varepsilon_i$ if $y_i^* > 0$ (that is, if $\varepsilon_i > -x_i'\beta/\sigma$) and $\eta_i = -x_i'\beta/\sigma$ if $y_i^* \leq 0$ (that is, if $\varepsilon_i \leq -x_i'\beta/\sigma$). The result in (6.34) shows that, for given value of x_i,

$$E[\eta_i] = \frac{1}{\sigma}\big(E[y_i] - x_i'\beta\big) = \frac{\Phi_i - 1}{\sigma}x_i'\beta + \lambda_i.$$

In general, $E[\eta_i] \neq 0$, and the distribution of η_i depends on x_i, so that OLS is inconsistent. More precisely, define $\omega_i = \eta_i - E[\eta_i] = \eta_i + \frac{1-\Phi_i}{\sigma}x_i'\beta - \lambda_i$, then $\eta_i = E[\eta_i] + \omega_i$ with $E[\omega_i] = 0$, and we can write the data generating process as

$$y_i = x_i'\beta + \sigma\eta_i = x_i'\beta + \big(\Phi(x_i'\beta/\sigma) - 1\big)x_i'\beta + \sigma\frac{\phi(x_i'\beta/\sigma)}{\Phi(x_i'\beta/\sigma)} + \sigma\omega_i, \quad E[\omega_i] = 0.$$

So in regressing y_i on x_i we neglect additional regressors, and, as the omitted regressors are correlated with x_i, this produces a systematic bias in OLS (see Section 3.2.3 (p. 142–3) on omitted variables bias). As the regressors x_i are not orthogonal to the error term η_i of the regression equation, OLS is not consistent.

Marginal effects in the tobit model

The *marginal effects* of the explanatory variables in the tobit model can be split into two parts. If $y_i = 0$ and $x_i'\beta$ increases, then the probability that $y_i > 0$ increases—that is, the probability of a positive response increases. Second, if $y_i > 0$, then the mean response will increase. More formally, it follows from (6.33) that

$$\frac{\partial E[y_i]}{\partial x_i} = \frac{\partial P[y_i > 0]}{\partial x_i}E[y_i|y_i > 0] + P[y_i > 0]\frac{\partial E[y_i|y_i > 0]}{\partial x_i}. \tag{6.35}$$

For the case of the standard normal distribution, the first term is $\phi_i(z_i + \lambda_i)\beta$ and the second term is $\Phi_i(1 - z_i\lambda_i - \lambda_i^2)\beta$, where $z_i = x_i'\beta/\sigma$ (see Exercise 6.4). Substituting these results in (6.35) gives for the tobit model

$$\frac{\partial E[y_i]}{\partial x_i} = \Phi(x_i'\beta/\sigma)\beta.$$

So in this case the marginal effects are not β but smaller, with reduction factor $0 \leq \Phi_i \leq 1$. The difference is small for large values of $x_i'\beta/\sigma$, as in this case $\Phi_i \approx 1$, but the difference is large for small values of $x_i'\beta/\sigma$, as then $\Phi_i \approx 0$. This is also intuitively clear. The condition for an observation $y_i > 0$ is that $\varepsilon_i > -(x_i'\beta/\sigma)$. If $(x_i'\beta/\sigma)$ takes a large positive value, then this is hardly a restriction, so that $y_i = y_i^* = x_i'\beta + \sigma\varepsilon_i$ in most cases. If we increase x_i in such a situation, then the marginal effect on y_i will (in most cases) be β. On the other hand, if $(x_i'\beta/\sigma)$ takes a large negative value, then the condition $\varepsilon_i > -(x_i'\beta/\sigma)$ will not often be satisfied, so that in most cases $y_i = 0$. A marginal increase in x_i will have no effect in most cases, as $y_i = 0$ still has a large probability.

Estimation by maximum likelihood

The parameters of the tobit model can be estimated consistently by maximum likelihood. Assuming that the observations are mutually independent, the log-likelihood $\log(L) = \sum \log(p(y_i))$ is obtained from (6.32), so that

$$\log(L(\beta, \sigma)) = \sum_{\{i;\, y_i=0\}} \log(1 - F(x_i'\beta/\sigma)) + \sum_{\{i;\, y_i>0\}} \left(-\frac{1}{2}\log(\sigma^2) + \log\left(f\left(\frac{y_i - x_i'\beta}{\sigma}\right)\right)\right). \qquad (6.36)$$

If we substitute $f = \varphi$ and $F = \Phi$ of the standard normal distribution, then this becomes

$$\log(L) = \sum_{\{i;\, y_i=0\}} \log(1 - \Phi(x_i'\beta/\sigma)) + \sum_{\{i;\, y_i>0\}} \left(-\frac{1}{2}\log(\sigma^2) - \frac{1}{2}\log(2\pi) - \frac{1}{2\sigma^2}(y_i - x_i'\beta)^2\right).$$

The term for the observations $y_i > 0$ is as usual, and the first term corresponds to the contribution of the observations $y_i = 0$. Note that this term differs from the truncated sample correction term in (6.28). The *tobit estimates* are obtained by maximizing this log-likelihood—for instance, by Newton–Raphson. The tobit estimators have the usual properties of ML.

Remark on the censored observations ($y_i = 0$)

The censored data are mixed continuous-discrete. For the continuous data $y_i > 0$, the regression model $y_i = x_i'\beta + \sigma\varepsilon_i$ applies. However, β should not be estimated by regressing y_i on x_i on the subsample of observations with $y_i > 0$, for two reasons. First, the observations with $y_i = 0$ contain relevant information on the parameters β and σ, as is clear from the contribution of these observations in the log-likelihood (6.36). Second, in the subsample of observations with $y_i > 0$ the error terms do not have zero mean as they come from a truncated distribution. The results in Section 6.3.1 show that OLS on the truncated sample is not consistent.

The Heckman two-step estimation method

An alternative estimation method is based on the idea that censored data can be seen as a combination of a binary response (with possible outcomes $y_i = 0$ and $y_i > 0$), followed by a linear relation $y_i = x_i'\beta + \sigma\varepsilon_i$ on the truncated sample of observations with $y_i > 0$. For the tobit model, the binary response model is a probit model with $P[y_i > 0] = \Phi(x_i'\beta/\sigma)$ and $P[y_i = 0] = 1 - P[y_i > 0]$. Define the parameter vector γ by $\gamma = (1/\sigma)\beta$, and let $\tilde{y}_i = 1$ if $y_i > 0$ and $\tilde{y}_i = 0$ if $y_i = 0$. Then, as a first step, γ can be estimated consistently by ML in the probit model $P[\tilde{y}_i = 1] = \Phi(x_i'\gamma)$. As a second step, consider the truncated sample of observations with $y_i > 0$. The expected value of y_i over this truncated sample—that is, $E[y_i|y_i^* > 0]$—is given by (6.28). If we use the notation y_i^+ for the random variable y_i, conditional on the information that $y_i > 0$, this can be written as

$$y_i^+ = x_i'\beta + \sigma\lambda_i + \omega_i, \quad \lambda_i = \frac{\phi(x_i'\beta/\sigma)}{\Phi(x_i'\beta/\sigma)} = \frac{\phi(x_i'\gamma)}{\Phi(x_i'\gamma)}, \quad E[\omega_i|y_i > 0] = 0.$$

The unobserved regressor λ_i is replaced by the consistent estimator obtained by substituting the probit estimate $\hat{\gamma}$ of γ, so that $\hat{\lambda}_i = \phi(x_i'\hat{\gamma})/\Phi(x_i'\hat{\gamma})$. Then OLS in the above equation for y_i^+ on the truncated sample (with $y_i > 0$) gives consistent estimators of the parameters β and σ. This is called the *Heckman two-step method*, which can be summarized as follows.

Heckman two-step estimation method

- *Step 1: Estimate the bias correction term by probit.* Let $\tilde{y}_i$ be the binary variable with $\tilde{y}_i = 1$ if $y_i > 0$ and $\tilde{y}_i = 0$ if $y_i = 0$. Estimate γ by ML in the probit model $P[\tilde{y}_i = 1] = \Phi(x_i'\gamma)$. Estimate the *bias correction term* λ_i by $\hat{\lambda}_i = \phi(x_i'\hat{\gamma})/\Phi(x_i'\hat{\gamma})$.
- *Step 2: Perform OLS in model with the estimated bias term as additional regressor.* Estimate β and σ by applying OLS in the model $y_i = x_i'\beta + \sigma\hat{\lambda}_i + \omega_i$, using only the observations in the truncated sample with $y_i > 0$.

This two-step estimation method is relatively simple as compared to ML. However this method is not efficient, both because the two separate steps neglect the parameter restrictions $\gamma = (1/\sigma)\beta$ and because the error terms ω_i in the second step are non-normal and heteroskedastic. The Heckman two-step method is useful, however, to obtain consistent initial estimates for ML.

Diagnostic tests

The reliability of censored regressions depends crucially on the underlying model assumptions. The ML tobit estimators become inconsistent in case of omitted variables, heteroskedasticity, or wrong specification of the distribution of the error terms. A simple specification check is to compare the probit estimate of γ (in the first step of the Heckman method) with the estimated values of $(1/\sigma)\beta$ obtained by ML in the tobit model. If the outcomes are largely different, this indicates that the decision whether to be active or not may be driven by other factors than the magnitude of the response y_i (given that $y_i > 0$). In the tobit model, both the decision to respond and the magnitude of the response are modelled in terms of $x_i'\beta$. In the next section we consider models where the decision process and the magnitude of the response are modelled in different ways.

XM601DMF

Example 6.7: **Direct Marketing for Financial Product (continued)**

We return to Example 6.6 of the foregoing section on a new financial product. In Example 6.6 we considered only the customers of the bank who decided to invest in the financial product. However, we also know the individual characteristics of the customers who decided not to invest. We will, therefore, construct a tobit model for the invested amount of money. We will discuss (i) the data, (ii) the ML estimates of the tobit model, (iii) a comparison with the results obtained in Example 6.6 for the truncated sample, (iv) the estimates obtained by the Heckman two-step method, and (v) a diagnostic check on the empirical validity of the tobit model.

(i) The data

The data set consists of 925 individuals, of whom 470 responded by making an investment in the product and 455 did not respond. For individuals who responded, the amount of money invested in this product is known. The explanatory variables (gender, activity, age) are known for all 925 individuals, hence also for the individuals that did not invest in the product. So the dependent variable is censored, not truncated. As before, we take as dependent variable $y_i = \log(1 + \text{invest})$, where 'invest' is the amount of money invested. For individuals who did not invest (so that 'invest' is zero), we get $y_i = 0$.

(ii) ML estimates of the tobit model

The tobit estimates (ML in the censored regression model) are in Panel 2 of Exhibit 6.11. For comparison this table also contains the OLS estimates that are obtained if the censoring is erroneously neglected (see Panel 1). The two sets of estimates can be compared by the implied marginal effects—that is, the estimates themselves in the OLS model and the average multipliers in the tobit model obtained by averaging $b\Phi(x_i'b/s)$ over the sample. The tobit multipliers in Panel 2 of Exhibit 6.11 are somewhat larger than the OLS multipliers. The variables 'gender' and 'activity' have a positive effect on the amount of money invested, and age has a parabolic effect, with a maximum at an age of around 53 years (namely, where $0.196 - 2 \cdot 0.185 \cdot (\text{age}/100) = 0$).

(iii) Comparison of tobit estimates with results for truncated sample

We compare the results of the tobit model in Panel 2 of Exhibit 6.11 with the results for the truncated sample obtained in Example 6.6 (see Panel 2 of Exhibit 6.9). The effect of 'activity' now has the expected positive sign (instead of negative) and the maximum investments are around an age of 53 (instead of 62). Further, the tobit estimates indicate higher investments by males as compared to females, whereas the reverse effect was estimated in the truncated sample. As the information on individuals who do not invest is of importance in describing the general investment behaviour, the results obtained for the censored sample are more reliable than the ones for the truncated sample. This illustrates the general point that it is always advisable to include relevant information in the model. The truncated model of Example 6.6 neglects the information on non-investing customers, and this makes this model much less informative than the tobit model for the censored data.

(iv) Heckman two-step estimates

Panels 4 and 6 of Exhibit 6.11 show the estimates obtained by the Heckman two-step method. This gives much larger standard errors and less significant results than ML. Because the error terms ω_i in the second-step regression are heteroskedastic, the standard errors in Panel 6 are computed by the method of White (see Section 5.4.2 (p. 324–5)). The estimated bias correction terms $\hat{\lambda}_i$ obtained in step 1 of the Heckman method are much larger than the ones estimated in Example 6.6 (see the histograms in Exhibits 6.9 (*d*) and 6.11 (*e*)). The minimum value of $\hat{\lambda}_i$ is now 0.41 (whereas in the truncated model all values are around 0.00). We conclude that the bias terms are

(*a*)

Panel 1: Dependent Variable: LOGINVEST = LOG(1 + INVEST)				
Method: Least Squares				
Included observations: 925				
Variable	Coefficient	Std. Error	t-Statistic	Prob.
C	−1.110803	0.956974	−1.160745	0.2460
GENDER	0.967838	0.174920	5.533017	0.0000
ACTIVITY	0.874305	0.198665	4.400908	0.0000
AGE	0.103027	0.038399	2.683045	0.0074
AGE^2/100	−0.095076	0.036670	−2.592709	0.0097
R-squared	0.069073			
S.E. of regression	2.346782			

(*b*)

Panel 2: Dependent Variable: LOGINVEST = LOG(1 + INVEST)					
Method: ML - Censored Normal (TOBIT), left censoring at 0					
Included observations: 925					
Convergence achieved after 7 iterations					
Variable	Coefficient	Std. Error	z-Statistic	Prob.	Average multiplier
C	−5.936450	1.975280	−3.005371	0.0027	−4.096151
GENDER	2.126287	0.360378	5.900151	0.0000	1.479896
ACTIVITY	1.691490	0.373128	4.533269	0.0000	1.177277
AGE	0.195933	0.079056	2.478413	0.0132	0.136369
AGE^2/100	−0.184648	0.075808	−2.435718	0.0149	−0.128515
Error Distribution					
SCALE: SIGMA	4.159631	0.155950	26.67282	0.0000	
R-squared	0.060935				
S.E. of regression	2.358299				
Left censored obs	455	Right censored obs		0	
Uncensored obs	470	Total obs		925	

(*c*)

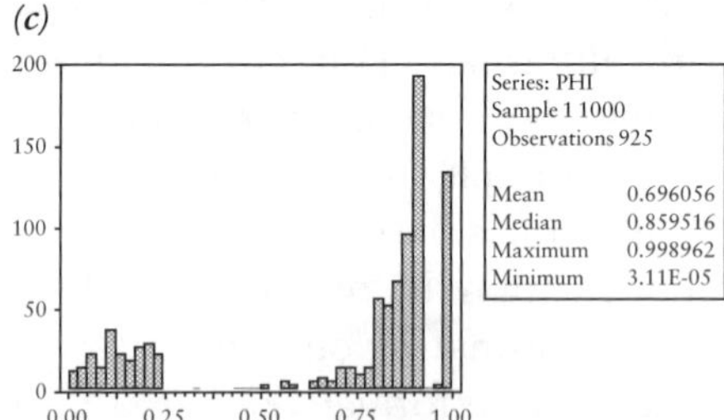

Exhibit 6.11 **Direct Marketing for Financial Product (Example 6.7)**

Models for invested amount of money based on data of 925 individuals (470 made an investment, 455 did not invest), OLS (Panel 1) and Tobit model (censored regression, Panel 2). (*c*) shows the histogram of the values of $\Phi(x'b_{ML}/s_{ML})$ (with sample mean 0.696; the average multipliers reported in Panel 2 for the Tobit model are obtained by multiplying the estimated coefficients by this factor).

underestimated in the truncated sample. As the values of $\hat{\lambda}_i$ for the censored data are quite large, this implies that OLS on the truncated sample is seriously biased. Hence also the truncated ML estimates in Panel 2 of Exhibit 6.9 are biased, as these estimates are nearly the same as OLS for these data. For instance, the effects of the variables 'gender' and 'activity' in the (consistent) second step of the Heckman method in Panel 6 of Exhibit 6.11 are

(*d*)

Panel 4: Dependent Variable: RESPONSE (1 = does invest, 0 = does not invest) Method: ML - Binary Probit Included observations: 925 Convergence achieved after 5 iterations				
Variable	Coefficient	Std. Error	z-Statistic	Prob.
C	−1.497584	0.536822	−2.789720	0.0053
GENDER	0.588114	0.096684	6.082811	0.0000
ACTIVITY	0.561167	0.111572	5.029656	0.0000
AGE	0.041680	0.021544	1.934636	0.0530
AGE^2/100	−0.040982	0.020607	−1.988730	0.0467

(*e*)

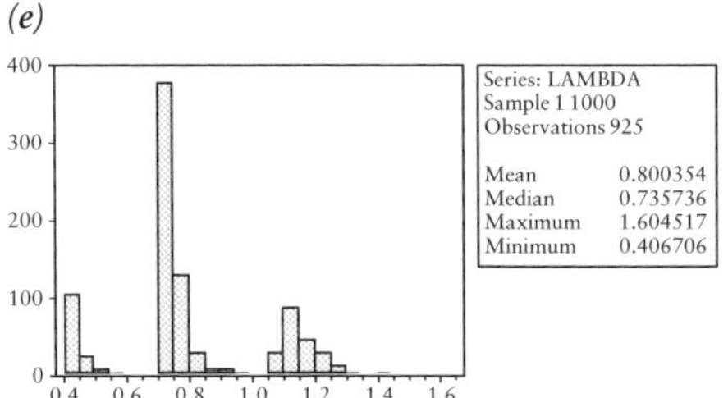

(*f*)

Panel 6: Dependent Variable: LOGINVEST = LOG(1 + INVEST) Method: Least Squares Sample(adjusted): 1 500 IF INVEST>0; Included observations: 470 White Heteroskedasticity-Consistent Standard Errors & Covariance				
Variable	Coefficient	Std. Error	t-Statistic	Prob.
C	−0.628395	5.993881	−0.104839	0.9165
GENDER	0.535657	1.317266	0.406643	0.6845
ACTIVITY	0.489967	1.065880	0.459683	0.6460
AGE	0.123239	0.093687	1.315437	0.1890
AGE^2/100	−0.108606	0.092892	−1.169162	0.2429
LAMBDA	1.951267	3.380174	0.577268	0.5640
R-squared	0.048679			
S.E. of regression	0.944855			

Exhibit 6.11 (*Contd.*)

Heckman two-step method, probit model for investment decision (step 1, Panel 4), histogram of the corresponding values of λ (inverse Mills ratio (*e*)), and OLS on the truncated sample with λ as additional regressor (step 2, Panel 6).

both positive, whereas these effects are negative if the bias correction term is neglected (see Panels 1 and 2 of Exhibit 6.9 for the truncated sample).

(v) A diagnostic check on the tobit model

Finally, as a diagnostic check we compare the estimates $\hat{\gamma}$ of the probit model in the first step of the Heckman method (Panel 4) with the tobit ML estimates $(1/s)b$ (obtained from Panel 2). Dividing the values of b by $s = 4.160$ gives (after rounding to three digits) the values $(1/s)b = (-1.427, 0.511, 0.407, 0.047, -0.044)'$. This does not differ much from $\hat{\gamma} = (-1.498, 0.588, 0.561, 0.042, -0.041)'$. So there is no indication that the factors that determine the decision whether or not to invest would be any different from the factors that determine the amount of invested money. This supports the use of the tobit model.

☞ Exercises: T: 6.4c, 6.5; S: 6.9c–e; E: 6.16.

6.3.3 Models for selection and treatment effects

A model for selection

In truncated samples, the values of the dependent variable are observed only in a certain interval ($y_i > 0$ in the standard model). More generally, let z_i be a selection dummy that takes the value $z_i = 1$ if the ith individual is in the sample and $z_i = 0$ if the individual is not in the sample. We assume that $y_i = x_i'\beta + \sigma\varepsilon_i$ applies for all individuals (observed and unobserved), and that this model satisfies all the standard assumptions. Then the observed sample can be described by

$$\begin{aligned} y_i &= x_i'\beta + \sigma\varepsilon_i && \text{if} \quad z_i = 1, \\ y_i &\text{ is not observed} && \text{if} \quad z_i = 0. \end{aligned} \tag{6.37}$$

OLS, that is, regressing y_i on x_i for the observations with $z_i = 1$, is consistent if and only if the selection is exogenous. This condition will be violated if the selection variable z_i depends on the error term ε_i. This is the case, for instance, in truncated regressions where $z_i = 1$ if and only if $y_i > 0$, since in this case $z_i = 1$ if and only if $\varepsilon_i > -(x_i'\beta/\sigma)$. In general, OLS on selected samples is inconsistent if the selection process is endogenous in the sense that the selection dummy z_i depends on the error term ε_i.

The tobit (type 2) model for selection effects

In truncated regression models, an individual is unobserved if the index function $y_i^* = x_i'\beta + \sigma\varepsilon_i$ takes negative values. That is, the factor $x_i'\beta$ that influences the probability of being observed is the same as the factor that influences the magnitude of the response $y_i = y_i^*$ for $y_i^* > 0$. In some cases these factors may be different. For instance, the decision to work or not may be based on considerations other than the number of hours worked, and the decision to buy a durable product or not may be influenced by factors other than the amount of money spent by the buyers of this product.

Let w_i be a set of variables that influences the chance that y_i is observed ($z_i = 1$) or not ($z_i = 0$). A possible selection model is as follows.

$$\begin{aligned} z_i &= 1 \quad \text{if} \quad w_i'\gamma + \omega_i > 0, \\ z_i &= 0 \quad \text{if} \quad w_i'\gamma + \omega_i \leq 0. \end{aligned} \tag{6.38}$$

The combined model (6.37) and (6.38) is called the *tobit type 2* model. It differs in the following respects from the standard (or *tobit type 1*) model (6.31) of Section 6.3.2. First, in the tobit type 1 model the dependent variable is censored (with $y_i = 0$ for $z_i = 0$ and $y_i > 0$ for $z_i = 1$), whereas in the tobit type 2 model y_i is not observed for $z_i = 0$ and y_i can take both negative and positive values if $z_i = 1$. Second, the selection variables w_i are (partly) different from the regressors x_i, whereas in the tobit type 1 model $w_i = x_i$, $\gamma = \beta$, and $\omega_i = \sigma\varepsilon_i$.

It is assumed that the data set consists of n observations of the variables (x_i, w_i, z_i), whereas the dependent variable y_i is observed only for the observations with $z_1 = 1$. For instance, we may have data of n individuals of whom some have a job ($z_i = 1$) and others not ($z_i = 0$). If the dependent variable of interest y_i is the wage that an individual with characteristics x_i would normally earn, then y_i is not observed for the individuals without a job. Relevant characteristics x_i that may affect wage are, for instance, age and education, and factors w_i that may affect the chance that an individual works are, for instance, age, education, and family composition. As another example, y_i may be the price of the new car bought by customer i during an action period. A relevant explanatory variable x_i may be the price of the current car of the customer, and w_i may be the age of the current car and the marketing effort for this customer. The sales revenue y_i is observed only for the customers who decide to buy a new car ($z_i = 1$), whereas the characteristics (x_i, w_i) are known for all customers.

Distinction between truncated and censored selection

Until now we have assumed that the dependent variable in the tobit type 2 model is truncated in the sense that y_i is not observed if $z_i = 0$. Sometimes one assigns instead the value $y_i = 0$ if $z_i = 0$, so that the dependent variable becomes censored instead of truncated. For instance, the wage of non-working people is zero, and the amount of money spent by non-buying customers is zero. In estimation it does not matter which convention one follows as, conditional on $z_i = 0$, the fact that $y_i = 0$ is a matter of definition that provides no additional information. However, the truncated sample interpretation is often more natural, since in this case y_i can be seen as the natural response that corresponds to x_i. For individuals with $y_i = 0$, this response is due not so much to x_i, but to w_i that causes $z_i = 0$. For instance, for non-working individuals the wage is 'zero' because they do not to work ($z_i = 0$), and it is better to say that we do not observe the wage that would normally be earned by individuals with the same characteristics x_i.

Derivation of selection bias of OLS

The regression of y_i on x_i in the observed sample (with $z_i = 1$) provides consistent estimates if the error terms ω_i in the selection equation are independent from the error terms ε_i in the regression model. Otherwise OLS is inconsistent. To investigate this in more detail, we assume that the values of (w_i, x_i) are fixed and that the error terms $(\omega_i, \varepsilon_i)$ are independent for different observations, with joint normal distribution with mean zero, variances $E[\omega_i^2] = 1$ and $E[\varepsilon_i^2] = 1$, and covariance $E[\omega_i \varepsilon_i] = \rho$. In this case

$$\begin{pmatrix} \omega_i \\ \varepsilon_i \end{pmatrix} \sim \text{NID}\left(\begin{pmatrix} 0 \\ 0 \end{pmatrix}, \begin{pmatrix} 1 & \rho \\ \rho & 1 \end{pmatrix} \right), \quad i = 1, \cdots, n.$$

As was discussed in Section 6.1.1, the variance of the error term ω_i should be fixed, as otherwise the parameters γ of the selection equation are not identified. The variance of ε_i should also be fixed, because of the term σ in the model (6.37). Let $\eta_i = \varepsilon_i - \rho\omega_i$, then η_i is normally distributed with mean zero, and, since $E[\eta_i \omega_i] = 0$, it follows that η_i and ω_i are mutually independent. Writing $\varepsilon_i = \rho\omega_i + \eta_i$, it therefore follows that $E[\varepsilon_i | z_i = 1] = E[\varepsilon_i | \omega_i > -w_i'\gamma] = \rho E[\omega_i | \omega_i > -w_i'\gamma]$. According to (6.27), the last term can be written as $\rho\lambda_i$, where $\lambda_i = \phi(w_i'\gamma)/\Phi(w_i'\gamma)$. This shows that for observations in the sample (with $z_i = 1$) there holds

$$E[\varepsilon_i | z_i = 1] = E[\omega_i | \omega_i > -w_i'\gamma] = \rho\lambda_i.$$

Also note that in the observed sample (with $z_i = 1$) $x_i'\beta$ is not equal to the mean of y_i, as

$$E[y_i | z_i = 1] = x_i'\beta + \sigma E[\varepsilon_i | z_i = 1] = x_i'\beta + \rho\sigma\lambda_i. \tag{6.39}$$

Therefore OLS in $y_i = x_i'\beta + \varepsilon_i$ is inconsistent, as this neglects the regressor λ_i, unless $\rho = 0$—that is, unless the selection variable z_i is independent of the error term ε_i.

Derivation of log-likelihood in case of sample selection

The parameters $(\beta, \gamma, \sigma, \rho)$ can be estimated consistently by ML. The likelihood function is equal to the joint probability distribution of the dependent variables z_i (for $i = 1, \cdots, n$) and y_i (for $z_i = 1$). If the observations are assumed to be mutually independent, we get $L = \prod_{\{i; z_i = 0\}} p(z_i) \prod_{\{i; z_i = 1\}} p(y_i, z_i = 1)$, and as $p(y_i, z_i = 1) = p(y_i) P[z_i = 1 | y_i]$ it follows that

$$\log(L(\beta,\gamma,\sigma,\rho)) = \sum_{\{i;\, z_i=0\}} \log(p(z_i)) + \sum_{\{i;\, z_i=1\}} \log(P[z_i=1|y_i]) + \sum_{\{i;\, z_i=1\}} \log(p(y_i)).$$

The last term in this expression stands for the contribution of the observed values $y_i \sim \mathrm{N}(x_i'\beta, \sigma)$. The first term in the log-likelihood can be evaluated by using the fact that $P[z_i=0] = P[\omega_i \le -w_i'\gamma] = \Phi(-w_i'\gamma) - 1 - \Phi(w_i'\gamma)$. For the second term in the log-likelihood we use that $P[z_i=1|y_i] = P[\omega_i > -w_i'\gamma|y_i]$ where $y_i = x_i'\beta + \sigma\varepsilon_i$, so that $(\omega_i,\, y_i)$ follows the bivariate normal distribution

$$\begin{pmatrix}\omega_i\\ y_i\end{pmatrix} \sim \mathrm{N}\left(\begin{pmatrix}0\\ x_i'\beta\end{pmatrix}, \begin{pmatrix}1 & \rho\sigma\\ \rho\sigma & \sigma^2\end{pmatrix}\right).$$

It follows from (1.22) that $\omega_i|y_i \sim \mathrm{N}(\frac{\rho}{\sigma}(y_i - x_i'\beta),\, 1-\rho^2)$, so that

$$P[z_i=1|y_i] = P[\omega_i > -w_i'\gamma|y_i] = P\left[\frac{\omega_i - \frac{\rho}{\sigma}(y_i - x_i'\beta)}{\sqrt{1-\rho^2}} > \frac{-w_i'\gamma - \frac{\rho}{\sigma}(y_i - x_i'\beta)}{\sqrt{1-\rho^2}}\right]$$
$$= 1 - \Phi\left(\frac{-w_i'\gamma - \frac{\rho}{\sigma}(y_i - x_i'\beta)}{\sqrt{1-\rho^2}}\right) = \Phi\left(\frac{w_i'\gamma + \frac{\rho}{\sigma}(y_i - x_i'\beta)}{\sqrt{1-\rho^2}}\right). \qquad (6.40)$$

Because of these results, the log-likelihood of the model with selection effects can be expressed as follows.

$$\log(L(\beta,\gamma,\sigma,\rho)) = \sum_{\{i;\, z_i=0\}} \log(1 - \Phi(w_i'\gamma)) + \sum_{\{i;\, z_i=1\}} \log\left(\Phi\left(\frac{w_i'\gamma + \frac{\rho}{\sigma}(y_i - x_i'\beta)}{\sqrt{1-\rho^2}}\right)\right) + \sum_{\{i;\, z_i=1\}} \left(-\frac{1}{2}\log(\sigma^2) - \frac{1}{2}\log(2\pi) - \frac{1}{2\sigma^2}(y_i - x_i'\beta)^2\right).$$

Heckman two-step method

Consistent estimates of β can again also be obtained by means of a Heckman two-step method. According to (6.39), for observed values of y_i (that is, for $z_i = 1$) the bias term is equal to $E[y_i|z_i=1] - x_i'\beta = \rho\sigma\lambda_i$. Let $\eta_i = y_i - E[y_i|z_i=1]$; then we can write

$$y_i = x_i'\beta + \rho\sigma\lambda_i + \eta_i, \quad E[\eta_i] = 0 \quad (\text{for } z_i = 1).$$

The two-step method is similar to the one described in Section 6.3.2 for censored data. In the first step we use all n observations (w_i, z_i) to estimate the parameters γ of the probit selection model (6.38). Let $\hat{\gamma}$ be the obtained estimates; then the inverse Mills ratios are estimated by $\hat{\lambda}_i = \phi(w_i'\hat{\gamma})/\Phi(w_i'\hat{\gamma})$. In the second step consistent estimates of β and $\rho\sigma$ are obtained by regressing y_i on x_i and $\hat{\lambda}_i$, using only the subsample of observations with $z_i = 1$. A test on the significance of selection bias (that occurs only if $\rho \neq 0$) can be performed by testing whether the coefficient of the inverse Mills ratio $\hat{\lambda}_i$ is significant. Since the error terms η_i are heteroskedastic, the conventional OLS formulas for the standard errors are not valid. Consistent standard errors can be obtained by White's method (see Section 5.4.2 (p. 324–5)).

Remark on the explanatory variables w_i and x_i

It may well be that some of the variables w_i that affect the selection variable z_i are also relevant in explaining the response y_i. For instance, someone's age may influence the decision whether to work or not and, for someone who is working, it may also affect the wage level. To avoid excessively large correlations between the regressors x_i and λ_i, one usually requires that w_i contains at least one variable that is not present in x_i.

Model for treatment effects

The above selection model can also be used for the analysis of *treatment effects*. Consider the model

$$y_i = x_i'\beta + \alpha z_i + \sigma\varepsilon_i, \quad \varepsilon_i \sim \mathrm{NID}(0, 1),$$

where z_i is a dummy variable with the value 0 (no treatment) or 1 (treatment). It is assumed that the treatment selection can be described by (6.38). For instance, y_i may be the amount of money spent in a store and the treatment z_i may indicate whether the customer owns a credit card for the store or not. The coefficient α is the treatment effect—that is, the additional purchases that a customer makes because he or she owns a credit card for the store.

Derivation of treatment bias of OLS

If the treatment effect is estimated by regressing y_i on x_i and z_i, then this gives inconsistent estimators if the error term ω_i in the treatment selection is correlated with the error term ε_i in the regression model. To analyse this in more detail, let $\phi_i = \phi(w_i'\gamma)$, $\Phi_i = \Phi(w_i'\gamma)$, and $\lambda_i = \phi_i/\Phi_i$; then under the same assumptions as before we have $E[\varepsilon_i|z_i = 1] = \rho\lambda_i$. Further, $E[\varepsilon_i|z_i = 0]$ can be obtained from the fact that

$$0 = E[\varepsilon_i] = P[z_i = 1]E[\varepsilon_i|z_i = 1] + P[z_i = 0]E[\varepsilon_i|z_i = 0]$$
$$= \Phi_i \rho \lambda_i + (1 - \Phi_i)E[\varepsilon_i|z_i = 0],$$

so that $E[\varepsilon_i|z_i = 0] = -\rho\lambda_i\Phi_i/(1 - \Phi_i)$. Combining the results for $z_i = 1$ and $z_i = 0$, we can write

$$E[\varepsilon_i|z_i] = z_i(\rho\lambda_i) + (1 - z_i)\frac{-\rho\lambda_i\Phi_i}{1 - \Phi_i} = \rho\lambda_i\frac{z_i(1 - \Phi_i) - (1 - z_i)\Phi_i}{1 - \Phi_i}$$
$$= \rho\frac{\lambda_i(z_i - \Phi_i)}{1 - \Phi_i}.$$

For given x_i and z_i, let $\eta_i = \varepsilon_i - E[\varepsilon_i|z_i]$. Then $E[\eta_i|z_i] = 0$ and $\varepsilon_i = \eta_i + E[\varepsilon_i|z_i]$, so that the model with treatment effects can be written as

$$y_i = x_i'\beta + \alpha z_i + \sigma E[\varepsilon_i|z_i] + \sigma\eta_i$$
$$= x_i'\beta + \alpha z_i + \rho\sigma\frac{\lambda_i(z_i - \Phi_i)}{1 - \Phi_i} + \sigma\eta_i, \quad E[\eta_i|z_i] = 0.$$

The additional term $E[\varepsilon_i|z_i]$ is the treatment bias term. Regression of y_i on x_i and z_i is inconsistent because the omitted regressor is correlated with the treatment variable z_i (note that λ_i, ϕ_i, and Φ_i also depend on z_i). OLS is consistent only if $\rho = 0$—that is, if the random effects ω_i in the treatment selection are independent of the random effects ε_i in the outcome of y_i. For instance, if individuals with higher than average expenditure ($\varepsilon_i > 0$) also have a larger than average chance of owning the store's credit card ($\omega_i > 0$) so that $\rho > 0$, then OLS will overestimate the treatment effect. This is because the OLS estimate of α will incorporate part of the effect of the omitted bias term that has a coefficient $\rho\sigma > 0$ in this case.

Estimation of treatment effects by ML and by the Heckman two-step method

T

As before, consistent estimates can be obtained by ML. Again, we assume that the values of (w_i, x_i) are fixed, or, equivalently, we use the likelihood function conditional on the observed values of (w_i, x_i). The likelihood function is equal to the joint probability distribution of the dependent variables z_i and y_i, $i = 1, \cdots, n$. If the observations are assumed to be mutually independent, we get $L = \prod_{i=1}^{n} p(y_i)\, p(z_i|y_i)$ and hence

$$\log(L(\alpha, \beta, \gamma, \sigma, \rho)) = \sum_{i=1}^{n} \log(p(y_i)) + \sum_{i=1}^{n} \log(p(z_i|y_i)).$$

As the selection model is again given by (6.38), the log-likelihood can be evaluated in the same way as discussed above for the model with selection effects. By using (6.40) for $P[z_i = 1|y_i]$ and the fact that $P[z_i = 0|y_i] = 1 - P[z_i = 1|y_i]$, we get

$$\log(L(\alpha, \beta, \gamma, \sigma, \rho)) = \sum_{\{i;\, z_i=1\}} \log\left(\Phi\left(\frac{w_i'\gamma + \frac{\rho}{\sigma}(y_i - x_i'\beta - \alpha)}{\sqrt{1-\rho^2}}\right)\right)$$
$$+ \sum_{\{i;\, z_i=0\}} \log\left(1 - \Phi\left(\frac{w_i'\gamma + \frac{\rho}{\sigma}(y_i - x_i'\beta - \alpha)}{\sqrt{1-\rho^2}}\right)\right)$$
$$+ \sum_{i=1}^{n}\left(-\frac{1}{2}\log(\sigma^2) - \frac{1}{2}\log(2\pi) - \frac{1}{2\sigma^2}(y_i - x_i'\beta - \alpha z_i)^2\right).$$

Maximum likelihood estimates can be computed by maximizing this log-likelihood. A simpler way to get consistent estimates of the treatment effect α is again to apply a Heckman two-step method. As before, in the first step we use the observations (w_i, z_i) to estimate the parameters γ of the probit selection model (6.38). This gives consistent estimates of the bias term $\lambda_i(z_i - \Phi_i)/(1 - \Phi_i)$. In the second step y_i is regressed on the variables x_i, z_i, and the estimated bias terms.

The overall difference between treated and non-treated subjects

The above analysis shows that, for an individual with characteristics x_i, the overall difference of the response y_i between treated and untreated individuals will in general not be equal to α, unless the treatments are applied randomly over the sample (so that $\rho = 0$). The expression for the overall difference in response is

$$E[y_i|z_i = 1] - E[y_i|z_i = 0] = \alpha + \rho\sigma\left(\frac{\lambda_i(1 - \Phi_i)}{1 - \Phi_i} - \frac{\lambda_i(0 - \Phi_i)}{1 - \Phi_i}\right)$$
$$= \alpha + \frac{\rho\sigma\lambda_i}{1 - \Phi_i}. \qquad (6.41)$$

Here α is the actual treatment effect. If $\alpha = 0$, so that treatment has no actual effect, then there is still a difference between treated and untreated individuals if $\rho \neq 0$. For instance, if $\rho > 0$, then treated individuals already have a tendency for higher responses, since $E[\varepsilon_i|z_i = 1] = \rho\lambda_i > 0$ and $E[\varepsilon_i|z_i = 0] < 0$ in this case. If we neglect this bias and apply OLS of y_i on x_i and z_i, then in this case (with $\alpha = 0$) we might in general find misleading significant values for $\hat{\alpha}$, which would wrongly suggest that treatment matters.

Example 6.8: **Student Learning (continued)**

In this example we will analyse the (treatment) effects of additional calculus courses on the grades that students obtain in intermediate micro- and macroeconomics. For this purpose we consider data on student learning that were analysed by J. S. Butler, T. A. Finegan, and J. J. Siegfried in their paper 'Does More Calculus Improve Student Learning in Intermediate Micro- and Macroeconomic Theory', *Journal of Applied Econometrics*, 13/2 (1998), 185–202. Part of these student learning data was used as a leading example in Chapter 1 (see in particular Example 1.1, where this data set was introduced).

We will discuss (i) the data and the model for the grades, (ii) a selection model for the attained level of calculus, (iii) the results for grades in microeconomics, and (iv) the results for grades in macroeconomics.

(i) **Data and model for the grades**

We are interested in the question whether more calculus improves student learning in intermediate micro- and macroeconomic theory. The data consist of the results of 609 students in intermediate microeconomics and of 490 students in intermediate macroeconomics of the Vanderbilt University. The dependent variable y_i is the obtained grade (in intermediate microeconomics or macroeconomics). These grades range from 0 to 4, and the sample mean is 2.65. The explanatory variable of interest (z_i) is the level of calculus attained by the student prior to following the intermediate economic theory course. This variable has the interpretation of a treatment variable. We distinguish two levels of calculus, ordinary (3 or 4 credit hours, denoted by $z_i = 0$) and high (6 to 12 credit hours, denoted by $z_i = 1$). The effect of the level of calculus z_i on the grades y_i is modelled by the linear relation

$$y_i = x_i'\beta + \alpha z_i + \sigma\varepsilon_i, \quad \varepsilon_i \sim \mathrm{NID}(0, 1).$$

The explanatory variables (z_i, x_i) are listed in Exhibit 6.12. The treatment variable z_i is denoted by 'mathhigh', and the grade deflator is used to compensate for possible differences between the different instructors who graded the exams in intermediate economic theory.

(ii) **Selection model for level of calculus**

Because of possible selection bias, a direct regression of the grade y_i in the intermediate theory course on the explanatory variables (x_i, z_i) may give an inconsistent estimate of the (treatment) effect α of additional courses in calculus. This is because similar aptitudes and interests may lead students to enrol and do well in both mathematics and economics. The level of

(*a*)

x_i and z_i	Explanatory variables for grade in economics
C	Constant term
MATHHIGH	'Treatment', $z_i = 0$ if 3 or 4 credit hours, $z_i = 1$ if 6 to 12 credit hours
GRADELOW	Grade in last calculus course if 3 or 4 credit hours
GRADEHIGH	Grade in last calculus course if 6 to 12 credit hours
GRDFINT	Grade deflator of instructors in intermediate theory course
GRMACRO1	Grade in introductory macroeconomics
GRMICRO1	Grade in introductory microeconomics
FRESHMAN	Freshman grade point average
FEMALE	Gender dummy, 1 for females and 0 for males
SATMATH/100	SAT mathematics score, divided by 100
SATVERB/100	SAT verbal score, divided by 100

(*b*)

w_i	Explanatory variables for level of calculus
C	Constant term
SATMATH/100	SAT mathematics score, divided by 100
FEMALE	Gender dummy, 1 for females and 0 for males
MAJORESH	1 if expected major in economics, social science, or humanity, 0 otherwise
MAJORNAT	1 if expected major in natural science, 0 otherwise
ADVMATH1	1 if 1 year of high school advanced maths, 0 otherwise
ADVMATH2	1 if 2 years of high school advanced maths, 0 otherwise
ADVMATH3	1 if > 2 years of high school advanced maths, 0 otherwise
PHYSICS	1 if physics in high school, 0 otherwise
CHEMISTRY	1 if chemistry in high school, 0 otherwise

Exhibit 6.12 Student Learning (Example 6.8)

Explanatory variables (x_i, z_i) for obtained grade in economics (*a*) and explanatory variables w_i for attained level in calculus (*b*). The variable MATHHIGH is the treatment variable z_i.

calculus chosen by the student is explained by means of the probit model (6.38), with $\omega_i \sim \mathrm{N}(0, 1)$ and with the explanatory variables w_i listed in Exhibit 6.12 (*b*).

(iii) Results for grades in microeconomics

The parameters $(\alpha, \beta, \gamma, \sigma, \rho)$ of the joint model are estimated by the Heckman two-step method. In the first step we estimate γ by a probit model for z_i in terms of the explanatory variables w_i. The results are used to estimate the bias correction terms $\lambda_i(z_i - \Phi_i)/(1 - \Phi_i)$. In the second step, the grade y_i is regressed on the explanatory variables (x_i, z_i) and the estimated bias correction terms as additional regressor. The standard errors in the second-step regression are computed by the method of White (see Section 5.4.2 (p. 324–5)), because the error terms in this regression are heteroskedastic. The results for microeconomics are given in Exhibit 6.13 (*a–c*).

(*a*)

Panel 1: Dependent Variable: MATHHIGH				
Method: ML - Binary Probit				
Included observations: 609 (MATHHIGH = 0(1) for 224(385) observations)				
Convergence achieved after 4 iterations				
Variable	Coefficient	Std. Error	z-Statistic	Prob.
C	−3.233952	0.694970	−4.653367	0.0000
SATMATH/100	0.443273	0.099780	4.442485	0.0000
FEMALE	0.158684	0.116379	1.363505	0.1727
MAJORESH	−0.214143	0.137400	−1.558537	0.1191
MAJORNAT	0.386246	0.178288	2.166418	0.0303
ADVMATH1	0.173933	0.248937	0.698701	0.4847
ADVMATH2	0.878933	0.253796	3.463152	0.0005
ADVMATH3	0.691171	0.621522	1.112063	0.2661
PHYSICS	0.326966	0.118983	2.748005	0.0060
CHEMISTRY	0.139247	0.220568	0.631311	0.5278

(*b*)

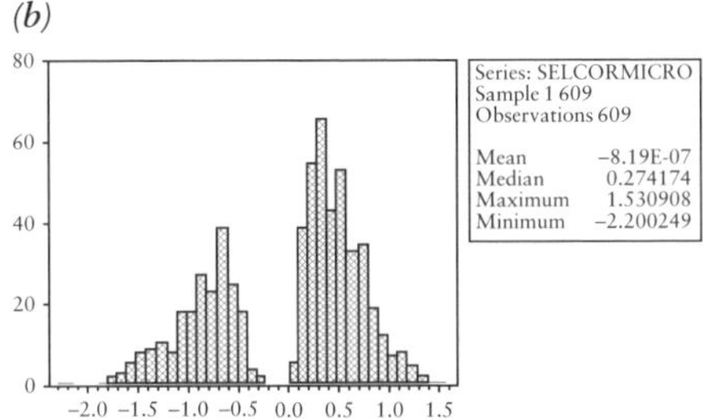

(*c*)

Panel 3: Dependent Variable: GRINTERMICRO				
Method: Least Squares; Included observations: 609				
White Heteroskedasticity-Consistent Standard Errors & Covariance				
Variable	Coefficient	Std. Error	t-Statistic	Prob.
C	−1.313984	0.386882	−3.396346	0.0007
SELCORMICRO	0.022413	0.037716	0.594255	0.5526
MATHHIGH	0.987359	0.215678	4.577921	0.0000
GRADELOW	0.292158	0.065798	4.440232	0.0000
GRADEHIGH	0.060555	0.051076	1.185590	0.2363
GRDFINTMICRO	0.839083	0.102980	8.148048	0.0000
GRMACRO1	0.176453	0.052557	3.357358	0.0008
GRMICRO1	0.290380	0.046338	6.266522	0.0000
FRESHMAN	0.324305	0.101163	3.205755	0.0014
FEMALE	0.082313	0.059692	1.378972	0.1684
SATMATH/100	0.088795	0.054408	1.631999	0.1032
SATVERB/100	0.055464	0.041474	1.337304	0.1816

Exhibit 6.13 Student Learning (Example 6.8)

Heckman two-step estimate of the effect of additional courses in calculus (MATHHIGH, 0/1) on grades in intermediate microeconomics, probit model for level of calculus (step 1, Panel 1) with histogram of estimated bias terms (denoted by SELCORMICRO, i.e. $\lambda_i(z_i - \Phi_i)/(1 - \Phi_i)$ in (*b*)) and OLS in model with this bias correction term included (step 2, Panel 3).

(*d*)

Panel 4: Dependent Variable: MATHHIGH				
Method: ML – Binary Probit				
Included observations: 490 (MATHHIGH = 0(1) for 167(323) observations)				
Convergence achieved after 4 iterations				
Variable	Coefficient	Std. Error	z-Statistic	Prob.
C	−2.534435	0.786598	−3.222019	0.0013
SATMATH/100	0.382440	0.110370	3.465072	0.0005
FEMALE	0.095552	0.133248	0.717101	0.4733
MAJORESH	−0.116509	0.154365	−0.754767	0.4504
MAJORNAT	0.325960	0.201677	1.616247	0.1060
ADVMATH1	−0.050933	0.269884	−0.188723	0.8503
ADVMATH2	0.721165	0.276831	2.605076	0.0092
ADVMATH3	0.336540	0.661922	0.508429	0.6112
PHYSICS	0.330657	0.133081	2.484635	0.0130
CHEMISTRY	0.061545	0.284738	0.216147	0.8289

(*e*)

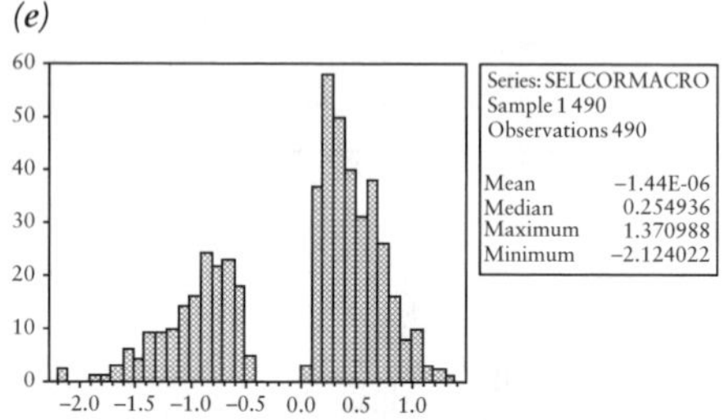

(*f*)

Panel 6: Dependent Variable: GRINTERMACRO				
Method: Least Squares; Included observations: 490				
White Heteroskedasticity-Consistent Standard Errors & Covariance				
Variable	Coefficient	Std. Error	t-Statistic	Prob.
C	−0.086512	0.366548	−0.236019	0.8135
SELCORMACRO	0.034281	0.043518	0.787743	0.4312
MATHHIGH	0.021387	0.070944	0.301467	0.7632
GRDFINTMACRO	0.919443	0.161693	5.686344	0.0000
GRMACRO1	0.206147	0.054263	3.798994	0.0002
GRMICRO1	0.307535	0.050872	6.045269	0.0000
FRESHMAN	0.564736	0.089483	6.311126	0.0000
FEMALE	0.028948	0.063046	0.459166	0.6463
SATMATH/100	0.006629	0.054836	0.120892	0.9038
SATVERB/100	−0.022063	0.047101	−0.468414	0.6397

Exhibit 6.13 (*Contd.*)

Heckman two-step estimate of the effect of additional courses in calculus (MATHHIGH, 0/1) on grades in intermediate macroeconomics, probit model for level of calculus (step 1, Panel 4) with histogram of estimated bias terms (denoted by SELCORMACRO, i.e. $\lambda_i(z_i - \Phi_i)/(1 - \Phi_i)$ in (*e*)) and OLS in model with this bias correction term included (step 2, Panel 6).

The explanatory variables w_i in the probit model have the expected signs. The second-step regression in Panel 3 indicates that the selection effects (the bias correction term denoted by 'selcormicro' in Panel 3) are not significant (P-value 0.55). Further, a higher level of calculus has an estimated payoff of 0.99 (the coefficient of the treatment variable denoted by 'mathhigh' in

Panel 3). This means a whole letter grade (the grades in the sample range from 0 to 4 with sample mean 2.65). That is, additional calculus gives significantly better results in intermediate microeconomics. The other explanatory variables have the expected signs.

(iv) Results for grades in macroeconomics

The last three panels in Exhibit 6.13 (*d–f*) show the results for intermediate macroeconomics. The results of the probit model are comparable to that for microeconomics. The second-step regression in Panel 6 indicates that selection effects (the bias correction term denoted by 'selcormacro' in Panel 6) are again not significant (*P*-value 0.43). Further, a higher level of calculus has no payoff (the coefficient of 'mathhigh' in Panel 6 is 0.02, with *P*-value 0.76). That is, additional calculus does not affect the results in intermediate macroeconomics. The other explanatory variables have the expected signs (the variables 'gradehigh' and 'gradelow' are omitted because of missing data for this group of students). In the paper of Butler, Finegan, and Siegfried the above questions are studied in more detail, with more explanatory variables and with a finer distinction of the attained level of calculus (with seven ordered levels instead of the above two levels). A further analysis of the data is left as an exercise (see Exercise 6.15).

☞ **Exercises:** T: 6.4d; E: 6.15b.

6.3.4 Duration models

Duration data

A *duration* measures the amount of time that elapses before a certain event takes place, or the amount of time that has passed since a certain event took place. Examples are the time it takes for an unemployed person to find a job (or the time of unemployment if a job has not yet been found), the time that elapses between two purchases of the same product, and the length of a strike. Exhibit 6.14 (*a*) shows the duration (measured in days) of 62 finished strikes—that is, the number of days between the start and the end of strikes (these data will be further described and analysed in Example 6.9 (p. 516)). The mean duration is 43 days, the median duration 27 days, and the durations are positively skewed. Exhibit 6.14 (*b*) shows the histogram of the logarithmic strike durations, which are more normally distributed.

Censoring aspect of duration data

In many cases duration data are right censored—namely, at the time of measurement the duration may not yet be finished. This is the case, for

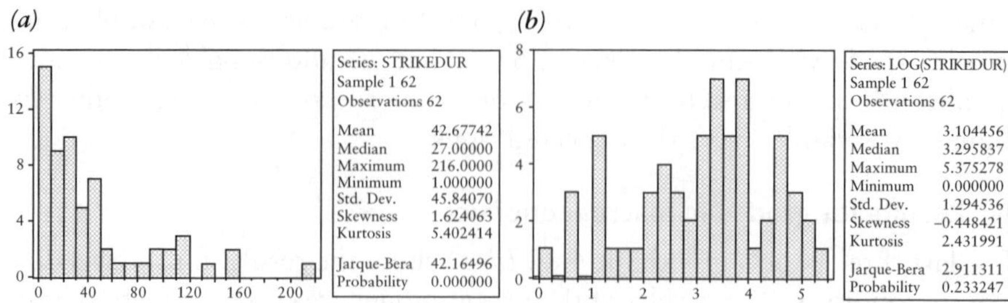

Exhibit 6.14 Duration data

Histogram of strike durations (measured in days (*a*)) and of logarithm of strike durations (*b*).

instance, if the observed person is still unemployed, if the observed customer has not bought the product again, or if the observed strike is still going on. It follows from the results in Sections 6.3.1 and 6.3.2 that the application of OLS to explain durations in terms of explanatory variables is inconsistent, for two reasons. First, some of the durations may be censored (if the event had not taken place at the time of measurement). Second, if the sample is restricted to the durations that have finished (so that the event has taken place before the time of measurement), then the effect of this truncation should be taken into account.

The hazard rate

In practice the main interest often lies in the question of how long the duration will continue, given that it has not finished yet. The *hazard rate* measures the chance that the duration will end now, given that it has not ended before. In the above examples, this can be interpreted as the chance to find a job, to purchase a product, or the end of a strike. Duration models are expressed in terms of hazard rates, and the econometric question is to estimate hazard rates from observed duration data. Let the data consist of a sample of n durations $y_1, \cdots, y_n$. It is assumed that these durations consist of a random sample from a population with density function f and corresponding cumulative distribution function F. The *survival function* $S(t)$ and the hazard rate $\lambda(t)$ are defined by

$$S(t) = P[y_i > t] = 1 - F(t),$$

$$\lambda(t) = \lim_{\delta \downarrow 0} \frac{P[t < y_i \leq t + \delta \mid y_i > t]}{\delta}.$$

Instead of estimating the density function f of the durations, one usually estimates the hazard rate λ, as this is of more practical interest. The survival function and the density function can then be obtained as follows from the hazard rate. Since

$$\lambda(t) = \frac{f(t)}{S(t)} = -\frac{d\log(S(t))}{dt},$$

it follows that

$$f(t) = \lambda(t)S(t), \quad S(t) = e^{-\int_0^t \lambda(s)ds} \tag{6.42}$$

(see Exercise 6.6).

Models for the hazard rate

Several models for the hazard rate can be formulated according to whether the hazard is constant or increases or decreases over time. For instance, the probability of finding a job or purchasing a product may be constant over time, but it may also increase or decrease as time progresses. The model with constant hazard rate

$$\lambda(t) = \gamma \quad \text{(for all } t\text{)}$$

corresponds to the density $f(t) = \gamma e^{-\gamma t}$—that is, the exponential distribution. This is called the *exponential hazard model*. Several models with positive or negative time dependence can be formulated. For example, the *Weibull distribution* with density $f(t) = \alpha\gamma t^{\alpha-1}e^{-\gamma t^{\alpha}}$ corresponds to the (Weibull) hazard model

$$\lambda(t) = \alpha\gamma t^{\alpha-1} \tag{6.43}$$

(see Exercise 6.6). In this model, the hazard rate increases over time if $\alpha > 1$, it decreases if $\alpha < 1$, and it remains constant if $\alpha = 1$. It may also be that the hazard rate first increases and later decreases. This can be modelled, for example, by the *log-normal distribution*, where the log-duration $\log(y_i)$ is normally distributed with mean μ and variance σ^2. The corresponding hazard rate is given by

$$\lambda(t) = \frac{\phi\left(\frac{\log(t)-\mu}{\sigma}\right)}{\sigma t\left(1 - \Phi\left(\frac{\log(t)-\mu}{\sigma}\right)\right)} \tag{6.44}$$

(see Exercise 6.6). In this case the hazard rate first increases and later decreases, with turning point given by the solution of the equation $t\sigma\lambda(t) = \sigma + (\log(t) - \mu)/\sigma$ (see Exercise 6.6). Exhibit 6.15 shows graphs of some of the above hazard rates.

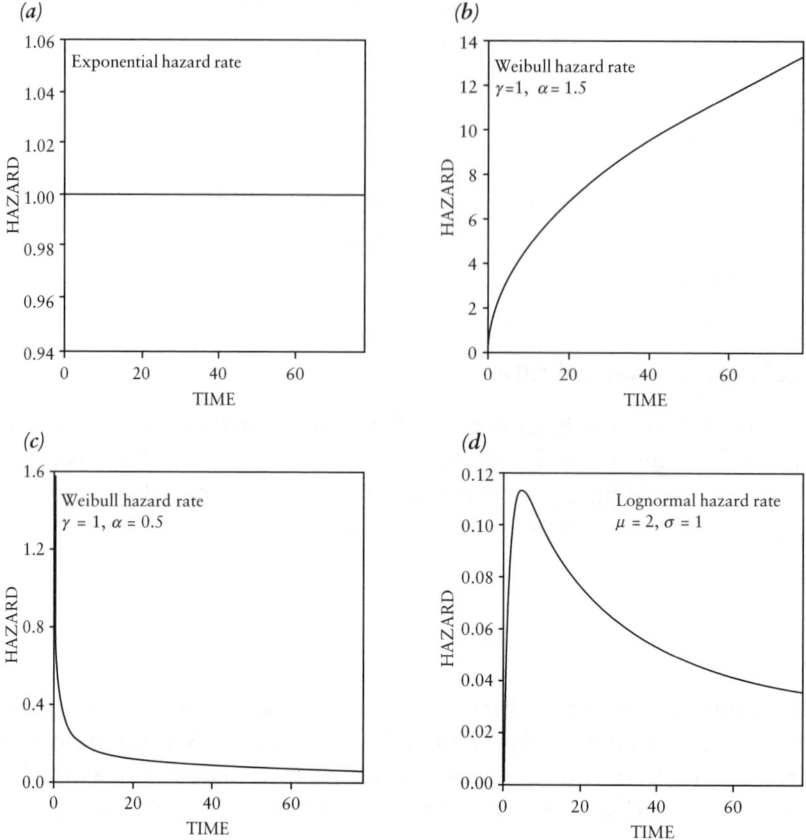

Exhibit 6.15 Hazard rates

Hazard rates, exponential with constant hazard rate $\lambda(t) = \gamma = 1$ (*a*), Weibull with $\gamma = 1$ and $\lambda(t) = \alpha t^{\alpha-1}$ with $\alpha = 1.5$ ((*b*), increasing hazard rate) and with $\alpha = 0.5$ ((*c*)), decreasing hazard rate), and hazard rate corresponding to the log-normal distribution with $\mu = 2$ and $\sigma = 1$ (*d*).

Proportional hazard model

The hazard rates may not be the same for all individuals and may depend on individual characteristics. Let $\lambda_i(t)$ be the hazard rate that applies to the ith duration y_i. We assume that the individual hazard rates can be expressed as $\lambda_i(t) = g_i\lambda(t)$, where the factor $g_i > 0$ stands for the individual-specific effects. If these effects are modelled by $g_i = e^{x_i'\beta}$, where x_i are observed variables that affect the hazard rate, then

$$\lambda_i(t) = e^{x_i'\beta}\lambda(t).$$

This is called the *proportional hazard model*. As the *baseline hazard* rate $\lambda(t)$ often contains a scale parameter, the constant term should be excluded from x_i. If we take logarithms, we get

$$\log(\lambda_i(t)) = x_i'\beta + \log(\lambda(t)),$$

so that the log-hazard depends linearly on the explanatory variables. This resembles the linear regression model somewhat, but a crucial difference is that the log-hazard is not directly observed. The individual characteristics x_i are assumed to be constant over time. The parameters β measure the marginal relative effects of the explanatory variables on the hazard rate—that is,

$$\beta = \frac{\partial \log(\lambda_i(t))}{\partial x_i} = \frac{1}{\lambda_i(t)}\frac{\partial \lambda_i(t)}{\partial x_i}.$$

The survival function of the proportional hazard model is given by $S_i(t) = [S(t)]^{e^{x_i'\beta}}$, where $S(t)$ is the survival function of the baseline hazard rate $\lambda(t)$. For larger values of $x_i'\beta$ the hazard $\lambda_i(t)$ increases, and as $0 \leq S(t) \leq 1$ the survival function $S_i(t)$ decreases in this case. That is, larger values of $x_i'\beta$ correspond on average to shorter durations. If the baseline hazard rate $\lambda(t)$ corresponds to the Weibull distribution in (6.43), then the expected durations of the proportional hazard model are given by $E[y_i] = e^{-x_i'\beta/\alpha}\mu_0$, where μ_0 is the expected duration of the baseline. hazard with $x_i = 0$ (see Exercise 6.6).

Estimation of the hazard rate model by maximum likelihood

T

The parameters of a (proportional) hazard model can be estimated by maximum likelihood. To derive the likelihood function, it should be realized that some of the observed durations $y_1, \cdots, y_n$ may be finished (the person found a job, or made a purchase, or the strike ended, indicated by $z_i = 1$), but others may be censored (the person is still unemployed, or has still not made a purchase, or the strike still continues, indicated by $z_i = 0$), so that the finished duration will be larger than y_i. The probability that the ith duration is still unfinished is given by $P[z_i = 0] = S_i(y_i)$, and the density for finished durations is given by $p_i(y_i) = \lambda_i(y_i)S_i(y_i)$. Assuming that the n observations are mutually independent, the log-likelihood is therefore given by

$$\begin{aligned}
\log(L) &= \sum_{\{i;\, z_i=1\}} \log(p_i(y_i)) + \sum_{\{i;\, z_i=0\}} \log(S_i(y_i)) \\
&= \sum_{\{i;\, z_i=1\}} \log(\lambda_i(y_i)) + \sum_{i=1}^{n} \log(S_i(y_i)) \\
&= \sum_{\{i; z_i=1\}} (x_i'\beta + \log(\lambda(y_i))) - \sum_{i=1}^{n}\left(e^{x_i'\beta}\int_0^{y_i} \lambda(t)dt\right).
\end{aligned} \qquad (6.45)$$

Here we used the fact that $S_i(t) = [S(t)]^{e^{x_i'\beta}}$, so that $\log(S_i(y_i)) = e^{x_i'\beta}\log(S(y_i)) = -e^{x_i'\beta}\int_0^{y_i}\lambda(t)dt$. The log-likelihood (6.45) can be maximized to obtain ML estimates of the parameters β and of the parameters of the baseline hazard rate $\lambda(t)$. For instance, for a constant baseline hazard rate $\lambda(t) = \gamma$, the log-likelihood becomes

$$\log(L(\beta, \gamma)) = \sum_{\{i; z_i = 1\}} (x_i'\beta + \log(\gamma)) - \sum_{i=1}^{n} \left(e^{x_i'\beta}\gamma y_i\right).$$

The estimated model can be visualized by making plots of the estimated hazard rate functions $\lambda_i(t)$ against the time variable t, for different choices of the values of the explanatory variables x_i.

Diagnostic checks on hazard rate models

To describe a test on the correct specification of the model, let $m \leq n$ be the number of finished duration times in the sample. Suppose that the data are ordered so that the first m observations are finished and the remaining $n - m$ observations are censored. Then the *generalized residuals* are defined in terms of the survival function by

$$e_i = -\log(S_i(y_i)) = e^{x_i'\beta} \int_0^{y_i} \lambda(t)dt, \quad i = 1, \cdots, m,$$

where the ML estimates are substituted for β and for the parameters of the baseline hazard rate λ. If the model is correctly specified, then the random variable $S_i = S_i(y_i)$ has a uniform distribution on the unit interval and e_i follows the unit exponential distribution with density e^{-t} (see Exercise 6.17). Note that this result does not depend on the functional form of the hazard rate.

If the model is correctly specified, then the sample cumulative distribution function of the outcomes $S_i(y_i)$, $i = 1, \cdots, m$ should be close to the 45° line. Alternatively, the sample distribution of the generalized residuals may be compared with the unit exponential distribution. The (uncentred) sample moments $\sum_{i=1}^{m} e_i^k / m$ can be compared with the corresponding moments of the unit exponential distribution that has kth population moment $k! = k \cdot (k-1) \cdots 2 \cdot 1$ (see Exercise 6.17). If the sample contains no censored observations—that is, if $m = n$—then ML gives $\sum_{i=1}^{n} e_i / n = 1$, so that the comparison should be based on the second and higher order moments (see Exercise 6.17).

Example 6.9: **Duration of Strikes**

We consider data on the duration of contract strikes in US manufacturing. The data are taken from J. Kennan, 'The Duration of Contract Strikes in US Manufacturing', *Journal of Econometrics*, 28 (1985), 5–28. We will describe (i) the data, (ii) results of the log-normal distribution for the strike durations, (iii) the results of different hazard models, (iv) a diagnostic check in terms of the generalized residuals, and (v) the effect of censoring.

(i) The data

The data set consists of $n = 62$ durations y_i (measured in days) of finished strikes. A histogram of these durations is given in Exhibit 6.14 (*a*). As possible explanatory variable, an indicator x_i of general economic activity during the strike is used. Exhibit 6.16 (*a*) shows a histogram of this production indicator and (*b*) a scatter diagram of log-durations against this indicator. This indicates that strikes may last longer if economic conditions are worse.

(ii) Log-normal distribution for the durations

The histogram of the log-durations $\log(y_i)$ in Exhibit 6.4 (*b*) shows that the null hypothesis of normality is not rejected, as the Jarque–Bera test for normality has a *P*-value of $P = 0.23$. This motivates the use of the log-normal density for the strike durations. The sample mean of the log-durations is $\hat{\mu} = 3.10$ and the sample standard deviation is $\hat{\sigma} = 1.29$ (see also Panel 3 in Exhibit 6.16). The expected duration time of strikes is then estimated as $E[y_i] = E[e^{\log(y_i)}] = e^{\hat{\mu}+\frac{1}{2}\hat{\sigma}^2} = 52$ days (using the result in Exercise 5.2 (*e*) for

(*a*)

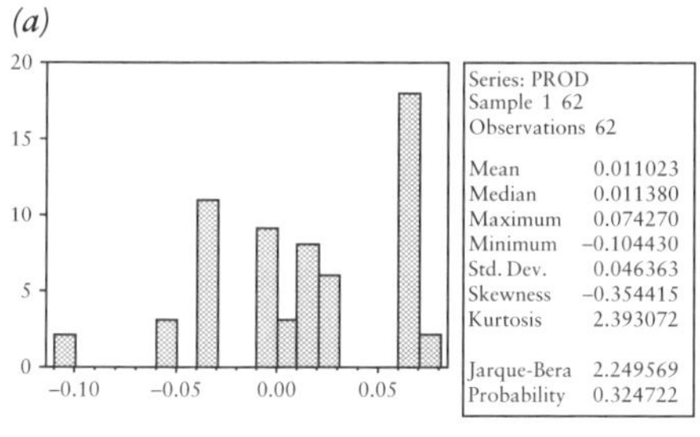

(*b*)

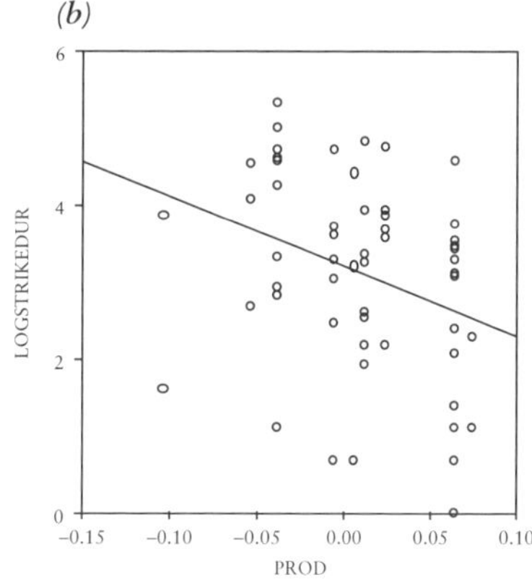

(*c*)

Panel 3: Least Squares; Dependent Variable: LOG(STRIKEDUR)				
Variable	Coefficient	Std. Error	t-Statistic	Prob.
C	3.101156	0.164406	18.88284	0.0000
S.E. of regression	1.294536			

(*d*)

Panel 4: Least Squares; Dependent Variable: LOG(STRIKEDUR)				
Variable	Coefficient	Std. Error	t-Statistic	Prob.
C	3.205657	0.160988	19.91236	0.0000
PROD	−9.180774	3.404293	−2.696822	0.0091
S.E. of regression	1.232705			

Exhibit 6.16 Duration of Strikes (Example 6.9)

Histogram of a production index (*a*), scatter diagram of strike durations (in logarithms) against the production index (*b*), regression of strike durations (in logarithms) on a constant (Panel 3) and on a constant and the production index (Panel 4).

(*e*)

Panel 5: ML: EXPONENTIAL without explanatory variable				
Parameter	Coefficient	Std. Error	z-Statistic	Prob.
GAMMA	0.023432	0.002793	8.389152	0.0000
Log likelihood	−294.7275	Akaike info criterion		9.539598

(*f*)

Panel 6: ML: EXPONENTIAL with production index as explanatory var.				
Parameter	Coefficient	Std. Error	z-Statistic	Prob.
GAMMA	0.022902	0.003185	7.189665	0.0000
BETA (coef PROD)	9.333815	2.977868	3.134395	0.0017
Log likelihood	−289.7647	Akaike info criterion		9.411765

(*g*)

Panel 7: ML: WEIBULL without explanatory variable				
Parameter	Coefficient	Std. Error	z-Statistic	Prob.
ALPHA	0.924688	0.111835	8.268300	0.0000
GAMMA	0.032183	0.015191	2.118483	0.0341
Log likelihood	−294.4027	Akaike info criterion		9.561377

(*h*)

Panel 8: ML: WEIBULL with production index as explanatory var.				
Parameter	Coefficient	Std. Error	z-Statistic	Prob.
ALPHA	1.007855	0.122542	8.224586	0.0000
GAMMA	0.022160	0.011101	1.996139	0.0459
BETA (coef PROD)	9.405522	3.071885	3.061808	0.0022
Log likelihood	−289.7617	Akaike info criterion		9.443926

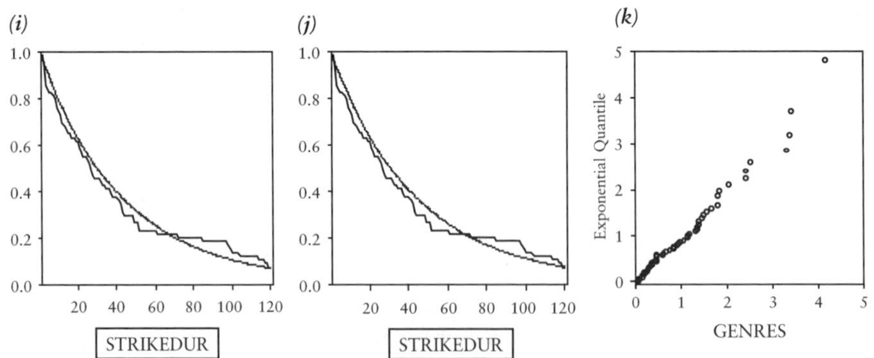

Exhibit 6.16 (*Contd.*)

Estimated hazard rate models without explanatory variable (exponential model in Panel 5 and Weibull model in Panel 7) and proportional hazard models with the production index as explanatory variable (exponential model in Panel 6 and Weibull model in Panel 8). (*i*) shows the empirical survival function of the durations and the survival function of the estimated model of Panel 5, (*j*) shows the survival function of the estimated proportional model of Panel 6 (for given value PROD = 0 of the index), and (*k*) shows the scatter diagram of the quantiles of the generalized residuals of the model of Panel 6 (on the horizontal axis) against the theoretical quantiles (of the unit exponential distribution, on the vertical axis).

(*l*)

Panel 12: TOBIT (censored normal); Dep. Var.: LOG(STRIKECENS80) Right censoring at value 80				
Variable	Coefficient	Std. Error	z-Statistic	Prob.
C	3.026027	0.150206	20.14582	0.0000
Error Distribution				
SCALE: SIGMA	1.182725	0.106212	11.13553	0.0000
S.E. of regression	1.202275	Akaike info criterion		3.238035

(*m*)

Panel 13: TOBIT (censored normal); Dep. Var.: LOG(STRIKECENS80) Right censoring at value 80				
Variable	Coefficient	Std. Error	z-Statistic	Prob.
C	3.113678	0.146893	21.19691	0.0000
PROD	−7.951562	3.106232	−2.559874	0.0105
Error Distribution				
SCALE: SIGMA	1.124777	0.101008	11.13556	0.0000
S.E. of regression	1.153019	Akaike info criterion		3.169821

(*n*)

Panel 14: ML: EXPONENTIAL hazard (right censoring at value 80)				
Parameter	Coefficient	Std. Error	z-Statistic	Prob.
GAMMA	0.023596	0.003000	7.865414	0.0000
Log likelihood	−237.3338	Akaike info criterion		7.688188

(*o*)

Panel 15: ML: EXPONENTIAL PROP. hazard (right censoring at value 80)				
Parameter	Coefficient	Std. Error	z-Statistic	Prob.
GAMMA	0.021726	0.003073	7.070767	0.0000
BETA (coef PROD)	10.18983	2.979147	3.420386	0.0006
Log likelihood	−232.5119	Akaike info criterion		7.564900

(*p*)

Panel 16: ML: WEIBULL hazard (right censoring at value 80)				
Parameter	Coefficient	Std. Error	z-Statistic	Prob.
ALPHA	0.890842	0.123693	7.202063	0.0000
GAMMA	0.035919	0.018397	1.952408	0.0509
Log likelihood	−236.8438	Akaike info criterion		7.704639

(*q*)

Panel 17: ML: WEIBULL PROP. hazard (right censoring at value 80)				
Parameter	Coefficient	Std. Error	z-Statistic	Prob.
ALPHA	0.950645	0.127085	7.480377	0.0000
GAMMA	0.026287	0.013733	1.914126	0.0556
BETA (coef PROD)	9.915412	3.134831	3.162981	0.0016
Log likelihood	−232.4195	Akaike info criterion		7.594179

Exhibit 6.16 (*Contd.*)

Hazard models (without and with explanatory variable) for strike duration data censored at a maximum of eighty days, lognormal hazard models (Panels 12 and 13, corresponding to tobit), exponential hazard models (Panels 14 and 15), and Weibull hazard models (Panels 16 and 17).

the mean of a log-normal distribution). The result of regressing $\log(y_i)$ on a constant and the production indicator is given in Panel 4 of Exhibit 6.16. The production indicator is significant ($P = 0.009$) and has the expected negative sign (-9.18). That is, the average duration of strikes is shorter in periods of high production than in periods of low production, possibly because strikes are relatively more costly in periods of high economic activity.

(iii) Results of different hazard models

Next we estimate exponential and Weibull hazard models by maximizing the corresponding log-likelihood (6.45). As the data are not censored, the term in (6.45) with the summation over $\{z_i = 1\}$ runs over all n observations. It is clear from the outcomes in Panels 5–8 of Exhibit 6.16 that the hypothesis of a constant hazard rate ($\alpha = 1$ in the Weibull models) is not rejected. The exhibit shows the survival functions $S(t) = e^{-\hat{\gamma}t}$ of the exponential hazard model (in (*i*), corresponding with Panel 5, that is, without x_i) and of the proportional exponential hazard model (in (*j*), corresponding with Panel 6, that is, with explanatory variable x_i; the plot is for $x_i = 0$). Exhibit 6.16 (*i*) and (*j*) also show the empirical survival function—that is, $S_{\text{emp}}(t) =$ (number of $y_i > t)/n$. The survival functions of the estimated models are quite close to the empirical survival function.

To obtain somewhat more insight into the estimated proportional exponential hazard model we compute the expected duration of strikes for three values of the economic indicator—that is, when economic activity is minimal ($x_i = -0.10$), neutral ($x_i = 0$), and maximal ($x_i = 0.07$). The expected durations are given by $E[y_i] = e^{-\beta x_i}\mu_0 = e^{-\beta x_i}/\gamma$. This gives expected durations of 111, 44, and 23 days respectively, so that the differences are quite considerable. Further, the probability that a strike will end today (that is, the hazard rate) is $\hat{\gamma}e^{\hat{\beta}x_i} = 0.023e^{9.33x_i}$—that is, around 1 per cent if economic activity is minimal, 2.3 per cent if economic activity is neutral, and 4.5 per cent if economic activity is maximal.

(iv) Diagnostic check in terms of generalized residuals

Exhibit 6.16 (*k*) shows the generalized residuals of the proportional exponential hazard model—that is, with the production index as explanatory variable so that $e_i = 0.023y_ie^{9.33x_i}$. In Exhibit 6.16 (*k*), the quantiles of these residuals e_i, $i = 1, \cdots, 62$ are compared with the (62) quantiles of the unit exponential distribution. In case of a perfect fit these quantiles should be the same, and the diagram shows that the deviations are not large as the plot of the two quantiles lies close to the 45° line. This provides support for the proportional exponential hazard model. The first three sample moments of the generalized residuals are respectively 1, 1.91, and 4.88. This is quite close to the corresponding population moments of the unit exponential distribution, which are respectively 1, 2, and 6.

(v) The effect of censoring

As discussed before, in many applications part of the durations are censored. To illustrate the effect of censoring, we now suppose that all strikes with a duration of eighty days or more are censored at the value of 80. In the data set there are twelve such durations. For the log-normal model we estimate tobit models (without and with explanatory variable) with known censoring from above at eighty days. The outcomes do not differ much from those obtained without censoring. We also estimate the exponential and Weibull hazard models (both without and with the economic indicator) on the censored data set. In this case the first term in the log-likelihood (6.45) runs over the fifty uncensored durations (with $y_i < 80$) and the second term runs over all sixty-two durations (where the largest twelve durations all have the value $y_i = 80$). The results in Panels 12–17 of Exhibit 6.16 show that censoring does not lead to significant biases in the involved hazards. As an illustration we compare the proportional exponential hazard models $\lambda_i(t) = \gamma e^{\beta x_i}$. For the original (uncensored) data, the estimates in Panel 6 are $\hat{\gamma} = 0.023$ (0.003) and $\hat{\beta} = 9.334$ (2.978), with standard errors in parentheses. For the censored data, the tobit estimates in Panel 15 are $\hat{\gamma} = 0.022$ (0.003) and $\hat{\beta} = 10.190$ (2.979). Although the censored data obviously contain less information than the original data, this has hardly any effect on the estimates and their standard errors in this example. The differences are so small because the exponential hazard model provides a good description both for shorter ($y_i < 80$) and for longer ($y_i > 80$) strike durations.

Some further aspects of these data are left as an exercise (see Exercise 6.17).

☞ **Exercises:** T: 6.6; E: 6.17.

6.3.5 Summary

We considered different situations where the dependent variable y_i in the regression equation $y_i = x_i'\beta + \varepsilon_i$ is limited in some sense. The model should be based on the relevant type of limited dependent variable. OLS is not consistent for this type of data. The models can be estimated consistently by maximum likelihood. In some cases also a two-step method is possible, where in the first step the bias term of OLS is estimated and in the second step y_i is regressed on x_i and the estimated bias term. We paid attention to the following types of data.

- In truncated samples the observed data come from a selective part of the population. This can be modelled in terms of truncated distributions for the error term. The bias term of OLS can be expressed in terms of the inverse Mills ratio.

- Censored data arise if the dependent variable cannot take values below (or above) a certain threshold value. This can be modelled by means of the tobit (type 1) model in terms of distributions that are mixed continuous-discrete. The continuous part applies to the non-censored outcomes, and the discrete part to the censored outcomes. The tobit model can be estimated by ML or by a Heckman two-step method.
- Sometimes the selection process that determines which data are observed can be modelled by means of a probit model with additional explanatory variables. This is called the tobit type 2 model, which can be estimated by ML or by a two-step Heckman method. This model is also useful to estimate treatment effects in case the assignment of treatments is not blind but correlated with the dependent variable y_i.
- A duration variable measures the time that elapses before a certain event takes place. Such a variable can take on only non-negative values. The observed values are censored if the relevant event has not yet taken place at the time of observation. Durations are modelled in terms of hazard rates that may depend on relevant explanatory variables.
- Some care is needed to interpret the estimated parameters in models for truncated or censored data. It is more informative to determine (average) marginal effects. The marginal effects differ from (and are actually smaller than) the estimated parameters. This is caused by the fact that truncation and censoring lead to non-linearities in the observed relations between y_i and x_i. The difference $E[y_i] - x_i'\beta$ is called the bias correction term, and we derived explicit expressions for this term.

Summary, further reading, and keywords

SUMMARY

This chapter discussed econometric models for dependent variables that are restricted in their domain of possible outcomes. Data of this type become more and more widespread in empirical economic work on choices of individual economic agents. In the year 2000, the Nobel prize in economics was awarded to McFadden and Heckman, two pioneers in the econometric modelling of this type of economic data. For binary data we discussed logit and probit models, with extensions for (unordered or ordered) multinomial data. Truncated and censored data can be described by truncated and mixed continuous-discrete probability distributions, in particular tobit models. We also described models for duration data and methods to estimate the hazard rate. All models discussed in this chapter can be estimated by maximum likelihood, and in some cases regression methods can be used by incorporating bias correction terms. As the models are non-linear, the marginal effects of the explanatory variables on the dependent variable are in general not constant over the population. We derived expressions for these marginal effects. Further we paid attention to the intuitive interpretation of the models and to methods for testing the empirical adequacy in practical applications.

FURTHER READING

Some of the textbooks mentioned in Chapter 3, Further Reading (p. 178–9), contain chapters on the topics discussed here, in particular the three volumes of the *Handbook of Econometrics*. Further there are many textbooks that deal specifically with qualitative and limited dependent variables. Introductory textbooks are Cramer (2003) and Franses and Paap (2001), more advanced texts are Maddala (1983), Amemiya (1985), and Ben-Akiva and Lerman (1985). Duration models are discussed in Kiefer (1988) and Lancaster (1990).

Amemiya, T. (1985). *Advanced Econometrics*. Cambridge, MA: Harvard University Press.

Ben-Akiva, M., and Lerman, S. R. (1985). *Discrete Choice Analysis*. Cambridge, MA: MIT Press.

Cramer, J. S. (2003). *Logit Models*. Cambridge: Cambridge University Press.

Franses, P. H., and Paap, R. (2001). *Quantitative Models in Marketing Research*. Cambridge: Cambridge University Press.

Kiefer, N. M. (1988). 'Economic Duration Data and Hazard Functions', *Journal of Economic Literature*, 26: 646–79.

Lancaster, T. (1990). *The Econometric Analysis of Transition Data*. Cambridge: Cambridge University Press.

Maddala, G. S. (1983). *Limited-Dependent and Qualitative Variables in Econometrics*. Cambridge: Cambridge University Press.

KEYWORDS

Exercises

THEORY QUESTIONS

6.1* (☞ Section 6.1.4)
Consider the binary logit model with heteroskedastic error terms where $\sigma_i = e^{-z_i'\gamma}$ (here we use this expression instead of $\sigma_i = e^{z_i'\gamma}$ of the text as this simplifies some of the derivations, both models are of course equivalent by reversing the signs of all entries of the parameter vector γ). By $\theta = (\beta, \gamma)$ we denote the vector of unknown parameters of the model. We derive the LM-test for the null hypothesis of homoskedasticity ($\gamma = 0$).

a. Compute the score vector $s(\theta)$ consisting of the subvectors $\partial \log(L)/\partial\beta$ and $\partial \log(L)/\partial\gamma$. Evaluate $s(\theta)$ at the ML estimators under the null hypothesis that $\gamma = 0$.
b. Compute the Hessian matrix $H(\theta)$ consisting of the second order derivatives of $\log(L)$ with respect to the parameters (β, γ). Next compute the information matrix $\mathcal{I}_n(\theta) = -E[H(\theta)]$, evaluated at the ML estimators under the null hypothesis that $\gamma = 0$.
c. Show that the LM-test $LM = s'\mathcal{I}_n^{-1}s$ amounts in large enough samples to $LM = nR^2$ of the auxiliary regression (6.14), in the sense that $\text{plim}\left(s'\mathcal{I}_n^{-1}s - nR^2\right) = 0$.

6.2 (☞ Sections 6.1.2, 6.1.3)
In direct mailings the fraction of respondents is often relatively small. To limit the database, one sometimes keeps only a fraction f_1 of the respondents (with $y_i = 1$) and a fraction $f_1 f_2$ of the non-respondents (with $y_i = 0$) in the sample, where $0 \leq f_1 \leq 1$ and $0 \leq f_2 \leq 1$ are known. Let z_i be the selection variable with $z_i = 1$ for selected observations and $z_i = 0$ for deleted ones. The selection is supposed to be random.

a. Show that the sample probabilities $p_i^s = P[y_i = 1|z_i = 1]$ are related to the population probabilities $p_i = P[y_i = 1]$ by $p_i^s = p_i/(p_i + f_2\,(1 - p_i))$.
b. Suppose that the population probabilities p_i satisfy the logit model (with parameters $\beta_1, \beta_2, \cdots, \beta_k$, where β_1 is the constant term). Show that the sample probabilities p_i^s then also satisfy the logit model, with parameters $\beta_1 - \log(f_2), \beta_2, \cdots, \beta_k$.
c. Show that the individual rankings in the logit model are not affected by selecting a subsample—that is, if $p_i > p_j$ then also $p_i^s > p_j^s$.
d. Show that ML in selected subsamples remains consistent, but that it is not efficient.
e. Suppose that there are relatively few respondents (so that p_i is close to zero). In the sample of size n, let there be m respondents who are all kept in the subsample, whereas from the $n - m$ non-respondents only m are chosen randomly. So the sample size is reduced by a factor $2m/n$. Argue why the standard errors of the logit estimators will in general increase by much less than the factor $\sqrt{n/2m}$, by using the expression (6.11) for the information matrix.

6.3 (☞ Section 6.2.2)

a*. Prove the expressions for the probabilities p_{ij} in (6.20) for the multinomial and the conditional logit model when the error terms ε_{ij} follow the extreme value distribution with cumulative distribution $e^{-e^{-t}}$.
b. Prove the expressions given in Section 6.2.2 for the marginal effects $\partial P_{MNL}[y_i = j]/\partial x_i$ in the multinomial logit model and $\partial P_{CL}[y_i = j]/\partial x_{ij}$ and $\partial P_{CL}[y_i = j]/\partial x_{ih}$ in the conditional logit model.
c. Prove that the log-likelihood for the multinomial logit model is given by (6.21). Prove also the expressions for the gradient and Hessian matrix given below (6.21).
d. Prove that the log-likelihood for the conditional logit model is given by (6.22). Prove also the expressions for the gradient and Hessian matrix given below (6.22).

6.4 (☞ Sections 6.3.1–6.3.3)

a. Illustrate the bias term $\sigma\lambda_i$ in (6.28) by simulating a truncated sample from the model $y_i = 1 + \varepsilon_i$, where $x_i = 1$ is constant and the ε_i are random drawings from N(0, 1). The sample is truncated by considering only the observations with $y_i > 0$ and deleting all observations with $y_i \leq 0$. Compare the sample mean of the remaining observations with the theoretical value of the inverse Mills ratio $\lambda_i = \lambda$ in this case.

b*. Prove the expression (6.30). Prove that the correction factor in front of β lies between zero and one.

c. Compute the two terms in (6.35) for the case of the standard normal distribution. Prove that, when added, this gives $\Phi_i\beta$.

d. Illustrate, by means of a suitable simulation experiment, that OLS is an inconsistent estimator of treatment effects if the treatments are not applied randomly. Use this simulation also to check the result mentioned in Section 6.3.3 that $E[y_i|z_i] = x_i'\beta + \alpha z_i + \rho\sigma\frac{\lambda_i(z_i-\Phi_i)}{1-\Phi_i}$ (which leads to (6.41)), by computing the sample means of y_i over the two subsamples (with $z_i = 1$ and with $z_i = 0$) and by averaging the terms $x_i'\beta + \alpha z_i + \rho\sigma\frac{\lambda_i(z_i-\Phi_i)}{1-\Phi_i}$ over these two subsamples.

6.5 (☞ Section 6.3.2)

a. Suppose that the latent variable y_i^* satisfies $y_i^* = x_i'\beta + \sigma\varepsilon_i$ with all the standard assumptions (in particular, with $\varepsilon_i \sim$ NID(0, 1)), and that we observe $y_i = y_i^*$ if $c_0 < y_i^* < c_1$ but that $y_i = c_0$ for $y_i^* \leq c_0$ and $y_i = c_1$ for $y_i^* \geq c_1$, with c_0 and c_1 given constants. Derive the expression for the log-likelihood of this model.

b. Propose a consistent method to estimate the model described in **a** when the threshold values c_0 and c_1 are unknown.

c*. In some applications (for instance, in income and budget studies of households) the data are censored in the sense that a group of large values is summarized by their sample mean. Suppose that the data y_i satisfy the following model, where c_0 is a known threshold value and the error terms ε_i are NID(0,1). For $y_i^* = x_i'\beta + \sigma\varepsilon_i \leq c_0$ we observe $y_i = y_i^*$, but for $y_i^* = x_i'\beta + \sigma\varepsilon_i > c_0$ we observe only the sample mean of the values y_i^* and the sample mean of the corresponding values of the explanatory variables x_i. Also the number of these large observations is given. Derive the expression for the log-likelihood of this model. What condition is needed on c_0 to be able to estimate the parameters β and σ by maximum likelihood?

d. Suppose that the threshold value c_0 in the model of **c** is unknown. Propose a consistent method to estimate the parameters (β, σ, c_0) of the resulting model.

6.6 (☞ Section 6.3.4)

a. Show the expressions in (6.42) concerning the relations between the hazard rate, the survival function, and the density function of duration data.

b. Show the expression (6.43) for the hazard rate corresponding to the Weibull density.

c. Show the expression (6.44) for the hazard rate corresponding to the log-normal density. Derive the equation given below (6.44) in Section 6.3.4 for the time instant where this hazard rate reaches its maximum.

d. Prove that the expected duration in the proportional Weibull hazard rate model is equal to $E[y_i] = e^{-x_i'\beta/\alpha}\mu_0$, where μ_0 is the expected duration in the baseline hazard model with $x_i = 0$.

EMPIRICAL AND SIMULATION QUESTIONS

6.7 (☞ Sections 6.1.2, 6.1.3)

a. Simulate a sample of $n = 200$ data where $x_i = i$ and $y_i^* - -10 + 0.1x_i + \varepsilon_i$ with ε_i independent drawings from N(0, 1), $i = 1, \cdots, 200$. Generate observed choices y_i by $y_i = 0$ if $y_i^* < 0$ and $y_i = 1$ if $y_i^* \geq 0$.

b. Compute the theoretical odds ratio $P[y = 1]/P[y = 0]$ for the following five values of x: 60, 80, 100, 120, and 140. Compare this with the odds ratios in the sample for the observations with x respectively in the intervals $55 \leq x \leq 65$, $75 \leq x \leq 85$, and so on, to

$135 \leq x \leq 145$. Clarify these results with a scatter diagram of y_i^* against x.

c. Perform a regression of y_i on the constant and the variable x_i, with result $\hat{y}_i = a + bx_i$. Compute the estimated odds ratios $\hat{y}_i/(1 - \hat{y}_i)$ for the five values of x in **b**, and compare the outcomes with those in **b**.

d. Estimate a probit model for the data (x_i, y_i), $i = 1, \cdots, 200$. Compute again the estimated odds ratios for the five values of x in **b** and compare the outcomes with those in **b** and **c**.

e. Estimate a logit model for the data (y_i, x_i), $i = 1, \cdots, 200$. Compare the estimated parameters of this model with those obtained for the probit model in **d**.

f. Using the logit model in **e**, compute the estimated odds ratios for the five values of x in **b**. Compare the outcomes with those of the probit model in **d**.

6.8 (☞ Sections 6.1.3, 6.1.4)
Consider the following data generating process. The variable x_i consists of independent drawings from N(100, 100), and $y_i^* = -10 + 0.1x_i + \varepsilon_i$ with ε_i independent drawings from N(0,1) that are independent of x_i. The choices y_i are generated by $y_i = 0$ if $y_i^* < 0$ and $y_i = 1$ if $y_i^* \geq 0$. The observed data consist of the values of (x_i, y_i) for $i = 1, \cdots, n$.

a. Generate samples with $n = 100$, $n = 1000$, and $n = 10{,}000$ from this process. For the resulting three data sets, estimate the parameters of the probit model. Compare the estimates with the theoretical values of the data generating process.

b. Estimate logit models for the three data sets. Compare the estimated logit parameters with the probit estimates. Explain why the logit estimators are not consistent.

c. Perform heteroskedasticity tests on the standardized residuals of the 6 models estimated in **a** and **b**. Use the following specification of the standard deviation: $\sigma_i = e^{\gamma x_i}$, with null hypothesis $H_0: \gamma = 0$.

d. Now generate ε_i by independent drawings from the distribution $N(0, \sigma_i^2)$, where $\sigma_i = e^{x_i/100}$, and generate corresponding new values of y_i^* and y_i. Estimate logit and probit models for a sample of $n = 10{,}000$ observations from this process.

e. Comment on the outcomes in **d**. Why are the probit estimators no longer consistent?

f. How can the parameters be estimated consistently in this case, if it is given that $\sigma_i = e^{x_i/100}$? Estimate the parameters by adjusting for this heteroskedasticity and compare the resulting estimates with the parameter values of the data generating process.

6.9 (☞ Sections 6.3.1, 6.3.2)
Consider the following data generating process. The variable x_i consists of independent drawings from N(100, 100), and $y_i^* = -10 + 0.1x_i + \varepsilon_i$, with ε_i independent drawings from N(0, 1) that are independent of x_i. In Exercise 6.8 we considered binary data related to y_i^*, but now we will consider truncated and censored data, where $y_i = 0$ for $y_i^* \leq 0$ and $y_i = y_i^*$ for $y_i^* > 0$.

a. Suppose that the sample is truncated, so that the data consist only of the observations (x_i, y_i) with $y_i > 0$. Generate a sample of $n = 100$ truncated observations. Estimate the parameters α (the constant), β (the slope), and σ (the variance of ε_i) by regressing y_i on a constant and x_i. Estimate the parameters also by ML by maximizing (6.29).

b. Relate the bias of the OLS estimator of the slope parameter ($\beta = 0.1$) in **a** to the result (6.30) on marginal effects for truncated data.

c. Now suppose that the sample is censored, so that the data consist of observations (x_i, y_i) including also the cases where $y_i = 0$. Generate a sample of $n = 100$ censored observations. Estimate the parameters α, β, and σ by regressing y_i on a constant and x_i. Estimate the parameters also by ML using the standard normal distribution—that is, by maximizing (6.36).

d. Relate the bias of the OLS estimator of the slope parameter ($\beta = 0.1$) in **c** to the result (6.34) that implies that for censored data $\partial E[y_i]/\partial x_i = \Phi(x_i'\beta/\sigma)\beta$.

e. Compare the results of the ML estimates for the truncated sample in **a** and for the censored model in **c**. Which method produced the smallest (finite sample) bias, and which the smallest (large sample) standard errors? Could this be expected or not?

6.10 (☞ Section 6.1.4)
We consider a (simulated) data set of 100 employees in the ICT sector who responded to a questionnaire on teleworking. For each employee we know the answer to the question whether she or he wants to

make use of teleworking ($y_i = 1$ if yes, $y_i = 0$ if no), the gender ($x_{2i} = 1$ for females and $x_{2i} = 0$ for males), and the travel distance between home and work (x_{3i}, in miles).

a. Estimate the logit model $P[y_i = 1] = \Lambda(\beta_1 + \beta_2 x_{2i})$. Does gender have a significant effect? What is the hit rate of this model?

b. Estimate the logit model $P[y_i = 1] = \Lambda(\beta_1 + \beta_2 x_{2i} + \beta_3 x_{3i})$—that is, including travel distance as additional explanatory variable. Does gender have a significant effect? What is the hit rate of this model?

c. Explain the possible cause of the differences in the significance of the variable 'gender' in **a** and **b**.

d. Perform a Likelihood Ratio test on the significance of the variable 'travel distance'.

e. Make two plots (in a single diagram) of $P[y = 1]$ as a function of the travel distance, one for females and a second one for males. Comment on the outcomes.

6.11 (☞ Section 6.1.3)

Consider the direct marketing data of Example 6.1.

a. Let $\hat{p}_i = \Lambda(x_i' b)$ where b are the logit estimates. Make a plot of $\hat{p}_i$ against the age of active males (that is, with $x_{2i} = 1$ and $x_{3i} = 1$) and also against the age of inactive males (with $x_{2i} = 1$ and $x_{3i} = 0$). Do there exist segments in the sample that show distinct response behaviour?

b. Answer the same questions as in **a** for the probit model.

c. Plot the probit log-odds for active and inactive males against their age, and compare this with the corresponding curves estimated from the logit model.

d. The data set in Example 6.1 contains 470 observations with $y_i = 1$ and 455 with $y_i = 0$. This data set is drawn randomly from a much larger set that contains 4988 observations with $y_i = 1$ and 100,321 observations with $y_i = 0$. What estimated values of β would you expect if a logit model were to be estimated for the set of all 105,309 observations (use the result in Exercise 6.2 **b**)?

6.12 (☞ Section 6.1.5)

Consider again the direct marketing data of Example 6.1.

a. Divide the 925 individuals into ten age groups, with the youngest group having ages of 30 years or less, the oldest with ages 71 or more, and the other eight groups with ages in the five-year intervals ranging from 31–35 to 66–70. Determine the group sizes and the group means of the explanatory variables (gender, activity, age) and the explained variable (the fraction of respondents in each group).

b. Estimate a logit model based on the $G = 10$ observations of the grouped data in **a**. The explanatory variables in this model are a constant, the three group mean variables for gender, activity, and age, and finally the square of the mean age per group.

c. Perform an LR-test on the five restrictions of the logit model—that is, $p_j = \Lambda(\overline{x}_j' \beta)$, $j = 1, \cdots, 10$, where $\overline{x}_j$ contains the values of the five explanatory variables for group j and β contains the five model parameters.

d. Estimate the parameters of the logit model also by applying FWLS to the grouped data.

e. Compare the outcomes in **b** and **d** with those of the logit model for the individual data in Example 6.2.

6.13 (☞ Sections 6.1.3, 6.1.4, 6.2.2, 6.2.3)

Consider the salary data (of male employees) of Examples 6.4 and 6.5. Instead of considering three alternatives, let the job categories 1 (administration) and 2 (custodial) be joined in one alternative, and define the binary variable y_i by $y_i = 0$ if the ith individual has an administrative or custodial job and $y_i = 1$ for a management job.

a. Estimate a logit model for the binary variable y, including as explanatory variables a constant and the variables education, minority and previous experience.

b. Distinguish between minority and non-minority males, and compute the marginal effects (averaged over the relevant subsamples) of education on the probability to get a job in management.

c. Estimate the logit model of **a** without the variable 'previous experiencc'. Test for the significance of the variable 'previous experience', both by the t-test and by the LR-test. Also test for the possible presence of heteroskedasticity with the model $\sigma_i = e^{\gamma z_i}$ where z_i is the variable 'education'.

d. Compute the R^2 and the hit rate (with corresponding z-value) for the estimated logit model of **c** (that is, without the variable 'previous experience').

e. Compare this binary logit model with the multinomial logit model in Example 6.4. Which model do you prefer to predict the probability that a male employee will have a management position?

f. The probability of a minority male having a management job depends on his education. Compute this probability for two levels of education, 12 years and 16 years, for the following three models: the logit model of **c** (without the variable 'previous experience') and the multinomial and ordered logit models in Examples 6.4 and 6.5. Comment on the outcomes.

6.14* (☞ Section 6.2.2)

In Example 6.4 we considered a multinomial logit model for the attained job category of male employees. There are three job categories, $y_i = 1$ for administrative jobs, $y_i = 2$ for custodial jobs, and $y_i = 3$ for management jobs. Female employees were excluded from the analysis because there are no female employees with a custodial job. We now consider two possibilities to investigate the attained job categories for males and females jointly. The first one is to formulate a multinomial model for males and females, with gender as additional explanatory variable, the second one is to combine the multinomial model for males with a binomial model for females (excluding the custodial jobs for females).

a. Formulate the multinomial logit model (for the data set of all 474 employees, males and females) for the attained job category, in terms of the explanatory variables gender (with value 0 for males and 1 for females), education, and minority. Take administration (the first job category) as reference category.

b. The probability p_{i2} for a custodial job can be made arbitrarily small for females by giving the corresponding gender coefficient in β_2 very large negative values (where β_2 is the 4×1 vector of parameters for custodial jobs). Explain that the ML estimate of this coefficient in the multinomial model is equal to $-\infty$. Describe a practical method for estimating the remaining seven parameters of this model.

c. As an alternative, write down the log-likelihood of the combined multinomial logit model (for males) and binary logit model (for females, with job categories 1 and 3 alone). Take the first job category as reference category, and assume that the parameter values in management jobs for education and minority are the same for males and females (so that the model contains in total seven parameters, two for 'education', two for 'minority', two constants for males, and one constant for females).

d. Estimate the parameters of the models in **b** and **c** and compare the outcomes.

e. Perform diagnostic tests on the two models of **d** and compare this with the results for males alone in Example 6.4. In particular, compare the signs and significance of coefficients and the hit rates of the three models.

6.15 (☞ Sections 6.2.2, 6.2.3, 6.3.3)

In this exercise we consider some further aspects of the data set on students of the Vanderbilt University discussed in Example 6.8. We consider the data of 609 students following an intermediate course in microeconomics.

a. In Example 6.8 the attained level of mathematics was taken as a binary variable ('mathhigh'). The data in the file are more refined because seven ordered levels of calculus courses are distinguished (see the variable 'levelmath' in the data file). Estimate an ordered logit model for the attained level of mathematics, with the variable 'levelmath' as dependent variable and with the same explanatory variables w_i as in Example 6.8 (see Exhibit 6.12 **b** for the list of variables).

b. Compare the estimates of the ordered logit model in **a** with the binary probit model in Example 6.8 (see the results in Exhibit 6.13, Panel 1).

c. In Example 6.8 three expected majors were distinguished—namely in natural science, in the areas of economics, social science, and humanity, or in another field or an unknown major (the reference category). The data are more refined, as the file contains five majors by distinguishing between majors in economics, social science, and humanity. Estimate a multinomial logit model for the expected major in terms of the following explanatory variables: the SAT scores mathematics (SATM) and verbal (SATV), the Freshman grade point average (FGPA), and gender (FEM).

6.16 (☞ Section 6.3.2)

Consider the direct marketing data. In Example 6.7 a tobit model is estimated for the amount of money invested, whereas in Example 6.2 a binary probit model is estimated for the decision to invest.

a. Compare the estimated parameter vector $(1/\sigma)\beta$ of the censored regression model with the estimated parameter vector in the binary probit model (that we denote by γ). Do you find the restrictions $\gamma = (1/\sigma)\beta$ of the tobit model acceptable for these data?

b. Discuss possible methods to obtain a better model for the joint decision to invest and how much to invest.

6.17 (☞ Section 6.3.4)

In this exercise we consider some theoretical results for duration models and their application on the strike data of Example 6.9.

a. Show that for finished duration data the survival values $S_i(y_i)$ as defined in Section 6.3.4 are uniformly distributed.

b. Show that the corresponding generalized residuals $e_i = -\log(S_i(y_i))$ have an exponential distribution with density e^{-t} and with kth moment $k! = k \cdot (k-1) \cdots 2 \cdot 1$.

c. Show that, if the sample contains no censored durations, ML in (6.45) always gives a sample mean of the generalized residuals of $\sum_{i=1}^{n} e_i/n = 1$.

d. For the censored duration data in Example 6.9 (with censoring from above at eighty days), compute the generalized residuals of the model with exponential hazard rate both for the case without and for the case with explanatory variable.

e. Make plots of the sample cumulative distribution functions of the generalized residuals for the two models of **d**, and compute the first three sample moments of the generalized residuals. What is your conclusion?

f. For the log-normal model $\log(y_i) = \alpha + \beta x_i + \varepsilon_i$ estimated in Example 6.9, determine the hazard rates after $t = 10$ days for the values $x_i = -0.10$, $x_i = 0$, and $x_i = 0.07$ of the production index. At what time instant does the hazard rate reach its maximum when $x_i = 0$ (it may be helpful to plot $\lambda(t)$ as a function of t to determine the location of the maximum graphically)?

7 Time Series and Dynamic Models

This chapter treats the modelling of variables that are observed sequentially over time. The main focus is on univariate time series models for a single economic variable, but we also discuss regression models with lags and multivariate time series models. Time series analysis consists of several phases. First, the dynamic structure of the model is selected and then the parameters of the model are estimated. Diagnostic tests are performed to test the model assumptions, and the outcomes may suggest alternative specifications of the model. When an acceptable model has been obtained, it can be used, for example, to forecast future values of the variables. Many economic time series contain trends that are of major importance in forecasting. The series may also exhibit seasonal variation or a variance that changes over time. Therefore we pay special attention to the modelling of trends, seasonals, and the variance of economic time series.

Sections 7.1–7.3 are the basic sections of this chapter that are required for the material discussed in Sections 7.4–7.7. Sections 7.4 and 7.5 can be read independently from each other, Section 7.5 is required for Sections 7.6 and 7.7.

7.1 Models for stationary time series

☞ Uses Chapters 1–4; Section 5.5.

7.1.1 Introduction

To get an idea of economic time series we consider two series that are used as leading examples in this chapter.

E

XM701INP

Example 7.1: Industrial Production

In this section and in following sections we will consider a time series that measures the quarterly industrial production in the USA. The data are taken from the OECD main economic indicators. We will discuss (i) the data and (ii) some useful transformations of the data.

(i) The data

Exhibit 7.1 (*a*) shows the quarterly index of total industrial production in the USA. In time series plots, the horizontal axis always measures time (here the years and quarters) and the vertical axis measures the values of the time series. If we would follow the convention of scatter diagrams, the horizontal axis should be labelled as 'time' and the vertical axis as the 'observed series'. However, in time series plots one usually places the name of the observed variable on the horizontal axis as this is easier to read, but note that the values of this variable are measured on the vertical axis. The series is indexed so that the average of the four quarterly values of industrial production over 1992 is equal to 100. The sample period runs from 1950.1 to 1998.3. In our analysis of this series, the data prior to 1961.1 are used as starting values and the data from 1995.1 to 1998.3 are left out to evaluate the out-of-sample forecasting performance of proposed models. Therefore, in modelling this series the effective sample ranges from 1961.1 to 1994.4 and contains $n = 136$ observations. We denote the industrial production index by x_t. Here we follow the convention in the time series literature to use the index t (instead of i), because the observations are naturally ordered with time.

(ii) Transformations of the data

The series x_t shows exponential growth over time. Therefore we will consider models for the logarithm of this series. We denote the resulting series by $y_t = \log(x_t)$. The series y_t is shown in Exhibit 7.1 (*b*). It contains a clear upward trend and some fluctuations that may be due to seasonal effects. Models for the trend of this series are described in Examples 7.13 and 7.14 and the seasonal effects are discussed in Example 7.16. Exhibit 7.1 (*c*) shows the quarterly series of annual growth rates, defined by

$$\Delta_4 y_t = y_t - y_{t-4} = \log\left(\frac{x_t}{x_{t-4}}\right) = \log\left(1 + \frac{x_t - x_{t-4}}{x_{t-4}}\right) \approx \frac{x_t - x_{t-4}}{x_{t-4}}.$$

This series contains no trend anymore and moves with gradual upward and downward fluctuations around a long-term mean. Such fluctuations

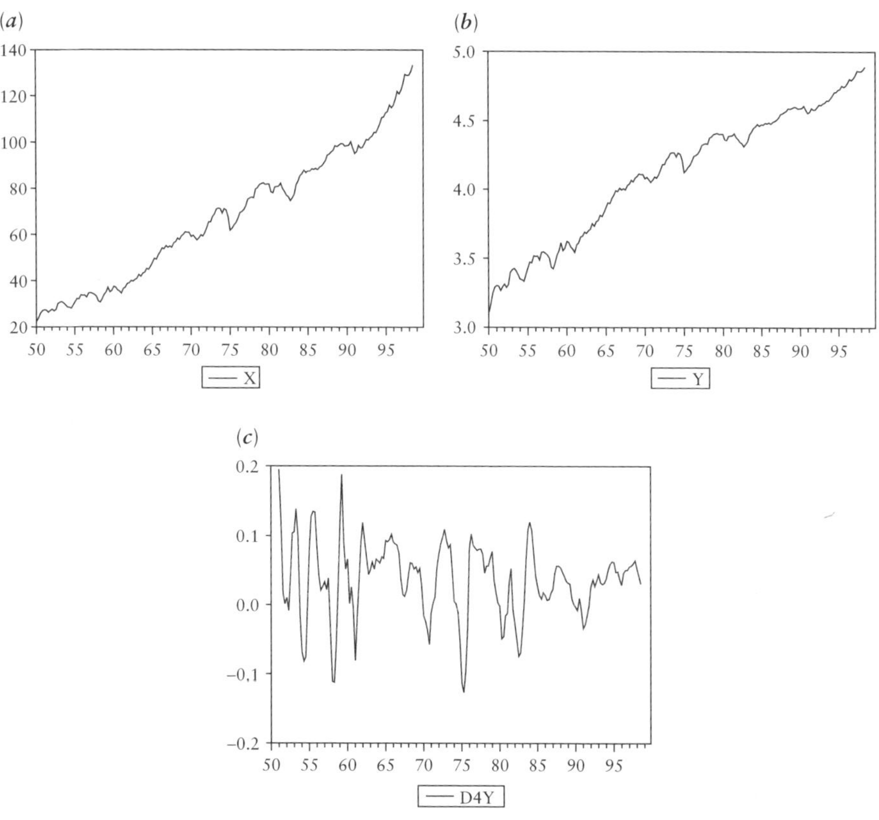

Exhibit 7.1 Industrial Production (Example 7.1)

Quarterly series of US industrial production (X in (*a*)), in logarithms (Y = log (X) in (*b*)), and the corresponding yearly growth rates (D4Y = Y − Y(−4) in (*c*)).

correspond to a business cycle with negative growth rates in the recession periods, for example around the periods 1974–5 and 1980–2. This series of quarterly growth rates will be further analysed in later examples in Sections 7.2.2–7.2.4.

XM702DJI

Example 7.2: **Dow-Jones Index**

As a second example we consider the Dow-Jones Industrial Average. The data are taken from the Internet database 'Economagic'. We will discuss (i) the data and (ii) some useful transformations of the data.

(i) **The data**

The observed series consists of the daily close of the Dow-Jones index over the period 1990 (2 January) to 1999 (31 December). The series (denoted by

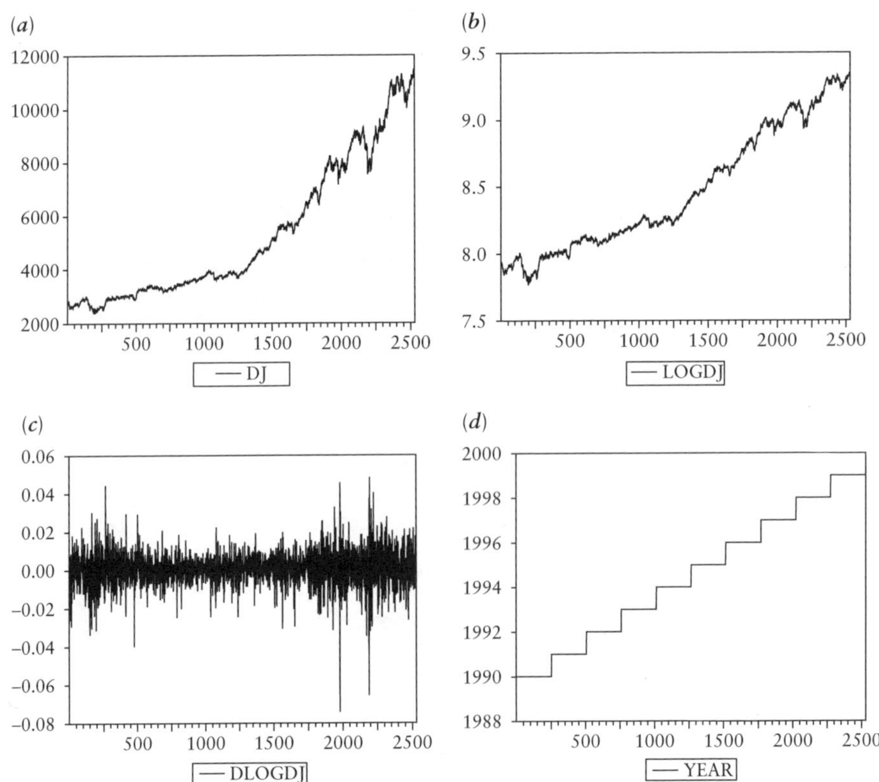

Exhibit 7.2 Dow-Jones Index (Example 7.2)

Dow-Jones Industrial Average (DJ in (*a*)), series of logarithms of the Dow-Jones (LOGDJ in (*b*)), series of daily returns (DLOGDJ, the series of first differences of LOGDJ in (*c*)) and years ((*d*); the observation number is measured on the horizontal axis).

DJ_t) contains $n = 2528$ observations and is shown in Exhibit 7.2 (a). The days are numbered consecutively so that closing days (weekends and holidays) are not taken into account. Exhibit 7.2 (d) shows the years that correspond to the observation numbers.

(ii) Transformations of the data

The Dow-Jones index shows an exponential trend with fluctuations that become more pronounced for higher levels of the index. Exhibit 7.2 (b) shows the logarithm of the index (which we denote by $y_t = \log(DJ_t)$). The fluctuations around the trend are now more stable. Exhibit 7.2 (c) shows the series of daily returns of the index, defined by

$$\Delta y_t = y_t - y_{t-1} = \log\left(\frac{DJ_t}{DJ_{t-1}}\right) = \log\left(1 + \frac{DJ_t - DJ_{t-1}}{DJ_{t-1}}\right) \approx \frac{DJ_t - DJ_{t-1}}{DJ_{t-1}}.$$

The variance of the series of daily returns changes over time, with volatile periods followed by periods with smaller fluctuations. The nature of the trend in the Dow-Jones index is analysed in Section 7.3.3, and models for changes in the variance are discussed in Section 7.4.4.

Structure of Sections 7.1–7.4

The actual modelling of univariate time series like the ones in the above two examples is described in Sections 7.2 (for stationary series), 7.3 (for time series with trends and seasonals), and 7.4 (for time series with non-linear aspects). This requires some basic models and tools in time series analysis, which are now discussed.

7.1.2 Stationary processes

Time series

When a variable is observed sequentially over time, the observations constitute a time series. Such a time series consists of a set of realized values of the relevant business or economic process that evolves over time. The frequency of observation can, for example, be annual, quarterly (as in Example 7.1), monthly, or daily (as in Example 7.2). Time series data are often strongly correlated over time. For example, if the current industrial production index has a value of 100, then it is more likely that the next quarter this index will be somewhere between 90 and 110 than that it will be as high as, say, 200.

Stationarity

A time series is called stationary if its statistical properties remain constant over time. This means that, when we consider two different time intervals, the sample mean and sample covariances of the time series over the two time intervals will be roughly the same. More precisely, a time series y_t is called (*second order*) *stationary* if the following conditions are satisfied:

$$E[y_t] = \mu, \quad E[(y_t - \mu)^2] = \gamma_0, \quad E[(y_t - \mu)(y_{t-k} - \mu)] = \gamma_k \text{ (for all } t).$$

Here μ, γ_0, and γ_k are finite-valued numbers that do not depend on time t. So the mean has to be constant over time, and, if the series has a trend, this should be removed (see Section 7.3). Also the variance has to be constant, and, if the series contains seasonal fluctuations or changing variance, this should also be removed (see Sections 7.3.4 and 7.4). Finally, the covariances are constant over time—for instance, the covariance between the industrial production in two consecutive quarters is the same for all quarters and over all years.

Autocorrelations of a stationary process

The *autocorrelations* of a stationary process are defined by

$$\rho_k = \frac{\gamma_k}{\gamma_0}.$$

These correlations describe the short-run dynamic relations within the time series, in contrast with the trend, which corresponds to the long-run behaviour of the time series. A time series model summarizes the correlations between y_t and the past values y_{t-k}, $k \geq 1$, in terms of a limited number of parameters. This differs from the models discussed in the foregoing chapters, where the outcomes of the dependent variable were explained in terms of other, independent variables. For instance, in the regression model the explained part of y_t is given by $x_t'b$, where $b = (X'X)^{-1}X'y$, which involves the correlations between the dependent and the independent variables. In a univariate time series model, it is the correlation with lagged values of the explained variable that is of interest.

Time series prediction and the innovation process

To describe the correlations, we imagine that our observed time series comes from a stationary process that existed before we started observing it. For instance, in Examples 7.1 and 7.2 we use data on US industrial production from 1961 to 1994 and on the Dow-Jones from 1980 to 1999, but both processes existed before the start of our observations. We denote the past of the stationary process y_t by $Y_{t-1} = \{y_{t-1}, y_{t-2}, \cdots\}$, where the 'dots' mean that there is no clear-cut beginning of this past. Here Y_{t-1} is called the information set available at time point $(t-1)$. The least squares predictor of y_t based on the past Y_{t-1} is the function $f(Y_{t-1})$ that minimizes $E[(y_t - f(Y_{t-1}))^2]$. This predictor is given by the conditional mean $f(Y_{t-1}) = E[y_t|Y_{t-1}]$ with corresponding (one-step-ahead) *prediction errors*

$$\varepsilon_t = y_t - f(Y_{t-1}) = y_t - E[y_t|Y_{t-1}]. \tag{7.1}$$

The process ε_t is also called the *innovation process*, as it corresponds to the unpredictable movements in y_t. If the observations are jointly normally distributed, then the conditional mean is a linear function of the past observations — say,

$$E[y_t|Y_{t-1}] = \alpha + \pi_1 y_{t-1} + \pi_2 y_{t-2} + \cdots.$$

Here α is included to model the mean $E[y_t] = \mu$ of the series. From the above equation we get $\mu = \alpha + \sum \pi_k \mu$, so that $\mu = (1 - \sum \pi_k)^{-1}\alpha$. As the process is assumed to be stationary, the coefficients π_k do not depend on time and the innovation process ε_t is also stationary. It has the following properties (see Exercise 7.1):

$$\begin{aligned} E[\varepsilon_t] &= 0 && \text{for all } t, \\ E[\varepsilon_t^2] &= \sigma^2 && \text{for all } t, \\ E[\varepsilon_s \varepsilon_t] &= 0 && \text{for all } s \neq t. \end{aligned}$$

Here the variance σ^2 is constant over time. Such a process, with all autocorrelations equal to zero, is called *white noise*. It has all the properties (zero mean, homoskedastic, uncorrelated) of the disturbance term in the standard regression model.

Autoregressive model for stationary time series

We can rewrite (7.1) as

$$y_t = \alpha + \pi_1 y_{t-1} + \pi_2 y_{t-2} + \cdots + \varepsilon_t. \tag{7.2}$$

This can be interpreted as a regression model with disturbance terms that satisfy the standard assumptions of the regression model — that is, Assumptions 2, 3, and 4 of Section 3.1.4 (p. 125). The above model is called an autoregressive model. The regressors consist of time lags of the dependent variable and are therefore stochastic. The regressors in this model are exogenous, because, for all $k \geq 1$, y_{t-k} belongs to the information set Y_{t-1}, so that

$$\begin{aligned} \operatorname{cov}(y_{t-k}, \varepsilon_t) &= E[(y_{t-k} - \mu)(y_t - E[y_t|Y_{t-1}])] \\ &= E[(y_{t-k} - \mu)y_t] - E[E[(y_{t-k} - \mu)y_t|Y_{t-1}]] \\ &= E[(y_{t-k} - \mu)y_t] - E[(y_{t-k} - \mu)y_t] = 0. \end{aligned}$$

General idea of estimation of time series models

The model (7.2) has many parameters, in principle as many as the number of periods since the beginning of the process. In practice the data generating process is unknown and the data consist of observations y_t on a limited time interval $t = 1, \cdots, n$. To estimate a time series model, the model (7.2) should be approximated by models with fewer parameters. That is, the unknown optimal prediction function $f(Y_{t-1})$ has to be approximated by a model of our choice. We denote the model by $f(Y_{t-1}, \theta)$, where f is a specified function containing a limited number of unknown parameters θ. In Sections 7.1.3 and 7.1.4 we discuss models that are often used for this purpose—namely, ARMA models. The parameters θ of the model can be estimated, for instance, by minimizing the sum of squared prediction errors

$$S(\theta) = \sum_{t=1}^{n} \left(y_t - f(Y_{t-1}, \theta)\right)^2.$$

If the model is properly specified in the sense that $f(Y_{t-1}, \hat{\theta}) \approx E[y_t|Y_{t-1}]$, then the prediction errors will be close to the innovations ε_t. This can be used as a basis for diagnostic testing, by testing whether the model residuals are uncorrelated and have constant variance. Estimation, diagnostic tests, and model selection are discussed in Section 7.2.

☞ Exercises: T: 7.1a.

7.1.3 Autoregressive models

Autoregressive process of order p: AR(p)

A simple model for a time series y_t is obtained by choosing a specific finite length of the autoregression (7.2). If p past values are included in the regression, this gives the model

$$y_t = \alpha + \phi_1 y_{t-1} + \phi_2 y_{t-2} + \cdots + \phi_p y_{t-p} + \varepsilon_t, \quad t = p+1, 2, \cdots, n. \quad (7.3)$$

Here α and ϕ_1 to ϕ_p are unknown parameters. The process ε_t is white noise with the property that $E[\varepsilon_t y_{t-k}] = 0$ for all $k \geq 1$. So the regressors y_{t-k} in (7.3) are exogenous, $k = 1, \cdots, p$. As the time series y_t is observed for $t = 1, \cdots, n$, the lagged explanatory variable y_{t-p} is available only from time $t = p + 1$ onwards. This model is called an *autoregressive model* of order p, also written as AR(p).

The lag operator

For ease of notation one uses the *lag operator* L defined by

$$Ly_t = y_{t-1}.$$

Repetitive application of this operator gives $L^k y_t = y_{t-k}$. The AR(p) model can then be written in a more concise form as

$$\phi(L)y_t = \alpha + \varepsilon_t, \quad \phi(L) = 1 - \phi_1 L - \cdots - \phi_p L^p. \quad (7.4)$$

Stationarity condition

The statistical properties of the process (7.4) are determined by the values of the parameters $\phi_1, \cdots, \phi_p$. For instance, the condition for stationarity can be expressed in terms of the roots of the polynomial $\phi(z)$ by factorizing this polynomial in terms of its p (possibly complex valued) roots $z = 1/\alpha_i$ as

$$\phi(z) = (1 - \alpha_1 z)(1 - \alpha_2 z) \cdots (1 - \alpha_p z). \quad (7.5)$$

The process is *stationary* if and only if $|\alpha_k| < 1$ for all $k = 1, \cdots, p$—that is, all the solutions of $\phi(z) = 0$ should lie outside the unit circle in the complex plane. Here we will clarify this in more detail for the case of an AR(1) model; the general AR(p) model is left as an exercise (see Exercise 7.1).

Derivation of stationarity condition for an AR(1) process

We consider the first order autoregressive model

$$y_t = \phi y_{t-1} + \varepsilon_t, \quad t = 2, \cdots, n. \quad (7.6)$$

Here ε_t is the innovation process and for simplicity of notation we write ϕ for the parameter ϕ_1 and we assume that $\alpha = 0$. By recursive substitution of the lagged values of y_t this can be rewritten as

$$y_t = \phi^{t-1} y_1 + \sum_{j=0}^{t-2} \phi^j \varepsilon_{t-j}, \quad t = 2, \cdots, n. \tag{7.7}$$

An innovation at time $t - j$ therefore affects the value of y_t with multiplier ϕ^j. If $|\phi| > 1$, then the impact of the innovations grows over time and the time series displays explosive behaviour, whereas for $|\phi| < 1$ the impact dies out over time. We will now show that the AR(1) process is stationary if and only if $|\phi| < 1$.

First we suppose that the process y_t is stationary with mean μ and variance γ_0, and we will prove that $|\phi| < 1$. Recall that ε_t has mean zero and variance σ^2, that ε_t is uncorrelated with y_{t-1}, and that $\gamma_0 = E[(y_t - \mu)^2] = E[y_t^2] - \mu^2$. It then follows from (7.6) and (7.7) that

$$\mu = E[y_t] = \phi^{t-1}\mu,$$
$$\gamma_0 + \mu^2 = E[y_t^2] = \phi^2 E[y_{t-1}^2] + \sigma^2 = \phi^2(\gamma_0 + \mu^2) + \sigma^2.$$

The first equality implies that $\mu = 0$ or $\phi = 1$, but in the last case the second equality has no finite solution for γ_0 (because $\sigma^2 > 0$). So we conclude that $\phi \neq 1$ and $\mu = 0$. Then the second equality becomes $\gamma_0 = \phi^2\gamma_0 + \sigma^2$ or $\phi^2 = (\gamma_0 - \sigma^2)/\gamma_0$, so that $|\phi| < 1$. This shows that for a stationary process $|\phi| < 1$.

Now we prove the reverse—that is, if $|\phi| < 1$, then (7.6) has a solution process y_t that is stationary. We prove this by constructing the process y_t. Let y_1 be a random variable with mean zero and variance $\sigma^2/(1 - \phi^2)$ and let ε_t be IID$(0, \sigma^2)$ for $t \geq 2$ and independent from y_1. Further let y_t for $t \geq 2$ be defined by (7.7). Then it follows that $E[y_t] = 0$ for all $t \geq 1$, so that the mean $\mu = 0$ is constant over time. It remains to prove that the variance and covariances of this process are constant over time. Using the fact that $E[\varepsilon_s \varepsilon_t] = 0$ for all $s \neq t$, that $E[y_1 \varepsilon_t] = 0$ for all $t \geq 2$, and that for $|\phi| < 1$ there holds $\sum_{h=0}^{\infty} \phi^{2h} = 1/(1 - \phi^2)$, we obtain from (7.7) that for $0 \leq k \leq t - 1$

$$\begin{aligned}
E[y_t y_{t-k}] &= E\left[\left(\phi^{t-1} y_1 + \sum_{j=0}^{t-2} \phi^j \varepsilon_{t-j}\right)\left(\phi^{t-k-1} y_1 + \sum_{h=0}^{t-k-2} \phi^h \varepsilon_{t-k-h}\right)\right] \\
&= \phi^{2t-k-2}\mathrm{var}(y_1) + \sigma^2 \sum_{h=0}^{t-k-2} \phi^{k+2h} \\
&= \sigma^2 \frac{\phi^{2t-k-2}}{1 - \phi^2} + \sigma^2\phi^k \left(\sum_{h=0}^{\infty} \phi^{2h} - \sum_{h=t-k-1}^{\infty} \phi^{2h}\right) \\
&= \sigma^2 \frac{\phi^{2t-k-2}}{1 - \phi^2} + \sigma^2\phi^k \frac{1 - \phi^{2(t-k-1)}}{1 - \phi^2} = \sigma^2 \frac{\phi^k}{1 - \phi^2}.
\end{aligned}$$

This shows that the variance of y_t (obtained for $k = 0$) is constant over time and that the covariance between y_t and y_{t-k} does not depend on time t. This means that the AR(1) process is stationary for $|\phi| < 1$, which concludes the proof.

Variance and autocorrelations of an AR(1) process

The above derivation shows that the variance of a stationary AR(1) process (with $|\phi| < 1$) is equal to

$$\gamma_0 = \frac{\sigma^2}{1-\phi^2}.$$

The autocorrelations are given by

$$\rho_k = \frac{\gamma_k}{\gamma_0} = \phi^k.$$

The correlations tend exponentially to zero for $k \to \infty$ with a speed that depends on ϕ. If this coefficient is very close to one, then the correlations die out only very slowly. For $\phi = 1$ the process y_t is no longer stationary, it does not have a finite variance, and it has trending behaviour, as will be further discussed in Section 7.3.

Mean of an AR(p) process

The constant term α in (7.3) is included to allow for a non-zero mean of the time series. Note, however, that this parameter is not equal to the mean $\mu = E[y_t]$ of the process. By taking expected values in (7.3) it follows that $(1 - \sum_{k=1}^{p} \phi_k)\mu = \alpha$, or $\mu = \alpha/(1 - \sum_{k=1}^{p} \phi_k)$. This can also be written as

$$\mu = E[y_t] = \alpha/\phi(1),$$

where $\phi(1) = 1 - \sum_{k=1}^{p} \phi_k$ is the value obtained by evaluating the polynomial $\phi(z)$ of (7.4) at $z = 1$. If $\phi(1) = 0$—that is, if the polynomial $\phi(z)$ of the AR(p) model has a root at $z = 1$ (called a unit root)—then the mean of the process is not defined. This is in line with the fact that the process is not stationary in this case.

Example 7.3: **Simulated AR Time Series**

E

As an illustration we consider three simulated time series. The series are generated respectively by the white noise process $y_t = \varepsilon_t$, by the stationary AR(1) process $y_t = 0.9y_{t-1} + \varepsilon_t$, and by the stationary AR(2) process $y_t = 1.5y_{t-1} - 0.6y_{t-2} + \varepsilon_t$. Exhibit 7.3 shows time plots of the three simulated time series. The white noise process is uncorrelated, whereas the AR(1) process is strongly correlated over time with $\rho_k = (0.9)^k$, $k \geq 0$.

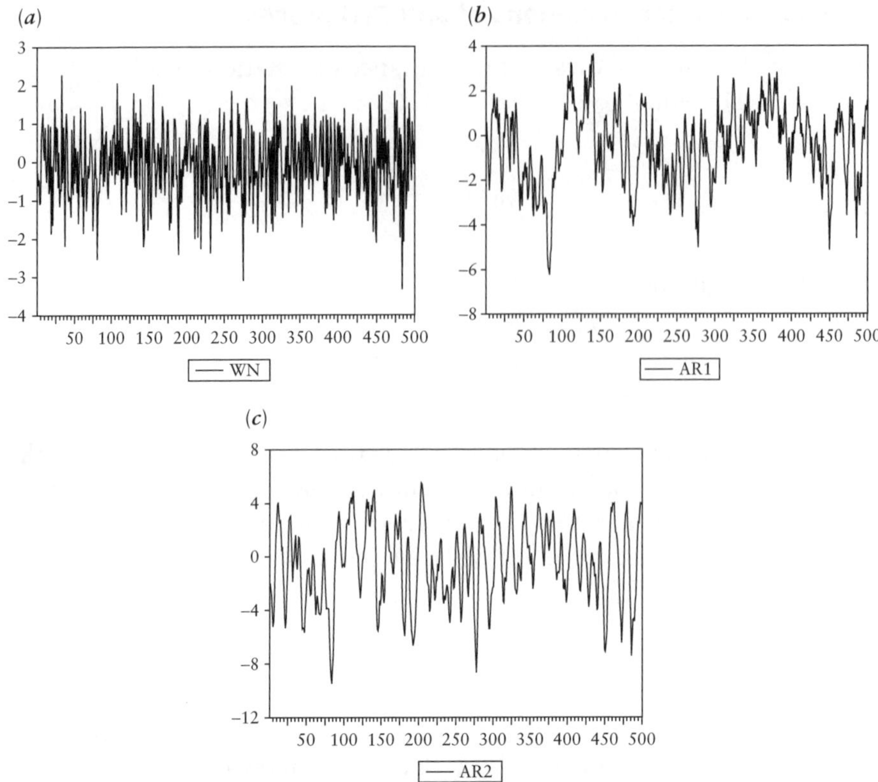

Exhibit 7.3 Simulated AR Time Series (Example 7.3)

Simulated time series, white noise (*a*), AR(1) process (*b*), and AR(2) process (*c*).

The AR(2) process shows more or less steady oscillations. This is related to the fact that the corresponding polynomial $\phi(z) = 1 - 1.5z + 0.6z^2$ has complex roots $z = 1.25 \pm 0.32i$ (where i is the complex number defined by $i = \sqrt{-1}$).

☞ Exercises: T: 7.1b.

7.1.4 ARMA models

Moving average process of order *q*: MA(*q*)

A process y_t is called a *moving average* process if it can be described by

$$y_t = \alpha + \varepsilon_t + \theta_1 \varepsilon_{t-1} + \cdots + \theta_q \varepsilon_{t-q}, \tag{7.8}$$

where ε_t is white noise. This is called an MA(q) process. This process is always stationary, with mean $\mu = E[y_t] = \alpha$, variance $\gamma_0 = \sigma^2(1 + \sum_{j=1}^{q} \theta_j^2)$, and covariances $\gamma_k = \sigma^2(\theta_k + \sum_{j=k+1}^{q} \theta_j \theta_{j-k})$ for $k \leq q$ and $\gamma_k = 0$ for $k > q$.

Invertibility condition

In an MA model, the observed series y_t is expressed in terms of current and past values of the error terms ε_t. In a sense, this is the inverse of the autoregressive model (7.2), where ε_t is expressed in terms of current and past values of y_t. If an MA model can be expressed as an (infinite order) autoregressive model (7.2), then the MA model is called *invertible*. In this case the error terms ε_t in (7.8) are equal to the innovations (or one-step-ahead prediction errors) $\varepsilon_t = y_t - E[y_t|Y_{t-1}]$, so that

$$E[y_t|Y_{t-1}] = \alpha + \theta_1 \varepsilon_{t-1} + \cdots + \theta_q \varepsilon_{t-q}.$$

Invertibility requires some restrictions on the parameters in (7.8). If the MA polynomial is factorized as $\theta(z) = (1 - \beta_1 z)(1 - \beta_2 z) \cdots (1 - \beta_q z)$, then invertibility is equivalent to the condition that $|\beta_j| < 1$ for all $j = 1, 2, \cdots, q$. Stated otherwise, all the solutions of $\theta(z) = 0$ should lie outside the unit circle. Here we will explain this condition in more detail for the MA(1) model; the general case (with $q \geq 2$) is left as an exercise (see Exercise 7.1).

Derivation of invertibility condition for MA(1) process

T

We consider the MA(1) model with mean $\alpha = 0$ described by

$$y_t = \varepsilon_t + \theta \varepsilon_{t-1}.$$

Invertibility requires that ε_t can be written in terms of current and past values of the observed process—that is, in terms of y_{t-k} with $k \geq 0$. Now $\varepsilon_t = y_t - \theta \varepsilon_{t-1}$, and similarly $\varepsilon_{t-1} = y_{t-1} - \theta \varepsilon_{t-2}$, and by further substitutions it follows that

$$\varepsilon_t = y_t - \theta y_{t-1} + \theta^2 y_{t-2} - \cdots + (-\theta)^{t-2} y_2 + (-\theta)^{t-1} \varepsilon_1. \qquad (7.9)$$

Assuming that the process was the same before the observations started (that is, for $t \leq 0$), this substitution can be continued. Invertibility requires that, in the limit, the error term on the right-hand side vanishes. This is the case if and only if $-1 < \theta < 1$. Under this condition the process is therefore invertible.

Autoregressive moving average process: ARMA(*p*, *q*)

Every stationary process can be approximated with any desired degree of accuracy by means of autoregressive models (by taking the order p of the AR(p) model large enough) and also by means of moving average models (by taking the order q of the MA(q) model large enough). However, good approximations may require very large orders and hence many parameters. It may then be more convenient to describe the process y_t by the ratio of two polynomials of relatively low order as $y_t = \frac{\theta(L)}{\phi(L)}\varepsilon_t$. The resulting model is written as

$$\phi(L)y_t = \alpha + \theta(L)\varepsilon_t, \tag{7.10}$$

with AR polynomial $\phi(L) = 1 - \phi_1 L - \cdots - \phi_p L^p$, MA polynomial $\theta(L) = 1 + \theta_1 L + \cdots + \theta_q L^q$, and where ε_t is white noise. The above model is called an *autoregressive moving average* model of order (p, q), also written as ARMA(p, q). The constant term α is included to allow for a non-zero mean $\mu = E[y_t] = \alpha/\phi(1)$. An ARMA process is stationary if all the solutions of $\phi(z) = 0$ lie outside the unit circle, just as in the case of AR processes. An ARMA model is invertible if all the solutions of $\theta(z) = 0$ lie outside the unit circle, just as in the case of MA processes.

In many cases, low order ARMA models provide an accurate approximation of much higher order AR and MA models. That is, ARMA models need relatively few parameters to describe the process, so that ARMA models are parsimonious in this sense.

Example 7.4: **Simulated MA and ARMA Time Series**

As an illustration we simulate three time series—namely, from the MA(1) model $y_t = \varepsilon_t + 0.9\varepsilon_{t-1}$, from the MA(2) model $y_t = \varepsilon_t + 0.9\varepsilon_{t-1} + 0.8\varepsilon_{t-2}$, and from the ARMA(1,1) model $y_t = 0.9y_{t-1} + \varepsilon_t + 0.8\varepsilon_{t-1}$. All three processes are stationary and invertible. Exhibit 7.4 contains graphs of the three simulated series. Comparing the graphs in Exhibit 7.4 with those in Exhibit 7.3, we see that it may not be easy to determine the appropriate ARMA model from a time series plot. The next section discusses a tool to select the orders of AR and MA models.

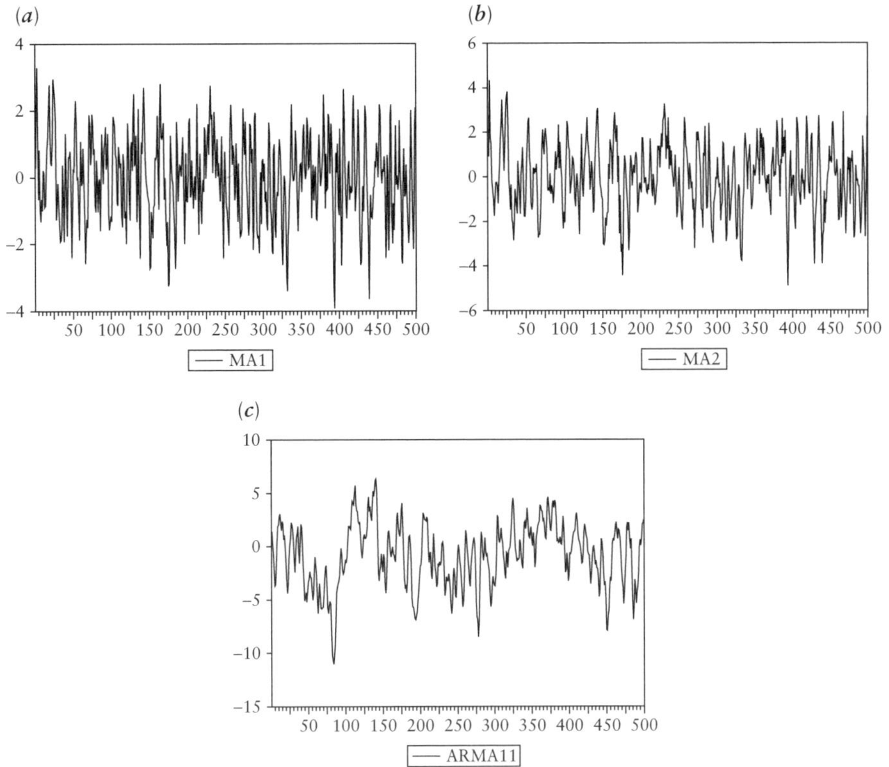

Exhibit 7.4 Simulated MA and ARMA Time Series (Example 7.4)

Simulated time series, MA(1) process (*a*), MA(2) process (*b*), and ARMA(1,1) process (*c*).

☞ Exercises: T: 7.1c.

7.1.5 Autocorrelations and partial autocorrelations

Autocorrelation function

As mentioned before, the correlations between successive values of a time series are of key interest in forecasting the future movements of the series.

Therefore it is of interest to get insight in the correlations that are implied by an ARMA model. The correlations have a direct meaning in terms of time series properties, whereas the parameters in the ARMA model have only a less direct interpretation. The *autocorrelation function* (ACF) of a time series model is defined by the sequence of autocorrelations (for k ranging from $-\infty$ to $+\infty$)

$$\rho_k = \operatorname{corr}(y_t, y_{t-k}) = \frac{\gamma_k}{\gamma_0},$$

where $\gamma_k = E[(y_t - \mu)(y_{t-k} - \mu)]$. There holds $\gamma_k = \gamma_{-k}$ and hence also $\rho_k = \rho_{-k}$, and $\rho_0 = 1$ always. So it suffices to consider the ACF only for $k \geq 1$.

Derivation of autocorrelations of an ARMA process

A white noise process ε_t is characterized by the property that $\rho_k = 0$ for all $k \geq 1$. Now we consider the ACF of an ARMA model (7.10) that is stationary and invertible, so that the roots of the polynomials $\phi(z) = 0$ and $\theta(z) = 0$ all lie outside the unit circle. The stationarity condition on $\phi(z)$ implies that y_t can be written as a linear function of ε_{t-k}, $k \geq 0$—say,

$$y_t = \mu + \varepsilon_t + \psi_1 \varepsilon_{t-1} + \psi_2 \varepsilon_{t-2} + \psi_3 \varepsilon_{t-3} + \cdots. \tag{7.11}$$

This can be written as $y_t = \mu + \psi(L)\varepsilon_t$ where $\psi(z) = \sum \psi_k z^k$ with $\psi_0 = 1$. As y_t also satisfies the ARMA model equation $\phi(L)y_t = \alpha + \theta(L)\varepsilon_t$, it follows that $\alpha + \theta(L)\varepsilon_t = \phi(L)y_t = \phi(1)\mu + \phi(L)\psi(L)\varepsilon_t$, where we used the fact that $\phi(L)\mu = (1 - \sum \phi_k L^k)\mu = (1 - \sum \phi_k)\mu = \phi(1)\mu$. It follows that $\mu = \alpha/\phi(1)$ and

$$\phi(z)\psi(z) = \theta(z).$$

So the coefficients ψ_k in (7.11) can be obtained from the parameters $(\phi_1, \cdots, \phi_p, \theta_1, \cdots, \theta_q)$ of the ARMA model by solving the equations $\phi(z)\psi(z) = \theta(z)$ (for all powers z^k, $k \geq 0$). Once the values of ψ_k are determined, the ACF can be computed by

$$\gamma_k = E[(y_t - \mu)(y_{t-k} - \mu)] = E\left[\sum_{j=0}^{\infty} \psi_j \varepsilon_{t-j} \sum_{h=0}^{\infty} \psi_h \varepsilon_{t-k-h}\right] = \sigma^2 \sum_{h=0}^{\infty} \psi_{k+h}\psi_h.$$

Here we used the fact that ε_t is white noise, so that $E[\varepsilon_{t-j}\varepsilon_{t-k-h}] = 0$ for all $j \neq k + h$.

Autocorrelations of AR(1) and MA(1) process

As an illustration, for the AR(1) model (7.6) with $y_t = \phi y_{t-1} + \varepsilon_t$ we have $\phi(z) = 1 - \phi z$ and $\theta(z) = 1$. Then the equation for $\psi(z)$ becomes $(1 - \phi z)\psi(z) = 1$, so that $\psi(z) = 1/(1 - \phi z) = \sum \phi^k z^k$ and $\psi_k = \phi^k$. It then follows that $\gamma_k = \sigma^2 \sum \psi_k^2 = \sigma^2 \phi^k/(1 - \phi^2)$ and $\rho_k = \phi^k$. This agrees with earlier results in Section 7.1.3 for the AR(1) process.

As another illustration, for the MA(1) model $y_t = \varepsilon_t + \theta\varepsilon_{t-1}$ we have $\phi(z) = 1$ and $\theta(z) = 1 + \theta z$. Then the equation for $\psi(z)$ simply becomes $\psi(z) = 1 + \theta z$. So the coefficients are directly obtained as $\psi_0 = 1$, $\psi_1 = \theta$, and $\psi_k = 0$ for all $k \geq 2$. So $\gamma_0 = \sigma^2(1 + \theta^2)$, $\gamma_1 = \sigma^2\theta$, and $\gamma_k = 0$ for $k \geq 2$. The autocorrelations are $\rho_1 = \theta/(1 + \theta^2)$ and $\rho_k = 0$ for all $k \geq 2$. This agrees with earlier results in Section 7.1.4 for MA processes.

Further cases are treated in the exercises (see Exercise 7.2).

Characterization of MA processes in terms of autocorrelations

In the MA(q) process (7.8) the terms ε_t are uncorrelated. This implies that the ACF has the property

$$\rho_k = 0 \quad \text{for all } k > q \quad (MA(q)).$$

That is, the ACF of an MA(q) process cuts off after lag q. The reverse also holds true—that is, if the ACF of a process has the property that $\rho_k = 0$ for all $k > q$, then it can be written as an MA(q) process (see Exercise 7.3). Therefore the ACF can be used to select the order of an MA model. If the ACF of a process is zero for $k > q$, then it can be described by an MA(q) model.

Characterization of AR processes in terms of partial autocorrelations

For AR processes the ACF decays to zero exponentially, but the order of the model cannot easily be detected from the ACF. The order of AR models can be selected by considering the so-called *partial autocorrelation function* (PACF). The partial autocorrelation at lag k, denoted by ϕ_{kk}, is defined as the correlation between y_t and y_{t-k} that remains after the correlation due to the intermediate values y_{t-j} $(1 \leq j \leq k-1)$ has been removed. Formally, let $y_t^- = y_t - E[y_t|y_{t-1}, \cdots, y_{t-k+1}]$ and $y_{t-k}^+ = y_{t-k} - E[y_{t-k}|y_{t-1}, \cdots, y_{t-k+1}]$ be the 'residuals' of predicting y_t and y_{t-k} from the intermediate values $\{y_{t-1}, \cdots, y_{t-k+1}\}$; then the *partial autocorrelation* $\phi_{kk} = \text{corr}\,(y_t^-, y_{t-k}^+)$ is the correlation between these two residuals. The two involved conditional expectations are obtained by regressing y_t and y_{t-k} on the set of intermediate values. It follows from the result of Frisch–Waugh in Section 3.2.5 (p. 146) that ϕ_{kk} can also be obtained from the regression

$$y_t = \alpha + \phi_{k1}y_{t-1} + \phi_{k2}y_{t-2} + \cdots + \phi_{kk}y_{t-k} + \omega_t \tag{7.12}$$

(see Exercise 7.3). So ϕ_{kk} is obtained by an autoregression of lag length k—that is, for each partial autocorrelation we need a different regression. An AR(p) process is characterized by the following property (see Exercise 7.3).

$$\phi_{kk} = 0 \quad \text{for all } k > p \quad (AR(p)).$$

That is, the PACF of an AR(p) process cuts off after lag p. The intuitive explanation is that, for the AR(p) process (7.3), y_t is expressed in terms of $y_{t-1}, \cdots, y_{t-p}$, so that additional lagged regressors y_{t-k} with $k > p$ in (7.12) have coefficient zero.

Sample (partial) autocorrelations

In practice the (partial) autocorrelations are unknown and have to be estimated from the observed time series. The so-called sample autocorrelation function (SACF) is obtained by replacing ρ_k by the sample correlations

$$r_k = \frac{\sum_{t=k+1}^{n} (y_t - \overline{y})(y_{t-k} - \overline{y})}{\sum_{t=1}^{n} (y_t - \overline{y})^2},$$

where $\overline{y} = \sum_{t=1}^{n} y_t/n$ is the sample mean of the series. The sample partial autocorrelation function (SPACF) is obtained by replacing ϕ_{kk} by the estimated coefficient $\hat{\phi}_{kk}$ of y_{t-k} in the regression (7.12). Note that this involves a different model for each coefficient—that is, $\hat{\phi}_{kk}$ is obtained by a regression in an AR(k) model.

E

Example 7.5: **Simulated Time Series (continued)**

As an illustration, we consider the six simulated time series that were generated in Example 7.3 (see Exhibit 7.3) and Example 7.4 (see Exhibit 7.4). Panels 1 and 2 of Exhibit 7.5 show the SACF and the SPACF of these six series. For the white noise series, the theoretical ACF and PACF are both zero, and the SACF and SPACF are relatively small. Statistical tests for the significance of sample (partial) autocorrelations are discussed in Sections 7.2.3 and 7.2.4. For the two generated AR series, the SPACF is small for lags $k > 1$ for the AR(1) process and for lags $k > 2$ for the AR(2) process. For the two generated MA series, the SACF is small for lags $k > 1$ for the MA(1) process and for lags $k > 2$ for the MA(2) process. For the ARMA(1,1) process

Panel 1	WN		AR(1)		AR(2)	
Lag	SACF	SPACF	SACF	SPACF	SACF	SPACF
1	−0.010	−0.010	0.833	0.833	0.907	0.907
2	0.008	0.008	0.681	−0.045	0.713	−0.618
3	−0.114	−0.114	0.534	−0.072	0.481	−0.049
4	−0.074	−0.077	0.433	0.059	0.262	0.045
5	−0.034	−0.035	0.365	0.043	0.080	−0.056
6	0.038	0.026	0.312	−0.001	−0.060	−0.064
7	−0.087	−0.105	0.247	−0.062	−0.158	−0.017
8	−0.076	−0.096	0.215	0.076	−0.206	0.083
9	0.018	0.018	0.213	0.092	−0.211	−0.023
10	−0.001	−0.018	0.206	−0.022	−0.193	−0.081

Panel 2	MA(1)		MA(2)		ARMA(1,1)	
Lag	SACF	SPACF	SACF	SPACF	SACF	SPACF
1	0.543	0.543	0.688	0.688	0.911	0.911
2	0.050	−0.347	0.353	−0.229	0.742	−0.513
3	0.002	0.248	0.014	−0.254	0.593	0.295
4	−0.025	−0.231	−0.017	0.325	0.480	−0.116
5	−0.037	0.162	−0.020	−0.118	0.401	0.126
6	0.018	−0.069	−0.012	−0.138	0.336	−0.137
7	0.009	0.012	−0.026	0.152	0.278	0.101
8	−0.075	−0.117	−0.074	−0.160	0.244	0.068
9	−0.080	0.064	−0.086	−0.017	0.233	0.023
10	−0.050	−0.094	−0.103	0.039	0.228	−0.021

Panel 3: Dependent Variable: AR1
Method: Least Squares
Sample(adjusted): 2 500; Included observations: 499

Variable	Coefficient	Std. Error	t-Statistic	Prob.
C	−0.077447	0.044504	−1.740224	0.0824
AR1(−1)	0.835782	0.024710	33.82336	0.0000

Panel 4: Dependent Variable: AR1
Method: Least Squares
Sample(adjusted): 3 500; Included observations: 498

Variable	Coefficient	Std. Error	t-Statistic	Prob.
C	−0.080056	0.044741	−1.789344	0.0742
AR1(−1)	0.874953	0.044910	19.48236	0.0000
AR1(−2)	−0.046516	0.044931	−1.035273	0.3010

Exhibit 7.5 Simulated Time Series (Example 7.5)

First ten sample autocorrelations (SACF) and partial autocorrelations (SPACF) of time series of length $n = 500$ simulated from a white noise process (WN), an AR(1) process, and an AR(2) process (Panel 1) and from an MA(1) process, an MA(2) process, and an ARMA(1,1) process (Panel 2). The regressions in Panels 3 and 4 illustrate the computation of the first SPACF (Panel 3, value 0.836) and second SPACF (Panel 4, value −0.047) of the series AR1 (the reported numbers in Panel 1 are 0.833 and −0.045, as EViews uses a slightly different method to compute the SPACF).

the SACF and SPACF decay relatively slowly. Panels 3 and 4 of Exhibit 7.5 contain two regressions to illustrate the calculation of the SPACF for the AR(1) time series. The first sample partial autocorrelation $\hat{\phi}_{11} = 0.836$ is obtained by regressing y_t on a constant and y_{t-1}, and the second one $\hat{\phi}_{22} = -0.047$ by regressing y_t on a constant, y_{t-1} and y_{t-2}. Clearly, the variable y_{t-2} in the last regression is not significant, as expected.

Exercises: T: 7.2b, c, 7.3a–c.

7.1.6 Forecasting

One-step-ahead and multi-step-ahead forecasts

In this section we describe general methods to forecast future values of an ARMA process by exploiting the correlation structure of the process. We assume that the process is known, in the sense that all the parameters are known and hence the correlations of the process are also known. We suppose that the time series is observed on the time interval $t = 1, \cdots, n$ so that the available information is given by $Y_n = \{y_1, \cdots, y_n\}$. The (least squares) one-step-ahead forecast $\hat{y}_{n+1} = f(Y_n)$ is given by $f(Y_n) = E[y_{n+1}|Y_n]$, and the h-step-ahead forecast is $\hat{y}_{n+h} = E[y_{n+h}|Y_n]$. We will restrict the attention to linear forecasts—that is, to functions $f(Y_n)$ that are linear in the observations y_t, $t = 1, \cdots, n$.

Forecasting an AR process

First we consider forecasting in the stationary AR(p) model (7.3) with $y_t = \alpha + \phi_1 y_{t-1} + \cdots + \phi_p y_{t-p} + \varepsilon_t$. The stationarity condition on the AR polynomial implies that y_t is a function of the past innovations (ε_{t-k}, $k \geq 0$), as in (7.11). For y_{n+1} this means that ε_{n+1} is uncorrelated with all observations in Y_n, so that the optimal one-step-ahead forecast is given by

$$\hat{y}_{n+1} = \alpha + \phi_1 y_n + \cdots + \phi_p y_{n+1-p}.$$

The corresponding forecast error is $y_{n+1} - \hat{y}_{n+1} = \varepsilon_{n+1}$ and the forecast error variance is σ^2. In a similar way, the two-step-ahead forecast is given by

$$\hat{y}_{n+2} = \alpha + \phi_1 \hat{y}_{n+1} + \phi_2 y_n + \cdots + \phi_p y_{n+2-p}.$$

The corresponding forecast error is $y_{n+2} - \hat{y}_{n+2} = \varepsilon_{n+2} + \phi_1(y_{n+1} - \hat{y}_{n+1}) = \varepsilon_{n+2} + \phi_1 \varepsilon_{n+1}$ with variance $\sigma^2(1 + \phi_1^2)$. Forecasts for three and more steps ahead can be constructed in a similar way (see Exercise 7.4).

Forecasting an ARMA process

For a stationary and invertible ARMA model $\phi(L)y_t = \alpha + \theta(L)\varepsilon_t$, the forecasts can in principle be computed from the moving average representation (7.11). The first step is to compute the parameters ψ_k of this representation by solving the equations $\phi(z)\psi(z) = \theta(z)$ (where $\phi(z)$ and $\theta(z)$ are given). Then we can write

$$y_t = \mu + \varepsilon_t + \psi_1\varepsilon_{t-1} + \psi_2\varepsilon_{t-2} + \cdots,$$

with $\mu = \alpha/\phi(1)$ known. As the process is invertible, the innovation process has the property that ε_t is a function of the observations y_{t-k}, $k \geq 0$. Assuming for the moment that the process has been observed since the infinite past, this means that the innovations ε_t are known for all times $t \leq n$. It follows from the above moving average representation that any linear h-step-ahead forecast $\hat{y}_{n+h}$ (that is, any linear function of y_t, $t \leq n$) can be written in the form $\beta + \sum_{k=0}^{\infty} \beta_k \varepsilon_{n-k}$. As the process ε_t is uncorrelated, the mean squared prediction error of such a forecast is equal to

$$E[(y_{n+h} - \hat{y}_{n+h})^2] = (\mu - \beta)^2 + \sigma^2 \left(\sum_{k=0}^{h-1} \psi_k^2 + \sum_{k=h}^{\infty} (\psi_k - \beta_{k-h})^2 \right),$$

where $\psi_0 = 1$. This is minimized by taking $\beta = \mu$ and $\beta_{k-h} = \psi_k$ for all $k \geq h$. So the optimal h-step-ahead forecast is given by

$$\hat{y}_{n+h} = \mu + \psi_h\varepsilon_n + \psi_{h+1}\varepsilon_{n-1} + \psi_{h+2}\varepsilon_{n-2} + \cdots. \tag{7.13}$$

The corresponding h-step-ahead prediction error $(y_{n+h} - \hat{y}_{n+h})$ gives a forecast variance of

$$\text{SPE}(h) = E[(y_{n+h} - \hat{y}_{n+h})^2] = \sigma^2 \sum_{k=0}^{h-1} \psi_k^2.$$

The one-step-ahead prediction error is equal to the innovation ε_{n+1}. Therefore the innovation process is also called the process of prediction errors. The forecast variance increases if the forecast horizon h becomes larger. This is natural, as the past observations contain more information for the immediate future than for the future far ahead. For $h \to \infty$ the forecast variance converges to the variance of the process y_t. That is, in the long run all information from the past eventually dies out. This is because the correlations ρ_k of a stationary process converge to zero for $k \to \infty$, so that the past information is uncorrelated with the infinitely far ahead future. Forecast intervals can be constructed if the process is assumed to be normally distributed. For instance, a 95 per cent forecast interval for y_{n+h} is given by the interval

$$\hat{y}_{n+h} - 1.96\sqrt{\text{SPE}(h)} \leq y_{n+h} \leq \hat{y}_{n+h} + 1.96\sqrt{\text{SPE}(h)}.$$

The forecast intervals are wider for larger horizons h, as the variance SPE(h) increases for larger values of h.

Forecasting an MA process

The above forecasting method becomes particularly simple for an MA(q) model, as $\phi(z) = 1$ in this case, so that $\psi(z) = \theta(z)$ and $\psi_k = \theta_k$ for $k \leq q$ and $\psi_k = 0$ for $k > q$. For example, for an MA(2) model $y_t = \alpha + \theta_1 \varepsilon_{t-1} + \theta_2 \varepsilon_{t-2}$, the one-, two-, and three-step-ahead forecasts are

$$\hat{y}_{n+1} = \alpha + \theta_1 \varepsilon_n + \theta_2 \varepsilon_{n-1}, \quad \hat{y}_{n+2} = \alpha + \theta_2 \varepsilon_n, \quad \hat{y}_{n+3} = \alpha.$$

An MA(2) process contains no information (apart from the mean) on future values for $h > 2$. This is sometimes expressed by saying that an MA(q) process has a memory of length q.

Forecasting in practice

In the foregoing analysis we assumed that the process was observed since the infinite past and that the ARMA parameters are known. In practice we do not know these parameters and the time series is observed only on a finite time interval. In the next section we discuss methods to estimate the ARMA parameters from the observed time series. The forecast function (7.13) can then be approximated as follows. Estimates of the coefficients ψ_k are determined from the estimated ARMA parameters. Further, the infinite sum in (7.13) is replaced by a finite sum $\sum_{k=0}^{n-1} \hat{\psi}_{k+h} \hat{\varepsilon}_{n-k}$, where the terms $\hat{\varepsilon}_t$ are the residuals (the estimated innovations) of the estimated ARMA model.

Example 7.6: **Simulated Time Series (continued)**

As an illustration, we consider forecasts of three simulated time series of foregoing examples—namely, for the AR(2) series of Example 7.3 (see Exhibit 7.3 (c)) and for the MA(2) and ARMA(1,1) series of Example 7.4 (see Exhibit 7.4 (b) and (c)). Exhibit 7.6 shows the forecasts and 95 per cent forecast intervals for estimated models for these three time series. The models are estimated using the first $n = 450$ values using methods to be discussed in Section 7.2.2, and the estimated models are then used to forecast the last fifty values of the series. The outcomes are as expected. The forecasts are more accurate for short forecast horizons h, especially for the MA model, and the forecast intervals become wider for larger forecast horizons. The intervals contain the majority of the actual values in the forecast period.

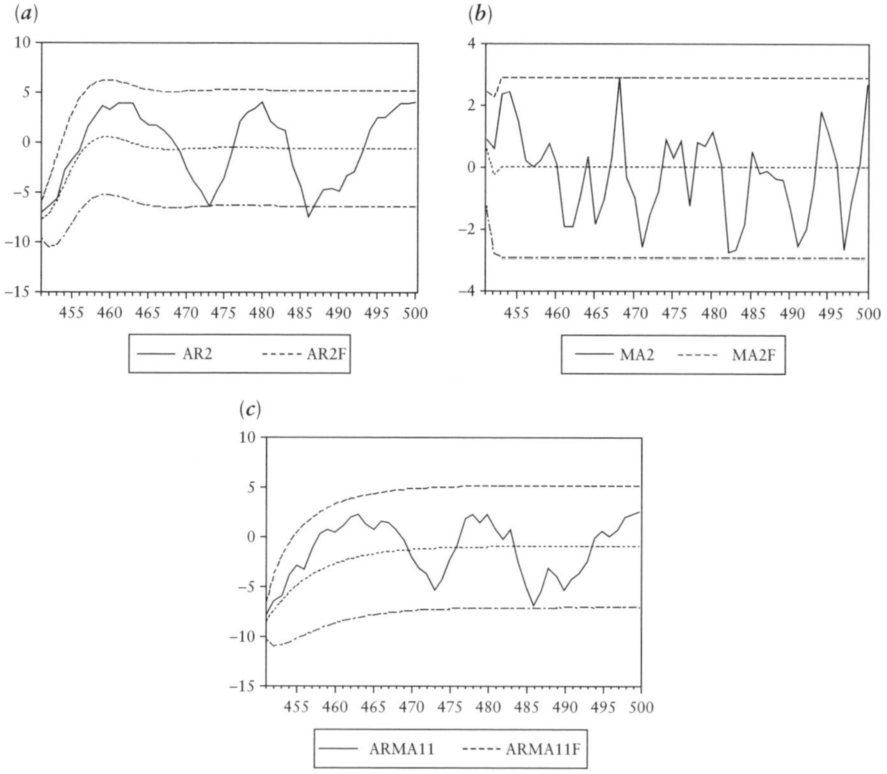

Exhibit 7.6 Simulated Time Series (Example 7.6)

Actual series, forecasts (1- to 50-step-ahead), and 95% forecast intervals for three time series, AR(2) (*a*), MA(2) (*b*), and ARMA(1,1) (*c*).

☞ Exercises: T: 7.4.

7.1.7 Summary

In this section we have discussed some concepts, models, and results that are needed in later sections to construct econometric models for observed time series.

- A time series is stationary if its mean, variance, and autocorrelations are constant over time. Stationary time series can be described by autoregressive models, by moving average models, and by mixed ARMA models.
- Stationarity requires restrictions on the autoregressive parameters (all roots of the autoregressive polynomial should lie outside the unit circle). Invertibility, which means that the error terms in an ARMA model have

the interpretation of one-step-ahead forecast errors, requires restrictions on the moving average parameters (all roots of the moving average polynomial should lie outside the unit circle).

- The properties of stationary time series can be summarized in terms of the autocorrelations of the process. A moving average process has the property that the autocorrelations become zero after a certain lag. An autoregressive process is characterized by the fact that the partial autocorrelations become zero after a certain lag.
- For given parameters of the ARMA model, future values of the time series can be forecasted from past values by exploiting the correlations that are present between successive values in the process.

7.2 Model estimation and selection

☞ Uses Chapters 1–4; Section 5.5; parts of Sections 5.2, 5.3, 5.6; Section 7.1.

7.2.1 The modelling process

Iterative steps in modelling

In empirical time series analysis, a model is often obtained in an iterative process of model specification, diagnostic testing, and model adjustments. This was discussed in Section 5.1 for regression models (see Exhibit 5.1 (p. 276)). Exhibit 7.7 summarizes the main steps in time series modelling. Here we assume that the purpose of the model is to produce forecasts, as is often the case in time series analysis. Further we assume that the investigated time series is stationary. In practice, stationarity is often achieved after appropriate data transformations, as will be discussed in Section 7.3.

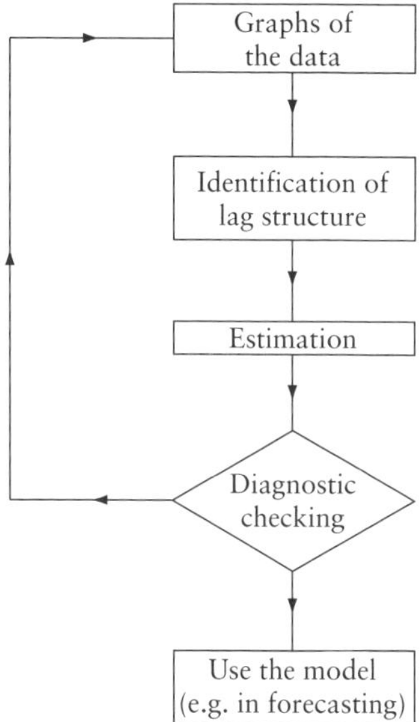

Exhibit 7.7 Steps in modelling

Iterative method of ARMA time series modelling.

Iterative method to model stationary time series

- *Step 1: Graphs of the data.* Make graphs of the time series (time plots, scatter plots against lagged values) and of transformations (like logarithms and first differences). This gives a first impression of the properties of the series — for instance, the presence of trends and cyclical fluctuations. In the next steps it is assumed that the modelled time series is stationary, which sometimes requires appropriate transformations of the original series.
- *Step 2: Choice of lag structure.* Compute the sample autocorrelations and the sample partial autocorrelations to get an impression of the nature of the correlations in the time series. This gives a first indication how to choose the orders p and q of a possibly adequate ARMA(p, q) model.
- *Step 3: Estimation of the model parameters.* For the selected orders p and q, estimate the parameters of the ARMA(p, q) model.
- *Step 4: Diagnostic checking.* Evaluate this model by diagnostic tests. In particular, investigate whether the model captures the main correlations in the time series and whether the model is able to produce reliable forecasts.
- *Step 5: Improve the model.* If the results of step 4 indicate that the model is not satisfactory, then repeat steps 1–4 (graphs of the data, choice of lag structure, estimation, and diagnostic checking). The model can be adjusted along the lines suggested by the outcomes of the diagnostic tests. This may lead to models other than ARMA — for instance, models with trends (see Section 7.3) or non-linear models (see Section 7.4).
- *Step 6: Use the model.* Finally, when the final model performs well enough, it can be used, for instance, to produce out-of-sample forecasts.

Steps 1 and 2 in this process constitute the so-called *model identification* phase. This is an important phase, as the main problem in time series modelling is often to find a good specification of the model. In practice the diagnostic tests in step 4 help to construct a sequence of models where each new model improves upon the former ones.

Overview of Section 7.2

Parts of steps 1 and 2 of the above iterative modelling method were discussed in Section 7.1 (see in particular Section 7.1.5 on the identification of the lags of AR and MA models). Section 7.2.3 describes some additional methods for model identification. In Section 7.2.2 we consider step 3, the estimation of a given ARMA model. Steps 4 and 5, diagnostic tests and their use in model improvement, are discussed in Section 7.2.4. Finally, the forecasting of time series in step 6 has already been treated in Section 7.1.6. In Section 7.2.4 we present diagnostic tools to evaluate the forecast performance of the model on a set of evaluation data, prior to the actual application of the model in forecasting the future.

Example 7.7: Industrial Production (continued)

We return to the series of industrial production in the USA described in Example 7.1. We will discuss (i) step 1 and (ii) step 2 of the above modelling method.

(i) Step 1: graphs of the industrial production data

This first step has already been made in Example 7.1 (see Exhibit 7.1). The original series shows exponential growth. After we have taken logarithms, the resulting series y_t shows a more or less linear growth path with some seasonal fluctuations. A time series that looks more like a stationary series is obtained by considering the quarterly series of yearly growth rates, denoted by $\Delta_4 y_t = y_t - y_{t-4}$. A time plot of this series was given in Exhibit 7.1 (*c*), and the series shows more or less regular fluctuations around a stable mean.

(ii) Step 2: identification of lag structure

To get some idea of the involved correlations in the time series, Exhibit 7.8 shows the first twelve sample autocorrelations and sample partial autocorrelations of this series. The SACF dies out more slowly than the SPACF, and the SPACF values are small from lag three onwards. As a first guess, this suggests specifying an AR(2) model for the series $\Delta_4 y_t$ of growth rates. We will investigate in the rest of this section whether this model gives an acceptable description of this time series (see Examples 7.8, 7.10, and 7.11).

Lag	SACF	SPACF
1	0.851	0.851
2	0.594	−0.466
3	0.319	−0.119
4	0.072	−0.083
5	−0.082	0.117
6	−0.176	−0.134
7	−0.236	−0.104
8	−0.264	−0.030
9	−0.234	0.159
10	−0.182	−0.098
11	−0.152	−0.186
12	−0.121	0.062

Exhibit 7.8 Industrial Production (Example 7.7)

Sample autocorrelations (SACF) and partial autocorrelations (SPACF) of quarterly series of yearly growth rates of US industrial production ($\Delta_4 y_t$).

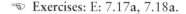

7.2.2 Parameter estimation

OLS estimator of AR(1) model

In this section we discuss the estimation of ARMA(p, q) models with given orders for p and q. For simplicity of the exposition we restrict the attention to processes with zero mean. The results can easily be extended to time series with non-zero mean by including a constant term in the model. First we consider the stationary AR(1) model

$$y_t = \phi y_{t-1} + \varepsilon_t, \quad t = 2, \cdots, n. \tag{7.14}$$

Here $-1 < \phi < 1$, and we assume for simplicity that the innovations ε_t are normally distributed. This model has the form of a regression model, but the regressor y_{t-1} is stochastic. The OLS estimator of ϕ is given by

$$\hat{\phi} = \frac{\sum_{t=2}^{n} y_{t-1} y_t}{\sum_{t=2}^{n} y_{t-1}^2}.$$

Derivation of asymptotic distribution of OLS estimator

As the finite sample distribution of ϕ is rather involved, one usually takes the asymptotic distribution as an approximation in sufficiently large samples. By substituting the expression (7.14) for y_t, it follows that

$$\sqrt{n}(\hat{\phi} - \phi) = \frac{\frac{1}{\sqrt{n}} \sum_{t=2}^{n} y_{t-1} \varepsilon_t}{\frac{1}{n} \sum_{t=2}^{n} y_{t-1}^2}. \tag{7.15}$$

Some details of the next steps are left as an exercise (see Exercise 7.12). The term $\frac{1}{n}\sum_{t=2}^{n} y_{t-1}^2$ in the denominator of (7.15) is the sample mean of the correlated terms y_{t-1}^2. As the correlations $\rho_k = E[y_t y_{t-k}] = \phi^k$ converge to zero exponentially fast, the probability limit of this term exists and $\text{plim}\left(\frac{1}{n}\sum_{t=2}^{n} y_{t-1}^2\right) = E[y_{t-1}^2] = \gamma_0$. Next we consider some properties of the sample average $\frac{1}{n}\sum_{t=2}^{n} y_{t-1}\varepsilon_t$ related to the numerator of (7.15). This is the sample mean of uncorrelated terms, because for $t > s$ the error term ε_t is uncorrelated with y_{t-1}, y_{s-1}, and ε_s, so that $E[y_{t-1}\varepsilon_t y_{s-1}\varepsilon_s] = E[y_{t-1} y_{s-1}\varepsilon_s] E[\varepsilon_t] = 0$. Each term has expected value $E[y_{t-1}\varepsilon_t] = E[y_{t-1}]E[\varepsilon_t] = 0$ and variance $E[y_{t-1}^2 \varepsilon_t^2] = E[y_{t-1}^2]E[\varepsilon_t^2] = \gamma_0\sigma^2$. Then the central limit theorem (see Section 1.3.3 (p. 50)) implies that the numerator of (7.15) has the property that

$$\frac{1}{\sqrt{n}} \sum_{t=2}^{n} y_{t-1}\varepsilon_t = \sqrt{n}\frac{1}{n}\sum_{t=2}^{n} y_{t-1}\varepsilon_t \xrightarrow{d} \text{N}(0, \gamma_0\sigma^2).$$

Combining the above results on the numerator and denominator of (7.15), and using the fact that $\gamma_0 = \sigma^2/(1-\phi^2)$, we conclude that $\sqrt{n}(\hat{\phi} - \phi)$ converges in distribution to a normal distribution with mean zero and variance $\gamma_0\sigma^2/\gamma_0^2 = \sigma^2/\gamma_0 = 1 - \phi^2$. That is,

$$\sqrt{n}(\hat{\phi} - \phi) \xrightarrow{d} \mathrm{N}(0, 1 - \phi^2). \tag{7.16}$$

So the least squares estimator is *consistent* and has an *asymptotic normal* distribution.

Approximate distribution of OLS estimator

It follows from the foregoing results that the approximate finite sample distribution of the OLS estimator $\hat{\phi}$ in the AR(1) model is given by

$$\hat{\phi} \approx \mathrm{N}\left(\phi, \frac{1-\phi^2}{n}\right).$$

The hypothesis that the time series y_t is uncorrelated—that is, that $\phi = 0$—can be tested by the t-test. The correlations are not significant (at an approximate 5 per cent significance level) if $\hat{\phi}$ is less than $2/\sqrt{n}$ in absolute value. Note that for values of $\phi \approx 1$ the asymptotic variance $1 - \phi^2$ approaches zero. This suggests that for $\phi = 1$ the OLS estimator converges at a higher speed than $\sqrt{n}$. This is indeed the case, as will be further discussed in Section 7.3.3.

Estimation of AR(*p*) models

The parameters of a stationary AR(p) model

$$y_t = \phi_1 y_{t-1} + \phi_2 y_{t-2} + \cdots + \phi_p y_{t-p} + \varepsilon_t, \quad t = p+1, \cdots, n$$

can also be estimated by OLS. The stationarity condition means that the model can be written as an infinite moving average as in (7.11). This implies that the error term ε_t is uncorrelated with the $p \times 1$ vector of regressors $x_t = (y_{t-1}, \cdots, y_{t-p})'$. Therefore the orthogonality condition is satisfied—that is, the regressors y_{t-k} in the AR(p) model are exogenous for all $k = 1, \cdots, p$. Further, as the process y_t is stationary, the matrix of second order moments $Q_n = \frac{1}{n}\sum_{t=p+1}^{n} x_t x_t'$ converges in probability to the corresponding matrix Q of population moments that is non-singular (see Exercise 7.3). It follows from the results in Section 4.1.4 (p. 197) that the OLS estimators are consistent and that the covariance matrix can be approximated by $\sigma^2\left(\sum_{t=p+1}^{n} x_t x_t'\right)^{-1}$. Under the assumption of normality, the OLS estimators coincide with the ML estimators (or, better, the conditional ML estimators, treating the initial values $y_1, \cdots, y_p$ as fixed).

Estimation of MA(1) model

The estimation of models with moving average terms is somewhat more involved. To illustrate this we first consider the MA(1) model

$$y_t = \varepsilon_t + \theta\varepsilon_{t-1}$$

with $-1 < \theta < 1$. The parameter θ cannot be estimated by regressing y_t on ε_{t-1}, because the regressor ε_{t-1} is not directly observed. Since $-1 < \theta < 1$, the model is invertible, so that we can express ε_{t-1} in terms of the past observations y_{t-k}, $k \geq 1$, by means of (7.9). Substituting this expression for ε_{t-1} (that is, applied at time instant $t-1$) in the MA(1) model, we obtain

$$y_t = (\theta y_{t-1} - \theta^2 y_{t-2} + \theta^3 y_{t-3} - \cdots) + \varepsilon_t.$$

This is a non-linear regression model. The parameter θ can be estimated by NLS after truncating $\sum_{k=0}^{\infty} (-\theta)^k y_{t-1-k}$ to the finite sum $\sum_{k=0}^{t-2} (-\theta)^k y_{t-1-k}$.

Estimation of ARMA models by NLS and ML

Stationary and invertible ARMA models can be estimated in a similar way. The ARMA(p, q) model $\phi(L)y_t = \theta(L)\varepsilon_t$ can be written in the form of the (infinite) regression model (7.2) so that

$$y_t = \sum_{k=1}^{\infty} \pi_k y_{t-k} + \varepsilon_t.$$

The parameters π_k are (non-linear) functions of the $(p+q)$ ARMA model parameters. If we write $\pi(z) = 1 - \sum_{k=1}^{\infty} \pi_k z^k$, then $\pi(L)y_t = \varepsilon_t$ so that $\phi(L)y_t = \theta(L)\varepsilon(t) = \theta(L)\pi(L)y_t$. So the relation between the regression parameters π_k and the $(p+q)$ ARMA model parameters ϕ_k and θ_k are given by

$$\phi(z) = \theta(z)\pi(z).$$

This equation (in terms of polynomials) can be used to compute the values of π_k for given values of the ARMA parameters ϕ_k and θ_k. If the infinite regression is truncated to a finite regression $y_t \approx \sum_{k=1}^{m} \pi_k y_{t-k} + \varepsilon_t$ (with $m \geq p+q$), then the

ARMA parameters of $\phi(z)$ and $\theta(z)$ can be estimated by NLS. If the innovations ε_t are assumed to be normally distributed, then asymptotically NLS is equivalent to ML. Indeed, suppose that $\varepsilon_t \sim \text{NID}(0, \ \sigma^2)$ and that the ARMA model is rewritten as $\pi(L)y_t = \varepsilon_t$ as before. Then the conditional log-likelihood of the ARMA model (treating the initial values as fixed) is given by

$$\log(L(\phi_1, \cdots, \phi_p, \theta_1, \cdots, \theta_q, \sigma^2)) = -\frac{n-p}{2}\log(2\pi) - \frac{n-p}{2}\log(\sigma^2) - \frac{1}{2\sigma^2}\sum_{t=p+1}^{n} \varepsilon_t^2.$$

Conditional ML corresponds to maximization of this function with respect to the parameters. So the ARMA parameters are obtained by minimizing $\sum \varepsilon_t^2$, which shows that ML in this case is equivalent to NLS for $n \to \infty$ (as the effect of treating the initial values as fixed then vanishes, provided that the roots of the MA polynomial are not too close to the unit circle, as otherwise the effect of initial values vanishes only very slowly). Standard errors of the estimates can be obtained as usual from the information matrix, and tests (such as t-, F-, and LR-tests) can be performed in the usual way.

Iterative estimation methods

T

Instead of direct optimization of the (non-linear) log-likelihood, one can also apply simpler iterative methods. As an illustration we consider the stationary and invertible ARMA(1,1) model

$$y_t = \phi y_{t-1} + \varepsilon_t + \theta \varepsilon_{t-1}.$$

The main idea is to estimate the parameters by two iterative regression steps, a first step, where ϕ is estimated for given value of θ, and a second step, where θ is estimated for given value of ϕ. The model can be written as $y_t = \phi y_{t-1} + \theta(L)\varepsilon_t$, where $\theta(L) = 1 + \theta L$. As the model is invertible, so that $-1 < \theta < 1$, it follows that $\theta(z)\alpha(z) = 1$, where $\alpha(z) = 1/(1 + \theta z) = \sum_{k=0}^{\infty} (-\theta)^k z^k$. In the first step it is assumed that the MA parameter θ is known. Define the process x_t by $x_t = \alpha(L)y_t$, so that $x_t = -\theta x_{t-1} + y_t$. As starting condition we take $y_0 = 0$, so that $x_t, \ t = 1, \cdots, n$, can be computed from the observed time series $y_t, \ t = 1, \cdots, n$, for given value of θ. Then x_t follows an AR(1) process, since $x_t - \phi x_{t-1} = (1 - \phi L)x_t = (1 - \phi L)\alpha(L)y_t = \alpha(L)\theta(L)\varepsilon_t = \varepsilon_t$—that is,

$$x_t = \phi x_{t-1} + \varepsilon_t.$$

In this AR(1) model, ϕ can be estimated by OLS. Let the corresponding OLS residuals be denoted by $e_t = x_t - \hat{\phi} x_{t-1}$. In the second step, for given value of $\hat{\phi}$, the MA parameter θ can be estimated by regressing $y_t - \hat{\phi} y_{t-1}$ on e_{t-1} in the regression model

$$(y_t - \hat{\phi} y_{t-1}) = \theta e_{t-1} + \varepsilon_t.$$

The estimated value of θ can be used to perform step 1 again to obtain a new estimate of ϕ, which can be used to perform step 2 again, and so on until the estimates converge. To start the iterations, we can take $\theta = 0$ in step 1, so that $x_t = y_t$ in this first round. The advantage of the above method is that the estimates are obtained by iterative (linear) regressions, whereas ML and NLS need non-linear optimization methods. Similar methods can be followed for ARMA models with higher orders p and q.

XM701INP

Example 7.8: **Industrial Production (continued)**

We continue our analysis of the quarterly series of yearly growth rates $\Delta_4 y_t$ of US industrial production. In Example 7.7 we discussed steps 1 and 2 of the modelling process of Section 7.2.1. Now we consider step 3—that is, the estimation of the model parameters. We will discuss (i) the estimates of the AR(2) model and (ii) an interpretation of the estimated model.

(i) **Estimates of AR(2) model**

For reasons discussed in Section 7.2.1, an AR(2) model is postulated for the series $\Delta_4 y_t$. Therefore we estimate an AR(2), and we include an intercept because the average growth rate is non-zero. The parameters of the AR(2) model are estimated by regressing $\Delta_4 y_t$ on a constant and the two lagged values $\Delta_4 y_{t-1}$ and $\Delta_4 y_{t-2}$. The result is in Exhibit 7.9 and can be summarized as follows (asymptotic standard errors of the parameters are in parentheses).

$$\begin{aligned} \Delta_4 y_t = \underset{(0.002)}{0.007} + \underset{(0.072)}{1.332}\Delta_4 y_{t-1} - \underset{(0.072)}{0.546}\Delta_4 y_{t-2} + e_t. \end{aligned} \tag{7.17}$$

The considered data period is 1961–94, with $n = 4 \cdot 34 = 136$ observations. As was mentioned in Example 7.1, the values of y_t are also known prior to 1961. This allows us to estimate the above regression equation using $n = 136$ observations, since in the initial period the values of the required lagged regressors (which involve values of y_t back to 1959.3 to compute the first value of $\Delta_4 y_{t-2}$) are known.

(ii) **Interpretation of the estimated model**

The estimated AR(2) polynomial $\phi(z) = 1 - 1.332z + 0.546z^2$ can be factorized as in (7.5). This gives $\phi(z) = (1 - \alpha_1 z)(1 - \alpha_2 z)$ with $\alpha_{1,2} = 0.68 \pm 0.32i$, so that $|\alpha_{1,2}|$ lies well below 1. This provides some support for the stationarity of the series $\Delta_4 y_t$. The stationarity of this series will be investigated by means of statistical tests in Example 7.16. The AR(2) model can be used to determine the average annual growth rate—that is, to estimate $E[\Delta_4 y_t]$. It follows from (7.17) that this growth rate (in percentages) is estimated as

Dependent Variable: D4Y				
Method: Least Squares				
Sample: 1961:1 1994:4				
Included observations: 136				
Variable	Coefficient	Std. Error	t-Statistic	Prob.
C	0.007147	0.002161	3.307447	0.0012
D4Y(−1)	1.332025	0.072094	18.47633	0.0000
D4Y(−2)	−0.545933	0.072174	−7.564120	0.0000
R-squared	0.821380	Mean dependent var		0.032213
Adjusted R-squared	0.818694	S.D. dependent var		0.049219
S.E. of regression	0.020958	Akaike info criterion		−4.870824
Sum squared resid	0.058416	Schwarz criterion		−4.806574
Log likelihood	334.2160	F-statistic		305.7993
Durbin-Watson stat	2.050254	Prob(F-statistic)		0.000000

Exhibit 7.9 Industrial Production (Example 7.8)

AR(2) model for the quarterly series of yearly growth rates of US industrial production.

$$100 \cdot \frac{0.007}{1 - 1.332 + 0.546} = 3.34\%.$$

The quality of the AR(2) model for this series will be further evaluated in the next two sections, where we will also consider alternative ARMA models (see Examples 7.10 and 7.11).

☞ Exercises: T: 7.2a, 7.3d; S: 7.12a–e.

7.2.3 Model selection

Identification of ARMA model orders

The estimation of ARMA models requires first that the orders p of the autoregressive part and q of the moving average part are chosen. The choice of these orders is called the *identification* of the ARMA model (see step 2 of the modelling method described in Section 7.2.1). We will now discuss some tools for selecting the model orders p and q; related diagnostic tests are described in the next section. The results in Section 7.1.5 show that the sample (partial) autocorrelations are helpful for selecting the orders of MA and AR models. The theoretical ACF becomes zero for an MA process and the theoretical PACF becomes zero for an AR process. These correlations can be estimated from the sample by the SACF (denoted by r_k) and SPACF (denoted by $\hat{\phi}_{kk}$) (see Section 7.1.5). To select the orders we can plot the correlations r_k and $\hat{\phi}_{kk}$ against the time lag k. The plot of r_k is called the *correlogram*.

Significance of the first order sample autocorrelation coefficient

One way to select the orders of an AR or MA model is to test whether the (partial) correlations differ significantly from zero. For this purpose we need to know the (asymptotic) distribution of the sample (partial) autocorrelations. We derive this distribution for the first order sample autocorrelation r_1 of a white noise process. The value of r_1 is obtained by regression in the AR(1) model $y_t = \alpha + \phi y_{t-1} + \varepsilon_t$, and the asymptotic distribution is given in (7.16). A white noise process has $\phi = 0$, so that in large enough samples there holds

$$r_1 \approx \mathrm{N}\left(0, \frac{1}{n}\right) \quad \text{if } y_t \text{ is white noise.}$$

The null hypothesis of no autocorrelation ($\rho_1 = 0$) can be tested against the alternative $\rho_1 \neq 0$. At (approximate) 5 per cent level, the null hypothesis is rejected if

$$|r_1| > \frac{2}{\sqrt{n}}.$$

In this case the first order autocorrelation is significant.

Significance of S(P)ACF for AR and MA processes

The first order sample partial autocorrelation $\hat{\phi}_{11}$ is obtained by the regression (7.12) with $k = 1$—that is, by regression in the model $y_t = \alpha + \phi_{11} y_{t-1} + \varepsilon_t$. This means that $\hat{\phi}_{11} = r_1$, so that $\hat{\phi}_{11} \approx \mathrm{N}(0, 1/n)$ if the process is white noise. Similar results hold true for higher order sample (partial) autocorrelations. It can be shown that, for an MA(q) process, the SACF r_k for $k > q$ are approximately normally distributed with mean zero and variance

$$\mathrm{MA}(q): \quad \mathrm{var}(r_k) \approx \frac{1 + 2\sum_{j=1}^{q} r_j^2}{n} \quad \text{for all } k > q.$$

The significance of r_k can be tested by the t-test. If the SACF are not significant beyond lag q, this indicates that an MA(q) model may be appropriate for the time series. For an AR(p) process, the SPACF for $k > p$ are, for large enough samples, approximately normally distributed with mean zero and variance

$$\mathrm{AR}(p): \quad \mathrm{var}(\hat{\phi}_{kk}) \approx \frac{1}{n}, \quad \text{for all } k > p.$$

The significance can again be tested by the t-test. If the SPACF are not significant beyond lag p, this means that an AR(p) model can be appropriate to describe the time series.

Model selection by means of tests and information criteria

The foregoing methods can be used to select the order of an AR model or of an MA model. In general it is not easy to select the orders of a mixed ARMA model from the S(P)ACF. One can instead estimate a collection of ARMA models, for different orders of p and q, and then select a model from this collection. Competing models can be compared by tests or by using information criteria. If two competing models are nested, in the sense that one model is a restriction of the other model (for example an AR(2) model versus an ARMA(2,2) model), then one could select the best model by performing an F-test or an LR-test on the parameter restrictions. If competing models are not nested in this way, then one can use information criteria like AIC and SIC, as discussed in Section 5.2.1 (p. 279), where the number of parameters of an ARMA(p, q) model (with constant term) is $k = p + q + 1$. One then chooses the model that minimizes AIC or SIC.

Example 7.9: **Simulated Time Series (continued)**

To illustrate step 2 of the modelling process, we use the S(P)ACF of the six simulated time series of Examples 7.3 and 7.4 to identify the model orders. The SACF and SPACF of these six time series are given in Panels 1 and 2 of Exhibit 7.5. The simulated time series have length $n = 500$, so that the approximate 5 per cent critical value for S(P)ACF is $2/\sqrt{500} = 0.089$. For the white noise series, some of the correlations (for instance, r_3 and $\hat{\phi}_{33}$) are marginally significant, but none of the correlations is far above 0.089. The S(P)ACF indeed suggests that the series is white noise. For the AR(1) process only the first SPACF is highly significant, and for the AR(2) process only the first and second SPACF are highly significant. So the AR processes are well identified by the SPACF. Similar results hold true for the SACF of the MA(1) and MA(2) process. For the ARMA(1,1) process many of the S(P)ACF are significant, so that this series is not well described by (low order) AR or MA models. This indicates that the model is of mixed ARMA type.

Example 7.10: **Industrial Production (continued)**

We continue our analysis of the quarterly series of annual growth rates in US industrial production (see also Examples 7.7 and 7.8). We now consider step 2 of the modelling process of Section 7.2.1 in more detail for this series. We will discuss (i) the sample (partial) autocorrelations of the series and (ii) a comparison of two models: AR(2) and ARMA(2,5).

(i) Sample (partial) autocorrelations

Exhibit 7.8 contains the first twelve S(P)ACF of the quarterly series of yearly growth rates in US industrial production. The quarterly data are considered over the years 1961–94, giving $n = 136$ observations. Therefore the standard error of the SPACF is approximately $1/\sqrt{n} = 0.086$, and SPACFs are significant if they are (in absolute value) larger than 0.172. The SACF in Exhibit 7.8 displays a somewhat cyclical pattern, and the SPACF suggests that an AR(2) model is a good starting point because the SPACFs for lags 3–12 are relatively small. Only the eleventh SPACF is significant, but this has no intuitive meaning and may be due to random effects. Note that, at 5 per cent significance level, on average one out of twenty sample correlations may be significant if the theoretical correlations are zero.

(ii) Comparison of two models: AR(2) and ARMA(2,5)

The AR(2) model was estimated in Example 7.8. As an alternative we consider an ARMA(2,5) model for these data, so that $\phi(L)\Delta_4 y_t = \alpha + \theta(L)\varepsilon_t$,

Panel 1: Dependent Variable: D4Y
Method: Least Squares
Sample: 1961:1 1994:4
Included observations: 136
Convergence achieved after 23 iterations
Backcast: 1959:4 1960:4

Variable	Coefficient	Std. Error	t-Statistic	Prob.
C	0.001657	0.000607	2.729598	0.0072
D4Y(−1)	1.395914	0.136396	10.23425	0.0000
D4Y(−2)	−0.460286	0.126571	−3.636585	0.0004
MA(1)	−0.076816	0.125279	−0.613155	0.5409
MA(2)	0.054674	0.037878	1.443424	0.1513
MA(3)	−0.049391	0.035496	−1.391466	0.1665
MA(4)	−0.867788	0.037032	−23.43334	0.0000
MA(5)	−0.022209	0.115754	−0.191859	0.8482
R-squared	0.880726	Mean dependent var		0.032213
Adjusted R-squared	0.874203	S.D. dependent var		0.049219
S.E. of regression	0.017457	Akaike info criterion		−5.201129
Sum squared resid	0.039008	Schwarz criterion		−5.029796
Log likelihood	361.6768	F-statistic		135.0226
Durbin-Watson stat	1.979721	Prob(F-statistic)		0.000000

Panel 2: Wald Test
Null Hypothesis: C(4) = 0, C(5) = 0, C(6) = 0, C(7) = 0, C(8) = 0

F-statistic	12056652	Probability	0.000000
Chi-square	60283262	Probability	0.000000

Exhibit 7.10 Industrial Production (Example 7.10)

ARMA(2,5) model for the quarterly series of yearly growth rates of US industrial production (Panel 1; the two lagged values of D4Y before 1961.1 are available and the five lagged values of the error terms before 1961.1 are 'backcasted' from the model) and test on the joint significance of the 5 MA terms (Panel 2).

where the AR polynomial $\phi(z)$ has degree 2 and the MA polynomial $\theta(L)$ has degree 5. Panel 1 of Exhibit 7.10 shows the ML estimates of this model. If we compare the AIC and SIC of the ARMA(2,5) model in Panel 1 of Exhibit 7.10 with the AIC and SIC of the AR(2) model in Exhibit 7.9, we see that both these selection criteria favour the ARMA(2,5) model. As the AR(2) model is a restriction of the ARMA(2,5) model, we can test the null hypothesis of an AR(2) model (the restricted model) against the alternative of an ARMA(2,5) model. Panel 2 of Exhibit 7.10 shows the outcome of the F-test on the joint significance of the five MA terms. This test has the $F(g, n-k)$ distribution, where $g = 5$ is the number of restrictions (the five MA terms), $k = 8$ is the number of parameters of the ARMA(2,5) model (including a constant term), and $n = 4 \cdot 34 = 136$ is the number of observations (note that pre-sample values before 1961 are available; see also our remarks on this point in Example 7.8). The test shows that the five MA terms are jointly significant. If we use the log-likelihood values in Exhibit 7.9 and Panel 1 of Exhibit 7.10, the LR-test gives $LR = 2(361.68 - 334.22) = 54.92$ with P-value (obtained from the $\chi^2(5)$ distribution) equal to $P = 0.0000$. So this leads to the same conclusion—that is, the ARMA(2,5) model is preferred above the AR(2) model. However, as we shall see in Example 7.11, the ARMA(2,5) model corresponds to over-fitting, which leads to worse performance in prediction as compared to the AR(2) model.

7.2.4 Diagnostic tests

Overview

Once the model orders have been selected and the parameters of the model have been estimated, the resulting model should be tested to see whether the model is correctly specified. Here we discuss some of the main diagnostic tools for time series models. Some of these tools are based on the diagnostic tests for regression models discussed in Chapter 5, in particular tests based on the model residuals and tests based on the predictive performance of the model. The discussion of some specific time series tests is postponed till later sections. In Section 7.3.3 we consider tests for the presence and nature of trends, and in Section 7.3.4 we discuss tests for outliers in time series and for time varying variance.

Check on stationarity

As a first step one should check that the modelled time series is stationary, as all tests discussed below are based on this assumption. A time plot of the series is useful to see whether the mean level and the variance are more or less stable over time. One can also split the time series into two parts and check whether the mean, variance, and autocovariances are comparable in the two periods. Many time series in business and economics show changes in levels due to trends and seasonals. Such aspects should then first be modelled by methods to be discussed in Section 7.3.

Graphical inspection of residuals

The model selection methods of Section 7.2.3 and the estimation methods in Section 7.2.2 are based on the assumption that the error terms of the ARMA model satisfy the standard assumption that $\varepsilon_t \sim \mathrm{NID}(0,\ \sigma^2)$. That is, the error terms are assumed to have constant mean zero and constant variance, and they are *uncorrelated* and *normally distributed*.

It is always helpful to use graphical tools as a first step to analyse the residuals, as this may indicate possible defects of the model. The time plot of the residuals shows the mean and variance over time, the correlogram can be used to check for residual correlation, and the histogram of the residuals can be compared with the normal distribution.

Check for serial correlation

As the time series model tries to capture the correlations over time, it is of particular importance to test for serial correlation of the model residuals $e_t,\ t = 1, \cdots, n$. The residual autocorrelations $r_k(e)$, for $k \geq 1$, are given by

$$r_k(e) = \frac{\sum_{t=k+1}^{n} e_t e_{t-k}}{\sum_{t=1}^{n} e_t^2}.$$

In a correctly specified model the parameters are estimated consistently and the residuals e_t converge to the innovations ε_t. Asymptotically, the residuals are then uncorrelated and $r_k(e)$ has mean zero and variance $1/n$. The autocorrelations are not significant (at approximate 5 per cent significance level) if they are within the interval

$$-\frac{2}{\sqrt{n}} \leq r_k(e) \leq \frac{2}{\sqrt{n}}.$$

Serial correlation test of Ljung–Box

The joint significance of the first m residual autocorrelations can be tested by the *Ljung–Box* test of Section 5.5.3 (p. 365)—that is,

$$LB(m) = n \sum_{k=1}^{m} \frac{n+2}{n-k} r_k^2(e) \approx \chi^2(m-p-q).$$

Under the null hypothesis that the estimated ARMA(p, q) model is correctly specified, this test asymptotically follows the $\chi^2(m-p-q)$ distribution. Note that, in contrast with this test for the regression model in Section 5.5.3, now $(p+q)$ degrees of freedom are lost. This is because the ARMA(p, q) model has $(p+q)$ parameters that affect the serial correlation of the model residuals.

Serial correlation test of Breusch–Godfrey

Another useful test for residual autocorrelation is obtained by applying the *Breusch–Godfrey LM*-test for serial correlation in regression models, described in Section 5.5.3 (p. 364). If the estimated model is an AR(p) model with residuals e_t, then the test for serial correlation is based on a regression of the type

$$e_t = \alpha + \beta_1 y_{t-1} + \cdots + \beta_p y_{t-p} + \gamma_1 e_{t-1} + \cdots + \gamma_r e_{t-r} + \omega_t.$$

Here r is chosen to incorporate possibly relevant correlations up to lag r. The LM-test is given by $LM = nR^2$ of this regression, which is asymptotically distributed as $\chi^2(r)$ under the null hypothesis that the AR(p) model is correct. It is also possible to use the F-test on the joint significance of the parameters $\gamma_1, \cdots, \gamma_r$, and this is asymptotically equivalent to the LM-test. In a similar way one can test for residual autocorrelation in ARMA(p, q) models by adding lagged values of the residuals e_t as explanatory variables. For instance, for an ARMA(1,1) model the test equation for second order residual autocorrelation becomes

$$e_t = \alpha + \beta_1 y_{t-1} + \gamma_1 e_{t-1} + \gamma_2 e_{t-2} + \omega_t + \beta_2 \omega_{t-1}.$$

This auxiliary equation corresponds to the general principle of the Breusch–Godfrey test in Section 5.5.3 to add lagged residuals to the model equation under the null hypothesis. Here the 'regressors' y_{t-1} and ω_{t-1} correspond to the chosen ARMA(1,1) model, and the lagged ARMA(1,1) residuals e_{t-1} and e_{t-2} are the added regressors to test for the presence of serial correlation. To perform the Breusch–Godfrey test for ARMA models, one first estimates the postulated ARMA(p, q) model by ML, with residuals e_t, and then estimates the test equation (again by ML, because of the presence of MA terms, with corresponding fitted values $\hat{e}_t$). Then $LM = nR^2 = n(SSE/SST) = n\left(\sum \hat{e}_t^2 / \sum e_t^2\right)$ of the test equation.

Forecast performance on a hold-out set of data

It is always of interest to compare alternative models by their *forecast performance*. In many situations the main purpose of a time series model is to produce out-of-sample forecasts. To simulate this situation, one should leave out a part of the available observations, as was discussed in Section 5.2.1 (p. 280). Suppose that in total $(m + n)$ observations are available and that the last m observations are left out for evaluation purposes. Models are then identified, estimated, and tested on the basis of only the first n observations y_t, $t = 1, \cdots, n$, and forecasts are produced for the time moments $t = n + 1, \cdots, n + m$. These forecasts can be made in two ways. One method is to predict y_{n+h} h-steps-ahead ('dynamic' forecasts), using only the observations until $t = n$ in producing the forecasts. Another method is to predict y_{n+h} one-step-ahead ('static' forecasts), using the observations until $t = n + h - 1$ in forecasting y_{n+h}. Here we will consider the case of dynamic forecasts, as this is more relevant in actually predicting the future multiple steps ahead.

Forecast evaluation criteria

The forecast performance may be checked, for instance, by the percentage of the m observations in the hold-out sample that are within the 95 per cent forecast intervals of the model. As was discussed in Section 5.2.1, different models may, for instance, be compared by their *root mean squared prediction error* (RMSE) and their *mean absolute prediction error* (MAE), that are defined by

$$\text{RMSE} = \left(\frac{1}{m} \sum_{h=1}^{m} (y_{n+h} - \hat{y}_{n+h})^2 \right)^{1/2}, \quad \text{MAE} = \frac{1}{m} \sum_{h=1}^{m} |y_{n+h} - \hat{y}_{n+h}|.$$

Two competing models can also be compared by the number of times B that the absolute error $|y_{n+h} - \hat{y}_{n+h}|$ of the first model is smaller than that of the second model. If the models forecast equally well, then B has the binomial distribution with m trials and with chance of success equal to $\frac{1}{2}$. The first model is preferred if B is significantly larger than $\frac{1}{2}$, and the second model is better if B is significantly smaller than $\frac{1}{2}$. One can test the hypothesis that both models forecast equally well (that is, that this chance is $\frac{1}{2}$) by means of the binomial distribution. If m is large enough, then $\frac{1}{\sqrt{m}}(B - \frac{m}{2})$ is approximately normally distributed with mean zero and variance $\frac{1}{4}$. That is, under the null hypothesis of equal forecast quality

$$\frac{1}{\sqrt{m}}(2B - m) \approx \text{N}(0, 1).$$

For instance, one may choose for the first model if $(2B - m)/\sqrt{m} > 2$ and for the second model if $(2B - m)/\sqrt{m} < -2$.

Summary of diagnostic tests

Summarizing, in time series analysis the following diagnostic tests are useful to check the empirical validity of the model. The model should be adjusted if some of the tests lead to rejection of the null hypothesis that the time series model is correctly specified. If several models pass the diagnostic tests, then a choice can be based on the forecast performance of the models.

- Test the stationarity of the time series (time plot and correlogram of the series, and tests described in Sections 7.3.3 and 7.3.4).
- Test for outliers and constant variance (time plot and histogram of the series and of the model residuals, Jarque–Bera test and Breusch–Pagan test on the model residuals; further tests described in Section 7.4).
- Test the lag structure of the ARMA model (S(P)ACF, *t*- and *F*-tests on additional lags, AIC and SIC).
- Test for residual autocorrelation (SACF, Ljung–Box test, Breusch–Godfrey test on model residuals; note that the Durbin–Watson test should not be used, as the regressors are stochastic in a time series model).
- Evaluate the forecast performance (especially dynamic forecasts on a hold-out sample), and compare this performance between competing models.

We shall now illustrate this by means of an example. As most time series in business and economics are characterized by trends and seasonal effects, further empirical applications of the methods treated in Section 7.2 (that are valid for stationary time series) are postponed until Sections 7.3.3 and 7.3.4.

Example 7.11: **Industrial Production (continued)**

We continue our analysis of the quarterly data of yearly growth rates of industrial production in the USA. In terms of the modelling steps described in Section 7.2.1, steps 1–3 were discussed in previous examples (see Examples 7.7, 7.8, and 7.10). Now we consider steps 4–6 and discuss (i) diagnostic tests for the AR(2) model of Example 7.8, (ii) diagnostic tests for two alternative models, ARMA(2,5) and AR(5), (iii) the forecast performance of the AR(2) model, (iv) a remark on the computed forecast intervals, and (v) a comparison of the forecast quality of the three considered models.

(i) Diagnostic tests for the AR(2) model

First we perform diagnostic tests on the AR(2) model that was our first guess in Example 7.7 (see also Example 7.8). Exhibits 7.11 (*a*) and (*b*) show the time plot and the histogram of the residuals of this model. The assumption of normally distributed error terms is clearly rejected by the

Jarque–Bera test. The residuals have excess kurtosis (around 5.9, as compared with 3 for the normal distribution), which is due to some outlying observations. The influence of outliers is further discussed in Example 7.17. Panel 3 of Exhibit 7.11 shows the correlogram of the residuals. There are $n = 136$ observations, so that correlations are significant (at 5 per cent significance level) if they are larger than $2/\sqrt{136} = 0.172$ in absolute value. There is some evidence of residual correlation at lags 3, 4, and 8. The Ljung–Box test has P-values close to 0.05 if eight or more lags are included. The Breusch–Godfrey test for serial correlation, with four lags included, has P-value 0.06 (see Panel 4).

(ii) Diagnostic tests for the ARMA(2,5) and AR(5) models

Because the residuals of the AR(2) model have some significant autocorrelations (for instance at lag 4, corresponding to a lag of one year), it is worthwhile comparing this model with other models that allow for a richer correlation pattern in the time series. This is achieved by adding extra lags to the model. We consider the ARMA(2,5) model of Example 7.10 (with parameter estimates in Panel 1 of Exhibit 7.10) and the AR(5) model (with parameter estimates given in Panel 5 of Exhibit 7.11). Panel 6 of Exhibit 7.11 summarizes the outcomes of diagnostic tests for the three models—that is, AR(2), ARMA(2,5), and AR(5). Of these three models, the ARMA(2,5) model is preferred by the selection criteria AIC and SIC. However, normality of the residuals is rejected for all models and the AR(5) model performs relatively best in this respect. The non-normality is due to outliers, as will be further investigated in Section 7.4.1.

(iii) Forecast performance of the AR(2) model

Next we consider the forecast performance of the AR(2) model estimated in Example 7.8 (see (7.17)). This model was estimated with the data over the years 1961–94, and now we will forecast the series over the period 1995.1–1998.3 (this period contains fifteen quarters). First we consider the quality of the model in forecasting the growth rate in the next quarter. Exhibit 7.12 (*a*) shows the fifteen one-step-ahead point forecasts and corresponding 95 per cent forecast intervals of $\Delta_4 y_t$ for 1995.1 to 1998.3, together with the actually realized growth rates. These forecasts are quite accurate and the 95 per cent forecast intervals include all the actual values. Next we consider multi-step-ahead forecasts of the growth rate, ranging from one quarter ahead (for 1995.1) to fifteen quarters ahead (for 1998.3). Exhibit 7.12 (*b*) shows these fifteen h-step-ahead forecasts of $\Delta_4 y_t$. The forecasts converge to the mean value of 3.34 per cent for increasing values of the horizon h. For longer horizons the 95 per cent forecast intervals become very wide and even include substantial negative growth rates.

(a)

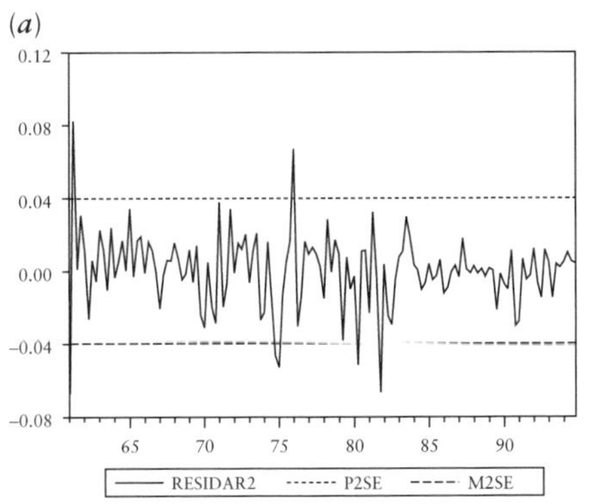

(b)

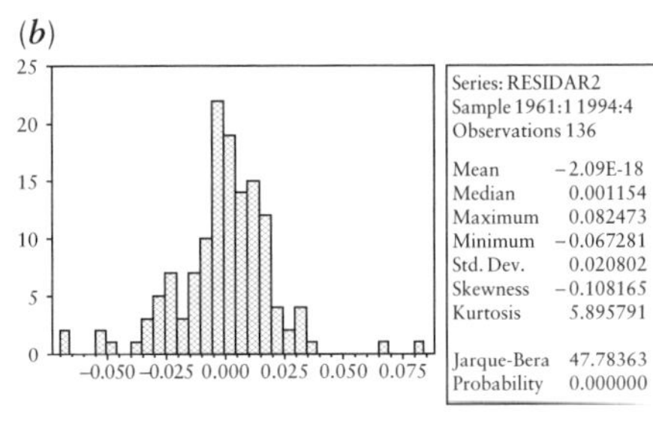

(c)

Panel 3: Correlogram RESIDAR2			
Sample: 1961:1 1994:4; Included observations: 136			
Lag	SACF	LB-Statistic	P-value
1	−0.064	0.5700	0.450
2	0.010	0.5850	0.746
3	0.172	4.7681	0.190
4	−0.191	9.9534	0.041
5	0.013	9.9777	0.076
6	0.066	10.599	0.102
7	0.023	10.676	0.153
8	−0.194	16.181	0.040
9	−0.053	16.596	0.055
10	0.116	18.613	0.045
11	−0.106	20.301	0.041
12	0.029	20.426	0.059

(d)

Panel 4: Breusch-Godfrey Serial Correlation LM Test (4 lags included)				
F-statistic	2.289063	Probability		0.063290
Obs*R-squared	9.013347	Probability		0.060767
Test Equation:				
Dependent Variable: RESIDAR2				
Method: Least Squares				
Variable	Coefficient	Std. Error	t-Statistic	Prob.
C	−0.001508	0.005028	−0.299866	0.7648
D4Y(−1)	0.152125	0.292653	0.519812	0.6041
D4Y(−2)	−0.106304	0.183270	−0.580037	0.5629
RESID(−1)	−0.191041	0.308317	−0.619624	0.5366
RESID(−2)	−0.079094	0.258568	−0.305893	0.7602
RESID(−3)	0.116781	0.195341	0.597830	0.5510
RESID(−4)	−0.181992	0.140802	−1.292540	0.1985

Exhibit 7.11 Industrial Production (Example 7.11)

Diagnostic tests on the residuals of the AR(2) model for the series D4Y of yearly growth rates of US industrial production, time plot (*a*), histogram (*b*), correlogram and Ljung–Box test (Panel 3), and Breusch–Godfrey test (Panel 4).

(*e*)

Panel 5: Dependent Variable: D4Y				
Method: Least Squares				
Sample: 1961:1 1994:4; Included observations: 136				
Variable	Coefficient	Std. Error	t-Statistic	Prob.
C	0.006444	0.002295	2.807883	0.0058
D4Y(−1)	1.360621	0.082194	16.55380	0.0000
D4Y(−2)	−0.650037	0.130812	−4.969235	0.0000
D4Y(−3)	0.365532	0.131069	2.788851	0.0061
D4Y(−4)	−0.536124	0.121923	−4.397234	0.0000
D4Y(−5)	0.269831	0.078028	3.458135	0.0007
R-squared	0.844584	Mean dependent var		0.032213
Adjusted R-squared	0.838607	S.D. dependent var		0.049219
S.E. of regression	0.019773	Akaike info criterion		−4.965862
Sum squared resid	0.050827	Schwarz criterion		−4.837363
Log likelihood	343.6786	F-statistic		141.2934
Durbin-Watson stat	1.902114	Prob(F-statistic)		0.000000

(*f*)

Panel 6: Overview of diagnostic tests				
Criterion	Diagnostic test	AR(2)	AR(5)	ARMA(2,5)
Model fit	R-squared	0.821	0.845	0.881
	St.Dev. residuals	0.021	0.020	0.017
Sel. Crit.	AIC	−4.871	−4.966	−5.201
	SIC	−4.807	−4.837	−5.030
Normality	Skewness	−0.108	−0.300	−1.007
	Kurtosis	5.896	4.936	5.738
	Jarque-Bera	47.784	23.280	65.490
Ser. Corr.	Ljung-Box (12 lags)	P = 0.059	P = 0.055	P = 0.113
	Breusch-Godfrey (4 lags)	P = 0.063	P = 0.025	P = 0.004
RMSE	one-step (95.1–98.3)	0.0085	0.0076	0.0093
	multi-step (95.1–98.3)	0.0167	0.0152	0.0251

Exhibit 7.11 (*Contd.*)

AR(5) model for the series D4Y of yearly growth rates of US industrial production (Panel 5) and overview of diagnostic tests for the AR(2), AR(5), and ARMA(2,5) models (Panel 6).

The model can also be used to forecast the 'levels' y_t (in logarithms) instead of the growth rates $\Delta_4 y_t$ of industrial production. Exhibits 7.12 (*c*) and (*d*) show respectively the one-step (static) and multi-step (dynamic) forecasts of the series y_t obtained by this model. This shows that the AR(2) model provides relatively good short-term forecasts (up to six quarters) but that the model may be less useful in long-term forecasting as the uncertainty becomes very large. For instance, fifteen quarters (around four years) ahead, Exhibit 7.12 (*d*) shows that the 95 per cent forecast interval of y_t (in logarithms) has a width of 0.4. This corresponds to a factor of $e^{0.4} = 1.5$ in the actual level of industrial production—that is, an uncertainty of around 50 per cent.

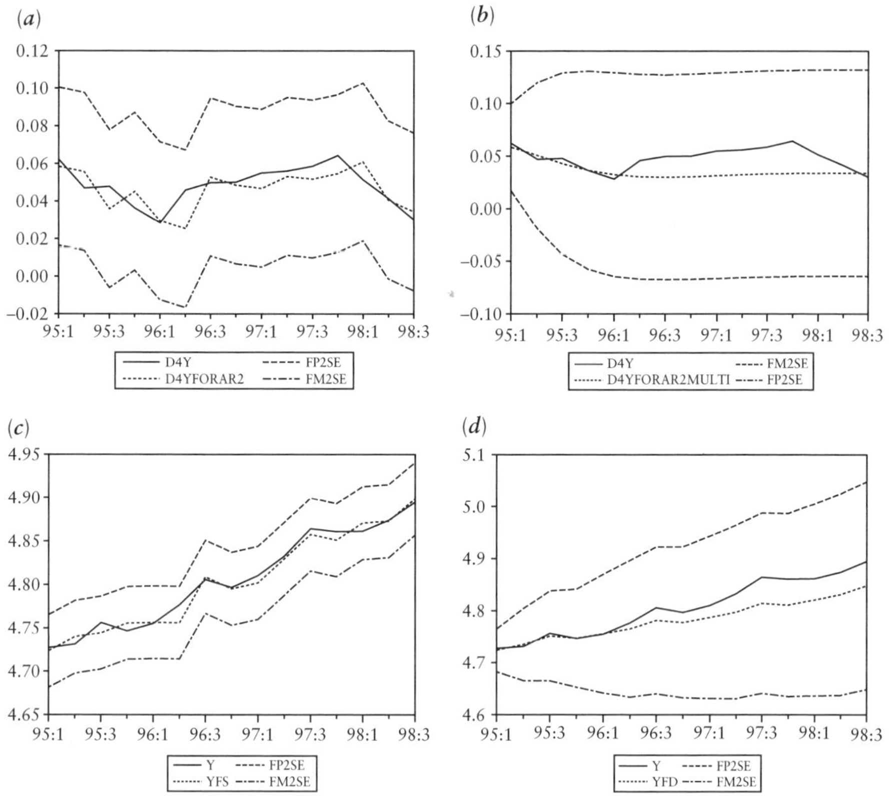

Exhibit 7.12 Industrial Production (Example 7.11)

One-step-ahead forecasts (*a*) and multi-step-ahead forecasts (*b*) of the yearly growth rates of US industrial production (D4Y) generated by the AR(2) model, together with the 95% forecast intervals and the actually realized growth rates. Further, implied forecasts of the logarithmic levels (Y) of US industrial production: static forecasts (one-step-ahead (*c*)) and dynamic forecasts (multi-step-ahead (*d*)), together with the 95% forecast intervals and the actual values of Y.

(iv) Remark on the computed forecast intervals

The forecast intervals for $\Delta_4 y_t$ are computed as discussed in Section 7.1.6, by substituting the estimated values of the AR(2) model. These parameter estimates are themselves uncertain, but this is not taken into account in constructing the uncertainty bounds of the forecasts. For the case of regression models, the effect of parameter uncertainty on prediction intervals was discussed in Section 3.4.3 (p. 171). For time series models this is more complicated, as the regressors are themselves stochastic. Forecast intervals can be estimated by simulation. However, in large samples the effect of parameter uncertainty vanishes, and in practice one often neglects this effect. The forecast intervals for y_t are computed from those of $\Delta_4 y_t$.

(v) Comparison of forecast quality of three models

Finally we compare the out-of-sample forecast quality of the three models, AR(2), AR(5), and ARMA(2,5). Panel 6 of Exhibit 7.11 reports the RMSE of the three models for static and dynamic forecasts of the series $\Delta_4 y_t$ of growth rates over the period 1995.1 to 1998.3. The AR(5) model gives the best predictions. Note that this model did not perform best from the point of within-sample residual diagnostics and that it was not selected by AIC and SIC. This shows that within-sample criteria need not always give the best model for out-of-sample purposes. It is therefore of importance to keep some data out of the specification, estimation, and diagnostic phases for later model selection purposes. This may in particular prevent the data from being over-fitted by models that contain too many parameters. Such models improve the fit over the estimation sample but provide worse forecasts. The ARMA(2,5) model seems to suffer from this kind of over-fitting (see Panel 6 of Exhibit 7.11). The ARMA(2,5) model has the smallest in-sample residuals (the standard deviation of the residuals is 0.017, which is smaller than that of AR(2) and AR(5)), but it gives the worst forecasts (the RMSE of dynamic forecasts is 0.0251, which is considerably larger than that of AR(2) and AR(5)).

The overall conclusion is that the AR(5) model performs best in forecasting, with the AR(2) model as a good alternative. The ARMA(2,5) model seems to be somewhat less useful.

☞ Exercises: E:7.20e

7.2.5 Summary

In this section we have discussed a sequence of steps to obtain adequate models for observed stationary time series.

- The modelling starts with graphical inspection of the time series and possible transformations to obtain stationarity.
- Next the orders of an ARMA(p, q) model are chosen, with the help of the sample (partial) autocorrelations.
- If the chosen model is purely autoregressive, then it can be estimated by OLS, and, if the model contains MA terms, it is estimated by ML (or by NLS or other asymptotically equivalent methods).
- One should check whether the estimated model is adequate. In particular, it is of interest to test whether the model residuals are uncorrelated and whether the model performs well in producing forecasts on a hold-out sample.

- If the model does not perform well enough, one can improve the model by selecting other orders of the ARMA model. The outcomes of diagnostic tests and model selection criteria help in finding better models.
- Finally, if one is satisfied with the obtained model, this model can be used, for instance, to predict future values of the time series. In general, the forecasts will perform better for the nearer future than for more distant times.

7.3 Trends and seasonals

☜ Uses Chapters 1–4; Section 5.5; parts of Section 5.3; Sections 7.1, 7.2.

7.3.1 Trend models

Deterministic trends

Many economic time series tend to grow over time—that is, they display trending behaviour. This is the case, for example, for the level of industrial production in Example 7.1 (see Exhibit 7.1 (*a*)) and for the Dow-Jones index in Example 7.2 (see Exhibit 7.2 (*a*)). The logarithm of both series also contains trends. Such time series do not satisfy the assumption of stationarity that is required for the methods discussed in Sections 7.1 and 7.2. If the series shows a more or less steady upward or downward trend, this can be modelled by a *deterministic trend*. The simplest model is

$$y_t = \alpha + \beta t + \varepsilon_t, \quad t = 1, \cdots, n. \tag{7.18}$$

This corresponds to a linear trend. This model is clearly non-stationary (for $\beta \neq 0$), because the mean $E[y_t] = \alpha + \beta t$ varies over time. The non-stationarity may also be detected from the autocorrelation function. For $n \to \infty$ all sample autocorrelations converge to one, and in finite samples the SACF tends to zero very slowly (see Exercise 7.13). Other trend specifications may also be of interest—for example, a quadratic trend with trend function $f(t) = \alpha + \beta t + \gamma t^2$ or a trend with saturation such as $f(t) = \alpha + \beta t^{-1}$. The above trend models can be extended by including (stationary) AR terms and (invertible) MA terms. For instance, an ARMA model with linear deterministic trend is described by

$$\phi(L) y_t = \alpha + \beta t + \theta(L)\varepsilon_t, \tag{7.19}$$

where $\phi(z)$ and $\theta(z)$ have all their roots outside the unit circle.

Estimation of models with deterministic trends

In the models (7.18) and (7.19) the trend term t is non-stationary and the stability condition on the regressors that was used in the asymptotic theory of

Chapter 4 is not satisfied. More precisely, Assumption 1* in Section 4.1.2 (p. 193) requires that the probability limit of $\frac{1}{n}X'X$ exists. However, for the regressor $x_t = t$ we get $\frac{1}{n}\sum_{t=1}^{n} x_t^2 \to \infty$ for $n \to \infty$. The consequence is that the OLS estimator of the slope coefficient β is consistent at a speed that is higher than the usual speed $\sqrt{n}$—namely, $n\sqrt{n}$ (see Exercise 4.2).

A simple two-step estimation method is the following. First regress the time series y_t in the model (7.18), neglecting possible AR and MA terms. If the trend is modelled correctly, the residuals are stationary and can be modelled in the second step by ARMA models as discussed in Section 7.2. Instead of this two-step approach, one can also directly estimate the ARMA model (7.19) with the deterministic trend included. The asymptotic statistical properties of the estimated ARMA parameters are the same as in the stationary case discussed in Section 7.2.2, provided that the trend has been modelled correctly.

The random walk model

The above trend models are called deterministic, as they impose a deterministic pattern on the time evolution of the mean of the time series. That is, every time step the mean of the series increases by the same amount β. Another type of trend models contains so-called *stochastic trends*. The simplest model is the *random walk*

$$y_t = y_{t-1} + \varepsilon_t. \tag{7.20}$$

Here ε_t is white noise. The name 'random walk' originates from the fact that the trend direction cannot be predicted, because for given value of y_{t-1} it is equally likely that $y_t > y_{t-1}$ as that $y_t < y_{t-1}$. Indeed, the expected change $\Delta y_t = y_t - y_{t-1} = \varepsilon_t$ in the time series, conditional on the past information $Y_{t-1} = \{y_{t-1}, y_{t-2}, \cdots\}$, is equal to

$$E[\Delta y_t | Y_{t-1}] = E[\varepsilon_t] = 0.$$

So we cannot predict whether the time series will move upward or downward. This differs from stationary series. For instance, for a stationary AR(1) model $y_t = \phi y_{t-1} + \varepsilon_t$ with $-1 < \phi < 1$ we get $\Delta y_t = (\phi - 1)y_{t-1} + \varepsilon_t$, and as $(\phi - 1) < 0$ it follows that

$$E[\Delta y_t | Y_{t-1}] < 0 \text{ if } y_{t-1} > 0, \quad E[\Delta y_t | Y_{t-1}] > 0 \text{ if } y_{t-1} < 0.$$

As $E[y_t] = 0$, this means that a stationary series has the tendency to return to the mean value of the process. A stationary process is, therefore, said to be *mean reverting*. The random walk does not have this property.

Stochastic properties of the random walk

A random walk series does not have a steady trend direction. However, during some time intervals a sequence of particular values of ε_t may lead to local trendlike movements in the series y_t. This can be explained by recursive substitution in (7.20), which gives

$$y_t = y_1 + \sum_{s=2}^{t} \varepsilon_s.$$

This shows that a large value of ε_s affects the values of the time series y_t for all $t \geq s$. The impact of a shock ε_s on y_t does not diminish over time. One therefore says that the shocks in this model are persistent, in contrast with stationary processes, where the effect of innovations eventually dies out. The random walk process is non-stationary. For instance, if $y_1 = 0$ is given, then the mean of the series is $E[y_t] = 0$, but the variance is equal to $\text{var}(y_t) = (t-1)\sigma^2$, which increases over time. For large values of t, the correlation between y_t and y_{t-k} is approximately equal to $\frac{t-k}{t}$. So the SACF will have values that are very close to 1 and that die out only very slowly (see Exercise 7.13).

Integrated processes and ARIMA models

The AR polynomial of the model (7.20) is given by $\phi(z) = 1 - z$, which has a root $\phi(z) = 0$ at $z = 1$. For this reason the random walk model (7.20) is said to have a *unit root*. This shows once more that the random walk is not stationary, as in Section 7.1.3 we derived the condition that all the roots of the AR polynomial should be outside the unit circle for a stationary process. The process y_t is called *integrated* of order one, as y_t is non-stationary but the series of first differences $\Delta y_t = (1-L)y_t = y_t - y_{t-1} = \varepsilon_t$ is stationary.

The random walk model can be extended by including a constant term and by incorporating (stationary) AR and (invertible) MA terms. An ARIMA(p, d, q) model has the property that $\Delta^k y_t$ is non-stationary for all $k < d$ and that $\Delta^d y_t$ is stationary and follows an ARMA(p, q) model. Such models are described by

$$\phi(L)(1-L)^d y_t = \alpha + \theta(L)\varepsilon_t,$$

where $\phi(z)$ and $\theta(z)$ are polynomials of degrees p and q respectively that have all their roots outside the unit circle. Such a process is called integrated of order d, and the process is said to have d unit roots. Because series that are integrated of order $d = 1$ have the property that the difference $y_t - y_{t-1}$ is stationary, such series y_t are called *difference stationary*. For time series in business and economics, the cases $d = 0$ and $d = 1$ are of most importance. Stationary series have $d = 0$, and non-stationary series often become stationary after taking first differences. In some applications one may encounter series that are integrated of order $d = 2$—for instance, some nominal price series may have this property. Higher orders of integration are very rare in practice.

Estimation and diagnostic tests of models with trends

An ARIMA(p, d, q) model can simply be estimated and evaluated by applying the results of Section 7.2 on the suitably differenced stationary series $(1 - L)^d y_t$. The question whether the trend is deterministic or stochastic and, in the latter case, the question what is the order of integration is treated in Section 7.3.3. The conventional statistical tests (such as t-tests and LR-tests) and the diagnostic tests of Section 7.2.4 remain valid after the trend has been appropriately removed (by regression in the case of a deterministic trend or by differencing the data in the case of a stochastic trend). However, if the model is misspecified because a deterministic trend is wrongly excluded or because the data are not properly differenced, then the results of Section 7.2 do not apply anymore. That is, the conventional tests no longer follow the standard distributions of the stationary case. This affects all standard inference procedures. It is, therefore, of major importance to model the trend appropriately before any further analysis of the data is performed.

Random walk with drift

If a constant term is added in the random walk model (7.20), then we get

$$\Delta y_t = \alpha + \varepsilon_t.$$

This is called a *random walk with drift*, and α is the drift term. By recursive substitution this can be written as

$$y_t = y_1 + \alpha(t - 1) + \sum_{s=2}^{t} \varepsilon_s.$$

So the constant term α becomes the coefficient of a deterministic trend component in the time series. This shows that the role of the constant term in a model with a unit root is different from the one in stationary models. The constant term has a similar trend interpretation in more general ARIMA(p, 1, q) models that are integrated of order one. The key difference from the deterministic trend model (7.19) is the stochastic trend term $\sum_{s=2}^{t} \varepsilon_s$.

We summarize some of the properties of the random walk with drift by comparing this model with the general AR(1) model $y_t = \alpha + \phi y_{t-1} + \varepsilon_t$. If $-1 < \phi < 1$, then the series y_t is stationary with mean $\mu = \alpha/(1 - \phi)$. So in this case $\alpha = (1 - \phi)\mu$, and we can rewrite the model as $y_t - \mu = \phi(y_{t-1} - \mu) + \varepsilon_t$ and also as $\Delta y_t = \Delta(y_t - \mu) = (\phi - 1)(y_{t-1} - \mu) + \varepsilon_t$. As $\phi - 1 < 0$ for the stationary series it follows that

$$E[\Delta y_t | Y_{t-1}] < 0 \text{ if } y_{t-1} > \mu, \quad E[\Delta y_t | Y_{t-1}] > 0 \text{ if } y_{t-1} < \mu.$$

This shows again that a stationary series is mean reverting. On the other hand, in the random walk with drift model we get

$$E[\Delta y_t | Y_{t-1}] = E[\alpha + \varepsilon_t] = \alpha.$$

So in this case we always expect the series to move forward (upward if $\alpha > 0$ and downward if $\alpha < 0$). This shows that the process is not stationary. Further, by writing the random walk with drift as $y_t = y_1 + \alpha(t - 1) + \sum_{s=2}^{t} \varepsilon_s$, it follows that $E[y_t | y_1] = (t - 1)\alpha$ and $\text{var}(y_t | y_1) = (t - 1)\sigma^2$, so that both the mean and the variance are unbounded.

Trend stationary processes

Next we consider the model

$$y_t = \alpha + \beta t + \phi y_{t-1} + \varepsilon_t. \tag{7.21}$$

This model contains as special cases the stochastic trend model (7.20) (for $\alpha = \beta = 0$ and $\phi = 1$) and the deterministic trend model (7.19) (if $-1 < \phi < 1$). We consider the model with $-1 < \phi < 1$ in more detail. In this case the AR polynomial $\phi(z) = 1 - \phi z$ is stationary. Define $z_t = y_t - \delta_1 - \delta_2 t$, where $\delta_2 = \beta/(1 - \phi)$ and $\delta_1 = (\alpha - \phi\delta_2)/(1 - \phi)$; then it follows by direct substitution in equation (7.21) that $z_t = \phi z_{t-1} + \varepsilon_t$ and hence

$$(y_t - \delta_1 - \delta_2 t) = \phi(y_{t-1} - \delta_1 - \delta_2(t - 1)) + \varepsilon_t.$$

Because $-1 < \phi < 1$, the process z_t is stationary, so that the effect of the innovations ε_t eventually dies out. So in this case $f(t) = \delta_1 + \delta_2 t$ is the long-term trend in the series and deviations from this trend are transient. The series returns to the trend $f(t)$ in the long run. Therefore the series y_t is called *trend stationary* in this case. More generally, every process (7.19) with stationary AR polynomial $\phi(z)$ is trend stationary. On the other hand, if $\phi = 1$ and $\beta \neq 0$ in (7.21), then we can rewrite this as $\Delta y_t = \alpha + \beta t + \varepsilon_t$, so that $E[\Delta y_t | Y_{t-1}] = \alpha + \beta t$. In this case the series is expected to exhibit changes that become larger as time progresses. This corresponds to quadratic trend behaviour, and the model contains both a stochastic trend (as $\phi = 1$) and a deterministic trend (as $\beta \neq 0$).

A model with latent trend

As an alternative for deterministic and stochastic trend models, the trend can also be modelled by a so-called *latent trend* variable. For example, let

$$y_t = \mu_t + \varepsilon_t, \quad \mu_{t+1} = \alpha + \mu_t + \eta_t, \tag{7.22}$$

where $\varepsilon_t \sim \mathrm{N}(0, \sigma_\varepsilon^2)$ and $\eta_t \sim \mathrm{N}(0, \sigma_\eta^2)$ are independent white noise processes. The trend component μ_t is unobserved and follows a random walk with drift. If $\sigma_\eta^2 = 0$, this model reduces to a deterministic trend, as $\mu_t = \mu_1 + \alpha(t-1)$ in this case. If $\sigma_\varepsilon^2 = 0$, then the model reduces to a random walk with drift $y_t = \alpha + y_{t-1} + \eta_t$. If $\sigma_\eta^2 > 0$, then the trend can be eliminated by taking first differences. This gives

$$\Delta y_t = \alpha + \varepsilon_t - \varepsilon_{t-1} + \eta_{t-1}.$$

As the correlations of the composite error term on the right-hand side are zero for all lags $k > 1$, it follows that Δy_t is an MA(1) process. So y_t is an ARIMA(0,1,1) process and can be written as

$$\Delta y_t = \alpha + \omega_t - \theta\omega_{t-1}. \tag{7.23}$$

The parameter θ can be derived from σ_ε^2 and σ_η^2, as follows. As ε_t and η_t are independent white noise processes, it follows that Δy_t has variance $\gamma_0 = 2\sigma_\varepsilon^2 + \sigma_\eta^2$ and first order covariance $\gamma_1 = -\sigma_\varepsilon^2$. On the other hand, from the ARIMA(0,1,1) model it follows that $\gamma_0 = (1+\theta^2)\sigma_\omega^2$ and $\gamma_1 = -\theta\sigma_\omega^2$. Let $\lambda = \sigma_\eta^2/\sigma_\varepsilon^2$ be the so-called signal-to-noise ratio of the model; then the first order autocorrelation of Δy_t is given by

$$\rho_1 = \frac{E[(\Delta y_t - \alpha)(\Delta y_{t-1} - \alpha)]}{E[(\Delta y_t - \alpha)^2]} = \frac{\gamma_1}{\gamma_0} = \frac{-\theta}{1+\theta^2} = \frac{-\sigma_\varepsilon^2}{2\sigma_\varepsilon^2 + \sigma_\eta^2} = \frac{-1}{2+\lambda}.$$

Because $\lambda > 0$, it follows that $\theta > 0$, and the (invertible) solution (with $\theta < 1$) for θ in terms of λ is given by $\theta = 1 + \frac{1}{2}\lambda - \frac{1}{2}\sqrt{\lambda^2 + 4\lambda}$. In the next section we consider the use of this trend model in trend estimation and forecasting.

Example 7.12: Simulated Series with Trends

We give a graphical illustration of the differences between trend stationary and difference stationary processes by simulating time series from the model (7.21), for different values of the parameters (α, β, ϕ). Exhibit 7.13 shows graphs of the following five simulated time series.

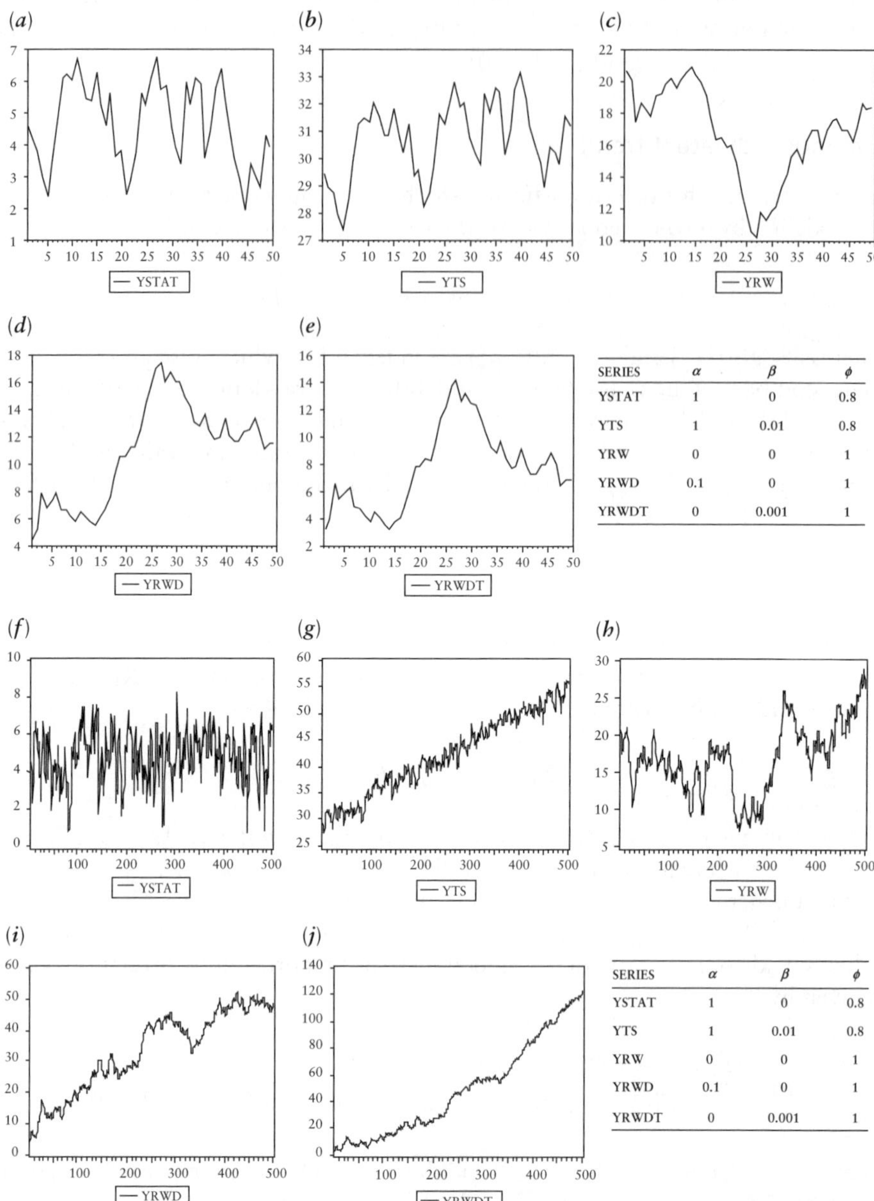

SERIES	α	β	ϕ
YSTAT	1	0	0.8
YTS	1	0.01	0.8
YRW	0	0	1
YRWD	0.1	0	1
YRWDT	0	0.001	1

SERIES	α	β	ϕ
YSTAT	1	0	0.8
YTS	1	0.01	0.8
YRW	0	0	1
YRWD	0.1	0	1
YRWDT	0	0.001	1

Exhibit 7.13 Simulated Series with Trends (Example 7.12)

Simulated series of length 500 ((*f*)–(*j*)) and first fifty observations ((*a*)–(*e*)) generated by the model $y_t = \alpha + \beta t + \phi y_{t-1} + \varepsilon_t$, where ε_t are NID(0,1), for different values of the parameters (α, β, ϕ).

- The first series has parameters $(\alpha, \beta, \phi) = (1, 0, 0.8)$. This is a stationary series without trend.
- The second series has parameters $(\alpha, \beta, \phi) = (1, 0.01, 0.8)$. This series is trend stationary. The series shows some short-term fluctuations but it always returns to the long-term trend $1 + 0.01t$.
- The third series is the random walk with parameters $(\alpha, \beta, \phi) = (0, 0, 1)$. This series has prolonged periods of up- and downward movements, but there is no clear overall trend direction.
- The fourth series is a random walk with drift with parameters $(\alpha, \beta, \phi) = (0.1, 0, 1)$. This series shows an upward trend but the location of the trend is not stable.
- The fifth series has parameters $(\alpha, \beta, \phi) = (0, 0.001, 1)$. This series contains a stochastic trend (as $\phi = 1$) and a deterministic trend (as $\beta = 0.001$). The combination of these two trends results in quadratic trend behaviour, since the growth $\Delta y_t = 0.001t$ increases over time.

Exhibit 7.13 (*f*)–(*j*) show the series over a sample period of length $n = 500$ where the differences are quite pronounced; (*a*)–(*e*) show the series for the first fifty observations, and the differences are much less clear in this case. Obviously, differences in trends can be distinguished only after a sufficiently long observation period.

☞ **Exercises:** S: 7.13a, b.

7.3.2 Trend estimation and forecasting

Forecasting a deterministic trend

If a time series shows trending behaviour, this is of major importance in forecasting. We consider the estimation and forecasting of the trend models of the foregoing section—that is, trends that are deterministic, stochastic, or latent. First we consider the linear deterministic trend model (7.18)—that is,

$$y_t = \alpha + \beta t + \varepsilon_t, \quad t = 1, \cdots, n.$$

We suppose that the time series y_t is observed at times $t = 1, \cdots, n$, and we wish to forecast y_t at time $t = n + h$. Let a and b denote the OLS estimates of α and β, based on the data $(y_1, \cdots, y_n)$. The h-step-ahead forecast is given by

$$\hat{y}_{n+h} = a + b(n + h).$$

If we neglect the errors in the parameter estimates—that is, if we assume that $a = \alpha$ and $b = \beta$—then the forecast error variance is σ^2 for all forecast horizons. If the trend is deterministic, then the uncertainty about the future does not depend on the forecast horizon. If the parameter uncertainty is taken into account, then the results in Section 2.4.1 (p. 105) show that the forecast variance is equal to

$$E[(y_{n+h} - \hat{y}_{n+h})^2] = \sigma^2 \left(1 + \frac{1}{n} + \frac{n + h - \frac{n+1}{2}}{\sum_{t=1}^{n} \left(t - \frac{n+1}{2}\right)^2} \right) \approx \sigma^2.$$

Here the last approximation is valid if the number of observations n is large compared to the forecast horizon h. This motivates the usual practice to neglect the parameter uncertainty in constructing prediction intervals.

Forecasting a stochastic trend

Next we consider the random walk with drift

$$y_t = \alpha + y_{t-1} + \varepsilon_t, \quad t = 2, \cdots, n.$$

Let a be the OLS estimate of α. This estimate is obtained by regression in the model $\Delta y_t = \alpha + \varepsilon_t$, so that a is the sample average of Δy_t with variance $\sigma^2/(n-1)$. The h-step-ahead forecast is given by

$$\hat{y}_{n+h} = y_n + ah.$$

If $a = \alpha$, then the forecast error is equal to $y_{n+h} - \hat{y}_{n+h} = \sum_{j=1}^{h} \varepsilon_{n+j}$ with forecast variance $h\sigma^2$. Therefore, in contrast with a deterministic trend, for series with a stochastic trend the forecast uncertainty grows for larger forecast horizons. If the parameter uncertainty is taken into account, then the forecast error is given by $y_{n+h} - \hat{y}_{n+h} = h(\alpha - a) + \sum_{j=1}^{h} \varepsilon_{n+j}$. As the estimate of a is based on the observations y_t with $t \leq n$, all terms in this error are uncorrelated. It follows that

$$E[(y_{n+h} - \hat{y}_{n+h})^2] = \sigma^2 \left(h + \frac{h^2}{n-1} \right) \approx h\sigma^2,$$

where the last approximation is valid if n is large compared to h. This again motivates the usual practice of neglecting the parameter uncertainty in constructing prediction intervals for the series y_t.

Forecasting of ARMA models with deterministic trends

The foregoing trend models are concerned only with the long-run trend and neglect possible short-run fluctuations in the series. Now we consider forecasts for the ARMA model with deterministic trend

$$\phi(L)y_t = \alpha + \beta t + \theta(L)\varepsilon_t.$$

Here $\phi(z)$ satisfies the stationarity condition and $\theta(z)$ the invertibility condition. As in our analysis of (7.21) in Section 7.3.1, we can write the model in the form

$$\phi(L)z_t = \theta(L)\varepsilon_t, \quad z_t = y_t - \delta_1 - \delta_2 t.$$

Here the parameters δ_1 and δ_2 are chosen in such a way that $\phi(L)(\delta_1 + \delta_2 t) = \alpha + \beta t$. The parameters (δ_1, δ_2) are obtained from (α, β) by solving the equation $\phi(L)(\delta_1 + \delta_2 t) = \phi(1)\delta_1 + (t - \sum \phi_k(t-k))\delta_2 = \alpha + \beta t$. To obtain forecasts of y_t, we can first forecast the stationary series z_t by the methods discussed in Section 7.1.6. Then forecasts for y_t are computed by

$$\hat{y}_{n+h} = \hat{z}_{n+h} + \delta_1 + \delta_2(n+h).$$

If the parameter uncertainty in δ_1 and δ_2 is neglected, then the forecast error variance of y_t is the same as that of z_t, because $y_{t+h} - \hat{y}_{t+h} = z_{t+h} - \hat{z}_{t+h}$ in this case.

Forecasting of ARIMA models

Next we consider the forecasting of time series that are integrated of order 1 and that are described by the ARIMA$(p, 1, q)$ model

$$\phi(L)(1-L)y_t = \alpha + \theta(L)\varepsilon_t.$$

The methods of Section 7.1.6 can be used to forecast the stationary variable $z_t = (1-L)y_t$. As $y_{n+h} = y_n + \sum_{j=1}^{h} z_{n+j}$, it follows that the h-step-ahead forecast of y_t is given by

$$\hat{y}_{n+h} = y_n + \sum_{j=1}^{h} \hat{z}_{n+j}.$$

The forecast error is $\sum_{j=1}^{h}\left(z_{n+j} - \hat{z}_{n+j}\right)$. Using the notation of Section 7.1.6, the forecast variance is given by $\text{SPE}(h) = \sigma^2 \sum_{j=1}^{h}\left(\sum_{k=0}^{h-j}\psi_k\right)^2$ (see Exercise 7.5).

Trend forecasts by exponential smoothing (EWMA)

Next we consider trend forecasting in the model (7.22) with latent trend variable μ_t. To derive the forecast formula we rewrite this model as the ARIMA(0,1,1) model (7.23). For simplicity we assume for the moment that the model contains no drift, so that $\alpha = 0$. The MA(1) model for $z_t = \Delta y_t$ is then given by $z_t = \omega_t - \theta\omega_{t-1}$, where $0 < \theta < 1$. Because the MA model for z_t is invertible, the results in Section 7.1.6 show that $\omega_t = z_t - \hat{z}_t$, where the one-step-ahead forecast $\hat{z}_t$ of z_t is equal to $\hat{z}_t = -\theta\omega_{t-1}$. Since the value of y_{t-1} is known at time $(t-1)$, it follows that $\hat{z}_t = \widehat{\Delta y_t} = \hat{y}_t - y_{t-1}$, where $\hat{y}_t$ is the forecast of y_t based on the observations $(y_{t-k},\ k \geq 1)$. The foregoing results for z_t and $\hat{z}_t$ imply that $\omega_t = z_t - \hat{z}_t = y_t - \hat{y}_t$ and that $\hat{y}_t = y_{t-1} + \hat{z}_t = y_{t-1} - \theta\omega_{t-1}$. So the one-step-ahead forecasts of y_t are related by

$$\hat{y}_{t+1} = y_t - \theta\omega_t = y_t - \theta(y_t - \hat{y}_t) = (1-\theta)y_t + \theta\hat{y}_t.$$

Here $1 - \theta$ is called the *smoothing factor*. If this factor is small (that is, if θ is close to one), then the old forecast $\hat{y}_t$ has relatively more weight than the most recent observation y_t. If the smoothing factor is large (so that θ is close to zero), then the new observation y_t has a relatively large weight. By repetitive substitution, the above forecast equation can be written as

$$\hat{y}_{t+1} = (1-\theta)\sum_{j=0}^{\infty}\theta^j y_{t-j}.$$

In the trend model (7.22) the term ε_t is white noise, so that $\hat{\mu}_t = E[\mu_t | Y_{t-1}] = \hat{y}_t$ and hence

$$\hat{\mu}_{t+1} = (1-\theta)y_t + \theta\hat{\mu}_t = (1-\theta)\sum_{j=0}^{\infty}\theta^j y_{t-j}.$$

So in this latent trend model the trend is forecasted as a weighted average of the past observations, with exponentially declining weights that sum up to unity. This is called the *exponentially weighted moving average* (EWMA) method of trend estimation. One also says that the trend is estimated by *exponential smoothing*. The above forecast formula can also be used for h-step-ahead forecasts, as $\hat{y}_{n+h} = \hat{\mu}_{n+h} = \hat{\mu}_n$. So the forecasts are the same for all horizons. This shows that EWMA should be used only for series that do not have a clear trend direction.

Choice of smoothing factor in EWMA

In practice the infinite summation of the EWMA is truncated (as the time series is not observed for $t \leq 0$). Further, the smoothing parameter θ should be specified by the user. Smooth trend estimates are obtained by choosing small values for the smoothing factor — that is, for $\theta \approx 1$. For $\theta \approx 0$ the trend follows the fluctuations in the time series quite rapidly. One possible method to choose θ is by minimizing the sum of squared one-step-ahead forecast errors $\sum_{t=2}^{n}(y_t - \hat{y}_t)^2$. If the error terms ω_t are normally distributed, this corresponds to the ML estimate of θ in the MA(1) model for Δy_t. As this criterion focuses on one-step-ahead forecasts, the obtained trend is often only suitable for short-run forecasts. If long-run forecasts are needed, then other values of θ with smoother trends may provide better results.

Holt–Winters trend forecasts

In the above derivation of the EWMA we assumed that $\alpha = 0$ in (7.22), so that the time series y_t has no drift term in the trend. If the time series has a clear overall trend direction, then this can be modelled by taking $\alpha \neq 0$ in (7.22), but instead one often uses a more flexible model that allows for variations in the trend component α. This leads to the model

$$y_t = \mu_t + \varepsilon_t, \quad \mu_{t+1} = \alpha_t + \mu_t + \eta_t, \quad \alpha_{t+1} = \alpha_t + \zeta_t.$$

Here the three noise processes $(\varepsilon_t, \eta_t, \zeta_t)$ are assumed to be mutually independent and normally distributed white noise processes. Least squares forecasts and trend estimates can be determined in a way similar to the method discussed before for EWMA. This gives the so-called *Holt–Winters* trend estimate

$$\hat{\mu}_{t+1} = (1-\theta_1)y_t + \theta_1(\hat{\alpha}_t + \hat{\mu}_t), \quad \hat{\alpha}_{t+1} = (1-\theta_2)(\hat{\mu}_{t+1} - \hat{\mu}_t) + \theta_2\hat{\alpha}_t.$$

To apply this method one should specify two smoothing factors, $0 < 1-\theta_1 < 1$ for the 'level' μ_t and $0 < 1-\theta_2 < 1$ for the 'slope' α_t in the series. These parameters can be estimated, for instance, by ML in the corresponding ARIMA(0,2,2) model for y_t (see Exercise 7.5). Whereas the EWMA forecasts are the same for all horizons, so that they lie on a horizontal line, the Holt–Winters forecasts lie on a straight line (see Exercise 7.5).

Example 7.13: **Industrial Production (continued)**

We continue our analysis of the data on industrial production in the USA. In Section 7.2 we considered the quarterly series $\Delta_4 y_t$ of yearly growth rates. The fourth difference removes the trend of the series, so that $\Delta_4 y_t$ could be modelled as a stationary series by means of ARMA models (see for instance

Example 7.11). Instead of this differenced series, we will now consider the series y_t consisting of the logarithms of the index of US industrial production. This time series was plotted in Exhibit 7.1 (*b*) in Example 7.1. We will discuss several models for the trend of this series—namely (i) a deterministic trend model, (ii) a stochastic trend model, and (iii) EWMA and Holt–Winters trend estimates.

(i) Deterministic trend model

First we fit a deterministic linear trend. Exhibit 7.14 (*b*) and (*c*) show that the series moves around this trend line but that deviations persist for relatively long periods. This strong positive serial correlation is also indicated by the very low value for the Durbin–Watson statistic (0.08) of the regression in Panel 1 of Exhibit 7.14. Exhibit 7.14 (*b*) also shows the (dynamic) out-of-sample forecasts over the period 1995.1 to 1999.4. Comparing these forecasts with the actual values over the period 1995.1 to 1998.3, we see that the general direction is predicted quite accurately but that the forecast intervals are quite wide. The intervals are equally wide for all horizons. The RMSE over the period 1995.1 to 1998.3 is 0.0249.

(ii) Stochastic trend model

Next we estimate a random walk with drift. Panel 4 of Exhibit 7.14 shows the corresponding regression, with residuals in (*f*), and (*e*) shows the (dynamic) out-of-sample forecasts. The point forecasts are comparable to those of the deterministic trend model. For short forecast horizons the forecast intervals are narrower than for longer horizons. The RMSE over the period 1995.1 to 1998.3 is 0.0348. So the model with stochastic trend performs worse in this respect as compared with the deterministic trend model.

(iii) EWMA and Holt–Winters trend estimates

Exhibit 7.15 (*a*) and (*b*) show the trend estimates obtained by EWMA. If the smoothing factor is estimated by ML, this gives a value of $1 - \theta = 0.97$ in (*a*)—that is, the past is forgotten very fast. If we set this smoothing factor at $1 - \theta = 0.20$ in (*b*), then the estimated trend becomes much smoother and trend deviations in the series are followed only after longer delays. Further note that in the EWMA the estimated trend always lags behind the observed series. This indicates once more that this method is not suitable for trending series. Exhibits 7.15 (*c*) and (*d*) show the Holt–Winters trend estimates, with ML smoothing factors ($1 - \theta_1 = 1.00$ and $1 - \theta_2 = 0.02$) in (*c*) and with both smoothing factors equal to 0.20 in (*d*). The last trend estimate is relatively smooth and it lags behind much less than the smooth EWMA trend.

(*a*)

Panel 1: Dependent Variable: Y				
Method: Least Squares				
Sample: 1961:1 1994:4; Included observations: 136				
Variable	Coefficient	Std. Error	t-Statistic	Prob.
C	3.781132	0.012345	306.2982	0.0000
@TREND(61.1)	0.007140	0.000158	45.16380	0.0000
Durbin-Watson stat	0.082816			

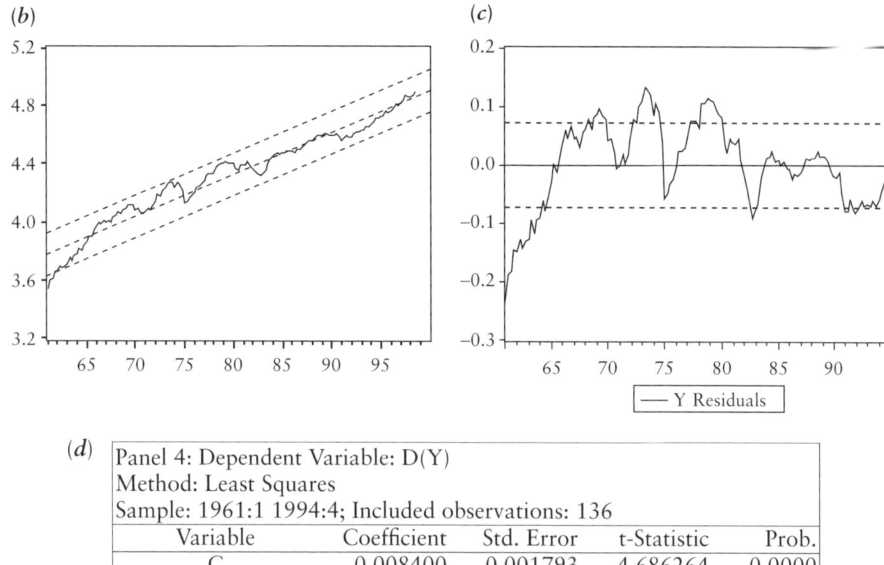

(*d*)

Panel 4: Dependent Variable: D(Y)				
Method: Least Squares				
Sample: 1961:1 1994:4; Included observations: 136				
Variable	Coefficient	Std. Error	t-Statistic	Prob.
C	0.008400	0.001793	4.686264	0.0000

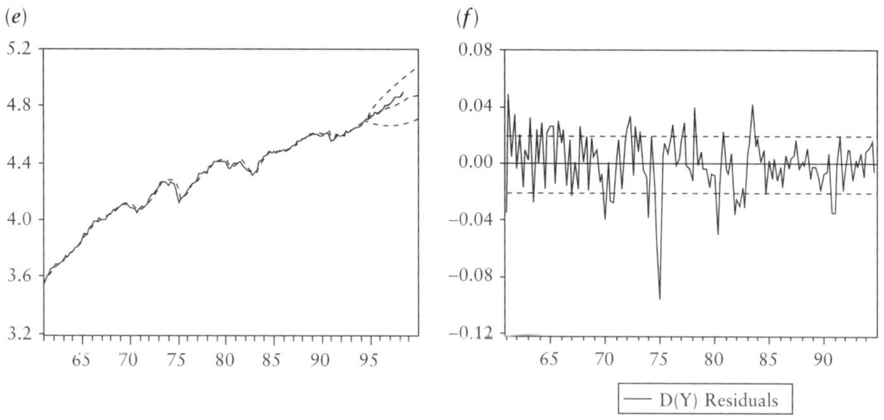

Exhibit 7.14 Industrial Production (Example 7.13)

Deterministic trend model for the logarithm of US industrial production (Panel 1) with fitted values over 1961.1–1994.4 and with forecasts for 1995.1–1999.4 with 95% forecast intervals (*b*) and with corresponding residuals (*c*). Stochastic trend model (Panel 4) with similar graphs ((*e*) and (*f*); the fitted values in (*e*) lag closely behind the actual values).

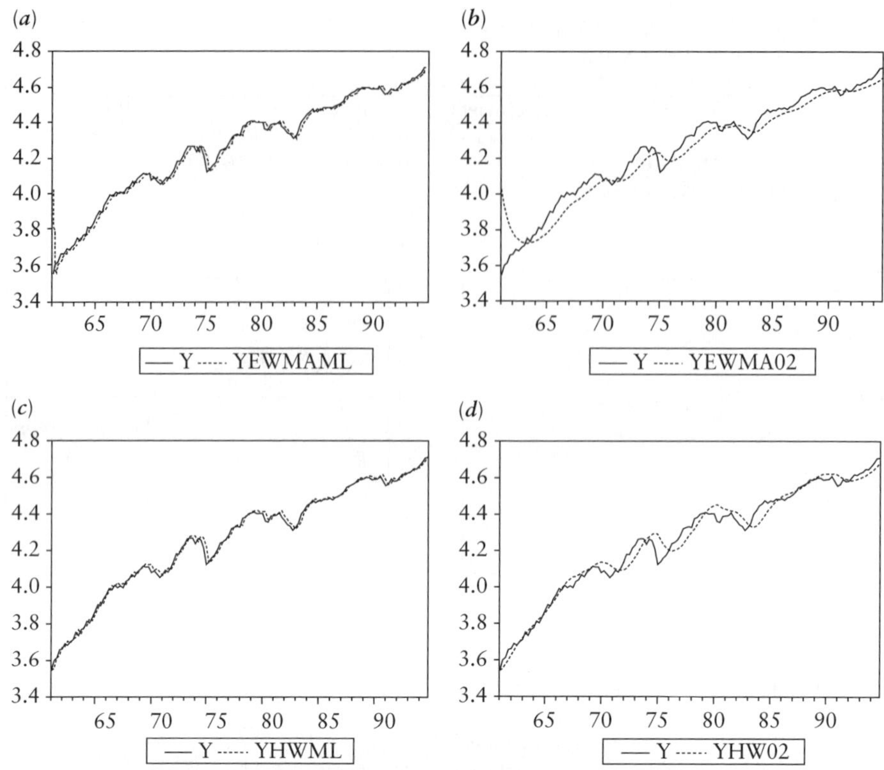

Exhibit 7.15 Industrial Production (Example 7.13)

Trend estimates obtained by EWMA ((*a*)–(*b*), with ML smoothing factor $1-\theta = 0.97$ in (*a*) and with $1-\theta = 0.2$ in (*b*)) and by Holt–Winters ((*c*)–(*d*), with ML smoothing factors $1-\theta_1 = 1.00$ and $1-\theta_2 = 0.02$ in (*c*) and with $1-\theta_1 = 1-\theta_2 = 0.2$ in (*d*)).

☞ Exercises: T: 7.5a–c; E: 7.17b, 7.18e, 7.20c, d.

7.3.3 Unit root tests

Formulation of the testing problem

The analysis in the two foregoing sections shows that it is of importance to model the trend in an appropriate way. In particular, one should distinguish deterministic from stochastic trends. If the trend is deterministic, then the series reverts to the trend line in the long run, innovation shocks have an effect that diminishes over time, and the forecast variance is constant for all horizons. On the other hand, if the trend is stochastic, then the series does not revert to a long-term trend line, innovation shocks have a permanent and non-vanishing effect, and the forecast variance increases for larger horizons. In this section we discuss tests for the nature of the trend. In formulating the testing problem, we should make sure that the models under the null hypothesis and under the alternative hypothesis are reasonable competing alternatives.

As a first step we can make a time plot of the series to see if it has any trending pattern. In many cases it has. A simple test on the nature of the trend can be based on the model (7.21)—that is,

$$y_t = \alpha + \beta t + \phi y_{t-1} + \varepsilon_t,$$

where ε_t is white noise. This model corresponds to a deterministic trend if $-1 < \phi < 1$ and $\beta \neq 0$, and it corresponds to a stochastic trend if $\phi = 1$ and $\beta = 0$. The case $\phi = 1$ and $\beta \neq 0$ is somewhat less relevant, as this corresponds to a quadratic trend pattern that does not occur so much in practice. As the test of parameter restrictions is much easier than that of parameter inequalities, one usually takes as null hypothesis that the trend is stochastic and as alternative that the trend is deterministic. By subtracting y_{t-1} from both sides of the above test equation, it can be rewritten as

$$\Delta y_t = \alpha + \beta t + \rho y_{t-1} + \varepsilon_t, \qquad (7.24)$$

where $\rho = \phi - 1$. The null hypothesis of a stochastic trend and the alternative hypothesis of a deterministic trend can be formulated in terms of the following two parameter restrictions:

$$\begin{aligned} &H_0 : \rho = 0 \text{ and } \beta = 0 && \text{(stochastic trend)},\\ &H_1 : (-2<)\ \rho < 0 \text{ and } \beta \neq 0 && \text{(deterministic trend)}. \end{aligned}$$

The case $\rho \leq -2$, or equivalently $\phi \leq -1$, is of little practical importance, so that the relevant alternative situation of a (trend) stationary time series corresponds to $\rho < 0$.

Dickey–Fuller *F*-test

The above two parameter restrictions can be tested by the usual *F*-test. Because of the lagged regressor y_{t-1}, the equation has $n - 1$ effective observations and $k = 3$ parameters under the alternative hypothesis. So the *F*-statistic is given by

$$F = \frac{(e_R' e_R - e'e)/2}{e'e/(n-4)}.$$

Here $e'e$ is the residual sum of squares in the model (7.24) without parameter restrictions and $e_R' e_R$ is the residual sum of squares in the stochastic trend model with $\beta = \rho = 0$—that is, in the random walk with drift. The null hypothesis of a stochastic trend is rejected for large values of the F-statistic. However, the distribution of this statistic is *non-standard* as it is not equal to the conventional $F(2, n-4)$ distribution, not even asymptotically. The reason is that, under the null hypothesis, the series y_t contains a unit root, so that the regressor y_{t-1} in the test equation is non-stationary. That is, the stability condition of Section 4.1.2 (p. 193) is not satisfied as $\text{plim}\left(\frac{1}{n}\sum_{t=2}^{n} y_{t-1}^2\right) = \infty$ for series with a stochastic trend.

Critical values for the test were obtained by Dickey and Fuller. The 5 per cent critical values for this test are given in Exhibit 7.16 (*a*). For large samples, the 5 per cent critical value of the standard $F(2, n-4)$ distribution is 3.00, but in our trend testing problem the critical values are larger than 6. The 1 per cent critical values range from 9.8 for $n = 50$ to 8.2 for large samples, and these values are also around twice as much as the 1 per cent critical value of the $F(2, n-4)$ distribution that is 4.61 in large samples. Exhibit 7.16 also contains critical values for other tests that will be explained below.

Unit root test and Dickey–Fuller *t*-distribution

Instead of the above F-test, in practice one often tests the single restriction that $\phi = 1$ against the alternative that $\phi < 1$. This is called a *unit root test.* Then the null hypothesis of a stochastic trend against the alternative of a deterministic trend corresponds to the one-sided test

$$\begin{aligned} &\text{H}_0 : \rho = 0 \quad \text{(stochastic trend)}, \\ &\text{H}_1 : \rho < 0 \quad \text{(no stochastic trend)}. \end{aligned}$$

The test is based on the t-value of ρ in the regression (7.24). This t-value is denoted by $t(\rho)$. The null hypothesis of a stochastic trend is rejected if $t(\rho)$ is significantly smaller than zero—that is, if it falls below the relevant (negative) critical value. For the same reasons as before, $t(\rho)$ does not follow the t-distribution, not even asymptotically. The distribution of $t(\rho)$ in the test equation (7.24) depends on the value of β. If the DGP actually has $\rho = 0$ and $\beta = 0$, which is the relevant case under the null hypothesis of a stochastic trend, then the distribution of $t(\rho)$ in the test equation (7.24) is called the *Dickey–Fuller distribution.* The 5 per cent critical values are given in Exhibit 7.16 (*a*). Whereas the one-sided critical value of the conventional t-distribution is around -1.645 in large samples, the Dickey–Fuller critical

(*a*)

DATA: TREND
Test equation: $\Delta y_t = \alpha + \beta t + \rho y_{t-1} + \varepsilon_t$

Sample size (n)	F-test: $H_0: \beta = \rho = 0$	t-test: $H_0: \rho = 0,\ H_1: \rho < 0$ DGP has trend parameter $\beta = 0$
50	6.73	−3.49
100	6.49	−3.45
500	6.30	−3.42
∞	**6.25**	**−3.41**

The critical values apply for the DGP with $\beta = \rho = 0$ and do not depend on α.
The Dickey–Fuller t-test corresponds to the last column.
Bold numbers indicate the asymptotic test values that are used most often.

(*b*)

DATA: NO CLEAR TREND
Test equation: $\Delta y_t = \alpha + \rho y_{t-1} + \varepsilon_t$

Sample size (n)	F-test: $H_0: \alpha = \rho = 0$	t-test: $H_0: \rho = 0,\ H_1: \rho < 0$ DGP has constant term $\alpha = 0$
50	4.81	−2.92
100	4.74	−2.89
500	4.65	−2.86
∞	**4.60**	**−2.86**

The critical values apply for the DGP with $\alpha = \rho = 0$.
The Dickey–Fuller t-test corresponds to the last column.
Bold numbers indicate the asymptotic test values that are used most often.

Exhibit 7.16 Unit root tests

Critical values (for 5% significance level) of unit root tests for data with a clear trend direction (*a*) and for data without a clear trend direction (*b*). The critical values are obtained by simulation.

value is around −3.41 in large samples—that is, it is about twice as large again. Simulation evidence of this large shift in the distribution is left as an exercise (see Exercise 7.14). It has been shown that $t(\rho)$ in the test equation (7.24) has asymptotically the standard normal distribution if $\rho = 0$ and $\beta \neq 0$. However, this situation is not so relevant in unit root testing because under the null hypothesis (with $\phi = 1$ and $\beta \neq 0$) the series would contain a quadratic trend.

Test for data without a clear overall trend direction

If the data show prolonged upward and downward patterns but no clear overall trend direction, then the deterministic trend term can be dropped from (7.24), so that the test equation simplifies to

$$\Delta y_t = \alpha + \rho y_{t-1} + \varepsilon_t.$$

In Section 7.3.1 we showed that, for the stochastic trend model with $\rho = 0$, the parameter α introduces a deterministic trend in the series. As we started from the assumption that the series has no clear overall trend direction, the relevant parameter restrictions for a stochastic trend are that $\rho = 0$ and $\alpha = 0$. The alternative of a stationary process corresponds to $-2 < \rho < 0$, and in this case α is included to model the possibly non-zero mean of the process. So the testing problem becomes

$$\begin{aligned} &H_0 : \rho = 0 \text{ and } \alpha = 0 && \text{(stochastic trend)}, \\ &H_1 : (-2<)\ \rho < 0 \text{ and } \alpha \neq 0 && \text{(no trend)}. \end{aligned}$$

This can again be tested by the F-test. The distribution is again non-standard, and the critical values differ from the ones obtained for the test (7.24) where a deterministic trend is included. The 5 per cent critical values are in Exhibit 7.16 (*b*) and range from around 4.8 to 4.6 in large samples. This is approximately midway between the conventional F-values (≈ 3) and the F-values (≈ 6) that apply for the test equation (7.24) with trend term included.

Also in this case one often uses a t-test instead of the F-test, so that $H_0 : \rho = 0$ is tested against $H_1 : \rho < 0$. Under the null hypothesis of a stochastic trend ($\rho = \alpha = 0$), the t-value of $\hat{\rho}$ in the test equation $\Delta y_t = \alpha + \rho y_{t-1} + \varepsilon_t$ again follows a non-standard distribution. The relevant Dickey–Fuller distribution differs from the one that applies for the test equation (7.24), as the deterministic trend term (βt) is now omitted. The 5 per cent critical values are now around -2.9, well below the conventional value of -1.645 (see Exhibit 7.16 (*b*)). We mention that for $\rho = 0$ and $\alpha \neq 0$ the t-test of $\hat{\rho}$ asymptotically has the standard normal distribution. However, the case $\rho = 0$ and $\alpha \neq 0$ is not so relevant here, as in this case the series contains a clear trend direction so that (7.24) with the deterministic trend term (βt) included would be the correct test equation.

Choice of appropriate test equation

In practice it is sometimes not so clear whether the time series has a clear overall trend direction or not. Then the question arises whether the trend term (βt) in (7.24) should be included in the test regression or not. A possible method is to start with this term included and to drop it if it is not significant. However, if the series has a stochastic trend so that $\rho = 0$ in (7.24), then the t-statistic of β in (7.24) (with a constant, the deterministic trend t and y_{t-1} included as regressors) does not follow the standard t-distribution. The (two-sided) 5 per cent critical value for β is around 3.1 instead of the conventional value of 2.0.

In practice, often the best way to proceed is to plot the data and to exclude the trend term (βt) only if there is no overall upward or downward trend. In particular, one should make sure not to exclude the trend term if the series has a clear direction, as otherwise the alternative hypothesis of the test corresponds to a stationary time series, so that the test has little chance of rejecting the null hypothesis of a stochastic trend. Simulation evidence of this is left as an exercise (see Exercise 7.14). Sometimes, for time series without clear trend direction that move around the value zero, the test equation is simplified even further by excluding both the constant and the trend so that the test regression becomes

$$\Delta y_t = \rho y_{t-1} + \varepsilon_t.$$

The null hypothesis of a stochastic trend corresponds to $\rho = 0$ and the alternative of a stationary process to $-2 < \rho < 0$. This test equation makes sense only if the series has no clear trend direction and the series moves around a mean level zero. The reason is that, under the alternative hypothesis, the series has mean zero. The (one-sided) 5 per cent critical value is around -1.95 (instead of the conventional value of -1.645).

Overview of unit root testing

We summarize the above results. In most cases where one is interested in investigating the nature of the trend in a series, the relevant test regression is (7.24) or its generalization (7.25), which will be discussed in the sequel. The null hypothesis of a stochastic trend is tested by the F-test on $\rho = \beta = 0$. As an alternative, one can apply the Dickey–Fuller t-test on the single restriction that $\rho = 0$ against the alternative that $\rho < 0$. The null hypothesis of a stochastic trend is rejected in favour of the alternative of a deterministic trend if the F-test takes large values, or if the t-test takes large negative values. The tests do not follow the conventional F- and t-distributions. In large enough samples ($n \geq 100$) the critical values of the F-test are roughly around 6.5 and those of the t-test around -3.5. As a rule of thumb, the presence of a stochastic trend is rejected for $F > 6.5$ or for $t < -3.5$. Critical values are given in Exhibit 7.16 (*a*).

For time series with prolonged up- and downswings but without clear trend direction, the trend term (βt) can be dropped from the test equation (7.24). The null hypothesis of a stochastic trend can then be tested by the F-test on $\rho = \alpha = 0$ or by the one-sided t-test on $\rho = 0$ against $\rho < 0$. The relevant critical values of these tests are in Exhibit 7.16 (*b*), with values (for $n \geq 100$) of roughly 4.7 for the F-test and -2.9 for the t-test.

Phillips–Perron test

The above tests are valid under the assumption that the error terms ε_t in the relevant test equation are normally distributed white noise. In practice, time series are often also characterized by short-term fluctuations in the sense that the detrended series is correlated over time. The above models neglect this, so that the residuals will be serially correlated and the critical values will not be valid. For the Dickey–Fuller t-test, we can apply a Newey–West correction for serial correlation to compute the standard error of the estimated parameter ρ. This correction is based on the GMM method, as was discussed in Section 5.5.2 (p. 359–60). If this correction is applied, the Dickey–Fuller critical values remain valid asymptotically. The t-test based on the Newey–West standard error of ρ is called the *Phillips–Perron* test.

Derivation of augmented Dickey–Fuller test equation

An alternative method is to model the short-run correlations by including lagged values of y_t in the test equation so that

$$\phi(L)y_t = \alpha + \beta t + \varepsilon_t,$$

where the AR-polynomial $\phi(z) = 1 - \phi_1 z - \cdots - \phi_p z^p$ has degree p. We assume that the series y_t is either integrated of order 1 or trend stationary. The null hypothesis of a stochastic trend corresponds to the case where $\beta = 0$ and y_t is integrated of order 1. In this case, the AR polynomial $\phi(z)$ should have a unit root, so that $\phi(1) = 0$. Then the polynomial can be factorized as $\phi(z) = (1 - z)\psi(z)$, so that y_t is an ARIMA process. The alternative is that y_t is trend stationary—that is, $\beta \neq 0$ and the AR polynomial is stationary, so that all the roots of $\phi(z) = 0$ lie outside the unit circle. As $\phi(0) = 1$, the requirement that $\phi(z) = 0$ has no solutions for $|z| < 1$ implies that $\phi(1) > 0$ in this case. Therefore the testing problem can be formulated as follows in terms of the parameters β and $\phi(1) = 1 - \sum_{k=1}^{p} \phi_k$:

$$\begin{aligned} &\mathrm{H}_0 : \phi(1) = 0 \text{ and } \beta = 0 \quad \text{(stochastic trend)},\\ &\mathrm{H}_1 : \phi(1) > 0 \text{ and } \beta \neq 0 \quad \text{(deterministic trend)}. \end{aligned}$$

For the case of an AR polynomial of order $p = 1$ we have $\phi(1) = 1 - \phi$, so that $\phi(1) = 0$ corresponds to $\phi = 1$ and $\phi(1) > 0$ to $\phi < 1$, which is the case discussed before in terms of the test equation (7.24).

The following technical results are helpful to write the above testing problem for AR(p) models in a more convenient form. Define the polynomial $\psi(z) = \phi(z) - \phi(1)z$; then $\psi(1) = 0$, so that $\psi(z)$ can be factorized as $\psi(z) = (1 - z)\rho(z)$ for some polynomial $\rho(z) = 1 - \rho_1 z - \cdots - \rho_{p-1} z^{p-1}$ of degree $(p - 1)$. Now define $\rho = -\phi(1)$ and rewrite the polynomial $\phi(z)$ as

$$\begin{aligned} \phi(z) &= \psi(z) + \phi(1)z = \phi(1)z + (1 - z)\rho(z)\\ &= -\rho z + (1 - z) - (1 - z)\sum_{k=1}^{p-1} \rho_k z^k. \end{aligned}$$

If we use this result, the test equation $\phi(L)y_t = \alpha + \beta t + \varepsilon_t$ can be written as follows:

$$\Delta y_t = \alpha + \beta t + \rho y_{t-1} + \rho_1 \Delta y_{t-1} + \cdots + \rho_{p-1} \Delta y_{t-p+1} + \varepsilon_t. \quad (7.25)$$

Augmented Dickey–Fuller test

As $\rho = -\phi(1)$, the testing problem can be formulated as follows in terms of the augmented Dickey–Fuller test equation (7.25):

$$\begin{aligned} &\mathrm{H}_0 : \rho = 0 \text{ and } \beta = 0 \quad \text{(stochastic trend)},\\ &\mathrm{H}_1 : \rho < 0 \text{ and } \beta \neq 0 \quad \text{(deterministic trend)}. \end{aligned}$$

The test can be performed by the F-test, or by the t-test on ρ. This is called the *augmented Dickey–Fuller* (ADF) test. The test equation is simply obtained from the basic test equation (7.24) by adding lagged values of Δy_t as additional regressors. Note that, under the null hypothesis of a stochastic trend, the series y_t is integrated of order 1, so that the added regressors Δy_{t-k} are all stationary. The asymptotic critical values (for $n \to \infty$) of the ADF test are the same as the ones for the Dickey–Fuller test reported in Exhibit 7.16. Although the finite sample critical values are different, they are still approximately valid provided that the lag length p is relatively small compared to the sample size n.

The lag order p in the ADF test equation can be selected, for instance, by starting with a large value for p and then sequentially reducing the order by testing for the significance of the coefficient ρ_{p-1} of the largest lag. As the regressors Δy_{t-k} are stationary, it can be shown that the t-tests for these coefficients follow the standard t-distribution. Another method to select the lag order p is to start with equation (7.24) and then to increase the order p until the residuals have no significant autocorrelation anymore.

Testing for integration of order 2

The above results hold true for testing the null hypothesis that the process has a single unit root against the alternative that it is stationary around a deterministic trend. If the process Δy_t is possibly non-stationary—that is, if y_t is possibly integrated of order 2—then one can proceed as follows. First test the null hypothesis that y_t is integrated of order 2 against the alternative that it is integrated of order 1. This can be tested by considering the differenced series z_t, which is integrated of order 1 under the null hypothesis and (trend) stationary under the alternative. For instance, one can apply the ADF test equation (7.25) for the series z_t. If the null hypothesis is rejected—that is, if z_t is trend stationary—then y_t is integrated of order at most 1. As a second step, one can test whether y_t is integrated of order 1 against the alternative that it is (trend) stationary by applying the ADF test for the series y_t.

Remark on critical values in unit root tests

Exhibit 7.16 shows that critical values of unit root tests depend on the inclusion of deterministic components (constant, trend) in the equation. The critical values also depend on other possible deterministic components, such as breaks in the level α or in the trend slope β or the presence of seasonal components. Therefore one should first make sure that such components are modelled in an appropriate way before unit root tests are applied, as otherwise the test outcomes may be misleading. The effect of breaks is further discussed in Section 7.4.1.

Example 7.14: **Industrial Production (continued)**

E

XM701INP

We continue our analysis of the series y_t consisting of the logarithm of US quarterly industrial production. We will discuss (i) the data, (ii) the results of Dickey–Fuller tests, and (iii) the results of Phillips–Perron and augmented Dickey–Fuller tests.

(i) The data

Exhibit 7.1 (*a*) in Example 7.1 shows that this series is characterized by an upward trend. In Example 7.13 we considered different trend models, and now we will test for the nature of the trend of this series. Because of the clear overall trend direction, we should always include a deterministic trend term in testing the null hypothesis of a stochastic trend. Otherwise, if this trend term is omitted, the alternative hypothesis would correspond to a stationary process and there would be no chance of rejecting the null hypothesis in favour of the alternative. We use quarterly data over the period 1961–94, so that there are $n = 136$ observations.

(ii) Dickey–Fuller tests

We start with the basic test equation (7.24). The results are in Panels 1 and 2 of Exhibit 7.17. The test values are $F = 5.46$ (which is smaller than the 5 per cent critical value of around 6.45) and $t = -2.80$ (which is larger than the critical value of around -3.44). Therefore the null hypothesis of a unit root is not rejected (at 5 per cent significance). However, this test equation is not well specified, as the residuals show serial correlation. Panel 3 of Exhibit 7.17 shows the values of the first five S(P)ACF of the OLS residuals of the regression (7.24). For instance, the correlations at lags four and five are significant, indicating the possible presence of seasonal effects. Such effects could well be present for quarterly production figures.

Panel 1: ADF Test Statistic	−2.797508	5% Critical Value	−3.4433
Dickey-Fuller Test Equation; Dependent Variable: D(Y)			
Sample: 1961:1 1994:4; Included observations: 136			
Variable	Coefficient	Std. Error	t-Statistic
Y(−1)	−0.065763	0.023508	−2.797508
C	0.261410	0.088632	2.949402
@TREND(1961:1)	0.000397	0.000175	2.263446

Panel 2: F-test on Y(−1) and TREND	
Null Hypothesis:	C(1)=0, C(3)=0
F-statistic	5.459897

Panel 3: S(P)ACF of residuals of Dickey-Fuller regression				
Sample: 1961:1 1994:4; Included observations: 136				
Lag	SACF	SPACF	Q-Stat	Prob
1	0.086	0.086	1.0180	0.313
2	0.196	0.190	6.3727	0.041
3	−0.123	−0.160	8.5222	0.036
4	0.310	0.318	22.176	0.000
5	−0.298	−0.379	34.894	0.000

Panel 4: Phillips-Perron Test	−2.897757	5% Critical Value	−3.4433

Panel 5: ADF Test Statistic	−2.879186	5% Critical Value	−3.4433
Augmented Dickey-Fuller Test Equation; Dependent Variable: D(Y)			
Sample: 1961:1 1994:4; Included observations: 136			
Variable	Coefficient	Std. Error	t-Statistic
Y(−1)	−0.062996	0.021880	−2.879186
D(Y(−1))	0.267290	0.080354	3.326419
D(Y(−2))	0.111804	0.077854	1.436074
D(Y(−3))	−0.150127	0.076845	−1.953643
D(Y(−4))	0.345637	0.076304	4.529756
D(Y(−5))	−0.289789	0.079154	−3.661092
C	0.247258	0.081971	3.016418
@TREND(1961:1)	0.000397	0.000166	2.398142

Panel 6: F-test on Y(−1) and TREND	
Null Hypothesis:	C(1)=0, C(8)=0
F-statistic	5.493062

Panel 7: S(P)ACF of residuals of Augmented Dickey-Fuller regression				
Sample: 1961:1 1994:4; Included observations: 136				
Lag	SACF	SPACF	Q-Stat	Prob
1	0.001	0.001	6.E-05	0.994
2	−0.104	−0.104	1.5259	0.466
3	0.049	0.049	1.8584	0.602
4	0.013	0.002	1.8826	0.757
5	−0.015	−0.004	1.9127	0.861

Exhibit 7.17 Industrial Production (Example 7.14)

Tests on the nature of the trend in the series of US industrial production (in logarithms): Dickey–Fuller *t*-test (Panel 1) and *F*-test (Panel 2), S(P)ACF of residuals of test equation (Panel 3), Phillips–Perron test (Panel 4), ADF *t*-test (Panel 5) and *F*-test (Panel 6), and S(P)ACF of residuals of ADF test equation (Panel 7).

(iii) Phillips–Perron and augmented Dickey–Fuller tests

The foregoing results show that we should correct for the short-run correlations that are present in the time series. Panel 4 of Exhibit 7.17 shows the result of the Phillips–Perron test. The computed t-value is slightly lower (-2.90 as compared to an OLS t-value of -2.80). Still, this is well above the critical value of -3.44, so that the null hypothesis of a stochastic trend is not rejected. Panels 5 and 6 of Exhibit 7.17 show the result of the augmented Dickey–Fuller test with five lagged terms Δy_t included in the test equation. The relevant t-value is now -2.88, and again we cannot reject the presence of a unit root. The F-test has value $F = 5.49$, which is below the 5 per cent critical value (6.45), so the presence of a unit root is also not rejected by the F-test. Panel 7 of Exhibit 7.17 contains the S(P)ACF of the residuals of this ADF test equation. These residuals do not contain any significant correlation anymore, so that this test equation is well specified. The overall conclusion is that the logarithmic series of industrial production contains a unit root—that is, the trend is stochastic. The modelling of the seasonal components of this series is further discussed in Example 7.16 in the next section.

E

XM702DJI

Example 7.15: **Dow-Jones Index (continued)**

As a second example we consider the series y_t consisting of the logarithm of the daily Dow-Jones index. This series is shown in Exhibit 7.2 (b) in Example 7.2. The series contains a clear upward trend and consists of $n = 2528$ observations. We will (i) test for the presence of a unit root, and (ii) test for the presence of two unit roots.

(i) Test for the presence of a unit root

We use the ADF test equation (7.25) with five lagged terms. This is because the series consists of daily data, so that the five lagged terms can pick up possible weekly effects. Because of the large number of observations we can use the asymptotic critical values (for $n = \infty$) in Exhibit 7.16. The results in Panels 1 and 2 of Exhibit 7.18 show that the null hypothesis of a stochastic trend cannot be rejected, as $F = 4.20 < 6.25$ and $t = -2.54 > -3.41$. Panel 3 shows that the residuals of the test equation are not serially correlated.

(ii) Test for the presence of two unit roots

Exhibit 7.2 (c) shows that the series of first differences Δy_t does not display a clear trend direction. We can test whether the series y_t has two unit roots by testing whether the series Δy_t has a unit root. The ADF test equation (7.24) in Panels 4 and 5 of Exhibit 7.18 give test values $F = 1189$ and $t = -48.77$. So the presence of a second unit root is clearly rejected. The S(P)ACF of the

Panel 1: ADF Test Statistic	−2.539298	5% Critical Value	−3.4142
Augmented Dickey-Fuller Test Equation; Dep. Variable: D(LOGDJ)			
Sample(adjusted) 7 2528; Included obs 2522 after adjusting endpoints			
Variable	Coefficient	Std. Error	t-Statistic
LOGDJ(−1)	−0.004428	0.001744	−2.539298
D(LOGDJ(−1))	0.030979	0.019923	1.554888
D(LOGDJ(−2))	−0.016979	0.019930	−0.851933
D(LOGDJ(−3))	−0.044691	0.019907	−2.245021
D(LOGDJ(−4))	−0.006859	0.019923	−0.344270
D(LOGDJ(5))	−0.013512	0.019916	−0.678443
C	0.034227	0.013418	2.550807
@TREND(1)	3.04E-06	1.09E-06	2.787442

Panel 2: F-test on LOGDJ(−1) and TREND	
Null Hypothesis:	C(1)=0, C(8)=0
F-statistic	4.201230

Panel 3: S(P)ACF of residuals of ADF regression for LOGDJ				
Sample: 7 2528; Included observations: 2522				
Lag	SACF	SPACF	Q-Stat	Prob
1	0.000	0.000	0.0002	0.988
2	0.000	0.000	0.0004	1.000
3	−0.002	−0.002	0.0148	1.000
4	−0.001	−0.001	0.0167	1.000
5	−0.001	−0.001	0.0174	1.000

Panel 4: ADF Test Statistic	−48.76587	5% Critical Value	−3.4142
Augmented Dickey-Fuller Test Equation; Dep Variable: D(DLOGDJ)			
Sample(adjusted) 3 2528; Included obs 2526 after adjusting endpoints			
Variable	Coefficient	Std. Error	t-Statistic
DLOGDJ(−1)	−0.970458	0.019900	−48.76587
C	0.000128	0.000355	0.361549
@TREND(1)	3.27E-07	2.43E-07	1.342188

Panel 5: F-test on DLOGDJ(−1) and TREND	
Null Hypothesis:	C(1)=0, C(3)=0
F-statistic	1189.055

Panel 6: S(P)ACF of residuals of ADF regression for D(LOGDJ)				
Sample: 3 2528; Included observations: 2526				
Lag	SACF	SPACF	Q-Stat	Prob
1	0.001	0.001	0.0008	0.978
2	−0.018	−0.018	0.7986	0.671
3	−0.046	−0.046	6.2523	0.100
4	−0.009	−0.010	6.4792	0.166
5	−0.013	−0.015	6.9391	0.225

Exhibit 7.18 Dow-Jones Index (Example 7.15)

Augmented Dickey–Fuller test on a unit root in the logarithms of the Dow-Jones (LOGDJ), *t*-test (Panel 1), *F*-test (Panel 2), S(P)ACF of residuals of the ADF test equation (Panel 3), and Dickey–Fuller test on a unit root in the series of first differences (DLOGDJ), *t*-test (Panel 4), *F*-test (Panel 5), S(P)ACF of residuals of the DF test equation (Panel 6).

residuals of this test equation in Panel 6 of Exhibit 7.18 indicates no serial correlation, which justifies the use of the simple equation (7.24).

☞ **Exercises:** S: 7.12f, 7.14a–d; E: **7.17c, d, 7.20a, b, 7.21b, 7.23a, d, 7.24a.**

7.3.4 Seasonality

Time series components

When time series are measured for instance every month or every quarter, they may contain pronounced seasonal variation. The *seasonal component* in a time series refers to patterns that are repeated over a one-year period and that average out in the long run. The patterns that do not average out are included in the constant and the trend components of the model. Whereas the trend is of dominant importance in long-term forecasting, the seasonal component is very important in short-term forecasting as it is often the main source of short-run fluctuations. Seasonal effects may be detected from plots of the time series, and also from plots of the seasonal series that consist of the observations in the same month or quarter over the different years. The autocorrelations of seasonal time series often show positive peaks at the seasonal lag and its multiples—that is, at lags 12, 24, 36 (and so on) for monthly series and at lags 4, 8, 12 (and so on) for quarterly series.

If trend and seasonal components are *additive*, then the time series may be decomposed as

$$y_t = T_t + S_t + R_t.$$

Here T_t denotes the trend component and S_t the seasonal component. The component R_t stands for a stationary process that consists of transient deviations from the trend and seasonal components. If the effects are *multiplicative* this is modelled as $y_t = T_t S_t R_t$—that is, the three components multiplied with each other produce the observed series. The multiplicative model can easily be transformed to an additive model by taking logarithms, so that $\log(y_t) = \log(T_t) + \log(S_t) + \log(R_t)$. In this section we will therefore discuss only additive models.

Decomposition of time series and the Census X-12 method

Stated in general terms, for series with additive components the trend T_t can be obtained by long-term moving averages of the series y_t. After the trend has been estimated, the seasonal components can be obtained by averaging the detrended values $(y_t - T_t)$ that pertain to the same period of the year (the same month or the same quarter). Finally, the stationary remainder $(y_t - T_t - S_t)$ can be modelled by an ARMA process to take care of short-term deviations of the series y_t from the trend and seasonal patterns. Forecasts of the series y_t can then be computed by adding the forecasts of the trend, the seasonal component, and the stationary part. A well-known method of this type is the so-called *Census X-12* method to construct the seasonal component S_t and the corresponding seasonally adjusted time series $(y_t - S_t)$. For quarterly data with additive trend and seasonal components, the idea is as follows. A simple first estimate of the trend is given by the centred yearly average $T_t = \frac{1}{4}(\frac{1}{2}y_{t-2} + y_{t-1} + y_t + y_{t+1} + \frac{1}{2}y_{t+2})$. The seasonal index Q_j of quarter j is then defined as the sample average of all values of the trend-adjusted series $(y_t - T_t)$ that fall in the jth quarter, $j = 1, \cdots, 4$. The seasonal component is defined by $S_t = (Q_j - \overline{Q})$, where j is the quarter of observation t and $\overline{Q}$ is the average of the four seasonal indices. The value of $\overline{Q}$ is subtracted in computing the seasonal component S_t because this component then sums up to zero over a year. The seasonally adjusted series is defined by $(y_t - S_t)$. This adjusted series may be used as a starting point in a second round to construct a new (longer term) estimate of the trend and corresponding new estimates of the seasonal components. This method is much used in practice, with modifications to take care of many kinds of possible special properties of observed time series. A disadvantage of this method is that it does not specify a statistical model, so that it is not possible to apply statistical tests on the outcomes.

Model with deterministic seasonals

Now we discuss some parametric models for seasonal time series. As in the case of trends, one should distinguish deterministic from stochastic seasonals. For simplicity we consider again the case of quarterly data with additive seasonals. The results can be generalized for other observation frequencies (for instance, for monthly or weekly data) and for series with multiplicative seasonals.

Deterministic seasonals can be modelled by *seasonal dummies*. For instance, an AR(1) model for quarterly data with deterministic trend and seasonal components is given by

$$y_t = \alpha + \beta t + \alpha_2 D_{2t} + \alpha_3 D_{3t} + \alpha_4 D_{4t} + \phi y_{t-1} + \varepsilon_t.$$

Here D_{2t} is a dummy variable with $D_{2t} = 1$ if the tth observation falls in the second quarter of a year and $D_{2t} = 0$ otherwise, and the dummies D_{3t} and D_{4t} for the third and fourth quarters are defined in a similar way. If $-1 < \phi < 1$, then this model can be estimated and evaluated by conventional OLS methods, and more general ARMA models can be estimated as usual by ML. If the trend is stochastic—that is, if $\phi = 1$—then the parameters are easily estimated by regressing Δy_t on a constant, the trend t, and the three seasonal dummies. In order to perform a unit root test—that is, to test whether $\phi = 1$—the critical values of Dickey–Fuller also apply for this model with deterministic seasonal dummies.

Model with stochastic seasonals

The simplest model with *stochastic seasonals* is given by the seasonal random walk model

$$y_t = \alpha + y_{t-4} + \varepsilon_t.$$

This can be written as $(1 - L^4)y_t = \alpha + \varepsilon_t$. The AR polynomial $(1 - z^4)$ has a unit root at $z = 1$ and three so-called seasonal unit roots at $z = -1$ and at $z = \pm i$. As $1 - z^4 = (1 - z)(1 + z + z^2 + z^3)$, the series of fourth differences can be written as $(1 - L^4)y_t = (1 - L)x_t$, where $x_t = (1 + L + L^2 + L^3)y_t$ is the year-total of the series y_t over the last four quarters. So a model for y_t with stochastic seasonality implies that the series x_t of year totals has a unit root. This can be tested, for instance, by applying the ADF test on the series x_t of year-totals.

Seasonal ARIMA models and the 'airline' model

The above model with stochastic seasonal components can be generalized to the class of so-called seasonal ARIMA or SARIMA models. For quarterly data, a SARIMA(p, d, q) model is defined by

$$\phi(L^4)(1 - L^4)^d y_t = \theta(L^4)\varepsilon_t,$$

where $\phi(z)$ and $\theta(z)$ have all their roots outside the unit circle. This is an ARIMA model where the value of y_t is related only to the values of y_{t-4}, y_{t-8}, y_{t-12} (and so on) of observations in the same quarter in former years. This is motivated by the fact that seasonal time series often exhibit the strongest correlations at the seasonal lags. If non-seasonal correlations are also of importance, the seasonal model can be combined with an ARIMA model. For instance, the so-called '*airline model*' is given by

$$(1 - L)(1 - L^4)y_t = (1 + \theta_1 L)(1 + \theta_4 L^4)\varepsilon_t.$$

The right-hand side is an MA(5) process with parameter restrictions, as only lags 1, 4, and 5 are present. The advantage of this and other seasonal ARIMA models is that they contain relatively few parameters to model correlations over longer lags. Note that the above model contains a double root at unity—that is, the process is assumed to be integrated of order 2. This makes sense, for instance, if the series $(1 - L)y_t$ contains strong seasonal correlations that die out only very slowly. An alternative is to consider models with deterministic trends and seasonals or combinations of stochastic trends with deterministic seasonals.

Choice between deterministic and stochastic trends and seasonals

To choose among the various possible models, it is helpful to start by testing for the order of integration of the series y_t. In practice the order of integration does not exceed two, and two unit roots may be present in the case of a stochastic trend combined with a stochastic seasonal. However, in most cases the order of integration is either one or zero. We can first test the null hypothesis of integration of order 2 against the alternative of order 1. This can be tested by an ADF test on the series of first differences $(1 - L)y_t$. If the series contains two unit roots, this suggests incorporating a stochastic trend and a stochastic seasonal in the model. If second order integration is rejected, we can test the null hypothesis of first order integration against the alternative of (trend) stationarity. Deterministic components for trend and seasonals can be included in the test equation. If the series is integrated of order 1, then we can include either a stochastic trend with deterministic seasonals in the model, or a stochastic seasonal with a deterministic trend. If the series is trend stationary, we can include deterministic trend and seasonal terms in the model.

Note that, if the series is integrated of order 1, the transformation $x_t = (1 - L)(1 - L^4)y_t$ involves over-differencing. This means that the ARMA model for x_t is not invertible (see Exercise 7.13). An indication of possible over-differentiation can be obtained from the SACF of x_t, as the theoretical autocorrelations sum up to $-\frac{1}{2}$ in this case (see Exercise 7.13).

Example 7.16: **Industrial Production (continued)**

We continue our analysis of the quarterly series y_t of logarithms of US industrial production. We will discuss (i) the order of integration of this series, (ii) the nature of the seasonal component of this series, (iii) remarks on two alternative models, and (iv) the time series decomposition obtained by the Census X-12 method.

(i) Order of integration

In Example 7.14 in the foregoing section we concluded that the time series has a unit root (see Exhibit 7.17). Now we investigate whether the series has two unit roots—that is, we test whether the series Δy_t of quarterly growth rates has a unit root. For this purpose we apply the ADF test on the series $z_t = \Delta y_t$. Four lags are included to account for possible seasonal effects. As the series z_t does not have a clear trend direction, we exclude the deterministic trend component from the ADF test equation. The result is shown in Panel 1 of Exhibit 7.19. The relevant t-value is -5.67, which is much below the 5 per cent critical value of -2.88 (note that the test equation does not contain the deterministic trend term). This means that z_t does not have a unit root. So we conclude that the series y_t is integrated of order 1.

(ii) Nature of the seasonal component

Panel 2 of Exhibit 7.19 shows the correlogram of the series Δy_t. The SACF indicates the presence of seasonal effects. Panels 3 and 4 contain ADF tests for the series of year-totals $z_t = (1 + L + L^2 + L^3)y_t$. The null hypothesis of integration of order 2 is rejected (see Panel 4, the t-value is $-3.89 < -2.89$), and the null hypothesis of integration of order 1 is not rejected (see Panel 3, the t-value is $-2.49 > -3.44$). We conclude that the series z_t is integrated of order 1. So the series $(1 - L)z_t = (1 - L^4)y_t = \Delta_4 y_t$ is stationary. This result, together with the seasonal correlation that is present in the series Δy_t, motivates using a model with stochastic seasonal for the series y_t. This motivates our analysis of the quarterly series of annual growth rates $\Delta_4 y_t$ in foregoing sections.

The series $\Delta_4 y_t$ contains no trend and also no seasonal effects, as is clear from the SACF in Exhibit 7.8 (see Example 7.7). This means that the trend and the seasonal are both eliminated by transforming the series y_t to the series of annual growth rates $\Delta_4 y_t = (1 - L^4)y_t$. Models for the stationary series $\Delta_4 y_t$ were discussed in Example 7.11.

(iii) Remarks on two alternative models

It is left as an exercise (see Exercise 7.16) to estimate two alternative models—namely, an AR(p) model with deterministic seasonals for the series Δy_t and an 'airline' model for the series y_t. The models can be compared by diagnostic tests and by comparing their forecast performance, as described in Section 7.2.4.

(iv) Time series decomposition obtained by the Census X-12 method

Finally we describe the results of the Census X-12 method. We consider an additive model for the series y_t of logarithms of the industrial production. This corresponds to a multiplicative model for the original production index series. The seasonally adjusted series for the period 1980–94 is shown in Exhibit 7.20 (a). The estimated seasonal components are relatively small, as they are all below 0.01—that is, they are less than 1 per cent. As a consequence, the seasonally adjusted series is very close to the original one. The estimated seasonal components in Panel 2 of Exhibit 7.20 indicate some

Panel 1: ADF Test Statistic −5.668179 5% Critical Value −2.8827
Augmented Dickey-Fuller Test Equation; Dependent Variable: D(DY)
Sample: 1961:1 1994:4; Included observations: 136

Variable	Coefficient	Std. Error	t-Statistic
DY(−1)	−0.786100	0.138687	−5.668179
D(DY(−1))	0.070365	0.134332	0.523814
D(DY(−2))	0.160678	0.114100	1.408224
D(DY(−3))	−0.020794	0.099616	−0.208744
D(DY(−4))	0.322013	0.079909	4.029740
C	0.006605	0.001925	3.431268

Panel 2: Correlogram of DY

Lag	SACF	SPACF	Q-Stat	Prob
1	0.112	0.112	1.7472	0.186
2	0.212	0.202	8.0437	0.018
3	−0.098	−0.147	9.3999	0.024
4	0.325	0.332	24.430	0.000
5	−0.269	−0.372	34.775	0.000
6	0.059	0.082	35.272	0.000
7	−0.258	−0.159	44.928	0.000
8	0.091	−0.009	46.135	0.000
9	−0.295	−0.076	58.988	0.000
10	0.124	0.061	61.269	0.000
11	−0.193	−0.059	66.869	0.000
12	0.163	0.057	70.889	0.000

Panel 3: ADF Test Statistic −2.486805 5% Critical Value −3.4445
Augmented Dickey-Fuller Test Equation; Dep. Var.: D(YEARSUMY)
Sample(adjusted): 1962:2 1994:4; Included observations: 131

Variable	Coefficient	Std. Error	t-Statistic
YEARSUMY(−1)	−0.016469	0.006622	−2.486805
D(YEARSUMY(−1))	1.306777	0.087579	14.92109
D(YEARSUMY(−2))	−0.594846	0.145276	−4.094604
D(YEARSUMY(−3))	0.183889	0.144221	1.275052
D(YEARSUMY(−4))	−0.136339	0.085423	−1.596048
C	0.260355	0.099926	2.605466
TREND	0.000404	0.000192	2.102449

Panel 4: ADF Test Statistic −3.890236 5% Critical Value −2.8837
Augmented Dickey-Fuller Test Equation; Dep. Var.: D(DYEARSUMY)
Sample(adjusted): 1962:3 1994:4; Included observations: 130

Variable	Coefficient	Std. Error	t-Statistic
DYEARSUMY(−1)	−0.179666	0.046184	3.890236
D(DYEARSUMY(−1))	0.572717	0.078698	7.277444
D(DYEARSUMY(−2))	−0.080749	0.093386	−0.864676
D(DYEARSUMY(−3))	0.239245	0.090181	2.652941
D(DYEARSUMY(−4))	−0.203484	0.084778	−2.400198
C	0.005857	0.002188	2.676967

Exhibit 7.19 Industrial Production (Example 7.16)

ADF test on the series of first differences Δy_t (denoted by DY in Panel 1; here $H_0: y_t$ is I(2) is tested against H_1: y_t is I(1)), correlogram of Δy_t (Panel 2), ADF test on the quarterly series of year-totals (Panel 3; here H_0: YEARSUMY is I(1) is tested against H_1: YEARSUMY is I(0)), and ADF test on the first differences DYEARSUMY (Panel 4; here H_0: YEARSUMY is I(2) is tested against H_1: YEARSUMY is I(1)).

(*a*)

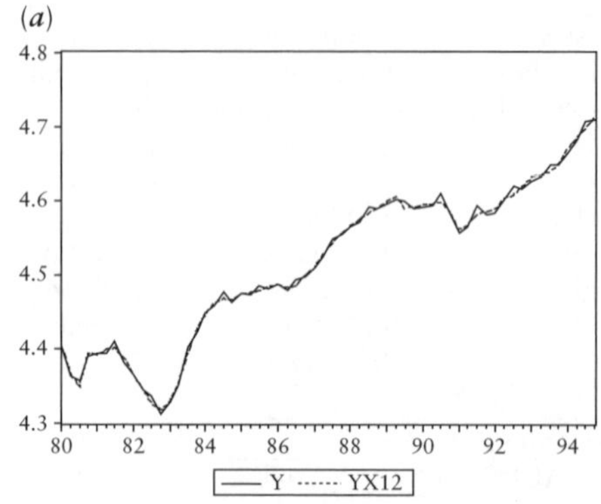

(*b*)

Panel 2: Estimated seasonal components				
Year	Quarter 1	Quarter 2	Quarter 3	Quarter 4
1980	0.002	−0.005	0.009	−0.005
1981	0.001	−0.005	0.009	−0.005
1982	0.001	−0.005	0.009	−0.005
1983	0.000	−0.004	0.008	−0.004
1984	0.000	−0.004	0.008	−0.003
1985	0.000	−0.004	0.007	−0.003
1986	0.000	−0.004	0.007	−0.002
1987	−0.001	−0.004	0.007	−0.002
1988	−0.002	−0.004	0.008	−0.002
1989	−0.004	−0.003	0.010	−0.002
1990	−0.005	−0.003	0.011	−0.003
1991	−0.005	−0.002	0.011	−0.003
1992	−0.006	−0.002	0.011	−0.003
1993	−0.005	−0.002	0.010	−0.003
1994	−0.005	−0.001	0.009	−0.003

(*c*)

Panel 3: Predicted Seasonal Components one year ahead (1995)					
Quarter	1	2	3	4	Average
Predicted Seasonal	−0.005	−0.001	0.009	−0.003	0
Actual Production (in logs)	4.727	4.731	4.756	4.746	4.740
Actual Production (level)	112.9	113.4	116.3	115.2	114.5
(Actual – Average) / Average	−0.014	−0.009	0.016	0.007	0

Exhibit 7.20 Industrial Production (Example 7.16)

Seasonally adjusted series obtained by Census X-12 for the logarithmic series y of US industrial production ((*a*), 1980–94), estimated additive seasonal components (Panel 2), and forecasts for 1995 together with the actual production (Panel 3).

trends in the seasonal components. For all years, the effect of the third quarter is positive and by far the largest. The effects of the second and fourth quarters are slightly growing over time, and the first quarter is falling back.

Panel 3 of Exhibit 7.20 shows the forecasts for the four quarters in 1995 for the series y_t. As the series consists of the logarithms of industrial production, we conclude that the production level is predicted to be around 1.5 per cent higher (0.009−(−0.005)) in the third quarter than in the first

quarter of 1995. The actual production indices for 1995 are also given in Panel 3 of Exhibit 7.20, which shows that the production in the third quarter of 1995 actually was around 3 per cent higher (0.016−(−0.014)) than that in the first quarter. Such deviations from previous patterns may be of interest to predict further future developments in industrial production.

☞ **Exercises:** T: 7.2d, 7.5d; S: 7.13c, d; E: 7.16a–e, 7.17e–g, 7.18b, f, g.

7.3.5 Summary

Many time series in business and economics are characterized by trends and seasonal fluctuations.

- To predict future developments one should make sure that the trend and the seasonal effects in the time series are modelled in an appropriate way.
- A time series with deterministic trend has the following properties. The time series reverts to the trend line in the long run, and the effect of shocks dies out when time progresses. Forecast intervals are equally wide for all forecast horizons.
- A time series with stochastic trend is not trend reverting, shocks have a permanent effect on the level of the series, the variance increases over time, and forecast intervals become wider for larger horizons.
- The (augmented) Dickey–Fuller test can be used to test the null hypothesis of a stochastic trend against the alternative hypothesis of a deterministic trend. The corresponding (F- and t-) tests do not have a standard distribution. The appropriate distribution depends on the inclusion of constant term and trend term in the test equation.
- Trends and seasonals can be estimated and predicted by parametric models with deterministic or stochastic trends and seasonal components. It is also possible to use other methods — for instance, exponential smoothing (EWMA), Holt–Winters, and Census X-12.

7.4 Non-linearities and time-varying volatility

☞ Uses Chapters 1–4; Section 5.5; parts of Sections 5.3, 5.4; Sections 7.1–7.3.

7.4.1 Outliers

Additive outliers

Trends and seasonals are the most dominant features of most time series in business and economics. In addition the series may have other striking features. For example, in Example 7.1 we considered the quarterly series of industrial production, and Exhibit 7.1 shows that the observations in 1975.1 and 1975.2 correspond with an excessive slump in US industrial production. Given the general pattern of the data before 1975, it seems unlikely that one could construct an ARMA model with trend and seasonals that could forecast these exceptionally large negative growth rates. Such observations are outliers. If one does not correct for such outliers, they may have an excessive impact on parameter estimates and forecasts.

One can distinguish different types of outliers in time series. Suppose that

$$y_t = z_t + \delta D_t(\tau),$$

where z_t is a stationary but unobserved time series and $D_t(\tau)$ is a dummy variable with $D_\tau(\tau) = 1$ and $D_t(\tau) = 0$ for $t \neq \tau$. Then the observation y_τ (at time $t = \tau$) is called an *additive outlier* and δ is the size of the outlier. An additive outlier affects the measured value of the time series at one specific point in time ($t = \tau$), but there are no effects on the observations afterwards. If additive outliers are neglected in modelling, then this may have serious effects. For instance, suppose that z_t follows a stationary AR(p) process. Then the additive outlier at time $t = \tau$ affects all forecasted values of y_t at times $t = \tau + 1, \cdots, \tau + p$. So not only will the model produce a bad forecast for the observation y_τ, but also the forecasts of the observations $y_{\tau+j}$ will be affected for $j = 1, \cdots, p$. So this may produce a sequence of comparatively large residuals. As a consequence, an additive outlier affects the estimated parameters (that are obtained by minimizing the squared residuals) and the quality of a sequence of forecasts. Additive outliers may also affect unit root tests, in the sense that the null hypothesis of a unit root is too easily rejected (see Exercise 7.14).

Test for additive outliers

If the time instant τ of the potential outlier is known, one can apply a t-test for the significance of δ. For instance, suppose that z_t follows a stationary AR(p) process, so that $\phi(L)z_t = \alpha + \varepsilon_t$. If we substitute $z_t = y_t - \delta D_t(\tau)$, it follows that the relevant test equation is

$$y_t = \alpha + \sum_{j=1}^{p} \phi_j y_{t-j} + \delta D_t(\tau) - \sum_{j=1}^{p} \delta\phi_j D_{t-j}(\tau) + \varepsilon_t$$

Here $D_{t-j}(\tau)$ is a dummy variable that has the value one at time $t = \tau + j$ and zero otherwise. This is a regression model with $(2p + 2)$ regressors $(1, y_{t-1}, \cdots, y_{t-p}, D_t, D_{t-1}, \cdots, D_{t-p})$ and $(p + 2)$ parameters $(\alpha, \delta, \phi_1, \cdots, \phi_p)$. The parameters can be estimated by non-linear least squares. If δ is significant, this indicates the possible presence of an additive outlier. One can also test whether the outlier is of this specific additive type. For this purpose estimate the unrestricted model with $(2p + 2)$ parameters, and test the p parameter restrictions corresponding to the additive outlier model.

Innovation outliers

Another type of outlier is an *innovation outlier* where the outlier occurs in the innovation process. An innovation outlier at time τ in an ARMA model is given by

$$\phi(L)y_t = \theta(L)(\varepsilon_t + \delta D_t(\tau)).$$

For instance, for an AR(p) model this gives

$$y_t = \phi_1 y_{t-1} + \cdots + \phi_p y_{t-p} + \delta D_t(\tau) + \varepsilon_t.$$

This shows that the forecast of y_t is affected only at time $t = \tau$. So an innovation outlier will lead to a single large residual and will in general have less severe effects on parameter estimates than an additive outlier. An innovation outlier may affect unit root tests (see Exercise 7.14). If the time τ of a possible innovation outlier is known, one can apply a simple t-test on the significance of δ. One should check whether neighbouring residuals are not also outliers, as otherwise an additive outlier may be more appropriate.

Level shifts

If the series contains a stochastic trend, then an innovation outlier has a permanent effect on the level of the series (see Exercise 7.14). For a stationary series, a *level shift* at time $t = \tau$ can be modelled by

$$\phi(L)y_t = \alpha + \delta D_t^+(\tau) + \theta(L)\varepsilon_t.$$

Here D_t^+ is a dummy variable with $D_t^+(\tau) = 0$ for $t < \tau$ and $D_t^+(\tau) = 1$ for $t \geq \tau$. The mean of the series y_t shifts from $\alpha/\phi(1)$ prior to the level shift to $(\alpha + \delta)/\phi(1)$ afterwards. Neglecting such a shift will lead to a sequence of large residuals around $t = \tau$. If the time τ of the potential shift is known, the presence of a level shift can simply be tested by the t-test on δ. In some cases the shift is more gradual and extends over several time periods. This can be modelled by replacing the step function $D_t^+(\tau)$ by a more smooth function of time.

Diagnostic checks

In practice one can detect possible outliers and breaks by considering plots of the observed time series y_t. It may also be instructive to estimate simple models and to inspect the time series plot and the histogram of the resulting series of residuals. Statistical tests can be applied by including appropriate dummy variables in the model and by testing their significance. If the outliers cannot be modelled in an acceptable way, then a possible alternative is to use robust estimation methods that assign less weight to outliers. This was discussed in Section 5.6.4 (p. 390).

Example 7.17: **Industrial Production (continued)**

We consider again the quarterly series $\Delta_4 y_t$ of yearly growth rates of US industrial production. We will discuss (i) a graphical inspection of outliers, (ii) a model with dummies for the outliers, and (iii) diagnostic tests for this model.

(i) **Graphical inspection of outliers**

Exhibit 7.1 (*c*) in Example 7.1 shows a time plot of the series $\Delta_4 y_t$ of yearly growth rates. This exhibit shows that the series quite often takes values that are far apart from the majority of observed growth rates. In Example 7.8 we estimated an AR(2) model for this series (see Exhibit 7.9), and in Example 7.11 we applied diagnostic tests (see Exhibit 7.11). The residuals of this model are not normally distributed. The time plot of the residuals is given once more in Exhibit 7.21 (*a*), together with the 95 per cent confidence bounds. This shows that there may be outliers in the quarters 1961.1, 1961.2, 1974.4, 1975.1, 1976.1, 1980.2, and 1981.4.

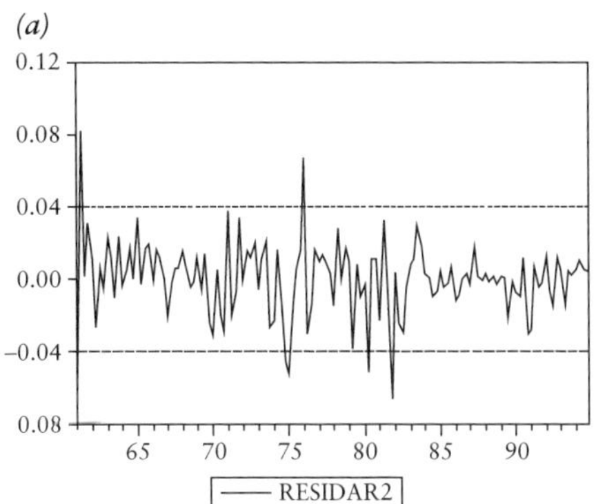

(b)

Panel 2: Dependent Variable: D4Y Method: Least Squares Sample: 1961:1 1994:4; Included observations: 136				
Variable	Coefficient	Std. Error	t-Statistic	Prob.
C	0.007652	0.001687	4.536416	0.0000
D4Y(−1)	1.318387	0.057799	22.80998	0.0000
D4Y(−2)	−0.515566	0.057037	−9.039201	0.0000
DUM611	−0.068627	0.015648	−4.385536	0.0000
DUM612	0.081021	0.016277	4.977700	0.0000
DUM744	−0.047186	0.015593	−3.026035	0.0030
DUM751	−0.054010	0.015859	−3.405648	0.0009
DUM761	0.069084	0.016130	4.282876	0.0000
DUM802	−0.052449	0.015568	−3.369090	0.0010
DUM814	−0.067683	0.015575	−4.345596	0.0000
R-squared	0.907760	Mean dependent var		0.032213
Adjusted R-squared	0.901171	S.D. dependent var		0.049219
S.E. of regression	0.015473	Akaike info criterion		−5.428742
Sum squared resid	0.030167	Schwarz criterion		−5.214576
Log likelihood	379.1545	F-statistic		137.7771
Durbin-Watson stat	2.035319	Prob(F-statistic)		0.000000

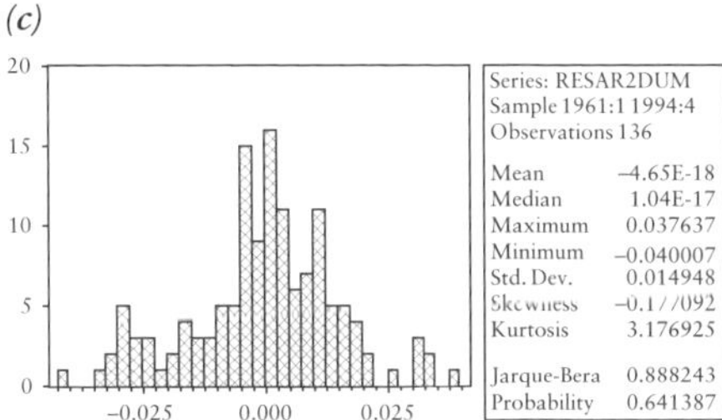

Exhibit 7.21 Industrial Production (Example 7.17)

(a) shows the time plot of the residuals of the AR(2) model (without dummies) for the series $\Delta_4 y_t$ of yearly growth rates (see also Exhibit 7.11), Panel 2 shows the results of the AR(2) model with seven outlier dummies, and (c) contains the histogram of the residuals of this model.

(ii) Model with outlier dummies

We include separate dummy variables for the seven possible outlier observations in the AR(2) model for $\Delta_4 y_t$. The resulting estimates are shown in Panel 2 of Exhibit 7.21. Each of the dummies is highly significant. The estimated autoregressive parameters (with standard errors in parentheses) are $\hat{\phi}_1 = 1.318$ (0.058) and $\hat{\phi}_2 = -0.516$ (0.057). If we compare these outcomes with the ones of the original AR(2) model in Exhibit 7.9 of Example 7.8, we see that the estimates do not change much, but that the standard errors become considerably smaller after correction for the outliers (the standard errors in Exhibit 7.9 are 0.072). Also the standard error of regression reduces considerably, from $s = 0.021$ in the model without dummies to $s = 0.015$ in the model with dummies. If the AR(2) model with dummies is used in forecasting, then the point forecasts of future values of the series are not much affected but forecast intervals are narrower.

(iii) Diagnostic checks on model with outlier dummies

The histogram of the residuals of the AR(2) model with dummies is given in Exhibit 7.21 (*c*). The assumption of a normal distribution of the residuals is not rejected (the Jarque–Bera test has *P*-value 0.64). The kurtosis is 3.177, which is close to 3, whereas the kurtosis of the residuals of the AR(2) model without dummies is equal to 5.896 (see Panel 6 of Exhibit 7.11 in Example 7.11). This indicates that the non-normality of the residuals of the AR(2) model may well be caused by outliers in the time series. It is left as an exercise to investigate whether some sequences of successive outliers may be due to additive outliers (see Exercise 7.16). Further non-linear aspects of this time series are analysed in Example 7.18 in the next section.

☞ Exercises: S: 7.14e–h; E: 7.16f, 7.23f.

7.4.2 Time-varying parameters

Parameter variations in ARMA models

A sequence of outlying observations may be due to changes in the ARMA parameters. Such changes can be caused, for instance, by different economic *regimes*. For example, the speed of dynamic adjustments of an economic process during a recession may differ from the speed in expansion periods. If expansions are more common than recessions, then estimated models will in general perform better for the expansion periods and may produce sequences of outliers for recession periods. In such a situation the model should be adjusted by allowing the parameters to vary over time.

In Section 5.3 we discussed methods to model parameter variations and to test for the presence of such variations. These methods—for instance, the CUSUM and Chow tests—can also be applied in stationary ARMA models. This is straightforward for AR models, as these models have the same structure as regression models. If MA terms are present, then the Chow tests can be performed by incorporating appropriate dummy variables under the alternative hypothesis of a break. The recursive residuals needed for the CUSUM test can be obtained from a sequence of ML parameter estimates, where the observations y_s for $s < t$ are used to estimate the model at time $(t-1)$ to make a one-step-ahead forecast for y_t.

Threshold model

There are many ways to specify parameter variations in ARMA models. For simplicity we consider the stationary AR(2) model to illustrate some possible models. If the parameters have changed at a single and known time moment $(t = \tau)$, then this can be modelled by

$$y_t = \alpha_1 + \phi_{11}y_{t-1} + \phi_{21}y_{t-2} + D_t^+(\tau)(\alpha_2 + \phi_{12}y_{t-1} + \phi_{22}y_{t-2}) + \varepsilon_t.$$

Here D_t^+ is a dummy variable with $D_t^+(\tau) = 0$ for $t < \tau$ and $D_t^+(\tau) = 1$ for $t \geq \tau$. So the regime switches abruptly at the time instant $t = \tau$. It may also be that the regime is determined by past values of the process y_t. For instance, if a recession corresponds to a negative value of y_{t-1}, then the regime may be defined by the sign (positive or negative) of y_{t-1}. A possible model with regime switches is then obtained by replacing the dummy variable $D_t^+(\tau)$ in the above model by the dummy variable $D_t(y_{t-1})$ defined by

$$D_t(y_{t-1}) = 0 \text{ if } y_{t-1} > 0, \quad D_t(y_{t-1}) = 1 \text{ if } y_{t-1} \leq 0.$$

The resulting model is

$$y_t = \alpha_1 + \phi_{11}y_{t-1} + \phi_{21}y_{t-2} + D_t(y_{t-1})(\alpha_2 + \phi_{12}y_{t-1} + \phi_{22}y_{t-2}) + \varepsilon_t. \quad (7.26)$$

This is called the *threshold autoregressive* (TAR) model. The above model is a TAR(2) model with switching variable y_{t-1} and with threshold value zero between the two regimes. This model can be extended to ARMA models with other switching variables and other threshold values.

Smooth transition model

In the TAR model the shifts of regime are abrupt, because the switching function $D_t(y_{t-1})$ is a discontinuous function of y_{t-1}. The transitions can also be modelled more smoothly by means of a *smooth transition autoregressive* (STAR) model. The STAR(2) model with switching variable y_{t-1} is given by

$$y_t = \alpha_1 + \phi_{11}y_{t-1} + \phi_{21}y_{t-2} + F(y_{t-1})(\alpha_2 + \phi_{12}y_{t-1} + \phi_{22}y_{t-2}) + \varepsilon_t. \quad (7.27)$$

Here F is a smooth switching function. For instance, the logistic STAR(2) model with switching variable y_{t-1} is defined by (7.27) with logistic switching function

$$F(y_{t-1}) = \frac{1}{1 + e^{-\gamma_1(y_{t-1}-\gamma_2)}}.$$

The parameter γ_1 determines the speed of the parameter switches due to variations in y_{t-1} around γ_2. For $\gamma_1 \to \infty$ the switching function becomes very steep and the model converges to the TAR model (7.26) (with $\gamma_2 = 0$). If γ_1 is relatively small, then the transitions are more smooth, and if $\gamma_1 = 0$ the parameters do not change at all. A Likelihood Ratio test for parameter variation of this type is obtained by comparing the log-likelihood value of the non-linear model (7.27) with the log-likelihood of the linear AR(2) model. One can also apply more general tests for non-linearities — for instance, the RESET of Section 5.2.2 (p. 285). The advantage of the STAR model is that it gives a clear economic interpretation of parameter variations in terms of different economic regimes.

XM701INP

Example 7.18: **Industrial Production (continued)**

We continue our analysis of the quarterly series of yearly growth rates in US industrial production. We will discuss (i) a smooth transition model, (ii) a threshold model, and (iii) an interpretation of the threshold model for this series.

(i) **Smooth transition model**

In Example 7.17 in the foregoing section we detected seven outliers in the series of yearly growth rates $\Delta_4 y_t$ in US industrial production. Six of these outliers fall in quarters after a quarter with negative growth — that is, at times t where $\Delta_4 y_{t-1} < 0$. This suggests modelling this series by means of two different regimes to allow for different production adjustments in recession periods. Instead of the AR(2) model considered in previous examples, we now estimate the logistic STAR(2) model for $\Delta_4 y_t$ with switching variable $\Delta_4 y_{t-1}$. The results are reported in Panel 1 of Exhibit 7.22. The value of $\hat{\gamma}_1 = 2361$ is very large. As the switching variable has mean 0.03 with standard deviation 0.05, the large value of γ_1 leads to very fast transitions. However, the estimates $\hat{\gamma}_1$ and $\hat{\gamma}_2$ do not differ significantly from zero.

(ii) **Threshold model**

Since the transitions in the STAR model are very fast, this motivates the use of a threshold (TAR) model with two regimes, expansion if the last observed growth rate $\Delta_4 y_{t-1}$ is positive and recession if this growth rate is negative. We model this by means of the dummy variable D_t^+, which has value 1 during

(a)

Panel 1: Dependent Variable: D4Y
Method: Least Squares
Sample: 1961:1 1994:4; Included observations: 136
Convergence achieved after 98 iterations
D4Y = C(1)+C(2)*D4Y(−1)+C(3)*D4Y(−2) + (C(4)+C(5)*D4Y(−1)+C(6)*D4Y(−2))/(1+ @EXP(−C(7)*(D4Y(−1)−C(8))))

Parameter	Coefficient	Std. Error	t-Statistic	Prob.
C(1)	−0.006696	0.005367	−1.247760	0.2144
C(2)	1.174642	0.138134	8.503617	0.0000
C(3)	−0.711489	0.113235	−6.283286	0.0000
C(4)	0.015946	0.006978	2.285306	0.0239
C(5)	0.069069	0.172454	0.400509	0.6894
C(6)	0.244899	0.145274	1.685779	0.0943
C(7) $(=\gamma_1)$	2360.688	10225.55	0.230862	0.8178
C(8) $(=\gamma_2)$	0.002389	0.001865	1.281076	0.2025

R-squared	0.836230	Mean dependent var	0.032213
Adjusted R-squared	0.827274	S.D. dependent var	0.049219
S.E. of regression	0.020456	Akaike info criterion	−4.884093
Sum squared resid	0.053559	Schwarz criterion	−4.712760
Log likelihood	340.1183	Durbin-Watson stat	2.172684

(b)

Panel 2: Dependent Variable: D4Y
Method: Least Squares
Sample: 1961:1 1994:4; Included observations: 136
D4Y=C(1)+C(2)*D4Y(−1)+C(3)*D4Y(−2) + DUMPLUS*(C(4)+C(5)*D4Y(−1)+C(6)*D4Y(−2))

Parameter	Coefficient	Std. Error	t-Statistic	Prob.
C(1)	−0.006937	0.005423	−1.279223	0.2031
C(2)	1.172922	0.138174	8.488734	0.0000
C(3)	−0.714031	0.112871	−6.326091	0.0000
C(4)	0.014694	0.006739	2.180352	0.0310
C(5)	0.092095	0.170993	0.538589	0.5911
C(6)	0.247076	0.144471	1.710210	0.0896

R-squared	0.834945	Mean dependent var	0.032213
Adjusted R-squared	0.828597	S.D. dependent var	0.049219
S.E. of regression	0.020377	Akaike info criterion	−4.905686
Sum squared resid	0.053980	Schwarz criterion	−4.777186
Log likelihood	339.5866	Durbin-Watson stat	2.158046

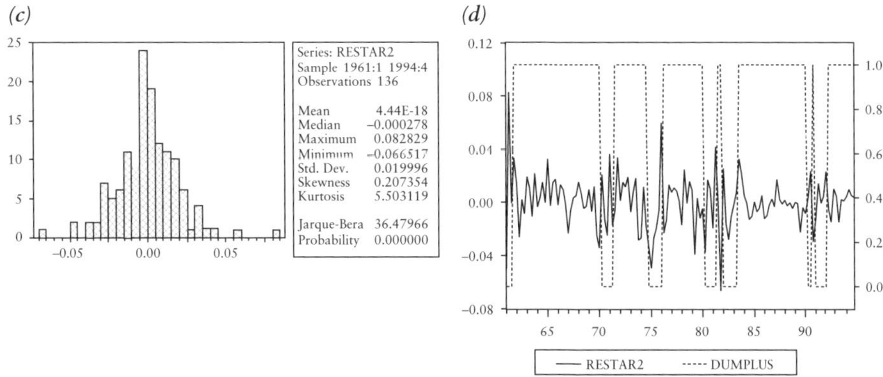

Exhibit 7.22 Industrial Production (Example 7.18)

STAR(2) model (Panel 1) and TAR(2) model (Panel 2) for quarterly series of yearly growth rates in US industrial production; (*c*) shows the histogram of the TAR(2) residuals; (*d*) shows the time plot of these residuals together with the expansion dummy D_t^+ (denoted by DUMPLUS).

expansions ($\Delta_4 y_{t-1} \geq 0$) and value 0 during recessions ($\Delta_4 y_{t-1} < 0$). The results of the TAR(2) model are shown in Panel 2 of Exhibit 7.22. The TAR(2) model is preferred above the STAR(2) model on the basis of AIC and SIC. We can also compare these two models by the *LR*-test, as the TAR corresponds to the two parameter restrictions $\gamma_1 = \infty$ and $\gamma_2 = 0$ in the STAR model (in this case $F(z) = 1$ for $z > 0$ and $F(z) = 0$ for $z < 0$, so that $F(\Delta_4 y_{t-1}) = D_t^+$). The test has value $LR = 2(340.12 - 339.59) = 1.06$, and the *P*-value corresponding to the $\chi^2(2)$ distribution is $P = 0.59$. So the TAR(2) model is not rejected. The TAR(2) model can also be tested against the alternative of the AR(2) model with constant coefficients. The AR(2) model is obtained from the TAR(2) model (7.26) by imposing the three parameter restrictions $\alpha_2 = \phi_{12} = \phi_{22} = 0$. The AR(2) model was estimated in Example 7.8 (see Exhibit 7.9). If we compare the log-likelihood values of both models, we obtain $LR = 2(339.6 - 334.2) = 10.8$, with *P*-value corresponding to the $\chi^2(3)$ distribution equal to $P = 0.013$. So the *LR*-test rejects the AR(2) model, and we conclude that the adjustment process in recessions differs from that in expansions.

(iii) Interpretation of the threshold model

The estimated TAR(2) model in Panel 2 of Exhibit 7.22 can be used to estimate the mean growth rates of industrial production during expansion and recession periods. The mean growth in recession periods (where $D_t^+ = 0$) is equal to $-0.007/(1 - 1.17 + 0.71) = -1.3$ per cent, whereas in expansion periods (where $D_t^+ = 1$) it is $0.008/(1 - 1.26 + 0.47) = +3.8$ per cent. Exhibit 7.22 (*d*) shows the plot of the expansion dummy D_t^+. This shows that expansions last for longer periods as compared to recessions. The recessions in the periods 1961, 1974–5, and 1980–2 contain the observations that were earlier detected as outliers in the AR(2) model in Example 7.17. Exhibit 7.22 (*c*) and (*d*) show the residuals of the TAR(2) model. These residuals still contain some outliers in recession periods (where $D_t^+ = 0$). Normality of the TAR(2) residuals is rejected because the kurtosis is still large (with a value of 5.503, as compared to 5.896 in the AR(2) model in Panel 6 of Exhibit 7.11).

Although the TAR model is not completely satisfactory from a statistical point of view, it is of economic interest as it distinguishes between recessions and expansions.

7.4.3 GARCH models for clustered volatility

Changing variance in time series

In the foregoing sections we considered lagged effects on the level $E[y_t|Y_{t-1}]$ of the observed time series. It has been assumed until now that the innovations ε_t all have the same variance σ^2. This is not always realistic, as there may exist lagged effects in the conditional variance $\sigma_t^2 = \text{var}(y_t|Y_{t-1})$ of the time series. As the variance is a measure of the uncertainty or risk on future values of the variable, this is of importance for decisions in business and economics that involve risk. For instance, in finance the price of options and other financial instruments depends on the variance or volatility of price movements in the market. Further, if the variance changes over time, then an appropriate model for the variance also leads to more accurate forecast intervals, with wider intervals in risky periods and narrower intervals in stable periods.

Empirical evidence for changing variance

Many time series in business and economics exhibit changes in volatility over time. This especially holds true for many financial time series. As an illustration, in Example 7.2 we considered the daily Dow-Jones index. The results in Example 7.15 indicate that the series of daily returns $\Delta \log(\text{DJ})$ is uncorrelated (see Exhibit 7.18). That is, the past returns contain no information on the returns of tomorrow. Exhibit 7.2 (*c*) in Example 7.2 shows the time plot of the returns. This shows that the variance in the returns changes over time. There exist quiet periods with relatively small returns, but also very volatile periods where large positive and negative returns follow each other. This property is called *clustered volatility*. In this case the variance or risk in the returns can be predicted to some extent. Exhibit 7.2 further indicates that there are relatively many large positive and negative returns that cannot be modelled well by the normal distribution.

Many financial time series have the above properties—that is, no autocorrelation in the level (white noise), time-varying variance (clustered volatility), and distributions with excess kurtosis (fat tails). In this section we describe time series models that account for these properties.

Autoregressive conditional heteroskedasticity (ARCH)

If the variance of a time series depends on the past, we say that the series is conditionally heteroskedastic. If this dependence on the past can be expressed by an autoregression, this gives the so-called model with *autoregressive conditional heteroskedasticity*, abbreviated as ARCH. For instance, the ARCH(1) model for a white noise series y_t is given by

$$y_t = \mu + \varepsilon_t, \quad \varepsilon_t|Y_{t-1} \sim \text{N}(0, \sigma_t^2), \quad \sigma_t^2 = \alpha_0 + \alpha_1 \varepsilon_{t-1}^2. \tag{7.28}$$

Here $\sigma_t^2 = \text{var}(y_t|Y_{t-1})$ is the conditional variance of the series, where $Y_{t-1} = \{y_{t-1}, y_{t-2}, \cdots\}$ denotes the available information set at time $t-1$. As variances are non-negative, we impose the conditions that $\alpha_0 \geq 0$ and

$\alpha_1 \geq 0$. If $\alpha_1 > 0$, then the conditional variances are positively related, as σ_t^2 is larger for larger values of the previous innovation ε_{t-1}. This makes it possible to predict the variance of the time series — that is, the risk that is involved in future movements in the series.

Properties of ARCH processes

It is left as an exercise (see Exercises 7.6 and 7.7 (*a*)) to prove that the ARCH(1) process (7.28) has the following properties if $\alpha_1 < 1$. It is a white noise process with $E[(y_t - \mu)(y_s - \mu)] = 0$ for all $t \neq s$. The mean is $E[y_t] = \mu$. For $0 < \alpha_1 < 1$ the (unconditional) variance $E[(y_t - \mu)^2] = \alpha_0/(1 - \alpha_1)$ is constant over time, and for $\alpha_1 = 1$ the process does not have a finite (unconditional) variance anymore. Further, the series of squared innovations ε_t^2 follows an AR(1) process — that is,

$$\varepsilon_t^2 = \alpha_0 + \alpha_1 \varepsilon_{t-1}^2 + v_t,$$

where $v_t = \varepsilon_t^2 - \sigma_t^2$ is a white noise process. This implies that the volatilities are clustered if $\alpha_1 > 0$. Finally, the (unconditional) distribution of ε_t is not normal and has kurtosis larger than 3. So the ARCH(1) process has the three aforementioned properties of many financial time series — that is, it is a white noise process with clustered volatility and with fat tails. Simulation evidence of these properties will be given in Example 7.19 at the end of this section.

In practice, extensions of the ARCH(1) model are needed because the squared innovations ε_t^2 often show correlation patterns that cannot be modelled well by an AR(1) model. The ARCH(p) model has p lags in (7.28), so that

$$\sigma_t^2 = E[\varepsilon_t^2 \mid Y_{t-1}] = \alpha_0 + \alpha_1 \varepsilon_{t-1}^2 + \cdots + \alpha_p \varepsilon_{t-p}^2. \qquad (7.29)$$

It is left as an exercise (see Exercise 7.6) to show that in an ARCH(p) model the squared innovations ε_t^2 follow an AR(p) process.

Generalized ARCH models (GARCH)

Still more general correlation patterns are obtained by using ARMA models for the series ε_t^2. This leads to the class of so-called *generalized ARCH* models (abbreviated as GARCH). For instance, the GARCH(1,1) model is described by

$$\sigma_t^2 = \alpha_0 + \alpha_1 \varepsilon_{t-1}^2 + \alpha_2 \sigma_{t-1}^2,$$

with all three parameters non-negative. As before, let $v_t = \varepsilon_t^2 - \sigma_t^2$; then v_t is a white noise process (see Exercise 7.6). By substituting $\sigma_t^2 = \varepsilon_t^2 - v_t$ in the above equation we get

$$\varepsilon_t^2 = \alpha_0 + (\alpha_1 + \alpha_2)\varepsilon_{t-1}^2 + v_t - \alpha_2 v_{t-1}.$$

So the process ε_t^2 follows an ARMA(1,1) process with AR polynomial $\phi(z) = 1 - (\alpha_1 + \alpha_2)z$ and MA polynomial $\theta(z) = 1 - \alpha_2 z$. The process ε_t^2 is stationary if $\alpha_1 + \alpha_2 < 1$, and it is integrated of order 1 if $\alpha_1 + \alpha_2 = 1$. In the latter case the (unconditional) variance of the innovations ε_t^2 is not constant over time if $\alpha_0 > 0$, because $E[\varepsilon_t^2] = \alpha_0 + (\alpha_1 + \alpha_2)E[\varepsilon_{t-1}^2] = \alpha_0 + E[\varepsilon_{t-1}^2]$ in this case. The general GARCH(p, q) model contains p lags of σ_t^2 and q lags of ε_t^2 in the above equation for the conditional variance σ_t^2. Then ε_t^2 follows an ARMA(m, p) process where $m = \max(p, q)$.

Combined models for level and variance

The foregoing models are pure (G)ARCH processes—that is, the variance of y_t is predictable but the level of y_t is not predictable (as y_t is a white noise process). We can also combine an ARMA model for the level of y_t with a GARCH model for the variance of the innovations $\varepsilon_t = y_t - E[y_t|Y_{t-1}]$. For instance, an AR(1)-ARCH(1) model is described by the equation $y_t = \alpha + \phi y_{t-1} + \varepsilon_t$ for the level, where $\varepsilon_t|Y_{t-1} \sim \mathrm{N}(0, \sigma_t^2)$ with variance equation $\sigma_t^2 = \alpha_0 + \alpha_1\varepsilon_{t-1}^2$. This model has four parameters and can be described by

$$y_t|Y_{t-1} \sim \mathrm{N}(\alpha + \phi y_{t-1}, \sigma_t^2) = \mathrm{N}\big(\alpha + \phi y_{t-1}, \alpha_0 + \alpha_1(y_{t-1} - \alpha - \phi y_{t-2})^2\big). \tag{7.30}$$

In a similar way we can formulate mixed ARMA–GARCH models. In some cases it is also of interest to consider clustered volatility models for the error terms in regression models $y_t = x_t'\beta + \varepsilon_t$. For example, suppose that $y_t = \alpha + \beta x_t + \varepsilon_t$ and that $\varepsilon_t|Y_{t-1} \sim \mathrm{N}(0, \sigma_t^2)$, where $\sigma_t^2 = \alpha_0 + \alpha_1\varepsilon_{t-1}^2$. Then we get

$$y_t|Y_{t-1} \sim \mathrm{N}(\alpha + \beta x_t, \sigma_t^2) = \mathrm{N}\big(\alpha + \beta x_t, \alpha_0 + \alpha_1(y_{t-1} - \alpha - \beta x_{t-1})^2\big).$$

The use of GARCH error terms in regression models will be illustrated in Example 7.22.

Example 7.19: **Simulated ARCH and GARCH Time Series**

E

We illustrate the above results by means of two simulations. The first time series is generated by the ARCH(1) process (7.28) with parameter values $\mu = 0$, $\alpha_0 = 1$, and $\alpha_1 = 0.9$. So $y_t = \varepsilon_t$ with $y_t|Y_{t-1} \sim \mathrm{N}(0, \sigma_t^2)$ where $\sigma_t^2 = 1 + 0.9y_{t-1}^2$. This series is simulated as follows. First we draw white noise terms $\eta_t \sim \mathrm{NID}(0, 1)$, and then the ARCH(1) process y_t is generated by recursively computing $y_t = \sigma_t\eta_t$ where $\sigma_t^2 = 1 + 0.9y_{t-1}^2$. The results are in Exhibit 7.23 (*a–f*). The series y_t shows clustered

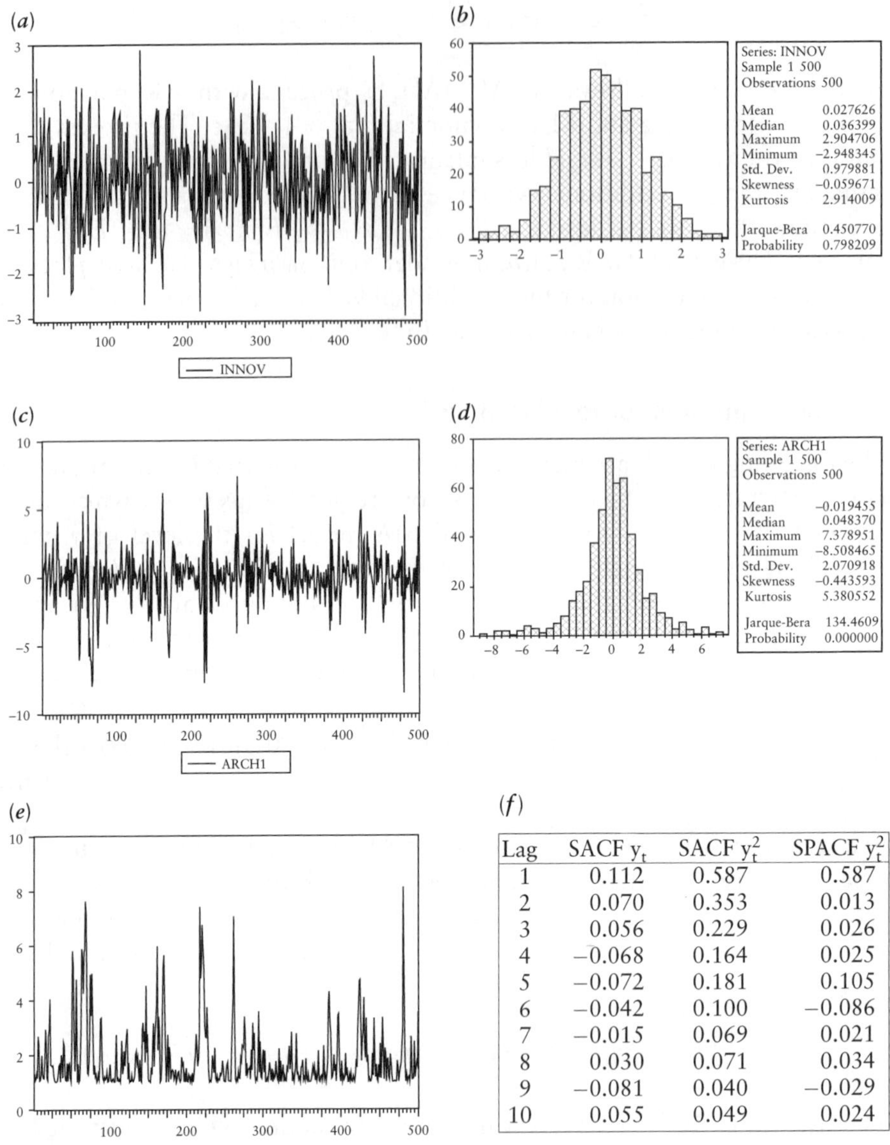

Lag	SACF y_t	SACF y_t^2	SPACF y_t^2
1	0.112	0.587	0.587
2	0.070	0.353	0.013
3	0.056	0.229	0.026
4	−0.068	0.164	0.025
5	−0.072	0.181	0.105
6	−0.042	0.100	−0.086
7	−0.015	0.069	0.021
8	0.030	0.071	0.034
9	−0.081	0.040	−0.029
10	0.055	0.049	0.024

Exhibit 7.23 Simulated ARCH and GARCH Time Series (Example 7.19)

Time series simulated by an ARCH(1) process, innovations η_t (denoted by INNOV ((*a*)–(*b*))), ARCH(1) series $y_t = \sigma_t \eta_t$ (denoted by ARCH1 ((*c*)–(*d*))), time plot of conditional standard deviation σ_t (where $\sigma_t^2 = 1 + 0.9 y_{t-1}^2$ (*e*)), and S(P)ACF of the ARCH(1) series y_t and of the squared series y_t^2 (*f*).

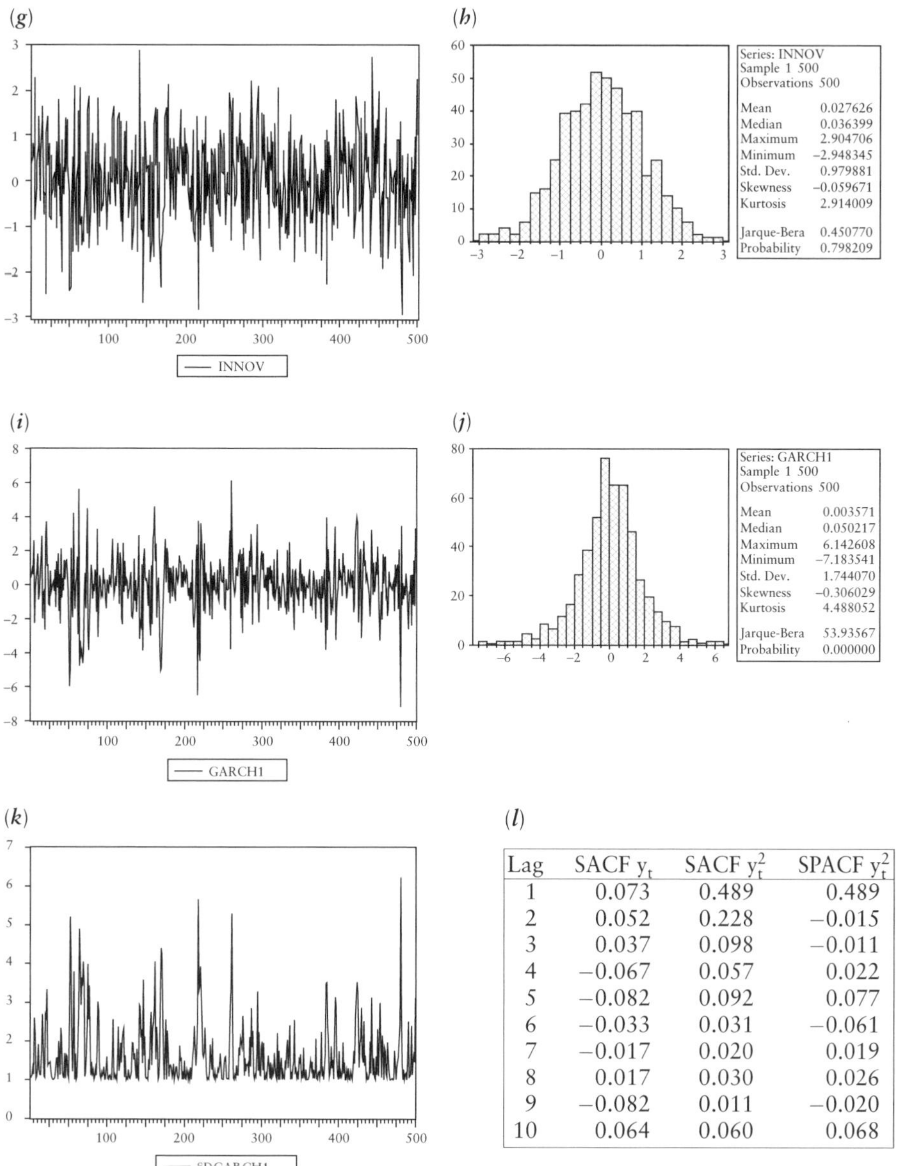

Lag	SACF y_t	SACF y_t^2	SPACF y_t^2
1	0.073	0.489	0.489
2	0.052	0.228	−0.015
3	0.037	0.098	−0.011
4	−0.067	0.057	0.022
5	−0.082	0.092	0.077
6	−0.033	0.031	−0.061
7	−0.017	0.020	0.019
8	0.017	0.030	0.026
9	−0.082	0.011	−0.020
10	0.064	0.060	0.068

Exhibit 7.23 (*Contd.*)

Time series simulated by a GARCH(1,1) process, innovations η_t (denoted by INNOV ((*g*)–(*h*))), GARCH(1,1) series $y_t = \sigma_t \eta_t$ (denoted by GARCH1 ((*i*)–(*j*))), time plot of conditional standard deviation σ_t (where $\sigma_t^2 = 1 + 0.2y_{t-1}^2 + 0.7\sigma_{t-1}^2$ (*k*)), and S(P)ACF of the GARCH(1,1) series y_t and of the squared series y_t^2 (*l*).

volatility (see (c)) and has a kurtosis of 5.38 (see (d)). The exhibit also shows the series of simulated conditional standard deviations σ_t (in (e)), as well as the correlograms of the series y_t and of the squared series y_t^2 (in (f)). The SPACF of the series y_t^2 indeed indicates that this is an AR(1) process.

In the second simulation we generate a time series from the GARCH(1,1) model with parameter values $\mu = 0$, $\alpha_0 = 1$, $\alpha_1 = 0.2$, and $\alpha_2 = 0.7$. The results are in Exhibit 7.23 (g–l). Again, the simulated series is white noise, it has clustered volatility, and it has excess kurtosis.

☞ **Exercises: T: 7.6, 7.7a.**

7.4.4 Estimation and diagnostic tests of GARCH models

Two-step estimation of ARMA–GARCH models

If the process y_t follows a GARCH process with mean μ, then the squared series $(y_t - \mu)^2$ follows an ARMA process. So the parameters of a GARCH model can be estimated by estimating an ARMA model for the series $(y_t - \mu)^2$ by the methods discussed in Section 7.2.2. If the mean μ is unknown, it can be replaced by the sample mean $\bar{y}$. More generally, if the process y_t follows an ARMA process with innovations that are GARCH, then the model parameters can be estimated in two steps. In the first step the parameters of the ARMA model for y_t are estimated as discussed in Section 7.2.2. Let the residuals of the ARMA model be denoted by e_t; then in the second step the parameters of the GARCH model are estimated by estimating an ARMA model for the series e_t^2 of squared residuals. For example, for the AR(1)–ARCH(1) model the first step consists of a regression of y_t on a constant and y_{t-1}, and the second step of a regression of the squared residual e_t^2 on a constant and e_{t-1}^2. This two-step method provides consistent estimators, but they are not efficient. This is because the error terms are not normally distributed. For instance, in the AR(1)–ARCH(1) model, the error terms ε_t in the AR(1) model for y_t are not normally distributed, so that the AR parameters are not estimated efficiently in the first step. Also the error terms $v_t = e_t^2 - \sigma_t^2$ in the AR model for e_t^2 are not normally distributed, so that the ARCH parameters in the second step are also not efficiently estimated.

Estimation by maximum likelihood

Consistent and efficient estimates are obtained by applying maximum likelihood in correctly specified models. As an illustration we derive the log-likelihood for the AR(1)–ARCH(1) model; the likelihood function for other models can be obtained in a similar way. The likelihood derived in Section 7.2.2 for ARMA models does not apply in this case, because the innovations ε_t are no longer normally distributed. To express the log-likelihood we use the fact that a joint density function can be factorized as $f(z_1, z_2) = f(z_1)f(z_2|z_1)$, where $f(z_2|z_1)$ is the conditional density of z_2 conditional on z_1. So the likelihood function can be factorized as

$$L = p(y_1, y_2, \cdots, y_n) = p(y_1)\, p(y_2|y_1)\, p(y_3|y_1, y_2) \cdots p(y_n|Y_{n-1}).$$

These conditional densities are normal (see (7.30)), so that

$$\begin{aligned}
\log (L(\alpha, \phi, \alpha_0, \alpha_1)) &= \sum_{t=1}^{n} \log p(y_t|Y_{t-1}) \\
&= -\frac{n}{2}\log(2\pi) - \frac{1}{2}\sum_{t=1}^{n} \log(\sigma_t^2) - \frac{1}{2}\sum_{t=1}^{n} \frac{\varepsilon_t^2}{\sigma_t^2} \\
&= -\frac{n}{2}\log(2\pi) - \frac{1}{2}\sum_{t=1}^{n} \log\left(\alpha_0 + \alpha_1(y_{t-1} - \alpha - \phi y_{t-2})^2\right) \\
&\quad - \frac{1}{2}\sum_{t=1}^{n} \frac{(y_t - \alpha - \phi y_{t-1})^2}{\alpha_0 + \alpha_1(y_{t-1} - \alpha - \phi y_{t-2})^2}. \qquad (7.31)
\end{aligned}$$

Because the values of $(y_t, t \leq 0)$ are unobserved, one often maximizes the conditional log-likelihood (where the observations y_1 and y_2 are treated as fixed). In this case the summations in (7.31) start at $t = 3$ instead of $t = 1$. The ML estimators have the usual asymptotic properties if the ARMA process y_t and the GARCH model are both stationary. For instance, the ML estimators of the AR(1)–ARCH(1) model are asymptotically normally distributed, provided that $-1 < \phi < 1$ and $0 \leq \alpha_1 < 1$.

Test for the presence of conditional heteroskedasticity

Correlations in the variance of a series can be exploited to forecast future risks and to adjust the width of forecast intervals. Therefore it is of interest to test for the presence of GARCH effects. This can be done, for instance, by estimating an ARMA–GARCH model and applying an *LR*-test or an *F*-test on the joint significance of the GARCH parameters. These tests have the usual asymptotic distributions if the ARMA model and the GARCH model are both stationary.

The Lagrange Multiplier test is somewhat simpler to perform. In this case we need to estimate an ARMA model only under the null hypothesis that no GARCH effects are present, so that we can apply the estimation methods of Section 7.2.2. As an example, suppose that we wish to test the following hypothesis on the disturbance terms ε_t of an ARMA model. The null hypothesis states that the terms ε_t are independent, so that $\varepsilon_t|Y_{t-1} \sim \mathrm{N}(0, \sigma^2)$. The alternative hypothesis is that the terms ε_t are conditionally heteroskedastic according to the ARCH(p) process (7.29), so that $\mathrm{var}(\varepsilon_t|Y_{t-1}) = \sigma_t^2 = \alpha_0 + \sum_{k=1}^{p} \alpha_k \varepsilon_{t-k}^2$. Then the null hypothesis of (conditional) homoskedasticity corresponds to the p parameter restrictions

$$\mathrm{H}_0 : \alpha_1 = \cdots = \alpha_p = 0.$$

It is left as an exercise (see Exercise 7.7) to derive that, in an ARMA model for y_t, the LM-test for ARCH(p) disturbances can be computed by the following steps.

LM-test for ARCH(p) error terms

- *Step 1: Estimate the ARMA model.* First estimate the ARMA model by ML—that is, by OLS (for an AR model) or by NLS (if MA terms are present). Let e_t be the corresponding series of (OLS or NLS) residuals.
- *Step 2: Estimate the ARCH model.* Regress the squared residuals e_t^2 on a constant and $e_{t-1}^2, \cdots, e_{t-p}^2$.
- *Step 3: $LM = nR^2$.* Then the LM-test can be computed as $LM = nR^2$ of the regression in step 2. Under the null hypothesis that no ARCH is present, the LM-test asymptotically has the $\chi^2(p)$ distribution, and the null hypothesis is rejected for large values of the LM-test.

ARCH LM-test as a general test for non-linearities

A significant value for $LM = nR^2$ in the ARCH LM-test does not necessarily imply that GARCH is the correct alternative model. A significant R^2 for the squared residuals may also be caused, for example, by unmodelled non-linearities in the functional relation (similar to the RESET) or by clusters of outliers. Therefore, the ARCH LM-test can also be used as a general test for possible non-linearities in the time series. If the interpretation of clustered volatility is attractive—for instance, in financial applications—then one can estimate a GARCH model. In other situations one may find other non-linear models more useful—for instance, the models discussed in Sections 7.4.1 and 7.4.2.

Standardized residuals as diagnostic tool

The purpose of a GARCH model is to represent changes in the variance. To check whether the volatility clustering is modelled correctly, let e_t denote the series of residuals of the estimated ARMA–GARCH model. The so-called *standardized residuals* are defined by $e_t/\hat{\sigma}_t$, where $\hat{\sigma}_t^2$ is the estimated conditional variance. If the model is correct, the standardized residuals should be approximately uncorrelated and normally distributed with constant (conditional) variance. This can be checked by applying the Jarque–Bera test for normality and the ARCH test for absence of heteroskedasticity on the series of standardized residuals.

Use of GARCH models in risk modelling

In a GARCH model the conditional variance changes over time, so that the forecast accuracy will also vary over time. The forecast interval can be based on the point forecast plus or minus $2\hat{\sigma}_t$. In very volatile periods, where the residuals e_t are large, the estimated conditional variances $\hat{\sigma}_t^2$ will also be relatively large, so that the forecast intervals are wider. This reflects the fact that in such periods there is more uncertainty about the future values of y_t. That is, large values of $\hat{\sigma}_t$ correspond to periods with higher risk. In Example 7.21 below we consider the use of GARCH models in predicting future risks.

Example 7.20: **Industrial Production (continued)**

We continue our analysis of the quarterly series of yearly growth rates in US industrial production (see also Examples 7.17 and 7.18). We will discuss (i) results of an AR–ARCH model and (ii) some diagnostic tests of this model.

(i) AR(2)–ARCH(1) model

In Example 7.17 we observed that some of the outliers in the yearly growth rates of US industrial production appear in clusters. Therefore we apply a test for the possible presence of volatility clustering. As the growth rates show correlations, we do not estimate a pure GARCH model for this series. We model the growth rates by an AR(2) model. This model was estimated in Example 7.8 (see Exhibit 7.9), but for convenience the estimated AR(2) model is shown once more in Panel 1 of Exhibit 7.24. The ARCH *LM*-test for ARCH(1) effects in the disturbances of the AR(2) process is obtained as $LM = nR^2$ of the regression of the squared residuals e_t^2 of this model on a constant and the lagged squared residuals e_{t-1}^2. This is shown in Panel 2 of Exhibit 7.24. The *LM*-test has value $LM = nR^2 = 135 \cdot 0.063 = 8.5$ with *P*-value $P = 0.003$ (one observation is lost of the 136 available residuals, because of the term e_{t-1}^2 in the test equation). We conclude that the residuals contain significant ARCH effects.

Panel 3 of Exhibit 7.24 shows the ML estimates of the AR(2)–ARCH(1) model for $\Delta_4 y_t$. The AR parameters do not change much as compared to the AR(2) model without ARCH, but the ARCH parameters are of interest in predicting uncertainties in US industrial production. The ARCH parameter $\hat{\alpha}_1 = 0.304$ is relatively small but significant ($P = 0.016$). Also the *LR*-test on ARCH has a significant value, as the results in Panels 1 and 3 of Exhibit 7.24

(*a*)

Panel 1: Dependent Variable: D4Y				
Method: Least Squares				
Sample: 1961:1 1994:4; Included observations: 136				
Variable	Coefficient	Std. Error	t-Statistic	Prob.
C	0.007147	0.002161	3.307447	0.0012
D4Y(−1)	1.332025	0.072094	18.47633	0.0000
D4Y(−2)	−0.545933	0.072174	−7.564120	0.0000
R-squared	0.821380	Log likelihood		334.2160
S.E. of regression	0.020958			

(*b*)

Panel 2: ARCH Test:				
F-statistic	8.973384	Probability		0.003268
Obs*R-squared	8.532634	Probability		0.003488
Test Equation: Dependent Variable: RESID^2				
Method: Least Squares				
Sample(adjusted): 1961:2 1994:4; Included observations: 135				
Variable	Coefficient	Std. Error	t-Statistic	Prob.
C	0.000298	8.16E-05	3.651675	0.0004
RESID^2(−1)	0.233622	0.077989	2.995561	0.0033
R-squared	0.063205			

(*c*)

Panel 3: Dependent Variable: D4Y				
Method: ML – ARCH				
Sample: 1961:1 1994:4; Included observations: 136				
Convergence achieved after 15 iterations				
Variable	Coefficient	Std. Error	z-Statistic	Prob.
C	0.007454	0.002138	3.485798	0.0005
D4Y(−1)	1.406509	0.071004	19.80898	0.0000
D4Y(−2)	−0.600541	0.076058	−7.895869	0.0000
Variance Equation				
C	0.000288	3.24E-05	8.895637	0.0000
ARCH(1)	0.303640	0.126185	2.406315	0.0161
R-squared	0.819478	Log likelihood		342.6833
S.E. of regression	0.021229			

(*d*)

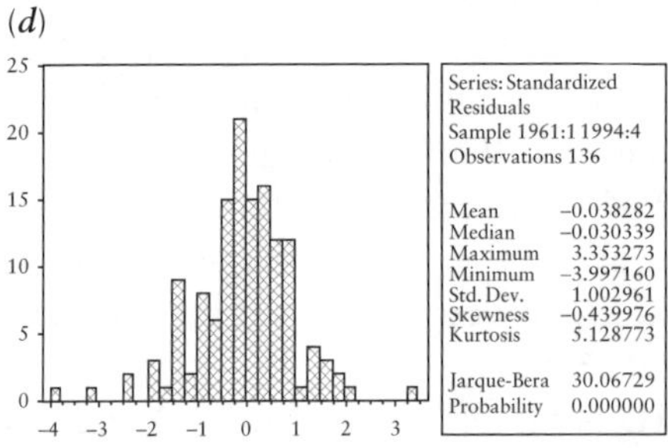

(*e*)

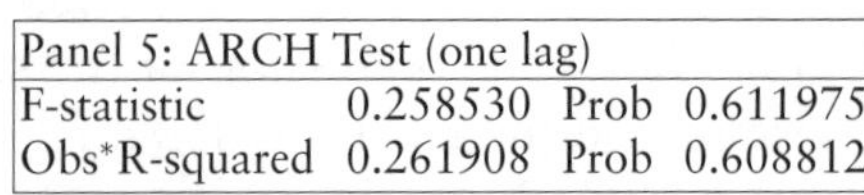

Panel 5: ARCH Test (one lag)			
F-statistic	0.258530	Prob	0.611975
Obs*R-squared	0.261908	Prob	0.608812

Exhibit 7.24 Industrial Production (Example 7.20)

AR(2) model for yearly growth rates in US industrial production (Panel 1), ARCH test on residuals of this model (denoted by RESID, Panel 2), AR(2)–ARCH(1) model (Panel 3), test on normality of the standardized residuals (*d*), and test on remaining ARCH in the standardized residuals of the AR(2)–ARCH(1) model (Panel 5).

give $LR = 2(342.7 - 334.2) = 17.0$ (with P-value according to the $\chi^2(1)$ distribution $P = 0.000$).

(ii) Diagnostic tests

Exhibit 7.24 (*d*) and (*e*) show some diagnostic tests on the standardized residuals of the AR(2)–ARCH(1) model. The ARCH test (with one lag) indicates that no ARCH effects remain in the AR(2)–ARCH(1) model ($P = 0.61$). However, normality is rejected ($P = 0.00$) because the kurtosis of 5.129 is still quite large. This is due to some isolated outliers that are not captured well by the ARCH(1) process.

Example 7.21: **Dow-Jones Index (continued)**

As GARCH models are of particular interest in finance we now consider data on the Dow-Jones index. We will discuss (i) some of the data properties of this series, (ii) results of two GARCH models, (iii) prediction of the risk in tomorrow's returns, (iv) an evaluation of the quality of the risk predictions, and (v) the prediction of high risks.

(i) Data properties

We consider the series of daily returns of the Dow-Jones index over the period 1990–9. Panel 1 of Exhibit 7.25 shows the sample (partial) autocorrelations of this series and of the squares of this series. The correlations in the returns are very small, so that the returns cannot be predicted from their past. However, the squared returns series contains significant correlations, so that the risk in the returns is predictable to some extent. Further, the histogram of the returns in (*b*) shows that the kurtosis is equal to 8.2, so that this series has fat tails. These properties (no correlation in levels, clustered volatility, and fat tails) motivate the use of GARCH models for the returns.

(ii) Results of two GARCH models

Panels 3 and 6 of Exhibit 7.25 show the results of two GARCH models. The models are of the form $y_t = \mu + \varepsilon_t$, where μ is the mean of the returns and ε_t follows an ARCH(5) process (in Panel 3) or a GARCH(2,2) process (in Panel 6). The ARCH and GARCH parameters are significant (except the first lagged GARCH term in the GARCH(2,2) model). Exhibit 7.25 (*d*, *e*, *g*, *h*) show histograms and ARCH tests (with five lags included) of the standardized residuals of these two models. The standardized residuals contain no ARCH anymore ($P = 0.47$ in Panel 4 for the ARCH(5) model and $P = 0.61$ in Panel 7 for the GARCH(2,2) model). The kurtosis has decreased (to around 5.4 for the ARCH(5) model (see (*e*)) and 5.5 for the GARCH(2,2) model (see (*h*))), but the standardized residuals are not normally distributed. This is because the series of returns contains some isolated outliers that cannot be modelled well by a GARCH model. Note that the sample mean

(*a*)

Panel 1				
Lag	SACF y_t	SPACF y_t	SACF y_t^2	SPACF y_t^2
1	0.030	0.030	0.208	0.208
2	−0.017	−0.018	0.151	0.112
3	−0.046	−0.045	0.069	0.018
4	−0.011	−0.008	0.091	0.062
5	−0.013	−0.014	0.178	0.149
6	−0.004	−0.006	0.066	−0.011
7	−0.047	−0.048	0.137	0.093
8	−0.012	−0.011	0.057	0.001
9	0.041	0.039	0.078	0.027
10	0.039	0.032	0.055	0.002

(*b*)

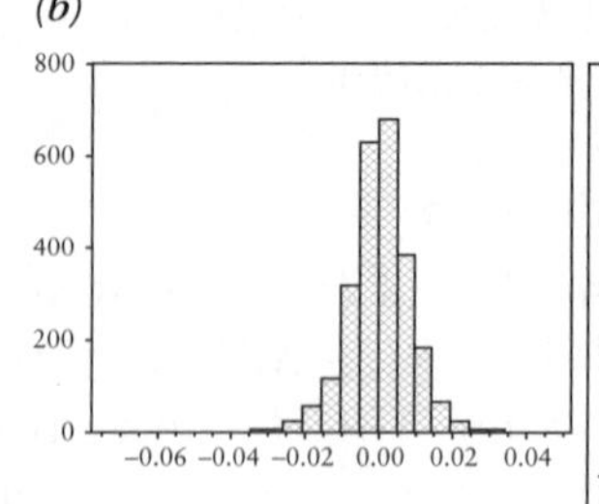

Series: DJRET	
Sample 2 2528	
Observations 2527	
Mean	0.000558
Median	0.000605
Maximum	0.048605
Minimum	−0.074549
Std. Dev.	0.008917
Skewness	−0.409383
Kurtosis	8.201159
Jarque-Bera	2918.942
Probability	0.000000

(*c*)

Panel 3: Dependent Variable: DJRET				
Method: ML – ARCH				
Sample(adjusted): 2 2528; Included observations: 2527				
Convergence achieved after 15 iterations				
Variable	Coefficient	Std. Error	z-Statistic	Prob.
C	0.000668	0.000165	4.044671	0.0001
Variance Equation				
C	3.97E-05	1.67E-06	23.86055	0.0000
ARCH(1)	0.085180	0.017965	4.741323	0.0000
ARCH(2)	0.127996	0.014382	8.899731	0.0000
ARCH(3)	0.064421	0.020266	3.178738	0.0015
ARCH(4)	0.124051	0.019582	6.334810	0.0000
ARCH(5)	0.104425	0.020429	5.111540	0.0000
S.E. of regression	0.008928	Akaike info criterion		−6.708544
Log likelihood	8483.245	Schwarz criterion		−6.692381

(*d*)

Panel 4: ARCH Test on STRESID of ARCH(5)			
5 lags included in the test equation			
F-statistic	0.907729	Prob	0.474914
Obs*R-squared	4.541276	Prob	0.474380

(*e*)

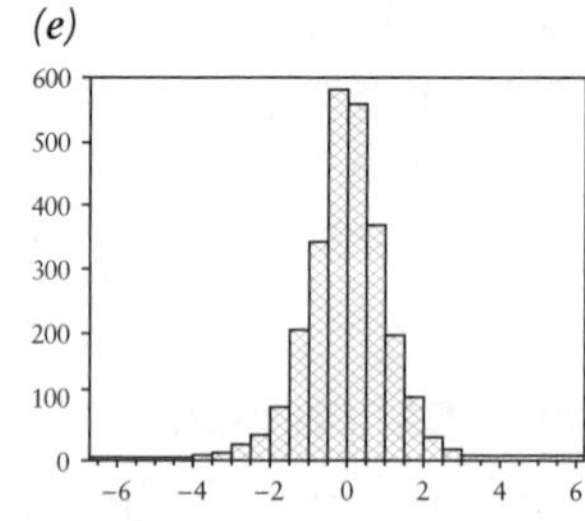

Series: Standardized Residuals of ARCH(5) model	
Sample 2 2528	
Observations 2527	
Mean	−0.021353
Median	−0.007114
Maximum	5.677472
Minimum	−6.188729
Std. Dev.	1.000002
Skewness	−0.332833
Kurtosis	5.425713
Jarque-Bera	666.2010
Probability	0.000000

Exhibit 7.25 **Dow-Jones Index (Example 7.21)**

S(P)ACF of the daily Dow-Jones returns and of the squares of this series (Panel 1), histogram of this series (*b*), ARCH(5) model (Panel 3), ARCH test on standardized residuals of this model (Panel 4), and histogram (*e*).

of the daily returns is 0.056 per cent (see the histogram of the returns series in Exhibit 7.25 (*b*)), but the mean daily return μ is estimated as 0.067 per cent in the ARCH(5) model in Panel 3 and as 0.062 per cent in the GARCH(2,2) model in Panel 6. The estimates of the ARCH and GARCH models are more

(*f*)

Panel 6: Dependent Variable: DJRET				
Method: ML – ARCH				
Sample(adjusted): 2 2528; Included observations: 2527				
Convergence achieved after 26 iterations				
Variable	Coefficient	Std.Error	z-Statistic	Prob.
C	0.000621	0.000154	4.040140	0.0001
Variance Equation				
C	1.86E-06	4.11E-07	4.515180	0.0000
ARCH(1)	0.037997	0.011418	3.327782	0.0009
ARCH(2)	0.070522	0.008987	7.847085	0.0000
GARCH(1)	0.117028	0.130196	0.898860	0.3687
GARCH(2)	0.752955	0.121789	6.182480	0.0000
S.E. of regression	0.008926	Akaike info criterion		−6.755778
Log likelihood	8541.926	Schwarz criterion		−6.741925

(*g*)

Panel 7: ARCH Test on STRESID of GARCH(2,2)			
5 lags included in the test equation			
F-statistic	0.722747	Prob	0.606318
Obs*R-squared	3.617159	Prob	0.605739

(*h*)

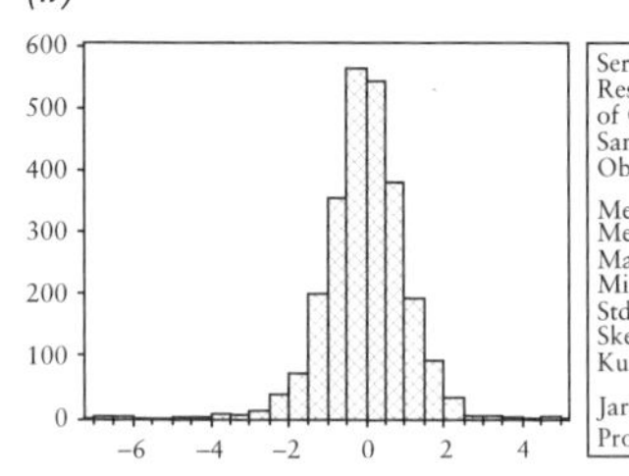

Exhibit 7.25 (*Contd.*)

GARCH(2,2) model for the daily Dow-Jones returns (Panel 6), ARCH test on standardized residuals of this model (Panel 7), and histogram (*h*).

reliable, because the returns are not normally distributed so that the sample mean is not an efficient estimator.

(iii) Prediction of tomorrow's risk

Next we consider the use of these two models in predicting whether the next day is risky or not. The models produce estimates of tomorrow's risk $\sigma_t^2 = \text{var}(y_t|Y_{t-1})$, which can be compared with the actually realized returns. The risks are predicted well if the estimated risk $\hat{\sigma}_t$ is positively correlated with the absolute return $|y_t|$. Exhibit 7.25 (*i*) and (*j*) contain plots of the estimated conditional standard deviations $\hat{\sigma}_t$ of both models. Panel 11 of Exhibit 7.25 shows the correlations between these forecasted standard deviations and the series of absolute returns. The correlations are positive (0.26 for the ARCH(5) model and 0.29 for the GARCH(2,2) model). So the models have some success in predicting the risks in the daily movements of the Dow-Jones index. If the forecasted standard deviation for tomorrow is large, then tomorrow the return will, on average, be relatively large (positive or negative).

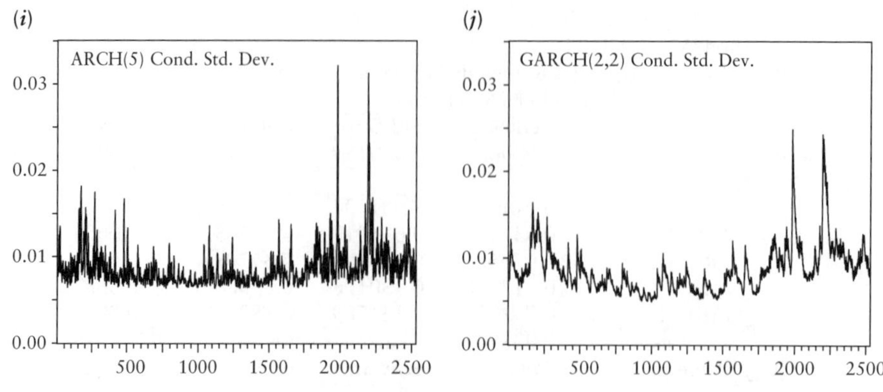

(*k*)

Panel 11: Correlations between absolute returns and conditional Std. Dev.			
	$\lvert y_t \rvert$	σ_t (ARCH5)	σ_t (GARCH22)
$\lvert y_t \rvert$	1.000000	0.255448	0.292503
σ_t (ARCH5)	0.255448	1.000000	0.782080
σ_t (GARCH22)	0.292503	0.782080	1.000000

(*l*)

Panel 12: Prediction–realization table for large (absolute) returns					
Real	Total	ARCH(5)		GARCH(2,2)	
		$\sigma_t < s$	$\sigma_t > s$	$\sigma_t < s$	$\sigma_t > s$
$\lvert y_t \rvert < s$	1900	1392	508	1352	548
$\lvert y_t \rvert > s$	627	352	275	306	321
$y_t > s$	355	193	162	166	189
$y_t < -s$	272	159	113	140	132

(*m*)

Panel 13: Prediction–realization table for very large (absolute) returns					
Real	Total	ARCH(5)		GARCH(2,2)	
		$\sigma_t < 2s$	$\sigma_t > 2s$	$\sigma_t < 2s$	$\sigma_t > 2s$
$y_t > 2s$	64	58	6	56	8
$y_t < -2s$	66	64	2	59	7
Total	130	122	8	115	15

Exhibit 7.25 (*Contd.*)

Estimated series of conditional standard deviations of ARCH(5) model (*i*) and of GARCH(2,2) model (*j*), correlations between absolute returns $|y_t|$ and one-step-ahead predicted standard deviations σ_t (Panel 11), prediction–realization table for small and large (absolute) returns against predicted standard deviations of the ARCH(5) and GARCH(2,2) model (Panel 12), and prediction–realization table for very large (absolute) returns (Panel 13).

(iv) Evaluation of the risk predictions

To evaluate the quality of the risk forecasts in more detail, Panel 12 of Exhibit 7.25 contains a prediction–realization table, which is constructed as follows. The sample mean and the sample standard deviation of the returns y_t are equal to $\bar{y} = 0.0558$ per cent and $s = 0.8917$ per cent. As the standard deviation is much larger than the mean, we take as one-day-ahead forecast

$\hat{y}_t = 0$. We call a day risky if the squared return is larger than average—that is, if $y_t^2 > s^2$ or equivalently if $|y_t| > s$. A day is predicted to be risky if the estimated conditional standard deviation $\hat{\sigma}_t > s$. As a benchmark we consider the forecasts generated by the model $y_t \sim \text{NID}(0, s^2)$. In this model we cannot predict tomorrow's risk from the past. But we can randomly predict that tomorrow is risky with probability $p = P[|y_t| > s]$ and that tomorrow is non-risky with probability $(1 - p) = P[|y_t| < s]$. In this model $y_t^2/s^2 \sim \chi^2(1)$, so that $p = P[y_t^2 > s^2] = P[\chi^2(1) > 1] = 0.317$. The benchmark model has an expected hit rate of correctly predicting risky and non-risky days equal to $p^2 + (1 - p)^2 = 0.567$. For the ARCH(5) model, 275 out of 627 risky days and 1392 out of 1900 non-risky days are predicted correctly, with hit rate $1667/2527 = 0.660$. For the GARCH(2,2) model, 321 of the risky days and 1352 of the non-risky days are predicted correctly, with hit rate $1673/2527 = 0.662$. Both hit rates are larger than the benchmark, so that both models are successful in predicting the amount of risk one day ahead.

It is also of interest to distinguish between large positive returns $y_t > s$ and large negative returns $y_t < -s$, as this corresponds to different types of risks. The ARCH(5) model correctly predicts 162 of the 355 large positive returns (45.6 per cent) and 113 of the 272 large negative returns (41.5 per cent). For the GARCH(2,2) model these numbers are 189 out of 355 (53.2 per cent) and 132 out of 272 (48.5 per cent) respectively. So the GARCH(2,2) model performs somewhat better than the ARCH(5) model in this respect.

(v) Prediction of high risks

In practice it is most relevant (and most difficult) to predict large future risks. Panel 13 of Exhibit 7.25 contains results for very large returns ($y_t > 2s$ and $y_t < -2s$). Of the 2527 observed daily returns, 130 days involve such large risks (64 days with $y_t > 2s$ and 66 days with $y_t < -2s$). The ARCH(5) model correctly predicts eight out of these 130 days (6.2 per cent), in the sense that $\hat{\sigma}_t > 2s$ for such days. The GARCH(2,2) model correctly predicts fifteen out of these 130 days (11.5 per cent). The hit rates are small, but still better than what would be obtained by random predictions from the model $y_t \sim \text{NID}(0, s^2)$. In this model there holds $P[|y_t| > 2s] = P[y_t^2/s^2 > 4] = P[\chi^2(1) > 4] = 0.046$. If we randomly predict tomorrow to be very risky with probability $p = 0.046$ and not very risky with probability $(1 - p)$, then the hit rate for very risky days would be 4.6 per cent. Summarizing, (G)ARCH models help in evaluating the risk of tomorrow's returns in financial markets.

☞ **Exercises:** T: 7.7**b–f**, 7.8; E: 7.18c, **d**, 7.19, 7.22, 7.23e.

7.4.5 Summary

In this section we have considered different non-linear aspects that may be relevant in time series modelling. The modelling of non-linear aspects like switching regimes and changing volatilities helps to understand the dynamical structure of the process. The outcomes of estimates, diagnostic tests, and forecasts depend on the proper modelling of such non-linear aspects. We discussed

- outliers in time series (additive outliers, innovation outliers, level shifts) and the modelling of outliers by means of dummy variables;
- changes in the parameters of ARMA models (sudden parameter breaks or more smooth transitions);
- changes in variance (conditional heteroskedasticity) and the use of (G)ARCH models in modelling financial time series, in constructing forecast intervals, and in predicting future risks;
- the ARCH test for conditional heteroskedasticity, which can also be used as a general test for the presence of non-linearities in observed time series.

7.5 Regression models with lags

☞ Uses Chapters 1–4; Sections 5.5, 5.7; Sections 7.1–7.3.

7.5.1 Autoregressive models with distributed lags

Time series models with explanatory variables

In the foregoing sections we considered the modelling of time series data of a single variable y_t, where the value of y_t is explained in terms of lagged values of this variable and possibly lagged values of the error term. If an explanatory variable x_t is available, then y_t can in addition be explained by this variable and its lagged values. If we add x_t and r lagged values of x_t to an ARMA(p, q) model for y_t, we obtain the model

$$y_t = \alpha + \sum_{k=1}^{p} \phi_k y_{t-k} + \sum_{k=0}^{r} \beta_k x_{t-k} + \sum_{k=1}^{q} \theta_k \varepsilon_{t-k} + \varepsilon_t. \tag{7.32}$$

This is a dynamic regression model that incorporates both the autocorrelation between successive observations of y_t and the correlation of y_t with the explanatory variable x_t and its lags. The model extends the regression model of Chapters 2 and 3 (which is obtained if $\phi_k = 0$ and $\theta_k = 0$ for all k) and the ARMA model of Section 7.1.4 (which is obtained if $\beta_k = 0$ for all k).

Autoregressive model with distributed lags

Of particular interest is the model without MA component—that is, with $q = 0$. This is called the *autoregressive model with distributed lags*, also denoted as ADL(p, r). In this model, the effect of the explanatory variable x_t on the dependent variable y_t is distributed over time. The model can be written as

$$\phi(L) y_t = \alpha + \beta(L) x_t + \varepsilon_t,$$

where $\phi(z) = 1 - \sum_{k=1}^{p} \phi_k z^k$ and $\beta(z) = \sum_{k=0}^{r} \beta_k z^k$. We assume that the AR polynomial is stationary—that is, that $\phi(z) = 0$ has all its solutions outside the unit circle. A change in x_t has an effect on y_t that is distributed over time. The instantaneous or short-run multiplier is β_0. The *long-run multiplier* (that we denote by λ) measures the long-run effect on $E[y_t]$ of a permanent change in the level of x_t. If the level of x_t increases by one unit for all times, then the mean of y_t increases by $\lambda = \sum_{k=0}^{r} \beta_k / (1 - \sum_{k=1}^{p} \phi_k) = \beta(1)/\phi(1)$ units. Note that $\phi(1) \neq 0$, as it is assumed that the AR polynomial has all its roots outside the unit circle.

The model (7.32) is easily extended to the case of more than one explanatory variable, but for simplicity we will restrict ourselves to a single explanatory variable. A special case of the ADL(1,1) model was discussed in Section 5.5.4 (p. 369)—namely, the regression model with AR(1) errors. This corresponds to the ADL(1,1) model with the parameter restriction $\beta_0\phi_1 + \beta_1 = 0$, see (5.52) in Section 5.5.4. This model is sometimes used to reduce some of the serial correlation in (static) regression models, but in practice the residuals of this model often still contain much serial correlation. In this section we discuss some other special cases of the model (7.32) that have an interesting economic interpretation.

Partial adjustment

One of the possible reasons for dynamic effects in business and economic processes is that economic subjects adjust themselves only gradually to changing conditions. For instance, consumption habits are adjusted only gradually to changes in income levels and prices. Similarly, the sales of a new brand of a product may reach its equilibrium level only after a certain period of time, when the brand has established its position in the market. For given value of the independent variable x_t, let the corresponding equilibrium level of y_t be given by $y_t^* = \gamma + \delta x_t$. Suppose that the actual level of y_t is only partially adjusted in the sense that

$$y_t = y_{t-1} + \lambda(y_t^* - y_{t-1}) + \varepsilon_t,$$

where $0 \leq \lambda \leq 1$. For instance, if the current level y_{t-1} is smaller than the equilibrium value y_t^*, then the series tends to be adjusted upwards. The adjustment is complete if $\lambda = 1$, it is partial if $0 < \lambda < 1$, and there is no adjustment if $\lambda = 0$. Substituting $y_t^* = \gamma + \delta x_t$ in the above equation gives the model

$$y_t = \alpha + \phi y_{t-1} + \beta x_t + \varepsilon_t,$$

where $\alpha = \lambda\gamma$, $\phi = (1 - \lambda)$, and $\beta = \lambda\delta$. This is an ADL(1,0) model. It is called the *partial adjustment* model.

Adaptive expectations

It may also be that economic subjects decide on the level of y_t on the basis of expected values of x_{t+1}, denoted by x_{t+1}^*. For instance, expenses on durable goods may depend on expected income, and the production of a new product may be based on expected sales. The model is given by

$$y_t = \gamma + \delta x^*_{t+1} + \varepsilon_t.$$

The expectation of the future value of x_{t+1} can be adjusted according to the actual values of x_t. The *adaptive expectations* model postulates that

$$x^*_{t+1} = x^*_t + \lambda(x_t - x^*_t),$$

where $0 \leq \lambda \leq 1$. For instance, if the current value x_t is larger than expected (so that $x_t > x^*_t$), then this leads to an upward correction in future expectations. The adaptation is complete if $\lambda = 1$ (as $x^*_{t+1} = x_t$ in this case), it is partial if $0 < \lambda < 1$, and expectations are not adapted if $\lambda = 0$ (as $x^*_{t+1} = x^*_t$ in this case). In this model the expectations are obtained by exponential smoothing (with smoothing factor $1 - \theta = \lambda$), so that this gives the optimal forecasts if x_t is an ARIMA(0,1,1) process (see Section 7.3.2). The unobserved variable x^*_{t+1} in the above equation for y_t can be eliminated by using $y_t - (1-\lambda)y_{t-1} = \lambda\gamma \ + \delta(x^*_{t+1} - (1-\lambda)x^*_t) + \varepsilon_t - (1-\lambda)\varepsilon_{t-1}$, where $x^*_{t+1} - (1-\lambda)x^*_t = \lambda x_t$, so that

$$y_t = \alpha + \phi y_{t-1} + \beta x_t + \varepsilon_t - \phi\varepsilon_{t-1},$$

where $\alpha = \lambda\gamma$, $\phi = (1-\lambda)$, and $\beta = \lambda\delta$. This model is of the form (7.32) with orders $p = 1$, $r = 0$, and $q = 1$. The only difference with the partial adjustment model is that the adaptive expectations model contains an additional MA(1) term.

Error correction model

The ADL model can be rewritten in terms of changes of the variables—that is, in terms of the first differences $\Delta y_t = y_t - y_{t-1}$ and $\Delta x_t = x_t - x_{t-1}$. We consider this reformulation first for the ADL(1,1) model—that is, the model (7.32) with $p = 1$, $r = 1$, and $q = 0$. By subtracting y_{t-1} from both sides of the equation (7.32), we can write this model as $\Delta y_t = \alpha + (\phi - 1)y_{t-1} + \beta_0\Delta x_t + (\beta_0 + \beta_1)x_{t-1} + \varepsilon_t$, or equivalently

$$\Delta y_t = \beta_0\Delta x_t - (1-\phi)(y_{t-1} - \lambda x_{t-1} - \delta) + \varepsilon_t, \tag{7.33}$$

with $\delta = \alpha/(1-\phi)$ and where $\lambda = (\beta_0 + \beta_1)/(1-\phi)$ is the long-run multiplier. Note that the equilibrium relation $y = \delta + \lambda x$ is obtained if in the ADL(1,1) model $\varepsilon_t = 0$ and the values of $y_t = y_{t-1} = y$ and $x_t = x_{t-1} = x$ are fixed, as in this case $y = \alpha + \phi y + \beta_0 x + \beta_1 x$, so that $y = \frac{\alpha}{1-\phi} + \frac{\beta_0+\beta_1}{1-\phi}x = \delta + \lambda x$. The ADL(1,1) model written in the form (7.33) is called an *error correction model* (ECM). This shows that there are two systematic effects on the changes Δy_t of the dependent variable. The first effect is the instantaneous multiplier effect $\beta_0 \Delta x_t$ that is due to changes in the explanatory variable. The second effect concerns deviations from the long-run equilibrium relation $y_{t-1} = \delta + \lambda x_{t-1}$. For instance, suppose that $y_{t-1} > \delta + \lambda x_{t-1}$, so that the value of y_{t-1} is above the long-run equilibrium value corresponding to x_{t-1}. The stationarity assumption implies that $\phi < 1$, so that $(1 - \phi) > 0$, and hence this provides a negative effect on Δy_t—that is, y_t will tend to move downwards in the direction of equilibrium. Therefore the term $-(1 - \phi)(y_{t-1} - \lambda x_{t-1} - \delta)$ takes care that deviations from equilibrium (the 'errors') are corrected. If $\phi = 1$—that is, if the series y_t has a unit root—then the error correction term drops out from (7.33). In this case there exists no long-run equilibrium for y_t and the long-run multiplier is infinitely large.

It is left as an exercise (see Exercise 7.9) to show that for higher order lags the ADL model can also be written in error correction form. That is, the ADL(p, q) model with stationary AR polynomial $\phi(z)$ can be written as

$$\Delta y_t = \beta_0 \Delta x_t - \phi(1)(y_{t-1} - \lambda x_{t-1} - \delta) + \sum_{k=1}^{p-1} \phi_k^* \Delta y_{t-k} + \sum_{k=1}^{r-1} \beta_k^* \Delta x_{t-k} + \varepsilon_t, \tag{7.34}$$

with $\phi(1) = 1 - \sum_{k=1}^{p} \phi_k > 0$, $\delta = \alpha/\phi(1)$, and where $\lambda = \beta(1)/\phi(1)$ is the long-run multiplier. As before, the relation $y = \delta + \lambda x$ corresponds to the long-run equilibrium relation. Since $\phi(1) > 0$, deviations from this equilibrium are again corrected in this model.

☞ **Exercises: T: 7.9a, b.**

7.5.2 Estimation, testing, and forecasting

Model assumptions

To estimate the parameters of the ADL model $\phi(L)y_t = \beta(L)x_t + \varepsilon_t$, we make the following assumptions. First, the disturbance terms ε_t satisfy all the usual assumptions—that is, they have mean zero and constant variance σ^2, and they are mutually independent and jointly normally distributed. If this is not the case, then the model should be adjusted (by including more lagged terms of y_t and x_t or by including MA terms as in (7.32). Second, the explanatory variables are *exogenous*, in the sense that all current and past values

$\{x_{t-k}, k \geq 0\}$ are uncorrelated with the error term ε_t. If this is not the case, then one should instead specify a multiple equation model—for instance, a vector autoregressive model, as will be discussed in Section 7.6. Finally, the AR polynomial $\phi(z)$ is *stationary*—that is, it has all its roots outside the unit circle—and the process x_t is stationary. These conditions imply that y_t is a stationary process. If the AR polynomial contains unit roots, then y_t contains stochastic trends and ADL models are not appropriate. The modelling of series with stochastic trends is discussed in Section 7.6.3.

Estimation of ADL models

The ADL(p, q) model—that is, (7.32) without MA terms—is a regression model with stochastic regressors. Under the above model assumptions, the parameters can be estimated by least squares and the OLS estimators have the standard statistical properties discussed in Section 4.1.4 (p. 197). That is, under the above assumptions OLS is consistent and the conventional t- and F-tests are valid asymptotically. Because the error terms are assumed to be normally distributed, OLS is equivalent to ML and hence it is asymptotically efficient. To analyse this in more detail, we consider for simplicity the ADL(1,1) model. Let $z_t = (1, y_{t-1}, x_t, x_{t-1})'$ be the vector of regressors in this model. Then the stability and orthogonality conditions for stochastic regressors formulated in Section 4.1 can be formulated as

$$\text{plim}\left(\frac{1}{n}\sum_{t=2}^{n} \varepsilon_t z_t\right) = 0, \quad \text{plim}\left(\frac{1}{n}\sum_{t=2}^{n} z_t z_t'\right) = Q_{zz},$$

where Q_{zz} is an invertible matrix. The first (orthogonality) condition is satisfied because the explanatory variable x_t and its lagged values are assumed to be exogenous. The second (stability) condition requires the variables to have finite variances and covariances, and this is satisfied because the processes y_t and x_t are assumed to be stationary. It is sufficient that the process x_t is stationary and that $-1 < \phi < 1$. If the process y_t has a unit root, then the stability condition is not satisfied. This is because in this case y_t has infinite variance for $t \to \infty$ (see Section 7.3.1). Then the OLS estimators do not have the standard properties discussed in Section 4.1 (see also the discussion in Section 7.3.3 on unit root tests).

Estimation of models with MA terms

If the model (7.32) contains moving average terms, then least squares is no longer consistent. For instance, in the case of single lags (so that $p = q = r = 1$) and with exogenous regressors x_t and x_{t-1}, the covariance between the regressor y_{t-1} and the error term $\varepsilon_t + \theta\varepsilon_{t-1}$ in (7.32) is equal to

$$\mathrm{cov}(\alpha + \phi y_{t-2} + \beta_0 x_{t-1} + \beta_1 x_{t-2} + \varepsilon_{t-1} + \theta\varepsilon_{t-2},\ \varepsilon_t + \theta\varepsilon_{t-1}) = \theta\sigma^2 \neq 0.$$

Models with MA terms should be estimated by maximum likelihood. The standard asymptotic theory for ML estimators applies, provided that the processes x_t and y_t are stationary.

Diagnostic tests

If the processes x_t and y_t are stationary, then the diagnostic tests described before (in Chapter 5 for regression models and in Section 7.2.4 for stationary time series) can all be applied to models of the form (7.32). For instance, the lag lengths p, q, and r can be chosen by means of t-tests and F-tests on the significance of additional lagged terms, and also by means of the selection criteria AIC and SIC. The Breusch–Godfrey LM-test on serial correlation and the ARCH LM-test on heteroskedasticity can be performed as before on the residuals of the estimated model.

Forecasting

To use the model (7.32) in one-period-ahead forecasting we need to know or to estimate the value of x_{n+1} and we have to estimate the value of ε_n. The best we can do is to replace the unknown parameters by their ML estimates and to take the resulting residual series as an estimate of the error terms ε_t. For instance, in the model with single lags ($p = q = r = 1$), the forecast is then given by $\hat{y}_{n+1} = \hat{\phi} y_n + \hat{\beta}_0 \hat{x}_{n+1} + \hat{\beta}_1 x_n + \hat{\theta} e_n$, where $e_n = y_n - \hat{y}_n$. The required forecast $\hat{x}_{n+1}$ of the explanatory variable can be obtained, for instance, from a (univariate) time series model for x_t as discussed in Section 7.1.6. For multi-period-ahead forecasts, the future values of y_t that appear as regressors on the right-hand side in (7.32) are themselves forecasted. Combined with the additional uncertainty in the forecasts of the explanatory variables x_t, this implies that the forecast intervals will be wider than in the case of known, non-stochastic regressors considered in Sections 2.4.1 (p. 106) and 3.4.3 (p. 171).

Example 7.22: **Interest and Bond Rates (continued)**

To illustrate the use of the regression model with lags, we consider the relation between the monthly changes y_t in the AAA bond rate and the monthly changes x_t in the three-month Treasury Bill rate. These data were also used in Chapter 5; see Example 5.11 (p. 322) for further motivation. The data cover the period 1950–99, leading to $n = 600$ monthly observations. We will subsequently discuss (i) the simple regression model, (ii) an ADL model, (iii) an ADL model with GARCH error terms, (iv) interpretation of the GARCH effects, and (v) some important remarks on further relevant data properties.

(i) The simple regression model with AR(1) errors

In Chapter 5 we considered the simple regression model $y_t = \alpha + \beta x_t + \varepsilon_t$ for these data. This model was analysed in Examples 5.19 (p. 354), 5.21 (p. 360), 5.22 (p. 365), and 5.24 (p. 370). The conclusion of this analysis was that the residuals of the simple regression model show significant serial correlation and that an AR(1) model for the error terms ε_t is too limited to remove this serial correlation. Therefore other models are needed that reflect the dynamical relations between the two variables. For later comparison the estimation results of the simple regression model (in Panel 1 of Exhibit 5.30 (p. 360)) are given once more in Panel 1 of Exhibit 7.26.

(ii) ADL model

To model the dynamical relations between the bond rate y_t and the interest rate x_t we now estimate ADL models. We start with an ADL(p, r) model that contains enough lags so that the residuals are not serially correlated anymore. It turns out that it is sufficient to include $p = r = 6$ lags. Next we try to reduce the number of lags, by considering the significance of lagged terms, by comparing SIC values, and by checking for serial correlation in ADL models with lower orders for p and r. This leads to the ADL model with $p = 3$ lags of y_t and $r = 4$ lags of x_t. The estimation results of the ADL(3,4) model are given in Panel 2 of Exhibit 7.26. The correlations of the residuals of this model are small, with a largest correlation of 0.078 at lag 6 (see Panel 3). The Breusch–Godfrey test on serial correlation gives P-values of $P = 0.07$ (with one lag included) and $P = 0.03$ (with twelve lags included). So, at the 1 per cent significance level (which is a reasonable choice for $n = 600$ observations), there is no significant serial correlation. We conclude that the dynamic correlations between the changes in the AAA bond rate and the three-month Treasury Bill rate are captured well by this model. The short-run multiplier (the coefficient of x_t) in the ADL(3,4) model is 0.24. This is quite close to the estimated value of 0.27 in the simple regression model.

It is of interest to test whether changes in the interest rate in the long run lead to equal changes in the bond rate — that is, to test whether the long-run multiplier is equal to 1. This corresponds to the parameter restriction $\lambda = \sum_{k=0}^{4} \beta_k / \left(1 - \sum_{k=1}^{3} \phi_k\right) = 1$, or, equivalently, to $\sum_{k=0}^{4} \beta_k + \sum_{k=1}^{3} \phi_k = 1$. Panel 4 of Exhibit 7.26 shows the outcomes of the F-test for this hypothesis. The hypothesis is clearly rejected ($F = 119$ with $P = 0.00$).

(iii) ADL model with GARCH error terms

The residuals of the ADL model are not serially correlated, but they exhibit clustered volatility. This is clear from the time series plot of the residuals in Exhibit 7.26 (*e*). The ARCH test (with four lags) on the residuals is very significant (see Panel 6). Therefore we now estimate the ADL(3,4) model with GARCH(1,1) error terms, with results in Panel 7 of Exhibit 7.26. The residuals of the ADL(3,4)-GARCH(1,1) model do not contain clustered volatility anymore (the ARCH *LM*-test with four lags gives $P = 0.087$, see Panel 8). Further note that the lagged values of x_t have become jointly insignificant in this model (the corresponding *F*-test has $P = 0.58$, see Panel 9). This means that the dynamic effects, which were attributed in the ADL model to past changes in the Treasury Bill rate, are better described in terms of clustered volatility of the AAA bond rate changes.

(iv) Interpretation of the GARCH effects

Exhibit 7.26 (*j*) shows the time series plot of the predicted standard deviations obtained from the GARCH(1,1) model. The conditional standard deviation shows much variation over time. In particular there seems to be a break in the volatility around 1980. The GARCH(1,1) model captures the variations in the volatility of the series much better than the models discussed in Example 5.18 (p. 350–2) for these heteroskedastic data. Exhibit 7.26 (*k*) shows the scatter plot of the absolute changes in the AAA bond rate against the predicted standard deviation. These variables are positively correlated. On average, if the predicted standard deviation is relatively large (small) then the (absolute) change in the AAA bond rate is also relatively large (small). So this model is helpful in predicting risky months—that is, months where the AAA bond rates contain much uncertainty.

(v) Remarks on further relevant data properties

We will return later to these data to answer two remaining questions. The first is why the model is formulated for the changes and not for the levels of the two rates. The reason is that, in estimating the ADL model, it is assumed that the series are stationary. We will analyse this issue further in Example 7.25 in the next section and especially in Example 7.27 in Section 7.6.3. It will turn out that it is better to model the levels of the two time series, and not the series of first differences. The second question is related to the possible endogeneity of the Treasury Bill rate. Indeed, in Example 5.33 (p. 414–16) we concluded that x_t is endogenous. This means that a fundamental assumption of the ADL model is violated, so that the results of the ADL model may be misleading. Models that account for the joint endogeneity of both time series are considered in Examples 7.26 and 7.32.

(a)

Panel 1: Dependent Variable: DAAA				
Method: Least Squares				
Sample: 1950:01 1999:12; Included observations: 600				
Variable	Coefficient	Std. Error	t-Statistic	Prob.
C	0.006393	0.006982	0.915697	0.3602
DUS3MT	0.274585	0.014641	18.75442	0.0000
R-squared	0.370346	Mean dependent var		0.008283
S.E. of regression	0.171002	Akaike info criterion		−0.690952
Sum squared resid	17.48658	Schwarz criterion		−0.676296
Log likelihood	209.2857	F-statistic		351.7282
Durbin-Watson stat	1.446887	Prob(F-statistic)		0.000000

(b)

Panel 2: Dependent Variable: DAAA				
Method: Least Squares				
Sample: 1950:01 1999:12; Included observations: 600				
Variable	Coefficient	Std. Error	t-Statistic	Prob.
C	0.004909	0.006518	0.753160	0.4517
DAAA(−1)	0.376847	0.042230	8.923663	0.0000
DAAA(−2)	−0.229060	0.044907	−5.100809	0.0000
DAAA(−3)	0.087534	0.042553	2.057033	0.0401
DUS3MT	0.240321	0.015169	15.84308	0.0000
DUS3MT(−1)	−0.084951	0.018208	−4.665701	0.0000
DUS3MT(−2)	0.080341	0.018521	4.337855	0.0000
DUS3MT(−3)	−0.061728	0.018403	−3.354288	0.0008
DUS3MT(−4)	0.055952	0.014510	3.856226	0.0001
R-squared	0.459580	Mean dependent var		0.008283
S.E. of regression	0.159358	Akaike info criterion		−0.820443
Sum squared resid	15.00839	Schwarz criterion		−0.754489
Log likelihood	255.1329	F-statistic		62.82430
Durbin-Watson stat	2.022425	Prob(F-statistic)		0.000000

(c)

Panel 3: correlograms of residuals of ADL(0,0) and ADL(3,4)						
Sample: 1950:01 1999:12; Included observations: 600						
	ADL(0,0)			ADL(3,4)		
Lag	SACF	Q-Stat	Prob	SACF	Q-Stat	Prob
1	0.276	45.932	0.000	−0.013	0.1064	0.744
2	−0.076	49.398	0.000	0.014	0.2288	0.892
3	0.008	49.441	0.000	−0.030	0.7695	0.857
4	0.034	50.126	0.000	0.021	1.0323	0.905
5	0.055	51.939	0.000	0.011	1.1061	0.954
6	0.101	58.189	0.000	0.078	4.8142	0.568
7	0.035	58.934	0.000	−0.013	4.9128	0.671
8	0.049	60.412	0.000	0.059	7.0251	0.534
9	0.044	61.610	0.000	0.032	7.6697	0.568
10	0.008	61.646	0.000	0.012	7.7540	0.653
11	0.032	62.289	0.000	0.045	8.9743	0.624
12	−0.062	64.624	0.000	−0.037	9.8041	0.633

Exhibit 7.26 Interest and Bond Rates (Example 7.22)

Simple regression of DAAA on DUS3MT (ADL(0,0) model, Panel 1) and ADL(3,4) model (Panel 2) with correlograms of residuals (Panel 3).

(*d*)

Panel 4: Wald test on long-run multiplier			
Null Hypothesis: C(2)+C(3)+C(4)+C(5)+C(6)+C(7)+C(8)+C(9)=1			
F-statistic	119.0438	Probability	0.000000
Chi-square	119.0438	Probability	0.000000

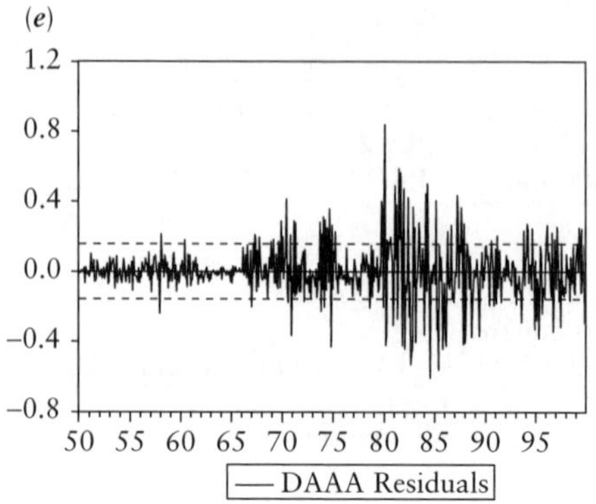

(*f*)

Panel 6: ARCH Test on residuals of the ADL(3,4) model			
4 lags of squared residuals included in the test equation			
F-statistic	28.63848	Probability	0.000000
Obs*R-squared=596*0.162360	96.76672	Probability	0.000000

(*g*)

Panel 7: Dependent Variable: DAAA				
Method: ML - ARCH				
Sample: 1950:01 1999:12; Included observations: 600				
Convergence achieved after 33 iterations				
Variable	Coefficient	Std. Error	z-Statistic	Prob.
C	0.001375	0.002852	0.482058	0.6298
DAAA(−1)	0.395604	0.048109	8.223042	0.0000
DAAA(−2)	−0.194726	0.045298	−4.298749	0.0000
DAAA(−3)	0.054381	0.042720	1.272948	0.2030
DUS3MT	0.144789	0.012544	11.54285	0.0000
DUS3MT(−1)	−0.002217	0.016460	−0.134683	0.8929
DUS3MT(−2)	0.020133	0.016000	1.258328	0.2083
DUS3MT(−3)	−0.020644	0.015003	−1.375931	0.1688
DUS3MT(−4)	0.000278	0.012548	0.022179	0.9823
Variance Equation				
C	9.97E-05	2.09E-05	4.776163	0.0000
ARCH(1)	0.183616	0.028026	6.551611	0.0000
GARCH(1)	0.836600	0.021622	38.69214	0.0000
R-squared	0.389533	Mean dependent var		0.008283
S.E. of regression	0.169803	Akaike info criterion		−1.560654
Sum squared resid	16.95374	Schwarz criterion		−1.472716
Log likelihood	480.1962	F-statistic		34.10875
Durbin-Watson stat	1.991229	Prob(F-statistic)		0.000000

Exhibit 7.26 (*Contd.*)

Wald test on unit long-run multiplier (Panel 4), plot of residuals of the ADL(3,4) model (*e*), ARCH(4) test on these residuals (Panel 6), and ADL(3,4) model with GARCH(1,1) disturbances (Panel 7).

(*h*)

Panel 8: ARCH Test on residuals of the ADL(3,4) - GARCH(1,1) model			
4 lags of squared residuals included in the test equation			
F-statistic	2.045773	Probability	0.086559
Obs*R-squared = 596*0.013657	8.139619	Probability	0.086596

(*i*)

Panel 9: Wald Test on significance of lagged terms of DUS3MT			
Wald Test	C(6)=0, C(7)=0, C(8)=0, C(9)=0		
F-statistic	0.711700	Probability	0.584132
Chi-square	2.846801	Probability	0.583781

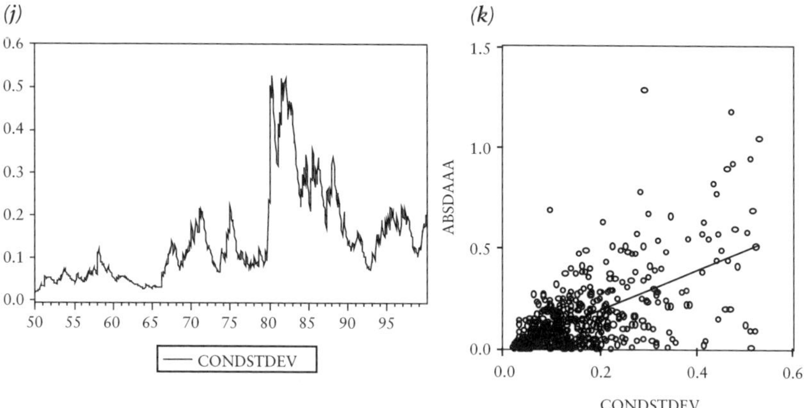

Exhibit 7.26 (*Contd.*)

ARCH(4) test on residuals of ADL(3,4)–GARCH(1,1) model (Panel 8), *F*-test on significance of the four lagged terms of DUS3MT in this model (Panel 9), plot of one-month-ahead predicted standard deviations of GARCH(1,1) (denoted by CONDSTDEV (*j*)), and scatter diagram of absolute monthly changes in the AAA bond rate (denoted by ABSDAAA) against the predicted standard deviation ((*k*), with regression line).

☜ Exercises: E: 7.21a, d–f.

7.5.3 Regression of variables with trends

Danger of spurious regressions

In the foregoing section we described the estimation and testing of regression models for time series data. The outcomes can be evaluated in the usual way, provided that the sample is large enough, the explanatory variables are exogenous, and both the dependent and the explanatory variables are stationary. If the variables contain stochastic trends, then the application of standard regression techniques may lead to misleading results. That is, regression may lead to *nonsense correlations* (seemingly significant correlations) or to *spurious regressions* (seemingly significant effects) that are due only to the presence of neglected trends in the variables. We will illustrate this by means of a historical example and by means of a simple simulation experiment.

XM723MOM

Example 7.23: **Mortality and Marriages**

First we consider data from a historically influential paper on spurious regressions. We will discuss (i) the data and (ii) the results of regressions with these trending data.

(i) **The data**

Exhibit 7.27 (*a*) shows yearly data on the standardized mortality (per 1000 persons) in England and Wales and on the proportion of Church of England

(*a*)

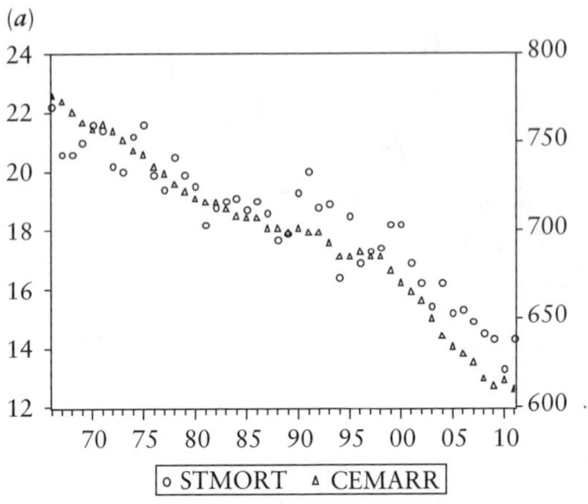

(*b*)

Panel 2: Dependent Variable: STMORT; Sample: 1866 1911; Method: OLS				
Variable	Coefficient	Std. Error	t-Statistic	Prob.
C	−13.88367	1.573472	−8.823593	0.0000
CEMARR	0.046137	0.002249	20.51460	0.0000
R-squared	0.905346			

(*c*)

Panel 3: Dependent Variable: STMORT; Sample: 1866 1911; Method: OLS				
Variable	Coefficient	Std. Error	t-Statistic	Prob.
C	−20.70949	9.400182	−2.203095	0.0330
@TREND(1866)	0.030870	0.041907	0.736640	0.4653
CEMARR	0.054920	0.012135	4.525843	0.0000
R-squared	0.906525			

(*d*)

Panel 4: Dependent Var: D(STMORT); Sample(adj): 1867 1911; Method: OLS				
Variable	Coefficient	Std. Error	t-Statistic	Prob.
C	−0.132989	0.210475	−0.631852	0.5308
D(CEMARR)	0.011539	0.042687	0.270319	0.7882
R-squared	0.001696			

Exhibit 7.27 Mortality and Marriages (Example 7.23)

Time plots of the standardized mortality per 1000 persons in England and Wales (STMORT) and of the proportion of Church of England marriages per 1000 of all marriages (CEMARR) ((*a*), left axis for STMORT, right axis for CEMARR, horizontal axis for years 1866–1911), regression without trend (Panel 2) and with deterministic trend (Panel 3) and regression of the variables in first differences (Panel 4).

marriages (per 1000 of all marriages) for the period 1866–1911. The data in the file are reconstructed from figure 1 in G. U. Yule, 'Why do we Sometimes Get Nonsense-Correlations between Time-Series', *Journal of the Royal Statistical Society*, 89 (1926), 1–64, at p. 3. The sample correlation between the two original variables reported in the paper is 0.9512, and for the reconstructed data this correlation is 0.9515, which indicates that the reconstructed data are quite close to the original ones.

(ii) Results of regressions

We perform a regression of mortality on the proportion of Church of England marriages (either with a constant included or with a constant and a deterministic trend included). The results are in Panels 2 and 3 of Exhibit 7.27. In both cases the effect of marriages on mortality is highly significant (the t-value is 20.5 in the model without deterministic trend and it is 4.5 in the model with deterministic trend). It seems quite unlikely that the way people marry has anything to do with the mortality in the same year. The positive association of both variables is due to their common decline over the sample period. This becomes clear if we regress the variables after taking first differences, to remove the stochastic trends in both variables. The results in Panel 4 of Exhibit 7.27 show that the effect of changes in marriages on changes in mortality is not at all significant (the t-value is 0.27 with $P = 0.79$). Results like the above ones have inspired the practice to take first differences of trended variables in order to prevent nonsense correlations.

Example 7.24: **Simulated Random Walk Data**

E

Next we illustrate the possibility of spurious regressions by means of a simulation. We generate two independent random walks, $y_t = y_{t-1} + \eta_t$ and $x_t = x_{t-1} + \omega_t$, where η_t and ω_t are two independent white noise processes. So the two variables y_t and x_t are completely unrelated. The two series are independent random walks. Exhibit 7.28 (*a*–*d*) show scatter diagrams of y_t against x_t and Panels 5–8 show the outcomes of regressions of y_t on x_t for different sample sizes ($n = 10$, $n = 100$, $n = 1000$, and $n = 10{,}000$). For larger sample sizes the effect of x_t on y_t becomes more and more significant if measured by the t-value of the slope coefficient. The R^2 is also quite large and suggests a significant relationship between x_t and y_t. Note, however, that the estimated slope is negative for sample size $n = 1000$ but positive for the other three sample sizes. That something is wrong with these regressions is indicated by the Durbin–Watson statistic, which comes very close to zero in large samples. The estimated effects are, of course, spurious for these data. To prevent this kind of nonsense regressions one can take first differences of variables that contain stochastic trends. In our simulation this gives the two white noise series η_t and ω_t, and the corresponding regressions are not at all significant anymore.

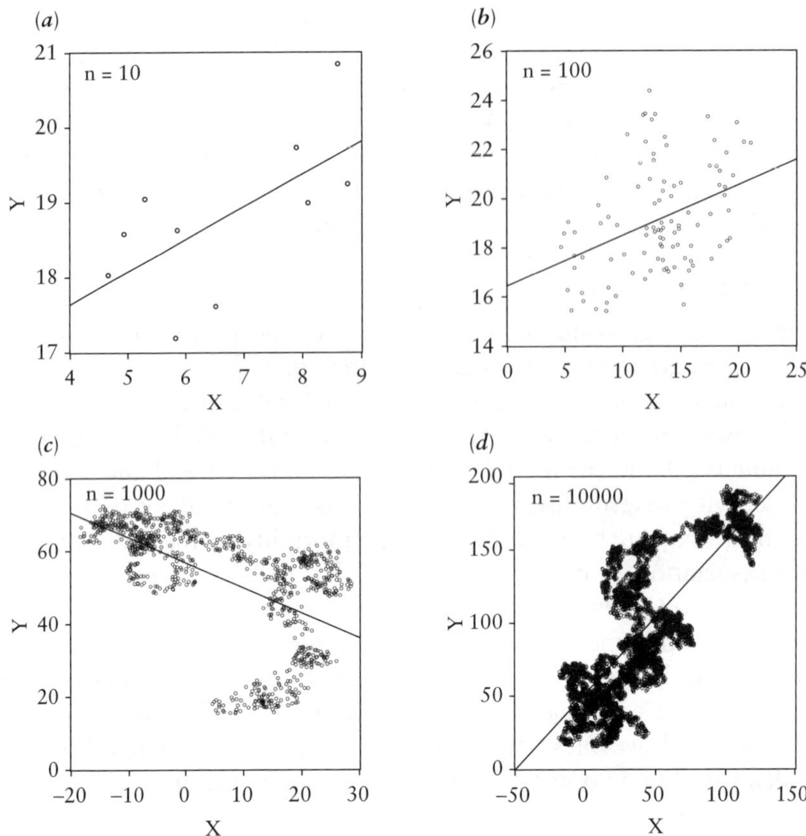

Exhibit 7.28 Simulated Random Walk Data (Example 7.24)

Scatter diagrams of two independent random walks for four sample sizes ($n = 10$ in (*a*), $n = 100$ in (*b*), $n = 1000$ in (*c*), and $n = 10,000$ in (*d*)).

Statistical causes of spurious regressions

To obtain some understanding of the statistical reasons for possible spurious results with trending variables we consider the above simulation in Example 7.24 in more detail. The data are generated by $y_t = y_{t-1} + \eta_t$ and $x_t = x_{t-1} + \omega_t$, and the regression model is given by $y_t = \alpha + \beta x_t + \varepsilon_t$. As the two processes are independent, the data generating process corresponds to $\alpha = 0$ and $\beta = 0$. So the error terms of the model are equal to $\varepsilon_t = y_t = y_1 + \sum_{k=2}^{t} \eta_k$. This implies that the error terms are very strongly correlated. For instance, if $y_1 = 0$ then $\text{var}(\varepsilon_t) = (t-1)\sigma^2$ and $\text{cov}(\varepsilon_t, \varepsilon_s) = (s-1)\sigma^2$ for $t \geq s \geq 2$. In the simulation this strong positive serial correlation was indicated by the Durbin–Watson statistic, which is close to zero. There are two reasons why the conventional *t*-test on significance is misleading in this case. The first is that, in the case of serial correlation, the *t*-value of the estimated slope does not follow the *t*-distribution anymore, as was discussed in Section 5.5.2 (p. 359). The second reason

(e)

Panel 5: Dependent Variable: Y; Sample: 1 10; Included obs. 10				
Variable	Coefficient	Std. Error	t-Statistic	Prob.
C	15.90026	1.241768	12.80454	0.0000
X	0.434657	0.182335	2.383839	0.0443
R-squared	0.415320	Durbin-Watson stat		2.217163

(f)

Panel 6: Dependent Variable: Y; Sample: 1 100; Included obs. 100				
Variable	Coefficient	Std. Error	t-Statistic	Prob.
C	16.47030	0.694868	23.70278	0.0000
X	0.204200	0.050861	4.014873	0.0001
R-squared	0.141249	Durbin-Watson stat		0.299211

(g)

Panel 7: Dependent Variable: Y; Sample: 1 1000; Included obs. 1000				
Variable	Coefficient	Std. Error	t-Statistic	Prob.
C	56.80644	0.428361	132.6135	0.0000
X	−0.689132	0.029447	−23.40248	0.0000
R-squared	0.354328	Durbin-Watson stat		0.009218

(h)

Panel 8: Dependent Variable: Y; Sample: 1 10000; Included obs. 10000				
Variable	Coefficient	Std. Error	t-Statistic	Prob.
C	51.78272	0.455985	113.5623	0.0000
X	1.041574	0.007875	132.2616	0.0000
R-squared	0.636319	Durbin-Watson stat		0.002408

Exhibit 7.28 (*Contd.*)

Regressions corresponding to the scatter diagrams in (*a–d*).

is that the regressor x_t is non-stationary. In Section 4.1.4 (p. 197) we concluded that, under the usual assumptions, the t-test is still valid asymptotically for stochastic regressors that are stable. However, in the simulation the variable x_t is a random walk that does not satisfy the stability condition because $\text{plim}\left(\frac{1}{n}\sum_{t=1}^{n} x_t^2\right) = \infty$. This also affects the distribution of the t-value, as was discussed in Section 7.3.3.

Differencing to remove stochastic trends

The foregoing results motivate the practice to take first differences of variables with trends, in order to prevent spurious results. This is to protect ourselves from claiming the existence of significant relations that are caused only by neglected trends in the observed variables. However, by taking first differences the interpretation of the model changes. The model is then concerned with the short-run relationship between the variables, as their long-run dependence is eliminated in this way. To explain this in more detail, suppose that the two variables y_t and x_t are both integrated of order 1—that is, they contain stochastic trends and the series Δy_t and Δx_t are stationary. Suppose that we initially specify an ADL model to explain y_t in terms of x_t.

This model can be written in error correction form (7.34). If $\phi(1) \neq 0$, then this model contains the error correction term $(y_{t-1} - \lambda x_{t-1})$, which has an interesting economic interpretation in terms of the long-run equilibrium between the levels of the two variables. If we were to follow the practice of removing the trends and making an ADL model for Δy_t in terms of Δx_t, then the error correction term would drop out of the model. This is a correct procedure if $\phi(1) = 0$, but we would omit an important regressor if $\phi(1) \neq 0$.

Cointegrated time series

If the two variables y_t and x_t are both integrated of order 1—that is, if they both contain stochastic trends—then the ECM model (7.34) has an interesting interpretation for $\phi(1) \neq 0$. In this case the term $(y_{t-1} - \lambda x_{t-1} - \delta)$ in (7.34) can be written as a linear combination of the stationary variables ε_t, Δy_t, and Δx_t and their lags. This implies that $(y_{t-1} - \lambda x_{t-1})$ is also stationary. That is, in this case the variables y_t and x_t are integrated of order 1, but the linear combination $(y_t - \lambda x_t)$ is stationary. The series y_t and x_t are then said to be *cointegrated*. Stated intuitively, if two series are cointegrated, then they share one *common trend* that drops out in the linear combination $(y_t - \lambda x_t)$. A regression of y_t on x_t is then not spurious, as the relation is caused by one trend term that is common to the two variables. The regression is even of the greatest interest, as it provides the long-run equilibrium relation between the two series. So we should not take first differences if the variables are cointegrated.

Summarizing, if the observed series contain stochastic trends, then we should proceed as follows. If the series are not cointegrated, then we should take first differences to prevent spurious results. But, if the variables are cointegrated, we should estimate an error correction model to incorporate the long-run relations between the variables. Tests for cointegration and the modelling of cointegrated time series are further discussed in Section 7.6.3.

Example 7.25: **Interest and Bond Rates (continued)**

We continue our analysis of the interest and bond rate data of Example 7.22 in the previous section. We will discuss (i) the data (levels and first differences), (ii) an error correction model for these data, and (iii) the interpretation of this model.

(i) The data

Exhibit 7.29 shows the monthly data on the AAA bond rate and the three-month Treasury Bill rate, both in levels (in (*a*) and (*c*)) and in first differences (in (*b*) and (*d*)). Both variables show prolonged upward and downward

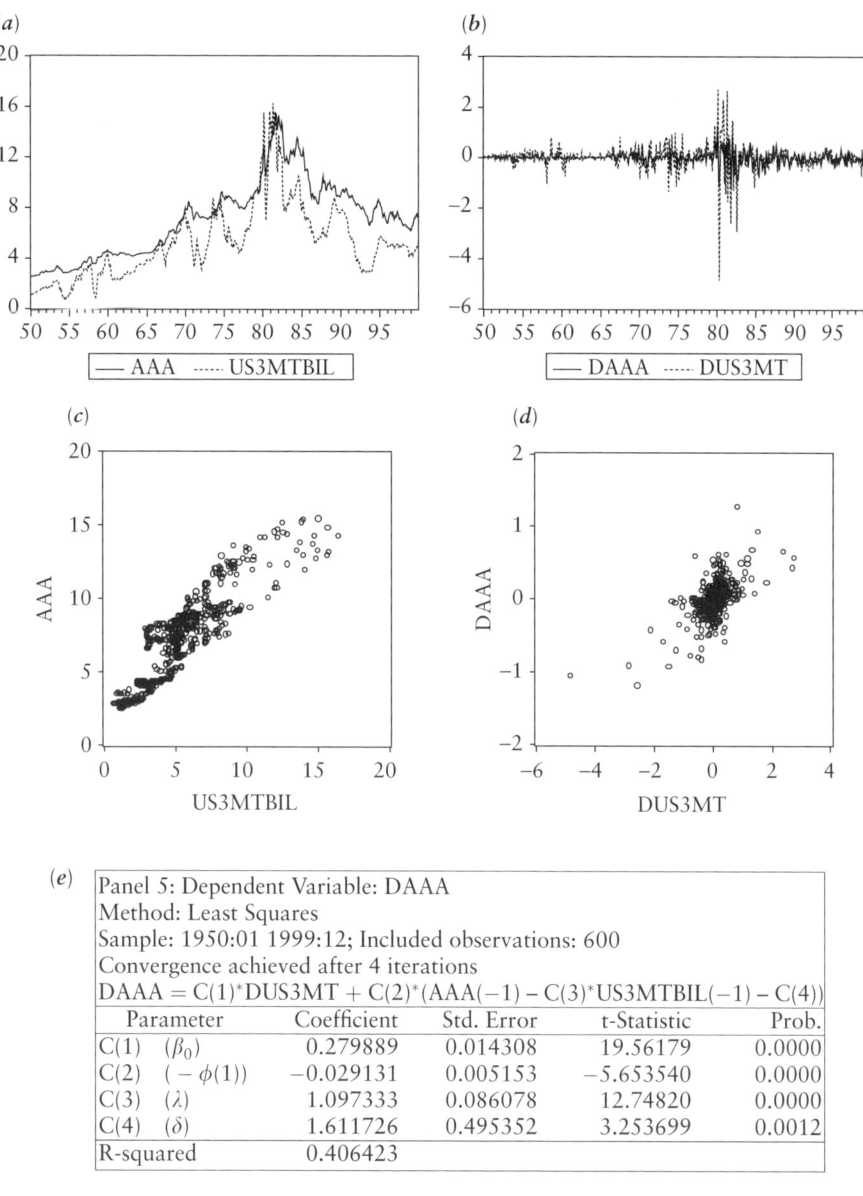

(e)

Panel 5: Dependent Variable: DAAA
Method: Least Squares
Sample: 1950:01 1999:12; Included observations: 600
Convergence achieved after 4 iterations
DAAA = C(1)*DUS3MT + C(2)*(AAA(−1) − C(3)*US3MTBIL(−1) − C(4))

Parameter	Coefficient	Std. Error	t-Statistic	Prob.
C(1) (β_0)	0.279889	0.014308	19.56179	0.0000
C(2) $(-\phi(1))$	−0.029131	0.005153	−5.653540	0.0000
C(3) (λ)	1.097333	0.086078	12.74820	0.0000
C(4) (δ)	1.611726	0.495352	3.253699	0.0012
R-squared	0.406423			

(f)

Panel 6: Wald Test: Null Hypothesis: C(3)=1			
F-statistic	1.278621	Probability	0.258610
Chi-square	1.278621	Probability	0.258156

Exhibit 7.29 **Interest and Bond Rates (Example 7.25)**

Monthly time series of AAA bond rate and US three-month Treasury Bill rate (*a*) and of the two series of first differences (*b*), two corresponding scatter plots ((*c*) and (*d*)), ADL(1,1) model in error correction form (Panel 5), and test on unit long-run multiplier (Panel 6).

movements and are non-stationary. However, the two series tend to stay near to each other in the long run, so that they possibly share a common trend. The series of first differences do not contain trends anymore. Clearly, modelling the (short-run) relation between the monthly changes in these rates is something different from the possible (long-run) relation between the levels of these two variables.

(ii) Error correction model

We estimate an ADL(1,1) model for these data. We estimate this model in the error correction form (7.34). Because in the ADL(1,1) model $p = r = 1$, the two summations in (7.34) are dropped in this model. The results are shown in Panel 5 of Exhibit 7.29. The long-run elasticity λ in (7.34) is estimated as $\hat{\lambda} = 1.097$. The F-test on the restriction of a long-run elasticity equal to one ($\lambda = 1$) in Panel 6 has $P = 0.26$, so that this hypothesis is not rejected. The coefficient of the error correction term in (7.34) is $-\hat{\phi}(1) = -0.029$ (see Panel 5). This differs significantly from zero, and the negative sign means that deviations from equilibrium are corrected.

(iii) Interpretation of the model

The above results suggest that the two series may be cointegrated and (as $\lambda = 1$) that a shift in the level of the three-month Treasury Bill rate leads, in the long run, to an equally large shift in the level of the AAA bond rate. However, these are only tentative conclusions, because the results could be spurious if the variables are not cointegrated. In the next section we will perform a statistical test for the presence of cointegration for these two series (see Example 7.27), and we will reconsider the nature of the equilibrium mechanism.

7.5.4 Summary

In this section we have considered the modelling of one time series variable in terms of another time series variable. This involves a combination of regression models (now with lagged dependent and lagged explanatory variables added) and univariate time series models (now with explanatory variables added).

- The autoregressive model with distributed lags can be estimated and evaluated in the usual way, provided that the time series are stationary and that the explanatory variables are exogenous.
- This model can be written in error correction form, with interesting interpretations in terms of long-run equilibria between variables and adjustments in case the variables are out of equilibrium.

- If the time series contain stochastic trends, then conventional methods may lead to spurious results. This can be prevented by differencing the variables until they are stationary. This should be done only if the variables are not cointegrated, as otherwise the model misses long-run equilibrium effects.

7.6 Vector autoregressive models

☞ Uses Chapters 1–4; Sections 5.5, 5.7; Sections 7.1–7.3, 7.5; Appendix A.5.

7.6.1 Stationary vector autoregressions

Joint model for multiple observed variables

In the foregoing section we discussed regression models with lags to explain the dependent variable y_t in terms of an explanatory variable x_t. A crucial assumption in such models is that the variable x_t is exogenous—stated intuitively, that it does not depend on y_t. Otherwise the parameters are not estimated consistently and standard procedures for diagnostic testing and forecasting are not valid anymore. This was discussed in Section 5.7, to which we refer for further background on endogenous regressors. If the variable x_t is endogenous (so that it depends on y_t), then we can try to make a joint model for the two variables x_t and y_t, so that we get two equations. Such models are called multiple equation models. In Section 7.6 we discuss the extension of univariate autoregressive models to the case of more than one endogenous variable. We consider stationary time series in Sections 7.6.1 and 7.6.2 and time series with trends in Section 7.6.3. In Section 7.7 we briefly discuss three other types of multiple equation regression models—namely, seemingly unrelated regressions in Section 7.7.2, models for panel data in Section 7.7.3, and simultaneous equation models in Section 7.7.4.

Importance of correct choice of endogenous variables

To illustrate the possible danger of neglecting the endogeneity of explanatory variables we consider a simple example. Suppose that the variables y_t and x_t are generated by the model

$$y_t = \phi y_{t-1} + \eta_t, \quad x_t = \gamma y_{t-1} + \omega_t.$$

We assume that $0 < \phi < 1$ and $\gamma \neq 0$ and that η_t and ω_t are independent white noise processes. Then y_t is an AR(1) process that is independent of x_t, and x_t depends on the past of y_t. In practice we do not know the DGP, and it may be that we are interested to see whether the variable y_t can be explained in terms of x_t. Suppose that we (wrongly) assume that x_t is exogenous in the regression model $y_t = \beta x_t + \varepsilon_t$ and that we estimate β by OLS. In large enough samples the regression coefficient then tends to $\text{plim}(b) = \text{cov}(x_t, y_t)/\text{var}(x_t) \neq 0$, because $\text{cov}(x_t, y_t) = \text{cov}(\gamma y_{t-1} + \omega_t, \phi y_{t-1} + \eta_t) = \gamma\phi\text{var}(y_{t-1}) \neq 0$. So, if the endogeneity of x_t is neglected, then this regression gives the wrong impression that the variable x_t would affect the variable y_t. This is caused by the fact that the regressor y_{t-1} is omitted in the regression model for y_t, whereas the wrong regressor x_t (that is correlated with y_{t-1}) is included instead of y_{t-1}.

Vector autoregressive model of order 1

Of course, in practice we do not know the data generating process. If the explanatory variable is possibly endogenous, it is better to start with a model that contains equations for both variables. In the above example the equations of the DGP can be written in matrix form as

$$\begin{pmatrix} x_t \\ y_t \end{pmatrix} = \begin{pmatrix} 0 & \gamma \\ 0 & \phi \end{pmatrix}\begin{pmatrix} x_{t-1} \\ y_{t-1} \end{pmatrix} + \begin{pmatrix} \omega_t \\ \eta_t \end{pmatrix}, \quad \begin{pmatrix} \omega_t \\ \eta_t \end{pmatrix} \sim \text{IID}\left(\begin{pmatrix} 0 \\ 0 \end{pmatrix}, \begin{pmatrix} \sigma_\omega^2 & 0 \\ 0 & \sigma_\eta^2 \end{pmatrix}\right).$$

In practice we do not know the parameter restrictions in this model, but we can estimate the parameters in the unrestricted model

$$\begin{pmatrix} x_t \\ y_t \end{pmatrix} = \begin{pmatrix} \alpha_1 \\ \alpha_2 \end{pmatrix} + \begin{pmatrix} \phi_{11} & \phi_{12} \\ \phi_{21} & \phi_{22} \end{pmatrix}\begin{pmatrix} x_{t-1} \\ y_{t-1} \end{pmatrix} + \begin{pmatrix} \varepsilon_{1t} \\ \varepsilon_{2t} \end{pmatrix},$$
$$\begin{pmatrix} \varepsilon_{1t} \\ \varepsilon_{2t} \end{pmatrix} \sim \text{IID}\left(\begin{pmatrix} 0 \\ 0 \end{pmatrix}, \begin{pmatrix} \sigma_{11} & \sigma_{12} \\ \sigma_{12} & \sigma_{22} \end{pmatrix}\right).$$

We use the following notation. Usually capital letters denote matrices, but in multiple equation models we will denote vectors of variables also by capital letters—for instance Y_t, to distinguish this from single variables like y_t. Let Y_t denote the 2×1 vector $(x_t, y_t)'$, α the 2×1 vector $(\alpha_1, \alpha_2)'$, ε_t the 2×1 vector $(\varepsilon_{1t}, \varepsilon_{2t})'$, Φ the 2×2 matrix of AR coefficients, and Ω the 2×2 covariance matrix of the disturbance terms. Then the above model can be written as

$$Y_t = \alpha + \Phi Y_{t-1} + \varepsilon_t, \quad \varepsilon_t \sim \text{IID}(0, \Omega). \tag{7.35}$$

This is called a *vector autoregressive* (VAR) model of order 1, because it is a direct generalization of the univariate AR(1) model to the case of a vector of variables. The VAR(1) model for m variables is defined in a similar way, in which case Y_t is the $m \times 1$ vector of variables, α is a $m \times 1$ vector of constants, and Φ and Ω are $m \times m$ matrices.

Stationary VAR(1) process

A VAR process Y_t is called stationary if it has a constant vector of means $E[Y_t]$ and a finite and constant covariance matrix $\text{var}(Y_t) = E[(Y_t - E[Y_t])(Y_t - E[Y_t])']$, and if the autocovariance matrices $\text{cov}(Y_t, Y_{t-k})$ depend only on the lag k and not on the time t. For the case of a single variable ($m = 1$), it was shown in Section 7.1.3 that the AR(1) process is stationary if and only if $-1 < \phi < 1$. In the multivariate model with $m > 1$ variables the stationarity condition is that Φ has all its eigenvalues within the unit circle. To clarify this result, we rewrite the VAR(1) model by repetitive substitution of the equation (7.35) as

$$Y_t = \Phi^{t-1}Y_1 + \sum_{j=0}^{t-2} \Phi^j \alpha + \sum_{j=0}^{t-2} \Phi^j \varepsilon_{t-j}.$$

The effects of the starting values Y_1 and of the disturbances die out over time if and only if $\Phi^j \to 0$ for $j \to \infty$. This is equivalent to the condition that Φ has all its eigenvalues within the unit circle. In this case the mean and variance of the process Y_t are obtained from the above equation (for $t \to \infty$), so that

$$E[Y_t] = \sum_{j=0}^{\infty} \Phi^j \alpha = (I - \Phi)^{-1}\alpha, \quad \text{var}(Y_t) = \sum_{j=0}^{\infty} \Phi^j \Omega (\Phi')^j.$$

The autocovariance matrix at lag $k > 0$ is equal to $\text{cov}(Y_t, Y_{t-k}) = \sum_{j=0}^{\infty} \Phi^{k+j}\Omega(\Phi')^j$. The stationarity condition can also be expressed in terms of the polynomial matrix $\Phi(z) = I - \Phi z$ for the VAR(1) model (7.35)—that is, $\Phi(L)Y_t = \alpha + \varepsilon_t$ where $LY_t = Y_{t-1}$. The stationarity condition is that all the m eigenvalues of the matrix Φ lie inside the unit circle—that is, all solutions of the equation $\det(\Phi - \lambda I) = 0$ should satisfy $|\lambda| < 1$. The roots of the polynomial matrix $\Phi(z)$ are the solutions of the equation $\det(\Phi(z)) = \det(I - \Phi z) = (-z)^m \det(\Phi - z^{-1}I) = 0$. So the roots of $\Phi(z)$ are the inverses of the eigenvalues λ, and the stationarity condition is that all roots of the VAR polynomial $\Phi(z)$ lie outside the unit circle. This generalizes the stationarity condition of Section 7.1.3 for univariate AR(p) processes.

Derivation of implied univariate ARMA processes

If Y_t follows a stationary VAR(1) process, then each of the individual components of Y_t follows a univariate ARMA(m, $m - 1$) process. To show this, we use some results of Appendix A.5 on matrices. For simplicity we assume that $\alpha = 0$ and we write the VAR(1) model as $(I - \Phi L)Y_t = \varepsilon_t$. Let $C(z)$ be the $m \times m$ matrix of cofactors of the matrix $(I - \Phi z)$. The elements of the matrix $C(z)$ consist of determinants of $(m - 1) \times (m - 1)$ submatrices of $(I - \Phi z)$, so that they are polynomials in z of degree (at most) $(m - 1)$. The matrix $C(z)$ further has the property that $C(z)(I - \Phi z) = \det(I - \Phi z)I = d(z)I$, where the (scalar) polynomial $d(z)$ is the determinant of $(I - \Phi z)$, which has degree (at most) m. If we premultiply the model $(I - \Phi L)Y_t = \varepsilon_t$ by $C(L)$, then using $C(z)(I - \Phi z) = d(z)I$ we obtain

$$d(L)Y_t = C(L)\varepsilon_t.$$

Note that $d(z)$ is a scalar polynomial and $C(z)$ is a matrix polynomial. In each of the m equations, the right-hand side is an MA process of order (at most) $(m - 1)$ (because all elements of $C(z)$ have degree at most $(m - 1)$), and the left-hand side is an AR expression (of order at most m) in a single variable. Therefore, each of the components of Y_t follows an ARMA$(m, m - 1)$ process (the orders may be lower if Φ satisfies certain parameter restrictions). The results in Section 7.1.3 show that the univariate processes are stationary if and only if the (scalar) AR polynomial $d(z) = \det(I - \Phi z)$ has all its roots outside the unit circle. As we concluded before, this is equivalent to the condition that Φ has all its eigenvalues within the unit circle.

Illustration for VAR(1) process with two variables

T

As an illustration of the above technical results, we consider the case of $m = 2$ variables $Y_t = (x_t, y_t)'$ with disturbance terms $\varepsilon_t = (\omega_t, \eta_t)'$. In this case the matrix of cofactors of $(I - \Phi z)$ is equal to

$$C(z) = \begin{pmatrix} 1 - \phi_{22}z & \phi_{12}z \\ \phi_{21}z & 1 - \phi_{11}z \end{pmatrix}.$$

The determinant of $(I - \Phi z)$ is equal to $d(z) = (1 - \phi_{11}z)(1 - \phi_{22}z) - \phi_{12}\phi_{21}z^2 = 1 - (\phi_{11} + \phi_{22})z + (\phi_{11}\phi_{22} - \phi_{12}\phi_{21})z^2$. Hence the implied univariate models—that is, the two components of $d(L)Y_t = C(L)\varepsilon_t$—become

$$\begin{aligned} x_t &= (\phi_{11} + \phi_{22})x_{t-1} + (\phi_{12}\phi_{21} - \phi_{11}\phi_{22})x_{t-2} + \omega_t - \phi_{22}\omega_{t-1} + \phi_{12}\eta_{t-1}, \\ y_t &= (\phi_{11} + \phi_{22})y_{t-1} + (\phi_{12}\phi_{21} - \phi_{11}\phi_{22})y_{t-2} + \phi_{21}\omega_{t-1} + \eta_t - \phi_{11}\eta_{t-1}. \end{aligned} \quad (7.36)$$

In both equations the composite error term is uncorrelated for lags 2 and larger, so that this is an MA(1) process, and the autoregression involves two lags. So the variables x_t and y_t follow ARMA(2,1) processes, and for some parameter restrictions on Φ the orders can be lower. The processes x_t and y_t are stationary if and only if the AR polynomial equation $1 - (\phi_{11} + \phi_{22})z + (\phi_{12}\phi_{21} - \phi_{11}\phi_{22})z^2 = \det(I - \Phi z) = 0$ has both its solutions outside the unit circle. This is equivalent to the condition that $\det(\Phi - \lambda I)$ has both its solutions inside the unit circle. This shows once more that stationarity is equivalent to the condition that the two eigenvalues of Φ lie inside the unit circle.

T

Stationary VAR(*p*) process

The VAR(1) model can be extended to the VAR(p) model by incorporating additional lags so that

$$Y_t = \alpha + \Phi_1 Y_{t-1} + \Phi_2 Y_{t-2} + \cdots + \Phi_p Y_{t-p} + \varepsilon_t, \quad \varepsilon_t \sim \text{IID}(0, \Omega). \tag{7.37}$$

Here Φ_j ($j = 1, \cdots, p$) and Ω are $m \times m$ matrices. The VAR(p) process Y_t is stationary if it has constant vector of means and constant autocovariances $\text{cov}(Y_t, Y_{t-k})$ that depend on the lag k but not on the time t. Stationarity is equivalent to the condition that the characteristic polynomial $\det(\Phi(z))$ has all its roots outside the unit circle, where $\Phi(z)$ is the $m \times m$ polynomial matrix $\Phi(z) = I - \Phi_1 z - \cdots - \Phi_p z^p$. Under this condition each of the individual variables is a stationary ARMA process with AR order (at most) mp and MA order (at most) $(m-1)p$. The mean of the process Y_t is equal to $\mu = (I - \sum_{j=1}^{p} \Phi_j)^{-1} \alpha = \Phi(1)^{-1}\alpha$. Note that $\Phi(1)$ is an invertible matrix if the characteristic roots of $\Phi(z)$ all lie outside the unit circle.

Derivation of vector error correction model

A stationary VAR(p) process can be written in error correction form. For the VAR(1) model (7.35) with $\alpha = (I - \Phi)\mu$ we can write

$$\Delta Y_t = (\Phi - I)(Y_{t-1} - \mu) + \varepsilon_t.$$

This shows that deviations of Y_{t-1} from the long-run mean μ are corrected by the multiplier matrix $(\Phi - I) = -\Phi(1)$, where $\Phi(z) = (I - \Phi z)$ is the VAR polynomial of the model. This shows some similarity with the error correction representation (7.33) of ADL models in Section 7.5.1, with the difference that now all m variables are corrected simultaneously. The VAR(p) model can be written in a similar form, as follows. The matrix polynomial $\Phi(z) - \Phi(1)z$ is the zero matrix for $z = 1$, which implies that it can be factorized as $\Phi(z) - \Phi(1)z = (1 - z)\Gamma(z)$. Here $\Gamma(z)$ is a $m \times m$ polynomial matrix of order $(p-1)$, and the value at $z = 0$ is equal to $\Gamma(0) = \Phi(0) - \Phi(1) \cdot 0 = I$. So we can write $\Gamma(z) = I - \sum_{j=1}^{p-1} \Gamma_j z^j$. With this factorization, and using the fact that $\Phi(z) = \Phi(1)z + (1 - z)\Gamma(z)$, the VAR model $\Phi(L)Y_t = \alpha + \varepsilon_t$ can be written as $\Phi(1)Y_{t-1} + \Delta Y_t - \sum_{j=1}^{p-1} \Gamma_j \Delta Y_{t-j} = \alpha + \varepsilon_t$. Here $\alpha = \Phi(1)\mu$, where μ is the vector of means of the process Y_t, and by rearranging terms we obtain

$$\Delta Y_t = -\Phi(1)(Y_{t-1} - \mu) + \sum_{j=1}^{p-1} \Gamma_j \Delta Y_{t-j} + \varepsilon_t. \tag{7.38}$$

This shows that the deviations of Y_{t-1} from the equilibrium value μ are corrected again by the multiplier matrix $-\Phi(1)$. The model written in this form is called a *vector error correction model* (VECM). It shows some similarities with the error correction model (7.34), with the difference that in general all the m variables are affected by the correction process.

☞ **Exercises:** T: 7.9c, d; S: 7.15a, b.

7.6.2 Estimation and diagnostic tests of stationary VAR models

Estimation of stationary VAR models

In the foregoing section we showed that the individual variables of a VAR(p) process follow (univariate) ARMA models. One could estimate these implied ARMA models by means of the techniques discussed in Section 7.2.2, but this is not efficient. The VAR(p) model contains $m + pm^2$ regression parameters, whereas the m univariate ARMA(mp, $(m-1)p$) models (each with a constant term) contain in total $m + pm^2 + pm(m-1)$ parameters. The difference arises because the estimation of models for the individual univariate series neglects the cross equation parameter restrictions between the different univariate ARMA models. For instance, in the foregoing section we saw that the AR polynomial is the same for each of the m individual time series. Moreover, this univariate approach also neglects the possible cross equation correlations between the error terms ε_t in case the covariance matrix Ω is not diagonal. Efficient estimates are obtained by applying ML to the system of m equations (7.37). Suppose that the disturbance terms are normally distributed so that $\varepsilon_t \sim \text{NID}(0, \Omega)$—that is, ε_t follows the m-dimensional multivariate normal distribution. The density $p(\varepsilon_t)$ of this distribution is given in (1.21) in Section 1.2.3 (p. 31), and it follows that $\log(p(\varepsilon_t)) = -\frac{m}{2}\log(2\pi) - \frac{1}{2}\log(\det(\Omega)) - \frac{1}{2}\varepsilon_t'\Omega^{-1}\varepsilon_t$. Therefore the conditional log-likelihood of the VAR(p) model (7.37) (treating the initial values as fixed) is equal to

$$\begin{aligned}\log(L) = & -\frac{(n-p)m}{2}\log(2\pi) - \frac{n-p}{2}\log(\det(\Omega)) \\ & -\frac{1}{2}\sum_{t=p+1}^{n}\left(Y_t - \alpha - \sum_{j=1}^{p}\Phi_j Y_{t-j}\right)'\Omega^{-1}\left(Y_t - \alpha - \sum_{j=1}^{p}\Phi_j Y_{t-j}\right).\end{aligned}$$

It is left as an exercise (see Exercise 7.10) to show that ML in this model is equivalent to applying OLS on each of the m equations in (7.37) separately. So the estimation of VAR models is quite straightforward. The covariance matrix Ω can be estimated by $\hat{\Omega} = \frac{1}{n-p}\sum_{t=p+1}^{n} e_t e_t'$, where e_t is the $m \times 1$ vector of residuals at time t. If some elements of the parameter matrices Φ_k are restricted in some way, then OLS is still consistent but not efficient anymore, and in large enough samples ML provides more accurate estimates in this case.

Model selection

The OLS or ML estimators have the usual asymptotic statistical properties, provided that the VAR process is stationary. So we can apply conventional

t- and F-tests on the significance of the coefficients. For instance, the lag order p of the VAR model can be selected by applying F-tests or LR-tests on the significance of additional lags. These tests follow (asymptotically) the standard F- and χ^2-distributions respectively. Another method to select the lag order is by minimizing the AIC or SIC, which are defined for VAR(p) models by

$$AIC(p) = \log\left(\det\left(\hat{\Omega}_p\right)\right) + 2\frac{pm^2}{n}, \quad SIC(p) = \log\left(\det\left(\hat{\Omega}_p\right)\right) + \log(n)\frac{pm^2}{n}.$$

Here pm^2 is the total number of coefficients of lagged regressors in the VAR(p) model and $\hat{\Omega}_p$ is the estimated covariance matrix of the disturbances in the VAR(p) model. In practice the order p of VAR models is often chosen relatively small, as otherwise the number of parameters pm^2 of lagged terms quickly becomes large.

VAR models are less useful for large numbers of variables. The total number of parameters in the VAR(p) model for m variables is $m + pm^2 + \frac{1}{2}m(m+1)$—namely, m for the vector of constants α, pm^2 for the $m \times m$ AR matrices Φ_j $(j = 1, \cdots, p)$, and $\frac{1}{2}m(m+1)$ for the symmetric $m \times m$ matrix Ω. Estimation becomes infeasible for large numbers m of variables, because the number of parameters increases with the square m^2. This is called the *curse of dimensionality* of multiple equation models.

Exogenous variables and model simplification

In practice VAR models are used only for a small number of variables, with $m = 2$ or $m = 3$ in many and $m \leq 10$ in almost all applications. One method to reduce the number of parameters is by considering the possible *exogeneity* of some of the variables. For instance, in our example at the beginning of Section 7.6.1, the variable y_t is exogenous in the equation for x_t, because in the bivariate VAR(1) model (7.35) there holds $\phi_{21} = 0$ and $\sigma_{12} = 0$. In this case the effect of y_t on x_t can be estimated simply by regressing x_t on y_t and neglecting the time series model for y_t. This reduces the number of parameters from in total nine for the VAR(1) model (two for α, four for Φ, and three for Ω) to four for the regression model (the constant, the two slope parameters ϕ_{11} and ϕ_{12}, and the variance of the disturbance term). This may improve the finite sample efficiency of the estimators. More generally, consider the VAR(p) model where the m variables are split in two groups, denoted by Y_t and X_t, so that

$$\begin{pmatrix} \Phi_{11}(L) & \Phi_{12}(L) \\ \Phi_{21}(L) & \Phi_{22}(L) \end{pmatrix} \begin{pmatrix} Y_t \\ X_t \end{pmatrix} = \begin{pmatrix} \alpha_1 \\ \alpha_2 \end{pmatrix} + \begin{pmatrix} \varepsilon_{1t} \\ \varepsilon_{2t} \end{pmatrix}.$$

Then the variables X_t are exogenous in the equations for Y_t if

$$\Phi_{21}(z) = 0 \quad \text{and} \quad \Omega_{12} = 0,$$

where Ω_{12} is the cross correlation matrix between ε_{1t} and ε_{2t}. Indeed, under these assumptions the process X_t is described by the VAR model $\Phi_{22}(L)X_t = \alpha_2 + \varepsilon_{2t}$, which is uncorrelated with the process ε_{1t} at all lags. Therefore the regressors $\Phi_{12}(L)X_t$ in the equations $\Phi_{11}(L)Y_t = \alpha_1 - \Phi_{12}(L)X_t + \varepsilon_{1t}$ are uncorrelated with the disturbance terms ε_{1t}, so that these regressors are exogenous in these equations. Consistent estimates are then obtained by regressing Y_t on the appropriate lags of Y_t and X_t. This reduces the number of involved parameters considerably. If $\Phi_{21}(z) = 0$, then it is also said that Y_t does not cause X_t. The corresponding F-test on the parameter restrictions $\Phi_{21}(z) = 0$ is called the *Granger causality test*.

Diagnostics for stationary VAR models

Diagnostic tests of VAR models can be performed in a similar way, as was discussed in Section 7.2.4 for univariate AR models. Since the main purpose of the VAR model is to express the dynamic correlations between the variables, it is of particular importance to check whether the m residual series are white noise. A simple check is to perform tests on serial correlation for the m residual series separately. Note that the model allows for cross equation correlations between the residuals of different equations at the same time (if the off-diagonal elements of Ω are non-zero), but the residuals should not be correlated with each other at different time moments.

One can apply further tests on the individual equations—for instance, on possible parameter breaks, outliers, and ARCH effects. Competing models can be compared by their forecast performance. For instance, for a VAR(1) model the one-step-ahead forecast is given by $\hat{Y}_{n+1} = \alpha + \Phi Y_n$ with covariance matrix of the forecast error equal to Ω. The two-step-ahead forecast is $\hat{Y}_{n+2} = \alpha + \Phi\hat{Y}_{n+1} = (I + \Phi)\alpha + \Phi^2 Y_n$, and the corresponding covariance matrix is $E[(Y_{n+2} - \hat{Y}_{n+2})(Y_{n+2} - \hat{Y}_{n+2})'] = \Omega + \Phi\Omega\Phi'$. Similar expressions can be derived for higher order VAR models and longer forecast horizons.

Example 7.26: **Interest and Bond Rates (continued)**

We continue our analysis of the interest and bond rates data. In Example 7.22 it was assumed that the changes in the Treasury Bill rate are exogenous in the model for the changes of the AAA bond rate. Now we will discuss (i) the motivation for a vector autoregressive (VAR) model for these data, (ii) the estimation and selection of a VAR model, (iii) a test on the exogeneity of the Treasury Bill rate, and (iv) some diagnostic checks on the model.

(i) Motivation for a VAR model

In Example 7.22 we estimated an ADL model for the (endogenous) changes in AAA bond rate in terms of the (supposedly exogenous) changes in the three-month Treasury Bill rate. However, as we remarked at the end of Example 7.22, the changes in the Treasury Bill rate are possibly correlated with the disturbance term in this equation. This is because the unobserved factors that influence the AAA bond rate may very well also influence the Treasury Bill rate. This was analysed in Example 5.33 (p. 414–16), where we concluded that the Treasury Bill rate is indeed endogenous. Therefore we now estimate VAR models that treat the changes in both the Treasury Bill rate and the AAA bond rate as endogenous variables.

(ii) Estimation and selection of a VAR model

Panel 1 of Exhibit 7.30 shows the first six autocorrelations of both variables and also the cross correlations between the two variables. Some of the lagged effects are significant, but it is not so easy to decide on the order of a VAR model on the basis of these autocorrelations. We estimate VAR models for orders $p = 1$, 2, and 3. The resulting estimates are in Panels 2–4 of Exhibit 7.30 (the t-values are in parentheses). The Schwarz criterion selects the VAR(2) model. By comparing the log-likelihoods we can test the null hypothesis of the VAR(2) model against the alternative of the VAR(3) model, which corresponds to four restrictions. The corresponding LR-test has value $LR = 2(-95.77 + 99.97) = 8.4$ with a P-value according to the $\chi^2(4)$ distribution of $P = 0.078$. This means that the VAR(2) model is not rejected (at 5 per cent significance level, this is sufficiently convincing for the relatively large sample size of $n = 600$).

(iii) Test on exogeneity of the Treasury Bill rate

The VAR(2) model can be used to check for the possible exogeneity of the Treasury Bill rate in the equation for the AAA bond rate. In the VAR(2) model, this corresponds to the following three restrictions. The two coefficients of the AAA bond rate (with lags 1 and 2) in the equation for the Treasury Bill rate are zero, and the disturbances of the two equations are uncorrelated. The results in Exhibit 7.30 can be used to test for these restrictions. In Panel 3 of Exhibit 7.30, the t-values of the two lagged AAA bond rate terms in the equation for the Treasury Bill rate are 6.94 and -4.94. The Granger causality test in Panel 6—that is, the F-test on the joint significance of the two coefficients—gives $F = 28.9$ with $P = 0.0000$. So we strongly reject the null hypothesis that the AAA bond rate does not affect the Treasury Bill rate. Further, the cross correlation between the two series of residuals is significant with a value of 0.54 (see Panel 5). We conclude that the Treasury Bill rate is not exogenous. This is in line with our earlier conclusion in Example 5.33 (p. 414–16).

Panel 1: autocorrelations and cross correlations Sample: 1950:01 1999:12; Included observations: 600				
Lag	DAAA	DUS3MT	DAAA with past DUS3MT	DUS3MT with past DAAA
0	1.000	1.000	0.6086	0.6086
1	0.371	0.273	0.1523	0.3377
2	−0.087	−0.106	−0.0329	−0.0964
3	−0.084	−0.089	−0.0763	−0.1248
4	0.042	−0.036	0.0577	−0.0451
5	0.151	0.044	0.1496	0.0683
6	0.010	−0.183	−0.0975	−0.1024

Panel 2: VAR(1) model Sample: 1950:01 1999:12; Included observations: 600		
Variable	Eq. for DAAA	Eq. for DUS3MT
DAAA(−1)	0.442465	0.605146
t-value	(9.27999)	(5.64462)
DUS3MT(−1)	−0.052705	0.106805
t-value	(−2.45113)	(2.20907)
C	0.005125	0.001369
t-value	(0.62954)	(0.07477)
R-squared	0.146332	0.121339
S.E. equation	0.199278	0.448077
Log Likelihood	−133.8794	
Akaike Information Criterion	0.466265	
Schwarz Criterion	0.510234	

Panel 3: VAR(2) model Sample: 1950:01 1999:12; Included observations: 600		
Variable	Eq. for DAAA	Eq. for DUS3MT
DAAA(−1)	0.529146	0.747457
t-value	(11.0142)	(6.93980)
DAAA(−2)	−0.318410	−0.547129
t-value	(−6.44597)	(−4.94054)
DUS3MT(−1)	−0.040867	0.165415
t-value	(−1.91532)	(3.45804)
DUS3MT(−2)	0.047549	−0.051966
t-value	(2.24003)	(−1.09198)
C	0.006676	0.004685
t-value	(0.84884)	(0.26573)
R-squared	0.206751	0.188312
S.E. equation	0.192419	0.431385
Log Likelihood	−99.97261	
Akaike Information Criterion	0.366575	
Schwarz Criterion	0.439858	

Exhibit 7.30 Interest and Bond Rates (Example 7.26)

Autocorrelations and cross correlations for the series of changes in the AAA bond rate and the series of changes in the three-month Treasury Bill rate (Panel 1), VAR(1) model (Panel 2), and VAR(2) model (Panel 3).

Panel 4: VAR(3) model (summary)	
Log Likelihood	−95.77027
Akaike Information Criterion	0.365901
Schwarz Criterion	0.468496

Panel 5	Covariances residuals		Correlations residuals	
	DAAA	DUS3MT	DAAA	DUS3MT
DAAA	0.036716	0.044631	1.000000	0.542195
DUS3MT	0.044631	0.184542	0.542195	1.000000

Panel 6: Pairwise Granger Causality Tests in VAR(2) model Sample: 1950:01 1999:12			
Null Hypothesis:	Obs	F-Statistic	Probability
DUS3MT does not Granger Cause DAAA	600	3.70414	0.02519
DAAA does not Granger Cause DUS3MT	600	28.8526	1.1E-12

Panel 7: autocorrelations of residuals of VAR(2) model Sample: 1950:01 1999:12; Included observations: 600						
Lag	SACF Eq 1 (DAAA)	Q-Stat	Prob	SACF Eq 2 (DUS3MT)	Q-Stat	Prob
1	0.021	0.2754	0.600	0.009	0.0462	0.830
2	−0.019	0.5019	0.778	−0.019	0.2534	0.881
3	0.050	2.0435	0.563	0.012	0.3351	0.953
4	0.011	2.1115	0.715	−0.090	5.2399	0.264
5	0.131	12.579	0.028	0.063	7.6752	0.175
6	−0.006	12.600	0.050	−0.181	27.597	0.000

Exhibit 7.30 (*Contd.*)

Summary of outcomes of VAR(3) model (Panel 4), covariance matrix and correlation matrix of the two residual series of the VAR(2) model (Panel 5), Granger causality tests (Panel 6), and correlogram of the two residual series of the VAR(2) model (Panel 7).

(iv) Some diagnostic checks

We check whether the VAR(2) model captures the correlations that are present in both series. Panel 7 of Exhibit 7.30 shows the first six autocorrelations for the two series of residuals of the VAR(2) model. The correlations at lags 1–4 are no longer significant, but some correlation at lags 5 and 6 remains present. Here we analysed the relation between the changes in the two variables — that is, the short-run relations between the variables. In the next section we will consider the long-run relationships between the levels of these two variables (see Example 7.27).

☞ **Exercises:** T: 7.10d; S: 7.15c, d.

7.6.3 Trends and cointegration

Multiple time series with stochastic trends

The analysis of VAR models in the foregoing section was based on the assumption that all m variables are stationary. If the variables contain deterministic trends, then this can be modelled by incorporating appropriate time functions as additional regressors in the VAR equations. However, if the variables contain stochastic trends, then the standard properties of ML and related tests are not valid anymore. This has already been discussed for univariate time series in Section 7.3.3. Further, regressions of variables with stochastic trends may lead to spurious results, as was discussed in Section 7.5.3. As many economic variables contain stochastic trends, this suggests that VAR models can be applied only after sufficient differencing of the variables to obtain stationarity. This is indeed the way to proceed, unless the variables are cointegrated. In this case the correlations between trended variables are not spurious, as was explained at the end of Section 7.5.3. In this section we consider this situation in more detail. We describe tests for cointegration and the modelling of cointegrated variables by means of vector error correction models.

Analysis of the VAR(1) model with two variables

To introduce the main ideas we first consider the VAR(1) model (without constant terms) for two variables. The model $Y_t = \Phi Y_{t-1} + \varepsilon_t$ can be written in the form of the VECM

$$\Delta Y_t = \Pi Y_{t-1} + \varepsilon_t, \quad \Pi = \Phi - I.$$

In this model there are three cases of interest, according to whether the rank of the 2×2 matrix Π is 0, 1, or 2. If the two variables in Y_t are stationary, this means that Φ has both its eigenvalues within the unit circle. This implies that $\det(\Phi - I) = \det(\Pi) \neq 0$, so that the matrix Π has rank 2. On the other hand, if Π has rank 0, then $\Pi = 0$ and hence $\Delta Y_t = \varepsilon_t$. Then both variables follow random walks. In this case one says that there exist two stochastic trends for the two variables. The variables are modelled in terms of their first differences. A final possibility is that Π has rank 1, so that $0 = \det(\Pi) = \det(\Phi - I)$. In this case the matrix Φ has one eigenvalue at $z = 1$ and another eigenvalue $\rho \neq 1$. As Π has rank 1, this means that the second column is a multiple of the first column, so that we can write

$$\Pi = \begin{pmatrix} \alpha_1 & -\theta\alpha_1 \\ \alpha_2 & -\theta\alpha_2 \end{pmatrix} = \begin{pmatrix} \alpha_1 \\ \alpha_2 \end{pmatrix} (1 \ \ -\theta) = \alpha\beta',$$

where $\alpha = (\alpha_1, \ \alpha_2)'$ and $\beta' = (1, \ -\theta)$. Let the two variables in Y_t be denoted by $Y_t = (y_t, \ x_t)'$; then the VECM becomes

$$\Delta y_t = \alpha_1(y_{t-1} - \theta x_{t-1}) + \varepsilon_{1t},$$
$$\Delta x_t = \alpha_2(y_{t-1} - \theta x_{t-1}) + \varepsilon_{2t}.$$

The rest of this section is devoted to the modelling of this kind of processes.

Cointegration in the VAR(1) model with two variables

We analyse the above VECM in more detail. This model corresponds to the case that Π has rank 1 and that the matrix Φ in the corresponding VAR(1) model has an eigenvalue at $z = 1$. We assume that the other eigenvalue $z = \rho$ is stable—that is, that $-1 < \rho < 1$ (if $\rho = 1$ then the process would have two unit roots). We will show that in this case (that is, with one unit root and one stable root) the individual variables y_t and x_t contain a stochastic trend, but that $(y_{t-1} - \theta x_{t-1})$ is stationary, so that the two variables are cointegrated. The fact that the variables y_t and x_t are not stationary can be derived as follows. The implied ARMA(2,1) models for y_t and x_t are given in (7.36), with AR polynomial $d(z) = \det(I - \Phi z) = z^2 \det(z^{-1}I - \Phi) = z^2(z^{-1} - 1)(z^{-1} - \rho) = (z - 1)(z - \rho)$. So both time series have a unit root—that is, y_t and x_t contain a stochastic trend. Since we assumed that $-1 < \rho < 1$, it follows that y_t and x_t are both ARIMA(1,1,1) processes. On the other hand, $(y_{t-1} - \theta x_{t-1})$ is stationary, which can be seen as follows. Because Π has rank 1, it follows that $\alpha_1 \neq 0$ or $\alpha_2 \neq 0$ (or both). The above VECM then shows that the linear combination $(y_{t-1} - \theta x_{t-1})$ is stationary, because it can be expressed in terms of Δy_t, Δx_t, ε_{1t}, and ε_{2t}, which are all stationary.

The above results show that the series y_t and x_t are cointegrated in this case. The relation $(y_t - \theta x_t)$ is called the *cointegration relation*, and $y_t = \theta x_t$ is the long-run equilibrium relation between the two variables. The parameters α_1 and α_2 are called the *adjustment coefficients*. They describe how y_t and x_t are adjusted if the variables are out of equilibrium. For instance, if $\alpha_1 < 0$ and $y_{t-1} > \beta x_{t-1}$, then this leads to a downward adjustment of y_t in the direction of equilibrium.

Cointegration in the VAR(*p*) model

Similar results hold true for VAR(p) models for m variables. Let $\Pi = -\Phi(1)$, where $\Phi(1)$ is the $m \times m$ matrix obtained by substituting $z = 1$ in the VAR polynomial $\Phi(z)$ of the model. We rewrite the VECM (7.38) as follows, where we define $\gamma = \Phi(1)\mu$:

$$\Delta Y_t = \gamma + \Pi Y_{t-1} + \Gamma_1 \Delta Y_{t-1} + \cdots + \Gamma_{p-1}\Delta Y_{t-p+1} + \varepsilon_t, \ t = p+1, \cdots, n. \quad (7.39)$$

As before, the existence of cointegration and the number of stochastic trends for the m series in Y_t depends on the rank of the matrix Π. We consider again three cases—namely, $\text{rank}(\Pi) = m$, $\text{rank}(\Pi) = 0$, and $\text{rank}(\Pi) = r$ with $1 \leq r \leq m - 1$. If the variables are all stationary this means that $\Phi(z)$ has all its roots outside the unit circle. In this case the matrix Π has full rank m. There are no stochastic trends in this case. On the other hand, suppose that $\Pi = -\Phi(1) = 0$. Then the VAR polynomial $\Phi(z)$ contains m unit roots, and (7.39) is a VAR($p - 1$) model in the variables ΔY_t. In this case there are m stochastic trends. Finally, if $\text{rank}(\Pi) = r$ with $1 \leq r \leq m - 1$, then the polynomial $\Phi(z)$ has $m - r$ unit roots. Assuming that the other r roots of $\Phi(z)$ all lie outside the unit circle, this means that the m variables have $(m - r)$ common stochastic trends and that there are r cointegration relations. This can be seen as follows. If the $m \times m$ matrix Π has rank r, it can be written as $\Pi = AB' = \sum_{j=1}^{r} \alpha_j \beta_j'$, where A and B are $m \times r$ matrices of rank r with $m \times 1$ columns α_j and β_j respectively, $j = 1, \cdots, r$. (In the literature one often writes this matrix decomposition as $\Pi = \alpha\beta'$ instead of $\Pi = AB'$, but here we do not follow this convention, and we write $\Pi = \alpha\beta'$ only if Π has rank 1, in which case the matrices A and B reduce to column vectors.) The VECM implies that each of the r linear combinations $\beta_j' Y_t$ is stationary, so that there exist r linearly independent cointegration relations. It should be noted that the matrices A and B in the decomposition $\Pi = AB'$ are not defined uniquely, because $\Pi = (AC^{-1})(BC')' = AB'$ for every invertible $r \times r$ matrix C. Therefore the r cointegration relations are also not unique, since every linear combination $\Sigma_{j=1}^{r} c_j \beta_j' Y_t$ is a cointegration relation for arbitrary constants c_j, $j = 1, \cdots, r$.

Summary of results for VAR(*p*) model

Summarizing the foregoing results, suppose that all individual variables in the $m \times 1$ vector Y_t are integrated of order at most 1. The appropriate way to model the series Y_t depends on the rank of the $m \times m$ matrix Π in the VECM (7.39). If the variables are jointly stationary, then the matrix Π has full rank m. In this case the series do not contain stochastic trends and one can estimate a VAR model. If the matrix Π has rank $r = 0$, so that $\Pi = 0$, then the series contain m stochastic trends and the variables are not cointegrated. One should estimate a VAR model for the differenced variables ΔY_t. If the matrix Π has rank $1 \leq r \leq m - 1$, then the variables are cointegrated. There exist r linearly independent cointegration relations and $(m - r)$ common stochastic trends. One should estimate the VECM (7.39) with the restriction that the matrix Π has rank r.

Estimation of VAR model with cointegration

For a given rank $1 \leq r \leq m - 1$ of the matrix Π, the parameters of the VECM in (7.39) can be estimated by ML. This is in principle similar to the estimation of stationary VAR models discussed in the foregoing section, but of course one should incorporate the rank restriction on Π. The corresponding log-likelihood can be maximized by so-called reduced rank regressions. It is beyond the scope of this book to treat the details of this optimization, but it is useful to know that no numerical optimization is needed and that the maximum can be obtained by means of regressions. The maximal value of the log-likelihood, for given rank r of the matrix Π, is equal to

$$\log(L_{\max}(r)) = c - \frac{n-p}{2}\sum_{j=1}^{r}\log(1-\hat{\lambda}_j).$$

Here c is a constant that does not depend on the chosen rank r, and the (eigenvalues) $\hat{\lambda}_j$ are ordered so that $1 \geq \hat{\lambda}_1 \geq \hat{\lambda}_2 \geq \cdots \geq \hat{\lambda}_m \geq 0$. The square root $\hat{\lambda}_j^{1/2}$ of these values are the so-called (sample partial) *canonical correlation coefficients* of the two $m \times 1$ vectors ΔY_t and Y_{t-1}.

Interpretation of the eigenvalues $\hat{\lambda}_j$

The eigenvalues $\hat{\lambda}_j$ in the above log-likelihood for the VECM have the following intuitive interpretation. The series are cointegrated if there exist linear combinations $\beta' Y_{t-1}$ that are stationary. This is expressed in the VECM (7.39) by the condition that $\Pi \neq 0$—that is, a non-zero (partial) correlation of Y_{t-1} with the stationary variables ΔY_t (for given values of ΔY_{t-j}, $j = 1, \cdots, p-1$). The number of cointegration relations—that is, the rank of Π in the VECM (7.39)—is equal to the number of non-zero correlations between linear combinations of Y_{t-1} and ΔY_t. The canonical correlations $\hat{\lambda}_j^{1/2}$ measure these correlations. The number of stochastic trends is equal to the number of zero canonical correlations. This means that in practice the number r of cointegration relations and the number $(m-r)$ of (common) stochastic trends can be determined by checking how many of the canonical correlations differ significantly from zero. That is,

$$r = (\text{number of significant } \hat{\lambda}_j), \quad m - r = (\text{number of } \hat{\lambda}_j \approx 0).$$

Note that the ADF test regression (7.25) for univariate time series resembles the VECM (7.39). The null hypothesis of a unit root in (7.25) (that is, the presence of a stochastic trend) corresponds to $\rho = 0$. In this case Δy_t and y_{t-1} are uncorrelated (for given values of Δy_{t-j}, $j = 1, \cdots, p-1$). In a similar way, the null hypothesis of no cointegration (that is, the presence of m stochastic trends) in the VECM (7.39) corresponds to $\Pi = 0$. In this case the vectors ΔY_t and Y_{t-1} are uncorrelated (for given values of ΔY_{t-j}, $j = 1, \cdots, p-1$). This corresponds to the null hypothesis that all the m eigenvalues λ_j are zero.

LR-test on the number of cointegration relations

The above results can be used for likelihood ratio tests on the number of cointegration relations. Because the constant c in the above expression for the log-likelihood does not depend on the postulated rank, the LR-test for the null hypothesis that $\text{rank}(\Pi) = r$ against the alternative that $\text{rank}(\Pi) \geq r + 1$ is given by

$$LR(r) = 2(\log(L_{\max}(m)) - \log(L_{\max}(r))) = -(n-p) \sum_{j=r+1}^{m} \log(1 - \hat{\lambda}_j). \tag{7.40}$$

This is called the *Johansen trace test* on the number of cointegration relations. The null hypothesis is not rejected if the LR-test gives sufficiently small values—that is, if the values of $\hat{\lambda}_j$ are sufficiently close to zero. In this case the last $(m - r)$ eigenvalues are not significant, so that there are at most r significant eigenvalues and hence at most r cointegration relations. The trace test can be used as follows to determine the number r of cointegration relations.

Testing for the number of cointegration relations

- *Step 1: Test $H_0 : r = 0$ against $H_1 : r \geq 1$.* First test the null hypothesis that there is no cointegration and that there are m stochastic trends. This corresponds to the hypothesis that $\lambda_1 = \cdots = \lambda_m = 0$, and the relevant test statistic is (7.40) with $r = 0$. If H_0 is not rejected, then there is no cointegration. If H_0 is rejected, continue with step 2.
- *Step 2: Test $H_0 : r = 1$ against $H_1 : r \geq 2$.* In a similar way as in step 1, apply the test (7.40) with $r = 1$. If H_0 is not rejected then there is a single cointegration relation and there are $(m - 1)$ common trends. If H_0 is rejected, continue with step 3.
- *Step 3: Iteratively test $H_0 : rank(\Pi) = r$ against $H_1 : rank(\Pi) \geq r + 1$.* Repeat the test (7.40) iteratively, increasing the value of r by one in each step. Continue until the first time that H_0 is not rejected. Then the number of cointegration relations is equal to r and the number of (common) trends is $(m - r)$.

The above LR-tests do not have the usual χ^2-distribution. This is because the regressors Y_{t-1} in the test equations (7.39) contain stochastic trends under the null hypothesis. The (asymptotic) distribution depends on the number of variables m and on the cointegration rank r, and also on the presence of deterministic components (such as constants and deterministic trends) in the VECM test equations.

Below we will discuss three variants of the test equations that are much used in practice. These three variants are based on considerations that are similar to those for the three types of unit root tests discussed in Section 7.3.3. Some critical values for the three types of cointegration tests

Data properties and VECM assumptions	$m-r=1$	$m-r=2$	$m-r=3$	$m-r=4$	$m-r=5$
Linear trend in data; constant and trend in CE	12.25	25.32	42.44	62.99	87.31
Linear trend in data; constant, no trend in CE	3.76	15.41	29.68	47.21	68.52
No clear trend in data; constant, no trend in CE	9.24	19.96	34.91	53.12	76.07

CE denotes the Cointegration Equations.
m is the number of variables and r is the number of cointegration relations.
$m-r$ is the number of unit roots—that is, the number of common stochastic trends for the m variables.

Exhibit 7.31 Cointegration tests

The 5% critical values for the Johansen trace test on the number of cointegration relations (r) for three types of DGP—that is, one for data with a clear trend direction and with a trend in the cointegration relations, another for data with a clear trend direction but without a trend in the cointegration relations, and finally one for data without a clear trend direction (and no trend in the cointegration relations). For trending data one should start by including constant and trend in CE (this trend term could be dropped if it is not significant).

(7.40) are given in Exhibit 7.31. The critical values are based on the assumption that the VECM is correctly specified and that the error terms are normally distributed. Under these assumptions, the critical values depend on the type of cointegration test and on the number $(m-r)$ of stochastic trends, but they do not depend on the order p of the VECM.

Test equations for data with clear overall trend direction

The Johansen trace test (7.40) is based on the VECM (7.39), possibly extended with deterministic trend terms. These trend terms and the constant terms require special attention, because the relevant critical values of the test (7.40) depend on the precise specifications of these deterministic components.

As a first case we assume that the data display a clear general trend direction. For such data we should include constant terms in the VECM and a deterministic trend in the cointegration equations. It is useful to rewrite the resulting VECM in another form. If the coefficient matrix Π of Y_{t-1} in (7.39) has rank r, it can be written as $\Pi = AB'$, where A and B are $m \times r$ matrices of rank r. Further we decompose the $m \times 1$ vector γ in the VECM as $\gamma = \gamma_1 - A\gamma_2$ where $\gamma_2 = -(A'A)^{-1}A'\gamma$ and $\gamma_1 = (I - A(A'A)^{-1}A')\gamma$, so that the two components γ_1 and $A\gamma_2$ are orthogonal as $\gamma_1' A\gamma_2 = 0$ (this corresponds to the OLS decomposition $y = Xb + e = Hy + My$ of Section 3.1.3 (p. 123), replacing y by γ, X by A, b by $-\gamma_2$, and e by γ_1). With this notation, $\Pi = AB'$ and $\gamma = \gamma_1 - A\gamma_2$, the relevant test equation for cointegration of trending data can be written as

$$\Delta Y_t = \gamma_1 + A(B'Y_{t-1} - \gamma_2 - \delta t) + \Gamma_1 \Delta Y_{t-1} + \cdots + \Gamma_{p-1} \Delta Y_{t-p+1} + \varepsilon_t.$$

The constants γ_1 are drift terms for the stochastic trends in the variables Y_t. The cointegration relations or long-run equilibria are described by the r equations $B'Y_{t-1} - \gamma_2 - \delta t = 0$. One usually expresses this by saying that there is a linear trend in the data (if $\gamma_1 \neq 0$) and a constant and linear trend in the cointegration equations (if $\gamma_2 \neq 0$ and $\delta \neq 0$). The *LR* cointegration test for data with clear trends is based on the above test equations, with trends in the data and in the cointegration equations.

Model for cointegration relations without trend

For the economic interpretation of equilibria it is sometimes relevant to consider the restricted model with $\delta = 0$, because in this case the linear combinations $B'Y_t$ move around a constant equilibrium value γ_2 in the long run. The corresponding VECM is given by

$$\Delta Y_t = \gamma_1 + A(B'Y_{t-1} - \gamma_2) + \Gamma_1 \Delta Y_{t-1} + \cdots + \Gamma_{p-1} \Delta Y_{t-p+1} + \varepsilon_t.$$

In this case one says there is a linear trend in the data and a constant but no trend in the cointegration relation. The best approach is to determine the cointegration rank r first by means of the VECM with deterministic trend included in the cointegration relations, as it is worse to omit relevant terms (if $\delta \neq 0$) than to include irrelevant ones (if $\delta = 0$). One can then test for the significance of the trend coefficients δ. If these are not significant, one can redo the tests and estimate a VECM without trend in the cointegration relations.

Test equations for data without clear trend direction

If the variables display no clear trend direction, then the drift terms γ_1 can also be removed from the model. So the relevant test VECM for non-trended data becomes

$$\Delta Y_t = A(B'Y_{t-1} - \gamma_2) + \Gamma_1 \Delta Y_{t-1} + \cdots + \Gamma_{p-1} \Delta Y_{t-p+1} + \varepsilon_t.$$

One says that there is no trend in the data and in the cointegration relation.

Overview of modelling of multiple time series with trends

We summarize the steps needed to model a set of trended variables. Here we assume that the variables are either integrated of order 0 (so that Y_t is trend stationary) or integrated of order 1 (so that ΔY_t is stationary).

- *Step 1: Test for the nature of the trends in the time series.* Test whether the trend of the variables is deterministic or stochastic, by the methods discussed in Section 7.3.3. If the null hypothesis of stochastic trends is rejected and the trends are deterministic, then estimate a VAR model with deterministic trend terms included as regressors. If the trends are stochastic, then continue with step 2.
- *Step 2: Test for the presence of cointegration.* If the variables contain stochastic trends, then test for the presence of cointegration by means of the Johansen trace test. Choose the relevant VECM test equation (with or without constant terms and deterministic trends), starting with constants and trends included. If the null hypothesis of no cointegration is rejected, then continue with step 3, and if this hypothesis is not rejected, continue with step 4.
- *Step 3: Estimation of VECM with cointegration.* If the series are cointegrated, then determine the number r of cointegration relations by applying the Johansen trace test iteratively until the null hypothesis of r relations against the alternative of at least $(r + 1)$ relations is not rejected. Estimate the corresponding VECM—that is, (7.39) where Π has rank r and with relevant constants and trend terms included.
- *Step 4: Estimation of VAR for ΔY_t in absence of cointegration.* If the series are not cointegrated, then take first differences of the data and estimate a VAR model for the stationary variables ΔY_t.

It is also possible to combine the tests in the above four steps, as follows. Perform the Johansen trace test iteratively, starting with $r = 0$ and increasing r until the null hypothesis is not rejected anymore. If $r = 0$ is not rejected, then the series are not cointegrated, so continue with step 4. If $r = m$ is not rejected, then the m series are jointly (trend) stationary, so continue with step 1 (VAR model). If $1 \leq r \leq m - 1$, then the series are cointegrated and continue with step 3 (VECM).

Example 7.27: **Interest and Bond Rates (continued)**

We continue our analysis of the monthly series of the AAA bond rate, denoted by y_t, and the three-month Treasury Bill rate, denoted by x_t. In Example 7.26 in the foregoing section we estimated a VAR model for the differenced series Δy_t and Δx_t—that is, we performed step 4 of the above approach without testing for the possible presence of cointegration. Now we investigate whether these two series are cointegrated. We follow the above steps and discuss (i) the nature of the trends in the two time series, (ii) the outcomes of cointegration tests, (iii) the results of a VECM with one cointegration relation, and (iv) an interpretation of the cointegration relation.

(i) Nature of the trends in both series

In step 1 we test for the presence and nature of trends in the data. The graphs of the levels of the two rates were given in Example 7.25 (see Exhibit 7.29 (*a*)). This indicates that the series are not stationary and that they do not have a clear long-term trend direction. The results of ADF *t*-tests are in Panels 1 and 2 of Exhibit 7.32, both for the test equation with deterministic trend included and for the test equation without deterministic trend term. Neither of the two tests can reject the presence of a unit root for the two series. The ADF tests on the series of differences Δy_t and Δx_t show that these series do not contain a unit root. We conclude that the series y_t and x_t are integrated of order 1.

(ii) Cointegration tests

In step 2 we apply the Johansen test on cointegration. We test this in two models. First we use the general VECM with linear trend in the data and deterministic trend in the cointegration relation. Next we consider the VECM without trend in the data and in the cointegration relation. The results are in Panels 3 and 4 of Exhibit 7.32. For the VECM with trends, the first eigenvalue $\hat{\lambda}_1 = 0.061$ differs significantly from zero but the second one $\hat{\lambda}_2 = 0.007$ not. For the VECM without trends the first eigenvalue $\hat{\lambda}_1 = 0.058$ is significant but the second one $\hat{\lambda}_2 = 0.006$ not. We conclude that the two series are cointegrated and that there exists one common stochastic trend.

(iii) VECM with one cointegration relation

In step 3 we estimate the VECM with one cointegration relation. Panels 5 and 6 of Exhibit 7.32 show the estimates for two VECMs, with and without trend terms. The trend in the cointegration relation is not significant ($t = -1.52$ in Panel 5) and the drift terms are also not significant (the *t*-values are 0.90 for the AAA equation and 0.23 for the Treasury Bill equation, see Panel 5). This motivates the use of the VECM without drift terms and with a constant (but no trend) in the cointegration relation. Panel 6 of Exhibit 7.32 shows the resulting estimated model:

$$\begin{pmatrix} \Delta y_t \\ \Delta x_t \end{pmatrix} = \begin{pmatrix} -0.0188 \\ 0.0338 \end{pmatrix} (y_{t-1} - 1.151x_{t-1} - 1.276) + \begin{pmatrix} 0.5137 & -0.0437 \\ 0.7780 & 0.1699 \end{pmatrix} \begin{pmatrix} \Delta y_{t-1} \\ \Delta x_{t-1} \end{pmatrix}$$
$$+ \begin{pmatrix} -0.3333 & 0.0364 \\ -0.5175 & -0.0324 \end{pmatrix} \begin{pmatrix} \Delta y_{t-2} \\ \Delta x_{t-2} \end{pmatrix} + \begin{pmatrix} e_{1t} \\ e_{2t} \end{pmatrix}.$$

In this model, the long-run equilibrium relation is estimated as $y_t - 1.15x_t - 1.28 = 0$ (where y_t and x_t are both measured in percentages), or

$$y_t = 1.15x_t + 1.28.$$

(a)

Panel 1: ADF t-tests for AAA and for Δ(AAA)				
AAA (const and trend)	t = −1.266009	1%	Critical Value	−3.9779
6 lags included		5%	Critical Value	−3.4194
AAA (const but no trend)	t = −1.615880	1%	Critical Value	−3.4437
6 lags included		5%	Critical Value	−2.8667
Δ(AAA) (const but no trend)	t = −8.770391	1%	Critical Value	−3.4437
6 lags included		5%	Critical Value	−2.8667

(b)

Panel 2: ADF t-tests for US3MT and for Δ(US3MT)				
US3MT (const and trend)	t = −1.974514	1%	Critical Value	−3.9779
6 lags included		5%	Critical Value	−3.4194
US3MT (const but no trend)	t = −2.053994	1%	Critical Value	−3.4437
6 lags included		5%	Critical Value	−2.8667
Δ(US3MT) (const but no trend)	t = −11.97861	1%	Critical Value	−3.4437
6 lags included		5%	Critical Value	−2.8667

(c)

Panel 3: Johansen test on cointegration
Test assumption: Trend in the data, trend and constant in coint relation
Series: AAA US3MT
Sample: 1950:01 1999:12; Included observations: 600; Included lags: 4

Eigenvalue (λ)	Likelihood Ratio test	5 Percent Critical Value	1 Percent Critical Value	Hypothesized No. of CE(s)
0.061070 (λ_1)	41.82298	25.32	30.45	None (r = 0)
0.006668 (λ_2)	4.014194	12.25	16.26	At most 1 ($r \leq 1$)
LR test indicates 1 cointegrating equation at 5% and at 1% significance level				

(d)

Panel 4: Johansen test on cointegration
Test assumption: No trend in the data, constant but no trend in coint relation
Series: AAA US3MT
Sample: 1950:01 1999:12; Included observations: 600; Included lags: 4

Eigenvalue (λ)	Likelihood Ratio test	5 Percent Critical Value	1 Percent Critical Value	Hypothesized No. of CE(s)
0.058389 (λ_1)	39.90205	19.96	24.60	None (r = 0)
0.006320 (λ_2)	3.804047	9.24	12.97	At most 1 ($r \leq 1$)
LR test indicates 1 cointegrating equation at 5% and at 1% significance level				

Exhibit 7.32 Interest and Bond Rates (Example 7.27)

Unit root tests for the series of the AAA bond rate (Panel 1) and for the three-month Treasury Bill rate (Panel 2), and Johansen cointegration tests (with trend in data and with constant and trend in cointegration relation in Panel 3, and without trends in Panel 4).

This means that, in equilibrium, the AAA bond rate is higher than the three-month Treasury Bill rate. For instance, if $x_t = 5$ per cent, then in equilibrium $y_t = 7.03$ per cent. The adjustment coefficients are -0.019 for the AAA bond rate and 0.034 for the Treasury Bill rate. For instance, if the two rates are out of equilibrium in the sense that $y_t > 1.15x_t + 1.28$, then this leads to a downward adjustment of y_t (of 1.9 per cent of the difference) and an upward adjustment of x_t (of 3.4 per cent of the difference). This means that the rates are adjusted in the direction of equilibrium. The adjustment is rather slow, as

(*e*)

Panel 5: VECM with trends and with 1 cointegration relation				
Sample: 1950:01 1999:12 (600 observations)				
Cointegrating Eq:	Coefficient	Std. Error	t-Statistic	
AAA(−1)	1.000000			
US3MTBIL(−1)	−1.051707	0.09014	(−11.6670)	
@TREND(1950:01)	−0.002080	0.00137	(−1.51513)	
C	−0.234493			
Error Correction Model	Equation for D(AAA)	t-Statistic	Equation for D(US3MT)	t-Statistic
Coint. Equation	−0.022650	(−3.43266)	0.039050	(2.62909)
D(AAA(−1))	0.513984	(10.7490)	0.773596	(7.18723)
D(AAA(−2))	−0.331826	(−6.75667)	−0.523998	(−4.74004)
D(US3MTBIL(−1))	−0.044806	(−2.11576)	0.172205	(3.61252)
D(US3MTBIL(−2))	0.034777	(1.62788)	−0.029947	(−0.62275)
C	0.007015	(0.89989)	0.004101	(0.23373)
R-squared	0.222181		0.197649	
Log Likelihood	−79.22656			
Akaike Information Criterion	0.314089			
Schwarz Criterion	0.424012			

(*f*)

Panel 6: VECM without trends and with 1 cointegration relation				
Sample: 1950:01 1999:12 (600 observations)				
Cointegrating Eq:	Coefficient	Std. Error	t-Statistic	
AAA(−1)	1.000000			
US3MT(−1)	−1.150871	0.08209	(−14.0192)	
C	−1.275931	0.46790	(−2.72690)	
Error Correction Model	Equation for D(AAA)	t-Statistic	Equation for D(US3MT)	t-Statistic
Coint. Equation	−0.018831	(−3.32220)	0.033829	(2.65473)
D(AAA(−1))	0.513660	(10.7291)	0.777986	(7.22849)
D(AAA(−2))	−0.333304	(−6.77534)	−0.517504	(−4.67940)
D(US3MT(−1))	−0.043715	(−2.06522)	0.169932	(3.57109)
D(US3MT(−2))	0.036440	(1.71060)	−0.032351	(−0.67553)
R-squared	0.220254		0.197719	
Log Likelihood	−80.26316			
Akaike Information Criterion	0.310877			
Schwarz Criterion	0.406144			

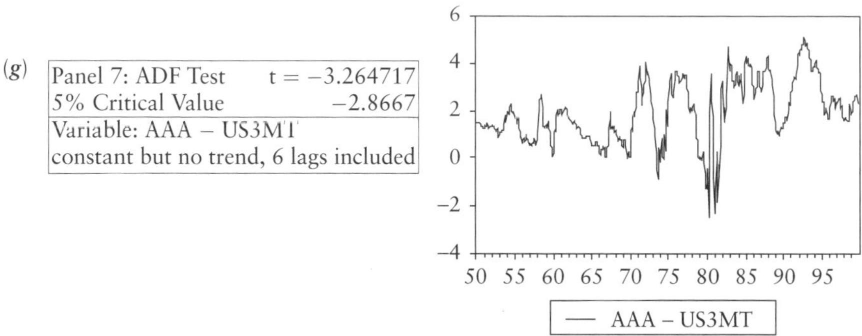
(*g*)

Panel 7: ADF Test	t = −3.264717
5% Critical Value	−2.8667
Variable: AAA − US3MT	
constant but no trend, 6 lags included	

Exhibit 7.32 (*Contd.*)

VECM for the series of the AAA bond rate and the three-month Treasury Bill rate (model with trends in Panel 5 and model without trends in Panel 6), unit root test on the difference of the two rates (AAA – US3MT, Panel 7) and time plot of this difference (*h*).

only around 5.3 per cent of the gap from equilibrium is adjusted within the period of one month.

(iv) Interpretation of the cointegration relation

The slope coefficient of 1.15 in the cointegration relation is quite close to 1, which suggests that the spread $(y_t - x_t)$ between the two rates may be stationary. This can be tested by an ADF test on this series. The results in Panels 7 and 8 of Exhibit 7.32 show that the spread $(y_t - x_t)$ is indeed stationary (at 5 per cent significance level). This equilibrium relation has a clear financial interpretation. In the long run the difference between the two rates stays constant. This means that the additional risk premium of AAA bonds, as compared to that of Treasury Bills, remains unaltered in the long run.

XM728TBR

Example 7.28: **Treasury Bill Rates**

As a second example we consider three series that we expect to be linked together in the long run—namely, Treasury Bill rates for three different maturities. We will discuss (i) the data, (ii) a test for the number of trends, (iii) a VECM with two cointegration relations (that is, with one common trend for the three series), and (iv) an interpretation of the two cointegration relations.

(i) The data

The three considered time series are the three-month, one-year, and ten-year Treasury Bill rates in the USA, with monthly observations over the years 1960–99. The data are measured in percentages and are taken from the Federal Reserve Board of Governors. The time plot of the three series is in Exhibit 7.33 (*a*). This graph suggests that the three series do not have a clear trend direction and that they possibly follow a random walk with one common stochastic trend.

(ii) Test for the number of trends

We test for the number of cointegration relations by applying the Johansen trace test. It turns out that the drift terms and the trend in the cointegration relation can be omitted. Therefore we present the results for the VECM without trends in Panel 2 of Exhibit 7.33. The test gives eigenvalues $\hat{\lambda}_1 = 0.078$, $\hat{\lambda}_2 = 0.041$, and $\hat{\lambda}_3 = 0.008$. The first two eigenvalues differ significantly from zero (at 5 per cent significance), but the third one does not. This means that the matrix Π in the VECM for these three series has rank $r = 2$. So there are two cointegration relations between the variables and there is one common stochastic trend that drives all three interest rates.

(*a*)

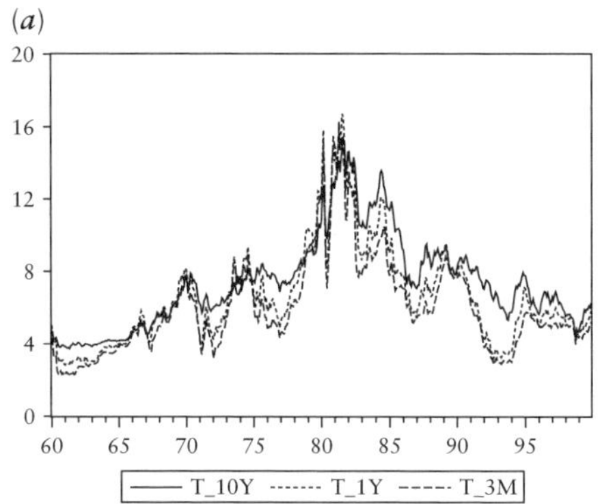

(*b*)

Panel 2: Johansen test on cointegration Test assumption: No deterministic trend in the data Series: T_3M, T_1Y, T_10Y Sample: 1960:01 1999:12; Included observations: 475; Included lags: 4				
Eigenvalue (λ)	Likelihood Ratio test	5 Percent Critical Value	1 Percent Critical Value	Hypothesized No. of CE(s)
0.077817 (λ_1)	62.51845	34.91	41.07	None (r = 0)
0.041226 (λ_2)	24.03773	19.96	24.60	At most 1 (r $\leq$ 1)
0.008470 (λ_3)	4.040461	9.24	12.97	At most 2 (r $\leq$ 2)
LR test indicates 2 cointegrating equations at 5% significance level				

(*c*)

Panel 3: VECM without trends and with 2 cointegration relations Sample(adjusted): 1960:04 1999:12 (477 observations)						
Cointegrating Equation:	Coefficients Coint Eq 1	Std. Error	t-Statistic	Coefficients Coint Eq 2	Std. Error	t-Statistic
T_3M(−1)	1.000000			0.000000		
T_1Y(−1)	0.000000			1.000000		
T_10Y(−1)	−0.882970	0.08490	−10.3999	−0.972623	0.07585	−12.8233
C	0.574733	0.65977	0.87111	0.595891	0.58941	1.01099
Error Correction Model	Equation for D(T_3M)	t-Statistic	Equation for D(T_1Y)	t-Statistic	Equation for D(T_10Y)	t-Statistic
CointEquation 1	−0.138592	−2.07326	0.052581	0.79810	0.116110	2.82168
CointEquation 2	0.124560	1.61478	−0.092694	−1.21928	−0.115427	−2.43089
D(T_3M(−1))	0.048494	0.41095	−0.114026	−0.98042	−0.082522	−1.13602
D(T_3M(−2))	0.011969	0.10133	0.170775	1.46689	0.136141	1.87226
D(T_1Y(−1))	0.362771	2.21719	0.401741	2.49133	0.070020	0.69520
D(T_1Y(−2))	−0.143895	−0.86784	−0.291773	−1.78547	−0.134795	−1.32065
D(T_10Y(−1))	0.156030	1.08619	0.322656	2.27904	0.398285	4.50414
D(T_10Y(−2))	−0.221795	−1.53246	−0.185207	−1.29841	−0.188165	−2.11202
R-squared	0.219135		0.214765		0.190565	

Exhibit 7.33 Treasury Bill Rates (Example 7.28)

Time plot of three US interest rates (three months, one year, and ten years (*a*)), Johansen cointegration test (Panel 2), and VECM (Panel 3).

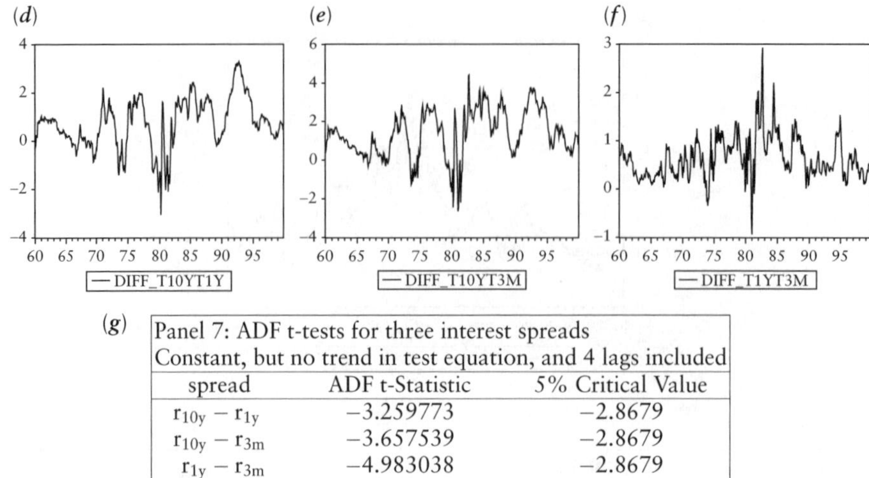

Panel 7: ADF t-tests for three interest spreads Constant, but no trend in test equation, and 4 lags included		
spread	ADF t-Statistic	5% Critical Value
$r_{10y} - r_{1y}$	−3.259773	−2.8679
$r_{10y} - r_{3m}$	−3.657539	−2.8679
$r_{1y} - r_{3m}$	−4.983038	−2.8679

Exhibit 7.33 (*Contd.*)

Time plot of three interest spreads ((*d*)–(*f*)) and unit root tests (Panel 7).

(iii) VECM with two cointegration relations

Panel 3 of Exhibit 7.33 shows the estimated VECM with two cointegration relations. The long-run equilibrium relations are estimated as

$$r_{3m} = 0.88r_{10y} - 0.57, \quad r_{1y} = 0.97r_{10y} - 0.60.$$

Here the index of the Treasury Bill rate r denotes the maturity, three months ($3m$), one year ($1y$), or ten years ($10y$). The outcomes are in line with financial theory, since in equilibrium the interest rates should be higher for longer maturities.

(iv) Interpretation of the two cointegration relations

The slope coefficients of the cointegration equations are quite close to one. Therefore we test whether the three series of interest spreads $(r_{10y} - r_{1y})$, $(r_{10y} - r_{3m})$, and $(r_{1y} - r_{3m})$ are stationary. We apply ADF tests, with a constant term but without deterministic trend in the test equation. The outcomes in Panel 7 of Exhibit 7.33 show that the null hypothesis of a unit root can be rejected for all three spreads. So the spreads are stationary and move up and down along a long-run equilibrium value. The graphs of the spreads in Exhibit 7.33 (*d*–*f*) indeed indicate the existence of such equilibria over long time horizons, although deviations may persist for considerable time. For instance, note that in the early 1980s the spreads were negative so that long-term interest rates were lower than short-term interest rates. However, this disequilibrium situation has been corrected over time.

☞ **Exercises:** S: 7.15e; E: 7.17**h**, **i**, 7.20f, 7.21c, 7.23**b**, **c**, 7.24**b**–**d**.

7.6.4 Summary

In this section we have considered the joint modelling of a set of mutually dependent time series variables.

- If the variables are (trend) stationary, one can estimate a vector autoregressive model by means of least squares. The estimated model can be analysed by means of the usual diagnostic tests for regression models and AR time series models. The model can be rewritten in error correction form, which provides insight in the correction mechanisms between the time series.
- If the variables contain stochastic trends, then one should investigate whether the variables are cointegrated. The appropriate cointegration test equation for the Johansen trace test depends on the data properties (clear overall trend direction or not, deterministic trend in cointegration relations or not).
- If the series are not cointegrated, then regressions of the variables in levels may lead to spurious results. Therefore the model should be estimated only after the stochastic trends have been removed by taking first differences of the data.
- If the series are cointegrated, then one should estimate a VECM (with reduced rank of the matrix Π of the regressor Y_{t-1}). If there are m variables and $\text{rank}(\Pi) = r$, then there are r cointegration relations and $(m - r)$ common trends. The estimated model has a clear interpretation in terms of long-run equilibria and adjustment mechanisms that preserve these equilibria.

7.7 Other multiple equation models

☞ Uses Chapters 1–4; Sections 5.4, 5.5, 5.7; Sections 7.1–7.3, 7.6.

7.7.1 Introduction

Combined cross section and time series data

Many data sets of practical interest consist of a large number of variables that are observed on a sequence of successive moments in time. Examples are yearly time series observations of the production of a large number of firms, weekly purchases of a large number of households, and quarterly developments in gross national product of a large number of countries. In such cases the data concern a cross section of units (firms, households, countries), and for each unit a time series of observations is available. If the information consists of such a combination of cross section and time series data, then one says that the data are *pooled*. Such data are also called *panel data*, where the panel refers to the cross section (of firms, households, countries, and so on).

The vector autoregressive model of Section 7.6 is an example of a model for a number of observed time series variables. However, as was discussed in Section 7.6.2, this model is not suitable for a large number of time series, because the number of parameters in the VAR model grows with the square of the number of time series. In practice, pooled data sets often contain a large number of units (dozens of countries, hundreds of firms, thousands of households). For instance, if the data set consists of fifty weekly observations of 1000 households, then a VAR(1) model for these 1000 series has more than a million parameters. Such data sets should be analysed in another way.

General model formulation

We suppose that the data set consists of time series observed at n time moments ($t = 1, \cdots, n$) for a number m of units ($i = 1, \cdots, m$). The variable to be explained is denoted by y_{it} and we assume that there are $(k-1)$ explanatory variables x_{it}, where i denotes the unit and t the time moment. In all that follows we exclude the constant term from x_{it}, as this term plays a special role in the models that we will discuss in this section. The considered models are of the following general form:

$$y_{it} = \alpha_{it} + x'_{it}\gamma_{it} + \varepsilon_{it}, \quad i = 1, \cdots, m, \quad t = 1, \cdots, n, \quad \text{var}(\varepsilon) = \Omega.$$

Here Ω denotes the $mn \times mn$ covariance matrix of the $mn \times 1$ vector ε of disturbances ε_{it}. This model is far too general to be of practical use, as it contains more parameters than observations. The number of observations is mn and the number of parameters is $kmn + \frac{1}{2}mn(mn+1)$ (namely, mn for the constants α_{it}, $(k-1)mn$ for the slopes γ_{it}, and $\frac{1}{2}mn(mn+1)$ for the symmetric matrix Ω). Therefore, to be practically useful we have to impose restrictions on the regression parameters $(\alpha_{it}, \gamma_{it})$ and on the covariance matrix Ω.

Three models of special interest

In the rest of this section we pay attention to three specifications that are of much practical interest. In Section 7.7.2 we consider the seemingly unrelated regression model that is characterized by the restrictions that

$$\alpha_{it} = \alpha_i, \quad \gamma_{it} = \gamma_i, \quad E[\varepsilon_{it}\varepsilon_{jt}] = \sigma_{ij}, \quad E[\varepsilon_{it}\varepsilon_{js}] = 0 \quad (\text{for all } i, j, \text{ and } t \neq s).$$

So the parameters differ between units, but they are constant over time for each given unit. Further, the error terms are uncorrelated over time, but the error terms are correlated between units at the same moment of time. This model contains in total $mk + \frac{1}{2}m(m+1)$ parameters. As we shall see in Section 7.7.2, this model can be used only if $n \geq m$—that is, the length of the time series should be at least as large as the number of units. In practice the number of units may be very large, in which case panel data models are appropriate. This is discussed in Section 7.7.3. The panel data model (with fixed effects) corresponds to the restrictions

$$\alpha_{it} = \alpha_i, \quad \gamma_{it} = \gamma, \quad \Omega = \sigma^2 I.$$

So the slope parameters are constant across units, and the error terms are uncorrelated (also between units at the same moment of time) and homoskedastic. In this way the number of parameters is drastically reduced, to $m + k$. Finally, in Section 7.7.4 we consider simultaneous equation models. These models have the same structure as the seemingly unrelated regression model. The crucial difference is that some of the explanatory variables are endogenous, as the dependent variable y_{it} of one unit plays the role of an explanatory variable in the equations for y_{jt} of other units.

In the following sections we briefly describe some of the salient features of these models. For further details we refer to the textbooks mentioned in the Further Reading section at the end of this chapter.

7.7.2 Seemingly unrelated regression model

Motivation of the SUR model

Suppose that the data set consists of time series for a number of units. It is assumed that the marginal effects of the explanatory variables differ per unit, but that these effects are constant over time. In terms of the general model in Section 7.7.1, this means that $\alpha_{it} = \alpha_i$ and $\gamma_{it} = \gamma_i$. Further it is assumed that the disturbances of each unit are not serially correlated. However, at a given time the disturbances of the different units may be correlated. This reflects the possibility that unobserved influences may affect all units simultaneously. The assumptions on the error terms are $E[\varepsilon_{it}\varepsilon_{js}] = 0$ for all $t \neq s$ and for all i, j, and $E[\varepsilon_{it}\varepsilon_{jt}] = \sigma_{ij}$ is possibly non-zero. One says that the error terms contain *contemporaneous correlation*. If the explanatory variables x_{it} are exogenous, the resulting model

$$\begin{aligned} y_{it} &= \alpha_i + x'_{it}\gamma_i + \varepsilon_{it}, \\ E[\varepsilon_{it}\varepsilon_{jt}] &= \sigma_{ij}, \quad E[\varepsilon_{it}\varepsilon_{js}] = 0 \text{ (for all } i, j, \text{ and } t \neq s), \end{aligned}$$

is called the *seemingly unrelated regression* (SUR) model. The equations for different units seem to be unrelated, as all parameters are different. However, the observations y_{it} and y_{jt} are related if $\sigma_{ij} \neq 0$. So the relations between the units are modelled implicitly via the correlation of the error terms. For instance, future expectations may influence the behaviour of all households in the data set, and changes in the state of the world economy may affect the profit of all firms or the national income of all countries in the data set. Influential factors like future expectations and worldwide prospects are difficult to measure, and their influence on all units is incorporated in the unobserved error terms ε_{it}.

Model formulation in matrix form

Let the observations be ordered per unit, and per unit let the observations be ordered with time. We denote the data for unit i by the $n \times 1$ vector y_i and by the $n \times k$ matrix X_i, with corresponding $k \times 1$ parameter vector $\beta_i = (\alpha_i, \gamma'_i)'$ and $n \times 1$ vector of disturbances ε_i. The model for unit i can then be written as

$$y_i = X_i\beta_i + \varepsilon_i.$$

The parameters β_i could be estimated by applying OLS per unit separately. However, this is not efficient if the disturbances contain contemporaneous correlation. By combining the models for the m units, the SUR model can be written in matrix form as follows, where $\varepsilon = (\varepsilon'_1, \cdots, \varepsilon'_m)'$ is the $mn \times 1$ vector of disturbances.

$$\begin{pmatrix} y_1 \\ y_2 \\ \vdots \\ y_m \end{pmatrix} = \begin{pmatrix} X_1 & 0 & \cdots & 0 \\ 0 & X_2 & \cdots & 0 \\ \vdots & \vdots & & \vdots \\ 0 & 0 & \cdots & X_m \end{pmatrix} \begin{pmatrix} \beta_1 \\ \beta_2 \\ \vdots \\ \beta_m \end{pmatrix} + \begin{pmatrix} \varepsilon_1 \\ \varepsilon_2 \\ \vdots \\ \varepsilon_m \end{pmatrix},$$

$$E[\varepsilon] = 0, \ \mathrm{var}(\varepsilon) = \Omega = \begin{pmatrix} \sigma_{11}I & \sigma_{12}I & \cdots & \sigma_{1m}I \\ \sigma_{12}I & \sigma_{22}I & \cdots & \sigma_{2m}I \\ \vdots & \vdots & & \vdots \\ \sigma_{1m}I & \sigma_{2m}I & \cdots & \sigma_{mm}I \end{pmatrix}. \tag{7.41}$$

Here I denotes the $n \times n$ identity matrix. This is a regression model in standard matrix form, but the error terms may be heteroskedastic and they may be correlated. Because of the block-diagonal structure of the matrix of explanatory variables, the OLS estimator of the mk parameters β_i, $i = 1, \cdots, m$, in the above model is equivalent to applying OLS per unit. However, this is not the best linear unbiased estimator, because the $mn \times mn$ covariance matrix Ω of the model is not of the form $\sigma^2 I$. In what follows we describe a general method to estimate regression models for which the covariance matrix Ω does not have the standard form (the SUR model is a special case).

The method of generalized least squares

T

An efficient estimator is obtained by transforming the model such that the covariance matrix becomes of the form $\sigma^2 I$. This is called *generalized least squares* (GLS). The idea is similar to the method of weighted least squares discussed in Section 5.4.3 (p. 327–30) for a diagonal covariance matrix Ω. As the covariance has another structure here, we need to apply another type of transformation to estimate the SUR model. The general idea is to transform the model $y = X\beta + \varepsilon$ (where ε has mean 0 and covariance matrix Ω) by means of an invertible matrix A to $Ay = AX\beta + A\varepsilon$ in such a way that the transformed error vector $A\varepsilon$ (that has mean 0) has covariance matrix I. As $A\varepsilon$ has covariance matrix $A\Omega A'$, the condition on A is that $A\Omega A' = I$, in which case $\Omega = A^{-1}(A')^{-1} = (A'A)^{-1}$. If we write $y_* = Ay$, $X_* = AX$, and $\varepsilon_* = A\varepsilon$, then $y_* = X_*\beta + \varepsilon_*$ with $E[\varepsilon_*] = 0$ and $\mathrm{var}(\varepsilon_*) = I$. Therefore, the best linear unbiased estimator of β is given by

$$b_{GLS} = (X_*'X_*)^{-1}X_*'y_* = (X'\Omega^{-1}X)^{-1}X'\Omega^{-1}y,$$

where we used the fact that $A'A = \Omega^{-1}$. This is called the generalized least squares estimator.

Methods to compute the transformation matrix

T

There are different methods to compute the transformation matrix A. A general method is the following. According to the matrix results in Appendix

A (Sections A.5 and A.6), the positive definite covariance matrix Ω can be written as

$$\Omega = VDV',$$

where D is a diagonal matrix with the positive eigenvalues λ_{it} of Ω on the diagonal and where V is an orthogonal matrix with columns that are eigenvectors of Ω and with the property that $V'V = I$. Now define $A = D^{-1/2}V'$, where $D^{-1/2}$ is the diagonal matrix with elements $1/\sqrt{\lambda_{it}}$ on the diagonal. Then $A\Omega A' = I$, which follows by writing out this matrix product and using that $V'V = I$ and $D^{-1/2}DD^{-1/2} = I$. This general method is not always the most convenient way to find a transformation matrix A, as the involved matrices Ω and A are of size $mn \times mn$. This is often too large to be practically feasible. Note that the $mn \times mn$ matrix Ω in (7.41) is sparse, in the sense that it contains many zero elements. Special methods have been developed to obtain transformations A for sparse matrices Ω, but here we will not discuss these computational aspects any further.

Feasible GLS

The above GLS estimator b_{GLS} can be computed only if the covariance matrix Ω is known, but this is not the case in practice. The *feasible* GLS estimator (FGLS) of the SUR model is computed in two steps. In the first step the matrix Ω is estimated by least squares methods, and in the second step this estimated covariance matrix is used in GLS. This approach is similar to the method of feasible WLS for heteroskedastic error terms discussed in Section 5.4.4 (p. 335–6).

Two-step feasible generalized least squares (FGLS)

- *Step 1: Estimate the covariance matrix* Ω. Apply m regressions, one per unit to estimate β_j by OLS, $j = 1, \cdots, m$. Let e_i be the $n \times 1$ vector of OLS residuals for unit i; then the (co)variances σ_{ij} are estimated by $s_{ij} = \frac{1}{n}\sum_{t=1}^{n} e_{it}e_{jt}$. The $mn \times mn$ matrix $\hat{\Omega}$ is estimated by replacing σ_{ij} in (7.41) by s_{ij}.
- *Step 2: Estimate the parameters* β_j *jointly by GLS*. The FGLS estimator is obtained by substituting the estimated covariance matrix $\hat{\Omega}$ of step 1 into the expression for the GLS estimator, so that

$$b_{FGLS} = (X'\hat{\Omega}^{-1}X)^{-1}X'\hat{\Omega}^{-1}y.$$

It can be shown that this estimator has the same (optimal) asymptotic properties as ML in (7.41) if the error terms are normally distributed, the number of time series observations $n \to \infty$, and the number m of units is fixed. In particular, if n is large enough then

$$b_{FGLS} \approx \mathrm{N}(\beta, (X'_* X_*)^{-1}) \approx \mathrm{N}(\beta, (X'\hat{\Omega}^{-1}X)^{-1}).$$

This can be used to perform t- and F-tests, provided that the length n of the time series is large enough. The first step in the above FGLS method is not efficient, as it neglects the fact that the error terms are heteroskedastic and correlated. One can iterate the FGLS steps, using the residuals of step 2 to make a new estimate of Ω in step 1 and a corresponding new GLS estimate in step 2. This can be iterated until the estimates converge. This is called *iterated FGLS*.

SUR requires a limited number of units

The SUR model can be estimated only if the number of units m is not larger than the number of time series observations n per unit. This can be derived as follows. To compute the SUR estimator b_{FGLS} (in step 2), the estimated covariance matrix $\hat{\Omega}$ (of step 1) should be invertible. Here $\hat{\Omega}$ is an $mn \times mn$ block-diagonal matrix with the $m \times m$ matrix S on the diagonal, where S has elements $s_{ij} = \frac{1}{n} e_i' e_j$ with e_i the $n \times 1$ vector of OLS residuals of unit i. Therefore $\hat{\Omega}$ is invertible if and only if S is invertible—that is, if and only if $\mathrm{rank}(S) = m$. Now define the $n \times m$ matrix $E = (e_1, \cdots, e_m)$; then $S = \frac{1}{n} E'E$ and $m = \mathrm{rank}(S) = \mathrm{rank}(E) \leq n$. So S and $\hat{\Omega}$ can be invertible and b_{FGLS} can be computed only if $m \leq n$. If the number of units present in the data set exceeds the length of the observation period per unit, then SUR cannot be applied. Models that are appropriate for such data sets are discussed in the next section.

Cases where OLS is efficient

There are two situations for which the GLS estimator in the SUR model boils down to the OLS estimator per unit. This happens if the different units are uncorrelated so that $\sigma_{ij} = 0$ for all $i \neq j$, or if all units have the same regressor matrix in the sense that $X_i = X$ is the same for all $i = 1, \cdots, m$ (see Exercise 7.10). In these cases OLS per unit is efficient.

The null hypothesis of uncorrelated units can be tested by means of the OLS residual vectors e_i. Let the sample correlation of the residuals of units i and j be defined by $r_{ij} = s_{ij}/\sqrt{s_{ii}s_{jj}}$, with s_{ij} as defined in step 1 of the FGLS method. If $\sigma_{ij} = 0$, then $r_{ij} \approx \mathrm{N}(0, \frac{1}{n})$, and the LM-test for the absence of cross-unit correlations ($\sigma_{ij} = 0$ for all $i \neq j$) is given by

$$LM = n \sum_{i=1}^{m-1} \sum_{j=i+1}^{m} r_{ij}^2 \approx \chi^2\left(\frac{1}{2}m(m-1)\right).$$

This is similar to the Box–Pierce test (5.50) for serial correlation. If the null hypothesis is not rejected, then one can apply OLS per unit without loss of efficiency; otherwise FGLS is preferred.

E

XM729PMI

Example 7.29: **Primary Metal Industries**

To illustrate some of the foregoing methods we consider yearly production data of $m = 26$ firms in the US primary metal industries (SIC33) over the period 1958–94, so that $n = 37$. The data are taken from the National Bureau of Economic Research (E. J. Bartelsman and W. Gray, The NBER Manufacturing Productivity Database, National Technical Working Paper 205, 1996). We will discuss (i) the data, (ii) the estimates of an SUR model for a subset of three firms, (iii) the SUR estimates for the full set of twenty-six firms, and (iv) comments on the outcomes.

(i) **The data**

The dependent variable y_{it} is the output (value added) and the explanatory variables are the input factors L_{it} (labour, production worker wages) and K_{it} (capital stock, both structures and equipment), all measured in millions of 1987 dollars. The Cobb–Douglas production function is $y_{it} = L_{it}^{\beta_i} K_{it}^{\gamma_i} e^{\alpha_i} e^{\varepsilon_{it}}$, and by taking logarithms this can be written as

$$\log(y_{it}) = \alpha_i + \beta_i \log(L_{it}) + \gamma_i \log(K_{it}) + \varepsilon_{it}.$$

The data (all in logarithms) are shown in Exhibit 7.34. Although some firms have a growing or declining output over time, this is by no means a general characteristic of the data. Here we will not incorporate trends in the model. Further, although the firms operate in the same industry sector, we allow for different labour elasticities (β_i) and capital elasticities (γ_i). The constants (α_i) represent the production efficiency of the firms — that is, the output for given levels of labour and capital, and this efficiency is also allowed to vary between firms.

(ii) **SUR estimates for a subset of three firms**

The full SUR model contains $mk = 26 \cdot 3 = 78$ parameters and will be discussed in part (iii) below. For simplicity we first consider the SUR model for a subset of three firms, neglecting the data of the other twenty-three firms. So in this case there are $m = 3$ units with $n = 37$ time series observations per unit. Panels 1 and 6 of Exhibit 7.35 show the results of OLS and of SUR (two-step FGLS) for the three firms. The OLS estimates are close to the SUR estimates, but most of the standard errors are smaller in the SUR model, so that the parameters are somewhat more efficiently estimated by

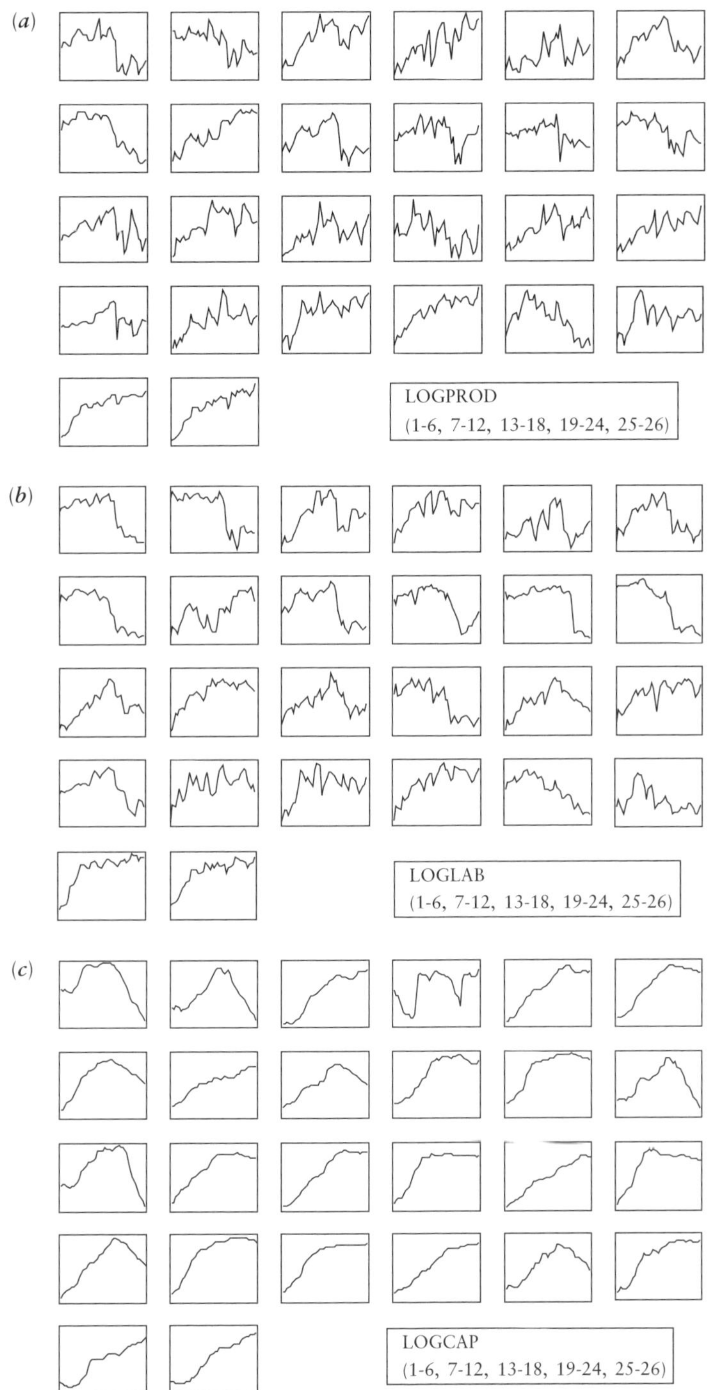

Exhibit 7.34 Primary Metal Industries (Example 7.29)

Yearly production data over the period 1958–94 of twenty-six firms in the US primary metal sector, value added (*a*), labour input (*b*), and capital stock (*c*), all in logarithms.

(a)

Panel 1: Dependent Variable: LOGPROD				
Method: Pooled Least Squares (OLS)				
Sample: 1958 1994; Included observations: 37				
Number of cross-sections: 3; Total panel (balanced) 111 obs.				
Variable	Coefficient	Std. Error	t-Statistic	Prob.
C_1	−1.087911	0.504532	−2.156275	0.0334
C_2	1.363460	0.500062	2.726584	0.0075
C_3	−0.339983	0.383163	−0.887306	0.3770
LOGLAB_1	0.961796	0.034245	28.08564	0.0000
LOGLAB_2	0.922977	0.169924	5.431716	0.0000
LOGLAB_3	1.330223	0.300807	4.422174	0.0000
LOGCAP_1	0.272703	0.074273	3.671644	0.0004
LOGCAP_2	0.005695	0.080226	0.070987	0.9435
LOGCAP_3	0.180628	0.074909	2.411288	0.0177
R-squared	0.950496	Log likelihood		62.90914
S.E. of regression	0.143215			

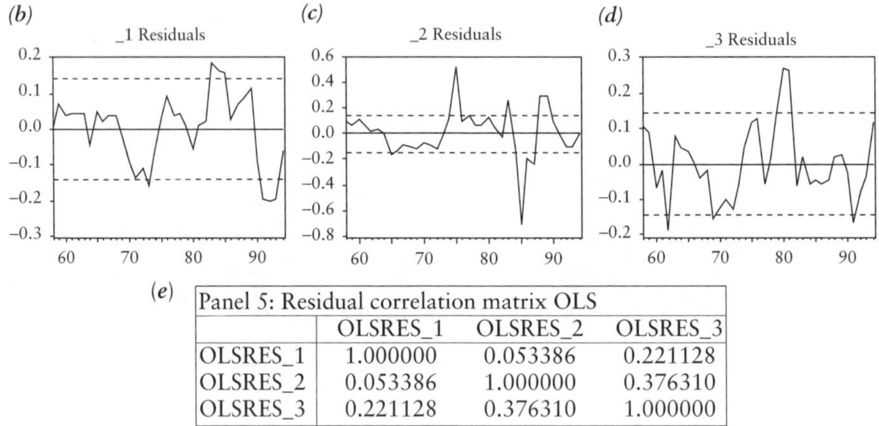

(e)

Panel 5: Residual correlation matrix OLS			
	OLSRES_1	OLSRES_2	OLSRES_3
OLSRES_1	1.000000	0.053386	0.221128
OLSRES_2	0.053386	1.000000	0.376310
OLSRES_3	0.221128	0.376310	1.000000

(f)

Panel 6: Dependent Variable: LOGPROD				
Method: Seemingly Unrelated Regression (2-step FGLS)				
Sample: 1958 1994; Included observations: 37				
Number of cross-sections: 3; Total panel (balanced) 111 obs.				
Variable	Coefficient	Std. Error	t-Statistic	Prob.
C_1	−1.048012	0.336424	−3.115150	0.0024
C_2	1.478908	0.634286	2.331612	0.0217
C_3	−0.394136	0.275345	−1.431427	0.1554
LOGLAB_1	0.960662	0.022609	42.49061	0.0000
LOGLAB_2	0.954174	0.214414	4.450154	0.0000
LOGLAB_3	1.355261	0.201169	6.736918	0.0000
LOGCAP_1	0.266874	0.049581	5.382560	0.0000
LOGCAP_2	−0.012646	0.101660	−0.124391	0.9013
LOGCAP_3	0.184460	0.052020	3.545939	0.0006
R-squared	0.950448	Log likelihood		77.99390
S.E. of regression	0.143284			

Exhibit 7.35 Primary Metal Industries (Example 7.29)

Cobb–Douglas production functions of three firms estimated by OLS (Panel 1) with time plots of the three corresponding residual series ((*b*)–(*d*)) and their correlation matrix (Panel 5), and model estimated by SUR (two-step FGLS, Panel 6); the firms (1, 2, and 3) are indicated by an underscore (_1, _2, and _3).

(*g*)

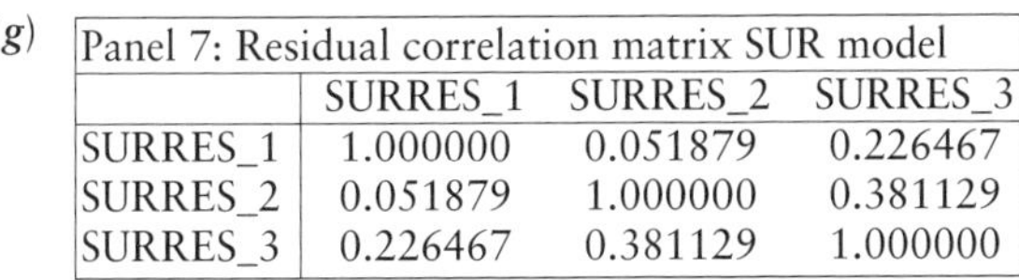

Panel 7: Residual correlation matrix SUR model			
	SURRES_1	SURRES_2	SURRES_3
SURRES_1	1.000000	0.051879	0.226467
SURRES_2	0.051879	1.000000	0.381129
SURRES_3	0.226467	0.381129	1.000000

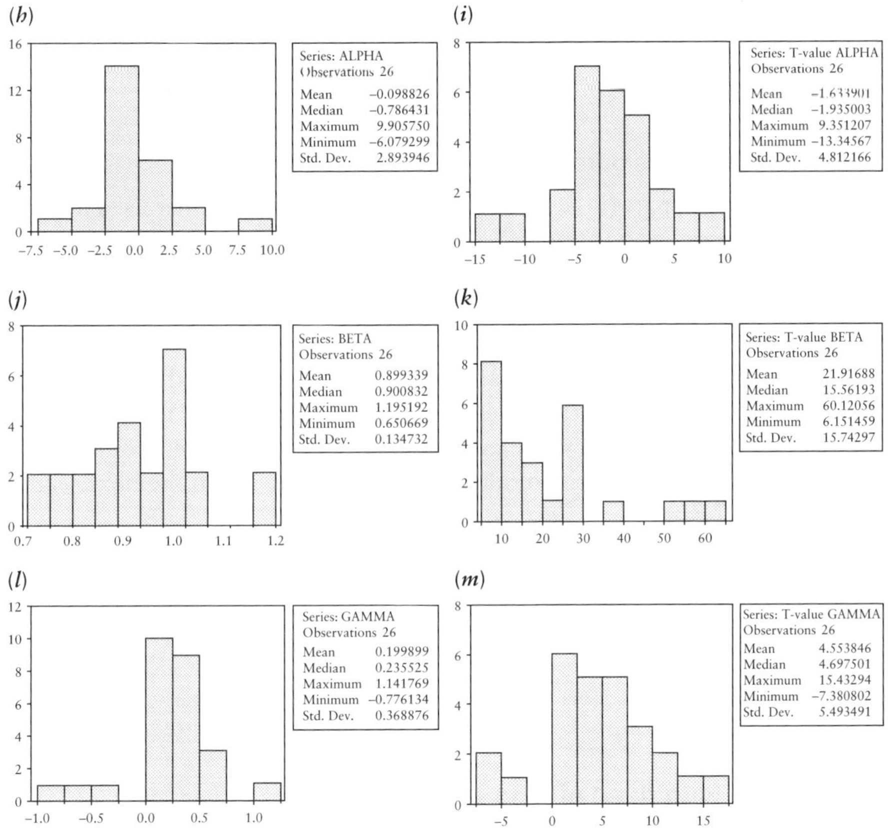

Exhibit 7.35 (*Contd.*)

Contemporaneous residual correlation matrix corresponding to the SUR model of Panel 6 (Panel 7) and SUR estimates (two-step FGLS) of Cobb–Douglas production functions of twenty-six firms, histograms of resulting twenty-six estimates of the constant term α (*h*), the labour elasticity β (*j*), and the capital elasticity γ (*l*), together with histograms of the twenty-six corresponding *t*-values ((*i*), (*k*), and (*m*)).

FGLS. Exhibit 7.35 (*b–d*) show time plots of the three series of OLS residuals. They follow different patterns and the cross correlations between the three series are relatively small (0.05, 0.23, and 0.38, see Panel 5). The *LM*-test for the significance of contemporaneous cross correlations is $LM = n(r_{12}^2 + r_{13}^2 + r_{23}^2) = 37(\,(0.05)^2 + (0.22)^2 + (0.38)^2) = 7.15 \approx \chi^2(3)$ with corresponding *P*-value $P = 0.07$. So the null hypothesis that $\sigma_{ij} = 0$ for $i \neq j$ is not rejected. This explains that the SUR and OLS estimates are close together.

(iii) SUR estimates for the full set of twenty-six firms

The results of SUR (two-step FGLS) on the full set of $m = 26$ firms are summarized in Exhibit 7.35 (*h–m*) by means of histograms of the resulting twenty-six estimates of α_i, β_i, γ_i, and their *t*-values. The estimated capital elasticities (γ_i) vary considerably across firms. Several of these coefficients are not significant and some are even negative (the minimum elasticity is -0.78, the maximum 1.14). The estimated labour elasticities (β_i) vary less (minimum 0.65, maximum 1.20) and are all significant.

(iv) Comments on the outcomes

The SUR model in part (iii) contains a large number of parameters. There are $mk = 78$ regression parameters. The $mn \times mn = 962 \times 962$ covariance matrix Ω is block-diagonal, with symmetric 26×26 matrices (with elements σ_{ij}) on the diagonal. This gives $\frac{1}{2}m(m+1) = 351$ additional parameters. In total, the SUR model uses $mn = 962$ data to estimate $(78 + 351) = 429$ coefficients. So the number of parameters is large as compared to the amount of data information, and this causes a lack of significance in some of the obtained estimates. More significant results can be obtained by imposing parameter restrictions on the model, as will be discussed in the next section (see Example 7.30).

☞ **Exercises: T: 7.10a–c; E: 7.25a, b.**

7.7.3 Panel data

Panel model with fixed effects

In some data sets — for instance, in consumer panels — the number of units (m) is much larger than the number of observations (n) per unit. In such situations one speaks of *panel data* or *longitudinal data*. For such data sets the SUR model cannot be applied, as this requires that $m \leq n$. The SUR model should then be simplified to reduce the number of parameters. One way to get a manageable model is to assume that the marginal effects of the explanatory variables on the dependent variable are the same for all units. This corresponds to the restriction that the slopes $\gamma_i = \gamma$ are constant across units. To account for differences between the units, the constant terms α_i are allowed to vary among units. These constant terms stand for all unobserved aspects that distinguish the units from each other. For instance, in a consumer panel this may capture differences in unobserved wealth of the households, and in a panel of firms it may represent differences in management style. A further simplification is obtained by the additional assumption that the random variables ε_{it} are homoskedastic and uncorrelated, both over time and across firms. Under the above assumptions, the model becomes

$$y_{it} = \alpha_i + x'_{it}\gamma + \varepsilon_{it}, \quad \varepsilon_{it} \sim \text{IID}(0, \sigma^2).$$

Here x_{it} is a $(k-1) \times 1$ vector of explanatory variables that does not include a constant term. This is called the panel model with *fixed effects*, as the difference between the units is modelled in terms of the unit-specific, fixed (but unknown) parameters α_i. The model has $(m+k)$ parameters (m for α_i, $(k-1)$ for γ, and 1 for σ^2). As compared with the SUR model, which has $mk + \frac{1}{2}m(m+1)$ parameters, this is a considerable simplification even for moderate values of m.

Fixed effects model in matrix form

T

The model can be written as a standard multiple regression model with constant coefficients by incorporating unit dummies, defined by $D_{it}(j) = 1$ if $i = j$ and $D_{it}(j) = 0$ if $i \neq j$. Then the model becomes

$$y_{it} = \sum_{j=1}^{m} \alpha_j D_{it}(j) + x'_{it}\gamma + \varepsilon_{it}, \quad \varepsilon_{it} \sim \text{IID}(0, \sigma^2).$$

This can also be written in matrix form, as follows. Let y_i be the $n \times 1$ vector with the values y_{it}, $t = 1, \cdots, n$, let ε_i be defined in a similar way in terms of ε_{it}, and let X_i be the $n \times (k-1)$ matrix with tth row x'_{it}, $t = 1, \cdots, n$. Further let ι be the $n \times 1$ vector with all elements equal to 1. Then the equation for the ith unit is $y_i = \iota\alpha_i + X_i\gamma + \varepsilon_i$. Now stack these equations for $i = 1, \cdots, m$, and write y for the $mn \times 1$ vector consisting of the stacked y_i, ε for the $mn \times 1$ vector of stacked ε_i, and X for the $mn \times (k-1)$ matrix of the stacked X_i. Further, let D be the following $mn \times m$ matrix built from the $n \times 1$ vectors ι and 0.

$$D = \begin{pmatrix} \iota & 0 & \cdots & 0 \\ 0 & \iota & \cdots & 0 \\ \vdots & \vdots & & \vdots \\ 0 & 0 & \cdots & \iota \end{pmatrix}.$$

Let $\alpha = (\alpha_1, \cdots, \alpha_m)'$; then the model can be written in matrix form as

$$y = X\gamma + D\alpha + \varepsilon, \quad \varepsilon \sim \text{N}(0, \sigma^2 I).$$

Fixed effects regression by numerically efficient methods

T

In the above model, the regressors x_{it} are assumed to be exogenous. As $\text{var}(\varepsilon) = \sigma^2 I$, efficient estimators of the parameters (γ and α) of this model are obtained by OLS. Direct application of OLS involves the inverse of the $(m+k-1) \times (m+k-1)$ matrix $(X\ \ D)'(X\ \ D)$. If the number m of units is large, then the computation of the inverse of such a large matrix is numerically cumbersome. We now describe a computationally simpler method that is based on the partial regression result of Frisch–Waugh in Section 3.2.5 (p. 146). This result states that the slope parameters γ can be estimated by means of the following two steps. In step 1, regress y and X on D and determine the 'cleaned' variables—that is, the residuals of these two regressions. These residuals are given by $M_D y$ and $M_D X$, where $M_D = I - D(D'D)^{-1}D'$. This is easy to compute, since $D'D = nI$, so that $(D'D)^{-1} = \frac{1}{n}I$. The 'cleaned' variable $M_D y$ has elements $y_{it} - \bar{y}_i$, where $\bar{y}_i = \frac{1}{n}\sum_{t=1}^{n} y_{it}$ is the average over the ith unit. In a similar way, $M_D X$ has elements $x_{it} - \bar{x}_i$. In step 2 of partial regression, the OLS estimates of γ are obtained by regressing $M_D y$ on $M_D X$. This gives

$$\hat{\gamma}_{OLS} = (X'M_D X)^{-1}X'M_D y$$

$$= \left(\sum_{i=1}^{m}\sum_{t=1}^{n}(x_{it} - \bar{x}_i)(x_{it} - \bar{x}_i)'\right)^{-1}\left(\sum_{i=1}^{m}\sum_{t=1}^{n}(x_{it} - \bar{x}_i)(y_{it} - \bar{y}_i)\right).$$

This regression involves only $(k-1)$ parameters, and we need to compute only the inverse of the matrix $X'M_D X$ that has size $(k-1) \times (k-1)$ that does not depend on the number m of units. This greatly simplifies the computations. The OLS estimates of the constants α_i can be obtained as follows. One of the normal equations in the matrix model reads $D'X\hat{\gamma} + D'D\hat{\alpha} = D'y$, so that $\hat{\alpha} = (D'D)^{-1}(D'y - D'X\hat{\gamma})$. By writing this out we obtain

$$\hat{\alpha}_i = \bar{y}_i - \bar{x}_i'\hat{\gamma}.$$

Properties of fixed effects estimators

Under the above assumptions, the OLS estimators have the usual properties discussed in Chapter 3. This means that t- and F-tests can be applied in the usual way. Here the variance s^2 should be estimated as $\frac{1}{mn-(m+k-1)}\sum_{i=1}^{m}\sum_{t=1}^{n} e_{it}^2$, as the regression model has mn observations and $(m+k-1)$ regression parameters. For instance, the null hypothesis of absence of unit-specific effects $(\alpha_1 = \cdots = \alpha_m)$ can be tested by the F-test with $(m-1)$ and $(mn - (m+k-1))$ degrees of freedom. If the above two-step estimation method is used, then the standard errors and t-values obtained in the second step should be corrected, as the second-step regression has only $(k-1)$ parameters instead of $(m+k-1)$ (see Exercise 3.9).

The OLS estimator of γ is consistent if $mn \to \infty$. It suffices that $m \to \infty$ with n fixed, so that the marginal effects γ can also be estimated accurately if the number of observations per unit is small. This is because these effects are assumed to be the same for all units. The OLS estimator of α is consistent only for $n \to \infty$, as increasing the number of units does not help to estimate the constant terms of previous units.

Panel model with random effects

In the panel model with fixed effects, all unit-specific characteristics that are constant over time are absorbed in the constant terms α_i. For instance, in a consumer panel that extends over a limited number of weeks we cannot discriminate between variables like the sex and the living area of the consumer. If we were to add these variables as additional regressors, we would obtain perfect collinearity, so these individual-specific effects cannot be estimated in the fixed effects model. In such situations it is helpful to adjust the model for the constant terms α_i—for instance, by assuming that they consist of independent drawings from an underlying population. This is a realistic assumption in many cases, because the units (say households) in the sample are often randomly drawn from a larger population of units. Suppose that $\alpha_i \sim \text{IID}(\alpha, \sigma_\alpha^2)$ and that these effects are independent of the disturbances ε_{it}. Then we can write $\alpha_i = \alpha + \eta_i$ with $\eta_i \sim \text{IID}(0, \sigma_\alpha^2)$, and

$$y_{it} = \alpha + x_{it}'\gamma + \omega_{it}, \quad \omega_{it} = \varepsilon_{it} + \eta_i.$$

This is called the panel model with *random effects*. As before, the $(k-1) \times 1$ vector of regressors x_{it} excludes the constant term. In this model the regressors x_{it} may contain variables that are constant over the observed time interval but vary between units, such as the sex and living area of consumers or the location and management style of firms. The above model has k regression parameters, as compared to $(k + m - 1)$ in the panel model with fixed effects. If the number of units is large, this leads to a considerable reduction in the number of parameters. However, compared to the fixed effects model, the disturbances ω_{it} are more complex, as (within units) they are correlated over time. Under the above assumptions there holds

$$E[\omega_{it}] = 0, \quad E[\omega_{it}^2] = \sigma^2 + \sigma_\alpha^2, \quad E[\omega_{it}\omega_{is}] = \sigma_\alpha^2 \quad (\text{for } t \neq s),$$
$$E[\omega_{it}\omega_{js}] = 0 \quad (\text{for all } t, s, \text{ and } i \neq j).$$

Random effects FGLS estimation by numerically efficient methods

T

The parameters (α and γ) in the random effects model can be estimated consistently by OLS. However, the OLS estimators are not efficient and the usual OLS formulas for the standard errors are not valid, because of the cross correlations between the disturbances for the same unit at different moments of time. Efficient estimates can be obtained by two-step FGLS. The general FGLS method was discussed in the previous section. Note, however, that the $mn \times mn$ covariance matrix Ω of the disturbances ω_{it} in the random effects model contains many zero elements and that Ω depends on only two parameters, σ^2 and σ_α^2. This simple structure of Ω can be exploited to compute the estimates in a numerically efficient way. We will illustrate this by considering the first step of the FGLS method in more detail. That is, we describe a simple method to estimate the two variance parameters σ^2 and σ_α^2. Once these two parameters are estimated, the second step of FGLS can also be performed in a straightforward way, but we do not present the computational details of this second step.

The unit-specific disturbance η_i is fixed for unit i, so it can be removed by taking the observations in the ith unit in deviation from the sample mean in this unit. This leads to the following relation between the de-meaned variables:

$$y_{it} - \overline{y}_i = (x_{it} - \overline{x}_i)'\gamma + (\varepsilon_{it} - \overline{\varepsilon}_i).$$

We can estimate this model by OLS, using in total mn de-meaned observations. For each unit, one degree of freedom is lost as the n de-meaned observations of the ith unit add up to zero. Let $\hat{\gamma}$ be the OLS estimator of γ obtained from the mn de-meaned data; then the variance σ^2 of the disturbances ε_{it} can be estimated by

$$\hat{\sigma}^2 = \frac{1}{m(n-1)}\sum_{i=1}^{m}\sum_{t=1}^{n}(y_{it} - \overline{y}_i - (x_{it} - \overline{x}_i)'\hat{\gamma})^2.$$

Next, to estimate the variance σ_α^2 between units, we consider the averages per unit so that

$$\overline{y}_i = \alpha + \overline{x}_i'\gamma + \overline{\varepsilon}_i + \eta_i, \qquad i = 1, \cdots, m.$$

The error terms of this equation have (between-units) variance $\sigma_B^2 = \mathrm{var}(\overline{\varepsilon}_i + \eta_i) = \frac{1}{n}\sigma^2 + \sigma_\alpha^2$. Let $\hat{\sigma}_B^2 = \frac{1}{m-k}\sum_{i=1}^{m}(\overline{y}_i - \hat{\alpha} - \overline{x}_i'\hat{\gamma})^2$ be the estimated variance in the above equation. Then the variance $\sigma_\alpha^2 = \sigma_B^2 - \frac{1}{n}\sigma^2$ can be estimated by

$$\hat{\sigma}_\alpha^2 = \hat{\sigma}_B^2 - \frac{1}{n}\hat{\sigma}^2.$$

The above estimates of σ^2 and σ_α^2 can be substituted in the covariance matrix Ω and used in the second step of FGLS to get efficient estimates of the parameters α and γ.

Comments on panel models

Panel data sets are becoming increasingly popular in many fields of business and economics. In this way, both common and individual characteristics of individuals (in marketing), of firms (in finance), and of countries (in international economics) can be measured and incorporated in one model.

The above panel models can be extended in several ways. For instance, time-specific effects that are the same for all units can be modelled by including n time dummies in the regression model. All the usual diagnostic tests discussed before are of equal importance in panel data models. Tests for exogeneity, heteroskedasticity, correlation, lagged effects, unit roots, and so on, can be performed in panel data models. The required methods and computations can often be simplified by exploiting the special structure of the panel models. Of special interest are possible selection effects, discussed in Section 6.3.3 (p. 500–4). In the random effects model it is assumed that the units that are present in the observed panel are randomly selected, but this is often not the case. For instance, firms that go bankrupt or individuals that stop buying a certain product fall out of the panel, and this selection may very well be endogenous. The models discussed in Section 6.3.3 can be extended to deal with selection effects in panel data.

Example 7.30: **Primary Metal Industries (continued)**

E

XM729PMI

We continue our analysis of the production data of $m = 26$ firms over $n = 37$ years, introduced in Example 7.29 in the foregoing section. We will discuss (i) the panel model with fixed effects, (ii) the panel model with random effects, (iii) the results of OLS on a restricted model, and (iv) comments on the obtained results.

(i) **Panel model with fixed effects**

We assume that the labour elasticity (β) and the capital elasticity (γ) are constant across firms. Then the panel data model with fixed firm effects becomes

$$\log(y_{it}) = \alpha_i + \beta \log(L_{it}) + \gamma \log(K_{it}) + \varepsilon_{it}.$$

Here α_i can be interpreted as a measure of production efficiency of firm i, because the larger it is the more the firm produces for given input levels of labour and capital. The estimated parameters of this panel model are shown in Panel 1 of Exhibit 7.36. The estimated labour elasticity is 0.84 (with standard error 0.021) and the estimated capital elasticity is 0.17 (0.020). The constants α_i differ significantly across firms. This is visualized by means of a histogram in Exhibit 7.36 (c), and the F-test for equal constants in Panel 2 has P-value $P = 0.000$.

(ii) **Panel model with random effects**

Next we estimate the panel model with random effects. The corresponding FGLS estimates are reported in Panel 4 of Exhibit 7.36. The estimated elasticity of labour is 0.82 (with standard error 0.019) and that of capital is 0.16 (0.018). These results are very close to the ones obtained in part (i) in the fixed effects model.

(*a*)

Panel 1: Dependent Variable: LOGPROD Method: Panel data model (FIXED EFFECTS) OLS Sample: 1958 1994; Included observations: 37 Number of cross-sections: 26; Total panel (balanced) observations: 962				
Variable	Coefficient	Std. Error	t-Statistic	Prob.
LOGLAB	0.839131	0.021278	39.43618	0.0000
LOGCAP	0.174129	0.020315	8.571613	0.0000
C_1	−0.242098	0.234578	−1.032058	0.3023
C_2	0.013008	0.149059	0.087267	0.9305
C_3	0.103623	0.149092	0.695030	0.4872
C_4	0.080292	0.155827	0.515261	0.6065
C_5	0.099636	0.152249	0.654429	0.5130
C_6	−0.283235	0.186157	−1.521489	0.1285
C_7	−0.331813	0.140583	−2.360265	0.0185
C_8	−0.008232	0.133647	−0.061594	0.9509
C_9	−0.187380	0.161702	−1.158795	0.2468
C_10	0.294013	0.153477	1.915677	0.0557
C_11	0.237625	0.115523	2.056952	0.0400
C_12	−0.086367	0.135793	−0.636019	0.5249
C_13	0.150745	0.177403	0.849735	0.3957
C_14	0.254307	0.141531	1.796823	0.0727
C_15	0.272252	0.150234	1.812182	0.0703
C_16	0.040844	0.161199	0.253374	0.8000
C_17	−0.138201	0.173634	−0.795935	0.4263
C_18	−0.132822	0.160190	−0.829154	0.4072
C_19	0.059361	0.127754	0.464654	0.6423
C_20	0.229970	0.149753	1.535659	0.1250
C_21	0.221035	0.170087	1.299545	0.1941
C_22	−0.163537	0.159114	−1.027793	0.3043
C_23	−0.045883	0.133522	−0.343636	0.7312
C_24	−0.004967	0.135952	−0.036532	0.9709
C_25	0.111176	0.143650	0.773934	0.4392
C_26	0.176474	0.135686	1.300602	0.1937
R-squared	0.954206			
S.E. of regression	0.247219			

(*b*)

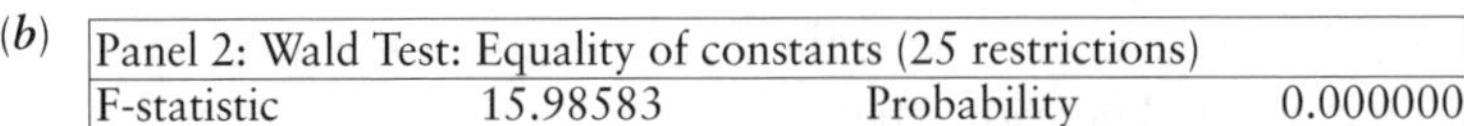

Panel 2: Wald Test: Equality of constants (25 restrictions)			
F-statistic	15.98583	Probability	0.000000

(*c*)

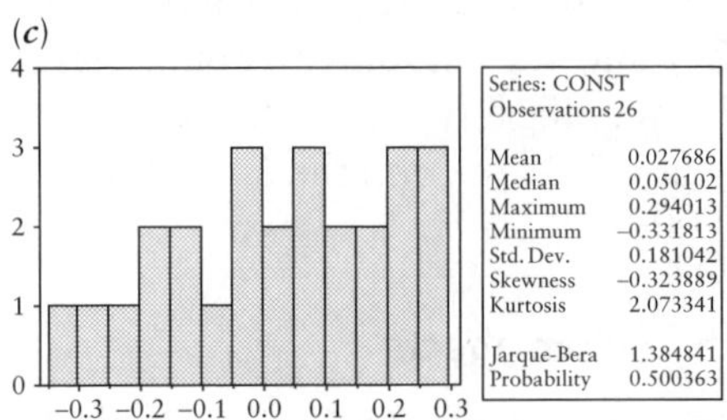

Exhibit 7.36 Primary Metal Industries (Example 7.30)

Estimated production function of twenty-six firms in panel data model with fixed effects (Panel 1, the constants α_i are denoted by C_i), *F*-test on equality of the twenty-six firm-specific constants (Panel 2), and histogram of these twenty-six constants (*c*).

(*d*)

Panel 4: Dependent Variable: LOGPROD Method: Panel data model (RANDOM EFFECTS) FGLS Sample: 1958 1994; Included observations: 37 Number of cross-sections: 26; Total panel (balanced) observations: 962				
Variable	Coefficient	Std. Error	t-Statistic	Prob.
C	0.133174	0.128244	1.038439	0.2993
LOGLAB	0.818331	0.018680	43.80877	0.0000
LOGCAP	0.162876	0.018043	9.027196	0.0000

(*e*)

Panel 5: Dependent Variable: LOGPROD Method: Pooled Least Squares (all coefficients constant across firms) Sample: 1958 1994; Included observations: 37 Number of cross-sections: 26; Total panel (balanced) observations: 962				
Variable	Coefficient	Std. Error	t-Statistic	Prob.
C	0.036817	0.094349	0.390220	0.6965
LOGLAB	0.764332	0.015065	50.73630	0.0000
LOGCAP	0.184513	0.014828	12.44331	0.0000

(*f*)

Panel 6: Dependent Variable: LOGPROD OLS; Sample: 1958 1958; Number of cross-sections: 26; Total obs: 26				
Variable	Coefficient	Std. Error	t-Statistic	Prob.
C	0.214441	0.341991	0.627037	0.5368
LOGLAB	0.804157	0.070529	11.40184	0.0000
LOGCAP	0.136557	0.058223	2.345402	0.0280

(*g*)

Panel 7: Dependent Variable: LOGPROD OLS; Sample: 1994 1994; Number of cross-sections: 26; Total obs: 26				
Variable	Coefficient	Std. Error	t-Statistic	Prob.
C	−0.159270	0.825574	−0.192920	0.8487
LOGLAB	0.730405	0.097399	7.499110	0.0000
LOGCAP	0.241949	0.120829	2.002401	0.0572

Exhibit 7.36 (*Contd.*)

Estimated production function of twenty-six firms in panel data model with random effects (FGLS, Panel 4), OLS estimates in panel model with all coefficients (including the constant term) fixed across firms for the full data period (Panel 5), for the first year (1958, Panel 6), and for the last year in the sample (1994, Panel 7).

(iii) Results of OLS on a restricted model

Next we impose the restriction that all firms are equally efficient, so that α_i is constant across firms. The corresponding OLS estimates (with $mn = 962$ observations) are given in Panel 5 of Exhibit 7.36. The elasticity of labour is estimated as 0.76 (with standard error 0.015), that of capital as 0.18 (standard error 0.015). Panels 6 and 7 of Exhibit 7.36 show the results of cross section regressions for the first year 1958 and for the last year 1994 in the sample (both with $m = 26$ observations). The results do not show large variations in the estimated elasticities for different years. In all cases, the labour elasticity is much larger than the capital elasticity.

(iv) Comments on the obtained results

The above results remain basically the same if trends are incorporated in the model. Note that simpler models—that is, models with less parameters—give more significant estimates (higher t-values) of the labour and capital elasticities. For the OLS model with all parameters fixed across firms the t-values are (50.7, 12.4), for the random effects model (43.8, 9.0), and for the fixed effects model (39.4, 8.6), whereas for the SUR model in Example 7.29 the averages of the t-values over the twenty-six firms are (21.9, 4.6). Smaller models often have larger t-values, because the use of less parameters provides a gain in degrees of freedom. However, the required parameter restrictions are not so much supported by the data. For instance, in Example 7.29 the elasticities vary considerably across firms, so that the panel data model is not supported. And the constants in the fixed effects panel model differ significantly, so that the regression model with fixed parameters (α, β, γ) involves unrealistic restrictions. For these data, the SUR model is most appropriate to model the differences between firms. Both panel models (with fixed or random effects) give a useful description of the average structure of production in primary metal industries and of possible differences in efficiency between firms.

☞ Exercises: E: 7.25c–f.

7.7.4 Simultaneous equation model

Model formulation

Historically, the first type of multiple equation models that was developed within econometrics is the *simultaneous equation model* (SEM). This model has the same structure as the SUR model $y_{it} = \alpha_i + x'_{it}\gamma_i + \varepsilon_{it}$, but the crucial difference is that in the equation for y_{it} some of the regressors x_{it} consist of endogenous variables y_{jt}, $j \neq i$. We split the set of all variables that appear in the m equations into two groups, the group of m endogenous variables y_{jt} and a group of k exogenous variables z_{jt} (including the constant term). Then the equations can be written as

$$y_{it} = \sum_{j \neq i} \gamma_{ij} y_{jt} + \sum_{j=1}^{k} \beta_{ij} z_{jt} + \varepsilon_{it}, \qquad i = 1, \cdots, m, \ t = 1, \cdots, n.$$

This model contains an equation for each of the m endogenous variables. If all the coefficients γ_{ij} are zero, then the model reduces to the SUR model. The model is called simultaneous if $\gamma_{ij} \neq 0$ for some $j \neq i$, because in this case y_{it} depends on the endogenous variable y_{jt} that itself is explained by another equation in the model. In particular, if for some $j \neq i$ both $\gamma_{ij} \neq 0$ and $\gamma_{ji} \neq 0$, then y_{it} and y_{jt} depend on each other simultaneously.

Inconsistency of OLS

Because the equations of the SEM contain endogenous regressors, OLS is not consistent. This was analysed for single equation regression models in Section 5.7. To illustrate this for the SEM, we consider the model with $m = 2$ equations where $\gamma_{12} \neq 0$ and $\gamma_{21} \neq 0$. The model equations are

$$y_{1t} = \gamma_{12} y_{2t} + \sum_{j=1}^{k} \beta_{1j} z_{jt} + \varepsilon_{1t},$$

$$y_{2t} = \gamma_{21} y_{1t} + \sum_{j=1}^{k} \beta_{2j} z_{jt} + \varepsilon_{2t}.$$

The regressor y_{2t} in the first equation is endogenous (that is, it is correlated with the error term ε_{1t}), as it depends on y_{1t} and hence on ε_{1t} because of the second equation. OLS is inconsistent because y_{1t} and y_{2t} depend on each other simultaneously.

Historically, SEM are mostly used for yearly macroeconomic data where variables like national income, consumption, imports, and exports depend mutually on each other. Before we discuss the general simultaneous equation model further, we first consider a simple simulation example to illustrate the main ideas.

Example 7.31: Simulated Macroeconomic Consumption and Income

E

We simulate data from a simple macroeconomic model that consists of two equations, a consumption equation and an income equation. We will discuss (i) the model and the parameter of interest, (ii) an analysis of the OLS bias, (iii) the simulated data, (iv) the results of OLS and IV, and (v) a graphical interpretation.

(i) The model and the parameter of interest

The variables are consumption (denoted by C_t), disposable income (denoted by D_t), and government expenditures (denoted by G_t), and the model is

$$\text{consumption equation:} \quad C_t = \alpha + \beta D_t + \varepsilon_{1t},$$

$$\text{income equation:} \quad D_t = C_t + G_t + \varepsilon_{2t}.$$

Here the government expenditures are assumed to be exogenous (that is, independent of ε_{1t} and ε_{2t}), and the (endogenous) dependent variables are consumption and income. The error terms ε_{1t} and ε_{2t} are mutually independent. The parameter of interest in this simple Keynesean model is the *multiplier*—that is, the average effect of government expenditures on income. To determine this effect, we substitute the first equation in the second one and solve for D_t, with the result that

$$D_t = \frac{\alpha}{1-\beta} + \frac{1}{1-\beta} G_t + \frac{\varepsilon_{1t} + \varepsilon_{2t}}{1-\beta}. \qquad (7.42)$$

So the multiplier is equal to $\frac{1}{1-\beta}$.

(ii) Analysis of the OLS bias

The multiplier can be obtained by estimating the marginal effect β of income on consumption. If we would neglect the income equation and estimate β simply by applying OLS to the consumption equation, then the resulting estimator is not consistent. The reason is that the regressor D_t in the consumption equation is not exogenous. This follows from (7.42), which shows that D_t is correlated with the error term ε_{1t}. The (asymptotic) bias of OLS—that is, $\text{plim}(b) - \beta$—follows from

$$\begin{aligned}\text{plim}(b) &= \text{plim}\left(\frac{\sum (D_t - \overline{D})(C_t - \overline{C})}{\sum (D_t - \overline{D})^2}\right) = \beta + \text{plim}\left(\frac{\frac{1}{n}\sum (D_t - \overline{D})(\varepsilon_{1t} - \overline{\varepsilon}_1)}{\frac{1}{n}\sum (D_t - \overline{D})^2}\right) \\ &= \beta + \frac{\text{cov}(D_t, \varepsilon_{1t})}{\text{var}(D_t)}.\end{aligned}$$

Let σ_1^2 be the variance of ε_{1t}, σ_2^2 that of ε_{2t}, and σ_G^2 that of G_t. Since $\text{cov}(G_t, \varepsilon_{1t}) = 0$ by assumption, as G_t is exogenous, and since ε_{1t} and ε_{2t} are assumed to be independent, it follows from (7.42) that $\text{cov}(D_t, \varepsilon_{1t}) = \sigma_1^2/(1-\beta)$ and $\text{var}(D_t) = (\sigma_G^2 + \sigma_1^2 + \sigma_2^2)/(1-\beta)^2$. We conclude that

$$\text{plim}(b) = \beta + \frac{(1-\beta)\sigma_1^2}{\sigma_G^2 + \sigma_1^2 + \sigma_2^2}.$$

So the inconsistency of OLS is relatively small if σ_G^2 is large compared to σ_1^2—that is, if the systematic variation (due to the variable G_t) is large compared to the random variation ε_{1t} in the consumption function.

(iii) Simulated data

We simulate $n = 100$ observations from this model, as follows. As parameter values we take $\alpha = 0$ and $\beta = 0.5$, so that the multiplier $\frac{1}{1-\beta} = 2$. The error

(*a*)

Panel 1: Dependent Variable: CONS Method: Least Squares Included observations: 100				
Variable	Coefficient	Std. Error	t-Statistic	Prob.
C	−3.041052	0.417545	−7.283168	0.0000
INC	0.656743	0.021417	30.66457	0.0000

(*b*)

Panel 2: Dependent Variable: CONS Method: Instrumental Variables Included observations: 100 Instrument list: C GOV				
Variable	Coefficient	Std. Error	t-Statistic	Prob.
C	−0.136355	1.018765	−0.133843	0.8938
INC	0.505148	0.052938	9.542177	0.0000

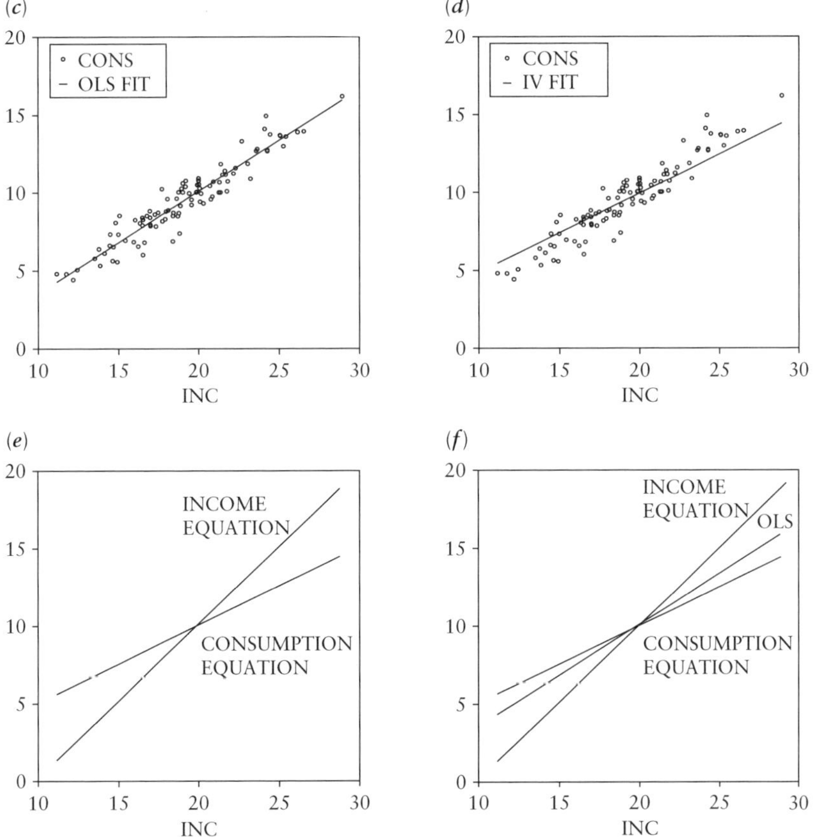

Exhibit 7.37 **Simulated Macroeconomic Consumption and Income (Example 7.31)**

Results of simulated consumption and income data in a simultaneous equation model, OLS estimate of the consumption function (Panel 1) and IV estimate (Panel 2); ((*c*)–(*d*)) show scatter diagrams of the consumption and income data and the lines fitted by OLS (*c*) and IV (*d*); ((*e*)–(*f*)) show the two DGP relations (*e*) and these relations together with the estimated OLS line (*f*).

terms ε_{1t} and ε_{2t} are independently drawn from the standard normal distribution, and G_t is independent from ε_{1t} and ε_{2t} and drawn from the normal distribution with mean 10 and variance 1. Then D_t is obtained from (7.42), and finally C_t is obtained from the consumption equation. As $\beta = 0.5$ and $\sigma_1^2 = \sigma_2^2 = \sigma_G^2 = 1$, it follows from (ii) above that $\text{plim}(b) = 0.5 + (0.5/3) = 0.67$. That is, if we estimate β by OLS, we can expect to find a multiplier $1/(1 - b)$ of around 3, whereas the actual multiplier is only 2. So OLS greatly overestimates the effects of government spending on income.

(iv) Results of OLS and IV

Panel 1 of Exhibit 7.37 shows the results of OLS for the simulated data. The estimated value of β is $b = 0.657$ with corresponding multiplier $1/(1 - b) = 2.9$. As was discussed in Section 5.7.2 (p. 404–5), consistent estimators can be obtained by the method of instrumental variables. As the consumption equation contains two parameters (α and β), we need two instruments. Since the government expenditures are assumed to be exogenous, we can take G_t and the constant term as instruments. The corresponding two-stage least squares estimates are shown in Panel 2 of Exhibit 7.37. The IV estimate of β is $b_{IV} = 0.505$ with multiplier $1/(1 - b_{IV}) = 2.0$, so that these estimates are much more reliable than OLS.

(v) Graphical interpretation

Exhibit 7.37 (*c*) and (*d*) show the scatter diagrams of the simulated consumption and income data, together with the fitted OLS and IV lines. Clearly, the IV line fits the scatter less nicely than the OLS line. However, the location of the points (C_t, D_t) in the scatter is determined not only by the consumption equation, but also by the income equation. Exhibit 7.37 (*e*) shows the two equations that result for $\varepsilon_1 = 0$, $\varepsilon_2 = 0$ and $G_t = 10$—that is, by substituting the mean values of these random variables in the two model equations. In our simulation example, these relations become $C_t = \alpha + \beta D_t = 0.5 D_t$ for the consumption equation, and $D_t = C_t + 10$ or equivalently $C_t = D_t - 10$ for the income equation. The data (C_t, D_t) satisfy both these equations (apart from random variations in ε_{1t}, ε_{2t} and G_t). The first equation has slope 0.5, but the second equation has slope 1. As OLS tries to find the line closest to the scatter, the resulting OLS line has a slope somewhere between 0.5 and 1. This is illustrated in Exhibit 7.37 (*f*).

Estimation by 2SLS and the order condition

Now we return to the general simultaneous equation model. In Section 5.7.1 (p. 398–400) we described the method of instrumental variables to get consistent estimators of the parameters of an equation with endogenous regressors. In an SEM this method can be applied per equation with the exogenous variables z_{jt} as instruments. This is called the *two-stage least squares* (2SLS) method. For each equation $i = 1, \cdots, m$, the parameters of that equation are estimated by the following two steps.

Estimation of simultaneous equation model by 2SLS

- *Step 1: Regress the endogenous regressors on the exogenous ones.* For each of the regressors y_{jt} that appear in the model equation (that is, for which $\gamma_{ij} \neq 0$), perform a regression of y_{jt} on the set of all k exogenous variables $(z_{jt}, j = 1, \cdots, k)$. Let $\hat{y}_{jt}$ be the fitted values of these regressions.
- *Step 2: Regress y_{it} on $\hat{y}_{jt}$ and z_{jt}.* In the equation for y_{it}, replace the regressors y_{jt} by the fitted values of step 1 and estimate the parameters by OLS in the equation $y_{it} = \sum_{j \neq i} \gamma_{ij} \hat{y}_{jt} + \sum_{j=1}^{k} \beta_{ij} z_{jt} + \varepsilon_{it}$, $t = 1, \cdots, n$.

As was discussed in Section 5.7.1, this method requires that the number of instrumental variables that do not appear in the equation is at least as large as the number of endogenous regressors in the equation—the so-called *order condition*. Let m_i be the number of endogenous regressors y_{jt} $(j \neq i)$ and let k_i be the number of exogenous regressors z_{jt} that appear on the right-hand side of the equation for y_{it}. Then the order condition is that

$$k - k_i \geq m_i.$$

Equivalently, the condition is that $(k - k_i) + (m - m_i - 1) \geq (m - 1)$, where $(k - k_i)$ is the number of exogenous variables and $(m - m_i - 1)$ is the number of endogenous variables that do not appear in the ith equation. In words, the order condition means that the total number of excluded variables from the ith equation should be at least $(m - 1)$. That is, for every equation at least $(m - 1)$ of the $(m - 1 + k)$ parameters appearing on the right-hand side of that equation should be set equal to zero. Such restrictions are called *exclusion restrictions* or *identification restrictions*. The restrictions should be based on economic theory.

Estimation by 3SLS

T

The 2SLS method is a single equation method that neglects the possible contemporaneous covariances $\sigma_{ij} = E[\varepsilon_{it}\varepsilon_{jt}]$ between the error terms ε_{it} and ε_{jt}. Therefore the 2SLS estimators are consistent but not (asymptotically) efficient. In the SEM, the error terms ε_{it} are assumed to be uncorrelated over time but possibly contemporaneously correlated across the m equations. The SEM then has the same structure as the SUR model (7.41) of Section 7.7.2, with the difference that some of the regressors are endogenous. The cross equation correlations can be treated in a similar way to that discussed in Section 7.7.2 for the SUR model, by applying two-step FGLS to the system of equations. This leads to the following system method for the joint estimation of the parameters of all m model equations.

Estimation of simultaneous equation model by 3SLS

- *Steps 1 and 2: Apply 2SLS.* Apply 2SLS to each of the m equations separately. Estimate the $mn \times mn$ covariance matrix of the system, as described in step 1 of the two-step FGLS estimator for SUR models in Section 7.7.2.
- *Step 3: Apply GLS to the system of equations.* Apply step 2 of the two-step FGLS estimator for SUR models in Section 7.7.2.

This is called the *three-stage least squares* (3SLS) method. This method is asymptotically efficient, as it is equivalent to ML (if the error terms are jointly normally distributed, as discussed in Section 7.7.2). Note that the 3SLS method uses the $\frac{1}{2}m(m+1)$ estimated cross covariances s_{ij} that are based on the 2SLS residual series of length n. If the sample size n is not so large, then these covariances may not be estimated very reliably. Therefore in practice, when the available sample size is not so large, one often uses 2SLS. The 2SLS method also has the advantage that the estimator for the ith equation remains consistent if another equation $j \neq i$ is not correctly specified. On the other hand, 3SLS uses all m equations to estimate the ith equation, and, if one equation is wrongly specified, then in general all parameters are estimated inconsistently. Summarizing, 3SLS is a good method if one has enough confidence in the specification of all the model equations and if sufficiently long time series of the variables are available. Otherwise 2SLS is preferred.

Dynamic simultaneous models

In some cases the SEM equations contain not only endogenous variables y_{jt} $(j \neq i)$ and exogenous variables z_{jt} as regressors, but also lagged values of y_{jt} $(j = 1, \ldots, m)$. This is called a dynamic simultaneous equation model. The lagged endogenous variables $y_{j,t-k}$ (with $k \geq 1$) are (contemporaneously) uncorrelated with the disturbance terms ε_{it} so that they provide proper instruments. The 2SLS estimates can be computed as before, taking as instruments all exogenous and all lagged endogenous variables. A dynamic SEM can also be written as follows, where we bring all current and lagged endogenous variables to the left-hand side of the equations:

$$\Phi(L)Y_t = Bz_t + \varepsilon_t, \quad \Phi(L) = \Gamma - \sum_{j=1}^{p} \Phi_j L^j,$$

where the $m \times m$ matrix Γ has elements 1 on the diagonal and elements $-\gamma_{ij}$ for $i \neq j$ (the sign changes because the current endogenous variables are shifted from the right-hand side to the left-hand side of the equations). This is a VAR model with m endogenous variables $Y_t = (y_{1t}, \ldots, y_{mt})'$ and with k exogenous variables $z_t = (z_{1t}, \ldots, z_{kt})'$. The only distinction is that in the standard VAR model the polynomial matrix $\Phi(L)$ is of the form

$\Phi(L) = I - \sum_{j=1}^{p} \Phi_j L^j$, whereas in the SEM the identity matrix is replaced by the unknown invertible $m \times m$ matrix Γ, which contains the parameters γ_{ij}, $j \neq i$. A standard VAR model is obtained if the matrix equations are premultiplied by the inverse of the matrix Γ. After this transformation, the resulting VAR model can be estimated as described in Sections 7.6.2 and 7.6.3. However, in case one is interested in the parameters γ_{ij}, then 2SLS provides more information, since the matrix Γ is lost in the transformed VAR model.

Example 7.32: **Interest and Bond Rates (continued)**

We continue our previous analysis of the changes in the AAA bond rate Δy_t and in the three-month Treasury Bill rate Δx_t. In Example 7.26 we considered a VAR model for these stationary data. Now we will discuss (i) the motivation of a simultaneous model for these data, (ii) estimation by 2SLS, and (iii) interpretation of the outcomes.

(i) Motivation of a simultaneous model

In Chapter 5 we considered the equation $\Delta y_t = \alpha + \beta \Delta x_t + \varepsilon_t$. We concluded that the residuals of this equation are serially correlated (see Example 5.22 (p. 365)) and that the regressor Δx_t is endogenous (see Example 5.33 (p. 414–16)). We add lagged variables to account for the serial correlation and we add an equation for Δx_t to account for the endogeneity of this variable. We consider the following dynamic SEM, which contains a constant and lagged endogenous variables (but no other exogenous variables) as explanatory variables:

$$\Delta y_t = \alpha_1 + \gamma_{12}\Delta x_t + \beta_{11}\Delta y_{t-1} + \beta_{12}\Delta x_{t-1} + \varepsilon_{1t},$$
$$\Delta x_t = \alpha_2 + \gamma_{21}\Delta y_t + \beta_{21}\Delta y_{t-1} + \beta_{22}\Delta x_{t-1} + \varepsilon_{2t}.$$

(ii) Estimation by 2SLS

We estimate the above equations by OLS (as would be appropriate if the two ADL equations would not be simultaneous) and by 2SLS, using the data over the period from January 1990 to December 1999 (so that $n = 120$). Both equations contain four parameters, and in 2SLS we use five instruments (the constant and Δy_{t-1}, Δy_{t-2}, Δx_{t-1}, and Δx_{t-2}). The results are in Exhibit 7.38. The OLS estimates of γ_{12} (in Panel 1) and γ_{21} (in Panel 3) suggest significant contemporaneous effects between Δx_t and Δy_t (the t-value is 4.08). However, if this is the case, then the OLS estimators are biased and the OLS standard errors are wrong. So the results of OLS cannot be trusted. On the other hand, the 2SLS estimates show that the contemporaneous effects are not at all significant ($\hat{\gamma}_{12}$ has $t = -0.03$ in Panel 2 and $\hat{\gamma}_{21}$ has $t = -0.08$ in Panel 4). Therefore the matrix Γ is diagonal, so that the model reduces to a VAR model. In Example 7.26 we estimated VAR models for these data (see Panels 2–4 of Exhibit 7.30).

(iii) Interpretation of the outcomes

The result of this example is illustrative for many applications. The mutual dependence between variables can often be modelled well in terms of a VAR, where each variable depends on the past of all other variables but not on the

Panel 1: Dependent Variable: DAAA
Method: Least Squares
Sample: 1990:01 1999:12; Included observations: 120

Variable		Coefficient	Std. Error	t-Statistic	Prob.
C		−0.003077	0.013533	−0.227360	0.8205
DUS3MT	$\hat{\gamma}_{12} =$	0.330442	0.080906	4.084257	0.0001
DUS3MT(−1)		−0.126609	0.084199	−1.503688	0.1354
DAAA(−1)		0.307879	0.090652	3.396253	0.0009

Panel 2: Dependent Variable: DAAA
Method: Two-Stage Least Squares
Sample: 1990:01 1999:12; Included observations: 120
Instrument list: C DAAA(−1) DAAA(−2) DUS3MT(−1) DUS3MT(−2)

Variable		Coefficient	Std. Error	t-Statistic	Prob.
C		−0.006983	0.015690	−0.445016	0.6571
DUS3MT	$\hat{\gamma}_{12} =$	−0.013614	0.524615	−0.025951	0.9793
DUS3MT (−1)		−0.033164	0.167148	−0.198409	0.8431
DAAA(−1)		0.385929	0.152556	2.529756	0.0128

Panel 3: Dependent Variable: DUS3MT
Method: Least Squares
Sample: 1990:01 1999:12; Included observations: 120

Variable		Coefficient	Std. Error	t-Statistic	Prob.
C		−0.008754	0.014502	−0.603618	0.5473
DAAA	$\hat{\gamma}_{21} =$	0.380471	0.093156	4.084257	0.0001
DAAA(−1)		0.081194	0.101716	0.798248	0.4264
DUS3MT(−1)		0.285623	0.087285	3.272314	0.0014

Panel 4: Dependent Variable: DUS3MT
Method: Two-Stage Least Squares
Sample: 1990:01 1999:12; Included observations: 120
Instrument list: C DAAA(−1) DAAA(−2) DUS3MT(−1) DUS3MT(−2)

Variable		Coefficient	Std. Error	t-Statistic	Prob.
C		−0.012350	0.021047	−0.586807	0.5585
DAAA	$\hat{\gamma}_{21} =$	−0.146298	1.938574	−0.075467	0.9400
DAAA(−1)		0.282863	0.749923	0.377190	0.7067
DUS3MT(−1)		0.266205	0.121696	2.187460	0.0307

Exhibit 7.38 Interest and Bond Rates (Example 7.32)

Two estimates of the equation that explains the changes in the AAA bond rate in terms of the changes in the three-month Treasury Bill rate and lagged values (OLS in Panel 1, 2SLS in Panel 2), and two estimates of the equation that explains the changes in the three-month Treasury Bill rate in terms of the changes in the AAA bond rate and lagged values (OLS in Panel 3, 2SLS in Panel 4).

present values of these variables. An advantage of VAR models is that they do not need the exclusion restrictions that are required in an SEM to satisfy the order condition for each equation. However, for models with a large number of endogenous variables, a VAR is not feasible anymore, as it contains too many parameters. In such situations a dynamic SEM may be preferred, provided that one can specify credible exclusion restrictions.

☞ **Exercises:** T: 7.11; E: 7.26.

7.7.5 Summary

In this section we have considered econometric models for data sets that consist of combined cross sections of time series variables.

- In SUR models, the effects of the explanatory variables on the dependent variable are different for all units. The relation between different units is modelled by the contemporaneous correlation between the error terms. This model requires that the number of units in the data set does not exceed the length of the observed time series per unit.
- Panel models are used for data sets with a large number of units. The effect of explanatory variables is the same across all units, and the differences between units are modelled by the constant term. In the fixed effects model each unit has its own parameter for the constant term; in the random effects model these parameters are supposed to be drawn from an underlying population.
- The simultaneous equation model consists of a set of equations for a number of endogenous variables that influence each other simultaneously. Estimation requires that the equations are identified in the sense that each equation excludes a sufficient number of variables.
- Apart from differences in the regression equations, the above models are each characterized by special structures of the covariance matrix of the error terms. A general estimation method for models with such covariance structures is (F)GLS. The actual computations can be simplified by exploiting the specific error structure of SUR models, panel models, and simultaneous equation models.

Summary, further reading, and keywords

SUMMARY

In this chapter we discussed the modelling of time series data. Many economic time series display trending behaviour and sometimes also seasonal fluctuations and structural breaks. These aspects of the data should be modelled in a proper way to be able to draw reliable conclusions from estimated time series models. In the year 2003, the Nobel prize in economics was awarded to Engle and Granger, two pioneers in the econometric modelling of trends and changing volatility in time series. For univariate time series we discussed methods to model trends, seasonals, parameter variations, and changing volatility. Further we considered the modelling of stationary time series by means of ARMA models. Several of the diagnostic tests of Chapter 5 can be applied to investigate the empirical adequacy of estimated time series models. We also considered time series models with exogenous variables and multiple time series models. The proper modelling of trends is again of crucial importance to obtain reliable results. If the variables contain stochastic trends, then one can estimate a vector autoregressive model for the first differences of the variables, unless they are cointegrated, in which case a vector error correction model is more appropriate. Finally we paid attention to data where the number of variables is large compared to the length of the observation period. We discussed the SUR model and the method of generalized least squares, models for panel data, and simultaneous equation models.

FURTHER READING

For further background on the topics of this chapter we provide some references. The three volumes of the *Handbook of Econometrics* mentioned in Chapter 3, Further Reading, contain chapters on panel data and simultaneous equation models. The fourth volume in this series, edited by Engle and McFadden (1994), contains chapters on many time series topics, including trends and unit roots, VAR models and cointegration, and ARCH models. From the many textbooks on time series we mention Brockwell and Davis (1997), Granger and Newbold (1986),

Franses (1998), Hamilton (1994), and Harvey (1991). A textbook with applications is Patterson (2000), the theory of VAR models is described in Lütkepohl (1991), and cointegration in Johansen (1995). The SUR model, panel data models, and SEM are discussed in most of the econometric textbooks mentioned in Chapter 3, Further Reading (p. 178–9), and Baltagi (1995) deals exclusively with panel data.

Baltagi, B. H. (1995). *Econometric Analysis of Panel Data*. Chichester: Wiley.

Brockwell, P., and Davis, J. (1997). *Time Series Analysis*. Berlin: Springer.

Engle, R. F., and McFadden, D. L. (1994). *Handbook of Econometrics, Volume IV*. Amsterdam: Elsevier.

Franses, P. H. (1998). *Time Series Models for Business and Economic Forecasting*. Cambridge: Cambridge University Press.

Granger, C. W. J., and Newbold, P. (1986). *Forecasting Economic Time Series*. 2nd edn. San Diego: Academic Press.

Hamilton, J. D. (1994). *Time Series Analysis*. Princeton: Princeton University Press.

Harvey, A. C. (1993). *Time Series Models*. 2nd edn. New York: Harvester Wheatsheaf.

Johansen, S. (1995). *Likelihood-Based Inference in Cointegrated Vector Autoregressive Models*. Oxford: Oxford University Press.

Lütkepohl, H. (1991). *Introduction to Multiple Time Series Analysis*. Berlin: Springer.

Patterson, K. (2000). *An Introduction to Applied Econometrics—A Time Series Approach*. New York: Palgrave.

KEYWORDS

Exercises

THEORY QUESTIONS

7.1* (☞ Sections 7.1.2–7.1.4)

a. Let $\varepsilon_t = y_t - E[y_t|Y_{t-1}]$ be the innovations of a stationary process y_t that is jointly normally distributed. Show that the process ε_t can be written as a linear function of the past observations $\{y_{t-k},\ k \geq 0\}$ and that it has mean zero and constant variance. Show that all the autocorrelations ρ_k $(k \neq 0)$ of the process ε_t are zero.

b. Show that an AR(p) process $\phi(L)y_t = \varepsilon_t$ (with ε_t the innovation process) is stationary if and only if all the roots $\phi(z) = 0$ lie outside the unit circle. (This was shown in Section 7.1.3 for $p = 1$; use this result to prove the statement first for order $p = 2$ by the factorization $\phi(z) = (1 - \alpha_1 z)(1 - \alpha_2 z)$, and then repeat this idea for orders $p > 2$.)

c. Prove that an MA(q) process $y_t = \theta(L)\varepsilon_t$ is invertible if and only if all the roots $\theta(z) = 0$ lie outside the unit circle. (This was shown in Section 7.1.4 for $q = 1$; use the factorization idea of **b** to show this for $q > 1$.)

7.2 (☞ Sections 7.1.5, 7.2.2, 7.3.4)

a. Show that the ACF of an MA(1) process with parameter θ is the same as that of an MA(1) process with parameter $1/\theta$. Discuss the relevance of this finding for maximum likelihood estimation of (AR)MA models.

b. Show that in a stationary AR(2) process $y_t = \phi_1 y_{t-1} + \phi_2 y_{t-2} + \varepsilon_t$ there holds that $\phi_2 \neq 1$, that $E[y_{t-k}\varepsilon_t] = 0$ for all $k > 0$, and that $E[y_t\varepsilon_t] = \sigma^2$. Use these results to prove that $\gamma_0 = \phi_1\gamma_1 + \phi_2\gamma_2 + \sigma^2$, $\gamma_1 = \phi_1\gamma_0 + \phi_2\gamma_1$, and $\gamma_k = \phi_1\gamma_{k-1} + \phi_2\gamma_{k-2}$ for $k \geq 2$. Show that the autocorrelations are given by $\rho_1 = \phi_1/(1 - \phi_2)$, $\rho_2 = \phi_1^2/(1 - \phi_2) + \phi_2$, and $\rho_k = \phi_1\rho_{k-1} + \phi_2\rho_{k-2}$ for $k \geq 3$.

c. Derive the first four autocorrelations of the (stationary and invertible) ARMA(1,1) process $y_t = \phi y_{t-1} + \varepsilon_t + \theta\varepsilon_{t-1}$.

d. Derive the ACF of $z_t = \Delta\Delta_4 y_t$ in the 'airline' model $z_t = (1 + \theta_1 L)(1 + \theta_4 L^4)\varepsilon_t$ and show that $\rho_2 = 0$ and that $\rho_3 = \rho_5$. Derive the ACF if $\theta_1 = \theta_4 = -1$.

7.3* (☞ Sections 7.1.5, 7.2.2)

a. If y_t is a stationary process with the property that the autocorrelations cut off (so that $\rho_k = 0$ for $k > q$), then show that y_t can be written as an MA(q) process. (The reverse statement was proven in Section 7.1.5.)

b. Show that a stationary process y_t can be written as an AR(p) process if and only if the partial autocorrelations cut off (so that $\phi_{kk} = 0$ for $k > p$).

c. Show that the regression in (7.12) provides the partial autocorrelations by using the result of Frisch–Waugh of Section 3.2.5.

d. If OLS is applied in an AR(p) model with constant term, then the regressors are given by $x_t' = (1, y_{t-1}, \cdots, y_{t-p})$. Show that, if the process is stationary, the matrix of second order moments $Q_n = \frac{1}{n}\sum_{t=p+1}^{n} x_t x_t'$ converges in probability to a non-singular matrix.

7.4 (☞ Section 7.1.6)

a. Derive formulas for the h-step-ahead forecasts of an AR(1) process $y_t = \alpha + \phi y_{t-1} + \varepsilon_t$ and for the corresponding forecast error variances, in terms of the parameters ϕ, α, and σ^2.

b. Derive formulas for the 3- and 4-step-ahead forecasts and corresponding forecast error variances of an AR(p) process.

c. Derive formulas for the h-step-ahead forecasts and forecast error variances $(h = 1, \cdots, 4)$ of a (stationary and invertible) ARMA(1, 1) process.

7.5 (☞ Sections 7.3.2, 7.3.4)

a. Section 7.3.2 states the formula $\text{SPE}(h) = \sigma^2\sum_{j=1}^{h}\left(\sum_{k=0}^{h-j}\psi_k\right)^2$ for the forecast error variance of an ARIMA(p, 1, q) process y_t in terms of the representation $z_t = \sum_{k=0}^{\infty} \psi_k \varepsilon_{t-k}$ of the stationary series $z_t = (1 - L)y_t$. Prove this result.

b. Show that the out-of-sample h-step-ahead forecasts produced by EWMA are constant, independent of the forecast horizon h.

c. Show that the Holt–Winters model with changing level μ_t and slope α_t can be written as an ARIMA(0, 2, 2) model by eliminating μ_t and α_t. Show that the h-step-ahead forecasts of this model lie on a straight line.

d. Consider the model with changing level μ_t and seasonal s_t defined by $y_t = \mu_t + s_t + \varepsilon_t$, where $\mu_{t+1} = \mu_t + \eta_t$ and $s_{t+1} = -s_t - s_{t-1} - s_{t-2} + \zeta_t$ and where all error terms are independently and normally distributed white noise processes. Show that $\Delta\Delta_4 y_t$ is an MA(5) process. Investigate whether the series y_t can be described by an 'airline' model.

7.6* (☞ Section 7.4.3)

a. Let ε_t follow an ARCH(1) process with conditional variance $\sigma_t^2 = \alpha_0 + \alpha_1 \varepsilon_{t-1}^2$. Show that ε_t has zero mean, that ε_t is a white noise process with (unconditional) variance $\alpha_0/(1 - \alpha_1)$, and that ε_t^2 follows an AR(1) process.

b. Let ε_t follow an ARCH(p) process. Show that ε_t is white noise and that ε_t^2 follows an AR(p) process.

c. Let ε_t follow a GARCH(1, 1) process with conditional variance $\sigma_t^2 = \alpha_0 + \alpha_1 \varepsilon_{t-1}^2 + \alpha_2 \sigma_{t-1}^2$. Show that ε_t is white noise and that ε_t^2 follows an ARMA(1, 1) process.

d. Show that the process ε_t^2 of **c** is stationary if $0 < \alpha_1 + \alpha_2 < 1$ but that it is integrated of order 1 if $\alpha_1 + \alpha_2 = 1$.

7.7* (☞ Sections 7.4.3, 7.4.4)

In this exercise we derive the ARCH LM-test of Section 7.4.4 for the null hypothesis of no ARCH against the alternative of an ARCH(1) process. The model for the observed time series y_t is formulated as $y_t|Y_{t-1} = \sigma_t \eta_t$ where $Y_{t-1} = (y_{t-s},\ s = 1, 2, \cdots)$ (for simplicity of the analysis we assume that this information extends infinitely far in the past), $\sigma_t^2 = \alpha_0 + \alpha_1 y_{t-1}^2$, and η_t is a series of independent variables with the N(0, 1) distribution. It is given that $\alpha_0 > 0$ and $0 < \alpha_1 < 1$. In Exercise 7.6 it was shown that y_t is a white noise process (so that $E[y_t y_{t-k}] = 0$ for all $k \neq 0$) and that y_t^2 is an AR(1) process.

a. Give a simple argument (without calculations) to prove that the process y_t cannot be normally distributed. Next show that the probability distribution of y_t has kurtosis larger than 3.

b. The log-likelihood is given by (7.31) with $\alpha = \phi = 0$. Derive the first and second order derivatives of this function with respect to α_0 and α_1.

c. Use the results in **b** to compute the LM-test for the null hypothesis of conditional homoskedasticity ($\alpha_1 = 0$) by means of the general formula (4.54) in Section 4.3.6 for the LM-test.

d. Show that this test can be computed as $LM = nR^2$ of the regression of y_t^2 on a constant and y_{t-1}^2.

e. Prove the validity of the following method for the ARCH LM-test for the error terms in the regression model $y_t = x_t'\beta + \varepsilon_t$. First regress y_t on x_t with residuals e_t, then regress e_t^2 on a constant and e_{t-1}^2 and let $LM = nR^2$ of this regression. (It may be helpful to prove first that the information matrix for the parameters $(\alpha_0,\ \alpha_1,\ \beta')'$, evaluated at the restricted ML estimates, is block-diagonal.)

f. Let $y_t = x_t'\beta + \varepsilon_t$, where ε_t follows an ARCH(1) process. Use the previous results to show that OLS is the best linear unbiased estimator of β but that it is not (asymptotically) efficient.

7.8 (☞ Section 7.4.4)

Consider the so-called bilinear process $y_t = \frac{1}{2}\varepsilon_{t-1} y_{t-2} + \varepsilon_t$, where ε_t are independent drawings from N(0, σ^2). As starting conditions are given $\varepsilon_0 = 0$ and $y_{-1} = y_0 = 0$.

a. Prove that y_t is an uncorrelated process. Is it also a white noise process?

b. Prove that y_t^2 is not an uncorrelated process.

c. Prove that y_t cannot be forecasted by linear functions of past observations y_{t-k} ($k \geq 1$) but that it can be forecasted by non-linear functions of these past observations.

d. Simulate $n = 200$ data from this process. Perform a Ljung–Box test and an ARCH test on the resulting time series. What is the relevance of this result for the interpretation of ARCH tests?

7.9 (☞ Sections 7.5.1, 7.6.1)

a. Rewrite the ADL model (7.32) (with $\theta_k = 0$ for all k) in error correction form (7.34). It is helpful to consider the AR polynomial $\phi(z) = 1 - \sum_{k=1}^{p} \phi_k z^k$ and to prove that $\phi(z) - \phi(1)z = (1 - z)\phi^*(z)$, where $\phi^*(z)$ is a polynomial of degree $p-1$ with $\phi^*(0)=1$.

b. Show that the coefficient $-\phi(1)$ of the 'error' $(y_{t-1}-\lambda x_{t-1}-\delta)$ in (7.34) is negative if the AR polynomial $\phi(z)$ is stationary (has all its roots outside the unit circle). Discuss why this is needed for error 'correction'.

c. In Section 7.6.1 we derived the general VECM (7.38). Compute this representation explicitly for a VAR(2) model.

d. Explain that stationarity of the VAR polynomial matrix $\Phi(z)$ corresponds to correction in the direction of equilibrium in the sense that deviations $(Y_{t-1}-\mu)\neq 0$ in (7.38) die out in the long run. Give an explicit proof of this fact for the VECM (7.38) with $p=1$ (so that the terms $\Gamma_j\Delta Y_{t-j}$ drop out of this equation).

7.10 (☞ Sections 7.6.2, 7.7.2)

a. Prove that GLS in the SUR model (7.41) with $\sigma_{ij}=0$ for all $i\neq j$ (so that Ω is diagonal) boils down to OLS per unit.

b. Prove this also in case Ω is non-diagonal but the regressor matrix $X_i=X$ is constant across all units $i=1,\cdots,m$. For simplicity consider only the case of $m=2$ units.

c. If **a** or **b** holds true, then explain why OLS is more efficient than FGLS for finite samples (and equally efficient asymptotically).

d. Write the VAR(p) model with m variables in terms of the SUR model—that is, with separate equations for each of the m variables y_{it}, $i=1,\cdots,m$, $t=p+1,\cdots,n$, and ordered as in (7.41). What is the structure of the $m(n-p)\times m(n-p)$ covariance matrix of the corresponding $m(n-p)\times 1$ vector of error terms? Explain that ML in the VAR(p) model is equivalent to applying OLS per equation.

7.11 (☞ Section 7.7.4)

Consider the simultaneous equation model

$$y_{1t}=\gamma_{12}y_{2t}+\varepsilon_{1t},$$
$$y_{2t}=\gamma_{21}y_{1t}+\beta_{21}z_{1t}+\beta_{22}z_{2t}+\varepsilon_{2t},$$

where y_{1t} and y_{2t} are endogenous variables and z_{1t} and z_{2t} are exogenous variables. The disturbances ε_{1t} and ε_{2t} are jointly normally distributed with mean zero and 2×2 covariance matrix Ω and they are uncorrelated over time. For $n=100$ observations, the following matrix of sample moments around zero is given (for instance, $\frac{1}{100}\sum_{t=1}^{100}y_{2t}z_{1t}=4$).

Variable	y_1	y_2	z_1	z_2
y_1	10	20	2	3
y_2	20	50	4	8
z_1	2	4	5	5
z_2	3	8	5	10

a. Prove that the first equation of this SEM satisfies the order condition but the second equation not.

b. Compute the 2SLS estimate of γ_{12}.

c. Compute the large sample standard error of this estimate, using formula (5.76) of Section 5.7.2 for the asymptotic distribution of the 2SLS estimator and replacing the error variance $\sigma_{11}=E[\varepsilon_{1t}^2]$ by the estimate $\hat{\sigma}_{11}=\frac{1}{n}\sum_{t=1}^{n}(y_{1t}-\hat{\gamma}_{12}y_{2t})^2$.

EMPIRICAL AND SIMULATION QUESTIONS

7.12 (☞ Sections 7.2.2, 7.3.3)

In this exercise we consider the properties of the OLS estimator $\hat{\phi}$ in the AR(1) model $y_t=\phi y_{t-1}+\varepsilon_t$ (discussed in Section 7.2.2) in some more detail. As a formal statistical analysis is involved, we perform a simulation study with $\phi=0.9$ and $\sigma^2=1$.

a. Generate a sample of length $n=1000$ of this process, with starting condition $y_0=0$ and with ε_t independent drawings from N(0, 1).

b. Compare the sample mean of y_t and of y_t^2 with the theoretical mean and variance of the AR(1) process.

c. Define the process $z_t=y_{t-1}\varepsilon_t$. Test whether there exists significant serial correlation in the process z_t.

d. Repeat the simulation experiment in a 1000 times. For each simulation, compute $\frac{1}{\sqrt{n}}\sum_{t=1}^{n}y_{t-1}\varepsilon_t$ and $\sqrt{n}(\hat{\phi}-\phi)$.

e. Compare the sample distributions of the two statistics in **d** with the distributions $N(0, \sigma^4/(1-\phi^2))$ and $N(0, 1-\phi^2)$ respectively that were mentioned in Section 7.2.2 (see (7.16)).

f. Repeat the 1000 simulations in **d** with $\phi = 1$ instead of $\phi = 0.9$. Compare the sample distributions of the two statistics in **d** with the normal distributions mentioned in **e**. Explain the outcomes.

7.13 (☞ Sections 7.3.1, 7.3.4)

a. Generate a sample of size $n = 400$ from the deterministic trend model $y_t = 1 + t + \varepsilon_t$, where ε_t is normally distributed white noise with mean 0 and variance $\sigma^2 = 2500$. Plot the time series y_t, the correlogram of y_t, and the scatter diagram of y_t against y_{t-1}. Plot also the differenced series Δy_t, the correlogram of Δy_t, and the scatter diagram of Δy_t against Δy_{t-1}.

b. Generate a sample of size $n = 400$ from the stochastic trend model $y_t = y_{t-1} + \varepsilon_t$, where $y_0 = 0$ and ε_t is normally distributed white noise. Make the same plots (for y_t and for Δy_t) as in **a** and compare the outcomes with those in **a**.

c. Suppose that y_t follows a stationary and invertible ARMA process. Show that the differenced series $x_t = (1 - L)y_t$ follows an ARMA process that is not invertible. Show also that the autocorrelations of x_t have sum $\sum_{k=1}^{\infty} \rho_k = -1/2$.

d. Illustrate the result in **c** by means of a suitable simulation experiment.

7.14 (☞ Sections 7.3.3, 7.4.1)

In this exercise we simulate data from the model $\Delta y_t = \alpha + \rho y_{t-1} + \varepsilon_t$, where $y_0 = 0$ and where ε_t are independent drawings from $N(0, 1)$.

a. Simulate a series of length $n = 100$ from the model with parameters $(\alpha, \rho) = (0, 0)$. Estimate ρ by OLS (including a constant in the equation) and compute the t-value of ρ.

b. Repeat **a** 10,000 times and make histograms of the resulting 10,000 estimates of ρ and of the t-values of ρ. Determine the left 5% quantile of these t-values and compare the outcome with the corresponding critical value in Exhibit 7.16.

c. Repeat **b**, for the DGP with $\alpha = 0.5$ and $\rho = 0$ (so that $\Delta y_t = 0.5 + \varepsilon_t$) and with test equation $\Delta y_t = \alpha + \beta t + \rho y_{t-1} + \varepsilon_t$ (including constant and trend term in the test equation).

d. For each of the 10,000 simulated data sets in **c**, estimate ρ and compute the t-value of ρ by regression in the (wrongly specified) model $\Delta y_t = \rho y_{t-1} + \varepsilon_t$ (that is, excluding both the constant and the trend term in the test equation). Determine the left 5% quantile of the resulting 10,000 t-values. Explain the relation of the outcomes with the possible dangers of misspecification of the Dickey–Fuller test equation.

e. Contaminate the 10,000 series of **b** by a single additive outlier of size 20 at time $t = 50$. How many times does the Dickey–Fuller test (with constant included) now reject the null hypothesis of a unit root (using a significance level of 5%)? Give an intuitive explanation of this difference with the outcomes in **b**.

f. Now contaminate the 10,000 series of **b** by an innovation outlier of size 20 at time $t = 50$. Answer the same questions as in **e**.

g. Generate 10,000 series of the model with parameters $(\alpha, \rho) = (1, -0.1)$ and with a single innovation outlier of size 20 at time $t = 50$. Answer the same questions as in **e**.

h. Illustrate, by means of a simulation, that an innovation outlier in a random walk model generates a time series with a permanent level shift.

7.15 (☞ Sections 7.6.1–7.6.3)

Consider the following VAR(2) model in the two variables x_t and y_t:

$$\begin{pmatrix} x_t \\ y_t \end{pmatrix} = \begin{pmatrix} 1 \\ 0 \end{pmatrix} + \begin{pmatrix} 0.5 & 0.1 \\ 0.4 & 0.5 \end{pmatrix} \begin{pmatrix} x_{t-1} \\ y_{t-1} \end{pmatrix} + \begin{pmatrix} 0 & 0 \\ 0.25 & 0 \end{pmatrix} \begin{pmatrix} x_{t-2} \\ y_{t-2} \end{pmatrix} + \begin{pmatrix} \varepsilon_{1t} \\ \varepsilon_{2t} \end{pmatrix},$$

where $(\varepsilon_{1t}, \varepsilon_{2t})' \sim \text{NID}(0, I)$ with I the 2×2 identity matrix.

a. Show that this process is stationary and compute the mean values of the two variables.

b. Simulate a series of length 105 from this VAR model by taking as starting values $x_t = y_t = 3$ for $t = 1, 2$ and computing the values for $t \geq 3$ by means of the two VAR equations and simulated values for the two independent white noise processes ε_{1t} and ε_{2t}.

c. Estimate a VAR(2) model and also a VAR(1) model, on the basis of the first 100 observations.

d. Compare the two models of **c** by means of an LR-test on the significance of second order lags and also by means of AIC and SIC. Compare also the forecast performance for the forecast period $t = 101, \cdots, 105$.

e. Perform an appropriate Johansen cointegration test and give an interpretation of the outcomes.

7.16 (☞ Sections 7.3.4, 7.4.1)

In this exercise we consider some alternative models for the series y_t of US industrial production (in logarithms) discussed in Example 7.16. For estimation use again the data over the period 1961.1 to 1994.4.

a. Estimate AR(p) models with deterministic seasonal dummies for the series Δy_t, for orders $p = 0, 1, \cdots, 8$. Which model is preferred by the AIC and SIC criteria? For the AR(5) model, perform tests on normality and serial correlation of the residuals.

b. Estimate an 'airline' model—that is, estimate the MA parameters in the model $\Delta\Delta_4 y_t = (1 + \theta_1 L)(1 + \theta_4 L^4)\varepsilon_t$. Perform tests on normality and serial correlation of the residuals. Check whether the series $\Delta\Delta_4 y_t$ is possibly overdifferenced.

c. Compute sequential one-step-ahead forecasts and also h-step-ahead forecasts (with $h = 1, \cdots, 15$) for the variable y_t over the period 1995.1 to 1998.3, for the AR(5) model of **a** and for the airline model of **b**.

d. In Section 7.2.2 an AR(2) model was estimated for the series $\Delta_4 y_t$. Use this model to compute sequential one-step-ahead forecasts and also h-step-ahead forecasts (with $h = 1, \cdots, 15$) for the variable y_t over the period 1995.1 to 1998.3.

e. Compare the forecast performance of the three models in **c** and **d**. Which model do you prefer?

f. In Section 7.4.1 an AR(2) model for $\Delta_4 y_t$ was estimated with seven dummies. Now add two dummies (one for 1961.3 and one for 1975.2) and estimate the corresponding AR(2) model with nine dummies. Test whether the two groups of three sequential outliers in the periods 1961.1–1961.3 and 1974.4–1975.2 can be modelled by means of two additive outliers (this gives in total four parameter restrictions on the nine dummy variables).

7.17 (☞ Sections 7.2.1, 7.3.2–7.3.4, 7.6.3)

The data file contains monthly production data of nine Japanese passenger car industries over the period 1980.1–2001.3. The data are taken from 'DataStream'. In this exercise we consider the largest industry, Toyota, and we denote the corresponding time series by y_t. The data over the period 1980.1–1999.12 should be used in estimation and diagnostic testing; the remaining observations are used to evaluate the forecast performance of models.

a. What conclusions do you draw from the time plot, the sample autocorrelations, and the sample partial autocorrelations of y_t? Argue why it does not seem necessary to take logarithms of this series.

b. Estimate the trend of this series by means of the Holt–Winters method. What are the estimated values of the level μ_t and the slope α_t in December 1999? Forecast the production of Toyota for the twelve months in 2000.

c. Perform an augmented Dickey–Fuller test for this series (include four lags, and motivate your choices concerning constant and trend term). Generate the residual series (with name 'resdf4') of the corresponding test equation.

d. In the Dickey–Fuller test in **c** you made use of critical values. What assumptions on the series 'resdf4' are needed to use these critical values? Which of these assumptions is clearly violated? Make use of the correlogram of 'resdf4'.

e. Regress y_t on a constant and eleven seasonal dummies. Generate the forecasted values (the seasonal components) of this model for the year 2000 (for later use in **g**). Generate also the residual series (with name 'restoy') and perform an ADF test on 'restoy'. Show that this test suffers less from the problems mentioned in **d**.

f. Follow the methodology of Section 7.2.1 to construct an ARIMA model for the series 'restoy'. Perform diagnostic tests on your favourite model.

g. Use the model of **f** and the estimated seasonal components in **e** to construct (dynamic) forecasts of the production of Toyota for the twelve months in 2000. Compare the quality of the forecasts with those obtained in **b**.

h. Let x_t be the monthly series of Japanese passenger car production, excluding Toyota. Test whether the series x_t and y_t are cointegrated, and provide an economic interpretation of the results.

i. The common movements in the series x_t and y_t could be caused solely by monthly patterns in production. Regress x_t on a constant and eleven seasonal dummies and let 'restot' be the residuals of this regression. Test whether the deseasonalized series 'restoy' and 'restot' are cointegrated, and compare the result with that obtained in **h**.

7.18 (☞ Sections 7.2.1, 7.3.2, 7.3.4, 7.4.4)

COMPANION WEB SITE XR718NEP

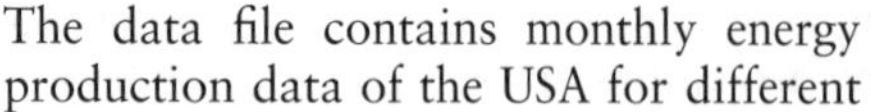

The data file contains monthly energy production data of the USA for different sorts of energy. The data are taken from 'Economagic'. Here we consider the series y_t of nuclear electric power generation with data from 1973.1 to 1999.11.

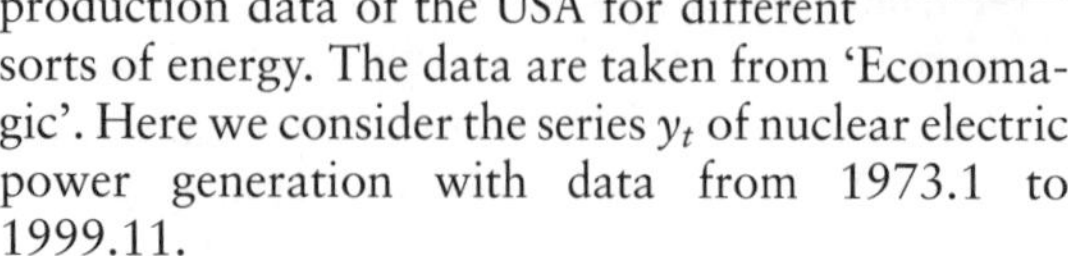

a. Plot the series over the full sample and also over the sample 1990.1–1999.11. What conclusions do you draw from this?

b. Regress the series $\log(y_t)$ on a constant, a deterministic trend, and 11 seasonal dummies, using the data over the period 1990.1–1998.12. Give an interpretation of the estimates of the seasonal effects.

c. Follow the method of Section 7.2.1 to construct an ARMA model for the series e_t of residuals of the model in **b**. Perform tests on normality, autocorrelation, ARCH effects, and parameter breaks on your favourite model.

d. Combine the models in **b** and **c**—that is, estimate the model of **b** including error terms that follow your ARMA model of **c**. Perform the tests of **c** also on this model.

e. Use the model of **d** to forecast the series $\log(y_t)$ over 1999.

f. Until now we have used a deterministic trend and seasonal for the series. Perform an appropriate test for this assumption. Estimate also a model for $\Delta_{12}\log(y_t)$ (that is, with stochastic seasonal), including (seasonal and non-seasonal) AR and MA terms in the model and using the observations over 1990.1–1998.12.

g. Use the model with stochastic seasonal in **f** to forecast the series $\log(y_t)$ over 1999 and compare the forecast quality of this model with that of the deterministic trend model in **e**.

7.19 (☞ Section 7.4.4)

Consider the monthly series of the three-month Treasury Bill rate r_t of Example 7.25 (in levels, as in Section 7.5.3) with the model $r_t - r_{t-1} = \beta_1 + \beta_2 r_{t-1} + \varepsilon_t$. In this exercise we consider ARCH models (7.29) for the error term ε_t. The data file contains monthly observations over the period 1950.1–1999.12, which are taken from 'Economagic'.

a. Estimate β_1 and β_2 by OLS and perform an ARCH test on the residuals. Also plot the correlogram of the residuals e_t and of the squared series e_t^2.

b. Estimate the parameters α_k of ARCH models (7.29) of orders $p = 1, \cdots, 4$, by regressing e_t^2 on a constant and $e_{t-1}^2, \cdots, e_{t-p}^2$. Which order of p do you prefer?

c. Now estimate β_1 and β_2 in the model with ARCH(p) error terms by maximum likelihood, for $p = 1, \cdots, 4$. Compare the estimates of β_1, β_2, and of α_k in (7.29) with those obtained in **a** and **b**.

d. Perform tests to choose the order p of the ARCH model, based on the outcomes in **c**.

e. Construct the series of estimated variances $\hat{\sigma}_t^2$ obtained from (7.29) by substituting the estimates of the parameters α_k of the preferred model in **d** and by replacing the terms ε_t^2 by $(e_t^*)^2$, where e_t^* is the series of residuals of the preferred model in **d**. Compare the series $\hat{\sigma}_t^2$ with the series $(e_t^*)^2$ to evaluate the quality of the forecasted risks in interest rate changes.

f. Perform a test on the presence of remaining ARCH effects and a test on normality of the standardized residuals $e_t^*/\hat{\sigma}_t$. What conclusions do you draw from these outcomes?

7.20 (☞ Sections 7.2.4, 7.3.2, 7.3.3, 7.6.3)

The data file contains yearly data on the gross national product (GNP) for a number of countries. We consider the series y_t consisting of the natural logarithm of US GNP over the period 1870–1993. The data are taken from A. Maddison, *Monitoring the World Economy 1820–1992* (OECD, 1995).

a. Investigate the nature of the trend in the series y_t over the full sample period, by means of ADF tests (both t and F).

b. Investigate the nature of the trend also over the three subperiods 1870–1929, 1900–49, and 1950–93.

c. Use the data over the period 1950–89 to estimate the yearly growth rate of US GNP by means of two simple models, the deterministic trend model $y_t = \alpha + \beta t + \varepsilon_t$ and the stochastic trend model $y_t = y_{t-1} + \alpha + \varepsilon_t$.

d. Use the two models of **c** to forecast y_t for the period 1990–3 and compare the forecast quality.

e. Try to improve on the forecast results of **d** by adding ARMA terms for the short-run fluctuations to the trend models for y_t. The model selection should be based on the data over the period 1950–89.

f. The data file also contains GNP data for Germany, Japan, and the UK. Investigate the presence of cointegration between the four GNP series (in logarithms), both for the period 1950–93 and for the period 1870–1993. Motivate your choice of cointegration test and comment on the outcomes.

7.21 (☞ Sections 7.3.3, 7.5.2, 7.6.3)

In this exercise we consider yearly data on gasoline consumption in the USA over the period 1970–99. The data file contains data on gasoline consumption (GC), gasoline price (PG), and disposable income (RI), all measured in real terms and taken in logarithms. These data were previously discussed in Examples 5.31 and 5.34 (p. 402–4, 416–18). In Example 5.31 we considered the regression $GC_t = \alpha + \beta PG_t + \gamma RI_t + \varepsilon_t$, and now we will consider whether this regression is possibly spurious due to trends and whether lags should be added to this model. Use a significance level of 5% in all tests of this exercise.

a. Regress GC on a constant and the variables PG and RI.

b. Test for the presence of stochastic trends in the variables GC, PG, and RI. Include a constant and deterministic trend in the test equations.

c. Test for the presence of cointegration between the three variables. Compare the price elasticity b of the estimated cointegration relation $GC_t = a + bPG_t + cRI_t + dt$ with the estimate of **a**.

d. Test for the presence of residual correlation in the model of **a**. Estimate two ADL models, including $p = 1$ or $p = 2$ lags of the variables GC_t, PG_t, and RI_t as additional regressors.

e. Which of the three models of **a** and **d** is preferred on the basis of LR-tests on the significance of the additional lagged terms? And which model is preferred by SIC? Test the selected model(s) for the presence of residual correlation.

f. Compute the long-run elasticities of price and income of the preferred ADL model(s) of **e** and rewrite this in error correction form. Give an interpretation of the outcome.

7.22 (☞ Section 7.4.4)

The data file contains monthly data for the UK on the returns in the sector of cyclical consumer goods (denoted by y_t) and in the market (denoted by x_t) over the period 1980.01–2000.03. The CAPM postulates a linear relation between the returns—that is, $y_t = \alpha + \beta x_t + \varepsilon_t$. The data are taken from 'DataStream' and were analysed previously in Examples 5.27 and 5.28 (p. 384–6, 387–8).

a. Estimate the CAPM, using data only over the period 1980.01–1999.12. Investigate the series of residuals e_t, in particular a time plot and the correlograms of e_t and of the squared series e_t^2.

b. Perform tests to show that e_t has no serial correlation but that it has significant ARCH. Estimate an ARMA model for the squared residuals e_t^2, with orders based on the test outcomes.

c. Obtain a new estimate of the CAPM $y_t = \alpha + \beta x_t + \varepsilon_t$ together with the GARCH model of **b** for the error terms ε_t. That is, estimate this combined model by ML (instead of the two-step approach in **a** and **b**). Use again the data over 1980.01–1999.12.

d. Test for normality, serial correlation, and ARCH effects in the (standardized) residuals of the model in **c**. Compare the outcome of the Jarque–Bera test on normality with the test results in Section 5.6.3 (p. 387–8) for the CAPM without GARCH, and explain the differences.

e. Compare the estimates of **c** with those obtained in **a** and **b**. Comment on the similarities and differences. Make scatter diagrams of the returns y_t against the predicted values $\hat{y}_t$ and of the risk $\hat{\varepsilon}_t^2$ against the estimated variance $\hat{\sigma}_t^2$ (the estimated value of the variance $\sigma_t^2 = E[\varepsilon_t^2]$ obtained from the model).

f. Use the model of **c** to forecast y_t and $\sigma_t^2 = E[\varepsilon_t^2]$ for the first three months in 2000 (use the actual values of x_t in these months). Use this model also to construct 95% forecast intervals and compare the outcomes with the actual values of y_t in these months.

7.23 (☞ Sections 7.3.3, 7.4.1, 7.4.4, 7.6.3)

The data file contains monthly data on price levels and exchange rates for a number of countries. The data are taken from 'International Financial Statistics'. We consider the data for Germany and the UK and we denote the consumer price indices by P_G and P_{UK}, the exchange rate of the Deutsche Mark to 1 US Dollar by X_G and the exchange rate of the British Pound to 1 US Dollar by X_{UK}. The nominal exchange rate of the Mark against 1 Pound is equal to X_G/X_{UK} and the relative price level of Germany against the UK is P_G/P_{UK}. The Purchasing Power Parity (PPP) hypothesis of international economics states that $X_G/P_G = X_{UK}/P_{UK}$, or equivalently that $X_G/X_{UK} = P_G/P_{UK}$. In the following questions we consider data for the four series P_G, P_{UK}, X_G and X_{UK} over the period 1975.1–1994.12. The PPP hypothesis is usually written as $\log(X_G/X_{UK}) = \log(P_G) - \log(P_{UK})$. Use a significance level of 5% in all tests of this exercise.

a. Make a plot of the two price series P_G and P_{UK} and also of the two exchange rate series X_G and X_{UK}.
b. Test for the presence of unit roots in the four series (all in logarithms) and test also for the presence of cointegration.
c. Perform the two tests of **b** also for the set of three series $\log(X_G/X_{UK})$, $\log(P_G)$, and $\log(P_{UK})$. For reasons of economic interpretation, do not include a trend in the cointegration equation.
d. The PPP can be formulated in econometric terms by the hypothesis that $\log(X_G/X_{UK}) - \log(P_G) + \log(P_{UK})$ should be a stationary time series. Test this hypothesis, compare the outcome with the one obtained in **c**, and give an economic interpretation.
e. Let $y_t = \Delta\log(X_G/X_{UK})$ be the series of monthly relative changes in the exchange rate between Germany and the UK. Perform tests for autocorrelation and for ARCH in the series y_t.
f. Test for the presence of outliers in the series y_t of **e**. Discuss the possible relevance of this for the analysis of PPP in **d**.

7.24 (☞ Sections 7.3.3, 7.6.3)

The data file contains yearly data on the Standard and Poor index y_t and dividends x_t, both in real terms, over the period 1871–1987. The data are taken from R. J. Shiller, *Market Volatility* (MIT Press, 1989). The Present Value theory of financial economics states that the stock price y_t is determined by the expected future dividends. Let δ be the discount factor; then this can be formulated as $y_t = \sum_{i=1}^{\infty} \delta^i E[x_{t+i}]$. If the expected dividends would be constant so that $x_{t+i} = x$ then the corresponding equilibrium value of y_t is $y = \sum_{i=1}^{\infty} \delta^i x = \frac{\delta}{1-\delta}x$. A further finding in financial economics is that stock prices often follow random walks, in which case the equilibrium relation $y = \frac{\delta}{1-\delta}x$ corresponds to the presence of cointegration between the series y_t and x_t.

a. Make a time plot of the series y_t and x_t. Test for the presence of unit roots in both series by means of appropriate ADF tests.
b. Test for the presence of cointegration between the series y_t and x_t. Include a deterministic trend in the cointegration relation.
c. Estimate a vector error correction model for the series $Y_t = (y_t, x_t)'$. Include an appropriate number of lagged terms ΔY_{t-k} and take as error correction term $(y_{t-1} - \theta x_{t-1} - \alpha - \beta t)$.
d. Give an interpretation of the adjustment coefficients of the VECM in **c**. Give also an interpretation of the estimated parameter θ by computing the corresponding value of the discount factor δ in the Present Value model.

7.25 (☞ Sections 7.7.2, 7.7.3)

The data file contains quarterly fashion sales data of a US retailer with multiple specialty divisions over the period 1986.1–1992.4. This is a panel data set with $m = 5$ units and $n = 28$ observations. The first two divisions specialize in high-priced fashion apparel, division 3 in low-priced clothes, and divisions 4 and 5 in specialities like large sizes, undergarments, and so on (the data of division 1 were previously analysed in Example 5.6 (p. 305–7)). The data consist of the quarterly sales S_{it} of the divisions, the purchasing ability A_t, and the consumer confidence C_t. Motivated by the results in Section 5.3.1 we formulate the model

$$\log(S_{it}) = \alpha_i + \alpha_{i2}D_{2t} + \alpha_{i3}D_{3t} + \alpha_{i4}D_{4t} + \beta_i \log(A_t) + \gamma_i \log(C_t) + \varepsilon_{it}$$

where $i = 1, \cdots, 5$ denotes the division and $t = 1, \cdots, 28$ the observation number and where D_{jt} are seasonal dummies ($j = 2, 3, 4$, the first quarter is taken as the reference season).

a. Estimate the above model (with thirty regression parameters) by OLS. Check that there exists significant contemporaneous correlation between the residual terms for the five divisions in the same quarter.

b. Estimate the model also by SUR. Compare the outcomes with **a**, and explain.

c. Estimate a panel model with fixed effects and with different parameters for the seasonal dummies. This means that the parameters β_i and γ_i are constant across the divisions, so that the model contains in total twenty-two parameters. Compare the results with **a** and **b**.

d. Estimate the model of **c** with the restriction of equal seasonal effects α_{ij} across the divisions but with different fixed effects α_i, so that the model contains in total ten regression parameters. Compare the estimated seasonal effects with the estimates in **c**.

e. Perform an LR-test of the twelve parameter restrictions that reduce the model in **c** to the model in **d**.

f. Explain why it would make little sense to estimate a random effects panel model for these data.

7.26 (☞ Section 7.7.4)

The data file contains fifty yearly data on the market for oranges in the USA over the period 1910–59. The data are taken from M. Nerlove and F. V. Waugh, 'Advertising without Supply Control: Some Implications of a Study of the Advertising of Oranges', *Journal of Farm Economics*, 43 (1961), 813–37. The variables are the quantity traded (Q), the price (P), real disposable income (RI), current advertisement expenditures (AC), and past advertisement expenditures (AP, averaged over the past ten years). First we assume that the supply Q is fixed and that the price is determined by demand via the price equation

$$\log(P_t) = \alpha + \gamma \log(Q_t) + \beta \log(RI_t) + \varepsilon_t.$$

a. Estimate the price equation by OLS. Test the null hypothesis of unit price elasticity ($\gamma = -1$).

b. Estimate the price equation also by IV, using as instruments a constant, $\log(RI_t)$, $\log(AC_t)$, and $\log(AP_t)$. Test again the null hypothesis of unit elasticity.

c. Perform the Hausman test for the exogeneity of $\log(Q_t)$ in the price equation.

d. Investigate the quality of the instruments—that is, whether they are sufficiently correlated with $\log(Q_t)$ and uncorrelated with the price shocks ε_t (take the IV residuals as estimates of these shocks).

e. Answer questions **b**, **c**, and **d** also for the $n = 45$ observations obtained by excluding the data over the period 1942–6.

Next we consider the simultaneous model for price and quantity described by the following two equations. We exclude the two advertisement variables (AC and AP) from the analysis in **f** and **g**.

$$\text{(demand)} \quad \log(P_t) = \alpha_1 + \gamma_1 \log(Q_t) + \beta_1 \log(RI_t) + \varepsilon_{1t},$$
$$\text{(supply)} \quad \log(P_t) = \alpha_2 + \gamma_2 \log(Q_t) + \varepsilon_{2t}.$$

f. Is the demand equation identified? Estimate this equation by OLS. What is your interpretation of the outcomes?

g. Is the supply equation identified? Estimate this equation by a method that you find most appropriate, and motivate your choice.

Appendix A. **Matrix Methods**

In this appendix we summarize some matrix methods and some results on functions of several variables. At the beginning of each section we state in which chapters or sections the discussed topics are used. For more background on these topics there exist numerous textbooks on linear algebra and calculus. See, for instance, G. Strang, *Linear Algebra and its Applications* (San Diego: Harcourt Brace Jovanovich, 1988); D. C. Lay, *Linear Algebra and its Applications* (Reading: Addison-Wesley, 1997); and J. R. Magnus and H. Neudecker, *Matrix Differential Calculus with Applications in Statistics and Econometrics* (Chichester: Wiley, 1999).

A.1 **Summations**

☞ Used in Chapters 1–7.

Sum notation

Many computations in econometrics involve summations of large amounts of numbers. For convenience of notation such summations are often denoted by the summation symbol $\sum$. The sum of the n numbers $y_1, y_2, \cdots, y_n$ is denoted by

$$\sum_{i=1}^{n} y_i = y_1 + y_2 + \cdots + y_n.$$

Sometimes, if the value of n is clear from the context, we write $\sum y_i$ instead of $\sum_{i=1}^{n} y_i$. In a similar way, $\sum_{i=1}^{n} y_i^2$ denotes the sum of the squared values $y_1^2 + y_2^2 + \cdots + y_n^2$, and $\sum_{i=1}^{n} y_i x_i$ is the sum of products $y_1 x_1 + y_2 x_2 + \cdots + y_n x_n$.

Properties of summations

By writing out the involved summations one can verify that, for any constants a and b that do not depend on i, there holds $\sum_{i=1}^{n} a = na$, $\sum_{i=1}^{n} a y_i = a \sum_{i=1}^{n} y_i$, and $\sum_{i=1}^{n} (a y_i + b x_i) = a \sum_{i=1}^{n} y_i + b \sum_{i=1}^{n} x_i$. We often work with numbers in deviation from their (sample) mean denoted by $\bar{y} = \frac{1}{n}\sum_{i=1}^{n} y_i$. The following properties are useful:

$$\sum_{i=1}^{n}(y_i - \bar{y}) = 0, \quad \sum_{i=1}^{n}(y_i - \bar{y})^2 = \sum_{i=1}^{n} y_i^2 - n\bar{y}^2, \quad \sum_{i=1}^{n}(y_i - \bar{y})(x_i - \bar{x}) = \sum_{i=1}^{n} y_i x_i - n\bar{y}\bar{x}.$$

XMA01SIM

Example A.1: **Simulated Data on Student Learning**

We consider (hypothetical) values of the scores of five students for their Freshman Grade Point Average (FGPA) and for their SAT mathematics test (SATM) and

Panel 1: scores

STUDENT	FGPA	SATM	SATV
1	1.8	4	4
2	2.4	6	5
3	2.9	6	7
4	3.0	7	6
5	3.5	8	7

Panel 2: operations on FGPA scores

STUDENT	FGPA	FGPA_M	FGPA_S	FGPA_MS
1	1.8	−0.92	3.24	0.8464
2	2.4	−0.32	5.76	0.1024
3	2.9	0.18	8.41	0.0324
4	3.0	0.28	9.00	0.0784
5	3.5	0.78	12.25	0.6084
SUM	13.6	0	38.66	1.6680
MEAN	2.72	0	7.732	0.3336

Panel 3: operations on FGPA and SATM scores

STUDENT	FGPA	FGPA_M	SATM	SATM_M	FGPA*SATM	FGPA_M*SATM_M
1	1.8	−0.92	4.0	−2.2	7.2	2.024
2	2.4	−0.32	6.0	−0.2	14.4	0.064
3	2.9	0.18	6.0	−0.2	17.4	−0.036
4	3.0	0.28	7.0	0.8	21.0	0.224
5	3.5	0.78	8.0	1.8	28.0	1.404
SUM	13.6	0	31.0	0	88.0	3.680
MEAN	2.72	0	6.2	0	17.6	0.736

Exhibit A.1 Simulated Data on Student Learning (Example A.1)

Panel 1 contains scores on FGPA (on a scale from 1 to 4) and on SATM and SATV (on a scale from 1 to 10) of five (hypothetical) students; Panel 2 shows the scores on FGPA, the scores in deviation from the mean (FGPA_M), the squares of FGPA (FGPA_S), and the squares of FGPA in deviation from the mean (FGPA_MS); and Panel 3 shows the scores on FGPA and SATM, the scores in deviation from the mean (FGPA_M and SATM_M), the products of the FGPA and SATM scores, and the products of the transformed values FGPA_M and SATM_M.

verbal test (SATV). The scores are in Panel 1 of Exhibit A.1, and Panels 2 and 3 report the results of some operations on these numbers. (For a real data set on student learning of 609 students, we refer to Example 1.1 (p. 12); here we restrict the attention to five students to get small matrices that are convenient as an introduction.) We denote the five students by the index $i = 1, \cdots, 5$, their FGPA by y_i, and their SATM by x_i. For instance, $y_2 = 2.4$ and $x_4 = 7$. The computations in Exhibit A.1 show that $\bar{y} = 2.72$, that $\sum_{i=1}^{5} (y_i - \bar{y}) = 0$, and that $\sum_{i=1}^{5} (y_i - \bar{y})^2 = 1.668$, which is equal to $\sum_{i=1}^{5} y_i^2 - n\bar{y}^2 = 38.66 - 5(2.72)^2$. The computations in Panel 3 of Exhibit A.1 further show that $\sum_{i=1}^{5} (y_i - \bar{y})(x_i - \bar{x}) = 3.68$ which is equal to $\sum_{i=1}^{5} y_i x_i - n\bar{y}\bar{x} = 88 - 5 \cdot 2.72 \cdot 6.2$.

A.2 Vectors and matrices

☞ Used in Chapters 1, 3–7.

Data table

In econometrics we are concerned with modelling observed data. In many cases the number of numerical data is large (several hundreds or thousands of observations on a number of possibly interesting variables) and all the data should be handled in an organized way. Many data sets are stored in a spreadsheet where each column corresponds to a variable and the length of the column is equal to the number of observations of that variable. For instance, the data on FGPA, SATM, and SATV of five students in the example in the foregoing section can be represented by the following table.

Student	FGPA	SATM	SATV
1	1.8	4	4
2	2.4	6	5
3	2.9	6	7
4	3.0	7	6
5	3.5	8	7

Data matrix

The real data information consists of the five paired scores on FGPA, SATM, and SATV and we can summarize these data by the following array of numbers:

$$\begin{pmatrix} 1.8 & 4 & 4 \\ 2.4 & 6 & 5 \\ 2.9 & 6 & 7 \\ 3.0 & 7 & 6 \\ 3.5 & 8 & 7 \end{pmatrix}.$$

Such a rectangular block of numbers is called a matrix. The above matrix has five rows and three columns. In econometrics we often work with matrices, and of course we should always remind ourselves and other users what is the meaning of the columns and rows (in this case, the correspondence between columns and variables and between rows and students, so that the number 2.9 in column 1 and row 3 is known to correspond to the FGPA of the third student).

Matrix notation

More generally, let A be a matrix with p rows and q columns; then we say the A is a $p \times q$ matrix and we denote the number in row i and column j by a_{ij}. The matrix is then of the form

$$A = \begin{pmatrix} a_{11} & a_{12} & \cdots & a_{1q} \\ a_{21} & a_{22} & \cdots & a_{2q} \\ \vdots & \vdots & \vdots & \vdots \\ a_{p1} & a_{p2} & \cdots & a_{pq} \end{pmatrix}.$$

For instance, the matrix in the student example has $p = 5$ rows and $q = 3$ columns and $a_{12} = 4$ and $a_{21} = 2.4$, and so on.

Matrix notation in econometrics

In this appendix we follow the convention of matrix algebra to denote the element on row i and column j by a_{ij}. However, in econometrics we often denote this element by $a_{j,i}$—that is, the first index refers to the variable (that is, the column) and the second index to the observation number (that is, the row), and for shorthand notation we then often even write a_{ji} for this number (see, for instance, Section 3.1.2 (p. 120)). This may be somewhat confusing in the beginning, but in essence it does not matter which convention we follow as long as we are clear what we mean by our notation. Therefore, in this appendix we follow the convention of matrix algebra books to make it easier to consult books that are specialized in this topic, but in the main text we follow the convention of most econometricians.

Special matrices

A square matrix is a matrix that has an equal number of rows and columns—that is, with $p = q$. A diagonal matrix is a square matrix with the property that $a_{ij} = 0$ for all $i \neq j$—that is, all elements are zero except possibly the elements a_{ii} on the diagonal (with equal row and column index). A special case of a diagonal matrix is the identity matrix that has $a_{ii} = 1$ for all $i = 1, \cdots, p$, and $a_{ij} = 0$ for all $i \neq j$. The $p \times p$ identity matrix is denoted by I_p or simply by I. A zero matrix is a (square or non-square) matrix with all its elements equal to zero—that is, $a_{ij} = 0$ for all i and j. The $p \times q$ zero matrix is denoted by O_{pq} or simply by O.

A matrix with only one column—that is, a $p \times 1$ matrix—is called a column vector, and a $1 \times q$ matrix is called a row vector. A column vector is often simply called a vector. Whereas matrices are denoted by capital letters (A, B, and so on), vectors are usually denoted by lower-case letters (a, b, and so on).

A.3 Matrix addition and multiplication

☞ Used in Chapters 1, 3–7.

Matrix addition

This section and the next one contain a number of operations on matrices that are much used in econometrics. Let A be a $p \times q$ matrix with elements a_{ij} and let B also be a $p \times q$ matrix with elements b_{ij}. Then the sum $C = A + B$ of the two matrices is defined by the $p \times q$ matrix with elements $c_{ij} = a_{ij} + b_{ij}$ in row i and column j ($i = 1, \cdots, p$, $j = 1, \cdots, q$). Note that A and B should have the same number of rows and also the same number of columns.

Matrix multiplication

Let A be a $p \times q$ matrix with elements a_{ij} ($i = 1, \cdots, p$, $j = 1, \cdots, q$) and let B be a $q \times r$ matrix with elements b_{jk} ($j = 1, \cdots, q$, $k = 1, \cdots, r$). Then the product $C = AB$ of the two matrices is defined by the $p \times r$ matrix with elements

$$c_{ik} = \sum_{j=1}^{q} a_{ij} b_{jk} = a_{i1} b_{1k} + a_{i2} b_{2k} + \cdots + a_{iq} b_{qk}$$

($i = 1, \cdots, p$, $k = 1, \cdots, r$). So the element in row i and column j of the product matrix AB is obtained by multiplying the ith row of A (element-wise) with the jth column of B. This requires that the number of columns of the matrix A is equal to the number of rows of the matrix B, otherwise the product AB is not defined.

If the $p \times q$ matrix A is multiplied with the $q \times 1$ vector b, then the product Ab is a $p \times 1$ vector. If in addition a is a row vector so that $p = 1$, then the product ab of a row vector with a column vector is a 1×1 vector—that is, a scalar number. Note that the product ba of the column vector b with the row vector a is a $p \times q$ matrix. Let A be a $p \times q$ matrix with elements a_{ij} ($i = 1, \cdots, p$, $j = 1, \cdots, q$) and let d be a real number; then the scalar multiple dA is defined as the $p \times q$ matrix with elements da_{ij} ($i = 1, \cdots, p$, $j = 1, \cdots, q$).

Calculation rules

The following calculation rules hold true for matrix products and scalar multiples (we use the notation ($p \times q$) to denote the number of rows and columns of a matrix).

$$\begin{array}{rl}
A(p \times q),\ B(q \times r),\ C(q \times r) & A(B+C) = AB + AC \\
A(p \times q),\ B(p \times q),\ C(q \times r) & (A+B)C = AC + BC \\
A(p \times q),\ B(q \times r),\ C(r \times s) & A(BC) = (AB)C \\
A(p \times q) & I_p A = A I_q = A \\
A(p \times q) & O_{rp}A = O_{rq},\ AO_{qr} = O_{pr} \\
A(p \times q),\ B(p \times q),\ d(\text{scalar}) & d(A+B) = dA + dB \\
A(p \times q),\ B(q \times r),\ d(\text{scalar}) & d(AB) = (dA)B = A(dB)
\end{array}$$

Although some of the operations on matrices have the same properties as corresponding operations on (scalar) numbers, this does not hold true for all operations. In particular, if A is a $p \times q$ matrix and B a $q \times r$ matrix, then AB (which is a well-defined $p \times r$ matrix) is not the same as BA. The product BA is not even defined if $r \neq p$, and even if $r = p$ then AB has p rows and columns whereas BA has q rows and columns, and even if in addition $p = q$ then still (except in special cases)

$$AB \neq BA.$$

Example A.2: **Simulated Data on Student Learning (continued)**

We illustrate the use of matrices and vectors as an efficient tool for data organization by considering again the data on scores of five students. Let y_i denote the FGPA score of student i and let x_i be the SATM score and z_i the SATV score of this student. As a simple model for the explanation of FGPA in terms of SATM and SATV we consider the linear relationship

$$y_i = b_1 + b_2 x_i + b_3 z_i, \quad i = 1, \cdots, 5.$$

If we substitute the numbers for y_i, x_i, and z_i given in Exhibit A.1 and collect the results for the five students in a 5×1 vector we obtain

$$\begin{pmatrix} 1.8 \\ 2.4 \\ 2.9 \\ 3.0 \\ 3.5 \end{pmatrix} = \begin{pmatrix} b_1 & + & 4b_2 & + & 4b_3 \\ b_1 & + & 6b_2 & + & 5b_3 \\ b_1 & + & 6b_2 & + & 7b_3 \\ b_1 & + & 7b_2 & + & 6b_3 \\ b_1 & + & 8b_2 & + & 7b_3 \end{pmatrix} = \begin{pmatrix} 1 & 4 & 4 \\ 1 & 6 & 5 \\ 1 & 6 & 7 \\ 1 & 7 & 6 \\ 1 & 8 & 7 \end{pmatrix} \begin{pmatrix} b_1 \\ b_2 \\ b_3 \end{pmatrix}.$$

Let y denote the above 5×1 vector of FGPA scores, let b be the 3×1 vector with elements b_1, b_2, b_3, and let X be the above 5×3 matrix with the first column consisting of ones, the second of the SATM scores, and the third of the SATV scores. Then the above model can be written in terms of the given data vector y and the given data matrix X as $y = Xb$ where

$$X = \begin{pmatrix} 1 & 4 & 4 \\ 1 & 6 & 5 \\ 1 & 6 & 7 \\ 1 & 7 & 6 \\ 1 & 8 & 7 \end{pmatrix}.$$

This is a system of five equations (one for each student) and three unknowns (the values of b_1, b_2, b_3). There does not exist a solution for the three unknowns so that all five equations are exactly satisfied. Approximate solutions can be obtained by least squares—that is, by minimizing $\sum_{i=1}^{5} (y_i - b_1 - b_2 x_i - b_3 z_i)^2$. Let $e_i = y_i - b_1 - b_2 x_i - b_3 z_i$ be the error of the equation for student i; then this corresponds to minimizing $\sum_{i=1}^{5} e_i^2$ by choosing appropriate values for b_1, b_2, b_3. We will later come back to this (see Example A.11).

A.4 Transpose, trace, and inverse

☞ Used in Chapters 1, 3–7.

Transpose of a matrix

Let A be a given $p \times q$ matrix with elements a_{ij}, $i = 1, \cdots, p$, $j = 1, \cdots, q$. Then the transpose of A, denoted by A', is the $q \times p$ matrix with the value of a_{ij} placed in row j and column i. For instance, the transpose of the 5×3 matrix X in Example A.2 is the 3×5 matrix

$$X' = \begin{pmatrix} 1 & 1 & 1 & 1 & 1 \\ 4 & 6 & 6 & 7 & 8 \\ 4 & 5 & 7 & 6 & 7 \end{pmatrix}.$$

A square $p \times p$ matrix A is called symmetric if $A' = A$—that is, if $a_{ij} = a_{ji}$ for all $i = 1, \cdots, p$, $j = 1, \cdots, p$. Some calculation rules for transposed matrices are

$$(A')' = A, \quad (A + B)' = A' + B', \quad (AB)' = B'A'.$$

If a is a $p \times 1$ vector, then $a'a = \sum_{i=1}^{p} a_i^2$ is a scalar number equal to the sum of the squares of the elements a_i of the vector a.

Partitioned matrix

In some cases it is convenient to work with partitioned matrices—that is, matrices that are split up in parts. For instance, let A be a $p \times q$ matrix and let A_1 be the $p \times s$ submatrix consisting of the first s columns of A and A_2 the $p \times (q - s)$ submatrix consisting of the remaining $(q - s)$ columns of A; then we write $A = (A_1\ A_2)$. Let the rows of the $q \times r$ matrix B be split in a similar way in the $s \times r$ submatrix B_1 consisting of the first s rows of B and the $(q - s) \times r$ submatrix

B_2 consisting of the remaining rows of B so that $B = \begin{pmatrix} B_1 \\ B_2 \end{pmatrix}$. Then $AB = A_1B_1 + A_2B_2$. More in general, let the jth column of the $p \times q$ matrix A be denoted by a_j (a $p \times 1$ vector) and let the jth row of the $q \times r$ matrix B be denoted by b'_j (a $1 \times r$ row vector), $j = 1, \cdots, q$, then $AB = \sum_{j=1}^{q} a_j b'_j$.

Trace of a square matrix

The trace of a square $p \times p$ matrix A, denoted by $\text{tr}(A)$, is defined as the sum of its diagonal elements—that is,

$$\text{tr}(A) = \sum_{i=1}^{p} a_{ii}.$$

The following calculation rules hold true (assuming that the shown matrix sums and products are square matrices):

$$\text{tr}(A + B) = \text{tr}(A) + \text{tr}(B), \quad \text{tr}(AB) = \text{tr}(BA), \quad \text{tr}(A') = \text{tr}(A).$$

Inverse of a square matrix

A square $p \times p$ matrix A is called invertible if there exists a $p \times p$ matrix B such that $AB = BA = I_p$, the $p \times p$ identity matrix. Such a matrix B is called the inverse matrix of A and is denoted by A^{-1}.

If A is a given invertible $p \times p$ matrix and b is a given $p \times 1$ vector, then there exists a unique $p \times 1$ vector c such that $Ac = b$—namely, $c = A^{-1}b$. The following computation rules apply, where A and B are square $p \times p$ invertible matrices:

$$(AB)^{-1} = B^{-1}A^{-1}, \quad (A')^{-1} = (A^{-1})', \quad (A^{-1})^{-1} = A.$$

Not every square matrix is invertible—for instance, if $A = O$ is a square zero matrix then it has no inverse. A square matrix A is invertible if and only if its determinant is non-zero, as is further discussed in the next section.

E

Example A.3: **Simulated Data on Student Learning (continued)**

In Example A.2 we mentioned that, for given observations collected in the 5×1 vector y and the 5×3 matrix X, least squares corresponds to choosing values for b_1, b_2, b_3, such that the sum of squares of the errors $e_i = y_i - b_1 - b_2x_i - b_3z_i$ is as small as possible. Let e be the 5×1 vector with elements e_i; then we can write $e = y - Xb$ and

$$\sum_{i=1}^{5} e_i^2 = e'e = (y - Xb)'(y - Xb).$$

This expression can be worked out by using $(y - Xb)' = y' - (Xb)' = y' - b'X'$ so that $(y - Xb)'(y - Xb) = y'(y - Xb) - b'X'(y - Xb) = y'y - y'Xb - b'X'y + b'X'Xb$. As y is a 5×1 vector, X a 5×3 matrix, and b a 3×1 vector, it follows that $y'Xb$ is a scalar (1×1 matrix), which is of course symmetric, so that $y'Xb = (y'Xb)' = b'(y'X)' = b'X'y$. Combining these results, the sum of squared errors becomes

$$(y - Xb)'(y - Xb) = y'y - 2b'X'y + b'X'Xb.$$

We can use the numerical values in Exhibit A.1 to compute $y'y = \sum_{i=1}^{5} y_i^2 = 38.66$ and

$$X'y = \begin{pmatrix} 1 & 1 & 1 & 1 & 1 \\ 4 & 6 & 6 & 7 & 8 \\ 4 & 5 & 7 & 6 & 7 \end{pmatrix} \begin{pmatrix} 1.8 \\ 2.4 \\ 2.9 \\ 3.0 \\ 3.5 \end{pmatrix} = \begin{pmatrix} 13.6 \\ 88.0 \\ 82.0 \end{pmatrix},$$

$$X'X = \begin{pmatrix} 1 & 1 & 1 & 1 & 1 \\ 4 & 6 & 6 & 7 & 8 \\ 4 & 5 & 7 & 6 & 7 \end{pmatrix} \begin{pmatrix} 1 & 4 & 4 \\ 1 & 6 & 5 \\ 1 & 6 & 7 \\ 1 & 7 & 6 \\ 1 & 8 & 7 \end{pmatrix} = \begin{pmatrix} 5 & 31 & 29 \\ 31 & 201 & 186 \\ 29 & 186 & 175 \end{pmatrix}. \qquad \text{(A.1)}$$

The matrix $X'X$ is symmetric, which also follows from $(X'X)' = X'(X')' = X'X$. The above results lead to the following expression for the sum of squared errors, which will be of later use.

$$\begin{aligned}(y - Xb)'(y - Xb) &= 38.66 - 2(b_1\ b_2\ b_3)\begin{pmatrix} 13.6 \\ 88.0 \\ 82.0 \end{pmatrix} + (b_1\ b_2\ b_3)X'X\begin{pmatrix} b_1 \\ b_2 \\ b_3 \end{pmatrix} \\ &= 38.66 - 27.2b_1 - 176b_2 - 164b_3 + 5b_1^2 + 201b_2^2 \\ &\quad + 175b_3^2 + 62b_1b_2 + 58b_1b_3 + 372b_2b_3. \qquad \text{(A.2)}\end{aligned}$$

The computation of the inverse of $X'X$ will be considered in the next section (see Example A.5).

A.5 Determinant, rank, and eigenvalues

☞ Used in Sections 1.2, 5.7, 7.6, 7.7.

As the results of this section are mostly of a computational nature, readers can skip the details without much cost and leave the actual computation of inverses, determinants, and eigenvalues to (matrix) software packages. Some of the details are needed in Section 7.6.

Determinant of a square matrix

A square $p \times p$ matrix A is invertible if and only if its determinant is non-zero. Here the determinant, denoted by $\det(A)$, is a scalar number that can be computed from the elements a_{ij} $(i = 1, \cdots, p, j = 1, \cdots, p)$. For a scalar (1×1) matrix $A = (a_{11})$ the determinant is simply defined by $\det(A) = a_{11}$. For a 2×2 matrix the determinant is defined by

$$\det\left(\begin{pmatrix} a_{11} & a_{12} \\ a_{21} & a_{22} \end{pmatrix}\right) = a_{11}a_{22} - a_{12}a_{21},$$

and for a 3×3 matrix the determinant is defined by

$$\det\left(\begin{pmatrix} a_{11} & a_{12} & a_{13} \\ a_{21} & a_{22} & a_{23} \\ a_{31} & a_{32} & a_{33} \end{pmatrix}\right) = a_{11}a_{22}a_{33} + a_{12}a_{23}a_{31} + a_{13}a_{21}a_{32}$$
$$- a_{11}a_{23}a_{32} - a_{12}a_{21}a_{33} - a_{13}a_{22}a_{31}.$$

E

Example A.4: **Simulated Data on Student Learning (continued)**

The determinant of the 3×3 matrix $X'X$ in (A.1) is equal to $5(201)(175) + 31(186)(29) + 29(31)(186) - 5(186)(186) - 31(31)(175) - 29(201)(29) = 107$.

Computation of determinant

The determinant of a $p \times p$ matrix A can be computed from the determinants of smaller-sized submatrices by expansion according to any of the rows or columns of A. Let A_{ij} be the $(p - 1) \times (p - 1)$ matrix obtained by deleting the ith row and the jth column of A and let the cofactor C_{ij} be defined by $C_{ij} = (-1)^{i+j}\det(A_{ij})$, then

$$\det(A) = \sum_{j=1}^{p} a_{ij}C_{ij} = \sum_{i=1}^{p} a_{ij}C_{ij}.$$

The first expression is valid for any choice of i and corresponds to an expansion according to the ith row of A, and the second expression is valid for any choice of j and corresponds to an expansion according to the jth column of A. Whatever choice we make for i or j, the above expansions always lead to the same numerical outcome. For example, the determinant of a 4×4 matrix A can be obtained by expansion according to the first row as $a_{11}C_{11} + a_{12}C_{12} + a_{13}C_{13} + a_{14}C_{14}$, where each of the four cofactors C_{1j}, $j = 1, \cdots, 4$, involves the determinant of a 3×3 submatrix of A that can be computed as indicated above.

Computation of inverse matrix

A matrix is invertible if and only if its determinant is non-zero, and the (i, j)th element of the inverse matrix can be computed by

$$C_{ji}/\det(A),$$

that is, the element on row i and column j of A^{-1} is equal to the cofactor C_{ji} divided by the determinant of the full $p \times p$ matrix A. For instance, the inverse of a 2×2 matrix A can be computed as follows. The cofactors are equal to $C_{11} = a_{22}$, $C_{12} = -a_{21}$, $C_{21} = -a_{12}$, and $C_{22} = a_{11}$, so that

$$\begin{pmatrix} a_{11} & a_{12} \\ a_{21} & a_{22} \end{pmatrix}^{-1} = \frac{1}{a_{11}a_{22} - a_{12}a_{21}} \begin{pmatrix} a_{22} & -a_{12} \\ -a_{21} & a_{11} \end{pmatrix}.$$

A direct computation shows that indeed $AA^{-1} = A^{-1}A = I_2$. Let C be the $p \times p$ matrix with elements C_{ij}; then $CA = AC = \det(A)I$—that is, the $p \times p$ diagonal matrix with the value $\det(A)$ on the diagonal.

The following computation rules apply for determinants, where A and B are square $p \times p$ matrices:

$$\det(A') = \det(A), \quad \det(AB) = \det(A)\det(B), \quad \det(A^{-1}) = 1/\det(A).$$

Example A.5: **Simulated Data on Student Learning (continued)**

As the determinant of the matrix $X'X$ is non-zero (see Example A.4), it has an inverse. Let the 2×2 cofactors of $X'X$ be denoted by C_{ij} $(i = 1, 2, 3,\ j = 1, 2, 3)$, then the (i, j)th element of $(X'X)^{-1}$ is equal to $C_{ji}/\det(X'X) = C_{ji}/107$. The nine cofactors are easily obtained from (A.1)—for instance, $C_{11} = (-1)^2(201 \cdot 175 - 186^2) = 579$, $C_{12} = (-1)^3(31 \cdot 175 - 186 \cdot 29) = -31$, and so on. This gives

$$(X'X)^{-1} = \frac{1}{107} \begin{pmatrix} 579 & -31 & -63 \\ -31 & 34 & -31 \\ -63 & -31 & 44 \end{pmatrix}. \tag{A.3}$$

From working out the matrix products it follows that $(X'X)(X'X)^{-1} = (X'X)^{-1}(X'X) = I_3$. Note that $X'X$ is a symmetric matrix and that $(X'X)^{-1}$ is also symmetric.

Rank of a matrix

If the determinant of a square matrix A is zero, then there does not exist an inverse matrix of A. Such a matrix is called non-invertible or singular.

The rank of a $p \times q$ matrix A is equal to the largest number r for which there exists a square submatrix of A of size $r \times r$ that has a non-zero determinant. Here square submatrices of size $r \times r$ are obtained by choosing the elements on the cross points of r chosen rows of the p rows of A and r chosen columns of the q columns of A. The rank of a $p \times q$ matrix A satisfies $\text{rank}(A) \leq \min(p, q)$ and the rank of the product of two matrices satisfies $\text{rank}(AB) \leq \min(\text{rank}(A), \text{rank}(B))$.

If a $p \times q$ matrix A has rank $r < q$, then there exists a non-zero $q \times 1$ vector b such that $Ab = 0$. One then says that the q columns of A are linearly dependent. If a square $p \times p$ matrix A has $\det(A) = 0$, then $\text{rank}(A) < p$ and there exists a

E

non-zero $p \times 1$ vector b such that $Ab = 0$. If A is invertible, then the only vector b for which $Ab = 0$ is $b = 0$. If a $p \times p$ matrix A has rank $r < p$, then there exist $p \times r$ matrices B and C with $\text{rank}(B) = \text{rank}(C) = r$ such that $A = BC'$.

E

Example A.6: **Simulated Data on Student Learning (continued)**

Consider the 3×5 matrix

$$X' = \begin{pmatrix} 1 & 1 & 1 & 1 & 1 \\ 4 & 6 & 6 & 7 & 8 \\ 4 & 5 & 7 & 6 & 7 \end{pmatrix}.$$

The 3×3 submatrix consisting of columns 2, 4, and 5 has determinant $(49 + 40 + 36 - 48 - 42 - 35) = 0$, but the submatrix consisting of the first three columns has determinant $(42 + 24 + 20 - 30 - 28 \ -24) = 4 \neq 0$. This shows that $\text{rank}(X') = 3$. As X' has five columns, there exists a non-zero 5×1 vector b so that $X'b = 0$. For instance, $b = (-2, 5, 1, -4, 0)'$ is such a vector. The five columns c_i (3×1 vectors, $i = 1, \cdots, 5$) of X' are linearly dependent—for instance, $c_3 = 2c_1 - 5c_2 + 4c_4$.

Eigenvalues and eigenvectors

A (possibly complex) number λ is called an eigenvalue of the square $p \times p$ matrix A if $\det(A - \lambda I_p) = 0$. When seen as a function of the (complex) variable $z, f(z) = \det(A - zI_p)$ is a polynomial in z of order p. This is called the characteristic polynomial of A and it has p (possibly non-distinct) roots $\lambda_i, i = 1, \cdots, p$—that is, values for which $f(\lambda_i) = 0$. These roots are the eigenvalues of A, and for each root λ_i there exists a (possibly complex-valued) non-zero $p \times 1$ vector v_i such that $(A - \lambda_i I_p)v_i = 0$—that is, such that $Av_i = \lambda_i v_i$. So if the vector v_i is multiplied by the matrix A, then the resulting vector is a multiple of v_i. Such a vector is called an eigenvector of the matrix A corresponding to the eigenvalue λ_i.

Let the square $p \times p$ matrix A have eigenvalues $\lambda_1, \cdots, \lambda_p$; then the determinant of A is equal to the product $\prod_{i=1}^{p} \lambda_i$ and the trace of A is equal to the sum $\sum_{i=1}^{n} \lambda_i$. Further, let A^k be the matrix product $A \times A \times \cdots \times A$ (with k terms A); then $A^k \to 0$ for $k \to \infty$ if and only if all eigenvalues λ_i lie inside the unit circle in the complex plane.

Eigenvalue decomposition of a symmetric matrix

If the matrix A (with a_{ij} real-valued for all i, j) is symmetric, then all its eigenvalues are real-valued. Moreover there exist p real-valued eigenvectors v_i such that $Av_i = \lambda_i v_i$ with the properties that $v_i'v_i = 1$ for all $i = 1, \cdots, p$, and $v_i'v_j = 0$ for all $i \neq j$. Let V be the $p \times p$ matrix with ith column v_i; then it follows that $V'V = I$ so that $V^{-1} = V'$. Such a matrix is called orthogonal. Further let D be the $p \times p$ diagonal matrix with the values $\lambda_1, \cdots, \lambda_p$ on the diagonal; then there holds $AV = A(v_1 \cdots v_p) = (Av_1 \cdots Av_p) = (\lambda_1 v_1 \cdots \lambda_p v_p) = (v_1 \cdots v_p)D = VD$ and hence $A = VDV^{-1} = VDV'$. Summarizing, every symmetric $p \times p$ matrix A (with real-valued elements a_{ij}) can be written as

$$A = VDV', \tag{A.4}$$

where D is a diagonal matrix and V an orthogonal matrix with the property that $V'V = VV' = I_p$.

Example A.7: **Simulated Data on Student Learning (continued)**

We consider the symmetric matrix $X'X$ in (A.1). If the calculation rule for the determinant of the 3×3 matrix $X'X - zI_3$ is applied, the characteristic polynomial is obtained as

$$f(z) = \det(X'X - zI) = -z^3 + 381z^2 - 657z + 107.$$

Exhibit A.2 shows the values of this polynomial for real values of z. It is seen that this polynomial has three positive roots. So the three eigenvalues are real and positive, with (rounded) values $\lambda_1 = 0.18208$, $\lambda_2 = 1.54946$, and $\lambda_3 =$

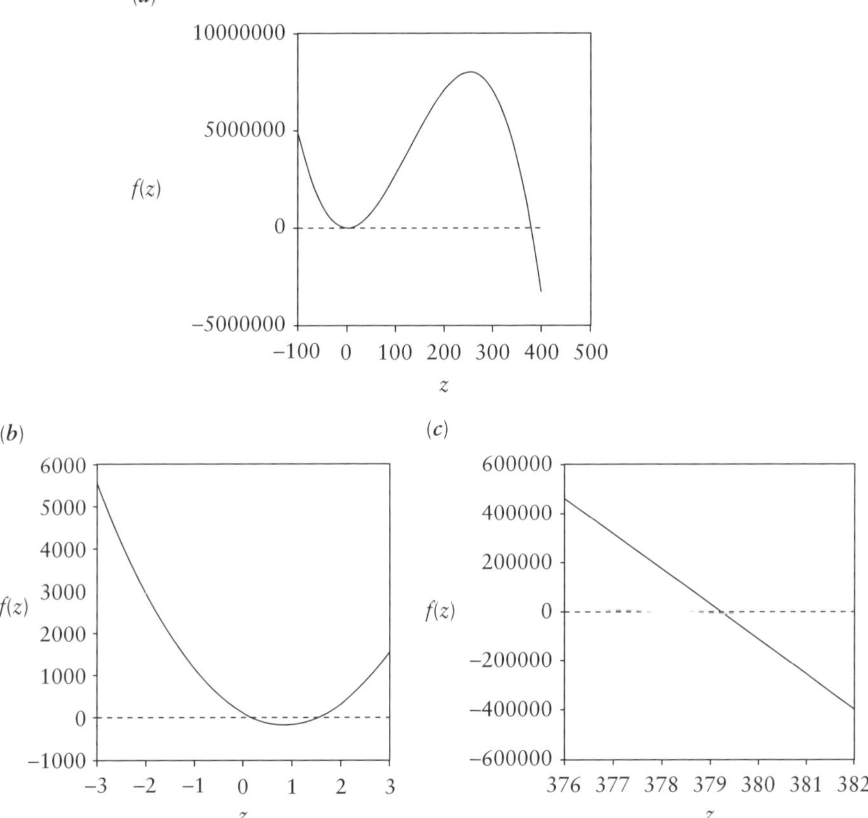

Exhibit A.2 Simulated Data on Student Learning (Example A.7)

Characteristic polynomial $f(z)$ of the 3×3 matrix $X'X$ (*a*) with details on two subintervals, one near the roots 0.18 and 1.55 (*b*) and the other near the root 379.27 (*c*).

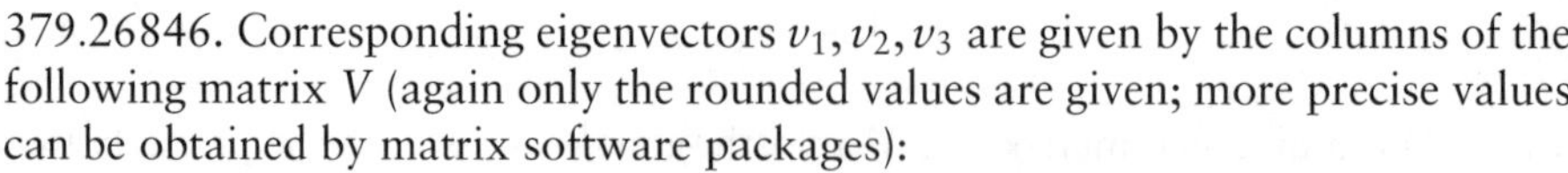

379.26846. Corresponding eigenvectors v_1, v_2, v_3 are given by the columns of the following matrix V (again only the rounded values are given; more precise values can be obtained by matrix software packages):

$$V = (v_1,\ v_2,\ v_3) = \begin{pmatrix} 0.99246 & 0.04813 & 0.11270 \\ -0.04929 & -0.68522 & 0.72667 \\ -0.11220 & 0.72675 & 0.67768 \end{pmatrix}.$$

By computing the respective matrix products one can directly verify that (up to rounding errors) $X'Xv_i = \lambda_i v_i$ $(i = 1, 2, 3)$ and that $V'V = VV' = I_3$ and $VDV' = X'X$, where D is the diagonal matrix with the elements $\lambda_1, \lambda_2, \lambda_3$ on the diagonal.

A.6 Positive (semi)definite matrices and projections

☞ Used in Chapters 1, 3, 5, 7.

Positive (semi)definite matrix

Let A be a square $p \times p$ symmetric matrix; then for every $p \times 1$ vector b the product $b'Ab$ is a 1×1 matrix—that is, this product is a scalar number. A symmetric matrix A is called positive definite if $b'Ab > 0$ for every non-zero vector b. It is called positive semidefinite if $b'Ab \geq 0$ for all vectors b. It is called negative definite if $b'Ab < 0$ for every non-zero vector b and it is called negative semidefinite if $b'Ab \leq 0$ for all vectors b. Let A be a $p \times q$ matrix; then AA' and $A'A$ are positive semidefinite matrices. For instance, for every $q \times 1$ vector b there holds $b'A'Ab = (Ab)'(Ab) = c'c = \sum_{j=1}^{p} c_j^2 \geq 0$, where c_j $(j = 1, \cdots, p)$ are the elements of the $p \times 1$ vector $c = Ab$. If $\text{rank}(A) = q$, then the $q \times q$ matrix $A'A$ has rank q and it is positive definite.

Square root of a positive definite matrix

If the symmetric matrix A is positive definite, then it has an inverse A^{-1} and this matrix is also positive definite. Further, if A is a $p \times p$ symmetric positive definite matrix, then there exist a $p \times p$ matrix B and $p \times p$ symmetric positive definite matrices C_1 and C_2, such that

$$BAB' = I_p,\ C_1C_1 = A,\ C_2C_2 = A^{-1}.$$

This can be proved by means of the decomposition $A = VDV'$ in (A.4), where V is an orthogonal matrix with $VV' = V'V = I_p$ and D is a diagonal matrix with elements $\lambda_1, \cdots, \lambda_p$. Let v_i be the ith column of V; then, because A is positive definite, it follows that $v_i'Av_i = \lambda_i > 0$. Let $D^{1/2}$ be the diagonal matrix with elements $\sqrt{\lambda_i}$ on the diagonal and let $D^{-1/2}$ be the diagonal matrix with elements $1/\sqrt{\lambda_i}$ on the diagonal. Then $B = D^{-1/2}V'$, $C_1 = VD^{1/2}V'$ and $C_2 = VD^{-1/2}V'$

have the properties mentioned above. The matrix C_1 is called a square root of the matrix A and C_2 is a square root of A^{-1}.

Example A.8: Simulated Data on Student Learning (continued)

The 5×3 matrix X has rank three, and the foregoing results imply that $X'X$ and $(X'X)^{-1}$ are positive definite. We check this for the matrix $X'X$ in (A.1) and leave the other one as an exercise (use the numerical values for $(X'X)^{-1}$ obtained in (A.3) in Example A.5). Let b be a 3×1 vector with elements b_1, b_2, b_3, then

$$\begin{aligned}
b'X'Xb &= 5b_1^2 + 201b_2^2 + 175b_3^2 + 62b_1b_2 + 58b_1b_3 + 372b_2b_3 \\
&= 5(b_1 + 6.2b_2 + 5.8b_3)^2 + (201 - 5(6.2)^2)b_2^2 + (175 - 5(5.8)^2)b_3^2 \\
&\quad + (372 - 10(6.2)(5.8)\,)b_2b_3 \\
&= 5(b_1 + 6.2b_2 + 5.8b_3)^2 + 8.8b_2^2 + 6.8b_3^2 + 12.4b_2b_3 \\
&= 5(b_1 + 6.2b_2 + 5.8b_3)^2 + 8.8\left(b_2 + \frac{6.2}{8.8}b_3\right)^2 + \left(6.8 - 8.8\frac{(6.2)^2}{(8.8)^2}\right)b_3^2 \\
&= 5(b_1 + 6.2b_2 + 5.8b_3)^2 + 8.8\left(b_2 + \frac{3.1}{4.4}b_3\right)^2 + \frac{10.7}{4.4}b_3^2.
\end{aligned}$$

As this is a sum of three squared terms with positive weights it follows that $b'X'Xb \geq 0$, and $b'X'Xb = 0$ if and only if all three terms are zero. The last term in the sum shows that then $b_3 = 0$, the middle term then implies that $b_2 = 0$, and subsequently the first term implies that also $b_1 = 0$. Stated otherwise, for $b \neq 0$ we have $b'X'Xb > 0$ and this shows that $X'X$ is positive definite.

Projection matrix

A square $p \times p$ matrix A is called idempotent if $AA = A$. A symmetric idempotent matrix is called a projection matrix. A projection matrix is positive semidefinite because $A = AA = A'A$. If A is a $p \times q$ matrix with $\text{rank}(A) = q$, so that $A'A$ is an invertible $q \times q$ matrix, then $P = A(A'A)^{-1}A'$ is a $p \times p$ projection matrix with $\text{rank}(P) = q$. Because $PA = A$ this means that every column of A remains unchanged when multiplied by P, so that P has q eigenvalues equal to one. The other $(p - q)$ eigenvalues of P are zero. A $p \times p$ projection matrix A with $\text{rank}(A) = r$ can be written as $A = K'K$ for an $r \times p$ matrix K with $KK' = I_r$. To construct K, let $A = VDV'$ be the decomposition (A.4), where the diagonal matrix D contains the eigenvalues of A—that is, the diagonal contains r times a one on the diagonal followed by $(p - q)$ times a zero. Let V_r be the $p \times r$ submatrix consisting of the first r columns of V; then $K = V_r'$ has the stated properties.

Example A.9: Simulated Data on Student Learning (continued)

The 5×3 matrix X that we considered before has rank 3 (see Example A.6). If we use the result for the inverse $(X'X)^{-1}$ in (A.3) in Example A.5, the matrix $P = X(X'X)^{-1}X'$ is equal to

$$P = \begin{pmatrix} 1 & 4 & 4 \\ 1 & 6 & 5 \\ 1 & 6 & 7 \\ 1 & 7 & 6 \\ 1 & 8 & 7 \end{pmatrix} \frac{1}{107} \begin{pmatrix} 579 & -31 & -63 \\ -31 & 34 & -31 \\ -63 & -31 & 44 \end{pmatrix} \begin{pmatrix} 1 & 1 & 1 & 1 & 1 \\ 4 & 6 & 6 & 7 & 8 \\ 4 & 5 & 7 & 6 & 7 \end{pmatrix}$$

$$= \frac{1}{107} \begin{pmatrix} 83 & 34 & 12 & 4 & -26 \\ 34 & 41 & -17 & 30 & 19 \\ 12 & -17 & 101 & -2 & 13 \\ 4 & 30 & -2 & 35 & 40 \\ -26 & 19 & 13 & 40 & 61 \end{pmatrix}.$$

Clearly, P is symmetric and one can check by direct computation that $PP = P$, so that P is also idempotent. So P is a projection matrix. According to earlier results $\text{tr}(P) = \sum_{i=1}^{5} \lambda_i = 3$, as P has three eigenvalues equal to one and two eigenvalues equal to zero. It is easily checked that the trace of the above matrix P is indeed equal to three. By applying a matrix software package to determine the eigenvectors of P, we can compute the following (rounded) 3×5 matrix K (here we do not show the calculation of the required eigenvalues and eigenvectors to compute $K = V_r'$):

$$K = \begin{pmatrix} -0.08169 & -0.53396 & 0.42535 & -0.52027 & -0.50657 \\ -0.84091 & -0.29451 & 0.08260 & 0.07297 & 0.44045 \\ 0.24880 & 0.10645 & 0.86959 & 0.22606 & 0.34566 \end{pmatrix}.$$

It is a matter of direct computation to check that (up to rounding errors) $K'K = P$ and $KK' = I_3$.

A.7 Optimization of a function of several variables

☞ Used in Chapters 1–7.

Notation

An econometric model often contains a number of unknown parameters that are estimated by optimizing a numerical criterion. Examples are least squares (discussed in Chapters 2 and 3) and maximum likelihood (discussed in Chapter 4). We denote the unknown parameters by the $p \times 1$ vector b and the criterion function by $f(b)$, where $f(b)$ is a real number that depends on the value of b. For instance, in our example of student scores the least squares criterion (A.2) is a function that takes on non-negative values that depend on the chosen values of the three parameters b_1, b_2, b_3.

Continuous and differentiable functions

First we summarize some concepts and results for functions of a single variable—that is, with $p = 1$. A function $f(b)$ of a single variable b is called continuous if, for every value of b_0, the function values $f(b)$ are close to $f(b_0)$ if b is close to b_0. This is written as $\lim_{b \to b_0} f(b) = f(b_0)$, and the formal definition is that for every number $\delta_1 > 0$ there exists a number $\delta_2 > 0$ with the property that $|f(b) - f(b_0)| < \delta_1$ for all $|b - b_0| < \delta_2$. The function f is called differentiable if, for every value of b_0, there exists a value (say a_0), such that

$$\lim_{h \to 0} \frac{f(b_0 + h) - f(b_0) - a_0 h}{h} = 0.$$

We will write this as $f(b_0 + h) - f(b_0) - a_0 h \approx 0$ if $h \approx 0$, or also as $f(b_0 + h) \approx f(b_0) + h a_0$ if $h \approx 0$. The value a_0 is called the derivative of f at b_0 and is written as $\frac{df}{db}(b_0)$, and the function $\frac{df}{db}(b)$, seen as a function of b, is called the derivative of f. Writing $b = b_0 + h$, we obtain from the foregoing that

$$f(b) \approx f(b_0) + \frac{df}{db}(b_0) \cdot (b - b_0) \text{ if } b \approx b_0.$$

For fixed value of b_0 the right-hand side of the above expression is a linear function of b, which is called the linear approximation of the function f at b_0.

Maxima and minima

The function f is said to have a global maximum at b_0 if $f(b_0) \geq f(b)$ for all values of b. The function f has a local maximum at b_0 if $f(b_0) \geq f(b)$ for all b close to b_0, formally, if there exists a $\delta > 0$ such that $f(b_0) \geq f(b)$ for all $|b - b_0| < \delta$. The function f has a global (local) minimum at b_0 if $f(b_0) \leq f(b)$ for all b (respectively for all b close to b_0). If f is differentiable, then

$$\frac{df}{db}(b_0) = 0$$

for all values of b_0 where f has a (global or local) maximum or minimum. This is called the first order condition for a maximum or minimum of the function f. To distinguish between maxima and minima we consider the second derivative of f—that is, the derivative of $\frac{df}{db}$, where we assume that this is a differentiable function. The second derivative is denoted by $\frac{d^2 f}{db^2}$. The function f has a local maximum at b_0 if $\frac{df}{db}(b_0) = 0$ and $\frac{d^2 f}{db^2}(b_0) < 0$, and it has a local minimum if $\frac{df}{db}(b_0) = 0$ and $\frac{d^2 f}{db^2}(b_0) > 0$.

Continuity of a function of several variables

Now we extend the concepts above to functions $f(b)$ of several variables—that is, where b is a $p \times 1$ vector with $p > 1$. The function $f(b)$ is called continuous if, for every given $p \times 1$ vector b_0, the function values $f(b)$ are close to $f(b_0)$ if b is close to b_0. Formally, the function is continuous at b_0 if for every $\delta_1 > 0$ there exists a

$\delta_2 > 0$ such that $|f(b) - f(b_0)| < \delta_1$ for all $\|b - b_0\| < \delta_2$. Here $\|b - b_0\|$ denotes the distance between the two $p \times 1$ vectors b and b_0, defined by $\|b - b_0\| = \left(\sum_{i=1}^{p} (b_i - b_{0i})^2\right)^{1/2}$, where b_i and b_{0i} denote the components of b and b_0 respectively.

Differentiability of a function of several variables

The function $f(b)$ is said to be partially differentiable with respect to the ith component b_i if, for every given $p \times 1$ vector $b_0 = (b_{01}, \cdots, b_{0p})'$, the function $g(b_i) = f(b_{01}, \cdots, b_{0i-1}, b_i, b_{0i+1}, \cdots, b_{0p})$ is a differentiable function of the (single) variable b_i. The ith partial derivative of f at b_0 is defined as $\frac{dg}{db_i}(b_0)$ and is denoted by $\frac{\partial f}{\partial b_i}(b_0)$. If the function f is partially differentiable with respect to all its p components, then the gradient of f at b_0 is defined as the $p \times 1$ vector with the p partial derivatives as elements. The gradient is denoted by $\frac{\partial f}{\partial b}$, so that

$$\frac{\partial f}{\partial b}(b_0) = \begin{pmatrix} \frac{\partial f}{\partial b_1}(b_0) \\ \frac{\partial f}{\partial b_2}(b_0) \\ \vdots \\ \frac{\partial f}{\partial b_p}(b_0) \end{pmatrix}.$$

From the results for functions of a single variable it follows that $f(b) \approx f(b_0) + \frac{\partial f}{\partial b_i}(b_0) \cdot (b_i - b_{0i})$ if $b_i \approx b_{0i}$ and $b_j = b_{0j}$ for all $j \neq i$—that is, if only the ith component of b varies. The function f is called differentiable if for every $p \times 1$ vector b_0 there exists a $p \times 1$ vector a_0 such that

$$\lim_{h \to 0} \frac{f(b_0 + h) - f(b_0) - a_0' h}{\|h\|} = 0.$$

Here h denotes a $p \times 1$ vector and $h \to 0$ means that $\|h\| = \left(\sum_{i=1}^{p} h_i^2\right)^{1/2} \to 0$. In particular, if we take $h = (0, \cdots, 0, h_i, 0, \cdots, 0)'$ with a single element h_i on the ith position and zeros elsewhere, then $f(b_0 + h)$ is a function only of the ith component of b, so that $a_{0i} = \frac{\partial f}{\partial b_i}(b_0)$ and a_0 is the gradient of f at b_0. Let $b = b_0 + h$; then we can write the above result as

$$f(b) \approx f(b_0) + \left(\frac{\partial f}{\partial b}(b_0)\right)'(b - b_0) \text{ if } b \approx b_0.$$

This is called the linear approximation of the function f at b_0.

E

Example A.10: **Simulated Data on Student Learning (continued)**

We consider the sum of squares $f(b) = (y - Xb)'(y - Xb)$ of $p = 3$ variables defined in (A.2) in Example A.3—that is,

$$f(b) = 38.66 - 27.2b_1 - 176b_2 - 164b_3 + 5b_1^2 + 201b_2^2 + 175b_3^2 + 62b_1b_2 + 58b_1b_3 + 372b_2b_3.$$

The gradient of f at b is equal to

$$\frac{\partial f}{\partial b} = \begin{pmatrix} \frac{\partial f}{\partial b_1} \\ \frac{\partial f}{\partial b_2} \\ \frac{\partial f}{\partial b_3} \end{pmatrix} = \begin{pmatrix} -27.2 + 10b_1 + 62b_2 + 58b_3 \\ -176 + 402b_2 + 62b_1 + 372b_3 \\ -164 + 350b_3 + 58b_1 + 372b_2 \end{pmatrix}$$

$$= \begin{pmatrix} -27.2 \\ -176 \\ -164 \end{pmatrix} + \begin{pmatrix} 10 & 62 & 58 \\ 62 & 402 & 372 \\ 58 & 372 & 350 \end{pmatrix} \begin{pmatrix} b_1 \\ b_2 \\ b_3 \end{pmatrix}. \qquad \text{(A.5)}$$

If we compare this with (A.1) in Example A.3, then we see that the gradient of the least squares criterion $(y - Xb)'(y - Xb) = y'y - 2b'X'y + b'X'Xb$ can be written as

$$\frac{\partial (y - Xb)'(y - Xb)}{\partial b} = -2X'y + 2X'Xb.$$

Maxima and minima of functions of several variables

The function f is said to have a global (local) maximum at b_0 if $f(b_0) \geq f(b)$ for all b (respectively for all b close to b_0), and a global (local) minimum if $f(b_0) \leq f(b)$ for all b (respectively for all b close to b_0). If the function f is differentiable, then it satisfies the following p first order conditions in all points b_0 where f has a local maximum or minimum:

$$\frac{\partial f}{\partial b}(b_0) = 0.$$

This corresponds to p equations in the p variables b_0. To distinguish between maxima and minima we assume that the function f is twice differentiable—that is, that each of the p functions $g_i(b) = \frac{\partial f}{\partial b_i}(b)$ is a differentiable function of b. Then the p^2 second order partial derivatives of f are defined by $\frac{\partial^2 f}{\partial b_j \partial b_i} = \frac{\partial g_i}{\partial b_j}$ for $i = 1, \cdots, p$, $j = 1, \cdots, p$. The Hessian matrix of f at b_0 is the $p \times p$ matrix of second order derivatives defined by

$$\frac{\partial^2 f}{\partial b \partial b'}(b_0) = \begin{pmatrix} \frac{\partial^2 f}{\partial b_1 \partial b_1}(b_0) & \frac{\partial^2 f}{\partial b_1 \partial b_2}(b_0) & \cdots & \frac{\partial^2 f}{\partial b_1 \partial b_p}(b_0) \\ \frac{\partial^2 f}{\partial b_2 \partial b_1}(b_0) & \frac{\partial^2 f}{\partial b_2 \partial b_2}(b_0) & \cdots & \frac{\partial^2 f}{\partial b_2 \partial b_p}(b_0) \\ \vdots & \vdots & \vdots & \vdots \\ \frac{\partial^2 f}{\partial b_p \partial b_1}(b_0) & \frac{\partial^2 f}{\partial b_p \partial b_2}(b_0) & \cdots & \frac{\partial^2 f}{\partial b_p \partial b_p}(b_0) \end{pmatrix}.$$

The function f has a local maximum at b_0 if it satisfies the first order conditions at b_0 and the Hessian matrix at b_0 is negative definite. This maximum is global if the Hessian matrix is negative definite for all $p \times 1$ vectors b. The function has a local minimum at b_0 if it satisfies the first order conditions at b_0 and the Hessian matrix at b_0 is positive definite, and the minimum is global if the Hessian matrix is positive definite for all values of b.

XMA01SIM

Example A.11: **Simulated Data on Student Learning (continued)**

We continue our analysis of Example A.10 of the sum of squares function $f(b) = (y - Xb)'(y - Xb)$ in (A.2). To determine the minimum of this function we first solve the first order conditions $\frac{\partial f}{\partial b} = 0$. According to the foregoing analysis in Example A.10, the gradient can be written as $-2X'y + 2X'Xb = 0$. So the first order conditions correspond to the three linear equations $X'Xb = X'y$. These are called the normal equations. We saw before that $X'X$ is an invertible matrix and we computed the inverse matrix in Example A.5 (see (A.3)). The vector $X'y$ was computed in Example A.3 (see (A.1)). If we use these results, it follows that the first order conditions are satisfied for the unique vector b given by

$$b = (X'X)^{-1}X'y = \frac{1}{107}\begin{pmatrix} 579 & -31 & -63 \\ -31 & 34 & -31 \\ -63 & -31 & 44 \end{pmatrix}\begin{pmatrix} 13.6 \\ 88.0 \\ 82.0 \end{pmatrix} = \frac{1}{107}\begin{pmatrix} -19.6 \\ 28.4 \\ 23.2 \end{pmatrix}.$$

To prove that these values of b provide a minimum of $f(b)$ we have to prove that the Hessian matrix at this point is positive definite. From the gradient in (A.5) in Example A.10 we obtain

$$\frac{\partial^2 f}{\partial b \partial b'} = \begin{pmatrix} \frac{\partial^2 f}{\partial b_1 \partial b_1} & \frac{\partial^2 f}{\partial b_1 \partial b_2} & \frac{\partial^2 f}{\partial b_1 \partial b_3} \\ \frac{\partial^2 f}{\partial b_2 \partial b_1} & \frac{\partial^2 f}{\partial b_2 \partial b_2} & \frac{\partial^2 f}{\partial b_2 \partial b_3} \\ \frac{\partial^2 f}{\partial b_3 \partial b_1} & \frac{\partial^2 f}{\partial b_3 \partial b_2} & \frac{\partial^2 f}{\partial b_3 \partial b_3} \end{pmatrix} = \begin{pmatrix} 10 & 62 & 58 \\ 62 & 402 & 372 \\ 58 & 372 & 350 \end{pmatrix}.$$

So the Hessian matrix is equal to $2X'X$ with $X'X$ given in (A.1). We have already checked in Example A.8 that $X'X$ is positive definite. As the Hessian matrix does not depend on the value of the 3×1 vector b, it follows that the computed value of $b = \left(-\frac{19.6}{107}, \frac{28.4}{107}, \frac{23.2}{107}\right)'$ is a global minimum of the least squares criterion $f(b)$. The

Dependent Variable: FGPA Method: Least Squares Included observations: 5	
Variable	Coefficient
CONSTANT	−0.183178
SATM	0.265421
SATV	0.216822
Sum Squared Residuals	0.014766

Exhibit A.3 Simulated Data on Student Learning (Example A.11)

Output of an econometric software package for the least squares coefficients and the corresponding sum of squares for the data of Exhibit A.1 on the scores FGPA, SATM, and SATV of five students.

vector b is called the least squares estimate of the parameters b_1, b_2, b_3 for the score data of the five students, and the corresponding model is given by $y = -\frac{19.6}{107} + \frac{28.4}{107}x + \frac{23.2}{107}z \approx -0.183 + 0.265x + 0.217z$, where y stands for FGPA, x for SATM, and z for SATV. The corresponding minimum sum of squares is obtained from (A.2) in Example A.3, with (rounded) value $f(-\frac{19.6}{107}, \frac{28.4}{107}, \frac{23.2}{107}) \approx 0.0148$.

For comparison, Exhibit A.3 contains the output of an econometric software package.

A.8 Concentration and the Lagrange method

☞ Used in Chapter 4.

Method of concentration in optimization

To determine the maximum or minimum of a function of several variables it is sometimes helpful to use the so-called concentration method. Let $f(b)$ be a function of the $p \times 1$ vector b and let this vector be split in two parts, a $p_1 \times 1$ vector b_1 and a $(p - p_1) \times 1$ vector b_2, so that $f(b)$ can be written as $f(b_1, b_2)$. For given values of b_1 the function $f(b_1, b_2)$ can be viewed as a function of b_2. Let $m(b_1) = \max_{b_2} f(b_1, b_2)$ be the maximum (with respect to b_2) of $f(b_1, b_2)$ for given values of b_1; then the maximum value $m(b_1)$ is a function of b_1 that can be maximized (with respect to b_1). There holds

$$\max_{b_1, b_2} f(b_1, b_2) = \max_{b_1} \{\max_{b_2} f(b_1, b_2)\}.$$

A similar result holds true for the minimum of a function. The advantage of the concentration method is that the two minimizations involve less variables ($(p - p_1)$ and p_1 respectively) than the one-shot minimization of f with respect to all its p components.

Method of Lagrange

As a final topic we consider the maximization or minimization of functions under restrictions. Let f and g_j $(j = 1, \cdots, r)$ be differentiable functions of p variables b, and suppose we wish to determine the maximum or minimum of the function $f(b)$ under the restrictions that $g_j(b) = 0$ for all $j = 1, \cdots, r$. We suppose that the derivatives of f and g_j $(j = 1, \cdots, r)$ are all continuous functions and that the $p \times r$ matrix with columns $\frac{\partial g_j}{\partial b}$ $(j = 1, \cdots, r)$ has rank r. The method of Lagrange states that the constrained maxima and minima of $f(b)$ satisfy the first order conditions for the Lagrange function $\Lambda(b, \lambda)$ defined by

$$\Lambda(b, \lambda) = f(b) - \sum_{j=1}^{r} \lambda_j g_j(b).$$

The corresponding set of first order conditions is given by

$$\frac{\partial \Lambda}{\partial b_i} = \frac{\partial f}{\partial b_i} - \sum_{j=1}^{r} \lambda_j \frac{\partial g_j}{\partial b_i} = 0, \quad i = 1, \cdots, p,$$

$$\frac{\partial \Lambda}{\partial \lambda_j} = g_j(b) = 0, \quad j = 1, \cdots, r.$$

Solutions for this set of $(p+r)$ equations in the $(p+r)$ unknowns (b, λ) can be obtained by numerical methods.

Interpretation of the Lagrange multipliers

Let (b_0, λ_0) be a solution of the above set of $(p+r)$ equations; then the Lagrange multipliers λ_{0j} have the following interpretation. Let h be a $p \times 1$ vector with small entries such that $g_1(b_0 + h) = \alpha_1 \neq 0$ and $g_j(b_0 + h) = 0$ for all $j = 2, \cdots, r$. This corresponds to relaxing the first restriction. As h is small, it follows that $\alpha_1 = g_1(b_0 + h) \approx \left(\frac{\partial g_1}{\partial b}(b_0)\right)' h$ and $0 = g_j(b_0 + h) \approx \left(\frac{\partial g_j}{\partial b}(b_0)\right)' h$ for $j = 2, \cdots, r$, and from the first p first order conditions of the Lagrange function it follows that

$$f(b_0 + h) \approx f(b_0) + \left(\frac{\partial f}{\partial b}(b_0)\right)' h = f(b_0) + \left(\sum_{j=1}^{r} \lambda_{0j} \frac{\partial g_j}{\partial b}(b_0)\right)' h \approx f(b_0) + \lambda_{01}\alpha_1.$$

That is, λ_{01} measures the marginal effect on the value of the function f when the first restriction is relaxed. In a similar way, λ_{0j} measures the marginal effect on the function value due to relaxing the jth restriction. For this reason, in business and economics the Lagrange multipliers λ_0 are also called the shadow prices of the r restrictions.

E

Example A.12: **Simulated Data on Student Learning (continued)**

We consider again the scores of the five students and we minimize the sum of squares $f(b) = (y - Xb)'(y - Xb)$ in (A.2) of Example A.3 under the two restrictions that $b_2 = 0$ and $b_3 = 0$. That is, we impose the model restriction that SATM and SATV do not affect the FGPA scores. The corresponding Lagrange function is $\Lambda = f(b) - \lambda_1 b_2 - \lambda_2 b_3$, and, using the expression (A.5) in Example A.10 for the gradient of f, we obtain the following first order conditions:

$$\frac{\partial \Lambda}{\partial b_1} = \frac{\partial f}{\partial b_1} = -27.2 + 10b_1 + 62b_2 + 58b_3 = 0,$$

$$\frac{\partial \Lambda}{\partial b_2} = \frac{\partial f}{\partial b_2} - \lambda_1 = -176 + 62b_1 + 402b_2 + 372b_3 - \lambda_1 = 0,$$

$$\frac{\partial \Lambda}{\partial b_3} = \frac{\partial f}{\partial b_3} - \lambda_2 = -164 + 58b_1 + 372b_2 + 350b_3 - \lambda_2 = 0,$$

$$\frac{\partial \Lambda}{\partial \lambda_1} = b_2 = 0,$$

$$\frac{\partial \Lambda}{\partial \lambda_2} = b_3 = 0.$$

Substituting $b_2 = b_3 = 0$ in the first equation gives $b_1 = 2.72$ with corresponding sum of squares $f(2.72, 0, 0) = 1.668$. The second and third equation give $\lambda_1 = -7.36$ and $\lambda_2 = -6.24$. For instance, if we relax the first restriction to $b_2 = \alpha_1 = 0.001$, then $f(2.72, 0.001, 0) = 1.660841$ and the 'increase' in the sum of squares is $1.660841 - 1.668 = -0.007159 \approx -0.00736 = \lambda_1 \alpha_1$. In a similar way, relaxing the third restriction to $b_3 = \alpha_2 = 0.001$ gives $f(2.72, 0, 0.001) = 1.661935$, with corresponding 'increase' in the sum of squares $1.661935 - 1.668 = -0.006065 \approx -0.00624 = \lambda_2 \alpha_2$.

Exercise

Consider the data on FGPA (denoted by y), SATM (denoted by x), and SATV (denoted by z) of the five students in Exhibit A.1. In the text we discussed the model $y = b_1 + b_2 x + b_3 z$. In this exercise we analyse this model without the constant term—that is,

$$y = c_1 x + c_2 z.$$

a. Write this model in the form $y = Zc$ where y is the vector of FGPA scores and Z the matrix with SATM and SATV scores and where c is the 2×1 vector with the coefficients c_1 and c_2.

b. Compute the matrix $Z'Z$ and its inverse $(Z'Z)^{-1}$.

c. Check that the matrices $Z'Z$ and $(Z'Z)^{-1}$ are both positive definite.

d. Compute the two eigenvalues of the matrix $Z'Z$ and check that the sum and product of these two eigenvalues are respectively equal to the trace and the determinant of this matrix.

e. Write $f(c_1, c_2) = (y - Zc)'(y - Zc)$ as a function of c_1 and c_2. Derive the gradient and the Hessian matrix of this function.

f. Use the results in **e** to compute the minimum of the function $f(c_1, c_2)$ and prove that this is a global minimum.

g. Check that the global minimum in **f** is obtained for $c = (Z'Z)^{-1} Z'y$.

h. The model of this exercise corresponds to the original model $y = b_1 + b_2 x + b_3 z$ under the restriction that $b_1 = 0$. The values of c_1 and c_2 computed in **f** minimize the function $g(b_1, b_2, b_3) = \sum_{i=1}^{5} (y_i - b_1 - b_2 x_i - b_3 z_i)^2$ under the restriction that $b_1 = 0$. Write down the Lagrange function $\Lambda(b_1, b_2, b_3, \lambda)$ that corresponds to this restricted minimization problem, and derive the four first order conditions for a minimum of the function Λ.

i. Solve the four equations of **h** and check that the restricted estimates of b_2 and b_3 are equal to the computed values of c_1 and c_2 in **f**. What is the shadow price of the restriction $b_1 = 0$? Give an interpretation of the shadow price, using the results of Example A.11.

j. Use a software package to check the computed values of c_1 and c_2 in **f**.

Appendix B. **Data Sets**

This appendix describes the data sources and the definitions of the variables of all empirical data sets used in the examples and in the empirical exercises.[1] The numerical data can be downloaded from the web site of the book. All econometric analysis in the examples and exercises in the book is performed with the software package EViews (version 3 suffices), but other packages can also be used in most cases.

The names of the data files start with XM for examples and with XR for exercises, followed by three digits indicating the chapter and the example or exercise number, and concluded with three letters to indicate the data content. For instance, the file XR210COF contains the data of Exercise 2.10 on coffee sales. If a data set is used in different chapters, then separate data files are included for each chapter, because in some cases different variables are analysed in the different chapters. Some of the original data sources contain additional variables that are not mentioned if they are not used in this book. Missing values in the original data sources are not deleted.

The list on p. 748 facilitates the use of this appendix. For instance, if you need further information on the data in the file XR210COF, the list shows 'COF' (Coffee Sales) as the 4th data set described in this appendix. For each data set, this appendix gives information on

- the topic of the data set,
- the type of data,
- the source of the data,
- the meaning of the variables,
- a list of examples and exercises where the data are used in the book.

The data sets are ordered according to their first appearance in the book.

[1] In this appendix we do not discuss simulated data sets (which have extension SIM) because the main text describes the simulation set-up explicitly for each case. Some simulated data sets can be downloaded from the web site of the book—that is, the data needed for Exercises 4.12, 5.23, and 6.10, and for the examples in Appendix A.

List of Data Sets

(The chapters where the data set is used are in parentheses.)

1. STU: Student Learning (Chapters 1–3, 6).
2. BWA: Bank Wages (Chapters 1–6).
3. SMR: Stock Market Returns (Chapters 2, 4, 5, 7).
4. COF: Coffee Sales (Chapters 2–5).
5. PMI: Primary Metal Industries (Chapters 3, 7).
6. MGC: Motor Gasoline Consumption (Chapters 3, 5, 7).
7. FEX: Food Expenditure (Chapters 4, 5).
8. FAS: Fashion Sales (Chapters 5, 7).
9. IBR: Interest and Bond Rates (Chapters 5, 7).
10. INP: Industrial Production (Chapters 5, 7).
11. TOP: Salaries of Top Managers (Chapter 5).
12. USP: US Presidential Election (Chapter 5).
13. DMF: Direct Marketing for Financial Product (Chapter 6).
14. DUS: Duration of Strikes (Chapter 6).
15. DJI: Dow-Jones Index (Chapter 7).
16. MOM: Mortality and Marriages (Chapter 7).
17. TBR: Treasury Bill Rates (Chapter 7).
18. CAR: Car Production (Chapter 7).
19. NEP: Nuclear Energy Production (Chapter 7).
20. GNP: Gross National Product (Chapter 7).
21. EXR: Exchange Rates (Chapter 7).
22. STP: Standard and Poor Index (Chapter 7).
23. MOR: Market for Oranges (Chapter 7).

1. Student Learning (STU)

Topic. Scores of students of the Vanderbilt University in the USA.

Type of data. Cross section, 609 observations, 4 variables.

Source. J. S. Butler, T. A. Finegan, and J. J. Siegfried, 'Does More Calculus Improve Student Learning in Intermediate Micro- and Macroeconomic Theory?', *Journal of Applied Econometrics*, 13/2 (1998), 185–202 (data obtained from the journal data archive on the Internet site qed.econ.queensu.ca/jae).

Variable	Meaning
FGPA	overall grade point average at end of freshman year (on a scale from 0 to 4)
SATM	score on the SAT Mathematics test divided by 100 (on a scale from 0 to 10)
SATV	score on the SAT Verbal test divided by 100 (on a scale from 0 to 10)
FEM	gender (1 for females, 0 for males)

Datafile	Used in
XM101STU[2]	Examples 1.1–1.7, 1.12, 1.13
XR111STU[3]	Exercises 1.11, 1.12, 2.14
XR314STU	Exercise 3.14
XM608STU[4]	Example 6.8
XR615STU[5]	Exercise 6.15

[2] Some examples use the variable SATA, the average SAT score defined by SATA = 0.5(SATM + SATV).

[3] This is a subset of ten randomly selected students out of the group of 609 students.

[4] Whereas the previous data sets of 609 students concerned the microeconomics course, this data set contains additional data of 490 students on the macroeconomics course (the data for microeconomics and those for macroeconomics are contained in two separate files). The data set contains several additional variables, such as GRINTERMICRO and GRINTERMACRO (obtained grades in microeconomics and macroeconomics, on a scale from 0 to 4) and MATHHIGH (the level of calculus of the student, 0 if 3–4 credit hours, 1 if 6–12 credit hours). See Exhibit 6.12 for a complete list of the variables.

[5] This is basically the same data set as the data set for microeconomics (with 609 students) in XM608STU, with the difference that this data set distinguishes seven attained levels of mathematics (instead of two) and five majors (instead of three).

2. Bank Wages (BWA)

Topic. Wages of employees of a bank in the USA.
Type of data. Cross section, 474 observations, 8 variables.
Source. SPSS, version 10, 2000, data file bank2.sav (with thanks to SPSS).

Variable	Meaning
SALARY	current yearly salary (in dollars)
LOGSALARY	(natural) logarithm of SALARY
EDUC	education (number of finished years)
SALBEGIN	yearly salary at employee's first position at same bank (in dollars)
LOGSALBEGIN	(natural) logarithm of SALBEGIN
GENDER	gender variable (0 for females, 1 for males)
MINORITY	minority variable (0 for non-minorities, 1 for minorities)
JOBCAT	job category (1 for administrative jobs, 2 for custodial jobs, 3 for management jobs)

Datafile	Used in
XR113BWA[6]	Exercise 1.13
XM202BWA[7]	Examples 2.2, 2.6, 2.9, 2.11; Section 2.1.4
XM301BWA[8]	Examples 3.1–3.3, 4.1; Sections 3.1.1, 3.1.7, 3.3.2, 3.3.4, 3.4.2, 3.4.4; Exercises 3.13, 3.16
XR414BWA	Example 4.1; Exercises 4.14, 4.15
XM501BWA[9]	Examples 5.1, 5.2, 5.4, 5.5, 5.8–5.10, 5.12, 5.15, 5.17; Exercises 5.24, 5.25
XM513BWA[10]	Examples 5.13, 5.17
XM604BWA[11]	Examples 6.4, 6.5
XR613BWA[12]	Exercise 6.13
XR614BWA[13]	Exercise 6.14

[6] Contains only the data on current salary and education.
[7] Contains only the data on current salary and education.
[8] For simplicity the logarithm of current salary is denoted by LOGSAL (instead of LOGSALARY).
[9] This data set contains dummy variables (DUMJCAT2 and DUMJCAT3) to denote the job category, where the first category is taken as reference category.
[10] This file contains grouped data obtained by dividing the 474 employees into twenty-six groups. The group mean of LOGSALARY is denoted by MEANLOGSAL and that of EDUC by MEANEDUC.
[11] This file contains the data of the 258 male employees. Example 6.5 uses the ordinal variable ORDERJOBCAT for the job category (instead of the nominal variable JOBCAT), with values 1 for custodial jobs, 2 for administrative jobs, and 3 for management jobs.
[12] Contains only the data for the 258 male employees and contains the additional variable PREVEXP, the previous experience (in months).
[13] This file is comparable to XM604BWA and contains the data of all 474 employees. As males are the reference category in this exercise, the variable GENDER is now redefined as 0 for males and 1 for females.

3. Stock Market Returns (SMR)

Topic. Monthly excess returns in the UK for the sector of cyclical consumer goods.

Type of data. Time series, monthly data over the period 1980–99 (240 observations), 2 variables.

Source. DataStream (data obtained from this database in 2000, with thanks to Ronald van Dijk).

Variable	Meaning
RENDCYCO	excess returns on an index of 104 stocks in the sector of cyclical consumer goods (household durables, automobiles, textiles, and sports) in the UK (in percentages)[14]
RENDMARK	excess returns on an overall stock market index of the total market in the UK (in percentages)

Datafile	Used in
XR201SMR	Examples 2.1, 2.5; Exercises 2.1, 2.2, 2.11, 2.12
XR215SMR[15]	Exercise 2.15
XM404SMR	Examples 4.4, 4.5, 4.7; Section 4.4.6
XR417SMR[16]	Exercise 4.17
XM527SMR	Examples 5.27, 5.28
XR530SMR[17]	Exercise 5.30
XR722SMR	Exercise 7.22

[14] The excess returns are defined as follows. Let p_i be the closing price of the index at the last trading day in month i and let r_i be the one-month interest rate at the start of month i. Then the return v_i of the index over month i is defined by $v_i = (p_i - p_{i-1})/p_{i-1}$ and the excess return is defined by $v_i - r_i$. The reported numbers in the data file are percentages—that is, $100(v_i - r_i)$. For r_i we take the so-called middle rate.

[15] This file also contains the excess returns of stock indices of three other sectors—namely, Noncyclical Consumer Goods (RENDNCCO), Information Technology (RENDIT), and Telecommunication, Media and Technology (RENDTEL).

[16] This file contains the excess returns for the sector of Noncyclical Consumer Goods (RENDNCCO) and the market returns (RENDMARK).

[17] This file also contains the excess returns of the stock index for the sector of Noncyclical Consumer Goods (RENDNCCO).

4. Coffee Sales (COF)

Topic. Effect of price reductions on coffee sales in suburban areas in Paris.

Type of data. Cross section data of weekly coffee sales for two brands of coffee in a controlled marketing experiment, 12 observations, 3 variables.

Source. A. C. Bemmaor and D. Mouchoux, 'Measuring the Short-Term Effect of In-Store Promotion and Retail Advertising on Brand Sales: A Factorial Experiment', *Journal of Marketing Research*, 28 (1991), 202–14 (data for two brands of regular ground coffee (RGC1 and RGC2) are obtained from table 3 on p. 206).[18]

Variable	Meaning
QUANTITY	quantity of coffee sold (weekly total unit sales of the considered shops)
PRICE	price of coffee (indexed, usual price has value 1, price is 0.95 for 5% price reduction and 0.85 for 15% price reduction)
DEAL	deal rate (with values 1, 1.05, and 1.15, defined by DEAL = 2 − PRICE)

Datafile	Used in
XR210COF[19]	Examples 2.3, 2.7; Exercise 2.10
XR317COF[20]	Exercise 3.17
XM402COF[21]	Examples 4.2, 4.6; Section 4.2.5
XR413COF[22]	Exercise 4.13
XM507COF[23]	Example 5.7
XR526COF[24]	Exercise 5.26

[18] The experiment contains six weeks with no actions, six weeks with price reductions without advertisement, and six weeks with price reductions combined with advertisement. The basic data set considers the twelve weeks without advertisement.

[19] This file contains data for the second brand of coffee (RGC2) for the twelve weeks without advertisement.

[20] This file contains data for the first brand (RGC1) with eighteen observations (instead of twelve), including the six observations for weeks with advertisement. The file also contains the variable A (advertisement dummy with value 1 in weeks with advertisement and 0 in weeks without advertisement).

[21] This file contains twenty-four observations, twelve observations for each of the two brands of coffee (RGC1 and RGC2) for the twelve weeks without advertisement. It contains as additional variables LOGQ1 and LOGQ2 (the logarithms of the sold quantities for the two brands), D1 and D2 (the deal rates for the two brands) and LOGD1 and LOGD2 (the logarithms of D1 and D2).

[22] This file contains the data for the second brand of coffee (RGC2) for the twelve weeks without advertisement.

[23] This file contains the same twenty-four observations as the file XM402COF. Apart from the variables QUANTITY, PRICE, and DEAL, it also contains the variables LOGQ (the logarithm of the sold quantity) and DUMRGC1 and DUMRGC2 (dummy variables that indicate the brand).

[24] This file contains data for the first brand (RGC1) for the twelve action weeks, six weeks with price reductions without advertisement and six weeks with price reductions combined with advertisement. It contains as additional variables A (advertisement dummy, 1 in weeks with advertisement and 0 otherwise) and DP (price dummy, 1 in weeks with 15 per cent price reduction and 0 in weeks with 5 per cent price reduction).

5. Primary Metal Industries (PMI)

Topic. Production in the US Primary Metal Industries (SIC33).

Type of data. Pooled annual data of 26 firms over the period 1958–94 (37 observations per firm), 3 variables.

Source. E. J. Bartelsman and W. Gray, 'The NBER Manufacturing Productivity Database', National Bureau of Economic Research, NBER Technical Working Paper 205 (1996), 30 pp. (data obtained from the Internet site www.nber.org in 1998, with thanks to Piet Lesuis).

Variable	Meaning
PRODUCTION	value added (in millions of 1987 dollars)
LABOUR	total payroll of production worker wages (in millions of 1987 dollars)
CAPITAL	capital stock, both structures and equipment (in millions of 1987 dollars)

Datafile	Used in
XR315PMI[25]	Exercise 3.15
XM729PMI[26]	Examples 7.29, 7.30

[25] Contains the three variables in logarithms, denoted by LOGY (for production), LOGL (for labour), and LOGK (for capital). The data set consists of a cross section of the twenty-six firms for the single year 1994.

[26] Pooled data set; contains the logarithms of the three variables (denoted by LOGPROD, LOGLAB, and LOGCAP) and the nominal variable ID (indicating the firm, ranging from 1 to 26).

6. Motor Gasoline Consumption (MGC)

Topic. Consumption of motor gasoline in the USA.

Type of data. Time series, yearly data over the period 1970–99 (30 observations), 7 variables.

Source. Economic Report of the President 2000 (statistical tables obtained from the Internet site w3.access.gpo.gov/eop in 2000)[27] and Census Bureau and Department of Energy (data obtained from the database Economagic at the Internet site www.economagic.com in 2000).[28]

Variable	Meaning
SGAS	nominal retail sales of gasoline service stations (in millions of dollars)
PGAS	motor gasoline retail price (US city average, in cents per gallon)
INC	nominal personal disposable income (in billions of dollars)
PALL	consumer price index (indexed so that the average value over the years 1982–84 is equal to 100)
PPUB	consumer price index of public transport (indexed in the same way)
PNCAR	consumer price index of new cars (indexed in the same way)
PUCAR	consumer price index of used cars (indexed in the same way)

Datafile	Used in
XR318MGC[29]	Exercises 3.18, 3.19
XM531MGC[30]	Examples 5.31, 5.34; Exercise 5.31
XR721MGC[31]	Exercise 7.21

[27] The variable INC is taken from file b29, the variable PALL from file b60, and the variables PPUB, PNCAR, and PUCAR from file b59b.

[28] The variable SGAS is obtained from the Census Bureau (retail sales by kind of business, gasoline service stations) and the variable PGAS from the Department of Energy (energy prices, motor gasoline retail prices, all types). The original monthly data for SGAS are aggregated to yearly data and the original monthly data for PGAS are averaged to yearly data. The data for PGAS are given in Economagic for the years 1978–99; the values for 1970–77 are obtained from W. H. Greene, *Econometric Analysis* (3rd edn., Prentice Hall, 1997), p. 328, after appropriate scaling.

[29] The exercises use several variables that are defined directly in terms of the variables mentioned above, by taking variables in real terms (instead of nominal) and by taking logarithms.

[30] This file contains the following variables in real terms, and taken in logarithms: GC = log (SGAS/PGAS) (gasoline consumption), PG = log (PGASS/PALL) (real price of gasoline), RI = log (INC/PALL) (real income), RPT = log (PPUB/PALL) (real price of public transport), RPN = log (PNCAR/PALL) (real price of new cars), and RPU = log (PUCAR/PALL) (real price of used cars).

[31] This file is the same as XM531MGC.

7. Food Expenditure (FEX)

Topic. Household expenditure on food and beverages.

Type of data. Cross section, 54 observations,[32] 5 variables.

Source. J. R. Magnus and M. S. Morgan (eds.), 'The Experiment in Applied Econometrics', *Journal of Applied Econometrics*, 12/5 (1997), 651–61, special issue (data obtained from Experiment Information Pack of the editors, file BS50US, see the journal data archive at the Internet site qed.econ.queensu.ca/jae).

Variable	Meaning
TOTCONS	total consumption expenditure (in 10,000 dollars per year)
FOODCONS	food and beverage consumption expenditure (in 10,000 dollars per year)
FRACFOOD	fraction of expenditure spent on food (FOODCONS/TOTCONS)[33]
AHSIZE	household size (average in the group of households)
SAMPSIZE	number of households in the group
Datafile	**Used in**
XR416FEX	Example 4.3; Exercise 4.16
XM520FEX[34]	Examples 5.20, 5.23, 5.25; Exercise 5.27

[32] The data are group averages of 12,448 households (divided into fifty-four groups). The household data are obtained by an interview survey in 1951 in the USA on income and expenditure over the whole year of 1950.

[33] The original data source contains the variables TOTCON and FOODCON measured in dollars per year, here we use TOTCONS = TOTCON/10,000 and FOODCONS = FOODCON/10,000.

[34] Contains restricted data set of forty-eight groups obtained by deleting the six smallest groups (with SAMPSIZE < 20). The data set is ordered in segments according to the variable AHSIZE, and for groups within the same segment according to the variable TOTCONS (for details see Example 5.20 (p. 356–8)). The data can also be ordered randomly, and the random ordering discussed in the book corresponds to the variable RAND in the data file.

8. Fashion Sales (FAS)

Topic. US retail sales of high priced fashion apparel.

Type of data. Time series, quarterly data over the period 1986–92 (28 observations), 3 variables (and 6 derived variables).

Source. G. M. Allenby, L. Jen, and R. P. Leone, 'Economic Trends and Being Trendy: The Influence of Consumer Confidence on Retail Fashion Sales', *Journal of Business and Economic Statistics*, 14/1 (1996), 103–11 (data obtained from the journal data site ftp://www.amstat.org/ JBES_View/).[35]

Variable	Meaning
SALES	real fashion sales (in millions of dollars per thousand square feet of retail space)
PURABI	purchasing ability (real personal disposable income divided by consumer price index for apparel)
CONFI	consumer confidence (an index of consumer sentiment of the University of Michigan Survey Research Center)
LOGSALES	logarithm of SALES
LOGA	logarithm of PURABI
LOGC	logarithm of CONFI
D2, D3, D4	quarterly dummy variables for quarters 2, 3, 4
Datafile	**Used in**
XM506FAS	Example 5.6
XR725FAS[36]	Exercise 7.25

[35] The original monthly data are aggregated to quarterly data. See p. 105 of the article for a detailed definition of the variables.

[36] Pooled data with twenty-eight quarterly sales data for each of five speciality divisions. The divisions 1 and 2 specialize in high-priced fashion apparel (division 1 corresponds to the data set XM506FAS), division 3 in low-priced merchandise, and divisions 4 and 5 in specialities like large sizes, undergarments, and so on.

9. Interest and Bond Rates (IBR)

Topic. Treasury Bill rate and AAA bond rate in the USA.

Type of data. Time series, monthly data over the period 1950–99 (600 observations), 2 variables.

Source. Federal Reserve Board of Governors (data obtained from the database Economagic at the Internet site www.economagic.com in 2000).[37]

Variable	Meaning
DUS3MT	monthly change in the three-month US Treasury Bill rate (in percentages)[38]
DAAA	monthly change in the AAA corporate bond yield (in percentages)

Datafile	Used in
XM511IBR[39]	Examples 5.11, 5.12, 5.14, 5.16, 5.18, 5.19, 5.21, 5.22, 5.24, 5.30, 5.32, 5.33
XR528IBR[40]	Exercise 5.28
XM722IBR[41]	Examples 7.22, 7.25–7.27, 7.32; Exercise 7.19

[37] The Treasury Bill rate is the three-month rate (auction average) and the AAA bond rate is Moody's Seasoned AAA, a monthly average over long-term bonds of firms with AAA rating.

[38] If the value of the rate in month i is denoted by r_i and that of the previous month by r_{i-1}, then the change DUS3MT_i in month i is defined by $r_i - r_{i-1}$.

[39] This file also contains the dummy variable DUM7599 with value 1 for 1975–99 and value 0 for 1950–74, which is used in Examples 5.16 and 5.18.

[40] This file contains the monthly levels (in percentages) of the three-month Treasury Bill rate, denoted by US3MTBIL, so that $\text{DUS3MT}_i = \text{US3MTBIL}_i - \text{US3MTBIL}_{i-1}$. The data period is January 1985 to December 1999 (180 observations).

[41] Apart from the first differences DUS3MT and DAAA, this file also contains the level US3MTBIL of the three-month Treasury Bill rate and the level AAA of the AAA bond rate that are used in Examples 7.25 and 7.27 and in Exercise 7.19 (both levels are in percentages). This file contains monthly data over the period 1948–99, so that the values in 1948 and 1949 can be used as pre-sample values to estimate models for the period 1950–99.

10. **Industrial Production (INP)**

Topic. Index of total industrial production in the USA.

Type of data. Time series, quarterly data over the period 1950.1–1998.3 (195 observations),[42] 1 variable.

Source. OECD Main Economic Indicators (data obtained from the database DataStream in 1999).

Variable	Meaning
IP	total industrial production index (indexed so that the average value over the four quarters of 1992 is equal to 100)
Datafile	**Used in**
XM526INP	Example 5.26; Exercise 5.29
XM701INP[43]	Examples 7.1, 7.7, 7.8, 7.10, 7.11, 7.13, 7.14, 7.16–7.18, 7.20; Exercise 7.16

[42] In most of the analysis the data prior to 1961.1 are used as starting values and the data from 1995.1–1998.3 are left out for forecast evaluation purposes, in which case the effective sample ranges from 1961.1 to 1994.4 with 136 observations.

[43] This file contains the variables X (this is IP, the level of the index), Y (defined by $Y = \log(X)$, the logarithm of the series IP), and D4Y (defined by $D4Y = Y - Y(-4) = \log(X/X(-4)) \approx (X - X(-4))/X(-4)$, the yearly growth rate of the series IP). In addition, in Example 7.16 we use the variable YEARSUMY (the year total $Y + Y(-1) + Y(-2) + Y(-3)$ over the last four quarters) and in Example 7.17 we use some dummy variables for specific observations (for instance, the dummy variable DUM611 has value 1 for the first quarter of 1961 and value 0 for all other quarters).

11. Salaries of Top Managers (TOP)

Topic. Salaries of top managers and profits of the 100 largest firms in the Netherlands in 1999.[44]

Type of data. Cross section, 100 observations, 3 variables.

Source. Annual reports of firms (data obtained from the Dutch newspaper *Volkskrant* at the Internet site www.volkskrant.nl in 2000).

Variable	Meaning
SALARY	average yearly salary in 1999 of top managers of the same firm (in thousands of Dutch guilders)
PROFIT[45]	profit of the firm in 1999 (in millions of Dutch guilders)
TURNOVER[46]	turnover of the firm in 1999 (in millions of Dutch guilders)

Datafile	Used in
XM535TOP[47]	Example 5.35; Exercise 5.32

[44] The set includes firms such as ABN–AMRO, Ahold, ING, Philips, Shell, and Unilever.

[45] One missing value (in sector of social services), three firms with negative profits (in telecommunication sector), ninety-six firms with positive profits.

[46] Thirteen missing values (in banking and insurance sector).

[47] The model is formulated in terms of logarithms of the variables (denoted by LOGSALARY, LOGPROFIT, and LOGTURNOVER). In most cases the analysis is restricted to the ninety-six firms with positive profits, the total turnover of the four dropped firms is less than 1 per cent of the total turnover of the 100 firms. In one case we use the variable TURNOVER; this leaves eighty-four observations.

12. US Presidential Election (USP)

Topic. US presidential election in 2000, results for the state Florida.

Type of data. Cross section, observations for 67 counties in Florida,[48] 10 variables (and 2 derived variables).

Source. CBS (data obtained via the Internet site www.cbsnews.com in 2000, with thanks to Ruud Koning).[49]

Variable	Meaning
BROWNE	number of votes for candidate Browne
BUCHANAN	idem for Buchanan
BUSH	idem for Bush
GORE	idem for Gore
HAGELIN	idem for Hagelin
HARRIS	idem for Harris
MCREYNOLDS	idem for McReynolds
MOOREHEAD	idem for Moorehead
NADER	idem for Nader
PHILLIPS	idem for Phillips
TOTAL	total number of votes in the county[50]
DUMPALM	dummy variable for the county Palm Beach (1 for county 50 (Palm Beach), 0 for the other 66 counties)

Datafile	Used in
XR533USP	Exercise 5.33

[48] The reported values are the number of votes on each candidate counted automatically, before recounting by hand, and excluding votes by mail.

[49] Similar data, of the 10 November recount, are discussed by B. E. Hansen (see the Internet site www.ssc.wisc.edu/~bhansen/vote for further information). The data differ somewhat because of the recounts.

[50] Defined as the sum of the number of votes on the ten mentioned candidates.

13. Direct Marketing for Financial Product (DMF)

Topic. Response of customers of a commercial bank to direct marketing campaign for a new financial product ('click funds').

Type of data. Cross section, 925 observations,[51] 5 variables.

Source. P. H. Franses, 'On the Econometrics of Modeling Direct Marketing Response', RIBES report 97–15, Rotterdam, 1997 (with thanks to Robeco).

Variable	Meaning
RESPONSE	response (dummy variable, 1 if customer invests in the new product and 0 otherwise)
INVEST	amount of money invested by the customer in the new product (in hundreds of Dutch guilders)
GENDER	gender (1 for males, 0 for females)
ACTIVITY	activity indicator (1 if customer already invests in other products of the bank and 0 otherwise)
AGE	age of customer (in years)

Datafile	Used in
XM601DMF[52]	Examples 6.1–6.3, 6.6, 6.7; Exercises 6.11, 6.12, 6.16

[51] The original database contains more than 100,000 observations.
[52] The file contains the additional variable LOGINV defined by LOGINV = log(1 + INVEST).

14. **Duration of Strikes (DUS)**

Topic. Duration of contract strikes in US manufacturing.

Type of data. Cross section, 62 observations, 2 variables.

Source. J. Kennan, 'The Duration of Contract Strikes in US Manufacturing', *Journal of Econometrics*, 28 (1985), 5–28 (the data are in table 1 on pp. 14–16 of this paper).[53]

Variable	Meaning
STRIKEDUR	strike duration (length of finished strikes, measured in days)
PROD	index of unanticipated industrial production in manufacturing (the value 0 corresponds to normal conditions)

Datafile	Used in
XM609DUS[54]	Example 6.9; Exercise 6.17

[53] The data concern official strikes in US manufacturing industries for the period 1968–76, involving 1000 workers or more, with major issue classified as general wage changes by the Bureau of Labor Statistics. Attention is restricted to strikes beginning in June of each year to remove seasonal effects (see Kiefer (1988), listed in the Further Reading of Chapter 6 (p. 524)).

[54] The file contains the additional variable STRIKECENS80, which is obtained by censoring the actual durations at a maximum of 80 days, so that STRIKECENS80 = min(STRIKEDUR, 80).

15. **Dow-Jones Index (DJI)**

Topic. Dow-Jones industrial average.

Type of data. Time series, daily data from 1990 (2 January) to 1999 (31 December), 2528 observations, 1 variable.

Source. Economagic (data obtained from the stock price indices at the Internet site www.economagic.com in 2000).

Variable	Meaning
DJ[55]	Dow-Jones Industrial Average index (daily close)
Datafile	Used in
XM702DJI[56]	Examples 7.2, 7.15, 7.21

[55] The days are numbered consecutively so that closing days are not counted.

[56] The file contains variables derived from the Dow-Jones index—namely, LOGDJ (the logarithm of DJ) and DLOGDJ (the daily differences of LOGDJ—that is, the daily returns on the Dow-Jones index). For the purposes of Example 7.21 it also contains the derived variables DJRET (the daily returns; this is the same series as DLOGDJ but the two names are useful in different settings) and DJABSRET (the absolute returns, defined as the absolute value of DJRET). The file further contains the auxiliary variables DD (day of the month, 1–31), MM (month of the year, 1–12), and YEAR (year, 1990–1999) to relate the time series to calendar time.

16. Mortality and Marriages (MOM)

Topic. Mortality in England and Wales and proportion of Church of England marriages.

Type of data. Time series, yearly data 1866–1911 (46 observations), 2 variables.

Source. G. U. Yule, 'Why do we Sometimes Get Nonsense-Correlations between Time-Series?', *Journal of the Royal Statistical Society*, 89 (1926), 1–64 (the data are reconstructed from figure 1 on p. 3 of this paper; see the comments in Example 7.23 (p. 648–9)).

Variable	Meaning
STMORT	standardized mortality in England and Wales (per 1000 persons)
CEMARR	proportion of Church of England marriages (per 1000 of all marriages)

Datafile	Used in
XM723MOM	Example 7.23

17. Treasury Bill Rates (TBR)

Topic. Treasury Bill rates in the USA for three different maturities.

Type of data. Time series, monthly data over the period 1960–99 (480 observations), 3 variables.

Source. Federal Reserve Board of Governors (data obtained from the database Economagic at the Internet site www.economagic.com in 2001).[57]

Variable	Meaning
T_3M	3-month Treasury Bill rate (measured in percentages)
T_1Y	1-year Treasury Bill rate (measured in percentages)
T_10Y	10-year Treasury Bill rate (measured in percentages)
Datafile	**Used in**
XM728TBR[58]	Example 7.28

[57] The 3-month Treasury Bill rate is the secondary market series; the 1-year and 10-year Treasury Bill rates are the constant maturity series.

[58] The file also contains the three spreads between the Treasury Bill rates—that is, the three differences DIFF_T10YT1Y = T_10Y − T_1Y, DIFF_T10YT3M = T_10Y − T_3M, and DIFF_T1YT3M = T_1Y − T_3M.

18. Car Production (CAR)

Topic. Production of Japanese passenger cars.

Type of data. Time series, monthly data over the period 1980.1–2001.3 (255 observations), 2 variables.

Source. DataStream (data obtained from this database in 2001).

Variable	Meaning
TOYOTA	production volume of passenger cars by Toyota (number of cars)
JPOUTPUT	total volume of produced passenger cars in Japan (number of cars)

Datafile	Used in
XR717CAR[59]	Exercise 7.17

[59] The file also contains the variable ALLMINTOY = JPOUTPUT − TOYOTA. In addition it contains production volumes of passenger cars of eight other industries (Daihatsu, Fuji, Honda, Isuzu, Mazda, Mitsubishi, Nissan, and Suzuki) that are not used in the exercise but that can be analysed in a similar way as the series of Toyota.

19. Nuclear Energy Production (NEP)

Topic. Generation of electricity from nuclear electric power in the USA.

Type of data. Time series, monthly data over the period 1973.1–1999.11 (323 observations), 1 variable.

Source. Department of Energy (data obtained from the database Economagic at the Internet site www.economagic.com in 2000).

Variable	Meaning
NUCEP	net generation of electricity from nuclear electric power (in Tbtu)

Datafile	Used in
XR718NEP[60]	Exercise 7.18

[60] The file also contains some additional energy production series (of petroleum, of natural gas, and of electricity generated by geothermal energy and by hydropower, as well as a total energy production series for the USA). These series are not used in the exercise but they can be analysed in a similar way as the series of nuclear electric power.

20. **Gross National Product (GNP)**

Topic. Gross national product of four countries.

Type of data. Time series, yearly data over the period 1870–1993 (124 observations), 4 variables.

Source. A. Maddison, *Monitoring the World Economy 1820–1992* (OECD, 1995) (the data are taken from table C.16 on pp. 180–3).

Variable	Meaning
GERMANY	real gross domestic product of Germany (in millions of Geary–Khamis dollars)
JAPAN[61]	real gross domestic product of Japan (same units)
UK	real gross domestic product of UK (same units)
USA	real gross domestic product of USA (same units)

Datafile	Used in
XR720GNP[62]	Exercise 7.20

[61] The series for Japan has missing values for 1871–84, leaving 110 observations.

[62] The file also contains the logarithms of the four GNP series, denoted by LOGGER, LOGJAP, LOGUK, and LOGUSA.

21. Exchange Rates (EXR)

Topic. Exchange rates and price indices of Germany and the UK.

Type of data. Time series, monthly data over the period 1957.1–1998.4 (496 observations, the exercise uses only the 240 observations of the years 1975–94), 4 variables.

Source. International Financial Statistics (data obtained from the database DataStream in 2000).

Variable	Meaning
X_UK	nominal exchange rate of British Pound to 1 US dollar
X_G	nominal exchange rate of Deutsche Mark to 1 US dollar
P_UK	consumer price index for the UK (indexed so that the average over 1990 is equal to 100)
P_G	consumer price index for (Western) Germany (indexed in the same way)

Datafile	Used in
XR723EXR[63]	Exercise 7.23

[63] The file also contains the logarithms of the four series (denoted by LOG_X_UK, LOG_X_G, LOG_P_UK, and LOG_P_G), as well as nominal exchange rates and consumer price indices for Canada, France, Japan, and the Netherlands, together with the consumer price index of the USA.

22. **Standard and Poor Index (STP)**

Topic. Standard and Poor composite stock price index.

Type of data. Time series, yearly data 1871–1987 (117 observations), 2 variables.

Source. R. J. Shiller, *Market Volatility* (MIT Press, 1989) (the data are taken from tables 26.1 and 26.2 on pp. 440–3).

Variable	Meaning
REALSP	stock price of Standard and Poor index (January, in real terms)
REALDIV	yearly dividends on Standard and Poor index (in real terms)
Datafile	**Used in**
XR724STP[64]	Exercise 7.24

[64] The file contains several other variables, in particular SP (nominal stock price), DIV (nominal yearly dividends), and PP (producer price index). The real variables are defined by REALSP = SP/PP and REALDIV = DIV/PP. The file also contains the series of earnings (EAR), interest rate (INT), real consumption (RC), and consumer price index (CPI).

23. Market for Oranges (MOR)

Topic. Relation between price of oranges and quantity traded in the USA.

Type of data. Time series, yearly data 1910–59 (50 observations), 5 variables.

Source. M. Nerlove and F. V. Waugh, 'Advertising without Supply Control: Some Implications of a Study of the Advertising of Oranges', *Journal of Farm Economics*, 43 (1961), 813–37 (data obtained from table 1 on p. 827). See also E. R. Berndt, *The Practice of Econometrics: Classic and Contemporary* (Addison-Wesley, 1991), 417–20.

Variable	Meaning
QTY	quantity of oranges sold (number of boxes per capita)
PRICE[65]	real price of a box of oranges (year average, in dollars)
INC	real disposable income per capita (in dollars)
CURADV[66]	current year real advertising expenditures (in cents per capita)
AVEADV	average real advertising expenditures (in cents per capita, averaged over the ten preceding years)

Datafile	Used in
XR726MOR[67]	Exercise 7.26

[65] This variable is defined by PRICE = REV/QTY, where REV is the per capita real revenue from sales of oranges (in dollars).

[66] The variables CURADV and AVEADV concern advertising expenditures for oranges by Sunkist Growers and the Florida Citrus Commission.

[67] This file contains some additional variables—namely, REV (per capita real revenue from sales of oranges), POP (population of the USA, in millions), and CPI (consumer price index used to produce the real series). Further it contains the logarithmic variables LOGQT (the log of QTY), LOGPT (the log of PRICE), LOGRIT (the log of INC), LOGAC (the log of CURADV), and LOGAP (the log of AVEADV).

Index